MY LI

Richard Wagner

Translated by
Andrew Gray

Edited by
Mary Whittall

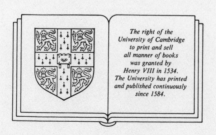

The right of the
University of Cambridge
to print and sell
all manner of books
was granted by
Henry VIII in 1534.
The University has printed
and published continuously
since 1584.

CAMBRIDGE UNIVERSITY PRESS

Cambridge

New York   New Rochelle

Melbourne   Sydney

Published by the Press Syndicate of the University of Cambridge
The Pitt Building, Trumpington Street, Cambridge CB2 1RP
32 East 57th Street, New York, NY 10022, USA
10 Stamford Road, Oakleigh, Melbourne 3166, Australia

Originally published in German as *Mein Leben*
by Paul List Verlag, Munich, 1963
and © Paul List Verlag, 1963

First published in English by Cambridge University Press 1983
as *My Life*
First paperback edition 1987
Reprinted 1988

English translation © Cambridge University Press 1983

Printed in Great Britain by the University Press, Cambridge

Library of Congress catalogue card number: 82-23568

British Library Cataloguing in Publication Data

Wagner, Richard
My life.
1. Wagner, Richard
2. Composers–Germany–Biography
I. Title   II. Mein Leben. *English*
782.1′092′4   ML410.WI
ISBN 0 521 22929 4 hard covers
ISBN 0 521 35900 7 paperback

CONTENTS

FOREWORD

The chronicle contained in these volumes has been taken down directly from my dictation over the course of various years by my friend and wife,[1] who wished me to tell her the story of my life. The desire arose in both of us to preserve this information regarding my life for our family as well as our trusted and true friends, and thus, to preserve the one copy of the manuscript against loss, we decided to have it reproduced in book form at our expense in a very limited number of copies. As the value of an autobiography put together this way depends upon its unvarnished truthfulness, which under the aforementioned circumstances had to be the sole justification for the undertaking and thus also necessitated my providing precise names and numbers, there could consequently be no question of its publication, assuming our descendants still evince interest in it, until some time after my death; and on this point I intend to leave directions for my heirs in my will. If we now nonetheless do not refuse a few reliable friends a look at this chronicle, it is done on the assumption that their interest in the subject is one of pure sympathy, and that they in particular would find it unthinkable to communicate anything further from its contents to anyone with respect to whom this presupposition would not be warranted.

Richard Wagner

PART ONE

1813–41

Born* May 22nd 1813 in Leipzig, two flights up in a house on the Brühl known as "The Red and White Lion", I was christened[1] two days later in St Thomas' Church with the name Wilhelm Richard. My father[2] Friedrich Wagner, at the time of my birth the registrar of police in Leipzig with the expectation of becoming director of police, died in October of the same year, following the great exertions imposed by an overwhelming load of official duties during the wartime unrest and the battle of Leipzig, after catching typhoid fever in what had become an epidemic. As to his own father's[3] situation in life, I learned much later that he had distinguished himself among compeers in his humble municipal post of toll collector at the Ranstädter Gate by giving both his sons a higher education, having one of them, my father Friedrich, study law, and the younger one, Adolf,[4] study theology. My uncle subsequently came to exert a not insignificant influence on my development; we will meet him again in a decisive phase of the story of my youth. About the father whom I lost so early I learned later that he was in general very much interested in poetry and literature, and particularly accorded an almost passionate devotion to the theater, at that time much patronized by the educated classes. My mother[5] told me among other things that he took her to Lauchstädt to the first performance of *Die Braut von Messina* and pointed out Schiller and Goethe to her on the promenade, enthusiastically setting her straight as to her ignorance of these great men. He seems to have been not entirely free of a certain amorous interest in actresses. My mother used to complain jokingly that she frequently had to hold lunch for him while he was paying rapturous visits to a certain famous actress of the day;†[6] whenever she scolded him, he asserted that official business had detained him, and to prove it pointed to supposedly ink-stained fingers, which upon enforced closer inspection always turned out to be completely clean. His fondness for the theater was also evidenced by his selection of the actor Ludwig Geyer[7] as an intimate friend of the family. While his choice of such a friend was surely attributable mainly to this love of the theater, he thereby bestowed upon his family a most noble benefactor, inasmuch as this modest artist, through heartfelt concern with the destiny of the numerous offspring of his unexpectedly deceased friend Wagner, was moved to devote the rest of his life most strenuously to the support and upbringing of this family. Even while the police official was spending

---

* At the head of the page, in Cosima's hand, the inscription "Munich, July 17th 1865" and the entwined initials R.C.W.

† Footnote in the original edition: "Mme Hartwig".

3

his evenings in the theater, this admirable actor generally filled his place in the bosom of his family, and it appears that he was often obliged to soothe my mother when she complained, rightly or wrongly, about the flightiness of her husband. How deep was the need of this homeless, hard-pressed, and buffeted artist to be at home within a sympathetic family environment was proved a year after his friend's death, when he married the widow and henceforth became a most solicitous father to the seven surviving children.[1] In this difficult undertaking he was favored by an unexpected improvement in his career. As a so-called character actor, he obtained an advantageous, honorable, and permanent position in the newly established Dresden Court Theater. His talent for painting, which at one time had helped him to get by in life when forced by the most extreme poverty to interrupt his university studies, again stood him in good stead in his position in Dresden. He complained, it was true, even more than his critics of having been deprived of systematic and academic training; nonetheless his extraordinary gifts, particularly for portraiture, brought him such important commissions that, alas, his two-fold exertions as painter and actor prematurely exhausted his strength. Once, when he was invited to Munich for a guest performance at the Court Theater, he obtained from the Bavarian court, through favorable references from the Saxon nobility, such important orders for portraits of the royal family that he considered it wise to interrupt his engagement and give it up entirely. But he also had poetic talent; after writing a number of occasional pieces, often in very finely wrought verse, he also penned several comedies, one of which, *The Massacre of the Innocents*, in rhymed Alexandrines, was often performed, appeared in print, and was praised by Goethe in a most friendly fashion. This excellent man, whom my family followed to Dresden in my second year, and by whom my mother had yet another daughter (Cäcilie),[2] also took my upbringing in hand with the greatest solicitude and love. He wished to adopt me entirely as his own son, and therefore, when I was first admitted to school, he gave me his name, so that until my fourteenth year I remained known to my boyhood companions in Dresden by the name Richard Geyer. Not until some years after the death of my stepfather, when my family returned to Leipzig, did I, once more in the home town of my blood relations, resume the name Wagner.

The earliest recollections of my childhood are fixed on this stepfather and pass from him to the theater. I remember well that my father would have been very happy to see a talent for painting develop in me; his studio, with the easels and paintings upon them, did not, to be sure, fail to make an impression on me; I remember, in fact, that I tried to copy a portrait of King Friedrich August of Saxony, with a child's eagerness to imitate; but as soon as I was expected to go beyond this simple playing with paint to a serious study of drawing, I did not persevere, possibly scared off by the pedantic ways of my teacher (a boring cousin of mine). After one of the common ailments of infancy, which made me so sick that my mother, as she later told me, almost wished me dead owing to my seemingly hopeless condition, I seem to have surprised my parents by thriving. On this occasion as well, I was told, my admirable stepfather played a splendid part, never despairing despite the cares and complaints of such a large family, remaining patient, and never giving up the hope that I could be pulled through.

My imagination was now dominated by acquaintance with the theater, with which I was brought into contact not only as a juvenile spectator from the concealed loge with its entrance from the stage, and by visits to the wardrobe with its fantastic costumes and all the paraphernalia of illusion, but also by taking part in performances myself. After being terrified by *The Orphan and the Murderer* and *The Two Galley Slaves* and similar horrific works, in which I saw my father play the villains, I was obliged to appear in some comedies. In an occasional piece entitled *The Vineyard on the Elbe*, written to welcome the King of Saxony upon his return from captivity, with music by Kapellmeister Carl Maria von Weber, I recall figuring in a tableau vivant as an angel, entirely sewn up in tights and with wings on my back, in a graceful, though laboriously learned, pose. I also remember on this occasion being given a large sugar cake, which I was assured the King had intended for me personally. Lastly, I remember playing the part of a child and speaking a few words in Kotzebue's[1] *Misanthropy and Misery*, which furnished me with an excuse at school for not having done my homework, as I declared myself to have been overburdened by the obligation to learn by heart a vast role in *Mr and Mrs Antropy*.

To show how seriously my father regarded my education, on the other hand, he took me, when I had completed my sixth year, to a clergyman in the country of Possendorf near Dresden, where I was to receive an excellent, sober and healthy education in the company of other boys from good families. From the short period of my stay date many first recollections of impressions of the world; in the evening the pastor*[2] would tell us of Robinson Crusoe, accompanied by instructive discussion.

* Footnote in the original edition: "Wetzel".

His reading aloud of a biography of Mozart made a great impression on me, whereas the newspaper and magazine reports of the contemporary events of the Greek War of Independence excited me dreadfully. My love for Greece, which later fell with enthusiasm upon the mythology and history of Ancient Hellas, thus originated in intense and painful interest in the events of the present. In later years, the story of the struggle of the Greeks against the Persians always revived my impressions of this modern revolt against the Turks.

One day, after scarcely a year of this stay in the country had elapsed, a messenger arrived from the city, notifying the pastor that he should accompany me to Dresden, where my father lay dying. We made the three-hour return trip on foot; exhausted when I arrived, I scarcely comprehended the tearful behavior of my mother. The following day I was conducted to my father's bedside; the extreme weakness with which he talked to me, together with all the preventive measures taken in the last desperate treatment of his acute emphysema, came over me only as visions in a dream; I believe my uneasy amazement was so great that I was unable to cry. My mother invited me into an adjoining room to demonstrate what I had learned on the piano in the hope that it would provide some distraction for my father: I played "Üb' immer Treu' und Redlichkeit"; then father asked mother: "Could it be that he has a talent for music?"

The next morning my mother came to our beds in the children's large bedroom at break of day and informed us, sobbing, of father's death, telling each of us, like a blessing, some things he had said; to me she said: "He wanted to make something of you." Pastor Wetzel arrived that afternoon and took me back to the country. We again went by foot and reached Possendorf only at dusk; on the way I asked him a lot about the stars, concerning which he gave me my first reasonable information. A week later the deceased man's brother appeared, having come from Eisleben to attend the burial ceremonies; he had agreed to try to help support the again destitute family and undertook to care for my future education. I took leave of my schoolmates and from the affable pastor, to whose own funeral I returned to Possendorf for the first time several years later; I paid the village only one more visit, many years later, on one of the rambles I often used to take in the countryside when I was conductor of the orchestra in Dresden; it moved me greatly that I could not find the old parsonage but found a more pretentious modern structure in its place, which so prejudiced me against the location that I never again directed any of my excursions into the area.

This time, my uncle brought me back to Dresden by carriage; I found my mother and sisters in dress of deep mourning and remember being received for the first time with a tenderness unusual in our family and similarly treated at my leavetaking, when I was taken along to Eisleben by my uncle after a few days. This uncle, a younger brother of my stepfather, had settled there as a goldsmith; he had already taken one of my elder brothers (Julius) into apprenticeship; he was a bachelor and the old grandmother still lived with him. Her son's death had been concealed from the old lady, whose own decease was anticipated in the near future; I too was instructed to keep it to myself. The servant girl carefully removed the mourning crêpe from my clothing and explained that she would retain it to be used for the grandmother after she was dead, as was soon to be expected. I was obliged to talk often of father to his mother; I had no trouble concealing his death, as I myself had no clear idea of it. She lived at the rear of the house in a dark room looking out on a narrow courtyard, and loved to have robins fluttering freely around her, for which she always kept fresh green twigs strewn by the stove. I once succeeded in snaring her a few to replace some that had been killed by the cat: she was highly delighted by this and in return kept me clean and tidy. Her expected death came to pass shortly: the carefully preserved mourning crêpe was now worn openly in Eisleben; the little back room with the robins and green bushes saw me no more. I soon made myself at home in the family of a soap-boiler, to whom the house belonged, and became popular with them by telling entertaining stories. I was sent to a private school whose headmaster Weiss left upon me an impression of seriousness and dignity. I was touched to read a report in a music magazine in the late 1850s of a performance in Eisleben of selections from *Tannhäuser*, at which my former master, who had not forgotten his pupil, had been present.

The quaint little town with the house where Luther lived and the manifold memorials to the time he spent there has often recurred to me in dreams, even to the present day; I have always wanted to visit it again[1] to find the clarity of my recollections confirmed; but curiously enough I have never done so. We lived near the market-place, which frequently offered me strange spectacles, as, for example, the performances of a team of acrobats, in which they walked on a cord drawn taut from tower to tower across the square, a feat which awakened in me an enduring bent for similar feats of daring. Indeed, I got so far as to walk upon twisted cords stretched out across our courtyard and, aided by a balancing pole, did quite well at it; even today I still feel a desire to do justice to my acrobatic inclinations. Most important of all for me was the band music of a regiment of Hussars garrisoned in Eisleben. One of the pieces played by this band awakened unheard-of attention as a curiosity: it was the Huntsmen's Chorus from *Der Freischütz*, which opera had just had its première in Berlin. Uncle and brother eagerly quizzed me about its composer, whom I surely must have seen in my parents' house in Dresden as Kapellmeister Weber. At the same time the Bridesmaids' Chorus was being zealously played and sung by daughters in a neighboring family. These two pieces now dispelled my liking for the Ypsilanti Waltz,[1] which I had considered until then as the most marvelous piece of music. I recall also having to withstand numerous battles with the autochthonous juvenile population, which I provoked to continuing mockery by wearing my square hat. Beyond that I also recollect a fondness for adventurous outings on the rocky cliffs on the banks of the Unstrut.

My uncle now married at last and established a new household, which seems to have caused a marked change in his relationship to my family. After a year, I was brought by him to Leipzig, where I was given over for a few days to the relatives of my father (Wagner). These were my uncle Adolf and his sister, my aunt Friederike Wagner. This very interesting man, who later had an even more stimulating influence upon me, makes his entrance in my recollections, with his strange entourage, at this point. Along with my aunt, he maintained a very close friendship with a strange old spinster, Jeannette Thomé, co-owner of a large house on the market square, in which, if I do not err, ever since the time of Augustus the Strong, the Saxon royal family had rented and furnished the first two floors for their use whenever in Leipzig. As far as I know, the third floor was owned by Jeannette Thomé, in which she kept for herself only a modest apartment overlooking the courtyard. As the King made use of the rented rooms at the most only a few days a year, Jeannette and her household usually occupied these splendid quarters, and it was in one of these stately rooms that a place to sleep was allocated to me. The furnishings of these rooms dated from the time of Augustus the Strong; they were magnificent with rich rococo furniture and heavy silk materials, by then all much worn and torn with age. I think I must have felt very grand in the vast fantastic rooms, from which one could look outward over the bustling Leipzig market-place, among whose denizens the students in alley-wide processions, in their old-German club attire, particularly fascinated me. Only one aspect of the decoration of these rooms caused me considerable anguish: this consisted of the

8

various portraits, particularly those of aristocratic ladies in hooped petticoats, with youthful faces and white (powdered) hair. These struck me as completely ghostly creatures, who, whenever I was alone in the room, seemed to come to life and filled me with terror. To sleep alone in such a large and remote room, near one of these fearsome pictures, in a sumptuous old bed, was horrible for me: I tried, it is true, to conceal my fear from my aunt when she lighted the way for me to bed in the evening; but never a night passed without my being bathed in sweat at the fear caused by these frightful ghostly apparitions.

The characteristics of the three principal occupants of these quarters were admirably suited to turn the phantom impressions of this stay into something strange as a fairy-tale: Jeannette Thomé was very short and fat, wore a blond Titus wig,[1] and appeared to be comfortable in the consciousness of former elegance. Her faithful friend and attendant, my aunt, who had also become an old maid, was remarkable for her height and extreme leanness. The oddity of her otherwise very pleasant face was increased by an exceedingly pointed chin. My uncle Adolf had set up his study once and for all in a gloomy room on the courtyard. I saw him there for the first time amid a chaotic mass of books in dowdy indoor attire, the most striking feature of which was a high and pointed felt cap, such as I had seen worn by a clown belonging to the troupe of acrobats in Eisleben. A strong inclination to independence had driven him to this strange retreat. Originally destined for theology, he soon gave this up to devote himself solely to philosophical and philological studies. Profoundly disinclined to function as a professor or in any formal teaching capacity, he tried from early on to make a meager living from literary work. Gifted with social abilities and particularly with a fine tenor voice, imbued as well with interest for the theater, he seems in his youth to have been welcome as a literary figure among a fairly wide circle of acquaintances in Leipzig. On an excursion to Jena, during which he and a friend appear to have found their way into some musical and oratorical associations, he also visited Schiller; for this purpose he had armed himself with an errand for the management of the Leipzig Theater, which wanted to acquire rights to perform the recently completed *Wallenstein*. He later described to me the enchanting impression made upon him by Schiller, with his tall trim figure and irresistibly winning blue eyes. His only complaint was that, as a result of a well-intentioned trick played on him by a friend, he was caused great and humiliating embarrassment. This friend had actually managed to send Schiller in advance a volume of Adolf Wagner's poems; the stricken young poet was thus obliged to accept friendly words of praise from Schiller, deeply convinced that he owed them solely to Schiller's humane generosity. In later years he concentrated more and more on philological studies. One of his best known works in this field is his publication, *Parnasso Italiano*,[1] which he dedicated to Goethe with an Italian poem, of which experts told me, as a matter of fact, that it was written in stilted and perfervid Italian, but which nonetheless procured for him from Goethe a nice letter of acknowledgement and a silver goblet from the poet's own pantry. The impression on me in my eighth year made by his appearance in the surroundings I have described was utterly puzzling and singular.

After a few days I was summarily removed from these influences and brought to my family in Dresden. In the meantime, under the guidance of my again widowed mother, my family had done its best to establish residence there. My eldest brother (Albert), originally destined to study medicine, had, on the advice of Weber, who admired his tenor voice, begun a theatrical career in Breslau. My second-eldest sister (Luise) soon followed him, dedicating herself to the theater as an actress. My eldest sister (Rosalie) had obtained an excellent engagement at the Dresden Court Theater itself, and she became from then on the focal point of the remaining younger part of the family, just as she remained the principal support of her careworn mother. I found them in the same large and pleasant quarters my father had previously provided for them; but now several superfluous rooms were always being let to strangers, including Spohr at one time. Thanks to my mother's great energy, and the help of some mitigating circumstances (among which should be mentioned the continuing kindness of the court in remembrance of my stepfather), my family managed to get along reasonably well, so that there was also no neglect of my education.

After yet a third sister (Klara), owing to her exceptionally beautiful voice, decided to go on the stage, my mother took pains to let me know that I was not to develop any such inclination for the theater as well. She never ceased reproaching herself for having consented to my eldest brother's stage career; inasmuch as my second brother showed no talents other than those that had fitted him to be a goldsmith, she was now very much concerned to see progress toward fulfillment of the hopes and wishes of my stepfather, who had "wanted to make something of me". After I had completed my eighth year, I was sent to the Kreuz Grammar School in Dresden; I was supposed to get a formal education. There I was placed at the bottom of the lowest class, and started my academic training under the most modest auspices. My mother noted with great interest whatever signs I showed of mental liveliness and talent.

For all who knew her, this remarkable woman, utterly without a formal education, represented a characteristic combination of practical domestic efficiency and great spiritual sensitivity. None of her children ever heard her speak in any detail about her origins. She came from Weissenfels and admitted that her parents had been bakers there. Even in regard to her maiden name she expressed herself with a curious reserve, giving it out as "Perthes", whereas, as we discovered no doubt by pestering her, it was really "Petz".[1] Strangely enough, she had been placed in a select boarding school in Leipzig and enjoyed there the protection of one whom she called "a fatherly friend", and to whom she afterwards referred as a Weimar prince[2] who had been very kind to the family in Weissenfels. Her education in that establishment seems to have been interrupted as a result of the death of this fatherly friend. She met my father at a very early age and married him, who had also matured early and already had a job, in the first bloom of maidenhood. Her dominant trait seems to have been a wry sense of humor and an amiable temperament, so that it should not be supposed that solely his sense of duty toward the family of his deceased friend, but rather a really sincere affection as well, impelled the admirable Ludwig Geyer to enter into matrimony with a woman no longer entirely youthful. A portrait of her painted by Geyer during her first marriage represents her appearance very advantageously. By the time my recollection of her is first distinct she was already compelled by a head ailment to wear a cap continually, so that I have no remembrance of her as a young and pretty mother. The anxious and trying relations with a large family (of which I was the seventh surviving member), the difficulties in providing the necessities of life, and the fulfillment of a certain desire to keep up appearances even with very limited means, were not conducive to a comforting tone of motherly solicitude in her; I hardly remember ever being caressed by her, just as outpourings of affection did not take place in our family at all; on the contrary, quite naturally a certain impetuous, even loud and boisterous manner characterized our behavior. In these circumstances I remember it as epoch-making one night being taken to bed and looking up at her with tearful eyes when she gazed back at me fondly and spoke of me to a visitor with a certain amount of tenderness. What particularly struck me about her was the strange zeal with which she spoke, in almost histrionic tones, of the great and beautiful in art. She would never let me suppose that she included dramatic art in this category, but rather solely poetry, music and painting, and often in fact came close to threatening me with her curse if ever I too were to think of going into the theater. At the same time she was of a very religious turn of mind; she would often subject us to long, sermon-like orations, spoken with great emotion, about God and the divine quality in man, during which, once in a while, she would change her tone suddenly and humorously interrupt her discourse with a rebuke to one of us. Indeed, since the death of my stepfather she assembled the rest of the family around her bed every morning where she would drink her coffee, but not before one of us had recited something from the hymnal, wherein we had a considerable latitude of choice until one day my sister Klara mistakenly recited a "Prayer in Time of War" so movingly that my mother interrupted her with the words, "Oh, stop it! God forgive my sins, there is no war on at the moment!"

In spite of our modest means, we now and then had merry evening parties, and, as it appeared to me as a boy, actually brilliant ones. From the time of my stepfather, who in his last years had raised his income through his success as a portrait painter to quite a respectable level for those days, there remained to us pleasant acquaintances from the best circles who even then still got together at our house once in a while. The members of the Court Theater in particular constituted a pleasant and stimulating group, of which I found no living trace later in Dresden. Especially popular were the picnics in the lovely surroundings of Dresden, brightened by the communal gaiety of the artists. I remember one such excursion to Loschwitz, where a gypsy camp of sorts was set up, in which Carl Maria von Weber did his part as a cook. We also had music: my sister Rosalie played the piano; Klara began to sing. Among the different theatrical performances formerly given at my parents' birthdays, to their mutual surprise and often with lengthy preparations, there remained in my memory even at that time only the performance of a parody of Grillparzer's *Sappho*, in which I myself participated in the chorus of street urchins running ahead of Phaon's triumphal carriage. I tried to refresh these memories by means of a puppet theater, which I found among the effects of my father, and for which he had painted the decorations himself. I intended to surprise my relatives with a spectacular performance in this theater. After I had carved several dolls with the greatest clumsiness and provided them with exiguous costumes from bits of clothing filched from my sisters, I began writing the chivalric drama in which my dolls were to be trained in their roles. When I had completed the first scene my sisters discovered the manuscript and accorded it howls of laughter; one line of the frightened lover, "I hear the knightly footsteps falling", was to my rage frequently thereafter recited to me by them with great pathos.

I now turned once again enthusiastically to the theater, to which my family remained very close. In particular *Freischütz*, though mainly because of its spooky plot, affected my imagination with characteristic intensity. The excitement of horror and fear of ghosts constitute a singular factor in the development of my emotional life. From earliest childhood certain mysterious and uncanny phenomena produced undue effects on me; I remember, whenever I was alone in a room for any length of time and looked fixedly at such inanimate objects as pieces of furniture, suddenly bursting into a loud shriek, because they seemed to me to come alive. Until late in my boyhood no night passed without my awakening with a frightful scream from some dream about ghosts, which would end only when a human voice bade me be quiet. Severe scoldings or even corporal punishment would then seem to me redeeming kindnesses. None of my brothers and sisters wanted to sleep near me; they tried to bed me down as far from the others as possible, not stopping to think that by so doing my nocturnal calls to be saved from the ghosts would become even louder and more enduring, until they finally accustomed themselves to this nightly calamity.

What attracted me so strongly to the theater, in which I include the stage itself, the compartments behind the scenes, and the dressing-rooms, was not so much the desire for entertainment and diversion, such as motivates today's theatergoers, but rather a tingling delight in finding myself in an atmosphere that represented such a contrast to normal life by its purely fantastic and almost appallingly attractive quality. Thus a set, or even a flat – perhaps representing a bush – or a costume or even only a characteristic piece of one, appeared to me to emanate from another world and be in a certain sense interesting as apparitions, and contact with all this would serve as a lever to lift me out of a monotonous everyday reality into that fascinating demoniacal realm. Everything connected with the theater had for me the charm of mystery, an attraction amounting to intoxication, and while I tried with playmates to imitate performances of *Freischütz*, and devoted myself with great zeal to the production of costumes and masks through grotesque painting, it was the more delicate costumes of my sisters, on which I often observed my family working, that exerted a more subtly exciting effect on my fantasy; touching these objects could cause my heart to beat wildly. Despite the fact that, as I have mentioned, there was little tenderness in our family, particularly as expressed in caresses, the predominantly feminine element in my surroundings must have had a strong impact on my emotional development. Perhaps it was precisely because members of my immediate family were restless and impetuous that the other attributes of femininity, particularly insofar as they were connected with the imaginary world of the theater, filled me with an almost passionate delight.

Luckily these fantastic moods, in which grotesquerie often lost itself in mawkishness, were counterbalanced strongly by the more serious influence derived at school from my teachers and schoolmates. But here also it was principally the realm of fantasy that aroused my keen interest. Whether or not I was a "bright" student in the usual sense I cannot judge; on the whole I believe that I could grasp whatever subject particularly attracted me almost without real study, whereas I scarcely devoted any effort to those which lay outside these immediate interests. This quality showed itself most clearly in arithmetic and later in mathematics; in both these fields I did not even succeed in bringing my mind seriously to bear on the tasks assigned me. With regard to the ancient languages I was also able to concentrate only as much as absolutely necessary to learn through them about subjects that stimulated me to reproduce their most characteristic aspects for myself. In this I was particularly attracted by Greek, because the stories from Greek mythology seized my imagination so strongly that I wanted to imagine their heroic figures speaking to me in their original tongue, in order to satisfy my longing for complete familiarity with them. Under these circumstances it can easily be imagined that the actual grammar would only be considered a tiresome obstacle and not an academic subject with its own attraction. That I was never very thorough with my language studies probably explains why it was so easy for me to drop them later. It was not until a much later period that I gained an authentic interest in the study of languages, when I grasped their physiological and philosophical aspects, as revealed to modern Germanic scholars by the pioneer work of Jacob Grimm. As it was then too late for me to dedicate myself to a thorough study of a subject I had at last learned to appreciate, I can only regret that this new way of studying languages had not yet found acceptance in our grammar schools when I was younger. Nevertheless my successes in the philological field brought me the preferential attention of a young teacher at the Kreuz Grammar School, Magister Sillig. This man permitted me to visit him frequently and to

communicate to him my creations, which consisted of metrical translations as well as my own poems. My declamatory exercises seem to have
especially attracted him, and what he thought of me may best be judged
by the fact that I, a boy of about twelve at the time, was required to
recite from the lectern not only "Hector's Farewell" from the *Iliad* but
also even the famous soliloquy of Hamlet.

Once, when I was in the Third form, a classmate named Starke died
suddenly, and this event aroused so much sympathy that not only was
the entire class permitted to attend the funeral, but the headmaster also
commissioned a poem, which was to be published, to enhance the burial
ceremony. Of the various poems submitted, including one hastily drafted
effort of my own, none appeared to the headmaster worthy of the
intended distinction, so that he announced in advance his intention to
compose a speech himself to replace the rejected attempts. Much
distressed, I hurriedly went to see Magister Sillig to urge him to
intervene on behalf of my poem; we then went over it; the well-
constructed and well-rhymed eight-line stanzas induced him to revise
its contents carefully. The poem had contained an agglomeration of
strange images that went far beyond what a boy of my age could handle.
I remember that in one part I had drawn heavily on the monologue in
Addison's *Cato* spoken just before the protagonist's suicide, having come
upon this passage in an English grammar. The words "The stars shall
fade away, the sun himself grow dim with age, and nature sink in years",
which were lifted directly from that monologue, made Sillig smile,
somewhat to my discomfiture. Nonetheless I owed to the care and
celerity with which he knocked such excesses out of my poem that it
was finally accepted by the headmaster, actually published, and distributed in numerous copies.

The impact of this distribution among my classmates and in particular
on my family was extraordinary; my mother folded her hands devoutly,
and in my own mind my future profession seemed clear. Beyond
question I was destined to be a poet. Magister Sillig now wanted to see
me attempt a major epic poem, and suggested as material "The Battle
of Parnassus", after Pausanias. This was the legend that the Muses
themselves had descended from Parnassus in the second century B.C.
to aid the combined Greek armies against the marauding Gauls by
provoking a panic among them. I actually began an heroic epic in
hexameters but did not get beyond the first canto. Being not far enough
advanced in my studies to master the Greek tragedians in their own
language, I was greatly influenced in my imitative attempts by the

discovery of August Apel's[1] striking poetic efforts in this direction, in particular his *Polyïdos* and *Die Aitolier*. To these ends, I selected as material the death of Odysseus according to a fable of Hyginus, in which the aged hero is murdered by his son, the offspring of his union with Calypso. But I did not get very far with this work either.

From the direction my mind was taking it is obvious that I did not devote much zeal to ordinary scholastic work. Greek mythology, legend, and, finally, history were all that interested me. An outgoing sort, I was always lively in the company of my schoolmates and ready to participate in any sort of wild prank. At that time, I was constantly forming almost passionate friendships with one or another of my comrades. My rapidly changing selection depended mainly upon the extent to which they could go along with my fantastic hobbies. It could be poetizing and versifying, or else theatrical undertakings, or even just the inclination to ramble around and be up to some mischief. Besides, now that I had reached my thirteenth year, a considerable change took place in my family life; my sister Rosalie, who had meanwhile become the bread-winner, obtained an advantageous engagement at the theater in Prague, and my mother and the rest of the family moved there in 1826 and gave up our Dresden home entirely. I alone was left behind to be able to complete without interruption my courses at the Kreuz Grammar School up to the point of being ready for the university. For this purpose, I was deposited for room and board with the Böhme family, whose sons were school-friends of mine and in whose house I had already felt quite at home. The period I spent in this rather rough, not very well off, and loosely disciplined family represents the beginning of my salad days. I no longer enjoyed the repose needed for concentrated work nor the gentler imaginative impulses produced by association with my sisters. In their place came turbulence, scrimmaging, and quarrelsomeness. On the other hand it was here that I began to feel the charm of the female sex in a previously unknown way; grown-up daughters and their friends often filled the shabby, narrow rooms. My first recollections of falling in love in a boy's way date from this period. I recollect a very beautiful, well-bred young lady named Amalie Hoffmann, if I am not mistaken, coming in immaculate dress to pay one of her rare Sunday visits, whose entrance struck me with such amazement that for a long time I was bereft of speech. On other occasions, I remember pretending to be in a state of stupified sleepiness in order to induce the girls to carry me to bed, as I had noticed to my excited surprise that their attention in similar circumstances brought me into delightfully intimate contact with the female being.

16

The most important event in this year of separation from my family, however, was the visit I paid them in Prague. In the middle of winter my mother came to Dresden to take me back with her for a week. Traveling with my mother was a wholly unusual experience: to the end of her life she preferred an adventurous trip with a hired carriage to a quicker trip with the mail coach. To get from Dresden to Prague we were underway in bitter cold for three full days. Passing over the Bohemian hills often seemed to involve outright danger, and after happily surviving the most exciting perils we finally arrived in Prague, where I found myself suddenly transplanted into an entirely different world. For a long time, my visits to Bohemia, and particularly Prague, from Saxony exercised a poetic charm upon me. The foreign nationality, the broken German that the people spoke, the curious headgear of some of the women, the native wine, the girls playing the harp and other musicians, and finally the ubiquitous signs of Catholicism, the many chapels and pictures of saints, always combined to produce a strangely exhilarating impression, no doubt in large part allied to my love for the theater as opposed to bourgeois everyday life. Above all the ancient magnificence and beauty of the incomparable city of Prague itself made an ineradicable imprint on my mind. And in my family surroundings as well I found things completely new to me. For instance my sister Ottilie, only two years older than I, had gained the intense friendship of a family from the nobility, that of Count Pachta.[1] Two of his daughters, Jenny and Auguste, who were counted for a long time among the outstanding beauties in Prague, had taken her to their hearts with fervent fondness. Such creatures and such a relationship were entirely new and enchanting to me. Moreover, some of the city's leading beaux esprits, among them W. Marsano, a splendidly handsome and affable man, found their way to our house. They often heatedly discussed Hoffmann's tales, which were then still fairly new and of great interest. I got my first, rather superficial impression of this master of fantasy at the time and conceived an interest which over the years grew to a mania and caused me to adopt the most eccentric way of looking at the world.

In the following spring of 1827, I repeated my visit from Dresden to Prague, this time making the trip on foot and in the company of my friend, Rudolf Böhme. The journey was full of adventures; we got within an hour of Teplitz on the first night but owing to sore feet had to proceed by carriage the next day, though only as far as Lowositz, where we completely ran out of money. Under a burning sun, hungry and half-fainting, we roamed along by-paths through entirely unknown terrain until at evening we again reached the main road, just at the moment when an elegant traveling carriage came upon us. I mastered myself sufficiently to pretend to be a traveling journeyman and to ask its illustrious occupants for alms, while my friend hunched timorously in the roadside ditch. For a place to spend the night we elected to try our luck in a welcoming wayside tavern, where we debated whether to spend the money we had just received on supper or bed: we decided upon supper, with the intention of camping in the open for the night. While we were enjoying the refreshments a bizarre wanderer entered: he was wearing a black velvet beret with a metal lyre pinned on as a cockade and had a harp on his back. He unloaded this instrument in good humor, settled down comfortably, and demanded something good to eat, intending to spend the night before proceeding onward to Prague, where he lived and to which he was returning from Hanover. The jovial character of the fellow, evidenced by his use of a favorite motto, "non plus ultra", at every opportunity, aroused my approval and trust: the acquaintanceship was soon struck up and my good wishes were reciprocated by the itinerant musician in a display of almost tender affection. We decided to march off together on our way the following day; he lent me two twenty-kreutzer pieces and let me enter our Prague address in his notebook. This little triumph delighted me enormously. My harpist became wildly merry: we drank a lot of Czernosek wine; he sang and played the harp like a madman, uttered his "non plus ultra" continually, and finally sank down stupefied on the straw spread on the floor for our communal bed. When the sun shone in on us he was immune to being awakened, and we had no choice but to start out bright and early in the morning, convinced that the sturdy fellow would overtake us sometime during the day. Yet we looked in vain for him on the route that day, as well as during our stay in Prague: it was only several weeks later that this strange fellow turned up at my mother's, less for the purpose of demanding repayment of his loan than to find out how his young friends were, whereupon he showed himself quite disconsolate to learn that we were no longer there.

The remainder of our tramp tried our young legs severely. My joy when we first glimpsed Prague from a hill at about an hour's distance was indescribable. As we approached the outskirts we met yet another luxurious carriage: from within came the surprised greeting of my sister Ottilie's two charming friends; they had recognized me immediately, despite the ravages of a sunburn and my blue linen blouse together with a bright red cotton cap. Shamefaced and with a thumping heart, I could hardly get out a word and rushed onward in order to get to my mother's house and begin above all to restore my incinerated complexion. I spent two whole days at this task, during which I kept my face continually poulticed with parsley. Thereafter, I could again devote myself to worldly pleasures. When I looked back on Prague from the same hill on the return journey, I dissolved in tears, threw myself on the ground, and could not be persuaded by my astonished friend to go on for some time. I remained solemn and there were no adventures en route this time.

I indulged my liking for long excursions on foot once again that year by accompanying a large group of schoolboys of different classes and ages that had decided to undertake a communal ramble to Leipzig during the summer vacation. This journey also stands out vividly among my memories of youth. The chief characteristic of this group consisted in our pretending to be much more advanced than we were; we postured and clothed ourselves like college students. After getting as far as Meissen by boat, we left the main road and tramped through a number of little villages yet unknown to me. In the village tavern of one such place, where we slept in a large barn after making merry, we discovered a large marionette show with puppets nearly life-sized. Of course we all plunked ourselves down in front of the stage and thereby caused the presenters great embarrassment, as the show was intended only for an audience of peasants. They were playing *Genovefa*;[1] the unceasing jokes, catcalls and jeering interruptions our smart-alecky corps of would-be students permitted itself finally aroused the displeasure of the rustic audience, which had come in order to be moved by the piece. I think I was the only one among us who found our impertinence painful, and despite involuntary laughs at the witticisms of my companions, nonetheless defended the play as well as the simple public for which it was originally intended. One popular idiom used in the play has remained unforgettable to me: Golo, instructing the inevitable Kaspar how to treat the returning Count Palatine, emitted the order, "Tickle him in the rear so that he will feel it in the front"; Kaspar betrayed his commission word for word to the Count, who then reproached the unmasked villain with virtually the same words uttered with the greatest dramatic emotion: "O Golo, Golo! You have told Kaspar he should tickle me in the rear so that I would feel it in the front." From Grimma the youthful party rode on into Leipzig in an open carriage, not without having previously removed all emblems of student status out of fear of being roughly handled for our presumption by the real students we might meet.

Since my first visit, when I was in my eighth year, I had returned to Leipzig only briefly and in the same circumstances as the first time; the fantastic impressions left by the Thomé house had been renewed, but this time, owing to the more advanced state of my schooling, I was already able to establish a more intelligent relationship with my Uncle Adolf. The occasion was provided by my joyful astonishment upon learning from him that the bookcase in his large anteroom, with its collection of volumes from my father's estate, belonged to me. I went through all the books with my uncle, immediately selected a number of Latin authors in the handsome Zweibrücken edition, together with other attractive-looking poetic and belletristic works, and arranged for them to be sent to Dresden. During this latest visit I was particularly interested in studying the characteristics of the students themselves. To my impressions of the theater and of Prague was now added another fabulous element by what was then termed student braggadocio. A tremendous change had taken place in their behavior. When I had first seen college students as a boy of eight, I had been vividly struck by their old-German costumes, with black velvet berets, long hair, and shirt collars flopping outward round bare necks. Since then the old student associations affecting these fashions had vanished in the wake of political persecution, and in their place the no less typical clubs representing the different German states were now flourishing. The costumes of the club members reflected even exaggeratedly the prevailing fashions; but they were clearly distinguishable from all other classes by a certain gaudiness and by display of the various club colors. The "Code", that compendium of pedantic rules of conduct for preservation of the defiantly exclusive esprit de corps against the townspeople, had its bizarre aspects, as do, at bottom, the most philistine traits of the Germans in general. For me it represented the idea of emancipation from school and family. My longing to become such a student unfortunately coincided with a growing distaste for the drier aspects of academic work and an increasing infatuation with the more bizarre types of literary emanation. The results were soon evident in my stubborn attempts to change my situation.

By the time I was confirmed at Easter in 1827, I had a rather desolate view of this ceremony and felt a noticeable diminution of my reverence for church rituals. The boy who had gazed with painful longing at the altarpiece of the Kreuzkirche only a few years before, yearning to take the place of Our Saviour on the cross, had by now lost his respect for the clergyman whose confirmation classes he attended, being inclined to make fun of him, and even joining a conspiracy of classmates to withhold a part of the collection money intended for him and squander it on sweets. How I really felt, however, was revealed to me, almost to my own dismay, when I walked with fellow confirmands in procession to the altar, and choir, organ, and singing burst forth at the partaking of holy communion. The shudder of emotion with which I received the bread and wine remained so unforgettable to me that in order not to spoil this impression I never again went to communion, which was easy for me because such participation is not compulsory among Protestants.

Soon thereafter, I used a rather far-fetched pretext to force a breach with the Kreuz Grammar School, in order to compel my family to allow me to return to Leipzig. In protest against what appeared to me an unjust punishment meted out by Rector Baumgarten-Crusius, for whom I otherwise had great respect, I pretended to him that I had received an unexpected summons to join my family in Leipzig, in order to procure permission to leave the school immediately. I had already left the Böhme household three months before and was living alone in a garret, where I was cared for by the widow of a court silver-washer, who provided me with virtually my only nourishment in the form of a constant supply of the characteristically thin Saxon coffee. In this garret, I did nothing but write verses and also began there a stupendous tragic play, which later caused my family consternation. The irregular habits I had acquired in this premature domestic independence induced my anxious mother to agree readily to my transfer to Leipzig, all the more so because a part of our widely scattered family had again landed there.

My longing for Leipzig, originally aroused by the fantastic impressions I had received there, and abetted by my enthusiasm for student life, had recently been stimulated still further. My sister Luise, then a girl of twenty-two, had been until then almost unknown to me, as she had gone into the theater in Breslau shortly after the death of my stepfather. A short while before, however, she had come through Dresden for a few days on her way to Leipzig, where she had accepted an engagement at the theater. My meeting with this unknown relative, her tender and delicate demonstrations of pleasure at seeing me again, as well as her sprightly and cheerful character, made the most delightful impression on me. To live with her, whom my mother and Ottilie were also joining for a time, seemed very alluring. For the first time one of my sisters showed some affection for me. When I arrived there at Christmas of the same year (1827) and found my mother together with Ottilie and Cäcilie (my stepsister), I was in the seventh heaven. But a great change had already taken place. Luise had become engaged to the respected and well-to-do bookseller Friedrich Brockhaus. This foregathering of the relatives of his utterly impecunious bride did not seem to bother the exceptionally good-natured bridegroom and husband, as he soon became; yet it may well have been the circumstance which began to worry my sister, who soon showed herself to me in a less endearing light. The need to establish herself in higher social circles led furthermore to a noticeable change in the behavior of my sister, formerly so merry and impulsive, of which in the course of time I became aware, causing such bitterness in me that on one occasion at a later date I broke with her completely for a time. But alas I soon gave good grounds for that criticism of my conduct which so offended me. The collapse of my studies and my complete turnabout from the path of formal academic training dates from my arrival at Leipzig, and the arrogantly pedantic system of instruction may have been to blame for it.

There are two advanced secondary schools in Leipzig: the older one, St Thomas', and the other and more modern, St Nicholas'. The latter at that time enjoyed a better reputation than the former; accordingly, I had to try to get into it. But the board of admissions, before whom I appeared early in 1828 to take an examination, thought it more in keeping with the dignity of their school to place me, who had already reached the Fifth form at the Kreuz School in Dresden, in the Upper Fourth form for a time. My disgust at having to lay aside Homer, of whom I had already produced a written translation of twelve books, in order to take up again the easier Greek prose writers, was indescribable and wounded me deeply. I henceforth comported myself in such a manner as never to win the friendship of a teacher at this school. The hostile treatment I was accorded in return made me even more stubborn, as new factors in my development reinforced this attitude. While the student life I saw unfolding day by day before my eyes filled me for now with an ever increasing love of rebellion for its own sake, I found yet another and more serious motive for despising scholastic pedantry. By this I mean the influence of my uncle Adolf Wagner, who for a long time remained unaware of it, yet whose company became tremendously significant for the curious education of the maturing adolescent.

The fact that my bizarre inclinations were not merely caused by a desire for superficial amusement was shown by the zeal with which I attached myself to this learned relative. Admittedly, he was highly winning in conversation and manner; his manifold knowledge, which embraced not only philology but also philosophy and belles lettres with equal warmth, made his conversation extremely appealing, as many people freely conceded. On the other hand, the fact that he was denied the gift of writing as winningly, or even with adequate clarity, was one of the curious imperfections of this man, which markedly weakened his impact on the literary world, and at times even subjected him to ridicule on account of the incomprehensible and pompous sentences which were to be found in his occasional polemical writings. This weakness did not, however, frighten me away, because for one thing I was in the thick of a murky period of my own development in which literary bombast appeared to me all the deeper if I could not understand it, and because, in the second place, I conversed much more with my uncle than I read of his works. He too appeared to enjoy the company of the ardently attentive boy. Unfortunately, he forgot in the fervor of his discourses, which perhaps he delivered with a certain self-satisfied zeal, that he went far beyond my youthful powers of comprehension, both in substance and in manner of expression. Every day I picked him up for his afternoon constitutional around the gates of the city. I imagine that we frequently provoked the amusement of passers-by, who overheard our profound and frequently heated discussions. The subject was essentially everything serious and exalted in the realm of knowledge. His huge library had excited me to feverish reading in all directions, so that I jumped avidly from one area of literature to another, without achieving a basic grounding in any of them. My uncle was delighted to find in me a very willing listener for his readings of classical tragedies, having himself begotten a translation of *Oedipus the King*; for he could justifiably flatter himself, in the opinion of his good friend Tieck, with being a superb reader. I remember once, when the two of us were alone and he was sitting at his lectern reading from a Greek tragedy, that, far from being annoyed when I fell fast asleep, he afterwards pretended not to have noticed it. The evenings spent with him also brought me friendly and comforting hospitality on the part of his wife. Since my earliest acquaintance with my uncle in the Thomé house his life had undergone a significant change. The haven he and his sister Friederike had then been accorded by his friend seems to have entailed a number of irksome obligations as time went on. As his literary work assured him a modest income, he eventually found it more consonant with his dignity to establish a household of his own. A lady friend of comparable age, sister of the not unfavorably regarded aesthetician Wendt[1] of Leipzig, was selected by him to be mistress in his own house. Without saying a word to Jeannette, instead of going for his usual afternoon walk he went off to church for a hastily arranged marriage ceremony with his chosen bride, announcing upon his return that he would be leaving and would have his things out of the house by nightfall. He managed to meet the consternation and perhaps also the reproaches of his older friend with quiet composure, and to the end of his life continued his daily visits to "Mamselle Thomé" who continued to sulk coyly from time to time. Only poor Friederike seems to have been obliged to atone at times for the unexpected inconstancy of her brother.

What attracted me most strongly in my uncle was his blunt yet still humorously expressed contempt for the modern pedantry of state, church, and school. While his other views on life were quite moderate, he nonetheless impressed me as a truly free spirit. I was transported by his loathing for academic pedantry. One day, when I had gotten into serious trouble with the faculty of the St Nicholas' School and the rector himself had directed a grave complaint about my behavior to my uncle as the only male representative of my family, he asked me very casually and with a smile during one of our communal walks around the town, as if addressing someone of his own age, what I had against the people at the school: I explained the case to him and told him about the punishment to which I was condemned and which I considered unjust. He calmed me down and exhorted me to be patient, telling me to console myself with the Spanish proverb, "Un rei no puede morír", which he construed as meaning that the monarch of a school must necessarily always be in the right.

Sooner or later, or course, he could not help noticing to his alarm the effect upon me of this kind of conversation, which I was far too young to grasp fully. Although I had been annoyed one day to be told, when I wanted to take up Goethe's *Faust*, that I would not yet be able to comprehend it, nonetheless our lengthy discussions of great poets, even of Shakespeare and Dante, had made me, in my opinion, so familiar with these noble paragons that for some time I had secretly been busy writing the great tragic drama I had conceived in Dresden. After falling out with the school, I devoted to the accomplishment of this task all the energies that should have gone into my schoolwork. In this secret activity I had only one accomplice, my sister Ottilie, who now lived with me at our mother's. I remember the misgivings and alarm which my first confidential communication of this great poetic undertaking caused in my good-hearted sister; she nevertheless willingly endured the ordeals to which she was subjected by my reciting to her, clandestinely but by no means without emotional emphasis, portions of my work as it progressed. Once, while I was reading her one of the most gruesome scenes, a heavy thunderstorm broke out: when lightning struck in our neighborhood and the thunder crashed, my sister felt bound to implore me to stop; yet she soon discovered the impossibility of convincing me to do so and endured it with touching devotion to the end.

Far more ominous storm clouds were now gathering on my life's horizon. My neglect of school reached the point that it would certainly lead to expulsion. While my mother had no presentiment of the approaching catastrophe, I awaited it with longing rather than with fear. To meet this crisis with dignity I finally decided to surprise my family by disclosing the recent completion of my tragedy. They were to be made aware of this great event by my uncle; I thought I could rely upon his cordial recognition of my predestined greatness as a poet as a result of our wide areas of agreement in all the important aspects of life, knowledge, and art. I therefore transmitted my voluminous masterpiece to him along with a comprehensive letter, in which I communicated my unshakable intention not to allow my free development to be hampered by academic pedantry one day longer, feeling certain that he would be vastly pleased by this announcement. It turned out differently. It was a great shock. My uncle, fully aware of his own guilt in the matter, paid a visit to my mother and my brother-in-law in order to excuse himself for what would perhaps be regarded as his pernicious influence by reporting about the misfortune that had thereby befallen the family. To me he wrote a serious letter of reproof, and to this day I cannot understand why he showed so little humor in his verdict on my aberration, for he concentrated exclusively on his own sense of guilt for driving me to such eccentricity by our incongruous association, without attempting at all to set me straight as to where I had gone wrong.

The crime the fifteen-year-old boy had committed was, as I said, a vast tragic drama entitled *Leubald und Adelaïde*.

The manuscript* of this piece has unfortunately been lost,[1] but I can still see it clearly before me: the calligraphy was stylized to the highest degree: the high letters, bent diagonally backwards in order to lend a distinctive patina to the whole thing, had been compared by one of my teachers to Persian cuneiform. In this work, I had put together a drama to which Shakespeare, principally through *Hamlet*, *Macbeth*, and *Lear*, and Goethe, through *Götz von Berlichingen*, had contributed. The plot was essentially a variation of *Hamlet*; my alteration consisted in the fact that my hero, upon the appearance of the ghost of a father murdered in similar circumstances and calling for vengeance, is galvanized into

---

* Note in the margin of the manuscript, in Cosima's hand: "Interruption due to Schnorr's death (July 21st 1865). Reprise au commencement de Novembre."

immediate action and goes mad after a series of murders. Leubald, whose character was a mixture of Hamlet and Hotspur, has sworn to his father's spirit to exterminate the clan of Roderich (such was the name of his goodly father's ruthless slayer). After he has killed this Roderich, then his sons, and finally all other partners in crime among his relatives in this wild vendetta, there remains only one obstacle to the fulfillment of his fondest wish, which is to be united with the shade of his father in death: one child of Roderich still lives. The daughter of the miscreant has been carried away to safety during Leubald's storming of the castle by a faithful suitor whom she, however, detests. I was inspired to call this girl Adelaïde. As even at that early age I leaned toward things purely teutonic, I can only explain my choice of the palpably un-Germanic name of my heroine by my enthusiasm for Beethoven's *Adelaïde*, whose sentimental refrain struck me as the ultimate evocation of love. The rest of my drama was concerned with strange delays in the accomplishment of this last but necessary propitiatory murder, the main difficulty consisting of a prompt and fiery love affair between Leubald and Adelaïde. I succeeded in representing the nascence and avowal of this love in the most extraordinarily adventurous circumstances. Adelaïde has been again abducted from the suitor sheltering her by a robber knight. After Leubald has immolated the first suitor, together with all his family, he heads for the abductor's castle, by now driven less by thirst for blood than by longing for death. Thus he deplores being unable to storm the castle at once, night having fallen and the castle being well situated for defense; he has to pitch a tent; after some further ravings he finally collapses in exhaustion; just as in *Hamlet* his father's ghost appears and urges him to fulfill the vow of vengeance, when suddenly his enemy makes a nocturnal attack and takes him prisoner. In the subterranean dungeons of the castle he meets the daughter of Roderich for the first time, also a prisoner but craftily preparing her escape, who strikes him under these circumstances as a heavenly vision. They fall in love, flee into the wilderness, and recognize one another as mortal enemies. The incipient insanity, already noticeable in Leubald earlier, breaks out all the more violently after this discovery; whatever can be done to intensify it is effected by the father's ghost, who interrupts the lovers unceasingly. But it is not his spirit alone that disturbs the conciliatory love between Leubald and Adelaïde: the ghost of Roderich also makes an appearance, and according to the method adopted by Shakespeare in *Richard III*, he is joined by the ghosts of all the other members of the clan slaughtered by Leubald. Hard-pressed by all these aggressive spirits, Leubald seeks to protect himself by enlisting the services of a debauched villain called Flamming and resorting to sorcery. One of Macbeth's witches is summoned to dispel the ghosts: as she fails to bring this off, the enraged Leubald sends her to her reward, but not before she has dispatched the whole crowd of spirits serving her to join those already pursuing him. Tormented beyond endurance, Leubald now finally turns in direst madness upon his beloved, the apparent cause of all this misery. He stabs her in his frenzy, finds himself suddenly at peace, sinks his head in her lap, and enjoys her last caresses while her life-blood streams over their dying bodies.

I can guarantee having omitted nothing that could give this material the most manifold coloration; nothing I had gathered from tales of chivalry, nor anything I had garnered from *Lear* and *Macbeth*, was left out in my attempt to furnish my drama with evocative scenes. One of the main ingredients of my poetic fancy I owed to Shakespeare's mighty diction, emotional and humorous. The boldness of my grandiloquent and bombastic expressions particularly upset and amazed my uncle Adolf. He could not imagine how I could have taken only the most extravagant forms of speech to be found in *King Lear* and *Götz von Berlichingen* and used them with the most incredible exaggeration. There remained to me, even after everybody had deafened me with their reproaches about my wasted time and perverted talent, a marvelous inner consolation in the face of the calamity having befallen me: I knew what no one else could understand, namely that my work could only be judged rightly when provided with the *music* I had now decided to write for it and which I intended to start composing immediately.

I must now go back and trace from the beginning what had happened to me with respect to music.

In our family two of my sisters were musical: Rosalie, the eldest, played the piano without getting very far with it; Klara, on the other hand, was more gifted and along with a good musical sense and a lovely warm tone at the piano, possessed a beautiful voice, which developed so precociously and significantly that my sister, trained by the then well-known voice teacher Mieksch,[1] appeared ready even before completing her sixteenth year to be a prima donna, as which she made her debut at the Italian opera in Dresden as Cenerentola in Rossini's opera of the same name. Incidentally, this premature development proved injurious to her vocal organ and the poor girl suffered for it for the rest of her life. As I have said, music was represented in our family by these two sisters. It was Klara's career, though, that brought Kapellmeister

Carl Maria von Weber to our house for repeated visits. His visits were interspersed with those of the fabulous male soprano Sassaroli; in between these two representatives of German and Italian music were sandwiched some visits by the voice teacher Mieksch. On such occasions I heard as a child my first discussion of German as opposed to Italian music and gathered that whoever wished to win the favor of the Court would have to cast himself in the Italian mould, a fact that had very practical impact on our family councils. Klara's talent, as long as her voice remained intact, was the object of a tug-of-war between German and Italian opera. I remember well being a partisan of German opera from the beginning; perhaps the stark contrast between the figures of Sassaroli and Weber influenced me in this respect. The Italian soprano, a monstrous, pot-bellied colossus of a man, terrified me by his very high feminine voice, by his astonishing volubility, and by his incessant screeching laughter. Despite his good humor and popularity, particularly in my family, he was profoundly antipathetic to me; to hear Italian spoken and sung struck me as the diabolical work of this spectral instrument, and after my sister's misfortune, when I heard them often talking about Italian intrigues and cabals, I conceived such a strong dislike for things Italian that even many years later I would get carried away by passionate abhorrence as a result. Weber's rare visits, on the other hand, seem to have produced in me those feelings of ineradicable sympathy I would keep for a lifetime. As opposed to Sassaroli's repulsive figure, Weber's utterly refined, delicate and spiritual appearance filled me with ecstatic admiration. His narrow, exquisite face with the sparkling yet often half-closed eyes captivated me irresistibly; his heavy limp, which I often observed from my window when the maestro went by our house on the way home for lunch from the morning's exhausting rehearsals, marked in my mind the great composer as an exceptional, super-human being. When my mother once introduced the nine-year-old boy to him, and he asked what I wanted to become and hinted that it might even involve music, my mother said that, while I was wild about *Der Freischütz*, she had nevertheless noticed nothing in me that might suggest a talent for music. In this she had observed quite accurately: nothing moved me more strongly than the music of *Freischütz*, and I tried in many ways to reproduce the effect it had on me, but curiously enough least of all by formal study of music. I was content to listen to excerpts from *Freischütz* played by my sisters. Yet in time the passion for this music grew so strong that I recall befriending a younger fellow named Spiess solely because he could play the overture to *Freischütz*, which I demanded he do whenever we met. It was the beginning of the overture in particular that finally drove me to the point of trying, even without any previous instruction on the piano, to play this piece for myself. For, surprisingly enough, I was the sole member of the family who had received no piano lessons, a fact no doubt attributable to my mother's anxious desire to keep me away from any exercises that could stimulate a love for the theater. When I was about twelve my mother nonetheless engaged a teacher by the name of Humann for me, from whom I received some actual but scanty training. Equipped with the most rudimentary knowledge of fingering, I pressed forward immediately to practising four-handed transcriptions of overtures, of which those of Weber remained the target of my ambition. When I had finally gotten far enough to play the *Freischütz* overture, if only haltingly, all by myself, I considered the purpose of my training fulfilled and saw no reason to devote further efforts to perfecting my piano-playing. Yet, I had learned enough to be no longer dependent for music on the playing of others; and from now on I tried to play in my seriously flawed way any piece with which I wanted to become familiar. Thus, I tried this also with Mozart's *Don Giovanni*, without yet being able to get much out of it, particularly because the Italian text in the piano transcription placed the music in a frivolous light, and much of it seemed to me trifling and unmanly. (I remember that whenever my sister sang Zerlina's arietta "Batti, batti, ben Masetto" the music repelled me, as it seemed so mawkish and effeminate.)

On the other hand my inclination to busy myself with music grew stronger and stronger, and I now sought to master my favorite pieces by transcribing them. I remember my mother's hesitation when she first had to give me money to buy music paper, on which I copied *Lützows Jagd* by Weber as my first piece of transcription. Music still remained a secondary occupation with me, however; yet I recollect that the news of Weber's death and the longing to know his music for *Oberon* fanned my enthusiasm into flame once more. This feeling was particularly nourished by the afternoon concerts in Dresden's Grosser Garten, where Zillmann's town band often performed my favorite music, with great virtuosity as I thought. The mysterious joy I felt at hearing an orchestra play from close up remains with me as a voluptuous memory to this day: even the orchestra's tuning up excited me fantastically: I remember particularly that the striking of fifths on the violin struck me as a greeting from another world – which incidentally had a very literal meaning for me. When I was still scarcely beyond infancy the sound of these fifths had been associated with the ghosts and spirits that had always excited me. I remember in later years never passing by the small palace of Prince Anton[1] at the end of the Ostallee[2] in Dresden without a shudder: in this area I had heard at close quarters a violin being tuned, the sound appearing to emanate from the stone figures with which this palace is decorated, and among which some are provided with musical instruments. (It made a strange impression on me, upon taking up my post as conductor in Dresden, to pay a call on concertmaster Morgenroth, an elderly man who had lived for many years opposite this palace, and to find that the player of fifths who had so strongly impressed my musical fantasy as a boy was anything but a spectral creature.) And when I saw the well-known picture in which a skeleton plays the violin to a dying old man, the ghostly quality of these sounds imprinted itself all the more strongly on the child's fantasy. Now at last grown to boyhood, I luxuriated nearly every afternoon in the Grosser Garten around Zillmann's band, and one can imagine the voluptuous shudder with which I drank in all the various chaotic sounds to be heard when an orchestra is tuning up: the sustained A of the oboe, awakening the other instruments like a call from the dead, never failed to strain my nerves to fever pitch; and when the swelling C of the *Freischütz* overture announced to me that I had stepped with both feet into the magic realm of awe, anyone observing me at the time could hardly fail to see what the nature of my case was, despite my dismal piano playing.

Another work also attracted me just as strongly: it was the overture in E major to *Fidelio*, in which the introduction gripped me especially. I asked my sisters about Beethoven and learned that news of his death[3] had just been received. Still obsessed by the terrible grief caused by the death of Weber, this new loss of a great master who had just entered my life filled me with a strange anguish, a feeling somewhat akin to my childish dread of the ghostly fifths on the violin. I now wanted to learn more about Beethoven: I went to Leipzig and found on my sister's piano the music for *Egmont*; then I tried to get hold of some of his sonatas; finally I heard a symphony of the master for the first time at a Gewandhaus concert: it was the A major Symphony. Its effect on me was indescribable. On top of this came the added impact of Beethoven's physiognomy, as shown by lithographs of the time, as well as the knowledge of his deafness and his solitary and withdrawn life. There soon arose in me an image of the highest supernal originality, beyond comparison with anything. This image melded with that of Shakespeare: in ecstatic dreams I met both, saw and talked to them; upon awakening

I was bathed in tears. Of Mozart I now got to know the Requiem: that was the beginning of my enthusiastic absorption with this master, who with his finale to the second act of *Don Giovanni* now joined my pantheon of spirits.

Just as I had also tried to write poetry, I now had to try to learn to compose: because this involves some highly complex techniques, there were many more difficulties than in the verses I tossed off so lightly; and it was these difficulties that led to my career taking on the outward appearance of that of a "musician", and later, more particularly, the stamp of "Kapellmeister" and "opera composer".

I now wanted to write incidental music for *Leubald und Adelaïde*, like Beethoven's for *Egmont*; the various categories of ghosts belonging to my spirit world would first receive their distinctive coloring from the corresponding musical accompaniment. To learn about composition quickly enough to do this I resorted to a book of Logier's[1] entitled *Thorough-Bass*, which was recommended to me in a lending library as a suitable textbook from which the art of composition could be easily mastered. The money troubles that have plagued my life began here: I borrowed Logier's manual on a weekly payment system in the fond hope of getting away with only a few such payments to be spared from my pocket-money. But the weeks stretched into months, and I still couldn't compose the way I wanted. Herr Friedrich Wieck,[2] Robert Schumann's future father-in-law and the owner of the library, kept sending me troublesome reminders of the money I owed, and by the time the bill had approached virtually the purchase price of Logier's book I found it necessary to disclose this to my family, who now learned of my new aberrations in the field of music along with my financial calamity and naturally expected at the very most nothing better than a repetition of *Leubald und Adelaïde*. The consternation at home was very great: mother, sisters and brother-in-law consulted one another with pained expressions to figure out how to supervise my studies and prevent my continually getting off the track. But they did not as yet know the real state of affairs at school and consoled themselves with the hope that I would soon abandon this path just as I had abandoned poetry.

Moreover, other domestic changes were taking place which necessitated my being left alone in our Leipzig apartment and entirely to my own devices during the summer of 1829. During this time my musical ecstasies reached a particularly fantastic apogee. I had secretly been taking some lessons in harmony from a capable musician of the Leipzig orchestra, Gottlieb Müller (later organist in Altenburg): while the accrual of his hourly fees would one day cause further domestic embarrassments, I was not even able to compensate my teacher for the failure to pay him by pleasure at palpable progress in my studies. His teaching and exercises soon filled me with great disgust owing to what I considered their dryness. For me music was demoniacal, a mystically exalted enormity: everything concerned with rules seemed only to distort it. For more congenial instruction than that of my Leipzig teacher I looked to Hoffmann's *Fantasies*; and now came the time when I really lived and breathed in Hoffmann's contrived atmosphere of ghosts and spirits. With my head quite full of Kreissler, Krespel, and other musical phantoms created by my favorite author, I now arrived at the happy belief that I had discovered one such odd type in real life: this ideal musician, in whom I saw for a time no less than a second Kreissler, was a certain Flachs. A tall, extraordinarily thin man with a particularly narrow head and a highly eccentric manner of walking, talking, and getting about, he showed up at all the town concerts, which remained for me the principal source of my musical education. He always sidled up to the members of the orchestra, spoke in eccentric haste first to this one and then to that, seemed to be well acquainted with all of them and welcome company to boot. That they were all making fun of him I was to learn to my humiliation much later. I remembered that I had previously seen this strange fellow during my early days in Dresden, and gathered from conversations I overheard that he really was equally well acquainted with all the musicians in Dresden. This circumstance alone would have made him highly interesting for me; but beyond this I was carried away by observing his behavior while listening to music: a certain convulsive nodding of the head and puffing of the cheeks as though by sighs I interpreted as demonic ecstasy; since I also noticed that he was invariably alone and obsessed solely with the progress of the concert music, I had no difficulty in identifying this odd creature with Kapellmeister Kreissler. I was determined to make his acquaintance, and I succeeded. Who can describe my elation when I first made my way to his apartment and found there incredible piles of musical scores! I had never before seen a score. To be sure, I discovered to my sorrow that he possessed nothing by Beethoven, Mozart or Weber, but rather a vast agglomeration of masses and cantatas by such composers entirely unknown to me as Staerkel, Stamitz, Steibelt,[1] and so forth, of whom Flachs nonetheless could speak so glowingly that the respect I felt for scores in general helped me over the disappointment at finding nothing from my favorite masters. I learned later, however, that the worthy

Flachs had come into the possession of precisely these scores through exploitation of his feeblemindedness on the part of unscrupulous operators, who had unloaded this worthless musical material on him for good money. In short, he had scores and that was good enough for me. Flachs became my bosom companion; people saw the slight sixteen-year-old running around everywhere with the strangely wobbly flax-pole, and the doors of my home, where, for the time being, I lived alone, were opened for this unusual guest, who had to listen to me play my compositions for him while he ate bread and cheese, and who in return once arranged one of my arias for wind instruments, which to my astonishment was played by the band in Kintschy's Swiss Chalet. That he really didn't have a thing to teach me did not occur to me, so strongly was I convinced of his originality that to demonstrate it he needed do no more than listen patiently to my outpourings. But as in the course of time other companions of my friend joined us, I could not avoid getting the impression at last that most people treated him as a nitwit and a fool; yet this discovery saddened me at first, until an odd event suddenly converted me to the general view of him. Flachs had a little money and for this reason was in the clutches of a questionable young damsel, by whom Flachs felt himself deeply adored: suddenly I found his door closed to me, and was amazed to learn that this resulted from jealousy. The ominous quality of this relationship, my first experience of such a case, filled me with strange horror. I suddenly saw the madness of my friend in a more lurid light than the facts justified: but I was so ashamed at having been deceived so long that I stopped attending the town concerts for some time for fear of again getting near my false "Kreissler".

During this period I had composed a first sonata in D minor. I had also begun a pastoral, proceeding to work it out in what was surely an unprecedented way. Guided by Goethe's *Die Laune des Verliebten* as far as form and content were concerned, I drafted little more than a synopsis of the text and began writing the poetry together with the music and its instrumentation one page at a time, without even figuring out the text for the next page in advance. I remember succeeding in this fantastic way, without having acquired the slightest knowledge how to write for instruments, in putting together a really lengthy number that turned into a scene for three female voices, followed by an aria for a tenor. My inclination to write for orchestra was so intense that, after I procured for myself the score of *Don Giovanni*, I set about writing a soprano aria, for which I produced what I considered a very carefully instrumented

33

accompaniment. I also wrote a quartet in D major, after sufficiently mastering the alto clef of the viola, the ignorance of which had greatly complicated my study of a Haydn quartet a short time before.

Armed with these works, I ventured forth that summer on my first artistic excursion. My sister Klara, married to the singer Wolfram,[1] had an engagement at the Magdeburg theater: I prepared myself for a journey there on foot in the old familiar manner. My short stay with these relatives brought many musical experiences: I found there yet another odd type, whose impression on me has remained unforgettable. This was the music director Kühnlein,[2] a real character and also an extraordinary human being; already rather old, sickly, and unfortunately drunk most of the time, he was distinguished by the striking, ardent mode in which he expressed himself. His salient characteristic was Mozart worship, combined with passionate denigration of Weber. He read only one book, Goethe's *Faust*, and there was no page in this work upon which he had not scribbled something in transfiguring tribute to Mozart or in disparagement of Weber. My brother-in-law submitted my compositions to this man, in order to get a verdict about my abilities. One evening, when we were sitting comfortably in a tavern, old Kühnlein came in and approached us with solemn but friendly mien. I thought I could read good news from his countenance; my brother-in-law asked him what he thought of my work. "Utter rubbish" came the calm reply. Accustomed to Kühnlein's eccentricity, my brother-in-law burst out laughing, which reassured me somewhat. I couldn't extract from Kühnlein any clear grounds for his judgment and reproof, but rather only further disparagement of Weber and commendation of Mozart alone, which nevertheless impressed me, given the warmth with which he delivered these sentiments. On the other hand, this visit brought me a wonderful acquisition, which was to lead me far from the path of Kühnlein's teaching: this was the score of Beethoven's great E flat Major Quartet, which was then relatively new and of which my brother-in-law ordered me a copy. Enriched by these experiences and this treasure, I returned to Leipzig, the incubator of my bizarre musical studies, but this time was unable to prevent my family, now reunited with Rosalie there, from learning how things really stood with me at school.

A notice found its way to our house, in fact, stating that I had not shown myself at the school for more than half a year; after the complaints previously directed by the rector to my uncle had elicited no adequate response, the school authorities seem to have given up further attempts to supervise me, which I had indeed rendered impossible by absenting myself entirely. A fresh council of war was held in the family to figure out what to do with me. Since I earnestly asseverated my love of music, my relatives were of the opinion that I should at least learn an instrument: my brother-in-law Brockhaus suggested sending me to Weimar to Hummel, who would turn me into a pianist. But as I passionately declared that "music" meant "composition" to me and not "playing an instrument", they gave in and decided that I should take regular lessons in harmony from the same musician Müller, whose bill for the previous clandestine lessons still remained unpaid. In return I pledged to take up my studies at the St Nicholas' School once again. Both soon oppressed me, for I felt coerced by everything and everybody; and this was unfortunately also true of my musical studies, in which the aridities of harmonic theory disgusted me more and more, whereas I continued to conceive and execute sonatas, overtures, and fantasias. Yet I was still spurred by ambition to show what I could do at school if I liked: on one occasion, when we Fifth-formers were assigned to write a poem, I produced a chorus in Greek about the most recent war of liberation. I suppose that this poem bore the same relationship to Greek language and poetics as my sonatas and overtures of the time to music by someone who had thoroughly mastered its elements. At any rate, my attempt was scornfully rejected as effrontery. From that point on, I recall no further impressions of the school: continuing to attend was to me purely a sacrifice for the sake of my family; I paid not the slightest attention to whatever was going on in the classes but rather busied myself with reading whatever attracted me at the moment.

Because, as I mentioned, instruction in music also availed me nothing, I went on with the process of arbitrary self-education by copying the scores of the masters I loved, whereby I acquired the graceful handwriting so much admired in later life. As far as I know, my transcriptions of the C minor and the Ninth Symphony of Beethoven have been preserved to this day as souvenirs. This Ninth Symphony became the mystical lodestar of all my fantastic musical thoughts and aspirations. What first attracted me to it was the opinion, prevalent not only among the Leipzig musicians, that this work of Beethoven's had been written in a state approaching insanity: it was considered the "non plus ultra" of all that was fantastic and incomprehensible, and this was grounds enough to arouse in me an impassioned desire to investigate this demoniac phenomenon. On first looking through the score, which I obtained only with great difficulty, I was struck at once, as if by force of destiny, with the long-sustained perfect fifths with which the first movement begins:

these sounds, which played such a spectral role in my earliest impressions of music, came to me as the ghostly fundamental of my own life. This symphony surely held the secret to all secrets; and so I got busy over it by painstakingly copying out the score. Once, after having spent a night at this task, I remember being startled by the dawn, which affected me so strongly in my excited condition that I buried myself under the bedclothes with a loud shriek as if terrified by an apparition. There was as yet no transcription of this work for piano solo; it had made so little impact on the public that the publisher saw no need to issue one. I got to work and actually produced a complete piano transcription for two hands, which I then tried to play myself. I sent my work to Schott,[1] the publisher of the score, in Mainz; in response I received word that the firm had, to be sure, not yet decided to bring out a piano transcription of the Ninth Symphony, but that the product of my labors would be kept on file, and I was offered in return the score of the great *Missa Solemnis*, which I then accepted with great pleasure.

Apart from this work I tried for a time to learn the violin, as my harmony teacher quite rightly contended that some familiarity with the technique of this instrument would be indispensable to the future orchestral composer. Indeed, my mother paid a man named Sipp,[2] who as of this writing (1865) is still functioning as a member of the Leipzig orchestra, eight talers for a violin; I don't know what became of it in the end, but for three months I inflicted from my strange little room unheard-of tortures on my mother and sisters with it. I got far enough to play some Mayseder[3] Variations in F major, but only to the second or third: from that point on my memory of these exercises fails me, and fortunately my family, probably from self-interest, did not insist on my continuing them.

But the time now arrived when the theater again took passionate possession of me. A new company had been formed in my home town under very favorable auspices through the efforts of the Dresden Court Theater management, which had taken over the running of the Leipzig theater for a period of three years. My sister Rosalie had become a member of this troupe; through her I had easy access to the performances, and that which had been in my childhood only the object of overheated curiosity now became the subject of a thoroughly conscious passion. *Julius Caesar*, *Macbeth*, *Hamlet*, Schiller's plays, and at last Goethe's *Faust*, all excited and enthused me deeply. The opera was giving the first performances of Marschner's *Vampyr* and *Templer und Jüdin*. The Italian opera company arrived from Dresden and delighted the Leipzig audiences by the display of their virtuosity. I too was almost carried away by the excitement they brought to Leipzig to the point of forgetting the childhood impressions Signor Sassaroli had once made upon me, when yet another miracle also coming to us from Dresden suddenly gave a new direction to my artistic sensibility and one which was to prove decisive for a lifetime.

This was a brief appearance as guest star by Wilhelmine Schröder-Devrient,[1] who stood then at the pinnacle of her career, young, beautiful and ardent as no woman I have since seen on the stage. She appeared in *Fidelio*.

When I look back across my entire life I find no event to place beside this in the impression it produced on me. Whoever can remember this wonderful woman at that period of her life will certainly confirm in some fashion the almost demonic fire irresistibly kindled in them by the profoundly human and ecstatic performance of this incomparable artist. After the opera was over I dashed to the home of one of my friends to write a short letter in which I told her succinctly that my life had henceforth found its meaning, and that if ever she should hear my name favorably mentioned in the world of art, she should remember that she had on this evening made of me that which I now vowed to become. I dropped this letter at Schröder-Devrient's hotel and ran wildly off into the night. When I came to Dresden in 1842 to make my debut with *Rienzi* and could often visit the home of this artist, who was amiably disposed towards me, she once surprised me by reciting this letter word for word, for it appears to have made an impression on her, and she had actually preserved it carefully.

Nowadays I am sure that the great confusion which prevailed for a time at this period in my life and particularly in my work was caused by the inordinate impact this artistic phenomenon made on me. I did not know where to turn or even how to begin to produce anything remotely commensurable with the impressions I had received; and everything that did not measure up to them appeared to me so stale and unprofitable that I could not bother to concern myself with it. I wanted to write a work that would be worthy of Schröder-Devrient: but as that was by no means within my power I abandoned all artistic efforts in headlong despair, and because academic work could certainly not enlist my attention, I let myself go, living rudderless from day to day in the company of a strange crew of companions, and indulged in all sorts of youthful dissipations. Now began the typically dissolute period of callow youth, the outward ugliness and inward emptiness of which amaze me still. My contact with those of my own age had always been purely haphazard; I do not recall any special inclination or affection determining my choice of friends. Whereas I can state with certainty that jealousy of anyone with superior gifts never held me back, I can only attribute my indifference in the choice of companions to the fact that I had never experienced a meaningful relationship and only wanted to have someone who would accompany me on my excursions and to whom I could pour out my innermost feelings to my heart's content, without worrying what effect it might have on him. The result was that after a stream of confidences for which my own excitement was the only reward, I would at length reach a point when I would finally stop and look at my friend: to my astonishment I usually found that there was no possibility of a response at all, and whenever I tried to force something commensurate out of the friend, and thus to stimulate him to some communication that was quite outside his character, the relationship usually broke up permanently and without leaving a trace on my life. In a certain sense my odd relationship with Flachs typifies the bulk of all my later ties. As no lasting bond of personal friendship ever came into my life by these means, it is easy to explain why I became so infatuated with the crass student life, because there the personal note is entirely submerged in mass activity. In the midst of drunken hubbub I remained entirely alone; and it is possible that these frivolities formed a protective crust around my inmost being, which needed time to grow to its natural strength and not be weakened by being tapped too soon. My life seemed to splinter off into all directions: I had to leave the St Nicholas' School at Easter 1830, for I was too deeply in disgrace with the masters ever to hope to be promoted from there to the university. It was now decided that I should be tutored for six months, in order to rematriculate at the St Thomas' School, where I would be in new surroundings and would supposedly be able to qualify for the university in a short time. My uncle Adolf, with whom I was constantly renewing my friendship, and who also encouraged and supported my interest in music, kept arousing in me, despite the deep degradation of my life in this phase, renewed interest in serious studies. I took private lessons in Greek from a scholar and read Sophocles with him. For a time, I hoped that this noble subject would reawaken my desire to learn the Greek language thoroughly; but it was all in vain: I hadn't found the right teacher; and besides, the living room in which we pursued our studies looked out upon a tannery, whose disgusting smell affected my nerves badly enough to spoil Sophocles and Greek for me completely.

My brother-in-law Brockhaus wanted to give me the chance to earn a little pocket-money and entrusted me with the correction of proof sheets of his new edition of Becker's *Universal History*,[1] as revised by Löbell. This afforded me the opportunity to improve by private study upon the superficial instruction generally given on all subjects at school, and this is the way that I have continued throughout my life to acquire the rudiments of those branches of learning imparted so boringly in the classroom. I should not omit to mention that the attraction exerted by my initial study of history was also greatly enhanced by the eight groschen I earned per proof sheet, thereby putting me for the first time in what was to be a rare position in my life, that of earning money; yet I would be unjust to myself if I did not mention the vivid impressions I now received from close consideration of those historical epochs of which I had previously only scanty knowledge: Marathon, Salamis, and Thermopylae had constituted the bounds of what interested me. Now for the first time, I became intimately acquainted with the Middle Ages and the French Revolution, as I was proofing the two volumes dealing with these two different periods. I recall being truly appalled by the heroes of the French Revolution as described in this volume; without knowledge of the prior history of France my human sympathies alone were outraged by the atrocities of the revolutionaries, and I was dominated by these purely human sentiments for so long that even in later years it cost me a real struggle to give due weight to the true political significance of those acts of violence.

Imagine my surprise when one day current events suddenly gave me personal experience of the kind of national upheaval I had glimpsed previously only distantly from my proof sheets. Special editions of the *Leipziger Zeitung* brought us news of the July revolution[2] in Paris. The King of France[3] had been driven from his throne; Lafayette,[4] who had recently been flitting through my imagination like some historical fairy-tale, was now once again riding through cheering crowds in the streets of Paris; the Swiss Guards had once more been butchered in the Tuileries; a new king[5] found no better way of commending himself to the people than by proclaiming his republican sympathies. To become suddenly conscious of living in an epoch when such things were actually happening could not fail to make a strong impression on a boy of seventeen. The world of history came alive for me from that day on; and naturally I became a fervent partisan of the revolution, which I now regarded as an heroic, popular and victorious struggle, unstained by the terrible excesses of the first French revolution. Since the whole of

Europe, including some of the German states, was soon more or less in uproar, I remained for some time in a feverish state of suspense and became aware for the first time of the causes of such movements, which I interpreted as struggles between the old and outmoded and the new and hopeful elements in humanity. Saxony was not spared: in Dresden it even came to street-fighting, which led to immediate political changes, with the co-regency of the future King Friedrich and the granting of a constitution. I was so excited by this event that I sketched a political overture with an introduction depicting dark oppression, during which a theme emerged under which I wrote, to make it easier to understand, the words "Friedrich and Freedom": this theme was supposed to be developed ever more gloriously into a closing triumph, which I hoped to see materialize in one of the Leipzig Garden Concerts.

But before I was able to develop my musico-political ideas any further, disorders broke out in Leipzig itself and summoned me from the realm of art to direct participation in affairs of state. Affairs of state in Leipzig took the form of antagonism between students and police; the police were the arch-enemy against which the youthful love of liberty tested itself. Some students had been arrested in a street brawl: these were now to be freed. The undergraduates, who had been in a state of turmoil for some days, assembled one night in the market square; the national clubs got together and formed a circle around their leaders, the proceedings being marked by a certain measured solemnity that impressed me deeply: they sang *Gaudeamus igitur*, formed columns, and marched determinedly off, reinforced by all other young men who sympathized with them, heading for the university building to spring the arrested students from their cells there. My heart beat wildly as I marched with them to this storming of the Bastille. But it turned out differently: in the courtyard of the Paulinum the solemn procession was halted by Rector Krug,[1] who had come to meet it, his grey head bared; his assurances that the students had already been released by his intervention brought him thunderous applause, and the whole thing seemed settled and done.

But the tense revolutionary expectations had grown too great to do without some kind of victim. Suddenly a yell was heard, summoning us to a certain notorious back-street to go after a hated town councillor, who had supposedly been protecting a house of ill fame. When I got to the place at the tail end of the crowd I found the house had been broken into and all sorts of violence committed. I recall with horror the intoxicating effect of this unreasoning fury and cannot deny that, without the slightest personal provocation, I shared, as if possessed, in the onslaught of the students, who were madly shattering furniture and crockery. I do not believe that the ostensible motive for these excesses, supposedly residing in a menace to public morals, carried any weight with me; on the contrary, it was the purely demonic element in such mass outbursts that drew me into its vortex. The fact that such outbursts do not subside quickly but rather come to a characteristic end by degenerating into a frenzy I was to learn for myself. No sooner had another voice beckoned us to a different house of this sort than I found myself in a tide surging toward the opposite end of the city; the same heroic acts were performed there, and the most ludicrous depredations perpetrated. I do not recall that alcoholic beverages contributed to my intoxication, or that of my immediate companions; but I do know that I finally arrived at the condition that usually follows a drinking spree. On the following morning I awakened as if from a hideous nightmare only to be forcibly reminded that I had indeed taken part in the events of the prior evening by seeing the trophy, in the form of a tattered red curtain, which I had brought home as a token of my heroism. The fact that public opinion, and my family in particular, took a lenient view of these youthful escapades reassured me considerably: this youthful madness was attributed to righteous indignation at really serious scandals, and I was able to own up to my part in these excesses without diffidence.

The dangerous example set by the students, however, incited the lower classes, especially the workers, to indulge in similar depredations against factory owners and the like: now things got more serious: property was threatened, and a struggle of poor against rich stood grinning at our doors. It was the students who were now summoned to help against the proletariat, for Leipzig was without armed militia and its police utterly disorganized. Then began such a glorious time for the students as I had scarcely dared dream of in my schoolboy fantasies. The student became the guardian angel of Leipzig; convoked by the authorities and armed for the protection of property, these same young men who had yielded to a frenzy of destruction two days before now assembled in the university quadrangle. The otherwise tabooed names of the national clubs and student associations were now to be heard in the mouths of town councillors and police officials, summoning the young men, armed with their extraordinary equipment and drawn up in a naive medieval order of battle, to take their posts throughout the city, man the gates, and place detachments on the property of several rich businessmen and other seemingly threatened places, among which taverns became notably popular locations for this protective work. Unfortunately not yet a student myself, I anticipated the delights of academic status by half-impudent, half-obsequious importuning of those leaders of the student body I admired most. I had the good fortune to gain the favor of one of the ringleaders through my relationship with Brockhaus, on whose property the main body of these matadors were encamped for a time. My brother-in-law, too, had been seriously threatened; only by great presence of mind and strong nerves had he succeeded in protecting his printing plant, and particularly his high-speed presses which had been specifically earmarked for destruction. To defend his property against further attack student platoons were dispatched to his premises; the lavish hospitality dispensed by this liberal host in his comfortable garden pavilion to the merry crew of watchmen attracted the cream of the student corps; my brother-in-law was guarded day and night against any conceivable incursion by the rabble for several weeks, and there I celebrated a veritable saturnalia of my student ambition as the admired and honored middleman in the provision of this extravagant hospitality. For a still longer period the job of guarding the city gates was entrusted to the students; the spectacular flowering of the student body in these events lured other undergraduates from near and far; every day huge chartered vehicles unloaded hordes of the most foolhardy students from Halle, Jena, Göttingen, and even from the most distant provinces. They plunked themselves down at the city gates and for several weeks never set foot in an inn or any other house: they lived there at the expense of the town council, drew bills on the police for food and drink delivered to them, and knew only one anxiety, namely the possibility that things would calm down and their services would be no longer needed. I never missed a day on guard, and unfortunately not a night either, while I tried to convince my family of the necessity of such persistence. Of course, the quieter, serious students soon withdrew from these guard duties, and only the hard core remained so dedicated that it became difficult for the authorities to relieve them of their responsibilities. I stuck with it to the end, and made the most astonishing friends for my age. Many of the wildest characters stayed on in Leipzig even without any guard function and peopled the town with a quite extraordinary bunch of desperate and dissipated types, who had been expelled from various universities for rowdyism and bad debts and who now, thanks to the exceptional circumstances, had found a refuge in Leipzig, where they had been at first received with open arms.

In the midst of all this I felt as if an earthquake had upset the order of things. My brother-in-law Friedrich Brockhaus, who was entirely justified in accusing the previous authorities in Leipzig of inability to maintain peace and quiet, became involved in a formidable opposition movement. A bold speech he delivered to the members of the town council at city hall made him popular; he was named vice-commandant of the newly formed Leipzig Municipal Guard. This body soon ousted my adored students from the guard rooms at the town gates; we were no longer accorded the right to stop itinerant workers and inspect their passports; at the same time I flattered myself into comparing this new citizens' militia with the French Garde Nationale and considering my brother-in-law Brockhaus as a Saxon Lafayette, all of which nourished my characteristically overexcited state. I began to read the newspapers assiduously and get involved in politics; associating with members of the establishment, however, did not attract me sufficiently to abandon my student relationships; I followed them faithfully from the guard rooms to the taverns, to which they now repaired in all their glory.

My chief ambition was to become a student at last: this could only be effected by renewed matriculation at a secondary school. The St Thomas' School, under the rectorate of a feeble old man at the time, was the place where my wishes could be most speedily attained; I entered this school in the autumn of 1830 with the sole intention of qualifying myself to take the final examinations by merely nominal attendance there. My chief activity consisted in establishing, together with some like-minded friends among the schoolboys, a bogus student association. It was organized with all possible punctiliousness, "The Code" instituted, fencing practice and dueling provided for, and an inaugural meeting, attended by several of the more prominent students and at which I presided as co-chairman in white buckskin trousers and large jack-boots, gave me a foretaste of the delights of student life to come. The masters of St Thomas', however, were not quite so willing to fulfill my desire to become a university student; at the end of the semester they concluded that I had paid no attention whatever to their pedagogical efforts and were not to be convinced that I had earned a title to academic citizenship by any new accretion of knowledge. Things now had come to a head; I advised my family that I had decided not to take up a formal course of study at the university but rather had decided to become a musician. There was nothing to prevent my matriculating as a "Studiosus Musicae"; without further quibbling with the monarchs of St Thomas' School, I therefore defiantly left that seat of learning unplundered in

43

order to present myself forthwith to the rector of the university, whose acquaintance I had made during the night of the riot, for enrollment as a student of music, which was accordingly done without further ado upon payment of the usual fee.

I was in a great hurry; Easter vacation would begin in a week, and the students would be leaving Leipzig, making it impossible for me to be admitted as a member of a club until after the vacation. To be stuck in my home town of Leipzig all these weeks without having the right to wear the coveted club colors seemed to me an unendurable torment. Straight from the interview with the rector, I ran as if shot from a gun to the fencing club, to present myself for admission to the Saxon club, flashing my registration card. I attained my object: I could wear the colors of Saxonia, which were then highly fashionable owing to the many congenial members in the club's ranks.

The oddest things were to happen to me during this Easter vacation, when I was really the only member of the Saxon club remaining in Leipzig. Originally, this association consisted mainly of the nobility, to which had been added the more dandified members of the student body; they all belonged to the more distinguished and well-to-do families of Saxony and particularly of its capital, Dresden, and they spent their vacations at home. There remained in Leipzig only those wandering students without real homes, for whom it was either always or never vacation time. Out of these had been formed a quite unusual congregation of the wildest and most desperate young reprobates, who had found a last refuge, as I have said, in Leipzig during the days of glory. These hooligans had greatly struck my fancy and I had already made their personal acquaintance while they were guarding the Brockhaus grounds. Although the regular term of study at university did not exceed three years, most of these men had not seen their homes for six or seven years. I was particularly dazzled by a certain fellow named Gebhardt, a person of incomparable good looks and strength; his slim, heroic figure towered head and shoulders above his companions. When he walked down the street arm in arm with two of his strongest comrades, he would suddenly take it into his head to lift them high into the air by a casual spreading of his arms and flutter along in this way as if he had a pair of human wings. He once stopped a hansom cab proceeding at a sharp trot through the streets by grasping a wheelspoke with one hand. People carefully avoided letting him know he was dumb for fear of his power, and thus his limitations in this respect were scarcely noticeable. His redoubtable strength, combined with a rather gentle temperament, lent him a majestic dignity, placing him beyond comparison with other mortals. He had come to Leipzig from somewhere in Mecklenburg together with a certain Degelow; strong and agile, but by no means of such gigantic proportions as Gebhardt, Degelow was interesting above all for his vivacity and unusually lively physiognomy. He had led a wild and dissipated life, in which drink, gambling, wild love affairs, and a constant readiness for dueling constituted the changing canon. A mixture of a fiercely hot temper and an ironic and pedantic coldness, schooled by club ceremony and testifying to his bold self-confidence, formed the personality of this fellow and others akin to him. In Degelow this wildness and passion produced a curious diabolical charm through the malicious humor he often turned against himself, whereas he treated others with a certain chivalrous decorum. These two extraordinary men were joined by others who could be considered paragons of dissipation, though not without authentic and defiant bravery. A certain Stelzer, a true wild man out of the *Nibelungenlied* with the nickname "Lope", was already in his twentieth semester. Whereas these men, decidedly and in full awareness, belonged to a world doomed to destruction and acted as they did from the belief that their inevitable ruin was imminent, I met one man from their group named Schröter, who especially attracted me by his friendly demeanor, his winning Hanover accent, and his refined wit. He did not belong to the real desperadoes but rather maintained a certain calm distance, while remaining welcome and popular among them. I got to know Schröter quite well, despite his being considerably older: through him I was introduced to the books and poems of Heinrich Heine; from him I acquired a certain frivolous elegance of diction, and I was inclined to be guided by Schröter in hope of improving my outward bearing. It was his company in particular that I sought every day; I usually met him in Kintschy's Swiss Chalet or in the Rosenthal, but never without the company of those odd giants who excited my aversion and admiration alike. They all belonged to national clubs on hostile terms with the one of which I had become a member. What that meant is well known to those familiar with the temper of those times: the mere sight of enemy colors sufficed to kindle the rage of even the most placid fellows, if there had been some prior provocation. As long as these roughnecks were sober, at any rate, they would look with good-natured complacency on a young and diminutive person like me, even if festooned with such provocative colors. I wore these colors in a very special manner: I had made use of the brief week during which my club was still in Leipzig to gain possession of a splendid Saxon cap, richly embroidered with silver, which I had seen on the head of a certain Müller, later a prominent police official in Dresden, and which had filled me with such avidity to own that I had managed to buy it from him, as he needed money for his trip home. Despite this provocative cap I was, as I have said, welcome in the tigers' lair; my friend Schröter saw to that. Only when the grog, the main beverage of these wastrels, began to take effect did I notice ominous glances and overhear threatening remarks, against the understanding of which I protected myself for some time by the fuzziness into which my senses were plunged by these stiff drinks.

As I was bound to get involved in quarrels sooner or later by behaving this way, I was pleased that the first pretext for one arose from an incident that reflected more credit on me than that needling I had half ignored. One day, Degelow approached Schröter and me in a grog shop we frequented; in a not disrespectful manner he confidentially confessed to us his fondness for a young and very pretty actress, whose talent Schröter disputed; Degelow retorted that, whatever the case, he still considered this young lady the most respectable woman engaged at the theater. At once, I asked him whether he deemed my sister less respectable. According to the student code of honor, Degelow, who had not by the remotest stretch of the imagination intended an insult, could only reply by assuring me that he did not consider my sister less decent but that he had to stand by his assertion concerning the young lady in question. At this there followed without delay the standard declaration of war with the words: "You're a young fool" – which sounded almost ludicrous to my own ears in the face of this seasoned hooligan. I recall that the same thought involuntarily struck Degelow too and his eyes glinted; yet he pulled himself together in the presence of our friend, and proceeded to observe the usual formalities of a challenge, choosing sabers for the duel. This case caused a great stir among our companions: but I felt even less constraint than before to continue my usual association with them; on the contrary, I grew more attentive with regard to the deportment of these roughnecks, and for several days no evening went by without producing a challenge between me and one of the fearsome thugs, until finally the only member of my own club who had as yet returned to Leipzig, Count Solms, paid me a friendly visit, inquired about these happenings, praised my conduct, but nonetheless advised me not to wear my colors until the return of our fellow members after the vacation and to keep away from the bad company into which I had plunged myself. Fortunately I did not have long to wait; university life quickened and the fencing grounds filled up again. My horrendous situation, in which I was "hanging", to use the student expression, with half a dozen of the fiercest duelers, earned me wide repute among freshmen and sophomore members of Saxonia, and even among some of its seasoned members. My seconds were duly appointed, the dates for the various duels settled, and the necessary period of time accorded me, through the solicitude of my seniors, to acquire some rudimentary skill in fencing. The light-hearted spirit with which I viewed my impending destiny, my life itself sure to be threatened in at least one of the duels, remained a mystery to me even at that time. The way destiny preserved me from the consequences of my rashness strikes me as truly miraculous to this day and is worthy of closer description.

Preparing for a duel also involved getting to know what went on by being present at some of these events. We freshmen got to attend by serving as weapons bearers, being entrusted with the corps rapiers (precious ceremonial weapons that belonged to the club), taking them first to the grinder for sharpening and then to the appointed place for the duel, a function that entailed some risk because it had to be carried out in secret inasmuch as dueling was against the law: for this reason we earned the right to observe the ensuing duels as spectators. When I first performed these honors the dueling site was the billiard room of a tavern on the Burgstrasse; the table had been shoved aside and upon it the accredited spectators planted themselves: I stood high among them with a thumping heart, looking forward to the audacious and fearful proceedings. On this occasion I was told of one of my companions (a Jew named Levy but known as Lippert) who had been obliged at this very spot to give ground so rapidly before his opponent that a door had to be opened behind him, while he backed hastily out into the alley, still thinking he was dueling all the while. After several bouts had been settled, two men came onto the dueling ground – Tempel, the senior member of the Markomans, accompanied by a certain Wohlfahrt, an eternal student already in his fourteenth semester with whom I was also booked to fight at a subsequent date. Because in such cases a man was ordinarily not allowed to watch, in order that potential weaknesses of his future opponent would not be betrayed to him, Wohlfahrt was asked by my seniors whether he insisted on my removal from the room, whereupon he replied with calm disdain that such a greenhorn should in God's name be allowed to stay. Thus, I became a witness to the disabling of a duelist who proved such a skillful and doughty fighter that I would have been justified in the most pessimistic appraisal of the outcome of any combat I might have had with him. His gigantic opponent severed the artery of his right arm; the doctor pronounced Wohlfahrt unfit to bear arms for years to come, under which circumstances my prospective bout with him was necessarily canceled. I do not deny that this event filled me with considerable cheer.

Shortly thereafter the first general assembly of our club took place at the Green Alehouse. These gatherings are a great place for hatching duels; I brought another one upon myself with a certain Tischer, to be sure, but learned at the same time that I had been relieved of two of the most monstrous previous engagements of this kind by the disappearance of my opponents, who had fled without trace because of their debts. The only one I ever heard of again was the fearsome Stelzer, alias Lope; he had taken advantage of the stream of Polish refugees passing through Germany to France to disguise himself as one of the freedom fighters and found his way into the Foreign Legion in Algiers. On the way home from the assembly Degelow, with whom I was scheduled to "go at it" in a few weeks, proposed a truce by suspension, a device which, if accepted as in this case, enabled the future combatants to accompany and talk to one another, something which otherwise had to be strictly avoided. Locked arm in arm, we ambled back to town: with chivalrous delicacy my highly interesting and formidable opponent declared that he was delighted at the prospect of crossing swords with me in a few weeks, considering it an honor and a pleasure in view of his esteem for me and my staunch conduct. Seldom has any personal success flattered me more: we embraced and parted amid effusions which by their ceremonial gracefulness made an unforgettable impression on me. Degelow had let me know that he first had to go to Jena, where a challenge with the rapier awaited him. A week later news reached Leipzig of the death of Degelow, who had been fatally stabbed in that duel in Jena.

I felt as if in a dream, from which I was awakened by the announcement of my encounter with Tischer. This man, a capable and energetic fighter, had been selected by my seniors for my baptismal passage-at-arms because he was rather short. Without being able to rely very firmly on my hastily acquired and by no means thoroughly schooled fencing talent, I nonetheless looked forward to this first duel with a light heart. I had a slight rash at the time, and although people told me that it made wounds particularly dangerous, and though I was modest enough to expect some, it did not occur to me to postpone the duel, as the rules required. My appointment was for ten o'clock one morning and I left the house smiling, thinking what my mother and sisters would say when I was brought back a few hours later in the frightful condition I expected. When I arrived at his house on the Brühl, my senior, Herr von Schönfeld, a pleasant, placid young man, greeted me from the window, a pipe hanging from his mouth, with the words: "You can go home, little man: nothing will come of it. Tischer is in hospital." When I went upstairs I found some club leaders assembled, from whom I learned that Tischer had gotten hopelessly drunk the night before, had been disgracefully mishandled by occupants of a house of prostitution, and had been delivered with terrible wounds to the nearest hospital by the police, which would necessarily entail his rustication and, most significantly, his expulsion from the student body.

I cannot recall clearly the twists of fate that removed from Leipzig the one or two remaining hooligans with whom I had gotten myself embroiled during that fatal vacation period, but I know that this aspect of my student notoriety now paled in the face of another. We were having a freshmen assembly, to which all who could manage it drove out in a four-in-hand in a long procession through the city. After the club president's suddenly assumed and sustained decorum had impressed me extraordinarily, I conceived the ambition to be among the last to return from the outing. Accordingly, I stayed away three days and three nights, which were mostly devoted to gambling: for this ensnared me in its devilish coils from the first night of the gathering. A bunch of the slickest members, perhaps half a dozen, got together at the Mercenary at early dawn and formed from then on the nucleus of a gambling club, reinforced during the day by returnees from the city. Many came just to see whether we were still at it; many went away again; only I and the rest of the original six stayed there steadfastly day and night. At the outset my motive for participation was the desire to win enough to pay my club dues (two talers): I succeeded in this and from then on was inspired by the hope of paying off all the debts I had contracted during this period by my gambling winnings. Just as I had tried to learn composing in double-quick time from Logier's *Thorough-Bass*, yet had unaccountably run into difficulties, so it went with my plan for speedy recoupment of my financial position: the profits did not accrue very rapidly, and for about three months I remained so helplessly addicted to gambling that all other preoccupations faded away. Neither the fencing grounds, nor the taverns, nor the dueling sites were graced by my presence again; my days were spent racking my brains to devise all conceivable ways and means of getting money to gamble away throughout the night. Without having the faintest idea of the real nature of my excesses, my mother tried her pitiful best to persuade me to come home at night. After leaving the house in the afternoon I never got back until dawn the next day, reaching my corner room by climbing over the courtyard gate, the key to which was denied me. My passion for gambling grew to almost manic intensity out of despair at my bad luck; insensible to everything that had previously attracted me in student life, senselessly indifferent to the judgment of my former companions, I disappeared entirely from their horizon and lost myself in the smaller gambling dens of Leipzig with the scum of the student body. I even bore with obtuse disregard the contempt of my sister Rosalie, who like my mother hardly deigned to accord the baffling young wastrel, whom she saw only at rare intervals, looking pale and wan, as much as a glance. In my growing despair, I finally seized the means to improve my lot by confronting my hostile fortune boldly. I was of the opinion that profits could only be achieved by upping the size of my stakes and to this end determined to make use of a not inconsiderable sum in cash that was in my safe-keeping, to wit my mother's pension, which I had collected for her. That night I lost it all, right down to one last taler: the excitement with which I staked that last coin on a card was something new for me, even after everything else I had experienced in my young life: without having eaten a bite, I was forced to leave the gaming table repeatedly to throw up. With this my last taler I staked my life: for there was no question of returning home; I could see myself in the grey dawn fleeing through fields and woods into the wide blue yonder like a lost prodigal. This despairing mood held me so forcibly that, when my card won, I left my winnings on the board and continued to do so time after time, until I had won a really substantial amount. I now began to win continuously. My luck became so reliable that I dared to gamble against the longest odds: for suddenly it occurred to me vividly that I was gambling for the last time. My luck became so conspicuous that the bank thought it best to close. I had actually regained not only all the money I had previously lost in this one night but also enough to pay all my past debts. The growing elation I felt during this whole process was utterly sacred. With the turn in my luck I clearly sensed God or His angels as if standing beside me and whispering words of warning and consolation. Once again I had to climb over the courtyard gate at daybreak to get into my home: there I fell into a deep and energizing sleep, from which I awakened late, strengthened and as if born again. No sense of shame deterred me from voluntarily telling my mother, to whom I remitted her money, about the events of this decisive night and of my dereliction with her property. She folded her hands and gave thanks to God for this sign of His grace, and expressed her confidence that I had been saved and would never again relapse into similar sins. And temptation really lost its power over me for all time. The world through which I had reeled and staggered now struck me as the most incomprehensible and unattractive one imaginable: the gambling mania had already made me indifferent to other student vanities; when I was liberated from this compulsion as well I found myself suddenly in another world, and to this world I belonged henceforth by devoting myself with previously unknown dedication to the new phase, that of truly serious study, upon which my musical education now entered.

Even in this wildest period of my life my musical development had not remained entirely at a standstill; on the contrary, music had become most decidedly the only direction for which I had a marked bent. But I had gotten entirely out of the habit of musical study. To this day it has remained incomprehensible to me how I had managed to find time to complete a number of compositions. Whereas I have only the faintest recollection of an overture in C major (6/8 time) and a sonata for four hands in B flat major, which I practised together with my sister Ottilie and scored for orchestra because it pleased us so much, another work from this period, an overture in B flat major, is etched indelibly on my memory. This composition grew out of my study of Beethoven's Ninth Symphony more or less the way *Leubald und Adelaïde* grew out of Shakespeare. I lent an especially mystical significance to my orchestra: this I divided into three contrasting and antagonistic elements. I wanted to characterize these elements for a reader of my score by an energetic display of colors, and only the fact that I could not get any green ink kept me from executing a gaudily painted score. I wanted to reserve black ink for the brass instruments alone; the strings were to be scored in red, and the woodwind green. I submitted this singular score to the musical director of the Leipzig Theater, Heinrich Dorn,[1] at that time a young man whose worldliness and wit as well as his musical proficiency impressed both me and the Leipzig public quite favorably. I still have no idea what moved him to grant my request for a public performance of this work. Later, along with others who were familiar with his fondness for leg-pulling, I was inclined to believe that he was making fun of me, but he always maintained that the overture had interested him and that if it had been introduced as a hitherto unknown work of Beethoven, it would have been received respectfully, if without understanding. It was Christmas of the fateful year 1830, and on Christmas Eve the theater gave, as usual, no performance but instead an always very sparsely attended charity concert. The first item on the program bore the exciting title "New Overture"; that was all. I had attended one of the rehearsals in anxious concealment and had been greatly impressed by Dorn's sang-froid in maintaining his composure in the face of an ominous rumble among the orchestra members when they were making their way through this enigmatic composition. The main theme of the allegro was in four bars; after every fourth bar, however, a fifth had been inserted, which had nothing to do with the melody and was distinguished by a loud bang on the kettle-drum on the second beat. As this drum-beat stood virtually alone, the drummer, who got the feeling he was continually making a mistake, became inhibited and did not give the note the accentuation the score called for; but this did not displease me as I listened in my invisible corner, as I had lost confidence in my original intention. To my great discomfiture, Dorn nevertheless brought this bashful drum-beat to the forefront and insisted that the player always give it the prescribed strength. When I communicated my concern to the conductor after the rehearsal, I did not succeed in converting him to a milder interpretation of the fatal drum-beat; he stuck to his view that the thing would sound very well as it was. Despite this reassurance I remained highly uneasy, and I did not have the confidence to tell my friends in advance that I was the composer of this new overture. My sister Ottilie, who had already been obliged to suffer through the clandestine readings of *Leubald und Adelaïde*, was the only one I told to get ready to come with me to the performance. It was on the evening when gifts were exchanged in the house of my brother-in-law Friedrich Brockhaus; my sister and I were both interested in attending this function. As a member of the household, she was particularly busy with the arrangements and could only get away with difficulty and for a short time, upon which our genial relative had the carriage readied for her so that she might get back more quickly. I took this opportunity to make my entrance into the musical world with a certain ceremony: the carriage drew up briskly outside the theater; Ottilie proceeded to my brother-in-law's box, while I was forced to find a place for myself in the parterre. I had forgotten to get a ticket and was turned back by the doorkeeper: hearing the orchestra tuning up with increasing intensity, I thought I would have to miss the beginning of my work and in my anxiety went so far as to reveal myself to the doorkeeper as the composer of the "New Overture", in order to induce him to admit me without a ticket, which he then did. I pushed my way to one of the front rows and sat down, discombobulated to insensibility. The overture began: after the theme of the "black" brass instruments had announced itself portentously, the "red" allegro theme made its entrance, punctuated at every fifth bar, as stated, by the drum-beat from the "black" world. Whatever effect the "green" theme for the woodwind, which joined in afterwards, together with the eventual commingling of the "black, red and green" themes, may have produced on the listeners, has remained lost to me, for that fatal drum-beat, executed with malevolent brutality, produced such an uproarious effect that I became deaf and blind to everything else. This persistent and regularly recurring effect soon began to excite the attention and then the amusement of the audience. I heard my neighbors calculating and announcing the returning beat in advance: my sufferings, knowing the correctness of these calculations, defy description. I lost consciousness. I came to finally when the overture, to which I had disdained to give anything so trite as a conclusion, came to a sudden standstill: none of the phantoms of Hoffmann's tales ever produced an effect upon me remotely comparable to that which now came over me when I noticed the astonishment of the audience at the close of my piece. I heard no boos or hisses, no criticism, not even any laughter, but rather sensed the simple amazement of everyone at such a singular occurrence, which seemed to them, and to me, no more than a strange dream. The most painful moment came when I had to leave the parterre hurriedly to accompany my sister home at once. To get up and sidle through the rows of seats to the exit was awful. But nothing approached the agony in which I now came face-to-face once again with the doorkeeper: the singular look he gave me made an ineradicable impression, and for a long time thereafter I avoided the parterre of the Leipzig Theater. The next step was to find my sister, who had gone through the whole thing in great sympathy, and then drive home to be present at the brilliant family festivities, which lit with grim irony the black night of my stupefaction.

I tried, indeed, not to surrender to this feeling and thought I could console myself with yet another overture I had on inventory, *Die Braut von Messina*, which I considered a better piece than the one performed. But there was no redress, for the directors of the Leipzig Theater henceforth regarded me, despite Dorn's friendship, as a doubtful risk. I still tried my hand at sketching some compositions for Goethe's *Faust*, some of which have been preserved to this day; but the beginnings of my wild student life soon inundated and swept away my inclination for serious work in music.

I now began to imagine that because I had become a student I ought to attend some lectures. From Traugott Krug, well known to us for his role in gently suppressing the student revolt, I tried to learn the first principles of philosophy; a single hour sufficed to make me give this up forever. Two or three times, nevertheless, I attended lectures on aesthetics given by one of the younger professors, a man named Weiss;[1] such exceptional perseverance was attributable to my personal interest in Weiss, whom I had met at the house of my uncle Adolf. Weiss had just translated Aristotle's *Metaphysics* and had dedicated it, with a polemical intent, to Hegel, if I remember correctly. On that occasion I had listened to a conversation between these two men about philosophy and philosophers, which impressed me very deeply. I recall that Weiss, whose distracted air, manner of speaking rapidly but in fits and starts, and above all interesting and pensive physiognomy greatly attracted me, justified the much criticized lack of clarity in his writing style by contending that the deepest problems of the human spirit could not be solved for the benefit of the mob. The maxim, which struck me as highly plausible, I at once accepted as the guiding principle for everything I wrote. I remember my eldest brother Albert being particularly incensed at the style of a letter I once wrote him on behalf of my mother and making known his fear that I was losing my wits. Although I thought I could count on Weiss to provide suitable intellectual nourishment, I did not succeed in continuing my attendance at his lectures, as my desires in those days drove me far from the field of aesthetic studies. Nevertheless, my mother's anxiety induced me to try to take up music again; that my former teacher Müller had not been able to kindle permanent enthusiasm in me for this was now clear to everybody: now it was necessary to find out whether a new teacher might prove better able to induce me to do serious work.

Theodor Weinlich[2] held at that time what was traditionally the most important musical post in Leipzig, that of organist and director of music at St Thomas' Church, occupied immediately before him by Schicht and long ago by Sebastian Bach himself. By musical temperament he belonged to the Old Italian school and had studied in Bologna under Padre Martini.[3] He had made a name for himself in this field by vocal compositions in which his beautiful handling of the parts was much praised: he himself once recounted to me that a Leipzig publisher had offered him very favorable terms if he would produce for his firm some books of vocal exercises similar to one which had proved very profitable to another publisher; when Weinlich let him know that he had no such

54

composition available at the moment but would be glad to offer him a new mass if he wanted to bring out something of his, the publisher refused with the comment: "Let him who got the meat gnaw the bones." The modesty with which Weinlich told me this little story characterized this excellent man in every sense. Very frail and sickly, he at first refused to take me on as a pupil when my mother approached him. After having long resisted the most heartfelt pleas, he seems finally to have taken a kindly pity on me because of the sorry state of my musical training, which he easily recognized from a fugue I had brought along; he then agreed to teach me, but only on the condition that I gave up all attempts at composing for six months and patiently followed his instructions. To this first part of my promise I remained faithful, thanks to the vortex of student dissipation into which I was drawn; but when I was requested to busy myself for any length of time with exercises in four-part harmony in the most disciplined style, the composer of overtures and sonatas as well as the frivolous student were alike extremely disenchanted. Weinlich had his complaints about me, too, and was on the point of giving up on me completely. It was then that the turning point of my life occurred, caused by the catastrophe of that terrible night in the gambling den. Weinlich's declaration that he wanted nothing more to do with me was almost as severe a shock as that experience. Humiliated and moved, I begged the gentle old man, to whom I was sincerely devoted, for his forgiveness and promised him greater persistence in the future. I was summoned by Weinlich to appear one morning at seven o'clock, in order to work out a fugue under his supervision by mid-day. He actually devoted the whole morning to me, giving each bar I wrote his closest and most instructive scrutiny. At about twelve o'clock he dismissed me with the assignment to complete the sketch at home by filling out all the contrapuntal voices. When I brought him the completed fugue he gave me in return his own version of the same theme for comparison. The joint work on fugues became the basis for the most productive affection between me and my genial teacher, for we both enjoyed further such tasks immensely. I was amazed to see how quickly the time flew. In eight weeks I had not only gone through a number of the most intricate fugues but had also waded quickly through the most difficult contrapuntal exercises, when one day, after I had handed him an extremely elaborate double fugue, he took my breath away by telling me I should have the piece framed because he had nothing more to teach me. As I had not been conscious of any great effort in doing all this, I often wondered for some time afterwards whether I could be considered a formally trained musician. Weinlich himself did not seem to attach much importance to what he had taught me: he said, "Probably you will never write fugues or canons. What you have achieved, however, is self-sufficiency. You now stand on your own two feet and know that you can use the most refined techniques if you need to."

One of the most important results of his influence on me, at all events, was the satisfaction I now found in clarity and fluidity, which he had taught me to value by his own example. Even when he gave me that first fugal exercise I had had to write proper vocal parts for it with the words written in below the stave; my feeling for vocal writing had been awakened in this manner. In order to keep me within bounds under his friendly tutelage, he had at the same time given me a sonata to write, which, as proof of my devotion, I was to build up under strict harmonic and thematic discipline along the lines of one of the most childlike sonatas of Pleyel,[1] which he had given me as a model. Anybody who knew my recently composed overtures would have been surprised that I could have mastered myself sufficiently to produce this sonata, which as of this writing has recently found its way into print once again through an indiscretion of the music publishers Breitkopf und Härtel:[2] to reward me for my self-discipline Weinlich had indulged himself by inducing that publishing house to let my feeble work see the light of day. From then on he gave me a free hand. As an initial reward I was allowed to compose a fantasia for piano in F sharp minor, in which I allowed myself complete formal freedom and treated the melody like recitative, and from which I derived great pleasure, as it won Weinlich's approval. Soon afterwards I wrote three overtures as well, all of which he praised. In the following winter (1831–2) I got the first of these, in D minor, performed at a Gewandhaus concert.

At that time this institution was run in a very casual manner: instrumental works were not led by any conductor but rather by the first violinist (Mathäi)[3] from his desk; but as soon as any singing began, the prototype of all fat and happy music directors, the highly popular Pohlenz,[4] would appear at the conductor's stand with a very imposing blue baton. One of the strangest events was the annual performance[5] of Beethoven's Ninth Symphony in this manner: after the first three movements had been played through like a Haydn symphony by the orchestra on its own as best it could, Pohlenz would appear, not to direct an Italian aria, a vocal quartet, or a cantata, but to undertake this most difficult test of a conductor's skill, the direction of this most complicated piece of music, which is, especially in its introductory instrumental section, so enigmatically liable to disintegrate. I will never forget the impression produced by an early rehearsal I attended, when Pohlenz conducted the fierce and shrieking fanfare with which this last movement begins in a cautious 3/4 time, whereby it was turned into a strangely limping galimatias. This tempo had been chosen to manage, in some way at least, the recitative of the bass instruments; but this never succeeded. Pohlenz sweated blood but the recitative never came off, and I really began to wonder uneasily whether Beethoven had not written nonsense after all: the contrabass player Temmler, an orchestral veteran of long service who was high-minded and blunt, finally persuaded Pohlenz to abandon the baton and give the recitative a chance; nevertheless, after having heard the last part in circumstances such as these, which it was outside my experience at the time to explain, a humiliating sense of doubt began to grow in me as to whether I had really understood this singular composition or not. For a long time I gave up brooding about it and turned without affectation toward clearer and calmer elements in music. My contrapuntal studies in particular had brought me a beneficial appreciation of the light and flowing manner in which Mozart handled the most complex technical problems in music, and the last movement of his great C major symphony served me as the most admirable model. After my overture in D minor, which had leaned heavily on Beethoven's *Coriolanus* overture, had been well performed and favorably received, thereby earning me the first hopeful smile from my mother, I came forward with a second overture in C major that closed with a real "fugato", which at the time I thought was the best I could possibly do in honor of my new paragon.

This overture too was soon performed, at a concert in which the popular singer Palazzesi[1] (of the Dresden Italian Opera) appeared as guest soloist. Prior to this I had given the work its first performance at a concert of the "Euterpe" musical society, when I conducted it myself. I recall the strange impression a remark by my mother made on me at that time; my piece, written in contrapuntal style and without any great emotional verve, had been received very coolly by her; she gave vent to her perplexity about it by extra-lavish praise for the *Egmont* overture, which had been played earlier at the same concert, and of which she asserted: "This kind of music is really much more moving than any stupid fugue." I also wrote (as my Opus 3) an overture to Raupach's[2] drama *King Enzio*, in which Beethoven's influence again made itself strongly felt. Through the efforts of my sister Rosalie I got this piece accepted by the theater to be played before one of the performances:

the management nevertheless took the precaution of not announcing it[1] on the program, although Music Director Dorn conducted it. As the performance went off smoothly and the public made no protest, my overture was played at subsequent performances during the run of the tragedy, which remained popular for some time, with my name boldly adorning the program. I now began work on a big symphony (in C major); in it I demonstrated all I had learned, and blended the influence of Beethoven and Mozart into the production of a really performable and intelligible work, in which the conclusion was again fugal, while the themes of all the movements were so constructed that they could be easily combined contrapuntally in strettos. Nevertheless, the passionate and bold elements of the *Sinfonia Eroica*, and particularly its first movement, were not without obvious influence on my conception. In the Andante there were even reminiscences of my earlier musical mysticism: a little figure jumping from the minor third to the fifth, like a constantly recurring question, connected this work, undertaken with the utmost desire for clarity, with the earliest period of my boyish extravagance. When I tried to get this symphony performed at the Gewandhaus the following year, and for this purpose visited Friedrich Rochlitz[2] (then the "Nestor" of musical life in Leipzig and chairman of the concert committee), this gentleman was amazed to find in me such a young fellow, having perused my score in advance and concluded that it was the work of an older and more experienced musician.

Before this performance took place, however, there was an intervening period in which I was subjected to several experiences in life which I must now describe more closely.

My short and stormy career as a student had submerged not only my sense of artistic development but also my interest in all other intellectual and spiritual matters. While I had nonetheless never quite given up music entirely, my reawakening interest in political events began to arouse disgust at the senseless student excesses, which soon were obliterated from my memory like some horrible nightmare. The Polish war of independence against Russian rule now filled me with growing enthusiasm. The victories achieved by the Poles during a short period in May of 1831 aroused my ecstatic admiration: it seemed to me as if the world had been created anew by some miracle. Conversely, news of the battle of Ostrolenka made me feel the world had once again come to an end. I was astonished how crudely my student tavern companions scoffed whenever I discussed my feelings about this: I began to understand the terrible shadow side of German student associations.

Every kind of enthusiasm was suppressed as a matter of principle and transformed into stylized bravado, which was characterized by coolness and the affectation of indifference. To get drunk and contract debts with a maximum of cold-bloodedness and without a trace of humor was considered almost as praiseworthy as bravery in dueling. It was only much later that I grasped the nobler aspect of German club life as against this corrupt student spirit; at that time I was personally infuriated by the insulting reproofs I brought down on myself, as stated, by openly bewailing the unhappy outcome of the battle of Ostrolenka. Such impressions as these, be it said to my credit, did their part to help me break with these degenerate student circles. My only self-indulgence during the period of study with Weinlich consisted of nightly trips to Kintschy's pastry parlor in the Klostergasse, where I eagerly devoured the first editions of the next day's newspapers. Many people of similar political views found their way here; I was particularly intrigued by listening to several older men heatedly discuss politics. Belletristic magazines began to interest me; I started to read a lot again, though not with much selectivity; but I now began to appreciate wit and intellect, whereas previously only the fantastic and the colossal had appealed to me. My principal preoccupation remained the outcome of the Polish struggle: the siege and capture of Warsaw struck me like a personal calamity.

My excitement when the remnants of the Polish army began passing through Leipzig on their way to France was indescribable, and unforgettable the sight of the first troop of these unfortunates, who were billeted at the Green Shield in the Fleischergasse. Much as this depressed me at first, I was soon roused to transports of enthusiasm when I was able to observe at close quarters in the foyer of the Leipzig Gewandhaus, on an evening when Beethoven's C minor symphony was performed, a group of heroic figures comprising the most distinguished leaders of the Polish revolution. I was especially captivated by Count Vincenz Tyskiewitsch, a man of exceptionally powerful physique and manly features, who impressed me by a combination of noble bearing and calm self-assurance I had not encountered before. To see a man of such regal quality in his frogged coat and red velvet cap made me realize at once my foolishness at having worshipped the ludicrously decked-out little rowdies from our student world. I was delighted to encounter this very man again in the home of my brother-in-law Friedrich Brockhaus and meet him there repeatedly, almost as one of the family. My brother-in-law distinguished himself by his great sympathy and dedication towards the unfortunate Polish fighters; he headed a committee which concerned itself with them over a long period, and he made substantial personal sacrifices on their behalf. The Brockhaus home now became tremendously appealing to me. Around Count Vincenz Tyskiewitsch, who remained the lodestar of this small Polish world, gathered a number of other exiles of some wealth, among whom I remember chiefly a cavalry captain Bansemer, characterized by boundless cheerfulness and equal frivolity, and possessor of a marvelous team of four horses which he drove at breakneck speed through the town, much to the fury of the Leipzig citizenry. I also recall finding myself at table one day with General Bem,[1] whose artillery had made such a gallant stand at Ostrolenka. Many other exiles passed through this hospitable home, impressing me in turn by their soldierly melancholy and supple refinement: but the only enduring impression was left by Vincenz Tyskiewitsch, whom I loved and revered as a paragon of true manliness.

This splendid man also took a real interest in me: nearly every day I found my way to him and often participated in the semi-military drinking bouts, from which he would withdraw with me for a time to some calm spot where he would give way to his melancholy and anxiety in my company. At the time he still had no news of the fate of his wife and small son, from whom he had been separated in Volhynia. Beyond this, he was under the shadow of a great misfortune that drew all sympathetic natures to him. To my sister Luise he had confided the terrible calamity that had once befallen him. He had been married before, and while staying at one of his remote castles, had seen a ghostly apparition one night at the window of his bedroom; having called out repeatedly to it, he finally grabbed his gun to protect himself and shot his own wife, who had indulged the eccentric idea of trying to tease him by pretending to be a ghost. I soon shared his joy when he learned that his family had been saved: his wife at last joined him in Leipzig with their beautiful three-year-old son Janusz. It saddened me not to be able to feel the same sympathy for this lady as I did for her husband, my unfavorable impression being based mainly on the unseemly way she painted her face in the curious attempt to conceal how much the exhaustion caused by the terrible strain she had been under had affected her drawn and sorrowful countenance. She soon went off to Galicia, to save what she could of their property there, while at the same time trying to wangle a passport from the Austrian government, by means of which her husband could follow her. Then came May 3rd. Eighteen of the Poles who were still in Leipzig got together for a banquet at an inn outside the town: they were celebrating the anniversary, so dear to Polish hearts, of the establishment of their constitution. The only others invited were the principal members of the Leipzig Polish Committee, and, as a mark of special distinction and affection, myself. It was an unforgettably impressive occasion. The dinner turned into an orgy: throughout the evening a brass band from the city played Polish folksongs uninterruptedly, in which the entire company, led by a Lithuanian called Zàn, joined in, jubilant and mournful in turn. The beautiful song, "The Third of May",[1] aroused particularly uproarious enthusiasm. Tears and shouts of joy commingled in a tremendous tumult, until the group went out onto the garden grass in widely dispersed pairs of lovers, whose extravagant endearments were keyed by the inexhaustible word "Oiczisna" (fatherland), the mantle of night finally enveloping this splendid debauch. The dreamlike evening later served me as the theme for an orchestral composition in the form of an overture with the title *Polonia*. I shall recount the fate of this work subsequently.

The passports for my friend Tyskiewitsch arrived; he was on the point of traveling to Galicia via Brünn, which his friends thought a rash thing to do. A yearning had grown up in me to see something more of the world. Tyskiewitsch offered to let me accompany him, which induced my mother to consent to my going to Vienna, a long-standing wish. With the scores of the three overtures already performed as well as that of my yet unperformed big symphony, I set out to accompany my friendly Polish patron in his comfortable traveling coach as far as the capital of Moravia. Upon stopping briefly in Dresden, the much beloved and admired count was given a friendly farewell dinner in Pirna by emigrants of noble and humbler rank, during which toasts were drunk to the future "Dictator of Poland" in rivers of champagne. We finally separated at Brünn, from which I was to continue my journey to Vienna the following day by mail-coach. During the afternoon and evening I spent alone in Brünn, I was strangely affected by a suddenly aroused fear of cholera. For the first time, I found myself in a place where I heard by chance that cholera was endemic. There I was, all alone in a strange place, newly separated from my reliable friend, knowing nothing whatever about the town where chance had brought me, and on receiving this information I felt as if some malicious demon had lured me into a trap to do away with me without a trace. I did not betray my feelings to people in the hotel; but when I was led to a bedroom in a remote wing of the house and suddenly left alone in this desolation, I buried myself fully clothed in the bed and relived all the terror of ghosts I had been through in my boyhood. Cholera stood personified before me: I saw her and could touch her; she came to my bedside, embraced me; my limbs turned to ice; I felt death at my heart. Whether I was asleep or awake I do not know; but I was utterly amazed to find myself at daybreak feeling completely healthy. Thus, I succeeded in getting away happily to Vienna, where I behaved as if totally immune to the epidemic that had reached there as well.

This was in mid-summer of 1832. Largely owing to introductions to some family friends, I soon found myself at home in this bustling city, where I stayed a full six weeks. As I didn't have any real business to transact, my mother's willingness to spare even a modest amount of money for a general pleasure trip could almost be considered extravagance on her part. I went to the theater, listened to Strauss,[1] made excursions and generally indulged myself, whereby some debts were contracted which I had to pay off later as conductor of the Dresden orchestra. The impressions of musical and theatrical life were certainly very stimulating, and Vienna remained for a long time my idea of creativity rooted in the originality of a people. In this sense, I was most contented with the performances at the Theater an der Wien, where a grotesque and farcical fairy-tale called *Fortunato's Adventures on Land and Water*,[2] in which one of the characters orders "a fiacre to the Black Sea", made a particularly vivid impression. As to music, I was caught in a vice between two forces. A young friend took me proudly to a performance of Gluck's *Iphigenia in Tauris*, which was particularly graced by a superb cast including the famous Wild, Staudigl, and Binder:[3] yet I must honestly confess that the work bored me as a whole, which was all the more painful as I did not dare admit it. My conception of Gluck had inevitably attained gigantic dimensions from my reading of Hoffmann's well-known tale: I assumed I would find in him, whose works I had not yet studied, an overpowering dramatic fire, and applied to my first hearing of his most famous work the standard set for me on that unforgettable evening when Schröder-Devrient had sung in *Fidelio*. With some effort I succeeded in bringing myself during the great scene of Orestes with the Furies into a halfway comparable state of ecstasy. I spent the rest of the opera waiting in solemn intensity for an effect that never came.

I found the vital nerve of Viennese theatrical taste in the opera *Zampa*,[4] which constituted at that time almost the sole daily repertory of both opera houses, at the Carinthian Gate and at the Josephstadt. Both houses competed fiercely in this vastly popular exercise: if the audience had appeared enthusiastic in *Iphigenia in Tauris*, they went genuinely wild in *Zampa*; no sooner would they leave the Josephstadt theater, in which *Zampa* had sent them all into transports of ecstasy, and proceed to the nearby coffee house called the "Sträusslein", than I would be assailed by Strauss' own febrile playing of a pot-pourri from *Zampa*, by means of which the audience would again be set palpably afire. I shall never forget the enthusiasm, bordering on derangement, generated in that extraordinary figure Johann Strauss whenever he played, no matter what the piece was. This demon of the Viennese musical spirit shook like a Pythia on her tripod whenever he began playing another waltz, and veritable whinnies of pleasure from the audience, indubitably attributable more to his music than to the drinks they had enjoyed, whipped up the ecstasies of this magician of the violin to heights that nearly frightened me. The hot summer air of Vienna was thus impregnated for me almost solely by *Zampa* and Strauss.

A very feeble rehearsal by pupils at the conservatory, in which parts of a mass by Cherubini were played, seemed to me like alms paid grudgingly to the cultivation of classical music. In that same rehearsal a professor to whom I had been introduced but whose name I have forgotten tried to lead the group through my D minor overture which had already been performed in Leipzig: I do not recall the reaction of the professor and his pupils to their attempts but remember only that they soon gave it up.

Thus diverted onto dubious byways of musical taste, I ended this first educational visit to a great European art center and began an inexpensive but very tedious trip to Bohemia by stage-coach. There, I was to visit the family of Count Pachta, of whom I had the most flattering boyhood memories, on their estate, Pravonin, eight miles from Prague. Very graciously received by the old gentleman and his lovely daughters, I enjoyed the most stimulating hospitality until late in the autumn. As a young man of nineteen, already with a solid little beard, about which the count's daughters had been forewarned in the letter of introduction from my sister, the constant and close association with such pretty and nice young ladies could scarcely fail to have an effect on my imagination. The elder one, Jenny, was slender and had black hair, dark blue eyes and an admirably noble profile; the younger, Auguste, was smaller and curvier, with a radiant complexion, blond hair, and brown eyes. Their uninhibited and sisterly good nature in all their dealings with me did not blind me to the fact that I was supposed to fall in love with one or the other. The two girls evidenced amused awareness of my embarrassment in having to make such a choice, and continual teasing was the reward for my zealous efforts. I unfortunately did not proceed very purposefully in my deportment with these young ladies: brought up in modest domesticity, they were condemned by their unusual parentage to swing back and forth between the hope for upper-class marriage or the necessity to accept a solid middle-class partner. The palpably limited, even medieval educational level of the typical Austrian gallant, which they themselves described to me slightingly at the time, had unfortunately also decisively affected the education of my two young friends. I soon noticed to my disgust their shallow knowledge in the whole area of aesthetics, while they evinced pronounced receptiveness to every kind of superficiality. None of my enthusiastic communications about the higher pursuits I had come to care about so much interested them in the slightest. I protested against the shabby circulating-library novels that constituted almost their sole reading matter, against the Italian opera arias Auguste sang, and finally against the horse-loving vacuous gallants who showed up from time to time and paid what was to me insulting court to both Jenny and Auguste. My outrage about this last point in particular soon gave rise to great unpleasantness: I became censorious and offensive, lost myself in harangues about the spirit of the French Revolution to the extent of giving the girls all sorts of fatherly sounding advice to accept a well-educated bourgeois "for God's sake", and to renounce the company of those crude, impertinent suitors whose company would only undermine their reputations. The indignation aroused by these homilies sometimes spurred me to hot retorts; but I never apologized, seeking rather by the feigned or perhaps real jealousy that possessed me to transmute the irritating elements in my outbursts into something more flattering and bearable. Undecided whether I was angry or in love, though still on good terms, I left these lovely girls one cold November day, soon to rejoin the family in Prague, where I stayed for some time without, however, taking up residence in the Count's house there.

This sojourn in Prague was supposed to further my musical education. I became acquainted with the director of the conservatory, Dionys Weber,[1] and through him my symphony was due to have its first performance. Apart from this, I spent most of my time with an actor named Moritz,[2] to whom I had been recommended as he was an old friend of my family. In his company I soon became friendly with another young musician by the name of Kittl.[3] Moritz, who noticed that scarcely a day passed without my badgering the redoubtable chief of the

conservatory with musical business of some sort, once dispatched me
with an improvised parody of Schiller's *Die Bürgschaft*:

> To Dionys the Director slunk
> Wagner, score under his tunic.
> "What are you up to with that music?" –
> The students hounded him like a skunk.
> The fearsome director told him "You're sunk,
> The town will never know why you do it,
> The reviewers will certainly make you rue it."

As a matter of fact, the man I had to deal with really did resemble
"Dionysius the Tyrant". Weber, who accepted Beethoven only as far
as his Second Symphony and termed the *Eroica* an utter aberration of
taste in the master, while exalting Mozart alone and beside him among
the newer composers solely Lindpaintner,[1] was no easy mark for me,
and I had to learn the art of bending tyrants to one's own purposes: I
dissimulated, professed to be struck dumb by the novelty of his
assertions, contradicted him in nothing, and, to underline the congruence
of our views, referred him to the closing fugues of my overture as well
as my symphony, both in C major and palpably influenced by Mozart.
I did not have to wait long for my reward: Dionys began rehearsing my
orchestral pieces with an almost youthful fervor. The pupils at the
conservatory were compelled to learn my new symphony meticulously
under his dry but frightfully noisy time beating; and in the presence of
several invited friends, among whom was my old friend Count Pachta,
who was there in his capacity as chairman of the conservatory's
governors, we actually brought off the first performance of the most
substantial work I had written to date.

While I was celebrating these musical successes, I continued my
strange wooing of the Pachta girls at their attractive home under the most
peculiar vicissitudes. As a colleague in this endeavor I had gained a
confectioner by the name of Hascha. He was a tall, thin, unusually
laconic young man, who, like most people in Bohemia, had taken up
music along with running his successful pastry shop, accompanied
Auguste when she sang, and, typically, fell in love as a result. Like myself,
he hated the visits of the gallants, which were even more frequent in
the capital: whereas my dissatisfaction generally took a humoristic turn,
his showed itself in darkest melancholy; in fact it even led him to open
boorishness, so that one evening, when the chandelier was to be lit for
the reception of one of the principal suitors, he bumped it with the tall

head that grew on his elongated body, broke it and thus eliminated the possibility of festive illumination, an act which brought down upon him the intense wrath of our friends' mother, so that he found it advisable to give up visiting the Count's house from then on. I well remember feeling in this period the first real pangs of love in the form of a curiously gnawing jealousy, which, however, was not actually rooted in true love: this happened one night when I wanted to pay them a visit and was held in an ante-room by the mother, while in the drawing room, as I could easily tell, the young ladies in especially exquisite dress were chattering away with the young noblemen I so loathed. All I had ever read in Hoffmann's tales of certain satanic love intrigues, obscure to me until then, now became vividly real, and I left Prague with an obviously exaggerated and unjust opinion of those people and things that had led me suddenly into a flux of hitherto unknown primal passions.

But I brought other booty back from this first extended excursion into the wide world: in Pravonin I had written poetry and composed. My musical work consisted of a setting of a poem by the friend of my youth Theodor Apel,[1] entitled *Glockentöne*.[2] While I had been able to compose a quite sizeable aria for soprano and orchestra in Leipzig the previous winter, and get it performed in a concert in the theater as well, this new work was my first vocal composition to be suffused with real emotion. Its general character was greatly influenced by Beethoven's vocal works, particularly his song cycle; nevertheless I recall it as a delicately romantic piece very much of my own making, with an especially expressive dreamy accompaniment. My poetic effort consisted of a draft for a tragic opera plot, which I worked out in its entirety during my stay in Prague under the title *Die Hochzeit*, without anyone noticing what I was doing, which had its difficult side, for I could not write in my unheated little hotel room but rather had to go to the apartment of Moritz and spend my mornings at it; I recall that I used to hide my manuscript behind the sofa whenever my host happened to enter the room.

The plot of this dramatic opus had a special significance for me. Several years before I had by chance come across a tragic story in Büsching's book[3] about medieval chivalry the like of which I have not since encountered. A lady of noble birth is assaulted one night by a man nursing a secret passion for her, and in the struggle to defend her honor she finds the strength to pitch him down into the courtyard. The riddle of his death remains unresolved until the day of his burial, also attended by this lady, who then suddenly sinks down in death as well. The mysterious strength of these passionate but unexpressed emotions imprinted itself with inextinguishable vividness upon my imagination. At first entirely under the spell of the way Hoffmann treats such phenomena in his tales, I sketched a novella in which my pet musical mysticism played its inevitable part. The action was to take place on the estate of a rich patron of the arts: a young couple about to be married invite a friend of the groom, an interesting but melancholy and introspective fellow, to the wedding. To this intimate group is added a strange old organist, who possesses intimate knowledge of everyone involved. The mystical relationships which gradually develop between the old musician, the melancholy young man, and the bride, were to be clarified by the unraveling of certain complications leading to the same event related in the above-mentioned medieval story. In addition to the young man mysteriously dead and laid in his coffin, and the bride of his friend also unaccountably dying at his side, the old organist was to be found dead on his bench at the organ, after playing an impressive requiem and expiring during an endlessly prolonged triad at its close. I did not complete this novella: but now that I wanted to write an opera text I again took up this subject and built upon it, in basic outline, the following dramatic plot.

Two great families have long lived in enmity and have now decided to end the vendetta. The aged head of one of these houses has invited the son of his former enemy to the wedding of his daughter to one of his loyal associates. The wedding feast is to be the instrument of reconciliation. Whereas the guests are still full of suspicion and fear of treachery, their young leader suddenly conceives a dark passion for the bride of his new ally. His somber glance strikes her to the heart, and when she has been led to the bridal chamber in a festive procession, to await the arrival of the groom, she suddenly sees this same look at the window of her chamber high in the tower, transfixing her with fearful passion, and realizes that it is a matter of life or death. When he penetrates her chamber and embraces her in wild abandon, she presses him to the balcony and pushes him over the parapet into the abyss, where his shattered body is found by his companions. They at once arm themselves in the face of this apparent treachery and shriek for revenge: tremendous tumult fills the courtyard; the interrupted wedding feast threatens to turn into a night of slaughter. The venerable head of the house nonetheless succeeds in averting the catastrophe; messengers are sent to the family of the victim of this mysterious accident; the corpse itself is to be the object of a ceremony of atonement for the inexplicable event, attended by all members of the suspected family as mourners, and

God's judgment is to be invoked, to discover whether any of them is guilty of the act of treachery. During the preparations for this funeral ceremony the bride shows signs of incipient madness; she flees from her bridegroom, denies the union and locks herself up in her room in the tower. She makes an appearance only at the funeral, which takes place at night in great splendor, pale and silent at the head of her maidens, participating in the solemn ritual which is suddenly interrupted by news of the approach of enemy forces and then by armed attack by the kinfolk of the murdered man. When the avengers of this supposed treachery finally burst into the chapel and call for the murderer, the horrified lord of the castle points to his dead daughter, who, turning her back on her bridegroom, has sunk lifeless upon the coffin of her victim.

This blackest nocturnal epic, through which echoed *Leubald und Adelaïde* from my distant youth in a somewhat more refined strain, was executed in black on black, with disdain for any ray of light and in particular for all operatic embellishments. Tender passages occurred here and there all the same; and the introduction to the first act (especially an adagio for vocal septet, in which the reconciliation of the warring families and the feelings of the bridal couple were expressed simultaneously with the somber ardor of the secret lover) brought me some encouraging praise for its clarity and singability from Weinlich, to whom I was able to show the beginning of the composition, which I had already started by the time I was back in Leipzig. But I was mainly interested in gaining the approval of my sister Rosalie for my undertaking. The poem, could not, however, find favor with her; she deplored the absence of everything I had intentionally left out, and wanted the stark circumstances of the story festooned with manifold and if possible more congenial subplots. I made a snap decision, coldly grasped my manuscript and destroyed it without a trace.

This action was not caused by wounded vanity, but rather evidenced a desire to prove to my sister how little I was impressed by my own work and how much I valued her judgment. If Rosalie enjoyed unusual respect and affection within our family from my mother and brothers and sisters, this was in no small part attributable to the fact that she had been its chief breadwinner for a number of years; the not inconsiderable salary she drew as an actress constituted the main source of funds from which household expenses were met. Her job gave her many other domestic perquisites. Her section of the apartment was always maintained with particular care and consideration for the peace and quiet she needed

for her studies; on market days, when the rest of us had to put up with
plain food, she alone did not have to do without the delicacies to which
she was accustomed. But more than any of these things, she was set apart
from the younger members of the family by her charming gravity, her
considered manner of expression and her refined, thoughtful deportment,
from which she rarely lapsed into the rather brisk tone that otherwise
prevailed among us. At any rate, I was the member of the family who
had caused the greatest anxiety in my mother and this motherly sister
alike. During my student dissipations her disapproval had hit me very
hard. That she finally began to believe in my future once again and
showed fresh interest in my studies filled me with comforting warmth.
The thought of inducing this sister who had virtually given up on me
to look kindly on my aspirations, and even to expect great things of me,
became a special spur to my ambition. In these circumstances I
developed a tender and almost romantic regard for Rosalie, which in its
innocence and purifying warmth can only be compared to the noblest
relationships between a man and a woman. Rosalie's special character
had, of course, a lot to do with this. She didn't have any real talent, and
certainly none for the theater; her acting was considered by most people
stilted and unnatural. Nonetheless her charming appearance and her
pure and dignified femininity earned her the hearty approval of nearly
everybody, and testimonials of the highest esteem remain in my memory
to this very day. But none of these tributes seemed to lead to any
permanent attachments, and a destiny still inexplicable to me brought
my sister finally to full womanhood with steadily dimming hopes of
making a suitable marriage. I thought I could detect hints at times that
Rosalie suffered deeply from this state of affairs. There was one
unforgettable evening, in particular, when I heard her, believing herself
to be alone, sobbing and moaning in her darkened room, which made
such an impact on me that I slunk unnoticed away and from then on
tried to be even more tenderly deferential in seeking to do her bidding
and particularly to please her by my successes. Not for nothing had our
stepfather Geyer given my gentle sister the nickname "little sprite"; if
her acting talent, as I have stated, was only modest, her imagination and
appreciation for art and everything exalted was all the more intense.
From her lips I first heard outpourings of admiration and delight about
the subjects that later were to excite me so much; she also created around
herself everywhere and continuingly a circle of serious and artistically
dedicated people, unspoiled by any admixture of affectation.

On my return from my long journey I met Heinrich Laube,[1] a newcomer who had been received most cordially by my family and Rosalie.

It was at this time that the after-effects of the July revolution made themselves felt in the activities of younger German intellectuals; among these Laube soon gained special attention. He was a young man, who came to Leipzig from Silesia, his principal object being to establish connections in this publishing center that would speed his progress towards Paris, from where Börne[2] was making a great sensation among us by his letters. In this connection Laube attended a performance of a play by Ludwig Robert[3] entitled *The Power of Circumstance* and was impelled to write a review in the *Leipziger Tageblatt* that caused such a stir by its sharp and vivacious execution that he was immediately offered the editorship of the *Zeitung für die elegante Welt*, along with a number of other literary commissions to boot. In our house he was hailed as a sparkling talent; his acerbic, short, often biting manner, which clearly had difficulty in giving poetry its due, made him appear both original and daring; his honesty, integrity and blunt impudence drew people to a character steeled by a harsh childhood. Laube had a very encouraging effect on me, and in particular I was wellnigh astonished to discover how highly he thought of me, as emerged from a piece he wrote in his paper about my musical talent after first hearing my symphony.

This performance took place early in 1833 at the Tailors' Arms in Leipzig: the "Euterpe" society had meanwhile withdrawn to these venerable premises. The room was dirty, cramped and feebly illuminated, and it was there that my work, most sloppily played by the orchestra, was introduced to the Leipzig public. I recall that evening as nothing more than an ugly nightmare: all the greater was my surprise, therefore, at the significance Laube accorded this performance. I now had high hopes of the performance which was to be given at a Gewandhaus concert, where in fact everything went off brilliantly and exactly as I had wished. Its reception was favorable; I got reviews in every paper; there was no real malice; on the contrary, most of the notices were encouraging, and Laube, having rocketed to fame, now declared his willingness to consign to me an opera text he had intended for Meyerbeer. This staggered me. I hadn't the slightest intention of trying to prove my worth as a poet, to be sure, but rather only to produce nothing more ambitious than an opera text for myself: but precisely as to how such a text had to be written I had my own definite and instinctive idea, which was immediately substantiated when Laube portentously revealed to me his subject. He announced his intention to write me a grand opera on no less a subject than Kocziusko.[1] Once again I was shaken: for I sensed immediately that Laube had a misconception about the nature of dramatic action. When I inquired about the plot, Laube was quite amazed that anything more should be required than the eventful life story of this heroic fighter for Polish freedom, out of which he would select enough incidents to typify the sufferings of an entire nation. Beyond that, of course, there was to be a Polish heroine falling in love with a Russian to provide the tragic amorous complications that would easily ensue. I told my sister Rosalie at once that I would not write the music for this subject; she backed me up, requesting only that I postpone answering him, which was greatly facilitated by my departure for Würzburg shortly thereafter, from where I eventually communicated my refusal to Laube by letter. He took this rebuff in good grace, but at no time in my life did he ever really forgive me for writing my own poems.

He was particularly contemptuous when he learned which subject matter I had chosen in preference to his brilliant political poem. I had borrowed the plot from a dramatic fable by Gozzi, *La Donna Serpente*, and had worked it out under the title *Die Feen*. The names of my heroes were culled from all kinds of Ossianic and similar poems: my prince was called Arindal; he was loved by a fairy called Ada, who held him captive away from his realm within her fairyland, until his friends at last found him after a long search and stirred him to return home by telling him his country was on the point of collapse, his capital city already in enemy hands. The loving fairy herself orders his return, for an oracle has decreed that she must subject her beloved to the sternest tests, by the mastering of which he alone can free her from the immortal world of the fairies and permit her to share his mortal destiny as a loving woman. At a moment when the prince is in deepest despair about the sorry state of affairs he finds in his country, Ada arrives and intentionally tries to shake his faith in her by deeds of the most cruel and inexplicable sort. Under the combined pressure of all these events, Arindal succumbs to the illusion that he has been seduced by an evil sorceress and tries to escape the magic spell by pronouncing a curse on Ada. Wild with sorrow, the unhappy fairy sinks down and reveals their mutual fate to her lover, who is now past all help, informing him that in punishment for having disobeyed the oracle, she is condemned to be turned to stone (this was a change I made to Gozzi's version, in which she becomes a serpent). At once it is revealed that all the terrors she had conjured up were only delusions: victory over the enemy as well as prosperity and welfare in the kingdom now set in with magical celerity; Ada alone is taken away by the servants of the oracle, and Arindal remains behind, completely out of his wits. The terrible sufferings of his insanity have not, however, propitiated the servants of the oracle: to destroy him entirely, they appear to the penitent Arindal and invite him to accompany them to the underworld under the false pretence of availing him the opportunity to break the magic spell which binds Ada. Through this ill-meant information Arindal's insanity is transformed into sublime exaltation; meanwhile one of his faithful followers, a magician, has equipped him with magic weapons and implements, armed with which he now follows the treacherous fairies. They are astounded and horrified to see Arindal win one struggle after another with the monsters of the underworld; only when they have led him to the vault in which they show him a stone in human form do they regain confidence that the bold invader will be vanquished: for this stone, which holds Ada herself, he is now compelled to disenchant if he is to avoid being transformed forever in the same way. Arindal, who has previously utilized the sword and shield given him by the magician, now uses an instrument the significance of which he has not yet understood, a lyre, also given him to take along, to the accompaniment of which he pours out his woe at the magic spell, his repentance, and his overpowering longing. The stone yields to this magic; his beloved is set free, the splendor of the fairy kingdom manifests itself, and the mighty mortal is informed that although Ada has lost her right to renounce immortality as a result of his previous tergiversations, he has now earned the right, by his own magic power, to live at Ada's side in this eternal abode.

While I had written *Die Hochzeit* without operatic embellishments and treated the material in the darkest vein, this time I festooned the subject with the most manifold variety: beside the principal pair of lovers I depicted a more ordinary couple and even introduced a coarse and comical third pair, which belonged to the operatic convention of servants and ladies' maids. As to the poetic diction and the verses themselves, I was almost intentionally careless about them. I was not nourishing my former hopes of making a name as a poet; I had really become a "musician" and a "composer" and wanted simply to write a decent libretto, for I now realized nobody else could do this for me, inasmuch as an opera book is something unique unto itself and cannot be easily brought off by poets and literati.

With the intention of setting this libretto to music, I now left Leipzig in January of 1833 to spend some time with my eldest brother Albert, who had an engagement at the theater in Würzburg. It was clearly time for me to try to begin to apply my musical skills to practical purposes, and to hunt for an appropriate opportunity to do so; in this my brother was to assist me at the little Würzburg theater. I traveled with the mail coach via Hof to Bamberg, spent a few days there in the company of a young man named Schunke, who had abandoned playing the horn to become an actor, and learned with immense interest the story of Caspar Hauser,[1] who at that time was creating a great stir and who, if I remember correctly, was pointed out to me personally; I also admired the unique regional dress of the women at market, recalled Hoffmann's stay in this place and how it had led to the writing of his tales, and went on my way to Würzburg on a farmer's cart, freezing all the way. My brother Albert, hitherto almost a stranger in my life, did his best to make me feel at home in his not very extensive quarters, was glad to find me less eccentric than the letter which I had sent him a while ago had led him to expect, and above all got me a job, exceptionally, as chorusmaster at the theater at a salary of ten guilders a month. The rest of the winter was devoted to my first practical exercises in musical management: I had to tackle in a very short time two new grand operas, in which the chorus played a major part, namely Marschner's *Der Vampyr* and Meyerbeer's *Robert le Diable*. At first I felt myself an utter tyro as a chorusmaster and made my debut with *Camilla* by Paër,[2] a score with which I was totally unacquainted. I remember having the feeling that I was embarking on something I had no right to do; I really considered myself no more than a dilettante. But soon the Marschner score began to interest me enough to make the arduous effort seem worthwhile. The score of *Robert* disappointed me greatly: to judge by the press reports, it should have been brimming with marvelous originality and unexpected innovation; I found nothing of the sort in this transparent work, and an opera with a finale like that to its second act could never be counted among the works I would place in my pantheon; I was impressed only by the subterranean key trumpets representing the voice of the mother's ghost in the last act. The aesthetic demoralization into which I was plunged by my continued daily dealings with this work was remarkable. My original distaste for this flat, completely uninteresting and, particularly for a German musician, repellent work lost itself gradually in the interest I felt I had to take in the success of the performance, until I ceased to be concerned with the shallow, affected and modishly derivative melodies except from the standpoint of their eliciting applause. Since my future career as a conductor of music was also at stake, my brother, who was very anxious on my behalf, was inclined to approve this lack of classical rigor on my part; and thus the groundwork was laid for that decline in my classical taste which was destined to last for some time. But it didn't happen quickly enough to prevent my evidencing my great lack of experience in lighter musical styles. My brother wanted to spatchcock into Bellini's *Straniera* a cavatina from his *Il Pirata*, the score of which was not available; he commissioned me to take care of the instrumentation for this aria. It was impossible for me to recognize from the piano transcription the original loud and heavy instrumentation of the musically extraordinarily thin ritornellos and bridge passages, and the composer of a big C major symphony with closing fugue could find no other way out than by recourse to a few flutes and clarinets playing in thirds. The cavatina sounded so ineffective and hollow in the orchestral rehearsal that my brother, who then decided to do without this insertion, reproached me bitterly for the expense of copying the parts. But I knew how to get my revenge: I added a new allegro section to Aubry's tenor aria in Marschner's *Vampyr*, to which I also wrote the words. My work turned out to be demoniacally effective, earning the applause of the public and enthusiastic recognition from my brother.

In the same German style I wrote the music to *Die Feen* during the course of the year 1833. My brother and his wife left Würzburg after Easter in order to give guest performances elsewhere, and I remained behind with the children, three little girls of the tenderest age, which placed me in the strange position of being the responsible guardian, a role in which I did not particularly distinguish myself. My time was divided between my work and boon companions, and so it was virtually inevitable that I would neglect the care of my wards. Among the friends I made there, Alexander Müller, a deft musician and pianist as well as a gay young blade, gained great influence over me: I was particularly impressed by his truly extraordinary talent for improvisation; he could captivate me for hours with fantastic variations on given themes. Together with him and other friends, among whom Valentin Hamm[1] with his grotesque figure, excellent violin playing, and particularly his enormous span at the piano (his hand stretched an octave and a half), entertained me hugely, I often undertook excursions into the surrounding country, during which we made merry with Bavarian beer and Franconian wine. A beer garden called The Last Chance, pleasantly situated on a hill, was the almost nightly scene of my wild carousing and fiery boisterousness; during the warm summer nights I never got back to my three foster children without having worked myself up into ecstasies over art and the world in general.

I remember doing a mean thing which has remained ever since a blot on my sensibility. Among my companions was a blond and unusually rapturous Swabian named Fröhlich, with whom I exchanged scores of the C minor symphony, which we had both copied out. This very weak but rather irritable character had conceived such an antipathy toward a youth named André, whose somewhat malign physiognomy did not please me either, that he declared this person was spoiling his evenings for him, wherever he met him. The unfortunate object of this hatred tried nonetheless to approach us whenever he could: friction developed; nevertheless André kept reappearing, more or less as a challenge. One evening Fröhlich lost his temper. After some insulting retort, he tried to chase him away from our table by whacking him with a stick; a fight ensued, in which Fröhlich's friends, who shared his antipathy, felt obliged to participate. A mad longing to join the fray came over me as well; I began belting our unhappy victim along with the others and heard the sound of one hard whack which I delivered as it struck André's skull, whereupon I caught the bewildered look he gave me. I relate this incident to be absolved from a sin that has weighed upon me unforgettably ever since. I can compare this sad memory only with one from my earliest childhood, comprising the frightful impressions left by the drowning of some puppies in a shallow pool behind my uncle's house in Eisleben. As the sufferings of others, and particularly those of animals, have always affected me almost too deeply, even to the point of filling me with a strange kind of disgust at life itself, these memories of my thoughtless cruelty have remained especially vivid.

The recollection of my first love affair is the more innocent by contrast. It was only natural that one of the young ladies in the chorus, whose voices I was training daily, would find a way to attract my attention. Therese Ringelmann, a gravedigger's daughter, led me by her beautiful soprano voice to believe that it was my duty to make a great singer of her. From the time I broached this subject with her, she became particularly attentive to the attire she wore to choral rehearsals and pleasantly excited my imagination by a string of white pearls which she wound through her hair. During the summer holidays, when I remained in town alone, I gave her regular singing lessons according to a method that has remained unclear to me to this day. I also paid a number of visits to her home, where I always found her mother and sister but never her eerie father. We also met quite often in the public gardens; but a rather unloverlike sense of shame kept me from confessing my infatuation to my friends. Whether her family's modest status, or her obvious lack of education, or my own doubt as to the sincerity of my affection was to blame for this I cannot precisely say; but I know that after I was pressed to make some formal declaration of my intentions, and was given grounds for jealous suspicions to boot, the relationship soon dissolved without a trace.

A deeper love affair developed with Friederike Galvani, the daughter of a mechanic and of pronounced Italian background. Very musical and gifted with a pleasant, easily trained voice, she had been taken under my brother's wing, and he had helped her make a successful debut in the theater. Very small in stature but with big black eyes and a sweet disposition, she had already inspired the enduring love of the first oboist of the orchestra, a solid and reliable musician. They were generally considered to be engaged: but, owing to some embarrassing incident in his past, he was not allowed to visit her parents' house before the marriage, which was continually being further and further postponed. When the autumn of this Würzburg year drew near, I received an invitation from friends, among whom were the oboist and his bride-to-be, to attend a rural wedding at several hours' distance from Würzburg. There was a lot of bumpkin merriment: there was drinking and dancing, during which I tried to refresh my long-forgotten skill on the violin, but without being able to handle even the part of second violin to the satisfaction of my fellow musicians. But my success with the gentle Friederike was all the greater, and I danced with her madly up and down the rows of peasants until in the general excitement we abandoned all restraint and, while her official lover was playing the dance music, began spontaneously hugging and kissing each other. That her fiancé, noticing all this, reacted with good grace and accepted his position with a touch of sadness but without any attempt to interfere aroused a certain self-satisfaction in me for the first time in my life. I had never had any reason to believe myself capable of making a favorable impression on girls. As regards my outward appearance, I could not nurse the slightest illusion of being handsome, and I really had never noticed a pretty girl paying any attention to me before. On the other hand, my dealings with men of my age were becoming more self-confident: my unusual vivacity and always quick excitability made me at last aware of a certain power over the slower-moving people I associated with, whether by carrying them away with my enthusiasm or simply by benumbing them. From my poor oboist's silent self-control upon becoming aware of Friederike's fiery advances, I acquired, as I have said, the first inkling that I could amount to something not only among men but also among women. The Franconian wine did its part in producing an ever increasing uproar, under the cover of which I began behaving openly as Friederike's lover. Far into the night, as day was already breaking, we all started home to Würzburg in an open wagon; this was the crowning triumph of my pleasant adventure; whereas all the rest, even at last the care-worn oboist, were sleeping it off in the face of the dawning day, I remained awake cheek-to-cheek with Friederike, listening to the warbling of the larks greet the rising sun.

During the days that followed we were hardly conscious of what had happened. A not unbecoming sense of shame kept us apart; but I soon gained access to her family and from then on was welcomed there daily, when I would linger for hours in openly amorous activity in the same domestic circle from which the unfortunate husband-to-be remained excluded. Not a word of this latter relationship was ever mentioned, and Friederike never for a moment thought of making any change in it; there was never any question of my taking the groom's place. The familiarity with which I was received by these people, and by Friederike most of all, had something of a natural force about it, just as when winter yields to spring; social consequences had no weight whatever, and this was precisely the most charming and flattering aspect of this first youthful love affair, which by no means ever degenerated into behavior that might have given rise to suspicion or concern. The relationship ended only with my departure from Würzburg, which was marked by a most touching and tearful farewell. I kept her in mind for a long time thereafter, but without trying to correspond with her. Two years later I visited her again on my way through the town: the poor child approached me with greatest diffidence. Her oboist had remained faithful to her; but without yet being in a position to marry him she had become a mother. Thereafter I heard nothing further of her.

Amid all these exciting events I plugged away at my opera. The good mood I needed for this was induced by the affectionate interest of my sister Rosalie. When my income as chorusmaster dried up with the oncoming of the summer season, my sister again undertook to provide me with adequate pocket money, so that I would not become a burden to anyone and could devote myself entirely to the completion of my work. Much later in life I found a long letter I had written to Rosalie at the time, which evidenced my tender, almost romantic devotion to this magnanimous being.*[1]

When winter was at hand, my brother returned and the theater reopened; I no longer had any official position there, but I was therefore all the more active in the concerts of the music society, under whose auspices I got my big C major overture and symphony performed, and eventually some excerpts from my new opera as well. An amateur singer with a fine voice, Fräulein Friedel, sang Ada's great aria; and in addition a trio was sung which made such a strong impact on my brother, who was taking one of the parts, that he admitted missing his entry at one particularly moving point.

My work was completed by Christmas, the score being copied out with the most commendable neatness, and now I intended to return to Leipzig early in the new year, in order to get my opera accepted by the theater there. On the trip home I stopped in Nuremberg, where I spent a week with my sister Klara and her husband, who were engaged at the local theater. I well remember how happy and comfortable I felt during this pleasant visit to the very same relatives who, when I had visited them in Magdeburg a few years before, had been skeptical of my determination to take up music as a career. Now I had really become a musician, had written a grand opera, and had brought many pieces to performance without suffering failure: awareness of all this did me much good and was no less flattering to my relatives, who now perceived that my apparent misfortunes had in the end been turned to my advantage. I was merry and relaxed, stimulated not only by the sociable house of my brother-in-law but also by the jolly taverns of Nuremberg. I got back to Leipzig in a confident and elated mood, where I was able to lay the three huge volumes of my completed score before my highly satisfied mother and my deeply delighted sister.

At that time my family was somewhat the richer through the return of my brother Julius from his long peregrinations. He had worked as a goldsmith in Paris for a quite long period and now intended to establish himself as such in Leipzig; he too, like the rest, was eager to hear something from my opera, which was no easy task, given my inability to play such things in an easily comprehensible manner and my need to work myself up into a state of complete ecstasy before it was possible for me to render a piece with any effect. Rosalie knew that I was hungry for something approaching a declaration of love on her part: I do not know whether the embrace and sisterly kiss with which she rewarded me after I had sung Ada's big aria for her were rooted in real emotion

* Note in the margin of the manuscript, in Cosima's hand: "Copy of the letter". See end-notes.

or tactful consideration. But there was no mistaking the zeal with which she went after the director of the theater, Ringelhardt,[1] as well as the conductor and the stage director, to induce them to accept my opera for performance, an effort in which she was soon successful. I was particularly interested to learn that the management wanted to settle the question of the proper costuming for my drama at once: to my astonishment I heard that this was deemed to be in the oriental genre, whereas I had supposed by my choice of names that the drama's nordic character had been clearly established: but it was precisely these names that were found inappropriate, on the grounds that fairies belonged not in the North but rather in the East, just as Gozzi's original evinced an unmistakably oriental tinge. Highly incensed, I fought against the insufferable turban and kaftan costumes and demanded energetically the knightly garb typifying the earliest period of the middle ages. Then I had to come to a precise understanding with Kapellmeister Stegmayer[2] about my score. This curiously small and fat little man, with a head of tightly curling blond hair and an exceptionally jovial disposition, was difficult to pin down on any subject. Over our wine at the tavern we could come to agreement quickly; yet whenever we sat down at the piano I had to listen to the most bizarre objections, the basis of which remained long unclear to me. As these vacillations greatly delayed the whole affair, I got together with the stage director of the theater, Hauser,[3] a singer and friend of the arts who was very popular in Leipzig at that period. I had the strangest experiences with this man as well: the man who had won public acclaim with his performances as the "Barber" and as the English tourist in *Fra Diavolo* suddenly revealed himself as the most fanatical adherent of the oldest music. I was amazed to hear him speak with barely disguised contempt of Mozart himself, and the only thing troubling him seemed to be that we had no operas by Sebastian Bach. After he had expostulated with me to the effect that no dramatic music worthy of the term had as yet been written and that only Gluck had shown any ability for it, he proceeded to what seemed an exhaustive examination of my own opera, but instead of giving me the requested verdict whether it was suitable for performance, he busied himself in trying to demonstrate the false tendencies in every one of my numbers: I sweated blood under the unparalleled torment of going through my work with this man. I told my mother and sister how discouraged I was. All these delays had already managed to make the performance of my opera at the originally scheduled date a pure impossibility; now it was postponed to August of the current year (1834).

An unforgettable experience infused me with fresh courage. Old

Bierey,[1] a veteran musician of great competence who had himself been a successful composer in his time, and who had gained in particular a splendid practicality from his long tenure as director of the theater in Breslau, was then living in Leipzig and was a good friend of my family. My mother and sister requested him to deliver a verdict as to the performability of my opera and submitted my score to him for this purpose. I was then deeply moved and shaken to see the old man appear one day at my family's house and to hear him excitedly assure everyone how he found it scarcely credible that such a young man as I could have written such a score as this. His testimony as to the size of my talent was truly irresistible and positively amazed me. When asked whether as a practical matter he considered the work performable and effective, he said he regretted only being no longer at the head of a theater, as otherwise he would consider it a great stroke of luck to win such a man as me as a permanent collaborator in all his ventures: this produced a truly blissful state of mind in my family, all the more firmly founded because they knew Bierey to be no amiable windbag but rather a hard-bitten practitioner schooled by a lifetime of experience.

I now could bear the postponement in good spirits and abandon myself for a while to hopes for the future. Among other things, I enjoyed renewing my acquaintance with Laube, who now, despite the fact that I had not set his *Kocziusko* to music, stood at the zenith of his fame. The first part of his epistolary novel *Das junge Europa* had appeared and, in conjunction with all the youthful aspirations I harbored at the time, stimulated me very greatly. Though his doctrine was really no more than a reflection of Heinse's *Ardinghello*,[2] he had certainly succeeded in giving eloquent expression to the forces surging among young people at that time. The movement was most prominent in literary criticism, which was directed chiefly against the apparent or real impotence of the semi-classical occupants of our literary thrones. Without the slightest clemency the old guard, to which Tieck was also relegated, was treated as a sheer encumbrance and hindrance to the evolution of a new literature. The palpable change in my estimate of the German composers I had revered and venerated that now took place was in part traceable to the influence of these so attractively cheeky critical skirmishes, but mainly attributable to my impressions from another guest performance of Schröder-Devrient in Leipzig, who carried everyone away with her interpretation of Romeo in Bellini's *Romeo and Juliet*. This was like nothing we had ever seen before. The sight of the boldly romantic figure of the young hero projected against a background of such obviously shallow and empty music prompted one, at any rate, to ruminate on the causes of the ineffectuality of most of the solid German music hitherto used in drama. Without yet losing myself in these meditations too deeply, I allowed myself to be borne along by the current of my excitable youthful sensibility and was instinctively impelled to shed that brooding seriousness which in my earlier years had driven me to such dramatic mysticism. What Pohlenz by his conducting of the Ninth Symphony, what the Vienna Conservatory, Dionys Weber, and many other clumsy performances, whereby classical music had been made to appear feeble, had not completely achieved was now accomplished by the inconceivable charm of this most unclassical, most Italian music as enhanced by the superbly incandescent characterization of Romeo by Schröder-Devrient. The influence*[1] exercised upon my judgment by these powerful impressions, the causes of which were a mystery to me, was revealed in the frivolous tone in which I tossed off a short review of Weber's *Euryanthe* for the *Elegante Zeitung*. This opera had been given by the regular Leipzig company shortly before Schröder-Devrient's appearance; cold and listless singers, among whom I particularly remember the heroine showing up in the wilderness wearing the hooped sleeves then in fashion, had simply gone through the motions of satisfying the classical demands of the work, thereby doing their utmost to dispel even the most enthusiastic impressions of Weber's music I had formed in my youth. I didn't know what to say to one of Laube's like-minded friends when he pointed out the agonies of this performance, particularly after it became possible for him to contrast it with the enchanting impression made by that Romeo evening. Here I found myself confronted by a problem I was inclined to solve for myself as easily as possible and proceeded to prove my courage in casting off preconceptions by the above-mentioned short review in which I simply scoffed at *Euryanthe*. Just as I had sown my wild oats as a student, I now boldly embarked on the same course in the development of my artistic tastes.

It was May, lovely spring weather, and a pleasure trip I planned with a friend into the promised land of my youthful dreams, Bohemia, was intended to bring the uninhibited "young-European" mood to full floration. This friend was Theodor Apel. I had known him for a long time and had always felt especially flattered at having won his cordial liking, for I rendered him, as the son of August Apel, the master of metrical forms and reviver of Greek verse forms, an admiring deference

* Note in the margin of the manuscript, in Cosima's hand: "Second interruption due to Will's absence!!" (see end-note) followed by the date of recommencement: "(March 9th 1866)".

of the kind I had never before been able to bestow on the offspring of a famous man. Well-to-do and a member of a respected family, his friendship also afforded me some contact, rather rare in my life, with upper-middle-class surroundings; while my mother was delighted to see me associating with such people, I was for my part extremely gratified by the realization of the cordiality with which I was received in such circles. Apel wanted very much to become a poet, and I took it for granted he had all that was needed for such a career, in particular the freedom given him by independent means from the need to earn his living and thereby from acquiring any utilitarian professional qualifications. Curiously enough his mother, who had married a Leipzig lawyer after the death of his distinguished father, was rather concerned on this point and wished to see her son follow a proper profession, as a lawyer, as she seemed to have no very elevated opinion of his poetic gifts. I owed my extremely friendly relationship with this lady to her efforts to convert me to her opinion in this matter, in order that I might use my intimate influence on my friend to avert the calamity of having yet another poet in the family. Her presumption succeeded only in stimulating me to encourage him in the choice of a literary career even more strongly than I would have done based solely on my opinion of his talent, thereby keeping him in a rebellious mood against his family. This was just what he wanted. As he was also studying music and could compose quite cutely, I soon reached a state of wide agreement with him. The fact that he had spent the very year in which I had sunk into the lowest depths of student madness in Heidelberg and not at Leipzig had kept him unsullied by any share in my excesses, and when we now met again in Leipzig in the spring of 1834, the only thing that shaped our friendship was our artistic ambition, to which we now endeavored experimentally to add some element savoring of the pleasure of life. We would have been delighted to launch ourselves into spectacular adventures, if only our immediate circumstances and the pressures of the bourgeois world had permitted. Despite the intensity of our impulses the best we could do was plan that excursion into Bohemia. At all events, it was worth something that we made the trip in our own carriage and not by mail coach, and our main enjoyment throughout, particularly in Teplitz, for example, where we stayed for several weeks, consisted in the lengthy outings we made daily in this lovely carriage. When we had eaten our trout at the Wilhelmsburg and drunk the good Czernosek wine with Bilin water, and beside that duly excited ourselves over Hoffmann, Beethoven, Shakespeare, Heinse's *Ardinghello*, and other matters of this sort, and then drove back to our hotel, The King of Prussia, where we had a big balcony room on the second floor, in the dusk of a summer evening, stretched comfortably in our carriage, we considered we had lived the day as young gods and in our exuberance found nothing better to do than quarrel with each other frightfully, which, particularly when the windows were left open, would attract numbers of alarmed listeners in the square in front of the inn.

On several lovely mornings I stole away from my friend to take breakfast alone at the Schlackenburg, and seized the opportunity to sketch in my notebook the draft for a new opera text. With this end in view I had closely studied the plot of Shakespeare's *Measure for Measure*, which, as befitted my mood at the time, I adapted very freely into an opera libretto to which I gave the title *Das Liebesverbot*. Abetted by the agitated state of mind in which I had rebelled against classical operatic music, *Das junge Europa* and *Ardinghello* now set the tone for my basic conception, which was directed in particular against puritan hypocrisy, thereby leading to a glorification of "free sensuality". I took pains to interpret the solemn Shakespearean text strictly in this manner; I could see only the somber, strait-laced governor, himself aflame with a frightful passion for the beautiful novice, who, while pleading with him to pardon her brother, condemned to death for illicit love, succeeds only in kindling in the rigid puritan an even more fiery and dangerous infatuation by infecting him with the lovely warmth of her human feelings. That these powerful aspects of the drama are so richly developed in Shakespeare solely that they may be in the end weighed all the more heavily in the scales of justice was no concern of mine; all I cared about was to uncover the sinfulness of hypocrisy and the artificiality of the judicial attitude toward morality. Thus, I departed from *Measure for Measure* entirely and let the hypocrite be punished only by the avenging power of love. I transferred the locus from a legendary Vienna to the capital of fiery Sicily, in which a German governor, incensed at the inconceivably loose morals of the citizenry, attempts to induce puritanical reforms and fails miserably in the process. Presumably *La muette de Portici*[1] contributed something to this plot, as did certain recollections of the Sicilian Vespers:[2] when I consider that even the gentle Sicilian Bellini constituted a contributing factor in this composition, I cannot help smiling at the strange medley in which the most extraordinary misinterpretations found their embodiment.

For the moment this remained only a draft. The real struggles with my work were scheduled to begin only after this merry excursion to

Bohemia was over. I led my friend to Prague in triumph to let him absorb the same impressions that had so vividly affected me. We met my lovely lady friends in Prague itself, for as a result of the death of old Count Pachta there had been many changes in the family and Pravonin was no longer inhabited by his daughters. My conduct was relaxed and highly exuberant, whereby a certain desire to avenge the bitter feelings with which I had previously left this circle expressed itself. My friend was well received. The changed family circumstances were forcing the girls ever more imperatively to come to some decision as to their future, and a rich bourgeois, so long as he was not a businessman but rather had inherited money, seemed to the distracted mother a good answer to her problem. Without the slightest malice aforethought I expressed my delight at the curious flutter caused by Theodor's introduction to this family by the merriest and wildest pranks, which comprised my entire relations with the young ladies. They could not understand why I seemed to have changed so much: no love of wrangling, no pedagogical fervor, no desire to proselytize, all these things that had so irritated them in me were no longer in evidence; but they also couldn't get a sensible word out of me, and now that they were seriously interested in discussion they got nothing in return but the most farcical responses. As I felt myself something of an uncaged bird in this situation, I allowed myself many a liberty against which they felt themselves helpless, and my spirits were excited all the more when my friend, who was carried away by my example, tried to imitate me, which was taken in very bad grace. Only once did it come to a serious approach to one another: I was sitting at the piano and overheard my friend telling the ladies that I had been impelled in a conversation at a tavern to respond very fiercely to someone who had expressed some reservations about the domestic and practical abilities of the two sisters. I was much moved to discover, as a result of their reaction to my friend's remarks, what unpleasant experiences these ladies had suffered in this respect, for what seemed to me a very natural act on my part touched them like some unexpected good turn. Jenny came up to me, embraced and kissed me with great warmth. By general consent I was now granted the right to behave with almost studied rudeness, and I even responded to Jenny's outpouring only with my usual banter and foolishness.

In our hotel, the then famous Black Horse, I found a terrain on which I could completely exhaust whatever exuberant spirits did not find expression in the Pachta house. Out of the casual company of table companions and fellow hotel guests we were able to form a group of followers who could be inspired nightly by us to the wildest pranks, to which a businessman from Frankfurt an der Oder, a timid and uncommonly small person, who nonetheless would gladly have passed himself off as a hothead, particularly incited me, as much because of the extraordinary circumstance of meeting someone from the Other Frankfurt as for any other reason. Whoever is familiar with the conditions prevailing in Austria at that time will get an idea of my recklessness when I report that I once managed to induce our convivial group in the dining hall to bellow the *Marseillaise* loudly out into the night. That I followed up this heroic act by going out half-dressed on the outer ledges of the roof in front of my third-story bedroom from one window to another naturally horrified all those who knew nothing of my childhood predilection for such acrobatic stunts. Whereas I had subjected myself to such dangers without fear, I was greatly sobered the following morning when I received a summons from the police, as my recollection of singing the *Marseillaise* worried me quite a bit. After I had been detained at the station for a long time as a result of some misunderstanding, the inspector supposed to examine me found the time too short in the end for a serious interrogation and, to my great relief, released me after a few perfunctory questions about the proposed length of my stay. Nevertheless, we thought it advisable henceforth to yield less frequently to the temptation to disport ourselves so recklessly under the wings of the double eagle. By means of a circuitous route* determined by our insatiable love of adventures, which as a matter of fact occurred solely in our heads and comprised no more than the usual diversions of travel, we finally arrived back in Leipzig. And with this homecoming my period of carefree youthfulness most definitely came to a close. While I had not been free of serious excesses and passionate excitement up to that time, *Care* now entered my life.

My family had been eagerly awaiting my return to let me know that I had been offered a position as music director of the theater in Magdeburg. During the current summer month this company was performing at the health spa Lauchstädt; the manager could get nowhere with the incompetent conductor assigned to the job and in this emergency had applied to Leipzig to get a replacement as soon as possible. Stegmayer, the conductor who was supposed to study the score of my *Die Feen* but showed little inclination to do so during the hot

---

* Note in the margin of the manuscript, in Wagner's hand: "(Still to add: adventure with the Uhlmann family in a little town whose name I have forgotten, on the way from Karlsbad to Teplitz. Apel in love – I out in the cold. Add all this. Dictator's note.)"

summer weather, hastily recommended me for this position and thereby
succeeded in getting rid of a nagging presence. For although I was hoping
to remain free to indulge my artistic predilections without restraint, I
was also gripped by a growing desire for the independence that could
be won only by earning my own living, a desire all the more under-
standable given my financial circumstances. But I had a premonition that
Lauchstädt would not be the place where I would gain such a foundation
in life; nor did I find it easy to give in to this little plot to delay the
production of my *Die Feen*. I therefore decided to make a preliminary
visit to the place to see how things stood.

The little spa had acquired a highly favorable reputation during the
time of Schiller and Goethe; its wooden theater had been built according
to Goethe's design; the first performance of *Die Braut von Messina* had
taken place there. Although I recounted all this to myself, the place still
made a rather dubious impression on me. I went to hunt for the director
of the company; he was out of the house; a dirty little boy, his son,
was dispatched with me to the theater to find "Papa". But we met him
along the way, an elderly man in a dressing-gown with a cap on his head.
He interrupted his expressions of pleasure at meeting me with a
complaint about a serious indisposition, to combat which he sent his son
to a nearby bar to bring him a Schnaps, after pressing a real silver coin
into his hand with an ostentation calculated to impress me. This director
was Heinrich Bethmann,[1] widower of the noted actress Bethmann,[2] who,
having flourished during the great era of German drama, had in
particular won such lasting favor from the King of Prussia[3] that this was
extended long after her death to include even her husband. Bethmann
regularly drew a good pension from the Prussian court and enjoyed its
protection, without ever quite succeeding in forfeiting these favors by
his irregular and dissipated way of life. At the moment he had reached
a low ebb through continuous involvement in theater management; his
diction and manners evidenced the saccharine refinement of a bygone
era, whereas everything he did and all his surroundings testified to the
most shameful decay. He led me back to his house, where he introduced
me to the "Directrix", who was lying with a lame foot on a curious couch
while an elderly basso, concerning whose excessive devotion Bethmann
complained to me quite unblushingly, smoked his pipe at her side. From
there the director took me to his stage director, who lived in the same
house. With this man, who was then engaged in a conference about the
repertory with the theater factotum, a toothless old bag of bones, he left

me to make all the necessary arrangements, upon which Herr Schmale,[1] the stage director, told me laughingly with a shrug of the shoulders that this was the way the director did things, generally leaving everything to him and paying attention to nothing: there he was now conferring with Kröge for more than an hour about what could be performed next Sunday; he was supposed to put on *Don Giovanni*, but how was he to arrange a rehearsal, seeing as the Merseburg municipal bandsmen, who made up the orchestra, were not willing to rehearse on Saturday? During all this Schmale was continually reaching through an open window to the branch of a cherry tree, picking and chewing cherries one after the other, and spitting out the cherry-stones with explosive noise. This last activity had a decisive effect on me, for curiously enough I have an inborn distaste for fruit. I informed the stage manager that there was no point in troubling himself about *Don Giovanni* on Sunday if the director was counting on me to make my debut at that performance, for I would have to disappoint him as I had first to return to Leipzig to take care of some matters there. This polite way of turning down the job, a decision I came to at once, caused me to indulge in some dissimulation by making it appear as if I really would do something to help them in Lauchstädt, a pretext that was really unnecessary considering my intention never to return there. They offered me help in finding a place to live, and a young actor I had by chance known in Würzburg undertook to be my guide in the matter. In taking me to the best house he knew, he told me I would thereby have the pleasure of living in the same abode with the prettiest and nicest girl to be found at the time in Lauchstädt: this was the leading lady of the troupe, Fräulein Minna Planer, of whom I must surely have heard before.

As luck would have it, the lady in question met us in the doorway of the house. Her bearing and appearance offered the most extreme contrast with all the unpleasant impressions of the theater I had formed during that fateful morning: looking very charming and fresh, the young actress was distinguished by great composure and solemn assurance in her movements and behavior, which lent a captivating air of dignity to her friendly face; her scrupulously clean and tidy dress completed the startling effect of this unexpected encounter. After I had been introduced to her in the hall as the new conductor and she had mustered with surprise the stranger who seemed so young for this title, she recommended me kindly to the landlady to be well taken care of and departed with proud and serene gait across the street to her rehearsal. I rented the apartment on the spot, agreed to conduct *Don Giovanni* that Sunday, regretted not having brought along my bags from Leipzig, and hastened back in order to be able to return to Lauchstädt all the sooner.

The die was cast. The serious side of life confronted me at once in significant experiences. In Leipzig I had to take uneasy leave of Laube; he had been banished from Saxony at the request of Prussia and could guess the deeper meaning of this act. The era of open reaction against the liberal movements of the early 1830s had arrived: that Laube had participated in no political activity but rather had engaged only in literary work in furtherance of aesthetic aims made the police measures appear quite incomprehensible for a time. The abhorrent doubletalk with which the Leipzig authorities answered all his inquiries as to the reasons for his banishment soon aroused his suspicions as to what they really had in mind for him. Because Leipzig was irreplaceably valuable terrain for his literary activity, it mattered a lot to him to be able to remain in the vicinity. My friend Apel owned a lovely estate on Prussian soil only a few hours' distance from Leipzig; we conceived the desire to see Laube hospitably harbored there; my friend, in whose power it lay to provide the persecuted man a place of refuge, without infringing upon the letter of the law, acceded to this plan at once, but confessed to us the next day, after having conferred with his family about the case, that he thought he might incur some unpleasantness if he took in Laube. At this Laube gave him an unforgettable smile, of the kind I have had frequent occasion in life to permit to glide across my own features. He bade farewell; and after a short time we got word that he had been arrested in the wake of new reprisals against the members of the students' league and was incarcerated in the Berlin municipal prison. With these two experiences weighing upon me like lead, I packed my scanty portmanteau, took leave of my mother and sister, and strode determinedly into my new career as a music director.

In order to get hold of the little room under Minna's abode as my new home, I had to play along with Bethmann's theatrical plans. There really was a performance of *Don Giovanni* straight away, for the director, who prided himself on his artistic courtesy, offered me the opera as a piece well-chosen for the debut of an aspiring young artist of good family. Although I had not yet done any conducting except for some of my own orchestral compositions, and certainly never an opera, both rehearsal and performance went quite well; there were only a few irregularities in the recitative of Donna Anna; yet this didn't cause any hostility towards me, and when I coolly and confidently took my place for *Lumpaci*

Vagabundus,[1] for which I had complete responsibility from the beginning, everybody seemed generally quite satisfied with this new acquisition. That I submitted without bitterness and even cheerfully to this abuse of my musical talent was attributable less to this period of indiscretion in my musical tastes, as I have termed it, than to my association with Minna Planer, who was cast in this fantastic farce as the Fairy Amorosa. In the midst of this dust cloud of frivolity and vulgarity, she seemed to me always like a fairy of whom one could not say why she had descended into this maelstrom, which in fact hardly seemed to suck her in or even affect her at all. While I could discover nothing in the opera singers beyond the familiar stage caricatures and grimaces, this lovely actress differed wholly from those around her by her unblemished sobriety and elegant tidiness, as well as the absence of all theatrical affectation or comical stiltedness. There was only one young man I could place beside Minna in respect of similar attributes: this was Friedrich Schmitt,[2] who had just begun his theatrical career with the hope of making his mark in opera, for which he felt well equipped by a splendid tenor voice. He too differed from the rest of the company, especially in the earnestness he brought to bear in his studies and his performances; the soulful, manly tone of his chest voice, his clear and noble enunciation, as well as his intelligent phrasing, remain exemplary in my memory. That he was without any acting gift and moved about the stage clumsily and awkwardly soon hampered his progress; but to me he remained a clever and original man of honest and reliable character, the only one worthy of my association.

But my association with my kindly housemate soon became a passionate addiction, and she returned the ingenuously impetuous advances of the twenty-one-year-old conductor with a certain tolerant amazement which, far from any coquetry or ulterior motive, soon permitted the establishment of friendly relations with her. When I returned one night late to my room on the ground floor, going through the window because I had not taken the housekey along with me, the noise of my entrance drew Minna to the window above mine; I asked her, still standing on the windowsill, to permit me to come and bid her goodnight; she had no objection whatever, but this had to be accomplished through her window because she always had her door locked by servants of the house and no one could get in that way; she facilitated my handshake by leaning out with the upper part of her body, so that I could grasp her hand from my place on the windowsill. When soon after I had an attack of erysipelas, from which I frequently suffered, and concealed myself from the world in my little room with swollen and distorted features, Minna visited me time after time, treated me and assured me that my ugly face didn't matter in the least. Once recovered, I thereupon visited her and complained about a sore spot on my mouth that had remained, which I considered so unpleasant that I apologized for showing it to her; she found nothing wrong with this either: then I opined that she would certainly not give me a kiss; whereupon she gave me practical proof that she didn't shrink from this either. All this was done on her part with a friendly calm and serenity that had something almost motherly about it and by no means suggested frivolity or heartlessness.

After only a few weeks the troupe had to leave Lauchstädt to spend the rest of the summer giving guest performances in Rudolstadt. I was very anxious to make what was then a rather bothersome journey in Minna's company; if I had succeeded in extracting from Bethmann my well-earned pay for my work as music director, there would have been no problem arranging this: but in this matter I encountered the most extraordinary difficulties, which in the course of fateful years grew in a chronic way into the strangest syndrome. I had already learned in Lauchstädt that there was only one man who got his salary paid punctually: this was the basso Kneisel, whom I had first met smoking his pipe beside the sofa where the directrix nursed her arthritic hip. I was assured that, if I really cared about seeing part of my salary, I could only achieve this by paying court to Madame Bethmann. On this occasion I preferred to go to my family for help and to this end went alone to Rudolstadt via Leipzig, where, to my mother's astonishment and distress, I had to replenish my funds from family coffers. On the way to Leipzig I had stopped off at the estate of Apel, who had come to join me in Lauchstädt for the trip. His arrival in Lauchstädt is etched in my memory by a wild party my wealthy friend gave in my honor at the local tavern. During this event one of my companions and I succeeded in completely demolishing an enormous tile oven of the massive type we had in our rooms at the inn. The next morning none of us could understand how it had happened.

On this journey to Rudolstadt I passed for the first time through Weimar, where on a rainy day I sought out Goethe's house with curiosity but without emotion; I had expected something different and looked forward to somewhat more lively impressions from the theatrical activities in Rudolstadt, to which I was now impelled with great haste. Although I was not scheduled to conduct there, this function being reserved for the director of the ducal orchestra specially engaged for our performances, I was so busy with rehearsals for the many operas and musical comedies with which the public of this principality, accustomed mainly to bird shoots, had to be regaled that I found no time for excursions into the little state's pleasant surroundings. Beyond these hard and poorly recompensed duties, I was captivated during my six weeks in Rudolstadt by two passions, one of which developed from my delight in writing the libretto for *Das Liebesverbot* and the other from my rapidly growing affection for Minna. At about this time I sketched, to be sure, one musical composition, namely a symphony in E major, whose first movement (in 3/4 time) was actually completed; in style and construction this work was greatly influenced by Beethoven's Seventh and Eighth Symphonies, and as far as I can recall I believe I would have had nothing to be ashamed of if I had managed to complete it or had even retained the fragment. But I had already begun at this time to come to the conclusion that to go beyond Beethoven in the symphonic area and to do anything new and noteworthy was an impossibility; whereas the opera, on the contrary, in which I increasingly felt myself to have no real predecessor, presented itself in varied and alluring shapes as a fascinating art form. In considerable excitement I thus completed my new opera libretto in the few hours of leisure available to me and this time was much more careful as regards diction and versification than with the preparation of my book for *Die Feen*, just as I also proceeded to the elaboration and even the invention of the various situations with far greater awareness than when writing the earlier work.

On the other hand, I now began to experience the first pangs and worries of a lover's jealousy. An inexplicable change had occurred in Minna's hitherto well-meaning and gentle demeanor towards me; it appeared that my naive attempts to gain her favor, which were in no sense directed toward an affair but in which a seasoned observer could rather have detected only the easily satisfied exuberance of a youthful infatuation, had caused the very respectable actress to be the target of some gossip. I was astonished to learn, first from her reserved manner and later from her own lips, that she felt compelled to inquire into the seriousness of my intentions and to consider their possible consequences. She was at that time, as I had already discovered, on very intimate terms with a young nobleman, whose acquaintance I first made at Lauchstädt where he used to visit her, and in whom I recognized an open and honest devotion to Minna. Within her circle of friends she was considered as already engaged to Herr von O.,[1] although it soon necessarily became clear that there could be no question of marriage, as the lover was without money yet came from such a distinguished family that his social position as well as his chosen career necessitated his sacrificing himself to a marriage of convenience. Some hint of all this seems to have reached Minna during this stay at Rudolstadt, which made her grave, even sad, and more inclined to treat my impetuous approaches with cool reserve. After riper consideration I recognized that *Das junge Europa*, *Ardinghello* and *Das Liebesverbot* were not on the programme, but rather that between the Fairy Amorosa in a playful theatrical mood and "the child of honest parents", who was looking for a safe position in life, there were certain palpable differences. Greatly discouraged and irritated, I proceeded to accentuate the wildest scenes in my *Liebesverbot* and during the evenings rioted with a few crass comrades in the sausage-scented atmosphere of the Rudolstadt public gardens, where my vexation even brought me once again in contact with the vice of gambling, although this time only the very innocuous form of the dice and roulette tables set up in the open market place.

I welcomed the time when we left Rudolstadt for the six-month-long winter season at the provincial capital, Magdeburg, chiefly because I could there resume my place at the head of the orchestra and in any case hope for a more worthy success from my musical efforts. But before reaching Magdeburg I had to go through a rather onerous interim in Bernburg, where Bethmann, in addition to his other commitments, had agreed to do some theatrical performances. I thus had to go there with a mere fraction of the troupe and arrange in passing for the performance of several operas, which were again directed by the local court conductor, and at the same time put up with a meager, almost farcical day-to-day existence that was enough to disgust me with the fatal profession of conducting music in the theater, at any rate for the time being. But I survived even this and – Magdeburg, as I believed, would now lead me to glory in my chosen profession.

The sensation of sitting at the conductor's desk from which not too long ago the great master Kühnlein had so impressed the confused young enthusiast by the weighty wisdom of his directorsmanship was not without its charm and soon made me feel like a master myself; for as a matter of fact I quickly succeeded in gaining complete confidence in my own conducting. I was soon gladly accepted by the capable members of the orchestra, and their well-balanced playing, particularly in the fiery overtures I always brought to a close at a spectacularly rapid tempo, often evoked intoxicating applause from the audience. The achievements of my inflammatory and often overly exuberant zeal won me the appreciation of the singers as well as the hearty approval of the public; as music criticism had not developed very far in Magdeburg, in that era at least, this general satisfaction with my work went around by word of mouth in the most encouraging manner, and at the end of the first three months of my Magdeburg tenure I flattered myself into the belief that I was really the kingpin of the opera. Considering its success a foregone conclusion under these circumstances, the stage director Schmale, who had meanwhile become quite friendly, wrote a festival play for New Year's Day for which I was supposed to write the music. All this happened very precipitously; a roaring overture, together with several melodramas and choruses, were speedily turned out and brought us such copious applause that we could even give a successful repeat performance, despite the fact that repetitions of occasional pieces like that without a specific festival to celebrate were virtually unprecedented.

With the advent of the new year 1835 there came a decisive turning point in my life. After Minna and I had broken off our relations in Rudolstadt and had more or less lost track of one another, our association was resumed upon our reunion in Magdeburg, but only in a rather cool and intentionally indifferent manner. I learned that she had made a great hit here at an appearance a year before, especially by her beauty, and that she had been particularly celebrated and visited by several young noblemen, a distinction to which she had shown herself not unreceptive. Although her reputation, thanks to her constantly earnest and dignified bearing, had remained truly beyond reproach, my repugnance against this kind of company, no doubt in part traceable to my recollection of unpleasant experiences in the Pachta house in Prague, grew very strong. While Minna assured me that these gentlemen behaved far more modestly and circumspectly than theater fans of middle-class background and particularly more so than certain young music directors, she never quite succeeded in conquering the bitterness and contentiousness with which I protested against these inclinations of hers. We thus spent three fruitless months in growing estrangement, while I pretended in half-despairing self-abandonment to enjoy the company of a motley crew and behaved in every way with such blatant frivolity that Minna, as she later told me, was moved to sympathetic concern for me. Moreover, as the ladies of the opera troupe were not adverse to paying court in a rather questionable way to their youthful conductor, and one young lady of dubious reputation in particular had cast her net in my direction, this solicitude on Minna's part seems to have ripened forcibly into a decisive commitment. I got the idea of treating the odd élite of our troupe to oysters and punch in my room on New Year's Eve. The men were invited with their wives, and now it became a question whether I could persuade the unmarried Fräulein Planer to participate in my little party: she accepted quite disingenuously and appeared, neatly and becomingly dressed as always, in my bachelor's quarters, where things soon became pretty lively. I had forewarned the landlord about the uproar he could expect and had promised to compensate him for any damage to his furniture. What the champagne did not succeed in doing, the punch finally accomplished: all restraints of the scanty conventionality which my companions sought to respect most of the time were exploded, and by unanimous consent general merriment ensued. And then it was that Minna distinguished herself by a calm and regal bearing from all her companions. She never lost her dignified composure; nobody dared take the slightest liberty with her; and even more meaningful, in fact utterly sobering, was the effect on everyone produced by the way Minna responded serenely to my kindly and solicitous attentions, whereby it became clear to the whole group that the link which bound us could not be compared to any usual affair. We had the particular satisfaction of seeing the young lady of doubtful repute,* who had so openly angled for me, have conniptions over this discovery.

From now on I remained continually on good terms with Minna. I do not believe she ever felt any sort of passion or genuine love for me, or was even capable of it, but can only describe her feelings for me as a kind of hearty good will, the sincerest desire for my success and prosperity, the friendliest interest and good-natured delight in characteristics of mine that often filled her with amazement, all of which finally blended into a constant and comfortable habit of mind. She obviously thought highly of my talent and was surprised and captivated by my unexpectedly quick string of successes; my eccentric nature, which she knew so well how to humor by genial moderation, stimulated her to continual exercise of this power, so flattering to her self-esteem, and without ever evincing any desire or real ardor herself, she never requited my impetuous advances with any coldness.

I had made at the Magdeburg theater the very interesting acquaintance of a no longer entirely youthful actress, who played the so-called duenna roles: this was Mme Haas,[1] who gained my deepest interest at once by revealing herself as an old friend of Laube, for whose destiny she

---

* Note in the margin of the manuscript: "(Mme Christiani, née Wunsch)".

continued to feel a sincere and notable concern. She was intelligent and very unhappy, to which her increasingly unprepossessing appearance, emphasized by her advancing years, contributed heavily. She lived with one child in modest circumstances and gave the impression of having known better days, which it pained her to recall. I visited her at first mainly to inquire about Laube, and soon thereafter became a regular caller. As she became friendly with Minna, we three often spent intimate evenings together: this intimacy was often disturbed, however, by a certain jealousy of the older woman for the younger one, and it particularly irritated me to hear her criticize Minna's talent and mental ability. One evening I had promised to take tea at Minna's in the company of the older friend. I had thoughtlessly promised to play a game of whist beforehand, which, although it really bored me, I had intentionally prolonged in order to arrive late for tea, expecting to find her irksome companion gone by the time I got there. I did this with the help of spirituous liquors, and thus I had the strange experience of rising completely intoxicated from the sober whist game, having reached this condition so imperceptibly that I refused to believe in it. This incredulity induced me to keep my belated appointment for tea; to my enormous irritation I found the older friend still there, which promptly caused a drunken outburst; for when the lady expressed astonishment at my crude and unseemly behavior in a few joking remarks, I replied with such vulgar mockery that she left the house at once in great indignation. I was only just conscious enough to perceive Minna's baffled amusement at my outrageous conduct. As soon as she realized that my condition precluded my going home without causing a great commotion, however, she rapidly formed a resolution which must indeed have cost her some effort, though it was carried out with the utmost calm and good humor. She must have pitied me as well; she provided me with everything I needed, and as I soon sank into the deepest sleep she unhesitatingly surrendered her bed to me, where I slept until awakened by a strangely graying day, which, when I realized where I was, illuminated for me with glowing clarity what was to become a long and boundlessly fateful lifetime relationship. Care had entered my life, as I had sensed it would. Without any light-hearted jokes, without showing any exuberance or gaiety of any kind, we breakfasted together quietly and decorously, and then at an hour when we could do so without attracting undue attention, I went off with Minna for a long walk beyond the city gates. After that we separated, from then on behaving openly as a pair of lovers and pursuing our tender interest without concealment.

The peculiar direction my musical activities had gradually taken was given further impetus by the successes as well as the failures which my efforts now harvested. In a concert for the subscribers I conducted my overture to *Die Feen* in a very winning manner and reaped a good deal of applause: at the same time I got confirmation of an ugly act by the Leipzig theater management in regard to the promised performance of my opera. But beginning the composition of *Das Liebesverbot* put me in a frame of mind in which I soon lost interest in the older work and could reject with proud disdain any furthur attempt to get it performed in Leipzig and consider myself well enough recompensed for my work on it with this successful performance of its overture. Meanwhile, in spite of numerous other distractions, I found time during the brief six months of this season in Magdeburg to write a large part of the new opera. In a concert which we gave in the theater I introduced two duets from it, which were received well enough to impel me to continue its composition in high spirits.

In the second half of the season I received a visit from Apel, who wanted to sun himself in my new theatrical glory. He had written a drama, *Columbus*, which I recommended to the management. Their approval was easily gained, for Apel offered to have the decorations representing the Alhambra painted at his expense and also promised many benefits to the actors taking part in his play, most of whom had been suffering under the preferential treatment accorded the basso Kneisel by the directrix in all matters involving pay. The piece itself struck me as containing some good things; it represented the struggles and aspirations of the great navigator up to the point of embarkation on his first voyage of discovery. The drama ended with the portentous departure of his ships from the harbor of Palos, the future results being known to everybody, and even in the judgment of my uncle Adolf, to whom Apel had submitted the manuscript at my prompting, it was distinguished by lively and authentic folk scenes, whereas a love subplot seemed weak and awkward. Apart from a little chorus for the Moors banished from Granada leaving their familiar home country and a little orchestral piece at the end, I also composed in exuberant celerity an overture to my friend's play. I sketched the whole thing one evening at Minna's, while I permitted my friend Apel to chatter to her to his heart's content, so long as I could hear what he was saying. The effect of this, alas, rather too hastily executed piece was based on a simple but rather startlingly developed basic idea: the orchestra depicted the ocean as well as the ship upon it, when necessary, in some not very carefully worked-out figuration; a mighty, passionately yearning theme was the only thing the ear could pick out in the whole tissue. This ensemble was then repeatedly and distractingly interrupted by a motive in a totally different mood, shimmering in the highest register of the violins, played at an extreme *pianissimo* and representing a Fata Morgana. I stipulated three pairs of differently pitched trumpets to give forth this exquisite, seductively dawning theme in the most delicate coloring and the most varied modulations: this was supposed to be the promised land toward which the hero's gaze is directed, which he always thinks is just across the horizon and which always disappears under the ocean rim, finally to rise in splendor in the morning sky as a vast continent of the future, unmistakably revealed to all the sailors to crown the hero's endless searching and struggling. My six trumpets were now to combine in the principal key to let the theme resound in the most splendid jubilation. Being familiar with the excellence of the Prussian regimental trumpeters, I had quite correctly counted on an overwhelming effect, particularly in the closing section: the overture dumbfounded everybody and got stormy applause. The play itself was done without any sense of occasion, the title role in particular being completely ruined by a conceited actor named Ludwig Meyer,[1] who also directed and made that his excuse for not learning his part adequately, even though he augmented his theatrical wardrobe at Apel's expense with an unreasonable number of magnificent costumes which he wore one after the other as the play's hero. Nonetheless Apel had succeeded in getting a play performed, which to be sure received no repeat performance but gave me the opportunity to increase my popularity with the Magdeburg audiences by repeating the overture at concerts in response to public demand.

The main theatrical event of this season, however, took place towards its close. I had prevailed upon Madame Schröder-Devrient, who was staying in Leipzig, to come over and do a few guest roles. I now had the great satisfaction and enjoyed the exciting experience of twice conducting operas in which she sang, thus entering into direct artistic collaboration with her. She appeared as Desdemona and Romeo: in the latter role, especially, she swept everybody off their feet once again and filled me anew with passion and fire. I got to know her better personally as well, whereupon she showed such a friendly interest in me that she offered on her own initiative to participate in a concert I wanted to arrange for my benefit, and for which she had to return after a brief absence. This concert, from which I felt justified in expecting under these circumstances the best possible results, had taken on vital importance for me. The essentially scanty salary which I was supposed to receive from the Magdeburg management had become altogether illusory, paid out as it was in small and irregular driblets, so that I had to pay for the necessities, and particularly my expenses for the frequent wining and dining of my odd singers and musical clientele, only by contracting what soon became a substantial amount of debt. I really didn't know how high this amount was, but I was equally vague about the supposedly large sum I would be getting from my concert and thus consoled all my creditors by reference to this fabulous bonanza, from which they were to be paid on the day after the concert, to which end I invited them all to call on me in the hotel where I had taken up residence at the close of the season on the morning of that happy day. There was, as a matter of fact, nothing unreasonable in my counting on the highest conceivable receipts when supported by so great and popular a singer, who was returning to Magdeburg solely for this purpose, and therefore I spared no expense whatever in regard to musical luxury by engaging a splendidly big orchestra and ordering many rehearsals. Unfortunately, nobody seemed to want to believe that this famous woman, who was entitled to regard her time as valuable capital, would be willing to return from far away merely on behalf of a little Magdeburg conductor. The advertisements blazoning her appearance were generally considered a deceptive maneuver, and there was indignation, in particular, at the high ticket prices. As a result it turned out that the hall was only scantily filled, and I had the painful experience of seeing my kindly patroness, who had punctually returned for the concert as I had expected, confronted by what was to her the unaccustomed sight of empty seats. Happily enough, she at least remained in good spirits (which, I later learned, was attributable to factors having nothing to do with me) and among other things sang Beethoven's *Adelaïde* gloriously and to my piano accompaniment, surprisingly enough. The concert was plagued by another unanticipated misfortune in the choice of the program pieces, which, given the undue resonance of the small hall in the City of London Hotel, turned out to be unbearably loud. My *Columbus* overture with its six trumpets had already scarified all the listeners; but now came as finale Beethoven's *Battle of Vittoria*, for which I had provided the most extensive orchestral armament possible, based on my enthusiastic estimate of the high receipts. Cannon and rifle-fire had been devised with the most ingeniously constructed and expensive machinery, arrayed with great care for both the French and the English sides; trumpets and bugles had been doubled and trebled; and now began a battle of such ferocity as has seldom been seen in a concert hall, because the orchestra launched its attack on the tiny auditorium with such overwhelming force that listeners eventually gave up completely and ran for their lives. Madame Schröder-Devrient, who had been kind enough to take one of the front row seats to hear the concert to the end, was unable to withstand it, in spite of all her experience of such alarums, even from friendship for me; during a particularly desperate attack by the British on the French positions she also finally took to her heels, wellnigh wringing her hands in dismay, and this became the signal for a panic-stricken stampede. Everybody rushed out, and Wellington's victory was celebrated in an exchange between the orchestra and myself alone.

Thus ended this memorable music festival. Schröder-Devrient departed at once, regretting the failure of her well-intended efforts, and abandoned me without rancor to my fate. After I had sought consolation in the arms of my distressed sweetheart and fortified myself for the following day's battle with the creditors, which seemed unlikely to end in a victorious finale, I went back to my hotel room the next morning, to which I could only proceed by running the gauntlet of a long double row of men and women who had all been invited there for the settlement of their myriad claims. Reserving the right to select individuals from among my visitors to interview one at a time, I first led to my room the second trumpeter of the orchestra, who had been responsible for ticket sales and procuring the music. From his calculations it emerged that, as a result of the high fees I had over-enthusiastically committed myself to pay the members of the orchestra, there would be a small deficit I would have to take care of in petty cash from my own pocket. When this was settled, the state of affairs was clear. I now invited in Madame Gottschalk, a trustworthy Jewess, to come to some agreement about the present crisis. She saw at once that drastic help would be necessary but did not doubt that I would be able to obtain it from my wealthy acquaintances in Leipzig, and thus she took it upon herself to appease the other creditors whom she criticized for their maladroit behavior in showing up this way, and finally succeeded in clearing the corridor to my room if only with great difficulty.

The theater season was now over, the company in dissolution, and I without a job; the theater director had gone from a state of chronic to acute bankruptcy; he met his bills with paper money, namely with strips of tickets to performances he assured everyone would one day take place. Minna, who had craftily managed to extract some return from these singular treasury bills, was living very frugally; moreover, as only the opera troupe was disbanded and the dramatic company remained active for as long as its members thought feasible, Minna could remain involved with the theater and dismissed me upon my unavoidable departure for Leipzig with the cordial wish to see us soon reunited, promising me to use her forthcoming vacation to visit her parents in Dresden, at which time she planned to visit me in Leipzig.

And so I fled home to my family early in May, in order to dig up some money to lighten the burden of debts I had incurred at Magdeburg during this first abortive attempt to become self-supporting. A very intelligent brown poodle accompanied me loyally from Magdeburg and was entrusted to my family for his board and keep as the sole tangible property I had acquired there. My mother and Rosalie nonetheless nourished hopes for my future career from the fact that I had proved able to conduct an orchestra. But to me the thought of returning to my former life within the family purview was discomforting; my relationship to Minna in particular spurred me to return to my career as quickly as possible. The great change that had come over me in this respect became most clear to me when Minna stopped off for a few days in Leipzig for my sake and through her confident, affectionate presence made me aware that my days of patriarchal family dependence were over. I conferred with her about the renewal of my engagement at the Magdeburg theater, promised to visit her in Dresden, and arranged for her to meet my mother and sister by obtaining their permission to ask her home one evening for tea. On this occasion Rosalie grasped at once how things stood: but she did nothing more than tease me about my infatuation. The affair didn't look very dangerous; but to me it appeared different, for my amorous attachment coincided with my desire for independence and my ambition to win a place for myself in the world of art.

My distaste for Leipzig itself was further strengthened by a change that took place in the state of music there at the time. While I was establishing myself as a conductor in Magdeburg by thoughtless submission to frivolous theatrical tastes, Mendelssohn-Bartholdy by his personal appearance as conductor at the Gewandhaus concerts had been inaugurating a momentous epoch for himself and particularly for the musical taste of Leipzig. His influence had put an end to the naivety with which the Leipzig public had hitherto judged its pleasant subscription concerts; and when I got my *Columbus* overture, which had been so stormily applauded in Magdeburg, performed at a benefit concert for the popular young singer Livia Gerhart[1] through the intervention of my old friend Pohlenz, who had not yet been altogether put on the shelf, I was amazed to find that the music lovers of Leipzig had undergone a change of heart which I could not assuage even with my six trumpets. This experience fortified me in my disgust at everything affecting a classical aroma, and I found myself in strange accord with the estimable Pohlenz, who sighed good-naturedly for the glory of bygone days.

A music festival in Dessau, under the baton of Friedrich Schneider,[1] offered me a welcome opportunity to get out of Leipzig. For this journey, which took about seven hours on foot, I had to get a passport valid for a week: this official document was destined to play a significant role in my life for many years; for it was and remained the only document I could later use in the most diverse European countries to establish my identity for police purposes, because inasmuch as I had evaded military service in Saxony, I was not able to get a regular passport from that state until I was appointed Kapellmeister in Dresden. The artistic enjoyment to which this passport conveyed me was of such little significance that it strengthened my hatred for everything classical. I heard Beethoven's C minor symphony conducted, by a man whose revolting physiognomy resembled that of a drunken satyr, so listlessly and meaninglessly, despite the battery of contrabass players with which such festivals festoon themselves, that once again the incomprehensible gulf I had so often observed yawning between my imaginative conception of these works and the only live performances I had ever heard presented itself to me as a bewildering and frightening problem, which I was too angry to try to solve. However, the experience of attending a performance of the oratorio *Absalom*, by the "old master" Schneider himself, turned my tortured mood into a parody of itself, and I was cheered up and calmed down for the moment.

In Dessau, where Minna had made her theatrical debut, I heard her talked about in the casual tone used by frivolous young people in discussing young and pretty actresses. My eagerness to contradict such chatter and shame the scandalmongers revealed to me ever more clearly the depth of the passion that drew me to her. I went back to Leipzig without showing myself to my relatives, and there managed to get enough money for an immediate trip to Dresden. When I was halfway there, on a journey that had to be taken by express carriage in those days, I met Minna in the company of one of her sisters already on her way back to Magdeburg. I got myself a ticket for the mail coach to Leipzig at once and joined my beloved; by the time we reached the next station I had succeeded in persuading Minna to turn back for Dresden, but by this time the mail coach was already far ahead of us and we had to travel in a special post-chaise. My convoying had amazed the two sisters and put them in a good mood. The extravagance of my conduct had obviously aroused in them the expectation of an adventure, the fulfillment of which I now had to undertake. I got the necessary money from a Dresden acquaintance in order to lead my two companions grandly off into the Saxon Alps, where we spent several truly merry days, full of innocent delight, interrupted only once by an outbreak of my jealousy, for which there was in fact no pretext, but which nourished itself on past memories as well as premonitions based on the experience I had already gained with women. Nevertheless this excursion, and especially one evening we sat together throughout almost the entire night in glorious summer weather in Bad Schandau, lingers in my memory as virtually the sole unalloyed happiness I enjoyed in my years of young manhood. Indeed, my subsequent and long relationship with Minna, marred as it was by so many of the most painful and bitter experiences, has often seemed to me one long expiation for the harmless and fleeting pleasure of those few days.

After I had accompanied Minna to Leipzig, from where she continued on to Magdeburg, I presented myself once again to my family, to whom I told nothing of the Dresden trip, and from then on, as if burdened by a strange and deep sense of guilt, was driven by a desire to arrange my affairs so that I could get back to my beloved as rapidly as possible. To this end, I had to extract a new engagement from Director Bethmann for the next winter season. While these negotiations were going on I couldn't stand to stay in Leipzig, so I availed myself of Laube's presence in Bad Kösen near Naumburg to pay him a visit there. A short time previously Laube had been released from nearly a year's painful investigatory detention in the Berlin municipal jail; on giving his word not to leave the country until a verdict had been rendered, he had been permitted to go to Bad Kösen, from where he paid us a clandestine visit of one evening in Leipzig. The signs of suffering in his appearance, his manly yet despairing and resigned attitude toward all his earlier aspirations to change things for the better, made an impression upon me in my highly excited state that has remained one of the saddest and most foreboding recollections of my life. In Bad Kösen I showed him some of the verses from my *Das Liebesverbot*, to which he accorded some praise and encouragement despite the disapproval with which he regarded my efforts to write my own libretti. I was impatient for letters from Magdeburg; not because I doubted that I would get the job, for I had good reason to regard myself as a good catch for Director Bethmann, but rather because anything that would bring me together with Minna again could not happen fast enough. No sooner did the news arrive than I hurried away to put forward on the spot all the proposals that would make the forthcoming opera season in Magdeburg a particularly dazzling success. The permanently bankrupt director had once again benefited from the inexhaustible favor of the King of Prussia; His Majesty had made available a not insubstantial sum to a committee composed of leading citizens of the town, with the proviso that it be applied to theatrical undertakings under Bethmann's management. What this meant, and the fresh dedication it suddenly inspired in me for the artistic enterprises of Magdeburg, can easily be imagined by considering the forlorn and neglected condition in which most small theaters wear out their contemptible lives. I immediately volunteered to travel around in search of good singers; I intended to find my own money for this trip but requested in return the guarantee of a benefit performance as compensation. This offer was gladly accepted and the director, in his most orotund vein, bestowed on me full powers to carry out this purpose, together with his special blessing. During this short stay I had been on terms of closest intimacy with Minna, who now had her mother living with her, and again took leave of her to carry out my adventurous undertaking.

In Leipzig it turned out to be difficult to dig up the necessary funds, so liberally counted on in Magdeburg, to finance my projected recruiting trip. The glamour of royal sponsorship for our theatrical efforts, which I described to my worthy brother-in-law Brockhaus in glowing terms, failed to impress him in the slightest, and it required great pains and humiliating exertions on my part to launch my ship of discovery. Naturally, I was drawn first of all to my old stamping ground in Bohemia, although I stopped off only briefly in Prague and did not see my lovely lady friends, proceeding directly to Karlsbad to observe the opera personnel then performing during the watering season there. Impatient to discover as much talent as I could as quickly as possible, in order that my funds should not be dissipated in vain, I attended a performance of *La Dame Blanche*, sincerely hoping to find the whole thing first-class. I didn't really recognize how bad all the singers were until the one basso I selected, Gräf, who had sung Gaveston, made his debut in Magdeburg, on which occasion he flopped so resoundingly and, as I was forced to admit, so rightly that I could not find a serious defence to the mockery which this acquisition brought upon me. But if the fruits of this first part of my trip were meager, the excursion itself pleased me all the more. The journey through Eger over the Fichtelgebirge and the entry into Bayreuth, pleasantly illuminated in the evening sun, have remained happy memories to this day.

My next goal was Nuremberg, where my sister Klara and her husband were still engaged at the theater, from whom I expected to get favorable tidings about my prospects for finding what I was looking for there. I was particularly glad to be received so hospitably in the house of my relatives, which gave me a chance to replenish my heavily depleted traveling money. To this end, I was counting on the proceeds of the sale of a snuff-box I had received as a present from a friend and which for obscure reasons I was convinced was made of platinum; beyond this I could throw in a golden signet ring my friend Apel had bestowed on me for the composition of the overture to his *Columbus*. The value of the snuff-box unfortunately proved chimerical, but by pawning these, the only two trinkets I possessed, I was able to generate the modest amount needed to meet the cost of continuing my trip to Frankfurt. All the advice I had received pointed me in the direction of that city and the Rhineland area; for after I had succeeded in persuading my brother-in-law and my sister to accept an engagement in Magdeburg, I still lacked a first tenor and a leading soprano, both of which had proved very elusive so far.

My stay in Nuremberg was most agreeably prolonged by another encounter with Madame Schröder-Devrient, who arrived there for a guest performance at precisely that time. Meeting her again dispersed the clouds that had hung over my artistic activities ever since we had last parted. The Nuremberg opera troupe did not offer her a very wide selection of roles; apart from *Fidelio* there was nothing else but *Die Schweizerfamilie*,[1] about which the singer complained that it had been one of the operas of her early youth which she had long outgrown and had moreover performed ad nauseam. I was also unenthusiastic and even apprehensive about *Die Schweizerfamilie*, as I could only conclude that this feeble opera and the mawkishly old-fashioned role of Emmeline would manage to weaken the exalted impression both the public and I had formed of her achievements as an artist. My emotion and absolute amazement were all the greater, therefore, when I found myself discovering that evening for the first time the truly overwhelming greatness of this incommensurable artist. That anything as marvelous as her embodiment of the Swiss maiden cannot be preserved and handed down to posterity as a monument for all time I have to recognize as one of the sublime sacrifices demanded by dramatic art, and whenever such phenomena appear our reverence for them cannot be great enough, nor deep enough our sacred awe.

Apart from this new soul-shaking experience, which was to be so profoundly meaningful for my whole life and my artistic development, my Nuremberg stay produced other impressions which, though their cause was apparently insignificant or even trivial, left such indelible traces on my mind that they were to revive in me later, though in a curiously transfigured way. My brother-in-law Wolfram had become very popular in Nuremberg theatrical circles as a witty and sociable boon companion: on this occasion I received delightful evidence of the spirit of extravagant merriment that prevailed during evenings in the taverns, in which I also participated. A master carpenter named Lauermann, a thick-set little man no longer young, of comical appearance and speaking only the crudest dialect, was pointed out to me in one of the inns we visited as an especially popular if unwilling butt of practical jokes. Lauermann was convinced of his truly great prowess as a singer and based on this self-deception conceived a particular interest in turn for those in whom he thought he could detect singing talent. Despite the fact that he became the continual object of mockery and contemptuous jokes as a result of this peculiarity, he never failed to appear every evening among his laughter-loving persecutors; so often had he been laughed at and hurt by their scorn, however, that it became extremely difficult to induce him to give a demonstration of his artistic skill, and this could only be accomplished by laying the most artfully devised traps for his vanity. My appearance as a stranger triggered a maneuver of this sort; and the astonishingly low opinion everybody held of the poor mastersinger's common sense was evidenced by the fact that my brother-in-law introduced me to him as the great Italian singer Lablache.[1] To his credit I have to concede that Lauermann mustered me long in patent disbelief, expressing doubts stemming from my youthful appearance and even more from the obvious tenor timbre of my voice. But to induce this enthusiast to believe the unbelievable was the entertaining if arduous skill of these tavern companions. My brother-in-law succeeded in persuading the carpenter that I, who was being paid immense sums for my accomplishments, was trying to establish an incognito by frequenting these public places; and if it had now come to a meeting between Lauermann and Lablache the only interesting thing, naturally, would be to hear Lauermann, and not Lablache, as the latter could learn something from the former but not vice versa. An odd battle between incredulity and vanity in the poor carpenter challenged me: I began to play my role with all the guile at my command, and after two hours spiced with the strangest antics we achieved our goal of inducing the eccentric, who had long fixed his shining eyes on me in the greatest excitement, to begin working his muscles in that extraordinarily eerie manner we associate with musical automata when they have been wound up: his lips quivered, his teeth ground, his eyes rolled convulsively, until finally there broke forth, in a hoarse and viscous voice, a preposterously banal street-song. Its delivery, accompanied by a regular movement of his outstretched thumbs behind his ears, and during which his fat face turned brick red, soon produced inordinate hilarity among his listeners, which immediately provoked the unhappy master to utmost fury. With studied cruelty this fury was requited by those who had previously been flattering him most intensely with the most shameless mockery, which literally made the poor man foam at the mouth. As this sad fellow was about to leave the tavern amid a hailstorm of imprecations from my friends, I was suddenly struck by pity and ran after him to beg his forgiveness and seek in some way to mollify him, a task all the more difficult because he was especially bitter at me as the newest of his enemies, who had deprived him of the pleasure of meeting Lablache. Yet I succeeded in stopping him at the threshold; and now the revelers tacitly joined in an unparalleled conspiracy to induce Lauermann to sing yet again on that same evening. How this was eventually accomplished remains all the fuzzier in my memory for the effect of spirituous liquors, which were no doubt ultimately responsible for the winning of this final victory over Lauermann, on my own capacity to follow the bizarre events of this unbelievably long night in the bar-room. After Lauermann had been given another dose of the same mockery, the whole group felt obliged to escort the poor fellow home; this was done by means of a wheel-barrow we found in front of the house and in which we drove him in triumph to his own doorway in one of those marvelous little alleyways of the old town. Awakened from her sleep to receive her husband, Frau Lauermann enabled us by her torrent of curses to gain a clear insight into the way his domestic affairs stood. She was as adept as we were at deriding his singing; but to this she added the most frightful maledictions on the worthless bums who were diverting him from his bread-winning activities by encouraging him in his delusions and finally producing such scenes as this. But at this point the mastersinger's wounded pride reasserted itself: for while his wife was helping him painfully up the stairs he harshly denied her right to judge his singing at all and told her to be quiet.

Even now this extraordinary nocturnal adventure was by no means over. The whole bunch surged back to the tavern; in front of it we found some other fellows congregated, including some apprentices who had already been denied access because of the police closing hours: the regular patrons among our party, who were on close terms with the tavernkeeper, deemed it proper and possible to request admittance. The host was troubled at having to bar the door against his friends, whose voices he could recognize; but it was necessary in order to prevent the newcomers from storming in after them. Out of this situation evolved an uproar, which through shouting and clamor and an inexplicable growth of the number of participants in the struggle soon assumed a truly demoniacal character. It looked to me as if the whole town would break out into a riot, and I really thought myself to be once again involuntarily witnessing a revolution of which no one had the slightest idea what it was all about. Then suddenly I heard a heavy thump, and as if by magic the whole crowd dispersed in every direction. In order to put an end to the chaos and to open a path for himself to get home, one of the regular patrons, well versed in an old Nuremberg way of fighting, had felled one of the noisiest rioters, though not in a manner to cause injury, with a knockout punch right between the eyes; and it was the effect of this which scattered everybody so suddenly. Scarcely a minute after the fiercest tumult had been raging among hundreds of people I was able to stroll arm-in-arm with my brother-in-law through the lonely moonlit streets, laughing and joking, only to be told by him to my utter amazement that this sort of thing went on nearly every evening.

At last it was time for me to attend seriously again to the purpose of my journey. I stopped in Würzburg only for a day on the way through: of my reunion with my relatives and acquaintances I recall nothing except that melancholy visit I paid to Friederike Galvani. On reaching Frankfurt I was obliged to establish headquarters in a good hotel to await the result of my petition for a subsidy from the Magdeburg theater management. My hopes to secure some real stars for our operatic undertaking were focused on Wiesbaden, where, I was told, a good operatic ensemble was on the point of dissolution. I found it extremely difficult to make this short journey but finally succeeded in getting there for a rehearsal of *Robert le Diable* in which the tenor Freimüller performed brilliantly. I interviewed him at once and found him willing in principle to entertain my proposals for Magdeburg; we concluded the necessary agreements and of necessity I rushed back to my Frankfurt haven in the Hotel Weidenbusch. I had to spend another anxious week there waiting vainly for the traveling expenses I had requisitioned from

Magdeburg. To kill time I resorted among other things to a big red portfolio[1] I had been carrying around in my bag and began making notes in it for my future biography – the same document which I now have before me to refresh my memory and which I have continued without interruption ever since in different phases of my life. Through the negligence of the Madgeburg management my situation went from bad to worse and finally achieved utter chaos when a transaction in Frankfurt turned out more favorably than my financial condition could bear. I had heard a performance of *Die Zauberflöte* under the baton of Guhr,[2] then renowned as a "genius among conductors", and had been pleasantly surprised by the truly superb cast. Naturally, I could not expect to lure any of the principals into my net; but I gazed closely enough upon the youthful Fräulein Limbach, who sang the First Boy, to recognize in her a useful talent. She accepted my offer of an engagement and seemed so anxious to get out of her Frankfurt contract that she elected to abscond. She explained all this to me and asked for my help in carrying out her plan, which could suffer no delay for fear the local management got wind of it. I had so lauded the Magdeburg theater committee that the young lady presumed me to be in the possession of a lavish letter of credit to finance my official activities on their behalf. But I had already been compelled to pawn my scanty traveling gear merely to be able to continue my trip; I had managed to persuade my landlord to put up with this much; but I found him by no means willing to advance me the funds to finance the abduction of a young singer. To mask the shabby conduct of my directorate, I had to invent some tale of woe and leave the astonished and indignant young lady behind. Greatly ashamed at this escapade, I journeyed through rain and storm via Leipzig, where I picked up my brown poodle, back.to Magdeburg, where from September 1st I resumed my work as music director.

The pickings I had gleaned from my business trip afforded me little satisfaction; the director demonstrated triumphantly that he had in fact at last remitted five whole louis d'or to my address in Frankfurt: to my tenor and my young lady, however, he had sent only carefully drafted contracts and none of the travel advances I had requested. Neither of them showed up; but the basso Gräf arrived from Karlsbad with pedantic punctuality and immediately aroused the ribaldry of our theatrical wags. At a rehearsal of *Die Schweizerfamilie* he sang with such a school-masterly drone that I broke out in a sweat of embarrassment. The arrival of my capable brother-in-law Wolfram with my sister Klara was of greater benefit to musical comedy than grand opera and caused me a good deal of worry and distress to boot, because these two, who were accustomed to reliable management, were not long in perceiving the deficiencies of Bethmann's unscrupulous management, royal patronage or no royal patronage, and recognized that their domestic circumstances were going to be considerably worse. My courage had already begun to sink when chance brought us as guest singer a young woman, Madame Pollert née Zeibig,[1] who was passing through Magdeburg with her actor husband and whose beautiful voice and talented singing suited her for leading roles. Necessity had also at last driven the management to take the necessary steps that brought us the tenor Freimüller at the eleventh hour; and I was particularly gratified when a sudden infatuation he had conceived for the young Limbach in Frankfurt impelled this enterprising tenor to undertake her successful abduction, the task in which I had failed so miserably. Both arrived beaming with pleasure; Madame Pollert, who impressed everyone, was also engaged despite her pretentions; a well-trained and musically competent baritone named Krug,[2] later chorusmaster in Karlsruhe, had also turned up, and thus I stood suddenly at the helm of a tolerably good opera company, in which only the basso Gräf had to be blanketed by a good deal of painful hushing up. We soon brought off a string of operatic performances a little outside the usual run of the mill, and our repertory encompassed virtually the whole genre: I was especially delighted with our presentation of Spohr's *Jessonda*, which really was touched with greatness and earned us the esteem even of the more knowledgeable opera-goers. I was tireless in inventing means to raise our performances above the usual standard dictated by the meager resources of the provincial theaters. I gained the enmity of Director Bethmann by continually augmenting the orchestra, for which he had to pay; but then I won his approval back again by enlarging the chorus and the stage music, which cost him nothing but lent our performances such glamor that subscriptions and casual attendance increased enormously. I did this by securing the participation of the Prussian regimental band and the superbly drilled Prussian army singers solely in return for free passes to the theater gallery for their relatives. Thus I managed to furnish the full complement of the particularly large on-stage band required by Bellini's score for *Norma* and was able to dispose of a body of voices for the opening *unisono* of the male chorus, which impressed me very much at the time, even bigger than the largest theaters could normally command. Much later I had the opportunity to assure M. Auber, whom I used to meet regularly at the Café Tortoni in Paris to eat ice-cream, that under my baton the chorus of the mutinous soldiers hatching their conspiracy in his *Lestocq* had been sung by a full military company, for which he thanked me in astonished delight.

Under such encouraging circumstances the composition of my *Liebesverbot* made rapid strides toward completion. I intended this work to be introduced at the benefit performance promised me as a means of recouping my expenses and worked hard at it in the hope of establishing my fame and achieving the no less hopefully anticipated betterment of my overall financial position. Even the few hours I could snatch from my official duties to spend at Minna's side were devoted with unparalleled zeal to the completion of my score. My diligence even touched Minna's mother, who had stayed on after the summer to take care of her daughter's house and who otherwise took a rather dim view of our love affair; through her intrusive presence a new and serious tension had developed in our relationship and demanded some resolution. It was only natural that the question what all this would lead to now became acute. I must confess that the thought of marriage, if simply because of my extreme youth, filled me with great anxiety; without actually reflecting much on the matter or seriously weighing the pros and cons, I had a naive and instinctive feeling that prevented me from considering the possibility of such a serious step, with all its consequences for my future life. Moreover, our financial affairs were in such precarious shape that even Minna was no doubt more inclined to hope for an improvement in this direction rather than for the conclusion of a marriage contract. But she was soon driven to pay attention to her own problems owing to some trouble that arose with regard to her position at the Magdeburg theater. A rival had popped up there in her own speciality who was particularly dangerous for her inasmuch as her husband had achieved supreme power as principal stage director. As Minna now, at the beginning of the winter, received an attractive offer from Berlin's Königstadt theater, which was doing a booming business, she used this pretext to break off her relationship with the Magdeburg theater entirely, whereby I, whom she did not seem to consider in the matter, was plunged into deepest anxiety. I could not prevent Minna from breaking her contract and leaving for Berlin to give guest performances. And so she departed, leaving me behind in agony and despair at her conduct. In my intense distress I bombarded her with letters urging her to return, and in order to induce her not to separate her fate from my own I came forward with formal declarations of intent to marry her. At the same time my brother-in-law Wolfram, having had a row with Bethmann and canceled his contract with him, had also proceeded to the Königstadt theater. My good sister Klara, who had stayed behind in Magdeburg under these disagreeable circumstances, soon perceived the anxious and troubled mood in which her normally cheerful brother was eating his heart out. One day she thought it advisable to show me a letter from her husband with news from Berlin, and especially about Minna, in which he earnestly deplored my infatuation with this girl, who was behaving quite unworthily of me and, as he could easily see from living in the same hotel with her, was keeping scandalous company and was guilty of the worst misconduct. The extraordinary impression made by this frightful communication upon me impelled me to abandon the reserve I had heretofore shown my relatives in regard to my love affair: I wrote my brother-in-law in Berlin how things were with me, how devoted I was to Minna, and how important it was to me to learn the unvarnished truth about the woman he had so much maligned. From my usually dry and sardonic brother-in-law I received a reply that filled my heart to overflowing. He admitted having accused Minna too hastily and regretted having allowed idle gossip, which proved to be without foundation, to lead him into slandering her and asserted that, after getting to know and conversing with Minna, he had become convinced of her honesty and decency and that he hoped with all his heart I might find my way to marrying her. And now there was no stopping me. I implored Minna to return at once and was pleased to learn from her that she no longer thought of extending her engagement at the Berlin theater, having become better acquainted with certain frivolous aspects of life there. All that remained for me, then, was to facilitate the resumption of her Magdeburg engagement. To this end I confronted the director and the detested chief stage director at a meeting of the theater committee and defended Minna against the wrong done her by both of them with such passionate warmth that all the members present, astonished at this frank revelation of my affection for her, gave in to my wishes without further ado. Then I set off by special mail coach in the depth of night and in deepest winter to meet my returning beloved, greeting her with tears of profoundest joy and leading her in triumph back to the cosy Magdeburg home of which I had become so fond.

While our life together became ever more closely entwined, following this brief separation, I finished the score of *Das Liebesverbot* toward New Year 1836. I based not a few of my hopes for the future on the success of this work; Minna too did not seem disinclined to share my expectations in this regard. We had reason to be concerned how things would pan out for us at the beginning of a new year, always a dangerous time for such fragile theatrical undertakings. Despite royal support and interventions of the subscribers' committee in the management of the theater, our venerable director remained perennially bankrupt, and there was really no question of his theatrical enterprise continuing on for long in any form whatsoever. Consequently the performance of my work while I still had at my disposal a truly first-rate company of singers would, I thought, inaugurate a fundamental change in my unsatisfactory circumstances. I had the right to arrange a benefit performance to recoup my traveling expenses of the previous summer: quite naturally I selected my own work for this purpose and endeavored in so doing to make this favor as inexpensive to the management as possible. But as there was no way of avoiding some expenses in putting on the new opera I agreed that the proceeds of the first performance should be retained by the management, whereas I would take those of the second. I did not consider it altogether unfavorable that the rehearsal period was postponed until toward the end of the season, for I thought I could safely assume that the final performances of a company so often heartily applauded by the public would be received with special attention. Contrary to our expectations, we unfortunately never reached this closing period of the season fixed for the end of April, because by the end of March, owing to the unpunctuality in the disbursement of their salaries, the most popular members of the company, having found better employment elsewhere, turned in their resignations to the management, which, lacking the means to pay them, was powerless to prevent them. Now I began to get really worried: it seemed more than questionable whether my *Liebesverbot* would be performed at all. I owed it entirely to the cordial feelings entertained toward me by the members of the company that the singers could be persuaded to stay on not only to the end of March but also to undertake the arduous task of learning my work in such a short time. In order for two performances to be squeezed in, we could only spare ten days for rehearsals. As the work was by no means a light musical comedy but rather, despite the airy character of the music, a grand opera with many large and complex ensembles, this undertaking was close to foolhardy. Nevertheless I counted on the extraordinary exertions which the singers would make on my behalf by studying early and late; and even though it was completely impossible to achieve with these hard-pressed artists any degree of perfection, particularly with respect to the memorizing of parts, I still felt capable of bringing off a miracle from the skill I had acquired in conducting. The special ability

I possessed to help singers and to make things seem to flow smoothly despite great uncertainty on their part was amply demonstrated in the few rehearsals, in which, by dint of continual prompting, loud singing along, and shouting drastic directions concerning the necessary movements, I held the whole thing together well enough so that it appeared quite possible that the performance would turn out acceptably after all. Unfortunately, we did not bear in mind that during the public performance all these drastic methods of moving the musico-dramatic machinery would be reduced to the wavings of my baton and the workings of my facial muscles. As a matter of fact, the singers, especially the men, were so exceptionally unsure of themselves that from beginning to end their embarrassment crippled the effect of every one of their roles. The tenor Freimüller, equipped with the feeblest memory, tried to supplement the lively and engaging character of his role as the madcap Luzio by resorting to routines adapted from *Fra Diavolo* and *Zampa*, and especially by the aid of an enormously thick, brightly colored and fluttering plume of feathers. Nevertheless, one could not blame the public for remaining completely in the dark about the outlines of the action as sung to them throughout, because the management had failed to come up with booklets containing the text. With the exception of a few parts sung by the ladies and in fact favorably received, the whole thing, for which I had relied entirely on crispness and energy of action and language, remained no more than a musical shadow-play, to which the orchestra contributed inexplicable effusions, often of an overly loud nature. As characteristic of the treatment accorded my tonal colorings, I might mention that the director of a Prussian military band, who had actually been very pleased by the work, felt impelled to offer me some well-meant advice for the handling of the Turkish drums in my future works. Before relating the subsequent destiny of this strange work of my youth, I will pause a brief moment to describe its character, particularly that of the poem.

Shakespeare's fundamentally deeply serious play got the following treatment in my libretto:

An unnamed King of Sicily leaves his country, presumably on a trip to Naples, and hands over to a Viceroy of his choice – named simply Friedrich in order to characterize him as a German – full authority to exercise all royal powers to attempt a complete reform of moral conditions in the capital, which have severely provoked the stern town council. At the beginning of the play we see the agents of the public weal busily employed either in shutting up or pulling down houses of public amusement in a suburb of Palermo, and in carrying off the occupants, proprietors and servants alike, as prisoners. The populace opposes these initial measures; a big riot; the chief of the Sbirri, Brighella (basso buffo), reads out in the thick of the throng, after a preliminary ruffle of drums for silence, a proclamation of the Viceroy according to which these acts are declared necessary to raise the moral tone of the people. A general outburst of indignation and a mocking chorus sets in; Luzio, a young nobleman and jovial wastrel (tenor), seems inclined to assume the role of mob leader, and at once finds a reason for playing a more active part on behalf of those being persecuted upon seeing his friend Claudio (tenor) being carted off to prison and learning from him that, according to some musty old law unearthed by Friedrich, he is to suffer the death penalty for an amorous escapade. His beloved, whom he has been prevented from marrying through the enmity of the parents, has had a child by him; to the hatred of her relatives is now added the puritanical zeal of Friedrich; he fears the worst and hopes only for a pardon, if his sister Isabella succeeds in mollifying the harsh Viceroy. Luzio swears to his friend that he will seek out Isabella in the convent of the Sisters of St Elisabeth, which she has recently entered as a novice.

There, within the silent walls of the convent, we now get to know this sister better in intimate conversation with her friend Marianne, who has also just become a novice there. Marianne discloses to her friend, from whom she has long been separated, the sad fate that has brought her there. She had been lured into a secret liaison with a man of high rank through promises of eternal fidelity; but in the end she found herself, when in great need, abandoned and even persecuted by him; for her betrayer revealed himself to her as none other than the most powerful man in the state, the present Viceroy. Isabella gives vent to her indignation at all this, and she calms down only with the resolution to depart from a world where such vile deeds can go unpunished. When Luzio brings her news of the fate of her own brother, her disgust at her brother's misconduct is at once transformed into the purest fury at the villainy of the hypocritical Viceroy, who now presumes to punish this lesser offense, unstained by treachery at least, with such cruelty. Her passionate outburst makes her, quite inadvertently, highly attractive to Luzio; smitten with sudden love, he urges her to leave the convent forever and take his hand in marriage. She contrives with dignity to keep his boldness within bounds, but decides at once to accept his offer to conduct her to the Viceroy. Here begins a courtroom scene, which I introduced by a farcical interrogation by the Sbirri chief, Brighella, of several people charged with crimes against public morality. The seriousness of the situation becomes all the more evident by contrast when the intimidating figure of Friedrich strides commandingly through the wildly inrushing crowd and he undertakes to examine Claudio with great severity. Unrelenting, he is about to pronounce the verdict when Isabella arrives and in front of everybody demands a private audience with the Viceroy. Face to face with the man who is so dreaded, yet whom she so despises, she controls her feelings and, showing noble restraint, appeals at first solely to his mildness and mercy. His interjections stimulate her ardor: she represents her brother's offense in the most moving light and begs forgiveness for such a human and by no means unpardonable misstep. Noting that her heated representations are making an impression, she continues with increasing fire to work on the personal feelings of this hard-hearted judge, who can surely not have been entirely immune to such sentiments as motivated her brother and whose own experience she now summons as testimony in support of her plea for pity. This now breaks the ice in his heart: Friedrich, pierced to the depths by Isabella's beauty, can no longer contain himself; he promises Isabella whatever she may wish in return for her love. Scarcely has she grasped this unexpected effect when, in highest revulsion at such incomprehensible villainy, she summons the people from door and window so that she may unmask the hypocrite before the world. The crowd is already pouring tumultuously into the hall when Friedrich, in a desperate outburst, succeeds with a few sharp words in making Isabella realize the impossibility of her scheme: he would flatly deny her accusations, boldly pretend that his offer was made up just to test her, and no doubt be believed to the extent it became a question of simply rebutting a charge of a frivolous proposal of love. Ashamed and confused, Isabella herself recognizes the rashness of her initiative and gnashes her teeth in silent despair. When Friedrich once again announces to the people his stern resolution and pronounces sentence on the prisoner, it suddenly occurs to Isabella, prompted by the painful memory of Marianne's fate, that the rescue she has failed to achieve by open force might possibly be attained by deceit. This thought dispels her misery at once and transforms it into utmost gaiety: turning to her sorrowing brother, their astonished friend and the baffled crowd, she assures them all that she will provide them with the merriest of adventures and declares that the carnival festivities, which the Viceroy has just strictly forbidden, will be celebrated this time with unusual abandon: for the dreaded ruler is only pretending to be so cruel in order to surprise everyone all the more pleasantly by his own gay participation in everything he has banned. Everyone thinks she has gone out of her mind, and Friedrich especially reproaches her with passionate severity for her incredible madness: a few words from her, however, suffice nevertheless to send the Viceroy into transports of ecstasy; for she promises him in intimate whispers to fulfill all his wishes and to send him a message presaging happiness for the following night. And so ends the first act in greatest excitement.

The nature of the heroine's hastily conceived plan we learn at the beginning of the second act, when she turns up in her brother's prison to test him in turn as to whether he is worthy to be saved. She discloses to him the shameful advances of Friedrich and asks him if he wishes to save his life at the price of his sister's dishonor? Claudio's fury and fervent declaration of his readiness to die, as he takes leave of his sister for this life and entrusts her with the most heart-rending greetings to his beloved who will survive him in mourning, is followed at last by an ambivalent mood which leads the unfortunate man through melancholy to weakness. Isabella, who has been on the point of announcing his rescue to him, stops in dismay as she sees her brother slide from these proud heights of noblest inspiration down to a muttered confession of unabated love of life and toward a shy query whether the suggested price of his rescue is impossibly high for her after all. Appalled, she springs to her feet, thrusts the unworthy man from her, and declares to him that he must now accept her deep contempt in addition to the shame of his death. After she has handed him over to his cell-keeper again, her mood at once changes to great exuberance: she decides, it is true, to let the waverer languish in uncertainty as to his fate for some time as a punishment, but nonetheless stands by her vow to rid the world of the most foul hypocrite that ever wished to impose laws upon his fellow men. She has notified Marianne to take her place at the assignation that night with Friedrich, who had been faithless to her and desires Isabella, and she now sends an invitation to Friedrich to this rendezvous, which, in order to entangle the latter more deeply in the web, is to take place in masks and at one of the houses of amusement he himself has been suppressing. To the madcap Luzio, whom she also desires to punish for his crass advances to the novice, she communicates Friedrich's desires and her allegedly forced acquiescence in their fulfillment in such an incomprehensibly carefree way that the normally frivolous fellow is struck serious with amazement and falls into a desperate rage: he swears that, even if the noble maiden is willing to suffer this unheard-of disgrace, he will strive by every possible means to avert it and if necessary arouse the whole of Palermo with fire and clamor. And he actually arranges for all his friends and everybody he knows to assemble that evening, as if to inaugurate the forbidden carnival festivities, at the exit to the Corso.

At nightfall, when things are already beginning to get out of hand, Luzio arrives and attempts to stir the crowd to open and bloody revolt by a wild carnival song with the closing refrain: "Who does not love our merry jest shall get a dagger in his breast". When a band of Sbirri led by Brighella approaches to break up the motley throng, the projected revolt seems on the point of being accomplished. But for the present Luzio advises them to yield and amuse themselves in the neighborhood, for he first has to find here the real leaders for this undertaking: this is, after all, precisely the place which Isabella has over-confidently revealed to him as the spot for her pretended tryst with the Viceroy. Luzio now lies in wait for him there: he manages to recognize him in his careful disguise, blocks his path, and as Friedrich breaks violently away, is about to pursue him with a loud shout and drawn sword when, upon a sign from Isabella, who is hidden in a bush, he himself is seized and led away. Isabella then steps forth, delighted at the thought of having restored the faithless bridegroom to the betrayed Marianne, and, as she supposes she has the promised decree of pardon for her brother already in her hands, she is on the point of generously renouncing any further revenge when, breaking open the document and reading it by torchlight, she finds to her horror that it contains an even harsher order for the death penalty, which, owing to her desire not to disclose the fact of his pardon to her brother, chance has now delivered to her by the hand of a jailer she has bribed. After a hard fight with the tempestuous passion of love, Friedrich had in fact already given in and, recognizing his helplessness in the face of this force undermining his peace of mind, had decided to face his ruin, if still as a criminal yet also as a man of honor. An hour on Isabella's bosom, then his own death according to the same law by which Claudio's life must also irrevocably be forfeited. Isabella, perceiving in this conduct only a further pile-up of hypocritical villainies, breaks out once more in a frenzy of agonized despair. Upon her outcry for an immediate revolt against this most scandalous tyrant a motley crowd forms in uproarious confusion, among them Luzio, who counsels the mob with stinging bitterness to pay no attention to the raging woman, who is surely deceiving them, just as she has deceived him: for he is insanely convinced that she has been disgracefully unfaithful. Fresh confusion, heightened desperation of Isabella: suddenly from the background comical cries for help are heard from Brighella, who, himself suffering from pangs of jealousy, has by mistake arrested the masked Viceroy and thus caused him to be discovered. Friedrich is recognized, and the trembling Marianne at his side is also unmasked; amazement, indignation and rejoicing intermix; the obligatory explications are soon accomplished; Friedrich darkly petitions to be conducted before the tribunal of the returning King to be condemned to death. Claudio, released from prison by a jubilant populace, informs him that the death penalty is not intended for every kind of amatory peccadillo: new messengers announce the unexpected arrival of the King in the harbor; it is decided to march in full masked procession to meet and pay joyous homage to the beloved Prince, who surely will recognize in the goodness of his heart how ill-suited the dank puritanism of a German must be for fiery Sicily. Of him it is said: "Merry feasting pleases him more than harsh decrees or legal lore." Friedrich, newly wedded to Marianne, is obliged to lead the procession, followed by Luzio and the novice, now forever lost to the convent.

These spirited and in many respects boldly devised scenes I had clothed with commensurate diction and meticulous verses which had already won Laube's approval. The police first of all objected to the title of the work, which, if I had not changed it, would have caused the complete collapse of all my plans for a performance. We had arrived at the week before Easter, and the theater was forbidden to present comedies, let alone frivolous pieces, during this time. Fortunately the sitting magistrate with whom I had to negotiate had not gone into the poem at all, and as I assured him that it had been adapted from a very serious Shakespearean play, it was deemed to be sufficient if I changed the title, which was startling in any circumstances, whereas the title *The Novice of Palermo* aroused no suspicions and its inaccuracy caused no scruples. It was different in Leipzig a short while later, where instead of my *Die Feen*, which had been dropped, I tried to insinuate my new work for performance. Director Ringelhardt, whom I had hoped to win for my undertaking by assigning to his daughter, who was about to make her debut in opera, the part of Marianne, took what he understood to be its propensities as an ostensibly unexceptionable pretext for rejecting the work. He asserted that if the Leipzig City Council were to permit its performance, which he in his esteem for that body greatly doubted, he would in any case not permit his daughter to sing in it.

In Magdeburg, strange to say, I suffered not at all from this questionable aspect of my opera libretto, for the material, as I have said, remained utterly obscure to the public as a result of the totally muddled performance. This circumstance, together with the fact that consequently no opposition had been raised to its propensities, thus paved the way for a second performance, against which there came no objection from any quarter as nobody was paying the slightest attention to it. Easily guessing that my opera had produced no impression and had left the public utterly in the dark as to what the whole thing was all about, I counted on the fact that this was to be the last performance by our company to produce nonetheless good or even large takings and as a consequence I did not hesitate to charge the so-called "full" price for admission. Whether a few people might have found their way into the auditorium before the beginning of the overture I cannot accurately state: but about a quarter of an hour before the scheduled starting time I saw in the parterre seats solely Frau Gottschalk with her husband and a very conspicuous Polish Jew in full costume. Despite this I was still hoping for some more customers, when suddenly behind the curtain the most extraordinary scenes began taking place. There, Herr Pollert, the husband of my leading lady (who was taking the part of Isabella), had run across the second tenor Schreiber,[1] a very young and handsome man who was to sing my Claudio, against whom the offended husband had long nursed a secret rancor born of jealousy. It appeared that the singer's husband, who had been surveying the composition of the audience with me from behind the drop curtain, now decided that the hour had struck in which he could, without damaging any theatrical undertaking, avenge himself upon his wife's lover. My Claudio took such a pasting from him that the unfortunate fellow had to retreat into the dressing-room, his face bloodied. Isabella received news of this, and plunged after her raging husband in desperation, only to be so soundly cuffed by him that she went into a fit. The uproar among the ensemble soon knew no bounds: people took sides, and it wouldn't have taken much more to produce a free-for-all, for it seemed that this unhappy evening offered everyone a suitable occasion to pay off mutual grievances once and for all. It was soon evident that the two who had been subjected to Herr Pollert's "ban on love" were quite incapable of mounting the stage that day. The stage director was sent before the curtain to advise the curiously select gathering in the auditorium that "owing to unforeseen difficulties" the performance of the opera could not take place.

That was the end of my career as conductor and composer of operas in Magdeburg, begun with much promise and undertaken with many sacrifices. The serenity of art now gave way to the earnestness of earning a living. My situation required some serious thought and the outlook was not cheerful. All the hopes I had shared with Minna based on the success of my work had been annihilated without a trace. All my creditors, who had been relying on the income I had told them would be forthcoming, now lost faith in my talent and counted solely on going after me personally, which they soon accomplished with a string of hastily lodged legal proceedings. My little apartment in the Breiter Weg had become highly antipathetic to me, for every time I came home I found a summons nailed to the door; henceforth I avoided it completely, especially because my brown poodle, which had brightened this refuge until then, had vanished without a trace, which I interpreted as a bad sign indicating the complete degeneration of my position. It was then that Minna, with truly comforting assurance and firmness of bearing, became a tower of strength to me and all I had left to fall back on. She had first resourcefully looked after her own future and was on the point of signing a not unfavorable contract with the director of the theater in Königsberg in East Prussia. It was now a question of finding me an appointment in the same place as music director: this post was already filled; but because the Königsberg director could no doubt gather from our correspondence that Minna's acceptance of the engagement depended upon my being employed at the same theater, he held out the prospect of a vacancy in this position before long and expressed willingness to hire me to fill it. We thereupon came to an agreement that Minna should go in advance to Königsberg and pave the way for my arrival as music director elect. Before these plans could be carried out we went through a dreadful period within the walls of Magdeburg, etched in my memory as a time of acute anxiety. I made, it is true, one more attempt to better my situation by personally going to Leipzig, upon which occasion I conducted the aforementioned negotiations with the director of the theater in regard to my new opera. But I soon saw that it was no longer sensible for me to stay in my native city and in the disquieting proximity of my own family, from whom I felt the restless desire to get away. My relatives recognized my irascible and deeply depressed mood: my mother begged me by all that was holy – whatever else I might do – not to be drawn into marriage at my early age. I was silent. As I departed, Rosalie accompanied me to the head of the stairs; I pretended that I would soon be coming back after taking care of some business matters and wanted to bid her only a casual adieu: she grasped my hand, looked long into my eyes, and said: "God knows when I will see you again." This cut me to the heart, yet still seemed mainly to hit my guilty conscience: that she was simultaneously expressing a presentiment of her early death dawned on me only when, after scarcely two years had passed, and without having seen her again, I received word of her sudden decease.

I now spent a few more weeks with Minna in Magdeburg in strictest seclusion; she helped to the best of her ability to ameliorate the worst of my straits. In view of our approaching separation and its uncertain duration, I hardly left her side, and our only recreation consisted of long walks to the more distant countryside around the town. Heavy forebodings weighed upon us: the warm May sun, which, as if to mock our forlorn condition, lighted for us the sad streets of Magdeburg, clouded over one day more deeply than I have ever since experienced and filled me with palpable dread. On our way home from one of these walks, as we were approaching the bridge over the Elbe we caught sight of a man who had just leapt from it into the water: we went to the river bank, called for help and induced a miller, whose mill abutted the river, to hold out a rake to the drowning man struggling with the current and being swept in his direction, so that he could save himself. With indescribable anxiety we awaited the decisive moment – saw how the drowning man grasped for the rake yet missed it and in the same instant vanished under the mill, never to be seen again. On the morning that I brought Minna to the stage-coach, to bid her what was for me a most unhappy farewell, the whole populace was streaming out of one of the city gates toward a big field to witness the execution of a man who was to be broken "on the wheel from below". The criminal was a soldier who had willfully killed his bride out of jealousy. When I returned for my last lunch at the inn I heard from all sides nothing but grisly descriptions of this atrocious Prussian method of execution. A young lawyer and a lover of music told us of a conversation with the executioner who had been brought in from Halle and with whom he had discussed the most humane method of hastening the death of the victim, and in relating all this he recalled with a shudder the elegant dress and bearing of this fearful person. These were the final impressions I took away from the scene of my first artistic endeavors and of my attempts to earn an independent living. These impressions have ever since often returned to me with singular persistence whenever I have left places with the feeling I would never return, and where I had expected to find fair weather for my art or personal prosperity. I have always had somewhat similar feelings upon leaving every place where I have stayed in the hope of improving my position.

Thus, I arrived in Berlin for the first time on May 18th 1836 and got to know the unique physiognomy of this imposing royal capital. My own prospects being anything but imposing, I took the most modest room I could find in the Crown Prince Hotel on Königsstrasse, where Minna had stayed a few months before. It was a great source of strength to find Laube again in Berlin, where he was awaiting the results of the legal proceedings against him and busying himself with teaching and literary work. He had a soft spot for the fate of *Das Liebesverbot* and gave me good advice as to how I might use some personal connections to get my opera accepted at the Königstadt theater. This theater was under the management of one of the most singular products of the population of Berlin: he went by the name of Cerf[1] and had been empowered by the King of Prussia to use the title of "Commission Councillor". This special favor on the part of the court was attributed to some not very savory reasons: through this patronage he had succeeded in vastly expanding the privileges enjoyed by this suburban theater. The decline of grand opera at the royal theater brought light opera, which was performed at the Königstadt theater, to greater public favor. Puffed up by these successes, the director with undisguised self-satisfaction fell in with the judgment of those who really thought that a theater could be properly managed only by a lower-class and uneducated person and thus held himself to be the right man in the right place, and continued to demonstrate his blissful ignorance on all sides in the most hilarious manner. Relying entirely on his instincts, he had become a little dictator over the artistic staff in his theater: he could do exactly as he wished. This characteristic seemed to work in my favor: Cerf announced at my first visit that I pleased him but he wished he could engage me as tenor; he had not the slightest objection to my application for a performance of *Das Liebesverbot* and promised it immediately. But he seemed particularly desirous of engaging me as music director. He was busily reinforcing his opera company and foresaw that his conductor, Gläser,[2] the composer of *Des Adlers Horst*, would make trouble by taking sides with the older singers, and thus he wanted to induce me to join his group in order to have someone "who would take the part of the new singers". All this seemed to go so swimmingly that I could scarcely be pardoned for believing my destiny had taken a decisive turn for the better and for feeling a sense of lightheartedness at the thought of such rosy prospects. No sooner had I permitted myself a few modifications in my standard of living which these circumstances seemed to justify than I perceived that my expectations were built on sand. With true horror I began to realize quickly how Cerf had deceived me, apparently merely for his own pleasure. In the manner of a despot he had granted me his favors directly and autocratically: the withdrawal and annulment of his promises, however, he made known to me through his clerks and secretaries by letting his exceptional relationship to me be detoured suddenly into the usual track of a potentate's alleged dependence on his bureaucracy. As Cerf wanted to get rid of me without offering any compensation, I was forced to deal with precisely those people against whom he himself had warned me and against whom he had wanted me to become his ally, and to come to some understanding regarding all that had been arranged between us with the disadvantage of being now to some extent a petitioner. The conductor, stage director, secretary and other gentlemen of that ilk were obliged to make it clear to me in turn that my wishes could not be fulfilled, and that the director owed me nothing whatsoever for the time he had made me waste while waiting for him to make good on his promises. I recall that this painfully prolonged process was an experience which filled me with prescient woe concerning my entire life.

My situation had gone from bad to worse as a result of all this. Minna now wrote me frequently from Königsberg as to the status of my hopes, but she had nothing of an encouraging nature to tell me; the local theater director seemed to be involved with his conductor in a murky relationship about which I could only later receive sufficient clarification, but which for the moment seemed to make my chances of obtaining the coveted position bafflingly remote. Yet it seemed certain that I would be able to begin work in Königsberg that autumn: as I was lolling around in Berlin at a loose end and under no circumstances would consider going back to Leipzig, I conjured up from these fragile hopes the ship that would transport me from the sandy marshes of Berlin to a safe haven on the Baltic.

This became possible, however, only after I had fought out and resolved within myself some difficult and serious inner conflicts produced by my relationship with Minna. An incomprehensible aspect of the character of this otherwise apparently straightforward female had thrown my young heart into turmoil. A good-natured, well-to-do merchant of Jewish descent named Schwabe, who until then had been established in Magdeburg, made friendly overtures to me in Berlin, and I soon discovered that his friendship was chiefly due to the passionate interest he took in Minna. It later became clear to me that a relationship had existed between this man and Minna, which could hardly have been construed as a breach of faith with me, since it had ended in a decided repulse of the rival's wooing in my favor: but the fact that the episode had been kept so secret that I had gotten no earlier inkling of it, and also the suspicion that Minna's comfortable circumstances were in part attributable to the friendship of this man, filled me with gloomy misgivings. But although, as stated, I could discover no real infidelity, I felt rather more of an anxious unease which drove me to the half-desperate resolve to regain my equilibrium in this respect by winning full possession of Minna. It seemed to me that my stability as a citizen as well as my artistic development would be assured by a totally committed union with Minna. The two years I had already spent in the theater world had kept me in a constant state of distraction, which made itself felt in an almost painful manner in my most inward being: I had a dark premonition that I was on a terribly wrong tack; I longed for self-possession and rest and hoped to find these most readily by bringing that relationship which had caused me so much unrest to a culmination. Laube had no trouble guessing from my untidy, emotional and peaked condition that something was wrong with this young man: it was in his company, which I always found comforting, that I gained my only halfway compensatory impressions of Berlin. The most important artistic experience came from a performance of *Fernand Cortez* under the baton of Spontini himself: the spirit of his conducting astonished me in a way virtually unknown to me before. If the actual performance, most particularly as regards the principal figures, who as a group could no longer be considered the cream of the Berlin opera ensemble, left me cold, and although it never produced an effect remotely comparable to that which Schröder-Devrient had made on me, yet the exceptionally precise, fiery and superbly organized way the whole work was brought off was entirely new to me. I gained a fresh insight into the inherent dignity of major theatrical undertakings, which in all their parts could be elevated by alert rhythmic control into a singular and incomparable form of art. This very intense impression remained vividly with me and guided me particularly in the conception of my *Rienzi*, so that from an artistic point of view Berlin can be said to have carved its traces on my development.

For the present, however, my chief concern was to extricate myself from my utterly helpless situation. I was determined to turn to Königsberg and communicated my decision, and the hopes upon which it was founded, to Laube. My splendid friend took it upon himself without further ado to use his connections to free me from my destitution in Berlin and assist me to reach my immediate goal, which was accomplished by the united efforts of some people friendly to Laube.

As we parted, my friend warned me with penetrating insight not to let myself get bogged down in the superficialities of theatrical life and, after exhausting rehearsals, not to go womanizing but rather to take a serious book in hand, in order that my greater gifts would not lack due cultivation. I did not tell him that I had it in mind to take an early and decisive step to protect myself against the more exciting distractions of the theater world. On July 7th I thus set out on what was then an extremely troublesome and fatiguing journey to far-away Königsberg.

It seemed to me as if I were departing this world as I rolled on day after day through the wilds of the marches. And then came the sad and depressing initial impression of Königsberg, where, in one of the poorest suburbs, Tragheim, near the theater and in such a lane as one would expect to find in a village, I found the decrepit house in which Minna had taken up residence. Her inborn equanimity soon had a highly soothing and domesticating effect on me. She was very popular at the theater and was respected by the management and the patrons; her bridegroom, which was now my public status, seemed the inevitable beneficiary of all this. Although there were as yet no definitive prospects for my getting an appointment, we nonetheless agreed that I should stick around for a while; it would all pan out in the end. This was in particular the opinion of a distinguished patron of the theater in Königsberg, the singular Abraham Möller, who took a friendly interest in Minna and eventually also in me. Möller, who was already well along in life, belonged to that breed of enthusiastic theater fans now totally extinct in Germany, but of which many stories are told in the history of actors of earlier times. One could not spend an hour in the company of the man, who was otherwise occupied in the boldest speculative deals, without having to listen to his account of the glories of the stage in past epochs in terms that were by no means discouraging. As a man of means from early in his career, he had contrived to get to know nearly all the great actors and actresses of the day and even to win their friendship as well. Through his inordinate generosity he had unfortunately suffered a serious depletion in his fortune, and he was now obliged to enter into all sorts of strange transactions in which profits could supposedly be made without any initial investment, in order to glean enough money to indulge his love of the theater by giving members of the company some support, which, however meager, was nonetheless in keeping with the company's decrepit condition. This strange man, who gave the theater director Anton Hübsch grounds to fear him, undertook to set my appointment straight. The obstacle was the following situation:

Louis Schubert,[1] a highly capable musician known to me from earlier times as the first cellist of the Magdeburg orchestra, had come to Königsberg from Riga, where he had left his wife and where the theater had been temporarily dissolved, to take the job of music director until the new theater in Riga reopened and he could return. The reopening of the Riga theater, scheduled for Easter of that year, had been postponed, and he was now in no hurry to leave Königsberg; since Schubert was unquestionably competent in his position, the director now faced the embarrassing situation of having to secure someone who would be willing to stand by before receiving his appointment until Schubert, whose comings and goings were beyond his control, found it convenient to leave. Consequently, a young music director who was anxious to remain in Königsberg at any price could only be highly welcome as a reserve and a replacement at the very shortest notice, when the need arose. Indeed, the director declared himself willing to pay me a small retainer until the time should arrive when I could assume my new duties. Conversely, Schubert was anything but pleased at my arrival, for the need to go back to Riga had vanished with the indefinite postponement of the reopening of the theater there. He had, moreover, developed a special reason for wanting to stay in Königsberg, because he had conceived a passion for the leading soprano of the opera, which had greatly cooled his desire to return to his wife. Thus he clung with considerable ferocity to his Königsberg job, viewed me as a mortal enemy and used all weapons of self-preservation to make my stay in Königsberg, as well as the inherently painful task of waiting in the wings, a veritable hell for me. Whereas previously in Magdeburg I had enjoyed the most cordial relationship with musicians and singers, and had always been accorded the greatest respect of the public, I here found it necessary to defend myself against the most dismaying hostility from all sides. This unpleasant situation, which soon made itself felt, went a long way toward making me regard my stay in Königsberg as a kind of banishment. That I should nonetheless go through with my marriage to Minna under such circumstances struck me even in my enamored state as a hazardous undertaking.

At the beginning of August the company went to Memel for a time to open its summer season: I followed Minna there a few days later. We went most of the way by sea, crossing the Kurisches Haff in a sailing vessel in terrible weather and with the wind against us, one of the most melancholy trips I have ever experienced. As we were sailing along beside the thin strip of sand separating the Haff from the Baltic Sea, the castle of Runsitten, where Hoffmann had laid the scene of one of his most gruesome tales (*Das Majorat*), was pointed out to me. The fact that in these desolate environs I should after such a long interval be confronted again by some of the fantastic impressions of my youth had a singular and chilling effect on my mood. My sad stay in Memel and the pitiful role I played there combined to make me seek my sole consolation in Minna who, after all, was the cause of my having gotten once again into such an unpleasant situation. Our friend Abraham joined us from Königsberg and seemed to be up to all kinds of tricks on my behalf, openly trying to sow discord between the manager of the theater and his music director. One day Schubert, following an argument with Hübsch in a tavern the night before, reported himself sick for an orchestral rehearsal of *Euryanthe*, in order to compel the manager to summon me to the conductor's desk, whereat my rival maliciously presumed that I would flounder about, the opera being seldom performed and very difficult, and thus expose weaknesses welcome to him. Although, as a matter of fact, I had never before had the score of *Euryanthe* before me, his wishes received so little gratification that he decided to recuperate in time for the performance in order to conduct it himself, something he would not have done if my incapacity had made it necessary not to give this opera. In this wretched position, irritated and sensitive to a raw climate which even on summer evenings bore frostily upon me, I was occupied in warding off the most painful and mundane troubles and gained nothing for my artistic development; at last, upon our return to Königsberg, the question of what to do next was seriously weighed, particularly under the guidance of friend Möller. Minna and I finally received a not unadvantageous offer from Danzig, through the influence of my brother-in-law Wolfram and my sister, who had gone there. Our theater friend seized upon this development to induce Director Hübsch, who was particularly anxious to retain Minna's services, to conclude a favorable contract with us both, according to which I would definitely become music director of his theater by the following Easter and we would be accorded a benefit performance, for which I selected *La muette de Portici*, to be given under my baton. For, as Möller now particularly urged us, it was high time to celebrate our marriage; it couldn't go on this way much longer. Minna had nothing against it, and I seemed to have demonstrated to myself by my endeavors and decisions up to that moment that I wanted nothing more eagerly than to reach that safe and restful haven. But in spite of all this, I had strange inner qualms the whole time.

I knew enough about Minna's life and character to be as clear about the salient divergencies in our two natures as the important step I was about to take required, if only I had by then achieved sufficient maturity to reach such judgment. The woman I was about to marry stemmed from parents who struggled to make a living in Oederan in the Erzgebirge in Saxony. Her father, an odd man of great vitality who in his later years evinced serious signs of mental disturbance, had been in his younger years a Saxon military trumpeter and had participated in a campaign in France as well as the battle of Wagram; thereafter he had taken up mechanical work and produced wool-carding combs, from which he earned a good living for a time, as he invented an improved process for manufacturing them. A rich industrialist in Chemnitz once gave him a large order to be delivered at the end of the year; the children, whose delicate fingers were extremely useful in this task, had to work night and day, their father having promised them an exceptionally lavish Christmas in his expectation of large profits. When the longed-for time arrived, however, he received news of the bankruptcy of his customer: everything previously delivered was lost and the inventory on hand was unsaleable. The family never recovered from the state of confusion caused by this misfortune: they went to Dresden, where the father hoped to find remunerative employment as a skilled mechanic, particularly in the construction of pianos, for which he could produce separate components. He also brought along a large quantity of fine wire originally intended for carding combs, which he hoped to sell there as profitably as possible. The ten-year-old Minna was given the job of offering swatches of it to milliners for the production of artificial flowers: she set out with a heavy basketful of wire and demonstrated such a gift for persuading people to buy that she had soon disposed of the whole supply at favorable prices. From this time on she conceived the intense desire to be of active assistance to her increasingly impoverished family, and to earn her own living as soon as possible and remove the burden of her care from the shoulders of her parents. As she grew up and developed quickly into a strikingly attractive young woman, she soon drew the attentive gaze of men. A certain Herr von Einsiedel fell desperately in love with her and in an unguarded moment succeeded in ruining the inexperienced girl. It was accomplished half by force and half by seduction. Her family was plunged into consternation: solely the mother and an older sister could be told of the terrible position in which Minna found herself; her father, from whose anger they all expected the worst, was never informed that his barely seventeen-year-old daughter had become a mother and, in circumstances perilous enough to threaten her life, had brought a daughter[1] into the world. From then on Minna, who could obtain no redress from her seducer, was doubly anxious to achieve independence and get out of her parental home. Through some friends she got involved with an amateur theatrical society: at one of their performances she attracted the attention of some members of the Royal Court Theater, and above all the interest of the director of the Dessau Court Theater, who at once offered her a job. She gladly grasped this chance to escape her sad situation, for the prospect of a brilliant career in the theater offered her at the same time the possible means to provide amply for her family at some point. Without being in the slightest stage-struck, and devoid of any coquetry or love of applause, she looked upon a theatrical career strictly as a means to earn a quick and possibly even a substantial livelihood. As she had no previous training predisposing her to artistic sensitivity, the theater to her meant merely the company of actors and actresses. Whether she pleased or not was important to her only to the extent it bore upon her achievement of economic independence: to use all the means at her disposal to reach this goal seemed to her as appropriate as it is for a merchant to display his wares as attractively as possible in a window. To make friends with the director, the stage director, and the most popular members of the company seemed to her the most elementary wisdom; those theatergoers whose judgement and taste influenced the public, and more importantly, the management were recognized by her as creatures upon whom the attainment of her inmost desires depended; never to make enemies of them seemed to her so natural and so necessary that she preferred to sacrifice her self-respect rather than lose their approbation. In so doing she developed a special skill in avoiding any breath of scandal while at the same time appearing to excuse anything that might seem wrong; at bottom she was unaware of doing anything really wrong, and this created certain apparent inconsistencies in her behavior, which she was nonetheless incapable of grasping. It was clear she had no inherent sense of delicacy; in its place she evinced only a sense of what is proper, by which she meant "doing the right thing", without being able to see that this accomplishes nothing if delicacy is violated. She lacked any feeling for art, as she had no sense of the ideal; she also had no talent for the stage: she pleased people by her winsome appearance; whether time and experience would have made her a good actress I cannot say. The characteristic power she exercised over me was by no means rooted in the deep idealism that had affected me so deeply, but rather to the contrary in the stability and sobriety of her character, which had seemed to complement what I felt to be lacking in my own in my disjointed quest for ideal goals. I had soon become accustomed never to appeal to Minna on any idealistic grounds; baffled by this, I always made a point of glossing over this aspect of things by laughter and jokes, yet still became naturally all the more sensitive to qualms about those aspects of womanly character in which I had accorded Minna a superiority profoundly beneficial to me. Her odd tolerance of certain intimacies and importunities, even with respect to her own person, on the part of those she regarded as her patrons in the theater irritated me severely; and I was incensed to find her responding to my reproaches about all this with an expression on her countenance of deep offense. The chance discovery of letters from the merchant Schwabe, of whose relationship with her I had received a first intimation in Berlin, astonished me by the revelation of much that had previously been unknown to me. All the pent-up jealousy, together with all my deep-seated doubts about Minna's character, now welled up in a precipitate decision to abandon the girl at once. We had one of those boundlessly fierce scenes that set the pattern for all our future altercations of this sort. In my outburst I obviously went too far toward a woman who had become attached to me through no real amorous passion, but who had more or less yielded good-naturedly to my advances and who basically did not belong to me, by behaving as if I really had exclusive right to her. To bring me up short, Minna needed only to remind me that from a worldly point of view she had refused several good offers in order to give way to the impetuosity of a penniless and ill-situated young man, whose talent had as yet to be proved to the world, with sympathetic kindness and devotion. But I did myself the most damage by the raging vehemence of my tone and diction, through which the target of it all felt herself so deeply wounded that I, realizing to what excesses I had gone, had to rely on admission of my own guilt to pacify the injured party and beg her forgiveness. Thus ended the fight, like all those to follow, with an outward victory for the female side. But peace had been undermined once and for all, and Minna's character in particular underwent a serious transformation as a result of the frequent recurrence of such incidents. Just as in later times she became increasingly perplexed at my seemingly incomprehensible conception of art and its relative importance, which caused her profound uncertainty in the judgment of everything connected with it, at this period she grew more and more confused by my feelings, so very different from hers, on the subject of higher delicacy in regard to moral questions, which, because she was unable to understand and approve my freedom of thought in some matters, roused a feeling of passionate resentment in her otherwise essentially equable nature. That this vehemence, increasing over the years, expressed itself in a manner commensurate with the tone and education of a lower-class family, was scarcely surprising, since the poor girl had gotten only a thin coating of civilized decorum instead of any real culture. The true torment of our subsequent life together lay in the fact that, as a result of this vehemence on her part, the support previously afforded by Minna's basic nature necessarily disappeared. At that time I got the first vague inklings of the fateful results my decision to marry Minna would bring. Her comforting and soothing qualities still had such a beneficial effect on me, however, that I managed to silence the inner voice foretelling dark disaster by the great frivolity characteristic of me and by the obstinacy with which I always confronted such warnings.

My family, meaning Rosalie and my mother, had been left entirely in the dark since my departure for Königsberg; I gave no one the slightest advance notice of the step I had decided to take. Under the reckless guidance of my old friend Möller I swept aside all legal difficulties standing in the way of the marriage. According to Prussian law, a man who had reached his majority did not need the consent of his parents to the marriage contract; but as I had not, according to this same law, as yet reached my majority, I had recourse to the laws of Saxony, to which I belonged by birth and by whose statutes I had come of age at twenty-one. Our banns had to be published at the place where we had been staying for the past year; and this formality was carried out in Magdeburg without any objections being raised. As there was no problem getting Minna's parents to approve, it remained only for us to pay a visit together to the pastor of the church in Tragheim to put everything in order. This proved to be a rather strange visit. It took place on the morning of the day fixed for our benefit performance, in which Minna was to assume the mime role of Fenella; her costume was not yet ready; there were other arrangements to be made and errands to be run; the cold, rainy November weather made us ill-humored, and we were kept waiting in the open vestibule of the parsonage for what seemed an unreasonably long time. This led to an extremely heated exchange of words between us, so that we were about to run off in different directions when the pastor opened the door and, abashed by the quarrel he had just witnessed, bade us enter. We were thus obliged to put a good face on the matter; the odd situation began to amuse us both; the pastor was appeased and the wedding fixed for eleven o'clock the following day.

Another source of irritation, which often led to the most intense disputes between us, was the furnishing of our abode, from which I intended to derive the maximum possible comfort and ease as a guarantee of the expected domestic happiness. Against the sensible views of my bride I reacted with impatience: the inauguration of the years of growing prosperity I saw stretching out before me was to be celebrated with commensurate symbols of household luxury. Furniture, utensils, and everything else were obtained on installment credit. There was not the slightest question of a dowry, a trousseau or any of the other amenities that make a bourgeois marriage the foundation of future prosperity. Our witnesses and wedding guests were drawn from the company of actors and actresses brought together by chance engagement at the Königsberg theater at the time: yet our friend Möller still managed to produce a silver sugar-box, to which another patron of the theater, a singular young man named Ernst Castell who remains a not uninteresting figure in my memory, added a silver cake-dish. The benefit performance of *La muette de Portici*, which I conducted with great fire, went off well and produced as large a sum as we had counted on. What remained of our wedding-eve, after the theater, we passed in silence and exhaustion, and then I took possession of our new quarters, without using the bridal bed decorated for the occasion but rather stretching out on a hard sofa, scantily covered and valiantly freezing while awaiting the happiness of the coming day. I was pleasantly excited the next morning by the arrival of Minna's belongings, packed in boxes and baskets; the rainy weather had vanished completely, and the sun shone brightly; only our sitting room refused to get duly warm, which brought me for a long time reproaches from Minna for having supposedly failed to look after the heating arrangements. At last I got dressed in the new suit, with a dark-blue cutaway with gold buttons. The carriage drove up, and I set out to fetch the bride. The blue sky had put us all in good spirits; in high good humor I found Minna in the splendid new gown I had chosen for her; she greeted me with real warmth and a sparkle in the eyes. Deeming the fine weather to be a good omen, we started off to what now seemed to us a merry wedding ceremony. We enjoyed the satisfaction of seeing the church crowded to overflowing, as if for a brilliant theatrical performance; we had trouble getting to the altar where a similarly worldly group consisting of our witnesses received us dressed in their theatrical finery. There was not a true friend among them all, for our good friend Möller was absent, on the grounds that there was no suitable partner for him.

I was not for a single moment insensible to the chilling frivolity, the profound cheerlessness of the congregation and its inevitable influence on the tone of the ceremony. I listened as if in a dream to the nuptial address of the parson, who, I later heard, had been not entirely dissociated from the bigotry that had stirred Königsberg in the past. A few days later I was told of a rumor going about town that I had proceeded legally against the parson for some gross personal insults contained in his sermon: I didn't understand what this was all about and could only suppose the exaggerated rumor arose from a passage I had absorbed with some puzzlement. In speaking of the future sufferings which we were to share, the preacher spoke of a friend whom we both did not know; anxious to learn more of this benevolent but secret protector who had chosen such an odd way of announcing himself to me, I looked inquiringly up at the parson: reproachfully, and with punitive emphasis, he disclosed to me the name of this unknown friend – Jesus. But I didn't interpret this, as most people thought, as an insult but rather felt it only as a disappointment, assuming that such remonstrances belonged to the ritual of such nuptial speeches. Yet my distraction in what was to me a basically incomprehensible act was in fact so great that when the parson held out the closed prayer-book for us to place our wedding rings upon it, Minna had to nudge me severely in order to induce me to follow her example. At this moment it suddenly became clear to me as if by a vision that my nature was caught in two cross-currents dragging me in entirely different directions: the upper one, facing the sun, bore me forward as if in a trance, while the lower one gripped me in some deep and inexplicable anxiety. The extraordinary levity with which I knew how to dispel the conviction surging repeatedly upward in me of commiting a two-fold sin against my own nature was absolved and supported by the truly warm affection with which I looked upon the young girl, so exceptional in her way and so uncharacteristic of her surroundings, who had now thus bound herself so unconditionally to a young man without any real means of support. It was eleven o'clock in the morning of November 24th 1836: I was twenty-three years and six months old. During and after the return from church my good mood overcame all doubts. Minna immediately took over the reception and provisioning of our guests. The table was set and a lavish feast, in which Abraham Möller, the promoter of our marriage, also took part despite being rather put out at his exclusion from the church ceremonies, had to compensate for the chilliness of the room, which to the distress of the hostess refused for a long time to get warm.

Everything went off in a rather tawdry and quickly forgotten way: but I nonetheless retained my good spirits until the following morning, when I was obliged to make my first trip to the city court to respond to the lawsuits instigated by my Magdeburg creditors which had pursued me to Königsberg. My friend Möller, whose help I had enlisted in defending myself against these attacks, had given me the sophistical advice to meet all my creditors' demands by pleading infancy under Prussian law for as long as proved necessary to get tangible assistance in settling the claims. The clerk of the court to whom I presented the grounds I had been advised to adopt for defense was greatly startled, for he had learned, presumably, of my marriage the previous day, which in turn could have taken place only after submission of documentary proof of my majority. I naturally gained only a brief respite by this, and the troubles which were to beset me from this source for a long time to come had their origin on the first day of my married life.

The period during which I remained without any function in the theater brought me a number of humiliations; yet I still hoped to make the most of the peace of the haven I had reached on behalf of my art; I composed a few pieces, among them a big overture based on *Rule Britannia*. While still in Berlin I had written the overture entitled *Polonia*, already mentioned in connection with the Polish feast. *Rule Britannia* was a further step in the direction of a type of composition calculated to make the most overwhelming effect; at the close of this work a large military band was to be added to an already overmanned orchestra, and I intended to have the whole thing performed at the Königsberg music festival scheduled for the following summer. To these two overtures I added a supplementary work, an overture with the title *Napoléon*: the choice of special effects for this work was particularly challenging, and I weighed the aesthetic dilemma whether I could represent the annihilating stroke of destiny that hit the Emperor in Russia by a thump on the tam-tam. I think it was my scruples about the admissibility of this thump which held me back from carrying out my plan for the time being.

On the other hand, thinking over the failure of *Das Liebesverbot* in performance, I was induced to plan a theatrical work in which the demands made upon chorus and soloists would be more commensurate with the acknowledged limitations of the local company, which was the only one at my disposal. A quaint tale from *The Arabian Nights* gave me the material for a lighter work of this kind: its title there, if I remember correctly, is *Men are better deceivers than women*. I transported the action from Baghdad to our times and modern costuming. A young goldsmith has offended the pride of a young woman by placing the above motto – "Men are better deceivers than women" – on the sign over his shop: heavily veiled, she shows up in his shop to solicit from him, who has always shown such excellent taste in his work, an opinion of her physical charms, beginning with her feet and hands and finally, as she notices the effect being produced upon him, ending with her face, which she suddenly discloses by removing the veil. To the jeweler, carried away by her beauty, she now complains that her father, who has kept her in strictest seclusion, describes her to every suitor as an ugly monster, in order, she supposes, to save the dowry; the young man vows not to be frightened off by this foolish objection of the father, if he should encounter it in his own wooing. No sooner said than done. The trusting jeweler is promised by the strange old man the hand of his daughter and when she is brought to the bridegroom after all the papers are signed, he recognizes that the father has indeed spoken the truth, for the genuine daughter is an absolute scarecrow. The beautiful young lady now returns to the despairing bridegroom to exult in his misery and promises to help him out of the terrible marriage if he is willing to remove the motto from his sign. At this point I departed from the original plot and proceeded as follows: the furious jeweler is already on the point of tearing down the offending sign, when a strange apparition leads him to desist; a tamer of bears appears on the street, making his clumsy beast perform a dance, in whom he at once recognizes his own father, who has been separated from him by the curious vicissitudes of fate. He suppresses his emotion at this encounter, for in a flash a scheme occurs to him whereby he can exploit this discovery to free himself from the marriage bonds with the daughter of the snobbish old man. He engages the bear-tamer to come that evening to the garden, where the ceremonies of betrothal will be celebrated before a select group of guests. To his young lady adversary, however, he announces his intention to let the sign hang over his shop for a while longer, for he hopes that the motto can still be substantiated. After the marriage contract, containing a lot of fictional titles he has awarded himself, has been read off to the assembled company, composed as I conceived it of the élite of the aristocratic French émigrés during the revolutionary period, the bear-tamer's whistle is suddenly heard and in he comes, together with his dancing beast. Angered by this tasteless spectacle, the astonished company becomes actually indignant, when the groom, now giving vent freely to his emotion, falls into the arms of the bear-tamer and loudly proclaims him as his long-lost father. The consternation of the group becomes even more intense when the bear himself embraces the man they suppose to be of aristocratic pedigree; for the bear is really his brother, who, upon the death of the actual bear used in the act, has enabled the poverty-stricken pair to continue to earn a living in the only way they know how by donning the skin of the deceased. The sudden discovery of his lowly origins dissolves the marriage at once, and the young lady, declaring herself outwitted by a man, offers the newly free jeweler her hand in compensation. I gave this unpretentious subject the title *Die glückliche Bärenfamilie* and equipped it with dialogue that later won high praise from Holtei:[1] I was now about to begin setting it to music in a light neo-French style. But the complications of my situation, growing worse from day to day, prevented any further progress on the work.

In this respect my strained relations with the music director of the theater were a source of constantly recurring trouble. Without being afforded the opportunity or means to prove myself, I was compelled to see myself maligned and abused on all sides by an antagonist who dominated the field, wherein his principal objective was to spoil my appetite for the position of conductor contractually assured me by next Easter. Though I did not lose my self-confidence in this fray, the oppressive and humiliating aspects of the situation pained me very much. When at last, at the beginning of April, the time finally came when music director Schubert had to resign and I could take his place, he had the melancholy satisfaction of knowing not only that the opera company had been seriously weakened by the departure of the prima donna but also that its continued existence had itself been rendered entirely questionable. This Lenten month, a bad time for all theatrical enterprises in Germany, had its depopulating effect on the Königsberg theater as well. The director made every possible effort to fill the gaps in the ensemble by guest appearances and new engagements, and in this I and my hyperactivity were of great assistance to him; I devoted all my energy to buoying up by word and deed the battered theatrical ship, in which I now could take a hand for the first time. For a considerable period I had to try to keep cool in the face of rough treatment at the hands of a clique of students among whom my predecessor had recruited enemies for me. I also had to overcome initial resistance on the part of the orchestra, upon whom Schubert had also worked, by the unerring certainty of my conducting. Having laboriously laid the foundation of a good reputation, I was soon obliged to recognize that the business methods of Director Hübsch had already entailed sacrifices too great for the theater to survive the adversities of the season successfully. He disclosed to me in May that he was on the point of being compelled to close the theater: by exerting all my eloquence and presenting plans calculated to improve the fortunes of his undertaking, I was able to induce him to persevere; but this was made possible only by the support of the members of the troupe, who were required to forgo part of their salaries for a time. This aroused general bitterness on the part of the uninitiated, and I found myself in the curious position of being forced to pacify those affected by this measure on behalf of the director, while I and my personal situation were so deeply affected that it became from day to day more and more difficult for me to carry on under the burden of difficulties rooted in my past activities. While I myself did not lose courage even then, Minna, who as my wife was deprived of all the means previously at her disposal in such situations, found this turn of events unbearable.

The quarrel long smoldering between the young married couple was not long in bursting out afresh under such melancholy circumstances, and our battles took as their point of departure the same issues that had troubled me so intensely before our marriage and had led to the fiercest scenes between us. The less I was able during the winter to maintain our standard of living by my own work and by making the most of my talents, the more Minna felt, to my unsupportable humiliation, obliged to take this burden upon herself by exploiting her personal popularity; frequent experience of such condescensions, as I used to call them, led repeatedly to the ugliest scenes, and only her peculiar conception of her position in the theater and the exigencies it involved made it possible to interpret her behavior charitably. I was utterly unable to bring my young wife to see my point of view, or to make her grasp my own feelings resulting from these unpleasant occasions; but what put any understanding between us irretrievably beyond reach was the bitterness and violence of language and behavior in which I indulged myself. These scenes frequently sent my wife into paroxysms so alarming that the satisfaction of reconciling her became, as can easily be imagined, the sole success I enjoyed from them. It was clear that we both found our conduct increasingly incomprehensible and inexplicable. The strength of any affection that Minna was able to feel for me was no doubt diminished by these ever more frequent and distressing quarrels; yet I had no idea that it needed only a suitable pretext for her to embark on a desperate action.

To replace the missing tenor in our company, I had summoned

Friedrich Schmitt, a friend from my first year in Magdeburg whom I
have already described in some detail; he was cordially attached to me
and helped me as best he could in coping with the difficulties which
plagued the theater as well as my own personal situation. The necessity
of winning friends among the general public made me, particularly in
his company, less reserved and choosy in developing new social
relationships. A wealthy merchant named Dietrich had a short time
before constituted himself a patron of the theater, and especially of the
ladies belonging to it: he made a practice of inviting the pick of these
ladies, duly including their menfolk, to dinners at his house at which
things were conducted according to the precepts of the English style of
comfort that he affected – the ideal of all German businessmen in the
northern centers of commerce. I had already shown myself to be less
than enchanted by the idea of accepting the first such invitation
addressed to us – at first simply because I didn't like his looks; Minna
found, on the contrary, that I was wrong. I remained decidedly against
broadening our relationship with this man; and although Minna did not
insist on our accepting visits from him, my conduct toward the intruder
was grounds for angry scenes between us. My friend Schmitt considered
it his duty to inform me one day that this Herr Dietrich had spoken of
me at a public dinner in such a way as to suggest that he enjoyed a
questionable intimacy with my wife. I in turn had reason to suspect that
Minna, in some way unknown to me, had told this fellow about my
conduct toward her and about our precarious position as well. Accompanied by Schmitt, I called the dangerous man to account in his own
home, which led first of all to the usual denials on his part and
subsequently to secret communications with Minna on the subject, who
now felt my intervention to be new grounds for her resentment against
me. Our behavior now took a serious turn for the worse: some things
were simply passed over in silence. At the same time – it was toward
the end of May 1837 – the business affairs of the theater reached the
aforementioned critical point: the management had to bank on the
self-sacrificing spirit of the company to assure the continued existence
of the theater. And as stated, my own situation at the end of such a
disastrous year for my personal finances was even more ruinously
affected than that of anyone else; yet there seemed to be nothing for it
but to persist in the face of these difficulties, and I took it upon myself,
without any intervention on Minna's part but with the help of the
faithful Friedrich Schmitt, to make the necessary arrangements to shore
up my position in Königsberg. Together with my unceasing participation

in the day-to-day work of the theater, this kept me so busy and away from the house so frequently that I really could not pay much attention to Minna's silent and reserved deportment during those days. On the morning of March 31st I took leave of Minna, expecting to be detained by rehearsals and business matters until late in the afternoon. Some time before, she had, with my hearty approval, summoned her daughter Nathalie, whom she let everyone believe was her younger sister. When I was about to say my usual quiet goodbye, both women rushed after me to the door and embraced me passionately, Minna and her daughter both bursting into tears, so that I became alarmed and immediately inquired about the meaning of all this, but receiving no answer from them I was obliged to leave and then ponder this strange conduct, the true reason for which I did not come close to guessing. I arrived home late in the afternoon, worn to a frazzle by my exertions, irritated, dead-tired, pale and hungry, only to find the table not laid and Minna not at home, the maid telling me that she had not yet returned from a walk with Nathalie. I collected myself to wait patiently and sat down exhausted at the sewing table, which I proceeded to open absent-mindedly. To my astonishment it was empty. Struck by frightful foreboding, I sprang up and went to the clothes closet and realized at once that Minna had left the house. Her departure had been so cunningly planned that even the maid had known nothing about it. With death in my heart I rushed out of the house to investigate Minna's disappearance; old Möller, Dietrich's sworn enemy, soon found out with his practised eye for such things that he had left Königsberg that morning by special coach in the direction of Berlin. The horrible truth now stared me in the face. I simply had to try and overtake the fugitives; this seemed possible with a lavish expenditure of money; but that was lacking and first had to be laboriously collected. On Möller's advice, I took along the silver wedding presents for possible emergency use, and after a delay of several horrible hours, set off with my distressed old friend, also by special coach. It seemed certain that we would overtake the ordinary mail-coach that had left a short time before, and it appeared a foregone conclusion that Minna would use this to continue her journey, once it had reached a safe distance from Königsberg. But this proved impossible: reaching Elbing at dawn the following day we found our funds depleted by the extravagant use of the special coach and saw ourselves forced to turn back, discovering that, even to return by regular coach, it would be absolutely necessary to sell the sugar-box and cake-dish. This journey back to Königsberg justifiably remains as one of the saddest memories of my young life. Of course I did not think for a minute of staying in the place but only of how to get away. Caught between the lawsuits of my Magdeburg creditors and the Königsberg tradesmen who had claims on me for installment payments on my household furnishings, my departure necessarily had to be carried out in secret: but for this I again needed money, particularly considering the distance from Königsberg to Dresden, where I had to go in search of my wife. This held me back for two terrible days. There was no news for me from Minna; it was only through Möller that I learned that Minna had gone to Dresden, accompanied by Dietrich part of the way supposedly as a friendly demonstration of helpfulness. In the belief that she had really only wished to escape from a situation that filled her with desperation, accepting for this purpose the assistance of a man who had been moved to sympathy at her predicament, and that she was now seeking asylum with her parents, my initially furious reaction at this step softened to such an extent that I even began to reproach myself for my behavior and for having brought her such unhappiness, and to feel increasing commiseration with her despair. I became so convinced of the correctness of this way of looking at it during the tedious journey to Dresden via Berlin, which I eventually undertook on June 3rd, that when at last I found Minna in the humble abode of her parents I was quite unable to express anything other than repentance and heartbroken sympathy. It turned out that Minna had indeed felt herself ill-treated by me and declared that she had been forced to take this drastic step solely because of our untenable situation, to which she thought me both blind and deaf. Her parents were not pleased to see me: their daughter's over-wrought condition seemed to give ample justification for her complaints about me. Whether my own sorry state, my hasty pursuit, and all my outpourings of grief made a favorable impression on her I can hardly say, so confused and even incomprehensible was her ambivalent attitude toward me. Yet it did impress her when I told her there were good prospects of my getting the job of music director in a theater soon to be opened in Riga under the most promising auspices. I didn't think it wise to press her at the time for further decisions concerning the resolution of our future relationship but rather concluded I must strive all the more earnestly to provide a better foundation for them. With this in mind, and after spending a miserable week together under the most trying circumstances, I went off to Berlin to conclude the urgent business of signing my contract with the newly appointed director of the Riga theater. This was accomplished, and in fact under not unfavorable conditions which offered me the possibility of setting up house in such a way that Minna could withdraw from the theater entirely and thereby be in a position to spare me humiliation and anxiety in the future.

Returning to Dresden,* I found Minna ready to lend a not unwilling ear to my plans and persuaded her to leave the cramped parental home for the moment and take up residence at Blasewitz, in the country not far from Dresden, until it was time for me to begin my work in Riga. We took modest lodgings at the inn on the Elbe, whose garden restaurant I had often visited as a child. Minna's mood seemed to improve greatly; she had asked me not to press her too hard and I responded by sparing her as much as possible, with the result that after a few weeks had elapsed I thought I could safely assume the worst period of trial would soon be over. But it upset me very much to find her mood deteriorating again, and seemingly without explicable cause: Minna started talking about advantageous offers she was receiving from various theaters, and startled me one day with the announcement of a little pleasure trip she proposed to take with the family of a childhood friend. As I felt obliged not to put any constraints on her, I made no objection to this plan, whereby she was to leave me for a week, and even accompanied her back to her parents' house, promising to await her return calmly in Blasewitz. Several days later her eldest sister paid me a visit and asked me for the requisite written assent for the issuance of a passport for my wife. Startled by this, I went to Dresden to ask my in-laws what their daughter had in mind; to my surprise I got a particularly rude reception there and received coarse reproaches about my conduct toward Minna, whom they contended I was not even able to support; as my only response was to persist in requesting information as to the whereabouts and intentions of my wife, I was rebuffed with some improbable stories. Tormented by the bitterest forebodings and understanding nothing of all that had happened, I returned to my little village. There I found a letter from Möller in Königsberg, which explained my misery: Herr Dietrich had journeyed to Dresden; the hotel where he stayed was specifically named. The frightful light which this cast on Minna's conduct flashed upon me like lightning: I hurried into the city to make the appropriate inquiries in that hotel; it appeared the man had actually spent some time there but had since left; Minna was likewise nowhere to be found. I now knew enough to demand of Fate why it had sent me, at such an early age, an experience so terrible that it bade fair to poison the rest of my life.

* Note in the margin of the manuscript, in Cosima's hand: "Triebschen May 17th 1866".

In my boundless suffering I turned for solace to my sister Ottilie and her excellent husband, Hermann Brockhaus, to whom she had now been married for a number of years; at the time they lived in a lovely summer villa in the beautiful Grosser Garten on the outskirts of Dresden. I had looked them both up immediately upon my arrival in Dresden; still in great uncertainty as to my situation, I had told them nothing about it and showed myself only infrequently: now I was driven to overcome my pride and tell them almost everything about my misfortunes. For the first time I was in a position to appreciate the advantages of family relationships and the direct and intimate communication between blood relatives. There was no need for long explanations; brother and sister remained two who had lived in closest communion in their earliest childhood; we understood each other without lengthy discussion; I was unhappy and she was happy: consolation and help were forthcoming as a matter of course.

This was the same sister to whom I had once, amid thunder and lightning, read *Leubald und Adelaïde*, who had listened with astonishment and sympathy to the fateful performance of my first overture on that Christmas Eve, and whom I found married to a splendid fellow, Hermann Brockhaus, the youngest brother of my older brother-in-law Friedrich Brockhaus, who was now making a name for himself as an orientalist. Their marriage had already been blessed with two children; being comfortably off, they led a carefree life, and whenever I arrived from Blasewitz on one of my long walks, as now happened almost daily, and stepped into one of those much sought-after villas in the Grosser Garten, where I knew the family was always ready to accord me a friendly welcome, it was like going from a hopeless desert into paradise. Not only did my sister's company calm me down considerably but the society of my brilliant and scholarly brother-in-law reawakened my long dormant desire for higher learning. My youthful marriage, it was brought home to me without in any way hurting my feelings, was a pardonable error, yet still in need of remedy, and my mind regained sufficient buoyancy to attempt artistic creation, which this time was not calculated solely to meet the frivolous standards of the theatrical world as I had come to know it. During the miserable days of my last stay with Minna in Blasewitz I had read Bulwer's novel[1] about Cola Rienzi; while I was recuperating in the bosom of my sympathetic family, I worked out a plan for a grand opera to which this subject had inspired me. Even though I was compelled for the time being to return to work in a relatively small theater, I nevertheless determined to aim at enlarging my sphere of action in the future. I sent my overture on *Rule Britannia* to the Philharmonic Society in London and tried to get in touch with Scribe[1] in Paris about material for a drama I had extracted from a novel of Heinrich König[2] entitled *Die hohe Braut*. That is how I spent the rest of the unforgettably pleasant summer of this year, leaving for Riga at the end of August to take up my new appointment. Although I knew Rosalie had shortly before followed the inclination of her heart and married Professor Oswald Marbach, I avoided going via Leipzig, no doubt in some foolish way seeking to spare myself humiliation, and went straight to Berlin, where I was to receive some additional instructions from my future director and also acquire a passport. There I met one of Minna's younger sisters, Amalie Planer,[3] a singer gifted with a beautiful voice whom we had drawn to our opera company in Magdeburg for a short time. This extremely good-natured girl was deeply shaken by my report about Minna; during a performance of *Fidelio* we attended together we both broke out into tears and sobs. Strengthened by this consoling thought, I now traveled via Schwerin, where I had an erroneous idea I would find some trace of Minna, to Lübeck, to wait for a merchant ship going to Riga. We had already gotten out to Travemünde when an unfavorable wind set in, which delayed our departure for a week. I was forced to live out this trying period in a miserable seamen's saloon; without funds for entertainment I took up, among other books, the reading of the popular version of *Till Eulenspiegel*, which first gave me the idea of a real German comic opera. When I finally came to write the poem for *Der junge Siegfried* many years later, I remember having many vivid recollections of this melancholy sojourn in Travemünde and my reading of *Till Eulenspiegel*. After four days at sea we finally arrived at the port of Bolderaa, and I felt at first a strange unease at coming into contact with Russian officialdom, which I had instinctively detested ever since the days of my sympathy with the Poles as a boy. It seemed to me almost as if the harbor police could read my enthusiasm for Poland on my face and would send me to Siberia without further ado: I was thus all the more agreeably surprised, upon reaching Riga, to be enveloped at last by a thoroughly familiar German element, which pervaded in particular everything connected with the theater.

After my unhappy experiences with the conditions at the smaller German theaters, the nature of the new theatrical venture there made an initially reassuring impression. A group of wealthy theater fans and rich merchants had founded an association to raise sufficient money by voluntary subscription to provide a solid foundation for the kind of good theater management they wanted: the management itself had been put in the hands of a man with a certain reputation in the theatrical world, the not unpopular dramatist Karl von Holtei. An adherent of a school of drama already on the wane at that time, Holtei combined extraordinary social gifts with an unusual acquaintance with all the leading personalities in the theater for the past twenty years. He counted himself as one of a circle of so-called "likeable libertines", who were fond of being considered brilliant and witty and looked upon the theater as a publicly licensed arena for their wild eccentricities, but against whom the more normal people held themselves just as aloof as the intelligentsia of the nation, which was rapidly retreating with ever-increasing hopelessness from its previous support for the theater as a whole. The Königstadt theater in Berlin, at which Holtei's first wife[1] had long ago glittered as a popular actress, had, at the time of the ascendancy to which it had risen precisely owing to the presence in the company of the famous Henriette Sontag,[2] schooled audiences in the taste for Holtei. Apart from his musical comedies, among which *Der alte Feldherr* had achieved a certain poularity, his melodrama *Lenore*, adapted from Bürger's ballad,[3] had in particular won for him a wide-ranging reputation as a dramatic craftsman. Possessed by the desire to throw himself completely into the life of a theater, the invitation to Riga had been especially welcome to him, as he could justifiably hope to indulge his predilections without restraint in such an out-of-the-way place. His peculiar familiarity of manner, his inexhaustibly amusing store of conversation, and uncommonly light way of doing business gave him a remarkable hold on the businessmen of Riga, who wanted nothing more than the kind of entertainment he was ready and willing to provide. They gave him whatever resources he wanted and bestowed upon him in every respect their unconditional confidence. My appointment to his venture had come about with extraordinary facility: he wanted to keep surly old pedants off his neck and thus chose young people just for their youth's sake; in my case it had sufficed that he knew me to come from a family that he knew and liked, and as he had also gathered that I had become a fiery partisan of modern French and Italian opera, he had decided that I was the right man for him. He had ordered the scores of all the operas of Bellini, Donizetti, Adam and Auber in bulk; I was now to give the good people of Riga the benefit of hearing them at the earliest opportunity.

At my first visit to Holtei's apartment I met my old Leipzig acquaintance and former protector, Heinrich Dorn, who had accepted a steady job as municipal director of church and school music. He was delighted to find the bizarre youth he had known transformed into a conductor in an independent position and was even more astonished to discover in me, once the fervent Beethoven partisan, now an ardent champion of Bellini and Adam. He took me to his summer house, which in Riga jargon lay "in the greenery", that is, in point of literal fact, among the sand dunes. While I was telling him something of what had happened to me, I grew conscious of the strangely deserted look of the place, and my initial uneasiness grew from a feeling of homelessness into passionate longing to escape from the vortex of theatrical activity that had carried me to such inhospitable regions. Unease and longing gradually dispelled the casual frivolity with which in Magdeburg I had allowed my musical taste to be dragged down at the same time as I had contented myself with the most unworthy kind of theatrical society. In turn I developed new tastes during the period of my activity in Riga, which brought me into growing estrangement from the theater, thereby causing Director Holtei the anger born of disappointment in me.

At the outset, however, I found no trouble making the best of a bad bargain. We had to open the theater before all the members of the company had shown up; this was done with a performance of a little comic opera by Carl Blum[1] called *Marie, Max und Michel*. For insertion in this work I set to music an aria written by Holtei for the capable basso Günther; it consisted of a sentimental introduction together with a merry military rondo and was a great hit. Later I composed another, prayer-like song for the basso Scheibler for insertion in *Die Schweizerfamilie*, and this pleased not only the public but myself as well, as it showed signs of the great changes taking place in my musical development. I was also entrusted with the composition of a tune for a National Anthem written by Brakel for the birthday of Tsar Nicholas, to which I tried to give as darkly despotic and patriarchal a coloring as possible and once again I reaped some glory, as it was performed every year on the same day for a time. Holtei tried to persuade me to write a light and pleasing opera, or even better, a Singspiel suitable for performance by the existing company; I took another look at the text of my *Die glückliche Bärenfamilie*, and found Holtei, as previously stated, favorably inclined toward it; yet when I unearthed the small amount of music I had composed for it in Königsberg I was overcome with lively disgust at this kind of writing. I presented the text to my good-natured but rather feckless friend Löbmann,[2] my assistant as conductor, and never gave it another thought from that day to this. On the other hand, I now started to work on the text for *Rienzi* that I had sketched out in Blasewitz and in so doing proceeded on such a grandiose theatrical scale that with this work I deliberately cut off all possibility of being tempted by circumstances to produce my work anywhere other than on one of the largest stages in Europe.

While this strengthened the desire to escape from the petty degradations of work at a small theater, new complications entered my life which affected me more and more seriously and placed new obstacles in the way of these aforementioned endeavors. The prima donna Holtei had engaged had not shown up; we found ourselves without a singer for the more serious operatic works. In these circumstances Holtei gladly accepted my suggestion that we should waste no time in summoning to Riga Amalie, Minna's sister, who was pleased to accept an engagement that would let her work with me. From Dresden, where she was staying at the time, she also notified me in her answer of Minna's return to her parents, as well as of the sorrowful and suffering condition, aggravated by severe sickness, in which she now was. I naturally took this piece of news very coldly; what I had learned of Minna, since she had last left me, had necessarily impelled me to give my old Königsberg friend the task of commencing divorce proceedings on my behalf. It was certain that Minna had spent quite a long time in a hotel in Hamburg with that accursed Herr Dietrich and had proclaimed our separation with such disregard for the consequences that the whole theatrical world, in particular, was buzzing about the subject in a manner most dishonorable for me. I simply informed Amalie of this and asked her to spare me any further reports about her sister.

Minna* herself appealed to me with a truly shattering letter, in which she openly confessed her unfaithfulness. Just as she had been driven to this by despair, so had she now been brought back from this path by despair over the misery into which she had plunged herself. Certain hints led to the conclusion that she had been duped as to the character of her seducer and through recognition of her frightful situation had fallen into a debilitated condition morally as well as physically, from which, sick, suffering and admitting her guilt, she now turned back to me in order to beg my forgiveness and to assure me that she had now for the first time become fully aware of her love for me. I had never heard such words from Minna before and I was never to hear them again, except in one touching moment many years later, in which the same avowal moved me to such a change of heart as happened this time with the receipt of

---

* Note in the margin of the manuscript, in Cosima's hand: "Triebschen October 5th 1866".

146

her letter. I wrote her back telling her that I gave myself most of the blame for what had happened, and promised that the subject would never be mentioned between us again; and I can say with some pride that I carried out this vow to the last syllable.

As the appointment of her sister was settled in a satisfactory manner, I invited Minna to accompany her at once to Riga. Both gladly accepted my invitation and arrived from Dresden at my new home on October 19th, the raw weather having meanwhile already set in. I saw immediately to my sorrow that Minna's health had truly suffered and so did everything in my power to provide her with the domestic comfort and quiet she needed. This was not easy, because I had only my modest income as music director, and we were both resolutely determined not to let Minna go back into the theater. Carrying out this resolve, with all its attendant inconveniences, produced strange complications, the nature of which was revealed to me only later when startling developments disclosed the true moral character of Holtei. For the moment I had to be content to be regarded as jealous of my wife; that this was accompanied by a general feeling that I had grounds for this jealousy I managed to take in my stride and rejoiced at the restoration of a satisfactory married life, particularly as Minna had begun to develop her talent for running our modest household as comfortably as our circumstances allowed, to the benefit of us both. Inasmuch as our marriage always remained childless and we were compelled to enliven our hearth by enlisting the help of a dog, we this time hit upon the eccentric idea of taking in a baby wolf, which had been brought to our door as a tiny cub. As we found that this experiment did not augment our domestic felicity, we gave it up after a few weeks. We were more successful with sister Amalie, whose good-natured and unaffected manner for a time compensated very pleasantly for what was lacking in our family circle. The two sisters, who had enjoyed no real education, often lapsed back into their childhood ways in the most amusing manner; when they sang folksong duets and Minna, who had no musical training to speak of, ably seconded her sister, and when we partook of Russian salad, salted salmon from the Dvina, or even fresh caviar for supper, we all three felt quite cheerful and comfortable in our far-away northern home.

Amalie's lovely voice and true singing talent brought her at first a very favorable reception by the public, which pleased all three of us hugely. Small in stature and without much acting ability, the scope of her powers was nevertheless quite limited, and as she was soon surpassed by more gifted rivals, it was a great stroke of luck for her that a young officer of the Russian army, then Captain and now General Carl von Meck, fell head over heels in love with the simple girl and married her a year later. This relationship brought a number of difficulties with it, however, and cast the first shadow over the life we three were leading together. In time the two sisters quarreled irreconcilably, and I had to go through the unpleasant experience of living for a full year in the same apartment with two relatives who neither looked at nor spoke to each other.

We spent the winter that ushered in the year 1838 in a cramped, cheerless dwelling in the old part of the city; it was not until spring that we were able to get a better place to live in the more spacious Petersburg suburb, in which, despite the breach between the two sisters, we led quite an active social life, as we made a point of entertaining our friends as often as possible. Beside members of the theater company, I now and then cultivated some acquaintanceships in the city; we received and visited the family of music director Dorn, with whom I swore brotherhood; but it was my second in command at the theater, the not very gifted but worthy Franz Löbmann, who remained loyalest to me. Nevertheless, I did not attempt to make much of a splash in wider circles and in accordance with what now increasingly established itself as my lifelong propensity, soon saw less and less of people, so that when I left Riga after a stay of not quite two years, I departed almost as a stranger and with as much indifference as I had left Magdeburg and Königsberg. What particularly embittered me about my departure, however, was a series of experiences so disagreeable that I determined henceforth to cut myself off from contact with the sort of people I had met in my previous attempts to carve out a position for myself in theaters.

But I only began to realize all this gradually, whereas at the outset, given the resuscitation of a marital happiness that had been so badly disrupted in its earliest days, I felt distinctly better off in my artistic activities than I had before. The solid financial foundation of this theatrical undertaking exercised a healthy influence on the performances. The theater itself was squeezed into a very small space; there was as little room for scenic display on its tiny stage as there was accommodation for lavish musical forces in the extremely cramped orchestra pit. In both respects strict limitations were imposed, yet I successfully contrived to introduce in time substantial reinforcements into a pit actually designed for a string section consisting of no more than two first and two second violins, two violas, and one contrabass, thereby bringing down upon myself Holtei's wrath. For the opera we soon put together a good ensemble. I was particularly stimulated by the preparation of Méhul's opera *Joseph in Egypt*, whose noble and uncomplicated style, together with the touching and exciting effect of the music, contributed a good deal toward the favorable change in the direction of my taste, heretofore badly warped by the theatrical customs of the time. It was also most gratifying to feel my old and serious predilection for the spoken drama reawakened by some extremely good dramatic performances. I remember in particular a production of *King Lear*, of which I attended with huge interest not only the performances themselves but also the rehearsals. Yet it was just these stimulating experiences that caused me to feel more and more dissatisfied with my work at the theater, for on the one hand I found the members of the company increasingly distasteful and on the other I was becoming more and more dissatisfied with the policies of the management. In regard to the ensemble, I soon discovered the hollowness, vanity and impudent selfishness of this uneducated, entirely undisciplined class of people, for I had by now lost that former indiscriminate liking for casual company I had indulged in Magdeburg. There were soon very few members of the opera with whom I had not quarreled in combating one or more of the above-mentioned character-istics. But my saddest experience was that, in spite of my being drawn into such disputes in truth solely from my desire to promote the overall artistic success of the performances, I not only received no support whatever from the Director Holtei, but thereby even made an enemy of him. He in turn went so far as to state in all frankness that our theater had taken on a much too respectable character for his taste and sought to educate me to the view that theatrical achievements presuppose a promiscuous company. Just as he declared the concept of any inherent dignity in theatrical art to be pedantic nonsense, he also deemed vaudeville, with its mixture of sentimentality and farce, to be the only type of performance really worth considering. He hated serious grand opera, and particularly lavish musical ensembles, and my demands in this direction aroused his scorn and harvested his malicious rebuffs. It gradually became clear to me, much to my horror, that there was a strange connection between his artistic prejudices and his predilections touching upon the terrain of morality. For the present I felt so repelled by the revelation of his artistic antipathies that I felt increasingly justified in my growing distaste for any truck with the theater. I still took pleasure in some good performances we got up in the larger theater at Mitau, to which the company repaired for a time at the beginning of the summer. But it was there, while spending most of my time reading Bulwer's novels, that I formed the secret resolve to sever my connection with the theater in the sole form I had as yet been able to know it.

I looked to the composition of my opera *Rienzi*, the text of which I had finished in the early days of my sojourn in Riga, to bridge my way to that more glorious world I intensely longed for. While I had abandoned *Die glückliche Bärenfamilie* because, among other reasons, the execution of such a light piece would have involved me in precisely those theatrical practices I despised, it now elevated and consoled me to plan *Rienzi* as a work so recklessly elaborate in the artistic resources it would demand as well as in other respects that my desire to see it on the boards would compel me to break out of the narrow confines of the small theaters to which I was accustomed and seek a new connection with one of the larger theaters. After our return from Mitau in mid-summer 1838, I began the composition, keeping myself thereby in a mood of enthusiasm that took on the quality of bravado in the light of my real situation. Everyone to whom I communicated my plan saw from the first glance at the subject that my primary intention was a breach with my present position, which offered no possibility of producing my work, and in the eyes of my acquaintances I seemed both arrogant and frivolous.

I was also considered impractical and eccentric for turning away from my recent unthinking indulgence in a taste for trivial opera, particularly by the former defender of my remarkable Leipzig overture. He gave uninhibited vent to this opinion in a review written for the *Neue Zeitschrift für Musik* of a concert I had given at the close of the winter season, in which he openly ridiculed that Magdeburg *Columbus* overture and the aforementioned overture based on *Rule Britannia*. I myself had taken no pleasure in the performance of these two overtures, and the predilection for trumpets ubiquitously evident in them did me some mischief, as I had obviously expected too much of our Riga musicians and had to endure all kinds of slips in the execution of the music. In complete contrast to the extravagant scale on which my *Rienzi* was conceived, the same Heinrich Dorn had set to work on an opera devised with the practical intent of using only the existing resources of our Riga theater. *The Juror of Paris*, a comic-historic opera from the period of the siege of Paris under Joan of Arc, was rehearsed and performed by our company to the full satisfaction of the composer. The success of this work gave me no compelling reason to depart from my plan for the completion of *Rienzi*, and I was inwardly pleased to find how little I envied this success. Utterly disinclined to rivalry, I withdrew more and more from artistic society in Riga, confined myself strictly to carrying out my contractual duties, and worked out the first two acts of my opera without concerning myself in the slightest as to whether the work would ever be performed.

The reversion of my innermost inclinations to the passionately serious side of my being that had been dominant in my earliest youth was undoubtedly determined in part by the deadly serious experience I had garnered so early in life, and this had recently been colored even more darkly by especially melancholy sensations. Not long after I had been reunited with Minna came news of the death of my sister Rosalie.[1] For the first time in my life I experienced the death of one near and dear to me. The death of this sister hit me as a particularly significant stroke of fate; she had been the one for whose love and sympathy I had renounced my youthful excesses so drastically, and to earn whose respect I had devoted such splendid care and energy to my early works. When the passions and cares of life had taken possession of me and driven me from the parental home for good, she had been the one to look into my darkly tormented heart and to bid me that prophetic farewell upon my last departure from Leipzig. During the time when I had vanished from sight, when news of my headstrong marriage and the unfortunate consequences it entailed reached my family, she had been the one, as my mother later told me, who had never lost faith in me, but rather clung to the hope that I should one day come into my own and amount to something. Now, upon the news of her death, along with the memory of our last leave-taking, the whole scope of the immense value of my sister's relationship to me was illuminated as if by lightning, and the influence she exercised on me became clear to me later when, after my first notable successes, my mother tearfully lamented that Rosalie had not lived to see them. Now it really did me good to get into contact with my family again. My mother and sisters had received news of my doings through the grapevine; I was deeply moved to find no reproaches whatever in the letters that now resumed their flow concerning my headstrong and apparently heartless behavior, but on the contrary solely sympathy and heartfelt solicitude. My family had also received reports of my wife's good qualities, and this was particularly beneficial as it spared me the painful and difficult necessity of defending her dubious conduct towards me. This produced a salutary calm in my innermost being, until then a prey to the worst anxieties. All the forces that had driven me in such impulsive haste to an improvident and premature marriage, all that had as a consequence so disturbed and oppressed me now seemed appeased and pacified; and although the ordinary cares of life weighed upon me for many years to come, often in their ugliest and most vexatious forms, the worries of my distraught youth had been calmed and subdued in such a way that from then on until I reached my artistic independence I was able to concentrate my energies solely on that ideal goal, which now, since the conception of *Rienzi*, was the only influence governing me in all my decisions.

It was only later that I first grasped the real nature of my life in Riga, when a comment by a native was relayed to me expressing astonishment at hearing of the successes of a man of whose importance during his entire two-year stay in the Livonian capital – by no means a large city – he had noticed nothing whatsoever. I met no one there of the slightest interest. Thrown entirely on my own resources, I remained a stranger to everybody. As stated, I withdrew from contact with the personnel of the theater out of increasing disgust, and so it turned out that, when the management gave me notice of dismissal at the end of March 1839 at the close of my second season there, I was in complete accord with this compulsory change in my career, even though the action surprised me greatly for other reasons. The circumstances surrounding this dismissal, however, were such as to make me regard it as one of the ugliest experiences of my life. I had already received depressing evidence of Holtei's hostility to me on the occasion of a very dangerous illness. I had caught a bad cold at rehearsal in the depths of winter, and given the effect of my constant annoyance and gnawing irritation at the worthlessness of the oppressive theater business on my already highly strained nervous system, this soon took on a very serious character. But we were scheduled at precisely that time to give a guest performance of the opera *Norma* in Mitau. Holtei managed to compel me to rise from my sick-bed and undertake the wintry journey, thus exposing me to the danger of serious aggravation of my illness in the icy Mitau theater. The result was typhoid fever, which wore me down so quickly that Holtei, when he learned of my condition, bruited about in the theater that I would very likely never again conduct and that I was perhaps "on my last legs". I owed my rescue and recuperation to a splendid homeopathic doctor named Prutzer. Soon thereafter Holtei left our theater and Riga for good; his work there, coping with what he termed "the much too respectable conditions", had become intolerable to him; beyond that, however, certain circumstances in his private life, which had been severely shaken shortly before by the death of his wife, appear to have made it advisable for him to get out of Riga. But to my astonishment I now became aware that I too had been an unwitting sufferer from the troubles he had brought upon himself. When Holtei's successor as director, the singer Joseph Hoffmann,[1] notified me officially that he had inherited the obligation to honor a contract Holtei had made with Heinrich Dorn appointing him to the post I had hitherto held, thereby precluding my reappointment, my wife met my astonishment at the news by explaining the reasons, of which she had been well aware for some time, for Holtei's deep antipathy toward both of us. What I now learned from Minna, of events that she had considerately concealed from me in order not to cause me to think ill of my superior, cast a horrifying light on the whole affair. I well remembered that soon after my arrival in Riga I had been strongly urged by Holtei not to oppose the engagement of my wife at the theater; I asked him to talk things over quietly with her, in order that he might learn that Minna's avoidance of the theater rested on a mutual understanding and by no means on any one-sided jealousy on my part. I had intentionally arranged the times for these meetings to coincide with my rehearsals in the theater; after these meetings I had often found Minna, upon my returning home, in a very excited state, and finally obtained from her the categorical assurance that she would not accept a job from Holtei in any circumstances. Moreover I noticed in Minna's demeanor towards me an inexplicable inclination to search timidly for the reasons for my willingness to permit Holtei to try to persuade her. I now learned after the catastrophe that Holtei had used these occasions to make blatant advances to her, the character and purpose of which remained difficult to account for in light of further knowledge of his idiosyncrasies, yet which finally became comprehensible when I learned of other attempts of this nature by Holtei, who found it advantageous to provoke gossip about his relations with women in order to distract the attention of the public from other and far more disreputable vagaries. Beyond this, Minna was absolutely infuriated when Holtei, after being rebuffed in his own amorous pursuit, stepped forward as agent for another suitor, telling her that while he thought none the worse of her for rejecting him, already greying and without money, he would be happy to refer her to a handsome, youthful and also very rich man, the merchant Brandenburg. His fierce anger at the double rebuff and his humiliation at having revealed himself for what he was to no avail seems, to judge from Minna's observations, to have been vast. I now understood that his frequently repeated outbursts of passionate contempt for the "overly respectable conditions in the theater" were by no means spirited exaggerations, but that on the contrary he had often been given reason to complain of the most irritating reverses in this respect. That playing such games as he did with my wife could not in the long run serve to conceal his really dirty activities from the ever-increasing scrutiny of observers seems to have dawned on him at last, and friends of his in the show who discussed the matter with me openly admitted that fear of further very damaging disclosures had motivated him to abandon his position in Riga so precipitately. Right up to very recently I have continued to get wind of the passionate hostility toward me with which Holtei, among other things, has fulminated against "the music of the future"[1] and its propensity to endanger the simplicity of pure emotions. As I have mentioned, he already showed an equal degree of personal feeling in the manifestations of his animosity during the latter part of the time we were in Riga together, but until then I had attributed this to the divergence in our respective views on artistic matters.

Having learned to my dismay that purely personal considerations had been at the bottom of it all, and feeling a bit humiliated to find my knowlege of people so rudimentary as to have permitted me to place unreserved confidence in a character I had thought incomparably upright, the revelation of the true character of my friend Heinrich Dorn now baffled me almost more. During our continuing association in Riga he had proceeded from treating me good-naturedly as a younger brother to becoming an open and intimate friend; we saw and visited one another almost daily, quite often with our families; I kept no secrets from him, and the performance of *The Juror of Paris* went off as well under my baton as it would have done under his. Hearing now that my job had been given to him, I believed that I had only to ask him about the matter to discover that he was laboring under some error as to my intentions concerning the post that had hitherto been mine in the theater. From a written reply, however, I could see that Dorn had really exploited Holtei's hostile attitude toward me to wring from the departing director a commitment that would bind the successor, to his advantage. That as my friend he should only have made use of this commitment in the event I was truly ready to resign my position in Riga seems to have occurred to him dimly enough to make him carefully avoid touching upon the possibility of my going or staying. He contended, on the other hand, that Holtei had revealed to him that I would not be rehired, on the grounds that I could not get along with the singers; accordingly he, whose inclinations for the theater had been newly aroused by the success of *The Juror of Paris*, could scarcely be blamed for grasping the opportunity to fill the vacancy. Moreover, he had gathered from our confidential talks that I was in an awkward situation and, considering my small salary, which Holtei had always paid short, could hardly cope with the demands of my Königsberg and Magdeburg creditors, who had engaged a lawyer to press their claims who was at the same time a close friend of Dorn. This had brought him to the assumption that I would really not be able to maintain myself in Riga. Therefore even as a friend he had felt no compunction in accepting Holtei's offer. In order not to leave him undisturbed in these self-delusions, I put it to him in all conscience that he could not have been unaware of the salary increase due me upon commencing my third year on the job, and also of my prospects, now that all the initial difficulties of moving in and getting established were over, of meeting my long-standing debts by giving orchestral concerts, which had already gotten off to a good start. I asked him how he would comport himself if I declared that I saw it would be to my advantage to remain in my present position and thereupon asked him to abrogate the agreement with Holtei, who had by then left Riga anyway and thus removed the reason for my departure. To this I received no answer from Dorn right down to the present day, but in the summer of 1865, I was startled to see him turn up unannounced in my house in Munich and, noticing to his great pleasure that I recognized him at once, stride toward me with a movement indicating his intention to embrace me; while I managed to evade this, I immediately saw the difficulty in avoiding his addressing me with the brotherly "Du", as the attempt to do so would have involved me in all sorts of explanations that would have been a needless addition to the exertions I was making at the time. (It was the time of the performance of my *Tristan*.) Such a man was Heinrich Dorn, who, although at that time, after the failure of three successive operas, he had retired from the theater in disgust to devote himself entirely to the purely commercial side of music, had nonetheless achieved a permanent position among the dramatic composers of Germany through the local success in Riga of his comic-historic opera *The Juror of Paris*. Across the bridge of betrayal of a friend, aided by that virtue personified in Director Holtei, and thanks to a magnanimous oversight on the part of Franz Liszt, Dorn had been rescued from obscurity. The interest of King Friedrich Wilhelm IV in church affairs eventually helped to win for him his important position at the largest lyric theater in Germany, the Royal Opera in Berlin; at first he was prompted far less by the call of the dramatic muse than by the simple desire to find a good job in one of the larger German cities, and following Liszt's recommendation he was appointed director of music at Cologne Cathedral. On the occasion of a celebration connected with the construction of the cathedral he had managed to work on the religious sensibilities of the Prussian monarch in such a way as to induce him to accord Dorn the dignity of Kapellmeister at his Court Theater, in which capacity, together with Wilhelm Taubert,[1] he has for a long time upheld the honor of German dramatic music.

I must give credit to Joseph Hoffmann, manager of the Riga theater from this time forward, for being considerably shaken by the manner in which I was betrayed; he let me know that he felt himself obligated to keep Dorn only for one year and indicated his intention to sign a new contract with me at once for the year after next. In addition, some patrons in Riga offered to compensate me for the loss of my salary as music director by enabling me to give music lessons, arranging concerts, and the like. However pleased I was by these signs of recognition, I was so deeply possessed, as already stated, by the desire to get completely away from the theater world as I had known it so far that I grasped this involuntary but by no means unwelcome necessity to leave the path of my previous career and to plunge myself into a new one with decided eagerness. Not without some skill, I played upon my wife's indignation at the treachery I had suffered to induce her to accede to my rather eccentric plan to go to Paris. While I already had my eye on only the most grandiose of theaters in the conception of my *Rienzi*, I now wanted also to jump over all intermediate steps and land immediately at the center of grand opera in Europe. In Magdeburg, I had already extracted an opera plot from the novel *Die hohe Braut* by Heinrich König, to be carried out in five acts on the most lavish French scale. Having worked out the scenario in full, I had it translated into French and sent it from Königsberg to Scribe in Paris. I accompanied this submission with a letter to the renowned librettist, in which I recommended his acceptance of my draft on the condition that I would receive a commission from the Paris Opera to write the music. In order to convince him of my ability to write opera music in Parisian style, I sent him at the same time the score of my *Liebesverbot*. But beyond that I also wrote to Meyerbeer, in order to inform him of my plans and to enlist his support for them. I was not disconcerted at receiving no answer whatever to all this; what mattered to me, on the contrary, was solely the possibility of saying that I was "in touch with Paris". I really had, upon embarking on such a bold expedition from Riga, a reasonably solid point of departure, and my Paris plans were not entirely built on air. A new factor now was that my youngest sister Cäcilie had become engaged to a bookseller, Eduard Avenarius, who worked for the Brockhaus company and had just taken over the management of the branch this German firm had established in Paris. I turned to him to get something out of Scribe in regard to my application, now of several years' standing. Avenarius went to see Scribe and extracted from him an acknowledgement of my previous submission. Scribe also evinced recollection of the subject in question, in which, he remembered, there was a "joueuse de harpe" who was mistreated by her brother: from the fact that this single episode had stuck in his memory I was led to the conclusion that in fact Scribe had not gotten beyond the first act, in which this event occurred; that he also had nothing more to say about my score beyond the comment that he had caused excerpts to be played for him by a student at the conservatory could not move me to the flattering assumption that he had reached a clear and conscious rapport with me. And yet I nonetheless had palpable evidence in the form of a letter from Scribe to Avenarius, forwarded by him to me, that Scribe had actually busied himself with me and that I was in communication with him. The letter of Scribe had such a significant effect on the otherwise by no means sanguine outlook of my wife that she found herself increasingly able to overcome the terrors of setting out with me on the Parisian adventure. We finally decided without further ado that we would travel directly from Riga to Paris upon expiration of the second year of my contract, in the coming summer of 1839, in order that I might try my luck there solely as a composer of operas.

Now it became all the more important to complete my *Rienzi*: the second act was finished before our departure, complete with a heroic ballet on the most extravagant scale. It also became obvious that I would have to learn French in a hurry, a subject I had cast aside most contemptuously during my classical studies at school. Now that only four weeks remained to make up for all I had missed, I took on a capable teacher of French; but as I soon saw I would not be able to achieve the desired results in so short a time, I utilized the lessons solely to pry from the teacher, on the pretext of doing necessary exercises, a prose translation of the text of *Rienzi*; I wrote this down at once in red ink in the score of those parts of my music that were ready, in order to be in a position to display my half-finished opera to the arbiters of music in France immediately upon my arrival in Paris.

Thus everything seemed conveniently arranged for my undertaking, and it only remained to raise enough money to carry it out. The prospects for this were not good: the sale of our modest household effects, the proceeds of a benefit concert, together with some miscellaneous savings, were just sufficient to settle with the creditors from Magdeburg and Königsberg who were now suing me. If I had been obliged to devote my money to this purpose, there would not have been a heller left. Here was a case for some desperate measures, and our old friend from Königsberg, Abraham Möller, showed up to offer characteristic but by no means easily evaluable advice. It was at this critical time that he came to visit us in Riga for the second time; I explained my sorry situation to him and the obstacles standing in the way of carrying out my plan to go to Paris. He advised me in his pointed and laconic way to use all my money for our trip and settle with the creditors only after my Paris successes had given me the means to do so. To facilitate this, he offered to take us in his traveling carriage at top speed over the Russian border to an East Prussian port; this border-crossing would have to be accomplished without passports, for ours had been impounded on behalf of our foreign creditors. He said the execution of this highly hazardous plan would be very easy, as he had a friend on a Prussian estate near the border who would give him the most effective assistance. The desire to get away from my present situation at any price and to reach the terrain on which I expected to fulfill my most ambitious wishes blinded me to all the unpleasant complications the adoption of this course of action would necessarily entail. Director Hoffmann, who felt obliged to help me as best he could, facilitated my departure by permitting me to leave several months before the expiration date of the contract. After I had conducted the performances of the June season in Mitau, we began our secret journey right from Mitau, under Möller's protection and in his carriage furnished with extra horses, the goal of which was Paris and which we would ultimately reach only after the most unheard-of tribulations.

The sense of contentment instinctively awakened by our passing through fruitful Courland in the luxuriant month of July, and by the illusion that I had cut myself loose from an utterly hateful existence to enter upon a boundlessly new path of fortune, was disturbed at the very outset of the trip by the tormenting inconveniences caused me by the presence of a huge Newfoundland dog called Robber. This extraordinarily handsome creature, originally the property of a merchant in Riga, had, quite against the grain of this particular breed, formed a strong attachment to my person. After I had left Riga, during my prolonged stay in Mitau, Robber laid siege to my now empty dwelling and by his obvious devotion so touched the hearts of my landlord and his neighbors that they sent the dog along after me to Mitau, by the conductor of the mail coach, where I received him with genuine emotion and swore to myself, despite all complaints, never again to turn him away. Whatever might happen, the dog had to go with us to Paris; but even finding a place for him in the carriage seemed utterly impossible; all means whereby I attempted to secure a place for him in or on the carriage came to nothing, and to my growing dismay I had to watch the heavily furred nordic animal run along beside the carriage all day long in the burning summer heat until I, moved beyond endurance by pity at his exhaustion, finally hit upon a most ingenious way to get the huge dog into the fully occupied carriage in such a way that he could hold out. On the evening of the second day we reached the Russo–Prussian frontier; Möller's anxiety about the outcome of our secret border-crossing made us realize that this was really a most dangerous undertaking; the trusted friend from the other side met us as agreed with a small carriage, in which he conveyed Minna, myself and Robber away from the main road and by various detours to a point from which he conducted us on foot to a house of highly suspicious appearance, leaving us there after handing us over to the care of a guide. We were supposed to wait there until after sundown and had ample leisure to realize that we found ourselves in a smugglers' den, which gradually filled to bursting with Polish Jews of the most filthy aspect. Finally, we were instructed to follow our guide. Several hundred paces away, at the foot of a slope, there was the trench which extends along the entire Russian border and which is guarded by Cossack sentries at very close intervals. It was a question of using the very few minutes after the relief of the watch, during which time the sentries were otherwise occupied. We therefore had to run very quickly down the slope, clamber across the trench, and then run on again quickly until we had gotten out of the line of fire; for the Cossacks, as soon as they saw us, were under orders to send bullets after us even when we were over the trench. Despite my deep solicitude for Minna, I had observed to my great delight the intelligent behavior of the dog who, as if he sensed the danger, stuck silently to us, utterly dispelling my worry that he would cause us trouble during the dangerous crossing. At last we were met by the trusted helper; he was so moved that he clasped us in his arms and then conducted us again in his carriage to the tavern in the Prussian border town, where our friend Möller, sick with anxiety, leapt up from his bed to greet us with sobs and rejoicing. It was then that I had time to think over the extent of the danger into which I had plunged not only myself but also poor Minna at my side, and the folly of which I had been guilty through my ignorance of the frightful

circumstances of the surreptitious border-crossing Möller had so frivo-
lously recommended. I found no words adequate to express my regret
about the whole affair to my totally exhausted wife.

And yet the obstacles we had just overcome were only a prelude to
the fresh difficulties which accompanied this adventurous trip that was
to have so decisive an effect on my life. While we were driving through
the bounteous plain of Tilsit to Arnau, with our courage already restored,
we determined that the next stage of the journey would be undertaken
by sailing-ship from the Prussian port of Pillau bound for London. This
was arranged mainly out of consideration for our dog, as it was the easiest
way to take him along; to transport him by carriage from Königsberg
to Paris was obviously out of the question, and railroads had not yet been
heard of. Beyond this, however, our decision was influenced by the state
of our purse; the total proceeds from my arduous labors amounted to
a little less than one hundred ducats, which not only had to finance the
trip but also our stay in Paris until I was able to earn something.
Therefore, after several days' rest at the hostelry in Arnau, we journeyed
on, once again accompanied by Möller, in one of the open wagons typical
of the district, not unlike a break in appearance, through small villages
and over bad roads in order to avoid Königsberg, to the little port of
Pillau. Even this shorter trip was destined not to go by without an
accident. The clumsy carriage tipped over in a farmyard, and Minna was
so badly shaken up internally by her fall that we had to spend a night
in a farmhouse, to which I had to drag her, lame and totally helpless,
with the greatest difficulty. The people were dirty and surly, and the
night was highly unpleasant for my suffering wife. The delay of several
days in the departure of the vessel from Pillau was thus very welcome
in these circumstances, as we thereby gained some respite for Minna's
recovery. Since the captain had to take us on board without passports,
the embarkation itself was also fraught with special difficulty for us. We
had to try to slink past the harbor police in a little boat and board ship
before daybreak; once we got there, and after having hauled Robber up
the steep shipside with great effort and without causing a ruckus, we had
to go and hide below deck, in order that those visiting the ship before
it sailed would not notice us. At last the anchor was weighed, and as
we saw the land slowly recede from view we thought we could breathe
more easily and feel more comfortable.

We were on board a merchant vessel of the smallest class; it was called
the Thetis, had a bust of the nymph at the bowsprit,[1] and had a
complement, including the captain, of seven men. Given the good

weather to be expected in the summertime, it was thought that the voyage
to London would take eight days. But we were already held back by
prolonged calm before we had gotten out of the Baltic; I used my leisure
to proceed a little further in my knowledge of French by studying a novel
of George Sand entitled *La dernière Aldini*. Our association with
members of the crew also provided us some entertainment. We especially
had our eye on one taciturn old sailor named Koske, chiefly because our
otherwise good-natured Robber had taken an irreconcilable dislike to
him, a fact that was to cause us some preposterous trouble in a moment
of danger. After seven days' sailing we had gotten no further than
Copenhagen, where we took the opportunity, without leaving the vessel,
of supplementing our meager ship's rations by various purchases of food
and drink. In cheerful spirits we sailed on past the beautiful castle of
Elsinore, the sight of which brought back my youthful impressions of
Hamlet, and now proceeded hopefully through the Kattegat to the
Skagerrak, when the wind, which at the outset had been merely adverse
and had forced us to a lot of arduous tacking, suddenly on the second
day of this leg turned into a storm. For a full twenty-four hours we had
to struggle against it, while Minna and I endured sufferings quite outside
our previous experience. Cooped up in the captain's pitifully small cabin,
without a berth adequate even for one of us, we were a prey to sea-sickness
and every kind of fear. Unfortunately, the brandy cask, at which the crew
from time to time fortified themselves, was stowed under the bench on
which I lay; and it happened to be Koske who came most frequently to
pester me in search of this refreshment, despite the necessity each time
of engaging in mortal combat with Robber, who went after him, and him
only, with inexhaustible fury whenever he came clambering down the
narrow steps. This in turn compelled me, quite worn out as I was by
sea-sickness, to exertions that rendered my condition virtually catastrophic. At last, on July 29th, the captain was forced by a fierce westerly
wind to put in at a port on the Norwegian coast. With a feeling of
profound relief I beheld the extended rocky coast toward which we were
being driven with great speed, and after a Norwegian pilot, who had come
out to meet us in his small craft, had assumed the helm of the Thetis
with his practised hand, I was treated to one of the most marvelous and
beautiful experiences of my life. What I had taken to be the shore-line,
composed of an unbroken chain of rocky cliffs, turned out, as we
approached them, to be a line of separate conical rocks rearing up out
of the sea; sailing past them we could see that these reefs were not only
in front of and beside us, but behind us as well, and these latter were

bunched together so tightly that once again they seemed to form a single chain of rocks. These rocks at our back broke the waves in such a way that the further we pressed on into the labyrinth of conical rocks the calmer the sea became, and at last, upon entering one of those long waterways through a gigantic ravine, as the Norwegian fjords appeared to me, the ship glided smoothly and peacefully into port.

A feeling of indescribable well-being came over me as the granite walls of the cliff echoed the chantings of the crew as they cast anchor and furled[1] the sails. The sharp rhythm of their call stuck with me as an omen of good fortune and soon resolved itself into the theme of the sailors' chorus in my *Der fliegende Holländer*, the idea for which I already carried within me at the time and which now, under the impressions I had just gained, took on its own characteristic musico-poetic coloring. Our next move was to go on shore. I learned that the little fishing village serving as our haven was called Sandwike and was some miles away from a bigger town called Arendal. We were allowed to put up at the house of a ship's captain away at sea at the time, and the stormy winds that continued to rage on the open seas kept us there for two days, which we sorely needed to restore ourselves. On July 31st the captain insisted on putting out to sea again, despite contrary advice from the pilot. Once more on board the Thetis, we were devouring a lobster for the first time in our lives a few hours after leaving land, when I heard the captain and the crew suddenly cursing the pilot, whom I saw at the tiller trying desperately to avoid a reef jutting up only slightly above sea level and toward which we were being driven. Great was our terror at this passionate tumult, and we could only believe that we were all in extreme danger. The ship then actually received a heavy jolt, which I imagined at once to be the shattering of the hull; fortunately it turned out that the vessel had only scraped the side of the reef, and there was thus no immediate danger. Nevertheless, the captain felt he had to turn back to port to have the hull examined. Having gotten back to another point on the coast, we again cast anchor, and the captain invited us to go along with him and two crew members in a small boat to a somewhat larger town several hours distant named Tromsond, where he had to fetch members of the port authority to inspect his ship. This little trip was again extremely alluring and impressive; the view of one fjord in particular, stretching away far inland, struck my imagination as an unknown, grim, yet still majestic waste land. A long walk from Tromsond up to the highland plain augmented this impression by the frightful melancholy of the dark moors, treeless, even without bushes, covered at most with thin moss, and extending off to the horizon and losing itself in a gloomy sky of identical color. Returning from this expedition late at night in the small boat, much to my wife's anxiety, we were at last able on the following morning of August 1st, after being reassured about the ship's condition, to put to sea with fair winds and without hindrance.

After four days of calm sailing a stormy north wind caught us and drove us forward in the right direction at uncommon speed. We thought we had already gotten through the worst of the trip when on the evening of August 6th the wind changed, and the storm began to rage with vastly increased violence. It was on August 7th, a Wednesday, at two-thirty in the afternoon that we felt death would be upon us at any moment. It was not the terrible force pitching the ship uncontrollably about, entirely at the mercy of a sea showing itself now as a darkest abyss and now as a steep mountain peak, that awakened in me the fear of death; rather my premonition of our approaching end was based on the despondency of the crew, from whom I caught despairing and malevolent looks, as if we were to be blamed in some superstitious way for the threatening disaster. Uninformed about the relatively trivial reason for keeping our trip secret, they no doubt assumed that our reason for flight was attributable to some serious or even criminal act. Even the captain seemed at the moment of greatest extremity to regret having taken us on board, as we had apparently brought him, who made this trip so often, particularly in summer, in a short time and without any trouble, such obvious misfortune. And as at this aforementioned fateful time of day the storm was accompanied by thunder and lightning, Minna expressed the heartfelt desire to die with me, if need be, by a bolt of lightning rather than by sinking while yet alive into the vasty deep. She also requested me to tie her to me with some cloths, so that we would not be parted as we sank. We spent yet another entire night amid these incessant terrors, which only our extreme exhaustion helped to alleviate. On the next day the storm had subsided, but the wind remained unfavorable though weak; the captain made an effort to take our bearings with his astronomical instruments; he complained about the sky, overcast for so many consecutive days and nights, swore he would give anything for a single glimpse of the sun or stars, and did not conceal the uneasiness he felt at not being able to fix precisely the nautical position in which we found ourselves. He consoled himself, however, by following a ship sailing some sea-miles ahead in the same direction, and whose movements he observed with close and continuing attention through the ship's telescope. Suddenly he jumped up in alarm and commanded in great agitation a change in our course. He had seen the ship ahead of us driven onto a sand bar, from which, he assured us, it would not be able to free itself, because he now realized clearly that we were in the vicinity of the most dangerous part of the Dutch coast, beset with extensive sand-bars. By very skillful sailing it now became possible to maintain an opposite course directly toward the English coast, which we finally sighted in the area of Southwold on the evening of August 9th. I felt new life coursing through my veins when I spotted in the distance the pilots racing out toward our vessel, for on the English coast they compete freely with one another and sail out to meet the incoming ships even when the risks are very great. A powerful, grey-haired man succeeded in reaching us first, but it was only after much fruitless struggling with the waves tossing his light smack away from our vessel, that at last, his hands dripping with blood from repeated attempts to grasp and hold the line we had thrown him, he boarded the Thetis. For such was still the name of our poor, severely tried ship, although the storm in the Kattegat had ripped away the wooden figure representing our guardian nymph and hurled her into the waves, an event interpreted even then by the crew as an evil omen. Knowing the helm to be now in the firm possession of this calm English sailor, whose every aspect impressed us most agreeably and in whom we saw a redeemer from all our dreadful trials, filled us with a religious sense of well-being. But we were as yet by no means out of danger; for now began a trip accompanied by countless perils along the sand-banks of the English coast, on which, I was told, around four hundred vessels founder annually. For a full twenty-four hours, from the evening of August 10th to the evening of the 11th, we had to fight our way through a westerly gale along these banks, and this delayed us so badly that we reached the mouth of the Thames only in the night of August 11th–12th. Up to that point my wife had been so distracted by the numerous danger signals, consisting chiefly of bright red lightships, their bells ringing continuously owing to the fog, that she had not gotten a wink of sleep in her anxiety at watching them and pointing them out to the crew. To me, on the other hand, these heralds of human proximity and deliverance were so reassuring that, despite Minna's lively reproaches, I indulged myself in long and refreshing sleep. When we were finally anchored in the mouth of the Thames, calmly awaiting the break of day, I was overcome with exuberance, and while Minna and all the exhausted crew lay sleeping, gave thought to my dress, changed my linen, shaved on deck leaning against the mast, and watched the increasing traffic on this famous waterway with intense interest. Our longing to be totally released from the miserable confinement on the ship impelled us, after we had begun the slow trip up the estuary, to board a passing steamship at Gravesend to take us all the more quickly to London. The approach to London on the river teeming with ships of all sorts, along riverbanks crowded ever more densely with houses, streets, the famous docks, and other maritime constructions, filled us with growing astonishment, and when we finally reached London Bridge, in the midst of the inconceivable bustle of this incomparable metropolis, and set foot there upon firm ground after more than three horrible weeks at sea, we became pleasurably giddy, as our sea legs carried us staggeringly through the deafening uproar. Even Robber seemed possessed by this feeling, as he ran wildly around every street-corner and seemed every minute to be lost forever. But we all three soon found safety in a hansom cab, which took us, on our captain's recommendation, to the Horseshoe Tavern, a sailors' inn near the Tower of London, where we now had to make our plans for the conquest of this monster of a city.

The neighborhood into which we had penetrated was such that we elected to leave it with all possible haste. A friendly little hunchbacked Jew from Hamburg suggested better quarters in the West End, and I remember vividly our drive there, which took a full hour in one of the tiny cabs in use at the time, designed only for two passengers to sit opposite each other, and in which we had to place the huge dog across our laps and sticking out both windows. Everything we saw during the drive from our strange vantage point surpassed all our previous conceptions of the overwhelming dimensions and life of a great city. We arrived at our boarding house in Old Compton Street in an excited mood. Although as a twelve-year-old boy I had gotten far enough in English to make what I supposed was a translation of a soliloquy from Shakespeare's *Romeo and Juliet*, whatever I had retained from those studies was of no help to me now when I tried to make myself understood of the landlady of the house, which was called the King's Arms. Yet this lady, the widow of a ship's captain, felt called upon to try to communicate with me in French, and her attempts made me wonder which of us knew the least of this language. A most disturbing event now occurred, however, as we suddenly noticed that Robber had not followed us into the house but had slipped away from us at the door. Our concern and misery at having immediately lost the dog we had dragged along to this point with such vast difficulty occupied us exclusively during our first two hours in a house on terra firma, until, keeping constant watch at the window, we suddenly saw to our immense joy Robber walking unconcernedly around the corner of an alley toward the house. We later learned that our dog had wandered as far as Oxford Street in search of novelty, and I have always remembered his incomprehensible return to a house he had not even entered as strong proof of the astonishing certainty of animal instinct.

We now had time to realize the bothersome after-effects of our voyage. That the ground continued to heave under us, and that we went to the most absurd lengths to have something to hold on to at every step we took struck us as almost hilarious; but when we came to take our rest in the huge English double-bed, and found that it too rocked up and down, and, just as we were getting to sleep, it seemed to sink into a terrible abyss so that we leaped up crying for help, things became finally unbearable, for we thought that this horrible sea voyage would continue in this way for the rest of our lives. Added to this, we felt miserably ill because, after the atrocious fare on board ship, we had been only too ready to indulge, with less discretion than enjoyment, in the most exquisite food.

Much weakened by all these tribulations, we forgot to consider what was, after all, the vital question, namely how much all this was going to cost us in hard cash, but rather, fascinated by the marvels of the metropolis, set out in a cab the following day on manifold explorations as if pleasure was the sole object of our journey, following a plan I had sketched on a map of London. In our wonder and delight we entirely forgot all we had been through. The eight-day stay in London that proved so damaging to our budget I justified on the one hand from the need to give Minna a chance to recuperate, and on the other hand from the opportunity afforded me to make some acquaintances in the art world. The *Rule Britannia* overture composed in Königsberg I had already sent during my stay in Dresden to Sir John Smart,[1] Chairman of the Philharmonic Society; he had, it is true, never acknowledged my submission; but I felt this to be all the more reason to look him up and make him account for himself. While I was pondering which from my panoply of languages I would use to make myself understood by him, I spent several days trying to find out where he lived, the efforts of which were crowned by finding out that he was not in London. I then spent several days entertaining the idea that it would be a good thing if I looked up Bulwer, to come to some agreement with him concerning the musical treatment I was going to give his novel *Rienzi*, which I had dramatized. As I had already learned on the continent that Bulwer was a Member of Parliament, I asked for him at the Houses of Parliament themselves. In this my utter ignorance of the English language helped me to get an unexpectedly considerate reception. Inasmuch as none of the lower officials I met in this huge building could made head or tail of what or whom I was after, I was conducted up the ladder to people of progressively higher rank. With Minna ever at my side and only Robber left behind at the King's Arms, I was then introduced, evidently as an utterly incomprehensible person, to a man of aristocratic appearance, who had just stepped out of a large hall. In response to his polite question in French as to what I wanted, my inquiry as to the whereabouts of the famous Bulwer seemed to make a not unfavorable impression. He was obliged to inform me that the gentleman in question was not in London; but as I pressed on and asked whether I might be permitted to attend a sitting of Parliament, the man advised me that, as a result of the old Houses of Parliament having burned down, there was only very limited space available for visitors in the hall being used temporarily for this purpose, and that tickets to get in were available only to the favored few; but as I pressed him even more urgently my patron, whom I had every reason to take for a Lord inasmuch as we were outside the Upper House, relented and shortly thereafter let us be ushered through a door directly into the strictly reserved strangers' gallery of the House of Lords. This interested me tremendously. I heard and saw the then prime minister, Lord Melbourne,[1] and Brougham[2] (who seemed to take a very active part in the proceedings, often prompting Lord Melbourne); and also the Duke of Wellington, who looked so comfortable in his grey beaver hat, his hands in his trouser pockets, and who, particularly by the way his body shook at certain points of special emphasis in a speech that sounded quite relaxed and conversational, dispelled all feelings of excessive awe. I was also interested in Lord Lindhurst, Brougham's special antagonist, and I was amazed to see the latter go over several times to his opponent in the course of his speech, sit down beside him, and, as it seemed to me, try to help him out. The question before the house, as I later determined from the newspaper, concerned measures to be taken against the Portuguese government to enforce the bill banning the slave trade. The Bishop of London,[3] whom I had also had the chance to hear on this occasion, was the only one among these men whose tone and bearing made an unpleasant impression, but possibly this was because of my prejudice against the clergy in general.

After this pleasing adventure I imagined that I had exhausted the attractions of London for a time, for although I was not allowed to attend a session of the Lower House, my untiringly obliging patron, whom I met by chance on the way out, showed me the room where the Commons sat, explained as much as was necessary, gave me a glimpse of the Speaker's woolsack, as well as this dignitary's mace lying hidden under the table. After this I thought I knew all there was to know about the capital of the British empire. I didn't think for a minute of attending the Italian Opera, perhaps because I took it for granted that the seat-prices would be ruinously high. Having thoroughly explored the city's main streets on foot, frequently to the point of dropping in our tracks, shuddered through a ghastly and ghostly London Sunday, and finally taken, together with the captain of the Thetis, the first train ride of our lives to the park in Gravesend, we embarked, on August 20th, by steamship for France, where we took leave of the sea, with the fervent wish that it would be forever, in Boulogne-sur-mer.

We both felt a certain anxiety in the premonition of the disappointments that awaited us in Paris, yet we concealed this from one another. But it was partly on this account that we decided to linger for a few weeks in or near Boulogne. At any rate, it was too early in the season for the various important people I had to see in Paris for my purposes to be available there; conversely, it seemed to me most fortuitous to learn that Meyerbeer was staying in Boulogne at precisely this time. I also had to finish scoring the second act of *Rienzi*; it was very important to me to be able to present half of my work fully completed immediately upon my arrival in expensive Paris and it seemed to us that we ought to find a cheaper place to spend this time in the vicinity of Boulogne. To find such quarters we hunted first of all in the immediate surroundings, and on the main road to Paris, half an hour's distance from Boulogne, we found two virtually unfurnished rooms in the exposed house of a rural wine merchant, which we rented for a short period and proceeded to furnish sparsely enough but adequately for our purposes, a task in which Minna excelled. Apart from a bed and two chairs, we dug up a table on which, as soon as I had cleared away my work on *Rienzi*, we partook of meals we prepared at our own fireside.

While we were here I paid my first call on Meyerbeer. I had often read in journals of his proverbial amiability and complaisance; I forgave him easily for his failure to reply to my previous letter and found my favorable opinion confirmed by the fact that I was soon admitted to his presence and received in a friendly manner. The impression he made upon me was good in every respect, to which his very reassuring countenance, particularly the finely chiseled setting for his eyes, contributed decisively, for his face had not yet, as unfortunately happens with most Jewish physiognomies, assumed a flabby look from advancing years. He did not regard my plan to seek success in Paris as a dramatic composer as a desperate undertaking. He let me read him the text of my *Rienzi*, and really listened all the way to the end of the third act, taking the two completed acts of the composition for perusal, and at a subsequent visit promised me his unflagging support for my work, though it bothered me somewhat that he kept reiterating his praise for my decorative handwriting, wherein he thought he recognized the Saxon in me. He promised me letters of recommendation to the Director of the Grand Opéra, Duponchel, and to the principal conductor of the same, Habeneck.[1] I thus felt I had every reason to congratulate myself upon a fate that had led me through the most dangerous adventures to precisely this place in France. What greater success could I have achieved than to have secured, in so short a time, the sympathetic interest of the most famous composer of French opera? Meyerbeer also introduced me to Moscheles,[2] who was in Boulogne at the time, as well as to Mlle Blahedka,[3] a celebrated performer whose name had been familiar to me for many years. I attended several intimate musical soirées in the houses of both and thus found myself for the first time in the company of celebrities of the music world, an element entirely foreign to me up to then.

After I had written to my future brother-in-law Avenarius in Paris to try to find suitable accommodations for us, we began the trip on September 16th by stagecoach, with Robber, whom I had to stow on top of it, causing me the customary trouble. Having looked forward to our arrival in Paris with the most intense excitement, I was at first disappointed at not being able to be awed by the city's magnificence, as I had been in London. It all seemed much narrower, more confined, and I had visualized the famous boulevards in particular as being far more vast. I was furious, when the huge coach put us off in the Rue de la Jussienne, to realize that I was obliged to first set foot in Paris in such a wretched little alley. Nor did the Rue de Richelieu, where my brother-in-law had his bookshop, seem very imposing after the streets in the West End of London. When I was directed from there to the furnished rooms rented for me in the Rue de la Tonnellerie, one of the tiny back alleys connecting the Rue St Honoré with the Marché des Innocents, I really felt quite degraded. I needed all the consolation I could get from the inscription in my hotel, under a bust of Molière, reading: " Maison où naquit Molière ", a good omen which did something to dispel these melancholy impressions. Small but friendly and comfortably furnished, the little room reserved for us on the fourth floor was very inexpensive, and from its windows we were soon looking down with growing trepidation upon the frightful bustle in the market-place below, unable to grasp quite what we were doing in such a place.

Avenarius, who had to return to Leipzig for a short time to marry[1] his fiancée, my youngest sister Cäcilie, and conduct her back to Paris, introduced me to his only musical acquaintance, a German holding a job in the music department of the Bibliothèque Royale, called E. G. Anders.[2] He soon came to visit us in the Molière house and I quickly recognized him as one of those rare people who, however little they have affected my fortunes, have made an indelible imprint on my memory. He was unmarried, in his fifties, and soon confessed to me that he had been the victim of some terrible experiences that had driven him from prosperous and comfortable circumstances to the dismal necessity of earning a living in Paris entirely unassisted, in which his previous hobby, which had involved amassing extraordinary bibliographical knowledge particularly in the field of music, became his source of support. He never revealed his true name to me; this, like the details of his misfortune, he wanted to withhold until after his death; for the time being he told me only that his name was "Anders" ("other"), that he was of noble birth, and had owned property on the Rhine which he had lost, along with almost everything else, by blackest betrayal of his good-natured gullibility. All he had managed to save was his very voluminous library, the size of which I was able to see for myself, as it covered all the walls of his modest apartment. Even here in Paris, to which he had repaired, it seems, with a significant letter of recommendation, he soon thought he had reasons to complain of bitter enemies; for despite the length of his service in the library, and despite his vast knowledge, he still had not risen above the lowest level of employee, whereas he had to stand by and watch while ignoramuses climbed to the higher positions promised to him. I discovered later that the real reason probably lay in his general helplessness and lack of backbone, no doubt traceable to a spoiled childhood, for he was no longer capable of any systematic effort. Thus he led a weary and anxious existence on a miserable pittance of fifteen hundred francs per year. Growing old in loneliness, and looking forward, as he thought, to the probability of death in a poorhouse, he was visibly revived by the company of people who, though as indigent as he, nonetheless looked to the future boldly and hopefully. My vivacity and unshakable energy filled him with hopes for my success, to the promotion of which he now devoted himself with a touching interest and dedication. Although he was a contributor to the *Gazette Musicale* of Maurice Schlesinger,[1] he had never known how to gain the slightest influence there, as he was without the versatility of a publicist and was entrusted by the editors with little more than the preparation of bibliographical notes. It was with this most unworldly and least resourceful of men, anxiously enough, that I now had to discuss my plan for the conquest of the musical terrain of Paris, consisting as it did of elements of the most inconceivable worthlessness, wherein we really didn't get very far beyond encouraging each other in the hope that some unforeseen stroke of luck would help my cause.

To assist in these deliberations he drew in his friend and neighbor, the philologist Lehrs,[2] thereby enabling me to make an acquaintance that was to lead to one of the most beautiful friendships of my life. Lehrs, the younger brother of a celebrated Königsberg scholar, had come from there to Paris several years previously to try to win an independent position for himself through philological studies, a course he greatly preferred, whatever the difficulties, to a job as a salaried teacher, the only way such a person can get by in Germany. He had soon found himself a position with the book dealer Didot to work on a large edition of Greek classics, wherein the publisher, who exploited the helpless situation of the young scholar, was far more concerned with the success of his venture than with the condition of his poor collaborator. Thus Lehrs had to wage a constant battle against poverty, yet always retained an even temper and proved in every way a model of unselfishness and willingness to put himself out for others. Without any knowledge of music, and without any interest in the subject, he at first saw in me only a person in need of advice, but before long a fellow sufferer in his Parisian miseries as well. We soon became so intimate that I saw him turn up with Anders at our dwelling every evening. For Anders the companionship of a friend was particularly necessary, for he was somewhat uncertain on his feet, and though armed invariably with both umbrella and walking stick, was particularly fearful of crossing busy streets in the evening hours. He also liked to send Lehrs to reconnoiter at my doorstep and drive off Robber, of whom he was so terrified that the otherwise good-natured animal was actually moved to a hearty dislike of Anders and soon assumed as aggressive an attitude toward him as toward the sailor Koske on board the Thetis. Both lived in a hotel on the Rue de Seine and complained heavily of their landlady, who confiscated so much of their income that they were entirely in her power. In order to emancipate himself from her, Anders had been nurturing a plan to move for several years, but without ever having been able to carry it out. There were soon no secrets between us as to the nature of our common plight, so that, although living under separate roofs, we and our friends kept house together, bound by ties of shared suffering.

The various ways by which I might obtain recognition in Paris formed the chief topic of our conversation at that time. The arrival of Meyerbeer's promised letter of recommendation immediately excited our hopes. The director of the opera, M. Duponchel, actually received me in his office; he read Meyerbeer's letter after fixing a monocle in his right eye, and betrayed while going through it not the slightest sign of emotion. Of course he had opened many such letters of recommendation from Meyerbeer in the past. After he had dismissed me I heard nothing whatever from him again. On the other hand, the old conductor Habeneck received me with more than just a perfunctory show of interest and at my request expressed willingness to let his orchestra play through a piece of mine at some point in the future when there was nothing much to do at one of the regular orchestral rehearsals. Unfortunately I had no suitable example of my purely orchestral works at hand other than my strange *Columbus* overture, which I still considered the most effective work that had flowed from my pen, given the immense applause it had earned in the Magdeburg Theater through the agency of the brave Prussian military trumpeters. I handed over score and parts to Habeneck and thus was able to report to the evening session of our little committee that at least one project had been formally launched.

I was held back by the advice of my friends from seeking to see Scribe on the basis of our previous communications, for they made it clear to me from their own experience that it was out of the question for such an exceptionally busy author to occupy himself seriously with a young and unknown musician. Anders, however, introduced me to another acquaintance, a certain M. Dumersan.[1] This gentleman, already advanced in years, was the author of about a hundred vaudeville pieces and before his death would have been glad to see one of his works performed on a larger lyric stage. Devoid of any vanity of authorship, he had nothing against adapting an existing opera and fitting it out with French verses; we thus suggested to him the adaptation of my *Liebesverbot* for a third lyric theater existing at the time, terming itself the Théâtre de la Renaissance and performing in the new Salle Ventadour, restored after its destruction by fire. On the basis of a literal translation, he immediately turned out some pleasant little French verses for three numbers from this opera which I hoped to use in an audition. Beyond this, he asked me to compose a chorus for a vaudeville sketch entitled *La Déscente de la Courtille*, which was to be given at the Variétés theater during carnival season. This was a second prospect.

My friends now strongly advised me to write something on a smaller scale in the way of songs, which I could then offer to popular singers for performance at their frequent concerts. Lehrs and Anders produced texts for these; Anders brought me some very innocent verses, *Dors, mon enfant*, written by a young poet he knew, and this was the first French-language piece I set to music; it turned out so well that, when I went through it softly on the piano several times late one night, my wife called out to me from bed that it was heavenly music to be put to sleep by. In addition, I composed *L'Attente* from Hugo's *Les Orientales* and a romance by Ronsard, *Mignonne*. These small pieces, of which I had no reason to be ashamed, I published subsequently as supplements to Lewald's[1] journal *Europa*, where they appeared in the 1841 edition. I now hit upon the idea of composing for Lablache a grand bass aria with chorus to be introduced into his part as Oroviso in Bellini's *Norma*; Lehrs was obliged to dig up an Italian political refugee and extract from him the text for such an aria; this was done and I executed an effective composition in Bellini's style, which is still somewhere among my papers and which I at once set out to offer personally to Lablache. The courteous blackamoor who received me in the singer's antechamber was on the point of letting me in to see his master unannounced. Having anticipated some difficulty in approaching such a celebrity, I had put my request in writing beforehand, whereby I thought I would have a better chance of making myself understood than through oral explanations. The amiability of this black servant disconcerted me somewhat; I pressed my score and letter upon him for transmission to his master, paying no attention to his friendly astonishment at my repeated refusal to enter his master's presence and chat with him, and rushing off hastily with the intention of coming back in a few days to hear his response. When I returned Lablache received me most cordially and assured me the aria was well-executed, but that it was impossible to insert it at this late date in an opera given as often as Bellini's. This retrogression into the field of Bellinian opera which I had permitted myself in the composition of this aria remained thus without its reward, and I soon became convinced of the fruitlessness of my efforts in that direction. I saw that I would need personal introductions to leading singers if I expected to see my other works performed.

I was delighted, therefore, when Meyerbeer at last arrived in Paris. The lack of success of his letters of introduction, which I reported to him, did not surprise him in the least, but on the contrary he felt it necessary to point out to me that things were all very difficult in Paris and that I would do best to look around for some remunerative employment. For this purpose he referred me to his publisher, Maurice Schlesinger, and, leaving me at the mercy of this monstrous acquaintance, went off to Germany. At first, Schlesinger had no idea what to do with me, and as the acquaintances I made in his office at his instigation, including that of the violinist Panofka,[1] also led to nothing, I returned to our domestic council of war, which had meanwhile been cooking up other things for me, including a translation of Heine's *Die beiden Grenadiere* by a Paris professor, which I set to music for a baritone voice in a satisfactory way. At Anders' suggestion, I now began searching for singers for my new compositions. Mme Pauline Viardot,[2] to whom I first turned, went through my pieces very amiably, did not fail to express approval of them, yet assured me she saw no occasion for performing them. The same thing happened to me with Mme Widmann, who sang my *Dors, mon enfant* for me most tenderly in her lovely contralto, yet still couldn't figure out what more she might do. A certain M. Dupont, third tenor at the Opéra, tried my Ronsard setting but opined that the linguistic style would not appeal to the modern Paris public. M. Géraldy, a very popular concert singer and teacher, pronounced my *Deux Grenadiers*, which I offered him, to be impossible on the grounds that the *Marseillaise*, which I had blended into the close of the song, was at present customarily heard in Paris only in the streets and to the accompaniment of cannon fire and gunshots.

Habeneck alone fulfilled his promise by playing my *Columbus* overture for me and Anders at one of his orchestral rehearsals, which was really a kindly act of encouragement on the part of the old fellow inasmuch as there was no question whatever of attempting to include the work in the program of one of the famous Conservatoire concerts. Yet it seemed for the moment to exclude any further gestures of the kind, for I could clearly see that this uncommonly perfunctory work of my youth only perplexed the orchestra. Nonetheless, at one of these rehearsals, I unexpectedly had such a profound experience that I must regard it as a major influence on an important change of direction that now took place in my artistic development. It came about through hearing Beethoven's Ninth Symphony, which this renowned orchestra played with the finish that came from incomparably long study, a performance so perfect and so moving that the conception of this marvelous work which I had dimly formed in the enthusiastic days of my youth, before its execution (in both senses) by the Leipzig orchestra under the baton of the worthy Pohlenz had effaced it, suddenly stood before me bright as day and as palpable to my touch. Where formerly I had seen only mystic constellations and soundless magic spirits, I now found, flowing from innumerable sources, a stream of inexhaustible melody, gripping the heart with ineluctable force.

That whole period of deterioration in my musical taste, which dated precisely from the time I went astray about Beethoven's last compositions and had grown so much worse during all my superficial theatrical activities, now sank away before me as if into an abyss of shame and remorse.

While this inner change of direction had been gradually prepared by the painful experiences of the past few years, it was nevertheless the inexpressible effect of the Ninth Symphony, in a performance I had previously not dreamed possible, which revived my former spirit and gave it new life and strength. I can thus compare this event in my life with the similarly decisive impression which, as a youth of sixteen, I gained from the Fidelio of Schröder-Devrient.

The immediate upshot, in the midst of my growing awareness of the misery of my situation in Paris, and my profound inner despair of ever achieving success along the path I had chosen, was an intense desire to create something which would give me equivalent inner satisfaction. So I sketched an overture to *Faust*, which I initially planned to be only the first part of an entire *Faust* symphony, for I already had a treatment for Gretchen in my head to make a second movement. This was the composition, parts of which I revised fifteen years later, after having forgotten about it, in response to the sensible advice and urgings of Liszt, and which, since then, under the title *A Faust Overture*, has often been performed in public by me and has been favorably received by others as well. At the time, I nursed the hope that the Conservatoire Orchestra would be willing to accept such a composition for one of its concerts, but I found out that people there were of the opinion they had already done enough for me and wanted to be rid of me for a time.

Having failed everywhere else, I now turned to Meyerbeer and wrote to ask him for more letters, recommending me this time to singers. I was immensely surprised when, as a result of my request, Meyerbeer referred me from Berlin to a strange man, M. Gouin, a postal official and his general agent in Paris, with the statement that he had instructed him to do his utmost for me. Meyerbeer especially recommended that I get to know M. Anténor Joly, director of the aforementioned Théâtre de la Renaissance. With an ease that seemed almost suspicious, M. Gouin induced this man on my behalf to promise to produce my *Liebesverbot*, which had only to be translated. The only precondition was to have a few numbers from my opera sung to a theater committee at a special audition to obtain their verdict. When I then suggested that singers engaged at the theater should undertake to learn the three numbers that had already been translated by Dumersan, I was refused with the excuse that the singers were all at present far too busy. But Gouin found a way out of this as well: using the power of attorney granted him by the "Master", he got hold of several singers who were especially obligated to Meyerbeer. Mme Dorus-Gras,[1] an authentic prima donna of the Opéra, together with Mme Widmann and M. Dupont, already known to me from my vain attempts to enlist them on behalf of my smaller compositions, were compelled to consent to help me in the planned audition.

Such were my achievements after six months, as Easter 1840 approached, and on the basis of my negotiations with Gouin, and the solid hopes to which I felt entitled, I now decided, acting mainly on some foolhardy advice of Lehrs, to make some changes in the style in which we had so far lived in Paris, and to move from the obscurity characterizing the Quartier des Innocents to a part of Paris closer to its artistic center. What this change meant to me will be clearly evident from the following description of the circumstances under which we had dragged ourselves along through our Paris existence until then.

Although we had been living in the cheapest possible way ever since our arrival in Paris, dining at a very small restaurant at one franc per person, it was impossible to prevent the rest of our ducats from melting away. Our friend Möller had given us to understand that we could apply to him as soon as we were in need, for he intended to put aside for us the proceeds of his next favorable business speculation. There was nothing else for it but to turn to him now; meanwhile we pawned all the trinkets we possessed of any value. As I was shy about inquiring after a pawnshop, I hunted in the dictionary for the French term for such an establishment in order to be able to recognize one by its street sign when I saw it: in my little pocket dictionary I could not find any word for it other than "Lombards"; on the map of Paris I discovered a little alley named Rue des Lombards, situated in an indecipherable maze of streets. I wandered around this area at random for some time without getting any useful information. Yet I often ran across the inscription "Mont de Piété" on the transparent globes of lamps and became curious to find out what this might mean; when I inquired of my domestic councillors what this "Mountain of Piety" might signify, I was informed to my joyful surprise that this was precisely the place where I should seek my salvation. To the guardian of this Mont de Piété we now carried all we possessed in the way of silver, namely our wedding presents. Then followed my wife's costume jewelry, as well as the remains of her former theater wardrobe, among which was a lovely long robe replete with silver embroidery that had once belonged to the Duchess of Dessau. We still heard nothing from our friend Möller; it was a question of living from hand to mouth, awaiting the sorely needed help from Königsberg, and thus one day both our wedding rings had to go to the Mont de Piété as well. When still no help was forthcoming, I discovered that the pawn-tickets themselves represented one last source of succour, as they could be sold together with the right to redeem the pawned articles. At last we had to resort to this, and the Dessau robe was lost in this manner for good. We actually never heard from Möller. When he visited me later when I was in Dresden, he confessed to having been embittered about us as a result of reports of derogatory and slighting remarks we had supposedly made about him and for this reason had felt impelled to terminate our friendly relationship. We realized we had, without doubt, been the victims of slander and thus robbed of a seemingly sure source of assistance in an hour of need.

While all these troubles were piling up, we sustained a loss which seemed to us another evil omen: we lost the dog we had transported to Paris with such immense effort and who, because he was clearly a valuable animal and attracted much attention wherever he went, had undoubtedly been lured away from us. In spite of the terrible Parisian traffic, he had always been able to find his way home in the same clever manner he had mastered the difficulties of the London streets. In the early days after our arrival he had often gone off by himself to the gardens of the Palais Royal, where he met all kinds of other dogs and entertained the urchins by retrieving objects from the waters of its artificial pond, but he had always come back safely. On the Quai du Pont-Neuf he usually implored us to let him swim and used to attract such increasing crowds of spectators, who loudly and delightedly applauded the way he would dive down and retrieve miscellaneous articles of clothing and other objects from the bottom, that the police requested us to put an end to this potential cause of public disorder. When I let him out one morning

as usual for a short run in the street, he never returned, and despite all
the wiles I employed to get him back, no trace of him was to be found.
To many of those concerned about our welfare this loss appeared
fortunate, as everybody seemed, reasonably enough, to be amazed that
we, who had no visible means of support, had undertaken to feed such
an unusually large dog.

It was about this time, perhaps in the second month of our stay in
Paris, that my sister Luise arrived from Leipzig to join her husband
Friedrich, who had already been waiting for her there for some time.
They intended to go to Italy together on a pleasure trip, and Luise made
use of this opportunity to buy all sorts of expensive things. I found it
quite natural that they should feel in no way sympathetic with or
responsible for our apparently foolish move to Paris and, without trying
to give a false impression of our true circumstances, I did not try to derive
the slightest benefit from this family relationship. Minna was even kind
enough to assist my sister in making her extravagant purchases, while
we were concerned only to prevent our wealthy relatives from thinking
that we were anxious to arouse their pity.

My sister did in fact help me to make one strange acquaintance, who
soon began to take an intense interest in everything I did. This was the
young painter Ernst Kietz[1] from Dresden, an exceptionally loyal,
good-natured and unaffected person, whose facile talent for portraiture
in his chosen medium of bright pastels had made the young man so
popular in his home town that his financial success had led him to try
to obtain advanced training in his field in Paris, where he had been for
almost a year working in the studio of Delaroche.[2] With his curious,
almost childlike disposition, and his lack of all serious education,
combined with a certain weakness of character, this particular course was
one that would, in spite of all his talent, lead him inevitably to disaster,
an unfortunate fact which I regretfully realized as I began to see more
and more of him. At that time, however, the kindness and open-hearted
devotion of this young man was very welcome to us, particularly to my
often very lonely wife, and his friendship even became for me a source
of help in a period of uttermost need. He soon became a member of our
nocturnal family circle, proving in every respect a striking contrast with
the old, timid Anders and the serious, dignified Lehrs. His congeniality
together with his frequently hilarious notions soon made him indispensable to us all; he particularly convulsed us by his French, into which
he would launch with confident zeal and without the slightest embarrassment, despite his incapacity to put two words together correctly, a

disability which a subsequent twenty-year stay did nothing to remedy. His studies with Delaroche were supposed to teach him how to handle oils; he showed much palpable talent in this direction, yet this turned out to be the reef on which he foundered. It developed, in fact, that mixing the colors on his palette and especially cleaning the brushes took up so much of his time that he rarely came to do any actual painting. As the winter days were always so short, and because, whenever he was ready with palette and brushes, there was generally no longer light enough to see by, he never, to the best of my knowledge, completed a single portrait. Strangers to whom he had been recommended and whose portraits he had been commissioned to paint were always obliged to leave Paris without seeing them more than half done; at length he even began complaining that his clients were dying off before he could finish their portraits. His landlord, to whom he was continually in arrears with the rent, was the only one who managed to extract a complete portrait from Kietz, and to top it off he was very ugly; as far as I know this was the sole portrait finished by Kietz. On the other hand, he succeeded beautifully with little sketches of any subject suggested by our evening conversations, and in these he displayed both originality and facility of execution. During that first winter he completed a fine pencil portrait of me, which he touched up two years later after getting to know me better, finishing it as it remains today. He was pleased to sketch me in the mood I often assumed during our evening chats, when he could observe my spirits comfortably quickening. And indeed no night went by without my succeeding in dispelling the depression caused by the fruitless efforts and burdensome worries of the day and gradually regaining completely my characteristic joviality; and the cheerful Kietz was anxious to portray me in this difficult period of my life as a man utterly confident of his eventual success and smiling above and through all my troubles.

Before the end of the year[1] 1839 my youngest sister Cäcilie had also arrived in Paris with her husband Eduard Avenarius. I found it quite natural that she would be somewhat shy at meeting us here in Paris, to which we had repaired without any solid means of support, under what she could easily guess were painful circumstances, and all the more so because her husband was not particularly well off either. Consequently, instead of calling on them all the time, we preferred to wait until they came to see us, which took quite a while to happen.

On the other hand, we were much heartened by a renewal of our acquaintance with Heinrich Laube, who came to Paris at the beginning of the new year 1840 with his wife, née Iduna Budäus, a young widow of a wealthy Leipzig doctor whom Laube had married under extraordinary circumstances, and who now proposed to spend a few pleasurable months there. During the long period while he was in prison awaiting trial, which I have already mentioned, the young lady had been so moved by his misfortune that without knowing him at all well she had evinced great interest and sympathy in his case. Laube's sentence was pronounced soon after I left Berlin and it turned out to be unexpectedly light, one year's confinement in a municipal jail. He was allowed to serve it in a prison of his choice, in Muskau in Silesia, where he had the advantage of being near his friend Prince Pückler,[1] and, as a special favor granted by the prison governor, who was the Prince's subordinate, he had the consolation of corresponding with the Prince and even being able to see him. The lady had elected to marry him at the beginning of the prison term, so that she might be near him in Muskau to provide what solace she could. To see my old friend once again in such a comfortable situation was really very pleasing to me, and all the more so because of the satisfaction I felt at finding his previous regard for me entirely undiminished. We were often together; our wives also got on well, and Laube was the first person who was able to contemplate my audacious move to Paris with a degree of humor. In his house I also made the acquaintance of Heinrich Heine, and both of them made such good-natured jokes about my strange situation that I was glad to laugh along with them. Laube could not bring himself to believe seriously in my plan to get somewhere in Paris, because he could see that I regarded my own position, built on such wispy hopes, with a humor that charmed him even against his better judgement. Yet he was concerned to find a way, without raising any objections against the goals I had set myself, to help me as best he could, and wanted only to see me draw up some remotely plausible plan for my subsequent under-takings, so that he could do something on my behalf in our native land, to which he would soon be returning. This happened to be the time when I had arrived at my seemingly promising agreement with the management of the Théâtre de la Renaissance; this appeared to offer a solid starting point, and I thought I could honestly state that, if I could be assured of enough money to support myself for a period of six months, I would certainly get somewhere during that time. Laube promised to do this for me and kept his word. He induced one of his wealthy Leipzig friends to provide me with an allowance for half a year, an example which also spurred the well-to-do part of my family to help, to be paid to me in monthly installments through Avenarius.

We thereupon decided, as stated, to leave our furnished rooms and take an apartment for ourselves in the Rue du Helder. My prudent and careful wife had already become anxious and nervous as a result of the careless manner in which I treated the more mundane aspects of life and was only persuaded to this step by the assumption that she would be able to run an independent household at less expense than the hotel and restaurant existence was costing us. Success substantiated this assumption; but the only trouble was the necessity of establishing this household without any possessions whatsoever, with the attendant requirement to purchase everything needed to keep house before we had dug up the money to pay for it. In this matter Lehrs, well versed in the peculiarities of Parisian life, was able to give us some valuable advice. In his view the sole justification for everything I had ventured here in Paris up to then would be a success commensurate with my boldness; as I did not possess the resources to finance long years of patient waiting, I either had to count on extraordinary good luck or give the whole thing up completely. Either the anticipated success would come within a year, or I would be ruined: thus it boiled down to an act of daring, and he was sure that my name "Wagner" had more to do with the German word for daring, "wagen", than with the word "waggoner". Meanwhile, I had to pay annual rent of twelve hundred francs for the new apartment in quarterly installments; for the furniture and fittings he recommended me through his landlady to a carpenter, who provided everything in return for what seemed to be a comfortable series of installment payments. Lehrs stuck to his guns: if I did not show outward self-confidence I would get nowhere in Paris. The audition was scheduled for the near future; I was sure of getting the Théâtre de la Renaissance for it; Dumersan was keenly anxious to make a complete French verse translation of *Das Liebesverbot*. So we decided to run the risk. On April 15th we moved into the house on the Rue du Helder, much to the amazement of the concierge, who saw us arrive in the comfortable new apartment with virtually no baggage.

The very first visit I received in the rooms I had rented with such bold hopes brought Anders with the intelligence that the Théâtre de la Renaissance had just gone into bankruptcy and had closed. This news, which struck me like a thunderbolt, seemed to me much more than just another stroke of bad luck: it illuminated for me as if by a flash of lightning the absolute emptiness of my prospects. My friends speculated openly that Meyerbeer had presumably known all about the condition of the theater to which he referred me, away from the Opéra. I didn't bother to pursue this line of reasoning to where it might lead, as I had grounds enough for bitterness when I tried to think what I could do with my nicely furnished apartment under these circumstances.

As my singers had by now sufficiently rehearsed the pieces from *Das Liebesverbot* intended for the audition, I at least wanted the benefit of having them performed in the presence of some influential people. As there was clearly no obligation attached to attending the modest audition, M. Edouard Monnaie,[1] who after Duponchel's departure had been named acting director of the Opéra, had little reason to refuse my invitation, particularly as the singers belonged to his institution. Beyond this I went and visited Scribe, inviting him to the audition as well; he accepted with the friendliest willingness. Accordingly, my three pieces were performed before these two gentlemen one day in the green-room of the Opéra, with me accompanying at the piano; they found the music "charmant". Scribe expressed readiness to put together a text for me as soon as the administration of the Opéra saw fit to commission its composition, to which M. Monnaie had nothing much to reply apart from the statement that such a commission would not be soon forthcoming. I was under no illusion that these were anything more than polite phrases, and I found it really quite kind, particularly of Scribe, to have showed up and to have considered me worth even a casual word or two.

But in my heart of hearts I was rather ashamed at having once again seriously concerned myself with this frivolous work of my youth, from which I had excerpted the three pieces, and naturally had done so only in the opinion that I could win success in Paris by indulging its light musical tastes. My turning away from this direction for good and all, a step for which I had long been preparing myself, coincided with the abandonment of all my hopes for Paris. That my situation was such as to preclude me from discussing this important inner transformation with anyone, and most especially not with my wife, put me in a melancholy mood. If I still continued to put a good face on things, I nonetheless no longer believed inwardly in any sort of possible success in Paris. Foreseeing the boundless misery to come, I shuddered at the smiling aspect with which Paris presented us in the luxuriant sunshine of May. This was the least favorable time for any artistic undertaking in Paris; at every door where I knocked with feigned hope I was turned away with the terribly monotonous "Monsieur est à la campagne". During long walks, when we felt ourselves so utterly alone amid the merry and bustling crowds, I used to fantasize for my poor wife about free countries in South America, where we could be entirely removed from all these disconcerting apparitions, where people knew nothing of opera and music, and where we could easily earn a decent living through diligent labor. I referred Minna, who didn't quite understand what I had in mind, to a story I had just read by Zschokke,[1] entitled *The Founding of Maryland*, in which the experience of tormented and persecuted European emigrants in feeling able to breathe easily at last is conveyed in a very seductive way. Being of more practical temperament, she insisted on the necessity of finding a way to sustain ourselves in Paris, to which end she devised all kinds of economies in our style of living. For my part, I was sketching out the draft of the poem for *Der fliegende Holländer*, still having in mind the possibility of a production in Paris. I shaped the material into a single act, primarily because the subject itself called for it, for in this way I could render the straightforward dramatic action between the principal figures without any of the operatic accessories I had come to loathe so much. From a practical standpoint, moreover, I thought a one-acter, to be given as a curtain-raiser preceding a ballet at the Opéra, would have the best chance of being accepted. I wrote Meyerbeer in Berlin about this and requested his support. In addition, I again took up the composition of *Rienzi*, upon which I now labored uninterruptedly until it was completed.

Meanwhile our situation got worse and worse; I was soon compelled to draw upon the subsidy I had obtained through Laube in advance of the stipulated payments, whereby I increasingly alienated my brother-in-law Avenarius, who found our stay in Paris more and more incomprehensible. One morning, after we had been debating in great anxiety how we were to meet the first quarterly rental payment, a postal messenger appeared with a package for me from London; I took this for a providential sign and broke open the seal, while at the same moment the receipt-book was thrust in my face, from which I saw at once that I was supposed to pay seven francs postage due. To my horror I recognized in the contents of the package the score of my *Rule Britannia* overture, which was being returned to me by the London Philharmonic Society. In a rage, I told the messenger that I would not accept the parcel, whereby he demonstrated most vociferously that I had already opened it. But there was no help for him: I didn't have the seven francs; I declared that he had not communicated to me in time that there was postage due and thus compelled him to send the only existing copy of my overture back to the firm of Messrs Laffitte[2] & Gaillard, to be disposed of as they wished as their property. I do not know what happened to this manuscript and was never interested in trying to find out.

Kietz now found a way to help us in this calamitous situation. He had been asked by an elderly Fräulein Leplay, a very rich and extraordinarily miserly old maid from Leipzig, to find inexpensive quarters in Paris for her and Kietz's own stepmother, in whose company she was planning to travel. As our by no means large apartment was still bigger than we needed, and had already become a painful burden to keep up, we didn't hesitate a second to rent the better part of it to her for the duration of her stay in Paris, which was to last about two months. In addition, my wife made breakfast for the guests just as if they were in a hotel, and was pleased to consider the few sous derived from this activity as being earnings of her own. However trying we found the company of this strange sample of old-maidenhood, the arrangement nonetheless helped us to get through a difficult time, and despite the household disturbance, I was able to continue my work on *Rienzi* without interruption. This became more difficult after Fräulein Leplay's departure, when we again sublet a room in our apartment, this time to a German traveling salesman, who in his leisure time played untiringly on the flute. His name was Brix, and he was a modest, decent fellow who had been referred to us by a new friend, the painter Pecht.[1] I had gotten to know Pecht through Kietz, who was studying together with him in the studio of Delaroche. He was Kietz's exact opposite; obviously endowed with less talent, he nevertheless tackled the task of learning to paint in oils under difficult circumstances in the shortest possible time with unusual diligence and earnestness; beyond this, he was well-educated, highly receptive to further learning, and proved in every respect to be principled, serious and reliable. Without attaining the same degree of intimacy with us as our three other friends, he nevertheless belonged from then on to those few who stuck with us in our troubles and spent nearly every evening in our company.

One day, I received fresh and surprising proof of Laube's continuing solicitude for me. The factor to a certain Count Kushelew called on me and after some inquiries concerning my situation, about which the count had learned in Karlsruhe through Laube, informed me without further ado that his employer wanted to be useful to me and therefore wished to make my acquaintance. He was intending, it seemed, to put together in Paris a comic opera troupe, which was to follow him to his estate in Russia; for this he was searching for a music director experienced enough to be of assistance in recruiting the ensemble. I willingly obeyed the summons to the Count's hotel and found there an already rather elderly and smoothly cordial gentleman, who good-naturedly let me play some of my little French songs for him. Having a shrewd eye for human nature, he realized at once that I was not his man, and amid polite phrases of regret refused to pursue any further negotiations concerning his operatic undertaking. Yet on that same day he sent me, together with a friendly note, ten gold napoleons, a payment the purpose of which I could not figure out. I therefore wrote to him to ask what he wanted of me and requested him to commission a composition, as I assumed he had paid me the honorarium in advance. When I received no answer, I tried in vain to see him again. Through other channels I learned that Count Kushelew preferred exclusively the operatic genre of Adam, and that in regard to the recruitment of the opera troupe his tastes ran more to establishing a little seraglio than an artistic institution!

So far I had gotten nowhere with the music publisher Schlesinger. It was impossible to persuade him to publish my little French songs. In order to do something to make myself known in this direction, however, I decided to have my *Deux Grenadiers* engraved by him at my expense. Kietz was to lithograph a magnificent title-page for it. When it was done, Schlesinger charged me fifty francs. This publication had a curious destiny: the work bore Schlesinger's imprint, and as I had defrayed all the costs, any proceeds were, of course, to be credited to me. I had to take it on trust from the publisher later that not a single copy had been sold. After my sudden rise to fame with *Rienzi* in Dresden, the music publisher Schott of Mainz, whose catalogue consisted almost exclusively of works translated from French, found it advisable to publish *Les Deux Grenadiers* for Germany. Below the text of the French translation he printed the original poem of Heine line for line, but as the French version was a very free paraphrase, and in a meter differing entirely from that of the original, Heine's text fitted so grotesquely to my music that, in a fury at the dishonor it did me, I felt obliged to protest the publication by Schott as an unauthorized pirating of my work. Schott responded by threatening an action for libel, as he contended that according to his agreement his edition was not a reprint but simply a reimpression. In order to avoid further annoyance, I was induced to publish an apology for not having realized this delicate distinction. When in the year 1848[1] I inquired of Schlesinger's successor, Herr Brandus, as to the fate of my little work, having meanwhile been told that a new edition had been put out, it was denied that I had any rights to it whatsoever. As I really had no desire to spend my own money to purchase a copy, I have had to get by to the present day without possessing something that is my own. The scale to which later similar remunerative enterprises relating to the publication of my works grew will be shown in due course.

For the present it was a question of finding a way to pay Schlesinger the fifty francs he had charged me; he suggested I do some work for the *Gazette Musicale*, which he published; since I was by no means adept enough in French to use the language for literary purposes, I was obliged to have my articles translated and split the fee with the translator. Yet I was consoled by the assurance that I would receive sixty francs per printer's sheet of completed work; what was meant by such a sheet I was soon to learn, when I presented myself to obtain payment from the publisher, always highly irritated at such things, who proceeded to apply to the article an abominable iron instrument, on which the lines in the columns were marked off numerically, and by means of which, after carefully deducting space for title and author's name, he calculated the number of lines, whereby it turned out that what I had considered a full sheet was in reality only half of one. At any rate, I began writing articles for Schlesinger's strange magazine. The first was a lengthy essay entitled *De la musique allemande*, in which I could not help, at that time, holding forth with enthusiastic exaggeration about the intimate and deep nature of German music, so that my friend Anders felt called upon to observe how nice it would be if it were all in fact true. I had the unexpected satisfaction of seeing this article subsequently reproduced in an Italian translation in a music magazine published in Milan, whereby I was amused to find myself termed "dottissimo musico tedesco", an error which most probably no one would make today. My essay seemed to attract some favorable comment even then; Schlesinger now asked me to write an article, to be favorable in any case, about the adaptation of Pergolesi's *Stabat Mater* by the Russian General Lvov,[1] which I tried to make as long as possible, in my own interests. On my own initiative I wrote a somewhat more congenial essay entitled *Du métier du virtuose et de l'indépendance du compositeur*.

Meanwhile I was surprised in mid-summer by the arrival of Meyerbeer, who came to Paris for two weeks. He showed himself very sympathetic and obliging. When I told him of my idea to write a one-act opera to precede the ballet and asked him to introduce me to the newest director of the Opéra, M. Léon Pillet,[2] for this purpose, he eventually decided there was no objection to visiting this gentleman with me and recommending me to him. Unfortunately I had the unpleasant surprise, when listening to the two men seriously debate what might be done with me, to hear Meyerbeer hit upon the suggestion that I might consent to compose one act of a ballet, together with another composer. Naturally, I didn't want any part of that, and instead handed over to M. Pillet my brief scenario for *Der fliegende Holländer*. This was as far as I had gotten when Meyerbeer again left Paris, this time for an extended period.

As I heard nothing from M. Pillet for a long time, I now continued to work industriously at the composition of *Rienzi*, but to my gnawing distress was often obliged to interrupt that task, in order to do some work for Schlesinger, to enable us to keep our heads above water. Since my collaboration in the *Gazette Musicale* produced so little cash, Schlesinger one day suggested that I might devise a better method for learning to play the *cornet à pistons*. He countered my bewilderment at how to go about this task by sending me five different published "methods" for the *cornet à pistons*, at that time the favorite musical instrument among the younger male population of Paris. From these five methods I was supposed to devise a new sixth one by blending the rest of them, because Schlesinger was interested only in having one in his own list. I had actually begun to ruminate seriously on how I could do it when Schlesinger freed me from the task because a new "method" had just been submitted to him from another source. Instead I was told to write no fewer than fourteen suites for the *cornet à pistons*; by this he meant operatic excerpts arranged for the instrument, and to provide me with material for the work, Schlesinger sent to my residence no fewer than sixty complete operatic vocal scores. I now scavenged among these for suitable melodies for my suites, marked the appropriate places in each volume with slips of paper, and constructed from the sixty volumes an odd edifice around my desk, in order to have the maximum amount of melodious material within my immediate reach. To my great relief, though to my poor wife's dismay, Schlesinger informed me while I was in the midst of my labors on this project that Monsieur Schiltz, the leading cornet player in Paris, to whom he had showed my studies before having them engraved, had let it be known that I obviously knew nothing of the instrument and had written everything in keys so high that the Parisians would never be able to produce the notes. The work already completed was accepted, however, as Schiltz had agreed to emend it, but on the condition that I should surrender half my fee to him; the rest of the work was then taken off my hands, and the sixty vocal scores made their way back to the singular shop in the Rue Richelieu.

Thus my income was again in poor shape; distress at home grew, although at the same time I had the chance to put the finishing touches to my *Rienzi*. On November 19th I finally finished this most voluminous of all operas. I had already decided to offer it to the Dresden Court Theater for its first performance, in the hope of building myself a bridge back to Germany if it should be successful. I had decided upon Dresden in the knowledge that I would find there in Tichatschek[1] the best tenor for the leading role; I also counted on my acquaintance with Schröder-Devrient, who had been favorably inclined toward me from old times, and who had already vainly tried, out of consideration for my family, to induce the Dresden Court Theater to accept my *Feen*. I also knew that the secretary of the theater, Councillor Winkler[2] (known as Theodor Hell), was an old friend of my family; the chief conductor, Reissiger,[3] was also known to me personally from the time of my youthful excursion to Bohemia with Apel, when we spent a merry evening together in Dresden. To all these people I now addressed urgent and eloquent letters, wrote an official application to the intendant, Herr von Lüttichau,[4] and even went so far as to include a formal petition to the King of Saxony. I now got everything ready to send off.

Before packing it, I had not omitted to indicate the precise tempi for my opera with the help of a metronome; as I owned no such instrument, I had been obliged to borrow one and set off one morning, the metronome concealed under my thin little coat, to return it to its owner. The day on which this happened was one of the most extraordinary of my life, for into it the whole misery of my situation at the time was compressed in the most ghastly way. Apart from the fact that I didn't know from one day to the next how to scrape together the few francs necessary to allow Minna to meet our household expenses, several of the bills of exchange which I had issued, according to Parisian custom, at the time when we were fitting out our apartment, had now fallen due. Hoping for help from one source or another, I had to try first to persuade the holders of the bills to extend the maturity dates; such bills, being commercial paper, naturally went through many hands, and I had to hunt down the holders across the length and breadth of the city; on this particular day I was out to pacify a cheesemonger in a fifth-floor apartment in the Cité. At the same time I also intended to apply for help to the brother of my two Brockhaus brothers-in-law, Heinrich,[5] who had arrived in Paris shortly before; from Schlesinger I hoped to squeeze out enough money to pay the postal service to dispatch my score that day. As I also had to deliver the metronome, I set out early in the morning after an anxious farewell from Minna, who knew from experience that whenever I went out in quest of money she would not see me again until late in the evening. A thick fog covered the streets when I stepped outside the house, and the first thing I recognized was my dog Robber, who had been taken from me a year before. At first I thought I was seeing a ghost, but then yelled to him hastily in a shrill and piercing voice; the animal seemed to recognize me and approached rather near; when I strode quickly toward him with outstretched arm, however, the fear of a punishment, such as I had foolishly administered to him once or twice during the latter part of the time he was with us, seemed to dispel every other recollection; he drew back timidly, and when I ran hastily after him, he fled me each time at greater and greater speed. That he had recognized me became clearer and clearer, for I could see him pause at street-corners to look anxiously back at me before setting off again with renewed energy. Thus, I followed him through a labyrinth of streets, hardly distinguishable in the thick mist, until breathless and dripping with sweat, burdened by my metronome, I lost sight of him near the church of St Roch, never to see him again. For a time I stood glued to the spot, staring into the fog. I wondered what the ghostly reappearance of the companion of my adventurous travels on this horrible day could possibly signify. That he had fled his old master with the terror of a wild beast filled my heart with a strange bitterness and seemed to me a terrible omen. Deeply shaken, I set out again with wobbly knees to look after my various melancholy transactions. After he had assured me that he could do nothing on my behalf, I left Heinrich Brockhaus humiliated and attempting to conceal from him how painful this humiliation was for me. My other errands turned out so hopelessly that, after having been kept waiting for hours in Schlesinger's office listening to his intentionally protracted and trivial conversations with his visitors, I finally reappeared after nightfall entirely without money under the windows of our house, in one of which I spotted Minna peering anxiously out after me. Sensing that I would have no luck, she had delicately petitioned our fellow tenant and table companion, the flute-player Brix, whom we patiently tolerated for his good nature despite all inconvenience, for a small cash advance and thus could at least set before me a nourishing meal. Further help was to be forthcoming for a time, if under great sacrifices on my part, from the success of a Donizetti opera.

La favorite, a very weak work of the Italian maestro which had nonetheless been received enthusiastically by a Paris public whose tastes had already sunk very low, for the sake of two cabalettas, had been purchased by Schlesinger, who had lost money on the last two operas of Halévy. Exploiting what he knew to be my helpless position, he stormed into my apartment one morning, beaming grotesquely, and demanded pen and paper to calculate before my very eyes the enormous amounts he had determined to pay me. He wrote "*La favorite* – complete arrangement for pianoforte, piano arrangement without words for two hands, ditto for four hands, complete arrangement for quartet, the same for two violins, ditto for *cornet à pistons*. For these works eleven hundred francs. Immediate cash advance of five hundred francs." I could see at a glance the immense amount of work acceptance of this order would entail but I did not hesitate for a moment. When I had brought home the five hundred francs and piled the hard five-franc pieces on the table to our delight, my sister Cäcilie Avenarius happened to drop in to see us. The sight of our riches effectively counteracted the anxiety she had previously felt about associating with us, and from then on we saw each other often and were frequently invited to Sunday dinner. But I was no longer interested in distractions of any kind; I had been so badly shaken by events of the recent past that now, as if in expiation of all my bygone sins, I willingly imposed upon myself the penance of utter dedication to this humiliating yet still lucrative job. To economize on heating we restricted ourselves to our bedroom, making it serve simultaneously as living room, dining room and study; with two steps I could get from my bed to my work table, from which I could swivel my chair to the dinner table, leaving my seat only to go to bed late at night. Every fourth day I allowed myself a short constitutional. As these penitential rites continued throughout most of the winter, I thereby contracted those abdominal disorders that have plagued me more or less ever since.

I increased my earnings by undertaking the extremely time-consuming and painstaking task of reading the proofs of the score of Donizetti's opera, for which I managed to extract three hundred francs from Schlesinger, who had no one else to do the job. While doing all this I still had to find time to write out the orchestral parts for my *Faust* Overture, which I continued to hope would be played at the Conservatoire; and in order to preserve myself in the face of this shameful musical drudgery, I wrote a little novella, *A Pilgrimage to Beethoven*, which appeared in the *Gazette Musicale* under the title *Une visite à Beethoven*. Schlesinger admitted to me frankly that this little work had created an unusual stir and had met with marked approval, being reprinted in whole or in part in a number of popular magazines. He asked me to continue producing such pieces. By means of a sequel entitled *The End of a Musician in Paris*, or, in French, *Un musicien étranger à Paris*, I avenged myself for all my humiliations. It pleased Schlesinger much less, but earned me touching evidence of approval from his poor assistant, as well as an encomium from Heinrich Heine: "Hoffmann himself could not have written such a thing". Even Berlioz bestirred himself and mentioned it favorably in one of his articles in the *Journal des Débats*. He also expressed his approval, if only in personal conversation, of yet another essay on musical aesthetics, *Concerning Overtures*, being particularly pleased that I had illustrated my principle by singling out Gluck's overture to *Iphigenia in Aulis* as a model for compositions of this type.

Encouraged by these signs of interest on his part, I tried to get to know Berlioz more intimately. I had been introduced to him some time before in Schlesinger's office, where I had seen him from time to time since then. I had presented him with a copy of my *Deux Grenadiers* but could elicit nothing more from him about it beyond the statement that he could only strum the guitar a bit and was unable to play it on the piano for himself. Yet his great orchestral works, which I had heard during the previous winter under his baton, had made a tremendously exciting impression on me. During that winter of 1839–40, he had conducted three performances of his new *Romeo and Juliet* symphony, one of which I had attended. This was a completely new world for me, in which I had to try to find my way in an unprejudiced manner commensurate with these impressions. At first it was the impact of orchestral virtuosity, such as I had never before dreamed of, that nearly overwhelmed me. The fantastic boldness and sharp precision with which the most audacious orchestral combinations pressed almost tangibly upon me, over-awed my own musico-poetic sensibility and drove it with irresistible force back into my innermost being. I was all ears for things I had until then had no conception of and which I now had to try to explain to myself. In *Romeo and Juliet* I had nevertheless found long and frequent stretches that were empty and shallow, which pained me all the more considering that this work of art, despite being truly marred by its construction and its undue prolongation, overpowered me in its manifold brilliant moments to the point of extinguishing all reservations. Berlioz followed this new symphony with repeat performances of his *Harold en Italie* and his *Symphonie fantastique* during that winter. While I had listened to these works with rapt astonishment, being particularly impressed by the musical genre painting in the *Symphonie fantastique* and in almost every respect by *Harold*, the latest work of this extraordinary master, *Grande Symphonie Funèbre et Triomphale*, which he scored in the most brilliant and imaginative way for an immense military band and performed in the summer of 1840 at the ceremonial interment under the column in the Place de la Bastille of those who had fallen in the July Revolution, had thoroughly acquainted me with the greatness and energy of this unique and quite incomparable artist. But I had nonetheless been unable to shake off an odd, profound and serious feeling of oppression provoked by his work as a whole. There remained in me a residue of reserve, as if toward a foreign element with which I could never become entirely familiar, and this reserve took on the character of serious reflection as to why I could be so carried away by one of Berlioz's longer works and yet at times so undeniably repelled or even bored by it. It was only much later that I succeeded in bringing this problem, which caused me for years a certain painful tension toward Berlioz, out into the light and resolving it.

There is no question that at the time I felt myself a mere schoolboy beside Berlioz; and thus I was particularly embarrassed when Schlesinger now decided to exploit the success of my novellas on my behalf and requested me to perform one of my own compositions at a big concert to be sponsored by the publishers of the *Gazette Musicale*. I realized that none of my compositions to hand at the time would be in any way suitable for such an occasion. I was not yet confident about my *Faust* Overture because of its delicate and quiet close, which I presumed would be appreciated only by an audience already prejudiced in my favor. Since it had also been indicated to me that only a second-rate orchestra, that of Valentino from the Casino in the Rue St Honoré, would be available, and that there could be only one rehearsal, I felt I was confronted by the choice of abandoning this chance or resorting to that hasty product of my youthful years in Magdeburg, the *Columbus* overture. I elected the latter course. When I went to fetch the orchestral parts for this composition which were still stored in the archives of the Conservatoire, I was warned by Habeneck somewhat dryly but not without kindness about the danger of going before the Paris public with this work, for it was, in his words, too "vague". A huge difficulty to be overcome was to find six trumpeters, as this instrument, on which the Germans are such virtuosi, is only rarely well represented in Parisian orchestras. The man who had corrected my suites for the *cornet à pistons*, M. Schiltz, good-naturedly offered his advice: I would have to reduce the number of trumpets to four, of which he then assured me I could count on good playing from only two of them. At the rehearsal the prime source of my composition's effect proved very disheartening; not *once* were the high and delicate passages blown without cracking. Moreover, since I was not allowed to conduct, I had to deal with a *chef d'orchestre* whom I clearly perceived to be inwardly convinced my work was nonsense, a view that seemed to be shared by all the members of the orchestra. Berlioz, who attended this rehearsal, remained silent throughout; he gave me no encouragement, yet also did not try to dissuade me, but rather let me know with a weary smile that things were very difficult in Paris. On the evening of the performance (February 4th 1841) the public, consisting mainly of subscribers to the *Gazette Musicale* and therefore familiar with my novellas, seemed rather favorably inclined toward me. I was assured that my overture, even if it had bored everybody, would certainly have been applauded, if only the trumpeters had not excited the public to barely suppressed disgust by the repeated cracking in the higher passages, for in Paris it is generally only the virtuoso parts of a composition, i.e. successful production of certain hazardous notes, that are followed with close attention. I did not try to conceal from myself that I had failed completely, that after this calamity Paris no longer existed for me, and that I could do nothing more at the moment than lock myself away in my universal bedroom and resume my work of arranging Donizetti's operas.

My renunciation of the world was so extreme that, like a penitent, I no longer shaved and grew a long beard, much to my wife's dismay, for the first and only time in my life. I tried to bear everything with equanimity, but a piano player living next door, who practised Liszt's fantasy on *Lucia di Lammermoor* throughout the day, threatened to drive me to despair. To give him some of his own medicine, I moved our old piano, which was frightfully out of tune, from the living room to the bedroom one day, placed it right up against the wall nearest my neighbor, and requested Brix to dig out his piccolo and accompany me in the overture to *La favorite*, which I had just finished arranging for piano and violin or flute. The effect seems to have truly terrified my neighbor, a young piano teacher; some days later the concierge told me he was moving to another apartment, about which I then felt somewhat ashamed. The wife of our concierge had developed a discreet and useful relationship with us; at first we had taken her in occasional service to help out with the most necessary household duties, especially in the kitchen, in cleaning clothes, and in polishing shoes; at last even the modest salary we were paying her caused us trouble, and Minna had to take it upon herself to dimiss her from our service and do all the meanest household chores by herself. As we didn't want our sub-tenant to know anything of all this, my wife, who not only did the cooking but also washed all the dishes, found it necessary to polish our guest's shoes as well. But we considered the humiliation we felt in regard to our concierge the most difficult thing to bear; yet in this we were proved wrong: the couple showed us their esteem by heightened politeness, in which admittedly a certain amount of familiarity was mixed. Thus, I frequently discussed politics with the man; at the time, the quadruple alliance[1] against France had been concluded, and as the situation under Thiers'[2] short-lived government was regarded as extremely tense, my concierge consoled me one day with these words: "Monsieur, il y a quatre hommes en Europe qui s'appellent: le roi Louis Philippe, l'empereur d'Autriche, l'empereur de Russie, le roi de Prusse; eh bien, ces quatre sont des couillons; et nous n'aurons pas la guerre."

I seldom lacked entertainment in the evening; but my few loyal friends had to accustom themselves to communicating with me while I went on with my musical scribbling until far into the night. On New Year's Eve of the year 1840, I was given a most touching surprise party they had arranged among themselves. Lehrs rang the doorbell and appeared with a large leg of veal; Kietz came with rum, sugar, and lemons; Pecht came with a goose; but Anders arrived with two bottles of champagne taken from a supply he had been given by an instrument-maker for a favorable article about his pianos and which he saved for only the most ceremonial occasions. At once I threw aside the degrading *Favorite* and plunged with the greatest enthusiasm into the business of celebrating a feast of friendship. Everybody had to help in the preparations, first in heating the living room, assisting my wife in the kitchen, and then getting whatever was still lacking from the grocer. The supper developed into a dithyrambic carousal; when the punch began to supplement the effect of the champagne, I delivered a fiery speech, which provoked such unbroken hilarity in my friends that it found no end and carried me away to the point that I, who had already mounted a chair in heightened emotion, finally got up on the table itself, and from this vantage point preached to my transported listeners a gospel of the most nonsensical contempt for the world, together with a eulogy of the South American Free States, the whole thing ending only in sobs of laughter, with everyone so overcome that we had to put them up for the night, as they would certainly not have been able to go home. On New Year's Day 1841, I was again doing penance working on my *Favorite*. I recall a second, considerably less boisterous evening party, occasioned by a visit from the violin virtuoso Vieuxtemps, who happened to be a childhood friend of Kietz. We had the pleasure of having the young virtuoso, at that time the toast of Paris, entertain us throughout the evening by his beautiful playing, which gave my salon an unusual touch of dignity; Kietz rewarded him for his kindness by carrying him home from my apartment to his nearby hotel on his shoulders.

We were hit hard early in this new year by a mistake I made as a result of my ignorance of Parisian regulations. It seemed only natural that I should give notice that we were leaving our apartment as soon as the proper term had expired. For this purpose I went to see the landlady, a young and very rich widow living in one of her houses in the Marais quarter. The lady received me with some embarrassment, and told me she would speak with her manager about my giving notice, referring me to him. I was then informed in writing that my notice would only have been valid if it had been delivered no later than the previous evening, and that as a result of this slip-up I would be obliged, according to the terms of our contract, to pay the rent for the apartment for an additional year. Greatly alarmed, I went to see the manager himself; I was admitted to his presence only after much difficulty and found an elderly man stretched out limply before me, seemingly crippled by a painful malady; after I had told him my tale of woe and begged him heartrendingly to use his influence to abrogate my contract, I got no reply other than that it was my fault, not his, that I had given notice one day too late, and that I would somehow have to come up with the rent for the following year. My concierge, to whom I gave an agitated report of this scene, responded with the following consolatory remark about this man: "J'aurais pu vous dire cela, car voyez, monsieur, cet homme ne vaut pas l'eau qu'il boit."

This entirely unforeseen misfortune destroyed our last hopes of redemption from our untenable situation. For a time we soothed ourselves with the hope of finding another tenant. This was not fulfilled; we saw Easter come and with it the beginning of the new contractual year. At last the concierge was able to recommend to us a foreign family willing to take our apartment, furniture included, for a few months. We eagerly grasped this means of meeting at least the next rental payment to fall due and thought that if we could only get away from this unlucky dwelling, we would find some way to rid ourselves of it altogether. Therefore we began hunting for an inexpensive summer place in the outskirts of Paris. We were referred to Meudon for this purpose and decided to take lodgings there on the avenue connecting Meudon with nearby Bellevue. The apartment in the Rue du Helder was entrusted to the concierge, to whom I gave full powers to re-let, and we established ourselves as best we could in our temporary asylum, in which we were at first obliged to include our former subtenant, the good-natured flute-player Brix, as the poor man was short of cash himself and in the absence of his money would have been in dire straits if we had excluded him from our household. Our improvident move took place on April 29th, being actually a flight from the impossible into the incomprehensible; for how we were going to survive the summer was entirely unclear to us, as Schlesinger had dried up as a source of funds and no other seemed to be open to us.

However unremunerative it might be, there seemed nothing for me to do other than continue my journalistic efforts, which had afforded me the few successes I had achieved. In the previous winter, I had produced for the *Gazette Musicale* a fairly lengthy essay on Weber's *Der Freischütz*, designed to pave the way for the then forthcoming performance of the work in the Opéra, to be supplemented with recitatives by Berlioz. Apparently I managed to irritate Berlioz with this article. I could not help referring to the incongruousness of supplementing this of all works, whose form derived from the traditional Singspiel, with ingredients bound to distort its original dimensions solely for the purpose of adapting it for the luxuriant repertory of that theater. That the results completely justified my foreboding in no way diminished the hostility of the participants to me. But I had the almost flattering satisfaction of finding that my article had attracted the attention of the famous George Sand. In the introduction to a legendary tale of French provincial life, she tried to dispel doubts about the capacity of the French to appreciate such characteristically mystical, mythical folk stories, as I had demonstrated *Der Freischütz* to be; in this connection she referred to my article. I was spurred to further journalistic activity by my efforts to have *Rienzi* accepted in Dresden. The secretary of the theater there, the afore-mentioned Winkler, reported to me at length about the state of the matter; in his capacity as editor of the *Abendzeitung*, a paper that had gone far down hill at the time, he seized the opportunity to enlist me as an unpaid correspondent, soliciting frequent communications from me for publication; whenever I wanted to discover more about the state of my application, I first had to send in something more for the paper. As the negotiations with the Court Theater became immeasurably protracted, I had to deliver an inordinate number of articles from Paris, which threw me into some perplexity, as I had for some time withdrawn completely to my bedroom and knew nothing of what was going on in Paris.

I had serious reasons for keeping away from Parisian artistic or social life. In part it was my painful experiences, but also in part the growing antipathy, deeply rooted in my inner development, toward the entire artistic and social bustle I had once found so attractive, that had driven me with truly frightening speed away from any contact with it. The production of *Les Huguenots*, which I heard here for the first time, had dazzled me very much indeed; the beautiful orchestral playing and the extremely meticulous and effective staging gave me an enticing foretaste of the great resources inherent in such well-trained artistic means. But curiously enough, I was not impelled to attend repeat performances of such works; I soon found the singing style a caricature of itself and developed the knack of mimicking the latest Parisian singing techniques and their tasteless excesses, thereby delighting and entertaining my friends exceedingly. The composers themselves, who achieved their successes by pandering to these ridiculous fashions, could not fail in time to attract my critical mockery. That such a flat and basically un-French potboiler as *La favorite* could monopolize this once proud theater for so long exhausted the last reserves of patience I had maintained with the accomplishments of the "leading lyric theater in the world". During my entire stay in Paris I do not believe I went to the Opéra more than four times. The productions of the Opéra Comique, because of the characteristic coldness of the acting style as well as the degenerate quality of the music produced there, had repelled me from the start. The same coldness on the part of the singers also drove me away from the Italian Opera. The very famous names of most of these singers, who sang in the same four operas year after year, could not compensate me for the complete absence of even the simplest theatrical emotion that I had so profoundly appreciated in the performances of Schröder-Devrient. I saw clearly that everything was going downhill here, but at the same time felt neither the desire nor the hope of seeing this degeneration halted and reversed. I preferred the little theaters in which the French talent showed itself to me in its true light; but I had so much trouble trying to relate myself to the Parisian environment that I could not spare much sympathy or attention for casual observance of excellence that did not really interest me. Moreover, my misery and need had been so great from the outset, and the realization of the fruitlessness of my Paris endeavors so vivid, that I soon began declining all invitations to see this or that, either from indifference or annoyance. Several times I sent back tickets for performances by Rachel at the Théâtre Français, much to Minna's regret, and in fact saw this famous theater only once, when I had to go there professionally for my Dresden patron, who was always anxious for articles.

To fill the columns of the *Abendzeitung*, I adopted the shameful practice of patching together whatever I was told in the evenings, based on newspaper stories and restaurant conversations, by Anders and Lehrs, who themselves never had any experiences worth telling about, and seasoning all this in the piquant style made popular in recent journalism by Heine. I couldn't help fearing that my good Councillor Winkler would one day inevitably uncover the secret of my wide knowledge of Paris. I had also delivered to him a lengthy article for his moribund publication about the actual performance of *Der Freischütz*, which was of particular interest to him as guardian of Weber's children. As he now promised me he would not rest until he had given me the most binding assurances as to the acceptance of *Rienzi*, I sent him, in my effusive gratitude, the German original of my Beethoven story. The 1841 volume of this publication, then published by Arnold in Dresden but long since defunct, contains the only printed version of this manuscript.

A further sphere for my transitory literary activity opened to me with a request by Lewald, editor of the belletristic monthly *Europa*, to write for him. This man was the first who had from time to time mentioned my name to the public at all; as he was accustomed to publish musical supplements to his elegant and for a time quite widely circulated magazine, I had sent him two of my compositions from Königsberg, to get them before the public in this manner. These consisted of a musical setting of a melancholy poem by Scheuerlin,[1] *Der Knabe und der Tannenbaum* (a work I am still pleased to call my own), and my ripping Carnival Song from *Das Liebesverbot*. When I now hit upon the idea of publishing my little French compositions in this way, and therefore sent Lewald *Dors, mon enfant*, the *Attente* of Hugo, and the *Mignonne* of Ronsard, he not only sent me a small fee – the first I had ever received for one of my compositions – but also commissioned me to produce a series of long articles based on my impressions of Paris, to be written as entertainingly as possible. For his paper I now wrote *Paris Amusements* and *Paris Fatalities*, in which I gave vent, in Heine's fashion and employing all kinds of stylistic tricks, to my disappointments and my contempt for Parisian life in general. In the second I exploited the misadventures of a certain Hermann Pfau, a strange good-for-nothing whom I had gotten to know better than I should have during my Leipzig student days, and who had been hanging around in Paris as a vagabond since early the previous winter. The paltry income I derived from my work on *La favorite* was often partly consumed in helping this completely broken-down and pitiful fellow. Thus there was a certain economic justice in my using his Parisian adventures to recoup a few francs by writing about them for Lewald.

My literary work took a different turn through my negotiations with the director of the Opéra, Léon Pillet. After endless inquiries I had finally learned he had taken a liking to my scenario for *Der fliegende Holländer*; he revealed this to me while simultaneously requesting me to sell him this material, as he had contractual obligations to supply several different composers with subjects of this type for short operas. I now tried to convince Pillet orally and by letter that I was really the only one who could complete the text and compose the music with any prospect of success, for with it I had come upon my own terrain for the first time, to which he had been led solely by my guidance. But reasoning of that sort availed nothing; the director felt obliged to tell me honestly what I had really gained by Meyerbeer's recommendation to him on my behalf: there could be no question of my receiving a commission to compose the music even for a light opera for at least seven years, as his existing commitments to others sufficed to cover that period; I should therefore be reasonable and sell my material to an "auteur" of his choice, and if I still wished to try my luck as a composer for the Opéra, he counselled me to speak with the *maître de ballet*, who might want some music for an extra number. When I rejected this proposal with undisguised revulsion, he abandoned me to my own devices, until, after endless unsuccessful attempts to do better, I finally begged the theater commissioner Edouard Monnaie, with whom I had struck up a friendship through his being the editor of the *Gazette Musicale*, to intervene on my behalf. After acquainting himself with my scenario, he candidly confessed that he did not understand how Pillet could possibly have taken to it; but inasmuch as he had done so – which would assuredly have detrimental consequences for him – Monnaie advised me to take advantage as quickly as possible of whatever might be offered for it, for he had heard that Pillet had already turned it over to Monsieur Paul Foucher,[1] a brother-in-law of Victor Hugo, and Foucher had moreover asserted that he had found nothing new in the plot, since the subject of "le vaisseau fantôme" was quite familiar in France as well. Now I saw where I stood, declared myself willing to oblige M. Pillet, and participated in a conference with M. Foucher, at which, as a result of Pillet's advocacy, the value of my scenario was fixed at five hundred francs, a sum paid to me by the theater cashier as an advance on any author's royalties.

Our summer refuge in the Avenue de Meudon now took on a specific look: those five hundred francs had to be used at once to allow me to write the poem and the music of *Der fliegende Holländer* for Germany, while I abandoned "le vaisseau fantôme" to its Gallic fate.

With the completion of this transaction, I had succeeded to some extent in bolstering my increasingly shaky finances. The months of May and June had brought steadily augmented cares and worries. The beauty of the season, the refreshing country air, the sensation of freedom following my deliverance from the shameful musical hack-work at which I had spent the winter, all initially raised my hopes and inspired the little novella *A Happy Evening*, which appeared in French in the *Gazette Musicale*. But soon our lack of any means of support began to make a profoundly disheartening impact upon us. It came home to us with particular bitterness when my sister Cäcilie persuaded her husband to follow our lead and they took a summer residence nearby. Not well-to-do, but at least financially secure, my relatives lived side-by-side with us and saw us every day without our ever finding it apposite to let them know the true extent of our boundless embarrassment. One day it all came to a bitter climax. As we were totally without funds, I set out for Paris at daybreak on foot, for we did not have the money for the train fare, to spend the whole day there, dragging myself from street to street, trying to hunt down the sum of five francs, until late that afternoon, without having achieved the slightest success, I was compelled to undertake the long and painful walk back to Meudon. When I got back and announced these results to Minna, who had dashed out to meet me, she informed me in despair that the aforementioned Hermann Pfau had taken refuge with us, in the most pitiful condition, in the hope of at least a morsel of food; she had thus been obliged to give him the last bread the baker had delivered to us that morning. Yet we still had the hope that our sub-tenant Brix, who had become our companion in misery as a result of an odd turn of fate, would return from Paris, where he had gone that morning on a similar venture, with at least some small success. At last he returned, exhausted and dripping with sweat, driven by the need of a meal he had not been able to obtain in the city, because he had not been able to find a single one of his acquaintances there; he now desperately entreated my wife for a piece of bread. This climax to the situation finally inspired my wife with heroic resolution; she felt it her sacred duty to do battle against the hunger of her menfolk. For the first time during her stay in France she persuaded butcher, baker, and wine merchant with plausible excuses to supply her without immediate cash payment, and Minna's eyes beamed when, an hour later, she was able to put before us a superb meal, during which it just happened that the Avenarius family stopped by to see us, being visibly relieved to find us so well provided for.

This extreme distress was mitigated for a time at the beginning of July by the sale of my "Vaisseau fantôme", and thus by my final renunciation of hopes for success in Paris. As long as the five hundred francs lasted, I had breathing space for my work. The first expense was for the rental of a piano, which I had done without for several months. It was supposed to serve to reawaken in me the belief that I was still a musician, after I had been exercising my wits since the autumn of the previous year solely as a journalist and transcriber of operatic arrangements. The poem of *Der fliegende Holländer*, which I completed at great speed during the trials we had just survived, excited the particular approval of Lehrs; he declared I would never do anything better, and that *Der fliegende Holländer* would be my *Don Giovanni*. Now it was a question of finding the music. At the time during the previous winter when I still had hopes of adapting the subject for French opera, I had already worked out some of the lyrical parts both poetically and musically and had gotten them translated by Emile Deschamps for an audition that never actually materialized. These were: Senta's ballad, the song of the Norwegian sailors, and the spectral singing of the crew of the Dutchman's ship. Thereafter, I had been forced to become such a stranger to music that now, upon arrival of the piano in my summer haven, I did not dare even to touch it for a whole day. I was really frightened of finding out that I would be unable to have any more ideas, when I suddenly had the feeling that I had forgotten to set down the song of the helmsman in the first act, although as a matter of fact I could not remember having composed it at all, since I had just written the actual lyrics. I now proceeded to do this successfully, and the result pleased me. It went the same way with the Spinning Song; and when I had finished writing down these two pieces and had concluded that both had in fact come to me at that time and not earlier, I was beside myself with joy. It took me seven weeks to complete all the music for *Der fliegende Holländer*, except for the orchestration.

After that everything took a turn for the better; my exuberance astonished everyone, and my Avenarius relatives in particular came to the conclusion that I must be prospering very well, inasmuch as I was always such merry company. I took long walks in the woods around Meudon, where I even agreed to help Minna hunt for mushrooms on numerous occasions, that being unfortunately the principal pleasure she derived from our bosky retreat. It always horrified our landlord when he saw us returning with our booty, for he was certain we would poison ourselves when we ate them. My destiny, which almost invariably led me into strange adventures, once again confronted me with one of the oddest types to be found not only in the vicinity of Meudon, but also in all of Paris. This was M. Jadin, who was in fact so old that he insisted he remembered seeing Madame de Pompadour in the flesh at Versailles, yet was still of the most unbelievable vigor. He seemed to want to keep the world in continual and excited conjecture as to his real age; just as he did everything else for himself, he had manufactured a large number of wigs, ranging in the most delicate nuances from youthful blond to venerable white, together with shades of gray pleasantly interspersed, and he would wear any one of these, depending upon his mood at the moment. As he dabbled in virtually everything, I was pleased to see him especially enchanted by painting. That he had covered the walls of his room with the most juvenile caricatures of animal life and had even embellished the outside of his window blinds with the most ludicrous paintings did not disturb me in the slightest. On the contrary, I took this as welcome proof that he was not an amateur musician; until I discovered, to my horror, that the strangely discordant harp tones wafting up to me from some inexplicable nether region originated in his basement apartment, where he had two harp-pianos of his own invention. Unfortunately, as he assured me, he had long neglected to play them but now wanted to start practising in earnest to be able to give me a little pleasure. I succeeded in dissuading him by stating that the doctor had forbidden me to listen to the harp as my nerves were too delicate. I recall the last time I saw him he struck me as an apparition from the world of Hoffmann's tales. When we were moving back to Paris late that autumn, he requested us to take along on our furniture waggon a colossal stove-pipe, which he promised to pick up a short time later. On a very cold day Jadin did in fact appear in our new Paris apartment, in the most preposterous costume of his own manufacture, consisting of very thin light yellow trousers, a very short pale green dress jacket with conspicuously long tails, projecting lace shirt frills and cuffs, a very pale wig, and a hat so small it was constantly falling off; on top of all this he wore an enormous amount of costume jewelry, his whole appearance being based on the obvious assumption that he could not show himself in elegant Paris dressed as simply as in the country. Then he asked for his stove-pipe; we asked him who was going to help him carry it; he smilingly expressed astonishment at our helplessness, grasped the

colossal stove-pipe under his arm and refused flatly to accept the help
we proffered to get it down the staircase, a maneuver that took him a
full half-hour, despite all his vaunted skill; everyone in the house
assembled to watch the operation; but he did not let himself be
distracted, brought the pipe deftly through the front gate and sailed
gracefully down the street until he vanished forever from our sight.

During this short though eventful period I was free to obey my
innermost dictates and devote myself to the consolations of artistic
creation, and I recall that, when it came to an end, I had made such
progress that I could look forward with cheerful composure to the much
longer and more trying period of trouble and distress I could see ahead
of me. This set in with unerring punctuality; for I had just managed
to finish the closing scene when the five hundred francs gave out; they
did not suffice to give me the necessary peace and quiet to compose the
overture; I had to postpone that until my situation took a turn for the
better, and meanwhile I was forced to struggle once again for a bare
subsistence, with exertions that left me neither leisure nor time for
reflection. The concierge from the Rue du Helder brought us the news
that the mysterious family to whom we had sublet our rooms had now
left, and that we were once more obligated for the rent. I now had to
tell him flatly that I would no longer trouble myself about the matter
and would leave it to the owner to recoup whatever she could by the
sale of the furniture we had left there. This was arranged at a very painful
loss to us, and the furniture, the greater part of which was still unpaid
for, was sacrificed to pay the rent for an apartment we no longer
occupied.

Under the stress of the most indescribable privations I still tried to
keep a free hand to work on the instrumentation of my *Holländer*. The
raw fall weather came exceptionally early, and everyone returned to Paris
from their summer resorts, the Avenarius family as well. We were the
only ones unable to do so, as we did not have the funds to pay for the
move. I told M. Jadin, who was concerned about us, that I was in the
grip of my work and had to avoid the slightest interruption, in spite of
the cold that penetrated through the thin walls of the house. In this
condition I awaited help from a Königsberg acquaintance of earlier years,
Ernst Castell, a young and wealthy merchant who had looked us up in
Meudon a short time before, taken us out to a lavish meal, and had
promised at the time to help us out of our difficulty with what would
be for him, we knew, a painless cash advance. In order to provide us
with distraction and company in our unpleasant rustic abandonment,

Kietz arrived one day with his huge sketchbook and a pillow under his arm; he wanted to cheer us up by working on a huge caricature representing me and my luckless adventures in Paris, and the pillow was supposed to enable him to get some rest on our hard couch, which he had noticed lacked a head-rest. Since he knew we had difficulty getting firewood, he brought along several bottles of rum, so that we could warm ourselves with punch during the cold evenings; on these occasions I used to read aloud to him and to my wife from Hoffmann's tales. At last came news from Königsberg, from which I gained the knowledge that the young wastrel had not meant his promise to be taken seriously. We now looked forward in total despair to the chilly mists of the oncoming winter. Then Kietz suddenly declared it was up to him to get help; he packed up his sketches, taking them under his arm together with the pillow, and left for Paris, to return the next day with two hundred francs, which he had drummed up in the most self-sacrificial manner. At once we set out to Paris to find a little apartment to rent, choosing one in our friend's vicinity in the back part of the building at 14 Rue Jacob. I later learned that Proudhon[1] took these rooms shortly after us.

Thus we got back to the city on October 30th. It was a very small and cold apartment, its chilliness being unfortunately bad for our health. We furnished it with the scanty remains we had saved from our shipwreck in the Rue du Helder, and there we settled to await the results of my efforts to have my works accepted and performed in Germany. For the moment the main thing was to find peace and quiet for the short time it would take me to compose the overture to *Der fliegende Holländer*; I told Kietz that he would have to find the money to keep us above water until I had completed the composition and dispatched the full score of the opera. With the help of a parsimonious uncle, who had also established himself in Paris as a painter a long time ago, he succeeded in providing me with the necessary subsidy, five and ten francs at a time. During this period I often pointed with amused pride to my boots, which became literally only an apparent cover for my feet, as the soles eventually disappeared entirely.

As long as I was at work on the *Holländer* and Kietz was taking care of me, that was no problem, for I never went out; but when my completed score had finally been dispatched to the management of the Berlin Court Theater[2] at the beginning of December, the bitterness of my position could no longer be ameliorated; I had to try to get help once again for myself. What this meant in Paris I learned at this very time from the pitiful fate of the worthy Lehrs. Driven by money troubles such as I had had to survive a year earlier, he had been compelled on a broiling hot day in the previous summer to run breathlessly around various quarters of the city to get his bills of exchange, which had now fallen due, extended. He foolishly took a very cold drink, which temporarily robbed him of his voice, and from that time on he became increasingly hoarse, and the seeds of consumption, no doubt latent in him, ripened into mortal sickness with terrifying rapidity. For months he had been growing weaker and weaker, filling us with the most dreadful anxiety: he alone believed that his supposed catarrh would finally go away if he could only succeed in heating his room a bit better. One day I visited him in his lodgings, finding him cowering behind his work table in the freezing room; he complained that the work for Didot was very hard for him, which was all the more painful as he had been living from cash advances on account of which his employer was now pressing him. He declared that if he did not enjoy the consolation in these doleful hours of knowing that my *Holländer* had been completed, thus opening a prospect of success to our little circle of friends, his misery would prove almost impossible to bear. In my own great suffering I begged him at least to share the warmth of our fireplace and work in our room; he smiled at my foolhardiness in still trying to be of help to others, especially as my room scarcely afforded enough space for my wife and myself. Then one evening he came to see us and showed us speechlessly a letter from the then Minister of Education Villemain, in which he expressed in the warmest terms his great regret at having only just learned that such a distinguished scholar, whose brilliant and comprehensive collaboration in Didot's edition of the Greek classics had given him a share in a work that would contribute to the glory of the nation, should be in such bad health and difficult circumstances. Whereas unfortunately the amount of public funds at his disposal for furtherance of scholarly purposes only permitted him to offer the sum of five hundred francs, which he enclosed with apologies, he asked him to accept it as a token of esteem on the part of the French Government, adding that he would give earnest consideration as to how he might further improve his financial position. This struck us all, in addition to filling us with thankfulness on poor Lehrs' account, as a pure miracle; even on the assumption that Monsieur Villemain had been prompted by Didot, who by this means wanted to assuage his guilty conscience at having exploited Lehrs and also be freed from any necessity to help Lehrs, we nonetheless had to admit to ourselves, as was amply to be confirmed by my later experience, that such a kind, considerate and effective act on the part of a minister would have been impossible in German countries. Lehrs could now heat his room and work again, yet without being able to allay our fears as to the state of his health. When we left Paris the following year, the certainty that we would never see our faithful friend again made our parting particularly painful.

In my own great distress I was subjected to the annoyance of being forced to write more unpaid articles for the *Abendzeitung*, for my patron, Councillor Winkler, was still not able to come through with any binding assurance concerning the fate of my *Rienzi* in Dresden. In these circumstances I had to consider it as a stroke of luck that at last Halévy wrote another successful opera. Schlesinger arrived beaming with joy at the triumph of *La Reine de Chypre*, promising me heaven on earth if I would produce a vocal score and various other arrangements of music from this new star in the operatic firmament. So I was forced to sit down and do penance for having composed *Der fliegende Holländer* by fiddling with Halévy's opera. But the toil was easier for me this time. Apart from the well-founded hope of being at last rescued from my Paris exile, and thus being able to consider this last battle with poverty as the decisive one, the arrangement of Halévy's score was an incomparably more interesting piece of hack-work than the shameful labor at Donizetti's *Favorite*. After a long lapse of time I again visited the Opéra to hear this *Reine de Chypre*; although it gave me much to smile at, and although my eyes were open to the weakness of the whole genre and particularly to the elements of caricature in performance, I took an honest pleasure in recognizing once more the better side of Halévy, whose *La Juive* had taught me to like him and of whose powerful talents I had formed a very favorable opinion. At Schlesinger's prompting, I held forth at considerable length in an article for his magazine on this new work of Halévy. In it I particularly stressed the hope that the French school might not again allow the benefits obtained by the study of the German style to be lost by a relapse into the shallow Italian manner. I made this the opportunity to encourage the French school by pointedly referring to the special significance of Auber and his *La muette de Portici*, contrasting it with the overloaded melodies of Rossini, which often somewhat resembled solfège. In reading through the proofs of my article I found that this passage about Rossini had been omitted; M. Edouard Monnaie admitted to me, in his capacity as editor of a musical publication, that he had felt compelled to cut this part, for if I wanted to express my doubts about Rossini, I was free to do so in every other kind of journal, but not in one dedicated to the interests of music, as no such sentiments could be expressed there without appearing absurd. That I had singled out Auber for praise annoyed him a bit, it seemed, but he nonetheless let it stand. I learned a lot from this of permanent value concerning the decay of operatic music and its connection with the general decline of present-day French taste in artistic matters. I wrote another long article about the same opera for my dearly bought friend Winkler in Dresden, who was still unwilling to come forth with a definitive acceptance for my *Rienzi*. In this I particularly made fun of a mishap that had occurred to Kapellmeister Lachner.[1] The then director of the Munich theater, Küstner,[2] had commissioned a libretto for him from Saint-Georges[3] in Paris, with a view to doing something in a fatherly manner to further his protégé's career. This was the highest happiness a German composer could dream of. When Halévy's *Reine de Chypre* appeared, however, it turned out that it used the same subject as Lachner's supposedly original and meanwhile completed work. It mattered little that the libretto as delivered was really a pretty good one, for the value of the commission lay in the intention that the subject be transfigured by Lachner's music alone. Saint-Georges had, as a matter of fact, apparently altered the text he had sent to Munich somewhat, but only by the omission of several interesting features. Küstner's fury knew no bounds; Saint-Georges, on the other hand, was astounded that anyone would think he would get a text from him with exclusive rights for the German theater for so paltry a price as that at which the German commission had been contracted. As I had come to my own conclusions concerning the worth of French opera texts, and as nothing in the world would have induced me to set to music even the most effective piece by Scribe or Saint-Georges, this occurrence delighted me immensely, and in the best of spirits I indulged myself in writing about it for the readers of the *Abendzeitung* among whom, it is to be hoped, my future "friend" Lachner was not included.

A consequence of my work on Halévy's opera was a closer acquaintance with the composer himself, which occasioned many a spirited conversation with him. He was good-natured in his odd way and basically an unpretentious person who had unfortunately slackened off too early; Schlesinger in particular was beside himself at the man's laziness. After having looked through my vocal score, Halévy wanted to make several alterations for the purpose of simplification; but he didn't get on with the task; Schlesinger couldn't get the proofs back, found the whole edition thereby delayed, and was afraid the opera's success would be a thing of the past by the time the edition came out. So he got after me to go and see Halévy early in the morning at his flat and nail him down to make the alterations together with me. The first time, I arrived at ten o'clock in the morning, found him just out of bed, and was informed by him that he would really have to have his breakfast first. Following his invitation, I sat down to quite a copious repast; he seemed to like my company; friends began dropping in, and eventually Schlesinger as well, who exploded with rage at finding that Halévy was not busy doing the corrections he considered so urgent, all of which did not make the slightest impression on Halévy. In the best of moods, he contented himself with a complaint about his latest success, stating he had never enjoyed such peace and quiet as during the recent period when his operas were regularly failing, for after each failure he had been able to wash his hands of the work. He also didn't seem to have any idea why *La Reine de Chypre* in particular had been a success; he expressed the opinion that Schlesinger had engineered it on purpose, in order to be in a position to hound him. When Halévy began speaking a little German with me, one of the visitors expressed amazement, whereat Schlesinger explained that all Jews could speak German. Then Schlesinger was asked whether he was a Jew, to which he responded that he had been formerly but had become a Christian for the sake of his wife. The casual manner in which this subject was discussed astonished me pleasantly, for in Germany any such conversation would have been anxiously avoided for fear of offending the person concerned. But as we still did not get started on the corrections, Schlesinger made me promise to stay on Halévy's heels until we had gotten them done. The secret reason for Halévy's indifference to his successes became clear to me in the course of further conversation, when I learned that he was on the point of making a rich marriage. At first I was inclined to consider this a shameful confession that solely the desire to make a fortune could stimulate such talents as his in their youth, and it also seemed to account for the fact that so often such people could only produce one work surpassing the bounds of the ordinary; but in Halévy's attitude there was in addition a certain characteristic element of modesty regarding his achievements, in that he clearly didn't consider himself one of the great composers, and it was also an expression of his fundamental disbelief in the value of the works brought forth for the French theater of the time by successful authors inspired only by their ceaseless ambition. In him I met for the first time frankly admitted skepticism as to the true worth of all our modern creations in this problematic genre, a view, I have since observed, that serves all Jews as their pretext for participating in our artistic endeavors, although unfortunately none have expressed it with such modesty. Only once did Halévy speak to me with real earnestness, when, on the occasion of my eventual departure for Germany, he wished me the success he thought my works deserved. In the year 1860 I saw him again. I had learned that, while the Paris music critics were making the most acidulous remarks about the concerts I was then giving, Halévy had expressed his approval; this induced me to visit him in the Palais de l'Institut, of which he had been for some time permanent secretary. He seemed particularly curious to learn from me what my new theory of music was all about, as he had heard so much blather about it. For his part, he assured me, he had always heard my music simply as music, but with the difference that mine had generally struck him as very good. This gave rise to some jovial comments on my part, to which he responded in good humor, once again wishing me success in Paris; but this time he did so with less conviction than when bidding me farewell on my way to Germany, a fact I attributed to his doubts about the possibility of my succeeding in Paris at all. I took away from this final visit a depressing impression of the moral and aesthetic enervation that had overcome one of the last significant French composers, and I could not help sensing the dominant hypocrisy and even overt exploitation of the overall degeneracy in all those who could be considered as Halévy's successors.

While I was finishing this new piece of hack-work, all my thoughts were focused on a return to Germany, which now appeared to me in a wholly new and ideal light. I sought contact in various ways with the things that drew me back and filled me with longing for the return. My association with Lehrs had already been nurturing my former inclination to grapple seriously with matters, a tendency which my close contact with the theater had somewhat dissipated. Out of this came the basis for closer study of philosophical subjects. I had been astonished to hear the grave and virtuous Lehrs at times openly and quite as a matter of course expressing the profoundest doubts about any kind of life after death. He asserted that this skepticism, even though unspoken, had been the real incitement to the great acts of great men. The conclusion to which such a belief leads speedily dawned on me, yet without causing me any shudders of anxiety; on the contrary, I found in the idea a fascinating temptation to see boundless regions of meditation and knowledge opening before me, whereas previously I had skipped by them lightly. Lehrs dissuaded me from any efforts to study the Greek classics in the original, consoling me with the well-intentioned statement that, given the way I was and the music I had in me, I would find a way to extract knowledge from them even without grammar and dictionary; whereas Greek, if it were to be studied seriously, was no joke and could not be treated as a secondary matter.

Instead, I was strongly drawn toward a closer acquaintance with German history than I had been able to gain at school. I started with Raumer's[1] history of the Hohenstaufens; all the great figures in his book arose in my mind's eye before me, and I was particularly captivated by the figure of that brilliant emperor Friedrich II, whose fortunes aroused my deepest interest and stimulated me to a vain attempt to find appropriate artistic expression for them; on the other hand, the fate of his son Manfred struck me as a counterpart of comparable meaning and easier to handle dramatically. Accordingly, I drafted the plan for a vast five-act dramatic poem, which was intended also to be ideally suited for musical composition. My inspiration for the invention of a principal female character of highly romantic significance was derived from the historical fact that Manfred, during his flight through Apulia and the Abruzzi, having been betrayed at every turn, excommunicated by the church and deserted by all his followers, was received in Luceria with enthusiasm by the Saracens, who supported the youthful hero from victory to victory until he attained his final triumph. I was delighted even in those days to find in the German mind the capacity to transcend national barriers and appreciate purely human qualities, no matter in what guise they might present themselves, a faculty that seemed akin to the Greek spirit. Friedrich II embodied this quality at its highest; the fair-haired German of old Swabian stock, heir to the Norman realm of Sicily and Naples, who gave the Italian language its first polish and laid the groundwork for the evolution of knowledge and art where previously ecclesiastical fanaticism and feudal brutality had alone contended for dominance, a monarch who gathered at his court the poets and sages of Eastern countries and surrounded himself with the grace of the Arabian and Persian spirit and way of life, he who had been betrayed by the Roman clergy to the infidel on his crusade but who, to their fury, had nevertheless succeeded in bringing it to a close with a pact of peace with the Sultan, from whom he obtained a more generous grant of privileges to the Christians in Palestine than the bloodiest victory could have brought, this marvelous emperor who, excommunicated by that same church, struggled in vain against the raging bigotry of his century, seemed to me the highest embodiment of the German ideal. My poem concerned the fortunes of his favorite son, Manfred.

After the death of his elder brother, his father's empire had disintegrated, while he had been left under Papal auspices in nominal possession of the throne of Apulia. We see him first in Capua attended by a court in which the spirit of his great father has survived only in an enfeebled, almost degenerate form. In despair of ever restoring the imperial power of the Hohenstaufens, he seeks the solace of forgetfulness in poetry and song. Into this circle now enters a young Saracen woman straight from the East, who, invoking the memory of the pact binding East and West concluded by his great father, implores the son to uphold the imperial heritage, instead of sinking further into dejection. Her demeanor is always that of an inspired prophetess, and though the Prince immediately falls in love with her, she inspires him with a reverence that restrains his ardor. By a skillfully contrived flight, always leading him from afar, she snatches him not only from the clutches of rebellious Apulian nobles, but also from the dangers consequent upon a Papal edict deposing him from the throne; accompanied by only a few loyalists, she guides him across the wildest mountains, in which the spirit of Friedrich II, passing through the Abruzzi with his feudal train, appears one night to the exhausted son, to lead him to aforementioned Luceria. To this district, part of the Papal States, Friedrich had transferred by peace treaty the remnants of the former Saracen rulers, who had been wreaking havoc in the mountains of Sicily, by giving over this city to them completely, much to the fury of the Pope, and thereby providing himself with a loyal ally in the middle of treacherous enemy territory. There Fatima (as I named my heroine) with the help of trusted friends has prepared a reception for Manfred, who now, after the Papal viceroy has been done away with in a rebellion, steps through the gate into the city, is recognized by the entire populace as the son of the beloved emperor and, amidst the wildest enthusiasm, is placed at their head to lead them in battle against the enemies of their deceased benefactor. While Manfred now advances from victory to victory, winning back all of Apulia, the relationship I had invented between him, in his ever more tempestuous passion, and the strange heroine has remained nonetheless the tragic focal point of the action. She is herself the product of the love uniting the great emperor with a noble Saracen lady; her mother dispatched her from her deathbed to Manfred with the prophecy that she will work wonders on his behalf provided she never yields to his love (whether Fatima should ever realize that she was Manfred's sister was something I left unresolved in the scenario). True to her vow, she has been careful to show herself to Manfred only at critical moments and solely in such a way as to remain unapproachable; and now when she at last witnesses his coronation in Naples, she considers her work done and decides to slip secretly away from the newly anointed king, the better to meditate in the solitude of her distant home on the success of her mission. A childhood Saracen friend Nurreddin, to whose help she has chiefly owed her success in rescuing Manfred, is to be her only companion in the flight. This man, to whom she has been promised since earliest childhood, who loves her with consuming fire and to whom she has now resigned herself to belong, is carried away by raging jealousy when, shortly before their secret departure, she pays a final visit to the slumbering king in order to bless him, thus giving an apparent indication of infidelity to her betrothed. The last farewell look that Fatima casts from the distance at the young monarch, upon his return from the coronation, inflames the jealous lover to wreak instant vengeance for the supposed loss of his honor; he strikes the prophetess down, whereupon she thanks him with a parting smile for having delivered her from an unbearable existence. At the sight of her corpse, Manfred recognizes that happiness has deserted him forever.

I had festooned this subject with many opulent scenes and tangled situations, so that in its execution I thought I could count on it to be rather convincing, effective and interesting, particularly in comparison with other dramatic subjects I had known of a similar type. Yet, I couldn't really bring myself to get started seriously in working it out; on the contrary, I was suddenly gripped by a quite different subject. This came to me quite by chance through a folk book about the Venusberg.

All I regarded as inherently German had attracted me with ever-increasing force and impelled me to look for its deepest meaning with enthusiastic longing, and here I suddenly found it in the simple re-telling of the legend, based on the ancient, well-known ballad of Tannhäuser. Of course I already knew the basic outlines of the story from Tieck's version in his *Phantasus*; yet his conception of the subject had led me back in the direction of fantasy, as evoked for me by Hoffmann, and I had in no way felt myself tempted to attempt an adaptation of the material for dramatic purposes. The element in the folk book which made such an impact on me was the connection, if only fleetingly set forth, of Tannhäuser with the contest of song at the Wartburg. I was also familiar with this through Hoffmann's story in his *Serapionsbrüder*; but I felt that the writer had a distorted view of this old material and I now wanted to form a more authentic picture of this attractive legend for myself. Then Lehrs brought me the annual proceedings of the

Königsberg Germanic Society, which included Lukas's[1] critical study of the "Wartburg War", even giving the text in the original language. Although I could use virtually none of the material from this authentic version for my own purposes, it nonetheless showed me the German Middle Ages in a significant coloring I had not yet dreamed of.

In the same volume I also found, as a continuation of the Wartburg poem, a piece of criticism about the poem *Lohengrin*, together with a lengthy narrative of the principal contents of this rambling epic.

This was a completely new world for me, and for the moment I was unable to find the form in which to master the Lohengrin material; yet the image lived inextinguishably within me from then on, so that when I later became acquainted with various ramifications of the Lohengrin legend, I could visualize it with a clarity equal to that of my picture of Tannhäuser when I first began to think about that subject.

Under these influences my longing to get back to Germany as quickly as possible and enjoy the homeland I hoped to win in the leisure necessary for creative work was greatly intensified. I still could not think of getting started on the work I wanted to do; the struggle with the sordid necessities of life kept me in Paris. While doing this, I nonetheless found a way to employ my talents in a more congenial manner. During one of my early trips to Prague, I had made the acquaintance of a certain Herr Dessauer,[2] a Jewish musician and composer not devoid of talent, and who in fact achieved a certain reputation, but who was best known to his friends for his hypochondria. He had prospered and now was under Schlesinger's wing, to the extent of the latter seriously trying to get him a commission from the Opéra. Dessauer had come across my poem for *Der fliegende Holländer* and now insisted that I should draft a similar plot for him, as M. Léon Pillet's *Vaisseau fantôme* had already been allocated to his chorusmaster, M. Dietsch,[3] for him to set to music. Dessauer had been promised a similar commission by Pillet, and now promised me two hundred francs if I would cede to him a comparable plot suitable for his hypochondriacal temperament. I rummaged around in my recollections of Hoffmann and easily came upon the idea of adapting his *Die Bergwerke von Falun*. I succeeded in moulding this attractive and singular material precisely as I wished, and Dessauer too was convinced that this subject was worthy of being set to music by him; all the greater, therefore, was his disappointment when Pillet rejected our draft on the grounds that the staging, particularly for the second act, would prove too onerous, and would have caused insuperable difficulties for the ballet that had to follow it every time. Then Dessauer wanted me to write a text for an oratorio on Mary Magdalene. As on the day he revealed this desire to me he seemed to be experiencing a particularly severe bout of hypochondria, telling me that he had seen his own head lying beside his bed that morning, I thought it well not to reject his request; but I asked him to give me some time to think it over, and I have taken my time right down to the present day.

Amid such diversions that winter finally ebbed away, while slowly, and very tryingly for my patience, my prospects for Germany neared a more satisfactory state. I had been corresponding uninterruptedly with Dresden about *Rienzi* and finally had found there in the person of the chorusmaster Fischer[1] a decent, honest and well-intentioned man, who provided me with reliable and confidence-building communications concerning the state of my application. After being advised at the outset of January 1842 that there would be some further delay, I at last received news that *Rienzi* was to be ready for production by no later than the end of February, which alarmed me greatly as I did not believe I could arrange to get there that soon. But this communication was soon revoked, and the trustworthy Fischer notified me that the performance of my opera had necessarily been postponed until the autumn of the current year. I knew, of course, that it would never see the light of day if I were not in Dresden myself. When eventually in March Count Redern,[2] director of the Royal Opera in Berlin, notified me that *Der fliegende Holländer* had been accepted for performance there, I thought I had sufficient grounds to get back to Germany as soon as possible.

German theater managers were, I had already found, of disparate views about *Der fliegende Holländer*. Relying on the subject itself, which had so pleased the director of the Paris Opéra, I had sent the poem to the director of the Leipzig theater, Ringelhardt, well known to me from earlier days. But ever since *Das Liebesverbot* he had been nursing an unconcealed dislike for me. As this time he could not charge me with "frivolity" in the choice of my subject, he now found fault with its gloomy solemnity and refused to accept it. As I had gotten to know Councillor Küstner, the director of the Munich Court Theater, when he was in Paris ordering the text for *La Reine de Chypre*, I also sent the libretto of *Der fliegende Holländer* to him with the same request. Assuring me that it was not suitable for German stage conditions and did not correspond to the taste of the German public, he too sent it back to me. Since he had commissioned a French libretto for Munich, I could easily figure out what he meant. When the score had finally been completed I sent it, together with an accompanying letter to Count Redern, to

Meyerbeer in Berlin, asking him, inasmuch as his efforts on my behalf in Paris had proved unavailing despite the best will in the world, to be kind enough to use his influence in Berlin in favor of my work. I was genuinely astonished and delighted at the prompt acceptance of my work two months later, accompanied by highly gratifying assurances by the Count, and I saw in it proof of Meyerbeer's sincere and energetic interest in me. But amazingly enough, I soon found out upon my return to Germany that Count Redern had been for some time on the point of resigning his position as director at the Berlin Opera, and that Herr Küstner from Munich had already been chosen as his eventual successor; this meant that Count Redern's acceptance, while very polite, had by no means been seriously intended, for its realization depended not upon him but upon his successor. The upshot of all this will soon be seen.

The circumstance that facilitated my long-desired return to Germany, now justified by my good prospects, was the tardily awakened interest in my situation on the part of the wealthier members of my family. Just as M. Didot may have had reasons of his own for applying to Minister Villemain on behalf of Lehrs, my Paris brother-in-law Avenarius now felt himself impelled by the realization of the nature of my struggle against poverty to surprise me with unexpected assistance through his intervention in my favor with my sister Luise. On December 26th of the waning year 1841, I was the one who came home to Minna carrying a goose, and this goose contained a five-hundred franc note in its beak, which had been transmitted to me through Avenarius by a rich merchant named Schletter[1] at the instigation of his friend, my sister Luise. This welcome addition to our extremely straitened domestic resources might not in itself have sufficed to put me in high good humor had I not clearly seen the prospect of escaping completely from my situation in Paris which this gift now clearly opened for us. Since I already had two clear acceptances for my works from major German theaters, I now thought I could seriously get after my brother-in-law Friedrich Brockhaus, who the year before, when I had turned to him in direst need, had rejected my appeal on the grounds of "disagreement with your direction in life", with greater success for the financing of my return trip. In this I was not mistaken; when the time approached, I got my traveling money from this source.

With these prospects and my situation thus improved, I found myself spending the second half of the winter of 1841-2, from the New Year onwards, in high spirits, which often benefited the small circle of people who gathered around me through my relationship with Avenarius.

Minna and I spent many pleasant evenings with this family and others, among whom I have pleasant recollections of Herr Kühne, headmaster of a private school, and his wife. I contributed to the merriment of these evenings not only by my conversation but also by my good-natured willingness to improvise music on the piano for everyone to dance by, and these soirées were such a success that I began to enjoy in this respect an almost burdensome popularity.

At last the hour of redemption came; the day arrived on which, as I devoutly hoped, I would be turning my back on Paris forever. It was April 7th; Paris was already festooned with the first luxuriant buddings of spring. In front of our windows, which throughout the winter had looked out upon a bleak and desolate garden, trees were greening and birds singing. Great, even overwhelming was our emotion at parting from our poor, faithful friends Anders, Lehrs, and Kietz. Anders seemed destined for imminent death, for his health had been severely shaken, and he was already of advanced age. As to the condition of Lehrs, there could be, as aforementioned, no illusions, and it was dreadful for me, during the two and a half years of struggle Paris had cost me, to see the ravages wrought by poverty among these good, noble, and to some extent even distinguished men. Kietz, about whose future I was concerned more on grounds of morals than of health, moved us once again by his boundless and almost child-like good nature. He concluded, in fact, that I couldn't possibly have enough travel money, and pressed upon me, despite all protestations to the contrary, yet another five-franc piece, just about the substance of his own fortune at that moment; he also stuffed a package of good French snuff for me into the side compartment of the coach in which we at last were borne away across the boulevards and to the city gates, of which we this time saw nothing, for our eyes were blinded with tears.

PART TWO

1842–50

The journey from Paris to Dresden in that era took five full days, including the intervening nights. At the German border near Forbach we ran into snow and raw weather, a very inhospitable greeting after the springtime we had enjoyed in Paris. And indeed, as we continued our journey through our native land, we found much that disconcerted us, and it occurred to me that the French travelers who, upon their return from Germany, always unbuttoned their coats and breathed more freely after stepping on French soil, as if coming from winter into summer, were not entirely wrong, for we were compelled to do the precise opposite to protect ourselves against the palpable drop in temperature by the most ingenious use of our clothing. But our ordeal by the bad weather reached its apogee when we later, on the road from Frankfurt to Leipzig, fell into the stream of travelers on their way to the Leipzig Easter Fair, who so overburdened the mail coach facilities that for two days and a night, amid unceasing storm, snow, and rain, we had to change from one decrepit relief carriage to another, thereby turning our journey into an adventure almost comparable to our previous voyage at sea. The one real ray of light was our view of the Wartburg, past which we drove during the only sunlit hour of this journey. The sight of the mountain-top castle, clearly visible at great distance to those approaching from the Fulda side, stirred me very warmly. I at once mentally christened a neighboring ridge the "Hörselberg" and thus constructed, as we drove through the valley, the scene for the third act of my *Tannhäuser* in an image so clear that I could always recall it vividly and later was able to give Despléchin,[1] the Paris scene-painter, precise instructions to execute my design. Whereas I had already sensed the deep significance of the fact that I had crossed the legendary German Rhine for the first time on my way home from Paris, it seemed a particularly prophetic indication that I should first sight the Wartburg, so rich in history and myth, at precisely this moment. The view so warmed my heart against wind and weather, Jews and Leipzig Fair, that I at last arrived safe and sound, together with my poor battered and frozen wife, on April 12th 1842, in that same city of Dresden which I had last seen upon that melancholy separation from Minna, when I departed for my exile in the North.

We put up at the City of Gotha inn. The city in which I had spent such meaningful years of childhood and boyhood made a chilling and deadening impression on me under the influence of the gloomy and raw weather; everything that might remind me of my youth seemed to have passed away; there was no hospitable home to receive us; we found my wife's parents living in cramped, dingy quarters and in pitiful shape financially; we were at once obliged to look around for a small place for ourselves, finding it eventually in the Töpfergasse at a rental of seven talers per month. After making the necessary round of polite visits in connection with *Rienzi* and making provision for Minna during my short absence, I went off on April 15th to Leipzig, where I saw my mother and sisters for the first time in six years. During what had been such a fateful period for me, my mother's domestic situation had undergone a substantial transformation as a result of Rosalie's death; she was now living in a friendly and spacious apartment near the Brockhaus family, free of all those household cares to which she had devoted so many anxious years in caring for a large family. The energetic and even harsh elements in her character had yielded completely to the innate cheerfulness with which she now participated in the family doings of her married daughters. She owed the blissful calm of this happy old age mainly to the affectionate consideration of her son-in-law, Friedrich Brockhaus, to whom I also expressed my heartfelt gratitude for what he had done. She gave a start of astonished pleasure as she saw me enter her room unannounced; any bitterness that had ever existed between us had vanished, and her sole complaint was that she could not put me up in her flat in place of my brother Julius, the unsuccessful goldsmith, who was not much of a companion for her. She had faith in the success of my undertakings and felt herself buttressed in these hopes by the last prophecies of the gentle Rosalie, who had spoken of me favorably shortly before her death.

For the present, however, I stayed only a few days in Leipzig, in order to proceed right away to Berlin, where I had to come to some agreement with Count von Redern about the production of *Der fliegende Holländer*. As previously stated, I learned immediately upon arrival that the count was on the verge of retiring, and accordingly I was referred by him for any arrangements that had to be made to the new director, Herr von Küstner, who had not yet reached Berlin. I suddenly grasped the significance of this strange circumstance and realized that, as far as my Berlin affairs were concerned, I could just as well have stayed in Paris. This impression was more or less confirmed by my visit to Meyerbeer; I found that he considered my trip to Berlin a sign of over-zealousness. Yet he was friendly and well-disposed to me, regretting only that he was "about to leave", a condition in which I invariably found him later, whenever I visited him in Berlin. Mendelssohn was also in Berlin at this time, to which he had been summoned by the King of Prussia as one of the general music directors. As I had already introduced myself to him in Leipzig, I looked him up as well; from him I learned that he did not believe his work would prosper in Berlin and would prefer to go back to Leipzig. I did not inquire about the fate of the score of my symphony, performed during my youthful years in Leipzig, which I had pressed upon him so long ago; and in turn, he gave no indication whatever of remembering this singular gift. In his luxurious domestic surroundings he struck me as being somewhat cold, yet it was not so much that he rebuffed me, but rather that I slipped away from him. I also visited Rellstab,[1] to whom I had a letter of introduction from his trusty publisher, my brother-in-law Brockhaus. Here I did not encounter such smoothness, but rather felt rebuffed, which was doubtless his intention, as he showed not the slightest sign that it could ever even occur to him to become interested in me. I began to feel miserable in Berlin; I could almost have wished old Councillor Cerf back again. Despite the ugly times I had experienced here years before, I had at least come upon one person who, notwithstanding his blunt manner, had accorded me true friendliness and solicitude; I tried in vain to summon up that Berlin through which I had meandered, with all the ardor of youth, together with Laube. Now that I had gotten to know London and particularly Paris, this city, in which empty lengths pretended to grandeur, had a depressing effect, and I told myself that if I got nowhere in life, I would rather fail in Paris than in Berlin after all.

Returning from this utterly fruitless mission, I stopped off again for several days in Leipzig, staying this time with my brother-in-law Hermann Brockhaus, now Professor of Oriental Languages at the University. His family had been further swelled by the birth of two daughters, and the atmosphere of unruffled content, transfigured by mental alertness and casual yet lively participation in all activities belonging to an elevated way of life, greatly moved me, homeless as I was and driven from pillar to post. One evening, after my sister had gently put her well-behaved children to bed and we had gathered in the large and richly stocked library for the evening meal and an intimate chat, I broke down completely and began crying; it seemed as if my kindly sister, who had known me five years before in the bitter troubles of my early married life, understood me. And then, at the suggestion of Hermann Brockhaus, my family got together and offered me a loan to tide me over the waiting period until the performance of *Rienzi* in Dresden. This was done, I was told, out of a sense of obligation and I was not to have any compunctions about accepting it. The loan consisted of two hundred talers, to be paid to me in monthly installments for half a year. As I had no other plausible source of income for this period, it was perfectly clear that Minna's talent for domestic economies would be taxed to the utmost; but still it would be possible to get by, and I could go back to Dresden feeling entirely satisfied. At the home of my relatives I had played and sung the *Holländer* for the first time connectedly; it appeared to me to arouse considerable interest, and when my sister Luise later saw an actual performance of the work in Dresden, she complained that in many places she did not receive the impression that I had made in that earlier performance. I also looked up my old friend Apel again; the poor man had gone completely blind, yet surprised me by his cheerfulness and contentedness with his condition, whereby he deprived me once and for all of any reason to pity him; when he asserted he remembered very well the blue coat I was wearing, despite the fact I was wearing a brown one, I thought it best not to argue the point, and left Leipzig in a state of amazement at finding everyone there so happy and placid.

When I got back to Dresden on April 26th, I had to get busy again on my own affairs. Here I began to be increasingly stimulated by my dealings with people I needed to enlist for the performance of *Rienzi*. Admittedly, my meetings with the General Director of the theater, Herr von Lüttichau, as well as with Kapellmeister Reissiger, who were both amazed to see me turn up in Dresden, left me chilled and pessimistic, and even my patron, Councillor Winkler, whom I had bombarded so heavily with letters, would have preferred me to remain in Paris. As I had previously experienced, and have found ever since, advocacy for my cause came from the lower ranks, never from the upper regions; thus, I was first agreeably encouraged by the overwhelmingly cordial reception accorded me by the old chorusmaster Wilhelm Fischer, whom I had never met before but who had been the only one to have familiarized himself with my score, seriously hoping for the success of my opera and working energetically to secure its acceptance. When I first stepped across the threshold of his room and told him my name, he rushed forward to embrace me with a loud cry of delight, and in a second I was transported into an atmosphere of hope. In addition to him, I found in the actor Ferdinand Heine and his family an immediate source of heartily cordial, even deeply committed friendship. As a matter of fact, I had known him since childhood; he had been part of a small group of young people my stepfather Geyer liked to gather around him. Apart from a rather negligible talent for drawing, it was principally his social talents that had gained him access to our intimate family circle. Very small and

slight of build, he had been nicknamed "Davidchen" by my stepfather
and as such was included in those larger parties in which, as I have
already mentioned, even Carl Maria von Weber used to take a jocular
part, particularly in the merry excursions into the nearby countryside.
Belonging to the traditional "good" school of acting, he had become a
valued though not prominent member of the Dresden theater troupe;
he had all the makings of a good stage director but never quite knew
how to persuade the management to entrust him with this function. His
talents found other expression only in the field of costume design; in
this capacity he was included in the discussions concerning the
performance of *Rienzi* and thus found himself in the position of busying
himself with the work of an up and coming member of a family in whose
company he had spent many pleasant days as a youth. He took me into
his own family at once, and we two homeless people there found native
ground under us again for the first time in the homeland which had
become so completely strange to us. We spent most of our evenings at
Heine's house, together with Papa Fischer, and along with much hopeful
talk enjoyed the potatoes with herring, the staples of most such meals.

Schröder-Devrient was away on vacation; Tichatschek, who was also
about to go away for a time, was only available for a quick greeting and
a hasty look at some of his part in *Rienzi*. His brisk and lively nature,
together with his glorious voice and great musical ability, lent special
weight to his assurance that he was delighted by his role in *Rienzi*. Heine
also let me know that the prospect of having so many new costumes,
and especially new silver armor, had made the role particularly attractive
to Tichatschek, and that I could certainly count on him under any
circumstances. And so I could get started at once in preparing for the
rehearsals, which were to begin late in the summer after the principal
singers had returned from vacation. I had to make special efforts to oblige
my worried friend Fischer by agreeing to cuts in the overly voluminous
score. His intentions in the matter were so honest that I gladly sat down
with him to this wearisome task. On an old piano in the rehearsal room
of the Court Theater I played and sang my score to the astonished man
with such violent energy that he was ready to consign the piano to the
scrap heap, while remaining concerned only about the state of my lungs.
Amid hearty laughter we soon gave up any attempt to agree on the cuts,
for wherever he felt one was appropriate I would convince him with
irresistible eloquence that precisely this part was the core of the whole
work. He plunged head over heels together with me into the vast,
resounding chaos, against which he could only urge upon me the

testimony of his pocket-watch, the accuracy of which I eventually also disputed. With a light heart I surrendered to him as booty the big pantomime and most of the ballet in the second act, whereby I thought we had saved a whole half hour. And so the whole monstrous thing was handed over with our blessing to the copyists to write out the parts: everything else would take care of itself.

We then began looking around to see what we could do with the summer; I decided to spend several months in Teplitz, the goal of my first childhood excursions, whose pure air and waters would, I thought, simultaneously help restore Minna's shattered health. But before we could carry out this plan, the need to find out what was to be done with *Der fliegende Holländer* cost me a few days' trip to Leipzig. I went there on May 5th to speak to Councillor Küstner, the new Berlin intendant, whose recent arrival in Leipzig had been reported to me. He was now in the curious position of being required to produce in Berlin the same opera he had rejected for Munich, because it had been accepted by his predecessor. He promised to think over what to do in this unusual case. To learn the results of Küstner's deliberations, I decided to go and see him again, this time in Berlin on June 2nd; but in Leipzig, on my way, I found a letter in which he requested me to be patient for a while in regard to the whole matter. Being in the vicinity of Halle, I took advantage of the occasion to pay a visit to my eldest brother Albert. I was much grieved and depressed to find the poor fellow, whom I was obliged to credit with elevated aspirations and an authentic talent for dramatic singing, in such highly unworthy and narrow circumstances as those the theater in Halle afforded to him and his family. The recognition of such conditions, in which I had nearly been ensnared myself, repelled me unspeakably. But it was still more distressing to hear my brother speak of these conditions in a way that betrayed to me the hopeless resignation with which he had surrendered to them. There was only one encouraging aspect, namely the child-like nature and already remarkably beautiful singing voice of my brother's then fifteen-year-old stepdaughter Johanna,[1] who sang for me in a particularly moving manner Spohr's song *Rose, wie bist du so schön.*

From there I went back to Dresden to begin at last, together with Minna and one of her sisters, a pleasant trip in superb weather to Teplitz, where we arrived on June 9th and took up scanty lodgings at the Oak Inn in Schönau. Here we were soon joined by my mother, who paid her yearly visit to the warm baths all the more gladly in the knowledge of finding me there. Though she had long nursed a stubborn prejudice against Minna because of what she considered my far too early marriage, my mother now came to realize Minna's domestic abilities and thus had ample grounds for learning to appreciate and become fond of my companion in the Paris sufferings. I enjoyed my mother's company, although her vagaries occasionally demanded a good deal of tolerance, and what particularly delighted me was the great vivacity of her almost child-like imagination, which she had retained to such a degree that one morning she complained that my account of the Tannhäuser legend on the previous evening had given her a whole night of pleasant but exhausting sleeplessness.

Immediately after I had managed to do something for Kietz, who had remained behind in Paris in misery, by writing on his behalf to Schletter, the wealthy Leipzig patron of the arts, and then to arrange medical care for Minna as well as shore up my own precarious financial position somewhat, I set off in my old boyish way on several days' hiking over the Bohemian mountains. I intended to work out my treatment of the "Venusberg" material amid the agreeable sensations of such an outing. This tempted me to take lodgings for several days on the romantically situated Schreckenstein near Aussig, where I obtained a tiny room in which a bed of straw was made up for me to sleep on at night. Daily ascent of the Wostrai, the highest peak in the area, revivified me, and the fantastic loneliness excited my youthful spirits in such a way that, on one moonlit night, I clambered around the ruins of the Schreckenstein castle wrapped only in a sheet, thereby hoping to provide myself with the ghost that was otherwise lacking, and delighting myself with the thought that some nearby wanderer might see me and be terrified. On this trip I wrote down in my pocket-book a comprehensive draft of a three-act opera to be called *Der Venusberg*, and subsequently wrote the complete libretto entirely in accordance with this sketch. One day, while climbing the Wostrai, I was astonished, upon rounding a corner into a valley, to hear a joyful dance tune being piped by a shepherd from above on the hill. At once I found myself amid the chorus of pilgrims, wending their way past the shepherd in the valley. But later I could not for the life of me recall the melody he had been piping, and so I had to help myself out in the usual way. Enriched by this booty, I went back to Teplitz in high good humor and in the best of health, where news of the impending return of Tichatschek and Schröder-Devrient impelled me to leave once more for Dresden, not so much to avoid missing any of the early rehearsals for *Rienzi* as to make certain that the management would not get the idea of replacing it with another work. I left Minna behind for a time in the company of my mother and reached Dresden on July 18th.

I took up residence in an odd little house, since demolished, looking out on the Maximiliansallee and immediately got in touch with the principal singers in the opera. My old enthusiasm for Schröder-Devrient was rekindled when I saw her now perform again in the opera house. It had a curious effect on me to hear her in Grétry's *Barbe-bleue*, as I could not help but recall that this opera was the first theatrical piece I ever saw, at the age of five and likewise in Dresden, and retained all the wondrous impressions of it. Childhood memories came alive, and I remembered that it had been Bluebeard's aria, "Ha! Faithless wife! The door ajar!", that I had often sung at home with tremendous verve, much to the amusement of my family, with a paper helmet on my head. My friend Heine still remembered it. The rest of the operatic performances did not make a very favorable impression on me; I particularly missed the sonorous tone of the full strength of the Paris strings. I noticed that at the opening of the fine new theater no provision had been made to increase the number of strings in proportion to the increase in the size of the auditorium. In this, as well as in the equipment for the stage itself, I sensed a certain poverty in German theatrical efforts, most evident whenever operas from the Parisian repertory were given, in feeble translations to boot. Although I had already felt profound dissatisfaction with this kind of opera during my Paris days, the feelings that had formerly driven me from the German theaters to Paris now came back to me, so that I again felt degraded, and nursed in my innermost being a contempt already so strong that I didn't even want to think of binding myself permanently even to one of the best German opera houses, but rather wondered to myself sadly what I could plausibly do to get somewhere in a world in which I teetered between disgust and ambition.

In this mood, it was the sympathy I received from some exceptionally gifted individuals which made me strong enough to overcome my scruples. This was true above all of that marvelous artist Mme Schröder-Devrient, and indeed to work with her one day had been the most burning ambition of my youth. Of course, quite a few years had elapsed since my youthful impression of her had been formed. Her looks were already such as to prompt Berlioz, who came to Dresden in the following winter, to pronounce the unfavorable verdict, in a review published in Paris, that her somewhat "maternal" embonpoint made her unsuitable for youthful parts, especially those requiring male attire as in *Rienzi*, and tended to overtax the imagination of the public. Her voice, which had never been a truly outstanding organ, was often not up to par, and while singing she was obliged consistently to drag the tempo a bit. But beyond these physical disadvantages, her achievements were diminished by the fact that her repertory consisted of a limited number of leading roles, all of which she had sung so frequently by now that there was a certain sameness in the carefully calculated effects, often to the point of mannerism, which at times, given her predilection for exaggeration, bordered on the embarrassing. While I could not fail to see all this, I was, after all, more qualified than anyone else to look beyond these weaknesses to the grand and incomparable element still present in her performances and grasp it with a clarity that never failed to give me profound delight; and it really required only the stimulus of such excitements as her exceptionally eventful life continued to afford her to arouse in this artist the full creative powers of her prime; I was later to receive the most uplifting demonstrations of this faculty. Yet my ardor was cooled when I reflected on the destructive influence of the theater world on the once assuredly great and noble character of this artist. Out of the same mouth that gave forth the most inspired dramatic musical utterances I had to listen to just about the same language one hears, with few exceptions, from all leading ladies of the theater. She could not endure rivals in the public favor, whether by the mere gift of a beautiful voice or even simple physical attributes; far from receding to the dignified resignation that befits a great artist, her jealousy increased over the years in a most painful manner. For the time being I could take note of this without suffering from it. The fact that she did not learn music easily and had great trouble studying a new part caused much more difficulty and provided many arduous hours for a composer trying to familiarize her with his work. That she was slow to grasp a new role was particularly evident in the case of the part of Adriano in *Rienzi* and caused her frustrations that later made great trouble for me.

Whereas with her it was a question of handling a great and touchy nature tactfully, I had a delightfully easy time with Tichatschek, who for all his extraordinary gifts was a bit innocent and superficial. He didn't learn his roles very well by heart, because he could sight-read the most complicated music and thus concluded that any preliminary study was a waste of time, whereas for most other singers learning to hit the notes was the sum of their study. If he had sung a part often enough at rehearsals to impress it on his memory to some extent, the rest of it, particularly everything pertaining to vocal art or dramatic delivery, was supposed to take care of itself. For this reason any errors written into the text of his part were irremediably learned by heart, and he would sing the wrong words with the same palpable verve as the correct ones. He would cheerfully dismiss any suggestions or attempts to interpret the text with the assertion: "Everything will turn out all right." And in fact I soon resigned myself completely to abandoning all efforts to tax his intellectual ability in the interpretation of my hero, and I was amply rewarded for this by the most heart-warming enthusiasm with which he approached his superb role, as well as by the irresistible appeal of his glorious voice.

Apart from the artists cast in the two leading roles, I had only mediocre forces to work with. But there was good will in abundance, and to induce even Kapellmeister Reissiger to hold regular piano rehearsals, I hit upon an ingenious scheme. He had complained to me of the difficulty he had always encountered in finding a good opera libretto and thus considered it very reasonable of me that I seemed accustomed to write them for myself. He had, as he said, neglected to do likewise for himself in his youth, and yet this was the only thing keeping him back from success as a dramatic composer, for, as he was confident I would admit, he had "a lot of melody"; but it seemed that somehow this was not enough to enthuse his singers sufficiently, inasmuch as he had to suffer through Schröder-Devrient singing the closing passage of his *Adèle de Foix* in a lacklustre manner, whereas in the comparable scene in Bellini's *Romeo and Juliet* she always sent the audience into transports of ecstasy. It just had to be a question of the material. And so I promised him immediately to deliver an opera text in which he could introduce this and similar melodies with the most splendid effect. He accepted this offer with immense joy; and I dug out the old draft of *Die hohe Braut*, adapted from König's novel, which I had once sent to Scribe, for versification on behalf of Reissiger. I guaranteed to bring him a page of verse at each piano rehearsal; and I fulfilled this obligation punctiliously, until the libretto was fully completed. I was thus highly astonished to learn some time later that Reissiger had requested yet another opera text, this one written by an actor called Kriethe[1] and entitled *Der Schiffbruch der Medusa*. I then found out that Frau Reissiger was very suspicious of my willingness to provide her husband with an operatic text. While they both thought my libretto was good enough and potentially effective, they concluded there must be some kind of snare in it, to avoid which the greatest circumspection was required. Thus it came that I got my libretto back and was subsequently able to hand it over to my old friend Kittl[2] in

Prague, who set it to music under the title *Die Franzosen vor Nizza*, and as I gathered, though I never heard his work myself, got it performed frequently and to great applause; all this spurred a critic in Prague to inform me that this text was proof of my true calling as a librettist, and that I was only going astray in attempting also to compose; whereas Laube asserted on the basis of my *Tannhäuser* that it was my bad luck not to have found a practised dramatist to produce a decent text for my music.

For the moment, this effort produced the desired result; Reissiger kept his nose to the grindstone with my *Rienzi*. Even more than my verses, what encouraged him was the growing interest of the singers, above all Tichatschek's genuine enthusiasm. The tenor, usually all too ready to abandon the rehearsals at the piano in the theater foyer to go off on a hunting expedition, soon turned the rehearsals for *Rienzi* into little celebrations, to which he invariably came with eyes beaming and in the most expansive mood. I soon felt myself in a state of constant exhilaration: certain special passages were invariably greeted by the singers with acclamation, and one group number in the third act, which later unfortunately had to be cut from all performances owing to the length, even became a source of income for me. For Tichatschek maintained its B minor was so lovely that everybody should pay something for it each time it was rehearsed, and he plunked down a silver coin with an invitation to the other singers to do likewise; everyone ponied up in good humor; whenever we got to it during the rehearsals the shout went up "Here comes the new groschen passage", and Mme Schröder-Devrient, when she too was obliged to open her purse, insisted that this work would bankrupt her completely. I was handed this curious gratuity conscientiously every time, and nobody guessed that this jocular honorarium constituted welcome help in putting a square meal on our table.

At the beginning of August, Minna had also returned from Teplitz to Dresden, accompanied for a time by my mother. We lived frugally in a chilly apartment, hopefully waiting for the deliverance that seemed so long delayed. Amid frequent interruptions caused by the fluctuating and shaky repertory of the German operatic theater, the months of August and September were consumed in the preparations for my work, and it was not until October that these reached that point from which an actual production would conclusively be forthcoming. With the commencement of orchestral and group rehearsals came a universally shared belief that a great success was in store. The dress rehearsals created a perfectly intoxicating effect. When we first performed the opening scene of the second act, with the arrival of the messengers of peace, on stage with sets and costumes, there was a general outburst of emotion, and even Schröder-Devrient, who was dissatisfied with her part because she was unable to be the heroine of the drama in it, could only respond to me in a voice stifled by her tears. I believe the whole crew of the theater, right down to the humblest employees, loved me as if I were some sort of miracle, and I am probably not far wrong in attributing much of this to sympathy for and interest in a young man whose difficult circumstances were all well known to them, and who now was to step from utter obscurity into sudden glory. During the interval at the final dress rehearsal, while members of the cast had dispersed to calm their exhausted nerves by getting something to eat, I remained seated on a pile of boards on the stage, in order not to let anyone notice my embarrassment at being unable to afford to do the same. A crippled Italian singer, who had a small part in the opera, seemed to notice this and generously brought me a glass of wine and a piece of bread. I was sorry to be obliged in the course of time to take his little role away from him, for its loss provoked such ill-treatment at the hands of his wife that by conjugal tyranny he was driven to join the ranks of my enemies. After my flight from Dresden in 1849, I learned that I had been denounced to the police for alleged complicity in the uprising in the city by this very same singer, and I recalled at once this little meal during the dress rehearsal for *Rienzi*, thinking that I had thus been punished for my guilt in having gotten him into trouble with his wife.

The frame of mind in which I looked forward to the first performance of my work compares with nothing I have since experienced and with nothing that preceded it. It was shared by my gentle sister Klara, who had come to visit us in Dresden from Chemnitz, where she was leading a straitened life financially. The poor woman, whose unquestionable artistic capacities had withered so early, and who now had to drag herself along through life as a wife and mother in trivial domesticity, gained a new lease of life through her heartfelt interest in my growing success. Together with her and the worthy chorusmaster Fischer, we spent our evenings with the Heine family, always with potatoes and herring, but in the most exalted mood. On the night before the first performance we crowned our happiness with a bowl of punch. Laughing and crying like little children we parted late that night to sleep away the time separating us from the day that was to bring such a decisive and clearly anticipated turn of events. On the morning of October 20th 1842, when I had sworn to myself not to bother any of the singers again with a visit, I nonetheless came across one of them, the somewhat stiff and philistine Herr Risse, a rather boring but competent singer who was taking one of the less significant basso parts in my opera. It was a rather cool but gloriously bright, sunny day that looked down upon us after the dank weather preceding it. Without a word this odd fellow stopped suddenly in front of me, saluted me and stood motionless, as if bewitched, gazing into my face with wonder and rapture in order to determine for himself, as he finally blurted out with unexpected emotion, how a man looked who that same day was proceeding toward such an unusual destiny. I smiled and thought that I must be something special after all, promising Risse to meet him the next day in the City of Hamburg tavern to drink with him a glass of the wine he had stammeringly recommended.

No subsequent experience has given me feelings even remotely similar to those I had on this day of the first performance of *Rienzi*. The only too well-founded anxiety as to their success has so dominated my feelings at all subsequent first performances of my works that I could never really enjoy them or even take much notice of the way the audience was behaving. What I later experienced at the dress rehearsal of *Tristan und Isolde* under such extraordinary circumstances was so profoundly different from the impression of the first performance of *Rienzi* that, in another sense, it was utterly incomparable. The initial success of *Rienzi* was no doubt assured beforehand. But the uproarious way in which the public declared its partiality for me was extraordinary insofar as audiences in cities like Dresden rarely trust their own judgment in regard to works of unknown authors and thus remain generally cold and inhibited. In this case, however, the public had been forcibly predisposed to accept it, because everyone connected with the theater had been spreading such favorable reports about it throughout the city that the entire population was looking forward to what was heralded as a miracle. I sat with Minna, my sister Klara, and the Heine family in a parterre box, and in trying to recall my condition during that evening, I can remember it only as possessing all the features of a dream. I felt no particular joy or emotion; I seemed to stand quite aloof from my work; on the other hand, the packed auditorium almost frightened me, so that I did not dare to cast a single look at the massive audience but rather felt its presence like some elemental force, something like an unceasing rainstorm, against which I had to protect myself by withdrawing into the farthest corner of the box as if under a protective roof. I never noticed the applause; and when after the finale of each act I too was summoned tempestuously, my friend Heine had to prompt me forcibly every time and shove me onto the stage. One tremendous worry filled me with increasing alarm; I noticed that at the close of the second act it had already grown so late that the whole of *Der Freischütz* could have been performed during the time elapsed; the third act started off with its tremendous uproar depicting warlike tumult, and when it finally came to a close the clock pointed to ten, so that the performance had already consumed four hours. I became completely desperate; that I was also called out on the stage boisterously after this act as well struck me as the final courtesy of the public, which would certainly now find it had absorbed enough and would desert the theater in droves. As we still had two acts to go, I considered it certain we would not be able to finish, and gave vent to my contrition at having failed to understand the need for copious cuts in time, as a result of which I now found myself in the unheard-of position of not being able to finish an opera which was otherwise being very well received merely because of its ludicrous length. That the singers were still in good shape, and Tichatschek in particular growing in gusto and verve the longer it lasted, I attributed to a kindly deception, where the inevitable catastrophe was being intentionally concealed from me. My amazement to see the entire audience still there for the last act, even toward midnight, turned into utter perplexity: I no longer trusted my eyes and ears and thought the whole evening a fantasm. It was past midnight when I finally obeyed the thunderous call of the public at the side of my singers for the final time.

My feeling of desperation about the unparalleled length of the work was intensified by the attitude of my relatives, whom I saw for a short time after the performance. Friedrich Brockhaus and his family had come over from Leipzig with some friends and had invited us to a tavern, in the expectation of being able to celebrate with a pleasant supper and toast my success. But we found kitchen and cellar closed when we arrived, and everybody was so exhausted that I heard only expostulations about how incredible it was that an opera performance could last from six until after midnight. That was the only comment that was made, and we slunk away from one another in complete stupefaction. At about eight the next morning I was already at the copyist's office to take care of what I deemed the necessary cuts, in the event there might be a second performance. Whereas in the previous summer I had fought with chorusmaster Fischer for every measure, and proved they were all indispensable, I now succumbed to a blind mania for excision. Nothing in the score seemed necessary to me any more; whatever the public had been compelled to swallow on the previous evening appeared to me a chaos of impossibilities, each and every one of which could be left out without disturbing anything in the slightest or detracting from its comprehensibility. My one thought was to reduce the volume of these monstrosities to bearable proportions. Through the great ruthlessness with which I ordered the copyists to carry out the cuts I hoped to meet a disaster halfway, because I assumed that the General Director would tell me on this very day, in agreement with the municipality and the administration of the theater, that anything resembling the performance of my *Last of the Tribunes* could be given only once as a curiosity, but certainly not again. During the whole day I thus sedulously avoided all contact with theater personnel, in order to await the beneficial effects of my heroic cuts, news of which was bound to get around in the meantime. But in the afternoon I looked in on the copyists again to make sure everything was being carried out in accordance with my instructions; here I learned that Tichatschek had been there as well, had ordered my suggested cuts to be shown to him, and had summarily forbidden them all. Chorusmaster Fischer wanted to speak to me about the cuts as well; the work was suspended; I saw great danger of confusion; I didn't know what it all meant and feared disaster if this onerous job were to be postponed. Finally, I went to look up Tichatschek that evening in the theater: without giving him a chance to say a word I began questioning him angrily as to why he had interrupted the work of the copyists. In a half choked voice he replied shortly and stubbornly: "I won't let anything be cut. It is all simply heavenly!" I just stared at him blankly and felt a sudden enchantment: such an unheard-of testimony to my success inevitably dispelled my anxiety. Others joined him; Fischer was radiant with pleasure and made fun of my worries; they all talked only of the enthusiastic sentiments rampant throughout the city; the General Director sent me a letter expressing special gratitude for my work. I could only embrace Tichatschek and Fischer and be on my way to tell Minna and Klara how things stood.

After a few days' rest for the singers, a second performance took place on October 26th, with a few cuts I had succeeded in wresting from Tichatschek. I heard no particular complaints about its scarcely diminished length and finally came to the same conclusion as Tichatschek that, if he could survive it, so could the public. Thus, I let things run their natural course for six performances, all of which harvested tremendous applause. My opera had also aroused the interest of the older princesses of the royal family, and while they found its exhausting length a difficult barrier, they nonetheless did not want to lose any of it. Herr von Lüttichau thus felt obliged to suggest to me that we continue giving the complete opera but in two halves on consecutive evenings. This was all right with me, and after an interval of several weeks we announced for the first night a performance of *Rienzi's Greatness* and for the second *Rienzi's Fall*. On the first evening we gave the first two acts, and on the second the last three, to which I had composed a special prelude. This corresponded precisely with the wishes of these exalted personages, particularly the two eldest members of the royal family, Princess Amalie and Princess Augusta. But the public simply calculated that it was now asked to pay for two tickets to hear what it had previously enjoyed for the price of one, and that the whole thing was clearly a form of extortion; dissatisfaction with this threatened to hurt attendance at *Rienzi*, and after three performances of the divided work, the management felt compelled to restore it to its former unity, which I willingly made possible by again introducing the cuts.

From then on *Rienzi* packed the house to bursting as often as it was given, and the persistence of its success became all the more obvious to me as I began to notice the envy it produced in various quarters. I had an initial and painful experience of this at the hands of the poet Julius Mosen[1] on the day after the first performance. I had looked him up upon my arrival in Dresden the previous summer; as I had a truly high opinion of his talent, I soon established friendly relations with him, and this gave me much instruction and pleasure. He gave me a volume of his plays, which on the whole appealed to me greatly; among them was a tragedy entitled *Cola Rienzi*, which treated the material in a way that was in part new to me, and, I thought, most effective. In regard to this work I had asked him to pay no attention to my opera libretto, as the quality of my poetry would bear no comparison to his; he did not have much difficulty in acceding to this request. But shortly before my *Rienzi* was performed, he had caused one of his least satisfactory dramas, *Bernhard von Weimar*, to be put on the boards in Dresden, and had scant satisfaction in the results, for it was a drama with little life in it and was largely made up of political harangues, with the result that it had shared the destiny of most such aberrations. He had therefore awaited the production of my *Rienzi* with some irritation and admitted to me his bitterness at not having been able to secure acceptance in Dresden for his tragedy of the same name, presumably, as he said, owing to its tendentious political character, an element that is always more noticeable in spoken drama than in an opera where, he stated, nobody pays any attention to the words. I had good-naturedly encouraged him in this deprecation of the operatic genre; so I was all the more upset when, upon meeting him at the house of my sister Luise the day after the first performance, he immediately overwhelmed me with an outburst of anger and scornful denigration of my success. Yet he struck a chord in me in strange harmony with his view of the inherent emptiness of the type of opera I had so triumphantly embodied in *Rienzi*, and in my secret shame I really didn't know how to contradict his unrestrained vituperation. Whatever arguments I could have used in my defense were not yet clear enough to me or sufficiently grounded in a clearly demonstrable product of my own special direction to enable me to speak up on the subject. I felt only a certain pity for the unhappy poet, which I considered all the more necessary to express, inasmuch as his furious outburst had given me the inner satisfaction of seeing him admit to a great success I had myself not quite realized as yet.

But beyond this, the first performance of *Rienzi* saw the beginnings of what was to become an ever-widening breach between myself and the music critics of the newspapers. I had already known Herr Carl Bank,[1] for some time the chief critic in Dresden, from my Magdeburg days, where he had once visited me to hear me play some substantial excerpts from *Das Liebesverbot*, to his considerable pleasure. Now that we had met again in Dresden, he could not forgive me that I had found it impossible to provide him with tickets to the first performance of *Rienzi*. I had the same experience with a Herr Julius Schladebach,[2] who had likewise settled in Dresden at about that time as a critic. However much I wanted to oblige people, I have always felt an invincible repugnance at showing any special consideration to a man simply because he was a music critic, and as time went on, I carried this principle almost to the point of systematic rudeness, with the consequence that I have been persecuted by journalists throughout my life in the most brazen manner. As yet this hostility was not very pronounced, for in those days journalism in general did not cut much of a figure in Dresden, and so little news emanating from Dresden appeared in outside publications that artistic occurrences there got only scant notice, a fact that was in turn not without its disadvantages for me. Thus for the present the unpleasant side of my success scarcely affected me at all, and, for the first and only time in my life, I felt pleasantly borne along on a wave of general good will and considered myself recompensed for all my past miseries.

Further and quite unexpected fruits of my success now began appearing with astonishing rapidity; yet this was not so much in the form of monetary gain, for that amounted for the time being to a mere three hundred talers paid me by the management as an exceptional honorarium instead of the usual twenty louis d'or. And also I could not hope to sell my opera to a publisher on favorable terms until it had been performed at several other major theaters. Then fate intervened through the entirely unexpected death of the Royal Music Director Rastrelli[1] shortly after the first performance of *Rienzi*, thereby vacating a position that made all eyes focus on me at once.

Although the negotiations on this matter lasted quite a while, on the other hand the theater management gave me proof of an almost impassioned regard for my talent. The first performance of *Der fliegende Holländer* was on no account to be granted to Berlin: Dresden wanted the honor for itself. As the Berlin management made no difficulties whatever about this, I willingly handed my most recent work to the Dresden theater as well, and whereas I had this time to do without Tichatschek's collaboration, in the absence of a so-called heroic tenor role, I could by way of compensation count on all the more help from Schröder-Devrient, because in the role of the heroine she would have a far more suitable part than in *Rienzi*. It was really rather pleasant for me to be able to rely on her so completely, for she had grown surprisingly irritated with me as a result of her insufficient contribution to the success of *Rienzi*; and I demonstrated to her the extent to which I pinned my hopes on her, in a move of excessive zeal that was in other respects much to the detriment of my work, by virtually forcing the male lead, despite his honest protests, on the baritone Wächter,[2] who, though formerly a competent executant, was by now no longer in good health and in no way suited to the role. To my great satisfaction, however, the artist I so much admired found that even my text on its own made a special appeal to her as we went through it together; and the period during which she studied the role of Senta, when I was with her most of the time, became, thanks to the genuine personal sympathy I felt for the character and destiny of this extraordinary woman under these unusual circumstances, one of the most exciting and, in many important respects, most instructive experiences of my life.

Although this great artist, especially through the influence of her famous mother, Sophie Schröder,[3] who was then staying with her, showed undisguised indignation with me at having composed so glamorous a work as *Rienzi* for Dresden without reserving the principal part for her, her inherently magnanimous nature triumphed over this particularism; she termed me openly "a genius" and evinced for me that special trust which, she contended, none but a genius should be accorded. I was soon to find that such confidence had its questionable aspect, for she proceeded to make me her confidant and adviser in the really horrendous affairs of her heart; but for the time being she found occasions to proclaim herself openly as my friend, singling me out in the most flattering manner.

First of all, I had to go with her on a trip to Leipzig, where she was giving a concert for her mother's benefit, which she thought to make particularly attractive by including on the program two numbers from *Rienzi*, Adriano's aria and Rienzi's Prayer (the latter to be sung by Tichatschek), both of them to be conducted by me. Mendelssohn, who was a good friend of hers, had also been enticed to this concert: he performed his new overture, *Ruy Blas*, at it. During the two busy days I spent in Leipzig on this occasion, I got to know him closely for the first time, for up to then my contact with him had been restricted to a few infrequent and utterly unproductive visits. At the home of my brother-in-law Friedrich Brockhaus, Mendelssohn and Schröder-Devrient made music for us, as he accompanied her in a wide assortment of Schubert songs. I noticed at this occasion a curious uneasiness and agitation in the way this still youthful master, then at the pinnacle of his fame and influence, observed me, or more accurately, reconnoitered me. It was clear to me that he didn't value an operatic success very highly, and most certainly not in Dresden, and no doubt I counted for him among that species of musician in whom he saw little merit and with whom he believed he would never be obliged to have anything to do. Yet it was precisely some of the characteristics of my success that held something alarming for him. Mendelssohn himself had for a long time ardently desired to write a successful opera; he was probably disgruntled to see such a success pop up rudely in his face, conveyed by a type of music he could justifiably contend was not good, and before he had been able to achieve one himself. He was doubtless no less irritated to hear Schröder-Devrient, whom he regarded as a marvel and who for her part was greatly devoted to him, openly and loudly advocating my cause as well. All this dawned on me when Mendelssohn made a very odd remark that virtually compelled me to such an interpretation. While I accompanied him home after the orchestral rehearsal and was expatiating with great warmth about music, this by no means loquacious man interrupted me with sudden agitation to state that the only bad thing about music was its capacity to excite not only the good but also the evil emotions, such as envy for example, more intensely than all the other arts. I blushed at the necessity of construing this as pertaining to his feelings toward me, for in deepest innocence I was conscious that I could not possibly think of remotely comparing my capacities and achievements as a musician with those of Mendelssohn. Yet, strange to say, at this very concert he did not show himself in the light that would have precluded any conceivable comparison with me; a performance of his *Fingal's Cave* overture, for example, would have spared me any embarrassment in standing at his side, for the distance between our achievements would have seemed palpably vast; apparently, however, he had been prompted to choose the *Ruy Blas* overture by his desire to get so near to the genre of operatic music that its effects would also spill over onto his work. The overture seemed designed for the Paris public; and how surprised everybody was about Mendelssohn was demonstrated in a naive way by Robert Schumann, who came up to the podium after the piece and smilingly expressed his amazement at such a "giddy piece for the orchestra". To give truth its due, however, it must be mentioned that neither of us harvested the success of the evening; we vanished into insignificance beside the tremendous impression made by the aged Sophie Schröder with her recitation of Bürger's *Lenore*. Before the concert the local newspapers had accused the daughter of resorting to all kinds of musical novelties in order to extort from the Leipzig musical public a benefit quite inappropriate to her mother, who had never had any associations with music, but on the evening itself we who were the musical accomplices in the scheme stood by as the idle supporting turns while this venerable, almost toothless lady declaimed Bürger's poem with truly awe-inspiring beauty and grandeur. And this gave me, like so much else I saw and heard during those few days, much to ruminate over and analyze.

A second excursion I took with Schröder-Devrient led me in December of the same year to Berlin, where she had been invited to participate in a big concert at court, and where for my part I wished to get after Küstner concerning *Der fliegende Holländer*. While I obtained no tangible results in that matter, this short visit to Berlin was memorable for my meeting with Franz Liszt, which subsequently proved to be of the greatest significance. It took place in singular circumstances, in mutual embarrassment brought about by an exasperating caprice on the part of the over-exuberant Schröder-Devrient.

I had already narrated to my patroness the story of an earlier encounter with Liszt. In that fateful second winter in Paris, during which I was obliged to consider myself lucky to keep my head above water with hack-work for Schlesinger, I was notified one day by a communication from the always solicitous Laube that Franz Liszt, to whom he had spoken in Germany, recommending me, would be coming to Paris; I should on no account, he advised me, neglect to look him up, for Liszt was "generous" and would surely know how to help me. When I learned of his actual arrival, I announced myself one day at his hotel. It was early in the morning; I was let in and found myself in a salon together with a few strangers, to be joined after some time by Liszt, who was friendly, talkative and casually dressed. Being unable to participate in the French conversation, which was mostly about Liszt's experiences during his most recent concert tour in Hungary, I listened for a while in thorough boredom, until I was at last affably asked by Liszt what he could do for me. He didn't seem to remember any recommendation from Laube; all I could answer was to say that I wished to make his acquaintance, to which he seemed to have no objection and he let me know that he would not forget to procure me a ticket for his next big matinée concert. My sole attempt to launch a conversation on artistic matters consisted in the question whether Liszt was familiar with Loewe's version of *Der Erlkönig*, in addition to Schubert's. His denial brought an end to this rather inhibited initiative, and the visit closed by my giving my home address, to which in due course came a ticket, transmitted by his secretary Belloni and accompanied by a few graceful lines, for a solo concert to be given by the Maestro in the Salle Erard. Having wended my way to the packed concert hall, I beheld a podium on which the piano stood beleaguered by the élite of Parisian female society grouped around it in a tight circle. After witnessing the frenzied ovations accorded to the world-renowned virtuoso, I listened to several of his most brilliant pieces, including his fantasia on *Robert le Diable*, and went away with nothing more than a feeling of stupefaction. This was precisely the time I was turning from the path which had led me away from my innermost nature and which I then drastically abandoned in silent bitterness. I was thus the last person in the world able to appreciate adequately the achievements of such a person who at the time was sunning himself in the brightest light of day, whereas I had turned my back and faced the night. I did not call on Liszt again.

As stated, I had recounted this tale briefly at some point to Schröder-Devrient; she had taken it all in with particular alertness, for it touched on her weak point of professional jealousy. Now that Liszt had likewise been invited by the King of Prussia to the big court concert, it happened that when she first encountered him he inquired of her with great interest about the success of *Rienzi*. As she noticed that its composer appeared to be entirely unknown to Liszt, she proceeded to taunt him with great relish for his alleged lack of perspicacity, inasmuch as the composer he was now asking about with such lively interest was the same poor musician he had "turned away so contemptuously" a short time before in Paris. She told me all this jubilantly, much to my dismay, and I tried at once to correct the false impression she had gained from my previous account. Just as we were discussing this point in her room, we were interrupted by the sound from the neighboring room of the famous bass passage from the "Revenge" aria of Donna Anna, rapidly executed in rippling octaves on the piano. "That's Liszt himself", she cried. In walked Liszt to accompany the singer to rehearsal. To my great embarrassment she introduced me to him maliciously as the composer of *Rienzi*, whom he had so wanted to meet, after booting him out the door in his grand surroundings in Paris. My solemn asseverations that Schröder-Devrient was making a bad joke by intentionally distorting my account of the previous visit in Paris apparently set him straight concerning me, for he no doubt had come to his own conclusions about the impetuous singer. He nonetheless was obliged to admit that he could remember nothing of my visit in Paris, although it had pained and disquieted him to learn that anyone could have any grounds for complaining of such rude treatment at his hands. The utterly cordial tone of the straightforward language in which Liszt expressed himself to me about this misunderstanding contrasted pleasantly and beneficently with the extraordinarily excited raillery of this incorrigible woman. The whole attitude by which he sought to disarm her relentless mockery was new to me and gave me an intimate insight into the character of this man, who was so profoundly sure of himself in his kindness and incomparable humanity. She finally got after him about the recent doctorate awarded him by the University of Königsberg, pretending to mistake his title and calling him a druggist. At last he stretched prostrate on the floor, as if to implore her mercy, declaring himself defenseless against the storm of her ridicule. After he had turned to me with the assurance that he would make every effort to hear *Rienzi* and give me grounds for a better opinion of him than his unlucky star had as yet permitted, we parted company for the moment. The almost naive simplicity and naturalness of his every word and phrase, and particularly its manner of expression, made as deep an impression on me as it had on everybody else, and for the first time I was able to account for the feeling of enchantment produced by Liszt in all who came within his sphere, and clearly saw how erroneous had been my former view as to its cause.

These two trips to Leipzig and Berlin were only brief interruptions in the preparations we were making back in Dresden for *Der fliegende Holländer*. In this regard I was particularly anxious to keep Schröder-Devrient in a state of enthusiasm for her task, as I knew that, given the weakness of the rest of the cast, it was from her alone that I could expect a performance commensurate with the spirit of my work. Beyond the fact that she really liked the role of Senta, there were several special circumstances unduly exciting this passionate woman at the time. I was abashed when she confided in me that she was on the point of breaking off a love affair of many years' standing with an earnest, devoted and very young man, the son of the former Minister of Education Müller, then a lieutenant in the Royal Guard, and in its place launch off on another and far less desirable one with all the haste of passion. Her new choice was, it seemed, a man she had recently met in Berlin, Herr von Münchhausen, also young, tall and slender, as was to be expected now that I was becoming familiar with her predilections. I thought her passionate way of confiding in me on this occasion had its source in a guilty conscience; she knew that Müller, whom I liked for his estimable qualities, had been devoted to her with all the fire of a first love, and that she was now betraying him in the most faithless way on the flimsiest pretext. She seemed also to be entirely aware that her new paramour was utterly unworthy of her and was only attracted to her for frivolous and selfish reasons. Thus she also knew that nobody, and most particularly none of her older friends, who had ample prior experience with her in these matters, would approve of her conduct; and so she now explained to me openly that she felt compelled to confide in me on the grounds that she considered me a genius, and I would necessarily grasp the compulsions of her temperament. This certainly put me in an odd position. While I was repelled by the object of her affections, I had to recognize to my own amazement that this to me highly distasteful passion had such a fierce grip on this singular woman that I could not withhold a certain sympathy and even a serious interest. She was pale and distracted, ate hardly anything and was in every way so unduly tense that I thought she could not escape a serious or even perhaps fatal illness. She had not been able to sleep at all for some time, and whenever I came to her with my unhappy *Holländer*, her looks so alarmed me that the scheduled rehearsal was the last thing I thought of. But she was the one who insisted on continuing, pushing me to the piano and plunging into her role as if there were no tomorrow. Because learning music was really rather difficult for her, she could only master her role by very frequent and long rehearsals. She would sing for hours on end with such passion that I would often jump up in alarm and try to get her to restrain herself; then she would point to her chest and flex the muscles of her still lovely body, in order to demonstrate to me that she was indestructible. In fact her voice at this time actually took on a youthful freshness and an enduring strength that often astonished me, and I had to admit to myself that her absurd infatuation for an insipid ne'er-do-well was very much to the advantage of my Senta. The endurance of this overly intense woman was so great that she even consented to do a dress rehearsal on the actual day of the first performance, thereby obviating a delay that would have been greatly to my disadvantage.

This performance now took place on January 2nd of the new year 1843. Its reception was extremely instructive and produced the turning point in my future career. In the first place, I had to learn from what was on the whole an unsuccessful performance how much care and forethought would be necessary to assure myself an adequate representation of my later works. I saw that I had been more or less of the opinion that my score would be readily intelligible in itself, and that my singers would be able to do things right instinctively. My good old friend Wächter, a popular "Barber of Seville" in the era of Henriette Sontag, had been, as I have already mentioned, of a much more modest opinion in this respect from the beginning. His total incapacity in the difficult role of my spectral, suffering mariner dawned on Schröder-Devrient unfortunately only after the rehearsals were too far along to make any change. Wächter's distressing corpulence, particularly his broad, round face and the curious way he moved his arms and legs like shriveled stumps, sent my Senta into transports of despair. In one rehearsal she broke off suddenly at the point in the second act when she steps toward the Dutchman in the guise of a guardian angel to offer him salvation, and whispered fiercely in my ear: "How can I come out with this when I look into those beady eyes? My God, Wagner, what have you done?" I tried to console her as best I could and relied secretly upon Herr von Münchhausen, who actually promised me to sit in the stalls in a place where Schröder-Devrient could not fail to see him. And the magnificent performance of this great artist did actually succeed, despite the fact she stood alone as in a desert on the stage, in rousing everyone to great enthusiasm in the second act. But the first act, which offered the public nothing more than a boring conversation between Herr Wächter and that Herr Risse who had invited me to share a glass of wine the day after the first performance of *Rienzi*, and then the third act, in which the mightiest tempest in the orchestra was unable to disturb the quiet sea nor budge the ghost ship from its meticulous mooring, evoked amazement in the public as to how I could possibly offer, after a *Rienzi* during whose every act there was so much going on and in which Tichatschek shone in repeated changes of costumes, such an utterly unornamented, meager and somber piece of work.

Since Schröder-Devrient soon left Dresden completely for a long period, *Der fliegende Holländer* got only four performances, at which the diminishing size of the audience gave ample evidence that I hadn't done right by the Dresdeners. The management saw itself compelled to prevent my reputation from being tarnished by putting *Rienzi* back on the boards in short order; and now I had to ponder the success of this opera, as well as the failure of the other. With singular dismay I had to admit to myself that, while the great flaws in the representation of *Der fliegende Holländer* were clear to me, I had actually not owed the success of *Rienzi* to any particular exactitude and correctness of the execution. While Wächter had fallen far short of my requirements for the Dutchman, I could not conceal from myself the fact that Tichatschek was almost equally inadequate in his characterization of the title role in *Rienzi*. His horrendous errors and faults in the performance of the part had never escaped me; Tichatschek had not for a moment been willing to lay aside his glittering manner as a heroic tenor to do justice to the gloomy, demonic strain in Rienzi's character, upon which I had placed great stress at the critical moments of the drama, until that point in the fourth act, when he would fall upon his knees in the most tearful manner upon pronouncement of the papal ban, abandoning himself to his fate in an outpouring of lyrical pathos; in opposition to my suggestion that Rienzi at this point should, though sunk in meditation, remain standing firmly as a statue, Tichatschek advised me that the great success of this closing scene was traceable to his interpretation, admonishing me by no means to change it. When I thus pondered what had really caused the success of my *Rienzi*, I concluded that it was the result of the glorious, electrifying voice of the tirelessly exuberant singer, of the stimulating effect of the choral ensembles, and of the constant bustling activity on the stage. I got a special indication of this when we played the opera in two parts, and the dramatically as well as musically much stronger second part was noticeably less well attended than the first, and for the simple reason, as I was frankly told on all sides, that the ballet came in the first part. I got an even more spontaneous demonstration of what was the really attractive element in the opera from my brother Julius, who came over from Leipzig to attend a performance. Since I was sitting

in a box with him in full view of the audience, I forbade him to give
the slightest applause, even if solely for the singers; he proved capable
of restraining himself from applauding throughout the whole evening;
only at a certain point in the ballet did his enthusiasm get the better of
him to the extent that he joined the audience in clapping his hands
violently, informing me that he simply could not hold back any longer.
Remarkably enough, when *Rienzi* was later given in Berlin, where it was
on the whole received with indifference, this same ballet secured for the
work the lasting esteem of the present King of Prussia,[1] who many years
afterward ordered a revival of the opera, although its dramatic substance
had failed entirely to enthuse the Berlin public. When I was obliged to
attend a performance of the opera in Darmstadt much later, I found that
while its best parts had been brutally cut, the ballet had even been
expanded by additions and repetitions. And yet I had tossed off the music
for the ballet in Riga in a matter of a few days, contemptuously and in
intentional haste, such was my lack of interest in it; it had such obvious
weaknesses that I was already thoroughly ashamed of it in Dresden,
particularly inasmuch as I had been compelled to cut its best feature,
the tragic pantomime. Furthermore, the resources available for the ballet
in Dresden did not even permit proper execution of my directions for
the entrance of ancient Roman gladiators or ritual dances, as later were
to be executed very well in Berlin. I had to reconcile myself shamefully
to two little *danseuses* executing some silly steps, until at last a company
of soldiers marched in, their shields held above their heads forming a
roof of sorts to remind the audience of an ancient Roman "testudo",
only to have the ballet master and his assistant, dressed in flesh-colored
tights, leap onto the shields and turn somersaults, a proceeding which
they considered redolent of gladiatorial combat. This was the instant
when the house invariably exploded in applause, and I had to regard
this moment, whenever it came, as the pinnacle of my success.

In this way I became increasingly conscious of the intrinsic divergence
between my inner aims and outer fortunes, and at the same time the
pressure of circumstances drove me to as fateful a step as my marriage
through my acceptance of the post of a Kapellmeister in Dresden. From
the beginning I had sought to prolong the negotiations in the matter by
a lukewarm attitude which was in no sense an affectation. My contempt
for the theater was already total; my closer acquaintance with the
would-be aristocratic system of management of court theaters, which
in its conceit and ignorance seems designed to conceal the shameful
fakery of the modern theater under a glossy veneer, was not calculated

to change my feelings. For a quarter of a century a man had stood at the head of the Dresden Court Theater and Orchestra whose lack of education and refinement was obvious to everybody. Many anecdotes about both these characteristics were current in Dresden at the time, and the slightest contact with him, either socially or on business, was sufficient to evoke amazement that a cultured monarch could entrust such a man to be his intermediary in his relations with an institution supposedly devoted to art. This was explicable almost solely by the fact that the King himself could not be considered entirely cultured, and it could thus be presumed that he didn't attach much importance to the interests of art. Thus it was also clear that no appeal would be possible to the monarch against the ignorance and crudity of his theater director, for precisely in those matters where great delicacy and finesse were needed to foster artistic interests, an arbitrariness would inevitably prevail bearing comparison with the most brutal Russian despotism. Under such a system, every noble impulse was stifled in those connected with the theater, and the whole enterprise boiled down to an agglomeration of vain and frivolous interests, held together by a ludicrously inflexible bureaucracy. I thus could see with the greatest certainty that any requirement to concern myself with the theater would be the most repellent thing I could think of; and when the aforementioned death of Rastrelli produced here at this time and place the temptation to be untrue to my inner promptings, I told my older, intimate friends at once that I had no intention of accepting the vacant position.

But everything capable of shaking human resolution combined against this decision. The prospect of gaining a secure livelihood through a permanent position with a fixed salary was tyrannically attractive. I fought this temptation by reminding myself of my success as an operatic composer which should, I hoped, bring in enough to rent two little rooms where I could live modestly and produce new works. But precisely on this point of the leisure to get on with my work, people told me that a steady job with no overwhelming demands on my time would be better, as a whole year had passed since the completion of the *Holländer* without my finding any leisure for composition. I stuck to my guns, however, and maintained that Rastrelli's post, which was that of Music Director and was subordinate to that of the Kapellmeister, was in every respect unworthy of me, and I firmly refused even to consider the job, thus compelling the management of the theater to look elsewhere for a candidate to fill it. But whereas that position was now out of the question, I was informed that the death of the conductor Morlacchi[1] some time ago had left another vacancy still unfilled, and this was a Kapellmeister-ship. It was to be expected that the King would probably be inclined to offer me this position. Inasmuch as court appointments are taken very seriously in Germany, especially in capital cities, and considering the "respectability" they confer, which makes most German musicians regard such a position with its lifelong tenure as the closest thing to heaven on earth, my good wife began to get very excited about the prospect. It would open many doors hitherto closed to us; domestic comfort and social prestige were highly alluring to the homeless wanderers, to whom a permanent place to live, under the most honorable royal patronage, seemed to offer the comfort and security so sorely missed in times of misery. Another important factor that finally softened my stubbornness was the influence of the widow of Carl Maria von Weber, the lively and likeable Karoline, to whose house I now often repaired and whose company was particularly attractive to me through the revivified memories of the master I still so deeply loved. She now implored me with truly touching tenderness not to resist this significant turn of fate. She had a right, she insisted, to demand that I settle in Dresden and fill the position that had been so lamentably empty since the death of her husband. "Just think", she told me, "how I am to look Weber in the face when the time comes for me to join him if I have to tell him that the work for which he made such sacrifices is being neglected in Dresden. Imagine my feelings when I see that lazy Reissiger standing in Weber's place, and when I hear his operas rattled off with less insight and imagination every year. If you love Weber, you owe it to his memory to take this job and continue his work." From the practical standpoint, too, drawing on her own experience of life, she urged me with energetic solicitude to take to heart my wife's need for security, for if I were to die suddenly, she would be amply provided for if I had accepted the position.

But more than the promptings of affection, ambition and prudence, what settled things was the intense conviction, which life has never succeeded in quite eradicating in me, that wherever fate had led me, even here in Dresden, this was perhaps the place where I might set in motion the transformation of the familiar and summon the unknown into being; for in the end all that was required was the advent of a fiercely aspiring person, if destiny were kind to him, to regenerate what had decayed, to gain a truly ennobling influence, and to achieve the deliverance of art from its shameful fetters. The marvelously rapid turnabout in my fortunes could not fail to encourage such a belief in me; and as I began to realize the curious change in the whole attitude of the General Director Herr von Lüttichau toward me, the effect was truly seductive. This singular man began evincing toward me a warmth of which no one had previously thought him capable, and even during my unceasing squabbles with him in later years, I never had reason to doubt his fundamentally good intentions toward me. Nevertheless, the final decision came about by my being more or less taken by surprise. On February 2nd 1843 I was summoned in a most amiable manner to the office of the intendant and found the general staff of the Royal Orchestra assembled there, in whose presence Herr von Lüttichau had my unforgettable friend Winkler, as Secretary of the Court Theater, read aloud in a most ceremonial manner the text of a royal decree by which I was appointed Kapellmeister to His Majesty with an annual salary for life of fifteen hundred talers. Herr von Lüttichau followed up this reading with a rather ceremonial address, in which he expressed his assumption that I would be grateful to the King for this mark of favor. Amid all this kindly solemnity, it did not escape my attention that with this announcement all possibility of negotiating my salary was eliminated, although admittedly the omission of the precondition that I serve a year's probation with the mere title of Royal Music Director, which had been enforced even on Weber in his time, constituted a significant exemption and was calculated to make me remain silent on the matter. My new colleagues began congratulating me at once, and Herr von Lüttichau accompanied me back to my own door amid the most congenial conversation, where I then fell into the arms of my poor wife, who was almost babbling with joy, so that I fully realized I would have to put the best face I could on the matter and, unless I wished to give unheard-of offense, had to congratulate myself upon becoming "Master" of His Majesty's "Chapel".

After I had been sworn in at a special meeting as a servant of the crown and introduced to the assembled members of the Royal Orchestra with a few ardent remarks from the General Director, I was summoned a few days later to an audience with the King. When I first glimpsed the features of this kind, courteous and straightforward monarch, I involuntarily thought of my youthful attempt at a political overture on the theme of "Friedrich and Freedom". Our somewhat strained conversation was enlivened when the King expressed his satisfaction with the two operas I had now given in Dresden. If there were one thing wanting in his view, he added after a polite hesitation, it was a somewhat clearer delineation of the principal figures in my dramas; it struck him that the elemental forces tended to overshadow them, the populace in *Rienzi* and the ocean in *Der fliegende Holländer*. I could well understand this and was pleased at this sign of serious attention and original judgment. Beyond that, he excused himself in advance for not attending my operas more frequently, which he attributed solely to a general distaste for the theater conceived during his early education, when he and his brother Johann,[1] who now felt exactly as he did, had been forced to attend performances regularly, whereas to tell the truth, he would have much preferred being left to follow his own pursuits irrespective of etiquette. As a characteristic instance of the spirit of the genus "courtier", I later learned that Lüttichau, who had been obliged to wait for me in the anteroom during this audience, had been greatly agitated at its long duration. In the course of the years, I came into close personal contact with the King on only two further occasions: the first time was upon my presentation to him of the dedicatory copy of the vocal score of *Rienzi*; the second was after my successful adaptation and performance of *Iphigenia in Aulis* by Gluck, whose operas he particularly liked, when he came up to me in a public promenade and congratulated me on my work.

That initial audience with the King marked the zenith of my hastily adopted career in Dresden; from then on cares began piling up again on all sides. I soon realized the difficulty of my financial position, for it turned out that the advantages gained by my permanent appointment were in no way commensurate with the sacrifices and obligations previously incurred from the moment I had come of age. The young music director of Riga, long since forgotten, now suddenly turned up in an astonishing reincarnation as the Royal Saxon Kapellmeister. The first fruits of this general awareness of my success consisted of threats of prosecution and urgent demands by those Königsberg tradesmen from whose clutches I had escaped by that incomparably miserable and painful flight from Riga. In addition, I began hearing from all the people who felt they had claims upon me of any kind, originating from any conceivable time or place, including some from my student and even my school days, so that at one point I cried out in dismay that I would no doubt soon get a bill from my wet-nurse for having suckled me. All this didn't add up to any vast amount, and in order to counteract all the malicious rumors circulating at the time that I first learned about in later years, let it be said that the thousand talers I borrowed at interest from Frau Schröder-Devrient not only entirely sufficed to pay these bills but also enabled me to repay Kietz for those sums he had given me without any thought of reimbursement during my Paris privations and even help him out a bit further. And where else could I have found this money, as my financial distress had been so great that I was obliged to urge Schröder-Devrient to hurry with the rehearsals for *Der fliegende Holländer* on the grounds that the fee I was going to receive was of boundless importance to me? I received no payment whatever for my setting up house in a manner befitting a person with the rank of Court Kapellmeister, and I even had to pay for a silly and expensive court uniform without any kind of compensation. Thus, without borrowing money at interest, I could not begin to get established, given the fact that I was without any money of my own. Yet no one who knew of the extraordinary success of *Rienzi* in Dresden could help believing that my works would soon spread among the German theaters with highly remunerative results for me; and my own relatives, particularly the sensible Ottilie, were so confident in this respect that they predicted I would receive double my salary in the income from my operas. And in fact it appeared at first as if all would go well; the Kassel Court Theater soon ordered the score of *Der fliegende Holländer*, as did the theater in Riga I knew so well. Both theaters evidently wanted to give something by me right away, and word had got about that this opera was on a smaller scale and demanded less in the way of staging than *Rienzi*. From both these places I got good news in May 1843 of successful performances. But that was the end of it for the moment, and the rest of the year went by without the slightest hint of an inquiry about one of my scores reaching me. An attempt to publish a vocal score of *Der fliegende Holländer* (I was withholding *Rienzi* for a more favorable occasion after further successes as a kind of capital reserve) to produce some additional income, foundered on the refusal of Messrs Härtel in Leipzig, who expressed themselves willing to publish my opera, but only if I would renounce any fee.

Thus for the moment I had to content myself with the less tangible aspects of my successes; my unmistakable popularity with the Dresden public and the respect they paid me was certainly part of this. But even in this respect my Arcadian dream was soon shattered. I think my appearance in Dresden ushered in a new era in the practice of journalistic music criticism, which found material in the anger caused by my successes to breathe life into what had hitherto been a rather feeble activity. The two aforementioned critics, Carl Bank and Julius Schladebach, for a fact took up permanent residence in Dresden only after my arrival; I know there were certain difficulties in regard to Bank obtaining a domiciliary permit that were resolved only after the intervention and recommendation of the man who was now my colleague, Reissiger. While the success of my *Rienzi* was clearly uncongenial to these gentlemen, who now obtained permanent employment as music critics for the Dresden papers, and all the more so because I made no effort to win their favor, it had nonetheless proved difficult for them to pour their vitriol over the head of a popular young musician, who had won the approval of the public in part as a result of the widespread knowledge of all the tribulations he had endured to date. With my "unheard-of" appointment as Royal Kapellmeister, however, the need for all humane restraint suddenly evaporated: now I was "doing well", indeed "on top of the world"; envy found ample nourishment; there was now a perfectly clear point of attack; and soon there radiated outward from Dresden throughout the German press, in those columns devoted to Dresden news, an estimate of me which has not changed its basic tone to this day, with the single exception of a certain modification, which proved transitory and took place solely in publications of a certain color, during the time I first took up residence in Switzerland as a political refugee. Yet this lasted only until, through Liszt's efforts, my operas began to be produced all over Germany, when even papers of this stripe reverted to the old tone. That two other theaters had ordered my score immediately after the Dresden performances I owed to the circumstance that up to then the destructive proclivities of my journalistic adversaries had been somewhat constrained; and I feel justified in attributing the cessation of new inquiries essentially to the effect of the calumnies in the papers. My old friend Laube had been, to be sure, immediately anxious to play his part as a journalist in introducing me to the world as favorably as possible: he reassumed the editorship of the *Zeitung für die elegante Welt* at the beginning of 1843 and requested me to provide an autobiographical sketch for one of his first issues. He was obviously pleased to be able in this way to lead me triumphantly into the literary world, and to this end he included in that number a lithograph of the portrait Kietz had made of me. But even he began to get worried after a time and became somewhat inhibited in his judgments about my achievements, for he began to grasp the systematic persistence and assurance with which they were increasingly belittled, depreciated and vilified. He admitted to me later he had not been able to conceive of such a hopeless position as that in which I found myself in relation to the whole journalistic world, and when he got to know my attitude in the matter, he smilingly blessed me as a doomed man.

But there was also a noticeable change in the attitude of those immediately connected with my work, and this provided welcome material for this journalistic campaign to boot. No motive of personal ambition had led me to request to be permitted to conduct the performances of my own work. But as I had found that Kapellmeister Reissiger had grown continually more careless in each performance of *Rienzi*, and that the whole production was slipping back into the well-known, expressionless routine, I had asked, particularly in view of my forthcoming appointment, to be given personal charge of the sixth performance of this work. I conducted it without having held a single rehearsal or having ever before stood at the head of the Dresden Court Orchestra; it went superbly, singers and orchestra being inspired with new life, and everyone came to the conclusion that this had been the most successful performance of *Rienzi*. *Der fliegende Holländer* was then willingly entrusted to me to rehearse and to conduct, one reason for this being that Reissiger found himself overwhelmed with work in consequence of the death of Music Director Rastrelli. In addition, I was requested to prove my capacity to direct works other than my own by conducting Weber's *Euryanthe*. I apparently filled the bill, and it was actually on the basis of this performance that Weber's widow justified her emphatic demand that I accept the Dresden conductorship, as she asserted that this was the first time since the death of her husband she had heard his work given in the right spirit, and particularly in the right tempo. The ensuing appointment upset Reissiger for a time, as he would have much preferred to have a music director subordinate to him, instead of which he had been provided with a colleague of equal rank. Whereas his natural inclination to indolence made him affable and relatively easy for me to get along with, his ambitious wife took pains to keep him in a state of anxiety about me. This never produced any overt altercations, however; it was just that I noticed from then on that certain indiscretions began appearing in the press, demonstrating to me that the amiability of my colleague, who never spoke to me without first kissing me, was not of the most honest order.

I also received quite unexpected proof that I had aroused the bitter envy of another man whose feelings of this kind I had no prior reason to suspect. This was the long-time principal concertmaster of the Royal Dresden Orchestra, Karl Lipinsky,[1] a violin virtuoso in his day and a person of ardent temperament and singular gifts, yet of the most incredible vanity, a quality his volatile, mistrustful Polish character had fostered to a most alarming extreme. I always found him difficult to deal with, for although he had an instructive and stimulating effect on the technical execution of the violinists, he was certainly completely out of place as concertmaster in a well-disciplined orchestra. This extraordinary man tried to justify in the most literal way General Director Lüttichau's encomium that his tone could always be heard within the orchestral sound; he always came in a little bit before the other violins, and thus was a leader in the double sense, being rhythmically always ahead as well. He acted in the same way with regard to nuances of intonation, and usually executed delicate inflexions in soft passages with fanatical sharpness. It was totally out of the question to try to remonstrate with him on this, as solely the most unguent flattery had any effect on him at all; I had to endure this as best I could and try to think of ways to minimize the damage he was doing to the orchestral performances by resorting to circumlocutions of the most enthusiastic friendliness. Nevertheless, he couldn't bear it that the orchestra got more applause whenever I conducted, because he took it for granted that any orchestra in which he played would always be at the top of its form no matter who might chance to stand on the conductor's podium. It now happened, as is usual whenever a new chief with fresh ideas embarks upon such a job, that members of the orchestra came to me with all sorts of suggestions for hitherto neglected improvements; a particular case of this nature was then utilized by Lipinsky, who was also annoyed about this circumstance, to a strange act of treachery. One of our most senior contrabass players had died, and Lipinsky had been after me not to fill this position in the usual manner by promotion from within the ranks, but rather by hiring a virtuoso on the contrabass whom he named to me, the distinguished player Müller, who was then in Darmstadt where he had been honored with the title of Chamber Musician to the Court. When the man whose seniority rights would have been affected by this step came to see me, I remained faithful to my promise to Lipinsky, expressed reservations about the seniority system in general, and declared that, in accordance with my oath to the King, I held it my paramount duty to consider the artistic interests of the institution above all else. I then found to my great astonishment, though it was silly of me to be surprised, that the whole orchestra turned against me to a man, and when it came to a dispute between Lipinsky and myself about several issues that had arisen, Lipinsky actually accused me of having threatened by my remarks in the case of the contrabass player to undermine the established rights of the members of the orchestra, whom we were morally obliged to protect. Lüttichau, who was on the point of leaving

Dresden for a time, was extremely uneasy, particularly because Reissiger was on vacation, at the prospect of leaving musical affairs in such an ominous position. The shameless deceit of which I had been the victim opened my eyes and gave me the necessary composure to reassure the harassed General Director in the most conclusive way that I now understood the people I had to deal with and would henceforth act accordingly. I kept my word faithfully; I never again got involved in any kind of conflict with Lipinsky or any other member of the orchestra; on the contrary, in the course of time all the musicians became so attached to me that I could pride myself on their dedication.

One thing became clear to me from that day on, however: I would not be spending the rest of my days as Kapellmeister in Dresden. From then on my job and all my activities in Dresden became a burden, which the occasional truly marvelous successes I achieved there made me feel all the more heavily.

Fate nonetheless brought me one very special friend through my appointment, whose close relationship with me long survived the period of our communal musical efforts in Dresden. In addition to the two Kapellmeisters, we had to hire a music director; in this capacity we needed not so much a musician of wide repute as an industrious worker and a tactful person, who above all had to be a Catholic, for much to the dissatisfaction of the clergy at the Catholic Court Church, in which the court musicians had to perform countless services, both the Kapellmeisters were Protestants. Proof that he had all these qualifications was furnished by August Röckel, a nephew of Hummel, who applied to us from Weimar for the vacant post. He belonged to an old Bavarian family; his father was a singer, had frequently sung the part of Florestan before Beethoven himself at the time of the first performances of *Fidelio*, and had even been on friendly terms with the master, many details of whose life had been preserved by him for posterity. His subsequent position as singing teacher had led him into the field of theatrical management; he had been the one who first performed German opera in Paris, and with such brilliant results that the great impact made by *Fidelio* and *Der Freischütz* upon a French public entirely unfamiliar with these works, through which Schröder-Devrient also became known to the Parisians, was attributable to his admirable enterprise. In this and similar undertakings the then very young August had helped his father and so gained practical experience as a musician. As his father's ventures also took him to England for a protracted period, August had also absorbed much other practical knowledge in his manifold experience of people and places, and in addition had learned English and French; yet his musical bent determined his choice of a career, and his great natural talent justified him in the highest hopes for success. He played the piano superbly, could read through a score with the utmost rapidity, and had an extremely good ear, thus possessing every qualification for a professional musician. As far as composition was concerned, he was impelled less by a strong productive drive than by the impulse to show what he was capable of and to see if he could score a success or two with popular works. He was not particularly interested in recognition as a significant composer but rather in a reputation as a skillful operatic craftsman. Armed with this modest ambition, he had put together an opera entitled *Farinelli*, for which he had himself written a libretto with no higher purpose in mind than to equal the achievements of his brother-in-law Lortzing. Then he came to me with his score, but first of all asked me, inasmuch as it was his first visit and he had heard none of my operas in Dresden, to play something for him from my *Rienzi* and *Der fliegende Holländer*. His frank, agreeable personality induced me to fulfill his request as best I could, and I soon found that I made such a significant and unexpectedly overwhelming impression that he decided on the spot not to bother me any further with the score of his own opera. It was only after we had become much more intimate and our mutual personal interests had deepened that he permitted himself, in his need for a verdict on his work, to ask me as a personal favor to take a look at his score. I gave him a number of suggestions as to how it might be improved; but soon he was so hopelessly disgusted by his own work that he not only put it aside completely but also could never again be induced to try his hand at a similar undertaking. After he had become familiar with my previous works and gotten to know something of my plans for new ones, he declared to me man to man that he felt it his duty to play the part of observer, help me loyally to gain widespread sympathy for my new works, to protect me entirely or relieve me as far as possible from the repugnant aspects of my professional activities or other dealings with the public, and to avoid placing himself in the ridiculous position of composing operas of his own while living on terms of close friendship with me. I tried, to be sure, to make him exercise his own productive capacities notwithstanding, and referred to him material I considered suitable for him to set to music. Among these subjects was a little French drama, *Cromwell's Daughter*, on a later occasion one derived from a sentimental peasant story I had found in a popular publication and for the adaptation of which I presented him with an extensive plan. All my efforts remained ultimately fruitless, and it turned out that the productive drive in him was weak, added to which he was soon involved in extremely trying domestic troubles, so that the poor man had to struggle along in support of a wife and a rapidly expanding bunch of children. Thus he began to need my help and sympathy in matters other than those pertaining to his artistic development. He was uncommonly open-minded, possessed a rare capacity for autodidactic development in every branch of knowledge and experience, and soon became through his unshakable loyalty and unvarying kindness an indispensable friend and comrade to me. He was and remained the only person who grasped the true character of my relationship to the world around me, and thus the sole person with whom I could discuss all the sufferings and cares arising from it with absolute frankness, and know that I would be understood. The dreadful trials and experiences, along with the most painful anxieties to which fate would before long lead us both will soon be seen.

I also obtained one other loyal and lifelong friend at an early date in my residence in Dresden, though by his nature not suited to exert such a decisive influence on my future development. A young doctor named Anton Pusinelli lived next to me; he seized the occasion of a little serenade sung in honor of my thirtieth birthday by the Dresden Glee Club to make my acquaintance and express his sincere and uncommonly deeply felt personal interest in me. We soon became steadfast friends, and he assumed the function of a solicitous family doctor who in the course of the years had ample opportunity, given the increasing difficulties of my stay in Dresden, to assist in the most self-sacrificial way. His financial position was very good and this permitted him to help me most substantially in this respect as well, thus obliging me to lasting recognition of his most valuable friendly services.

A further opportunity to develop my contacts with Dresden society was afforded by the generous attention of the family of Court Chamberlain Könneritz, whose wife, Maria von Könneritz née Fink, a friend of the Countess Ida Hahn-Hahn,[1] expressed particularly vivid appreciation and even passionate enthusiasm for my ventures as a composer. Through this family, which often invited me to their house, I seemed likely to be drawn into further association with the higher circles of the Dresden aristocracy; but matters never went beyond superficial contact; we didn't find many mutual interests of any significance. To be sure, I became acquainted there with Countess Rossi, the famous Henriette Sontag, by whom I was greeted to my genuine surprise with winning warmth, and also obtained the opportunity of visiting her later in Berlin among distinguished company. The peculiar disillusionment I experienced at this subsequent occasion will be described in detail in due course, but I will mention here only that, inasmuch as I had been steeled by my earlier experiences in the world against illusions about such people, my inclination to know them more intimately soon gave way to a complete hopelessness and utter renunciation of any comfort from these spheres. Although the Könneritz couple remained favorably disposed to me throughout my long stay in Dresden, this relationship did not have the slightest effect either on my development or on my position. Nonetheless Herr von Lüttichau, at a time when our relations were approaching a crisis point, told me that in his opinion the inordinate praise from Frau von Könneritz had gone to my head and made me forget my station as his subordinate. But in this he overlooked the fact that if any woman from the higher circles of Dresden society had exerted an invigorating influence on my inner pride, that woman was his own wife, Ida von Lüttichau née von Knobelsdorf. The impression I gained from this cultured, delicate and distinguished lady was new in my life and might have become of great importance if I had been able to see her more frequently and know her more intimately. It was not so much her position as the wife of the General Director of the Court Theater that held me back, but rather her continually precarious health and my singular reluctance to appear in any way importunate under those particular circumstances that permitted me to enjoy a closer association with her only at very infrequent intervals. In my memory her image blends somewhat with that of my sister Rosalie; for I remember being spurred by a subtle ambition to awaken the interest of this sensitive woman, who was painfully wasting away in coarse surroundings. The first evidence of fulfillment of this ambition I found in the attentiveness she accorded *Der fliegende Holländer*, despite the fact that, after *Rienzi*, it had so bewildered the Dresden public. She was thus the first who swam against the tide to meet me in my new direction. I was so delighted by this conquest that I dedicated this opera to her upon its subsequent publication. In the account of some particular events of my later years in Dresden I shall have more to say about the deep sympathy she showed for my development and my innermost artistic concerns. But, as stated, we really were never on close terms, and the manner in which I lived in Dresden was thus not affected by this in itself so important acquaintanceship.

On the other hand, my theatrical acquaintances spread themselves with irresistible importunity across the whole foreground of my life.

Strictly speaking, even after my great successes I was still basically confined to the same casual and domestic sphere in which I had prepared for them. In addition to my old friends Heine and Papa Fischer, the only new member of the circle was Tichatschek, who also brought along an odd retinue of household friends. Anyone who lived in Dresden in those days and happened to know the court lithographer Fürstenau[1] will be amazed to learn that, without really being aware of how it came about, I developed a close familial relationship with this intimate friend of Tichatschek, and the significance of this singular connection may be judged from the fact that my eventual estrangement from him coincided precisely with the collapse of my civic standing. My good-natured acceptance of election to a high position in the Dresden Glee Club also brought me further casual acquaintances. This club consisted of a moderate number of young merchants and officials intrinsically more interested in social intercourse than in music, yet sedulously held together for his special purposes by a strange and ambitious fellow, Professor Löwe, who believed that an authority such as I possessed at this time in Dresden was essential to the attainment of those ends. Chief among them was his interest in transferring the ashes of Carl Maria von Weber from London to Dresden; as this objective was profoundly congenial to me as well, I offered him whatever assistance I could, even though the Professor was no doubt only following the promptings of ambition in this effort. But his initial plan, as head of the musically entirely worthless Glee Club, was to summon all the male-voice choral societies of Saxony to a gala performance in Dresden. To carry out this design a committee was set up, and as the fur soon began to fly, Löwe transformed it into a regular revolutionary tribunal, over which he presided day and night as the great event approached, earning from me by his frantic zeal the nickname "Robespierre". Although I had been placed at the head of this undertaking, I was able to evade this reign of terror, for I had enough work to do in writing the composition I had promised for the festival. I had been given the job of writing a piece for male chorus, and it was supposed to be of approximately a half hour's duration. I decided that the monotony of such choral singing, which the orchestra would only enliven to a slight extent, could be made bearable solely through the introduction of some dramatic elements. I therefore conceived a quite large choral scene depicting the first feast of Pentecost and the outpouring of the Holy Ghost, and executed it in such a way that the whole thing would be sung by various choral groups in turn, completely avoiding any real solo parts in accordance with the dictates of the situation. What came out of this was my *Liebesmahl der Apostel*, a work that has been performed here and there in recent times and which, given the specific circumstances in which I had to produce it, I am content to assign to the category of "occasional" works. But I was not displeased by the success of this work, particularly in the rehearsals held under my direction with the Dresden choral societies alone. When, therefore, twelve hundred so-called singers from all over Saxony grouped themselves around me in the Frauenkirche, where the performance took place, I was astonished at the comparatively feeble effect produced upon my ear by this colossal mass of human bodies. This experience convinced me of the inherent foolishness of such gigantic choral undertakings, and produced in me a decided antipathy to concerning myself with them in any way in the future.

I had a good deal of difficulty getting out of the clutches of the Dresden Glee Club, and succeeded only when I was able to introduce Professor Löwe to another man of similar ambition, Herr Ferdinand Hiller.[1] The most glorious deed I accomplished in my work with this society was to effect at last the transfer of Weber's ashes, which took place before I had extricated myself from the club, and which I will describe in due course. Let me first cite yet another occasional composition, which was officially commissioned from me as Royal Kapellmeister. On June 7th of this year (1843), the monument to King Friedrich August executed by Rietschel[2] was unveiled in the Dresden Zwinger, and, together with Mendelssohn, I was given the honor of composing a festive song, as well as conducting the musical performance at the ceremony. I had produced a simple and unpretentious song for male voices, whereas Mendelssohn had been assigned the more complicated task of weaving into the male chorus he was to compose the anthem *God Save the King*, or, as it is called in Saxony, *Heil Dir im Rautenkranz*. He accomplished this by a contrapuntal tour de force, introducing the Anglo-Saxon folk-song on the brass as accompaniment, after the first eight measures of his own original melody. My simple song seems to have sounded quite nicely in the distance, whereas I learned the effect of the more audacious Mendelssohn composition had been entirely nugatory, because nobody had understood why the singers were not singing the same tune the brass was blowing. Nevertheless Mendelssohn, who was present at the affair, accorded me a written expression of thanks for the pains I had taken in the performance of his composition; I also received from the Festival Committee a gold snuff-box, which presumably was intended to reflect the value of my little song, for I found to my surprise a hunting scene so badly engraved upon it that the metal had been pierced in numerous places.

Amid all the distractions of this new and greatly changed way of life, I was concerned to pull myself together and, given my inner recognition of the true nature of my successes, steel myself against these impressions. I had completed the poem of the *Venusberg*, as I then still called my .*Tannhäuser*, as early as May, by my thirtieth birthday. But I had not yet arrived at any close study of medieval poetry: the classical side of the poetry of the Middle Ages had so far only faintly dawned on me, partly from youthful recollections and partly from the brief acquaintance with it I had made through the instruction of Lehrs in Paris. The establishment of a permanent home, which was supposed to be facilitated by my lifelong royal appointment, gained particular significance from the hope that it would now be possible for me to dedicate myself once again to serious and systematic studies of a productive character, an aim which my theatrical activities and the sufferings of my Paris years had almost entirely frustrated. This hope was strengthened by the nature of my official duties, for I was never overwhelmed with work from that quarter, and was treated with exceptional consideration by the theater management. Though I had been employed for only a few months, I was granted a vacation this first summer and spent it in Teplitz, which I had grown to like so much and to which I had dispatched my wife in advance.

The change in my condition since the previous year was an immense source of satisfaction, and I could now rent four spacious rooms in the same inn, the Oak at Schönau, where I had lived before in such frugal circumstances. My sister Klara paid us a visit at our invitation; my good mother, whose arthritic problems necessitated a water cure at Teplitz every year, also got together with us again. I too seized the opportunity of taking the mineral waters, in the hope of doing something about the gastric troubles that had plagued me ever since my Paris days. Unfortunately, the attempted cure had the opposite effect; and when I complained about the painful irritation it caused, I learned that I was evidently not a suitable subject for such a cure: I had been observed in particular during my morning walks, while I drank my water, marching hurriedly through the shady alleys of the adjacent Thurn gardens, and I was given to understand that such a cure could only be effective if I meandered along in a most leisurely manner. Beyond this, it had been noticed that I was always carrying around a rather thick book, with which I sat down to rest together with my mineral water in hidden places. This was Jacob Grimm's *Deutsche Mythologie*. Whoever knows this work will understand how the inordinate wealth of its contents, gathered from all sides and really intended almost solely for scholars, had an immediately stimulating effect on me, who was looking everywhere for expressive and meaningful symbols. Formed from the scanty fragments of a vanished world, of which scarcely any tangible monuments remain to testify, I discovered here a confusing construction which at first sight appeared to me as a huge rocky crevice choked with underbrush. Nothing in it was complete, nor was there anything resembling an architectural line, and I often felt tempted to abandon the seemingly hopeless effort to make something systematic out of it. And yet I was firmly in the power of its strange enchantment: even the most fragmentary legends spoke to me in a profoundly familiar tongue, and soon my entire sensibility was possessed by images suggesting ever more clearly the recapture of a long lost yet eagerly sought consciousness. There rose up in my soul a whole world of figures, which yet proved to be so unexpectedly solid and well-known from earliest days, that when I saw them clearly before me and could hear their speech I could not grasp the source of the virtually tangible familiarity and certitude of their demeanor. The effect they produced upon my innermost being I can only describe as a complete rebirth, and just as we feel a tender joy at a child's first sudden flash of recognition, so my own eyes now flashed with rapture at a world I saw revealed for the first time, as if by a miracle, in which I had previously moved blindly though presentient, like a child in its mother's womb.

The effect of all this did not particularly further my intention to sketch some of the music for *Tannhäuser*; I had set up a piano in the Oak, and had banged away until I had broken all its strings, but still nothing had come of it. With a good deal of arduous toil I wrote the initial Venusberg music, as fortunately I had been carrying the main motives for it around in my head for some time. Meanwhile, I was much troubled by irritability and sudden suffusions of blood to the brain, got the idea I was sick, and stayed in bed for days reading the German legends of Grimm as well as constantly returning to his disturbing *Mythology*, until I finally hit upon the idea of liberating myself from all these manias by an excursion to Prague. I made this pleasant journey in an open carriage with my wife, with whom I had already climbed the peak at Milischau, stopped again at the Black Horse, met my friend Kittl, now distinctly plump, made various side trips, and reveled in the antique marvels of the city. I learned to my delight that the lovely companions of my youth,

Jenny and Auguste Pachta, had married happily into the highest ranks of the aristocracy, found everything else wonderful, and headed back to Dresden to take up again my functions as Royal Saxon Kapellmeister.

We now set to work getting ourselves established in a roomy and nicely situated house on the Ostra-Allee, with a view of the Zwinger. We did a good and thorough job of it, as was only fitting for a thirty-year-old man who was settling down permanently in life. As I received no reimbursement whatever for these expenses, I naturally had to borrow the necessary funds at interest; yet the real fruits of my Dresden opera success were still to be plucked: what was more natural than to assume I would soon begin harvesting them? My nice little dwelling, fit for a royal Kapellmeister, was adorned by three treasures: a concert grand from Breitkopf & Härtel, of which I had made myself the proud possessor; then, hanging above a stately writing desk, now in the possession of Chamber Musician Otto Kummer,[1] the title page by Cornelius[2] for the *Nibelungenlied* in a beautiful gothic frame, the only object of the three which has remained faithfully in my hands to this day; but above all the house was transformed into a home by the presence of a library, which I had acquired in one fell swoop in accordance with the systematic plan of study I had in mind to undertake. Upon the collapse of my Dresden existence, this library through some odd vicissitudes came into the possession of Herr Heinrich Brockhaus, to whom I owed five hundred talers at the time, and who slapped a lien on it for this amount without telling my wife. I never succeeded in getting this unusual collection back from him. Old German literature formed the salient part of the collection, together with related medieval works, which led to my purchasing some expensive editions, as for example the very scarce old *Romans des douze pairs*. Beyond this there were the best historical works on the Middle Ages as well as on German history as a whole; at the same time I made sure to include the classical and poetic literature of all times and languages, among which I bought the Italian poets and also Shakespeare, as well as the French authors whose language I could cope with to some extent, in the expectation that I would one day find time to learn these languages I had neglected. I took the easier way with classical antiquity and purchased those translations that have themselves become classics, because I had already found in perusing Homer, whom I bought in the original Greek, that I would have to count on more leisure than I could plausibly expect from my conducting duties if I wanted to find time to polish up my former knowledge of the Greek language; then in addition I provided most thoroughly for a study of world history and to this end did not fail to equip myself with many multi-volume works in this field. Thus armed, I thought I could defy all the tribulations I clearly foresaw my career and my position would bring me, and in the hope for long and quiet enjoyment of the domesticity I had at last won for myself, I moved into my by no means luxurious but still substantial and solidly comfortable house in the best of spirits in October of the year 1843.

The first respite I could snatch from my official duties, as well as the studies upon which I had so enthusiastically embarked in the bosom of my new house, I devoted to the composition of *Tannhäuser*, of which the first act was completed in January of the new year 1844. This winter, during which I did nothing in Dresden worthy of special recollection, was marked by two expeditions, the first of which took me to Berlin at the beginning of the year for a production of *Der fliegende Holländer*, and the second to Hamburg in March for a production of *Rienzi*.

The impressions of the first expedition have remained more vivid. I had been utterly taken by surprise at being notified suddenly by the Berlin intendant, Herr von Küstner, of a forthcoming performance of my *Holländer*: inasmuch as the opera house that had burned down a year before was not yet available for performances, I had taken no soundings in Berlin about my work, as I was content to await its reconstruction. Because it had been performed in Dresden with very poor scenery, and I had learned how important a careful mise-en-scène was to my dramatic seascapes, I had been counting on the proven staging capacities of the Berlin theater to do much better and was thus highly upset at this use of my opera by the Berlin Intendant as a stop-gap for interim performances being given in the Schauspielhaus, a theater used otherwise only for spoken drama. But my remonstrances availed nothing, as I was not told the opera was about to be rehearsed, but rather that all preparations had been completed and it was ready to go on the boards within a few days. This arrangement obviously implied that my opera was condemned to a merely transitory appearance in the Berlin repertory, because I could not suppose that it would be staged anew at some later date in the rebuilt opera house. There was an attempt to rationalize the matter to me by combining the performances with a guest appearance of Schröder-Devrient, who would be singing in Berlin at the time, for everybody assumed I would be happy to see the great artist appear in it. But I could just as well contend that my opera had been dug out as a makeshift vehicle for this guest appearance, because they were evidently in a quandary with regard to her repertory, which consisted mainly of so-called "grand" operas, such as those of Meyerbeer, and suitable only for a big opera house, and these were precisely the works they wanted to reserve for a particularly brilliant future in the new house. Thus I recognized from the beginning that my *Holländer* was considered by the management of the Berlin Court Theater as falling in the category of "Kapellmeisters' operas" and was foreordained to share the same fate as all the rest of them. The treatment granted my work and myself accorded fully with this discouraging assumption. Nevertheless, since Schröder-Devrient was expected to take part, I struggled to overcome my distaste and went to Berlin to do my best to make the performances a success. I saw immediately that my presence was very necessary; at the conductor's podium I found a man who went by the name of Henning[1] (or Henniger), a functionary who had risen to this position out of the musical rank and file by scrupulous regard for seniority rights, but who had little idea how to conduct an orchestra and, as to my opera, not the faintest shimmer of comprehension. I therefore took up the baton, and conducted the general rehearsal and two performances, in which, however, Schröder-Devrient did not sing. Although I was upset by the under-manned string section and the consequently thin orchestral sound, I was nonetheless well satisfied with the performers, both as to their capabilities and to their enthusiasm for the task, and I was most pleasantly surprised by the superb staging under the direction of the truly brilliant stage director Blum, with the collaboration of his highly skilled and ingenious technicians.

Hence I was very curious to find out how all these, to me, pleasant and encouraging dispositions would strike the Berlin public at the first performance. What I experienced in this respect was very singular. It was obvious that the only thing that interested the audience was what particular fault or faults they were going to discover in me: in the course of the first act a consensus seemed to be forming that I belonged in the category of bores; there was no clapping, and later I was advised that this was very fortunate, as the slightest sign of applause would have been interpreted at once as evidence of a claque and would have been energetically opposed. Küstner nonetheless assured me later that he admired my courage in leaving the orchestra and coming out on the stage to show myself after this act, despite this purportedly auspicious absence of applause. But as long as I was content with the performance itself, I was certainly not disposed to let myself be discouraged by lack of public response, and of course I knew that the decisive effect of my opera lay in its second act. I therefore devoted my zealous efforts to making this act come off well rather than to analyzing the reasons for the attitude of the Berlin public. And this really broke the ice; the audience seemed to surrender its preconceived notions and let itself be carried away at the close of the second act in swelling applause, even to the point of stormy enthusiasm. Amid boisterous shouts I and my singers appeared in front of the curtain to tread the customary pavan of thanks, and inasmuch as the third act was too short to let boredom develop, and the scenic effects turned out to be novel and exciting, the renewed bursts of applause at the end of the work left us all in no doubt that we had scored a triumph. Mendelssohn, who was in Berlin together with Meyerbeer at the time in connection with their duties as general music directors, had attended the performance in a proscenium box, following its progress without expression on his pale visage, and he came up to me at the end to whisper to me in emotionless bonhomie, "Well, you should certainly be happy now!" I saw him on several other occasions during my short stay in Berlin and also spent one evening at his home enjoying some chamber music; but never did another word about *Der fliegende Holländer* escape his lips, except for an inquiry concerning the second performance, whether Schröder-Devrient would sing or someone else; I also found, moreover, that he responded with similar indifference to my genuinely enthusiastic allusions to his incidental music for *A Midsummer Night's Dream*, which was being given quite frequently in those days and which I had heard for the first time. The only point he discussed in any detail was the performance of the actor Gern, who played Bottom and, in his opinion, was over-acting.

A few days later came a second performance with the same cast, which I also conducted. What I experienced on this evening was even more singular than on the first. I had clearly gained a few allies from the first performance, who turned up again and began applauding after the overture; this aroused a lot of hissing, and throughout the entire evening nobody dared to applaud again. My old friend Heine had come from Dresden on behalf of the theater management to study the staging of *A Midsummer Night's Dream* and attended this second performance. He had persuaded me to accept an invitation from one of his Berlin relatives to have supper together after the performance in a little restaurant on Unter den Linden. Very weary, I followed him to an ugly and dimly lit tavern, gulped down the proffered wine in somewhat hasty discontent in the hope of warming myself, listened to the strained conversation of my good-natured friend and his companion, and stared fixedly at the daily papers, now having ample leisure to read the reviews of the first performance of *Der fliegende Holländer*, which had appeared that day. I felt pretty badly cut up when I saw for the first time my name and my work handled in the most contemptible tone and absolutely shameless, rampant ignorance. Our Berlin host, a thorough philistine, stated that he had known all along what would happen this evening, for he had read these reviews in the morning. The Berliners, he said, wait for the verdict of Rellstab and his cronies to determine how they should react. This singular fellow really wanted to cheer me up, and he ordered bottle after bottle of various wines; my friend Heine tried to evoke the happier memories of our *Rienzi* period in Dresden; staggering, and with my head spinning, I was finally conducted back to my hotel by the two of them. It was after midnight. When the night-clerk was lighting my way through the dark corridors to my room, a man suddenly stepped out in my path, dressed in black and of pale and distinguished countenance. He said he wanted to talk to me. He asserted he had been waiting for me since the end of the performance and in his determination to speak to me had remained here until now. I tried to excuse myself as being totally unfit for any kind of business for, as he could see, I had, without exactly giving way to unrestrained merriment, carelessly drunk a little too much wine. I got this out in a stammer; but my strange visitor was all the less willing to be rebuffed; he accompanied me to my room and declared it was now all the more imperative that he speak to me. We seated ourselves in the cold room to the feeble light of one candle, and he began telling me in fluid and impassioned speech that he too had attended that night's performance of *Der fliegende Holländer* and could well imagine the mood in which such experiences had left me; but precisely for that reason he had decided to stop at nothing to be able to speak to me tonight in order to tell me that with *Der fliegende Holländer* I had written an unprecedented masterpiece, and that it would be indeed terrible if I yielded to the slightest feeling of discouragement as a result of the unworthy reception accorded it by the Berlin public, as on this very evening he had made the acquaintance of a work that evoked new and undreamed-of hope for the future of German art. My hair began standing on end: one of Hoffmann's fantastic figures had entered my life in the flesh! I could think of nothing to say except to inquire his name, whereupon he seemed very surprised, as I had, he said, conversed with him the day before at Mendelssohn's house: it was there that my conduct and conversation had attracted his attention; he had suddenly regretted giving in to his general distaste for opera by not attending the first performance of *Der fliegende Holländer* and swore to himself not to miss the second; he was, he informed me, Professor Werder.[1] This didn't mean anything to me; he had to write it down. He hunted up pen and paper, did as requested, and we parted, after which I threw myself upon the bed, dead to the world, and enjoyed a deep and refreshing sleep. By the next morning I was relaxed and well, paid a parting visit to Schröder-Devrient, who promised to do all she could for my *Holländer*, collected my fee of a hundred ducats and went back to Dresden via Leipzig, where I used my ducats to reimburse my relatives for the cash advances they had made to me to keep me going during the previous waiting-period in Dresden, and arrived home to recuperate among my books and ponder the deep impression produced by Werder's nocturnal visit.

Before the end of the winter I received a genuine invitation to Hamburg for a production of *Rienzi* through the enterprising director Cornet,[2] who, as he admitted to me, was having a succession of disasters in his theater and needed a big success of the kind he thought he could expect from *Rienzi*, having heard the work in Dresden. So I set off on the journey in March, which in this era was still rather troublesome, as after Hanover we had to proceed by mail-coach, and crossing the ice-strewn Elbe was a risky business. The city of Hamburg was being rebuilt at the time after its great fire, and its center showed a lot of open spaces covered with ruins. The cold weather and a continually gloomy sky make my recollections of my rather prolonged stay there almost exclusively disagreeable. I was tormented so much by having to rehearse with resources suitable only for the poorest theatrical trumpery that I spent most of my free time, exhausted and subject to constant colds, alone in my hotel room. My earlier experiences of superficial and poorly founded theatrical doings came back to me afresh. It was particularly depressing to realize that I had made myself an unwitting accomplice in Director Cornet's least appetizing objectives. His one aim was to create a sensation, and he assumed this would be fine with me, inasmuch as he granted me only a small fee and a promise of large future royalties. The dignity of the stage presentation, a quality of which he for his part understood nothing, was utterly sacrificed to the most ludicrous and tawdry showiness, as he thought that pageantry was all that was needed to ensure my success. Thus he put together all sorts of processions, for which he dug out the costumes from all the fairy-tale ballets in the repertory, and thought that if everything looked gay enough and people were always bustling around the stage, I ought to be satisfied. But the sorriest part of the whole affair was the singer taking the title role, an elderly, flabby and voiceless tenor named Wurda,[1] who sang Rienzi with the same expression as in his favorite role, Elvino in *La Sonnambula*. He was so unbearable that I got the idea of making the Capitol crumble and collapse as early as the second act, in order to bury him under the ruins, a plan which would also have eliminated several of those processions so dear to the director's heart. The sole ray of light was the woman who sang Adriano, who delighted me with her verve; this was a Mme Fehringer who later, after she had already passed her best, was cast by Liszt in the part of Ortrud in *Lohengrin* in Weimar. There could be nothing more disheartening than my being compelled to busy myself with this opera of mine in these circumstances. Yet there were no outward signs of failure; at any rate the director hoped to keep *Rienzi* in the repertory long enough so that Tichatschek could come to Hamburg and give the people of the town a better idea of it. This actually happened the following summer.

Herr Cornet noticed my depression and bad mood, and having discovered my desire to present my wife with a parrot, he arranged to procure for me a very attractive example of this species of bird, which he presented to me as a little gratuity. I carried it with me in its tiny cage on the melancholy trip home and was very touched to notice that it quickly requited my solicitude with great attachment. Minna received me with great joy as a consequence, for this lovely gray parrot was a sure sign that I would certainly get somewhere in the world. We already had a pretty little dog, born in Dresden in our landlady's house on the first day of rehearsals for *Rienzi* and which, owing to its fierce devotion to me and other conspicuous characteristics, was familiar to and petted by all those who knew me and my home in those years. And now came this pleasant bird, which had no bad habits and was very teachable, to help enliven our house in the absence of children. My wife soon taught him a snatch of song from *Rienzi*, with which the friendly bird henceforth greeted me from the distance when it heard me coming up the stairs.

And so it seemed as if I had established my domestic hearth with the most comfortable prospects.

There were no further expeditions to performances of my operas principally for the reason that there weren't any such performances. As I now clearly saw that the diffusion of my works among the theaters was a slow process, I concluded that this was no doubt attributable to the lack of vocal scores to assist in making them known. I therefore thought I would be well advised to press energetically to get these published as soon as possible. In order to secure the expected profits for myself, I hit upon the idea of publishing them at my own expense. I therefore got hold of the Dresden Court music dealer F. Meser, who up to then had not gone beyond publishing a dance or two, and concluded a contract whereby he and his firm were to serve as nominal publisher, whereas in reality he would do the edition on a basis of cost plus ten per cent, while I would put up the capital to meet these costs. As it was a matter of publishing two operas, one of them as voluminous a work as *Rienzi*, and given the fact that they were unlikely to prove profitable unless, in addition to the vocal scores, I also published other arrangements, for piano duet as well as solo, with text and without, a fairly large capital sum turned out to be necessary. Thus, in order to get the income I expected from all this, with which to repay old debts and pay off the remaining costs of my household furnishings, I had to look around for much larger sums. I laid my project and my motives before Schröder-Devrient, who had just returned to Dresden at Easter 1844 to begin a new engagement. She believed in the future of my works, recognized the special aspects of my position as well as the correctness of my calculations, and expressed herself willing, without considering it any great sacrifice, to finance the publication of my operas by placing her Polish treasury bonds at my disposal for this purpose in a loan at the customary rate of interest. This went so easily and seemed so much a matter of course that I at once made the necessary arrangements with a Leipzig printer and set the publication of my two operas in train.

By the time enough material had been delivered to necessitate a substantial payment on open account, I went to see my friend to obtain an initial capital advance. But here I was confronted by a new phase in the life of this celebrity, which placed me in a position that proved as disastrous as it was unexpected. After she had broken completely with that unfortunate Herr von Münchhausen some time before, returning with penitent ardor, as it seemed, to her previous relationship with my friend Hermann Müller, it now turned out that she had found no real satisfaction in this renewed affair. On the contrary, the longed-for guiding light of her life had now appeared in the form of another lieutenant of the Guards, Herr von Döring; for with a vehemence that swept away any compunctions she might have felt about betraying her earlier friend, she drew to herself this slim young man, whose moral and intellectual worthlessness was patent to everybody, to become the touchstone of her life. This fellow in turn took his good fortune so seriously that he would put up with no joking and above all soon got his hands on his future wife's money, as he contended that it was very poorly and insecurely invested, and that he knew much better ways of putting it to work. Schröder-Devrient now revealed to me in considerable pain and embarrassment that she had renounced control of her capital and could not keep her promise to me. With this turn I fell into a series of entanglements which henceforth dominated my life and plunged me into worries that made their melancholy imprint on all my undertakings. It was clear, at any rate, that I could not retroactively cancel the publishing venture; a satisfactory solution to these perplexities was still possible only through the execution of the plan and the success I hoped would attend it. I was compelled, therefore, to dig up the money to continue the publication of my operas, to which *Tannhäuser* was necessarily added in due course, at first from my friends and acquaintances, but at length, when things were more pressing, from anybody, even at shortest term and usurious interest rates. So much for now, in order to set the stage for the catastrophes toward which my path so inexorably led me.

At first the hopelessness of my position did not reveal itself, for there seemed to be no reason to despair of the eventual diffusion of my operas among the German theaters, though experience with them indicated that this would be a slow process. To set against the unpleasant experiences in Berlin and Hamburg, there were a number of encouraging signs. Above all, *Rienzi* maintained its favored position with the Dresden public, a fact which took on much greater significance in the summer months, with the stream of visitors coming through the city. My opera, which could be heard nowhere else,[1] was in great demand among visitors from all German and some foreign countries, and was always received with noticeably surprised satisfaction, so that a performance of *Rienzi*, especially in summer, always enjoyed a certain festival character, all of which obviously had an encouraging effect on me.

On one occasion Liszt was included among these visitors. As *Rienzi* was not on the bill at the time of his arrival, he had successfully petitioned the theater management for a special performance. I met him during this performance in Tichatschek's dressing room and was greatly touched and heartened by his unreservedly expressed, almost amazed appreciation. While the kind of life Liszt led in those days kept him perpetually surrounded by distraction and commotion of all types and prevented us from closer intimacy on this occasion, I began hereafter receiving continually increasing evidence that I had made a lasting impression on him and that his interest in me led him to take action on my behalf. From then on people, mostly from elevated circles and from first one part of the world and then another, wherever Liszt's triumphant progresses took him, would come to me in Dresden, demanding to hear *Rienzi* as a result of Liszt's reports about it and of his having played excerpts from it, all of them convinced that they were to hear something of unparalleled significance. Beyond these indications of Liszt's enthusiastic interest there were some other deeply touching testimonials. The startling initiative represented by Werder's nocturnal visit after the second performance of *Der fliegende Holländer* in Berlin was followed by a similarly unsolicited approach in the form of an epistolary outpouring from a person equally unknown to me, Alwine Frommann,[1] who subsequently became my close friend. She had heard two of the performances in which Schröder-Devrient had sung Senta after my departure from Berlin, and the letter in which she related to me her impressions of my work conveyed to me for the first time the vivid and deep feelings of a great and confident appreciation, such as is rarely vouchsafed even to the greatest master and which will not fail to exercise a profound influence on his spirit and on his soul's need to believe in himself.

I have no vivid recollections from this first year as conductor in a sphere of activity that grew more and more routine. For a ceremonial beginning to my function at the theater I was given, somewhat as a mark of distinction, Gluck's *Armide* to conduct, and this was performed in March 1843 with Schröder-Devrient, before her departure from Dresden for a time. Great importance was attached to this production, as Meyerbeer was then inaugurating his term as general music director in Berlin with a performance of the same work. Berlin, indeed, was the point of origin of the extreme respect accorded any such undertaking with Gluck; I was told that Meyerbeer had gone with the score of *Armide* in hand to Rellstab to get some hints as to how it should be handled. As I learned not long afterwards of the strange anecdote concerning the two silver candlesticks with which this famous composer was said to have illuminated the score of his *Feldlager in Schlesien* for the no less famous critic, I elected to attach no undue importance to whatever instructions about *Armide* he might have received from this source, and I found my own way of going about it by carefully studying the somewhat stiff score and trying to give it some elasticity by a fluid and nuanced interpretation. I had the gratification of receiving an exceedingly warm endorsement of my reading of this score from Herr Eduard Devrient,[2] a Gluck connoisseur of the first rank. After hearing the opera as we gave it and comparing it with the Berlin performance, he praised the delicate modulations in the interpretation of pieces which in Berlin had been treated with the coarsest insensitivity. As a striking instance of this, he singled out the brief C major chorus of the nymphs in the third act. By taking it at a slower tempo and imposing a particularly delicate softness of tone I had eliminated the original crudity with which Devrient had heard it rendered, presumably true to tradition, in Berlin. My most innocent device, and one that I frequently adopted, to break the disturbing rigidity of the orchestral movement in the original was a painstaking modification of the basso-continuo going on incessantly in quarter time by alternatively introducing legato and pizzicato playing. The management had spent a lot on externals, particularly on the stage decorations, and the work drew fairly good audiences, more or less as a spectacle opera, thus earning for me the reputation of being a conductor with a special and even decisive affinity for Gluck. This resulted in large part from the fact that the much more noble *Iphigenia in Tauris*, despite the superb performance of Schröder-Devrient in the title role, had played to empty houses.

I had to live on this reputation for a long time, as it often happened that I had no choice but to conduct routine performances of the standard repertory, including Mozart operas, and these necessarily more mediocre productions were all the more disappointing to those who attended them with special hopes based upon my achievements with *Armide*. Even some of my friends in the audience concluded from this that I didn't think much of Mozart and didn't understand him, because they failed to realize how confoundedly impossible it was for me to exercise any influence on such desultory, stop-gap performances, which I was often summoned to conduct as a substitute and without any rehearsals. Indeed, this often put me in a false position I was powerless to remedy, and went a long way toward rendering my new position, through its involvement in an excess of the meanest theatrical routine work, even more unbearable than I had anticipated, despite my clear prior insight into the less appetizing aspects of this activity. My colleague Reissiger, to whom I occasionally confided my distress that the management did so little to uphold proper standards in the operatic field, consoled me with the observation that in time I would learn, as he had, to let these things take their own course and submit to the inevitable fate of a Kapellmeister. In so doing he proudly thumped his stomach and expressed the hope that I might soon be able to boast of one as round as his own.

I received further cause for my growing disgust with these sloppy practices by close acquaintance with the manner and spirit in which even eminent conductors undertook to perform our masterworks. During my first year Mendelssohn was invited to conduct his *St Paul* in one of the then famous Palm Sunday concerts of the Dresden orchestra. Getting to know this work under such auspicious circumstances pleased me very much, and I made a fresh attempt to approach the composer in a sincere and friendly way. But a strange conversation I had with him on the night of this performance quickly extinguished this impulse. After the oratorio, Reissiger performed Beethoven's Eighth Symphony. In the preceding rehearsal I had noticed that Reissiger had fallen into the error of all routine conductors in this work of turning the minuet tempo of the third movement into a thoughtless waltz time, whereby the piece not only completely loses its imposing character but the trio is rendered absolutely ludicrous by the impossibility of playing the cello figurations properly at such speed. I had approached Reissiger on the subject; he agreed with me and promised to take the movement in true minuet tempo, such as I had indicated to him, at the performance. I related the incident to Mendelssohn, who, after conducting his *St Paul* had seated himself next to me in the box to relax and listen to the symphony; he acknowledged I was right and agreed that it should be played as I said. Then the third movement began, and Reissiger, who clearly did not have the ability to impose such a striking tempo change on the orchestra at short notice, followed his old practice and took the "tempo di minuetto" in the customary waltz time. I was just on the point of expressing my dissatisfaction about this when Mendelssohn nodded at me in a friendly way in the opinion that this was just what I had in mind and I should be happy with it. I was so deeply astonished at this instance of insensitivity on the part of such a famous musician that I remained speechless and from then on formed my own special opinion of him, an opinion later confirmed by Robert Schumann, when he expressed his great satisfaction at my tempo in the first movement of Beethoven's Ninth Symphony, which he had previously been obliged to hear taken by Mendelssohn year after year in Leipzig in distorting haste.

While I was longing for every all too infrequent opportunity to exercise some influence on the spirit of the performances of our most imperishable masterpieces, I had to slog along mostly in the deep disgust caused by my involvement with routine theater repertory. It was not until the Palm Sunday before Easter of 1844, just after getting home from my unpleasant expedition to Hamburg, that I got the chance to satisfy my desire by performing the Pastoral Symphony, assigned to me for that day's concert. There were still a number of evils I could remedy only with great difficulty and by indirect methods. The placement of the orchestra at these concerts, whereby the members were seated in a long, thin row in a semi-circle enveloping the chorus, was, in particular, so incomprehensibly faulty that it required an explanation by Reissiger to make me grasp how something so idiotic could have happened. He informed me that all these dispositions stemmed from the deceased Kapellmeister Morlacchi, who as a composer of Italian opera had known nothing of the significance or requirements of an orchestra. When I then asked why he had been allowed to make such arrangements concerning matters he didn't understand, I was informed that since time immemorial, even when Carl Maria von Weber was in Dresden, this Italian had enjoyed the unconditional preference of the court and the General Director's office, against which all opposition was fruitless, and that we would now have enormous problems if we tried to do anything about these inherited errors, because at higher levels there was still an assumption that he must have known best. My childhood memory of the castrato Sassaroli flitted across my soul, and I remembered the admonition of Weber's widow in regard to the significance of my succeeding Weber in the office of conductor in Dresden. Nevertheless, the performance of the Pastoral Symphony exceeded all expectations, and the incomparable and marvelously stimulating enjoyment I was henceforth to derive from such concern with Beethoven's works in particular revealed its restorative powers to me for the first time. Röckel went along with me in all this, supporting me at every rehearsal with eye and ear, always at my side, listening with me, united with me in a single will.

If I had achieved here an encouraging success, yet another undertaking was to provide me that summer with a splendid satisfaction, which to be sure had no great musical significance, but was rather of social importance. The King of Saxony, for whom, as aforementioned, I had conceived a fondness when he was still Prince Friedrich, was expected to return shortly from a lengthy trip he had undertaken to England. The reports about his reception there had gratified my patriotic feelings. While our modest monarch, who hated all pompous display and demonstration, was in England, it happened that Tsar Nicholas also arrived there quite unexpectedly. In the Tsar's honor all kinds of festivities and military reviews had been held, in which our King, much against his will, was obliged to participate, and he was consequently compelled to receive enthusiastic acclamations from the English crowds, who were most demonstrative in showing their preference for him as opposed to the Tsar. The newspapers indulged this tendency as well, and thus a warm wind blew over from across the channel to our little Saxony, filling us with intense pride in our King. In this mood, which took possession of me completely, I learned that there were plans afoot to arrange a special reception for the returning monarch in Leipzig, enhanced by the musical collaboration of Mendelssohn. I made inquiries as to what Dresden was going to do and was told that the King did not intend to come through Dresden on his return trip, but rather would proceed directly to his summer seat at Pillnitz. A moment's reflection showed me that this circumstance would be highly convenient for the fulfillment of my desire to give him a hearty welcome, for as a servant of the crown I could not have rendered any such act of homage in Dresden without its taking on the character of an entirely inappropriate official parade. I hit upon the idea of getting together everybody who could sing or play, and going with them on the morning after his arrival to perform a song I would quickly compose. But there was first the special obstacle posed by the absence of my superior Lüttichau on one of his country estates; to confer with my colleague Reissiger on the matter would only have delayed it and given the whole undertaking an official flavor I wanted very much to avoid. As there was no time to be lost if anything were to come of it, for his arrival was to take place within a few days, I utilized my position as head of the Glee Club, and in this capacity called upon singers and musicians, including also the members of the theater troupe as well as the orchestra, to participate. I went quickly off to Pillnitz to take care of the necessary arrangements with the chamberlain in residence, whom I found favorably disposed to the project. This little trip there and back was the only opportunity I had to write my verses and compose the music, for by the time I arrived back in Dresden I had to hand them over to the copyist and lithographer at once. The agreeable sensation of speeding through the warm summer air and the lovely countryside, together with the sincere affection I felt for our German monarch which had prompted this effort, brought me to the high pitch of excitement in which I found the melismatic figurations of my *Tannhäuser* march. This royal greeting was already imbued with these, and in the more fully developed form they were one of the means through which that march was later helped to become my most popular piece to date. No later than the following day we had to hold a rehearsal with one hundred and twenty musicians and three hundred singers: I had permitted myself to summon everybody to the stage of the theater for this purpose; everything went perfectly there from the beginning; all were enjoying themselves, and I no less so, when a messenger appeared from Herr von Lüttichau, who had suddenly come back to town and wanted to speak to me. The General Director was furious beyond measure at my independent initiative in this matter, of which he had been informed just in time by friend Reissiger; if he had been wearing his baronial coronet at the time, it would certainly have fallen off. Particularly the fact that I had negotiated directly with Court authorities, and that, as I had to tell him, these dealings had led to a favorable result with extraordinary rapidity, put him in blackest rage, because his importance derived mainly from his capacity to pretend successfully that obtaining anything from that direction was boundlessly difficult. I was willing to cancel everything: this upset him once again; I asked him what he really wanted, if it were to take place after all: he didn't seem to have any clear idea about this but contended it was very inconsiderate of me to have bypassed not only him but also my colleague Reissiger in this venture. I at once expressed willingness to hand over my composition and the job of conducting it to Reissiger: this was also not quite to his liking, for when it came right down to it he had, as I knew, no very high opinion of Reissiger. The most unpleasant aspect of the whole thing to him was my having handled all the arrangements through the chamberlain, Herr von Reizenstein, who was a personal enemy of his: I could have no idea, he told me, of all the chicanery he had to endure from that quarter. These amiable outpourings made it easier for me to respond with an exhibition of almost unhypocritical emotion, which he then requited by dismissing the whole affair with a shrug of the shoulders.

But this general-directorial tempest was of far less danger to my undertaking than the really bad weather that now threatened us; it poured the entire day; if this rain were to last, as we had every reason to fear, it would be practically impossible to set out at five o'clock in the morning, as I had planned, on a specially chartered steamer with my hundreds of accomplices, to give a morning concert in Pillnitz two hours distant. I looked forward in dismay to disaster; Röckel alone consoled me; I could count on it, he asserted, tomorrow would be a good day, for I was inherently lucky. This assurance remained in my memory in later epochs when my undertakings so frequently suffered such huge reverses, and I would recall it as a wanton impiety. But this time my friend was right: from dawn to dusk August 12th 1844 was the loveliest summer day I can recall in my entire life. The sensation of blissful satisfaction when I saw my light-hearted legion of gaily dressed bandsmen and singers gathering in the auspicious morning mists on board our steamer swelled my breast with fervent belief in my lucky star. My friendly impetuosity had succeeded in overcoming Reissiger's sulks and persuading him to share the honors of the occasion with me by conducting the performance of my composition. Everything went off splendidly; the King and the royal family were visibly moved, and in the dark days to come the Queen of Saxony, or so I was told, still recalled that day and that morning with particular emotion as the most beautiful of her life. After Reissiger had wielded the baton with utmost dignity and I had sung along in the choir as a tenor, we two Kapellmeisters were bidden to approach the royal family, where the King expressed to us his heartiest thanks, while the Queen paid us the special compliment of stating that I had composed well, just as Reissiger had conducted well. The King requested a repeat performance of the last three verses only, for owing to a severely ulcerated tooth, he could not stay out of doors very long. I immediately devised an improvisation, the uncommonly successful execution of which gives me pride to this day. I repeated the whole song, but in accordance with the King's wish I had only one stanza sung in the original semi-circular formation; with the second stanza I had my unwieldy four-hundred-man group of musicians and singers file away, and the two last stanzas were performed so that, as they marched away into the distance through the garden, the final notes could only reach the royal ears as if echoing from a dream. Thanks to my ubiquitous, active, and unprecedentedly resourceful conducting, this entire retreat went off with such assurance that there was not the slightest variance in tempo and delivery, and the whole thing could just as well have been a carefully rehearsed theatrical maneuver. When we got to the castle courtyard, we found tables on the green lawn decked out for a huge breakfast for all guests, as arranged with greatest thoughtfulness by the Queen. We saw the King's animated wife herself zealously supervising the feast from the windows and in the corridors of the surrounding castle. All eyes beamed upon me as the fortunate instigator of this general good fortune, and it wouldn't have taken much, in the rapture of the moment, to proclaim paradise on earth. After we had roamed en masse through the pleasant surroundings, especially the Keppgrund so familiar to me from my childhood, we returned in highest spirits to Dresden late that night.

The next day I was again summoned to the General Director's office. There was something else bothering Herr von Lüttichau, it seemed. But when I got there and wanted to begin excusing myself for any anxieties I may have caused him, this tall man with the dry, hard face took me by the hand with a rapturous expression on his face, such as, I am sure, no one had seen on him before, and told me there could be no further question of having caused any anxiety; I was, he said, a great man; long after he had been completely forgotten I would be remembered and loved. Deeply shaken, I wished only to express my embarrassment at this unexpected outpouring, but he interrupted me in a kindly way and sought an escape from his own emotion in some friendly confidences. He smilingly discussed my self-abnegation in yielding the place of honor on so extraordinary an occasion to the undeserving Reissiger; when I assured him it had been the greatest satisfaction of all to have persuaded my colleague to take over the conducting, he admitted he understood my motives but did not comprehend how Reissiger could have accepted a position in which he clearly did not belong. For a long time Lüttichau's attitude to me remained dominated by the temper generated by these events, so that we did business together in an almost intimate tone; however badly things degenerated in the course of time, even to the extent that our relationship became one of open enmity, this singular man nonetheless preserved a perceptible tenderness toward me, and many of his subsequent harsh outbursts sounded strangely like the laments of unrequited love.

For my holiday this year, I went early in September to Fischer's vineyard, near Loschwitz, not far from the famous Findlater vineyard, where I rented a somewhat belated summer residence. Here, pleasantly stimulated and under the beneficent effect of a six-week stay in the open air, I completed the music for the second act of *Tannhäuser* by October 15th. During this period I went back to Dresden to conduct a performance of *Rienzi* before an audience of unusual distinction. Spontini, Meyerbeer, and General Lvov, the composer of the Russian national anthem, were all seated in the gallery. I made no effort[1] to ascertain the effect of my work on these musical magnates, fully entitled as they were to pass judgment on me; I contented myself with the curious satisfaction of having performed for them an often-repeated work before a packed house and to overwhelming applause. But I was particularly pleased at the end to find my dog Peps, who had chased after me all the way from the country, brought to me at the theater most considerately, and I went back with him at once, without greeting these European celebrities, to my little vineyard, where Minna received me with particular joy at the recovery of Peps, whom she had believed lost forever. Here I also received a visit from Werder, who had first offered his friendship in such spectral shape in Berlin but now presented himself as a creature of flesh and blood in broad daylight under friendly skies. I argued with him pleasantly about the worth of *Der fliegende Holländer*, against which, now that I had *Tannhäuser* in my head, I evinced a certain disapprobation. It was delightful to allow a friend to oppose me on this point and instruct me as to the significance of my work.

When we were again in winter quarters, I tried to avoid allowing as lengthy a period to elapse between the composition of the second and third acts as I had endured between the first and second, and I succeeded, particularly under the soothing influence of carefully planned solitary walks, and despite the distractions of other duties, in completing the music of this third act before the end of the year, on December 29th.

The principal external demands on me during that period were created by a lengthy visit to Dresden from Spontini, in connection with a new production of his *La Vestale*. The singular episodes and characteristic aspects of my association with this venerable and famous musician have remained so vividly imprinted in my memory that they are worth recounting at this point.

As we could rely, given the collaboration of Schröder-Devrient, on what would be on the whole a splendid performance of the opera, I had inspired Herr von Lüttichau with the idea of showing Spontini the well-intentioned and demonstrative courtesy of inviting him to direct his justly celebrated work in person, since he had recently left Berlin after having suffered great humiliations there. This was done and I, who had been entrusted with the conducting of the opera, was delegated the special task of reaching agreement about everything with the master. It appeared that my letter, although I had written it in French myself, had imbued him with an excellent opinion of my zeal in this undertaking, and in a highly majestic answer he expressed his special requests regarding the arrangements to be made in celebration of his own participation. As far as the singers were concerned, considering that the likes of Schröder-Devrient would be counted among them, he had no qualms whatever; as for chorus and ballet, he took it for granted that nothing would be lacking in the way of fully adequate resources; he also assumed that the orchestra would satisfy him completely, presuming that each instrument would be represented in sufficient numbers, so that the whole would, as he expressed it, be "garnished with twelve good contrabassists" ("le tout garni de douze bonnes contrabasses"). This phrase broke my heart, for the statement of this one number allowed me to calculate the exact, lavish proportions of all his other presumptions, and I now rushed to the General Director to warn him that the enterprise would not go off as lightly as we had thought. His alarm was great and unfeigned: we had to find a way of canceling the invitation. Frau Schröder-Devrient learned of our anguish: she, who knew Spontini, laughed impishly at the naive imprudence with which we had issued the invitation, and then found in a slight indisposition she was then suffering the means to help us, for we could use it as a pretext for a substantial delay in the whole thing. Spontini had, in fact, urged us to all possible dispatch in the execution of our project, for as he was impatiently awaited in Paris he could spare only a little time for the fulfillment of our wishes. I now had to weave the tissue of white lies whereby we hoped to deflect the master from a definitive acceptance of our invitation. Then we all breathed more easily, held our rehearsals, and had reached the day before what we expected to be an undemanding dress rehearsal when at about noon a coach stopped before my house. Out of it, clad in a long blue coat with a thick pile, stepped the master himself, who strode up to my room unattended and in a great passion that led him to abandon his normal deportment of a Spanish grandee. He produced my letters and proved to me from our correspondence that he had by no means rejected our invitation but, properly interpreted, had clearly acceded to all our wishes. In the tremendous pleasure of seeing this marvelous man in my house, and at the prospect of hearing his work under his direction, I forgot all the possible difficulties that might be in store for us and immediately vowed to do everything conceivable to satisfy him. I told him all this with the most honest enthusiasm: he smiled in almost childish delight as he perceived this; it was only when, in order to demonstrate my absolute sincerity, I simply came out with the request that he would conduct the next day's rehearsal himself that he became suddenly very pensive and began pondering a number of apparent difficulties. In his great excitement, however, he did not express himself clearly, and thus it was difficult for me to elicit from him under what conditions he would be willing to assume the direction of the rehearsal. After a further pause for thought, he asked me what type of baton we used: I indicated with my hands the approximate length and thickness of the medium-sized stick coated with white paper customarily served up to us by the orchestra's factotum. He sighed and inquired if it would be possible for me to provide him by the following morning with a baton of black ebony, of the very substantial length and thickness he indicated by pointing to his arm and open palm, and to make certain that a rather large knob of white ivory was affixed to each end. I promised to provide him at all events with an instrument that looked quite similar by the next rehearsal, and to have an authentic one produced from the requested materials in time for the actual performance. Visibly relieved, he stroked his brow, authorized me to announce his consent to conduct on the following day, and after once more making certain I understood how important it was to carry out his specifications for the baton with utmost exactitude, went to his hotel.

I thought I was half dreaming and rushed off to tell everybody what had happened and what was in store for us. We had been caught. Schröder-Devrient offered herself as the scapegoat, and I got in touch with the theater carpenter with precise instructions for the baton. This turned out well enough, to the extent it looked black, had the requisite dimensions, and two big white knobs on the ends. Then we got to the actual rehearsal. Spontini was patently disgruntled at his position in the orchestra and, above all, wanted the oboes placed behind him; but as this one readjustment in the ranks of the musicians would have caused terrific confusion, I promised him to arrange it after the rehearsal. He fell silent and grasped the baton. I understood at once why he endowed its form with such immense significance: he did not hold it, like other conductors, at the end, but rather clasped it in the middle with his full fist and moved it in such a way that one could clearly see he considered the device as a marshal's baton, using it not to beat time but to command. Then ensued during the first scenes a confusion that was only exacerbated by the fact that the master's communications to the orchestra and to the singers were effectuated in a German so unintelligible as to constitute a most severe obstacle to mutual understanding. But we soon noticed that his main objective was to dissuade us from the assumption that this could be the dress rehearsal, as he had, on the contrary, set his mind on a thorough restudying of the opera from the very beginning. Great was the despair of my good old chorusmaster and stage director Fischer, who had previously advocated inviting Spontini with the greatest enthusiasm, when he realized the now inevitable disruption of the program; this feeling swelled to open anger, in the blindness of which he interpreted all of Spontini's suggestions as pure harassment and responded to him only in the rudest German. At one point Spontini beckoned me over at the end of a certain chorus to whisper into my ear: "Mais savez-vous, vos choeurs ne chantent pas mal." Fischer, who had looked on suspiciously, then asked me fiercely: "What does the old buzzard want now?" I had a hard time of it trying to pacify this suddenly renegade enthusiast. The greatest delay was caused by the staging of the triumphal march in the first act; with the most vociferous emphasis the master expressed his supreme discontent at the seemingly indifferent reaction of the populace during the procession of the Vestal Virgins; he was quite unaware of the fact that, in accordance with our instructions, they had fallen on their knees at the appearance of the priestesses, for nothing was visible to the extremely short-sighted master; what he demanded was that the Roman army show its devout respect in a more drastic demonstration by an act of prostration, but most particularly by a simultaneous thumping of the spears on the ground. This had to be rehearsed countless times; but some spears would invariably clatter too soon or too late; he himself tried to demonstrate this maneuver several times by banging the baton on the conductor's desk; but there was no help for it; the sound was not sufficiently sharp and emphatic. This reminded me of the notably precise and almost frightening effect produced by a similar procedure in a performance of *Fernand Cortez*, which had made such a big impression on me when I had seen it in Berlin many years before, and I realized it would require much painstaking and time-consuming training to overcome our prevalent sloppiness in such matters if we were ever to satisfy these requirements of the master, who had been spoiled in this respect. After the first act Spontini strode onto the stage in order to provide a detailed explanation of his reasons for insisting on the postponement of the performance of the opera for some considerable interval to gain time for rehearsals in every department. He expected to find the artists of the Dresden Court Theater assembled in his vicinity, but everybody was beating a hasty retreat; the singers and the stage director had gone off in all directions to give vent in their own manner to their feelings about this miserable situation: only some workmen, lamp-cleaners, and a few members of the chorus stood in a semi-circle around Spontini to listen to the extraordinary fellow as he held forth to them with singular emotion about the requirements of true dramatic art. I intervened in this grotesque scene, gently and subserviently told Spontini that his remonstrances were superfluous, assured him that everything would be done to meet his standards, particularly inasmuch as Herr Eduard Devrient, who had a very exact recollection of the production of *La Vestale* which had satisfied him in Berlin, would be brought in to drill our chorus and supernumeraries for the properly ceremonial reception of the Vestal Virgins, and thus got him out of the undignified situation in which I had been horrified to find him. This calmed him down; we drew up a schedule for the rehearsals according to his wishes, and as a matter of fact I was the only one who regarded this turn of events as not entirely unwelcome, for looking through the almost burlesque characteristics of Spontini's behavior I could see the uncommon energy with which he pursued an ideal, strangely distorted in form yet still intelligible to me, that had long since disappeared from the theatrical art of our time.

We therefore began with a piano rehearsal, to enable the master to communicate his special wishes to the singers. We got very little that was novel out of this; he did not give us tips about details of delivery so much as general observations about interpretation, in the course of which, I noticed, he was accustomed to make decided allowances for such famous singers as Schröder-Devrient and Tichatschek. To the latter he only forbade the word "Braut", with which Licinius in the German translation is made to address Julia; this struck his ear as horrendous, and he could not comprehend how something as vulgar as the sound of this word could be used in connection with music. To a less gifted and rather untried singer in the role of the high priest, however, he gave a somewhat lengthy lecture about the interpretation of his character, the key to which he was supposed to find in the dialogue in recitative with the Haruspex; here, Spontini averred, he would recognize that the whole thing was based on priestly deception and the exploitation of superstition. The Pontifex should let it be known that he was unafraid of his enemy, even at the head of a Roman army, for if worst came to worst he had machines ready that could, if need be, miraculously rekindle the extinguished fire of Vesta, whereby, even if Julia were thus spared sacrificial death, the power of the priesthood would nonetheless remain unimpaired.

During a discussion about the orchestra, I asked Spontini why he had omitted using trombones during the splendid triumphal march in the first act, seeing as he usually made use of this instrument everywhere; utterly astonished, he replied with the question: "Est-ce que je n'y ai pas de trombones?" I showed him the place in the published score, whereupon he requested me to add trombones to the march so that they could be included at the next rehearsal. He also said to me: "J'ai entendu dans votre *Rienzi* un instrument, que vous appelez bass-tuba; je ne veux pas *bannir* cet instrument de l'orchestre: faites m'en une partie pour la *Vestale*." It gave me pleasure to fulfill this wish with discrimination and discretion. When he heard the effect for the first time at a rehearsal, he threw me a really affectionate look of gratitude, and the impression made by the rather simple enrichment I had given his score was so enduring that he later sent me a friendly note from Paris asking for the instrumental parts I had produced; but his pride did not permit him to request in so many words something I had written, and so he wrote: "Envoyez-moi une partition de trombones pour la marche triomphale et de la Basse-tuba, telle qu'elle a été executée sous ma direction à Dresde."

I demonstrated my special devotion to him by the zeal with which I completely rearranged the placement of the instruments in the orchestra according to his wishes. These wishes were rooted less in any system than in force of habit, and the extent to which he could not tolerate the slightest deviation from his habitual practice was disclosed to me when he explained the way he conducted: he directed the orchestra, so he said, solely with the look of his eyes: "My left eye is the first violin, my right the second violin; to be effective with one's glance one must therefore not wear spectacles, the way bad conductors do, even if short-sighted: I can scarcely see one step in front of me, and yet with my eyes I make certain that everything goes according to my wishes", he confided to me. It has to be said that some of the details in the orchestral placement to which he had quite by chance become accustomed were highly irrational; from one of the earliest orchestras he had in Paris, where it had been necessary for some reason or other, came his habit of placing the two oboists directly behind him: these were thus obliged to turn their instruments away from the ears of the audience, and our superb oboist was so incensed at this affront that I was only able to persuade him to accede to this arrangement for the moment by treating it as a joke. Apart from this, Spontini's custom in this respect was based on a rightly conceived and, by German orchestras, unfortunately still neglected system whereby the four string sections are spread evenly across the whole orchestra, flanked by brass and percussion, which are thereby prevented from being concentrated at one point and consequently producing an oppressive effect, with the more delicate woodwinds strung out at appropriate distances between the violins; in contrast, the custom of dividing the mass of instruments into two halves, string and wind, practised to this day by some of the biggest and most famous orchestras, denotes crudity and lack of sensitivity for the beauty of a balanced and blended orchestral sound. I was very happy to have the chance to introduce this excellent innovation in Dresden on this occasion, for as it had been demanded by Spontini himself, it proved simple to persuade the King to command that the change be made permanent. Nothing remained after Spontini's departure except to correct some of his arbitrary arrangements and modify some eccentric dispositions to achieve a satisfactory and highly effective orchestral balance.

Despite all the idiosyncrasies Spontini showed at the rehearsals, this extraordinary man nonetheless fascinated musicians and singers alike, so that they devoted the production an unusual amount of attention. Very characteristic was his emphatic insistence on what occasionally seemed unduly sharp rhythmic accentuation; in his dealings with the Berlin orchestra he had formed the habit of specifying the note to be accented with the word "*this*", which particularly pleased Tichatschek, a real genius of vocal rhythm, for he too was accustomed to insist on special precision at important choral entries and asserted that if the first note were hit correctly the rest would follow as a matter of course. All in all, therefore, an amicable and cooperative spirit toward Spontini gradually established itself; it was only the violas that nursed a grudge against him for a long time as a result of a fright he had given them; in the accompaniment to the lugubrious cantilena of Julia at the end of the second act, the execution of the eerily soft figure for the violas did not meet his expectations; he therefore suddenly turned to them and called out in a sepulchral voice: "Has death struck the violas?" The two pale and incurable old hypochondriacs who, much to my irritation and despite their right to a pension, clung tenaciously to the first desk in this section, looked up in horror at Spontini, interpreting this as some kind of threat: I then had to try to explain Spontini's demands without any melodramatics in order to bring them slowly back to life.

As to the staging, Herr Eduard Devrient helped out materially in fostering precision in the ensemble, and he also found a way to carry out yet another of Spontini's special requests that had us all in a quandary. In accordance with the cut in the score traditional in all German theaters, we too decided to close the opera with the fiery duet, accompanied by the chorus, for Licinius and Julia after their rescue: but the master insisted that the old finale deriving from the French *opera seria* tradition and consisting of a cheerful chorus and a ballet be tacked on to it. He was absolutely opposed to seeing his brilliant work end in the dingy and melancholy setting of the burial ground; the scene had to undergo a transformation to show the rose garden of Venus in resplendent light, at whose altar the long-suffering couple would be wedded by her rose-bedecked priests and priestesses amid the merriest dances and songs. We performed it this way, but unfortunately it did not enhance the successful effect we all hoped for.

In the course of the actual performance, which went off with great precision and spirit, we experienced a difficulty in regard to the principal role which none of us had anticipated. Our great Schröder-Devrient was obviously no longer the right age, especially considering her rather matronly appearance, to produce the desired effect as the youngest of the Vestal Virgins, particularly when contrasted, as was the case here, with a high priestess played by a young girl whose exceptional beauty could not be concealed. This was my niece Johanna Wagner, then seventeen years old, whose voice was overwhelmingly beautiful at this age; this, in addition to her looks, and allied with her superb acting talent, made everybody instinctively wish the roles reversed. This unfortunate fact did not escape Schröder-Devrient's attention, and she felt impelled to try to compensate by using every dramatic trick she knew to overcome her difficult position, all of which frequently led to some exaggeration and at one critical point even to a truly deplorable instance of over-acting. After the great trio in the second act, as she moves toward stage-front away from her lover, who has just rescued himself by flight, when in utter exhaustion she expresses the pent-up emotion in her heart by the words "He is free!", she let herself be tempted into speaking the words instead of singing them. She had often previously demonstrated what overwhelming effect can be produced by tones approaching pure speech in *Fidelio*, carrying the public away whenever, at the words "One more step and you are dead!", she brought out the word "dead" in her speaking rather than singing voice. The tremendous effect, to which I, of all people, was particularly sensitive, was derived from the strange shock, like the blow of an executioner's axe, which I received at being abruptly brought down from the exalted sphere into which music lifts even the most gruesome situations to the bedrock of harshest reality. This gave a direct sensation of the peak of sublimity which, in recalling this feeling, I can only describe as the instant like a flash of lightning which, at the moment when two utterly different worlds touch and yet are completely separate, illuminates them both for us simultaneously. The tremendous significance of such a moment, and the fact that there should be no trifling with it, was revealed to me in this performance by the complete failure of this great artist to produce the desired result. The toneless, hoarse sound she emitted at the critical point was like a pail of cold water poured over us all, so that everybody held it to be just another failed stage effect. Perhaps the expectations of the public, who had been obliged to pay double for the privilege of seeing Spontini conduct, were too high; possibly the whole style of the work with its frenchified view of antiquity inevitably seemed somewhat obsolete, despite the splendor and beauty of the music; or perhaps it was the unhappily weak ending, rather like the botched effect tried out by Schröder-Devrient, that dampened everybody's spirits – at any rate, there wasn't any real enthusiasm, and the evening boiled down to a somewhat lukewarm tribute to the world-famous master, who cut what was to me a rather embarrassing figure with his huge armory of medals as he came out on stage at the end to acknowledge the rather short-winded summons from the audience.

Spontini himself was under no illusion as to the not very cheering outcome of this venture. He decided nonetheless to put a good face on it and insisted on the adoption of a device he had been accustomed to employ in Berlin to assure that his operas would be played before packed houses and an animated public. This was the practice of performing his works solely on Sundays, for experience had taught him that on Sundays the house was always packed and the audience animated. As the next Sunday on which his *Vestale* could be scheduled for performance under his baton lay some time ahead, this new prolongation of his stay in Dresden gave us the repeated pleasure and special interest of seeing Spontini socially on frequent occasions. My memories of hours spent in conversation with Spontini at Frau Devrient's house as well as my own are so vivid that I will cite a few of them here.

I shall never forget a dinner at Frau Devrient's house, in the course of which we had long and interesting conversations with Spontini and his wife (a sister of the famous piano manufacturer Erard). His customary role in the conversation was to sit calmly in noble silence listening to the comments of others, an attitude which seemed to express his expectation to be solicited for his opinion. When he eventually spoke, it was with rhetorical ceremony and in sharply etched phrases of a categorical nature and in a tone suggesting that contradiction would be an insult. Herr Ferdinand Hiller happened to be among the other guests; he brought the conversation around to the subject of Liszt; after this had been batted back and forth for some time, Spontini rendered a verdict in his characteristic way that demonstrated amply to me how incapable he was of judging the world from the vantage point of his throne in Berlin with any degree of impartiality and benignity. Whenever he was making such oracular pronouncements he could not suffer being disturbed by the slightest noise; when dessert was served and the conversation became livelier, it happened that Frau Schröder-Devrient, seated beside him, laughed a bit right in the middle of one of Spontini's prolonged perorations. Spontini shot a furious look at his own wife; Madame Schröder-Devrient apologized at once, confessing that she had been the guilty party who had giggled involuntarily at a little joke printed on a candy wrapper. But Spontini replied: "Pourtant je suis sûr que c'est ma femme qui a suscité ce rire; je ne veux pas qu'on rie devant moi, je ne rie jamais moi, j'aime le sérieux." Nevertheless he thawed to some extent. It pleased him, for example, to amaze us all by his capacity to crack large lumps of sugar loudly with his splendid teeth. After dinner, however, when we drew closer together, he became quite excited. To the extent this was possible for him at all, he seemed to have formed a special affection for me; he openly expressed his fondness and stated he wanted to demonstrate it by redeeming me from the misfortune of further pursuing my career as a dramatic composer. It would be difficult, he admitted, to convince me of the value of this friendly service; but as he felt it incumbent upon himself to look after my future welfare in this regard he would be willing, he said, to stay in Dresden for another six months, during which time we could, of course, also perform all his other operas under his supervision, and particularly *Agnes von Hohenstaufen*.

To substantiate his views about the ruinous nature of a career composing operas as a successor of Spontini, he began by praising my *Rienzi* inordinately; he said: "Quand j'ai entendu votre *Rienzi*, j'ai dit, c'est un homme de génie, mais déjà il a plus fait qu'il ne peut faire." To explain what he meant by this paradox, he continued as follows: "Après Gluck c'est moi qui ai fait la grande révolution avec la *Vestale*; j'ai introduit le 'Vorhalt? de la Sexte'[1] dans l'harmonie et la grosse caisse dans l'orchestre; avec *Cortez* j'ai fait un pas plus avant; puis j'ai fait trois pas avec *Olympie*. *Nourmahal*, *Alcidor* et tout ce que j'ai fait dans les premiers temps de Berlin, je vous les livre, c'était des oeuvres occasionnelles; mais puis j'ai fait cent pas en avant avec *Agnès de Hohenstaufen*, où j'ai imaginé un emploi de l'orchestre remplaçant parfaitement l'orgue." Ever since that time, he went on, he had been trying to work out a draft entitled *Les Athéniennes*, and had even been urgently requested by the present King of Prussia to complete this opus – to prove which he immediately extracted from his billfold several letters from the monarch and passed them around for us to read. Not until he had given us ample opportunity to study them carefully did he go on to say that despite this flattering sponsorship he had given up the attempt to set this otherwise very fine material to music, because he had realized that he could not possibly go beyond his *Agnes von Hohenstaufen* and break new ground. His conclusion sounded like this: "Or, comment voulez-vous que quiconque puisse inventer quelque chose de nouveau, moi Spontini declarant ne pouvoir en aucune façon surpasser mes oeuvres précédentes, d'autre part étant avisé que depuis la *Vestale* il n'a point été écrit une note qui ne fût volée de mes partitions." To prove that this assertion was not mere idle chatter but rather was based upon the most exacting scientific research, he leaned upon the testimony of his wife, who had read, together with him, a voluminous dissertation by a famous member of the French Academy, whose essay, for certain reasons, had nonetheless never been published. In this vastly comprehensive work of the greatest scientific importance, he continued, it was demonstrated that without Spontini's invention of the suspended sixth in *La Vestale*, modern melody would simply not exist, and that every melodic form devised since then had been borrowed from his compositions. I was benumbed, yet nevertheless hoped to induce the inexorable master to form a more favorable opinion at least as to the possibilities still open to him. I conceded that this was all more or less true as the academician had demonstrated; but, I asked him, did he not believe that, if a dramatic poem of a type yet unknown to him came before him, he would not be stimulated by it to new heights of musical invention? With a pitying smile, he replied that my question was inherently erroneous: where, after all, could anything new be found? "Dans la *Vestale* j'ai composé un sujet romain, dans *Fernand Cortez* un sujet espagnol–mexicain, dans *Olympie* un sujet grec–macédonien, enfin dans *Agnès de Hohenstaufen* un sujet allemand: tout le reste ne vaut rien." He would certainly hope, he added, that I was not thinking of the so-called romantic genre à la *Freischütz*? No serious man concerned himself with such juvenilia; for art was a serious matter, and he, Spontini, had exhausted all the serious material. From which nationality could come a composer to surpass him? Surely not from the Italians, whom he characterized simply as "cochons", nor from the French, who merely imitated them, and not from the Germans, who would never get beyond their childish preoccupations, and who, if there had ever been talent among them, had now seen it spoiled for them by the Jews: "Oh croyez-moi, il y avait de l'espoir pour l'Allemagne lorsque j'étais empereur de la musique à Berlin; mais depuis que le roi de Prusse a livré sa musique au désordre occasionné par les deux juifs errants qu'il a attirés, tout espoir est perdu."

Our charming hostess now thought it would be a good idea to divert the attention of the excited master. The theater was only a stone's throw from her house; she invited him to step over there in the company of our friend Heine, who was also among the guests, and look in on a performance of *Antigone*, which had just begun and would surely interest him on account of the layout of the stage in authentic classical style, according to Semper's superb stage designs. He was on the point of rejecting this suggestion, for he asserted that he knew all that much better from his *Olympie*. But after a while he consented; only he came back after a very short time and explained with a condescending smile that he had seen and heard enough to be fortified in his views. Heine recounted to us that, shortly after he and Spontini had entered the virtually empty gallery, he had turned to him at the beginning of the Bacchus chorus and said: "C'est de la Berliner Sing-Academie, allons-nous en." Through the opened door a beam of light had fallen on a hitherto unnoticed and solitary figure behind one of the pillars; Heine had recognized Mendelssohn and concluded at once that he had overheard the master's remark.

From the master's highly excited comments we soon realized very distinctively that he was angling for an invitation to stay in Dresden for a much longer period and have all his operas performed. But Schröder-Devrient had already decided it would be best and in Spontini's own interest, as she wanted to spare him the disappointment of his eagerly cherished hopes with respect to the second performance of *La Vestale*, to prevent this performance during his stay in Dresden. She therefore faked another indisposition, and the management gave me the task of notifying Spontini about the apparently indefinite postponement. This visit was so distasteful to me that I was glad to be able to take Röckel along, as Spontini had gotten to like him as well, and also because he spoke much better French. We entered in great anxiety and assumed we were in for some rough going: but on the contrary, we were astonished to find the master, who had been given advance warning in a friendly note from Schröder-Devrient, in the most cheerful mood imaginable. He revealed to us that he had to be on his way to Paris at once, in order to go on from there to Rome, where he had been bidden by the Holy Father, by whom he had just been named Count of San Andrea. At the same time he showed us a second document by means of which the King of Denmark had "elevated him to the Danish nobility"; this turned out to be an appointment to knighthood in the Order of the Elephant, which did in fact involve status as a noble; but he mentioned the nobility aspect and not the medal, as this was too vulgar for him. He expressed almost childish satisfaction about all this; as if by a stroke of magic he had been emancipated from the bondage of the

Vestale operation in Dresden and transported to a glorious realm from which he could henceforth look down with angelic comfort on the tribulations of the operatic world. Röckel and I silently thanked the King of Denmark and the Holy Father from the bottom of our hearts. We bade an emotional farewell to the master, and to make his happiness complete I promised him I would give his friendly advice about composing operas the most serious consideration.

I learned later that Spontini had expressed a view about me once more, upon hearing that I had left Dresden as a political refugee and sought asylum in Switzerland; he was of the opinion that this had come about as a result of my participation in highly treasonable activities against the King of Saxony, whom he regarded on the basis of his having appointed me royal Kapellmeister as my benefactor, and he cried out in pained amazement: "Quelle ingratitude!" As to his eventual death, I learned from Berlioz, who had not left his deathbed until the end, that the master had struggled most fiercely against his decease; he had cried repeatedly: "Je ne veux pas mourir, je ne veux pas mourir!" When Berlioz tried to console him with the words: "Comment pouvez-vous penser mourir, vous, mon maître, qui êtes immortel!", Spontini had cut him off angrily: "Ne faites pas de mauvaises plaisanteries!" The news of his death, which reached me in Zürich, moved me very much, despite all these strange experiences and memories: I expressed these feelings and my judgment somewhat briefly in an article for the *Eidgenössische Zeitung*, in which I emphasized the fact that, unlike the now dominant Meyerbeer and even the aged but still existant Rossini, he had distinguished himself by an authentic belief in himself and his art. That this belief had degenerated into superstition, as I had seen for myself almost to my horror, was something I did not mention.

I do not recall, given my mood during those days in Dresden, having found occasion to analyze in any depth the highly singular impressions I had derived from my strange encounters with Spontini, in order to bring them into harmony with my nonetheless hereby augmented esteem for the great master. Obviously, I had gotten to know only a caricature of the man; the inclination to such palpable megalomania was no doubt rooted in characteristics preserved from his earlier and more active years. Equally demonstrable, however, seemed to me the influence upon him of the quite profound decay of the art of dramatic music during the period which saw Spontini grow old in such equivocal and worthless circumstances as his position in Berlin entailed. That he saw his principal achievements quite surprisingly in subsidiary matters showed that his judgment had grown childish; but this could not reduce the uncommon worth of his works in my eyes, however boundlessly he himself might exaggerate their value. That which had driven him to such monstrous excesses of self-adulation, the comparison of himself with those artistic eminences who had meanwhile usurped his place, could nonetheless serve, if I put myself in his shoes, to justify him; for I felt myself more deeply allied to him in his contempt for these figures than I was willing to admit openly at the time. Thus it happened that this encounter in Dresden, however ludicrous the events that characterized it, filled me with an almost frightening sympathy for this man, whose like I was never to meet again.

The immediately ensuing period brought me different experiences of leading artistic personalities of our epoch. These turned out to be an entirely different story, and on one of the best of them, Heinrich Marschner, I must now report.

Marschner had been summoned as a very young man by Weber to serve as music director of the Dresden orchestra. After Weber's death he seems to have flattered himself that he would succeed him; and it was apparently attributable less to his rather modest achievements up to then than to his somewhat crude and abrasive demeanor that he was disappointed in this expectation. On the other hand, he was surprised one day to find that his wife had come into some money, thus making it possible for him to embark on the career of an operatic composer without a salaried position. During the wild period of my youth when music first took possession of me, Marschner was living in Leipzig, and it was there that his well-known operas *Der Vampyr* and *Templer und Jüdin* were first performed. My sister Rosalie had once taken me to see him to get his opinion about me. He was not unfriendly, but there was no significant result. I also attended a first performance of his opera *Des Falkners Braut*, which did not meet with much success. Then he went to Hanover; his opera *Hans Heiling*, which had its initial performance in Berlin, I first got to know during my days in Würzburg; it showed me some vacillation in its style and a diminution of creative powers. Since then a number of operas had appeared, among them *Das Schloss am Aetna* and *Der Bäbu*, which got nowhere. He had been steadily neglected by the Dresden theater, as if because of an old grudge; only his *Templer* was given there from time to time. It was my colleague Reissiger who usually conducted this opera, but on one occasion I had to conduct it in his absence; it was during the period I was working on *Tannhäuser*. I recall that, although I had conducted the same opera before quite frequently in Magdeburg, the slovenly and incompetent instrumentation affected me so painfully on this occasion that I suffered severely under it and begged Reissiger most earnestly upon his return to keep the opera under his baton. On the other hand, more or less as a point of artistic honor, I had pushed for a performance of *Hans Heiling*. Inadequacies in the cast, as were unavoidable at the time, made a complete success impossible; in any event, the style of the work seemed noticeably obsolete. But then I learned that Marschner had a new opera ready, *Adolph von Nassau*; an advertisement that came to me, whose veracity I had no means to judge, particularly emphasized the "patriotic, noble and thoroughly German tendency" of this newest of Marschner's creations; I wanted to accustom the Dresden theater to taking the initiative, and I persuaded Herr von Lüttichau to order this opera at once for Dresden before any other house could get hold of it. Marschner, who seemingly had not been treated with any special favor by the theater authorities in Hanover, accepted the invitation with great enthusiasm, sent along his score and expressed willingness to come to Dresden in person. But Herr von Lüttichau did not want to see him at the head of the orchestra; and I too felt that summoning conductors from outside to conduct their own works would only lead to confusion that would not always prove as stimulating and instructive as Spontini's visit. So the decision stood that I would be personally entrusted with the work. How I regretted it! The score arrived: a miserable text by Karl Golmick[1] had been set to music by the composer of *Templer* in such a shallow manner that the culminating effect came in a four-part drinking song in which "the German Rhine" and "German wine" were celebrated in the manner of a glee club. My spirits sank like a stone; but the affair could not be canceled, and I had to try to induce the singers to keep at it by putting a serious face on the whole thing. This was difficult. Tichatschek and Mitterwurzer[2] had the two male lead roles; both of them, being eminently musical, sang everything at sight and peered at me after every number to discern what I thought about it. I asserted it was good German music; they should not let themselves be misled; they looked at me in astonishment and didn't know what to make of me. Finally it became too much for them, and when I still didn't crack a smile, they broke out into hearty laughter, in which I then inevitably had to join. I had to make them accomplices in my misery and make them vow, now that nothing could be changed, to play the game along with me and be serious. A coloratura of the latest style from Vienna, Frau Spatzer Gentiluomo,[3] who had come to us from Hanover and upon whose services Marschner greatly relied, was rather pleased by her part, as she found it afforded ample opportunity to display "brilliance" and in fact there was a finale in which my "German master" had tried to outdo Donizetti: the Princess has been poisoned by a golden rose, the gift of the evil Bishop of Mainz, and has become delirious; Adolph von Nassau and the knights of the German empire swear revenge and pour all this out, to a choral accompaniment, in a stretta of such amateurishness and vulgarity that Donizetti would certainly have thrown it at the feet of his humblest pupil.

Marschner now arrived for the dress rehearsals, was entirely satisfied and offered me ample grounds to practise the art of disguising my real opinions without actually lying, so that our guest could consider himself considerately treated and zealously attended by me. In the performance it went with the public about the same way it had gone with my singers during the rehearsals: we brought a still-born child into the world; yet Marschner was completely consoled by the fact that his drinking quartet, which somewhat resembled Becker's song[1] "They shall never take it, our free German Rhine", had been encored. After the performance I hosted a supper for the composer and a few friends, at which my singers, who had had enough, unfortunately distinguished themselves by their absence. Herr Ferdinand Hiller had the presence of mind to express himself in a toast to the effect that, whatever one might say, the accent here was on the *German* master and his *German* work. Amusingly enough, he was disputed in this by Marschner himself, who instructed us that, to the contrary, composing German operas was a tricky business, and that it would be necessary in the future to show more consideration for the needs of the singers and their capacity for brilliant singing than he had unfortunately been able to demonstrate to date.

It thus appeared that the terrible degeneration in this truly gifted German musician was based in large part on an actual fashion in operatic composition which had caused in the aging master an important and in his view highly beneficial change. In later years I saw him once again in Paris, at the time of my adventurous production of *Tannhäuser* there. I had little desire to get together with him at the time, for quite frankly, I wanted to spare myself the pain of witnessing the final consequences of the altered point of view he had documented for us in Dresden long before. I learned that he had arrived at a state of rather helpless dotage, kept in leading-strings by an ambitious and much younger wife who wanted him to conquer Paris for one last time. On this occasion I read in advertisements to foster Marschner's fame that the Parisian public should certainly not come to the conclusion that it was I who currently represented the German musical spirit; for this spirit, as everyone would soon be convinced if only Marschner were given his chance, was far more assimilable and more enjoyable for the French than anything to be found in my works. Marschner died before his wife was able to succeed in establishing this point.

Ferdinand Hiller, on the other hand, behaved in a particularly charming and agreeable manner during those days in Dresden. Meyerbeer also turned up in Dresden from time to time, but nobody could really figure out why: he once rented a little summer house in Pirna, set up a piano under a pretty tree in his garden, and worked there in idyllic isolation at his *Feldlager in Schlesien*. But he made himself remarkably scarce, and I saw and heard virtually nothing of him. Ferdinand Hiller, by contrast, assumed an incomparably more prominent position on the musical scene in Dresden, insofar as the terrain was not in the possession of the Royal Orchestra and its masters, and busied himself there to the best of his abilities for a number of years. As he had independent means, he took up residence in a comfortable house and set up what was soon widely renowned as a highly hospitable establishment, which became a popular meeting place for the numerous members of the Polish colony through the efforts of Frau Hiller, an extraordinary Polish Jewess who had caused herself to be baptized a Protestant together with her husband, and in Italy to boot. His debut in Dresden also consisted of a performance of an opera from his pen, *Der Traum in der Christnacht*. After my *Rienzi* had accomplished the unheard-of result of emancipating the Dresden public through the creation of a success that had proved lasting there, at least, the eyes of many an opera composer were directed for a time at our "Florence on the Elbe", of which Laube once remarked that anyone returning there was always smitten with remorse for finding so many good things there that one always completely forgot when away. *Der Traum in der Christnacht* was also considered by its creator an especially German work: a gruesome play by Raupach, *Der Müller und sein Kind*, in which father and daughter die in quick succession of consumption, had been adapted by Hiller as an opera text and furnished with dialogue and music in what he thought was a very popular manner. He met the same fate with it that Liszt once told me followed all of Hiller's undertakings. Despite musical achievements that had won the praise of Rossini, among others, he had found that his operas, whether produced in French in Paris or in Italian in Italy, always failed completely. On German soil he had tried the Mendelssohnian style and had actually brought into the world an oratorio called *Die Zerstörung Jerusalems*, which had the advantage of being ignored by the fickle public, thereby bringing its creator an indestructible reputation as a genuinely German composer. He also took Mendelssohn's place as director of the Leipzig Gewandhaus concerts when the latter was summoned to Berlin. But his chronic bad luck had caught up with him there once again: he couldn't keep the job, because of his wife, it was said, who was denied recognition as a concert prima donna. Mendelssohn returned and got rid of him; Hiller boasted of having quarreled with him. Dresden and the success of my *Rienzi* now weighed so heavily upon his mind that he naturally made another attempt to establish himself as an operatic composer. Through his bustling activity and the charm a scion of a rich banking family always exerts even upon the directors of court theaters, he was able to induce them to put aside my poor friend Röckel's *Farinelli*, the production of which had been promised for the near future, in favor of his *Christmas Night's Dream*. He was of the opinion that, in addition to Reissiger and myself, a man of greater musical repute than Röckel was needed in an official capacity. But Herr von Lüttichau found that he had enough celebrities on his hands with the two of us, considering that we got on so well together, and he turned a deaf ear to Hiller's importunities. Meanwhile, the opera itself caused me personally some difficulties; I had to conduct a repeat performance, which took place before an extremely empty house. Hiller now decided that he had been unwise to reject my previous advice to shorten the work by one act and change the ending, and he thought he would give me pleasure by announcing his intention to do precisely as I had wished as soon as he could be assured of yet another performance. I managed to arrange things so that this could be done. But the work was beyond rescue, and Hiller, who had examined my libretto for *Tannhäuser*, concluded that I really had a big advantage in writing opera texts for myself that always turned out so well. I had to promise him my friendly assistance in the selection and working-out of his next operatic subject. Not long after this Hiller attended a performance of my *Rienzi* before a house filled to overflowing with a highly excited audience. Hiller seized the moment at which I was rushing from the pit to the stage after the second act, in a haste occasioned by the boisterous calls from the public, to supplement his perfunctory congratulations with the urgent request: "Do give my *Christmas Dream* once again", something which I laughingly promised to do for him if I could. I do not recall whether we ever got round to it. Meanwhile, awaiting the birth of a suitable opera subject, Hiller devoted himself to the zealous study of chamber music, to which his large and well-furnished salon lent itself most admirably.

A beautiful and solemn event, neutralizing the distractions produced by my association with these other composers, helped to purify the mood in which I completed the composition of *Tannhäuser* before the end of the year. This was the successful transference in December 1844 of the mortal remains of Carl Maria von Weber from London to Dresden. As previously stated, a committee had been formed years before to agitate for this transference. A traveler had reported in the meantime that the modest casket in which Weber's ashes were preserved had been stored so carelessly in a remote corner of St Paul's Church[1] that there was danger it might soon become unidentifiable. My energetic friend Professor Löwe had exploited this news to spur the Glee Club, his special hobby, to attack the task of retrieving the ashes for Dresden. The choral concert arranged to raise funds for this purpose had been a fair success; now they wanted the theater management to do likewise, and here ran into the first serious resistance. The General Director's office advised them that the King had religious scruples about disturbing the peace of the dead. Nobody really believed this was the real reason, but they could do nothing against it, and so I was next approached in the hope that my new position would enable me to do something for the project. I consented to do my best with the greatest enthusiasm; I let myself be elected to the committee; Councillor Schulz, an authority on art and Curator of the royal antiquarian collection, was also co-opted, together with a Christian banker; agitation flared up afresh; appeals went around in every direction; comprehensive plans were drafted, and above all there were countless committee meetings. But here again, I got into trouble with my chief, Herr von Lüttichau: he would no doubt have liked flatly to forbid me everything, on the grounds of the purported royal scruples, if he had not found, given the experiences of the previous summer and the musical reception for the King, that thwarting me, according to a popular expression he often used himself, would "put a hair in his soup". While the royal objection to the transfer was most certainly not as decided as was being pretended, Lüttichau was also obliged to admit eventually that not even the royal will could prevent the execution of this plan by purely private means, but that on the contrary, any such resistance would only provoke severe unpleasantness for the Court if the Royal Theater, to which Weber had once belonged, assumed a hostile attitude, and so Lüttichau attempted to talk me out of my participation in the whole affair, without which, he thought, it would not have a chance of success. He tried to convince me that it would be inappropriate for him to accord the memory of Weber such excessive honor when nobody would even dream of retrieving from Italy the ashes of Morlacchi, who had served the Royal Court Theater for a much longer period. What would be the consequences? Suppose, he went on, Reissiger died on his next trip to a spa; his wife could then demand with as much justification as Frau von Weber (who had already given him enough trouble) that the body of her husband be transported back with the same pomp and circumstance. I tried to calm him down; while I did not succeed in making clear to him the distinctions he was still confused about, I nonetheless managed to convince him that things must be allowed to run their course, particularly as the Berlin Court Theater had already announced a benefit performance in support of our undertaking. Thanks to Meyerbeer, to whom the committee had turned for help, the work given for this benefit was *Euryanthe* and it produced a splendid result in the form of two thousand talers. Some lesser theaters followed this example; therefore the Dresden Court Theater could no longer remain aloof, and before long we found that we could remit to our banker a capital sum large enough to pay the transfer costs as well as purchase a suitable burial vault and gravestone, while still preserving some funds for a statue of Weber to be erected sometime in the future. The elder of the two surviving sons of the deceased master journeyed personally to London to bring back to us the ashes of his father. This was done by ship up the Elbe, finally arriving at the pier in Dresden where the ashes were to be first landed on German soil. This landing was to be carried out in a ceremonial torchlight procession in the evening; I had undertaken to provide funeral music for the occasion. I put this together out of two themes from *Euryanthe*; starting with the music of the overture depicting the ghostly visitation, I led into Euryanthe's cavatina "Hier dicht am Quell", likewise unchanged, though transposed into the key of B flat major, and finished the piece, as Weber had closed his opera, with a transfigured version of the initial theme. This created a well-turned symphonic piece, which I had scored specially for eighty selected wind instruments, and despite the numerical strength I had been particularly careful to exploit the most delicate registers of each; for the eerie viola tremolo in the overture I used twenty muffled drums playing with utmost softness. I achieved with the whole thing, even when we were rehearsing it in the theater, such an overwhelming effect, especially abetted by our thoughts of Weber, that Schröder-Devrient, who had known Weber personally, was carried away with the most exalted emotion, and I could honestly tell myself that I had never before achieved anything that corresponded so perfectly to its purpose. The actual performance of the music in the open streets during the ceremonial procession went off no less successfully: because the very slow tempo, devoid of any strong rhythmic accents, was bound to create extra difficulties, I had caused the stage to be completely cleared at the rehearsal in order to gain the necessary space to permit the musicians, once they had learned the piece, to move in circular file around me during its performance. Those who witnessed the procession from windows as it approached and receded assured me that its effect was indescribably sublime.

After we had placed the coffin in the little mortuary chapel of the Catholic cemetery in Friedrichstadt, where it was greeted in modest silence by Frau Schröder-Devrient with a wreath, we proceeded the following morning[1] to lower it formally into the vault we had prepared. To me, in addition to the co-chairman of the committee Councillor Schulz, fell the honor of making a funeral oration. In preparing it, I had been afforded an especially moving and new element through the death of the second son of the departed master, Alexander von Weber, just before the transfer of the ashes. His mother had been so badly shaken by the unexpected death of this flourishing youth that, had we not been so far along in all our arrangements, we would have been virtually compelled to cancel everything, for the widow seemed inclined to recognize in this tragic new loss a verdict of heaven, damning the desire to transfer the ashes of her long-deceased husband as an act of vanity. As the public in its unfathomable conventional wisdom also seemed inclined to harbor similar views, I got the job of counteracting this sentiment by placing our undertaking in the right light; and I succeeded to such an extent that I was subsequently assured on all sides that nobody had the slightest quarrel with my proffered justification. On this occasion I had a strange personal experience while making the first official speech of my life. Ever since then, whenever I have been called upon to give a public address, I have made it a rule to speak extemporaneously; but this first time I had written out my speech in advance, in order to condense it sufficiently, and then had memorized it line for line. As I was so full of my subject and the treatment I had accorded it, I was also so sure of my memory that I made no provision for prompting; by this omission I caused my brother Albert, who was standing near me during the ceremony, a moment of great embarrassment, so that he later admitted to having cursed me, despite the emotion of the occasion, for not having given him my manuscript in advance to act as prompter if need be. It happened in this way: after I had begun my speech in a full and clear voice I was suddenly affected so strongly by the almost frightening effect my own voice, its tone and its accent made upon me, that I became completely transported and felt as if I could not only hear but also see myself speaking before the breathlessly listening crowd as well, and while I thus appeared in objectivated form to myself, I fell completely into a state of tense expectation at the fascinating event about to take place before me, just as if I were not the one who was really standing there and was supposed to speak. I didn't feel the slightest anxiety or even distraction during this time; yet there occurred such an inordinately long pause after the opening lines that whoever was observing me standing there with my contemplative and absent gaze could not know what to make of it. At last my lengthy silence and the absolute stillness enveloping me reminded me that I was there to speak and not to listen; I started in again at once and carried my address through to its conclusion with such fluidity of expression that the famous actor Emil Devrient[1] told me afterward he considered it not only a most deeply moving funeral service but also astonishingly impressive from an oratorical standpoint. The ceremony closed with the performance of a poem I had written and set to music, and though it presented many difficulties for a male chorus, the combined efforts of our best opera singers achieved a splendid rendition. Herr von Lüttichau, who had attended the ceremony, now declared himself convinced of the justice of the enterprise.

This was a profoundly satisfying and inwardly fortifying success for me; any cloud that might have remained hanging over the affair was dispelled by Weber's widow, when I visited her after leaving the churchyard, with a most heartfelt outpouring of her gratitude. For me the deepest significance lay in the fact that I, who had been led to so intense a love of music by the living phenomenon of Weber in my childhood, and had been so greatly shocked by news of his death so long ago, could now as a mature man again establish, as it were, a personal relationship with him by means of this second and last burial. From all the reports I have given on the previous pages of my dealings with contemporary masters of the tonal art and the experiences they afforded me, it is easy to see from what source I had been obliged to quench my thirst for association with great masters. There was no consolation in turning outward from the grave of Weber to look at his living successors; yet it still took some time before I realized clearly how hopeless the situation truly was.

I spent the winter of 1844–5 partly distracted by these external activities and partly under the spell of my own inner experiences; by extreme diligence and using the early morning hours, even in the winter, I succeeded in completing the full score of *Tannhäuser* by April, after having already finished its composition by the end of the previous year. In writing out the fully instrumented score I caused myself considerable difficulty by doing it straight on to paper specially prepared for the subsequent copying process with all the extra trouble this entailed. I had every sheet of the score lithographed at once and drew off a hundred copies in the hope that they would serve the purpose of rapidly circulating my work. Whether or not these expectations would ever be fulfilled, I was at any rate poorer by the five hundred talers it had cost me to produce these copies. The actual fruits of this painstaking effort, involving as it did so many sacrifices, will no doubt be recounted later in my biography; at all events, I could greet the arrival of the month of May with the first new work I had completed since *Der fliegende Holländer*, about which even Hiller, when I showed him a few parts of it, showed himself ready to express a tolerably favorable opinion.

These arrangements to secure quick acceptance for my *Tannhäuser* were intended to obtain the sorely needed success that my hard-pressed position seemed to require. In the course of the year that had elapsed since I had first begun publishing my own works, much had been accomplished; I had already been able to deliver the complete vocal score of *Rienzi* to the King of Saxony in a lavishly bound dedicatory copy during the autumn of 1844; *Der fliegende Holländer* was also complete; two-hand and four-hand piano arrangements of *Rienzi*, as well as the separate vocal numbers from both these operas, had also appeared or were about to be published; in addition, I had also caused twenty-five copies of the full scores of these operas to be made in what we call "autograph reproduction" (though in the handwriting of a copyist). While these new and heavy expenses increased the overall cost of publication significantly, it nonetheless appeared absolutely necessary to me to stimulate theaters to perform my works by sending them the scores, for the costly publication of the piano arrangements would only be profitable if my works were widely and successfully disseminated among the theaters. I first sent the score of *Rienzi* to the most important theaters: from each of them I got it back in the mail, from the Munich Court Theater not even opened. Thus enlightened, I saved myself the costs of a similar attempt with the *Holländer*. As a business speculation the whole venture could now succeed only if *Tannhäuser* gained the triumph I hoped for and pulled the other operas along after it; the worthy music dealer Meser, my improbable and now somewhat mistrustful agent in the affair, also had no choice other than to indulge this hope. The publication of the vocal score of *Tannhäuser*, which I had produced myself, whereas Röckel had taken care of the one for *Der fliegende Holländer*, and a certain Klink the one for *Rienzi*, was immediately undertaken. But Meser remained so utterly opposed to the title, which was still "The Mount of Venus" at the time, that he really succeeded in talking me out of it; he told me I simply didn't get around enough to hear the frightful jokes made about this title, which seemed to originate primarily from the staff and students of the Dresden medical school, as they attained heights of obscenity prevalent only in those quarters. I was sufficiently disgusted by the mere intelligence of this trivial attitude to consent to the recommended change; to the name of my hero, Tannhäuser, I added a reference to the legendary event which I had from the outset connected with the Tannhäuser story, although originally it was entirely separate from it, and this unfortunately later caused Simrock,[1] a scholar and renovator in the field of myth and folklore whom I much admired, to take umbrage with me.

At any rate *Tannhäuser und der Sängerkrieg auf Wartburg* became the title under which the work was to be introduced to the public in the outward form of a vocal score decked out in a manner appropriate to the opera's medieval character, and for this reason I had my Leipzig printer use special gothic lettertype for the printing of the text, a not insignificant increase in the total cost by which I demonstrated to Meser quite emphatically my confidence in the success of this work. We were already in it so deeply, and the accumulation of the capital necessary for my undertaking had already involved so many sacrifices, that we really had no alternative other than to rely on a favorable turn in my fortunes. Apart from this, my hopes for *Tannhäuser* were completely shared by the management of the theater. A number of excellent stage sets produced for Dresden by the best scene-painters at the Opéra in Paris, which, compared to the usual style of German stage decor, looked like authentic art works of the highest order, had given me the idea of persuading Lüttichau to have the *Tannhäuser* scenery done by the same painters. The order had been given, and the negotiations with the Parisian painter Despléchin had already been carried out the previous autumn. All my requests were approved, including those pertaining to the provision of lovely and historically accurate medieval costumes according to the designs of my friend Heine; only the order for the Hall of Song in the Wartburg was repeatedly deferred by Herr von Lüttichau, because he contended that the great hall of Charlemagne, which the Parisian painters had recently delivered for *Oberon*, would suffice for my purposes quite admirably. I had to exert superhuman strength to prove to him that we did not want a brilliant throne room but rather the particular scenic vision I had conceived, which could only be called forth according to my specifications. When I finally got rather cross and irritable, he calmed me down and said he certainly had nothing against having this Hall of Song specially designed and intended to order that this be done at once. He had only thought, he said, to increase my pleasure by making it a bit more difficult for me, as any request readily granted is generally valued the less for it. This Hall of Song was going to cause me more serious trouble, but for the moment everything was proceeding smoothly; all circumstances seemed favorably united in a focal point and cast a hopeful light on the production of my new work which was scheduled to open the autumn season. There was a good deal of excitement about it as well; for the first time I saw myself favorably mentioned in an article in the *Allgemeine Zeitung*, and they spoke of the high expectations aroused by my new opera, whose text had been written "with an indisputably poetic understanding". In the fullness of these hopes, I left in July for my yearly summer vacation on a trip to Marienbad in Bohemia, where my wife and I were both to take the recommended water cure.

Once again I found myself on the volcanic soil of this singular and, for me, always stimulating country of Bohemia; a marvelous, almost overly hot summer served to heighten my spirits still further. I intended to abandon myself to a life of the utmost leisure, as is in any case essential when undergoing the exhausting regime of a cure. I had therefore chosen my summer reading with care: the poems of Wolfram von Eschenbach in the versions of Simrock and San Marte,[1] together with the anonymous epic of Lohengrin with the great introduction by Görres.[2] With a book under my arm I betook myself to the seclusion of the neighboring woods, where I would lie beside a brook communing with Titurel and Parzival in this strange and yet so intimately appealing poem of Wolfram. But soon the longing to create something of my own from what I found here became so strong that, although I had been warned against any stimulus of this kind while taking the waters of Marienbad, I had difficulty fighting off the impulse. This soon put me into a highly overwrought state of mind: *Lohengrin*, the first conception of which dates from the latter part of my time in Paris, stood suddenly revealed before me in full armor at the center of a comprehensive dramatic adaptation of the whole material. Among all the many strands in the complex of myths that I was studying at this time, it was the legend of the Knight of the Swan, occupying such a significant position in their midst, which now stimulated my fantasy inordinately. Mindful of the doctors' warnings, I struggled manfully against the temptation to put the plan down on paper and resorted to a most curious and strenuous means to that end. From a few remarks in Gervinus'[1] *History of German Literature*, I had formed a particularly vivid picture of Hans Sachs and the mastersingers of Nuremberg. I was especially intrigued by the institution of the marker and his function in rating master-songs. Without as yet knowing anything more about Sachs and his poetic contemporaries, I conceived during a walk a comic scene in which the popular artisan-poet, by hammering upon his cobbler's last, gives the marker, who is obliged by circumstances to sing in his presence, his come-uppance for previous pedantic misdeeds during official singing contests, by inflicting upon him a lesson of his own. To me the force of the whole scene was concentrated in two points: on the one hand the marker with his slate covered with chalk-marks and on the other Sachs holding the shoes aloft, completed as a result of his hammering the marks in, whereby both indicate that the singing has been a failure. To this picture I now added a narrow, twisting Nuremberg alley, with neighbors, uproar and a street-fight to close the second act – and suddenly my whole mastersingers comedy stood before me so vividly that, on the grounds that it was an especially merry subject, I felt justified in putting it on paper despite the doctors' instructions. This was done, and I hoped to have freed myself thereby from preoccupation with *Lohengrin*. But I was fooling myself: no sooner had I stepped into my noonday bath than I was seized by such desire to write *Lohengrin* that, incapable of lingering in the bath for the prescribed hour, I leapt out after only a few minutes, scarcely took the time to clothe myself again properly, and ran like a madman to my quarters to put what was obsessing me on paper. This went on for several days, until the entire dramatic plan for *Lohengrin* had been set down in full detail.

At this point the doctor told me it would be better if I gave up taking water and bath cures entirely and admitted that I was utterly unsuitable for such treatment. My excitement had increased so much that even the attempt to sleep at night led to a series of adventures. We made several excursions in search of distraction, among other places to Eger, where the reminiscences of Wallenstein and the unusual dress of its inhabitants pleased me highly. In mid-August we traveled back to Dresden; my friends were enchanted to find me in such a euphoric state: I felt as if I had wings.

And thus began, when our singers had all gotten back early in September, the preparations for *Tannhäuser*, which soon caused me ever-increasing concern. Before long the rehearsals got to the point that, insofar as the purely musical preparations were concerned, the first performance could take place in the near future. It was Frau Schröder-Devrient who first grasped the special difficulties that stood in the way of the realization of such a work as this, and she saw and felt these difficulties so clearly that she didn't hesitate to communicate them to me, much to my dismay and discomfiture. The poem itself was her point of departure: when visiting me she proceeded to read the principal passages of the last act with great beauty and emotion, only to ask me how in the world I could possibly expect such a childish fellow as Tichatschek to find the necessary nuances for this Tannhäuser. I tried to murmur something about the nature of my music and how it was exact enough to compel the singer to express the necessary accentuations, even if performed by a purely musical singer without dramatic sense. She shook her head and told me that this would do only if I were talking about an oratorio. Then she sang Elisabeth's prayer for me from the piano score and inquired if I believed that these notes could be struck by a nice young voice without a soul of its own, and if I thought that all these pangs of the most heartfelt suffering would be expressed of their own accord. I sighed and said that what was lacking would simply have to be compensated for by the freshness and youthfulness of this actress and her matching voice. I asked her, however, to help my niece Johanna, who had been given the part of Elisabeth, as best she could in all this. Unfortunately nothing of that or any other kind could be done to resolve the problem with the role of Tannhäuser himself, for my doughty friend Tichatschek would only have been hopelessly confused by any attempts to teach him anything. So I had to rely solely on the force of his voice and on his characteristic penetrating vocal tone.

Schröder-Devrient's anxiety about the principal roles arose partly out of concern for her own: she herself did not quite know what to make of the part of Venus, which she had undertaken despite its very modest size owing to the difficulty and significance of its interpretation and to her desire to contribute to the success of the performance. I later came to the conclusion that the part had been treated all too sketchily in my work, and when I came to adapt it for Paris, I supplied everything I felt had been hitherto lacking by completely remodeling the part. But for the moment there was no way the artistry of the performer could transform my sketch into a satisfactory representation of the idea behind the figure. The best way of achieving an effect would have been by an appeal to the simple, sensual instincts of the public through a particularly young and beautiful actress fully confident in the impact of her physical charms. The realization by the now rather matronly artist that she could no longer produce such effects caused her inhibitions that made her disdain the usual means of pleasing the public. With a despairing smile she once attributed the whole difficulty in acting the part of Venus to the impossibility of finding the right costume: "For heaven's sake, what shall I put on as Venus? It wouldn't do for her to wear a belt and nothing else! Instead she'll be dolled up like something at a fancy-dress ball; that'll please you!"

On the whole, I still banked entirely on the effect of the purely musical aspects of the work, and the orchestral rehearsals were highly encouraging. In glancing through the score, Hiller had been completely amazed and praised me with the assertion that it could not have been scored with greater restraint. I myself was especially pleased at the characteristically delicate sonority of the orchestra and felt vindicated in my intention to husband my orchestral effects with the utmost thrift, and thus gain the opportunity to achieve the abundance of combinations that would be needed for my subsequent works. Only my wife, at the rehearsals, missed the trumpets and trombones that resounded everywhere in *Rienzi* with inexhaustible brilliance. Whereas I could afford to be amused at this, I had to give more serious consideration to her great anxieties about the feeble effect produced by the contest of song in rehearsal. Approaching the matter from the standpoint of the public, which above all else wants to be continually entertained or diverted, she had touched upon an extremely vulnerable aspect of the performance we were preparing. I had no trouble recognizing immediately where the fault lay, and that my error was not so much in the conception itself as in the failure to oversee its proper realization attentively enough. In the creation of the scene I had found myself unconsciously confronted by the essential dilemma about which I had to make a decision one way or another for good and all. Should this contest of song be a concert of arias or a competition in dramatic poetry? The nature of the operatic genre itself (and to this day people are of this opinion whenever they have failed to obtain the right impression from a perfectly good rendering of the scene) required here a juxtaposition and contrasting of various types of song, and, indeed, the differentiation of those songs by tempo and rhythm in the same way as, for example, a concert program is put together with an eye toward entertainment through constant surprise at the very least. Yet that was by no means my intent; and my true goal could only be reached if I were able, for the first time in the history of opera, to interest the audience forcibly in the development of a poetic idea through all its necessary stages; for solely by virtue of this interest would it be possible to comprehend the catastrophe, which in this case was not brought about by external causes but rather had to be represented as the inevitable outcome of an inner spiritual process. That was the reason for the great restraint and apparent slowness in the rhythmic build-up of the scene, in itself no hindrance to the understanding of the poetic expression but in fact, as I saw it, absolutely necessary to assist it, and also the reason for my refusal to interrupt it with unnecessary modulations or rhythmic changes until the approach of the passionate climax dictated it; thus also the sparse orchestral accompaniment, and the intentional renunciation of all purely musical effects, which are only gradually brought into play as the situation becomes more tense, so that feeling replaces thought in grasping the meaning of the scene. Nobody could deny that I was able to produce the right effect whenever I went through the contest of song at the piano. But this was precisely the decisive difficulty that plagued all my future ventures: I couldn't induce the singers to execute things precisely the way I wanted them. The lack of experience that had caused me to neglect this problem in the instance of *Der fliegende Holländer* now came back to me with full realization of its damaging consequences; and I now bent all my efforts to find a way to teach my singers the right way to handle their parts. Unfortunately it was impossible to do anything with Tichatschek because, as I have stated, we could only expect the worst if we confused him with discussion of things entirely incomprehensible to him. He was well aware of his great talent for using his metallic voice to sing with rhythmic and melodic beauty and precision, while not sacrificing any of his superb clarity of enunciation. That all this was not enough was something I had to learn myself and to my own amazement; and when even during the first performance of *Tannhäuser* I discovered to my horror something that had unbelievably managed to escape my attention in the rehearsals, namely that Tannhäuser at the end of the contest of song coyly directed his ecstatic and oblivious hymn to Venus right at Elisabeth, toward whom he strode as he delivered it, I thought of the warning of Schröder-Devrient, rather like Croesus at the stake, when he cried "O Solon, Solon!"

Whereas everything of greater vividness and melodic distinction in the part of Tannhäuser in this contest of song thus went by the board, in spite of the singer's musical excellence, on the other hand I did succeed in bringing into being a new element which I think I might almost say had never been so clearly delineated in opera before. I had paid close attention to the baritone Mitterwurzer – then still a young man and a curiously reserved and unsociable fellow – in several of his roles and had discovered in his soft, beautiful voice the desirable ability to make the innermost tones of the soul vibrate. I had entrusted the role of Wolfram to him and had every reason to be content with the results of his study of the part and with his dedication. I thus had to rely on him to live up to my previously undisclosed standards of execution with all that that entailed, if I were to demonstrate the validity of my intentions and the correctness of my way of doing things, particularly in this crucial contest of song. I went through the opening song of the scene with him and, after I had interpreted it for him in my fashion as penetratingly as I could, was at first utterly amazed at how new and difficult it all seemed to him. He felt himself entirely incapable of imitating me, and at every attempt to do so fell back quickly into the same old banal way of singing that showed me clearly that until then he had recognized nothing more in the piece than an apparent recitative with a few scattered vocal inflections to be sung this way or that, as normal operatic practice dictated, depending upon the condition of the voice. He too was astonished at his incapacity to follow me, and at the same time was so taken by the novelty and correctness of my way and its attendant requirements that he asked me not to insist on further such rehearsals at the moment, in order that he could find his own way into the new world suddenly opened to him. In several of the rehearsals he sang his part at only half-voice, as if to get by the difficulty; but in the dress rehearsal he succeeded so admirably in meeting the requirements of his part in full that his performance has remained to this day and for the future an anchor of hope for the possibility of properly training the performers I need, despite the degeneration of our operatic practices. The impact of this song, in the rendition of which Mitterwurzer had undergone a transformation in his entire bearing and countenance, became most remarkably the point of departure for the public's understanding of the work as a whole; and indeed Mitterwurzer's beautiful and moving performance of the role of Wolfram throughout, an assumption which of itself transformed him into a complete artist, became the foundation of my work's success, threatened as it was by the inadequacies of the first performance.

By his side the figure of Elisabeth made the only other really sympathetic impression. The youthful appearance of my niece, her tall and slender build, the unmistakably German cast of her features, what was then an incomparably beautiful voice, and the often innocently expressed emotion, together with skillful direction of her undoubted theatrical (though not dramatic) talent, all helped her to win the hearts of the public decisively. She became famous almost overnight through this achievement; and even in later years, whenever I received reports about a *Tannhäuser* in which she had sung Elisabeth, I was invariably told that its success had been attributable almost solely to her. Strangely enough, on these occasions I heard virtually unanimous praise for her varied and highly winning acting while receiving the guests in the Wartburg; in this I recognized the enduring fruits of incredible efforts that I and my very experienced brother had devoted to this aspect of her performance. But alas, it remained forever impossible to teach her how to sing the prayer in the third act; here again, as with Tichatschek, I was tempted to cry "O Solon, Solon!", and after the first performance I was obliged to make a drastic cut in the piece, whereby in my view it lost its significance for good. As I gather, Johanna, who for a long time was considered a really great artist, never really mastered this prayer, whereas a French singer, Mlle Marie Sax, sang it in Paris to my full satisfaction.

By the beginning of October we had gotten so far in our preparations that the only obstacle in the way of an early performance was the late delivery of the stage decorations ordered from Paris. Of impressive effect and completely successful was the Wartburg valley. The Venusberg grotto, on the other hand, caused me a lot of trouble. The painter had not understood me, and had painted a lot of bushes and statues, reminiscent of Versailles, on the interior walls of a wild mountain cave, and altogether had had not the least idea of how to combine the eerie and the alluring harmoniously. I had to insist on substantial changes, in particular on the painting out of the bushes and statues, and this took time. The concealment of the grotto in a rosy haze, out of which the Wartburg valley suddenly emerges, had to be attempted anew with the help of a special trick I had devised for it. The main calamity, however, was the further delay in the arrival of the Hall of Song; with all kinds of flimsy excuses coming from Paris, day after day went by, while everything else had been tried out and tried out again and all was ready for the dress rehearsal. Every day I went down to the railroad station to look through all the crates and packages: no Hall of Song arrived. Finally I gave in, and in order not to delay the long heralded first performance still further, I consented to substitute Charlemagne's throne room from *Oberon*, which Lüttichau had wanted to foist upon me originally for my Hall of Song, a painful sacrifice in view of the specific poetic effect I was trying to achieve. And indeed when the curtain went up on the second act and everybody beheld the reappearance of scenery well known from many performances of *Oberon*, it contributed in no small measure to the disappointment of the public, which was expecting the most startling innovations from this opera in every respect.

The first performance took place on October 19th. That morning an elegant and beautiful young lady came to see me with an introduction from Concertmaster Lipinsky; it was Frau Kalergis, a niece of the Russian Chancellor Count von Nesselrode. Liszt had made her such an enthusiastic convert to my cause that she had come all the way to Dresden to attend the miraculous birth of my latest work. I rightfully took this flattering visit as a good omen. Although on this occasion she went away somewhat perplexed and disappointed as a result of the inadequacies of the performance and its somewhat doubtful reception, I had sufficient cause in later years to appreciate all that these first impressions had planted and nurtured in this remarkable and lively woman. Her visit provided a strange counterpart to the arrival of a singular fellow, Carl Gaillard, editor of a recently launched music periodical in Berlin, in which I had been astonished to read the first and only favorable and substantial essay on *Der fliegende Holländer*. However vast my indifference to the doings of music critics had inevitably become, this essay nonetheless made a great impression on me, and I invited its author, though entirely unknown to me, to come to Dresden and attend the first performance of *Tannhäuser*. This he now did, and I was moved to find him a young man struggling against extreme poverty and chronic ill-health who, without thought of claiming compensation or even bed and board, had considered it a question of personal honor to respond to my summons. I saw from his knowledge and capacities that he would never rise to a position of any great influence, yet his honorable nature and receptive mind filled me with true respect for the poor fellow; I was truly distressed when, a few years later, without having gotten very far, he succumbed to his illness, having remained faithful and devoted to me under the most trying conditions right to the end. In addition, Alwine Frommann, a friend I had won for myself in Berlin with the performance of *Der fliegende Holländer*, but whom I had also not yet been able to meet, had arrived in Dresden somewhat earlier. I made her acquaintance at the home of Frau Schröder-Devrient, who was already a friend of hers and smilingly introduced her to me as one of my greatest conquests. No longer young and without any pretension to facial beauty, her remarkably penetrating and expressive eyes were the only external evidence of her profound spiritual gifts. She was a sister of the Jena bookdealer Frommann, and knew a lot of intimate stories about Goethe, who had lived in her brother's house whenever he was staying in Jena. She held the position of reader to Princess Augusta[1] of Prussia, but according to those in the know about her relationship to that exalted lady, she was more of a confidante and bosom friend. Nevertheless, she lived extremely modestly and seemed to be very proud of the ability to earn an independent living of sorts as a painter of arabesques. She has always remained utterly faithful to me, and was one of the few who ignored the unfavorable impression produced by the first performance of *Tannhäuser* and expressed prompt, decided, and heartfelt appreciation of my new work.

As to the performance itself, the conclusions I drew from it were as follows: the true defect in the work, as I have already mentioned, lay in the sketchy and clumsy way the role of Venus had been written, which thus spoiled the whole introductory scene of the first act. The effect of this weakness on the performance was that the rest of the work never really got off the ground, and by no means reached that intense degree of passion, which, in my poetic conception, should have impressed itself so strongly on the audience that the eventual catastrophe portended by this scene would overshadow the further development of the drama with a sense of impending tragedy. This great scene failed completely, despite the fact that it was entrusted to as great an artist as Schröder-Devrient and as unusually gifted a singer as Tichatschek. Perhaps Schröder-Devrient's genius might have found a way to give this scene the right accent of passion if she had not been partnered by a singer without any capacity for serious drama, gifted as he was solely for joyous and declamatory effects and without the slightest capability of expressing pain and suffering. The public warmed up a bit only at Wolfram's moving song and in the closing scene of the act. Tichatschek produced such a tremendous effect in this finale with his exuberant voice that, as I was assured later, the audience had been left in a most excited mood. This continued and even increased in the course of the second act, in which Elisabeth and Wolfram made a very appealing impression, but the hero of the drama disappeared more and more into the background and failed so completely to captivate the audience that in the closing scene, as if himself depressed by this fact, his attitude was one of broken-down dejection. The decisive failure in his interpretation lay in his inability to find the proper expression for the passage in the great adagio section of the finale which begins with the words: "To lead the sinner to salvation, the heaven-sent messenger drew near." I have since written in great detail about the importance of this passage in my directions for the performance of *Tannhäuser*; because Tichatschek's expressionless rendering only made it sound protracted and tedious, I was obliged to cut it entirely from the second performance onward. Not wanting to wound Tichatschek, who was sincerely devoted to me and a truly estimable singer, within his limitations, I pretended I had come to the conclusion that the passage was poorly conceived; and inasmuch as Tichatschek was generally believed to be the singer I preferred above all others to portray the heroes of my operas, this excision of what was to me such a crucial part carried over into all future performances of *Tannhäuser* as something I had authorized and even demanded, and for that reason alone I have had no illusions about the significance of the subsequent general success of the opera on German stages. My hero whose joy and misery must always be expressed with the most extreme emphasis, crept away at the end of the second act in an attitude of gentle penitence, only to reappear in the third with an air of humble resignation and a demeanor designed to awaken amiable sympathy. His declamation of the Pope's excommunication, however, was delivered with his customary rhetorical amplitude of tone and with such force that it was a joy to hear the accompanying trombones completely dominated by the singer. While these basic inadequacies in the representation of the principal figure left the audience in a state of never satisfactorily resolved bewilderment as to the true significance of the whole drama, an error of my own, rooted in my inexperience in this entirely new field of dramatic conception, and pertaining to the execution of the final scene, contributed to a highly damaging uncertainty as to the meaning of the dramatic action itself. In the first version of the closing scene, as performed on the first night, I had represented the new temptation of Venus, her last attempt to win back her faithless lover, as only a vision in the mind of the frenzied Tannhäuser; only a reddish shimmer on the Hörselberg, visible in the distance, elucidated visually the horror passing through his mind. And the decisive announcement of Elisabeth's death by Wolfram was also conveyed only as an act of divinatory inspiration by him; his justification for this was indicated to the public solely by the faint sound of mourning bells from the distance and a scarcely discernible gleam of torches to attract attention to the remote Wartburg.

Moreover, there was a confusing element in the closing appearance of the chorus of young pilgrims, to whom I had not yet given the fresh greening stave to carry and who thus had to convey their announcement of the miracle by words alone, and the chorus itself did not go over well from a purely musical standpoint as a result of the rather extended and unbroken monotony of the accompaniment which I had provided.

When the curtain fell at last, it was not so much the behavior of the rather friendly and demonstrably approving public as what I had experienced myself that convinced me the performance had been a failure, due to inexperience and the inadequacy of the means employed. My limbs felt like lead, and I was unable to prevent myself from infecting the friends who got together with me after the performance, including my kindly sister Klara and her husband, with the same mood of dejection. That same night I made the decisions necessary to save what we could from this shaky performance for the repetition scheduled for the day after next. I knew, of course, where the main problem lay, but could not dream of mentioning it; the slightest attempt to enlighten Tichatschek about the nature of his task was, I knew, a pure impossibility: I could easily have made him so irritated and inhibited that he would have refused under some pretext ever to sing Tannhäuser again. I thus embarked upon the only course open to me if I wanted to assure repeat performances of the opera and took all the blame for the ineffectiveness of his role upon myself, in order to be able to make the decisive cuts whereby I drastically reduced the dramatic significance of the title role, yet nonetheless made it possible that its inadequate execution would not necessarily reduce the appeal of other and more easily assimilable parts in the work. I thus hoped, though in deep inward humiliation, to help my work along most effectively by a second performance, and I was tremendously anxious that this take place as soon as possible. But Tichatschek had gotten hoarse, and I had to be patient for eight long days.

I can scarcely describe how much I suffered during this interim period. It looked as if the delay would wind up being fatal to my work. With every day that elapsed between the first and second performances, the success of the first appeared increasingly problematic, until at length it was acknowledged generally to have been a failure. While the greater part of the public gave vent to its disgruntlement that, after the endorsement they had given my *Rienzi*, I had paid no attention to their tastes in writing my new work, even the more judicious and devoted friends of my art were truly perplexed about the ineffectiveness of the work, the most important elements of which they had been unable to grasp, and which now seemed to them poorly conceived and badly performed. The critics swooped down upon it in undisguised glee, like ravens upon a piece of carrion thrown out for them. The passions and prejudices of the day were dragged in to confuse the matter still further and do me damage in every possible way. This was the epoch when the German-Catholic agitation, instigated by Czersky and Ronge[1] as a purportedly liberal movement, was causing a commotion. People now hit upon the idea that I had adopted a reactionary and intentionally provocative course with my *Tannhäuser*, as it was supposedly obvious that, just as Meyerbeer's *Les Huguenots* was designed to glorify Protestantism, my *Tannhäuser* was supposed to do the same for Catholicism. The rumor that I had been bribed by Catholic interests stuck to me like a burr for a long time; while these efforts to undermine my popularity were going on, I had the curious distinction of having my friendship and alliance solicited first by letter and then in person by a certain Herr Rousseau, until then editor of the Prussian State newspaper and the author of a destructive critique of my *Holländer*. He informed me that he had originally been sent to Berlin from Austria to further the Catholic cause, but having found these efforts fruitless, he was now returning to Vienna, where he would henceforth devote himself undisturbed to support those interests I had shown myself in *Tannhäuser* to share so devoutly. That remarkable paper, the *Dresdener Anzeiger*, the local gossip and scandal sheet, came up with something new of the same kind every day in the attempt to injure me. At last I noticed that some short, witty and very emphatic rebuttals to these attacks were appearing there. This puzzled me for some time, as I believed that only enemies and never friends resort to the press in such cases, until I pried it out of Röckel amid great laughter that he and my friend Heine had been the sole perpetrators of this campaign of encouragement on my behalf.

The bad odor emanating from these journalistic quarters irritated me solely because I had been prevented during these unhappy days from letting my work speak for me once again. Tichatschek remained hoarse: there was talk that he did not want to sing in my opera again. I heard from Herr von Lüttichau that he was on the point of canceling the order for the Hall of Song scenery, or at least sending it back when it arrived, out of fear that *Tannhäuser* would not hold the boards. I was so upset by the lack of confidence shown by this that I myself really began to think *Tannhäuser* was almost dead. The implications of all this for my financial position can be easily judged from my descriptions of my publishing ventures.

The eight frightful days dragged on to a seeming eternity. I didn't want to look anybody in the face, but one day I had to go to Meser, the music dealer; there I met Gottfried Semper, who was in the act of buying a copy of the *Tannhäuser* libretto. A short time previously I had been having a heated discussion with him regarding my material; he had contended in particular that the Minnesingers and the pilgrimage-obsessed Middle Ages had no place in art and let me know that he despised me for having chosen such material. While Meser now gave me to understand that there had not been the slightest demand for the available editions of my *Tannhäuser*, it was certainly curious to learn that my ardent antagonist was the only person to acquire a copy and pay for it. With a rather stilted earnestness, Semper now told me that it was obviously advisable to get to know the work well in order to form an adequate judgment, and he could unfortunately do this only by means of the text. This meeting with Semper, unimportant as it may appear, has remained in my memory as a first really encouraging sign.

Röckel was my greatest consolation, however, and in those miserable days entered into a close and lifelong relationship with me. Without my noticing a thing, he had been untiringly active in disputing, explaining, quarreling, and proselytizing on my behalf, and had worked himself up into a state of profound enthusiasm for my *Tannhäuser*. On the evening before the long-delayed second performance we got together for a glass of beer; his truly transfigured countenance actually managed to amuse me; we began joking: after he had looked long and hard at my visage, he swore I was indestructible; there was something about me that must lie in my blood, for it showed itself in my otherwise so dissimilar brother Albert as well. To explain himself, he termed this the characteristic heat of my temperament; he believed that such heat would consume others, but that I always felt quite comfortable at its hottest, for he had seen me literally glowing at times. I laughed and didn't know what to make of all this nonsense. Yet, he insisted, this time I would see it with my *Tannhäuser*; for any idea I might have that this work would not survive was a patent absurdity; it was absolutely certain of success. On the way home I concluded it was quite true that if *Tannhäuser* really caught on and achieved wide popularity, then something of immense consequence would certainly be gained.

At last the time came for the second performance, for which I thought

I had suitably paved the way by diminishing the significance of the title role and relaxing my original, more ideal standards regarding certain important aspects of the execution in order to stress the more easily appreciated parts and thus induce general approval of the whole. I was particularly pleased at the new scenery for the Hall of Song in the second act, which finally arrived to be set up in time for this performance. Its beautiful and imposing effect struck us all as a good omen. Unfortunately, I had to bear the humiliation of seeing the theater very sparsely populated: this sight, more than anything else, sufficed to let me know most decidedly the prevailing opinion about my work. Although the audience was small, it consisted in large part, at any rate, of the more serious friends of my art. The work was very warmly received, and Mitterwurzer in particular aroused the most fervent enthusiasm. In regard to Tichatschek, my two friends Röckel and Heine had thought it advisable to resort to some tricks to keep him in a good mood about his role. To contribute to general enlightenment about the decisive climax of the final scene, obscure as it was in some respects, they had organized a group of young people, mainly painters, with the mission of bursting out into violent applause at places which the operatic public would otherwise not regard as worthy of any such demonstrative acclaim. Curiously enough, the outburst of applause which, in accordance with these arrangements, followed Wolfram's words: "An angel prays for you at the throne of God; she will be heard: Heinrich, you are redeemed!", suddenly illuminated the significance of the whole situation for the public. At all future performances this passage, unnoticed in the first performance, became one of the principal moments at which the audience expressed its approval. A few days later we put on a third performance, this time to a packed house. Schröder-Devrient, dejected at the small contribution she could make to the success of my work, looked on throughout the performance from a small stage box; she told me that Lüttichau had come to her radiant with pleasure, expressing the belief that we had now brought *Tannhäuser* through safely.

And that is how it turned out: we repeated it many times in the course of the winter; yet we still found that whenever we put two performances together within a short time span, the second one was always less well attended, a fact indicating that I had not yet really captured the bulk of the opera-going public, but only the more cultivated stratum of the general public. Among these true friends of my *Tannhäuser*, I gradually discovered, were people who usually did not go to the theater, let alone the opera. The interest of the new audience formed in this way grew continually more intense and expressed itself in an unprecedented manner by a strong endorsement of the author. I was especially embarrassed for Tichatschek's sake to be obliged to respond to the calls of the public directed solely at me after virtually every act of every performance; try as I might, I could not elude these calls, for my hesitancy only caused my singer fresh humiliation because, whenever he showed himself in front of the curtain accompanied only by the other singers, he would be deluged with loud shouts for me. How I wished that the converse were the case, and that the excellence of the performer would overshadow the author! That I could never achieve this with *Tannhäuser* in Dresden was an experience characteristic of all my future undertakings. At any rate, with the Dresden performance of *Tannhäuser* I had at least gotten far enough to acquaint the educated part of the public with myself and with the less obvious and traditional aspects of my art, by compelling a degree of reflection about and abstraction from the simple realities of the staging. But I had not succeeded in making my intentions so irresistibly and convincingly clear in the dramatic representation that the less sophisticated sensibilities of the bulk of the public could be directly affected and thereby accustomed to them as well.

Through an enlarged sphere of activity and interesting new acquaintances, I had ample opportunity throughout the winter to obtain further clarification of these matters, whereby I was both instructed and encouraged.*

I became at this time a close friend of Dr Hermann Franck of Breslau, who had been teaching in Dresden for some time and whose company was very enlightening and stimulating. Equipped with sufficient means, he belonged to that small class of people who have gained a great reputation within a carefully selected yet far-flung circle of friends by means of vast knowledge, discriminating judgment, and an able pen, without ever achieving any public renown on this account. He had tried to make his knowledge and abilities useful to the public and had been persuaded by Brockhaus to edit his *Deutsche Allgemeine Zeitung* from the date of its initial appearance a few years previously. But after a year at this he gave the publisher a most emphatic resignation and since then had been induced only in the rarest of cases to have anything whatever to do with a newspaper. His pithy remarks about his journalistic venture with the *Deutsche Allgemeine Zeitung* amply substantiated for me his

* In the margin of the manuscript, in Cosima's hand: "Interruption (*Evchen's birth*) (March 28th)". Below, in Wagner's hand: "Yes! Yes!" [Editor's note: Eva (Evchen), Wagner and Cosima's second daughter, was born February 17th 1867. March 28th was presumably the date on which dictation was resumed.]

disgust with the practices of our press. This was all the more reason for me to be grateful to him for writing, without the slightest prompting on my part, a comprehensive article about *Tannhäuser* for the *Augsburger Allgemeine Zeitung*, which appeared in a supplement to that paper in October or November of 1845, and which I consider, despite its being the first such report about a work that has been much discussed since, by far the most balanced, wide-ranging, and exhaustive essay that has ever been written on the subject. By this means my name appeared for the first time in that great political journal of Europe-wide repute, whose columns have ever since been open, as a result of a curious transformation in the goals of the publishers, to anyone wishing to indulge in mockery of me and my work.

What particularly attracted me to Franck was the delicate and tactful way he reached his judgments and discussed things in general. There was something aristocratic about it, not so much rooted in the character-istics of his class as attributable to a truly cosmopolitan outlook. The refined coolness and reserve he evinced charmed rather than repelled me, for it was a characteristic I had not yet encountered in life. When I caught him indulging in rather conventional judgments about people of great fame whose repute did not seem to me entirely merited, I was pleased to find in the course of our conversations that I had in many respects a stimulating and decisive effect on his views. Thus I did not, even in those days, let it pass unchallenged when this or that great man was praised for his "good nature" as if that justified refraining from any closer scrutiny of his true merits. In this I often drove my worldly-wise friend into a corner, and it amused me hugely to receive from him several years later some drastic revelations about Meyerbeer's "good nature", as he had originally termed it, at which point he smilingly recalled the peculiar questions with which I had first contradicted his assertion. Even in the early days of our acquaintance he was very disconcerted to hear from me an instructive example of Mendelssohn's purported dis-interestedness and self-sacrifice in the cause of art, for in a conversation about Mendelssohn he had just remarked how refreshing it was to find a man willing to make real sacrifices to get out of a false position in which art was not adequately served; the fact that Mendelssohn had renounced his salary of three thousand talers per year as a conductor in Berlin to go back to Leipzig simply as the director of the Gewandhaus Orchestra was, Franck said, a beautiful thing and demanded respectful recognition. I was particularly qualified at the time to give him some precise details about this supposed sacrifice by Mendelssohn; for only a short time before, when I had gotten after our management to raise the salaries of some poor members of our orchestra, Herr von Lüttichau had been obliged to notify me that the orchestra budget had been so heavily strained by the most recent dispositions of the King that we could not think of doing anything for our poor musicians at the moment. A Leipzig government official and a great fan of Mendelssohn's, Herr von Falkenstein,[1] had actually managed to persuade the King to appoint Mendelssohn to a sub rosa Kapellmeister-ship with a sub rosa salary of two thousand talers, whereby he thus received, counting his one thousand talers annual salary from the Leipzig Gewandhaus, full compensation for what he had given up in Berlin, and that was why he had been willing to move to Leipzig. As those administering the finances of the orchestra had to hush this matter up in real embarrassment, considering the damage it did to our institution, and also inasmuch as the appointment of a Kapellmeister without an actual function would affront the existing Kapellmeisters actually doing the work and being paid less well to boot, Mendelssohn found these circumstances not only constituted ample justification for keeping his special remuneration strictly secret, but also forced him to permit himself to be lauded by his friends for his transfer to Leipzig as a model of self-abnegation, something which they found easy to do, despite Mendelssohn's substantial private fortune. When I informed him of all this, Franck was astonished, and he admitted that it was one of the most unusual examples of false reputation he had ever run across.

We soon began making adjustments of a similar nature in our assessments of several other artistic celebrities we found in Dresden at the time. With respect to "one of the most good-natured of all", Ferdinand Hiller, this was particularly easy. As to the more prominent members of the so-called Düsseldorf school of painting, whom I had come to know as a result of *Tannhäuser*, I was really not equipped to pass judgment, letting myself be guided mainly by the reputations they had won. Here it was Franck's turn to disillusion me most decidedly. In the cases of Bendemann[2] and Hübner,[3] I was under the impression that Hübner was nothing compared to Bendemann, and the latter, who had just completed the frescoes for a room in the royal palace and had been rewarded for it by his friends with a ceremonial banquet, appeared to me rightfully worthy of honor as a great master. I was therefore appalled to hear Franck dispassionately express his pity for the King of Saxony for the reason that Bendemann had been permitted to "daub" one of his rooms. Nevertheless, there was no denying the fact that all these men were "good-natured"; association with them, to which I was increasingly attracted, offered a contrast to my theatrical acquaintances by their more refined and varied artistic discussions. But it never got to any point of real warmth or fruitful stimulation. The latter was something that Hiller seemed particularly anxious to cultivate, and during this winter he established a so-called "circle" which met each week in the house of a different member. In addition to Hübner and Bendemann, the group was augmented by the painter-poet Reinecke,[1] who underwent the misfortune of creating a new opera libretto for Hiller at that time, the fate of which I will describe later.

Hiller and I as the two musicians, however, were now joined by Robert Schumann, who had at that time cast his lot completely with Dresden, and was also busying himself with drafts of opera libretti, which finally led to his *Genoveva*. I had known Schumann in Leipzig: we had commenced our careers in music at approximately the same time; I had written little articles for the *Neue Zeitschrift für Musik*, which he had previously edited, the last one being a rather longer piece than usual about Rossini's *Stabat Mater*, sent to him from Paris. He had been invited to give a concert performance of his *Paradies und Peri* in our theater; his quite extraordinary incompetence as a conductor on that occasion had aroused my especially active sympathy for this profound and productive musician, whose work I much admired. Emphatic good will and friendly trust prevailed between us. The morning after a performance of *Tannhäuser* he had attended, Schumann paid me a visit and expressed decided approval of my work, his only objection being that the stretta in the second act finale seemed too abrupt. This demonstrated to me his keenness of perception, and I was able to show him from the score how I had been compelled to make a painful cut that had produced the precise evil he had pointed out. We met from time to time for walks, and to the extent it was possible with this singularly laconic fellow, we exchanged ideas about music. He was delighted that he would soon be hearing the Ninth Symphony of Beethoven under my baton, after he had previously been obliged to suffer the performances of the same work in Leipzig, with Mendelssohn getting the tempo of the first movement all wrong. But beyond that I didn't get any real stimulation from his company, and that he was too unreceptive to benefit from any serious views of mine was soon evident, particularly with respect to his conception of the text for *Genoveva*. In this it turned out that my example had affected him only superficially, and really amounted only to an endorsement of my practice of writing my own libretti. He did, to be sure, invite me once to listen to him read the text he had put together, drawn from Hebbel[1] and Tieck; but when I, being filled with real solicitude for him and in the hope of seeing his work succeed, pointed out the great defects in it and suggested the necessary changes, I learned what kind of a person he really was. He would permit me to be carried away by him; but he would resist any interference with his work and his inspiration in a most stubborn and prickly fashion. So we left it at that.

In the course of the winter Hiller's assiduously maintained circle expanded considerably; it now became a kind of closed corporation meeting every week in a separate room of Engel's restaurant on the Postplatz. By now the celebrated Julius Schnorr[2] had been brought from Munich to be director of the Dresden gallery and had also been greeted by us with a banquet. I had already seen some of his inordinately large cartoons, which had impressed me greatly on account of their dimensions as well as the subjects taken from old German history, which preoccupied me at the time; now I learned of the "Munich School", and of Schnorr as its master: my heart overflowed when I thought of everything that was coming together in Dresden, and such giants of German art clasping hands there. I was much struck by Schnorr's appearance and conversation, although I could not reconcile his rather whining, schoolmasterly manner with his mighty cartoons; yet I thought it a great stroke of luck that he too began showing up at the Saturday evening gatherings in Engel's restaurant. He was well acquainted with old German legends, and I was always pleased whenever this subject was raised. Our group also included the famous sculptor Hänel,[3] whose great talent I had been taught to respect highly, even though I had to rely more on accepted authorities than upon my own feelings in judging his work. I soon saw that his bearing and conduct were a pose; he was fond of expressing ideas and opinions about artistic matters, but I was unable to figure out whether there was anything behind them. To me it seemed to be mostly philistine braggadocio: it was only after my "long-time" friend Pecht finally settled in Dresden for a while and demonstrated to me clearly and decisively Hänel's significance as an artist that I overcame my skepticism and tried to gain some pleasure from his works. A complete antithesis to him was provided by Rietschel; this pale, sickly man with his whiny, nervous manner of speech, didn't look much like a sculptor to me; but inasmuch as similar characteristics of Schnorr had not prevented me from recognizing in him a great painter, I soon succeeded in making friends with Rietschel, all the more easily because he turned out to be entirely unaffected and had a refined spiritual warmth I found most attractive. I recall his immediate sympathy and even intense enthusiasm for my efforts, particularly as a conductor. I refer in this respect to something that otherwise was completely absent within this versatile group of artists, despite all that we had in common; it seemed basically just a case of nobody being much interested in anybody else. Thus, for example, Hiller had arranged some orchestral concerts and had been appropriately fêted for this by his friends, on which occasion his praises had been sung with lavish rhetorical extravagance. Nonetheless, I never otherwise found a trace of enthusiasm for Hiller's efforts in all my private conversations with these friends, but on the contrary, noticed only expressions of doubt and apprehensive shrugs. These celebrated concerts soon expired. At our evenings together we never discussed or even mentioned the works of the masters who were present, and it was soon evident that none of the members really knew what to say to one another.

Thus it fell to Semper to enliven our conversations in his extraordinary way, and he used to do this by arguing with me so violently that Rietschel, an interested bystander, was often horrified and complained of our lack of restraint. Curiously enough, we seem to have assumed from the outset that we were antagonists: he considered me the representative of a Catholic medievalism and fought against it with fury. It took me a lot of effort to convince him at length that my studies and inclinations were really concentrated on German antiquity and the discovery of the ideals inherent in the early Germanic myths. As soon as we got onto heathen territory, and I had demonstrated my enthusiasm for heroic epics, he became a different person, and from then on we shared a deep and abiding interest that simultaneously isolated us from the rest of the group. But of course nothing was ever settled without fierce dispute beforehand, and this was no doubt attributable not only to Semper's strange and chronic predilection for flat contradiction but also to his feeling that he was an alien body in this group. His paradoxical assertions, which were obviously designed to pick a fight, soon showed me quite clearly that he and I were the only ones who took what he was saying seriously, whereas everyone else was perfectly content to let matters drop.

A man of this latter opinion was Gutzkow,[1] who often joined us. He had been summoned to Dresden by our theater management as a drama consultant. Several of his plays had recently become hits; *Zopf und Schwert*, *Das Urbild des Tartuffe*, and *Uriel Acosta* had lent an unaccustomed glamor to the repertory, and Gutzkow's appointment now seemed to inaugurate for the Dresden theater, where my operas were also being launched, a new and highly significant era. There was certainly no denying the good intentions of the management in this. I was only sorry on this occasion to be disappointed in my hopes that my old friend Laube would get this job. Laube too had been diligently devoting himself to theatrical literature; even in my Paris days I had noticed how zealously he used to study Scribe in particular, hoping to acquire his theatrical facility, without which, Laube felt, all German poetic drama was doomed to failure. With his comedy *Rokoko* he asserted that he had made himself absolute master of Scribean technique, and now boasted of his capacity to turn any subject whatsoever into an effective theater piece. Yet he was still very concerned to evince similar skill in the selection of his subjects, and as I saw it, his theory was demolished by the fact that the only pieces of his that had any luck were those of purely topical interest, to which public attention was drawn by catch phrases. The "topical interest" was nearly always political; there always had to be some pointed allusion to "German unity" and "German liberalism"; inasmuch as these important bulletins for the German public had to be transmitted first of all to our Court Theater subscribers, it all had to be, as stated, worked out with consummate skill, in the manner which people thought could be learned only from the most modern French vaudeville writers. The fruits of all this, including Laube's plays, were perfectly all right with me, particularly as Laube, who often came to visit us in Dresden when his plays were being performed, was very frank about his intentions and did not pretend to be a real poet. In addition, he showed great skill and almost fiery zeal not only in the concoction of his pieces but also in rehearsing and producing them, so that his appointment to a position in Dresden, which had been dangled before his eyes, would have been of substantial practical benefit to the theater in any event. But in the end the management decided in favor of his rival Gutzkow, despite his palpable incapacity to carry out the practical functions of a drama consultant. It soon turned out that he owed his successful plays solely to his literary facility, for following the effective pieces we had seen hitherto there now came a long string of wearisome and undramatic creations that made us realize, to our astonishment, that he himself had not been aware of the skill he had formerly demonstrated. It was, however, precisely the more ethereal qualities of a literary man which gave him the nimbus of a great writer in the eyes of many people, and which induced Herr von Lüttichau to prefer Gutzkow to Laube, Lüttichau being more interested in the ostensible reputation than in the practical benefit to the theater, and believing that he was thereby giving an impetus to the cause of high culture. I was honestly upset by Gutzkow's appointment, particularly in view of the prompt revelation of his inability to run the dramatic side of things, and I expressed my opinion to Lüttichau with such frankness that it was probably the first step toward our subsequent breach. I was really bitter about the lack of discrimination and the frivolity on the part of those in absolute command of such important artistic institutions as our German court theaters. In order to prevent any confusion that would otherwise arise from this ill-advised appointment, I entered a most decided objection against Gutzkow interfering in any way in the management of the opera, a request that was readily granted and no doubt saved Gutzkow a good deal of embarrassment. Nevertheless, the result was a certain strain in the relations between us; to alleviate this as best I could I took every opportunity to chat with Gutzkow during our communal evenings with the circle of artists I have described. I would have been happy to induce this singular fellow, whose head sat so frighteningly close to his chest, to relax a bit and unburden himself: but this simply was not possible, given his constantly shy and circumspect attitude: he remained aloof. One pretext for a discussion with him was afforded by his request, which we had to grant, to have the orchestra accompany in the manner of a melodrama a certain scene in his *Uriel Acosta*, in which the eponymous hero recanted his alleged heresy. As he did so, the orchestra had to execute that well-known effect of a soft tremolando on several purportedly suitable chords and sustain it for a time. When I heard it, it struck me as absurd and debasing to music and drama alike. On one of these evenings I now tried to come to terms with Gutzkow about this and also about the use of incidental music in support of spoken drama, and set forth my views in accordance with my fundamental artistic principles. To all the points I made he responded solely with an embarrassed and mistrustful silence, but finally retorted that I went too far with my claims for the significance of music, and that he could not imagine how music could be debased by being used in small doses to support a play, when poetry was used in support of operatic music with a much greater loss to its own integrity. As a practical matter, he said, it was best for the playwright not to be too fastidious in regard to music: an actor could not always be given a brilliant exit; yet nothing was more painful than when a star performer was obliged to leave the stage without applause: in such cases some distracting noise from the orchestra happily diverted attention. I really heard Gutzkow say all this and recognized that he meant it seriously. I never had anything to do with him again.

It was not long before I had equally little to do with all the painters, musicians, and other paragons of art belonging to our society. Yet at this time I formed a rather closer relationship with Berthold Auerbach.[1] Alwine Frommann had already drawn my attention to Auerbach's stories of peasant life; I had been delighted with her account of the effect of these modest works, as she characterized them, on her circle of Berlin friends. It was, she had said, as if fresh country air had streamed through an open window into a perfumed boudoir, her simile for the kind of literature they had been reading until then. I now read these *Schwarzwälder Dorfgeschichten*, which had shot to fame, and I too was strongly attracted by the refreshingly new tone and contents of these rough anecdotes of small-town life with their vividly described and easily recognizable localities. Inasmuch as Dresden was becoming more and more of a magnet for literary and artistic celebrities of all kinds at this time, Auerbach too showed up in the city to stay for a time with his friend Hiller, who thus once again had an ally of equal notability and equal status. This short, burly, Jewish peasant lad, as he was pleased to represent himself, made an entirely winning impression; it was only later that I learned the by no means innocent significance of his green jacket, and above all his green hunting cap, which lent him the looks of an authentic author of Swabian peasant stories. The Swiss poet Gottfried Keller later once told me in Zürich that Auerbach, after deciding to take Keller under his wing and help him get his literary products into circulation and make some money, had advised him above all else to procure a similar jacket and cap, on the grounds that he, Keller, was also not handsome and tall, and thus would be well advised to give himself a rather rustic and quaint appearance; Auerbach had then adjusted the cap on his, Keller's, head in such a way as to make him look a bit rakish. But at first I didn't see anything affected about Auerbach; he had assimilated so much of the folkways and colloquialisms of the people, and with such skill, that one could only wonder why, with these delightful qualities, he nonetheless moved in entirely antipodal spheres with the greatest ease. At any rate, he always seemed to be in his element precisely in those circles which one would have thought antipathetic to those characteristics he continually emphasized: there he stood in his green coat, a bit crude, but sensitive and open, surrounded by members of polite society who flattered him, delighting to display letters from the Hereditary Duke of Weimar[2] to him, together with his replies, and all the time observing things from the standpoint of a Swabian peasant nature, which nonetheless suited him so well.

What especially attracted me to him was that I found in him the first Jew with whom I could discuss the whole subject of Judaism with a hearty lack of inhibition. He seemed to be particularly anxious, in fact, to remove in an agreeable manner any prejudices on this score, and it was touching to hear him talk of his childhood, when it seemed to him that he was the only German who had got through Klopstock's *Messias* in its entirety. He had read this, it seemed, secretly in his humble village home, and had one day been late to school on that account, for which he was greeted by the teacher when he finally arrived in the classroom with the words: "You god-damned Jew-boy. Where have you been? Lending money again?" Such experiences had only made him melancholy and reflective, but had not embittered him, and he had, as he asserted, even managed to feel pity for the crudity of those who tormented him. These were qualities that I found very estimable; yet in the course of time I began to be somewhat concerned that he didn't get beyond his preoccupation with similar ideas and relationships, so that it appeared to me as if the world and its history boiled down for him solely to the problem of what to do about Judaism. One day I turned to him in an amiably intimate way and advised him simply to let the whole Jewish question go hang; there were, after all, a number of other standpoints from which to judge the world. Curiously enough, he lost all his ingenuousness at that point, adopted what struck me as a not entirely authentic tone of whimpering emotion, and assured me he could never do that, as Judaism still contained too much that demanded his complete sympathy. Later I could not help recalling this surprising obsessiveness I had noticed in Auerbach when I learned that he had contracted in the course of time a series of Jewish marriages, of which the only favorable result that came to my ears was that they had brought him a fortune. When I saw him again in Zürich after a number of years, I found his countenance changed in a disconcerting manner: he looked extraordinarily common and dirty; his former refreshing liveliness had turned into the usual Jewish fidgetiness, and every word he spoke came out in such a way that one could see he regretted not having saved it for a newspaper article.

During that time in Dresden, however, Auerbach's warm support for my artistic intentions, even though it was offered from his Jewish–Swabian standpoint, did me a lot of good, especially as it came at a time when I was undergoing the, for me, novel experience of finding that I was being recognized as an artist by people of renown, acknowledged distinction, and demonstrable culture. Whereas the success of my *Rienzi* had really enhanced my standing only within the theatrical world, the more problematical success of my *Tannhäuser* now brought me into contact with these wider cultural circles too, and this had served to broaden my horizons considerably, even though I was thereby accorded some disconcerting impressions of the dubious and insubstantial nature of precisely these seemingly highest spheres of the literary and artistic world of the day. At any rate, I did not derive from any of those acquaintances *Tannhäuser* brought me that winter any real reward, or even pleasant diversion, but rather felt driven irresistibly back upon myself from all this hectic activity instigated mainly by Hiller, whose innate worthlessness I soon recognized. I felt I must quickly create something new, as that would be the only means whereby I could get rid of the painful and disturbing agitation caused by the *Tannhäuser* performances.

Just a few weeks after the first of these performances I had completed the poem for *Lohengrin*. As early as November I read this poem to my close friends, and shortly afterwards to Hiller's circle as well. It was praised and deemed "effective". Schumann also liked it, yet couldn't figure out the musical form I had in mind for it, as he couldn't find any passages suitable for traditional musical numbers. I then had some fun reading him different parts of my poem just as if they were in aria and cavatina form, so that in the end he smilingly conceded the point.

Serious reflection aroused some deeper reservations about the nature of the tragic material itself, as suggested delicately and thoughtfully to me by Franck. He considered the punishment of Elsa by Lohengrin's departure unseemly: he understood perfectly well that it was precisely the most characteristic element in the legend that was expressed in this highly poetic event, but he doubted whether it did full justice to the sense of tragedy when allowance was also made for dramatic realism. He would have preferred to see Lohengrin die before our eyes as a result of Elsa's betrayal. At any rate, as this did not seem permissible, he wanted to see him riveted to the spot by some powerful motivating force and prevented from leaving. As I naturally wouldn't even think of such a thing, I nevertheless began considering whether the cruel separation could not be eliminated, while still retaining Lohengrin's indispensable departure for distant realms. I tried to find a means of permitting Elsa to depart with him, to do some sort of penance which would require her too to withdraw from the world; this struck my friend as more hopeful. While

I was languishing in uncertainty about this, I gave my poem to Frau von Lüttichau for perusal and for consideration of the objections Franck had raised. In a little note expressing her delight with my poem, she stated flatly on this particular matter that Franck had to be utterly devoid of poetic sense if he thought *Lohengrin* could end in any other way than my text depicted. I heaved a sigh of relief; I triumphantly showed this letter to Franck; extremely embarrassed and hoping to excuse himself, he at once initiated an exchange of correspondence on the subject with Frau von Lüttichau, which certainly cannot have been uninteresting, though I never got to see any of it. But the result was that *Lohengrin* remained the way it had been. Curiously enough, a similar experience with respect to the same subject later plunged me once again into temporary uncertainty. When Adolf Stahr[1] put the same objection about the ending of *Lohengrin* to me with great vehemence, I was really taken aback by this uniformity of judgment, and because I was at that much later date, as a result of all kinds of adventures, far removed from the mood in which I had written *Lohengrin*, I was foolish enough to toss off a hasty letter to Stahr telling him I thought he was almost totally right. I didn't know that I was thereby causing Liszt great distress, for he had taken the same position with regard to Stahr as Frau von Lüttichau had taken with respect to Franck. Fortunately my great friend's dismay at my seeming act of self-betrayal did not last long; for even before I had learned of the anxiety I had caused, my own misgivings about the matter brought me to my senses within a few days. After it had dawned on me how silly I had been, I was able to hearten Liszt with this laconic dispatch from my haven in Switzerland: "Stahr is wrong, Lohengrin is right."

For the present I got no further with my poem than this literary and critical assessment of it; I could not as yet think of sketching any music for it. I first had to struggle with fate to win that peace and harmony of mind I always needed for composition and which was always so hard to come by. Whereas all my experiences with the production of *Tannhäuser* had made me vastly pessimistic about the prospects for my future artistic activity, it was also perfectly clear that for a long period my work would not get beyond the Dresden repertory, if indeed it could maintain itself there, and that there was not the slightest chance of its reaching other German theaters, which had not even accepted my resoundingly successful *Rienzi*. The effect of all this on my financial position, as I have already described it, was bound to be catastrophic. In preparing myself for the troubles ahead, I tried to immerse myself in those studies of history, legend and literature I had grown to love, and, as an alternative, to drug myself with all sorts of hectic artistic activities. As far as concerned the former, it was principally the German Middle Ages in which I tried to make myself at home in every way. While I could not go about this with any degree of philological precision, I was nonetheless very serious and, for example, studied the German legal records edited by Grimm with the greatest interest. As there was no way to apply the fruits of such efforts to immediate dramatic purposes, many people did not comprehend why I, as an "opera composer", should occupy myself with such crudities; no doubt some noticed later that there was something unusual about my *Lohengrin*; but this was always attributed to the "lucky choice of material", and I was generally congratulated on my cleverness in making such a choice. Medieval German subjects and, later on, stories of Scandinavian antiquity have therefore been dug up and used by a lot of composers, who then, in the end, have been surprised to find nothing of any real value come out of it all. Perhaps it would help if I now recommend that they take a look at Grimm's *Weistümer* and similar things. I neglected at the time to give Ferdinand Hiller, who had proudly pounced upon a Hohenstaufen subject, the benefit of this advice; as he got nowhere with the work, he will perhaps consider me deceitful if he now learns that I concealed the *Weistümer* from him.

In the field of external activities, my principal undertaking in this winter consisted of an extremely carefully prepared performance of Beethoven's Ninth Symphony, which involved me in a number of struggles and yielded experiences of immense impact on my subsequent development. The facts were these: each year the Royal Orchestra had only one opportunity, outside church or opera, to show itself off independently in a major concert; the old opera house, as it was called, was given over every Palm Sunday to what had originally been an oratorio performed for the benefit of the orchestra's widows and orphans pension fund. To make the affair more attractive, it had become the custom, eventually, to append a symphony to the oratorio; as previously mentioned, I had on one such occasion conducted the Pastoral Symphony, and later Haydn's *Creation*, the latter performance giving me great pleasure in a work I first really got to know only on this occasion. Because we two Kapellmeisters had reserved the right to alternate, it fell to me to conduct the symphony for Palm Sunday of the year 1846. I felt a great longing to do the Ninth; my choice was buttressed by the fact that the work was virtually unknown to the Dresden public. When the senior members of the orchestra charged with responsibility for the pension fund learned about this, however, they were so horrified that they went to our General Director, Herr von Lüttichau, and tried to convince him to use his supreme authority to get me off this track. They based their appeal on the assertion that the pension fund would suffer severely through the choice of this symphony, as it was held in low repute in Dresden and surely would keep the public away from the concert. Some years before, as a matter of fact, this Ninth Symphony had been performed in a benefit concert under Reissiger, and with the full collaboration of the conductor had been a complete failure. I needed all my verve and powers of persuasion to overcome the doubts of our chief. As for the pension fund trustees, for the time being I had no choice but to quarrel with them, as I heard they were going around filling the town with their cries of anguish about my frivolity. To beshame them a bit in their worries, I made up my mind to prepare the public for the performance I was insisting upon and for the work itself in such a way that the excitement provoked by it would certainly lead to a full house, and thus swell the purportedly threatened box-office receipts. The Ninth Symphony thus became a point of honor for me in every respect, whose success called forth all my resources. The committee was opposed to the disbursements necessary to procure the orchestral parts; so I borrowed them from the Leipzig Concert Society.[1]

But imagine how it was for me, who had spent nights of my earliest youth copying this score, and who now for the first time since then gazed at its mysterious pages, the sight of which had once sent me into mystical transports, and began to study it in detail! Just as hearing a rehearsal of the first three movements by the incomparable Conservatoire orchestra during my obscure Paris period had suddenly affected me as if by a magic spell, returning me at a stroke, miraculously, to my early youth across all the years of alienation and confusion, and strengthening the new turn taken by my inmost strivings, so now the sounds of that performance, the last I had heard, were reawakened with mysterious power when I first saw before me with my own eyes that which had remained for me in those earliest days likewise only a mystic vision. By this time I had gone through enough to have been driven, tacitly and in my innermost depths, to attempt to collect myself, and to inquire almost despairingly as to my destiny. What I did not dare to admit to myself was my knowledge of the utter lack of a solid foundation for my existence as an artist and as a member of society, headed as I was in a direction in which I could not help seeing myself without prospects and a stranger within

my profession and in my daily life. My despair over this, which I tried
to conceal from my friends, was now transformed by this marvelous
Ninth Symphony into brightest exaltation. It is simply not possible that
the heart of a pupil has ever been captivated with such rapturous force
by the work of a master as mine was by the first movement of this
symphony. Anyone who came upon me by surprise with the open score
before me, as I went through it thinking how best it could be performed,
would have been startled to hear my wild sobs and see my crying, and
would no doubt have asked themselves in some amazement whether this
was proper behavior for a Royal Saxon Kapellmeister. Happily I was
spared such surprise visits by our orchestral committee, their worthy
conductor Reissiger, or even that great authority on classical music,
Ferdinand Hiller.

I began by drawing up a program, for which the custom of publishing
the text of the choruses provided a convenient pretext, as a guide to easier
understanding of the work, not with the idea of influencing the
audience's critical judgement, but rather in the hope of appealing to its
feelings. This program, for which excerpts from Goethe's *Faust* proved
particularly helpful, was received well not only in Dresden at the time
but also in a number of other places later. I also resorted to the columns
of the *Dresdener Anzeiger* anonymously, publishing short and enthusiastic
spot items in order to call the attention of the public to this work which,
as I had been told, was in bad repute in Dresden. My efforts in this
external direction alone succeeded so well that the receipts for that year
not only surpassed all previous years, but also persuaded the orchestral
pension fund committee to avail themselves of my presence in Dresden
to ensure similarly large receipts by repeating the symphony every year
I remained there. In regard to the artistic aspects of the performance,
I aimed at making the orchestra give as expressive a rendering as possible
by writing whatever drastic accentuation marks I felt were necessary on
the orchestral parts myself. The custom, here, of doubling the wind
instruments led me to a particularly carefully considered use of this
advantage, generally exploited only in a rough and ready way in the
performance of large-scale works by having the parts marked *piano*
played by a single instrument, and the parts marked *forte* played by both.
My way of achieving clarity of execution in such matters is perhaps best
demonstrated by a passage in the second movement of the symphony
when, in C major for the first time, the whole string section plays the
rhythmic main theme in unison in three octaves, as a kind of
accompaniment to the second theme, which is rendered solely by the

weak woodwinds; as the score is here marked *fortissimo*, it happens in every conceivable performance that the melody in the woodwinds is completely inundated by the supposedly accompanying strings and remains virtually unheard. Inasmuch as no literalistic piety would induce me to sacrifice the master's intended effect to an erroneous marking, I here had the strings play only moderately loudly instead of *fortissimo* up to the point where they combine with the wind instruments to continue the new theme in alternation: the theme as played by the doubled wind instruments as loudly as possible could now be heard with great clarity, for the first time, I believe, since the symphony was written. I proceeded in this manner throughout, in order to achieve maximum exactitude in the dynamic orchestral effects. Everything, however seemingly difficult to grasp, was to be rendered in such a way as to appeal decisively to the emotions. For example, the fugato in 6/8 time following the choral passage "Froh wie seine Sonnen fliegen" in that part of the finale marked *alla marcia* had always caused a lot of trouble: in view of the stirring tone of the preceding stanzas, a veritable call to battle, I treated this fugato as literally a serious yet exuberant combat and took it in an extremely fiery tempo and with the greatest tension and force. On the day after the first performance I had the satisfaction of receiving the visit of Music Director Anacker[1] from Freiberg, who came to tell me, penitently, that although he had previously been in the ranks of my opponents, he had now become a true friend: what had utterly overwhelmed him, he said, was precisely my conception and rendition of that fugato. I also devoted close attention to that most unusual recitative-like passage for cellos and contrabasses at the beginning of the last movement, which had caused old Pohlenz such embarrassment long ago in Leipzig. Given the superb technical skill of our contrabassists in particular, I felt every confidence in aiming for perfection at this point. In twelve special rehearsals for these two string sections alone, I succeeded in producing a declamation of the melodic line that seemed to flow of its own accord, expressed with the tenderest delicacy as well as the greatest emphasis. From the outset in this venture I had recognized that the possibility of obtaining a popular success with this symphony depended upon the application of the highest ideal standards in overcoming the extraordinary difficulties presented by the choral part. I saw that demands were made here that could only be met by a great and dedicated mass of singers. Thus the first prerequisite was to secure the services of as large a chorus as possible; beyond the usual augmentation of our theater chorus with the rather feeble students of the Dreissig singing academy,[1] I managed to overcome many difficulties to obtain the choir of the Kreuz School with its superb boys' voices as well as the choir of the Dresden Seminary, which was well trained in church singing. When these singers, more than three hundred strong, now assembled for our many rehearsals, I tried in my own peculiar way to inspire them for their task; I succeeded in proving to the basses, for example, that the famous passage "Seid umschlungen, Millionen", and especially the "Brüder, überm Sternenzelt muss ein lieber Vater wohnen", could not possibly be sung in a normal way but had to be, as it were, proclaimed in highest ecstasy. I was so transported myself at this point that I think I really got everyone into quite a state, and I didn't stop until my own voice, which I had previously been able to hear through all the others, was no longer audible, and I could feel myself drowning in a warm sea of sound. It gave me great satisfaction to work on the baritone soloist's recitative "O Freunde, nicht diese Töne", generally almost impossible to render adequately owing to its unusual difficulties, with Mitterwurzer, whose glorious delivery of it was rooted in the mutual understanding we had previously established. But I also took great pains to achieve the best possible balance by having the hall re-arranged in order to be able to array the orchestra according to a wholly new scheme of my own. As can be imagined, there were terrific difficulties in getting any money allocated for this purpose; but I remained undeterred and finally got the whole podium rebuilt, so that we could concentrate the whole orchestra in the center and surround it by the chorus on steeply banked seats in the manner of an amphitheater. This was of immense benefit to the choral sound, while in the purely symphonic movements it abetted the precision and emphasis of the nicely grouped orchestra.

The hall was filled to bursting even at the general rehearsal. On this occasion Reissiger committed the incredible folly of attempting to denigrate the symphony with the public and point out how sad it was that Beethoven had gone astray; on the other hand Gade,[2] who had come over from Leipzig where he was then conducting the Gewandhaus concerts, assured me after this rehearsal that he would willingly pay double the price of admission to hear the recitative of the basses once again. Hiller opined that I had gone too far in modifying the tempi; what he meant by this I learned later when I heard him conduct some great orchestral works himself, and I will have more to say on that subject. Yet the overall success exceeded all expectations, and noticeably among non-musicians as well; among these I recall the philologian Dr Köchly,[3] who came up to me on this occasion and confessed that for the first time in his life he had been able to follow a symphonic piece from beginning to end with intelligent interest. My own gain on this occasion was the reinforcement of the gratifying feeling that I had the capacity and power to accomplish just about whatever I wished if I seriously devoted myself to it. This led me on to ponder why it was that I had not as yet been able to perform my own compositions with equal success. I had succeeded completely with Beethoven's Ninth Symphony, a work many still considered problematic, and which had never yet attained much popularity; but every time my *Tannhäuser* went on the boards in Dresden, it taught me that the secret of its success was yet to be found. How could I find it? This was and remained the unspoken question with which my future development was confronted.

I did not have much time to devote to meditations about the more theoretical aspects of this problem; for the practical consequences of the lack of success of which I was inwardly only too aware stood exposed before me, a terrifying portent of catastrophe that surely would strike in my financial affairs, if I did not take desperate steps without delay.

I was driven to action initially by an absurd omen. My agent and the nominal publisher of my three operas *Rienzi*, *Der fliegende Holländer* and *Tannhäuser*, that oddity of a Court music dealer, C. F. Meser, invited me one day to discuss our financial situation in a tavern known as The Spoiler; in great anxiety we weighed the possibilities of a good or bad outcome of our sales at the forthcoming Easter Trade Fair. I tried to buoy him up and ordered a bottle of the best Haut-Sauternes; a venerable looking flask appeared; I filled our glasses, we raised them to toast success at the fair, and drank – only to shriek suddenly like madmen and try to spit everything out in horror – for by mistake we had been served the strongest tarragon vinegar in the house. "My God," cried Meser, "this really did it!" "Yes indeed," I replied, "I think a lot of things will turn to vinegar for us!" My humor revealed to me in a flash that I would have to look elsewhere for my salvation than to the Easter Trade Fair.

Not only was it necessary to repay the capital advances I had scraped together with such ever-increasing sacrifices for the costly business of publishing my operas, but also rumors about my indebtedness had circulated so widely, as a result of my having been forced to avail myself of help from usurers, that even the friends who had assisted me to get established in Dresden became highly concerned. I now had a really sad experience with Frau Schröder-Devrient, who precipitated my catastrophe with an incomprehensibly inconsiderate action. As mentioned, I had borrowed one thousand talers from her at the beginning of my stay in Dresden to repay prior debts and also to take care of my friend Kietz in Paris. Jealousy of my niece Johanna, and suspicion that I had brought her to Dresden in order to make it easier for the theater management to dismiss a great artist like herself, had aroused toward me in this otherwise so generous woman that mean and hostile spirit one finds so often in the theater. She had now broken her contract and went around telling everybody I had helped to drive her out. Casting aside all friendly consideration for me, to whom she now did the uttermost injustice in every respect, she left the demand note I had given her in the hands of an energetic lawyer, who promptly proceeded to sue me for the amount owed. I was thus compelled to disclose how things stood to Herr von Lüttichau and ask for his help in applying for an advance from the King to shore up my shattered financial position.*

My chief expressed willingness to endorse an appeal in the matter to the King. To that end I had to submit in writing the precise amount of my debts; but as I was told at once that the sum I needed would be provided only in the form of a loan from the theater pension fund at an interest rate of five per cent per annum, and that I would also be obliged to take out a life insurance policy in favor of the fund at a cost of three per cent of the principal sum per annum, I was irresistibly tempted to understate the full amount I owed by leaving out those debts that were not of a threatening nature, and which I thought I would be able to repay from the income I would eventually receive from my publishing venture. The burden of repayment rose nonetheless so high that my truly quite modest salary as a conductor was thereby severely eroded. I also had unpleasant experiences arising from the need to obtain the requisite life insurance policy; I had to go repeatedly to Leipzig and try to overcome all kinds of doubts with respect to my health and future life span, about which those who had observed me casually in my present agitated state actually expressed, it occasionally seemed to me, malicious apprehensions. My friend Pusinelli, as my regular doctor, finally succeeded in providing sufficient evidence as to the state of my health, so that I at last got my life insured for three per cent a year.

The last of these painful expeditions to Leipzig, however, was partly

---

* Note in the manuscript at this point, in Wagner's hand: "Febr. 21st 68", referring to his correction of the manuscript. In the margin, in Cosima's hand: "Interruption due to leaving Triebschen April 15th 1867"; and on the line below: "Resumption: July 28th 1868 (on Triebschen)", referring to the dictation.

for a more pleasant reason, a friendly invitation on the part of the old master Louis Spohr, which made me particularly happy as it simultaneously constituted an act of reconciliation. Some time previously Spohr had written to me that the success of my *Der fliegende Holländer* in Kassel and his own pleasure in this work had stimulated him to make another attempt in his career as a dramatic composer, which had brought him repeated failures in recent years. His latest work was an opera entitled *Die Kreuzfahrer*, which he had sent to the Dresden Court Theater during the past year, in the opinion, as he told me, that I would do everything I could to have it performed. In commending his work to me he had called my attention to the fact that this work represented a new departure for him, and that he had sustained the most precise dramatic declamation throughout it, this being greatly facilitated by what he termed "the marvelous subject". Though not entirely taken by surprise, my horror was nonetheless great when I took a look at his score as well as the text; for obviously the old master had been absolutely mistaken about the assurances he had given with regard to his work. My great hesitancy to engage in any strong advocacy on behalf of a performance for this opera was abetted by the tradition that decisions of this nature as to which works were to be accepted were not made by one Kapellmeister alone, and also by the fact that it was the turn of Reissiger, who often boasted of being an old friend of Spohr, to select and produce a new work. Unfortunately, I had learned a short time later that the office of the General Director had sent the opera back to Spohr with an offensively brief note, about which he then complained bitterly to me. I had been genuinely concerned about this, and that I had managed to calm him down and make him feel better was evidenced by the aforementioned invitation; it would be, he wrote me, painful for him to go through Dresden on his present vacation trip, but inasmuch as he was very anxious to make my acquaintance, he asked me to meet him in Leipzig, where he would be spending a few days.

The meeting did not fail to produce a lasting impression on me. He was a tall, imposing man of distinguished appearance and a serious, temperate nature, who disclosed the essence of his cultural principles as well as his alienation from the latest tendencies in music, in a touching, almost apologetic way by stating that he had received his first and decisive impression as a young boy from Mozart's *Zauberflöte*, new at the time. Regarding my libretto for *Lohengrin*, which I left behind with him for perusal, and the general impression I made on him, he later expressed himself with almost surprising warmth to my brother-in-law

Hermann Brockhaus, at whose house we had been invited to lunch and where we had conversed in great animation. We also got together for musical soirées at the homes of Music Director Hauptmann and of Mendelssohn, on which occasions I heard the master take the violin part in one of his quartets. It was particularly in these circles that his calm and dignified manner made an impression on me of almost moving integrity. Yet I later heard from witnesses whose reliability I could not gauge that my *Tannhäuser*, when it was performed in Kassel, caused him pain and embarrassment, so that he declared he couldn't follow me on such a path and was afraid I had gone astray.

To recover from all my hardships and worries I had managed to extract, as a maximum sign of favor from the management, three months' vacation, in order to retreat to the country to recuperate and draw a deep breath before beginning a new work. For this purpose I chose a peasant cottage in the village of Gross-Graupe, half way between Pillnitz and the fringes of our "Saxon Switzerland". Frequent excursions to the Porsberg, to the adjacent Liebethal valley, and also to the more distant Bastei helped to strengthen my shattered nerves. When I wanted to get started on a first sketch of the music for *Lohengrin*, fragmentary echoes of melodies from Rossini's *Guillaume Tell*, the last opera I had been obliged to conduct, bothered me incessantly to my great irritation; in desperation I finally hit upon an effective antidote for this annoying intrusion by singing to myself quite fiercely on one of my lonely walks the first theme from the Ninth Symphony, which had also recently refreshed itself in my memory. That helped. At Pirna, where I went almost every evening to bathe in the river, I was startled on one occasion to hear the melody of the Pilgrims' Chorus from *Tannhäuser* being whistled by a bather whom I couldn't see. This first indication of possible popularity for a work I had been compelled to struggle so hard to put across in Dresden made a greater impact on me than any similar experience I have had subsequently. From time to time friends visited me from Dresden, among whom one day appeared the then sixteen-year-old Hans von Bülow in the company of Lipinsky, much to my delight as I had heard of his great interest in me. But in general I remained mostly with my wife, and sometimes on my longer walks solely with my little dog Peps. During this summer vacation, the first part of which was necessarily consumed in taking care of unpleasant business matters and restoring my health, I nonetheless succeeded in sketching the music for all three acts of *Lohengrin*, if only in very hasty outline form.

336

With this much in hand, I returned that August to Dresden to take up those duties as a Kapellmeister which yearly seemed ever more burdensome. Moreover, I was immediately plunged back into the old familiar troubles which had been only temporarily allayed. The business of publishing my operas, the success of which I was still counting on as the only means of liberating me from my oppressive situation, continually demanded fresh sacrifices if those prospects were not to be abandoned. But my income was now so much reduced that even the smallest outlays for this purpose necessarily led to new and increasingly painful complications, so that I soon began to lose all hope again.

To fortify myself, my only recourse was to resume work on *Lohengrin*. In so doing, I adopted a course of action I was never to repeat: I completed the third act first, a procedure dictated by the aforementioned criticism of the dramatic character of this act and its close, which had made me determined to establish the act, to my own complete satisfaction, as the core of the whole work, if only for the sake of the musical material of the Grail narration. But I did not succeed in completing the act before being subjected to a lengthy and significant interruption.

As a result of a prior initiative on my part, Gluck's *Iphigenia in Aulis* was scheduled for performance that winter. I felt myself under an obligation to devote even more attention and care to this work, which particularly appealed to me on account of its subject, than to the *Armide* I had produced previously. When I opened the score of the Berlin performing edition, my first reaction was of horror at the translation. I also found there some very crude augmentation of the instrumentation, to remedy which I sent to Paris for the original edition, and after undertaking, to begin with, a thorough revision of the translation alone, in order to get the vocal stresses right, my growing interest spurred me at last to revise the score itself as well. From the poem I tried to eliminate everything redolent of the French taste that turned the relationship of Achilles to Iphigenia into a sentimental love affair, and in particular I completely changed the ending, with its inevitable marriage, to make it more consonant with Euripides' play of the same name. To foster the dramatic interest, I sought to link the arias and choruses, which for the most part followed one behind the other without any form of mediation, by composing transitions, postludes and preludes, though all the time endeavoring to use Gluck's own motivic material, so that the interpolations of another composer would remain as imperceptible as possible. It was only in the third act that I had to interpose arioso recitatives of my own for Iphigenia as well as for Artemis, whom I had introduced into the action. Beyond that, I more or less completely recast the whole instrumentation, but only in the intention of bringing out what was already there most effectively. It was the end of the year before I had finished this time-consuming task, and thus I had to postpone the completion of the third act of *Lohengrin* until after the new year had begun.

The first external claim on my attention in this new year (1847) was the production of *Iphigenia*, wherein I had to prove myself as a stage director as well; indeed, I was even obliged to lend the most urgent aid to the scene-painters and the machinists. Since the scenes in this work were strung together clumsily and without apparent connection, I had to find new ways to enliven the staging, for the problem seemed to me to lie largely in the conventional treatment of such scenes prevailing at the Paris Opera during Gluck's time. Of all the performers, the only one who satisfied me by fully grasping what I had in mind and carrying out my suggestions and instructions was Mitterwurzer in the role of Agamemnon, who really did a superb and moving job in every respect. The outcome of the whole thing was favorable beyond expectation, and even the management was sufficiently amazed at this exceptional popular success of a Gluck opera to take the initiative and add my name to the posters from the second performance onward as the author of the adaptation. This put the press on my heels at once; but this time, I must say, they did me justice almost entirely: only my treatment of the overture, the sole piece from this work with which the critics were previously familiar from the traditional feeble renditions, aroused any great objection. I have recounted and analyzed all this in a special essay, *On Gluck's Overture to Iphigenia in Aulis*, and will add here only the information that the musician who uttered such extraordinary sounds on this occasion was Ferdinand Hiller.

As in prior winters, the meetings of the disparate artistic elements of Dresden continued under Hiller's sponsorship; yet from now on they assumed the character of soirées in Hiller's home, and seemed to me to be designed to prepare the terrain for a general recognition of Hiller's artistic greatness. Already, together with some wealthy patrons, chief among them the banker Kaskel,[1] he had founded a society to promote subscription concerts. As it was not feasible to obtain the Royal Orchestra for this purpose, he had to content himself with members of the town band and military musicians for his orchestra, and there is no denying that, through great persistence, he accomplished much that was praiseworthy in this activity, and by performing many new compositions unknown in Dresden at the time, he induced me to attend these concerts repeatedly. The general public, however, seemed to be attracted only by his engaging foreign singers (among whom Jenny Lind was unfortunately not to be found) and virtuosi (among whom I got to know the then very youthful Joachim). The true worth of his musical powers, however, was disclosed to me when he concerned himself with works I already knew very well. The slipshod rendition of a triple concerto by Sebastian Bach under his direction really shocked me. And as to the "tempo di minuetto" in Beethoven's Eighth Symphony, I had a more bizarre experience with Hiller than previously with Reissiger and Mendelssohn. I had promised him to turn up at his performance of this symphony if I could rely on him to take the third movement correctly, given the fact that it was usually so shamefully distorted; he assured me most decidedly of his agreement on this point; I was all the more astounded, therefore, to hear the same old waltz tempo in the performance. When I got after him on the subject, he excused himself with a smile on the grounds of a momentary distraction that had gripped him at the beginning of the movement and had made him forget his promise. As the instigator of these concerts, which expired after the second season, Hiller was given a ceremonial dinner, which I took great pleasure in attending.

In these circles people were amazed at that time to hear me talk with particular vivacity about Greek literature and history, but never about music. In the course of my reading, which I zealously pursued, and which drew me away from my professional activities into increasing solitude, I was soon impelled to turn my attention to a new and systematic study of this all-important source of culture, in the hope of filling the perceptible gap between my boyhood knowledge of these eternal elements of humanist education and my current desolation on the terrain caused by the distractions of the life I had been leading. In order to approach the real goal of these studies, Old and Middle High German, I began anew with Greek antiquity and was soon filled with such overwhelming enthusiasm for it that whenever I could be brought to talk, I would only show signs of animation if I could force the conversation around to that sphere. Once in a while I found someone was willing to listen to me; but in the main people only wanted to discuss the theater with me, because, especially after my production of Gluck's *Iphigenia*, they believed me to be an authority on the subject. I was shown particular respect by a man I was obliged to acknowledge, rightly I am sure, as at least my equal in knowledge of the theater. This was Eduard Devrient, who at that time, as a result of an intrigue against him fomented among the actors by his brother Emil, had seen fit to resign his position as chief director of productions in the non-musical repertory. We were brought into close sympathy by our agreement on the triviality and profound hopelessness of the theater as we knew it, and particularly by the ruinous and irremediable influence of the ignorant court officials running our major theaters. He also was highly complimentary about my achievements with the production of *Iphigenia*, which he contrasted very favorably with the Berlin production for which he had not one good word to say. For a long time he remained the only person with whom I could discuss, seriously and in detail, the real needs of the theater and the possible remedies for its desolation. There was much he could tell me, based upon his long and specialized experience; in particular he helped me to rid myself of the idea that the theater would benefit from the injection of purely literary intelligence, and buttressed me in the conviction that the theater could only be helped by its own resources, by the dramatic performers themselves, if it were to find a way to thrive. From this time onward and until I left Dresden I remained on close terms with Eduard Devrient, although his dry nature and palpable limitations as an actor had previously attracted me very little. His highly meritorious work, *Die Geschichte der deutschen Schauspielkunst*, which he was then working on and gradually published part by part, shed instructive light on matters of vital concern to me, and gave me some fundamental insights.

At last I managed to resume the composition of the third act of *Lohengrin*, after having been interrupted in the middle of the bridal scene, and finished it by the end of the winter. After I had refreshed myself with the repetition of the Ninth Symphony at the Palm Sunday concert, put on by popular demand, I tried to find comfort and stimulation for further progress on my new work, without taking any vacation, by changing my place of residence. In an outlying and thinly populated suburb of Dresden was located the old Marcolini palace, with its very large garden in old French style; it had just been sold to the municipal authorities, and part of it was available for rental. The sculptor Hänel, who had been a congenial acquaintance for some time, and had even given me, as a token of his esteem, an ornament for my room in the shape of a complete plaster cast of a bas-relief representing the Symphony from his Beethoven monument, had taken the extensive rooms on the ground floor of a side wing of this palace for his dwelling and studio. That Easter, I moved into the spacious rooms above him, at a very low rent, and thereby not only gained, by freely availing myself of the large garden with its glorious trees, and by the pleasant seclusion afforded by the entire neighborhood, the spiritual sustenance and whole way of life necessary to restore the strength of a battle-weary artist, but also achieved reduction in my expenditure and thus at the same time some help for my extremely hard-pressed financial position. As Minna took care of furnishing it most expeditiously and without undue expense, we soon found ourselves established quite comfortably in the straggling row of pleasant rooms, and the only inconvenience I felt was the inordinate distance from the theater, particularly onerous after fatiguing rehearsals and exhausting performances, for I often found the cab fare a serious problem. But we were favored by an exceptionally lovely summer, and this helped to overcome every inconvenience and keep us in a happy mood the whole time.

During this period I withdrew from any involvement with the management of the theater in an increasingly open and decisive manner, and I had the most cogent reasons to justify my conduct. Each of my attempts to do something constructive about the willful chaos prevailing in the use of the costly artistic resources at the disposal of this royal institution had been repeatedly thwarted, precisely because I had tried to justify my proposals on grounds of principle. In a carefully drafted pamphlet I had written during the past winter, in addition to all my other tasks, I had worked out a plan for the reorganization of the Royal Orchestra, and demonstrated how a more sensible administration of the royal funds earmarked for its maintenance, while achieving greater fairness in salaries, would also significantly raise productivity on the part of the artists. This increase in productivity would in its turn raise the general standard of artistic achievement, as well as improve the economic position of the orchestra members, in accordance with my proposal that the orchestra should at the same time be constituted an independent concert society. As such, it would be the society's function to present with high distinction categories of music until then entirely unknown to the Dresden public, and to the extent this society was favored by a number of external circumstances which I described in detail, it would assist Dresden at the same time to obtain the adequate concert hall which, as I understand, remains lacking to this day. To this end I had been involved in comprehensive consultations with architects and builders; the plans had been fully worked out according to which the scandalous rear range of the famous Zwinger where it faces on to the Ostra-Allee, consisting of a shed for the theater scene-painters and the Royal Court laundry, should disappear and be replaced by a beautiful building which, in addition to a large concert hall such as we needed, would also have other rooms suitable for lucrative rental for social occasions. The practicality of these plans was undisputed, as even the managers of the orchestra pension fund saw in them the possibility of making a safe and profitable capital investment. But after lengthy consideration by the office of the General Director, they were returned to me, with thanks and an acknowledgement of my efforts, and the summary decision that it was thought better to leave things as they were. I had similar experiences with every single proposal to do something about the useless waste of our artistic resources by more methodical arrangements. As I also had found over the years that everything decided in the exhausting meetings of the management committee, particularly decisions about the repertory, could be overturned at short notice or altered for the worse by the whim of a singer or the objection of a budget examiner, I finally abandoned, after countless tirades on the subject, any further effort in this respect and withdrew conspicuously even from my obligatory participation in this field of management by limiting my activity strictly to running rehearsals and conducting performances of operas assigned to me. While my relations with Herr von Lüttichau became increasingly strained on this account, he nonetheless had to put up with my stubbornness, for I remained in a position commanding respect thanks to the continuing success of *Tannhäuser* and *Rienzi*, which were still performing to packed houses on gala evenings, notably in the summer season when the audiences included significant numbers of visitors.

By thus going my own way and seizing what advantages I could, I succeeded during this summer, amid the delightful and almost complete seclusion of my new residence, in sustaining the highly favorable state of mind needed for the completion of my *Lohengrin*. The element that made the mood more intensely pleasurable than any I had enjoyed before was the continuation of the aforementioned studies concomitantly with my work on the opera. For the first time I now mastered Aeschylus with mature feeling and understanding. Droysen's[1] eloquent commentaries in particular helped to bring the intoxicating vision of Attic tragedy so clearly before me that I could see the *Oresteia* with my mind's eye as if actually being performed, and its impact on me was indescribable. There was nothing to equal the exalted emotion evoked in me by *Agamemnon*; and to the close of *The Eumenides* I remained in a state of transport from which I have never really returned to become fully reconciled with modern literature. My ideas about the significance of drama, and especially of the theater itself, were decisively moulded by these impressions. After working my way through the other tragedians, I reached Aristophanes. When I had spent a morning industriously working on the music for *Lohengrin*, I used to slink away into the depths of the shrubbery in the part of the garden allocated to me to take refuge from the increasingly obtrusive summer heat; there I would read, to my boundless delight, the plays of Aristophanes, after having been introduced by *The Birds* to the world of this ribald darling of the Graces, as he boldly called himself. Side by side with him, I read the best of Plato's dialogues, and from the *Symposium* in particular gained such an intimate insight into the wonderful beauty of Greek life that I felt myself palpably more at home in ancient Athens than in any circumstances afforded by the modern world.

As I was following my own course of self-education it did not occur to me to follow any path hacked out by some literary historian, but rather I made my own way through the historical works I considered suitable, among them Droysen's history of Alexander and Hellenism, as well as the works of Niebuhr[1] and Gibbon, and onward to German antiquity, where my old and trusty guide Jakob Grimm took over again. In my efforts to master the German myths more thoroughly than had been possible from my previous perusal of the *Nibelungen* and the *Heldenbuch*, I became especially attracted to the unusually rich pages of Mone's[2] investigations of these heroic legends, even though stricter scholars have criticized them as overly audacious. This drew me irresistibly to the nordic sources of these myths, and to the extent that it was possible without fluent knowledge of the Scandinavian languages, I now tried to get to know the Eddas, as well as the prose fragments comprising the basis for large parts of these legends. Viewed in the light of Mone's comments, the *Wälsungasaga* exerted a decisive influence on the manner in which I began to form this material to my own purposes. The consciousness of the close primeval kinship of these old myths, which had been shaping within me for some time, thus gradually gained the power to create the dramatic forms which governed my subsequent works.

All this was growing and ripening in me while I was finishing, in true transports of joy, the first two acts of *Lohengrin*, and the last to be completed. As I thus proceeded backwards to finish my opera and looked forwards into the new world I was fabricating for myself, which I now perceived with ever growing clarity and conviction would be my haven from all the miseries of modern opera and theater practices, my health and my frame of mind improved to such an extent that I became so merry

I could even forget all the difficulties of my situation for a lengthy period. Daily excursions into the vicinity of the hills stretching from the banks of the Elbe to the Plauen Valley, undertaken mostly in the company of Peps alone, were good for my concentration. At the same time, I found I had gained a capacity I had almost never before possessed for the most amiable conversation with friends and acquaintances, who liked to come from time to time to the Marcolini gardens to share my simple supper. These visitors often found me perched on a high branch of a tree, or on the back of Neptune, the central figure of a large statuary group in the middle of an old fountain, unfortunately always dry, dating from the glorious era when the palace was in its prime. I used to enjoy walking up and down with my friends along the broad sidewalk outside the main entrance to the central block of the palace, which had been laid down especially for Napoleon, when he had established his headquarters there in the fateful year 1813.

By the end of the last summer month of August, when I had completely finished the composition of *Lohengrin*, however, I was forced to realize that it was high time to start taking some serious steps to improve my situation, as otherwise I would soon be compelled to do so by drastic necessities. It became a matter of importance to consider once again how I could gain wider acceptance for my operas in German theaters.

Even the success of *Tannhäuser* in Dresden, which became more obvious with every passing day, had produced not the slightest reaction elsewhere. As the only base from which I could plausibly hope to exert a decisive effect on German theaters, my eye had inevitably fallen on Berlin. Everything I had heard about the special tastes of King Friedrich Wilhelm IV seemed to justify me in the assumption that, if I could only succeed in showing them to him in the right light, he would feel sympathetically inclined to my new works and the direction I was taking. On this assumption I had already thought of dedicating *Tannhäuser* to him; to obtain the requisite permission, I had been obliged to turn to the intendant in charge of music at the Prussian Court, Count Redern. From him I learned that the King would accept dedications only of those works which had previously been brought to his attention by performance; inasmuch as my *Tannhäuser* had been rejected by the Berlin theater intendancy on the grounds that it was "too epic", it now appeared to the Count that, if I were to insist upon my request, I would have no alternative other than to arrange some parts of the work for military band and perhaps play them for the King at a parade. This sufficed to make me change my Berlin strategy. After this experience I saw that I would have to open my campaign there with the work that had brought me the breakthrough in Dresden. I thus turned to the Queen of Saxony, sister to the Queen of Prussia, and after obtaining an audience with her, requested her to use her influence to secure a royal command performance in Berlin of *Rienzi*, a work that was such a favorite at the Saxon court. This succeeded; I soon got a notice from my old friend Küstner that my opera *Rienzi* would be scheduled for performance in the immediate future, together with an expression of his desire that I might personally conduct the performance of my work. Inasmuch as Herr Küstner had recently introduced in Berlin the very lucrative system of paying royalties, for the sake of his old Munich friend Lachner and his opera *Catarina Cornaro*, I thought a successful *Rienzi* in Berlin, if it did only half as well as in Dresden, would certainly provide a substantial improvement in my situation. But above all, I was guided by the desire to introduce myself personally to the King of Prussia, and particularly to read to him my poem for *Lohengrin*, in what various signs indicated to me was the justifiable hope that he would be won over to my cause, in which case I was prepared to petition him to give the order for the first performance of *Lohengrin* at his Court Theater. After my odd experiences of the way in which my Dresden successes had been concealed from the rest of Germany, it struck me as absolutely vital to shift the future point of departure for my artistic ventures to Berlin, which I felt obliged to consider the sole center from which any real influence was exerted. Inspired by the success of my petition to the Queen of Prussia, I thought I would at least be able to get through to the King himself at some point, and in this hope I set off for Berlin in September, in good spirits and confident that my fortunes would take a turn for the better, with the initial purpose of attending the rehearsals for *Rienzi*, a work that no longer really interested me.

Berlin made somewhat the same impression on me as on the occasion of my previous visit, when I set foot there for the second time, following my long absence in Paris. Professor Werder, my friend from *Holländer* days, had procured lodgings for me in advance near the famous Gendarme market, yet even the daily view of this could not convince me I was really in the center of Germany. However, I was soon completely absorbed in the task at hand. There had been no lack of official measures to satisfy my wishes in regard to *Rienzi*, but I soon saw that the work was regarded as just another "Kapellmeister's opera", and that the necessary resources had been made available solely as a matter of routine and without the intention of making any additional special effort. But all arrangements for the rehearsals were immediately upset when Jenny Lind announced her willingness to give some guest performances, thereby tying up the Royal Opera for some time for her exclusive use.

During this delay I tried to get closer to my main goal, an audience with the King. To this end I used my earlier connection with the intendant of court music, Count Redern. This gentleman received me at once with great condescension, invited me to dinner and a soirée, and chatted with me most cordially about the steps necessary to obtain what I wanted, promising to help me as best he could. Beyond this, I appealed repeatedly to Sanssouci, hoping to receive the opportunity to express my gratitude to the Queen in person. But I never got beyond interviews with ladies-in-waiting. I was advised to get in touch with the chief of the King's private cabinet, Herr Illaire. This gentleman seemed to take my request seriously and promised to do what he could to further my prospects of an audience with the King. He asked me just what it was I had in mind; I told him I wanted to gain royal permission to read my poem for *Lohengrin* to him. During one of the frequent visits I paid him, traveling out to Potsdam from Berlin each time, he finally asked me whether I didn't think it a good idea to secure a recommendation from Tieck for my work. I was able to tell him that I had already been in close and cordial touch on this matter with the venerable poet, who was then living in the vicinity of Potsdam as a royal pensioner.

I had remembered very well that, several years before, when the subject of *Lohengrin* was raised between us, Frau von Lüttichau had sent her celebrated friend that poem as well as the libretto of *Tannhäuser*. Thus, when I showed up to visit Tieck, I was received like an old, and even quite close acquaintance. My long conversations with him were of lasting value for me. While Tieck may well have been a bit too liberal in extending recommendations of dramatic works submitted to him, and had thus acquired a somewhat dubious reputation in this respect, I was nonetheless tremendously pleased by the special warmth with which he expressed his opposition to the current trend in our dramatic literature, based as it was on the desire to imitate modern French theatrical techniques: his lament over the loss of all poetic worth in these works was spoken in truly powerful elegiac accents. He assured me that he completely approved of my poem for *Lohengrin*; yet declared that he didn't understand how all this could be set to music without a fundamental change in the nature of opera, and was particularly concerned in this respect about such scenes as the one between Ortrud and Friedrich at the beginning of the second act. I thought that I was arousing him to utmost enthusiasm when I began to elaborate to him in my own way on how I proposed to solve these apparent difficulties and set forth my ideas concerning the ideal of music drama. The further I went in these elaborations, however, the sadder he became, especially when I revealed to him my hope of eliciting the help and interest of the King of Prussia in carrying out my idealistic plans. He did not doubt, to be sure, that the King would give me an attentive hearing and even grasp my ideas with some warmth, but if I were not to be subject to the cruelest disappointments, he said, I should not count on the slightest practical results from such an audience: "What do you expect of a man who today is enthusiastic about Gluck's *Iphigenia in Tauris*, and tomorrow is just as excited about Donizetti's *Lucrezia Borgia*?" For the moment, Tieck's views of that and similar subjects were far too entertaining for me to give more serious consideration to the bitterness that lay beneath them. He gladly promised to recommend my poem most forcibly to Cabinet Councillor Illaire and bade me farewell most beneficently with his hearty yet anxious blessing for my well-being.

The upshot of all my efforts was that the audience with the King was simply not forthcoming. As soon as the rehearsals for *Rienzi* were resumed in earnest, after surviving Jenny Lind, I decided to cease all these extracurricular activities until after the opera had been presented, as I expected the monarch to attend the first performance, which was after all taking place at his command, and which I thought would give me a favorable opportunity to fulfill my main desire. But the closer we came to the first performance, the deeper my expectations of its outcome began to sink. For the title role I had been obliged to content myself with an irredeemably untalented tenor[1] of a level far below mediocrity. He was a nice and willing fellow, and had even been commended to me by my more than genial lunch-time host, the not uncelebrated Meinhard. After I had taken great pains with him and, as often happened with me, come to nourish some illusions about him as a result, I had to capitulate, when the critical period of the dress rehearsals arrived, and admit the truth to myself. I saw that the scenery, chorus, ballet, and the supporting roles had for the most part worked out splendidly, but that the principal figure, around whom everything is grouped in this of all operas, melted away to a mere shadow. My forebodings turned out to be a fairly accurate reflection of the public response, when the work was performed late in October. The brilliant effect of many of the ensembles, and particularly the glittering reception accorded the achievement of Frau Köster as Adriano, meant that outwardly the production could not be regarded as unsuccessful: but I knew, better than anyone else, that there wasn't any real substance to it, for only the unessential elements of my work had penetrated the eyes and ears of the public, whereas the essential feeling had not been communicated. And of course the Berlin critics opened fire immediately in their familiar way in the attempt to annihilate any success my work might have enjoyed, so that after the second performance, which I also conducted, I really had to ask myself what all my desperate efforts amounted to.

This question, when I directed it to my few trusted friends, led to some instructive answers. Among these friends I might first mention Albert Franck,[1] whom I re-encountered to my great comfort in his new domicile. My best hours during this two-month stay were spent in his company, though as a rule I had the chance to enjoy it only for short periods. As in former times, our conversation ranged widely beyond theatrical subjects, so that I was almost ashamed to bother him with my complaints in this domain, especially because my efforts pertained to a work in which I could have only a strictly practical interest. For his part he did not hesitate long before expressing his regret that I had chosen *Rienzi* for Berlin, with which I could appeal only to the common mass of opera-goers, whereas with my *Tannhäuser* an attempt might have been made to form a group of partisans in sympathy with my higher aims. He asserted, in fact, that the very nature of the latter work would have aroused fresh interest in the theater in the minds of people who, like himself, could really no longer be counted as theater-goers, precisely because they had abandoned all hope of finding anything noble or exalted in it.

On the other hand the curious reports I received from Werder about the nature of artistic enterprise in Berlin were completely discouraging. In regard to the public, he told me once that I should expect nothing from front to back row at any performance of an unknown work other than that each member of the audience would take his seat curious only to discover in what respects the work could be faulted. Despite the fact that Werder did not wish to dissuade me from any of my immediate goals, he felt impelled to warn me continually against expecting anything, especially from higher circles in Berlin. When I once asked him, who always insisted on according the King the respect his finer attributes deserved, how the monarch would react if I gave him the benefit of my ideas on the ennoblement of opera, he answered, after listening to my fiery rhodomontade for some time: "The King would tell you to go talk to Stawinsky!" This latter was the stage director, fat, slothful, and mired in routine.

Everything else I saw and heard was calculated to discourage me in a similar way. I visited Bernhard Marx,[1] who had adopted a favorable attitude toward me as a result of the *Holländer* several years before, and was received in a highly cordial manner. Marx, who in his earlier writings and music criticism had seemed to me replete with fire and energy, now struck me as limp and listless, particularly as I saw him at the side of a young and radiantly beautiful wife. From our conversation I soon gathered that he too had given up all hope of the success of any serious efforts on the terrain we both knew, as a result of long years of experience with the incredible shallowness of all the officials in the chain of command. He told me, for instance, of the certainly quite extraordinary fate which had befallen a project he had submitted to the King for the establishment of a school of music. In a special audience, the King had evinced interest right down to the smallest detail, so that Marx felt justified in entertaining the most lively hopes for its realization. Since then, however, all his efforts and further discussions of the matter, in the course of which he was referred from one official to another, had remained utterly fruitless, until finally he had been bidden to an audience by a certain general, who had likewise, just as the King had done initially, listened to Marx's proposals in minutest detail and expressed his support for the undertaking most warmly. "And that", Marx closed his copious account of the affair, "was the end of it all; I never heard another word."

One day I learned that Countess Rossi, the famous Henriette Sontag, who had by then already gotten into the difficulties that drove her back to her stage career, was living very modestly in Berlin, remembered me in a friendly way from Dresden, and wanted me to pay her a visit. She too had a good deal to say about the apathy of the influential circles of Berlin in any artistic ventures. The King in particular, she thought, actually seemed to feel some kind of satisfaction at seeing the theater badly administered, because he never disputed any of the criticisms that reached him in this regard, but nor did he ever agree to any proposals for its improvement. She expressed a wish to learn something about my latest work; I first gave her my *Lohengrin* poem for perusal. On the occasion of my next morning visit, when she told me I would soon be receiving an invitation to a musical soirée she was going to have at her house in honor of the Grand Duke of Mecklenburg-Strelitz, her elderly patron, she also gave me back the *Lohengrin* manuscript with the assurance it had pleased her very much, and while reading it she "could see the little fairies and elves dancing before her". As I had otherwise been greatly heartened by the friendly warmth of this instinctively cultured woman, I felt suddenly as if a pail of cold water had been poured over my head, soon took my leave and never saw the Countess Rossi again. Indeed, the promised invitation never appeared, so that I had no special reason to do so.

Herr Ernst Kossak[1] wanted to make my acquaintance; without getting involved in a relationship that could lead to anything productive, I nonetheless formed a sufficiently favorable impression of him to leave him my *Lohengrin* poem to read as well. I met him one day in his room, which had just been scrubbed with hot water and was steaming unbearably, thereby having caused him a headache and being no less disagreeable to me. With an almost tender expression on his face, he scrutinized me closely as he returned the manuscript of my poem and assured me in a tone of absolute sincerity that he had found it "most agreeable". I derived a bit more entertainment from occasional meetings with Hieronymus Truhn,[2] which generally took place over a good glass of wine at Lutter and Wegener's,[3] where I went from time to time on account of its associations with Hoffmann. Truhn took an apparently increasing interest in my ideas about the possible evolution of opera and the goals we should aim at. His comments were generally witty and to the point; his mercurial, lively nature made a particularly favorable impression on me. Yet after the performance of *Rienzi* he fell back into the camp of the scoffers and demolition men. Only my poor friend Gaillard stuck by me through all the unpleasantness, but was entirely powerless to do anything about it. His little music shop was not doing well, and his music periodical had already perished: thus he could help me solely in very small matters. Unfortunately I discovered not only that he was the author of a number of highly dubious dramatic works, for which he tried to obtain my endorsement, but also that his pronounced disposition to hectic fever seemed likely to condemn him to an early death, so that even my limited association with him, despite all his fidelity and devotion, exercised only a melancholy and oppressive influence on my mood.

But since I had embarked on the Berlin venture solely to do something about my financial position against my innermost inclination, I also overcame my scruples and paid Rellstab a visit. As he had objected to the "nebulousness" and "formlessness" of *Der fliegende Holländer*, I thought I might point out to some advantage the brighter and clearer contours of my *Rienzi*. He seemed to take it well that I was apparently interested in his judgment; yet he told me at once of his firm conviction that all artistic production since Gluck had been hopeless, and that however hard they tried, the products of today's artists would at best only be "bombast". I saw that everybody had abandoned all hope in Berlin, a mood which, as I understood, only Meyerbeer had been able to relieve a little.

I met this past and purported present patron of mine in Berlin this time as well. I had looked him up immediately after my arrival: I ran across his servant in the anteroom packing his bags and learned that Meyerbeer was on the point of leaving, which he then confirmed to me together with his regret at being unable to do anything on my behalf. I was thus obliged to bid him farewell at the initial reception. I had thought him long since departed when I learned to my astonishment several weeks later that Herr Meyerbeer, without having further shown himself, was still in Berlin; he had even been seen at one of the dress rehearsals for *Rienzi*. What this signified I discovered only later from an opinion held by quite a number of the initiated, which was reported to me subsequently by Eduard von Bülow,[1] the father of my young friend. Without having the remotest idea of the origin of it all, I was told by the conductor Taubert at about the midpoint of my stay in Berlin that he had learned from many well-informed sources that I was a candidate for a conductorship at the Court Theater there, and moreover had highly favorable prospects of obtaining this position and being granted special authority to boot. I was then obliged, particularly in order to remain on good terms with Taubert, to provide the most decided assurances that I was by no means thinking of applying for such a position, nor would I consider accepting it even if offered. But at the same time all my efforts to reach the King were thwarted. My chief agent in this effort, to whom I continually turned for help, remained Count Redern, whose somewhat dubious complicity with Meyerbeer had been pointed out to me, but whose unbelievably frank and amiable conduct had always strengthened in me the belief in his fundamental honesty. I had finally pinned all my hopes on the impossibility of the King not attending the performance of *Rienzi* he had commanded; on this assumption I based my further hope to be able to approach him more closely. But then Count Redern announced to me with an expression of pure dismay that the King would be away hunting on precisely the day of the first performance. I then asked him once again to do everything he could to make certain that the King would at least attend the second performance. Finally my tireless helper reported to me that His Majesty, however incomprehensible it might seem, was definitely disinclined to fulfill my wish; he had been obliged to hear, he said, the following words from the royal lips: "O, do stop pestering me with your *Rienzi*!"

At this second performance I experienced a pleasant little incident. After the impressive second act the public showed signs of wishing to summon me in front of the curtain; when I stepped out of the orchestra pit toward the wings, in order to be ready to respond to the call, my foot slipped on the smooth floor, and I was on the point of what might have been a serious fall when I felt a strong hand grasp my arm: I recognized the Prince of Prussia,[1] who had emerged from his box and at once, having me literally in his clutches, took this opportunity to invite me to follow him to his wife, who wished to make my acquaintance. Having just arrived in Berlin, she told me that although she was hearing my opera this evening for the first time, she had previously been given most favorable reports about me and my artistic endeavors by our mutual friend, Alwine Frommann. The whole tenor of this interview, during which the Prince remained present, was unusually friendly and encouraging.

It was indeed my old friend Alwine who had followed all my Berlin vicissitudes with more than just a sympathetic heart and had done everything in her power to give me consolation and courage to stick it out. I visited her regularly in the evening for finer conversation than any afforded me during my official activities and to gain an hour's refreshment and replenishment for my combat against the vexations of the following day. I was especially pleased by the warm and intelligent interest she and our mutual friend Werder devoted to *Lohengrin*, the subject which really dominated my efforts at the time. After the belated arrival of her friend, the Princess of Prussia, she thought she could get some information about the status of my affairs with the King, even though she had to tell me that this exalted lady was in great disfavor with the monarch, and her dealings with him could take place only in accordance with the most icy conventions. But I got no response from this direction either, until finally I could postpone my departure no further.

As I had been induced to conduct yet a third performance of *Rienzi*, and while there was still a possibility I could be summoned suddenly to Sanssouci, I now fixed a specific date until which I would wait to see if fate had anything favorable in store for me with regard to my most important plans. But this deadline went by, and I now had to recognize that my hopes for Berlin had foundered completely.

I was in a terrible frame of mind when I had to make up my mind and reach this conclusion. I can seldom remember having been so horribly oppressed by cold, wet weather and eternally gray skies as in these wretched last weeks in Berlin, when everything I experienced outside my own little sphere of suffering weighed upon me with leaden discouragement. This was true of my conversations with Hermann Franck about the social and political conditions that had taken on a particularly dark coloration as a result of the failure of the national assembly summoned by the King of Prussia. I had initially been among those who had been inclined to attach hopeful significance to this undertaking; thus it was a real shock to have the whole inside story illuminated for me by a man as well-informed as Franck. From his dispassionate views on this affair and on the Prussian state itself, the knowledge of German affairs that I supposed him to possess and the assured and ordered grasp of public life that everyone attributed to him shattered all my previously favorable and hopeful opinions so badly that I found myself drowning in chaos whenever I tried to picture to myself how Germany could emerge from all this and prosper. Whereas I had looked hopefully from my Dresden misery to the possibility of getting some support for my ideas by winning the favor of the King of Prussia, I now could no longer ignore the frightful hollowness this state of affairs revealed to me on every side.

In this mood of deep despair, almost the only impression made upon me when Count Redern with a very sad face informed me, upon the occasion of my farewell visit, that he had just received news of the death of Mendelssohn[1] was one of the strangeness of the circumstance. I remained utterly uncomprehending as to what this stroke of fate might signify, which affected me initially only because of its obviously agonizing impact on Redern. At all events it spared him the necessity, at this in any case painful farewell, of giving any detailed explanations about my own situation, for which his sympathy had been so intimately enlisted.

The only thing left for me to do in Berlin was to try to make my material gains counterbalance my material losses. For a stay of two months, during which my wife and even my sister Klara had been with me, lured by the hope of a striking success for *Rienzi* in Berlin, it turned out that my old friend Küstner felt he owed me no compensation whatsoever. From our exchange of correspondence he was able to demonstrate with incontrovertible legalistic precision that he had initially expressed only the " desire " that I participate in the preparations for *Rienzi*, but that this by no means constituted an " invitation " to do so. Now that Count Redern's extreme desolation over Mendelssohn's death precluded my asking him to intervene on my behalf in such a mundane personal matter, I had no choice other than to be grateful to Küstner for his liberality in advancing me the royalties for the first three performances. In Dresden there was surprise that I was now obliged to write from Berlin to ask for an advance on my salary to extricate myself from this brilliant Berlin venture. While I was journeying home with my wife in the most horrible weather through the deserted terrain of the Mark Brandenburg, I fell into what I considered as black a melancholy as I will probably ever experience only that once and never again. Yet I was vastly amused at one point, while I was silently gazing out from the coach into the fog, to hear my wife get into an argument with a traveling salesman, who had casually expressed a very negative opinion about the "new opera *Rienzi*". With great warmth, indeed even passion, my wife began correcting all the misconceptions of this antagonistic gentleman, and to her great satisfaction managed to extract from him the confession that he himself had never heard the opera, but that he had arrived at his opinion solely on the basis of hearsay and newspaper criticisms. This brought him a sharp rebuke from my wife to the effect that in such cases, "nobody can ever know whose future might be injured by such comments".

After this single consolatory and amusing incident we arrived back in Dresden, where the special consequences of the unpleasantness I had endured in Berlin were brought home to me by the expressions of regret on the part of my friends. The newspapers had reported a flat failure of my opera. To my particular distress, I now had to confront these troubles by putting a good face on the matter and pretending that things were by no means as bad as they seemed, but that on the contrary, there had been many hopeful signs.*

These unaccustomed efforts placed me in a position which in certain respects paralleled that in which I found Ferdinand Hiller upon my return to Dresden. At about this time he had succeeded in getting his new opera *Konradin von Hohenstaufen* performed. This work, which had been concealed from me while it was being written, was supposed by its poet and its composer to combine the effects and tendencies of my *Rienzi* and *Tannhäuser* in a way that would ensure a particularly happy reception in Dresden, and after three performances in my absence, Hiller

---

* In the margin of the manuscript, in Cosima's hand: "voire Page 455." On the next line, before the new paragraph: "(*voire page 453*)." The pages of the manuscript had got into the wrong order.

felt he had established it as a definite success. As he was about to leave for Düsseldorf, where he had been appointed concert director, he commended his work to me with utmost confidence in its future care, his only regret being that he had not been able to have me designated to conduct it. He admitted that he owed the great success in part to the marvelously convincing performance, particularly that of my niece Johanna in the travesty role of Konradin; she in turn told me with equal conviction that Hiller's opera would certainly not have come across so extraordinarily well without her. I was now really curious to get to know this fortunate work and its splendid rendition, and the opportunity to do so arose when a fourth performance was announced, after Hiller and his family had left Dresden. When I entered the theater at the beginning of the overture to take my seat in the stalls, I was completely baffled to find, with few exceptions, all the seats empty. At the other end of the row in which I was seated I spotted the author of the libretto, the gentle painter Reinicke. We slid over unashamedly to the middle of the row to sit next to one another and discussed the strange position in which we found ourselves. He lamented the way Hiller had set his text to music; but in his dismay over its incontrovertible failure he did not disclose to me the secret of how Hiller had arrived at the erroneous conclusion his work was a success. I then learned from other sources how Hiller had managed to deceive himself so grandiosely. Frau Hiller, who herself came from Poland, had managed to enlist the support of a large number of her compatriots living in Dresden at the time, most of them zealous theater-goers, for the opera of her husband at their frequent gatherings. These friends had fired the public to bursts of applause at the initial performance, while themselves finding the work so unpalatable that they had stayed away from the sparsely attended second performance, whereby the fate of the opera seemed just about sealed. Then all resources had been scraped together to gain a third performance, this time on a Sunday, when the theater normally filled without any effort, and every Pole available was called on to help out with applause. This took place: the aristocracy of Polish theater-goers fulfilled their duty to the needy couple in whose salon they had spent so many pleasant soirées with accustomed chivalry. The composer was summoned repeatedly before the curtain. Everything went well, and now Hiller concluded that the third performance was the decisive one for success or failure of a new work, just as it had been with *Tannhäuser*. The artificiality of these proceedings was now uncovered by the fourth performance, at which I was present, but which no one felt obligated to attend out of deference to the departed composer. My niece also felt humiliated and found that even the most splendid performance by a singer could not keep such a boring work on the boards. Even while we were watching the wretched work, I was able to point out to the librettist a few of the more obvious weaknesses and defects inherent in the material; he reported these to Hiller, who then sent me a friendly letter from Düsseldorf admitting his mistake in having rejected my preliminary advice about the subject. He also hinted broadly that there was still time for me to revise the opera in accordance with these suggestions, thus affording me the opportunity to get the credit for saving a well-intentioned and in its way significant work for the repertory – something which I however did not do.

Then I obtained the small satisfaction of receiving a report about two additional performances of *Rienzi* in Berlin, the success of which, the conductor Taubert told me, was attributable to himself and the extraordinarily judicious cuts he had made. Nevertheless, I was convinced that there was no hope of any lasting and lucrative success from my Berlin venture, and so I could* no longer conceal from Herr von Lüttichau that, if I were to go on with the requisite courage, I would have to insist on a salary increase. I couldn't count on any significant external successes, nor any profit from my unhappy opera publication business, and so, given the inroads into my basically rather modest salary, I could not possibly survive. I asked for nothing more than parity with my colleague Reissiger, a prospect that had been held out to me from the first.

At this juncture Herr von Lüttichau now seemed to feel the time had come to make me feel my dependence on his good will, which could only be assured by due deference to his wishes. After I had gone to him to lay my case for appealing to the King's favor for the modest salary increase I desired, Herr von Lüttichau promised to make the necessary written recommendation on my behalf as commendatory as possible. How great, therefore, was my pain and humiliation when one day he handed me this report after it had been returned from the King prior to informing me of the decision. In this it was set forth that I had overestimated my talent, and had also formed the opinion, through foolish overpraise on the part of certain exalted friends (among whom he listed Frau von Könneritz), that I was entitled to success of the magnitude of Meyerbeer's; for this reason I had contracted such substantial debts that it was really a question of whether I should be dismissed, were it not that my industry and praiseworthy achievements,

---

* Here in the manuscript, in Cosima's hand: "(Page 453)".

as had been brought to the management's attention in particular by my adaptation of Gluck's *Iphigenia*, argued in favor of my being given another chance, in which case there would necessarily have to be some consideration given to improving my financial circumstances. At this point I could read no further, and dumb with amazement, handed his paper back to my patron; he tried at once to soften the terrible impression it had obviously made on me by telling me that my wish had been in fact granted, and that I could proceed to withdraw three hundred talers from the cashier's office immediately. I departed in silence and considered how I could respond to the disgrace inflicted upon me. I found it impossible to withdraw the three hundred talers.

While all these adversities were plaguing me, the visit of the King of Prussia to Dresden was announced one day in November, and at his special request a performance of *Tannhäuser* was arranged. He actually came to this performance, together with the Saxon royal family, and remained with apparent interest from beginning to end. A singular explanation for his failure to attend the Berlin performances of *Rienzi* offered by the King of Prussia on this occasion was reported to me subsequently: he had taken care not to hear any of my operas in Berlin, he stated, because he wanted to get a good impression of them and knew that they could only be given very badly in his theater. Nevertheless this odd event at least restored enough self-confidence to permit me to accept the three hundred talers I so sorely needed.

Herr von Lüttichau also seemed to want to make a point of regaining my confidence; I was obliged to conclude from his unruffled friendliness that this uncultivated man had no idea of the outrage he had done me. He returned to the proposal I had made in the rejected memorandum to give some orchestral concerts, with the intention of persuading me that they should be given in the theater and presented as if the initiative had come from the management, not from the orchestra itself. After I had first arranged for the proceeds to go to the orchestra members, I gladly embarked on this project. According to my own special plan, the stage of the theater was enveloped in an excellent wooden shell containing the whole orchestra, thereby converting the theater into what has ever since been recognized as a first-rate concert hall. In future there were to be six such concerts every winter season; but as we by then had only the second half of the season remaining to us, three subscription concerts were announced, and the public took up every seat in the theater at once. I found the preparations for these concerts an enjoyable diversion, and entered the fateful year 1848 in a somewhat more reconciled and optimistic frame of mind.

In the following January the first of these orchestral concerts was given, and its highly unusual program was in itself sufficient to earn me great praise. I had formed the opinion that if these concerts were to have any real distinction, by contrast with the usual heterogeneous assembly, offensive to any serious artistic taste, of numbers from every type of musical genre, there should be music from no more than two mutually complementary genres. My entire bill consisted of two symphonies and, between them, one or two large-scale but seldom heard vocal pieces. After a Mozart symphony (in D major), I had the orchestra leave the platform, to be replaced by an imposing group of singers, who performed Palestrina's *Stabat Mater* in a style I had carefully prepared with them, and Bach's eight-part motet *Singet dem Herrn ein neues Lied*; thereafter I had the orchestra resume their places to perform Beethoven's *Sinfonia Eroica* to end the concert.

Its success was very heartening, and opened up to me in particular the somewhat consoling prospect of increasing my influence as a conductor at a time when my disgust was growing stronger every day at any involvement with our opera repertory, where I was losing influence as a result of the prima donna ambitions of my niece, which were even being supported by Tichatschek. As I had begun the orchestration of *Lohengrin* immediately after my return from Berlin, and in all other respects had surrendered to a certain mood of resignation, I thought I was ready to face calmly whatever fate held in store for me, when suddenly I was deeply shaken by unexpected news.

Early that February I received word of my mother's death.[1] I rushed to Leipzig to her funeral and was deeply moved to behold the wonderfully peaceful and sweet expression on the countenance of the deceased. She had spent the last years of her life, which had once been so restless and active, in cheerful ease and, at the end, in an almost child-like, peaceable distraction. On her deathbed she had exclaimed, humbly and modestly, her face transfigured by a smile: "O, how beautiful, how lovely, how divine! How do I deserve such grace?" It was a bitingly cold morning when we lowered the casket into the grave in the churchyard; the frozen clumps of earth, which we scattered on the lid of the casket instead of the customary handfuls of loose soil, frightened me by their ferocious clatter. On the way back to the house of my brother-in-law Hermann Brockhaus, where the family got together for an hour, my sole companion was Heinrich Laube, who had been very fond of my mother. He expressed anxiety about my unusually exhausted appearance. Then he accompanied me to the railroad station, and here we found words to describe the overwhelming pressure which seemed to weigh upon every attempt to resist the tendency of the time to sink into utter worthlessness. On the short trip back to Dresden the realization of my complete loneliness came over me for the first time with full clarity, as I could not help recognizing that the death of my mother had severed all the natural ties with my family, whose members were all preoccupied with their own special affairs. So I went coldly and gloomily about the sole task that could warm and cheer me: the orchestration of my *Lohengrin* and my studies of German antiquity.

And then came the last days of February, which were to bring Europe a new revolution. Among all my acquaintances, I was one of those who least expected or believed in an imminent or even possible overthrow of the political establishment. My first sense of these things had been awakened in my youth by the July revolution and the long and systematic reactionary movement that followed it. Since then I had come to know Paris, and from all the political symptoms there had noticed nothing faintly resembling the beginnings of a great revolutionary movement. I had been present during the construction of the *forts détachés* around Paris at the instigation of Louis Philippe, had learned about the strategic dispersion throughout Paris of fortified sentry posts, and agreed with those who considered everything henceforth so disposed as to make even the attempt at an uprising by the Parisian populace impossible. Therefore, when the Swiss "Sonderbund" war[1] at the end of the previous year and the successful Sicilian revolution at the beginning of the new year made all eyes turn in great excitement to Paris to discern the effect of these revolts, I did not take the slightest interest in any of the hopes or fears that had been aroused. We did in fact get news of growing unrest in the French capital; but I disputed, particularly against Röckel, that any significance could be attached to it. I was sitting at the conductor's desk during a rehearsal of *Martha*, when Röckel came up to me during a break and, with singular pleasure at having been in the right against me, announced the news of Louis Philippe's flight and the proclamation of the Republic in Paris;[2] this naturally made a curious, even astonishing impression on me, although at the same time doubts as to the ultimate significance of these events enabled me to smile fleetingly. But finally, as excitement was spreading on all sides, it also took possession of me. The German March revolution arrived, and from everywhere came the most amazing news; even in the narrower confines of our own country there was a hailstorm of deputations and petitions, which the King, in subsequently admitted self-deception as to the true meaning of this movement and the feelings that accompanied it, stubbornly withstood for a long period. On the evening of one of these really anxious days, when the very air seemed heavy and full of thunderclouds, we gave our third big orchestral concert, which was attended, like the first two, by the King and his court. To open this one I had chosen an A minor symphony by Mendelssohn, as a kind of commemoration of his death; the mood of this piece, a gentle melancholy which persisted even at moments when joy tried to break through, corresponded in a very strange manner to the anxious mood of the public, particularly given the presence of the royal family. I did not conceal from Concertmaster Lipinsky my regrets that the selection of the day's program was perhaps mistaken, since this symphony in A minor would be followed by Beethoven's Fifth Symphony, which was also in a minor key; with a singularly merry look in his eyes, the Pole, who sometimes displayed an eccentric wit, consoled me with the response: "Oh, just let us play the first two bars of the C minor symphony, and then nobody will remember whether we played the Mendelssohn in major or minor!" Before we could play these first two bars, some patriot in the audience had the happy idea of leading a loud and unexpected cheer for the King, which was at once heavily seconded from all sides with unusual warmth. From then on Lipinsky was proven completely correct: the symphony, in all the stormy excitement of its first movement, swept along like a hurricane of rejoicing and has without doubt seldom affected an audience as deeply as on that night. This was the last of the newly inaugurated concerts I ever conducted in Dresden.

Shortly thereafter political events ran their inevitable course. The King dismissed his council of ministers[1] and appointed a new one in its place, consisting entirely of men reputed to be either liberals or truly zealous populists, who at once proclaimed exactly the same measures as in every other state for the establishment of true popular government. I was greatly moved by this outcome, and particularly by the heartfelt joy that seemed everywhere evident among the populace: I would have given a great deal to have been able to approach the King in some way and convince myself that he had the requisite confidence in the honest devotion of the people to him. In the evening the streets were gaily illuminated; the King drove through the streets in an open carriage: in greatest excitement I followed his progress through dense crowds, often running hastily to arrive in time at a point from which I thought a particularly hearty shout of approval would please and console the monarch. My wife was quite shocked when she saw me return late at night, frightfully exhausted and with a voice completely hoarse from yelling.

The events taking place in Vienna and Berlin,[1] with their apparently momentous results, amounted for me to little more than interesting newspaper reports; the establishment of a parliament in Frankfurt, in place of the dissolved federal assembly, sounded oddly pleasant to me. Yet all these impressions, however significant, did not succeed in interrupting for a single day the hours set aside for my work; with immense, indeed almost proud satisfaction I completed, in the last days of this so portentous month of March, the full score of *Lohengrin* with the orchestration of the music accompanying the Knight of the Grail as he vanishes into the remote and mystic distance.

At about this time a young Englishwoman, Mme Jessie Laussot,[2] who had married a Frenchman in Bordeaux, came to visit me, accompanied by Karl Ritter, who was then barely eighteen years old. This young man, born in Russia of German parents, was a member of one of those northern families who had settled permanently in Dresden on account of the many pleasant artistic enjoyments it offered. I remembered having briefly received him once before not long after the first run of *Tannhäuser*, when he asked me to autograph a copy of the score of that work obtained from the music dealer. I now learned that that copy really belonged to this Mme Laussot, who had recently gotten herself introduced to me and had been present at those early performances. Overcome with shyness, the young lady expressed her admiration for me in a way I had not previously encountered, at the same time telling me how much she regretted being called away by family duties from her favorite place, Dresden, where she was so well cared for by the Ritters, whose similar admiration for me she also conveyed. It was a singular and quite new sensation with which I bade farewell to these young friends; for the first time since my encounters with Alwine Frommann and Werder in the *Holländer* period I seemed to hear once again, as if from some remote yet long familiar source, that tone of sympathy which never reached me from my immediate surroundings. I invited young Ritter to visit me whenever he wished and to accompany me from time to time on my walks. His extraordinary reticence seemed to hold him back from doing so, however, to the extent that I recall seeing him only very rarely in my house. He used to turn up at times with Hans von Bülow, whom he knew quite well and who had already begun his studies of jurisprudence at Leipzig University. This far more fluent and communicative young man evinced a similar warm and sincere devotion to me, which was easier to reciprocate because it was expressed more openly. It was on him I first beheld the more tangible signs of the political enthusiasm that was now under way. On his hat, as on his father's, the black, red and gold cockade flaunted itself before me.

Now that I had finally completed *Lohengrin*, I had for the first time the leisure necessary to look about and study the course of events, and thus I could no longer remain personally indifferent to the lively ferment in which the idea of Germany and the hopes for its realization had plunged everybody. I had been sufficiently schooled by my old friend Franck, of course, to have my doubts that any productive results would emanate from the German parliament now being assembled; yet in the end the general atmosphere of confidence, however unfocused, the belief, everywhere evident, that it was impossible to return to the old conditions had their inevitable impact on me. But instead of speeches, I wanted deeds, specifically deeds from our princes whereby they would break irrevocably with their old ways, so injurious to wider German interests. To this end I got excited enough to write a popular appeal in verse, calling upon the German princes and their peoples to launch a great military undertaking against Russia, the apparent source of the pressure in favor of those policies of German princes that had so fatefully alienated them from their subjects. One stanza ran:

> It's the old war against the East
> Coming home to us today:
> The people's sword must never rust
> When freedom is at bay.

As I had no connection with political journals, and had learned by chance that Berthold Auerbach had published something in one in Mannheim, where everything was in an uproar, I sent him this poem, telling him to make whatever use of it he wished. That was the last I ever saw or heard of it.

While the parliamentary doings got going in Frankfurt, with nobody quite able to see what would come of all these tremendous speeches by utterly powerless people, I was highly impressed to learn of the behavior of the Viennese populace under the leadership of the unexpectedly aggressive Academic Legion, when, in the month of May of this year, the forces of reaction made their first counter-moves, of the kind that had succeeded in Naples while the issue was still undecided in Paris, but which the Viennese had withstood with triumphant vigor. As I had arrived at the conclusion that in matters concerning the people there was no point in relying on reason or wisdom, but rather solely on the real power to act, such as is aroused only by enthusiasm or the dictates of necessity, I was particularly heartened by these events in Vienna, given the fact that the educated youth was participating shoulder to shoulder with the working classes, and in my enthusiasm could not refrain from giving voice to this feeling in another popular appeal in verse. This I sent to the editors of the *Oesterreichische Zeitung*, who then actually printed it with my full signature.

In the wake of these rapid changes, two main political societies had been formed in Dresden: the first styled itself the German Union; its program called for "a constitutional monarchy with a broad base of democratic support". The inherent harmlessness of its aims was soon evidenced by the names of its principal founders, among whom, despite its broad base of democratic support, my friend Eduard Devrient and Professor Rietschel were included as loud and doughty advocates. This society, which enlisted everybody who was afraid of a real revolution, conjured up in opposition a second association, which called itself the Patriotic Union. In this one the "democratic base" seemed to be the main thing, and the "constitutional monarchy" only the requisite camouflage.

Röckel argued passionately in favor of the second club, for he seemed to have lost all faith in the monarchy. Things were really going rather badly for the poor fellow. He had long since abandoned all hope of earning a decent living from his musical career; his job as music director had become pure drudgery for him, and it paid so little that he could not possibly support his family, which grew in size every year, from his salary: as far as giving music lessons was concerned, quite a profitable activity in Dresden with its many wealthy families, he had an eternal and unconquerable aversion to it. So he had to plug along miserably, getting increasingly into debt, and for a long time had seen no alternative way to improve his situation as the breadwinner of a large family other than emigration to America, where he thought he could establish himself as a farmer, beginning if necessary in the wilds and, by dint of the labor of his hands and an inventive brain, slowly but surely win for himself and his family an independent existence. During our walks together he had for some years past been entertaining me almost exclusively with the fruits of his readings in books on political economy, whose teachings he zealously applied to the improvement of his own shattered finances. Such was the mood in which the political movements of the year 1848 found him, and he immediately went over to the extreme socialist camp, which was playing an ominously prominent role in Paris. All those who knew him were highly astonished at the sudden transformation taking place in him, for he now declared he had finally found his true calling, that of "agitator". His oratorical gift, with which he nonetheless never ventured out onto the speaker's podium, evolved in private conversation to a stupefying intensity. No objection made any impression on him, and whoever he did not succeed in converting he rejected irretrievably. In his excitement about the problems that occupied him day and night, he sharpened his intellect into a weapon capable of demolishing every banal objection, and suddenly he stood in our midst like a prophet in the wilderness. He was instantly at home in every subject. The Patriotic Union had established a committee to work on a draft proposal for a people's militia; beside Röckel and a few other pure-bred democrats, some military experts were also included, among whom was my old friend Hermann Müller, lieutenant of the guards and former fiancé of Schröder-Devrient. He and a second officer named Zichlinsky were the only members of the Saxon army who joined the political movement. I attended the meetings of this committee, as in all these things, as a friend of the arts. As far as I can recall, the draft finally produced set forth a very sensible basis for the establishment of a true people's militia, even though, given the political realities which continued to prevail, there was no possibility of carrying it out.

With a gradually growing zeal I found increasing incentive to make myself heard concerning all these political and ultimately social questions which occupied everyone's attention, fired by my realization of the frightful shallowness and platitudinous volubility displayed by the orators of the day at these meetings and also in all their private utterances. Although, so far as I could tell, some of the people who were really well informed about these things (including, to my great regret, as I frankly told him, my old friend Hermann Franck) refrained from making any public statements as long as this senseless chaos prevailed, I myself, on the contrary, as soon as a ready opportunity to do so presented itself, felt impelled to offer my own views on the essential nature of these questions and problems. The daily papers naturally played a horrifyingly provocative role in all this. The Patriotic Union, whose meetings I attended only occasionally, more or less as a spectator at a play, whenever they were held in a public garden, once selected as a subject for debate by its speakers the elucidation of the question: Republic or Monarchy? I was astounded to hear and read how incredibly trivial these proceedings were, and that they came up with no better conclusion than that a republic would be best, but that the monarchy, if it would only conduct itself decently, could be endured if need be. This induced me, as a result of many heated discussions on the subject, to put my own views on this matter down on paper in an essay which I published in the *Dresdener Anzeiger*, but without revealing myself as the author. My concern in this essay was to focus the attention of the few who were really serious about the subject on the actual substance of the state and away from its merely external form. After I had discussed and specified right down to the final idealistic conclusions everything I felt necessary for the perfection of social and political conditions, I put the question whether all this could not be achieved with a King at the head of the state, and even went so far as to declare of this hypothetical King that he would recognize it as being in his own best interests to establish a truly republican form of government in the pursuit of his own highest aims. I also deemed it advisable to recommend to this King that he find a more intimate relationship with his people than could possibly emerge from the foggy atmosphere of his court or the exclusive company of the nobility. I then specifically pointed to the King of Saxony as having been specially chosen by fate to blaze the trail for the rest of Germany's rulers along the path I had recommended. Röckel found this article inspired by the angel of reconciliation, and inasmuch as he feared that it would receive too little attention and recognition in the paper, he implored me to read it in public at the next meeting of the association, particularly as he considered me a very effective speaker. Entirely uncertain whether I could bring myself to do it, I nonetheless went to the meeting; and then it was the unbearable twaddle of a certain lawyer named Blöde and of a furrier named Klette, who were then honored in Dresden as modern counterparts of Demosthenes and Cleon, that finally spurred me to mount the rostrum with my paper and read it with fierce emphasis to the assembled throng of approximately three thousand people.

Its effect was simply appalling. The astounded audience seemed to grasp nothing of this address by a Royal Saxon Kapellmeister apart from my incidental blast at the officialdom of the royal court. News of this incredible event spread like a forest fire. The next day I was rehearsing *Rienzi*, which was to be given the following evening; I was congratulated from many quarters on my self-sacrificial boldness; the orchestra's factotum Eisolt reported to me on the day of the performance, however, that there had been a change in schedule, and indicated that this was no coincidence. The tremendous uproar I had caused was in fact so great that the management had become concerned at the probability of unheard-of demonstrations if my *Rienzi* were given. Then a hailstorm of derision and scorn broke out in the press, and I was set upon from all sides in a manner that made self-defense irrelevant. It seemed I had even insulted the Communal Guard of Saxony, and was confronted by its chief with a demand to make amends in an official apology. But the most remorseless enemies I made were the court officials, especially those at lower levels, and I have been subject to their persecution right down to the present day. I learned that, so far as they could, they had incessantly petitioned the King, and finally the General Director, to get rid of me at once. I thus found it advisable to write to the King myself, in order that my conduct be viewed as a temporary aberration and not as a criminal act. I submitted this letter to Herr von Lüttichau with the request to deliver it to the King and at the same time grant me a short vacation to get away from Dresden for a time while things calmed down. The striking kindness and good will evinced by Herr von Lüttichau on this occasion made a not insignificant impression on me, and I made no effort to conceal this from him. But in the course of time his still barely controlled rage at many things, including certain parts of my essay he utterly misunderstood, broke loose, and I then learned that it was not from any elemental humanity that he had been so conciliatory with me, but rather that he was expressing the will of the King, who, as was later reported to me, rejected every single demand, even those presented by Lüttichau himself, to have me dismissed, and had most decidedly forbidden anyone to bother him with the matter any further. After this encouraging experience I felt justified in flattering myself that the King had understood not only my letter, but also even my essay better than the majority of people.

For a moment (it was the beginning of the month of July) I decided to utilize my little vacation to make a pleasure trip to Vienna. I journeyed there via Breslau, where I looked up Music Director Mosewius,[1] an old friend of my family, spending an evening in his house in entertaining conversation that was unfortunately not entirely free of political acerbity. What interested me most was his unusually lavish and, if I remember correctly, complete set of the cantatas of Sebastian Bach, in superb manuscript copies. Many of his delightfully humorous anecdotes about musicians, which he recounted in his own inimitable way, also remained for a long time fondly in my memory. When Mosewius returned my visit later that summer in Dresden and I played some of the first act of

Lohengrin for him at the piano, he expressed true amazement at my conception in a manner that did me good. In later years I heard he had given vent to negative and derisive views about me, but I never felt impelled to find out whether these reports were accurate or to reflect on the true character of the man, for as time went on I had to accustom myself more and more to many incomprehensible things.

In Vienna I first went to see Professor Fischhof,[1] whom I knew to be the possessor of significant musical manuscripts, particularly of Beethoven; among these I was particularly struck by the original of the sonata in C minor, opus 111. From this new friend, whom I found rather dry, I proceeded to make the acquaintance of Herr Vesque von Püttlingen,[2] who, as the composer of an opera (*Jeanne d'Arc*) of the utmost triviality, which we had also performed in Dresden, had in cautious discretion adopted from Beethoven's name only the "Hoven" as a pseudonym. We went to dinner with him one day, and I learned he had once been a trusted official under Prince Metternich, who now, wearing the black, red and gold ribbon, apparently in all sincerity, followed the way the wind was currently blowing. I also made an interesting acquaintance in the person of the Russian State Councillor and attaché at the Russian Embassy, Herr von Fonton. I got together with him frequently in Fischhof's company, sometimes for excursions into the surrounding countryside: it was interesting to run up for the first time against one of those hard-bitten advocates of that pessimistic view of the world, which holds that only a thoroughgoing despotism can guarantee a tolerable order of things. Not without interest, and certainly not without intelligence (he boasted of having been educated in the most enlightened Swiss schools), he listened to my enthusiastic perorations about the great and decisive influence I felt could be exerted on mankind through my idea of art. Although he had to concede that despotic power could by no means achieve such an effect, and therefore that he foresaw no possible reward for my endeavors, he nonetheless thawed sufficiently by the time we got to the champagne to wish me the best of luck. I learned later that Fonton, of whose talent and energy I had at that time formed a not unfavorable opinion, had disappeared in some disgrace.

Just as I never undertook anything without some more serious object in view, so I had coupled my excursion to Vienna with the idea of promoting in some practical manner my ideas for theatrical reform. Vienna, which had five theaters of markedly distinct character, all of which were miserably stagnant at that time, seemed to offer me particularly suitable terrain. I had quickly worked out a draft proposal whereby all these theaters would be united under a kind of federal administration, to be composed of the active members of these theaters and the literary talents employed by them. With a view toward submitting my plan to them, I now inquired about authorities with the right kind of interests. Apart from Herr Theodor Uhl,[1] with whom I had become acquainted through Fischhof at the outset, and who supported me quite actively, I was told of a certain Herr Franck[2] (I assume he is the one who later published a large epic poem called *Tannhäuser*), as well as of a Dr Pacher,[3] whom I came to know in time not very favorably as a pettifogging mouthpiece of Meyerbeer's. The most attractive and no doubt most distinguished of the select group which assembled one day in Fischhof's house was certainly Dr Becher,[4] a passionate, widely cultured man, who was the only one to react with truly serious support to the draft proposal I then read aloud, even though he didn't believe it could be realized. I observed in him a certain inner strife and vehemence, an impression which returned to me forcibly a few months later when I learned that he had been shot as a participant in the October insurrection in Vienna. At any rate, for the moment I had to content myself solely with having read my plan for theatrical reform to a few attentive listeners. Everybody seemed to feel that this was no time to be concerned with such peaceful reform plans. Instead, Uhl thought he should give me an idea of the matters currently agitating the Viennese by taking me one evening to a political club of extremist tendencies. I heard a certain Herr Sigismund Engländer speak there, who some time later made a name for himself by publishing in political monthlies: the audacity with which he and others expressed themselves that evening about the most feared public figures in Austria astonished me almost as much as the shallowness of the political opinions they advanced. A much more gentle impression was made by Franz Grillparzer,[5] whose name had been like a fable to me from earliest childhood ever since his *Ahnfrau*, and whom I also approached in respect of my project for theatrical reform. He seemed reasonably well disposed to listen to what I had to say; but he did not try to conceal his surprise at the immediacy with which I went to work and addressed my demands even to him. He was the first playwright I had ever seen in official uniform.

After I had paid a fruitless visit to Herr Bauernfeld[6] on the same matter, I concluded there was nothing much I could do about Vienna and abandoned myself to the exceptionally stimulating impressions produced by the public life led by the city's variegated population which had lately undergone such a marked change. While the Academic Legion, everywhere to be seen in the streets, had lifted my spirits by the uncommon emphasis with which they flaunted the German colors, in the end my feelings were turned to amusement by the same effect, when I saw ice cream being served in the theaters by waiters dressed entirely in black, red and gold. At the Karl Theater in Leopoldstadt I saw a new farce by Nestroy, the cast of which even included Prince Metternich who, in response to a question whether he had poisoned the Duke of Reichsstadt, fled into the wings as an unmasked sinner. As a whole, what I saw of the imperial city, usually so addicted to pleasure, impressed me with its youthful and forceful confidence, an impression I had reason to recall a short time later, when I heard of the energetic participation of the younger members of the population in the defense of Vienna during those fateful October days[1] against the troops of Prince Windischgrätz.

On the return trip I stopped over in Prague, where I found my old friend Kittl, grown very much more corpulent, still in the most terrible fright about the tumultuous events that had just taken place there. He seemed to be of the opinion that the Czech opposition to Austrian rule was directed at him personally, and in particular, contradictorily, he thought himself in part responsible for this agitation because he had composed that opera libretto of mine *Die Franzosen vor Nizza*, from which a revolutionary chorus of sorts had become very popular and seemed to him to have triggered the terrible uproar of the time. To my pleasure I found a companion for the last stage of my journey, by steamer, in the sculptor Hänel. He had just completed his business with Count Albert Nostitz,[2] who was also traveling with us, following delivery of his statue of the Emperor Charles IV, and he was in the gayest spirits, because, as he told me, the extreme weakness of Austrian paper currency had created a highly profitable rate of exchange for his honorarium, which by contract had been paid him in silver. I was pleased to find him, thanks to this, in such a confident and unprejudiced mood that, after our arrival in Dresden, he accompanied me in an open cab over the rather long distance from the steamship landing to our home, despite the fact that he knew very well of the terrible commotion I had caused in this city several weeks before.

On the surface the storm appeared to have already entirely died down; I was able to resume my previous function and way of life without further disturbance. But unfortunately my old worries and anxieties also revived: I had to get money and didn't know from where. And so I now scrutinized more closely the written communication I had received during the winter in response to my application for a salary increase, which I had left unread at the time in my utter disgust at the modifications that had been made in it. While I had previously been under the impression that Herr von Lüttichau had obtained the requested supplementary pay for me in the form of an annual special payment, which was already mortifying enough, I now found to my truly horrendous humiliation that the document spoke only of one such payment, and that there were no provisions stipulating that it be repeated annually. Having discovered this, I was at an irredeemable disadvantage, because any remonstration now would come far too late, with the result that I could do nothing but silently submit to a disgrace for which I had been incomparably badly recompensed. While my feelings about Herr von Lüttichau, which had mollified a little shortly before owing to his seemingly benevolent attitude toward me during the most recent turmoil, took a turn for the worse in light of this, I soon received new grounds to revise even the favorable view I had taken of his behavior in that latest affair and finally became irrevocably embittered. He had informed me that members of the Royal Orchestra had sent a deputation to demand of him my immediate dismissal, giving as their reason that it was dishonorable to continue serving under a conductor who had so severely compromised himself politically, upon which he had given them an appropriate rebuke and had calmed them down. All this, of course, put Lüttichau in the favorable light which had inclined me to be friendly to him in recent weeks. But now I learned by chance through members of the orchestra, when it came to a dispute about the matter, that the facts of the case were almost exactly the reverse. The members of the Royal Orchestra, it seemed, had been besieged on all sides by officials of the court to take such an initiative in the matter, and threatened with the displeasure of the King and the suspicion of harboring similarly dangerous political views. To combat these machinations, and in order to protect themselves against harsh consequences if they did not take the requested step, the musicians had dispatched a deputation to the intendant to state that as a body of artists they felt no call to get mixed up in matters that did not concern them. That was the end of the halo with which my old fondness had enveloped Herr von Lüttichau, and it was chiefly my feeling of humiliation at being so upset over his devious conduct toward me that now made me a permanent enemy of this man. Yet more than by these insults I had suffered, my attitude was determined by the recognition of my utter inability to enlist his influence in the cause of theatrical reform. The mere continuation of my appointment as Kapellmeister, at an extraordinarily inadequate and eroded salary to boot, necessarily seemed less and less worth trying to preserve. From then on I treated my job as a necessary evil in what had turned out to be a miserable situation. I did nothing to make it worse, but also nothing whatever that might have tended to assure its prolongation.

As my hopes for an increased income had been so sadly deceived, I had to look around at once for help from every possible quarter. I hit upon the idea of discussing my difficulties with Liszt and asking for his suggestions as to how I might alleviate my hard-pressed situation. Shortly after the fateful March revolution, and just before the completion of my *Lohengrin* score, he had delighted me by a surprise visit at my home. He had come from Vienna, where he had lived through the days of the barricades, and was on his way to Weimar to take up permanent residence. We had spent an evening together at the house of Schumann; there we had had music and then a lot of arguments, which had led, given the vast gulf between the opinions of Liszt and Schumann about Meyerbeer and Mendelssohn, to an outburst of rage on the part of Schumann, who withdrew for a time to sulk in his bedroom, leaving us behind in a state of considerable embarrassment toward our host, which ultimately turned into amusement as we made our way home. I have seldom seen Liszt so expansive as on this evening, when he accompanied Concertmaster Schubert and me, protected against the bitter cold only by his thin swallow-tail coat, one after the other to our respective homes. Subsequently I took advantage of a few free days in August to go over to Weimar, where I found Liszt permanently and grandly installed in his well-known special relationship with the Grand Duke. While he couldn't do anything on my behalf beyond a personal recommendation to the Duke, which eventually turned out to be fruitless, our meeting on the occasion of this short visit was so friendly and splendidly stimulating that it left me somewhat cheered and encouraged. Upon my return to Dresden I tried as best I could to cut my coat according to my cloth, while at the same time, as every other source of help had failed, I communicated with my friendlier creditors by means of a circular letter, frankly disclosing my position and telling them that they would have to forgo their claims for an indefinite period, until there was a turnabout in my affairs, without which I would really never be able to reimburse them. At any rate, such a statement from them would deter any hostile moves on the part of the General Director, such as I had reason to fear from him, for he would gladly seize upon any adverse actions on the part of my creditors as a pretext to take the worst steps against me. My creditors agreed to this without delay; my friend Pusinelli and my motherly old acquaintance Frau Klepperbein even expressed willingness to cancel their claims entirely. Thus reassured and fortified in my position against Herr von Lüttichau, so that I could leave it to my own judgement when or whether I should give up my post completely, I continued to fulfill my duties strictly according to the letter of my contract, and industriously resumed those studies which were carrying me further and further onward.

From this vantage point I now had a chance to observe the strange transformation in my friend Röckel. Since every day brought fresh rumors about impending reactionary coups d'état and similar acts of violence, Röckel now thought it necessary to combat them, and to this end drafted an exhaustively argued appeal to the soldiers of the Saxon army, had it printed, and then distributed it in countless copies in all directions. This was too flagrant a misdeed for the public prosecutors; Röckel was arrested and spent three days in jail while charges of high treason were being drawn up against him, until finally the lawyer Minkwitz raised the requisite bail of ten thousand talers. His return home to his highly anxious wife and family was the occasion of a small street celebration arranged by the committee of the Patriotic Union, at which Röckel was greeted openly as a champion of the people's cause. On the other hand, the management of the Court Theater, having already suspended him temporarily, now handed him his final dismissal. Röckel now at once grew a huge beard, began publishing entirely on his own a popular paper called *Das Volksblatt*,[1] expecting for it a success which would also, incidentally, compensate him for the loss of his salary as music director, and established a distribution center for his venture in the Brüdergasse. The paper soon drew attention to its author from many quarters and showed his gifts in an entirely new light. He never got lost in mere prolixity or fogginess, but rather confined himself strictly to matters that lay immediately to hand, and to those questions touching upon common interests, his calm and sober discussion of which then logically led on to the consideration of the higher interests underlying them. The articles themselves were short and never contained superfluous material; and in addition they were written so clearly that they could instruct and convince even the least well educated intellects. By concentrating in this way always on the essential aspects of things, and never indulging in that kind of formal circumlocution that often causes such confusion among the uneducated masses in political matters, he soon won a substantial circle of readers, among the educated and uneducated alike. But the price of his little paper, which appeared twice weekly, was too small to yield him any profit. And he also had to anticipate that the reactionary forces, if ever they came to power, would never forgive him for these articles. His younger brother Eduard, who was visiting in Dresden at the time, expressed his readiness to accept an otherwise unattractive but lucrative appointment as a piano teacher in England, in order to be in a position to support Röckel's family, if he should fulfill expectations and go to his reward in the penitentiary or even to the gallows. Inasmuch as his other connections with all kinds of different clubs took up most of his time, my association with him was confined more and more to our infrequent walks together. On these occasions, I often lost myself in the most extravagant speculative discussions with this remarkably excited man, whose head really remained quite clear and sober the whole time. He had already worked out an entirely coherent idea of the changes that would overtake political and economic conditions, such as now appear normal to us, from the conclusions he had drawn in contemplation of the complete reform of their social foundations. On the basis of the socialist theories of Proudhon and others pertaining to the annihilation of the power of capital by direct productive labor, he constructed a whole new moral order of things to which, by some of his more attractive assertions, he little by little converted me, to the point where I began to rebuild upon it my hopes for the realization of my artistic ideals. Two of the points he made particularly struck me: for one thing, he wanted to do away completely with the institution of marriage as we knew it. But wouldn't we then, I asked him, find ourselves in promiscuous relations with girls of necessarily dubious reputation? With kindly exasperation he gave me to understand that we could have no idea of the purity of morals in general, and of the relationship between the sexes in particular, until we were able to free people completely from the yoke of trades, guilds, and other coercive institutions of that kind. I should consider, he said, what the only motive would be that would induce a woman to surrender to a man, after considerations of money, fortune, position and family prejudice, and all the pressures they exerted, had entirely disappeared. When I asked on another occasion where he would find his free spirits, let alone artists, if everyone were to be swallowed up into the one working class, he met my objection by replying that if everybody participated in the work at hand according to his powers and capacities, work would cease to be a burden, and would become an occupation which would eventually assume an entirely artistic character, just as it had already been proven that a field worked laboriously by a single peasant with the plough was infinitely less productive than when cultivated by several persons according to a horticultural system. These and similar notions, communicated by Röckel with really delightful enthusiasm, led me to further reflections of my own, and I took pleasure in developing conceptions of a possible form of human society which would correspond wholly, and indeed solely, to my highest artistic ideals.

For the moment I turned my attention in this regard to the matter concerning me most closely and examined our theater. The impetus to do so came not only from within, but also from external promptings. According to the new and utterly democratic electoral law, a new Saxon assembly was soon to be chosen; the election of extreme radicals as our representatives, as had happened virtually everywhere else, led to the expectation, if this movement lasted, of the most extraordinary changes in budgetary as well as other affairs. There seemed to be a general consensus that the royal civil list should undergo a drastic revision; everything considered superfluous in the budget of the court was to be eliminated; the theater, as a useless appendage for the entertainment of a corrupt part of the public, was threatened with withdrawal of its subsidy. I now felt it my duty, in view of the importance I attached to the theater, to suggest to the ministers that they try to make it clear to the representatives that the theater, even though in its present condition it might not be worth any sacrifice on the part of the state, would sink into a much greater degeneracy and become more dangerous to public morality if denied that protective supervision and orientation toward the ideal that the state provided for education and the schools. Thus my main concern was now to establish the foundations for a reorganization of the theater, in accordance with which the fulfillment of these nobler objectives would be facilitated and assured. I worked out a plan by which the same sum previously appropriated for the maintenance of the Court Theater would henceforth be allocated for the establishment and maintenance of a national theater for the Kingdom of Saxony. To demonstrate the practical nature of my carefully reasoned draft, I went into such precise detail that I was satisfied my work was capable of providing the ministers with adequate guide-lines for presenting the matter to the assembly. Now it was a question of getting together on the matter with one of the ministers. I was of the opinion that I should turn to the Minister of Education. At the time Herr von der Pfordten[1] was functioning in that capacity. Although he had the reputation of being something of a political trimmer, and desirous of concealing the origins of his political elevation during this stormy period, he was nonetheless considered, as a former professor, a man worth talking to on the subject I had at heart. But I learned that the recognized artistic institutions of the kingdom, such as the Academy of Fine Arts, to which I particularly wanted the theater to be added, were the province of the Minister of the Interior. This was Herr Oberländer, a worthy man but not very cultivated or artistically receptive, and to him I now submitted my draft, after I had paid a courtesy visit on Herr von der Pfordten to enlist his sympathy, for the reasons I have just indicated. Though apparently very busy, the latter received me courteously and with assurances of interest, but the impression conveyed by his whole character, even his physiognomy, deprived me of any hope of finding in him the understanding I was looking for. Minister Oberländer, on the other hand, reassured me immediately by the straightforward seriousness with which he promised me a thorough inquiry in the matter. Unfortunately, however, he had to tell me there and then that in simple candor he could offer very little hope of getting the King's authorization for any unusual measures in an area which had previously been treated as entirely routine: there was no question, he said, that the relationship of the King to his ministers, and particularly to himself, was constrained and lacking in confidence; he could never succeed in establishing any contact with the monarch beyond that which the most formal execution of his duties required. He therefore believed it would be better if my plan were brought forward by the assembly. Since my immediate concern was only to prevent the question of the continuation of the Court Theater, if it were to arise during debates on the civil list, from being treated from the ignorant and unsympathetic radical point of view, as I very much feared it would be, I did not spare myself the effort of making the acquaintance of several of the more influential members of the assembly. This took me into an entirely novel sphere, and I got to know people and attitudes whose existence I had not even suspected until then. It was somewhat trying to find these men always surrounded by a haze of tobacco smoke and seated before their beer glasses, and then to converse with them, to their great astonishment, about a matter so alien to them. After Herr von Trütschler,[1] a very handsome, energetic man of almost gloomy seriousness, had listened to me calmly for a while, only to advise me that the *state* meant nothing to him any longer, but only *society*, and that the latter would know well enough without him or me how it should act in regard to art and the theater, I abandoned for the present both my efforts and also my hopes in a feeling of somewhat baffled humiliation. I heard nothing more of the whole affair, other than that it came to the attention of Herr von Lüttichau, as he told me at a subsequent meeting, and filled him with fresh hostility toward me.

During my walks, which I now took utterly alone, I relieved my spirits by working out in my head,* in ever more elaborate detail, my conception of a state of human society, for which the boldest wishes and goals of the socialists and communists, then so actively constructing their systems, offered me a mere foundation. Their efforts would assume significance and value for me only when they had completed their political upheavals and reforms, for it was only at that point that I could begin to realize my new ideal of art.

At the same time I busied myself with the thought of a drama whose hero was to be the Emperor Friedrich Barbarossa. The idea of a ruler was to be grasped here in its most powerful and momentous significance; his dignified resignation at the impossibility of realizing his highest ideals was to lead, while arousing sympathy for the hero as well, to a true insight into the manifold complexity of all action in this world. This drama was to be in popular verse in the style of our Middle High German epic poets, with the poem *Alexander* by the priest Lambert[1] serving as a model. But I never got beyond sketching the barest outlines of the plot. The action of the drama was to be divided in five acts. First Act: Imperial Diet in the Roncaglian fields, with a declaration of imperial power, extending even to enfeoffment of water and air. Second Act: siege and capture of Milan. Third Act: Desertion of Henry the Lion and defeat at Lignano. Fourth Act: Imperial Diet at Augsburg, with the humiliation and punishment of Henry the Lion. Fifth Act: Diet and huge court at Mainz, peace with the Lombards, reconciliation with the Pope, taking of the Cross, and departure for the Orient. My interest in carrying out the massive plan, however, was at once overborne by the more powerful attraction exerted upon me by the Nibelungen and Siegfried legends, in their mythic treatment of material that struck me as somewhat similar. At first, the points of similarity I had discovered in history and legend induced me to write an essay on the subject, wherein a number of monographs I found in the Royal Library by people whose names I have forgotten helped and stimulated me by providing attractive insights into the ancient German conception of kingship. I later published this longish essay, which signalized my abandonment, once and for all, of any desire

---

* In the margin of the manuscript, a small drawing of a head, by Wagner, and beneath it the words: "(very good indeed!!) (My god, what a likeness!)"

to adapt historical subjects to spoken drama, under the title *Die Wibelungen*.

In direct connection with this I now proceeded to sketch a clear summary of the form, still very complex even when condensed to its principal elements, in which the original age-old Nibelung myth had shaped itself in my mind in close conjunction with the myths of the gods. Out of this work emerged the possibility of converting the principal part of the material into a drama with music. It was only by slow degrees and very hesitatingly, however, that I began to think this idea really feasible, as the practical prospects of realizing such a work in our theater struck me as truly preposterous. Only when I had fully despaired of ever doing anything more for our theater did I muster the courage to make an attack upon this new work. Until then I simply allowed myself to drift along almost indifferently among the other possibilities of getting along in the existing circumstances. In regard to *Lohengrin* I now hoped for nothing more than a decent performance at the Dresden theater and was prepared to be content in this respect for all time if I were successful in achieving even that. I had informed Herr von Lüttichau of the completion of the score at the time, but given the unfavorable conditions then prevailing had left it entirely up to him to decide about the performance of my work.

Meanwhile, the time was approaching when, as the keeper of the archives of the Royal Orchestra called to mind, it would be three hundred years since the founding of this princely institution, and thus we had an anniversary to celebrate. For this purpose a big festival concert in the theater was planned, at which compositions of Royal Kapellmeisters from every era since the establishment of the institution were to be performed. All the musicians, with their two conductors at the head, were first to present their grateful homage to the King in Pillnitz, at which occasion a musician was to be elevated for the first time to the rank of Knight of the Saxon Civil Order of Merit: this musician was my colleague Reissiger, who until then had been treated very shabbily by the court and the theater management, but whose vocal protestations of loyalty at this difficult time, particularly in contrast to me, had put him in a highly favorable light with our superiors. When he first appeared wearing the unprecedented decoration, he was received with a great ovation by the no less loyal audience that filled the theater for this festival concert. His overture to *Yelva* was also accorded uproarious applause of the kind he had never before encountered, whereas by contrast the finale to the first act of *Lohengrin*, the most

recently appointed Kapellmeister's contribution to the program, got a
rather lukewarm reception, such as I, too, found quite uncustomary from
the Dresden public. After the concert there was a banquet at which, since
all kinds of speeches were being made, I freely proclaimed my views to
the orchestra members as to what should be done to make things better
for them in the future. In this connection, Marschner, who had been
invited to participate in the festivities as a former Dresden Music
Director, advised me that I would do myself a good deal of harm by
entertaining too high an opinion of the musicians. I should always
remember, he said, how uncultivated these people were, and consider
that they were only concerned with their own particular instruments.
If they were subjected to talk about higher artistic goals, he asked,
wouldn't this inevitably cause confusion or even bad blood? A far more
pleasant memory for me than these festivities was the quiet memorial
ceremony for Weber, for which we assembled on the morning of the
anniversary at the cemetery to place flowers on his grave. As nobody
could find appropriate words for the occasion, and even Marschner was
able to utter only a dry and almost casual greeting to the deceased
master, I felt it incumbent upon me to say a few heartfelt words to give
the memorial ceremony its appropriate character.

This brief spell of artistic activity was quickly superseded by new
impressions which besieged us from all sides of the political world. The
events of October in Vienna aroused our most passionate sympathy; our
walls bristled daily with red and black placards, summoning us to march
on Vienna, cursing the "Red Monarchy" as contrasted with the taboo
"Red Republic", and making other inflammatory demands. Except
among those who were completely in the know about the course of these
events – and who certainly did not draw attention to themselves – these
happenings caused intense excitement and uneasiness. With the entry
of Windischgrätz into Vienna, together with the pardoning of Fröbel[1]
but the execution of Blum,[2] even Dresden seemed on the point of an
explosion. A vast demonstration of mourning was organized for Blum,
with an endless procession through the streets; all the ministers walked
at the head of this procession; there was particularly pleasure at seeing
the highly questionable Herr von der Pfordten participating in this ritual
with every appearance of grief. From that day onward forebodings of
a terrible outcome became increasingly prevalent on all sides. People
went so far as to denounce the death of Blum, who had made himself
both feared and hated through his previous activity as an agitator in
Leipzig, as a favor performed by the Archduchess Sophie[3] for her sister,

the Queen of Saxony. Bands of Viennese refugees, in the garb of the Academic Legion, found their way to Dresden and swelled the local populace with ominous figures, who from then on made themselves increasingly at home. One day, when I was about to go into the theater to conduct a performance of my *Rienzi*, the orchestral factotum informed me that some strange people were asking to see me; thereupon a half dozen of these figures appeared, greeted me as a fellow democrat, and asked me to get them free tickets to the performance. Among them I now recognized in a stooped little fellow with an enormous Calabrian hat cocked at a terrific angle a former poetaster named Häfner, to whom I had been introduced by Uhl shortly before on my visit to that political club in Vienna. However great my embarrassment may have been to be glimpsed in such company by the astonished members of the orchestra, I didn't feel the slightest compulsion to give in to any feeling of shame; I went calmly to the box office, got six tickets, and handed them over to these strange creatures, who then took leave of me in front of everybody with much hearty handshaking. I rather doubt whether this incident in any way strengthened my hold on my position as a Royal Kapellmeister in the eyes of our theater personnel or any other interested parties; but it is nonetheless a fact that on no other occasion was I so frantically called for after every act as at that performance of *Rienzi*.

Indeed, by this time I seem to have gained a wellnigh passionate group of adherents among the theater public, in opposition to the consortium which had showed me marked coolness at that anniversary concert. No matter whether it was *Tannhäuser* or *Rienzi*, I was always singled out for special applause, and although the interests of this group may have given our intendant some cause for alarm, yet he felt nonetheless forced to treat me with a certain degree of deference. One day Herr von Lüttichau disclosed to me his willingness to perform *Lohengrin* in the near future: I explained to him the reasons why I had not previously pressed my work upon him, and advised him that, as the opera company seemed well equipped for it, I would be glad to take charge of the performance. At about this time the son of my old friend[1] Ferdinand Heine had come back from Paris, where he had been sent by the Dresden management to learn the art of scene-painting under the masters Despléchin and Dieterle. It was now up to him, if he were to be permanently hired by the Dresden theater, to offer a sample of his work. To this end, he had requested to be entrusted with the scenery for *Lohengrin*, and this had focused Lüttichau's attention on my newest work; as I now gave my permission, young Heine's wish was granted.

I greeted this turn of events with great satisfaction, as I believed that the preparations for the performance of this work would constitute a healthy, as I hoped, and decisive diversion from all the excitement and confusion of the recent past. Thus I was all the more upset when one day young Wilhelm Heine came to me with the news that the order for the *Lohengrin* scenery had been canceled, and that he had been told to do the scenery for another opera instead. I didn't say a word and never inquired as to the reasons for this extraordinary conduct. Assurances given by Lüttichau to my wife much later, if they were completely true, necessarily made me regret placing the full blame for this affront on his shoulders, and thus causing a permanent alienation from him. Questioned about the matter many years later, he in fact affirmed that the attitude toward me prevailing at court at the time was so antagonistic that he had encountered insuperable obstacles in his well-meant attempt to perform my work. Whatever the case, the bitterness I now felt influenced my mood decisively, and in abandoning my last hope to become reconciled with the theater through a fine performance of my *Lohengrin*, I also turned my back on the theater absolutely and irrevocably from that point on and wanted to have nothing further to do with it. I expressed this feeling by my utter indifference as to the continuation of my employment as a Royal Kapellmeister, as well as by artistic projects which led me far away from any possible involvement with the modern theater as it then existed.

I now began work on the poem of *Siegfrieds Tod*, a plan which I had nurtured for some time, without revealing it to another soul. In taking it up I did not have the Dresden Court Theater, or indeed any court theater, in mind, but rather wanted to do something that would remove me for good from this senseless activity. When I read my poem aloud after its completion to Eduard Devrient, my sole partner in discussions about art and the theater now that I could get nothing more out of Röckel in this area, he expressed utter amazement. He saw that I was headed away from any prospect of contact with the world of the modern theater, and naturally he did not approve of this. He tried, however, to take a positive view of my work as something that would not necessarily be too alien in the end, and might even be practicable in the theater. He demonstrated his seriousness in this by pointing out a defect which lay in my demanding too much of the audience, by expecting it to supplement the material of the plot with so much information only hinted at in short epic passages. He showed me, for example, that before Siegfried and Brünnhilde could be displayed in bitter hostility to one another, it would be necessary first to let the audience become acquainted with this couple in their true relationship of prior harmony. I had actually begun the poem of *Siegfrieds Tod* precisely with those scenes which now form the first act of *Götterdämmerung*, and had explained everything bearing upon the previous relationship of Siegfried to Brünnhilde solely through a lyric–episodic dialogue between the heroine, left alone on her rock after his departure, and a band of Valkyries passing by. This hint by Devrient, to my delight, at once gave me the idea for the scenes which I have worked out as the prologue to this drama.

Through this and similar shared interests, my relationship with Eduard Devrient grew much closer and increasingly pleasant. He often invited a select group of listeners to his home for dramatic readings, which I was glad to attend, as to my surprise the gift that deserted him on the stage asserted itself unmistakably here. And it was also a consolation to be able to discuss my rapidly degenerating relationship with our General Director with someone who understood me. Devrient seemed particularly anxious in this respect to avoid a complete break; but there was little hope for that. After the court had returned to Dresden at the approach of winter, and its members resumed their regular attendance at our theatrical performances, I got repeated signs of disapproval from on high concerning my activities as a conductor. To the Queen it seemed on one occasion that I had "conducted poorly" in *Norma*, and on another occasion "had gotten the tempo wrong" in *Robert le Diable*; and inasmuch as it fell to Herr von Lüttichau to communicate these reprimands to me, the conversations between us on such occasions were scarcely calculated to restore amicable relations.

Despite all this, matters still didn't seem to come to a head, though everything continued in a state of fermentation and tense uncertainty. At any rate, the reactionary forces were still at least uncertain enough of the date of their eventual triumph to find it prudent to avoid attracting undue attention. Thus our management did not prevent the musicians of the Royal Orchestra from setting up an association, in accordance with the spirit of the times, to consider and protect their artistic and personal interests. One of the youngest players, Theodor Uhlig, had been particularly active in this. A member of the violin section, he was a young fellow in his early twenties, of strikingly delicate, intelligent and noble countenance, whose calm yet determined character, coupled with his great earnestness, made him stand out among his colleagues, but who had attracted my special attention by a few occasions when he had demonstrated to me his penetrating insight and comprehensive musical knowledge. As I recognized in him a keenly alert mind and unusual desire to develop himself culturally, I soon selected him as a companion for my continuing walks, in which Röckel had formerly been the companion at my side. He also induced me, in order to foster and enliven its more praiseworthy tendencies, to attend one of the meetings of the new orchestral association and to make some comments. They listened eagerly as I told them the details of my plan for reform of the orchestra, rejected by the General Director a year before, and also elucidated some of my other plans and aspirations in this regard. At the same time I had to admit to them that I had lost all hope that the management would help in carrying out such plans, and that now it was up to them to grasp the initiative firmly in the matter. This was greeted with enthusiastic applause. While Herr von Lüttichau, as previously stated, had indulged these musicians in their democratically orientated association, he nonetheless made certain of being kept continually informed of any treasonable activities on its part by the use of spies, in particular through the agency of one of his especially unpopular protégés, the odious horn player Levy. Thus he had obtained a full if exaggerated account of my appearance there and again considered the time had come to make me feel his authority. I was officially summoned to his presence and had to listen to an outbreak of his long-suppressed fury about a number of recent events, on which occasion I also learned he had been aware of the plan for theatrical reform I had submitted to the ministers. He disclosed this knowledge to me with a Dresden colloquialism I had not heard before: he knew, he said, that I had "laid myself against his shop", that is, I had tried to make trouble for him, with a submission about the theater. I did not hold back with my contrary views as to the relationship prevailing between us; when he then threatened to report me to the King and demand my dismissal, I calmly told him to do whatever he wished, as I had sufficient faith in the King's sense of justice to believe that he would permit me to respond to such an accusation, and that I would in fact welcome this step, as it would afford me an opportunity I would otherwise not enjoy to speak frankly to the King about all those matters that dissatisfied me in the interests not of myself alone but also of the theater and art in general. This was not precisely what Lüttichau had in mind, and so he then asked me what I might be willing to do, if he were also so inclined, to patch up things between us, especially as I had already stated openly that with him "everything was down the drain". We were obliged to terminate this conversation with a mutual shrug of the shoulders. This seemed to have nonetheless caused my former patron some pain; he turned to Eduard Devrient, hoping that in his tact and moderation he would persuade me to find a way to get along with him. Despite his earnestness, Devrient had to admit with a smile, after he had discussed his mission, that there was nothing much to be done, and as I stubbornly insisted that I would never again participate with him in theater business conferences, the Director would in the end have to see how he could manage by himself.

Throughout* the whole remaining period during which fate kept me in the position of Kapellmeister in Dresden, I felt the ubiquitous effects of the disfavor of court and theater management. The series of concerts I had established the previous winter was entrusted this year to Reissiger. They at once reassumed the routine insignificance of previous concerts; public interest soon fell off, and the whole undertaking was only kept alive with great difficulty. In the opera I had been unable to obtain a revival of *Der fliegende Holländer*, even though in Mitterwurzer, whose talents had now fully matured, I had an ideal performer for the title role. My niece Johanna, whom I had chosen for the role of Senta, found the part uncongenial, particularly inasmuch as it did not afford many changes of costume, whereas she greatly preferred *Zampa* and *La favorite*, partly to please Tichatschek, her new protector and former champion of my *Rienzi*, and partly because the management had promised to deliver her three new and brilliant costumes for each of these roles. Indeed these two, at that time the leading lights of the Dresden opera, had formed a regular conspiracy to resist my rigorous demands with respect to the operatic repertory, and this opposition was crowned, to my great discomfiture, by their success in securing the performance of precisely this *Favorite* of Donizetti, with the arrangements from which I had been obliged to struggle for Schlesinger during my Paris days. This opera, whose principal role lay in a range very comfortable for the voice of my niece, as her father agreed, I had at first flatly rejected; but then, as my squabbles with the management, my abdication of influence, and even my palpable disgrace in the eyes of the authorities became known, conditions were regarded as auspicious for compelling me, whose turn it happened to be, to conduct this abhorrent work myself. Apart from this, my principal activity at the Court Theater consisted in conducting the opera *Martha* by Flotow, a work which really didn't appeal much to the public but which was used with undue frequency as a repertory

---

* Note in the margin of the manuscript, in Cosima's hand: "(August 28th Rudi Liechtenstein's visit)" [Prince Rudolph Liechtenstein was a friend and admirer of Wagner's. His visit to Triebschen on August 28th caused a break in dictation. See below, p. 661.]

filler owing to its convenience. Thus, to look at the outcome of my activity in Dresden, now entering its seventh year, was more than humiliating, given the many energetic initiatives I knew I had taken with regard to the Court Theater. I now had to confess to myself that, if I were to leave Dresden, not the slightest trace of my efforts would remain. In addition, there were a number of indications that, if it came right down to a confrontation between myself and the Director before the King, while the judgment of the monarch might tilt in my favor, nevertheless, for the sake of good order, the courtier would be allowed to prevail against me.

Once again, on Palm Sunday of the new year 1849, I had a glorious satisfaction. In order to ensure maximum box office receipts, the orchestra again had recourse to a performance of Beethoven's Ninth Symphony; everybody made every effort to make this one of the best performances of all; the public received it with open enthusiasm. The general rehearsal had been attended, in secret and without knowledge of the police, by Michael Bakunin; after it was over he came up to me unabashedly in the orchestra in order to call out to me that, if all music were to be lost in the coming world conflagration, we should risk our own lives to preserve this symphony. Several weeks after the performance this "world conflagration" seemed about to be ignited in the streets of Dresden, and Bakunin, with whom I had become more closely associated in a strange and unusual way, seemed to want to assume the function of chief pyrotechnist in this act.

I had made the acquaintance of this highly unusual man some time before. I had seen his name in the newspapers years ago in connection with extraordinary circumstances. As a Russian he had stood up at a meeting of Poles in Paris, and declared that it didn't matter at all whether one was Polish or Russian, but only whether one wanted to be free or not. I later learned through Georg Herwegh[1] that in Paris at that time he had willingly renounced all help he might otherwise have received as a member of a distinguished Russian family, and that one day, when his entire capital was down to two francs, he had donated these to a beggar on the boulevard, on the grounds that its possession was only an irksome reminder of the continuing need to worry about the future. His arrival in Dresden was reported to me one day by Röckel, who was by then out in the wilderness himself and in whose house he was staying, coupled with an invitation to make his acquaintance there. As a result of his role in the events of the summer of 1848 in Prague, as well as his participation in the Slavic Congress that preceded these events there, the Austrian government was after him, and he now had to protect himself against this, while at the same time not getting too far away from Bohemia. The sensation he had created in Prague arose from the fact that he had told the Czechs, who were looking to Russia in particular for support against the Germanization they dreaded, to defend themselves with fire and sword against these very Russians, as well as against any other race, as soon as they found themselves under a despotism like that of the tsars. A superficial knowledge of Bakunin's views had sufficed to transform the otherwise purely nationalistic prejudices of the Germans against him into friendly sympathy. When I now met him, under the humble shelter of Röckel's roof, I was at first truly amazed by the strangely imposing personality of this man, who was then in the prime of his life, aged somewhere between thirty and forty. Everything about him was on a colossal scale, and he had a strength suggestive of primitive exuberance. I never got the impression that he set much store by my acquaintance, for by then he appeared to be basically indifferent to spiritually gifted people, preferring on the contrary ruthless men of action exclusively; as occurred to me later, he was also more profoundly dominated in such things by abstract theory than by personal feelings, and he could expatiate on these matters at great length: in principle, he had accustomed himself to the Socratic method in conversation, and he was immediately at ease when, stretched out on his host's hard sofa, he could hold forth before a motley group of people on the issues of revolution. On such occasions he always emerged victorious; it was impossible to counter successfully any of his confidently expressed arguments, which always overstepped by a bit the boundaries of the most extreme radicalism. He was so loquacious that he undertook on that first evening to inform me about the various stages of his personal development. A Russian officer of good birth, he had found the pressures of the most blinkered kind of military discipline so insufferable that, inspired by his reading of Rousseau's works, he had fled to Germany under the pretext of going away on vacation; in Berlin he had flung himself upon philosophy with all the zest of a barbarian newly awakened to culture; he found Hegel's philosophy ruling the field there at the time, and he became such an adept at it that he was able to unhorse the most renowned disciples of the master in an essay written strictly in accordance with the most rigorous Hegelian dialectic. After he had gotten philosophy off his chest, as he put it, he had gone to Switzerland, where he preached communism, and from there had wandered back via France and Germany to the borders of the Slavic world, from which he expected the regeneration of the world to begin on the grounds that the Slavs had been least corrupted by civilization. He based his hopes in this respect on the Russian national character as the most starkly defined Slavic type. Its basic element, he believed, was the naive brotherliness and the instinct of the animal hunted by man, which he perceived in the natural hatred of Russian peasants for the nobles who persecuted them. As proof of this, he cited the childishly demonic delight of the Russian people in fire, upon which Rostopshin had counted in his strategy against Napoleon in the burning of Moscow. He argued that the only thing necessary to conjure up a world-wide movement was to convince the Russian peasant, in whom the natural goodness of oppressed human nature had survived in its most child-like form, that the incineration of the castles of his masters, together with everything in them, was entirely just and pleasing in the eyes of God, and that the least to be expected from such a movement would be the destruction of all those things which, deeply considered, must appear even to Europe's most philosophical thinkers as the real cause of all the miseries of the whole modern world. To set this destructive force in motion seemed to him the only goal worthy of a reasonable person. (While Bakunin was preaching these horrendous doctrines at me, he noticed that my eyes were troubling me as a result of the bright light, and despite my protests, held his hand before it to shield me for a full hour.) The annihilation of all civilization was the objective on which he had set his heart; to use all political levers at hand as a means to this end was his current preoccupation, and it often served him as a pretext for ironic merriment. In his little retreat he now received people reflecting every shade of revolutionary opinion; those of Slavic nationality were closest to him, for he thought he could use them most readily in the destruction of Russian despotism. He thought nothing of the French despite their republic and their socialism à la Proudhon. As to the Germans, he never expressed an opinion to me. Democracies, republics, and anything remotely resembling them he considered scarcely worthy of serious attention; every objection advanced by those who were concerned with the reform of that which was to be destroyed was met with an annihilating critique. I recall a Pole, shocked by his theories, admonishing him to the effect that there really had to be some sort of state organization, in order to guarantee the individual the right to the fruits of his honest toil; to him Bakunin replied, "I see you will want to put a fence around your field and thus give the police a new lease on life." The Pole fell abashedly silent. Bakunin then offered the consolatory thought that the builders of the new world would turn up of their own accord; we, on the other hand, would have to worry only about where to find the power to destroy. Was any of us insane enough to believe he would survive after the goal of annihilation had been reached? It was necessary, he said, to picture the whole European world, with Petersburg, Paris, and London, transformed into a pile of rubble: how could we expect the arsonists themselves to survey these ruins with the faculty of reason intact? He used to bewilder anybody professing readiness for such self-immolation by telling them it was not the so-called tyrants that were so ghastly, but rather the smug philistines, as a symbol of which he set up a Protestant pastor, who would only become fully human, he contended, after he had been willing to consign his vicarage, together with his wife and children, to the flames.

Against such gruesome assertions I remained for some time all the more helpless, inasmuch as Bakunin also revealed himself to me as a truly likeable and sensitive person. None of my own despairing concerns about the eternal perils threatening my artistic ideals seemed alien to him. Yet he rejected any attempt to acquaint him with my artistic plans more closely. He was not interested in my Nibelung project. Inspired by a recent reading of the gospels, I had at that time just produced a sketch for a tragedy to be performed in the ideal theater of the future and to be entitled *Jesus von Nazareth*; Bakunin asked me to spare him any details about it; yet as I seemingly won him over by saying a few words about my general plan, he wished me luck but requested me with great vehemence to make certain Jesus would be represented as a weak character. As to the music, he advised me to compose only one passage but in all possible variations: the tenor was to sing: "Off with his head!", the soprano "To the gallows", and the basso continuo "Fire, fire!" And yet I felt again sympathetically drawn to this prodigious man when one day I got him to the point of letting me sing and play for him the first scenes of *Der fliegende Holländer*. When I paused for a moment, he exclaimed, after having listened more attentively than anyone else had ever done, "That is terribly beautiful!", and wanted to hear more and more of it. As he had to lead the rather sad life of a permanent fugitive, I invited him on several evenings to our home; my wife once set before him for supper some delicate slices of sausage and meat, which he promptly bolted down en gros, without first placing them sparingly on bread, as the Saxon custom is; when I noticed Minna's horror at this, I was actually weak enough to point out to him how we usually served our meat, to which he responded with a smile that he had gone through enough, and should be allowed to consume whatever was put before him in his own way. I was similarly surprised at the manner in which he drank wine from the traditionally small glasses; as a matter of fact he detested wine, on the grounds that it satisfied the need for alcoholic stimulation only in such paltry and hypocritically prolonged doses, whereas a solid shot of brandy produced much more efficaciously what was after all never any more than a temporary effect. Above all, he scorned any comfortable prolongation of enjoyment by conscious self-restraint, contending that a real man should expect nothing more in this than the satisfaction of an essential need, and that the sole pleasure in life worthy of a human being was love.

These and similar little characteristics demonstrated clearly that in this remarkable man the purest humanitarian idealism was combined with a savagery utterly inimical to all culture, and thus my relationship with him fluctuated between instinctive horror and irresistible attraction. I frequently called for him to accompany me on my lonely walks, something he was quite glad to do not only because he didn't have to worry about meeting his pursuers but also for the sake of the bodily exercise he needed. My attempts during our talks on these occasions to impress upon him a clearer understanding as to the significance of my artistic aims remained ineffective as long as we were unable to get beyond mere theoretical discussion. All this seemed to him too premature; he was by no means willing to concede that the laws governing the future could be construed from the needs of the inadequate present, for the future would have to evolve out of quite different social conditions. While he thus continued to insist solely on destruction and ever more destruction, I finally had to ask myself how my strange friend really intended to get this demolition job started; and here it turned out that, as I had already suspected and as events were to demonstrate, his principle of action at all costs rested upon absolutely baseless assumptions. Just as I necessarily appeared to him as being hopelessly lost in the clouds with my hopes for a future artistic reformation of human society, so too it was soon revealed that his own views about the indispensable annihilation of all existing cultural institutions were no less unfounded. My first assumption had been that Bakunin was the center of some vast international conspiracy; but his practical plans seemed to amount to no more, for the time being, than another uprising in Prague, where he was relying upon a mere handful of students.

When he considered the time ripe for action, he got ready one evening for the journey to Prague, an excursion that was not without danger for him and for which he provided himself with a passport identifying him as an English businessman. To this end, he was obliged to sacrifice his huge beard and bushy head of hair to bourgeois convention; inasmuch as no barber was available, Röckel had to assume the office; a small circle of acquaintances was present during this operation, which was carried out with a blunt razor under continuous pain, against which only the patient remained immune. People bade Bakunin farewell in the expectation of never again seeing him alive. But after a week he was back in Dresden, as he had recognized how ill-informed he had been about conditions in Prague, and telling us that he had found there nothing but a bunch of students hardly out of the nursery. These admissions made him the butt of some good-natured jokes by Röckel, and after this he got the reputation among us of being no more than a theoretician of revolution. Just like his expectations of the students in Prague, everything he expected of the Russian people also turned out to be based on arbitrary and groundless assumptions about the nature of things, so that I was obliged to explain the universal belief in the monstrous danger attaching to this man solely from the sporadic reputation of his theoretical views, and not from any actual familiarity with his practical activities. But I was soon to learn almost as an eye-witness that his personal conduct was never determined even for an instant by those considerations one is accustomed to find in people who are not really serious about their theories. This was to be demonstrated during the fateful uprising in May 1849.

With the changes I have described overtaking my position and oppressing my spirits, I had spent the winter and early spring of 1849 in a mood of dull inner ferment. That draft of a five-act drama *Jesus von Nazareth*, sketched out at year-end, had remained my last creative project. From then on I had lingered in a state of restless brooding, hoping for something, but not knowing quite what to wish for. I was fully aware that my artistic activity in Dresden had come to an end, and I was only waiting for circumstances to compel me to shake off a position I had long since felt as burdensome. On the other hand, the whole political situation, both in Saxony and in the rest of Germany, was plunging toward an inevitable catastrophe: with each day this drew closer and closer, and I was content to regard my personal fate as intertwined with the general situation. The final decisive battles, such as the forces of reaction revealing themselves ever more openly in every quarter seemed determined to provoke, were near at hand; I was by no means a passionate enough partisan to want to be accorded an active role in these struggles, but I was nonetheless inclined to let the tide of events carry me wherever it might.

Just at this moment, a very strange new influence affected my destiny, in a manner which at first caused me to smile dubiously about it: Liszt announced to me in March[1] a forthcoming performance in Weimar of my *Tannhäuser* under his baton, the first outside Dresden. He had very modestly described this undertaking to me solely as the fulfillment of his personal wish; to help assure a favorable outcome, he had managed to engage Tichatschek as guest singer for the first two Weimar performances; upon Tichatschek's return, he reported to me that the performance had been a real success, something which surprised me considerably. As my honorarium I received from the Grand Duke a gold snuff-box, which served me nobly up to the year 1864. This was all new and strange for me, and I remained inclined to see in this gratifying event no more than an episode, attributable to the friendly whim of a great artist. I asked myself what it all meant, happening at this time; had it come too early or too late? Yet a cordial letter from Liszt persuaded me to go to Weimar for a few days for the third performance of *Tannhäuser*, which was to be given in May solely with members of the local company, in the hope of establishing it permanently in the repertory. For this purpose I asked the management for time off during the second week in May. Only a few days remained before this little project was to be carried out; but those days were fateful.

On May 1st the newly appointed ministerial council led by Beust,[2] who had been charged by the King with the execution of his reactionary policy, dissolved the assemblies. This event at once imposed upon me the duty of a friend of caring for Röckel and his family. As a sitting deputy, Röckel had been previously immune from the criminal prosecution that threatened him. From the moment the assembly was dissolved, however, he lost this protection and had to flee to avoid being arrested again. As I could help him very little in this, I promised him at least to make certain that the *Volksblatt* would continue to be published, if only because the income from it would help somewhat to support his family. Röckel had scarcely gotten across the Bohemian border, and I was actually in the print shop racking my brains as to how to put together material enough for an issue of the *Volksblatt*, when the long-expected thunderstorm broke within Dresden. Emergency deputations, nocturnal mob demonstrations, stormy meetings of various associations, and all other such signs presaging a battle in the streets, now manifested themselves. On May 3rd, the appearance of the crowds streaming through our streets made clear enough that what everybody undoubtedly wanted was going to happen, for all petitions to obtain recognition of the German constitution, the main bone of contention, had been rejected by the government with a firmness it had hitherto failed to show. That afternoon, still acting on behalf of Röckel's *Volksblatt*, whose continued existence I felt bound to foster on humane and economic grounds, I attended a meeting of the executive committee of the Patriotic Union, solely as an observer. Here I was all at once absorbed, watching the conduct and attitude of those men whom popularity had placed at the head of such associations up to then. Now events had obviously overtaken these people, at the first signs of that terrorism which members of the lower but more active classes exert on such occasions toward the upholders of democratic theories. I heard a medley of wild suggestions and indecisive responses from every side; a principal topic was the need for defense preparations; arms and their procurement were discussed, though most confusedly, and when suddenly it was decided to end the proceedings, the impression left on me was one of utter chaos. I departed together with the painter Kaufmann, a young artist whose work I had observed at the Dresden art exhibition, where he had shown a series of drawings illustrating the "History of the Human Spirit". I had seen the King of Saxony pause in front of one of these drawings, which represented the torture of a heretic by the Spanish inquisition, and had noticed him turn away from this abstruse subject shaking his head in disapproval. I was on my way home in conversation with this man, whose pale and troubled countenance reflected his realization of the coming events, when, just as we reached the Postplatz in the vicinity of the recently erected fountain designed by Semper, the bells in the near-by tower of St Ann's Church suddenly began to clash out the signal for revolt. "My God, it has begun!" my companion shouted, and vanished from my side forthwith. I later heard that he was living as a political exile in Berne, but I never saw him again.

The sound of the bells, emanating from so close at hand, also made a decisive impression on me. It was a very sunny afternoon, and at once I began to experience almost the same phenomenon described by Goethe when he attempted to depict his own sensations during the cannonade at Valmy. The whole square before me seemed bathed in a dark yellow, almost brown light, similar to a color I had once experienced at Magdeburg during a solar eclipse. My most pronounced sensation was one of great, almost extravagant well-being; I suddenly felt the desire to play with something I had hitherto regarded as useless; I thus hit upon the idea, no doubt because it was near the square, to go to Tichatschek's residence and inquire after the guns kept there by this ardent weekend hunter; I found only his wife there, as he was on vacation; her anxieties about the impending events provoked me to the utmost merriment; I advised her to guard her husband's guns, which could be requisitioned very easily by the mob, by depositing them safely with the committee of the Patriotic Union against issue of a receipt. I later learned that this eccentric whim of mine was construed in a most dubious way as a crime. I now descended again into the streets to see what was going on in the city, apart from the clangor of the tocsin and the yellowish solar eclipse. I first reached the old market square and noticed a group there in the midst of which somebody was making an animated speech. To my almost delighted astonishment, I beheld Frau Schröder-Devrient, who had just come back from Berlin, and was standing in front of a hotel evincing tremendous excitement at the news immediately communicated to her that the populace had already been fired upon. She had just seen an attempted revolt crushed by force of arms in Berlin, and she was now highly indignant to see the same thing happening in what she regarded as her peaceful Dresden. When she turned to me, away from the utterly stolid mass of people who had been complacently listening to her passionate outburst on the subject, she seemed pleased to find someone to whom she could more plausibly direct her appeal to do everything possible to combat these outrages. I met her again the following day at the home of my old friend Heine, where she had taken refuge; there she once more implored me, inasmuch as she attributed to me the requisite sang-froid, to make every effort to stop the senseless and murderous struggle. Her behavior on this occasion, I later learned, brought Frau Schröder-Devrient an arraignment for high treason on the grounds of incitement to revolt; she had to sue to demonstrate her innocence and keep the pension contractually owing to her from her long years of service as an opera singer in Dresden.

On that third day in May I then went directly to that section of the city from where disquieting rumors of bloody battles had come to my ears. As far as I learned later, the replacement of the civil guard at the arsenal had come under discussion by the civil and military powers, and this had been used as an excuse by a mob under reckless leadership to try to take possession of it by force. Against this bunch there had been a display of military bravura by shooting off a few guns loaded with grapeshot. When I approached the scene of this action through the

Ramische Gasse, I met a company of the Dresden Communal Guards, who although apparently quite innocent, had been subjected to the effects of this gunfire. I noticed one of these civilian guardsmen hurrying along as best he could leaning on the shoulder of a comrade, while his right leg seemed to drag along helplessly. Some voices from the crowd yelled: "He's really bleeding" as soon as they noticed the drops of blood trailing behind him on the pavement. This sight excited me greatly, and I suddenly took in the cry I heard from all sides: "To the barricades! To the barricades!"; mechanically I followed the stream of people in its movement toward the Town Hall on the old market square. During this uproar in the streets I saw a particularly noteworthy group striding down the Rosmaringasse and taking up the whole of its width, which reminded me, though a bit exaggeratedly, of the bunch of people that had once accosted me at the theater and requested free tickets for *Rienzi*; among them was a hunchback, who immediately recalled Goethe's Vansen in *Egmont* to me, and whom I saw, as the rebellious yells resounded around him, rub his outstretched hands together in singular glee at the prospect of the revolutionary joys he had been awaiting for so long. From this point on I remember quite clearly being attracted by the unprecedented drama itself, without ever feeling the desire to join formally the ranks of the combatants. Yet the excitement derived from my spectator's role increased with every step I felt impelled to take: thus I managed to press through to the inner chambers of the city council, without being noticed amid the wild mob; here it appeared that the council was in collusion with the mob; I also entered the council chamber without being noticed; what I saw there was general disorder and perplexity. As evening and night came on, I wandered back slowly to my home in the distant Friedrichstadt section of the city, past hastily improvised barricades consisting mainly of market stalls, only to make my way back to the center of town the following morning to continue my observation of these unprecedented events. It was Thursday, May 4th,[1] and on this day I found the city hall gradually but surely taking on the character of the headquarters of a revolutionary movement. The news that the King and his entire court, following the advice of his minister Beust, had left the castle and gone by ship up the Elbe to the fortress of Königstein greatly alarmed that part of the populace still counting on a peaceful reconciliation with the monarch. In these circumstances the city council now decided it could no longer cope with the situation, and it proceeded to summon all those members of the Saxon assembly still in Dresden, who now gathered at the city hall to decide what measures appeared necessary to uphold the rapidly crumbling public order. A group of emissaries was dispatched to the ministerial council but returned with word that the ministerial council could not be found. At the same time it was affirmed on all sides that, in accordance with a prearranged treaty, troops of the King of Prussia would march in and occupy Dresden. Now a universal demand went up for appropriate measures against this incursion by foreign troops. Inasmuch as news arrived at the same time of the success of the all-German movement in Württemberg, where the troops themselves had frustrated the intentions of the government by their declaration of loyalty to the parliament and had thus compelled the ministerial council against its will to accept the German constitution, there was a widespread consensus among our politicians in the city hall that the whole affair could be peacefully settled here as well, if it were only possible to induce the Saxon troops to adopt a similar attitude, for the King would be thereby forced, to the advantage of all, at the very least as a good patriot to resist the Prussian occupation of his country. Thus it all seemed to depend on giving units of Saxon troops still in Dresden some conception of the decisive importance of their attitude; as I saw in this the only hope for an honorable peace out of the senseless chaos surrounding me, I must admit that on this single occasion I went so far as to instigate a demonstration, though it ultimately turned out to be fruitless. I induced the printer of Röckel's *Volksblatt*, which was really of no further use by then, to take all the paper and ink he would have used for the next issue of the newspaper and bring out, in the biggest possible format on single sheets of paper, the sole words: "Are you with us against foreign troops?" These sheets were then actually posted on all those barricades where imminent attack was awaited. They were intended to indicate to the Saxon troops, if these should be sent into combat first, how they should react. Naturally nobody paid any attention to these posters save the people who subsequently denounced me. The rest of this day passed in confused negotiations and chaotic agitation, without further clarifying the situation in the slightest. The old city of Dresden with its barricades afforded an interesting spectacle for an observer, and to me, who was following the drift toward armed resistance with continuing amazement, a unique distraction was the sudden sight of Bakunin, emerging from his hiding place, and wandering elegantly in a black dress coat among these obstacles in the street. I was very much in error, however, in my belief that he approved of what he saw; he beheld in all these defense measures only childish imperfections and stated that for him the only pleasant aspect of current conditions in Dresden was that he no longer had to look out for the police and could calmly consider where he was to go next; for here, he contended, there was no temptation for him to participate in events that were conducted with such laxity. While he went around with a fat cigar in his mouth making fun of the naivety of the Dresden revolution, I was struck by the sight of the Communal Guard assembled with their arms at the city hall by order of their commander. From the ranks of one of its most popular units, the riflemen's company as it was called, I was accosted not only by Rietschel, who was very worried about the nature of the movement, but also by Semper. He seemed to assume that I was better informed about these events than he was, and avowed that he felt his position a most embarrassing one. The élite company to which he belonged, he added, was of predominantly democratic persuasion; as he necessarily held a special position within it, thanks to his status as professor at the Academy of Arts, he didn't know how he could reconcile his duties as a citizen with the spirit of his company, whose views he actually shared. The word "citizen" struck me as irresistibly funny; I looked Semper sharply in the eye and repeated the word "Citizen!" to which he responded with a peculiar smile and withdrew from me without further comment.

The next day (Friday, May 5th),[1] when my strangely impassioned interest brought me back to the city hall once again as a spectator, things took a decisive turn. The rump of the Saxon parliament assembled there found it advisable, in the absence of any actual Saxon government with which to negotiate, to constitute a provisional government of their own. In view of his great rhetorical gifts, Professor Köchly was selected to proclaim the establishment of this government; this ceremonial act took place on the balcony of the city hall in the presence of the remaining loyal elements of the Communal Guard and before a not very numerous crowd of people. At the same time the German constitution was proclaimed as legitimate, and an oath to uphold it was administered to the people's militia. I remember that this activity did not make a particularly inspiring effect on me; on the contrary, the opinions of the still ubiquitous Bakunin as to its inherent futility became thereby gradually more comprehensible. Even from a purely technical standpoint these criticisms were substantiated when Semper, decked out to my great amusement and surprise in full rifleman's uniform with a cockade in his hat, asked for me at the city hall and told me of the highly faulty construction of the barricades at the Wilsdruffer Gasse and at the Brüdergasse that flanked it. To calm his artistic conscience as an engineer, I sent him to the office of the military commission entrusted with the defenses. He followed my advice in the manner of one fulfilling a duty; presumably he received there the necessary authorization to carry out the important construction of defensive positions at those poorly guarded points. I did not see him in Dresden thereafter, but presume he carried out whatever strategic tasks the committee gave him as a conscientious architect with the artistic dedication of a Leonardo or Michelangelo.

The rest of this day was consumed in continuous negotiations for an armistice, which was agreed upon with the Saxon high command to last until noon the following day; in all this I noticed the particularly vociferous contribution of an old university friend, Marschall von Bieberstein, a lawyer at that time, who distinguished himself in his capacity as a senior officer in the Dresden Communal Guard by his boundless zeal amid the tumult of a large band of fellow orators. A commander for the Dresden forces was appointed that day as well, in the person of a former Greek colonel named Heinz.[1] But none of this seemed to satisfy Bakunin, who kept showing up everywhere; whereas the provisional government placed all its hopes on reaching a peaceful settlement of the conflict by moral suasion, he foresaw clearly the opposite outcome in the form of a well-planned military offensive on the part of the Prussians, and believed that this could only be countered by superior strategic measures, for which reason he urgently recommended, inasmuch as the Saxon rebels seemed to lack any kind of military talent, enlisting the services of the experienced Polish officers who were to be found in Dresden. This appalled everybody; on the other hand, people seemed to expect a great deal from negotiations with the national assembly in Frankfurt, which was at its last gasp; everything was supposed to be done in a legalistic and parliamentary manner to the maximum extent possible. The time passed pleasantly enough; during the lovely spring evening elegant ladies promenaded with their cavaliers through the barricaded streets; it all seemed to be little more than an entertaining bit of play-acting. At this sight, I also experienced a sense of comfortable reassurance, in which was admixed the ironic idea that none of this was really serious, and that soon some kind of good-natured proclamation would put an end to this provisional government. So I strolled in a relaxed and leisurely way through the barriers back to my distant home, and on the way worked out a drama on the subject of Achilles about which I had been musing for some time. At my house I found both my nieces Klara and Ottilie Brockhaus, daughters of my sister Luise, who had been staying with a governess in Dresden for the past year, and whose weekly visits and good spirits on these occasions had cheered me considerably. Here everyone was in the most comfortable revolutionary mood; everybody was pleased with the barricades and had no scruples about wishing those manning them the victory. This mood remained undisturbed throughout the whole of Friday (May 5th)[1] under the protection of the armistice. From all quarters news arrived indicating that there was a general uprising going on in Germany: Baden and the Palatinate were in open revolt on behalf of the national constitution; similar rumors came from individual cities such as Breslau; in Leipzig volunteer students had formed contingents for a march on Dresden; their arrival created jubilation among the populace; at the city hall a full-scale defense department had been established, with the active participation of young Heine, who like me had been frustrated in his hopes for a production of *Lohengrin*; and from the Saxon Erzgebirge in particular came vigorous promises of support and announcements of armed detachments on the way. Thus everyone believed, if only the barricades in the Old City could be strongly held, it would be possible to defy the foreign occupation successfully.

On Saturday May 6th[2] it became clear very early that things were getting much more serious; the Prussian troops had entered the New City, and the Saxon military forces, which it had been considered inadvisable to use in an attack, were thereby held in strict discipline under their flag. At noon the armistice ended, and immediately the troops, supported by several cannon, opened an attack on one of the main positions held by the people's forces on the new market place. So far I had not seriously considered any outcome other than that, as soon as it came to real fighting, the issue would be very quickly decided, for I had no evidence, in my own mood or in anything I saw around me, of that passionate dedication without which such severe trials are never withstood. While listening to the sharp rattle of fire, I was only irritated that I couldn't actually see what was going on, and so I got the idea of climbing the tower of the Kreuzkirche for this purpose. Without being able to gain a clear picture even from this height, I nonetheless saw enough to grasp that, after an hour of heavy fire, the steadily advancing Prussian artillery had been obliged to pull back and finally fall completely silent, an event accompanied by a fierce cry of triumph from the people's forces; thus the first attack seemed to have been beaten off; and now my interest in these events began to take on an increasingly vivid color. To obtain better information, I rushed back to the city hall, but at first could gather nothing from the terrific confusion prevailing there, until I finally ran into Bakunin among a group of leaders, who described to me with extreme precision the following events: headquarters had received news from the barricades in the new market square, where the fighting had been most intense, that everybody was breaking and running at the onslaught of the troops; at this my friend Marschall von Bieberstein, together with Leo von Zichlinsky, who was also an officer in the people's militia, had called for volunteers and led them to the danger point. Unarmed and bare-headed, the Freiberg town councillor Heubner,[1] the only member of the provisional government remaining on the scene after the two other chiefs, Todt[2] and Tzschirner,[3] had disappeared at the first sign of panic, had mounted the barricade that had just been abandoned by all the defenders, and turning back to the volunteers had exhorted them to follow his example in stirring words. His success was complete. The barricade was retaken, and from there, as unexpected as it was fierce, fire was opened on the troops, thus causing the withdrawal I had observed. Bakunin, who had gone along with the volunteers, had observed this scene at close quarters; now he declared to me that, however narrow Heubner's political views might be (he belonged to the moderate left in the Saxon assembly), he was a noble person, to whom he had now dedicated his services. This example, he said, was all it had taken to make him see what he had to do; he was now determined to risk his neck for the cause and ask for nothing more. Heubner too now saw the necessity for the most drastic measures, and did not recoil from any of Bakunin's suggestions directed to that end. The commander, whose incapacity had not been slow to reveal itself, was given a group of experienced Polish officers as his war council; Bakunin, who stated he didn't really know much about strategy, no longer left the city hall but rather stayed at Heubner's side, distributing advice and information in every direction with remarkable sang-froid. For the rest of the day the battle was restricted to skirmishes between snipers in various positions; I was itching to climb the Kreuz tower again to get the best possible overall view of the whole situation, but to get there from the city hall it was necessary to cross a stretch of ground open to incessant fire from the troops positioned in the Royal Castle. At a time when this ground was utterly devoid of people, I indulged an exuberant impulse and strode slowly across it to the Kreuz tower, and as I did so it occurred to me suddenly that young soldiers are always told never to run on such occasions, as this attracts bullets. When I reached my exalted post, I met several others there, in part motivated by a similar interest, and in part in obedience to orders from the militia commander to reconnoiter enemy movements. Among them I became more closely acquainted with a teacher named Berthold, a calm, gentle yet utterly dedicated and determined man, with whom I soon lost myself in a serious philosophical discussion which extended to the remoter boundaries of religion. At the same time he was solicitous in an almost domestic way to place the straw mattress we had procured from the tower-keeper skillfully enough to protect us against the conical bullets of the Prussian sharpshooters positioned on the distant tower of the Frauenkirche, who had selected the enemy height occupied by us as their target. At nightfall I found it impossible to leave my interesting place of refuge and start for home; I therefore persuaded the keeper to dispatch his assistant with a note to my wife in Friedrichstadt, and also ask her to send along some necessary provisions for me. Thus, in the immediate vicinity of the frightful clangor of the tower bell and to the accompaniment of Prussian bullets splattering against the tower walls, I spent one of the most noteworthy nights of my life, taking turns with Berthold to stand guard and sleep.

Sunday May 7th[1] was one of the most beautiful days of that year; I was awakened by the song of a nightingale wafting up from the Schütze garden close beneath us; a sacred calm and tranquillity lay over the city and the broad expanse of its surroundings I could see from my vantage point: toward dawn a light fog settled on the outskirts: penetrating through it we suddenly heard, from the area of the Tharandt road, the music of the Marseillaise clearly and distinctly; as the source of the sound came closer, the mists dispersed and the blood-red rising sun glittered upon the guns of a long column marching into the city. It was impossible to resist the impression of this unfolding sight; suddenly that element I had long missed in the German people, the absence of any evidence of which had contributed in no small part to the mood which had dominated me until then, now pressed in upon me in the freshest and most palpable colors; these were no fewer than several thousand well armed and organized men from the Erzgebirge, mostly miners, who had arrived to help in the defense of Dresden. Soon we saw them march into the old market square, outside the city hall and, after a jubilant greeting by the people, encamp there to rest after their march. Similar contingents kept arriving throughout the day; and it appeared that the brave deeds of the previous day would now find a most heartening reward. The Prussian troops' plan of attack seemed to have undergone a change, as evidenced by numerous simultaneous assaults on various positions but without massive concentration on any one of them. The incoming detachments had four small cannon with them, the property of a certain Herr Thade von Burgk, who was already known to me from a well-meant but ludicrously boring speech he had made at an anniversary celebration of the founding of the Dresden Glee Club; inasmuch as his cannon were now to be fired from the barricades upon the enemy, that occasion now came back to me in singular irony. But I was afforded an incomparably deeper impression when, toward eleven o'clock in the morning, I saw the old opera house, in which I had conducted the last performance of Beethoven's Ninth Symphony a few weeks before, go up in flames. As I have mentioned before, this building, originally put up only as a temporary structure, and full of wood and canvas, had always occasioned terrible fear that it might burn down. I was informed that, in order to protect against a dangerous attack by the enemy troops on this exposed flank, and also to protect the famous Semper barricade from being overrun at the same time, it had been put to the torch for strategic purposes; from this I concluded that such purposes will always predominate in the world over aesthetic considerations, which had long since vainly called for the removal of this ugly building, such an eyesore opposite the elegant lines of the Zwinger. Filled with such easily combustible material, this building of very imposing size was soon an immense sea of flames. When these also reached the metal roof of the adjacent Zwinger gallery, on which strange bluish tongues of fire began to dance, the first expressions of regret made themselves audible among us spectators; people thought the natural history collection was in danger; others maintained it was the armory, at which a member of the communal rifle brigade exclaimed that in that case it wouldn't be a bad thing if the "stuffed noblemen" burned up completely. But it seemed that concern for art managed to bring the fire under control, which actually caused the Zwinger very little damage.

At length, our observation post, which until then had remained relatively quiet, filled up with a growing swarm of armed men, sent there to defend the approach to the old market square, as it was feared that an attack upon it from the weakly manned Kreuzgasse would soon be forthcoming. Unarmed men were now merely in the way; moreover, I had received a message from my wife, who had gone through agonies of worry and now wanted me home at once. After overcoming innumerable obstacles and after the most time-consuming detours, I finally got to my distant suburb, from which I had been cut off by the sections of the city where the fighting was going on, particularly by a cannonade emanating from the Zwinger. My dwelling was filled with agitated women who had gathered around Minna, among them the panic-stricken wife of Röckel, who suspected her husband was in the thick of the fight, having assumed that he must have returned to Dresden at the news of the uprising. I had indeed heard that Röckel had arrived that day but I had not yet seen him. Beyond that, I was again cheered by my two young nieces, whose delight at all the shooting had put them in a most exuberant mood and even infected my wife to some extent, after she had reassured herself as to my condition. They had all been infuriated by the sculptor Hänel, who had wanted the whole building kept locked so that no revolutionaries could get in. All the women were particularly full of mockery about his terror at the sight of some men with scythes he had seen in the street. Thus this Sunday ended in a kind of jolly family celebration.

On the following morning, Monday May 8th,[1] I tried to get back to the city hall from my residence, cut off as it was from the field of battle, to find out how things stood. When I came up to a barricade near St Ann's Church, a member of the Communal Guard called out to me: "Herr Kapellmeister, the spark of divine joy has certainly ignited everything, the rotten building has burned to the ground." Obviously this enthusiast had attended the last performance of the Ninth Symphony. Coming so unexpectedly, this dramatic cry had a curiously strengthening and liberating effect on me. A small distance further, in a lonely alley in the suburb of Plauen, I came upon Hiebendahl, to this day the highly praised first oboist of the Royal Orchestra; he was in the uniform of the Communal Guards, yet was unarmed, and was chatting with a fellow citizen in similar garb. As soon as he saw me, he felt impelled to seek my intervention against Röckel, who, accompanied by an ordnance officer of the revolutionary forces, had been making a house-to-house search for weapons in this quarter of the city. Since I at once responded with a sympathetic inquiry about Röckel, he recoiled in horror: "But Herr Kapellmeister, aren't you thinking of your position, and all you may lose by risking yourself in this way?" This warning had a drastic effect on me; I burst into loud laughter and told him my position wasn't worth much anyway. This indeed was my first open and almost joyful expression of a long suppressed belief. Then I saw Röckel coming toward me with two members of the militia, who were carrying several guns. He greeted me most cordially, but turned at once to Hiebendahl and his neighbor with a reproof about their lounging around in uniform away from their posts. As Hiebendahl tried to excuse himself by asserting that his gun had been requisitioned, Röckel responded: "You're a funny bunch!" and left them standing there with a laugh. He then told me briefly as we were walking along what had happened to him since I had last seen him, but spared me the necessity of reporting about his *Volksblatt*. The two of us were soon interrupted by an imposing troop of well-armed young athletes, who had been summoned from outside the town and wanted to be conducted to their assembly point. The sight of these serried ranks of several hundred youthful figures striding firmly to fulfill their duty could not fail to make the most heartening impression on me; Röckel undertook to lead them safely through the barricades to the mustering point in the square outside the city hall. On the way there he complained of the lack of real energy he had found so far among those in charge of the uprising. He had suggested, he said, defending the most vulnerable barricades by encircling them with pitch and, if the worst came to the worst, setting them alight; the mere suggestion had been enough, however, to send the provisional government into shivers of decorous horror. I let him go his way in order to take a short cut to the city hall on my own, and didn't see him again for thirteen years.

At the city hall I learned from Bakunin that the provisional government had decided to follow his advice and give up what had been from the beginning a hopeless, and in the long run untenable, position in Dresden, and undertake an armed retreat into the Erzgebirge to the south, where the detachments streaming in from all sides, and particularly from Thuringia, could concentrate in such strength that it would provide a favorable base for what would no doubt become an all-German popular war, whereas to continue fighting in the barricaded streets of Dresden would only result in giving this struggle, however bravely conducted, the appearance of an urban disturbance. I must admit that this plan struck me as glorious and meaningful; while up to this moment only my interest had been aroused in an event that I had greeted at first with an almost ironic incredulity and then with amazement, now what had hitherto appeared incomprehensible began to grow into a prospect of great and hopeful significance. Without feeling any desire, let alone a vocation, to be accorded any special role or function in all this, I nonetheless now quite consciously abandoned all personal considerations and decided to surrender myself to the stream of events, to bear me in that direction in which my feelings about life had urged me with an acquiescence born of despair. Yet I didn't want to leave my wife behind in Dresden without help, and I soon thought of a way to induce her to leave and follow me in my chosen direction, without immediately letting her know what this decision was all about. During my hasty return to Friedrichstadt I recognized that this section of the city had been almost completely cut off from the inner city by Prussian troops; predicting the occupation of our suburb and the worst effects of a military siege, I had an easy time convincing Minna to leave via the Tharandt road, which was still clear, to go with me to Chemnitz to visit my married sister Klara, who was living there. At this she set about putting the house in order at once and promised to follow me within the hour, together with our parrot, to the neighboring village, where I went in advance with my little dog Peps to rent a carriage for the rest of the trip to Chemnitz. It was a smiling spring morning when I set foot for the last time on the path of my frequent solitary walks, conscious that I would never again be doing so. While the larks fluttered around me and warbled from the furrows in the fields, guns and rifles thundered and crackled unceasingly from the streets of Dresden. The noise of this shooting, which had continued without interruption for days, had made such an indelible imprint on my cerebral nerves that it resounded within me for a long time thereafter, just as the motion of the ship that brought me to London had made me stagger for some time afterward. To the accompaniment of this frightful music I bade my formal farewell to this friendly city with its many towers, and thought to myself with a smile that, although my entrance seven years before had been quite obscure, my exit was now taking place with a certain amount of pomp and circumstance.

When I finally found myself with Minna on our way in a one-horse carriage into the Erzgebirge, we frequently met freshly armed contingents headed toward Dresden; the sight of them always gave us involuntary pleasure, and even my wife could not restrain herself from cheering them on with a statement to the effect that no barricade had yet been lost. On the other hand, a company of line soldiers made a rather dismal impression on us as it went silently on its way toward Dresden. Several of these soldiers responded to inquiries as to their destination with the laconic retort, which they had obviously been ordered in advance to give, that they were going to do their duty. When we at last arrived at the house of my relatives in Chemnitz, I gave all of them a shock by declaring my intention of going back to Dresden as early as possible the following day to find out how things stood. Despite all attempts to dissuade me, I carried out my resolve, always under the assumption that I would be meeting the armed forces of the people on the open road. But the closer I got to Dresden, the more confirmation was provided for the rumors that there was no thought as yet of giving up or withdrawing from Dresden, as on the contrary the battle was going very well for the people's side. This all struck me as one miracle after another; with intense excitement I pressed through the increasingly difficult terrain on that Tuesday, May 9th,[1] avoiding all the streets and finding the only safe way to advance was through shattered buildings, making my way toward the city hall on the old market place. It was already evening; what I saw offered a truly horrible picture, for I was passing through those parts of the city where everyone was prepared for house-to-house fighting. The unceasing roar of big and small arms fire made the other sounds of the armed men calling to one another from barricade to barricade, or from one shattered house to another, seem merely an uncanny murmur. Torches burned here and there, and pale, exhausted figures lay about close to the guardposts, while stern challenges met the unarmed intruder. But nothing I experienced can compare with the impression I received upon entering the chambers of the city hall. It was a subdued yet seemingly orderly and serious mass of people; utter exhaustion was to be read upon every face; no voice retained its natural timbre, but rather a hoarse, indistinct croak, produced only with great effort it seemed, was to be heard on all sides. The only pleasant sight was afforded by the servants, old clerks of the city council, in their odd but familiar uniforms and three-cornered hats; these men, so tall and awe-inspiring at normal times, I now discovered spreading butter on bread, and cutting slices of ham and sausage, while others distributed from baskets the copious provisions for the fighters at the barricades to the emissaries sent to receive them. They had decidedly become the house-wives of the revolution. When I proceeded further, I came at last upon members of the provisional government, among whom Todt and Tzschirner, after their initial panic-stricken flight, were once again to be found, and now flitted about like miserable shadows, chained to their heavy responsibilities. Heubner alone had retained his original energy; yet he was really a pitiful sight: an unearthly fire flickered in his eyes, which had not closed in sleep for seven nights. He was glad to see me again, as it seemed to him a good omen for the cause he was defending, whereas he had come into contact with some characters in the clamor of events about whom he hadn't been able to form any satisfactory opinion. In Bakunin I found an utterly unruffled assurance and unshakably calm demeanor, and his appearance had not changed in the slightest, despite the fact, later confirmed to me, that he too had not enjoyed a single night's sleep the whole time. He received me on one of the mattresses which had been spread out in the city hall council chamber, a cigar in his mouth and at his side a very young Galician Pole by the name of Haimberger, a young violinist whom he had referred to me recently for recommendation to Lipinsky for further training on his instrument, as he had not wanted this entirely green and inexperienced fellow, who had attached himself to him with such devotion, to be swept into the vortex of these events. But now he had nonetheless been glad to see him, when he arrived with gun in hand to take his place on the barricades. Bakunin had made a place for him on the mattress, and gave him a vigorous slap on the back every time he twitched at the sound of the heavy cannonfire. "You're a long way from your violin here," he called out to him, "you should have stayed with it, musician." I now learned from Bakunin summarily and with utmost precision everything that had happened since I had left him the previous morning. The proposed withdrawal had soon turned out to be inadvisable, because it would necessarily have disheartened all those new detachments that had just arrived in the city; the will to fight was so great, and the defenders' strength so substantial, that the invading troops had been everywhere successfully resisted; after reinforcement, however, the troops had recently mounted a combined attack on the strong Wildruff barricade, and that had been effective; the Prussian troops had given up fighting in the streets and had begun fighting from house to house through breaches in the walls; for this reason it was to be anticipated that the provisions adopted hitherto for defending the barricades would be rendered useless, and that the enemy, slowly but irresistibly, would approach the seat of the provisional government at the city hall. He had suggested, Bakunin continued, getting together all the reserves of gunpowder and putting them in the basement of the building, and blowing the whole thing up at the approach of the troops. The city council, which was still transacting its business in the back rooms, had protested most earnestly against this; while he, Bakunin, had continued to insist on this measure, he had been eventually outwitted by removal of all gunpowder reserves and by the council members' winning Heubner over to their point of view, as of course Bakunin could not oppose the latter in anything. So it had now been decided, inasmuch as everything was fully ready, that the retreat to the Erzgebirge originally planned for the previous day would now be carried out early the next morning, and young Zichlinsky had already been ordered to clear the road to Plauen and cover it for strategic purposes. I asked about Röckel; Bakunin replied laconically that he had not been seen since the previous evening and had probably let himself be caught; he had been "nervous".

I then reported what I had seen and heard on the road to and back from Chemnitz, in particular the large number of reinforcements marching towards Dresden, including the Chemnitz Communal Guard with several thousand men. In Freiberg, I added, I had come across a company of four hundred military reservists, who were on their way in highly disciplined ranks to support the people's militia, yet had been too exhausted to continue their march at the time. It seemed quite obvious that there had been insufficient zeal in the requisitioning of vehicles and that, if the bounds of special consideration were exceeded in this effort, it would be very helpful in amassing fresh forces. I was immediately requested to make my way back there to convey to everyone I knew that this was the opinion of the provisional government. My old friend Marschall von Bieberstein immediately volunteered to accompany me, which I very much welcomed, inasmuch as he, as a formal representative of the provisional government, was far more suited to give the necessary commands than I was. He too, after expending a superabundance of energy, was now utterly exhausted from lack of sleep and unable to emit a sound from his hoarse throat; together we left the city hall and made our way through all the aforementioned detours and obstacles to his dwelling in the suburb of Plauen, to procure a vehicle that night from a coachman he knew for the remainder of our trip, and to bid farewell to his family at the same time, as he had to assume he would not see them again for a long while. As we waited for the coachman, we drank tea and ate our supper, while conversing fairly calmly and composedly with the ladies of the house.

After a number of adventures, we got to Freiberg early the next morning, where I at once set off to find the leaders of the reservist detachments. Marschall told them they should requisition horses and carriages in the villages wherever they could; when everybody had started marching away toward Dresden, and I again felt impelled by my passionate interest in the fate of the city to return to it, Marschall expressed the desire to canvass the surrounding countryside more widely, and suggested we should separate. I turned my back on the Erzgebirge once more and was making my way in a special postal coach toward Tharandt, when the need for sleep overcame me as well, but I was awakened by loud shouts and the sounds of an argument with the postilion. When I opened my eyes, I found to my surprise the road filled with armed insurgents, who were headed not toward but away from Dresden, several of whom wanted to force our carriage to turn around and transport them in their exhaustion. "What's going on?" I called

out. "Where are you headed?" "Home" was the reply, "It's all over
in Dresden! There comes the provisional government close behind us
in that carriage there." I shot out of the coach like an arrow, abandoning
it to the exhausted men, and rushed down the steeply sloping road to
find the ill-fated governmental party. I met them, as reported, coming
slowly up the hill in an elegant hired carriage from Dresden: Heubner,
Bakunin, and the energetic postal secretary Martin,[1] both the latter
armed with muskets; on the box what I took to be the secretariat had
found places; at the back as many weary members of the people's militia
as could were struggling for seats. As I now swung myself quickly into
the carriage, I became an immediate witness to a strange conversation
between the coachman, who owned his carriage, and the members of the
provisional government. The former implored them most vehemently
to spare his carriage, which had most delicate springs and was by no
means designed to carry such weight, and to tell all those people that
they should not try to sit on the front and back. Undisturbed by all this,
Bakunin preferred to give me a short report about the retreat from
Dresden, which had gone off successfully without losses. Early that day
he had ordered the newly planted trees in the Maximilians-Allee to be
felled, so as to guard against a cavalry flank attack with these barriers.
He had been particularly entertained by the laments of the people living
on this promenade, who had all complained volubly about the fate of
their "beeyootiful trees". During all this the complaints of our coachman
were becoming increasingly insistent; he broke out into loud sobbing
and crying. Bakunin observed him with true satisfaction without
according him so much as a word, but remarked, "The tears of a
philistine are the nectar of the gods." It was only to Heubner and myself
that the scene was irksome; he asked me if we two should not at least
get out, as he didn't expect anyone else to do so. Actually, it was high
time to leave the carriage at this point, for new contingents of
revolutionaries were now surrounding the highway and assembling in
orderly ranks to greet the provisional government and receive its orders.
Heubner now reviewed the ranks with great dignity, informed their
leaders how things stood, and exhorted them to retain their faith in the
justice of the cause for which so many had already shed their blood;
everyone was now to withdraw to Freiberg to await further orders. At
this point a certain Metzdorff,[2] a serious young man and a German-
Catholic priest, whom I had met in Dresden, and who had first called
my attention to the writings of Feuerbach, stepped out of the ranks of
the volunteers and asked for the protection of the provisional government:

he had, he told us, instigated an armed march on Dresden by the Chemnitz Communal Guard, but the corps had dragged him along with them on the march, more or less a prisoner, and he had been severely maltreated by its commander, being freed only through a chance meeting with another and more favorably disposed contingent of volunteers. We now ourselves saw this Chemnitz Communal Guard positioned on a distant hill. They sent messengers across to get information from Heubner as to what was going on; after having been instructed about the intention to continue the struggle in every way as decisively as possible, they invited the provisional government to establish its seat in Chemnitz. When they had returned to their corps, we saw them all turn about and move off.

After many similar delays and interruptions, our rather disjointed train reached Freiberg, where we were met in the streets by friends of Heubner who urgently requested him not to make their native town the scene of desperate street-fighting by establishing the seat of the provisional government there; Heubner was silent at all this and asked Bakunin and me to come to his house and confer with him there. We first witnessed there his painful reunion with his wife, whom he informed in a few words about the seriousness and significance of the task that had fallen to him: it was, he said, for Germany and for its nobler future that he had risked his life. Breakfast was served, and after all of us were put in a better mood by this refreshment, Heubner now made a brief, calm and serious speech to Bakunin, whom he had known only so fleetingly that he had not even learned how to pronounce his name correctly: "My dear Bakanin," he began, "before we go any further, I must ask you to state whether your political goal really is the red republic that I have been told you advocate: tell me frankly, so that I know whether I can count on your friendship in the future." Without any circumlocution, Bakunin replied that he had no formal scheme for any particular form of government and would not risk his life for any of them. As far as his long-term hopes and wishes were concerned, these didn't have anything to do with the street-fighting in Dresden, and anything that might mean for Germany. He had considered the Dresden uprising a rather fatuous affair, worthy of mockery at best, until he had seen the effect of the noble and courageous example set by Heubner. From then on he had abandoned all political considerations and intentions that had mitigated against his sharing in this dedicated attitude, and he had immediately decided to attach himself as a loyal and active friend to so admirable a man, about whom he indeed knew that he belonged to the so-called moderate party, the political future of which he was not in a position to judge, as he had found little occasion to inform himself as to the condition of political parties in Germany. Heubner expressed himself completely satisfied at this and now asked Bakunin his opinion about the present state of things; wouldn't it be honorable and conscionable to dismiss all these people and give up what was probably a hopeless struggle? To this Bakunin responded in his accustomed dispassionate and straightforward way that anybody who wanted to might give up the fight, but certainly not Heubner. As the leading member of the provisional government, he had issued the call to arms, and his call had been obeyed; hundreds of lives had been sacrificed: to send the people away would be tantamount to an admission that all those sacrifices had been made on behalf of a vain illusion, and even if only the two of them were to be left, they should not leave their places; if the effort failed, their lives were ruined anyway, but their honor must remain unbesmirched, so that in the future people would not react to a similar call with despair. This convinced Heubner; he at once drafted an appeal for elections for a constitutional assembly for Saxony, to meet at Chemnitz. He assumed that he would be supported there not only by the populace but also by the many contingents of volunteers purportedly streaming in from all directions, and that he would thus be able to sustain a center for the provisional government until the general situation in Germany became clearer.

While this conference was going on, Stephan Born,[1] a typographer who had assumed the military command to Heubner's great satisfaction during the last three days in Dresden, entered the room to announce that he had conducted the retreat of the armed forces, in good order and without suffering any losses all the way to Freiberg. This straightforward young man and the effect of his announcement made a very heartening impression on us; but when Heubner asked him whether he would undertake to defend Freiberg against the expected attack by royalist troops, he demurred, stating he was not a military man and knew nothing about strategy; the job could only be done, he said, by an experienced officer. Under the circumstances it seemed best, even if only to gain time, to withdraw to the more heavily populated Chemnitz; but first it seemed advisable to take care of the provisioning of the masses of revolutionaries assembled in Freiberg. Born departed at once to take the initial steps to accomplish this. Heubner also excused himself to restore his exhausted spirits with an hour's sleep. I was left behind alone with Bakunin on the sofa; he was soon overcome by inexorable slumber, and as he sank sideways his huge head thudded heavily onto my shoulder. Realizing that he would not awaken if I freed myself from this burden, I pushed him to the side with much difficulty and left everybody to their slumbers in Heubner's house in order, as I had already been doing for so many days, to see for myself what appearance these extraordinary events had now assumed.

So I came to the town hall, in front of and within which the excited horde of passionate revolutionaries was being fed by the townspeople to the best of their ability. To my astonishment I found Heubner there, once again fully active, though I had thought him asleep back at home. He had not been willing to leave the men without guidance even for an hour. Under his direction a headquarters of sorts had been organized, and now he was again busily signing orders and drafting documents, while all the time enveloped by tumultuous noise from all sides. It wasn't long before Bakunin put in an appearance as well: he was on the look-out for a good officer; but no such man was available; an enthusiastic but elderly fellow, who had arrived in command of a detachment from the Vogtland, attracted Bakunin's attention by his energetic speeches: he recommended that this man be appointed commander-in-chief at once. Yet in the tremendous confusion no orderly decision-making seemed possible; only in Chemnitz was there hope of bringing this wild movement under control, and Heubner therefore issued orders to make ready to march on to Chemnitz as soon as everybody had been provisioned. Once this was settled, longing to be out of this chaos, I told my friends that I would go to Chemnitz in advance of these detachments, and I would meet them there again the following day. I actually managed to catch the mail coach which was scheduled to depart at this hour and got a seat in it. But as the volunteers were starting out on the same road at that moment, in order not to have the carriage become bogged down in a morass of people, it was decided to wait for some time after their departure before leaving. The delay was considerable. For a long time I observed the strange demeanor of the volunteers as they filed past; I was particularly struck by a troop from the Vogtland, who marched in a rather pedantic way; they were following the beat of a drummer who tried to vary the monotonous sound of his instrument artificially by alternatively striking the wooden rim of the drum. This unpleasant rattling noise reminded me in a spectral way of the rattling of the skeletons' bones in their nocturnal dance around the gallows, depicted by Berlioz in the last movement of his *Symphonie fantastique* with such frightening verisimilitude during that performance in Paris. Suddenly

410

I felt a desire to see again the friends I had left behind and go with them to Chemnitz, if possible; I found they were no longer at the town hall; when I reached Heubner's house, I found that he was sleeping. I went back to the coach; its departure was still being delayed by streets filled with revolutionaries; I walked up and down for some time uneasily; as I finally lost faith that the coach would ever leave, I went back to Heubner's house again, this time determined to offer myself as a traveling companion to him. But Heubner and Bakunin had already left the house and were nowhere to be found. I now returned in despair to the coach and discovered that it was actually ready to leave. I took it and eventually got to Chemnitz after a series of further delays and adventures late that night.

Upon leaving the coach, I went at once to the nearest hotel, where I slept for a few hours before proceeding at five o'clock the following morning to the home of my brother-in-law Wolfram, fifteen minutes' walk from the city. On the way I asked a sentry belonging to the Communal Guard whether he knew anything of the arrival of the provisional government. "Provisional government?" was the response: "Well, that is all over with!" I didn't understand him and was also unable, when I arrived at the house of my relatives, to learn anything further about the way things stood in Chemnitz, for my brother-in-law had been ordered into the city for police duties. It was only when he got back later in the morning that I learned everything that had happened in another hotel nearby, while I had been resting for a few hours in Chemnitz. Heubner, Bakunin, and the aforementioned Martin had arrived, before me as it seemed, in a private coach at the gates of Chemnitz; challenged for their names, Heubner had invoked his full authority in announcing who he was, and had summoned the authorities of the town to meet him in the hotel he specified. Once there, all three had collapsed from over-exhaustion, when suddenly policemen entered their rooms and arrested them in the name of the Royal Saxon district authority. Their first reaction was only to ask for a few hours' rest, on the grounds that it was obvious that in their condition there would be no thought of escape. I learned further that they had been escorted the following morning under heavy military guard to Altenburg; unfortunately, as my brother-in-law had to admit to me, the commanders of the Chemnitz Communal Guard, who had been compelled most unwillingly to march toward Dresden, and had done so only in the resolve to place themselves at the disposal of the King's forces immediately upon arrival, had deceived Heubner by their invitation to Chemnitz and had thus lured him into a trap. They had arrived in Chemnitz long before him and had placed sentries at the gate in the intention of finding out immediately when Heubner arrived in order to arrange for his arrest. My brother-in-law was also in great anxiety on my account, as he had been told by leaders of this detachment in furious tones that I had been seen consorting with the revolutionaries. At any rate, it seemed to him a miraculous stroke of fate that I had not traveled with them to Chemnitz and stopped at the same hotel, as otherwise I would certainly have shared their fate. Like a bolt of lightning it flashed upon my soul how miraculously I had escaped from almost certain calamity in duels with the most experienced swordsmen in my student days. This latest frightful experience made such an impact on me that I literally could not bring myself to utter a word about it and all the related events. At the particular urging of my wife, who was very worried about my personal safety, my brother-in-law undertook the task of conducting me in his carriage by night to Altenburg, from where I immediately continued on by mail coach to Weimar, where I had already planned to spend my little vacation, and where I now arrived after all, though by a bizarre and unexpected route.

The state of dream-like trance in which I then found myself is best evidenced by the fact that upon my renewed reunion with Liszt I gave the appearance of plunging into the only matter he considered important in regard to me, the forthcoming new production of *Tannhäuser* in Weimar. I found it difficult to tell my friend that I had not left Dresden as Royal Kapellmeister in an entirely regular way. To tell the truth, I had only an extremely hazy conception of my relationship to the laws of what was, in the narrower sense, my native country. Had I committed a criminal act according to these laws or not? I couldn't come to any real conclusion about it. Meanwhile a stream of new and shocking bulletins concerning the horrifying state of things in Dresden poured into Weimar; the stage director Genast[1] in particular aroused great excitement by spreading rumors about the arsonist activities of Röckel, who was very well known in Weimar. From my own forthright remarks Liszt could soon see that I myself had some kind of serious connection with these terrible events; my attitude misled him for a time in this respect, however, because I was unwilling, for a number of reasons that would have been of no interest to the law courts, to proclaim myself a combatant in the recent fighting. My friend thus remained in a delusion I had not intended. At the home of Frau Caroline, the Princess von Wittgenstein,[2] whom I had met during her flying visit to Dresden a year before, we were able to debate all sorts of artistic questions quite spiritedly. Thus one afternoon there was a lively discussion resulting from my description of the draft for a tragedy to be entitled *Jesus von Nazareth*, during which I saw Liszt lapse into doubtful silence, while the Princess protested vigorously against any plan to bring such material onto the stage. From the lukewarm attempt I made to support the paradoxical theories I had put forward in this respect, I could see for myself how things stood with me inwardly; I had been and remained, even though it was not easy for outsiders to see, shaken to the bottom of my being by the events I had experienced. Then we came to an orchestral rehearsal for *Tannhäuser*, which again stimulated me artistically in manifold ways. The manner in which Liszt conducted it, though orientated more toward its musical than dramatic aspects, filled me for the first time with that flattering warmth of emotion evoked by the consciousness of being understood and inwardly seconded by another person. At the same time I was able to assess critically, despite my dream-like state of mind, the capacities of our opera singers and their stage director. After this rehearsal I went to a small dinner with Liszt, together with Music Director Stör[1] and the singer Goetze,[2] at a different hotel from the one where he himself was living, and had occasion to be startled at the revelation of an aspect of Liszt's character hitherto unknown to me. Circumstances conspired to arouse him from the serenity, which was the face he normally presented to the world, to a truly alarming state in which, virtually gnashing his teeth in his rage, he inveighed against the same elements in society to which I was also fiercely opposed. Deeply stirred by this strange insight into this extraordinary man, yet unable to figure out what his frightful imprecations were really all about, I remained in astonished silence, while Liszt had to recuperate from this attack of nerves during the ensuing night. I was amazed to find my friend fully restored early the next morning and ready to undertake an unexplained but apparently necessary trip to Karlsruhe, upon which I was invited to accompany him with Music Director Stör as far as Eisenach. On the way to Eisenach we were accosted by Beaulieu, a Grand Ducal chamberlain, who wanted to know if I was prepared to be received at Eisenach castle by the Grand Duchess of Weimar,[3] a sister of Tsar Nicholas; as my excuse that I was only in traveling clothes was not accepted, Liszt said I would be willing. And so that evening I was received in a surprisingly benevolent way by the Grand Duchess, who chatted with me most amicably and recommended me most solicitously to her chamberlain's care. Liszt asserted later that his exalted patroness had already received news that I would be wanted for arrest by the authorities in Dresden within the next few days, and thus had hastened to make my acquaintance at this point in the knowledge that a short time later she would have compromised herself too heavily by doing so. Proceeding onward from Eisenach, Liszt left me to Stör and the Eisenach Music Director Kühmstedt,[1] a zealous and skillful contrapuntalist, to be looked after and fed. With these two I made my first visit to the Wartburg castle, at that time not yet restored. I had strange thoughts about my own destiny on first entering this building, foreknown to me so intimately, at the very time that my days in Germany were numbered. And indeed, when we got back to Weimar the next day, the most ominous news arrived from Dresden. When Liszt came back on the third day, he found a letter to him from my wife, who no longer dared to write to me directly; she informed him that the police had searched my Dresden apartment, to which she had since returned, and that she had also received a warning not to bring me back to Dresden, as a warrant for my arrest had been issued, and I would soon have the police after me. Liszt, from then on filled solely with anxiety for my personal safety, convoked a council of experienced friends, to weigh the question of what to do with me to avoid the threatening danger. Minister von Watzdorf,[2] whom I had already visited, had been of the opinion that, if an official request were made to Weimar, I should quietly submit to being taken to Dresden, where they would convey me in a seemly fashion in a special carriage. On the other hand, the rumors about the brutal manner in which the Prussian troops had gone about the business of laying siege to Dresden were so alarming that Liszt and his council of devoted friends urged my immediate departure from Weimar, where it would not be possible to protect me. But I insisted, before I would leave Germany, on saying good-bye to my terribly anxious wife, and therefore wanted to spend at least a little more time in the vicinity of Weimar. This consideration prevailed, and Professor Siebert suggested I take temporary shelter with a sympathetic steward of an estate in Magdala, three hours' journey away. There I went the following morning, armed with a letter of recommendation from Professor Siebert, to introduce myself to the steward as Professor Werder from Berlin, who wished to subject his cameralistic studies to a practical scrutiny by means of a visit to the estate being administered there. There I remained in rustic tranquillity for three days, and also was afforded some peculiar entertainment from a people's congress being held in the town, put on by the remnants of bands of volunteers that had set out for Dresden but had since returned in disarray. I listened with singular feelings, almost bordering on the preposterous, to the myriad speeches being given. On the second day of my stay there, my host's wife came back from market day in Weimar and told the strange story of an opera composer, whose work was to be performed there that same day, but who had been suddenly obliged to leave Weimar, as a warrant for his arrest had arrived there from Dresden. My host, who had been initiated in the secret by Professor Siebert, asked waggishly what his name might be. As his wife didn't really know, he helped her out by offering the name Röckel, well known in Weimar. "Yes," she said, "Röckel, that's the one, quite right." Then my host laughed hugely and said he would not be so dumb as to let them catch him, despite his opera. At last, on May 22nd, my birthday, Minna herself actually arrived in Magdala. Upon receipt of my letter, she had hurried to Weimar and, told where to find me, had come to convince me by any possible means that I should get out of Germany at once. None of my attempts to induce her to share my exuberant mood was successful; she persisted in regarding me as a rash, inconsiderate person, who had plunged himself and her into the most catastrophic situation. It was then agreed that, while she would go there via Weimar at the same time, I would proceed on foot the following evening to Jena, where I would meet her at the home of Professor Wolff[1] for a last farewell. I started accordingly on this six hours' walk, and entered the friendly little university town, where I had never been before, over a high plateau at sundown. I found my wife again, as arranged, at the house of Professor Wolff, whom I had already befriended through Liszt. Once more there was a conference as to what I should do next, with the special participation of a certain Professor Widmann;[2] a warrant for my arrest really had been issued in Dresden, on the grounds of strong suspicion of participation in the revolt, and thus I could no longer count on safe asylum in any of the German federal states. Liszt's recommendation was in favor of Paris, where he was sure I would be able to find a new terrain for my activities; but Widmann advised me not to take the direct route via Frankfurt and Baden, as the uprisings were still going on there, and any suspicious persons traveling through would certainly be scrutinized very closely by the police. The safest route would be through Bavaria, which was very quiet at the moment, proceeding first to Switzerland, from where the trip to Paris could be undertaken without any danger. As I needed a passport for this purpose, Professor Widmann offered me his, issued in Tübingen, but which had already expired. I then departed in the mail coach, after taking leave of my utterly despairing wife in truly great misery myself. Without any further hindrance I reached the

Bavarian border, going through Rudolstadt, a town not without its memories for me, and from there continued my journey without interruption in another mail coach[1] straight to Lindau. At its city gates my passport was taken away for inspection, together with those of the other passengers; I spent a feverishly agitated night awaiting the departure of the Lake Constance steamship the next morning. I vividly recalled the Swabian accent of Professor Widmann, on whose passport I was traveling; I tried to figure out how I should deal with the Bavarian police if I were compelled to discuss the irregularities in my passport with them. A prey to feverish unrest, I tried throughout the night to practise Swabian dialect, but to my great amusement without the slightest success. I had braced myself for the crucial moment early the next morning, when a policeman entered my room and, not knowing to whom the passports belonged, offered me three of them at random to choose from. With a heart full of joy, I grabbed my own and dismissed the dreaded messenger in the friendliest way imaginable. Once I reached the steamship I saw to my great satisfaction that I was already on Swiss territory; a marvelous spring morning afforded me a view across the broad lake of an expanse of Alpine scenery; when I set foot on Swiss soil at Rohrschach, I used the first few moments to direct a few lines homeward, whereby I announced my safe arrival in Switzerland and my liberation from any danger. The trip in the mail coach through the friendly little canton of St Gall to Zürich cheered me immensely: when I entered Zürich at six o'clock in the evening on the last day of May, driving down from Oberstrass, and saw for the first time the Glarner Alps adjoining the lake gleaming in the sunset, I decided immediately, without really being conscious of it, that nothing would prevent my establishing residence here.

My principal reason for accepting the suggestion of my friends that I travel to Paris via Switzerland was that I knew I would find an old acquaintance in Zürich, with whose help I thought I could obtain a passport for France, because I wanted to avoid arriving there as a political refugee. Alexander Müller, with whom I had been on friendly terms in my Würzburg days, had long since settled, as I learned, in Zürich as a music teacher. One of his pupils, Wilhelm Baumgartner, had visited me in Dresden some years before and brought me greetings from my old friend; I had given him a copy of the score of *Tannhäuser* at the time, to be presented to Müller as a memento. My little gesture had not fallen on barren soil: Müller and Baumgartner, both of whom I at once looked up, introduced me forthwith to the two cantonal secretaries Jakob

Sulzer and Franz Hagenbuch, as being those among their friends in the best position to fulfill my request with the greatest ease. I was received by them, together with some other intimate friends of theirs, with such respectful interest and sympathy that I felt myself instantaneously at ease in their company. The great and unpretentious assurance with which they expressed themselves about the persecution to which I had been subjected, as viewed from the republican standpoint they had imbibed with their mothers' milk, introduced me to an entirely new sphere of the bourgeois outlook on life. I felt so safe and secure here, whereas in my own country, because of the curious conjunction of my disgust at the public conduct of artistic affairs with the prevailing political unrest, without quite realizing how, I had come to be considered a criminal. In order to win over completely the two cantonal scretaries, of whom Sulzer in particular had enjoyed an excellent classical education, my friends had arranged an evening party at which I was prevailed upon to read my poem for *Siegfrieds Tod*. I can testify that, among men, I have never had more attentive listeners than on that evening. The immediate effect of this success was the issue of a fully valid Swiss passport to the man who was a wanted criminal in Germany, with which I then proceeded without anxiety onward to Paris after my short stay in Zürich. After having been moved and enthralled by the world-famous cathedral in Strassburg, I continued my journey to Paris in what was then the best conveyance available, the so-called *malle-poste*. I remember experiencing a curious phenomenon on this occasion: until then the sounds of cannon and musket fire from the battle for Dresden had been echoing in my ears, particularly whenever I was only half-awake; but now the humming of the wheels as we rolled rapidly along the highway cast such a spell over me that during the whole journey I thought I could hear in this sound, as if carried by deep bass instruments, the melody to "Freude schöner Götterfunken" from the Ninth Symphony.

From the time I entered Switzerland to the moment I arrived in Paris, my spirits, which had previously sunk into dream-like apathy, had risen to a sense of liberation and comfortable well-being I had not experienced before. I felt like a bird on the wing, whose destiny could not be to end in some morass. Soon after my arrival in Paris in the first week in June, however, a palpable reaction set in. I had been recommended by Liszt to his former secretary Belloni; in accordance with the instructions he had received, Belloni understood it to be his office to put me in touch with a literary man, one Gustave Vaisse, whom I nonetheless never met personally, with a view to providing myself with an operatic libretto to set to music for Paris. I was not very taken by this and found sufficient pretext to ward off the negotiations aimed at setting this in train in the news about the cholera epidemic raging in Paris at the time. In order to be in Belloni's vicinity, I had taken rooms in the Rue Notre Dame de Lorette; along this street, heralded by muffled drumbeats, the bodies of the dead were conveyed almost hourly, escorted by the National Guard. Despite the stifling heat, drinking the water was strictly forbidden me, and altogether the strictest dietary precautions had been prescribed. As if this was not already enough to make me despondent, the whole external physiognomy of Paris had moreover the most depressing effect on me. The motto "Liberté, Egalité, Fraternité" was still to be seen on all public buildings and similar establishments; yet I was appalled by the sight of the *garçons caissiers* from the banks, with their large money sacks slung over their shoulders and fat portfolios in their hands. They were never so ubiquitous as now, when the old rule of capital was zealously reasserting itself victoriously against the previously dreaded Socialist propaganda with almost insulting pomp in the attempt to regain public confidence. I had gone almost mechanically to pay a visit to Schlesinger's music shop, and found that he had been succeeded there by a far more pronounced Jew, M. Brandus, of the most repellent personality. The old clerk M. Henri was the only one to accord me a friendly greeting, and after I had chatted loudly with him for a while in the apparently empty store, he asked me in some embarrassment whether I had already greeted my teacher – "votre maître" – Meyerbeer. "Is M. Meyerbeer here?" I asked. "Certainly," came the even more embarrassed answer, "quite nearby, over there behind the desk." And sure enough, as I walked over toward it, Meyerbeer emerged in extreme embarrassment from the place where he had remained concealed and in silence for over ten minutes after he had first heard my voice, excusing himself on the grounds of having had to take care of some pressing corrections. This apparition and singular reunion were quite enough for me; they recalled so many dubious experiences involving him, particularly the significance of his recent conduct toward me in Berlin; yet as I now really had nothing more to do with him, I greeted him with a certain merry abandon, induced by the regret I felt at his obvious discombobulation upon learning of my arrival in Paris. He assumed I would now make another attempt to seek my fortune in Paris and seemed much surprised when I assured him that, to the contrary, I was sickened by the thought of doing any such thing. "But Liszt has published a brilliant article about you in the *Journal des*

Débats." "Ah, that," I said. "But I really hadn't thought that the enthusiastic advocacy of a friend should at once be interpreted as a shared speculation." "But the article has created quite a sensation. It is really unthinkable that you should not try to get some advantage out of it." This offensive meddling spurred me to a rather heated response, wherein I now assured Meyerbeer that, particularly the way things seemed to be going in the world under the rule of reactionary forces, I was thinking of anything rather than producing works of art for public performance. "But what do you expect from the revolution?" he replied. "Do you want to compose scores for the barricades?" I thereupon told him I had no intention of writing any scores whatsoever. We parted, obviously without having arrived at a mutual understanding. I then met Maurice Schlesinger on the street, who was also very much under the spell of Liszt's article and considered me something of a prodigy. He too believed that I was necessarily up to something in Paris, and thought I now had very good prospects. "Do you want to be my agent?" I asked him. "I have no money. But do you think the performance of an opera by an unknown can be anything other than an *affaire d'argent*?" "You are right," said Maurice, and left me standing there. From these unpleasant contacts with the plague-stricken capital of the world, I turned to inquire as to the fate of my colleagues from Dresden, some of the closest of whom had also proceeded to Paris. Upon a visit to Despléchin, the scene-painter for my *Tannhäuser*, I ran across Semper, who had also been washed up on these shores. The joy at this reunion was considerable, despite the fact that neither of us could help grinning at our grotesque situation. After the famous barricade he had designed and then kept continually under supervision, as its architect, had been circumvented (for he did not believe it could possibly be taken by force), he had withdrawn from the rest of the fighting. Yet he felt he had sufficiently exposed himself to denunciation that, after the Prussians had occupied Dresden and announced a state of siege, he no longer felt safe there. He considered himself lucky as a citizen of Holstein to have been dependent not on the German but on the Danish government for his passport, as this had helped him reach Paris without difficulty. When I expressed my sincere and heartfelt regret that this turn of events had torn him from the important professional undertaking on which he had just started, the completion of the construction of the Dresden Museum, he refused to take it very seriously and told me the job had given him trouble enough. Despite our dismal situation, I spent with Semper the sole cheerful hours of my stay in Paris. Soon young Heine, my former would-be scene-painter for *Lohengrin*, turned up as a refugee as well. He wasn't worried about his future, for his teacher Despléchin gladly offered to employ him. It was only I who felt myself pitched quite uselessly into Paris and was desperately anxious to get away from its cholera-laden atmosphere. For this Belloni offered me an opportunity which I seized at once: he invited me to follow him and his family to the country near La Ferté sous Jouarre, where I could recuperate in the clean air and utter quiet, and await a change for the better in my personal fortunes. After another week in Paris, I made the little trip out to Reuil, and stayed for the time being in the house of a wine merchant, M. Raphael, in the immediate vicinity of the village *mairie*, where the Belloni family was staying and where I found meager, temporary accommodation for myself in a sitting room with bed-recesses, in which I now gazed forward into my future.*

There was no news from Germany for some time, and I tried to busy myself as best I could with reading, and after occupying myself with Proudhon's writings, particularly with his *De la Propriété*, in a spirit that afforded me singularly rich consolation for my position, I then entertained myself for a long time with Lamartine's[1] diverting and compelling *Histoire des Girondins*. One day Belloni brought me news of the unsuccessful uprising of the Republicans under the leadership of Ledru-Rollin,[2] which had been attempted on June 13th against the provisional government then sailing along with the full reactionary tide prevailing in Paris. Great as was the indignation with which this news was greeted by my host and the mayor of the place, a relative of his at whose table we took our modest daily meals, on the whole it made less impression on me, as my attention was still focused in great excitement on German events taking place on the Rhine, and particularly on the Grand Duchy of Baden, which had come under a provisional government. But when word now reached us from there, too, of the defeat by the Prussians of this movement, which had at first appeared by no means hopeless, I felt peculiarly miserable: the dispassion with which I was now obliged to consider my situation overpowered me; I now lost sight of the unusual circumstances that had previously justified my excitement in the demeaning need to pay attention to simple practical matters. The communications arriving at last from my Weimar friends as well as from my wife should have sufficed to complete my disenchantment. From the

* Note in the margin of the manuscript, in Cosima's hand: "(Interruption Italy, Munich. Resumption November 19th 1868 [Union].)" [Cosima returned to Triebschen on November 16th 1868, and was never separated from Wagner again. She began her diaries, recording their life together, on January 1st 1869.]

former I got a rather dry verdict on my conduct in the recent past; it was found that nothing could be done for me at the moment, particularly not in Dresden or at the Grand Ducal Court, as there was no point in "knocking at doors that are already battered down": "On ne frappe pas à des portes enfoncées" (Princess von Wittgenstein to Belloni). I didn't know what to say to all this, as I had nurtured not the slightest idea that anything could be expected from those directions, and was, on the contrary, unreservedly satisfied that they had provided some money to tide me over. With these funds I decided to go to Zürich, to look for a temporary abode with Alexander Müller, in whose house I had noticed sufficient room. The saddest thing for me was a letter from my wife, who for a long while had not written me a word. She let me know that she could not entertain any thought of a reunion with me; for after I had so unconscionably thrown away and ruined a position and circumstances I would never be afforded again, a wife could scarcely be asked to participate in any undertakings I might consider for future earnings. I initially felt inclined toward a just appraisal of her bad situation; having been obliged to leave her behind entirely without help from me, I could do nothing at that time but advise her to sell our Dresden furniture and appeal to my Leipzig relatives. My impression of her oppressive position had been until then somewhat alleviated by a feeling that she had shared at least some of my passionate involvement, and there had been various signs of this during those extraordinary events. But she now denied this flatly, and professed to see in me only what public opinion at home saw, the only mitigating circumstance in her eyes being my unheard-of frivolity. After having besought Liszt to do his best for my wife, however, I soon managed to achieve a relatively calm state of mind concerning this entirely unexpected conduct on the part of my wife. To her statement that she did not want to write me again for the moment, I responded by deciding not to upset her further with any news of my very doubtful fate. The course of all the years of our life together, beginning with that first stormy and passionate year of our wedding, now passed before me for my critical review. Without any doubt, those youthful days of struggle in Paris had exerted a beneficent influence. The cares she had borne so continuously, and against which I had struggled so industriously, had bound the soul of what we had in common with iron bands. Minna had then received a lovely reward for all she had endured in my Dresden success, and particularly in what was there such an envied position. As "Frau Kapellmeisterin" she was obviously at the pinnacle of all she had ever hoped for from life, and all those things that eventually made my conducting activities so bitter for me she regarded merely as threats to her own comfort. Even with the direction I had taken with *Tannhäuser*, and through which she saw my theatrical success so gravely imperiled, she had really lost her courage and confidence in our future. The more I deviated from the sole course she considered profitable, whether in my artistic conceptions, which I never disclosed to her, or even in my attitude to the theater and its Director, the more she lost that community of interest with me which she believed she had maintained through the earlier years, citing my successes as the proof of it. She regarded my behavior in the Dresden catastrophe as the outcome of these deviations from the right path and recognized in it solely the influence of unscrupulous persons, the unfortunate Röckel in particular, who had supposedly flattered my vanity and thereby dragged me into his own ruin. Deeper than all these disagreements, which after all concerned only the external circumstances of our life, the consciousness of our innate incompatibility had held me firmly in its grip ever since our initial reconciliation. There had always been scenes of the fiercest vehemence between us: none of these had ever ended with conciliation, or any admission on her part of being in the wrong; the necessity of restoring domestic peace as quickly as possible, together with the realization coming to me after every outburst that given our two very divergent temperaments, and particularly the great difference in our level of culture, it was up to me to do my best to avoid such scenes, had always prevailed upon me to take the responsibility for the outbursts, each time they occurred, entirely upon myself and pacify Minna by a demonstration of remorse. Unfortunately, I had to see that in the long run I thereby lost all influence over her temperament, and especially over her character; for now that it came right down to a case in which I could not possibly adopt this means of reconciliation, inasmuch as it involved the complete consequences of my beliefs and actions, I encountered a female disposition that had been hardened by my previous leniency to the point that she would never under any conceivable circumstances admit to having misjudged me in any way. But enough, and suffice it to say that what had contributed to the collapse of my situation in Dresden, apart from my great irresponsibility concerning my position there, was the similar collapse of my married life, where, in the place of support, consolation and strength, I found only an unwitting ally of the inimical circumstances that beset me. I came now to this clear insight after I had succeeded in overcoming the first shock at my wife's palpably loveless behavior. Yet I recall that I was not really pained by this, but on the contrary, now that I was entirely without help in my life, the recognition that I had built my whole existence on sand produced in me a sense of almost exalted calm. It is true that this newly won calm afforded me nothing more than the consciousness of how completely alone I stood, but I now found consolation and strength in my extreme poverty. I therefore eagerly grasped at the help proffered at last from Weimar, in order to abandon a purposeless sojourn in which I was supposed to strive for goals that were inappropriate for me, and look for a place of refuge which had nothing to attract me except the complete lack of any prospects for continuing my previous paths. And that place was Zürich, a town devoid of any public artistic activity, where for the first time I had met some straightforward people who knew nothing of my artistic labors, yet still, as it seemed, had taken a friendly liking to my naked self.

I arrived at Müller's house, requested a room of some kind as my refuge, and handed over to him the rest of my fortune – twenty francs. I was soon obliged to note that my old acquaintance was a bit embarrassed by my open trust in him and became worried as to what to do with me. At once I voluntarily gave up the large room with piano he had placed at my disposal in the impulse of the moment, and retired to a modest little bedroom. The only troublesome matter was my participation in his daily meals, not because they were distasteful to me, but because my digestive organs couldn't cope with them. Outside my friend's house, on the other hand, I enjoyed what was, by the standards of the locality, the most lavish hospitality. The same young men who had been so kind to me during my former trip through Zürich continued to show great pleasure in my company. Before long Jakob Sulzer emerged as the most imposing member of the group. He had to wait for a number of years before he was eligible to become a member of the Zürich government, because the minimum age for this was thirty. Despite his youthfulness he exercised on everyone around him the influence of complete maturity. Whenever I was asked in later years whether I had ever in my life run across what is called, in the moral sense, true character and genuine honesty, I could upon reflection name no other than the friend that I made at this time, Jakob Sulzer. He owed his early promotion to one of the best jobs in the Canton of Zürich, that of cantonal secretary, to the need of the liberal party, which had just come to power under the leadership of Alfred Escher,[1] to keep a sharp eye out for especially talented younger people to fill the public offices, which it could not plausibly leave occupied by the men with experience of those posts, who were members of the older conservative party. Sulzer was regarded by everybody as one such younger person. He had just returned from the universities of Bonn and Berlin with the intention of establishing himself as a professor of philology in his native city, when he was offered an appointment as a member of the new government. To qualify for the post he had been obliged to go to Geneva for six months to polish up his French, which he had hitherto neglected during his serious philological studies. His great perspicacity and uncommon industry, as well as his independence and unbending firmness of character, impervious to political machinations of any kind, brought him within a few years to one of the most important positions in the government, which he served for a long time with great distinction as director of finance and in particular as a member of the federal council on education. His unexpected acquaintanceship with me seemed to place him in a dilemma of sorts; the unexpected governmental appointment had torn him, in a startling, almost numbing way, from his philological and humane studies, to which inclination had directed him. It almost seemed as if his meeting me made him regret this. My poem for *Siegfrieds Tod* disclosed to him, an adept in the subject, my studies of German antiquity, with which he too had busied himself, though with far greater philological precision than had been possible for me. Somewhat later, in particular, when he had become better acquainted with my whole approach to music, serious and reserved though he was by nature, he conceived so warm a sympathy for a sphere so far removed from his chosen profession that in the end, as he expressly admitted, he felt obliged to take conscious and intentionally abrupt steps to resist those disruptive influences. In these early days of my residence in Zürich, however, he let himself be carried in that direction with genuine and likeable abandon. The venerable official residence of the first cantonal secretary opened its doors, far more frequently than could benefit the prestige of a civil servant in this small Philistia, to the meetings of such a group as could only be formed with me at its center. The musician Baumgartner was especially attracted on such occasions by the products of Sulzer's vineyards in Winterthur, which the latter dispensed with great liberality. And if I too, in the mood of irresponsibility and merriment born of my despair at that time, let myself go in dithyrambic outpourings that took the theories of art and life that were forming in me to their most extreme conclusions, my listeners often responded in a manner which I was obliged to attribute, without going too far wrong, more to the effects of the wine than to my inspiration. Once, when

Professor Ettmüller,[1] the Germanist and Edda scholar, had been invited by Sulzer to listen to a reading of my *Siegfried*, and had been conducted home in a state of ponderous exaltation, those of us remaining behind gave way to an extraordinary fit of high spirits. I hit upon the idea of removing all the doors of the cantonal secretary's residence from their hinges; when Secretary Hagenbuch noticed the terrific effort this was costing me, he helpfully contributed his enormous strength to the enterprise, and after that, every single door was in fact lifted off and put to the side, with Sulzer smiling good-naturedly the whole time. But the next day he admitted in response to our inquiries that he had been busy the whole rest of the night putting the heavy doors back on their hinges by himself, as he naturally didn't want the sergeant-at-arms, who appeared every day very early, to learn of the wild activities of the previous evening.

The extraordinary bird-like freedom of my outlaw existence had the effect of making me increasingly excitable. I often became frightened myself at the excessive gusts of exaltation affecting my whole being, under the influence of which I was always ready to indulge the most singular eccentricities, no matter whom I might be with at the time. Immediately after my arrival in Zürich I began setting down on paper my views on the nature of things, as formed under the pressure of my artistic experience and of the political excitement of the era. As there seemed nothing else for me to do but to try to earn something with my pen as a writer, I had conceived the idea of producing a series of articles for a major French journal, such as the then still extant *National*, in which I would air my revolutionary ideas about modern art and its relationship to society. I sent six of these interrelated essays to my old acquaintance Albert Franck, brother of the more distinguished Hermann Franck, who had taken over as owner of the Franco-German bookstore previously managed by my brother-in-law Avenarius, and requested him to take care of having them translated and getting them published. I got these articles back in the mail with the comment, soon to be proved true, that the Parisian public, particularly at this time, would neither pay any attention to them nor be able to understand them. I gave the manuscript the title *Art and Revolution* and, without any other changes, sent it off to the book-dealer Otto Wigand in Leipzig, who then actually undertook to issue it as a brochure, and sent me five louis d'or as an honorarium. This exceptional success induced me to think of further exploitation of my literary gifts. I hunted around among my papers for the essay I had written the previous year as an outgrowth of my studies of the Nibelung legends, gave it the title *The Wibelungs, World History out of Legend*, and again tried my luck with Wigand by dispatching it to him. The provocative title *Art and Revolution*, as well as the tremendous notoriety surrounding a Royal Kapellmeister who had become a political refugee, had inspired this radically inclined publisher with the hope that the publication of my writings might give rise to a profitable scandal. In fact, I soon learned that he had immediately gone ahead with a second printing of *Art and Revolution*, without giving me any prior notice. My second manuscript was also accepted for another five louis d'or. This was the first time I had ever made money from the publication of my works, and I really thought I was now at the right point to do something about my misfortunes. Pondering the matter, I thought I would give some public lectures on similar subjects during the following winter in Zürich, and thus in this rather free and easy manner, without a steady job and particularly without involvement with music, at least keep body and soul together for the time being.

It seemed necessary for me to resort to these expedients, for the world had otherwise resumed its work-a-day ways to the extent that without some source of income I would not have known how to survive in it. Shortly after my arrival in Zürich, I had seen the remnants of the army of Baden that had been driven onto Swiss soil, together with some fugitive volunteers accompanying them, and this had made a lamentable and disquieting impression on me. News of Görgey's surrender[1] near Villagos crippled the last hopes for a victorious outcome of what was until then the still undecided struggle for European liberty. It was only then that, although deeply shaken and alarmed, I shifted my gaze from events in the outside world to those of my inner spirit. In the Café littéraire, where I was accustomed to drink my coffee every day after my heavy mid-day meal among a motley crew of men smoking and amusing themselves at dominoes or cards, I absentmindedly studied the rather vulgar wallpaper, which depicted landscapes of the ancient world and recalled to me in a strange way impressions I had received in my early youth at the house of my brother-in-law Brockhaus from a watercolor by Genelli,[2] representing the education of Dionysos by the Muses. I conceived there the ideas for my *Art-Work of the Future*, and it seemed a strange omen to me to be awakened from one such dream-like musing by seeing a written announcement that Frau Schröder-Devrient was staying in Zürich. I at once set off with the intention of calling on her at the nearby Cutlass hotel, but learned to my almost frightening dismay that she had just departed again by steamship. I never saw her again, but only learned of her painful death[1] many years later from my wife, who had again established contact with her in Dresden.

After I had spent two such unusual summer months in this singularly footloose situation, I again received some consoling signs of life from Minna, who had remained behind in Dresden. Although she had disassociated herself from me in such a blunt and wounding manner, I could not bring myself to regard her as lost to me. I inquired about her sympathetically of one of her relatives in a letter that I assumed would be passed along to her, having to do the best I could for her through repeated appeals to Liszt. I now received a direct answer to that letter, which, at the same time as it offered evidence of the doughty manner in which this active woman was coping with her difficult situation, demonstrated her earnest desire to be reunited with me. While she expressed great skepticism about all my prospects for making a living in Zürich, and in an almost contemptuous manner, she nonetheless felt that, inasmuch as she was after all my wife, she should give me another chance, clinging the while to the assumption that I would offer her Zürich only as a temporary place of refuge, and do my utmost to further my career as an operatic composer in Paris. Thus she announced to me her impending arrival on Swiss soil at Rohrschach on a certain day in September, to be accompanied by the little dog Peps, the parrot Papo, and her purported sister Nathalie. After I had rented some rooms for their reception and our mutual shelter, I set out from Rapperswyl on foot through lovely and celebrated Toggenburg and Appenzell to St Gall and Rohrschach, and felt much moved after all when I saw the singular family, consisting half of domestic pets, land at Rohrschach. I was particularly won over, I must admit, by the little dog and the bird. My wife poured cold water on my feelings by threatening immediately upon our reunion that she was ready to go back at any moment to Dresden, where she had been assured of protection and assistance, if I behaved badly to her. For my part, one look at Minna, who had obviously aged very much in a short time, sufficed to arouse the sympathy necessary to dissolve my bitterness at once. I tried above all to cheer her up and represent the present miseries as transitory. But I had a hard time accomplishing this at first; even the unprepossessing external appearance of the city of Zürich made her feel ashamed when she recalled the more imposing lineaments of Dresden. The friends to whom I introduced her impressed her not at all. She mistook "Staatsschreiber" Sulzer for a "Stadtschreiber", a mere "town clerk, who would be a nobody in Germany". And the wife of my former host Alexander Müller, to whom she complained of the miserable situation into which I had brought myself, aroused her full indignation by telling her that my greatness consisted precisely in my not having been afraid of such misery. But then Minna appeased me by announcing the arrival of some personal effects from our Dresden household, which she assumed would be indispensable for our future dwelling. These consisted of my old Breitkopf and Härtel piano, which looked better than it sounded, and Cornelius' frontispiece for the *Nibelungenlied* in a gothic frame, which formerly hung above my desk in Dresden. With the nucleus of household effects, we now decided to establish ourselves in a small apartment in the so-called Hintere Escherhäuser on the Zeltweg. With great skill, Minna had contrived to make some money from the sale of our Dresden furniture, in spite of the huge difficulties raised by the various parties who thought they had a claim on it, of which, upon her arrival, about one hundred talers were left to help toward setting up our new household. She believed that she had saved my small but carefully chosen private library by turning it over, upon his urgent request, to the brother of my brother-in-law, Heinrich Brockhaus, the bookdealer and member of the Saxon Assembly. Later, when she applied for return of the books from their custodian, she was highly dismayed to be told that he intended to withhold them as collateral for a debt of five hundred talers which I had contracted with him during my days of financial misery in Dresden. As over the course of the years, I never found myself in a position to repay this sum in cash, this library, tailored to my special needs, remained lost to me for good. Thanks to my good friend Sulzer in particular, the cantonal secretary whom Minna at the outset persisted in underrating through her misunderstanding of the significance of his title, and who, though he was far from well off himself, thought it only fitting and proper that he should help me out to the best of his ability, we soon succeeded in making our little home seem so cosy that our Zürich friends, who were all accustomed to simplicity, were soon quite at home there on their visits. My wife's undeniable talents in this direction showed themselves to great advantage; I especially recall how cleverly she converted the crate in which my music and manuscripts had been transported to Dresden into a sideboard.

But in the end the question was how I could earn enough money to support us. My idea of giving public lectures greatly insulted my wife's pride. She had but one idea in her head for me: to stick to the plan recommended by Liszt: to compose an opera for Paris. Partly in order to reassure her, and also because I couldn't see anything else on the horizon, I actually resumed my correspondence about this with my great friend and his secretary Belloni in Paris. All the same, something more immediate had to be done; I accepted the invitation of the Zürich Musical Society to conduct a classical work at one of their concerts and rehearsed the rather weak orchestra in Beethoven's Symphony in A major, with which I nonetheless made a lasting impression on the audience, while making all of five napoleons for myself. But this merely saddened my wife, as she could not help thinking of the far greater resources at my disposal, and the more splendid surroundings crowning my efforts in such an undertaking in Dresden only a short time before. She continually called for me to devote myself completely to a brilliant career in Paris, whatever the circumstances and despite any artistic scruples I might have to the contrary. As long as we were both necessarily in the dark as to where I would find the funds to pay for the trip to Paris and for my stay there, I again took refuge in that speculation on the philosophy of art that was the only sphere now congenial to me. Hard-pressed by the need to provide food, and in a continuing but vain struggle against the chilliness of a sunless ground-floor room, I wrote the whole of my more comprehensive work, entitled *The Art-Work of the Future*, in the months of November and December of that year. Minna had no objection to this activity, as I had been able to show her the success of my first pamphlet and convince her of my hopes for receiving better remuneration for this longer work.

Thus for a while I enjoyed comparative peace, able to surrender completely to the inner excitement nourished in me by my acquaintance with the principal work of Ludwig Feuerbach. I had always felt an inclination to try to fathom the depths of philosophy, rather as I had been driven by the mystical influence of Beethoven's Ninth Symphony to plumb the deepest recesses of music. My first attempts with philosophy had been a complete failure. None of the Leipzig professors had been able to hold my attention with their lectures on basic philosophy and logic. I had later obtained Schelling's *System of Transcendental Idealism*, which had been recommended by Gustav Schlesinger,[1] a friend of Laube, but upon reading even its first few pages had scratched my head in vain to make anything of it, and had always gone back to my Ninth Symphony. During the last period of my residence in Dresden I had nonetheless tried to do justice to this old, now newly awakened urge, and took as a point of departure the more searching historical studies which so greatly satisfied me at the time. For my introduction to the philosophy of Hegel I chose his *Philosophy of*

History. Much of this impressed me, and it appeared as if I would gain admittance to the inner sanctum by this route. The more incomprehensible I found many of the most sweeping and speculative sentences of this tremendously famous intellect, who had been commended to me as the keystone of philosophic understanding, the more I felt impelled to get to the bottom of what was termed "the absolute" and everything connected with it. The revolution interrupted this effort; the practical considerations involved in the restructuring of society distracted me, and, as I have already mentioned, it was a former student of theology, at the time a German-Catholic preacher and political agitator with a Calabrian hat, named Metzdorf, who first called my attention to "the sole adequate philosopher of the modern age", Ludwig Feuerbach. Now my new Zürich friend, the piano teacher Wilhelm Baumgartner, brought his *Thoughts on Death and Immortality* to my house. The widely praised, very stimulating, lyrical style of the writer greatly fascinated me as a total layman. The absorbing questions treated here with an appealing circumstantiality, as if it were the first time they had ever been raised, had occupied me ever since my initial association with Lehrs in Paris, just as they occupy the mind of every serious and imaginative person, yet my interest in them, while continual, had not been incessant, and I had on the whole contented myself with the poetic animadversions on the subject which are to be found here and there in the works of our great writers. The frankness which Feuerbach finally finds the courage to adopt in the mellower parts of his book, in treating these deeply interesting questions, pleased me greatly, as much for its tragic implications as for its social radicalism. I found it elevating and consoling to be assured that the sole authentic immortality adheres only to sublime deeds and inspired works of art. But it was a bit more difficult for me to maintain my interest in *The Essence of Christianity* by the same author, as the reading of it, willy-nilly, would not allow me to ignore the sprawl and rather unhelpful prolixity in the development of the simple basic idea, the interpretation of religion from a purely psychological standpoint. Nonetheless, Feuerbach became for me the proponent of the ruthlessly radical liberation of the individual from the bondage of conceptions associated with the belief in traditional authority, and the initiated will therefore understand why I prefaced my book *The Art-Work of the Future* with a dedication and an introduction addressed to him. My friend Sulzer, a well-schooled Hegelian, was vexed to see me so involved with Feuerbach, whom he did not count as a philosopher at all. The only good thing about it, he opined, was that Feuerbach had awakened ideas in me, whereas he himself had none. But what had really induced me to attach so much importance to Feuerbach was his conclusion, which had led him to abandon his original master, Hegel: namely, that the best philosophy is to have no philosophy at all, a theory whereby the study of it, which had hitherto deterred me, became immeasurably easier for me; and in addition, there was his conclusion that the only reality was that which the senses perceived. The fact that he proclaimed what we call "spirit" to lie in our aesthetic perceptions of the tangible world, together with his verdict as to the futility of philosophy, was what afforded me such useful support in my conception of a work of art which would be all-embracing while remaining comprehensible to the simplest, purely human power of discernment, that is, of the drama made perfect at the moment of its realization of every artistic intention in "the art-work of the future"; and this must have been what was on Sulzer's mind when he spoke deprecatingly of Feuerbach's influence on me. Admittedly, after only a short time it became impossible for me to return to his works, and I recall that one of his books appearing shortly thereafter entitled *On the Essence of Religion* scared me off by the monotony of its title alone to such an extent that, when Herwegh opened its pages in front of me, I closed the book with a bang before his very eyes.

Meanwhile, I was working with great dedication on a more coherent draft of my literary effort, and was very pleased one day to read the chapter on poetry to the father of my young friend Bülow, Eduard von Bülow, the author of novellas and disciple of Tieck, who had arrived in Zürich and paid me a visit in my little room. In so doing I noticed that he was greatly startled at my radical views on literary drama and on the Shakespeare to which every age had to give birth anew. All the better, I hoped, would be the reception the bookdealer Wigand would accord this new revolutionary book, and all the higher the honorarium, in accordance with its greater length. I asked for twenty louis d'or, and that, for the moment, was the sum that I was – promised.

These anticipated proceeds were counted on to help me carry out the plan necessity had at last forced upon me of going once again to Paris to try my luck as an operatic composer. But this plan had some very serious drawbacks: not only did I really loathe the idea, but I also realized that I was being dishonest with myself in doing it, because it was perfectly clear to me that I would never be truly serious about the enterprise. But everything combined to make me agree at least to attempt such a venture; Liszt in particular pressed me once more to take what seemed to him my only path to renown, and reopen the negotiations which had been set up in the previous summer by Belloni. How earnestly I tried to believe in the feasibility of this project I demonstrated by drafting a comprehensive sketch for an opera text, which the French poet[1] would only have to put in verses for me, as I could never remotely consider simply setting to music some subject he himself had invented and turned into a libretto. For this purpose I chose the legend of Wieland the Smith, which had figured so prominently in the last part of the book I had just completed, *The Art-Work of the Future*, Simrock's treatment of the subject from the Wilkyna-saga having attracted me greatly. I sketched a complete scenario with precise indications of the dialogue for all three acts, and decided I could now send it off with a sigh to my Parisian author for adaptation. Liszt thought he had found a way to make my music known in Paris through an arrangement he had made with Seghers, the conductor of the "Concerts de Ste Cécile" which were given in those days. In January of the new year he was supposed to perform the *Tannhäuser* overture, and it now seemed desirable that I be there in person for this event. My lack of funds remained a serious obstacle to the undertaking, but now unexpected support came from another quarter. I had tried to drum up some help from every former friend at home, but in vain. In particular, the family of my brother Albert, whose daughter was now embarked on a brilliant theatrical career, treated me in the manner of a diseased person being shunned for fear of contagion. In contrast, I was now moved by the discovery of the dedicated support of the Ritter family, who had remained behind in Dresden, and whom I had previously known only fleetingly through young Karl. Notified of my financial position by my old friend Heine, Frau Julie Ritter, the venerable matron of the family, had at once felt obligated to transmit to me through a business friend the sum of five hundred talers. At the same time I received a letter from that same Mme Laussot who had visited me the previous year in Dresden, and who now evinced her continued sympathetic interest in me in touching words that it did me good to read. These were the first symptoms of the new phase my life was about to enter, in which I accustomed myself to look upon the outward circumstances of my existence as a product of my inner dispositions, and which was to lead me out of the circle of narrow domesticity surrounding me up to then. This help had a bitter element in it for me at the time, as it deprived me of any excuse I might have been inclined to use for not undertaking the Paris project. When I nonetheless suggested to my wife that, on the basis of this favorable change in our finances, we might content ourselves with remaining in

Zürich after all, she flew into a rage about my weakness and vacillation; she declared that if I didn't make a truly serious attempt to accomplish something in Paris, she would give up hope for me and would no longer look on while I went down the drain as a miserable writer and conductor of obscure concerts in this town. We had entered upon the year 1850, and my trip to Paris, which I had finally decided to undertake if only to get some peace, was now further delayed by my bad health. The effects of the terrible excitements of the recent past had not failed to strain my overwrought nerves, and subsequent reaction to this protracted strain had produced complete exhaustion. The continual colds, resulting from the unhealthy quarters in which I was compelled to sit at my work, produced some disquieting symptoms. Chest pains developed, which my doctor, a political refugee, felt obliged to combat by application of pitch plasters: as a result of these and their exacerbating effect on my nerves, I lost the ability to speak in a normal tone of voice for a protracted period; yet the verdict remained that I must be off. When I was supposed to go out to purchase my coach tickets for the journey, I felt so weak that I collapsed in a heavy sweat and turned back to consult with my wife as to whether it would not be better in these circumstances to give up the journey after all. Yet she saw, perhaps rightly, that there was nothing really dangerous in my condition, that much of it was in the mind, and that if I could only get to where I was supposed to go I would soon feel better. An inexpressibly bitter sensation already assailed my nerves when I left the house with despairingly quick strides to go to the post office to pick up the fateful ticket. And so in the first days of February I actually departed for Paris, but with strange emotions which, even if they included hope, nourished it from a quite different region of my inner being and certainly not from any belief in my success in Paris as an opera composer, imposed upon me externally as it was.

My first worry was to find a noise-free apartment, which from now on became one of the most important criteria each time that I selected a place to live. The coachman, who had to drive me through street after street in the most distant sections of the city, and whom I was at length obliged to admonish that everything was still much too noisy for me to dwell in peace there, reproached me with the assertion that nobody comes to Paris to live in a monastery. I finally found a way out of the dilemma by hunting in one of the *cités*, where there was no vehicular traffic, and at last found in the Cité de Provence, Rue de Provence, two rooms to rent. True to the plan imposed, I first went to see Seghers about the proposed performance of the *Tannhäuser* overture. My belated arrival, it soon turned out, had not caused me to miss anything, as there was a good deal of head-scratching going on as to how to procure the orchestral parts for the overture. I had to write to Liszt, order the copying, and await the shipment. Belloni was not around; nothing could be accomplished, and I again had time to ruminate upon the purpose of my Parisian stay, to the accompaniment of the barrel-organs which beset my *cité*. I had trouble convincing an agent of the Ministry of the Interior, who promptly presented himself to inquire about that very purpose, in view of my dubious status as a political refugee, that I was here for purely artistic purposes. Fortunately, he was sufficiently impressed by my score, which I held before his nose, as well as by Liszt's article about the *Tannhäuser* overture published in the *Journal des Débats* the previous year, to leave with the polite invitation calmly and diligently to continue my peaceful undertaking, in which the police would not disturb me in the slightest.

I also looked up my older Paris acquaintances again. I met Semper in the hospitable home of Despléchin, where he was trying to make the best of his difficult situation with an assortment of menial artistic tasks. He had left his family behind in Dresden, from where we received only the most horrendous news. The prisons there were beginning to fill up gradually with the unhappy victims offered up by the recent Saxon movement. We could learn nothing of Röckel, Bakunin and Heubner, apart from the fact that they had been charged with high treason and could expect the death sentence. Various reports about the brutal cruelties visited upon the prisoners by the military made us recognize our present position as indeed fortunate notwithstanding. My relations with Semper, whom I saw frequently, were generally enlivened by a sort of reckless humor; he was determined upon a reunion with his family in London, where he had been told he might receive several commissions. My latest literary works and their salient thoughts interested him very much; this gave rise to animated conversations in which Kietz also participated, at first to our amusement but in time to Semper's irritation. I had found Kietz literally in the same position I had left him many years before: he still couldn't get anywhere with his brushes and had really been hoping that the revolution would have produced a more decisive outcome, as he would have liked to escape from his painful indebtedness to his landlord in the favorable climate resulting from a general collapse. Yet he managed to produce quite a nice pastel portrait of me, done in his earliest manner; on this occasion I was unfortunately obliged to explain the art-work of the future to him and thus caused a confusion that lasted for many years, as he got the idea that he should henceforth make propaganda for my ideas everywhere, even at those bourgeois Parisian homes where he was always welcome at the dinner table. Beyond that, he was still the same old loyal and good-hearted fellow, and even Semper had to learn to bear him with a smile. I also ran to earth my old friend Anders, by now much aged. Finding him was always rather difficult as, when not sleeping, he was holed up in the library, where he could not receive anybody, dozed away his leisure hours in the reading room, and usually took his supper at the house of one of the families where he gave piano lessons. Yet I was very pleased to find him in much better shape than I had been able to hope for at my previous departure from Paris, when he seemed destined to waste away as a consumptive. Curiously enough, the fact that he broke his leg had contributed substantially to the restoration of his health; his treatment had involved a stay at a hydropathic establishment that had been highly beneficial for his health in general. His one thought was to see me achieve a great success in Paris, and he was particularly anxious to make certain that he would have a specially comfortable seat at the first performance of whatever work I would produce, because, as he continually repeated, it was always very trying for him to occupy a place where he could be squeezed by the crowd. He didn't really see the use of my current literary activities; yet these again became my sole occupation, as I was soon informed that there wouldn't even be a performance of the *Tannhäuser* overture. Liszt had procured and sent the orchestral parts with great celerity; yet M. Seghers now explained to me that he and his orchestra formed a democratic republic with everyone having an equal vote, and they had elected to do without my overture for the rest of the winter season. This turn of events was enough to bring home to me how miserable my situation was. In addition, the fruits of my writings were hardly more encouraging; a copy of Wigand's edition of *The Art-Work of the Future* reached me, and I found it teeming with horrible typographical errors; instead of the fee of twenty louis d'or I had expected, my publisher told me he could pay me only half that amount; he had been, he averred, misled by the initially quick sale of *Art and Revolution* into attributing an unrealistically high commercial value to my writings, and had learned of his mistake through the utter absence of demand for my second brochure, *The Wibelungs*. On the other hand, I received an offer to do some well-paid writing from Adolph Kolatschek,[1] who was also a refugee and was about to bring out a German monthly magazine as an organ of the progressive party. In response to this

435

invitation, I wrote a long essay entitled *Art and Climate*, which, in my view, supplemented ideas already touched upon in my *Art-Work of the Future*. Beyond that, it was only after arriving in Paris that I had worked out my sketch for *Wieland der Schmied* in full. But this work had become entirely useless, and I now wondered grimly what I could write to my wife at home, now that all the desperately needed funds I had recently received had been sacrificed to absolutely no avail. The thought of returning to Zürich was just as distasteful as the thought of staying longer in Paris. My feelings as to the latter alternative were decidedly strengthened by the impressions received from a performance of Meyerbeer's new work *Le Prophète*, which I had not seen before. Rising upon the ruined hopes of new and nobler impulses imparted to all the better sort of people in the past year, I saw in this work of Meyerbeer, the sole tangible result of the initiatives taken by the provisional French government for the encouragement of art, the dawning of a shameful day of disillusionment for the world. I was so sickened by the performance that, although I had unfortunately been seated in the middle of the stalls, I did not shrink from causing the commotion, which one is normally anxious to avoid, attendant upon a member of the audience leaving during the course of an act. When it came to the point in this opera where the celebrated "mother" of the prophet expatiates upon her anguish in the well-known series of trite roulades, I became desperately infuriated that I should be compelled to listen to anything like this. I was never willing to accord this work the slightest attention again.

But what was I to do now? Whereas during the miseries of my first stay in Paris I had been attracted by the South American republics, this time I fixed my longing on the Orient, as a place where I might breathe my last in a manner befitting human dignity, utterly oblivious to the whole modern world. It was in this mood that I now had to answer an inquiry from Mme Laussot in Bordeaux as to how things stood with me. My response was such that it prompted an urgent and friendly invitation to recuperate by spending at least a short time at her home, and to forget all my present worries. Under all the circumstances such an invitation to explore southern regions as yet new to me and to visit people who, while utter strangers, were well disposed toward me, attracted me strongly; I accepted, settled my Paris account, and left by coach via Orléans, Tours, Angoulême, and down the Gironde for this unknown city, where I was received with respect and great warmth in the house of the young wine dealer Eugène Laussot, and so came into the presence of his wife, my compassionate young friend.

Our closer acquaintance, which was now increased by Mme Laussot's mother, Mrs Taylor, led first of all to a closer insight into the quality of the interest devoted to me in so kindly and astonishing a fashion by people who had until then been complete strangers. Jessie, as the young lady was called only in the family circle, had become very intimate with the Ritter family during her lengthy stay in Dresden, and I had no reason to doubt the assurances that a good part of this was traceable to her interest in my works and what was to become of me. Ever since my expulsion from Dresden, and from the time news of my difficult situation had reached the Ritter family, there had been a good deal of discussion between Dresden and Bordeaux as to how I could best be helped. Jessie attributed the initiative in all this solely to Frau Julie Ritter, whose financial circumstances were not comfortable enough to enable her to offer me a sufficient subvention on her own, and who had therefore tried to come to an arrangement with Jessie's mother, the quite wealthy widow of an English lawyer, whose fortune was also the sole support of the young couple in Bordeaux. These negotiations had recently reached the stage that Mrs Taylor could inform me shortly after my arrival in Bordeaux that both families had decided to ask me to accept from them jointly, pending the dawning of better days, an annual subsidy of three thousand francs. My sole concern at this point was to explain to my benefactors how things really stood with me, if I were going to accept this offer. Any further success as an opera composer, in Paris or elsewhere, was out of the question for me; what to do as an alternative I really didn't know; but I was determined, I told them, to preserve myself from the shame of sullying my life with any further attempts to attain such success. I am certainly not wrong in the assumption that only Jessie understood me, and although I was treated with unfailing kindness by the rest of the family, I soon noticed the gulf separating her, as well as myself, from her mother and her husband. While this handsome young man spent most of the day conducting his business, and while the mother was usually prevented by her poor hearing from participating in our conversations, Jessie and I soon established a comity of views on various and decisive questions and reached a degree of great intimacy. About twenty-two years of age at the time, Jessie bore little resemblance to her mother in any respect, from which it appeared that she inherited all her qualities from her father. I learned much that was very appealing about him. The large and multifarious library he had bequeathed to his daughter testified to the singular tastes of this man, who beside his lucrative legal practice sustained a discriminating interest in literature and erudition. Jessie had learned German from him as a child, and she spoke the language with utmost fluency. She had been brought up on *Grimms' Fairy Tales*, and had become very familiar with German poetic literature, just as she was quite naturally at home in English as well as French literature (on which, incidentally, she tended to look down) in a manner according fully with her very good education. Her quick receptivity was astonishing; things which I scarcely hinted at were immediately and apparently precisely comprehended by her. It was the same way with music; she read at sight with great facility and played with significant accomplishment. Having learned in Dresden that I was still looking for the pianist who could play Beethoven's big B flat major sonata for me, she now really surprised me with a superb rendition of this most difficult of all piano pieces. The emotion aroused in me at discovering such an exceptionally natural talent and what it could accomplish was suddenly transformed into anxiety when I heard her sing. Her sharp, shrill, falsetto timbre, in which vehemence but no real feeling was discernible, shocked me so much that I could not refrain from requesting her to give up singing from then on. When playing the sonatas she listened willingly and eagerly to my instructions as to how they should be correctly interpreted, but without quite convincing me that she would ever be able to render them entirely as I would wish. I read her my new literary works, and she seemed able to follow even the most audacious concepts quite easily. She was much moved by my poem for *Siegfrieds Tod*, yet preferred my sketch for *Wieland der Schmied*. She admitted to me later that she preferred to see the reflection of her personal destiny in the helpful role played in Wieland's fortunes by his swan-bride than in Gutrune's position and fate with respect to Siegfried. It followed inevitably that the presence of the other members of the family proved onerous whenever we wanted to converse about these matters. While we were somewhat troubled at having to admit to ourselves that Mrs Taylor would obviously never be able to understand just what was really at stake in helping to protect me, it was particularly painful to me to realize as time passed the utter disharmony prevailing between the young couple, especially in point of their intellectual characteristics. The fact that Laussot had been for some time well aware of his wife's lack of affection for him was evidenced one day when he forgot himself so far as to complain openly and vehemently that she would not even love a child she had conceived by him, and that he therefore considered it fortunate that she had not become a mother. Amazed and saddened, I suddenly beheld an abyss, hidden here, as so often, under the appearance of a tolerably happy marital relationship.

At this moment, and just as my stay was nearing its end after three weeks, a letter from my wife arrived that could not have had a more damaging effect on my state of mind; on the whole she was content with our having found new friends, but she declared that if I did not at once go back to Paris, and do my utmost to get my overture performed, and extract some kind of success from it, she would no longer know what to make of me, and at any rate would not comprehend my returning to Zürich empty-handed. Simultaneously a new horror intensified my mood when I read a newspaper report that death sentences had been pronounced on Röckel, Bakunin and Heubner,[1] and that these sentences would soon be carried out. I wrote to both these first two friends a laconic but at the same time passionate farewell letter, and as I saw no possibility of having this document delivered to the fortress of Königstein, I conceived the idea of sending it to Frau von Lüttichau to be forwarded, for I considered her the only person whose position would permit her to do this, while at the same time possessing enough emotional generosity and spirit of independence to respect my wish, despite all differences of opinion, and make certain it was fulfilled. I was told later that this letter was seized by Herr von Lüttichau, who cast it into the stove. For the moment the impact of this painful news helped lead me to the decision to break utterly with my past, to have nothing more to do with life or art, but simply to place myself, even if under extreme privations, beyond the reach of everybody, no matter where it might be. Of the small allowance granted me by my new friends I intended to allocate half to my wife, and to go off with the other to Greece or Asia Minor, whatever might happen and heaven alone knowing in what form, to try to forget and be forgotten. This I then communicated to her who was now my sole confidante, in particular with the intention of telling her that she would have to explain to my patrons how I proposed to use the income they had offered me. Her reaction to the news seemed to be one of joy, and the decision to embrace a similar destiny seemed to flow easily from the disgust she felt with her own situation in life. This was expressed by hints and words dropped here and there. Without knowing where all this would lead, and without having come to any understanding with her, I left Bordeaux in the last days of April, more agitated than soothed, full of anxiety and regret, in order to return to Paris, stupefied and entirely uncertain as to what to do next.

In miserable shape, exhausted yet irritable from prolonged sleeplessness, I spent a week in the Hotel Valois after my arrival, struggling for composure in my disjointed situation. Even if I had wanted to resume work on the projects that had forced me to come to Paris, I was soon convinced that there was nothing to be done in that area for the time being. My distress at being obliged to waste my energies in a direction utterly distasteful to me, merely to satisfy uncomprehending demands upon me, grew into bitterness. At last I had to respond to my wife's latest communication, and explained to her in a long, friendly but frank document, recapitulating our whole past life together, that I had irrevocably decided to release her from any further share in my fate, as I considered myself entirely incapable of shaping it according to her requirements. Whatever income I now had, or would enjoy in the future, would always be shared equally with her; she should, I implored, accede to this arrangement and accept that the circumstances had now arisen in which, at the time of our first reunion in Switzerland, she had declared she would leave me again. I restrained myself from bidding her a total farewell. I immediately notified Jessie in Bordeaux of this step, but without yet being able to announce any definite plan for my utter escape from the world, as I had to call it, because the means to do it were still too pinched. I received a reply announcing her determination to do likewise, and invoking my protection, under which she intended to place herself as soon as she had fully extricated herself from her present situation. Greatly shocked, I did everything in my power to make her realize that it was one thing for a person like me, in such a miserable and desperate position, to feel justified in cutting himself adrift, but quite another matter for a young lady, whose family circumstances appeared outwardly, at any rate, to be entirely orderly, to decide to break away violently for that one reason which probably no one but I was capable of understanding. With respect to the unconventionality of her resolve, she reassured me that it would be carried out in an inconspicuous way, for at first she planned merely to visit her friends, the Ritter family in Dresden. I felt so overwrought by all this that, before doing anything further, I yielded to a desire for seclusion by going to a place not far from Paris. Toward the middle of April I went to Montmorency, about which I had heard good things, and hunted for a little hiding place. I dragged myself wearily through the still wintry landscape outside the tiny town, and then stepped into the little garden of a *marchand de vin*, seldom patronized by visitors except on Sundays, hoping to refresh myself with bread, cheese and a bottle of wine. Hens clustered around me, with whom I industriously shared my bread; the rooster touched me by his self-sacrificing way of leaving all the food to his hens, despite my throwing it directly to him. The hens grew progressively bolder, flew up onto my table, and shamelessly attacked my victuals; the rooster jumped up after them, and now having noticed that order had collapsed completely, flung himself upon the cheese with an ardor born of long self-denial. Driven from the table by all this fluttering chaos, I was suddenly seized by merriment for the first time in a long while; I laughed aloud and looked up toward the signboard of the inn. There I perceived that my host was named Homo. This seemed to be a hint from fate: I would have to stay here at all costs; I was shown to a very small and narrow bedroom, which I immediately rented. Apart from the bed, it held a rough table and two wicker chairs. I constructed a washstand of sorts from one of them, and on the table spread out a few books, writing materials, and the score of *Lohengrin*. I was almost inclined to heave a sigh of content in these constricted quarters; though the weather remained unfavorable and the leafless trees offered only depressing walks, I nonetheless felt that I had at least found a place where I might be completely forgotten, and might in turn forget all those matters that had caused so much desperate anxiety in the recent past. The old creative instinct bestirred itself; I leafed through my *Lohengrin* score and quickly decided to send it to Liszt, and leave it to him to find a way to get it performed, as best he could. After I had dispatched the score, I really felt my outlawry to be freedom, and I was filled by an indifference as to what would become of me worthy of a Diogenes. So I even invited Kietz to visit me in Montmorency and share the pleasures of rustication. And he actually came, just as formerly to Meudon; only this time he found my establishment even more modest than before. Yet he was quite prepared to take pot luck and sleep on an improvised bed, and vowed to himself, upon his return to Paris, to keep me in contact with the world. I was abruptly roused from this condition by news that my wife had arrived in Paris and was looking for me. I had to do battle with myself for a painful hour as to what decision I was to take: I decided not to permit the step I had taken in regard to her to be interpreted as an ill-considered and pardonable vagary of temperament, and left Montmorency at once, went to Paris, summoned Kietz to my hotel, and instructed him to conceal from my wife, who had already been trying to hunt him down, that he knew anything more of me other than that I had left Paris. At this the poor fellow, who for his part could not restrain himself from pitying Minna as much as I did, became utterly bewildered, and declared he felt like "the axis on which all the world's misery turned". Yet he seemed to have a real sense of the seriousness and significance of my decision and succeeded in carrying out his by no means easy task shrewdly and tactfully. I left Paris that night by rail, to travel via Clermont-Tonnerre, where I was obliged to spend some time, to Geneva, where I intended to wait a while for news from Frau Ritter in Dresden. My exhaustion was so great that I could not think of undertaking a longer journey at the moment, even if I were to be provided with the necessary funds. To gain time to await further developments, I withdrew to Villeneuve, at the other end of Lake Geneva, where I put up at the Hotel Byron, which was still quite empty at this time of year. There I learned that Karl Ritter, as he had previously notified me, had arrived in Zürich to spend some time with me there. Impressing upon him the need for absolute secrecy, I summoned him to me at Lake Geneva, where we were reunited in the second week of May in the aforementioned Hotel Byron. He pleased me by his utter devotion, quick perception of my situation and of the necessity of my decisions, as well as by his readiness to accept whatever arrangements I made, without lengthy argument, even when they affected him. He was full of my recent publications, talked about the vivid impression they had made on his acquaintances, and thereby prompted me to use the few leisure days at my disposal to prepare for publication an edition of my poem for *Siegfrieds Tod*. I gave it a short foreword, in which I commended the poem to the attention of my friends as a relic of the time when I had hoped to devote myself to purely artistic works, and particularly to the composition of music. I sent this manuscript once again to Herr Wigand in Leipzig, who returned it to me a short while later with a comment to the effect that, if I insisted upon having it printed in Roman type, he would not be able to sell a single copy. I learned later that he had stubbornly refused to pay the additional ten louis d'or he owed me for *The Art-Work of the Future* and which I had instructed him to remit to my wife.

Disappointing as things remained in that area, I was still not able to think of getting back to work because, only a few days after Karl's arrival, the realities of life again made the most serious assault on my peace of mind in an unexpected manner. I received a wildly agitated letter from Mme Laussot, informing me that she had not been able to avoid disclosing her intentions to her mother, who promptly assumed that this was all my doing. As a result of her passing on this information to M. Laussot, he was now swearing to hunt me high and low and put a bullet through my head. I now realized where I was at, and decided to go to Bordeaux at once to set things straight with my antagonist. First and foremost I sat down and wrote a long letter to M. Eugène, to put the matter in the right light, and, naturally, I did not omit to express to him my amazement that a man could bring himself to attempt to bind a woman to him by force, when she wanted nothing more to do with him. In closing, I advised him that I would be arriving in Bordeaux at the very same time as this letter, and immediately upon my arrival would notify him of the hotel in which he could find me; beyond that, I specified that his wife should remain unaware of the step I was taking, and he could thus act according to his own lights in the matter. As was only too true, I did not conceal from him that I was undertaking the journey under considerable additional difficulties, inasmuch as I did not feel I even had the time to get a visa from the French embassy to make my passport valid for entry into France. At the same time I wrote a few lines to Mme Laussot, in which I appealed to her to maintain calm and composure, but true to my vow gave her no hint whatever of a change in my whereabouts. (When I told Liszt the whole story many years later, he expressed the view that I had acted very stupidly in not notifying the wife at the same time about my intention.) Meanwhile, I took leave of Karl that same evening, in order to leave the following morning from Geneva upon what was then a very arduous journey through the heart of France. At that stage I felt myself so utterly exhausted I could not help thinking that I would soon be dead. I wrote that night to Frau Ritter in Dresden in that frame of mind, telling her briefly of the incredible difficulties I had gotten into. In fact I did have great trouble with my passport at the French border; I had to give my precise destination, and it required my assurance that urgent family matters drew me there to convince the officials to make an exception in my case. I traveled via Lyon and through the Auvergne by *diligence* for three full days and two nights before reaching Bordeaux, which I finally saw spread out beneath me from a neighboring height, in the first gray of a mid-May morning, illuminated by a major fire that had broken out there. I stopped at the Hotel Quatre Soeurs, wrote a note to M. Laussot at once, and told him I would not leave the hotel until I had heard from him. It was about nine o'clock in the morning when I sent him this note; I waited vainly for results until late in the afternoon, when I got a summons from the police station, to go there immediately. I was first asked whether my passport was in order; I disclosed the difficulty in which I had placed myself in that respect, and that an urgent family matter had compelled me to do so. In response I was advised that it was precisely on account of the family matter that had brought me there that I could not be permitted to remain in Bordeaux. In answer to my queries, they did not conceal from me the fact that this action against me had been undertaken at the specific instigation of the family involved. This extraordinary revelation immediately restored my good humor. When I put it to the police commissaire that surely I could be allowed to spend about two days recovering from the fatiguing trip before starting back, he granted my request most affably, inasmuch as he was able to assure me that I would not be meeting the family, since it had already left Bordeaux that noon. In fact I used those two days to recuperate, and also to compose a lengthy letter to Jessie, in which I described all that had happened in great detail, without hiding my contempt for a man who would sacrifice the honor of his wife by a denunciation to the police. I told her I considered this so reprehensible that I could not consider any kind of relationship with her until she had extricated herself from those shameful circumstances. The next thing was to see this letter safely delivered; the information given me by the police was insufficient to let me know what had happened in the Laussot family, and whether they had left their house only for the day or for a longer period. I decided simply to go to the house myself; I rang the doorbell, and the door flew open; without meeting a soul, I stepped into the open ground floor, went from room to room until I reached Jessie's sitting room, found her work-basket and placed the letter into it; thereupon I went calmly back the same way without running into anybody. I received no sign of life in reply, and set out upon my return journey as soon as the period I was allowed to stay had expired. The fine May weather refreshed me, and the clear waters as well as the charming name of the Dordogne, along whose banks the mail coach traveled for some time, gave me great pleasure. I was also entertained by the conversation of two traveling companions, an officer and a priest, about the necessity of doing away with the French Republic, wherein the priest showed himself much more humane and liberal than the military man, who emitted only the one refrain: "Il faut en finir." I also had a chance to look at Lyon more closely, and in walking around the city tried to evoke the scenes in Lamartine's *Histoire des Girondins* so vividly describing the siege and surrender of the town during the period of the Convention Nationale.

After returning to Geneva, and finally to the Hotel Byron, I was met by Karl Ritter with good news from his family. His mother had reassured him immediately as to the state of my health, asserting that people with nervous troubles tend to see death at hand all the time, and that there was thus no reason to yield to fears about me. In addition, she had told him of her intention to look us up in Villeneuve within a few days, together with her daughter Emilie. This news heartened me considerably, and this devoted family, so solicitous for my welfare, seemed sent by Providence to lead me to the new life I so deeply longed for. Both ladies arrived in time to celebrate my thirty-seventh birthday on May 22nd. The mother, Frau Julie, made a particularly profound impression on me. I had met her only once before, in Dresden, when Karl had invited me to be present at the performance of a quartet of his own composition being given at his mother's house; I had been agreeably struck by the respect and devotion displayed whenever the members of the family met. The mother had spoken little that evening, but when it was time for me to leave, she thanked me for my visit with tears in her eyes. I was unable to fathom this at the time, but she now told me, in surprise at my query, that this had been the result of her emotion at my unexpected kindness to her son. The ladies spent about a week with us; we sought diversion in excursions into the lovely valley of Valais, but did not succeed in dispelling Frau Ritter's great anxiety both at the most recent events, about which she now learned, and at the shape my personal destiny had assumed. I later learned that it had cost this delicate woman, who suffered from her nerves, an extreme effort to decide to undertake this journey, and when I urged her to bring her family to live in Switzerland in order to be united with me, it was finally intimated to me that I ought not to conclude from this one undertaking, which was quite out of the ordinary for her, that she possessed reserves of strength which in fact were no longer hers. For the moment she commended to me her son, whom she wanted to leave in my care, and gave me the funds to maintain myself at his side for a time. As to her personal wealth, she told me that this was limited, and now that it was no longer possible to share the expense with the Laussot family, she was worried as to how she could possibly provide enough help to sustain my independence. After a week we took leave with great emotion of this worthy woman, who then started back to Dresden with her daughter, and whom I have since then never seen again.

Still bent on discovering some way or other to disappear from the world, I thought of choosing the wildest possible mountainous spot, where I could withdraw with Karl. For this purpose we selected the lonely Visp valley in the Canton of Valais; with considerable difficulty we made our way over paths that had hardly yet been cleared to Zermatt. There, at the foot of the immense and marvelously beautiful Matterhorn, we could indeed consider ourselves isolated from the rest of the world. I tried to make us as comfortable as possible in these innocent wilds; but all too soon I noticed that Karl could not reconcile himself to these surroundings. He confessed to me on the second day that he really found it ghastly here and thought it would certainly be more bearable beside one of the lakes. We studied the map of Switzerland and chose Thun for our next destination. Unfortunately, I too found myself again reduced to an alarming state of nervous prostration, in which the slightest physical exertion caused heavy and enervating perspiration. Only by an extreme act of will was I able to make my way back out of the valley; yet with renewed courage we at length reached Thun, where we rented a couple of modest but pleasant rooms overlooking the main road, and there sat down to wait and see if we would like it there. Despite a reserve that still betrayed his prior shyness, I found my young friend's conversation continually appealing and stimulating; this was especially true when I realized the fluency and vivacity to which he could attain, particularly at night before retiring, when he would squat beside my bed and, in the agreeable, pure dialect of German Baltic provinces, give free expression to whatever had excited his interest. I was exceptionally cheered during the time we spent there by the chance discovery of a copy of the *Odyssey*, which I reread for the first time in a long while. Homer's long-suffering hero, always homesick yet condemned to perpetual wandering, and nonetheless continually prevailing over all obstacles, was an image highly sympathetic to my soul. This peaceful state was shattered almost immediately by a letter arriving for Karl from Mme Laussot. He didn't know if he should show it to me, as he concluded Jessie must have gone out of her mind. I snatched the document from him and found that the young woman had felt herself obliged to let my friend know that she had learned enough about me to forgo any further dealings with me. I afterwards discovered, chiefly through the help of Frau Ritter, that in consequence of my letter and my arrival in Bordeaux, M. Laussot, together with Mrs Taylor, had immediately whisked Jessie away to the country, intending to remain there with her until news was received of my departure, for the acceleration of which they had appealed to the police department. There, it seems, concealing my letter and my journey to Bordeaux from her, they had prevailed upon the young woman to promise to take no action for a year, to give up her visit to Dresden, and above all to cease all correspondence with me; since they assured her that, if these conditions were fulfilled, she would be completely at liberty at the end of that period, she decided that she ought to give her word to that effect. But immediately the two conspirators set to work to slander me with great efficiency on all sides, and finally blackened me in the eyes of the young woman as well. It was generally believed that

446

I had been the instigator of a kind of abduction. Mrs Taylor had turned to my wife with a lament about my "intended adultery", expressing her sympathy and offering her support; poor Minna, who now inevitably attributed my decision not to return to her to a reason she had not previously suspected, wrote back to Mrs Taylor complaining about me. In all this a curious misunderstanding, twisted into an intentional lie on my part, played a large role: in the course of a playful conversation, Jessie had once told me she didn't belong to any formal religious denomination, because her father had been a member of a particular sect which baptized according to neither the Catholic nor the Protestant rite; at this I had consoled her with the remark that I had come into contact with far more dubious sects, for shortly after my wedding I learned that it had been solemnized by a bigot. God knows in what form this got back to the worthy English matron, but at any rate, she had reported to my wife that I had stated I was not legally wedded to her. In any case, my wife's response to this had no doubt furnished enough material to poison Jessie's mind against me; and it was to this I owed her peculiar letter to my friend. I must admit that, with this insight into the matter, I was at first upset only by the mistreatment of my wife; and while I was perfectly indifferent to what the rest of them thought of me, I at once accepted Karl's offer to go to Zürich, seek out my wife, and explain things in a way that would restore her peace of mind. While I was awaiting his return, I received a letter from Liszt telling of the decisive impression, not only as to his view of me but also with regard to my future, made upon him by a close inspection of the score of my *Lohengrin*. He notified me immediately that, inasmuch as I had already given him permission to do so, he intended to bend every effort to commence preparations for a performance of my work in celebration of the forthcoming Herder festival in Weimar. At almost the same time Frau Ritter wrote to urge me, with respect to the recent events she now fully understood, not to take the matter too seriously; she had already found it difficult, she said, to hide her real feelings about it during the time we spent together in Villeneuve; she had come to know the young lady so well on previous occasions, she added, that she had realized immediately upon learning of my acquaintanceship with her that, whereas I might think I had made an imprint on her heart, I had really made a mark solely on sand, where it would soon be entirely obliterated. Then Karl came back from Zürich and spoke with great warmth about the attitude of my wife. After failing to find me in Paris, he said, she had pulled herself together admirably, had rented and furnished a noise-free apartment on the lake at Zürich according to my previous prescription, and had remained there in the hope of finally hearing from me again. Beyond this, he had much to tell me of the good sense and amiability of Sulzer, who had stood by my wife with great sympathy. Suddenly Karl exclaimed: "Ah, these are real people. Who can do anything with a crazy Englishwoman like that?" To all this I said not a word, but at length asked him with a smile whether he would really prefer to move to Zürich. He jumped up. "Oh yes! Better today than tomorrow!" "Have it your way", I said, "let's pack; I don't see much point in anything, whether here or there." Without uttering another word about all these things, we left the next day for Zürich.*

* In the margin of the manuscript, in Wagner's hand: "End of Part II".

PART THREE

1850–61

Minna had been lucky enough to locate a dwelling in Zürich corresponding very closely to the wishes I had expressed so emphatically before
my departure. This was in the community of Enge, about fifteen
minutes' walk from the city of Zürich, on a plot of ground directly at
the lakeside, and in an old-fashioned house called The Evening Star
belonging to a pleasant old lady named Frau Hirzel. The top floor, which
was quite self-contained and very quiet, offered us scanty but adequate
accommodations for a modest rent. I arrived there early one morning,
found Minna still in bed, and while she was very anxious to make certain
that I had not come back to her merely out of pity, I soon succeeded
in convincing her never to try to discuss what had happened with me
again. As a matter of fact, she was quite in her own element as she showed
me all the progress she had made in settling in; and since we now entered
upon a period when our external circumstances began on the whole to
pick up as the years passed, even though various difficulties brought
occasional setbacks, our domestic life was soon marked by a tolerable
happiness, even though I could never from now on quite suppress an
uneasy, often vehement inclination to break away from everything
accustomed.

Our two pets, Peps and Papo, meanwhile made an extraordinarily
effective contribution to our domestic ease; both were vastly fond of me,
often to the point of becoming a nuisance: Peps would always lie behind
me on my chair while I was working, and Papo would often come
fluttering into my work-room, after vainly summoning me by calling the
name "Richard", if I remained away from the living room too long. He
would then settle down on my desk and vigorously ruffle my pens and
papers. He was so well trained that he never emitted a true bird-sound,
but rather expressed himself only in speech and song. As soon as he heard
my steps on the staircase, he would begin whistling the great march
theme of the final movement of the C minor Symphony, the beginning
of the Eighth Symphony, or even a festive theme from the *Rienzi* overture.
Our little dog Peps, on the other hand, was a highly nervous creature;
my friends used to call him "Peps the Excited", and there were times
when no one could throw him a friendly word without causing him fits
of howling and whining. These pets were obvious substitutes for the
children we lacked, and the fact that my wife shared an almost passionate
devotion to them constituted a not unimportant bond between us. A
continual source of bickering, on the other hand, was the conduct of my
wife toward the unfortunate Nathalie. In bizarre shamefacedness, she
concealed from the girl to her dying day that she was her daughter.

Nathalie, in turn, held herself to be Minna's sister the whole time, and as such could not comprehend why she was not treated as an equal. Just as Minna always assumed the authority of a mother, she also indulged herself in continual exasperation at the failings in the way Nathalie had grown up; she had been neglected in her formative years, at least, and her physical and her mental development alike had been stunted: short and inclined to be stout, she was clumsy and slow-witted. Though she was by nature placid, Minna's hot temper and increasingly brusque and scornful treatment made the girl stubborn and spiteful, so that the behavior of the two purported sisters toward each other gave rise to the most frightful disturbances of our domestic peace and quiet, while my patience was sustained only by my inner indifference to all personal relationships in my surroundings.

At first the presence of my young friend Karl enlivened our little household in a pleasant way; he occupied a tiny attic room above our apartment and shared our meals, as well as my walks, and for a time seemed quite content with it all. But I soon noticed a growing uneasiness in him; he had been given ample opportunity to recognize, from the unpleasant scenes that again became daily occurrences in our married life, where the shoe was pinching me that I had put on again in patient compliance with his wishes. He remained silent one day, when I had cause to remind him that what had prevailed upon me to come back to Zürich was not the hope of a pleasant family life. Beyond this, I noted another and stranger cause for his disquiet: his attendance at our meals was highly irregular, and he never seemed to have any real appetite, something which at first made me fear he might have found our modest repasts unappetizing, until I finally discovered that my young friend was so excessively devoted to the pastries sold in the local bakeries that I had reason to believe he might even injure his health by his inordinate consumption of these products. My remarks about this seemingly annoyed him greatly; for henceforth he remained away from the house for protracted periods, and so I soon came to the conclusion that, inasmuch as he didn't like his little lodgings, there was no point in my trying to prevent his looking for an apartment in the city.

As I saw that he was increasingly uneasy, I was glad to be able to offer him a significant respite in a stay that he obviously found unsatisfactory: I persuaded him to undertake an excursion to Weimar to attend the performance of *Lohengrin* scheduled to take place there at the end of August. At the same time, I invited Minna to accompany me on our first expedition to the Rigi, which we both ascended robustly on foot.

Unfortunately, I noticed on this occasion, in the wake of her exertions, the first symptoms of the heart trouble which was to develop ever more pronouncedly from now on. We spent the evening of August 28th, on which the first performance of *Lohengrin* was given in Weimar, in Lucerne in the Swan tavern, watching the clock and closely following the hour of its beginning and presumed end. But there were always some elements of worry, discomfort, and irritation whenever I tried to spend such pleasantly animated hours in the company of my wife. The reports I got as to the initial performance were, moreover, not such as to afford me any clear and reassuring picture of it. Karl Ritter soon came back to Zürich; he told me in particular of scenic deficiencies in the performance, as well as of a highly unfortunate casting of the title role, yet on the whole of a successful outcome. Liszt's reports were the most encouraging: he did not seem to think it necessary to go into the inadequacy of the resources at his disposal in such an audacious undertaking, but rather preferred to dwell on the spirit of the venture and its effect on the more receptive members of the audience, some of them people of consequence, whom he had invited with great care and attention.

While everything that ensued from this significant event gradually assumed a brighter aspect, its immediate impact on my situation was very slight. My most direct concern was what was to become of the young friend who had been entrusted to my supervision: on his trip to Weimar he had seen his family again, and immediately upon his return revealed to me his anxious desire to embark upon a career as a musician, and if possible, obtain an appointment as conductor in a theater. Up to then I had never had an opportunity to judge his musical aptitude; he refused to play the piano in my presence, yet he had nonetheless placed before me his musical setting to an alliterative poem of his own entitled *Die Walküre*, and although its execution was undeniably awkward, it evidenced thorough knowledge of the rules of composition. In it he showed himself clearly a pupil of Robert Schumann, who had told me long before that Karl possessed great musical gifts, and that he could not recall any other pupil with such a good ear and rapid power of comprehension. I thus had no reason to question his confidence that he had the necessary qualifications for a conductor. Now that the winter season was approaching, I inquired as to the whereabouts of the director of the theater that we were expecting to open in Zürich, and learned that he still had his being in Winterthur at the time. Sulzer, who was always ready with the most useful help or advice whenever needed, arranged a meeting with this Herr Kramer at a dinner in the Wild Man tavern in Winterthur, where it was then arranged, upon my recommendation, that Karl Ritter would be engaged as Music Director for the ensuing winter, starting in October and at a good salary to boot. As my protégé was confessedly a beginner, I naturally had to provide a guarantee for him, which I furnished through an unconditional undertaking to step in for him as conductor as soon and for as long as any inadequacies on his part caused any disruption in the conduct of the theater's business. Karl seemed quite content. As October drew near and the opening of the new season was announced as being "under fresh artistic initiatives", I finally considered it necessary to give some attention to my young friend with regard to his new post. To give him a very familiar work for his debut, I had chosen *Der Freischütz*. Karl had not the slightest qualms about his ability to master such a simple score; but when he was required to overcome his shyness with regard to playing the piano and go through the opera with me at this instrument, I was greatly shocked to discover that he had no idea of proper accompaniment, but played the piano score with the abandon characteristic of a dilettante, who doesn't mind lengthening a bar by a whole beat to compensate for a fingering difficulty. He also hadn't the remotest idea of rhythmic precision or knowledge of tempo, the crucial requirements in conducting. Since I didn't know what to say to all this, in some stupefaction I let things get as far as an orchestral rehearsal, counting on some incalculable explosion of the young man's talent, and above all else, equipping him for it with a large pair of spectacles; for I had noticed that he was obliged by unsuspected short-sightedness to place his nose so close to the music that he could not possibly keep his eyes on the singers or the orchestra. I only needed to see this strange and, until that moment, so uncommonly self-confident young man as he stood at the conductor's desk, staring fixedly at the score despite his conspicuous ocular weaponry, and waving his baton about mechanically, as if in a dream, while beating time for a measure he was murmuring to himself, to realize that I would have to perform under my guarantee. It was a difficult and wearing task for me to make young Ritter comprehend the necessity for my stepping in for him; but there was nothing else for it, and I had to inaugurate the winter season of Kramer's artistic enterprise by conducting the performance of *Der Freischütz*, the success of which placed me in a curious position toward the theater and the public, which proved hard to escape from.

It was out of the question for Karl to continue in the position of Music Director. But strangely enough, this trying experience coincided with a change in the destiny of another young friend I had known in Dresden, Hans von Bülow. I had met his father, Eduard von Bülow, in the previous year, when he visited Zürich just after having married again. He had settled down on Lake Constance, and from there I heard from Hans, who had previously announced his intention of visiting me in Zürich, that to his enormous regret he was prevented from fulfilling this most ardent wish. As far as I could see, it was his mother, the now divorced first wife of his father, who was trying by all the means at her disposal to prevent her son from embarking on a career in the arts, hoping to compel him to use the legal studies he had pursued hitherto as a springboard to a career in the civil service or in diplomacy. Yet his inclination and his talent impelled him toward music. It now appeared that his mother, while granting him permission to visit his father, had drummed into him the absolute necessity of avoiding any meeting with me. When I then heard that his father had also advised him not to go to Zürich, I had to conclude, since he had shown me good will otherwise, that he did so as a conciliatory gesture towards his former wife, being reluctant to enter on any new conflict with her when the strife surrounding their divorce was only recently at an end, even if the question of his son's future profession were at stake. I may have erred in this presumption about the father, which aroused a strong feeling of resentment in me; yet the despairing tone of the letter from Hans, clearly demonstrating how deeply he was repelled by the thought of being obliged to enter with open eyes upon a career he found detestable, and so to plunge himself for all time into a conflict that would destroy his soul, was sufficient to serve me as pretext, in the state I was in at that time of being easily aroused to indignation at such forms of compulsion, for intervening in his destiny in my own way. I wrote him a long letter in which I most emphatically pointed out that he was in a particularly critical phase of life. The distracted and desperate tone of the letter in which he had turned to me gave me the right, I felt, to let him know that this was not simply a question of his exterior life but of his whole spiritual and intellectual existence. I advised him what I would do in his situation: if I felt a profound and truly irresistible impulse in my soul toward an artistic career, and if I felt ready to accept the greatest hardships and trials rather than see my life take the wrong course, if anyone would extend a hand toward me, as I now was willing to extend mine toward him, I would embrace my decision with the utmost resolution. If he wished to come to me in spite of his father's injunction, I told him, let him come immediately upon receipt of my letter, and carry out his decision whatever the circumstances. Karl Ritter was happy when I gave him this communication to bring in person to the Bülow country villa. When he got there he summoned his friend out of the house, went off with him into the fields, and gave him my letter to read, whereupon Bülow decided immediately, as he stood there, in the storm and rain of the roughest part of the year, to walk all the way to Zürich, as neither had sufficient money to travel in any other manner. Thus they appeared at my door one day, wild and disheveled, marked by obvious signs of their adventurous journey. Ritter beamed with joy at the success of the expedition, whereas young Bülow evinced a great, even passionate emotion toward me. I at once realized the vast and deep obligation I had assumed with respect to his future, and felt at the same time a truly intimate sense of sympathy with such a highly overwrought young person; both these feelings determined my conduct toward him for a long time to come.

At the outset it was a question of bolstering his confidence by a cheerful demeanor. The external situation was soon put in order: Hans participated as an equal in Karl's contract with the theater management, thereby giving both a salary of sorts, while I remained the guarantor for the work of the two of them. There was a musical comedy to be taken in hand at once; without knowing in advance what this work was all about, Hans stepped up to the conductor's desk and wielded the baton with great surety and gusto. I felt immediately safe as far as he was concerned, and all doubts as to the capacities of the new Music Director were immediately overcome; but it was difficult to dispel Karl's great sense of humiliation, arising from this palpable evidence that he was not suited for a musical career, a revelation that would affect his whole life. From this point onward, in spite of all his other gifts, a growing reserve and secret antipathy toward me became increasingly obvious. It remained impossible to keep him in his position or to let him conduct again. On the other hand, Bülow encountered unexpected difficulties in his position in that the director and his staff, having been spoiled by my conducting at the first performance, felt themselves obliged to impel me to do so repeatedly. I actually conducted on several other occasions, in part to obtain through my authority some credit with the public for this perfectly adequate opera company, and in part to show my young friends, and particularly the eminently qualified Bülow, what was really important in conducting operas. While Hans fulfilled all his tasks so well that I could in good conscience eventually declare myself no longer obligated to step in for him, one very conceited singer, who had been spoiled by my praise, succeeded in making so much trouble for the youthful conductor that I was again compelled to take up the baton. After this state of things had caused me enough irritation, we came to an agreement with the management two months later, liquidating this contractual arrangement. Since Hans was simultaneously offered an unconditional appointment as Music Director in St Gall I sent the two young people off to try their luck in the neighboring town and thus gain time for further developments.

Herr Eduard von Bülow had wisely consented, though with some resentment at me, to the decision of his son; he did not reply to a letter I wrote him in justification of my conduct, but he paid a conciliatory visit to Hans in Zürich. I went several times to see the young men in St Gall during the course of the few winter months they spent there. Karl had again met defeat in an attempt to conduct Gluck's overture to *Iphigenia*, so that I found him lost in dark disgruntlement and without any practical activity, whereas Hans was tremendously busy trying to accomplish something with the abominable personnel, dreadful orchestra and shabby theater. When I saw all this misery, it was soon decided that Hans had for the moment done and learned enough to be confirmed beyond doubt in his calling as a professional musician, in this particular, important aspect of it as an orchestral conductor. It was now a question of finding him a sphere which would give him a more suitable scope for his talents. He told me that his father was about to recommend him to Freiherr von Poissl,[1] at that time the intendant of the Munich Court Theater. But soon his mother intervened with the request that he be sent to Weimar for further study under Liszt. I was certainly in full accord with this proposal; it reassured me vastly to be in a position to commend this young man to whom I felt such a burdensome responsibility to my distinguished friend. At Easter 1851 he left St Gall to spend an extended period under the wing of Weimar, and was thus released from my personal supervision. Meanwhile, Ritter remained behind in sad seclusion in St Gall, undecided whether he should return to me in Zürich, where memories of his failure would haunt him.

My young friends had a more pleasant artistic exercise than St Gall could offer them that winter when they paid a visit to Zürich, where Hans appeared as a pianist in one of the concerts of the local music society, at which I myself conducted a Beethoven symphony, to our mutual encouragement. People had been after me again that winter to participate in some way in the activities of this society; as the existing orchestral resources were very limited, I was induced to offer my support, which was restricted to the performance of Beethoven symphonies, solely upon the condition that some capable musicians, particularly for the string section, would be recruited from outside. As I insisted on at least three rehearsals for each symphony, and as part of the orchestra had to journey to Zürich for this special purpose from a considerable distance, these rehearsals assumed a rather ceremonial character; and inasmuch as the whole period normally spent on one rehearsal was available to me exclusively for the one symphony, I had the time to work out the most delicate details and finest nuances of interpretation, for the purely technical problems were not overly great. Thus I achieved a freedom of execution which had previously eluded me and which I sensed all the more vividly as a result of the unexpected effect it produced. I discovered in the orchestra some truly talented musicians, whom I had uncommon success in training. Among them I would especially mention the first oboist Fries, who had risen from a subordinate position to that rank, and whom I obliged to practise his extremely important parts in the Beethoven symphonies as if they had been written for the voice. When we first performed the C minor Symphony, I induced the strange fellow, who subsequently resigned from the orchestra as soon as I left it, and opened a music shop, to play the little adagio passage at the one fermata of the first movement of this symphony in a moving and meaningful way I have not heard equalled since then. In addition, we possessed in the cultivated Herr Ott-Imhof, a rich patrician and an amateur and patron of the arts, a not very vigorous but extremely soft and lyrical clarinettist. I must also mention the quite estimable Bär, who played the French horn, and whom I appointed head of the brass section, upon whose playing he exerted a very beneficial influence; I cannot remember ever having heard the sustained and mighty chords in the final movement of the C minor Symphony executed with such intense power as at that time in Zürich, and can compare my recollections of it solely with the earliest impressions derived from hearing the orchestra of the Paris Conservatoire playing the Ninth. The performance of the C minor Symphony made a tremendous impact on the audience, and most particularly on my intimate friend Sulzer, who had up to then held himself aloof from music, but who now was carried away to the point of replying to an unwarranted newspaper attack on me with a verse satire worthy of Platen's[1] art. At a second concert, in which I was scheduled to conduct the *Sinfonia Eroica*, Bülow was also invited to perform at the piano, as I have already mentioned. Boldly and in a sense rashly, he chose for this occasion Liszt's brilliant but difficult transcription of my overture to *Tannhäuser*; he created a general sensation with it and amazed me in particular, as I had not paid close enough attention to his astonishing development as a virtuoso, and this aroused in me the greatest confidence in his future. I had already recognized his exceptional abilities in conducting, as well as in accompaniment; during the previous winter there had been ample opportunity for this, apart from those external events in his life to which I have already alluded. My acquaintances would frequently gather at my house; a kind of club was formed among them, with the objective generally being entertainment, in which Bülow played a really indispensable part. I would sing suitable passages from my operas, with Hans accompanying me in a hearteningly understanding manner. On such occasions I also ventured to read from my manuscripts; in a continuing series of evenings I actually read the whole of my lengthy work *Opera and Drama*, written during the course of this winter, before a steadily increasing group of listeners.

As I had secured a certain degree of tranquillity and peace of mind following my return, I began to think of resuming my real work. But it did not occur to me to begin the composition of *Siegfrieds Tod*: the idea of sitting down deliberately to write a score that would never go further than the paper on which it was written repeatedly discouraged me; on the other hand, I felt the continuing desire to lay a foundation for the possibility of performing such a work at some time in the future, even though by an apparently very roundabout route. To do so, it seemed necessary first of all to provide those few acquaintances near and far who were seriously interested in my art with a fuller explanation of those problems demanding solution, which were clear enough to me but still scarcely familiar to them. I was given a special cause to do this when Sulzer showed me one day an article about opera in the current Brockhaus encyclopedia, in the opinion that the views expressed there prefigured my own. A fleeting look at this essay showed me immediately its utterly erroneous nature, and I tried hard to point out to Sulzer the fundamental differences between the accepted views, even of entirely sensible people, and my own conception of the essentials of the matter. Finding it naturally quite impossible, even with all my eloquence, to elucidate these ideas in such short order, I set about preparing a methodical plan for detailed treatment of the subject as soon as I got home. Thus I was led to work out the text of the book published under the title *Opera and Drama*, a job which kept me fully occupied for several months until February 1851. But I had to pay cruelly for the exhausting labor expended on its completion: just a few days before my work would be finished, according to my calculations, my good little parrot, who had usually perched on my desk observing me as I worked, got seriously sick. As the bird had already recovered from several similar attacks, I didn't pay much attention to this one: when my wife asked for me to look up a recommended veterinarian who lived in a distant community, I kept putting it off, in order not to be obliged to leave my desk, from one day to the next. Late one evening I finally was done with the fateful manuscript: on the following morning my good Papo lay dead on the floor. I was completely inconsolable at this sad event, and Minna shared this heartfelt grief; the devotion that we both felt toward our house-pets drew us closer together in a genuine sympathy that was not unimportant for our further life together.

Apart from these domestic pets, our older Zürich friends had remained faithful to us throughout the course of the catastrophe in my family life. Sulzer became without doubt the most important and valuable of these friends. The profound differences between us, both as to intellectual predilections and attributes of temperament, actually seemed to favor our relationship, as we were constantly being surprised at one another, and since the reasons for these surprises were always significant, this gave rise to the most stimulating and instructive experiences. Extremely excitable and of delicate constitution, Sulzer had gone against his original inclinations in entering government service, and had sacrificed his own wishes to the conscientious fulfillment of his official duties in the widest sense. Through his association with me he had been drawn more deeply into the sphere of aesthetic enjoyment than appeared advisable for him. Perhaps his indulgence in this direction would have been more relaxed had I myself not been so serious about art; that I attributed such immense significance to the artistic destiny of mankind, far beyond anything that politics could offer, often made him lose his composure completely; but it was just this great seriousness of mine that attracted him all the more strongly to my viewpoint. As all this led to much more than mere conversation and comfortable discussions, our mutual irascibility often produced the most violent explosions, and so it occasionally happened that, with trembling lips, he would grab his hat and cane and rush away without saying a word of goodbye. It was then nice to see him show up punctually the following evening with both of us having the feeling that nothing had happened. It was only when certain physical infirmities kept him completely cooped up for days on end that it was difficult to deal with him, for he would become infuriated whenever anyone inquired about his health; at such times there was only one way to put him in a good mood: one had to explain that the reason for the visit was to request a personal favor of him; pleasantly surprised, he would then show himself ready not only to perform any such service but also in truly the most cheerful and benevolent mood in the world.

The musician Wilhelm Baumgartner made a striking contrast to him: he was a merry and easy-going fellow without any real aptitude for concentration, who had learned to play the piano just well enough to earn a hand-to-mouth living by giving lessons, and who was easily enthused for aesthetic delights as long as they did not involve too much effort; he was a good fellow, and greatly admired Sulzer, all of which unfortunately could not restrain him from overly frequenting the local bars. Apart from him, there were two other friends of theirs who had also formed a part of our circle from the outset; these were Hagenbuch, the worthy and capable Deputy Cantonal Secretary, and Bernhard Spyri,[1] a lawyer and at that time the editor of the *Eidgenössische Zeitung*, a singularly good-natured man but not over-endowed intellectually, who, for that reason, was sometimes given a rough time by Sulzer. Alexander Müller soon disappeared from our circle, as he was increasingly engulfed by domestic calamity, illness, and the drudgery of giving music lessons. Despite his *When the Swallows Homeward Fly*, I did not feel drawn to the musician Abt;[2] he soon left us anyway, going on to a brilliant career in Brunswick.

Meanwhile, however, Zürich society had been vastly enriched from outside, mainly as a result of the political shipwrecks. On my return in the summer of 1850, I had already found Adolph Kolatschek, a socially not unprepossessing but rather boring man: he felt himself called to be an editor and had founded a German monthly, which was intended to offer those who had been defeated outwardly in the recent movement a forum in which to continue the struggle on the intellectual plane. I felt almost flattered at being singled out by him as an author, as he insisted that in order to unify in such an undertaking as his the requisite intellectual forces, "a power like mine" was indispensable. I had already sent him from Paris the essay *Art and Climate*; now he willingly accepted large fragments of the still unpublished *Opera and Drama*, for which he also paid me very handsomely. He remains in my memory as the only tactful editor I have ever run across; he gave me the manuscript of a review of my *Art-Work of the Future* by a certain Herr Palleske to look through, and declared to me that he would not think of printing it without my consent, which he also did not try to solicit. As I found it a superficial, uncomprehending, yet most arrogantly worded discussion, and knew that if it appeared in this journal I would be obliged to write a lengthy and exhaustive reply further expounding my true ideas – something I was vastly disinclined to do – I agreed to Kolatschek's proposal to return the manuscript to its author for use elsewhere. On the other hand, through Kolatschek I also got to know Reinhold Solger,[1] a truly excellent and interesting person; as it soon became intolerable to his restless and adventurous spirit to remain cooped up in Zürich, he left us and went to North America, where I heard he gave controversial lectures about the European situation. It was certainly sad that this talented man did not succeed in making a greater name for himself with more significant works; his writings for our monthly magazine during the short period he stayed in Zürich clearly belonged among the finest ever produced in this field by a German.

In the new year of 1851, Georg Herwegh also joined the group, and I was surprised to meet him one day in Kolatschek's apartment. The vicissitudes that had driven him to Zürich were brought to my attention only somewhat later and in a rather ugly form; for the present, Herwegh put on a rather aristocratic manner, presenting himself as a child of his times, accustomed to refinement and luxury, a demeanor that gained a particularly elegant, or at least pampered, air from the French expressions he frequently interpolated in his conversation. Yet there was something about his external appearance, his quick, flashing eyes and kindliness of manner which was well calculated to make an attractive impression. I was almost flattered when he gladly accepted my invitation to our rather rustic evening gatherings, which as a matter of fact generally turned out to be quite pleasant, particularly when Bülow was there to enliven things musically, even though they didn't really offer me anything. When I began the readings from my manuscripts, my wife told me that Kolatschek had gone to sleep, and Herwegh had resorted unduly to the punch bowl throughout. When I later read *Opera and Drama* on twelve different evenings to my Zürich friends and their acquaintances, Herwegh stayed away, on the grounds that he did not want to mix with the kind of people for whom such a work had not been written. But my association with him gradually grew more cordial, not only as a result of my regard for his poetic talent, which had been so acclaimed only lately, but also because I perceived in him the delicate and refined qualities of a truly cultivated intellect. In the course of time I found that Herwegh himself began to covet an association with me. My insistent preoccupation with those deeper and more serious interests that so possessed me seemed to arouse an ennobling sympathy even in a man who, as a result of his sudden leap to fame as a poet, had abandoned his original ways to such modish and trivial externalities, much to his disadvantage. Possibly this process was accelerated by the growing difficulties of his situation, which up to then he had believed to demand a good deal of outward show on his part. In short, I found in him at first a discriminating and sympathetic interpreter of my most audacious schemes and views, and soon had good reason to believe his assertion that he was busying himself exclusively with my ideas and more penetratingly than others could do.

This familiarity with Herwegh, in which an element of affection was certainly commingled, was strengthened by communications I was able to make to him regarding a new dramatic poem, with which I began busying myself at the approach of spring. Liszt's production of *Lohengrin* at the Weimar Court Theater the previous autumn had yielded results which no one could possibly have expected, given the modest resources at his command. These could only have been achieved by efforts of such a versatile and abundantly gifted friend as Liszt. While it was beyond his power to attract to Weimar at short notice the kind of singers necessary to do justice to *Lohengrin*, and since many aspects of the performance could only hint at what was really required, he therefore did his utmost to make certain that these hints were fully understood. First of all, he himself wrote a comprehensive report concerning the production of *Lohengrin*; seldom has a written discussion of a work of art won for it such attentive friends, commanding their enthusiastic support from the outset, as did this essay of Liszt, which treated the most delicate nuances of the work. Karl Ritter distinguished himself splendidly by delivering a superb German translation of the French original, which was first published in the *Illustrierte Zeitung*. Soon thereafter, Liszt published his original text in the French language, together with a similar article on *Tannhäuser*, and it was this brochure which, for a long time to come and particularly in foreign countries, aroused surprisingly intense interest, and an intimate knowledge of those works far beyond anything that could have been achieved by incomplete study of the vocal scores. Far from contenting himself with this, Liszt succeeded in attracting to the Weimar performances of my operas a continuing stream of intelligent people from outside such as were capable of hearing and seeing them correctly, in order to draw their attention to them in a friendly but forcible way. While his good intentions did not quite succeed with Franz Dingelstedt,[1] who produced only a rather confused and obviously reluctant review of the work for the *Allgemeine Zeitung*, his eloquent advocacy seems nonetheless to have utterly won over Adolph Stahr to my work. His circumstantial discussion of *Lohengrin* in the Berlin *National-Zeitung*, which attributed immense significance to my work, was clearly not without a lasting effect on the German public. And the narrower circle of professional musicians, too, seems to have been impressed to a not insignificant degree by the unmistakable enthusiasm with which Robert Franz[1] spoke of *Lohengrin*, after Liszt had dragged him to a performance almost by force. These examples had an invigorating influence on many sides, and for a time it looked as if the otherwise so lethargic musical press would concern itself with me in a vital and constructive way. I will soon have occasion to set forth the reasons why this did not happen, and why the movement took an entirely different direction; meanwhile, Liszt felt emboldened by all these favorable signs to encourage me to renew my creative activity, which had been interrupted for several years. His achievement with *Lohengrin* gave him confidence in his ability to undertake an even bolder venture and he asked me to set my poem *Siegfrieds Tod* to music for Weimar. At his instigation, Herr von Ziegesar, the director of the Weimar Court Theater, was obliged to offer me on behalf of the Grand Duke a formal commission to do so: I was supposed to complete the work within one year and be paid five hundred talers for it during this period. It was very curious that at about the same time the Duke of Coburg, also through Liszt, made me an offer of nine hundred talers to handle the instrumentation of an opera to be composed by him, and in fact this generous employer even wanted to invite me, a political outlaw, to his castle in Coburg, where I was to closet myself with him, the composer, and Frau Birch-Pfeiffer,[2] the librettist, and foster the creation of this work. Liszt quite naturally requested of me nothing more than a suitable excuse to reject this commission, and he thought it advisable to suggest that I use "physical and mental indisposition" as grounds for it. My friend later told me that the Duke had been impelled to express a desire for my collaboration in his score especially on account of my skillful use of trombones; when he had inquired of Liszt as to my rules for their use, he had replied my secret was that, before I wrote anything for the trombones, I always had an idea for them in my head.

Yet I felt strongly drawn toward accepting the offer from Weimar. Still weary from my labors on *Opera and Drama*, and exhausted by all kinds of depressing matters, I sat down again for the first time in a long while at my old Breitkopf & Härtel piano, which had been saved from the Dresden catastrophe, in order to try to figure out how to get started on the composition of my weighty heroic drama. I drafted a hasty sketch of the music for the song of the Norns, only hinted at in that initial version of the work; when I also attempted to turn Brünnhilde's first address to Siegfried into song, my spirits sank completely, for I could not help asking myself what singer this time next year could possibly bring this heroic figure of a woman to life. Then I thought of my niece Johanna, whom I had vaguely had in mind for the role in the Dresden days, mainly on account of her physical and vocal gifts. She had meanwhile embarked on her career as a prima donna in Hamburg, and according to all the reports I got, and especially judging by her and her family's quite unabashed indifference toward me, I was obliged to conclude that I must abandon even my modest hopes for her talent. At the same time, I had another misfortune in seeing unceasingly before my mind's eye not Johanna but the second Dresden prima donna, Madame Gentiluomo Spatzer, who had once inspired Marschner to Donizettian dithyrambs, so that I once jumped up furiously from the piano and swore I would never write anything more for such crinolined dodos. Whenever I thought about my being involved with the theater again in the remotest way, I was seized by a fit of indescribable despair I was powerless to withstand. It was almost a reassuring thought that my melancholy mood might be attributable in part to a physical infirmity, for I was surprised that spring by a skin disease which spread over my entire body. My doctor prescribed sulphur baths as a remedy, and I was supposed to take them regularly every morning. However much this treatment exacerbated my nervous condition, compelling me later to adopt the most drastic measures to restore my health, my regular morning walks into the city and back through the burgeoning flowers of May had an initially cheering effect on my disposition. I conceived *Der junge Siegfried*, a heroic comedy to serve as preface to the tragedy *Siegfrieds Tod*. As this inspiration quickened in me I tried to convince myself at once that this piece would be easier to set to music than that other powerful and serious work. I notified Liszt of this my new project and offered the new libretto and the music I would write for *Der junge Siegfried* to the management of the Weimar theater in return for the subvention of five hundred talers for one year, which I now seriously intended to accept. This was agreed upon without hesitation, and I withdrew to the little attic room Karl Ritter had abandoned the previous year in order to attempt, between sulphur and the month of May, to write the poem of *Der junge Siegfried*, which had been part of my original design, in the best of spirits and in the shortest possible time.

I must now give some account of the deeply cordial relationship I had maintained with Theodor Uhlig, the young member of the Dresden orchestra I mentioned earlier, ever since my departure from that city, and which in time evolved into a highly productive and beneficial association. His independent, even rather abrupt manner had been transformed into a warm and almost boundless devotion to me through his close acquaintance with my writings, as well as his personal interest in my fate. He too had been among the audience at the initial Weimar performance of *Lohengrin* and had sent me a very thoughtful and understanding report about it. As the music dealer Härtel in Leipzig had willingly accepted my proposal that he publish *Lohengrin* without paying me any honorarium, I also gave Uhlig the task of producing the vocal score. But it was mainly his concern with the theoretical questions propounded in my writings that kept us in frequent correspondence. I was almost touched by the wholeheartedness with which he, who I knew had received no more than a narrow musical education, grasped and, as a direct consequence of his understanding, adopted views which generally frightened musicians of apparently much wider culture as being dangerous to the practice of their art. He had soon acquired the literary skill to give expression to our concord of views and gave proof of it in a superb, lengthy essay about instrumental music, which was published in Kolatschek's *Deutsche Monatsschrift*. In addition, he sent me another rigorously theoretical work on the construction of musical themes and movements, which has remained unpublished to this day. This evidenced an original grasp and intensive study of the methods employed by Mozart and Beethoven, and particularly of their highly characteristic differences. In its thorough and exhaustive discussion of the subject, it seemed to me to constitute a suitable basis for a new theory of the more advanced aspects of musical structure, through which the mysterious process employed by Beethoven might be fully elucidated and worked out in greater detail to furnish a practical system for further use. His essays had attracted the attention of Franz Brendel, the publisher of the *Neue Zeitschrift für Musik*, who had instinctively recognized his talent. Invited to contribute to this publication, Uhlig soon succeeded in prying Brendel off the fence where he had sat until then, and inducing him, who always remained serious and honest in everything he did, to commit himself once and for all to the so-called "new direction", which was beginning to cause a stir in the musical world at the time. I also found myself contributing what turned out to be a fateful article to that publication. I had noticed that its pages contained a number of such ugly catch-words as "Jewish melismas", "synagogue music", and others, but without any palpable intention of doing more than cause a negligible irritation. I was now attracted by the thought of further investigating the intervention of Jews in modern music and their impact on it, while trying to describe the characteristic aspects of this phenomenon. I did this in a lengthy essay entitled *Judaism in Music*. While I was not disposed to deny, when and if asked, that I was its author, I nonetheless deemed it advisable to sign it with a pseudonym[1] at the outset, in order to avoid by this device having the whole affair, which I took very seriously, dragged down into the realm of petty personalities, thereby obscuring its true significance. The impact made by this article, indeed the real uproar that it caused, probably defies comparison with any other publication of its kind. The unheard-of enmity which has pursued me to this day from the newspapers of Europe is comprehensible only to those who took note of that article and the commotion it caused at the time, and remember now that the newspapers of Europe are almost exclusively in the hands of the Jews. Those who seek the reason for this unceasing and vicious persecution solely in some kind of theoretical or practical disapproval of my views or my artistic works can never get at the truth of the matter. The appearance of the essay caused an immediate storm, which soon was transformed into a concerted action against the innocent Brendel, who was scarcely aware of what he had done, with the ultimate objective of annihilating him. Another immediate result was that the few people who, upon Liszt's promptings, had declared themselves in my favor now wrapped themselves in safe silence, and even withdrew in open animosity after a time, as in any undertakings of their own it appeared highly advisable to demonstrate their dissociation from me. All the more faithful and steadfast, on the other hand, was Uhlig; he encouraged the meeker Brendel in his willingness to stand by me, and helped him continuously with articles for his journal, some of them profound, others witty and pointed. He went after one opponent in particular, a Cologne protégé of Ferdinand Hiller named Bischoff,[2] who had invented the term "Musicians of the Future" to describe my friends and myself, and got into a prolonged and delightful polemical exchange with him. The foundations were thus laid of the issue, soon to grow into a European scandal, of "Music of the Future", a term which Liszt was quick to accept with good humor and a certain pride. I had no doubt initially suggested the expression to its inventors with my *Art-Work of the Future*, but it became a war cry only after *Judaism in Music* had opened the flood-gates of wrath over me and my friends. The publication of *Opera and Drama* came only in the second half of this year, and insofar as its existence was noted by the leading musicians of the time at all, it naturally helped no small amount to further stoke the fury raging against me; yet from then on the opposition increasingly assumed the character of deceit and willful slander, for the movement was henceforth systematically organized by a master of such procedures, Herr Meyerbeer, who from then on and until his benighted end kept a firm grip on things.

In the first stages of the public uproar in which we now found ourselves, Uhlig had already managed to acquaint himself with *Opera and Drama*. In fact I had presented him with the original manuscript; as this was elegantly bound in red, I got the idea of dedicating it to him with the converse of Goethe's line "Gray, my friend, is all theory", in the words: "*Red*, my friend, is *my* theory." This communication too gave rise to a truly stimulating and pleasant exchange of correspondence with this young, quick and sharply penetrating friend, and I had a hearty desire to see him again after a separation of two years. It was no easy matter for a poverty-stricken violinist, who had only recently been established as a permanent member of the Court Orchestra, to accept my invitation; yet he jauntily overcame all obstacles and notified me of his forthcoming visit in the first days of July. I decided to go as far as Rohrschach on Lake Constance to meet him and then conduct him back to Zürich via an excursion through the Alps. I went there by a pleasant roundabout route through Toggenburg, traveling on foot as usual. In this way, cheerful and refreshed, I reached St Gall, where I looked up Karl Ritter, who had remained behind in odd seclusion after Bülow's departure. I could not really guess the reason for his solitude, though he told me of a pleasant association with a musician in St Gall named Greitel, of whom I subsequently never heard a thing. Still rather exhausted from the exertions of my walking tour, I could nevertheless not resist reading the manuscript of my recently completed poem for *Der junge Siegfried* to my intelligent and extremely receptive young friend, who thus became the first to hear it. Its impact on him pleased me very much, and I now persuaded him in good spirits to abandon his strange existence as an anchorite and come with me to meet Uhlig, so that all three of us might proceed on foot via the top of Säntis back to Zürich, there to enjoy a lengthy period in each other's company.

The first sight of my guest, as he landed at the by now familiar pier at Rohrschach, filled me with immediate anxiety for the health of this young friend, as his consumptive tendency was immediately recognizable. To spare him the effort, I wanted to give up the mountain-climbing plans, but he vehemently insisted on carrying them out, contending that such activities in the open air could only do him good after the tiresome drudgery of his detested service as a violinist. After the three of us had crossed the little canton of Appenzell, we then began the by no means easy ascent of the Säntis. This was the first time I had ever tramped through extended fields of snow in the middle of summer. After reaching our guide's hut, located in very craggy heights, and fortifying ourselves with some extremely frugal fare, we had to climb the precipitous pinnacle of rock towering several hundred feet above us, which constituted the actual summit of the mountain. At this point Karl suddenly refused to go on; to shake him out of his weakness, I sent the guide back to bring him along almost by force. As we now proceeded to climb from rock to rock up the steep cliff, I soon saw how foolish I had been to compel Karl to participate in this dangerous ascent. Vertigo obviously benumbed him completely; he stared blindly in front of him; we had to keep him between us with our staves, and I expected to see him collapse at any moment and plunge into the abyss. When we at last attained the summit, he sank senseless to the ground; and I now had to consider the frightful responsibility I had assumed, for the descent would be even more dangerous. In an agony of fear, which filled me with the vision of my young friend lying shattered on the rocks below, while at the same time making me forget my own peril altogether, we at last reached the guide's hut safely. As we two remained determined to carry out the further descent via the precipitous other side of the mountain, described by the guide as not without danger, having grown wise by my indescribably painful experience, I now convinced young Ritter that he should remain behind in the hut, await the guide's return, and in his company take the entirely safe path down the side by which we had come. Thus we separated here, as he had to return via St Gall, while we two roamed through the lovely Toggenburg valley, and the following day to Rapperswyl on the Lake of Zürich, and then home. Not until many days thereafter did Karl dispel our anxiety about him by his arrival in Zürich, where he remained with us only a short time before tearing himself away, possibly in order to flee from the temptation of accompanying us on another mountain-climbing expedition, which we were in fact planning to undertake. I heard from him again only after a long sojourn in Stuttgart, where he had been living in apparent happiness with a young actor whom he had quickly befriended there.

I was heartily delighted by the close association with the young

"Kammermusikus" from Dresden, whose gentleness in no way detracted from his manly firmness of character and exceptional gifts, while his bright blond hair and sparkling blue eyes made my wife think that an angel had come to stay with us. For me his physiognomy had a special and, considering his fate, touching interest, stemming from his striking resemblance to King Friedrich August of Saxony, my erstwhile patron, which seemed to substantiate a rumor I had formerly heard to the effect that Uhlig was his natural son. I was highly entertained by his reports about Dresden, the theater, and the musical life there. My operas, hitherto the glory of the theater, had vanished from the repertory completely; the attitude of my former colleagues toward me was characterized neatly by one anecdote: when *Art and Revolution* and *The Art-Work of the Future* had appeared and been discussed, one of them had exclaimed, "He'll have a lot of scribbling to do before it makes a Kapellmeister of him again." To describe the progress of music there, he recounted to me that Reissiger, when he had to conduct the A major Symphony that I had performed in the past, found a novel way out of a dilemma that confronted him. As is well known, the great closing development of the final movement was marked by Beethoven with a *forte* throughout, which he finally heightens slightly by a *sempre più forte*: at this point, in the old days before I conducted the symphony, Reissiger had always found it meet to introduce a *piano*, in order to be able to produce at least a crescendo; I had naturally done away with this at once, and instead had urged the orchestra to play with their utmost force throughout. When the symphony again fell into the hands of my predecessor, it proved a bit embarrassing to him to actually restore that unhappy *piano*; yet he had to try to rescue his authority, which was compromised by this; and so he decided that, instead of *forte*, the orchestra was to play *mezzo forte*.

But the saddest news he gave me concerned the unutterable desolation that had befallen my unhappy opera-publishing venture under the auspices of the court music dealer Meser, who was now pretending, inasmuch as no money was coming in and there were still bills to be paid, that he was a lamb I had led to the slaughter. Yet he still steadfastly refused any examination of his books, insisting that he was thereby protecting my property from immediate confiscation, as had happened to all my other goods. Our conversations about *Lohengrin* were pleasant, my friend having completed the vocal score and now busying himself with the correction of the engraver's proofs.

Uhlig also exerted what became for a long time a decisive influence upon me in an entirely different direction. This derived from his enthusiastic advocacy of hydrotherapy. He brought me a book on the subject by a certain Rausse, whose radical system, particularly with its tinge of Feuerbach, pleased me in an odd way. His bold rejection of all medical science and its quackeries in favor of the most simple and natural processes resulting from the methodical exploitation of the strengthening and refreshing properties of water soon won me as a fervent partisan. This doctrine held that medicaments could only affect the human organism if they were in some way poisonous and thus could not be assimilated by it; it was demonstrated that people who had been gradually enfeebled by protracted use of medicaments had been cured by the famous Priessnitz[1] through driving all the poison in their bodies toward the skin and thus expelling it completely. I immediately thought of the sulphur baths I had reluctantly taken the previous spring, and my continuing and fierce irascibility I ascribed, no doubt in part not without reason, to this treatment. For a long while after this I did my best to get rid of this and all other poisons I might have absorbed in the course of time, and to achieve a radical restoration of my health as a pristine human being. Uhlig asserted that he could certainly strengthen his own health by a strictly observed water regimen. My faith in this grew daily.

At the end of July we commenced an excursion on foot through the heart of Switzerland: from Brunnen on the Lake of Lucerne we went via Beckenried to Engelberg, and from there crossed the wild Surenen-Eck, on which occasion we learned how to slide over the snow passably well. When crossing the high mountain stream, however, Uhlig had the misfortune to fall into the water; my concern as to its consequences he immediately dismissed with the assurance that this was a very healthy way to continue his treatment: the need to dry his clothes and underwear caused him not the slightest embarrassment, as he simply spread these out in the sun while he took what he asserted was a highly salubrious promenade in the open air completely naked. We spent the time during the process discussing several important aspects of the manner in which Beethoven develops his themes, until I hit upon the joke of telling him that I suddenly saw Court Councillor Carus[2] and a group from Dresden coming up behind him, a piece of news that managed to startle him for a moment. Thus we arrived in the best of spirits at last in the Reuss valley near Attinghausen and continued on that evening until we reached Amsteg, from where we proceeded the next morning, despite our exhaustion, to visit the Maderan valley at once. There we got to the Hüfi glacier, from which we could survey the splendid mountain panorama crowned at this point by the summit of the Tödy. After returning the same day to Amsteg, we felt ourselves really tired enough at last, so that I succeeded in dissuading my companion, who was enthusiastic for the plan, from carrying out my proposal to ascend the Klausen pass in the Schächen valley, instead of which we took the easy way back via Flüelen. I could truly detect no signs of exhaustion in the always calm and composed young man at the time of his departure to go back to Dresden early that August. As a matter of fact, he was hoping to lighten his burdensome situation somewhat by taking over the job of conducting the musical interludes in the performances of spoken plays, to which he wanted to bring some artistic distinction, and by means of this free himself to some extent from his demanding and demoralizing work in the service of the opera. Yet I was greatly disquieted when I brought him to the mail coach; and he too seemed suddenly seized by a sense of foreboding; and that actually turned out to be the last time we saw each other.

But for the present we maintained a lively correspondence; and as his letters were always pleasant and entertaining, constituting for a long time the only conduit for my communication with the outside world, I asked him to write me as much as possible. As the costs of mailing letters were high at that time, and the voluminous letters were a burden on our exchequers, Uhlig came up with the ingenious idea of using the parcel post service for our communications; since only shipments of a certain minimum weight qualified to be sent in this way, an old German translation of Beaumarchais' *Figaro*, which Uhlig possessed in a dignified edition, fulfilled the bizarre function of ballast for the letters exchanged between us; thus, every time our epistles had swelled to the requisite size, we announced them with the words: "Figaro is bringing new tidings today." Meanwhile, Uhlig was delighted by another piece I had written just after our separation, entitled *A Communication to My Friends*, with which I prefaced an edition of the poems of my three operas, *Der fliegende Holländer*, *Tannhäuser* and *Lohengrin*. He was highly amused to learn that Härtel, who accepted the book for an honorarium of ten louis d'or, had objected so determinedly to several passages in the introduction, in which I had questioned the integrity and patriotism of publishers in general, that I was really inclined to give my book to another printer, until finally I was overcome by an inclination to compromise and pacified his anxious conscience by a few small changes.

With this rather wide-ranging preface, which had occupied me during the whole month of August, my excursion into literary terrain was now at an end, and for good and all, I hoped. Yet as soon as I seriously thought of beginning the musical composition of *Der junge Siegfried*, as promised for Weimar, I was seized by depressing doubts, which infected me with a positive antipathy for the work. Unclear as to the reason for this feeling, I first concluded that the state of my health was to blame; and so I decided one day to translate the theories about water cures I had adopted with such enthusiasm into practice, inquired after a nearby hydropathic institution, and then disclosed to my wife in mid-September that I was about to go off to Albisbrunn,[1] about three hours' trip from our home, and not return until I had been radically restored to health. Minna was very startled to learn of this project and thought she should interpret it as a new tendency on my part to get away from her whenever possible. But I told her to devote herself during my absence to the task of furnishing and arranging as comfortably as possible our newly rented, small but well situated apartment on the ground floor of the Vordere Escherhäuser on the Zeltweg, to which we had decided to move because of the inconvenience of spending a winter in a house located so far from the city. My plan to take a water cure so late in the year was greeted with general amazement; yet I nonetheless succeeded in securing a fellow-sufferer. I completely failed to win Herwegh for this purpose; but fate sent me Hermann Müller, ex-lieutenant in the Saxon Guards and Schröder-Devrient's former lover, who proved to be a decent and entertaining companion. He had been unable to retain his position in the Saxon army, and while he was not actually a political refugee, inasmuch as he could not pursue any career in Germany and had been obliged to turn to Switzerland in order to work out a new plan for his life, he enjoyed the status of an exiled patriot. As I had been accustomed to see him frequently during the Dresden years, he soon became a regular habitué of our household, where my wife was especially glad to see him. I had an easy time convincing him to follow me to Albisbrunn after a few days, in order to undergo thorough treatment for an ailment from which he was suffering. I established myself there as comfortably as I could, as I was looking forward to a really thorough success. The treatment was administered by a Dr Brunner, whom my wife, when she came to visit me, termed a "Water-Jew" and soon began to despise, according to the traditional surface method: at five a.m. every morning I was wrapped up and made to perspire for several hours, only to be plunged into a bath with a temperature of no more than four degrees, after which I could warm up by a brisk walk in the late-autumn air, which rapidly grew icy. The watery diet precluded wine, coffee or tea, and this regimen, in the dismal company of none but incurables, the dull evenings when the game of whist with which they ended was something to look forward to, the avoidance of any other kind of intellectual labor, soon resulted in growing strain and nervous irritation; such was the life I survived for nine weeks, and which I did not intend to break off until, as I expected, all the medicaments I had ever taken appeared on the surface of my skin. As I now considered wine inherently dangerous, I felt I also had to sweat out of me all the unassimilable substances I had imbibed at the many evening parties at Sulzer's house. The many privations of this life in a miserable room with the hard wooden furniture and all the other Spartan domestic appointments typical of a Swiss boarding house now evoked in me by way of contrast a longing for particularly lavish household comfort, and in the course of the years this yearning developed into something close to a passion. My imagination was continually conjuring up visions of the manner and style in which a house or an apartment should be furnished, if my spirit were to be free and pleasantly disposed for artistic creation.

At this time there were signs of the possibility of a gradual improvement in my situation. Unfortunately for him, Karl Ritter had sent me a letter from Stuttgart to Albisbrunn, telling me of his independent attempts to achieve a cure, not by baths but rather by drinking inordinate amounts of water. Now, I had learned that drinking too much water without the aid of the rest of the treatment could prove very dangerous, and thus demanded of Karl that he submit to a regular regimen, come at once to join me, and not shy away effeminately from privation. He actually obeyed me immediately and arrived in Albisbrunn a few days later to my surprise and delight. Although he was filled with similar enthusiasm for radical hydrotherapy, he was soon repelled by its practical requirements: he was disgusted at the indigestible cold milk, contending that in nature it was drunk warm, as with mother's milk. He found the cold packs and baths made him feel agitated, and soon felt a desire to treat himself, behind the doctor's back, in a more pleasant manner. For this purpose he found some miserable little bakeries in a nearby village; whenever he was caught making clandestine purchases there, it irritated him hugely, and soon he felt himself to be in a forced and highly disagreeable position, from which only a sense of honor prevented him from fleeing. Here he suddenly got news of the death of a rich uncle, who had left every member of Karl's immediate family a not insubstantial legacy. His mother notified him and me of this improvement in her financial position by a statement to the effect that she was now in a position to provide me by herself with the subsidy which originally had been offered by the Laussot and Ritter families together. Thus, by being granted a yearly stipend of eight hundred talers for as long as I needed it, I entered into the Ritter family.

This exhilarating turn of events gave a great fillip to my spirits, and at once the decision matured in me to realize my original sketch for the *Nibelungen* in its entirety, irrespective of whether any part of it would be actually performable in our theaters. To do this it was first of all necessary to get out of my contractual obligation to the Weimar theater management. I had already drawn two hundred talers from the fee guaranteed me: Karl rejoiced in being able to hand me this amount so that I could repay it to them. I accompanied this remittance to the Weimar theater management with a hearty note of thanks for their conduct toward me, and also by a letter to Liszt, in which I discussed my great project, and the inner reasons compelling me to undertake it, in an extremely comprehensive and detailed manner. Liszt's answer expressed nothing but joy at my now being in a position to get started on such an extraordinary work, and he seemed to consider the plan, already by virtue of its startling originality, entirely worthy of me. Now I could definitely breathe more easily: for the thought of being obliged to deliver *Der junge Siegfried* even to the best of the German theaters, with their utterly inadequate resources, had struck me as an act of self-deception I could scarcely conceal from the moment I had accepted the obligation to do so.

Now I too found the water cure increasingly distasteful; I wanted to get back to work and this desire, as long as I had to renounce it, succeeded in producing a growing and eventually serious state of agitation. That the cure had failed of its purpose, and had even begun to do me lasting harm, was something I stubbornly tried to conceal from myself: the drastic secretions I had expected had not taken place, but instead my whole body had grown frightfully thin. I contented myself with this result, and, thinking I had now accomplished enough to expect some beneficial effects later, left Albisbrunn at the end of November, from where Müller was to follow me a few days later. Karl, on the other hand, expressed the intention to remain there with due persistence until he could show the kind of results I pretended to have achieved. In Zürich I was pleased at the arrangements Minna had made in our new albeit very small apartment. She had procured a deep, wide sofa, some carpeting for the floors and a number of other comforts; in the back room my cheap deal desk had been covered with a green tablecloth and surrounded by light green silk curtains, which greatly delighted me and everyone else. The table decorated in this manner, at which I worked thereafter, went with me to Paris years later, and when I left it there, was given to Blandine Ollivier,[1] Liszt's elder daughter, who had it sent from there to her husband's little country estate in St Tropez, where, as I understand, it remains to this day.

I was glad to be able to receive my Zürich friends again in this more conveniently located new apartment; but I spoiled things for them for a long time by my passionate advocacy of a water diet, together with a corresponding polemic against wine and other narcotic beverages. For me this was something of a new religion: when, for example, Herwegh, who claimed some knowledge of chemistry and physiology, and Sulzer drove me into a corner on the untenability of Rausse's theory concerning the poisonous element in wine, I resorted to the moral and aesthetic argument, contending that the enjoyment of wine was a bad and barbaric surrogate for the kind of ecstasy which should be gained only through love. I asserted namely that whatever one was looking for in drinking wine, even if not done to excess, nevertheless entailed some degree of intoxication, and thus of ecstatic arousal of the spiritual powers, whereas such arousal was truly ennobling only when the abnormal excitation of the spirit was the result of the intoxication of love. This led on to criticism of the modern relationship between the sexes, to which I was provoked by my observation of the crude segregation of men and women which was the custom in Swiss society. Sulzer opined that he had nothing against being intoxicated by the company of women, but wondered "where to get them without stealing them?" Herwegh was more susceptible to my paradoxical arguments, but he contended that wine had nothing to do with the matter and was really just a form of nourishment, which also harmonized well with the ecstasies of love, as Anacreon had testified. When they examined my condition more closely, however, my friends had grounds to be worried for their part about my strange and stubborn extravagances: I had become increasingly pale and haggard, slept very little, and revealed in all things an alarming degree of over-excitement. While eventually I was deserted by sleep entirely, I continued nonetheless to insist that things had never been better with me, and went on with my cold morning baths on the iciest winter days, much to the anguish of my wife, who was obliged to light my way with a lantern when I set off on the walk that was the necessary sequel to my dip.

In this condition I received the printed copies of *Opera and Drama*, which I devoured, rather than read, in a quite exceptional burst of joy. This overly excited mood was no doubt attributable in large part to my awareness that I could now say to myself justifiably, and even with Minna's forced concurrence, that I was now completely free from my previous career as a conductor and composer of operas and all the torments it had caused me. No longer did anyone expect me to do the things that had made me so unhappy two years before. The income the Ritter family had promised me, which if need be could suffice to keep me alive, and which had precisely that purpose of keeping me free to do my own work, was the crowning factor in producing the exuberance with which I now surveyed everything I proposed to undertake. Although my plans seemed to preclude for the moment any contact with our execrable artistic institutions, I nonetheless nursed deep within me the conviction that I was by no means writing for my own amusement. I continued to assume that those institutions, like the whole social order of things, would very soon undergo an immeasurable transformation; new conditions would quickly come into being, with new needs, and I believed that the works I had conceived with such recklessness were exactly what would meet those needs, and would produce all at once a totally new relationship of art to artistic institutions. Such bold expectations, about which I naturally could not talk very frankly with any of my friends at the time, were rooted in the way I viewed the world situation at the time. The general failure of all the liberal political movements had definitely not put me off the track; on the contrary, I thought that the real reason for their failure was the insufficient recognition and open advocacy of their true cause: I now saw this to be the whole social movement, which despite its political defeats had not lost force but rather was rapidly spreading. This was the way I judged what I had observed during my most recent stay in Paris. Among other things, I had attended a voters' rally of the so-called social-democratic party, the whole conduct of which had impressed me greatly; it took place in a temporary "Salle de la Fraternité" in the Faubourg St Denis, and had been crowded with six thousand men, whose dignified behavior, far from involving any tumultuous agitation, gave me a highly favorable idea of the concerted and confident energy of this newest political party. The addresses by the principal speakers from the extreme left wing of the Assemblée Nationale surprised me by their rhetorical verve as well as by the unshakable confidence they evidenced. Inasmuch as this really radical party was gradually being strengthened by all those elements driven into opposition by the reactionary government, and all those former "liberals" now openly adopted the campaign platform of these so-called "social democrats", it seemed highly probable that, at least in Paris, they would gain the upper hand in the forthcoming new elections for the year 1852, particularly in the election of a new president of the republic. My own assumptions about this were, as is well known, shared throughout France, and the year 1852 seemed likely to go down in history as the date of an unprecedented turnabout, such as was also very certainly feared by the rival party, which viewed the trend of things with extreme horror. The situation in the rest of the European nations, in which every initiative had been suppressed with the crassest brutality, allowed the supposition that this state of affairs would not endure for very long, and everybody seemed to look forward in tense anticipation to the forthcoming year of decision. In addition to exchanging views on the virtues of hydrotherapy, I had also discussed this significant political situation with my friend Uhlig: coming to me directly from the Dresden theater and orchestral rehearsals, it had been very difficult for him to accept the probability that such bold hopes for a heroic reversal in human affairs would be realized. He told me I could really have no idea how pitiful people were; yet I managed to benumb him enough to convince him to go along with me in regarding the year 1852 as being pregnant with great decisions. Much of our correspondence, as diligently trans-mitted back and forth by "Figaro", was concerned with this subject. Whenever we found any baseness to complain about, I always cited the hopeful and fateful date, in the belief, more or less, that we should have to stand quietly by, watching the awaited turnabout take its course, until such time as nobody else knew what to do next, and then it would be our turn to act. I cannot say precisely how firmly this tower of hope was founded within me; I soon had to recognize, however, that my excited nervous condition had a lot to do with the over-confident exuberance of my assumptions and assertions. The news of the coup d'état of December 2nd[1] in Paris struck me as positively unbelievable: while the world seemed to have been preserved, for me it collapsed completely. When the success of the coup became apparent, and what nobody had previously regarded possible established itself apparently in perpetuity, I turned away indifferently, as if from a riddle whose solution seems scarcely worth the trouble, and no longer tried to figure out what was going on in this strange world. As a playful reminiscence of our former hopes for 1852, I suggested to Uhlig that we should act as if that year had never started, and henceforth date all our letters December 1851, a month that thereby received an improbable prolongation.

Before long I was overtaken by exceptional depression, in which disappointment at external events in the world was admixed with the reaction I now began to feel against the excesses of the water cure as they had affected my health. I now saw on every side the triumphant return of all those discouraging phenomena, the enemies of all higher aspirations in cultural life, which had seemed to have been forever dispelled by the upheavals of the last few years. I foresaw the time when it would go so badly with us that a new book by Heinrich Heine would be greeted as a sign of ferment: and indeed when a short time later the *Romancero* of that nowadays completely ignored author caused all the old familiar stir in the public prints, I had to laugh aloud; I really do belong to the probably very small number of cultivated Germans who have never opened the covers of that book, which nevertheless is said to have great merits. I had grounds enough to pay closer attention instead to my worrying physical condition which for the moment necessitated a complete change in my regimen.

The change occurred very gradually, however, and under the special influence of my friends. Our circle had increased at the beginning of the winter, even though Karl Ritter, who had fled Albisbrunn a week after my departure and then tried to find a dwelling near me, soon went back to Dresden, as he obviously found too little going on in Zürich to suit his youthful taste. But then a family named Wesendonck,[1] just settled in Zürich, sought to make my acquaintance, and this was accomplished in the same apartment in the Hintere Escherhäuser where I had first lived in Zürich through Marschall von Bieberstein, who had established residence there, and was well-known to me from the Dresden revolution. I recall on that evening that my over-excited state became particularly evident in a discussion with Professor Osenbrück;[2] by the time the meal was over I had provoked him by my passionately argued paradoxes to a genuine antipathy toward me; for he fled in terror from any encounter with me thereafter. The acquaintance that I made on the same occasion with the Wesendoncks gave me first of all an entrée into a residence whose welcoming comfort distinguished it most favorably among the other Zürich households. Herr Otto Wesendonck, several years younger than I, had earned quite a substantial fortune as a partner in a New York silk firm and seemed to be governed in his decisions in life entirely according to the wishes of his young wife, whom he had married only a few years before. Both came from the Lower Rhineland and had the bright and friendly countenance typical of that area. Out of necessity to establish himself in a European location that would be of advantage

479

to the firm in New York, he had given Zürich preference over Lyon, presumably on account of its German element. The couple had attended a performance of a Beethoven symphony under my baton the previous winter, and, considering the stir which this event caused in Zürich, it had seemed to them desirable in their new establishment to try to win me for inclusion in their circle of friends.

This winter I again let myself be persuaded to conduct three concerts of the Music Society, but only on what were now the accepted conditions that I would be given an augmented orchestra with which to rehearse and perform only a few selected pieces of undoubted excellence. I was myself greatly pleased to have Beethoven's *Egmont* music done for once with the proper attention to detail. Inasmuch as Herwegh was very anxious to hear some music of mine, I performed the *Tannhäuser* overture expressly for him and took this opportunity to write a special program note serving to make it better understood. I also succeeded in achieving a superb performance of the *Coriolanus* overture, for which I also wrote a program note. All this was received by my acquaintances with great interest, so that at last I finally succumbed to the pleas of Löwe, the director of the theater at the time, and consented to his request for a performance of *Der fliegende Holländer* for my friends' sake, and thus got myself involved again, if only temporarily, in the highly distasteful affairs of the theater. But there were also humane consider-ations at work; for the performance was supposed to be a benefit for the young conductor Schöneck, who had convinced me of his undeniable musical talent.

The strain imposed on me by this excursion into the regions of operatic rehearsals and so on, to which I had become a complete stranger, contributed in no small part to the exacerbation of my nervous exhaustion, so that in my extreme suffering I was disloyal to my radical views in regard to doctors and, at the recommendation of Wesendonck, entrusted myself to Dr Rahn-Escher, whose gentle manner and soothing ways succeeded in time in putting me on a new and better track.

In the end all I wanted was to get well enough to embark upon the completion of my plan for the combined Nibelung poem. Before I could summon the courage to do so, I thought it best to await the arrival of spring and for the moment spent my time in a number of smaller tasks, among which was an open letter to Liszt concerning the Goethe Foundation, offering my ideas as to the necessity of establishing a German national theater, as well as a second letter to Franz Brendel setting forth my opinions on the direction a musical journal should follow. I also recall a visit of Henri Vieuxtemps, who came to Zürich in the company of Belloni to give a concert there, and once again, since that occasion in Paris long before, delighted my friends by his violin playing. With the approach of spring I was also surprised by a visit from Hermann Franck, with whom I had an interesting talk about recent world events, during which he had disappeared from my sight completely. In his calm way he expressed his disapproval of the passionate manner in which I had involved myself in the Dresden uprising; as I quite misunderstood this remark, he further elucidated it with the comment that he had thought me capable of warmth and enthusiasm for anything, but not the foolishness to take an active part in such a worthless undertaking as that. I now learned of the prevailing climate of opinion in Germany concerning these much maligned events, and particularly with respect to my friend Röckel was able to dispel some of the slanders about him, some of which even represented him as a miserable, cowardly rogue, and thus at last to my great satisfaction bring Franck around to a different attitude on the subject, for which he expressed his forthright gratitude. With Röckel himself, who some time before had been "pardoned" to life imprisonment, I maintained a necessarily open exchange of letters from time to time, the upshot of which was that, particularly considering the resilient, even cheerful manner in which he was coping with imprisonment, I had to consider him a happier man than I myself in a freedom that seemed bounded on all sides by such hopeless prospects.

Finally the month of May arrived. I felt I needed some time in the country to strengthen my strained nerves and to begin at last realizing my poetic plans. We found a fairly comfortable place to stay on the Rinderknecht estate, situated half way up nearby Mount Zürich, and were able to celebrate my 39th birthday on May 22nd by a rustic meal in the open air, with a broad view of the lake and the distant Alps. Unfortunately a period of incessant rain set in, lasting almost the entire summer, and I had to expend great effort in fighting off its depressing influence. Yet I soon got to work, and having begun the execution of my great design from back to front, I continued in this direction, pressing onward toward the beginning, now that *Siegfrieds Tod* and *Der junge Siegfried* had been completed, by initially working out the first of the main dramas, *Die Walküre*, and then finally following it with the introductory prelude, *Das Rheingold*. The poem for *Die Walküre* was completed in these circumstances by the end of June. Apart from this, I also wrote some words dedicating my *Lohengrin* to Liszt, and also produced a rhymed reproof to a foolish critic of my *Der fliegende Holländer* for a Swiss paper. Beyond this, a very disagreeable incident concerning Herwegh disturbed my country seclusion. One day, a certain Herr Haug, who identified himself as a former "Roman General" from Mazzini's time, came to see me on behalf of a family which had purportedly been deeply insulted by this "unfortunate lyricist", in order to further some kind of conspiracy against him. But I showed him the door. Much more pleasant was the lengthy visit of Julie, the eldest daughter of my honored friend Frau Ritter, who had married the young Dresden orchestral player Kummer. His health seemed so badly undermined that they had come to this neighborhood on account of a doctor specializing in hydrotherapy, who was practising in a place a few hours' distance from Zürich. This gave me an opportunity to indulge in a polemic against hydrotherapy, much to the alarm of my young friends, who had thought me a fervent convert. Abandoning the young musician to his fate, we were pleased to spend a considerable time at the Rinderknecht estate with his friendly and winning young wife.

Satisfied at the progress of my work, we finally returned at the end of June, largely owing to the unprecedented spell of cold and rainy weather, to our more comfortable apartment in the city, where I decided to await the onset of real summer weather before undertaking a long excursion on foot over the Alps, which I expected would have a favorable effect on my health. Herwegh had promised to accompany me; but that unpleasant business seemed to detain him, so I set off alone in mid-July,[1] expecting that my companion would catch up with me in Valais. I began my walking tour at Alpnach, on the Lake of Lucerne, and my plan was to proceed through the Alps by special and seldom frequented paths, as well as visiting the principal landmarks of the Bernese Oberland. I mapped out quite a systematic route for myself, even taking in, in the Bernese Oberland, for example, the Faulhorn, which was then still a difficult climb. When I reached the hostelry on the Grimsel via the Hasli valley, I asked the innkeeper, a dignified-looking fellow, about the possibility of climbing the Siedelhorn. As a guide he recommended one of his own servants, a person of crude and sinister appearance, who, inasmuch as he did not take me up the snowy slopes in the traditional zig-zag pattern but rather in a bee-line, soon aroused in me the suspicion that he was intentionally trying to tire me out. Reaching the summit of the Siedelhorn, I was delighted first of all by the view inside the ring of giant peaks that otherwise show only their faces to the outside world, and also by the sudden sight of the Italian Alps, together with Mont

Blanc and Monte Rosa. I had been careful to take a small bottle of
champagne with me, in order to imitate Fürst Pückler when he made
the ascent of Snowdon; only I couldn't think of anyone to whose health
I should drink. Then we went down across the snow-covered slopes
again, my guide sliding at high speed on his Alpenstock: I contented
myself with a more cautious descent on my heels. Utterly exhausted, I
reached Obergestelen that evening, where I rested for two days and
waited for Herwegh to join me. But in his place a letter from him arrived,
dragging me down from my lofty Alpine impressions into the unpleasant
everyday world in which my unfortunate friend found himself involved
in the complications I have already mentioned. He was afraid I had been
prejudiced against him by his enemy and had formed an unfavorable
opinion of him. I notified him he should not let the matter cause him
any worry whatsoever and suggested he meet me if at all possible in the
Italian part of Switzerland. Thus I set off alone with my sinister guide
to climb the Gries glacier, and to cross the pass there leading to the
southern side of the Alps. While I was climbing it, I beheld a very sad
sight; an epidemic of foot-rot had broken out among the cows in the
upper Alps, and numerous herds passed me in long files heading down
to the valleys for the necessary treatment. The cows had grown extremely
thin, so that they looked like skeletons and slunk along miserably with
great effort; there seemed to be some element of savage delight in the
glorious surroundings and the luxuriant pastures as they watched over
this pitiful retreat. At the foot of the steep glacier wall I felt so completely
depressed and my nerves so strained that I wanted to turn back. For
this I received the crude mockery of my guide, who seemed to think this
an indication of my softness. My irritation at this caused me to collect
my resources, and I at once began to ascend the steep icy wall with utmost
speed, so that my guide was the one who this time had trouble following
me. The two hours it took us to cross the back of the glacier brought
us difficulties that at least made the Grimsel servant worry about his own
safety. Fresh snow had fallen, and this partly concealed the crevasses,
so that we could not make out the most dangerous places. Here my guide
had to take the lead and reconnoiter the paths. At last we reached the
opening of the pass leading out into the Formazza valley, to which a
precipitous slope full of ice and snow now led us. Here my guide again
began his perilous game by conducting me not in a safer zig-zag but in
a straight line down the steepest slopes; when, by this means, we reached
a patch of scree so steep that I foresaw danger as inevitable, I protested
to my guide most seriously and forced him to go back with me a long

way on the route we had come, in order to reach a less dangerous path I had spotted for the descent. He gave in, but very testily. I was then much moved by our emergence from the bare and rocky wilds into a first contact with civilization. The first grazing ground accessible to cattle there was called the Bettel-Matt, and the first human being we met was a marmot hunter. Soon the wild landscape was enlivened by the tremendous effect of the headlong downward surge of the mountain river Tosa, which at one place breaks into a three-pronged waterfall of overwhelming beauty. After the mosses and reeds had given way in the course of our descent to grassy meadows, and the short shrubs had yielded to pines and firs that grew steadily taller, we finally traversed a valley of increasing charm and so reached our goal for the day, the village of Pommath, called Formazza by the Italian populace. Here I had to eat roast marmot for the first time in my life. In my great weariness I slept but little and was insufficiently restored, but I went on alone the next morning down the valley, after paying my guide and sending him home. It was not until November of that year, when all of Switzerland was startled by news that the Grimsel hostelry had burned to the ground and had been put to the torch by no other than its keeper, who had hoped thereby to force the local authorities to renew his lease, that I realized I had been in real danger of losing my life in the care of this guide. The keeper had in fact drowned himself in the little lake bordering on the hostelry immediately after his crime had been discovered; but his servant, whom he had bribed to set the fire, had been arrested and delivered to the authorities for punishment. I learned by his name that this was the same one whom the considerate host had given me as a guide to lead me in my lonely excursion over the glacier pass, on which, as I now learned, two travelers from Frankfurt, shortly before my own trip, had met with an accident and had perished: thus I had another occasion to believe that I had escaped fatal danger in an extraordinary way.

I shall never forget my impressions of the descent through the valley. I was particularly surprised by the sudden surge of Mediterranean vegetation after I emerged from a narrow mountain pass through which the Tosa squeezed itself. I arrived at Domodossola that afternoon in the blazing sun; and there I recalled a nice little comedy, worthy of Platen but by an author I never knew, which had been called to my attention in Dresden by Eduard Devrient. The scene of this play was set in Domodossola, and it described precisely what I had felt upon coming down from the northern world of the Alps into the sudden luxuriance of Italy. My first Italian meal, simple but well-served, remains just as unforgettable. Although I was too tired to go any further on foot, I was so impatient to reach the banks of Lago Maggiore that I rented a one-horse carriage that took me to Baveno that night. I felt so merry and content as the little carriage bounced along that I was inconsiderate enough to refuse bluntly the request of an officer, who had asked the coachman if he might accompany me. In the delightful places through which I drove I admired the delicacy of the decorations on the houses, and the winning countenance of the people. A young mother strolling along, her child on her arm and singing while she spun flax, also made an indelible impression on my memory. Shortly after sundown I caught sight of the Borromean Islands, rising gracefully out of Lago Maggiore, and from sheer excitement about the impending pleasures of the next day I again could not sleep. My visit to the islands the following day enchanted me so much that I really couldn't grasp how I deserved this marvel and what I could make of it. I left the place after the one day with a feeling as if I could not properly stay where I didn't belong, and went around Lago Maggiore via Locarno to Bellinzona, where I was again on Swiss soil; from there I proceeded to Lugano, intending to spend a longer time there in accordance with my original plan. But I soon began suffering under the intolerable heat; even my swims in the sun-baked lake were no longer refreshing. Apart from the dirty furniture, among which figured something resembling the "thinking couch" from Aristophanes' *Clouds*, I was quite ceremoniously lodged in a palatial building which in winter sheltered the government of the Canton of Ticino but doubled in summer as a hotel. But soon I was back in that condition under which I had been suffering for so long, fluctuating between extreme excitement and depression, and which prevented me from getting any real rest. This was what usually happened to me whenever I made an attempt to remain pleasantly idle. I had taken along some reading material, and Byron in particular was intended to constitute my chief entertainment. But unfortunately I had to force myself to extract any pleasure from him, and the further I got in *Don Juan*, the more difficult it became. After a few such days I no longer knew what I was doing there, when suddenly I was notified by Herwegh that he would look me up in Lugano, together with several friends. A strange instinct made me telegraph my wife at once, asking her to come and join us. She obeyed my invitation with surprising alacrity and arrived unannounced by mail coach over the Gotthard late one night. She was so exhausted that she sank into immediate sleep on the "thinking couch", and even a thunderstorm of greater violence than I have ever experienced since was unable to awaken her. The next morning our friends arrived from Zürich.

Herwegh's principal companion was Dr François Wille.[1] I had first met him some time before at Herwegh's house: his chief characteristics were a face furrowed by student dueling scars and an unshakable proclivity for drastic and witty remarks. He had recently settled near Meilen on Lake Zürich with his family and had often induced me to visit him there in the company of Herwegh. Here we saw something of the habits of a Hamburg family, which was maintained in some degree of prosperity by his wife,[2] a daughter of the wealthy ship-owner Sloman.[3] Whereas he remained in one sense a student all his life, he had previously enjoyed the opportunity, while editing a political paper in Hamburg, of attracting wide notice and a broad circle of acquaintances. He knew a lot of stories to tell and thus won the reputation of being entertaining. He had now, it seemed, taken charge of Herwegh, in order to jar him out of his bad mood and indecision with regard to the Alpine excursion, and had set off with a Professor Eichelberger over the Gotthard on foot. This had displeased Herwegh inordinately, as he felt obliged to contend that excursions by foot should be taken only where it was impossible to drive, and not on well-made roads such as that one. After an expedition into the country surrounding Lugano, during which I had ample opportunity to get sick of the childish carillons that tinkle from church towers all over Italy, I persuaded the group to follow me to the Borromean Islands, to which I was again irresistibly attracted. During the trip by steamship on Lago Maggiore we met a fragile-looking fellow with a long Hussar moustache, whom we jokingly named General Haynau[4] among ourselves, and whom we treated with feigned distrust, also to our amusement. But we soon discovered him to be an extremely good-natured nobleman from Hanover, who had been traveling extensively in Italy for pleasure, and who could give us a lot of useful hints about dealing with Italians. His recommendations were extremely useful during our visit to the Borromean Islands, after which my acquaintances departed to return to Zürich by the most direct route, while my wife and I intended to travel via the Simplon and through Valais to Chamonix.

The fatigue this whole trip had cost me so far let me know clearly enough that I would not soon set forth on a similar venture, and I was thus anxious to see all I could of the sights of Switzerland on this occasion. And I was in general in the mood, as had been the case with me for some time, to look for some significant effect to be produced on me by new impressions. Thus I didn't want to miss Mont Blanc. The sight of it cost us tremendous effort, involving a nocturnal arrival in Martigny, where we could find no accommodations in the overcrowded hotels and were obliged to exploit a love affair between a postillion and a maidservant to obtain clandestine shelter in a private house, whose owners were temporarily away. In the valley of Chamonix we made the obligatory visits to the so-called Sea of Ice, as well as the "Flégère", from which the view of Mont Blanc impressed me immensely. But I was less taken with the idea of climbing it than with a crossing of the Col des Géants, being attracted not so much by the great height of the former as by the glorious wildness of the latter. For a long time I nursed the plan of undertaking one more venture of this singular kind. While descending the "Flégère", Minna fell and sprained her ankle, and the painful consequences deterred us from any further adventures; we were thus compelled to return via Geneva more quickly than we had anticipated.

But even this important and grandiose trip, almost the only one I had ever undertaken solely for my recreation, left me with an unsatisfied feeling, and I was still prey to longings for faraway places, and for anything that would give my life a decisively new turn. Instead, upon my arrival at home, I found the signs of a different type of new turn in my fortunes. These consisted of bookings and inquiries from various German theaters wanting to give *Tannhäuser*. First it was the Court Theater of Schwerin which let itself be heard from; Röckel's youngest sister, a young singer, who had eventually married the actor Moritz whom I had known in my earliest youth, and who had returned to Germany from England, where she had been educated, had reported enthusiastically about the impressions made upon her by a Weimar performance of *Tannhäuser* to many people including the accountant of the local theater, an honest man named Stocks. He in turn had studied the work with the greatest eagerness and had urged the management of the theater to undertake its performance. Soon the theaters of Breslau, Prague, and Wiesbaden followed suit, at the last of which the friend of my youth Louis Schindelmeisser[1] was working as Kapellmeister. These were followed a short time later by still other theaters; the greatest surprise of all, however, came when even the Berlin Court Theater asked for the work through its new intendant, Herr von Hülsen.[2] In respect of this last request, I was probably correct in assuming that it was the then Princess of Prussia who had instigated so unexpected an approach, for the efforts of my friend Alwine Frommann had kept her favorably disposed toward me, while the Weimar production of *Tannhäuser* had given her a new and powerful motive for taking my part.

While I was delighted by the orders from the smaller theaters, I was anxious about the larger German opera houses. At the smaller ones I knew there were zealous conductors, who were loyal to me and had themselves been instrumental in instigating the performance of my work; but it was different in Berlin. In addition to the highly vain but also highly untalented Taubert, whom I had known in the past, the theater had only one other Kapellmeister, Heinrich Dorn, of whom I retained recollections from the earliest part of my life and later from our sojourn in Riga, where we had been at the last on very bad terms. I had no inclination, nor did I regard it as possible, to involve myself with either of these two gentlemen in a performance of my work, and from my knowledge of their capacities, as well as their ill-will, I had ample grounds to doubt the possibility of a successful performance of my opera under their direction. Since I myself, being in exile, could not go to Berlin to supervise things, I at once asked Liszt's permission to suggest him as my representative and alter ego in Berlin, to which he readily assented. When I then made Liszt's engagement a condition for the performance, the Berlin management objected that calling in a Kapell-meister from Weimar would necessarily be construed as an outrageous insult to the Prussian Court Kapellmeisters, and that I would have to waive this condition. A lengthy correspondence on the matter went back and forth for some time, but ended with Berlin postponing the performance of *Tannhäuser* for the foreseeable future.

While *Tannhäuser* from then on spread rapidly among the medium-sized German theaters, I was greatly worried as to the character of these performances, about which I could never obtain a clear picture. As I was barred from being present at any of them, I got the idea of ensuring the proper understanding of the challenges presented by my work by writing a very comprehensive essay which I intended should serve as a guide to its production. It was quite a lengthy piece, and I had it printed and lavishly bound at my own expense, and sent a number of copies to every theater that had ordered the score, heartily recommending it for distribution to the conductor, the stage-director, and all the principal singers. Over the course of the years I have not heard of a single person who has read this guide, let alone followed its instructions. By the year 1864 all the copies of the brochure had been exhausted by my conscientious distribution of it, and I was therefore delighted to find all the copies I had once sent the Munich Court Theater carefully preserved and utterly untouched in its archives. This enabled me to provide the King of Bavaria, who had asked after it, with the missing document, as well as to transmit it to some friends and refresh my own recollection of it.

It was a strange destiny that made the growing desire to perform my opera in the German theaters coincide with my decision to carry out a work whose conception had been so decisively influenced by my recognition of the need for complete ruthlessness with regard to the requirements of these very theaters; yet this unexpected turn of events in no way affected my state of mind in undertaking that work. By sticking firmly to my plan I actually gained the peace of mind necessary to let everything else take its own appointed course, without even in the slightest trying to abet performances. Thus I let people do as they liked, and listened in some amazement when I heard of remarkable successes; but this didn't lead to any change in my judgments about our theater in general and the opera in particular. I remained unalterably determined to complete my Nibelung dramas just as if the operatic theater of the day did not exist, and as if the ideal theater I had in mind would one day arise for me of its own accord. And so I wrote the poem of *Das Rheingold* in October and November of that year, whereby I brought the whole cycle of my Nibelung dramas to completion in reverse order. At the same time I revised *Der junge Siegfried* and especially *Siegfrieds Tod* in such a way that they now related correctly to the whole, and this last work in particular was considerably expanded to reflect the palpable significance of the entire drama. Accordingly, I had to give this final drama in the cycle a new title that would correspond to this altered relationship; I called it *Götterdämmerung*, while I changed *Der junge Siegfried*, inasmuch as this work no longer represented merely an isolated episode in the life of its hero but rather showed him in relationship to the other principal characters of the dramas, simply to *Siegfried*.

The prospect of this substantial poem necessarily remaining for a long time entirely unknown to those whose interest I could be sure it would arouse troubled me considerably. As the theaters now to my amazement sent me from time to time the customary remittances for my *Tannhäuser*, I allocated part of my income to pay for some beautifully printed copies of my poem for my own use. I decided to have only fifty copies of this de luxe private edition drawn off. Before I had completed this pleasant task, however, I was overtaken by a great sorrow.

In my immediate surroundings, it is true, I found signs of interest in the completion of my vast poetic work, although most of my acquaintances considered it a chimera, and perhaps even only a presumptuous caprice. Herwegh was the only one who entered into the work with much warmth and comprehension, and I often discussed it with him, reading him the parts as I completed them. Sulzer was upset at the revision of *Siegfrieds Tod*, for he considered this work good and original, and felt that these qualities would be lost if it were judged desirable and expedient to make a number of alterations. Therefore he asked me to give him the manuscript of the original version to retain as a souvenir, in the belief that otherwise it would be lost for good. To obtain some idea of the effect of the poem when presented in its entirety in proper sequence and with as little interruption as possible, a few days after finishing it I decided to utilize a mid-December visit of several days to the Wille family at their country estate to read it to a small group of friends. In addition to Herwegh, who accompanied me, Frau Wille and her sister, Frau von Bissing,[1] were also present. I had often entertained these two ladies at the piano in my own peculiar fashion during my pleasant visits to the house at Mariafeld, about two hours' walking distance from Zürich. They formed a very attentive and even devoted audience, somewhat to the annoyance of Herr Wille, who freely admitted that music was a torment to him yet still knew how to take the whole thing lightly in his typically boisterous way. As I arrived toward evening, *Das Rheingold* was immediately taken in hand, and because it did not seem very late and no exertion was deemed capable of harming me, I followed it by a reading of *Die Walküre* ending nearly at midnight. The next morning after breakfast it was time for *Siegfried*, and that evening I ended with *Götterdämmerung*. I felt I had good reason to be content with its impact, and the ladies in particular were so awestruck by it that they couldn't speak at all. Unfortunately, the effort left me in a state of almost painful excitement; I couldn't sleep and was so taciturn the next day that nobody could understand my hurried departure. Herwegh alone, who accompanied me back to Zürich, appeared to sense my mood and share it by maintaining a similar silence. It was now to be a special pleasure for me to transmit the completed work to my faithful Dresden friend Uhlig, with whom I had corresponded continually and discussed every phase of the execution of the plan he knew so well. I hadn't wanted to send him *Die Walküre* until the preceding *Das Rheingold* had been completed; and then he was not to receive the entire work for perusal until I could sent him a copy of the de luxe edition. When autumn came, however, I began to sense in Uhlig's letters grounds for growing concern about the state of his health. He complained of increasingly serious coughing spells and finally of continuing hoarseness. He viewed all these symptoms as weaknesses he hoped to combat by strengthening his body through cold water and long walks; his work as a violinist in the theater, he said, got him down very badly; whereas after a stiff march of about seven hours' duration through the surrounding countryside, he always felt much better; yet the coughing and hoarseness would not go away; it had become difficult, he added, to make himself heard in conversation, even to those right next to him. Until then I had not wanted to alarm the poor fellow and had always hoped his condition would finally compel some doctor to prescribe a reasonable treatment for him. But now, as I continually received testimony from him evidencing his absolute fidelity to the principles of hydrotherapy, I could not restrain myself and urged him to cease his madness and put himself in the care of a good doctor, since given his condition it was clearly a case requiring forbearance rather than exertion of any kind. This frightened the poor man greatly, as he could clearly see that I suspected he was in an advanced stage of consumption. "What will become of my poor wife and children if this is really the way it is with me?" That was what he wrote me. Unfortunately, it was soon too late; with his last remaining strength he tried to write once again, and finally my old friend, chorusmaster Fischer, had to carry out Uhlig's instructions in this regard, bending down close to his lips when he could no longer speak with sufficient force to make himself understood. News of his death followed with frightful celerity: he had died on January 3rd of the new year 1853. Together with Lehrs, he was the second of my truly faithful friends carried off by consumption. The handsome copy of my *Der Ring des Nibelungen* I had intended for him lay useless before me; I bestowed it on his youngest son, my god-child, whom he had named Siegfried. I asked his widow to send me his unpublished theoretical papers and received a good deal of important material, particularly the essay on thematic development I have previously mentioned. While the job of editing these papers and the necessity of revising them thoroughly would have cost me considerable effort, I inquired of Herr Härtel[1] in Leipzig whether he would be willing to pay the widow a decent fee for such a work: the publisher replied that he could not consider undertaking the publication even for nothing, as such things didn't bring in any money. I had realized by that time how every musician who had been active on my behalf had attracted enmity from certain quarters.

491

Uhlig's sad demise gave my local friends heavy ammunition against my theories on hydrotherapy. Herwegh insisted to my wife that I should be compelled to take a glass of good wine after the exertions of the rehearsals and concerts I had again undertaken this winter. And gradually I accustomed myself again to the mildly stimulating enjoyment of coffee and tea, whereat my acquaintances noted to their pleasure that I became progressively more companionable. Herr Dr Rahn-Escher now became a welcome and reassuring friend of the household, who over the years took good care of my health and particularly knew how to assuage the worries caused by my overwrought nerves. He soon demonstrated his shrewdness when I undertook in mid-February to read my tetralogy aloud on four consecutive evenings to a rather large audience. I got a very bad cold after the first evening and awoke on the day of the second with heavy catarrh and a very sore throat. I told my doctor at once that I would be highly upset if the reading had to be cancelled. He required that I remain quiet the whole day, wrap myself warmly in the evening and have myself brought to the place where the reading was to be given, and then take a few cups of weak tea before beginning; everything would then take care of itself, he assured me, whereas I would probably become seriously sick from frustration at any interruption in my undertaking. The reading of this passionate piece went really excellently; on the third and fourth evenings I read again and felt perfectly well. For these readings I had secured a large and elegant room in the Hotel Baur au Lac and was surprised to find that with each successive evening the hall grew more crowded, even though I had only invited a small circle of friends, giving them the option of bringing any acquaintances who in their opinion would take a genuine interest in the subject and not come from mere curiosity. The effect again seemed to be entirely favorable, and I received assurances of the greatest appreciation and even some judicious comments from the most serious university men and from government officials, who appeared to understand my poem and its artistic intent. From the characteristic sober earnestness with which they gave expression to their views, I gained enough confidence to conceive the idea of attempting to find out to what extent this auspicious climate of opinion could be exploited for my higher artistic aims. Everybody seemed to think, laboring under the usual superficial view of the subject, that I should involve myself once again with the theater. I tried to think how it might be possible to convert even such scanty resources as those enjoyed by the Zürich theater into something respectable by adherence to sound principles, and put my ideas on paper in an essay with the title

A Theater in Zürich[1] for everybody's benefit. The edition of approximately one hundred copies was actually sold, but I never received the slightest indication that it made any impression; on one occasion much later, at a banquet of the music society, the worthy Herr Ott-Imhof responded to criticisms from some quarters that my proposals were no doubt very fine but unfortunately quite impracticable with the statement that he could certainly not agree with this view; yet he added that he missed the one element in my plan which in his eyes would assure its success, namely my willingness to take over the direction of the theater, because he could not conceive of anyone else being able to handle the job. When I then had to state that I would have nothing to do with such a position, the matter was dropped, and in my heart I could not help thinking these people were right.

Meanwhile, interest in me was intensifying; as I really had to refuse to surrender to the wishes of my friends with respect to the performance of my principal works in the theater, I finally offered to give at least a selection of characteristic excerpts suitable to be heard in concert form, as soon as the necessary support was forthcoming. Accordingly, a subscription list was circulated, and this produced the satisfactory result of inducing several well-known and rich patrons of the arts to guarantee the costs. I was obliged to undertake to engage an orchestra adequate for my requirements; from near and far capable musicians were summoned, and after unceasing toil I began to feel that something really satisfactory would be achieved. I had arranged things so that the musicians I had engaged had to stay from one Sunday to another and spend a full week in Zürich. Half this time was reserved exclusively for rehearsals. On Wednesday came the first performance, the concert being repeated on Friday and Sunday evenings. The dates were May 18th, 20th, and 22nd, the last being my fortieth birthday. I had the joy of seeing all my instructions scrupulously carried out; from Mainz, Wiesbaden, Frankfurt, and Stuttgart, as well as from Geneva, Lausanne, Basel, Berne and the chief towns in Switzerland, the select group of musicians arrived punctually that Sunday afternoon. They were directed immediately to the theater to become acquainted with their precise positions in the orchestral layout of the type I had previously designed for Dresden and which proved its worth here as well, so that the next morning they were able to begin the rehearsals at once without any delays or disturbance. As these people were at my disposal from morning to night, I had no trouble rehearsing them in sizeable excerpts from *Der fliegende Holländer*, *Tannhäuser*, and *Lohengrin* within two and a half days. With somewhat greater difficulty I had tried to put a chorus together, and this now managed to do very well after all. The only solo piece was Senta's ballad from the *Holländer*, which the wife of Herr Heim,[1] the conductor of the choral society, sang with commendable spirit and a good, if untrained, voice. The whole undertaking did not really have a public aspect but was rather patriarchal in nature: I assumed I was fulfilling the honest wish of a large number of my acquaintances by making them familiar with the essentials of my music as best I could in the circumstances. As some knowledge of the poetic foundations was required even for this purpose, I invited those proposing to attend the performances to come to the music society's concert hall on three evenings to hear me read the poems of the three operas from which they were to hear excerpts. This invitation met an enthusiastic response; and I was now able to conclude that my audience would come better prepared to hear the representative fragments from my operas than had ever been the case before. These three evening concerts were especially moving for me, for it was the first time I had been able to perform anything from my *Lohengrin* and thus gain an impression of the effect of my instrumentation of the prelude to this work. Between the performances I was tendered a banquet, the only one, apart from an occasion much later in Budapest, I have ever been accorded. I was truly touched by the speech of the old president of the music society, Herr Ott-Usteri; he drew the attention of all the musicians who had come together from so many different places to the significance of their meeting, as well as to its purpose and its consequences, recommending they take home with them the conviction that must have been gained by all of having entered upon a close and fruitful relationship with a great new phenomenon in the realm of art.

The excitement caused by these evening concerts reverberated throughout Switzerland; inquiries and demands for further repetitions poured in from distant places; I was assured that I could repeat the three concerts in the following week without having to worry about any diminution in the throng of listeners. When this project was discussed, I pleaded fatigue and also expressed the desire to let these concerts retain their unique character and not become a routine matter. I was pleased to be firmly and powerfully seconded in this view by my versatile friend Hagenbuch. The festival was concluded and the guests sent home at the appointed time.

I had hoped to be able to welcome Liszt among the visitors, as he had celebrated a "Wagner Week" in Weimar the previous March with performances of the same three operas from which I had given only excerpts. Unfortunately it had not been possible for him to pry himself away so early, but instead he had promised me a visit at the beginning of July. Among my German friends, only the two loyal ladies Julie Kummer and Emilie Ritter had arrived in time for the concerts. As these two had gone to Interlaken at the beginning of June and I also began to feel greatly in need of some rest, I went there at the end of the month with my wife on a short pleasure trip, but this was most dismally spoiled by incessant rain. However on July 1st, as we started out in desperation to return to Zürich with our friends, magnificent and unbroken summer weather set in, which we interpreted with amiable enthusiasm as Liszt's companion on his trip to Switzerland, and indeed he arrived in Zürich in the best of spirits immediately after our return. Now followed one of those weeks[1] in life in which every hour of the day produced a rich treasure of memories. I had already taken a larger apartment on the second floor of the same so-called Vordere Escherhäuser in which I had previously occupied an unduly confined ground-floor dwelling. Frau Stockar-Escher,[2] co-owner of the house and an artistically talented woman (an amateur water-colorist) who was devoted to me, had made every effort to furnish the new apartment as luxuriously as possible. The unexpected improvement in my situation brought about by the increased demand for my operas permitted me to indulge lavishly my desire for comfortable domestic surroundings, which the deprivations of the water cure had awoken in me and repression had intensified almost to a mania. I had the apartment so elegantly decked out with carpets and other pieces that Liszt himself was startled into admiration of what he termed my "petite élégance". Now for the first time I had the delight of getting to know my friend as a fellow-composer. In addition to many of his more recent and celebrated piano pieces, we went through several of his latest symphonic poems with great ardor, in particular his *Faust* Symphony. My impression of this work was communicated in detail on a subsequent occasion in a letter to Marie von Wittgenstein[3] which has been published. My joy in everything I heard by Liszt was as profound as it was genuine, but above all it was productively stimulating; for after such a long interval I was myself about to begin composing again. Nothing could have been more important or more promising than this long-desired meeting with my friend, who was now continuously engaged in the exercise of his own mastery and yet had dedicated himself so absolutely to my own works and their wider understanding. These almost bewilderingly delightful days with the inevitable onrush of friends and acquaintances were interrupted by an excursion we took to the Lake of Lucerne, accompanied only by Herwegh, to whom Liszt made the charming suggestion of drinking brotherhood with him and me from the three springs of the Grütli. But after this my friend left us, having arranged for another meeting with me in the autumn.

Although I felt quite disconsolate after Liszt's departure, the Zürich public took good care to provide me with a form of diversion I had not previously experienced. After long toil a calligraphic masterpiece in the form of an honorary diploma to be awarded me by the Zürich Choral Society was at last ready; this diploma was to be presented with the participation of all the corporate and individual elements of Zürich society favorably disposed toward me, in the course of a solemn torchlight procession. Thus, on one lovely summer evening, stately ranks of torch-bearers approached the Zeltweg with a sonorous musical accompaniment and offered me a spectacle such as I have never again beheld to this day. There was singing, and then the formal address of the president of the choral society wafted up to me. I was so much moved by this event that my invincible optimism quickly took possession of my imagination: in my response I indicated plainly that I saw no reason why Zürich should not in fact be destined, in its solid bourgeois way, to give an impetus toward the fulfillment of my highest aims with respect to the artistic ideals I cherished. I think they interpreted this as foretelling the special prosperity of their male choral society and were thus well satisfied with my bold predictions. Apart from this rather serious quid pro quo I had invoked, the spirit of the evening remained cheerful and its effect on my mood entirely beneficial.

But I still felt the same peculiar anxiety and uneasiness about resuming my musical production that I had previously experienced after any lengthy interruption in this activity. I was also much exhausted by all I had gone through and accomplished, and the recurrent longing that had plagued me ever since my departure from Dresden to make a clean break with everything, the desire to seek out a virginally new mode of life, was made big by that especial anxiety, and revived in me to a new, unsettling degree. I got the idea that, before I undertook such a monumental task as setting my Nibelung dramas to music, I should make one last try at finding a more harmonious existence in entirely new surroundings than was afforded me by the present one, with all its prior compromises. I projected a trip to Italy, at least to the extent this was possible for me as a political refugee. The funds necessary for the fulfillment of my wish were easily provided by my friend Wesendonck, who was now eager to be helpful. Since I obviously could not think of commencing the journey before the onset of autumnal weather, and also because my doctor had recommended some special treatment to strengthen my nerves, even if only the better to enjoy Italy, I decided to proceed first of all to visit the spa of St Moritz in the Engadine, to which I set off with Herwegh in the second half of July.

Often in my life I have had the strange experience of finding what others would only note in their diaries as a simple visit or a little trip taking on for me the quality of a great adventure. Thus it was with this trip to the spa, when we were detained at Chur in a frightful driving rainstorm as a result of overcrowding in the mail coach. We were compelled to while away the time in a highly uncomfortable hotel with our reading material: I resorted to Goethe's *West-Östlicher Diwan*, having prepared myself by going through Daumer's version of Hafiz.[1] To this day I cannot think of some of Goethe's remarks in the notes on these poems without being forcibly reminded of our painfully delayed expedition to the Engadine. We didn't do much better in St Moritz; the comfortable present-day spa hotel had not yet been constructed, and we had to make do with the most primitive accommodations, which upset me particularly on Herwegh's behalf, as he had come along on this trip solely for pleasure and with no curative purposes. Yet we were soon cheered up by the impressions gathered during our walks out of the upper valley, covered solely with mossy growth, over steep slopes and into the lower Italian valleys. We got down to serious business when we managed to secure the services of the school-master of Samaden as a guide for the Rosegg glacier. We confidently looked forward to an exceptional pleasure in pressing through to the cliffs of the uniquely splendid Pizzo Bernina, whose beauty we deemed superior to that of Mont Blanc; this pleasure was somewhat diminished for my companion by the tremendous exertions attendant upon the ascent and crossing of the marvelous glacier. Once again, and this time even more intensely, I felt the exalted sense of sublime desolation and the almost violently benumbing calm which the extinction of all vegetation produces on the pulsating life of the human organism. After we had walked for two hours into the midst of the glacier by way of the track across it, the meal we had brought along, together with champagne which we chilled in the ice fissures, had to strengthen us for the difficult trip back. I had to cover almost double the distance, as I had to demonstrate repeatedly for the surprisingly over-anxious Herwegh the safety of the path we were taking before he could bring himself to follow. Yet I myself had ample grounds to realize the exhausting quality of the air in this region when we stopped at the first herdsman's cottage we saw on the way back and refreshed ourselves with some wonderful milk. I consumed such a volume of this that we both were utterly amazed, especially as I felt no unpleasant after-effects whatsoever. As far as the use of the local water for drinking and bathing was concerned, famous as it was for its iron content, the result was no better than on previous attempts of this kind: my temperament, which was so strongly inclined to excitement, brought me more discomfort than relief. My sole reading matter during leisure hours was Goethe's *Elective Affinities*, which I had read before only in early youth. This time I devoured the book line by line; it also became a bone of contention between myself and Herwegh, who, with his extensive familiarity with the nature of our poetic literature, felt obliged to defend the character of Charlotte against my attacks. In my agitation over the matter, I suddenly realized how curiously things stood with me now that I had completed my fortieth year, and had to admit to myself that Herwegh judged Goethe's work more truly, objectively speaking, than I, who felt some persistent moral inhibitions which, if Herwegh had ever felt them, had been dispelled by his special relationship to his resolute wife. When our time at the spa came to an end and I realized that I couldn't hope for very much from the treatment, we left in mid-August to go back to Zürich, where I now eagerly prepared myself for the trip to Italy.[1]

September arrived at last,[2] which everybody had told me was the best month for visiting Italy. I therefore departed via Geneva, full of indescribable visions of what was awaiting me and the manner in which my hopes would be fulfilled. Once again subjected to the strangest adventures, I got to Turin over Mont Cenis by special mail coach. Entirely dissatisfied by my stay there, I rushed on to Genoa two days later. Here the long awaited miracle seemed about to take place. To this day, the impression created by the city outweighs all my longing for the rest of Italy. For a few days I was as if intoxicated; but it was no doubt my extreme loneliness amid all these impressions which soon made me feel the alien elements of this world and realize that I would never become part of it. Without any guidance or capacity to hunt down Italian art treasures according to any systematic plan, I abandoned myself rather to what might be called a musical way of sensing these new phenomena and above all else tried to find the point which would help me decide to remain there and calmly enjoy it. For I was still driven to seek some sort of asylum which would afford me the soothing harmony I needed for artistic creation. But soon, as a consequence of over-indulgence in ice cream, I got an attack of dysentery, which produced a sudden and depressing lassitude after the initial exaltation. I wanted to get away from the horrendous noise of the harbor, beside which my hotel was situated, and seek the most extreme tranquillity. For this purpose I believed an excursion to Spezia would be appropriate, and after a week I proceeded there by steamship. Even this voyage, which lasted only one night, turned into an arduous adventure as a result of violent head-winds. My dysentery was supplemented by seasickness, and by the time I reached Spezia I could hardly take a single step and went to the best hotel, which to my dismay was situated in a narrow and noisy alley. After a sleepless and feverish night, I forced myself to undertake a long walk the following day among the pine-covered hills of the surroundings. Everything seemed to me to be bleak and bare, and I asked myself why I had come. Returning that afternoon, I stretched out dead-tired on a hard couch, awaiting the long-desired onset of sleep. It did not come; instead, I sank into a kind of somnambulistic state, in which I suddenly had the feeling of being immersed in rapidly flowing water. Its rushing soon resolved itself for me into the musical sound of the chord of E flat major, resounding in persistent broken chords; these in turn transformed themselves into melodic figurations of increasing motion, yet the E flat major triad never changed, and seemed by its continuance to impart infinite significance to the element in which I was sinking. I awoke in sudden terror from this trance, feeling as though the waves were crashing high above my head. I recognized at once that the orchestral prelude to *Das Rheingold*, long dormant within me but up to that moment inchoate, had at last been revealed; and I also saw immediately precisely how it was with me: the vital flood would come from within me, and not from without.

I immediately decided to return to Zürich and begin setting my vast poem to music. I telegraphed my wife to inform her of this and have my work-room ready. That same evening I climbed into the coach, which was to take me back to Genoa via the Riviera di Levante. I still had an opportunity of gaining lovely impressions of the countryside on this trip, which lasted the whole of the next day; the coloration of everything excited me especially: the red mountain rocks, the azure of sky and sea, the pale green of the pines, even the dazzling white of a herd of cattle had such a drastic impact on me that I had to bemoan how sad it was that I could not remain and absorb all this for the ennoblement of my senses. In Genoa I felt once again so agreeably stimulated that I suddenly took it into my head that I had only given way to a foolish weakness, decided to carry out my original plan, and began making arrangements to travel to Nice along the celebrated Riviera di Ponente. But I had scarcely resumed my original resolve when it dawned on me that the factor which had refreshed and invigorated me was not a renewal of my delight in Italy but rather the decision to begin work. For as soon as I made any change in this latter decision, all the old symptoms of dysentery returned at once. I now understood my own condition and forgoing the trip to Nice returned by the most direct route via Alessandria and Novara and by the Borromean Islands, to which I was now supremely indifferent, and so over the Gotthard to Zürich.

Once I had returned, the only thing that could have made me happy would have been the immediate commencement of my work. Yet there was the immediate prospect of a major interruption, namely the rendezvous I had arranged with Liszt in Basel for the beginning of October. Restless and bad-tempered I whiled away the time in visits to my wife at Baden am Stein, where she had gone to take the waters, assuming I would be away for a long period. As I was easily persuaded to submit to such treatment whenever it was urged upon me with any conviction, I let myself be ensnared in a program of hot baths, which seriously intensified my distraught condition. Finally the time came for the reunion in Basel. At the invitation of the Grand Duke of Baden, Liszt had put on a music festival in Karlsruhe, devoting it largely to providing the public with adequate interpretations of our own works. I could not set foot on the soil of any state of the German Federation; therefore Liszt had chosen Basel as the point nearest the Baden border in order to bring some young friends, who had gathered around him in Karlsruhe, to meet me. I got there first and was sitting alone that evening in the restaurant of the Three Kings hotel, when I heard from the vestibule a not very numerous but lusty chorus singing the trumpet fanfare accompanying the King's summons in *Lohengrin*. The door opened, and Liszt entered at the head of his exuberant little band. For the first time since his eventful winter stay in Zürich and St Gall I saw Bülow again, and with him Joachim, Peter Cornelius,[1] Richard Pohl,[2] and Dionys Pruckner.[3] Liszt told me that his friend Karoline von Wittgenstein would be arriving the following day in the company of her young daughter Marie. Given the unusually joyful mood of this meeting, which in spite of all informality had the characteristics of a grand and notable occasion about it, like everything connected with Liszt, it was no surprise that the evening gave birth to the most eccentric hilarity. In the midst of all this merriment I suddenly missed Pohl, whom I had already known to be a champion of our cause through articles he published under the pseudonym

"Hoplite". I stole away and sought him out in his distant room, where I found him already in bed with a severe headache. But my hearty regrets at this made such an impression on him that he suddenly asserted he felt quite well, jumped out of bed, let me help him get dressed again quickly, and followed me to rejoin the company, where we talked together hilariously until far into the night.

Our festivities were crowned the following day, when the ladies we were expecting arrived and became the center of our attention for several days. As everybody who came into contact with Princess Karoline in those days will know, it was impossible to resist her uncommon vivacity and the wholeheartedness with which she involved herself and all about her in every activity. She was as vitally interested in the loftiest questions engaging our interest as in the most trivial details of our personal dealings in the world, and this interest flattered everyone to such an extent that he was transported into a state where he felt impelled to give of his very best at all times. Her daughter, who was barely fifteen years old, made a rather distant and dreamy impression by contrast; her demeanor and attire were those of the young girl just blossoming into maidenhood, and I awarded her the honorary title "The Child". Sometimes our discussions or excited outbursts would virtually boil over, and then she would look at us with her dark and pensive eyes with such a deep and knowing calm that we instinctively felt she represented the innocent way of understanding all these matters that concerned us so fiercely. I was easily persuaded to read aloud from my Nibelung dramas, inasmuch as I had a great weakness for doing so at the time (much to Herwegh's annoyance, incidentally), and I selected only *Siegfried* for this purpose, as the time for our departure was approaching. As Liszt had to go on to Paris to visit his children, we all accompanied him as far as Strassburg: I had decided to follow Liszt to Paris, whereas the Princess and her daughter felt they had to go back to Weimar. In the few free hours of our stay there I was supposed to read them some more, but no really suitable occasion arose. Yet on the morning of our scheduled parting, Liszt came to my bedside to inform me that the ladies had elected to go with us to Paris; he smilingly claimed Marie had brought her mother to this decision by her desire to hear me read the other Nibelung dramas. I was delighted by the smack of magnanimity and adventure imparted to our travel plans by the manner in which our party was to be enlarged. Unfortunately we had to take leave of our young friends; as to Joachim, Bülow explained his rather modest and defensive attitude as resulting from a certain melancholy shyness toward me, because of the opinions

I had expressed in my notorious article on "Judaism". In presenting Bülow with one of his compositions for perusal, he had asked him whether I might possibly find anything "Jewish" in it. This gentle, even rather moving trait in Joachim's character impelled me to give him a warm hug and a fond word of farewell. I have never seen him since then* but have heard the most astonishing tales over the years of his inimical attitude toward Liszt and myself, which he began to strike not long after this meeting. The other young men were victims on their return to Germany of a very funny though unfortunate contretemps with the police in Baden: they had gone along the open road there singing the resounding *Lohengrin* fanfare, were charged with disturbing the peace, and had a good deal of trouble explaining its significance to the populace there.

The journey that the rest of us took together to Paris was full of significant impressions stemming from our almost extravagant sense of friendship, and it was the same with our stay there. Having found rooms for the ladies with great difficulty in the Hotel des Princes after our arrival late one night, Liszt demanded that we take a walk together along the utterly deserted boulevards. I surmise that our feelings on this walk differed as widely as our memories. When I entered the sitting room the next morning, Liszt remarked with his characteristic smile that Princess Marie was already in a state of great excitement, hoping to assure herself of yet another reading. By that time I had rather lost my enthusiasm for Paris; Princess Karoline felt compelled to make herself as inconspicuous there as possible; Liszt had been summoned away by his personal affairs; thus oddly enough, it came about that even before setting foot on the streets of Paris we spent that first morning in a continuation of the readings begun in Basel. And in the days that followed there was no surcease until I had gone through all four parts of my *Nibelung's Ring*. But finally Paris claimed its due, and when the ladies went off to visit the museums, I was the one who withdrew to my lonely room, plagued by incessant nervous headaches. Yet Liszt managed to persuade me to take part in some of their activities. Right at the beginning of our stay he had taken a box for a performance of *Robert le Diable*, as he thought it necessary to acquaint the ladies with the magnificence of the famous Opéra in a favorable light. I believe my friends shared something of the miserable depression this prospective occasion produced in me; yet Liszt had other motives for attending as well: he asked me to appear in formal

* Footnote in the manuscript, in Wagner's hand: "This was written in 1869".

evening dress, and he was obviously pleased to see that I had fulfilled his request when he invited me to stroll with him in the foyer during an intermission. I could see that reminiscences of certain uncommonly delightful evenings spent there in younger days had misled him as to the aspect this foyer would present on an evening as dismal as this one. We slunk quietly back to our friends, hardly knowing why we had undertaken this boring promenade.

But I derived extraordinary artistic pleasure, almost comparable to that produced long before in Paris by the performance of Beethoven's Ninth Symphony by the orchestra of the Conservatoire, from an evening of chamber music by the Maurin-Chevillard Quartet, who had been invited by Liszt to play Beethoven's E flat major and C sharp minor quartets for us. I again had occasion to admire the uncommon benefits deriving from the zeal and dedication with which the French master these musical treasures, which are still handled so roughly in Germany. The C sharp minor quartet, I must admit, was here revealed to me in its true form for the first time, as its melos had hitherto been unclear to me. Even if I had no other memories from my stay in Paris at that time, I would have to single that out as unforgettable and significant.

But other memories remain as a residue of that trip that are no less meaningful. One day Liszt invited me to spend an evening with his children,[1] who lived a secluded life in Paris under the care of a governess. It was a new experience for me to observe my friend in the company of these girls, who were already growing tall, and his son, who was just entering adolescence. He himself seemed a bit bemused by his role as a father, from which over the years he had derived only the cares and none of the satisfactions. On this occasion, too, it came to a reading, namely the final act of *Götterdämmerung*, and thus the long-awaited close of the whole thing. Berlioz, who arrived while it was going on, behaved with admirable forbearance in the face of this misfortune. We spent the next morning with him, when he gave us a breakfast to bid us farewell; he had already packed his musical materials to embark on a concert tour of Germany. Here Liszt played for me from *Benvenuto Cellini*, and Berlioz accompanied by singing in his own rather dry way. I also met the essayist Jules Janin[2] on this occasion, without realizing who he was, and his casual and for me incomprehensible Parisian French was the only thing about him that struck me then as unusual. I also recall a soirée in the house of the famous piano manufacturer Erard. Here I again met Liszt's children, as well as at a dinner given by Liszt himself at the Palais Royal, and the youngest, his son Daniel, made a particularly vivid impression on me by his great vivacity and resemblance to his father, whereas of his daughters I noted only their invariable shyness. I also recall an evening at the home of Mme Kalergis, whom I saw again here for the first time since that earliest performance of *Tannhäuser* in Dresden. This singular woman made a rather chilling impression on me in these surroundings. The rumors reaching me about the intimate relations she enjoyed with General Cavaignac,[1] and supposedly even the President, Louis Napoleon, made her appear in a rather dubious light. When she happened to ask me during dinner a question about Louis Napoleon, I forgot myself to the point of declaring, in an over-excited mood to which some bitterness was admixed, that nobody could possibly expect anything great for the world from a man who was incapable of true love for a woman: that ended the conversation. While Liszt was playing a few things for us after dinner, the young Marie Wittgenstein noticed my especially melancholy reserve, caused in part by my headaches and in part by a feeling of inner alienation from such circles as now surrounded me. I was touched by her sympathy and palpable desire to cheer me up.

After what was for me a very exhausting week, my friends left Paris. As I had once again been held back from beginning my work, I was determined not to leave Paris before I had finally achieved that calm and collected frame of mind suitable for carrying out my great project. I had invited my wife to come from Zürich and join me for the return trip, wanting to offer her a renewed glimpse of the city in which we had suffered so much. After her arrival Kietz and Anders began showing up for dinner with us almost every evening; and also a young Pole, the son of my old and so greatly esteemed friend Count Vincenz Tyskiewitsch, came to visit us. This very young man, born after the period in which I had known his father, had devoted himself enthusiastically to music, as so many do these days. He had already caused a stir in Paris by declaring, after attending a performance of *Der Frieschütz* at the Opéra, that the cuts and alterations in the score constituted a swindle on the informed listener, and filing a lawsuit against the theater management to recover the price of admission. He also wanted to found a magazine with the avowed purpose of drawing attention to the slovenly conduct of musical affairs in Paris, which he regarded as an insult to public taste. There also remained from Liszt's circle the young Prince Eugen von Wittgenstein-Sayn, for whom I frequently sat while he painted a miniature of me in an amateur yet skillful manner and which under the guidance of Kietz turned out quite well. I also had an important consultation with a young doctor named Lindemann, a friend of Kietz, who tried to win me away from the theory of hydrotherapy to the toxic theory. He had attracted the attention of Parisian society by having inoculated himself with various poisons at the hospital in the presence of witnesses and having tested their effect on the human organism by close analysis of the results. As to my own nervous condition, he asserted it would be easy to alleviate as soon as it could be determined by experiment which metallic substance could control the reaction of my nervous system. For periods of acute suffering he recommended to me with calm conscience the use of laudanum. Beyond that, he seemed to consider valerian a suitable medicine for me.

Tired, restless, and exceedingly distraught, I left Paris with Minna at the end of October, without having any real idea to what purpose I had spent so much money there. Hoping for compensation from the propagation of my operas in Germany, I went back to my Zürich lodgings in a mood of increasing composure, vowing not to leave them until I had completed the music for at least some part of my Nibelung dramas. At the beginning of November I finally commenced this long-delayed work. Since the end of March 1848, five and a half years had elapsed in which I had completely renounced any musical productivity, and as I now actually succeeded in getting into the right frame of mind to resume it, I can best compare this resumption with a rebirth after a long wandering of the soul in other spheres. As far as the technical aspect of my work was concerned, I soon got into difficulty when trying to transcribe the orchestral prelude I had conceived in that trance-like condition in Spezia in my accustomed manner of sketching it out on two staves. I had to resort to scoring it in full from the very first; this led me to adopt an entirely new method of sketching, whereby I drafted the various orchestral parts extremely cursorily in pencil for immediate reworking in the full score. This later caused me serious difficulties, for the slightest interruption in my work often made me forget the meaning of my cursory sketches, and I then had to struggle to recall it. But I didn't let that problem arise in the case of *Rheingold*; the sketch for the whole composition was completed as early as January 16th 1854, and thus the plan for the musical structure of the entire four-part work was prefigured in this work's thematic relationships. For it was here, in this great prelude, that the thematic foundation for the whole had to be laid.

I recall a decided improvement in the state of my health during the writing of this work, and so I remember very little of the external life around me throughout that period. With the onset of the new year I again conducted in a few orchestral concerts. To fulfill a request of my friend Sulzer, I performed in one of them Gluck's overture to *Iphigenia in Aulis*, after previously providing it with a new finale of my own. The need for this minor revision that I felt when I contemplated Mozart's ending also induced me to produce an essay for Brendel's musical journal concerning the artistic problem involved. Yet all this didn't keep me from finishing the full score for *Rheingold*, which I first quickly executed in pencil on individual sheets. On May 28th the instrumentation of *Rheingold* was complete.

Meanwhile there was little change in my domestic routine; everything that had evolved during the past few years in this respect continued in a pleasant and peaceful manner. But my financial position was again subject to some strain, for in the previous year, particularly as far as my household furnishings and general standard of living were concerned, I had, I suppose, counted too much on the continuation and augmentation of my income from the theaters giving my operas. But alas, the bigger and better-paying theaters still held back. Now in this particular year I had to face the disagreeable fact that I was not getting anywhere with Berlin and Vienna: this created worries of more than one variety, which weighed upon me for the greater part of the year. I sought refuge from depression in new work, and instead of making the fair copy of the score of *Rheingold*, busied myself at once with the composition of *Die Walküre*. By the end of July I had finished the first scene, before interrupting my labors to undertake an excursion to the southern part of Switzerland.

I had received an invitation from the Helvetian Society of Music to direct its music festival in Sion that year. I had refused this, yet had promised to attend and, provided the resources available seemed satisfactory to me, to conduct Beethoven's A major Symphony at one of the gala concerts. I combined this trip with a plan to visit Karl Ritter at Montreux on Lake Geneva, where he had settled with his young bride. I spent about a week there, observed the curious quality of this young marriage, which did not seem to promise permanent felicity, with some anxiety, and then went with Karl to the music festival in the canton of Valais. En route, in Martigny, we were joined by a strange young fellow, who had been introduced to me the year before on the occasion of my big Zürich concerts as a budding enthusiast and musician. This was Robert von Hornstein: this very comical person was welcome, above all to my younger friend Ritter, as a further companion in our anticipated adventure; for it was actually the news that I would direct the Helvetian music festival which had lured him from Swabia to Valais. Unfortunately, upon arrival at the location of this music festival, I found, contrary to my expectations, such inadequate and scanty preparations for the artistic undertaking, that, particularly upon hearing the sound of the pitifully small orchestra in a diminutive church which was supposed to serve also as the concert hall, I became furious at the frivolity which had sought to involve me in such a venture, and after scribbling a few lines to the festival director, Herr Methfessel from Berne, left without further ado, just catching the next mail coach as it set off, while keeping my young friends in the dark about this act. I had special reasons for this last move, and as they were rather interesting from a psychological point of view, I have never forgotten them. Returning to lunch at the inn that day in a black mood after discovering all this evidence of artistic inadequacy, by my very ill-humor I aroused persistent and even insulting boyish laughter on the part of these two. I was obliged to assume that this was the continuation of a merry mood induced by a previous conversation about me. As none of my exhortations, or even my anger, could bring them to conduct themselves more sensibly, I left the restaurant greatly put out, made arrangements for my departure, and contrived to conceal it from them so completely that they learned of it only after I had gone. I went to Geneva and Lausanne for a few days, and then called on young Frau Ritter, who had remained behind in Montreux, on my way back; here I met the two young people once again: taken aback at my sudden departure, they had also abandoned the misbegotten musical festival and, in the hope of hearing something from me, had returned to Montreux. I did not breathe a word about their rude behavior; as Karl requested me very cordially to stay with them for a while, and because a recently completed poetic work of his greatly interested me, I yielded. This was a comedy called *Alcibiades*, which had been conceived and executed with a remarkable degree of formal refinement and freedom. Karl had first told me of this project in Albisbrunn and had also shown me an elegant dagger, on the blade of which the syllables "Alci" had been branded. He informed me that his young actor friend, whom he had left behind in Stuttgart, possessed a similar dagger, the blade of which showed the syllables "Biades". It now appeared that in the young booby Hornstein Karl had found, even without the symbolic help of such weapons, a similar complement to the element of Alcibiades in him, and on that occasion in Sion the two no doubt had thought themselves performing an Alcibiadesian scene in the face of Socrates. Happily, his comedy showed me that his talent was greater than his practical abilities in life.

I regret to this day that the decidedly difficult problems obstructing a performance of the piece have never been resolved. Hornstein now behaved with seemly restraint as well; I accompanied him on his trip home a part of the way on foot from Vevey to Lausanne, and his quaint appearance with his little satchel was most amusing and touching.

I then went directly via Berne and Lucerne to Seelisberg on the Lake of Lucerne, where my wife had already preceded me for the purpose of taking a whey cure. The signs of heart trouble I had observed previously had now multiplied, and this stay had been urgently prescribed for her health. I patiently endured several weeks of suffering in a Swiss boarding house, but unfortunately my wife seemed to look upon me as a disturbing element, as she had adapted herself entirely to the ways of the house and seemed utterly comfortable; yet the fine air and daily outings on the mountain paths helped me as well. In my thoughts I went so far as to choose an especially wild place on which I desired to have a little wooden house constructed for my use, in order to be able to work there undisturbed some day. At the end of July we went back to Zürich together, where I at once resumed the composition of *Die Walküre*, finishing the first act before the end of August. As I was hard-pressed by the aforementioned worries at this time, and as the prospect of peace and quiet in the house was just what I wanted for my work, I was glad to accede to my wife's wish to visit her friends and relatives in Dresden and Zwickau. At the beginning of September, she left me for a time and soon reported to me about a visit to Weimar as well, where she had been hospitably received by Princess Wittgenstein in the Altenburg. There she had also seen the wife of Röckel, whose brother was supporting her in a self-sacrificing way. In a burst of energy curiously characteristic of her, she got the idea of going from there to visit the prison in Waldheim to see Röckel himself, despite the fact that she had always found him antipathetic, in order to be able to provide his wife with some news of his condition. She succeeded in this mission and notified me in a curious, almost sarcastic manner that Röckel appeared quite sleek and cheerful and did not seem to be badly off at all.

Meanwhile, I plunged deeply into my work, and on September 26th completed the exquisite fair copy of the score of *Rheingold*. In the tranquillity and stillness of my house I now also became acquainted with a book, the study of which was to assume vast importance for me. This was Arthur Schopenhauer's *The World as Will and Idea*.

Herwegh told me about this book, which had in a certain sense been discovered only recently, though more than thirty years had elapsed since its initial publication. It was only through an article relating these circumstances, by a Herr Frauenstädt,[1] that his own attention had first been directed to the work. I felt myself immediately attracted by it and began studying it at once. I had repeatedly experienced an inner impulse to come to some understanding of the true meaning of philosophy. Several conversations with Lehrs in Paris during my earlier days had awakened this desire within me, which up to this time I had tried to satisfy by attempts to get something out of the Leipzig professors, then from Schelling, and later from Hegel; those attempts had all daunted me before long, and some of the writings of Feuerbach had seemed to indicate the reasons for it. But now, apart from the interest elicited by the strange fate of this book, I was instantly captivated by the great clarity and manly precision with which the most abstruse metaphysical problems were treated from the beginning. As a matter of fact, I had already been struck by the verdict of an English critic,[2] who had candidly confessed that his obscure but unconvinced respect for German philosophy had been attributable to its utter incomprehensibility, as represented most recently by the works of Hegel. In reading Schopenhauer, on the other hand, he had suddenly realized that it had not been his dim-wittedness but rather the intentional turgidity in the treatment of philosophical theories which had caused his bafflement. Everyone who has been roused to great passion by life will do as I did, and hunt first of all for the final conclusions of the Schopenhauerian system; whereas his treatment of aesthetics pleased me immensely, particularly his surprising and significant conception of music, I was alarmed, as will be everyone in my frame of mind, by the moral principles with which he caps the work, for here the annihilation of the will and complete self-abnegation are represented as the only true means of redemption from the constricting bonds of individuality in its dealings with the world. For those seeking in philosophy their justification for political and social agitation on behalf of the so-called "free individual", there was no sustenance whatever here, where what was demanded was the absolute renunciation of all such methods of satisfying the claims of the human personality. At first, this didn't sit well with me at all, and I didn't want to abandon the so-called "cheerful" Greek view of the world which had provided my vantage point for surveying my "Art-work of the Future". Actually it was Herwegh who made me reflect further on my own feelings with a well-timed word. This insight into the essential nothingness of the world of appearances, he contended, lies at the root of all tragedy, and every great poet, and even every great man, must necessarily feel it intuitively. I looked at my Nibelung poems and recognized to my amazement that the very things I now found so unpalatable in the theory were already long familiar to me in my own poetic conception. Only now did I understand my own Wotan myself and, greatly shaken, I went on to a closer study of Schopenhauer's book. I now saw that before all else I had to comprehend the first part of the work, which elucidates and enlarges upon Kant's doctrine of the ideality of the world, which hitherto had seemed so firmly grounded in time and space. I considered I had taken the first step toward such an understanding simply by realizing its difficulty. From now on this book never left me entirely through the years, and by the summer of the next year I had already gone through it for the fourth time. Its gradual effect on me was extraordinary and, at any rate, decisive for the rest of my life. Through it, I was able to judge things which I had previously grasped only instinctively, and it gave me more or less the equivalent of what I had gained musically from the close study of the principles of counterpoint, after being released from the tutelage of my old teacher Weinlig. All my subsequent occasional writings about artistic matters of special interest to me clearly demonstrate the impact of my study of Schopenhauer and what I had gained by it. Meanwhile, I felt impelled to send the esteemed philosopher a copy of my Nibelung poem; I appended to the title in my own hand only the words "With admiration", without any other communication. This was in part a result of the great inhibition I felt about confiding in him, and also due to the feeling that if Schopenhauer could not figure out from reading my poem what kind of person I was, the most comprehensive letter on my part would not help him to do so. Thus I also renounced any vain wish to be honored by a written response from him. Yet I learned later[1] through Karl Ritter and also through Dr Wille, both of whom looked up Schopenhauer in Frankfurt, that he had expressed himself very favorably and meaningfully about my poem.

In addition to these studies, I continued with the composition of the music for *Walküre*, living in great seclusion, and spending my leisure time in long walks in the surrounding countryside. As usually happened with me whenever I was actively engaged in musical production, my poetic impulses were also stimulated. It was no doubt in part the earnest frame of mind produced by Schopenhauer, now demanding some rapturous expression of its fundamental traits, which gave me the idea for a *Tristan und Isolde*. I had been quite familiar with the subject from my Dresden studies, but my attention had been drawn to it more recently by Karl Ritter's telling me of his plan to dramatize it. At the time I had pulled no punches in pointing out to my young friend where the defects in his draft lay. He had confined himself to the adventurous incidents of the romance, while I had been immediately struck by its innate tragedy and was determined to cut away all the inessentials from this central theme. Returning from a walk one day, I jotted down the contents of the three acts in which I envisaged concentrating the material when I came to work it out at some future date. I wove into the last act an episode I later did not use: this was a visit by Parzival, wandering in search of the Grail, to Tristan's sickbed. I identified Tristan, wasting away but unable to die of his wound, with the Amfortas of the Grail romance. For the moment I was able to force myself not to devote further attention to this conception, in order that my great musical project be not interrupted.

In the meantime I succeeded, mainly with the help of my friends, in putting my precarious financial affairs into a more satisfactory shape. My relations with the German theaters also picked up again substantially. Minna had been in Berlin and, by means of an introduction from our old friend Alwine Frommann, had also succeeded in meeting the intendant of the Court Theater there, Herr von Hülsen. Now that two years had gone by without any results, I was all the more willing to hand over my *Tannhäuser* for a Berlin production without any preconditions, inasmuch as the work had meanwhile established itself so firmly in the other theaters that a failure in Berlin would no longer hurt its reputation, but rather would probably injure that of the Court Theater itself. At the beginning of November Minna returned from her expedition, and upon receiving her report I decided to let things take their own course with respect to the Berlin production of *Tannhäuser*. The upshot was a lot of vexation at the miserable presentation given my work, but I nonetheless gained a continuing flow of income in the form of the royalties paid by that theater.

Soon the Zürich Music Society knocked at my door again with a request that I participate in its winter concerts. Once again I acceded to this, but with the declaration that I now expected them to concern themselves seriously with the improvements in the orchestra I had recommended. I had already submitted to these worthy gentlemen of the music society two proposals for the establishment of a good orchestra in Zürich; now I quickly drafted a more comprehensive third one, in which I gave the most precise instructions as to how they would, at relatively small cost, achieve a good orchestra in cooperation with the theater. I told them I would be working with them this winter for the last time if they did not put these very inexpensive proposals into practice. Apart from this, I agreed to supervise the activities of a string quartet, formed from the leaders of the string sections of the orchestra, who had approached me with a request for assistance in acquiring the correct performance style in quartets I had recommended to them. Above all, I was glad to be able to help these people gain another quite lucrative source of income from the public, whose interest was rapidly drawn to them. Their artistic accomplishments, admittedly, were a horse of a different color, for it became clear to me that merely insisting on the dynamic nuances, when the style of the separate players was so free, could not of itself afford compensation for that which only the individual development of high artistic taste in the handling of the instrument can bring forth. Yet I went so far as to train them for a performance of Beethoven's C sharp minor Quartet, a venture which cost me a good deal of persistent effort in countless rehearsals. I produced a program note for this remarkable work of Beethoven. Whether this or the actual performance made any impression on any member of the audience I was unable to find out.

When I say that in addition I completed the sketches for the composition of the entire *Walküre* by December 30th of this year, I am surely saying enough to indicate my active and earnest life during his period, as well as to demonstrate that I did not allow any external distractions to interrupt my strict regimen.

In January 1855 I began the instrumentation of *Die Walküre*. Yet I was compelled to interrupt it immediately by some interim work resulting from the fact that I had mentioned to some friends my *Faust* Overture composed fifteen years before in Paris, thus arousing in them the desire to hear it. That in turn induced me to take a closer look at the composition, which had marked a significant turning point in my musical development at the time. Liszt had performed it in Weimar on one occasion some while ago, but, in addition to the good things he wrote me on the subject, had expressed the wish to see certain elements in it worked out more decisively. So I now revised the work and followed the advice my friend had offered me with his very fine perception in the manner demonstrated by the version of the composition now published by Härtel. I also rehearsed our orchestra in the overture and performed it with success, or so I thought. Only to my wife did it seem that there was really not much in it, and she asked me, when I went to London later in the year, not to perform it there.

For there now came a most curious invitation, the like of which has never been repeated in all my life. In January, I had received an inquiry from the London Philharmonic Society as to whether I might be inclined to conduct their concerts for the current year; since I was slow to respond, wanting to find out in advance more about the circumstances, I was surprised one day to receive a visit from a certain Mr Anderson. He was a member of the board of management of the famous society, who had traveled from London to Zürich for the purpose of securing my assent. I would have to come to London for four months, there to conduct eight concerts of the Philharmonic Society, for which I was to be paid in all two hundred pounds sterling. I still didn't know quite what to decide, as it was obvious that, from a business standpoint, there would be no profit for me in this, and also because conducting concerts was not of interest to me, except when individual performances of special worth could be achieved, which constituted the sole justification of the enterprise. One factor weighed in favor of the venture, in that I would again have the opportunity, after long deprivation, of dealing with a first-class orchestra; and then I was attracted by the almost mysterious circumstances by which the eyes of such a distant musical world had been focused on me. I saw something of a beckoning of fate in all this, and at last, confronted by the stupidly affable, in short, English countenance of Mr Anderson, agreed to the proposition, whereupon he very contentedly left me, clad in a huge fur coat whose owner I was later to know, to return directly to London.

Before I could follow him, I first had to take care of a calamity that had befallen me as a result of my good nature. The highly importunate director of this year's theatrical undertakings had in fact managed to procure my consent to a performance of *Tannhäuser* by insisting that, inasmuch as I had given the work to every other theater, it would certainly constitute a grave disadvantage if the Zürich theater were to be denied it merely because I was living there at the time. In addition, my wife got mixed up in the affair, as the singers for the roles of Tannhäuser and Wolfram soon turned to her for support; and she found a way to enlist my sympathy for one of her protégés, a poor tenor who had been badly treated by the director up to then. I went through their roles with these two several times and thus found myself impelled to attend the rehearsals to supervise their work. Because I was forced into one intervention after another, this was tantamount to my assuming the baton, and I actually conducted the first performance[1] myself. From this the woman who sang Elisabeth lingers in my memory in particular, for having usually sung soubrette roles in the past, she played the part in white kid gloves, dangling a fan. But this time I had enough of these concessions, and when the public summoned me onto the stage at the end, I told my friends quite flatly that they had seen me in this kind of enterprise for the last time, and that I would henceforth leave it to them to do what they could in the future for a theater whose feeble condition had that day once again been demonstrated to them; whereupon everyone was very startled. I delivered a similar statement to the music society, in which I again, and also for the last time, conducted a concert before my departure. Unfortunately, all this seems to have been interpreted as just another of my jovial whims, and no one felt the slightest inclination to make any extra effort, with the result that it required another very serious and almost rude statement on my part the following winter to avoid being pestered in this way ever again. Thus I left my former Zürich patrons in a somewhat baffled state and departed for London on February 26th.

I travelled via Paris and spent a few days there, during which I saw only Kietz and his friend Lindemann, whom he supposed to be a miraculous healer. Arriving on March 2nd[1] in London, I turned first of all to Ferdinand Praeger,[2] a childhood friend of the Röckel brothers, who had told me many good things about him. He had been established in London for many years as a music teacher and showed himself to be an unusually considerate fellow, yet a bit over-excited for the level of his education. After spending the first night in his house, I found with his help the following day a nice place to stay in Portland Terrace in the neighborhood of Regent's Park, of which I had pleasant recollections from my past visit. I thought my stay there would certainly prove agreeable, considering the expected onset of spring and the immediate proximity of that part of the park where the paths were shadowed by beautiful copper beeches. Although I spent four months in London, the spring never seemed to appear; the foggy climate weighed heavily on all the impressions I received there. Praeger immediately began looking after me in the most considerate way, accompanying me on the customary courtesy calls, including one to Mr Costa,[3] whom I found to be the *chef d'orchestre* of the Italian opera and thus the real power in musical activity in London; for he was also director of the Sacred Music Society, which gave performances of Handel and Mendelssohn nearly every week.

Praeger also took me to his friend Sainton, the first violinist of the London orchestra. After a very hearty reception on his side, I now learned the strange story of how I came to be invited to London.

Sainton,[1] a southern Frenchman from Toulouse with a fiery and out-going disposition, was living with a bona fide German musician from Hamburg named Lüders, the son of a municipal bandsman, and a man of very dry yet agreeable temperament. I was touched to learn later how these two became lifelong friends. Sainton had been touring as a virtuoso, and after playing in St Petersburg had found himself stranded in Helsingfors in Finland; hard-pressed by the demon of financial misfortune, he had no idea how to get away from there when the entirely modest and unimposing figure of the Hamburg bandsman's son approached him on the steps of the hotel with an inquiry whether he might be willing to accept his friendship, together with half the cash he had available at the time, inasmuch as he appeared to be in a tight situation. From this moment the two were inseparable friends, made a concert tour through Sweden and Denmark, returning in the most adventurous circumstances via Hamburg to Havre, Paris, and Toulouse, from where they eventually moved to London, Sainton to assume a leading position in the orchestra, and Lüders to get by as best he could as a humble music teacher. I found the two of them living together in a nice apartment like man and wife, always concerned for one another in tender friendship. This Lüders had read my writings on art, and *Opera and Drama* in particular had moved him to exclaim: "By thunder! There's something in that!" Sainton had pricked up his ears at this, and when he was consulted by Mr Anderson, the Philharmonic Society's Treasurer, as to what should be done, following a dispute that had arisen before the season began, for reasons that remained shrouded in obscurity, between the Society and the man who had hitherto conducted the Philharmonic Concerts, the powerful Mr Costa himself, who now declared he would not direct them in future, Sainton advised him, on Lüders' urging, to engage me. I learned that this recommendation had not been immediately accepted, and that only after Sainton had sworn blind that he had seen me conduct in Dresden, did Mr Anderson set forth in the fur coat lent him by Sainton to seek me out in Zürich, as a result of which I now found myself here. As I also discovered, Sainton had acted with the rashness characteristic of his nationality; for Costa had not dreamed that his declaration to the Philharmonic Society would be taken seriously, and he was vastly upset that I had taken his place. As leader of the same orchestra which was used for the Philharmonic Society concerts, he henceforth exerted an inimical influence on all the undertakings directed by me, under which even my friend Sainton was obliged to suffer, but without realizing the reason for it.

This became ever more evident as time went on, while abundant and manifold unpleasantness assailed me from other quarters as well. Above all the music critic of *The Times*, Mr Davison, expressed instant antagonism toward me. His behavior showed me clearly and distinctly for the first time the effect of my essay, *Judaism in Music*. Apart from this, Praeger notified me that, given his extremely powerful position on *The Times*, Davison was accustomed to receiving flattering attentions from anyone coming to England for musical purposes. Even Jenny Lind had bowed to this demand, with great benefit to her public success, and only Henriette Sontag, as Countess Rossi, had felt herself to be above such obligations. Since I was now looking forward solely to the opportunity of working with a good and full-strength orchestra, and producing some fine performances with it, I was very depressed, on the other hand, to learn that I was not to have the number of rehearsals I considered necessary for these concerts; the economic plans of the Society allowed me only one rehearsal per concert, each of which included two symphonies and many other pieces. Yet I still hoped the impact of my conducting might produce some special efforts in this respect; but it was utterly impossible to get out of the usual rut here, and thus I saw that the obligations I had assumed would be an intolerable burden. In the opening concert we performed Beethoven's *Eroica*, and my conducting seemed to be so great a success that the committee of the Philharmonic Society evinced obvious willingness to do their utmost for the second concert. They requested some excerpts from my works, as well as the Ninth Symphony of Beethoven, and for this purpose made an exception and granted me two rehearsals. This concert went quite well. For my prelude to *Lohengrin* I had written a program note, but the words "Holy Grail" and "God" were solemnly excised, on the grounds that this sort of thing was not appropriate for secular concerts. For the chorus in the symphony I had to content myself with the personnel of the Italian Opera and for the great recitative put up with a baritone whose English phlegm, combined with Italian training, drove me to despair in the rehearsals. From the English translation of the text I understood only "Hail thee, joy" for "Freude schöner Götterfunken". The Philharmonic Society seemed to have staked everything on the success of this concert, which actually left nothing to be desired; so people were all the more horrified when *The Times* furiously disparaged and belittled this achievement as well. They turned to Praeger, in the hope that he could induce me to make some gesture of appeasement toward Mr Davison, and at the very least persuade me to attend a dinner to be given by Mr Anderson, where

I could be introduced to him in a friendly way. Praeger already knew me well enough to deprive these gentlemen of any hope that I would make any concession whatever in this direction. The dinner did not take place, and subsequently I saw from then on that the Society, realizing that they were dealing with an irretrievably stubborn person, sincerely regretted having engaged me.

As the Easter holidays began after the second concert, thus causing a considerable hiatus, I conferred with my friends as to whether it might not be more sensible to give up the whole business of conducting these Philharmonic concerts, which I had so quickly discovered to be fruitless and foolish, and quietly return to Zürich. Praeger assured me that such a step would by no means be interpreted as a condemnation of the situation, but would rather be considered a deplorable instance of rudeness on my part, and the blame for it would fall primarily on my friends. This last factor determined my course, and I remained, though without any hope of being able to impart any fresh impetus to London musical life. The seventh concert brought the only noteworthy occurrence: the Queen chose that evening for her annual visit to one of these functions, and through her husband, Prince Albert, asked to hear the *Tannhäuser* overture. The presence of the court lent a ceremonial atmosphere to that evening; and I also had the pleasure of quite an animated conversation with the Queen and her consort at their invitation. At one point the subject of possible performance of my operas at the theater came up, to which Prince Albert objected that the Italian singers could not possibly do justice to my music. I was delighted when the Queen met this objection by contending that a great number of these Italian singers were actually German. All this made a favorable impression and served as a demonstration of public support for me, though it did not change the situation in any way; for the leading newspapers continued to proclaim that all my concerts were fiascos, and at about this time Ferdinand Hiller, who was directing a Rhenish music festival, felt he had grounds to cheer his cronies with the statement that I was at the end of my tether in London and could be considered as driven from the city with my tail between my legs. Yet I still experienced a profound satisfaction at the end of the eighth and final concert I conducted, when one of those rare scenes occurred which now and then spring from the pent-up emotions of the participants. After my initial successes, it had soon become clear to the members of the orchestra that whoever wished to remain in the good graces of their irresponsible chief, Mr Costa, and not be summarily dismissed by him, should under no circumstances show themselves to be sympathetic with me; this was the explanation given me for the sudden hush that had descended on the orchestra, whose members had at first been quite demonstrative in their approval. But now, at the close of this series of concerts, the suppressed feeling of these musicians burst forth, and they crowded around me on all sides with deafening shouts, while the audience, generally accustomed to leaving the hall noisily even before the music was over, formed enthusiastic groups which also pressed upon me from all sides with hearty cheers and handshakes, so that my farewell to musicians and public alike was expressed in a style that could scarcely be surpassed.

But the most unusual aspect of my life during this stay in London consisted in the different personal relationships into which it led me.

Immediately after my arrival, a young pupil of Liszt named Karl Klindworth[1] came to see me, bearing the highest recommendations from his teacher. He became a faithful and congenial friend, not only during this time in London, but afterward as well. Young as he was, the short period of his stay in London had sufficed to enable him to reach a despairing verdict on English musical activities, which I was soon obliged to share. Incapable of blending into the strange cliques comprising English musical life, he immediately forfeited all hope and prospects of gaining due recognition there, and he had already resigned himself to survive in this desert as best he could by giving hourly lessons. He had been too proud to pay the slightest attention to the all-powerful critics, who had initially fallen upon him as a pupil of Liszt. He was a really superb musician and an excellent pianist as well. He got busy with me immediately by offering to produce a piano transcription of my *Rheingold*, though only for the use of virtuosos of the highest rank. Unfortunately he soon developed a chronic illness, which robbed me of his desired company for long periods at a time.

While Praeger and his wife remained faithfully at my side, the curious ménage of Sainton and Lüders soon became my real domestic base of operations. I had a standing invitation to dinner there, and I almost invariably found it convenient to take my meals with these no less devoted friends. Here, where Praeger frequently joined us, I customarily recuperated from the wearisome round of my London activities. Often we wandered in the evening through streets enshrouded in fog, and on such occasions Lüders was particularly adept at immunizing us against these London phenomena by a splendid punch, which he had somehow or other learned to concoct. On only one occasion we got separated, and that was when there was a fearful crowd in the street, accompanying the

Emperor Napoleon from St James' Palace to the Covent Garden Theater one evening. This was during one of the critical stages of the Crimean War, and he had come to London with his wife to visit Queen Victoria, whereupon the Londoners gaped at him no less avidly than people of other nationalities are apt to do in similar circumstances. When I tried to cross over from Haymarket to Regent Street, I was taken for an over-eager spectator and accordingly treated to some jabs in the ribs, all of which only amused me as an obvious misunderstanding.

The great annoyances which arose in part from the curious manner in which Costa goaded Sainton through Mr Anderson, and which deprived me of the possibility of winning any influence over the Society, also gave rise to a number of amusing incidents. This Anderson had used the influence of a coachman of the Queen[1] to have himself elevated to the directorship of the Queen's Band, but he was so utterly bereft of musical knowledge that the annual court concert he had to conduct served always as a source of hilarity for the irrepressible Sainton, who told me many funny stories on the subject. Another matter coming to light during one of these imbroglios was that Mrs Anderson, whom I had christened Charlemagne on account of her colossal embonpoint, had managed to procure for herself among other things the position and the salary of a court trumpeter. Through these and similar bits of news I soon regretfully gained the impression that my merry friend would come out second-best in his exposé of that well-entrenched clique, and in fact it soon turned out that the question of who was to yield, Anderson or Sainton, was decided to the detriment of the latter, all of which simply confirmed to me that things were not very different in free England from the way they were elsewhere.

Our little group received a very significant addition through the arrival of Berlioz, who had been invited by the more recently established New Philharmonic Society to conduct two of its concerts in London. As its regular conductor, the Society had appointed, though on whose recommendation I could never discover, a certain Dr Wylde, a typical fat-faced Englishman, extremely good-natured but almost ludicrously incompetent. He had taken lessons in conducting from the Stuttgart conductor Lindpaintner, who had brought him to the point where he could at least try, when beating time, to keep up with the orchestra, which played on entirely as it pleased. I heard him perform a Beethoven symphony in this manner and was amazed to hear the audience burst out in the same applause accorded to the fiery and highly precise reading of the score at one of my concerts. To give these concerts some prestige, however, Berlioz, as stated, had been engaged for some of them. Thus I heard him perform some classical pieces, among others a Mozart symphony, and was perplexed, having heard him conduct his own compositions with such energy, to find him on these occasions to be just another time-beater of the most ordinary kind. Several of his own pieces, including some highly effective excerpts from his *Romeo and Juliet* symphony, again made a significant impression on me here; but I now began to be more precisely aware of the characteristic weaknesses, inherent in even the loveliest creations of this extraordinary musician, than I had been in that earlier period in Paris, where I generally felt only a certain discomfort commensurate with the immensity of the impression. But it was a very stimulating experience to dine with Berlioz on several occasions at Sainton's. Suddenly I was brought face to face with this man who had endured so much torment, whose fine edge was by then already blunted in some respects, and who yet possessed such singular gifts. Having come to London myself more from a desire for distraction and stimulation, I was entitled to consider myself completely happy and floating on the clouds by contrast with him, a man considerably my senior, who had come to London merely in the attempt to earn a few guineas. His whole being expressed weariness and despair, and I was suddenly seized by deep sympathy for the man, whose gifts obviously, to me, far surpassed those of all his rivals. Berlioz seemed to like the merry spontaneity with which I responded to him; his customarily short and almost frosty manner thawed considerably during the hours we spent together. He told me a lot of amusing stories about Meyerbeer, and how impossible it was to escape his flattery, which in turn was dictated by his desire for incessant laudatory articles in the press. Before the first performance of *Le Prophète*, he told me, Meyerbeer had given the customary "dîner de la veille"; when Berlioz had excused himself from attending, Meyerbeer reproached him delicately, requesting him to compensate for the injury by writing "nice little articles" about the opera. Berlioz informed me that it was utterly impossible to get anything unfavorable to Meyerbeer accepted by a Paris paper. It was less easy to communicate with him on more serious artistic concerns, for on such matters he always showed himself to be the glib Frenchman, expressing himself with well-honed arguments, and in his own certainty never entertaining any suspicion that he might not have understood his interlocutor properly. Once, when I had warmed to the subject, and to my astonishment suddenly found myself a master of the French language, I tried to express myself to him on the mystery of "artistic conception". I sought by this term to designate the strength of the impressions life makes on our inner self, which hold us captive in their way until we disburden ourselves of them by the unique development of forms out of the innermost soul, which those external impressions have by no means summoned up but merely stirred from their deep slumber, so that the artistic form takes shape not as the effect of the impressions received from life but rather as a liberation from them. Hereupon Berlioz smiled in an understanding and condescending way and said: "Nous appelons cela: digérer." My amazement at this rather abrupt summary of my painstaking explanation was substantiated in due course by the outward behavior of my new-won friend. I invited him to my last concert and thereafter to a modest farewell supper which I gave for my few friends in my lodgings. He soon left this latter function, pleading illness; those friends remaining behind made no secret of their conviction that Berlioz had been annoyed by the enthusiastic farewell accorded me by the public.

The remaining acquaintances I gleaned during my stay in London were not especially profitable. I was pleased, however, by a Mr Ellerton,[1] a pleasant and dignified man, brother-in-law to Lord Brougham, who was a poet, a music-lover, and alas, a composer to boot. He had himself introduced to me at one of the Philharmonic Society concerts and made no bones about welcoming me in London, on the grounds that I might help to counterbalance the overesteem accorded Mendelssohn. He was also the sole Englishman who was willing to honor me with a social invitation. He entertained me, together with some of my friends, at the University Club, at which occasion I had the opportunity to observe the munificence of such an establishment. After we had enjoyed ourselves thoroughly, one of the weaknesses in such English hospitality revealed itself to me, though in a perfectly pleasant way. My host let himself be conducted homeward by two men, one at each shoulder, as if this were the most normal thing in the world, for he would scarcely have been capable of proceeding very far down the street on his own.

I also made the acquaintance of a rather old-fashioned but very amiable composer named Potter,[2] one of whose symphonies I was obliged to conduct. This work pleased me by its unassuming dimensions and its clean contrapuntal working, and was all the more enjoyable in that its composer, an elderly but sociable eccentric, clung to me with almost fearful modesty. I virtually had to compel him to let me play the Andante of his symphony in the right tempo, thus proving that it was really rather pretty and interesting, whereas he had so little faith in his own work that he believed only the adoption of an unduly rapid tempo could overcome the danger of its causing boredom. When I earned him an ovation by taking this Andante in my tempo, he literally beamed with gratitude and joy. I got on less well with a Mr MacFarren,[1] a pompous and melancholy Scot whose compositions, I was assured by the Committee of the Philharmonic Society, were very highly regarded. He seemed too proud to discuss the interpretation of any of his works with me, and I was therefore relieved when one of his symphonies, which I did not find very appealing, was laid aside and its place on the program taken by an overture entitled *Steeplechase*,[2] which had a curiously wild and passionate element that made it a pleasure to perform. My contacts with a businessman named Beneke and his family, to whom I had been recommended by Wesendonck in order that I might have access to at least one "house" in London, caused me considerable inconvenience. In response to their several invitations I had to travel a full German mile[3] to Camberwell, where I discovered that I had landed with the same family with whom Mendelssohn had stayed whenever he was in London. These good people didn't know what to do with me, and could only praise my conducting of Mendelssohn's compositions, rewarding me for it with descriptions of the "abundant soul" of the deceased. Howard, the Secretary of the Philharmonic Society and an agreeable old chap, also made some efforts to entertain me, believing himself to be the only one in my circle of English acquaintances to do so. I had to go with him and his daughter a few times to attend the Italian Opera at Covent Garden; I heard *Fidelio* there, given in a rather grotesque manner, with recitatives, by unwashed Germans and voiceless Italians. I was able to ward off too many visits to this theater. On the other hand, when making my farewell visit to Mr Howard at his home I was surprised to run into Meyerbeer who had just arrived in London to produce his *Etoile du Nord* there. When I saw him enter the room, it quickly occurred to me that Howard, whom I had known only in his capacity as Secretary of the Philharmonic Society, was also music critic for the *Illustrated News*, and it was in that capacity that the great opera composer had made such haste to call on him. Meyerbeer was utterly paralyzed when he spotted me, and this turn put me in a frame of mind which made it impossible for us to exchange so much as a word; this amazed Mr Howard, who had been sure that we knew each other. As we were leaving he asked me if I were not in fact acquainted with Herr Meyerbeer, to which I responded that he should ask him such a question about me. When I met Howard again later that evening, he assured me that Meyerbeer had spoken of me exclusively in terms of the greatest respect. I thereupon advised him to read a few back numbers of the Paris *Gazette Musicale*, in which M. Fétis[1] had reproduced Meyerbeer's views on me in less flattering terms. Howard shook his head and couldn't understand "how two great composers could behave so strangely".

I had a pleasant surprise, however, from a visit from Hermann Franck, who was living at the time in Brighton and came to London for a few days. We chatted a great deal, and I had to exert myself considerably to set him straight about me, as he had heard the most bizarre reports from German musicians during the years that had elapsed since we had last seen each other. He was astonished, in the first place, to find me in London, where he considered it impossible for me to find suitable terrain for my musical tendencies. I didn't understand what he meant by these "tendencies" and told him quite simply how I had come to accept the invitation of the Philharmonic Society, that I proposed to fulfill my contractual obligation for this year's concerts, and then return to my work in Zürich without further ado. This sounded very different from what he had assumed, for he had thought that the only possible reason I could have for coming to London was to look for a strong position from which to undertake a war of annihilation against all other German musicians; this, at any rate, was the universal opinion of the motive for my venture as reported to him from Germany. Nothing could be more astounding, he then observed, than the curious incongruity between the fictive figure in which I appeared to people and my true nature, which he had recognized at once upon seeing me again; after a few jokes we understood each other on the subject very well indeed. I was glad to see that he valued the work of Schopenhauer as much as I did, its renown being only of such recent date. He expressed an unusual opinion in decided terms, contending that the German spirit was destined either to deteriorate completely, together with its political institutions, or else enjoy a total regeneration, in which case Schopenhauer would have his day. He left me, only to meet a terrible and inexplicable fate shortly afterwards. A few months later, after my return to Zürich, I learned of his mysterious death. He had been living, as I stated, in Brighton, to prepare his son, who was about sixteen, for a career in the British Navy, a course upon which he was obstinately determined despite the fact that his father obviously found it repugnant. On the morning on which his ship was scheduled to sail, the body of Hermann Franck was found lying shattered on the street as a result of a fall from the window, while his son was discovered lying dead on his bed, apparently strangled. The mother had died several years before. There was no one left to clear up these terrible events, which to the best of my knowledge have remained unexplained to this day. Out of forgetfulness, he had left a map of London behind on his visit to me, which I kept, since I did not know his address, and it is still in my possession.

I have pleasanter, though not entirely unclouded, recollections of my relations with Semper, whom I also found in London, where he had been settled for some time with his family. He who had always struck me in Dresden as vehement and gruff now surprised and touched me by the relative calm and dedication with which he bore the terrible interruption of his active career as an artist, and by his readiness to adapt his unusually productive talent to the circumstances in which he was placed. Commissions for large buildings were out of the question for him in England, but he set some hope on the patronage accorded him by Prince Albert, whereby he had some prospects for the future. For the time being he was contenting himself with commissions for interior decoration and luxurious furniture, work which he took as seriously from an artistic point of view as the design of large buildings, and which was also quite lucrative. We saw one another quite often; I also spent some evenings at his home in Kensington, where the old mood was generated between us and in a curiously grim humor we could view the uglier aspects of life with some equanimity. The reports I made about Semper on my return to Switzerland did much to influence Sulzer in successfully summoning him to Zürich to teach at the new Polytechnic.

On various occasions I also visited some not uninteresting London theaters, while naturally strictly avoiding the opera houses. I was most attracted by the little Adelphi Theater in the Strand, to which Praeger and Lüders were often obliged to accompany me. This theater offered some dramatized fairy tales under the title *The Christmas*. One of the performances interested me particularly in that it consisted of an artfully connected conglomeration of the most familiar fairy tales played straight through without any intermissions. It began with *The Golden Goose*, transformed itself into *The Three Wishes*, then glided into *Little Red Riding-Hood*, where the wolf changed into a man-eater who sang a very funny refrain, the whole thing ending with a *Cinderella* into which many other ingredients had been mixed. These pieces were in every respect well mounted and played, and they gave me a good idea of how ordinary people could be entertained in an imaginative way. The performances at the Olympic Theater were somewhat less naive. Apart from some well-acted and witty salon pieces in the French style, they did such magical tales as *The Yellow Dwarf*, in which an uncommonly popular actor named Robson took the simian title role. I saw this same actor on another occasion in a little comedy called *Garrick Fever*, in which he ends up acting the role of a drunken man who, when people insist on taking him for Garrick, undertakes to play Hamlet in this condition. I was greatly astonished by the many audacities in his performance. A small out-of-the-way theater in Marylebone was trying to attract the public with Shakespeare's plays at the time. I attended a performance of *The Merry Wives* which astonished me by its correctness and precision. Even a performance of *Romeo and Juliet* at the Haymarket Theater impressed me favorably, in spite of the palpable inferiority of the company, on account of its accurate delivery and its staging, which no doubt still went back to the Garrick tradition. Yet I recall a curious illusion in connection with this: after the first act I told Lüders, who had accompanied me, how surprised I was the part of Romeo had been given to such an old man, who appeared to be at least sixty, and who seemed to try to retrieve his lost youth by laboriously adopting a rather sickeningly sweet, feminine air. Lüders then examined the program again and exclaimed, "By thunder! It's a woman!" And indeed it was the once famous American, Miss Curshman.[1] Despite all my efforts, I found it impossible to obtain a ticket for *Henry VIII* at the Princess Theater. This play had been put on with the full resources of modern realism as a particularly pompous theatrical spectacle and as such enjoyed sensational popularity.

In the sphere of music, which concerned me more closely, I attended several concerts of the Sacred Music Society in the large Exeter Hall. The oratorios performed there almost weekly have the advantage of the great assurance gained in the course of very frequent repetitions. Beyond that, I could not withhold my admiration for the great precision of the seven-hundred-voice choir, which performed quite respectably on several occasions, particularly in Handel's *Messiah*. I got to know the true spirit of English musical life here. It is closely intertwined with the spirit of English Protestantism, and thus such an oratorio performance attracts the public far more than the opera; there is a further advantage in that attendance at such an oratorio is considered the equivalent of going to church. Everybody in the audience holds their Handel piano scores in the same way church-goers hold their prayer-books. These scores are sold in shilling editions at the box office and are read very avidly, in order not to miss such celebrated nuances, it seemed to me, as the start of the "Hallelujah Chorus", where it is deemed appropriate for everyone to rise from their seats, a movement which probably originated as an expression of enthusiasm but is now carried out with punctilious precision at every performance.

All these memories, however, are submerged in the overriding recollection of almost incessant ill-health, caused no doubt primarily by the London climate at that time of year, which is notorious throughout the world. I had a perpetual cold, and on the evidence of my friends tried to counteract the effect of the air by adopting the heavy English diet, but without improving matters in the least. I was also not able to get my lodgings sufficiently heated, and the work I had brought along suffered heavily as a consequence. I had hoped to complete the instrumentation of *Die Walküre* here, yet only managed to advance it by a paltry hundred pages. But the main problem was that my composition sketches, according to which I intended to execute the instrumentation, had been written down without allowing for the effect of such a prolonged interruption of my working mood on their relationship to the completed work. I often sat before my penciled pages as if confronted by hieroglyphics I was incapable of deciphering. In utter despair I would then turn to reading Dante, becoming seriously acquainted with him here for the first time. The London atmosphere lent his *Inferno* an unforgettable verisimilitude for me.

At last came the hour of redemption from all these sufferings I had brought upon myself by this last illusion that I could gain something encouraging or even agreeable from the great world. The sole consolation was the heartfelt emotion of my new friends at my departure; then I hurried home via Paris, which I found in its summer glory, and where I again saw people promenading and not merely chasing along the streets on business. I got back to Zürich on June 30th in a cheerful mood, the profits from my venture being all of one thousand francs.

My wife had it in mind to resume her whey cure on the Seelisberg beside the Lake of Lucerne; I also thought the mountain air would do my impaired health some good, and so we decided to go there forthwith. We were held back for a short time by the mortal illness of our little dog Peps. With his thirteenth year he had begun to grow old, and suddenly he appeared so weak that we didn't think we could take him to the Seelisberg, for fear that he would no longer be able to bear the effort of the ascent. A few days later his agony increased palpably; he grew senile and suffered repeated convulsions; his sole activity consisted in rising abruptly from his bed, located in my wife's room, and stumbling over to my work desk, where he would sink down exhausted.

The veterinarian didn't think he could do anything for him, and as the convulsions gradually became more acute, I was advised to shorten the poor animal's agony by a small dose of prussic acid. We delayed our departure for his sake until such time as I convinced myself that a quick death would be an act of charity toward this pitiful creature, who was clearly beyond all hope. I hired a dory and took an hour's trip across the lake to a young doctor of my acquaintance named Obrist, whom I knew to be the possessor of a village apothecary's stock, which included an assortment of poisons. From him I acquired the fatal dose and went back across the water on a lovely summer evening in my solitary skiff. But I still didn't want to resort to this last expedient until the dying animal was in direst agony. He spent the night as usual in a basket next to my bed, from where he had always awakened me in the morning by scratching the floor with his paws as he shuffled toward me. Suddenly I was awakened by his moans, caused by an unusually violent attack of convulsions; then he sank down without a sound; and this moment seemed so strangely meaningful to me that I immediately looked at the clock to etch upon my memory the hour at which my lavishly devoted little friend had died: it was ten minutes past one a.m. on July 10th. We spent the following day arranging for his burial, weeping the most bitter tears: our landlady, Frau Stockar-Escher, donated a pretty patch of ground in her garden for this purpose, and there we buried him, together with his basket and cushions. His grave was shown to me many years later; but when I last went there I saw that everything had been transformed in a most elegant way, and there was no longer any sign of the grave of Peps.

After this we set off for the Seelisberg, accompanied this time only by our new parrot, which I had procured for my wife the previous year from the Kreutzberg menagerie as a replacement for good old Papo. This one was a very good and intelligent bird as well, but I left him entirely to Minna, treating him with unvarying kindness but not trying to make him my friend. Fortunately for us, our stay in the glorious air of this summer resort, of which we had become so fond, was favored by sustained good weather. Apart from my solitary walks, I spent all my free time making a fair copy of that part of the score of *Die Walküre* for which the instrumentation was complete, and again took up my favorite reading material, the study of Schopenhauer. I was also delighted by a nice letter from Berlioz, sending me a copy of his latest book *Les soirées d'orchestre*, which entertained and stimulated me despite the fact that its author's taste for the grotesque was as alien to me here as in his compositions. I also met young Robert von Hornstein again, who behaved in an intelligent and amenable manner. I was particularly interested in the rapid and obviously successful way he came to grips with the study of Schopenhauer. He informed me that he intended to settle in Zürich for a while, where Karl Ritter had also decided to establish winter quarters with his young wife. In mid-August we ourselves went back to Zürich, where I quietly devoted myself to the completion of the rest of the *Walküre* instrumentation, while relations with my previous acquaintances went on in the old way. From the outside world I received reports of the gradual but persistent spread of my *Tannhäuser* throughout the German theaters, followed after some hesitation by *Lohengrin* as well. Franz Dingelstedt, then intendant of the Munich Court Theater, undertook to introduce *Tannhäuser* on that terrain, which owing to Lachner's influence was not entirely auspicious for me, and seems to have brought off the venture quite successfully, even though its success, according to him, was not great enough to permit him to pay me punctiliously the royalties he had promised me. Yet my income now sufficed, under the conscientious management of my friend Sulzer, to enable me to devote myself almost entirely to my work without any worries in this regard. But the onset of raw weather caused me fresh misery. Obviously as a result of the ill effects of the London climate, I suffered from numerous attacks of erysipelas through-out the winter, which recurred with the most acute misery at the slightest dietary error or mildest cold. The most painful aspect of the whole thing was the frequent interruption of my work, for on days I was sick the most I could possibly accomplish was a little reading. Burnouff's *Introduction à l'histoire du Bouddhisme* was the book that stimulated me most; I even distilled from it the material for a dramatic poem, which has remained with me ever since, if only in a very rough outline, and might one day even be brought to fruition. I gave it the title *Die Sieger*; it was based on a simple legend of a Jandala maiden,[1] who is received into the elevated order of mendicants known as the Cakyamounis as a result of her painfully intense and purified love for Ananda, the chief disciple of the Buddha. Apart from the beauty and profound significance of the simple tale, I was influenced to choose it as much by its peculiar aptness for the musical procedures that I have since developed. To the mind of the Buddha, the previous lives in former incarnations of every being appearing before him stand revealed as clearly as the present. The simple story owed its significance to the way that the past life of the suffering principal characters was entwined in the new phase of their lives as being still present time. I perceived at once how the musical remembrance of this dual life, keeping the past constantly present in the hearing, might be represented perfectly to the emotional receptivities, and this decided me to keep the prospect of working out this task before me as a labor of especial love.

I thus had two new subjects, *Tristan* and *Die Sieger*, etched upon my imagination as a continuing preoccupation from then on, alongside the *Nibelungen*, the unfinished portion of which lay before me in gigantic dimensions. The more these projects absorbed me, the more I writhed with impatience at the continual interruptions of my work by these horrible attacks of illness. Liszt had proposed to pay me a visit at about this time that had been postponed from the summer. I had to request him not to come, for I could not be certain, given my most recent experiences, that I would not be chained to a sick-bed during the few days he could spare for me. Thus I spent this winter in calm and productive resignation, but so erratic and irascible toward the outside world that I caused my friends a good deal of suffering. Yet I was pleased to get somewhat closer to Karl Ritter again after he had settled in Zürich. His young and rather uncultivated wife seemed to be a great hindrance for him in his social life through the many embarrassments she caused; but it touched and reassured me in regard to much of his character that he was very discreet and delicate with respect to this. By choosing Zürich once again, if only for the winter season, he evinced a satisfying devotion to me sufficient to dispel a number of unpleasant memories. Hornstein too had actually showed up; yet it was soon over with him: he claimed to be so "nervous" that he could no longer touch a piano key, and also did not try to hide his fear, inasmuch as his mother had died insane, that he might go mad. While this made him somewhat interesting, his intellectual gifts were mingled with such weakness of character that we soon were in sufficient despair about him not to be utterly inconsolable at his sudden departure from Zürich.

Meanwhile my circle of acquaintances had gained considerably by the addition of Gottfried Keller, a native of Zürich whose literary work had won him a good reputation in Germany, and who had now returned to the welcoming arms of his fellow-townsmen. Sulzer had already called my attention, without undue exaggeration, to some of his writings, particularly his longer novel *Der grüne Heinrich*. I was surprised to find in Keller a conspicuously helpless and shy fellow, about whom everyone, at first acquaintance, was seized by anxiety as to how he would get on in life. This was the sticking point with him; all his works, which evinced considerable originality, seemed at the same time to be but the preliminaries in his artistic development, and the inevitable inquiry arose as to when he would produce a book that would really establish his reputation. Thus it came that my association with him consisted mainly of a persistent inquiry about what he was to do next. He informed me of all sorts of carefully conceived plans, but on close inspection it always turned out there was nothing of inherent substance. Fortunately, people finally found a government job for him, no doubt from patriotic motives, and in this capacity, being an honest man and no fool, he did solid and reputable work, even though his literary activity seemed to lapse after those early efforts.

My older friend Herwegh was unfortunately not so lucky. I had been worried about him for some time as well, trying to believe that his previous achievements constituted only a prelude to some really significant artistic creations. He himself did not deny that he could only suppose his best was yet to come; he believed that he possessed the necessary material for a large poetic work in a store of "ideas"; all that was lacking, he contended, was "the frame", within which he could proceed to depict all these on his canvas. In this regard he was expecting the proper inspiration daily; as this seemed to be taking too long, I set about trying to find the frame he was looking for. He obviously wanted to write a vast epic poem in which he could embody all the views he had acquired. He had once alluded to Dante's good fortune in finding such an apt subject as the path through hell and purgatory to paradise. This gave me the idea to suggest for the framework of his poem the myth of metempsychosis, which, from its source in the Brahmin religion, through Plato impinged even upon our classical culture. He found this idea not bad at all, so I went even further and sketched the form such a poem should take; he should divide it in three main acts, each in three cantos, thus nine cantos altogether. The first part would show the principal figure in his Asiatic homeland, the second in the Hellenistic–Roman world, and the third in his rebirth in the medieval and modern world. All this pleased him immensely, and he thought something good would probably come of it. But the rather cynical Dr Wille, at whose country estate and with whose family we often got together, was of a different opinion about it. He believed that we were expecting far too much of Herwegh; viewed close up, he said, Herwegh was really nothing more than a decent Swabian boy, who, through the Jewish nimbus he had acquired through his wife, had become far more famous and admired than his abilities justified. In the end I had to shrug my shoulders in silent acquiescence with these cheerless and unkind remarks, as I could see poor Herwegh sinking more deeply into apathy with each passing year, until finally he seemed incapable of doing anything.

Semper's eventual arrival in Zürich greatly enlivened our circle. The Swiss authorities had asked me to use my influence to induce him to accept an appointment as a teacher at the Federal Polytechnic. Semper soon showed up to look things over, got a good impression of everything, and found cause for delight when out walking among the unclipped trees that he could even see a caterpillar again. He decided to make the move, as a result of which he and his family became a permanent part of my circle of acquaintances. True, he had little prospect of obtaining commissions for major buildings and saw himself condemned, as he put it, to play the role of schoolmaster henceforth. But he was already deep in a significant book about art which he later published, after a number of vicissitudes and changes of publisher, under the title *Style*. I met him often while he was working on the drawings which were to appear as the plates in this work, and he always executed these on the stone himself with great precision. He grew so fond of these labors that he declared vast and unwieldy construction work did not interest him; as an artist his attention was more engaged by the smallest detail.

True* to my vow, I had withdrawn completely from the activities of the Music Society, and I never again conducted a public performance in Zürich. At the outset these gentlemen refused to believe I was serious about this, and I had to resort to some categorical statements in this regard, wherein I was obliged to point out their laxity and unwillingness to follow my repeated suggestions concerning the establishment of a decent orchestra. The excuse I always received was that, although there was enough money in the hands of the music-loving public, everyone was shy about stepping forward and leading the list of subscribers with a specific amount, as this would serve to call unpleasant attention to his wealth on the part of his fellow citizens. My old friend Ott-Imhof told me that he would have no difficulty in donating ten thousand francs annually for such a purpose, but for the fact that from this moment on everybody would be asking how Ott-Imhof could possibly behave this way with his money. He contended that this would cause so much commotion that he might easily be called to account about the management of his property. This brought to mind Goethe's outburst[1] at the beginning of the first of his *Letters from Switzerland*. And so my musical activities in Zürich definitely came to an end at that time.

But from time to time we still had music at home. Klindworth's piano

* In the margin of the manuscript, in Wagner's hand: "1856".

versions of *Das Rheingold*, and of some acts of *Die Walküre* as well, lay ready at hand in accurate and expensive copies. At first, Baumgartner was compelled to struggle with the horrible difficulties of the arrangement. Later, the musician Theodor Kirchner,[1] who had settled in Winterthur and often came over to Zürich, showed greater aptitude in playing excerpts from the vocal scores. The wife of our friend Heim, the conductor of the choral society, was pressed into service to take the female vocal parts whenever I attempted to sing any of the scenes. She possessed a truly lovely voice with great warmth of tone, having participated in the music festival of 1853 as the only soloist. But she was utterly unmusical, and I had my hands full helping her to hit the notes accurately, and in particular to keep the right tempo. Yet we brought off several excerpts and at least gave my acquaintances an occasional foretaste of my Nibelung music. But I had to exercise great restraint in this as well, for after any excitement I was threatened by a return of erysipelas. One evening we were assembled at Karl Ritter's house; I hit upon the idea of reading aloud Hoffmann's tale *Der goldene Topf*, during which I failed to notice that the room gradually grew much cooler. Before I had completed the reading, I sat there to the dismay of all the listeners with a swollen red nose and had to struggle homeward to treat this malady, which caused me severe discomfort every time. During these periods of suffering the poem for *Tristan* assumed increasingly clear form within me. During interim periods of convalescence, on the other hand, I worked zealously, if also laboriously, at the score for *Walküre*, finally completing the fair copy of the whole work in March of that year (1856). My illness and my exertions combined to put me in an extremely irascible condition. I remember the foul mood in which I received our friends, the Wesendoncks, when they paid me a congratulatory visit on the evening after my score had been completed. I gave vent on this occasion to such bitter feelings concerning this method of expressing interest in my works that my poor offended guests left in haste and great embarrassment. It cost me a number of laborious explanations during the following days to atone for the insult I had inflicted, wherein my wife helped splendidly to smooth things over. A special bond between her and our friends had been formed by the donation of a friendly little dog to our household, acquired by the Wesendoncks to be the successor to my good old Peps. He proved such a well-behaved and ingratiating animal that he soon won my wife's most tender friendship; I too was always well-disposed toward him. I left the choice of a name entirely to my wife, and, apparently for the sake of its likeness to the name Peps, she invented the name Fips, which I was quite willing to call him; yet he remained always more of a companion for my wife, just as, in spite of my strong sense of justice toward the good qualities of all animals, I was never again to establish such a close relationship with them as I had enjoyed with Peps and Papo.

At about the time of my birthday, toward the end of May, I had a visit from my old Dresden friend Tichatschek, who had remained loyal and enthusiastically devoted to me, to the extent this was possible for a person without much culture. On the morning of my birthday I was awakened in a most touching way by the strains of the adagio I loved so much, from Beethoven's E minor Quartet. My wife had invited the quartet I had coached to give me this treat, and with true delicacy of feeling they had chosen just this piece, about which I had once spoken to them with great emotion. That evening Tichatschek sang some things from *Lohengrin* to a circle of guests, and we were all truly amazed at the vocal brilliance he had preserved. Tichatschek's persistence had also succeeded in overcoming the court-inspired reluctance of the Dresden theater management to take my operas back into the repertory. These were now being performed once again, always with great success and to packed houses. On an excursion we made with our guest to Brunnen on the Lake of Lucerne, I managed to catch a light cold and thus cause the thirteenth recurrence of my erysipelas. On this occasion I suffered all the more by going through with the whole thing, in order not to spoil it for our guest by my turning back sooner, despite one of those terrible southern gales, making it impossible to heat our rooms in Brunnen at all. I was still in my sick-bed when Tichatschek left, and so I decided to try to bolster my health with a change of air by going south, because this devilish illness seemed to cling to me in Zürich especially. I chose Lake Geneva and decided to hunt for a well-situated country resort near Geneva to commence a cure, for which my Zürich doctor had provided me with detailed instructions. So I set off early in June for Geneva, having great difficulty on the way with Fips, who was supposed to be my companion in my rural seclusion, but who almost caused me to change my intended destination, as on one stretch of the journey he was not allowed to travel with me in the railway compartment. Thanks to the enormous energy I devoted to getting my way in this matter, I finally reached Geneva to begin the treatment, as otherwise I would probably have gone in an entirely different direction.

Arriving in Geneva I stopped first at the old familiar Hotel de l'écu de Genéve, which evoked many memories for me. Here I consulted Dr

Coindet, who directed me to Mornex on Mont Salève for the sake of its good air, recommending a boarding house for me there. When I got there I first looked for a place where I would be undisturbed, and I persuaded the lady running the house to let me have an isolated garden pavilion, which consisted only of one large room for social meetings. This took a lot of eloquence, because all the boarders, with whom I precisely did not wish to come into any contact whatever, were furious at the prospect of being deprived of the room originally intended for their social functions. I finally got my way; but I had to pledge to vacate this salon every Sunday morning, because it then had to be filled with benches and utilized for a church service, something which seemed to mean a good deal to the Calvinist boarders. I was quite contented here and punctiliously made my offering on the first Sunday by going to Geneva to read the newspapers. The next day, however, the landlady notified me that general irritation was too great in that, while they had been able to keep the salon for the church service, they had lost it for their weekday sessions of games. I had to get out, and so I began looking around for new lodgings with a neighbor.

This neighbor was a Dr Vaillant, who had turned another large boarding house and its grounds into an institution for hydrotherapy. I first made inquiries only after some warm baths, as my Zürich doctor had recommended I take these with sulphur; but there was no question of obtaining any such things here. Dr Vaillant's whole manner pleased me so much, however, that I told him of my troubles. When I told him of the hot sulphur baths and a certain stinking mineral water I was supposed to drink, he merely smiled and said to me: "Monsieur, vous n'êtes que nerveux. All this will only make you more excitable; you need nothing more than calming down; if you will confide in my treatment, I promise to restore you far enough within two months that you will never get erysipelas again." He kept his word.

I certainly gained a different view of hydrotherapy from this doctor than from the "Water-Jew" in Albisbrunn and other crude amateurs of that sort. Vaillant had previously been a popular doctor in Paris, where he had been consulted by Lablache and Rossini; but he had endured the misfortune of becoming paralyzed in both legs. After he had struggled along for four years, lost his entire practice and grown miserable, he came upon the primitive Silesian hydrotherapist Priessnitz, to whom he had himself conveyed and who cured him completely. There he learned the method that had proved so effective in his case, refined it, according to his own principles as a trained and fastidious medical man, of all the crudities imparted by its inventor, and tried to win over the Parisians by establishing a therapeutic institute at Meudon. But he met with no response; when he solicited his former patients to visit this establishment, they would only ask him whether there was dancing every evening. It was impossible for him to earn a living; and to this circumstance I owed my meeting with him in Geneva where he renewed his attempt to put his therapeutic theories into practice. He differed from other doctors even in the fact that he accepted only a very limited number of patients, for he claimed that a doctor could be responsible for the proper application and outcome of his treatment only by being in a position to observe the sick very precisely at all hours of the day. The advantage of his system, which benefited me so immensely, lay in the calming effect of the treatment, which consisted in particular of the most ingenious use of water at more moderate temperatures.

Beyond this, Vaillant took special care of my needs, particularly as far as peace and quiet were concerned. I was exempted from attendance at the communal breakfast table, which would have been onerous and irritating for me, and instead I was allowed to prepare and take tea in my own room; this was an unaccustomed treat for me, and under the mantle of secrecy (for the boarders were to learn nothing of it) I over-indulged a bit, usually drinking tea behind closed doors for two hours straight after the exertions of the matutinal therapy, while reading novels by Walter Scott. I had found some inexpensive and good French translations of these novels in Geneva and had brought a whole pile of them to Mornex. This reading material was admirably suited to my routine, which precluded any serious studies or actual work. Moreover, I also found Schopenhauer's high opinion of this writer, who had until then appeared to me in a somewhat dubious light, to be fully substantiated. On my solitary walks, it is true, I generally took along a volume of Byron, largely owing to the convenience of the miniature edition I possessed, intending to read it on some mountain height within sight of Mont Blanc: yet I soon left it behind, for I noticed that I rarely pulled it out of my pocket. The only work I permitted myself was sketching plans for a house I wanted to build, and I tried to make a very accurate final version with all the tools of an architectural draftsman. I had conceived this bold idea upon entering negotiations at the time with the music dealers Härtels in Leipzig, regarding the possible sale of my Nibelung compositions. I was asking a flat forty thousand francs cash for the four works, of which half was to be paid me as soon as construction of my house commenced. The publishers actually appeared quite favorably inclined to accept my demands to the extent necessary to make my project feasible. Very soon, however, their estimate of the marketability of my works underwent a highly adverse change; I have never been able to figure out whether this was the result of their having taken a closer look at my poem for the first time and deciding that it was impracticable, or whether that same influence from other quarters, which has always tried to block my undertakings and has been increasingly evident over the years, was brought to bear on them. At any rate, I soon had to abandon the hope of generating enough capital to build my house; yet my architectural efforts nonetheless went forward, and from then on I made it my aim to obtain the funds to execute them.

As the two months I had guaranteed Dr Vaillant to devote to his treatment were up on August 15th precisely, I left this resort, which had proved so beneficial, proceeding first to visit Karl Ritter, who had settled with his wife for the summer in a very modest cottage near Lausanne. Both had already paid me a visit in Mornex; they had been happy to participate in my morning tea ceremony; it was only when I tried to lure Karl into sharing part of my treatment that he declared, after a brief trial, that even the most relaxing procedure excited him too much. On the whole, though, we found ourselves pleasantly in agreement on most things, and he announced to me his intention to return to Zürich in the autumn. Thus I traveled with Fips, for whose sake I intentionally avoided the obnoxious stretch of the railway, arriving home by mail coach in a rather cheerful frame of mind. My wife had already gotten back from her whey cure, and I found my sister Klara there as well, the only relative who had ever visited me in my Swiss refuge. With her we immediately undertook an expedition to my favorite spot, Brunnen on the Lake of Lucerne, and spent an exquisite evening there enjoying a splendid sunset amid all the other glorious effects of the Alpine scenery. When night fell and the moon rose full over the lake, it turned out that a nicely planned little ovation had been arranged for me by our enthusiastic and attentive host, Colonel Auf-der-Mauer, whom I had often visited before. On two large skiffs, lighted with coloured lamps, the brass band of Brunnen approached the shores of the lake abutting our hotel. This band was composed entirely of amateurs from the countryside, and there, with Swiss forthrightness, and without any attempts at painful precision, they let loose with some compositions of mine, loudly and irrefragably. This was followed by a little speech in my honor and an equally hearty reply on my part, after which I shook a large number of calloused hands while we drank a few bottles of wine at the lakeside. For years afterward I could never pass these shores on my frequent visits without being greeted by friendly shouts or cordial handshakes; I was usually in doubt as to what this or that boatman wanted of me, but it always turned out I was dealing with one of the bandsmen, whose goodwill had been so amply demonstrated on that merry evening.

My sister Klara's lengthy stay in Zürich enlivened our domestic circle very agreeably. Among my brothers and sisters, she was really the most musical, and I enjoyed her company greatly; her presence was also highly beneficial in acting as a damper on the various household tiffs caused by Minna's increasing heart trouble, which made her much more mistrustful and self-willed. I was expecting a visit in October from Liszt, who proposed this time to stay for a longer period in Zürich, accompanied by a number of people. But I could not wait so long to begin the composition of *Siegfried*. On September 22nd I commenced the sketches. Then one of the main irritations of my life became a positive nuisance: a tinker had recently moved in at the house opposite ours, and he stultified my ears throughout the day with his resounding hammer strokes. In my misery about my inability ever to find lodgings free of noise and disturbance, I was about to give in and abandon all composing until such time as this indispensable condition could be fulfilled. But it was precisely my anger at this tinker that, in a moment of fury, gave me the theme for Siegfried's outburst of rage at the bungling of Mime: I played this childishly quarrelsome, rowdy theme in G minor to my sister at once, singing the accompanying text in accents of ire, and we all had to laugh so much that I decided I would continue for the moment. This went on until I had finished a large part of the first scene, when Liszt notified me of his impending arrival on October 13th.

Liszt arrived, unaccompanied for the time being, and immediately turned my house into a musical center. He had meanwhile completed his *Faust* and *Dante* symphonies, and it was almost miraculous to hear him play them on the piano, reading from the orchestral score. As I was sure Liszt recognized the great impression his compositions had made on me, I felt I could frankly point out the defect in the close of the *Dante* Symphony. If anything had convinced me of the masterly powers of poetic conception he possessed, it was the original finale of the *Faust* Symphony, which ended delicately and sweetly with a last, utterly compelling reminiscence of Gretchen, without any attempt to arouse attention forcibly. This seemed to me also entirely appropriate for the close of the *Dante* Symphony, in which the delicate introduction of the Magnificat in the same way gives only a hint of Paradise by its soft shimmering. Thus I was all the more startled to hear this lovely conception suddenly interrupted by a pompous plagal cadence which, I was told, was supposed to represent Domenico.[1] "No, no!" I exclaimed loudly, "Not that! Out with it! No majestic Lord God! Let's stick with the fine soft shimmer." "You are right," Liszt replied, "I thought so too; the Princess convinced me otherwise, but it shall be as you recommend." This was all well and good. But I was all the more dismayed to learn later not only that this close for the *Dante* Symphony had been retained, but also that the delicate ending I had liked so much in the *Faust* Symphony had been altered by the introduction of choruses in a manner calculated to produce a more ostentatious effect. This expressed everything I felt about Liszt and his lady friend, the Princess Karoline von Wittgenstein!

This lady, together with her daughter Marie, was now also expected for a visit, and the necessary arrangements for her reception had been made. Before the ladies arrived, there was a most painful incident at my home involving Liszt and Karl Ritter. Ritter's mere looks, as well as a certain abrupt and contrary manner of expressing himself, seemed to put Liszt into an irascible state. One evening Liszt was holding forth on the merits of the Jesuits; Ritter's inopportune smile at this seemed to annoy him very severely: at the dinner table the conversation turned to the French Emperor, Louis Napoleon, whose achievements Liszt summarily demanded we acknowledge, whereas on the whole we were anything but enthusiastic about the state of affairs in France. When Liszt in an attempt to underscore the significance of France for European culture, mentioned among other things the Académie Française, Karl again indulged in his fatal smile. This exasperated Liszt beyond all bounds, and his response included some such phrase as this: "If we do not admit this, what are we? Baboons!" I laughed aloud, while Karl only smiled once again, but this time in mortal embarrassment. I learned later from Bülow that during some rowdy juvenile argument Karl had been accused of having the physiognomy of a baboon. It soon became perfectly obvious that Ritter considered himself grossly insulted by "the learned Doctor", as he called Liszt; he left my house fuming, refusing to cross its threshold again for years. A few days later he sent me a letter telling me that before he would visit me again, he must have a formal apology from Liszt and, if this were not forthcoming, demanded the latter's exclusion from my home. I was very distressed to receive a complaint shortly thereafter from his esteemed mother as well, reproaching me for treating her son unjustly in not having helped to obtain satisfaction for the insult he had suffered at my house. For a long time my relations with this family, intimate as they had been, were painfully strained, as I found it impossible to induce them to view the incident in the proper light. When Liszt learned of all this in the course of time, he also regretted the quarrel and with laudable magnanimity took steps to make amends by paying Ritter a visit, during which not a word was mentioned concerning the incident, and which Ritter returned, not to Liszt, but to the Princess, who had meanwhile arrived. At this, Liszt decided he could do no more; Ritter withdrew from our circle from then on; he transferred his winter quarters from Zürich, and settled permanently in Lausanne.

Not only my own modest residence, but the whole town of Zürich as well was plunged into a turmoil when the Princess Karoline and her daughter established residence for a time at the Hotel Baur. The curious spell of excitement this lady cast over everyone she succeeded in drawing into her sphere of acquaintance particularly intoxicated my good sister Klara, who was still with us at the time. It was as if Zürich had suddenly become a kind of metropolis: carriages drove back and forth; footmen announced arrivals and departures; dinners and suppers abounded; we found ourselves suddenly surrounded by an increasing number of interesting people, whose existence in the environs of Zürich we had never even suspected, but who all now cropped up beyond the shadow of a doubt. A musician named Winterberger,[1] who felt the need to behave eccentrically on certain occasions, had been brought from Winterthur, by Liszt; Kirchner, the Schumann enthusiast from Winterthur, was almost always there, and he too did not fail to behave a bit oddly. But mainly it was the professors from the University of Zürich whom the Princess Karoline managed to coax into abandoning their secretive Zürich habits. Sometimes she would see them one by one, and sometimes serve them up to us en masse. If I dropped in to see her briefly during one of my mid-day promenades, I would find her one day lunching en particulier with Semper, on another with Professor Köchly, on a third occasion with Moleschott,[2] and so forth. Even my singular and self-possessed friend Sulzer was attracted and, as he had to confess, in a sense carried away by her. In all this a sense of freedom and spontaneity prevailed, and the more informal evenings at my home, when the Princess would help the lady of the house to serve the meal with a kind of Polish patriarchal good-naturedness, were really remarkably pleasant. Once, after we had enjoyed some music, I had to impart the substance of my two newly conceived dramatic poems, *Tristan* and *Die Sieger*, to a most certainly not unseemly group of people, half sitting and half lying on the floor around me. The pinnacle of our little festivities was represented by Liszt's birthday on October 22nd, which the Princess celebrated with immense pomp at her residence. Everybody who was anyone in Zürich showed up for this. From Weimar a poem was telegraphed by Hoffmann von Fallersleben,[1] and at the request of the Princess this was solemnly read aloud by Herwegh in a marvelously changed tone of voice. Then, with Liszt at the piano, and together with Frau Heim, I gave the first act of *Die Walküre*, plus one scene of the second act. As to the effect our performance produced, I could judge by Dr Wille's reaction, who said that he would like now to hear them rendered badly in order to form an accurate opinion of them, for he feared he had been seduced by the virtuosity of the presentation. Beyond that, excerpts from Liszt's symphonic poems were played on two grand pianos. At the banquet a dispute arose on the subject of Heinrich Heine, about whom Liszt had all kinds of captious things to say; in response, Frau Wesendonck asked if he did not believe that Heine's name would be inscribed in the temple of immortality. To this Liszt replied summarily, "Yes, but in filth", a remark that did not fail to cause a sensation.

Unfortunately our reunion soon suffered a severe interruption in Liszt's becoming bed-ridden for a considerable period with a skin infection. As soon as he was a little better, we quickly went back to the piano to go through my two completed scores, *Rheingold* and *Walküre*. Princess Marie was a good listener and was even able to help others understand some of the more difficult parts of the poem.

Princess Karoline also seemed extraordinarily eager to get to the bottom of the "intrigue" surrounding the fate of the gods in my *Nibelung's Ring*. She interviewed me en particulier one day, exactly like one of the Zürich professors, in order to have this point elucidated for her. I must confess I became absolutely persuaded that she really wanted to understand its most delicate and mysterious aspects, but only in a rather arithmetically precise sense, so that at the end I had the feeling I had explained the intrigues of some kind of French play to her. Her vivacity in all such things was just as vast as the peculiar amiability of her nature; for she was genuinely amused one day when I told her that, as far as the former quality was concerned, if I had to remain constantly in her company I would be dead at the end of four weeks. I had reason for sadness in contemplating the changes that had taken place in Marie. I had once termed her "The Child", but I could not now properly salute her as a "young girl". Some shattering experience seemed to have aged her beyond her years. Only when she was greatly aroused, particularly during evenings in society, did the winsome and dazzling elements in her nature assert themselves markedly. I recall one pleasant evening at Herwegh's house, when Liszt was as greatly transported by a piano that was abominably out of tune as by the ghastly cigars, which he passionately preferred to the finer sort at the time. We all thought more of witchcraft than of magic when he produced fantastic improvisations at that piano. To my great dismay, there were several more occasions, like that fateful scene with Ritter, when Liszt gave unmistakable evidence of ill-temper and irascibility, and almost seemed to be looking for trouble. In particular it was impossible to talk sensibly with him about Goethe, especially in the presence of the Princess Karoline. About *Egmont*, which Liszt affected to despise on the grounds that the protagonist had let himself be "duped" by Alba, we almost had a fight, as he seemed inclined to seek one, even with me. But I was forewarned and remained calm enough on this occasion to keep my friend's physiological disorder in mind, giving greater consideration to his state of health than to the actual subject of our debate. There never was a scene of real anger between us; but from then on I had a vague feeling that there might one day be such an encounter, and that it would then be a frightful one; and perhaps it was precisely this feeling that restrained me consciously from ever going too far, despite my reputation among my friends for irritability and sudden outbursts of anger.

After our illustrious visitors had been with us for more than six weeks, we got together finally to see them on their way by betaking ourselves to St Gall for a week, where we had been invited by a young conductor named Sczadrowsky to give our assistance at a music society concert there.

We were lodged together in the Pickerel Hotel, where the Princess acted as our hostess just as if we had been in her own home. Thus she had provided my wife and myself with a room right next to her private suite, which promptly caused us a highly difficult night. Frau Karoline got one of her bad attacks of nervous worry, and to drive away the hallucinations to which she was subject on these occasions, her daughter was compelled to read aloud to her in an intentionally piercing voice throughout the night. I got tremendously upset about this, especially at the seemingly incomprehensible lack of consideration it showed for the peace and quiet of a neighbor. At two o'clock in the morning I jumped out of bed, rang the bell steadily until the attendant awoke, and asked him to take us to a room in one of the remotest sections of the hotel where no reading was going on. We actually moved out at this hour: this was noticed next door, but produced no reaction. I was amazed the next morning to find Marie quite unperturbed and normal, without showing the slightest strain from the nocturnal adventure, and learned that people living in the entourage of the Princess were entirely accustomed to such excesses. Here as well the house was soon filled with all sorts of guests: Herwegh came with his wife, as did Dr Wille, Kirchner and several others; life in the Pickerel was soon in every way as hectic as in the Hotel Baur. All this had been instigated, as aforementioned, on behalf of the little concert society of the town of St Gall. To my delight Liszt rehearsed the orchestra in two of his compositions, *Orpheus* and *Les Préludes*, to a point of masterly perfection; despite the extreme limitations of the instrumental resources available, their execution left nothing to be desired in point of beauty or panache. I was especially taken with the restrained orchestral piece *Orpheus*, to which I have always accorded a special place of honor among Liszt's compositions; the public on the other hand preferred *Les Préludes*, of which the main parts had to be encored. I conducted Beethoven's *Eroica* Symphony, and suffered quite a bit, as I always caught a cold on such occasions and usually developed a fever to boot. My interpretation and rendering of Beethoven's work made a powerful and right impression on Liszt, whose opinion was the only one that counted for me. We watched each other at work with a sympathy and interest that proved highly instructive. That evening we had to attend a small banquet in our honor, at which time the worthy citizens of St Gall expressed some nice and well-intended sentiments about the significance of our visit. As I was accorded a special panegyric by one of the local poets, I had to respond with commensurate eloquence. Liszt in fact was so carried away in dithyrambic ecstasy that he proposed a toast to a model performance of *Lohengrin* in St Gall, with which the new theater was to open. Nobody offered any objection. The next day, November 24th, we were all united in various festivities at the house of one of the principal patrons of music in St Gall, the rich businessman Bourit. There we went back to the piano, and Liszt played for us, among other things, the great B flat major sonata of Beethoven, at the close of which Kirchner remarked bluntly that we could all now claim we had witnessed the impossible; for he would always have to believe what he had just actually heard an impossibility. On this occasion, we also commemorated the twentieth anniversary of my marriage to Minna, which fell on that date, and to the strains of the wedding music from *Lohengrin* we paraded charmingly through the various rooms as if dancing a polonaise.

Despite all these pleasant experiences, I would just as soon have brought these matters to a close and returned to my domestic peace and quiet in Zürich. But the indisposition of the Princess held my friends back from their return to Germany for several days, and thus we found ourselves compelled to spend some more needlessly strained time together, until I could accompany my visitors to Rohrschach on November 27th and bid farewell to them at the steamship there. I have never seen the Princess and her daughter since then and assume I never will.

It was not without some misgivings that I took leave of these friends, for the Princess was truly ill, and Liszt seemed to be very exhausted. I recommended they go back to Weimar as quickly as possible for recuperation; I was therefore greatly amazed to hear, a short time later, that they indulged in a long stopover in Munich, attended with much noisy festivity and artistic entertainment. Accordingly, I came to the conclusion that it was foolish for me to recommend anything to people who were so differently constituted. As for me, I returned to my Zürich lodgings utterly tired out, deprived of sleep, and tormented by the frosty weather of the cold season, fearing at the same time that the way we had been living would earn me another bout of erysipelas. But I was delighted to find on the following morning no signs of the dreaded illness, and from that day on began singing the praises of my wonderful Dr Vaillant. Soon I had recuperated to the point of resuming the composition of *Siegfried* at the beginning of December. Thus I was able to resume my old steady routine, which offered so little external diversion: work, long walks, reading, and in the evenings sometimes one of our old friends. The only thing still worrying me was the after-effect of my dispute with Ritter over that incident with Liszt. I now lost touch entirely with this young friend, who had been so close to me in several phases of life; he left Zürich before the end of the winter without seeing me again.

During the months of January and February of 1857 I completed the first act of *Siegfried*, this time in fully detailed copy rather than in fleeting pencil sketches, and got started at once on the instrumentation. Throughout all this I followed the regimen Dr Vaillant had prescribed with probably a little too much zeal: always apprehensive about a recurrence of erysipelas, I sought to ward it off by weekly hydrotherapy consisting of sweating it out in hot packs. While I succeeded in eluding the dreaded illness, the treatment exhausted me greatly, and I longed for the return of the warmer season, which would permit me to abandon this strict routine.

But at the same time the torments inflicted upon me by noisy, music-making neighbors grew in intensity. Apart from the tinker I mortally detested, and with whom I had a fight of sorts every week, more and more pianos infiltrated the house, topped off by the Sunday flute-playing of a Herr Stockar in the rooms below me. I gave up trying to compose any more. Then one day my friends the Wesendoncks came back from a long winter sojourn in Paris and unfolded to me the most welcome prospect of fulfilling my ardent wishes for a future place to live. Wesendonck had already been inclined to grant my wish in this respect by building a little house for me on a site of my choice. My plans, executed with deceptive skill, had actually been presented to an architect for scrutiny. Only the acquisition of a suitable plot had been and remained a particular difficulty. On the back of the hill in the parish of Enge, separating Lake Zürich from the Sihltal, I had long ago, in the course of my walks, spotted a little winter cottage which was called the Lavater House, as it had belonged to the famous phrenologist and had been frequently visited by him. I had persuaded my friend, the Cantonal Secretary Hagenbuch, to take a crafty look around for a way for me to acquire a few acres of land there as cheaply as possible. But this turned out to be the great problem. The terrain was checkered with various lots belonging to larger estates, and it turned out that in order to acquire my one plot it would have been necessary to buy out a number of owners. I bewailed my lot to Wesendonck and gradually stimulated in him the desire to acquire this land for himself and create a fine estate with a large villa for his family. One plot at the far end was to be reserved for me. The purchase of this land and the construction of his house, which was to be imposing and dignified, took up all his time for the moment; and he also no doubt felt that settling two families within the bounds of one fence could lead in time to mutual inconveniences. On the other hand, there happened to be a very small and modest cottage with a garden, separated only by a narrow carriageway from his estate, which I already had my eye upon and which Wesendonck now decided to buy for me. When this was communicated to me my pleasure virtually knew no bounds. All the greater, then, was the shock when the overly careful buyer learned one day that the present owner, with whom he had been negotiating too coyly, had sold the property to someone else. Fortunately it turned out that the buyer was a doctor for the insane, whose intention, following the purchase, was nothing less than to establish his lunatic asylum next to my friend; for this news and the horrible visions it evoked galvanized Wesendonck into devoting all his efforts toward regaining the land from the fateful mad-doctor at any price. Thus it finally came into my friend's possession, after many vexing vicissitudes and at a rather high price. He then turned it over to me at Easter of that year for my long-term use, charging the same rent I had been paying for my quarters on the Zeltweg, eight hundred francs per year.

Furnishing this little house, which occupied me heart and soul at the onset of spring, was not achieved without some annoyances. The cottage, which was designed only for summer occupancy, required first of all the installation of heating and other necessities for winter living. While the owner took care of the basic items, there remained enough things to be done, and what with the perennial differences between my wife and myself as to this and that, and my financial situation, which was still fundamentally one of utter insolvency, everything conspired to create difficulties which were never entirely resolved. In this latter respect, it is true, there were signs from time to time that might have inspired a sanguine temperament to firm confidence in the future: despite the bad performances accorded my opera there, the Berlin *Tannhäuser* brought me an unexpectedly good return. Now in Vienna, too, unusual steps had been taken to gain me an opening. I was still excluded from the Court Opera House there, being assured that, as long as an imperial court existed, there could be no question of performing my "treasonous" operas in Vienna. But this strange situation impelled the director of the Josephstadt Theater, my old director from Riga days, Hoffmann, to venture a performance of *Tannhäuser* outside the city limits of Vienna in a big summer theater he had built at Lerchenfeld and with a specially recruited ensemble. He offered me a royalty of one hundred francs for each performance I would allow him. As Liszt found this venture rather dubious when I reported it to him, I told him that in this affair I proposed to adopt the standpoint of Mirabeau who, when he was not elected to the national assembly by his peers, offered himself to the voters of Marseille as a drapery merchant. This amply satisfied Liszt; and I now entered the Austrian imperial city through the gates of the Lerchenfeld summer theater. As for the performances themselves, the most bizarre things were relayed to me: Sulzer, who had been through Vienna on a trip at the time and had attended one of them, complained chiefly of the darkness in the auditorium, which had not permitted people to read a word from their texts, but also that it had rained heavily right on the heads of the audience. I got a different report several years later from the son-in-law of the widow of the composer Hérold, who had been on his honeymoon in Vienna at that period and had also attended one

of the Lerchenfeld performances: he assured me that despite all its
inadequacies this production had really pleased him, and had been far
more moving than the incomparably worse performance in the Berlin
Court Theater, which he had seen subsequently. Meanwhile, this
forceful Vienna initiative of my old Riga theater director actually
brought me two thousand francs for the twenty performances he
succeeded in giving; and it was perhaps pardonable that, after such open
confirmation of my popularity, I became more confident about
incalculable effects, and perhaps even profits, emanating from my works
in the future.

While I was thus occupied fixing up the little house in the country
I had longed for, and also working on the instrumentation of the first
act of *Siegfried*, I plunged once again into Schopenhauer's philosophy,
and also read Scott's novels with deep involvement. In addition, I made
a serious effort to put my impressions of Liszt's compositions into
significant form; for this purpose I resorted to an open letter to Marie
Wittgenstein, which was published in Brendel's music journal.

Now that the time was imminent for the move to what I expected to
be my final place of refuge in life, I again considered how I might best
find a means of sustaining myself in this life. Once more I commenced
negotiating with the Härtels concerning my *Nibelungen*, but found them
coy and opposed to any such proposition regarding the work. I
complained about this to Liszt,[1] and frankly asked him to consider
putting all my difficulties before the Grand Duke of Weimar, who,
according to my friend, wished to be regarded as the patron of the
Nibelung enterprise. I added that whereas one could not expect an
ordinary music dealer to assume responsibility for such an extraordinary
undertaking, it was nonetheless sensible to ask a prince, who entertained
the notion of making the work the brightest jewel in his own crown, to
take a serious part in the necessary preliminaries attendant upon it, which
must reasonably include its actual execution. My idea was that the Grand
Duke should take the publisher's place, buy the work from me, and pay
me for it in stages as it was completed, whereby he would become its
owner and be repaid eventually, if he so desired, by selling it to a
publisher. Liszt understood me well,[2] but could not help advising me
against pursuing the matter with His Royal Highness.

On the other hand, my attention was now attracted by the young
Grand Duchess of Baden. Several years had passed since Eduard
Devrient had been summoned by the Grand Duke of Baden to become
Director of his Court Theater at Karlsruhe. Since my departure from

Dresden I had remained in contact with Devrient, though with frequent interruptions; he had responded very appreciatively by letter to my writings *The Art-Work of the Future* and *Opera and Drama*. As to his theater in Karlsruhe, he maintained that company was so weak that he could not plausibly consider performing my operas there. All this changed suddenly when the Grand Duke married the young daughter of the Crown Princess of Prussia, whom Alwine Frommann had won over to my cause and who, being now mistress in her own house, eagerly demanded to hear my works. Now my operas were actually going to be performed there, and Devrient had to report to me of the great interest evinced by the young princess, who often even attended the rehearsals. This made a highly agreeable impression on me; I expressed my gratitude on my own initiative by a missive I directed to the Grand Duchess, to which I appended some sheets of music comprising "Wotan's Farewell" from the close of *Die Walküre* as an album leaf.

Thus April 20th approached, on which day I had to vacate my former apartment in the Zeltweg, already rented to someone else, but without my being able to move into the country house, which was not quite ready. In the bad weather, in the course of our frequent visits to the little house, in which masons and carpenters had been making themselves negligently at home, we both caught colds. We spent a week at the inn in the worst possible mood, and I began wondering whether it was worthwhile to occupy this new place at all, for I had a sudden premonition that I would be moving on again from there at some point. At the end of April we at last established ourselves there, more or less forcibly; it was cold and damp, and the new heating didn't work; we were both sick and could scarcely leave our beds. Then came a good omen: the first letter to reach me there was a very conciliatory and friendly communication from Frau Julie Ritter, letting me know that the quarrel brought about by her son's behavior was now over. Beautiful spring weather now set in; on Good Friday I awoke[1] to find the sun shining brightly into this house for the first time: the garden was blooming, and the birds singing, and at last I could sit out on the parapeted terrace of the little dwelling and enjoy the longed-for tranquillity that seemed so fraught with promise. Filled with this sentiment, I suddenly said to myself that this was Good Friday and recalled how meaningful this had seemed to me in Wolfram's *Parzival*. Ever since that stay in Marienbad, where I had conceived *Die Meistersinger* and *Lohengrin*, I had not taken another look at that poem; now its ideality came to me in overwhelming form, and from the idea of Good Friday I quickly sketched out an entire drama in three acts.

In the midst of the still uncompleted task of setting up our household, into which I threw myself wholeheartedly, I nonetheless wanted to work: I went back to *Siegfried*[1] and began the composition of the second act. While I had been previously in doubt as to the name I would give my new refuge, I had to laugh when it occurred to me, when the beginning of this act came off quite nicely, that it should be called "Fafner's Repose". But this would not really do; and so it remained for me to call it simply the "Refuge",[2] as which it henceforth figured in the dates inscribed on my manuscripts.

The miscarriage of my hope for support from the Grand Duke of Weimar for my Nibelung work put me in a continuingly bad mood; I saw myself confronting a burden which I did not know how to get rid of. At the same time I had received a challenging communication: a person whose name had to be Ferreiro,[3] naturally, had gotten in touch with me in his capacity as Consul of Brazil in Leipzig and had notified me of the great fondness of the Emperor of Brazil for my music. This man knew how to dispel my dubiety about this peculiar happenstance in very adroit letters; the Emperor, it seems, liked everything German and would be pleased to have me with him in Rio de Janeiro, in order that I could perform my operas for him. As only Italian was sung there, it would be necessary to translate my texts, but he felt this would be very easy and at the same time beneficial for them. Curiously enough, the prospect this conjured up struck me as extremely pleasant, and I was sure that I could easily bring off a passionate musical poem that would turn out very well in Italian. The old and ever-recurring inclination revived, and I thought of *Tristan und Isolde*. But first I sent Senhor Ferreiro, in order to test the generous instincts of the Emperor of Brazil, the expensively bound editions of the vocal scores of my three earlier operas, expecting to hear something agreeable about their gratifying reception in Rio de Janeiro. I have never heard anything more about them, not a word from the Emperor of Brazil[4] or Senhor Ferreiro. Yet Semper managed to get involved in some architectural activity in that tropical country: a competition was announced for the construction of a new opera house in Rio; Semper entered for it and produced some splendid plans, which gave us a good deal of enjoyment and incidentally struck Dr Wille as particularly challenging, for he thought it would necessarily be an architectural novelty to design an opera theater for a black public. I never learned whether the result of Semper's efforts for Brazil was much more satisfactory than my own; at any rate, I know that he did not build the theater.

A severe cold caused me a very high fever for several days; by the time I recovered my birthday had arrived: sitting on the terrace once again that evening, I was surprised to hear the song of the three Rhine Maidens from the close of *Das Rheingold* wafting up to me across the gardens from a little distance. Frau Pollert, the same one whose marital troubles had stood in the way of a second performance of my *Liebesverbot* in Magdeburg, in itself a difficult enough undertaking, had reappeared in the Zürich theatrical skies that previous winter as a singer. She was also the mother of two daughters. As she still possessed a good singing voice and behaved with extreme cordiality to me, I persuaded her to rehearse the last act of *Die Walküre* and, together with both daughters, the Rhine Maiden scenes from *Das Rheingold*. In the course of the winter we had been able to offer our friends some modest excerpts from this music; and now, on this birthday evening the singing by my thoughtful lady friends surprised and touched me very much, and I suddenly felt a curious disinclination to continue the composition of my *Nibelungen*, and in its place an inclination all the more intense to start work on *Tristan* at once. I decided to yield to this long-held, secret desire and set to work at once on this new task, which I still insisted on considering a temporary interruption of the vaster one. In order to prove to myself that I was not being scared away from the older work by any feeling of weariness with it, I determined to complete the composition of the second act of *Siegfried* at all costs, despite the fact that I had only just begun it; this I did with great gusto, while I let *Tristan* ripen within me.

The decision to take up *Tristan* was also influenced in part by some external motives which made the enterprise of executing the work appear to me to be an attractive and advantageous prospect. These factors came to maturity when Eduard Devrient paid me a visit at the beginning of July[1] and stayed three days. He informed me that my submission to the Grand Duchess of Baden had been accorded a favorable reception. On the whole, I gained the impression that he had been commissioned to reach some kind of agreement with me concerning a major undertaking; I let him know that I had it in mind to interrupt my big Nibelung work with a drama which, by its scale and requirements, would again bring me into contact with theaters as they were then constituted. I would certainly be doing myself an injustice if I were to say that this external motive was the sole reason for my deciding to carry *Tristan* out; yet I must admit that a palpable change had taken place with respect to the mood in which I had set forth upon the other, vaster work several years before. At that time I had just completed my writings on art, in which

I had tried to explain the reasons for the decay of our public art forms, particularly the theater, by a broad investigation of the relationship between those reasons and the general conditions of culture. In those days it would have been impossible for me to commence a work for which I could contemplate immediate performance at any of our theaters. Only a complete renunciation of this prospect, as I have previously demonstrated, could induce me to take up my creative work once again. As to a performance of the Nibelung dramas, I had been obliged to face the fact squarely that such a performance could only take place under very special auspices of the kind that I later specified in the preface to the dramatic poem when it was published. Yet the successful diffusion of my older operas had colored my frame of mind in such a way that, as I approached the completion of this huge work with more than half of it behind me, I could not help seriously considering the possibilities for its production. Up to then, Liszt had nourished this secret hope in my heart by his confidence in the Grand Duke of Weimar; but the latest experiences had proved all these hopes entirely illusory, whereas on the other hand it was widely confirmed to me that, if I produced a new work similar to *Tannhäuser* or *Lohengrin*, it would be welcomed everywhere. The manner in which I finally executed the plan for *Tristan* shows clearly how little I thought of our theaters and their capacities while doing so. Yet inasmuch as I was forced to struggle with the difficulties of my financial situation the whole time, I managed to cajole myself into believing that by interruping the composition of my *Nibelungen* to attack *Tristan* I was acting in a practical way as a prudent planner should. Devrient in turn was very glad to hear about such an allegedly practical undertaking on my part; he asked me which theater I had in mind for the first performance of my new work; I replied that I could naturally select only a theater where I could personally be present to participate in the production. This might be either in Brazil, I thought, or, inasmuch as the territory of the German Federation was barred to me, possibly in a city near the German border where I could plausibly expect sufficient artistic resources to be put at my disposal. I had my eye on Strassburg for this purpose; but Devrient had many practical objections to such an undertaking; a performance in Karlsruhe, he opined, would be far more successful and easier to arrange. My only objection to this was that I could not personally attend to the preparations there. As to this point, Devrient felt I would be justified in entertaining some hopes, as the Grand Duke of Baden was so well disposed toward me and took such an active interest in my work. This was all very pleasant to hear.

Devrient also spoke with a good deal of enthusiasm about the young tenor Schnorr,[1] who was the possessor of splendid vocal resources and was, moreover, devoted to my works. In the best of moods I played host to Devrient as well as I could; on one morning I played and sang the whole *Rheingold* for him, which seemed to please him very much. Half joking and half in earnest, I told him I had thought of him when writing the part of Mime; for if it were not too late, he should have his chance to play this role some day. With Devrient available we could obviously not fail to have a reading by him; I invited my household friends, together with Semper and Herwegh, and Devrient read us Antony's scenes from Shakespeare's *Julius Caesar* in such a superb way that even Herwegh, who had been inclined to mock the whole thing, willingly attested to the impact achieved by this well-schooled actor. Devrient wrote the Grand Duke of Baden while still at my home, reporting to him what he had found and how things stood. Shortly after his departure I received a very encouraging letter from the Grand Duke in his own hand, thanking me first of all most flatteringly for the musical folio I had presented to his wife, and then at the same time declaring his intention of intervening on my behalf in the future, particularly with respect to my return to Germany.

From this time forward my resolve to get started on the composition of *Tristan* was inscribed in bold letters on my plan of life. For the moment I had to be grateful to all this for sustaining the good mood in which I now was able to bring the second act of *Siegfried* to a close. My daily walks on the bright summer afternoons were directed toward the tranquil Sihltal, in whose bosky surroundings I listened long and attentively to the song of the forest birds. In doing so I was astonished to hear entirely new melodies from singers whose forms I could not see and whose names were even less familiar. Whatever I brought home with me from their melodies I put into the forest scene of *Siegfried* in artistic imitation. By the beginning of August,[2] I had managed to complete the composition of this second act with meticulous sketches. I was glad that I had reserved the third act with the awakening of Brünnhilde for subsequent recommencement; for it seemed to me as if I had now solved the principal problems in carrying out the work, and that what remained was to extract the pure pleasure from doing it.

Thus armed with the conviction that I was correctly husbanding my artistic powers, I was ready to begin work on *Tristan*. A certain strain was put on my patience at this point by the arrival of my worthy friend Ferdinand Praeger from London, though I was actually rather pleased by his visit, knowing him to be a proven and durable friend. Only he seemed to be extremely nervous and imagined himself persecuted by fate. This was a bit annoying for me, as with the best will in the world I could not conceive much sympathy for him in that respect. So we resorted to an excursion to Schaffhausen, where I visited the famous Rhine waterfalls, which did not fail to impress me duly. At about this time the Wesendoncks moved into their new villa, which had finally been cleared of Parisian plasterers and paperhangers. Thus my relations with this family entered on a new phase, which, although not really important, had a considerable effect on the outward course of my life. Now that we were such close neighbors, in almost rural isolation, a marked increase in our connections could not fail to occur, if only by the fact of our daily encounters. I had already noticed that Wesendonck, in his straightforward but rather uncultivated manner, showed a certain uneasiness at my making myself at home in his house; in many things, including heating, lighting, and meal times, consideration was shown to me that seemed to encroach upon his rights as master of the house. It required some confidential discussion about this to reach an understanding that was half implied and half expressed, an arrangement which over the course of time tended to assume significance in the eyes of others. This in turn necessitated a certain measure of precaution in our now intimate relationship, such precautions being at times a source of amusement for the two initiates.

Strangely enough, the timing of this closer neighborly association coincided with the commencement of my work on the text of *Tristan und Isolde*. Meanwhile, Robert Franz arrived for a visit in Zürich and pleased me by the winning aspects of his personality, while his visit also reassured me that no deep significance needed to be attached to the tension that had developed between us since the time he had become active on my behalf with regard to *Lohengrin*. This misunderstanding had resulted mainly from the meddling of his brother-in-law Hinrich, who had written a pamphlet about me. We had some music; he accompanied me in singing some of his songs; my Nibelung compositions seemed to please him. Yet when the Wesendoncks one day proposed inviting both of us to dinner, he requested to be left alone with the family without any other guests, on the grounds that if I were present he would not be able to shine, and that was a matter of a little concern to him. We joked about this, and I did so all the more heartily because I was often quite grateful to be spared the need to converse with people so uncommunicative and short-winded as I found Franz to be. He left without ever letting us hear from him again.

By the time I had virtually completed the first act of my poem for *Tristan*, a newly married couple arrived in Zürich who had every right to claim my interest and attention. Toward the beginning of September, Hans von Bülow, together with his young wife, Liszt's daughter Cosima, arrived at the Raven Hotel. I went to meet them and brought them back to my little house for a lengthy visit, as it was principally on my account that they had come to Zürich.

The month of September was spent together in exhilarating activities. During that time I completed the text of *Tristan und Isolde*, while Hans made me a fair copy of each act as soon as it was finished. I had already read each act separately to my friends before I could finally hold a private reading of the whole work, which made a great impression on the few listeners, who were all close friends. As Frau Wesendonck seemed particularly moved by the final act, I consoled her with the statement that there was no reason to mourn, for in such serious instances this was the very best outcome that could be expected – wherein Cosima agreed. Beyond this, we made a good deal of music; for in Bülow I had finally acquired the right player for the frightfully difficult Klindworth arrangements of my Nibelung scores. And Hans also knew how to master the first two acts of *Siegfried*, which I had only completed in sketch form, in such a way as to appear to be playing from an actual piano arrangement. To this I sang, as usual, all the parts; sometimes we had a few listeners, among whom the most appreciative was Frau Wille. Cosima listened with lowered head and said nothing; when pressed for her reaction, she began to cry.

Toward the end of September my two young friends departed, in order to journey back to Berlin to begin the serious business of their married life.

By playing so much of it, we had accorded the *Nibelungen* a sort of temporary requiem, as I now laid it aside completely, and at subsequent occasions of this nature, when the music was extracted from my files, it had an increasingly yellowed look, as if it were a souvenir. At the beginning of October,[1] on the other hand, I made a quick beginning to the music for *Tristan*, completing the first act before the New Year, by which time I was already working on the orchestration of the prelude. During this period I developed into a rather dreamy and anxious recluse. Work, long walks in spite of the rough weather, and reading Calderón in the evening formed my regimen, any disruption of which caused me great annoyance. My dealings with the world were restricted almost entirely to my negotiations with the music dealer Härtel about the publication of *Tristan*; when I let him know that with this work, in contrast to the gigantic Nibelung undertaking, I had something practicable in mind which would require for its performance solely a few good singers, he evinced such great willingness to accept my offer that I went so far as to ask him for four hundred louis d'or.[1] In response Härtel wrote me that I should open his counter-proposal, contained in a sealed envelope he enclosed, only if I were inclined to abandon my initial demand entirely, for he could not agree that my new work would turn out to be easy to perform. In the sealed envelope I now found an offer of only one hundred louis d'or, but with the undertaking, after five years to share the receipts from the venture with me, or else to buy the residual rights from me for another hundred louis d'or. I had to accept this and began at once with the instrumentation of the first act, sending the score to the engraver fascicle by fascicle.

Apart from all this I was interested at that time in a crisis that developed in the American money market, as a result of which the whole wealth of my friend Wesendonck seemed imperiled for several ominous weeks. I recall that the affected parties bore the threatened catastrophe with great dignity; yet our conversations about the possible necessity of selling hearth, home and horses lent our evening get-togethers an unavoidable melancholy. Wesendonck then departed on a trip to settle matters with various foreign bankers; in the meantime, having worked in the mornings at the composition of *Tristan*, I regularly read aloud from Calderón in the evenings. It was at this time, after Schack's work[2] had sufficiently prepared me to make the acquaintance of the dramatic literature of Spain, that Calderón made upon me a deep and lasting impression. At length the American crisis took a turn for the better, and the result was that Wesendonck's wealth was considerably augmented by it. During these winter evenings I read *Tristan* aloud once again to a wider circle of friends. Gottfried Keller was especially pleased at the economical form of the whole work, which really consisted only of three well-developed scenes. But Semper became distempered about it; he reproached me with taking everything too seriously; the benefit of artistic treatment of such material, he insisted, lay in dispelling its seriousness in order to gain enjoyment even from the most deeply moving elements. What pleased him so much about Mozart's *Don Giovanni*, he added, was that there we find the tragic types only as if in a masquerade, where even a domino is preferable to the usual disguises characters adopt. I conceded that I could make it much easier for myself if I were more serious about life and less so about art; but there was simply nothing else for it with me, I said, and things would have to remain the way they were. At bottom everyone was puzzled. After I had sketched the composition of the first act and considered the nature of my musical realization more closely, I had to smile strangely at my initial presumption that I would be writing a kind of "Italian" opera with this work, and the fact that I heard nothing more from Brazil gradually disturbed me less and less.

On the other hand, toward the end of the year my attention was compelled toward certain events in Paris that seemed to affect my operas. A young author wrote me from there with a request to be entrusted with the translation of my *Tannhäuser*, inasmuch as the Director of the Théâtre Lyrique, M. Carvalho,[1] had it in mind to perform this opera in Paris. I was greatly alarmed at this, for I was afraid my rights in my works were unprotected in France and, what was really abhorrent to me, that people could do what they wanted with them there. The manner in which things were done at the Théâtre Lyrique itself had recently come to my attention in a report about a production of Weber's *Euryanthe* and the objectionable adaptation, or rather mutilation, it had undergone for that purpose. Since Liszt's elder daughter Blandine had recently married the renowned lawyer Emile Ollivier,[2] thus providing me with a highly valuable ally, I now came to the decision to go to Paris for about a week to look into these affairs on the spot, and at any rate assure myself of legal protection for my copyrights in France. Beyond this I was in a melancholy frame of mind anyway, no doubt largely as a result of overwork, and particularly my constant preoccupation with those works of which Semper criticized with some justice, at least with respect to the strain on my spiritual powers, the excessive seriousness. I gave written testimony to this state of mind, in which my reaction was to despise all characteristically worldly cares, in a letter to my old friend Alwine Frommann on New Year's Eve 1857, if I remember rightly.

With the onset of the new year 1858 the need for a break in my work became so manifest that I was truly reluctant to begin the instrumentation of the first act of *Tristan und Isolde* before I had permitted myself the expedition I desired. Unfortunately neither Zürich, nor my household, nor my circle of friends afforded me any further recreation. Even the agreeable and originally so promising proximity of the Wesendonck family only increased my unease, for it was really intolerable for me to devote my evenings to conversations and diversions in which my worthy friend Otto Wesendonck felt himself obliged to participate at least to the same extent I and everyone else did. His obvious worry that everything in his house would soon be adapted more to my needs than to his gave him that characteristically emphatic manner, whereby a person of relatively little culture throws himself forcibly into every conversation, driven by his fears, with much the same effect that the snuffer has on the candle. Before long everything was a burden to me; only those who evinced some comprehension of this could expect to arouse my interest, and even that, under the circumstances, was cold comfort for me. In the midst of a harsh winter I thus decided to go to Paris despite the fact that I was most certainly not provided with sufficient funds at this point and had to make all kinds of hasty arrangements to dig them up. Once more I felt a dark presentiment that I might be leaving never to return. Much too exhausted to continue the journey immediately, I arrived in Strassburg on January 15th and from there wrote Eduard Devrient in Karlsruhe, suggesting that he propose to the Grand Duke that I be met at Kehl by one of his adjutants upon my return journey from Paris and conducted on a formal visit to Karlsruhe; for above all else I wanted to become acquainted with the prospective singers for my *Tristan* there. I soon received a reprimand from Eduard Devrient for my presumption in supposing that grand-ducal adjutants could be placed at my disposal; from this I saw that he thought my purpose was solely to receive some meaningless mark of honor, whereas I had hit on the idea as the only practical way in which I, as one convicted of political crimes, could dare set foot in Karlsruhe for my purely artistic purposes. This misconception amused me; at the same time my astonishment at this evidence of shallowness on the part of a man who had been my friend for a number of years was sufficient to influence my thoughts about his future conduct toward me from thenceforth. Meanwhile I was trudging wearily in the twilight along the main public promenade of Strassburg to restore my overwrought nerves when suddenly I was startled by the name TANNHÄUSER appearing on a theater placard. Upon closer inspection this turned out to be the overture to *Tannhäuser*, which was to be performed before a French play. I hadn't any idea what all this could mean; but naturally I took my place in the theater, which was very sparsely populated: the orchestra looked all the larger by contrast as its members assembled in substantial numbers in a spacious pit and then proceeded to give a really very good rendition of my overture under the conductor's baton. As I was sitting rather near the front of the stalls, the timpanist, who had played in my Zürich concerts in 1853, was able to recognize me. News of my presence spread like wildfire through the orchestra to its conductor and caused great excitement. The tiny audience, which had obviously come solely for the French play and was not in the slightest inclined to pay any special attention to the overture, was greatly amazed when, at the conclusion of the music, the conductor and the whole orchestra turned toward my seat and gave vent to enthusiastic applause, which I then had to acknowledge with a bow. All eyes followed me intently as I left the hall after this incident to pay my respects to the conductor: his name was Hasselmann, he was a native of Strassburg, and seemed to be a very genial and well-intentioned fellow; he accompanied me to my hotel and among other things related to me the circumstances surrounding this surprising performance of my overture. According to the terms of a copious bequest from a citizen of Strassburg, a great patron of music who had already been the most generous contributor to the construction of the theater, the orchestra, whose quality was also due to his bequest, was required to play a substantial piece of instrumental music once a week before one of the regular theatrical performances. By coincidence the *Tannhäuser* overture had been on the program this time. My principal reaction to all this was envy of Strassburg at having brought forth such a citizen whose like was not to be found in all the cities where I had ever had anything to do with music, and most particularly not in Zürich.

While I was discussing the state of music in Strassburg with Hasselmann, Orsini's notorious assassination attempt[1] on the life of the Emperor took place in Paris; upon continuing my journey the following day I already heard some vague rumors, but when I reached Paris on January 16th I received full details about it from a waiter at my hotel. I looked upon this event as a malicious stroke of fate aimed at me personally; I feared that at breakfast the very next morning I would see my old acquaintance from the Ministry of the Interior walk in and demand my instant departure from Paris as a political refugee. I therefore supposed that as a guest of the grand Hotel du Louvre, which was newly opened at the time, I would be treated by the police with greater respect than at the little hostelry in a corner of the Rue des Filles St Thomas, where I had first gone for reasons of economy. As a matter of fact I had originally intended to take up residence in a hotel I knew from earlier days in the Rue le Pelletier; but it was from precisely that spot that the assassination had been attempted, and it was in that very hotel that the principal accomplices had been found and arrested. How strange if I had arrived two days earlier in Paris and taken rooms there!

After this consultation with the demon of my fate, I hunted down M. Ollivier and his young bride. In the former I at once discovered a very winning and active friend, who promptly and resolutely took in hand the matter which constituted my chief exterior objective in coming to Paris. One day we went to a notary public he knew, who seemed to be under obligation to him; there I gave Ollivier a much be-claused and iron-clad power of attorney over all my proprietary rights as author, and in spite of the many formalities involving the stamping of this document, I was treated very hospitably, so that I felt well sheltered under my new friend's protection. But then, as I walked with my friend Ollivier in the Palais de Justice, I was introduced to the most famous lawyers in the world, promenading there in cap and gown in the Salle des Pas Perdus. On the instant I struck up so good an acquaintance with them that I allowed myself to be persuaded to expound the subject of *Tannhäuser* to a circle of them that formed around me. All this pleased me very much. I was no less satisfied by my conversations with Ollivier about his political views and his own position. He still believed only in a republic which would be permanently reestablished after the inevitable overthrow of the Napoleonic rule. He and his friends did not intend to provoke a revolution but only to prepare themselves, to make certain that, when it unavoidably came, it would not again be subject to exploitation by conspirators. On matters of principle he agreed with the most radical conclusions of socialism; he knew and respected Proudhon, but not as a politician: yet nothing, he thought, could be permanently established except through the initiative of political institutions. By means of simple legislation, which had already ushered in important measures protecting the public interest against the abuses of privilege, even the apparently most audacious demands for the introduction of equal distribution of public benefits could gradually be realized. I here noted that I had made considerable progress in the development of my character, for I was able to listen and discuss these and other such topics without getting excited, as I formerly did.

Blandine in turn impressed me very pleasantly by her gentleness, cheerfulness, and a certain quiet wit, all of which was coupled with a keen understanding. We came to an immediate meeting of the minds; the slightest suggestion sufficed to bring us to a mutual understanding as to persons and things with which we came into contact. Sunday came and brought a concert at the Conservatoire, for which my friends managed to obtain me a seat, knowing that I had previously attended only rehearsals there and never performances. In fact, I was placed in the box of the widow of the composer Hérold, a very charming woman who immediately declared herself a warm partisan of my music. She had not yet heard any of it personally; but the enthusiasm of her daughter and her son-in-law, who, as I mentioned previously, had attended performances of *Tannhäuser* in Vienna and Berlin on their honeymoon, had won her over by the power of sympathy. All this constituted a strange but agreeable surprise. In addition I heard here for the first time in my life a performance of Haydn's *Seasons*, which the audience enjoyed immensely, as they considered the melismatic cadences with which Haydn so frequently closes his melodic phrases, and which are so seldom heard nowadays in modern music, especially original and charming. The rest of the day was spent in the bosom of the Hérold family in a most agreeable way; toward the end of the evening a man appeared there whose presence seemed to be accorded special significance, particularly on that day. This was M. Scudo, about whom I later learned that he exerted great influence on many publications in his capacity as the powerful music editor of the *Revue des deux Mondes*. His influence, in fact, had been used most decidedly against me up to then. My friendly hostess had wished me to make his acquaintance on this occasion, so that he might form a favorable impression of me. But I told her such an objective was not likely to be achieved through the medium of conversation in a salon, and later I was confirmed in my opinion that the reasons why a person of this type, possessing no knowledge of the subject, declares himself hostile to an artist have nothing whatever to do with his convictions, or even his personal approval or disapproval. On that subsequent occasion these kind people had to suffer for having put themselves out on my account, because, in a review by M. Scudo of one of my concerts, they were ridiculed as a family with "acute democratic principles".

I now looked up my newly won friend of London days, Berlioz, and found him on the whole disposed to be amiable. I let him know that I was in Paris just for a short excursion and for my own amusement. At that time he was busy working on the composition of a big opera, *Les Troyens*; to obtain some impression of this work I wanted above all to become acquainted with its text, which he had written himself. He devoted an evening to reading it aloud for me alone: as he proceeded I became greatly ill at ease, not only with the poetic conception itself but also with the curiously dry and theatrically affected manner in which the poem was delivered. I believed his manner to be indicative of the kind of music he had in mind for his text and became utterly disconsolate, as I could see that Berlioz regarded his work as his *chef d'oeuvre* and its eventual performance as the crowning purpose of his life.

Together with the Olliviers I was also invited to the home of the Erard family,[1] in which I again found my old friend, the widow of Spontini; we spent a rather lavish evening there, during which I had to provide the musical entertainment at the piano in a markedly unusual way. I produced reminiscences of my operas as best I could, and my listeners claimed that they well understood and hugely enjoyed them. At any rate, the splendid salon had never heard such relaxed music-making before. Beyond this, I made one great acquisition through the thoughtful courtesy of Mme Erard and her brother-in-law Schäffer, who was running the business since the death of her husband, in the form of one of the famous grand pianos of their manufacture. By this the obscure purpose for which I had come to Paris was suddenly illuminated; for I was so delighted that I recognized that every other outcome of my visit was chimerical, and that this was its sole true success.

After that I left Paris on February 2nd in a more cheerful mood, stopping off on my homeward journey to see my old friend Kietz in Epernay. There M. Paul Chandon, a casual acquaintance of his youth, had interested himself in the shipwrecked painter, had taken him into his home, and had offered him a series of portrait commissions. Upon my arrival I was drawn irresistibly into this hospitable house and could not refuse to spend two days there resting up; for in Chandon I found a passionate fan also of my operas, especially *Rienzi*, the first performance of which he had attended long ago in Dresden. Here I also visited that fabulous wine cellar, which extends for miles through the bowels of the rocky ground of Champagne. I found Kietz at work on an oil portrait, and to my particular interest, people were generally of the opinion that he would complete it.

After much superfluous entertainment I finally freed myself from this unexpected hospitality and arrived back in Zürich on February 5th, where I had arranged by letter for an evening party immediately after my return, as I thought I had much to tell everyone and wanted to avoid the usual wearying task of making detailed reports individually to my friends by communicating with them collectively. Semper, who was included in the company and who was annoyed at having been obliged to stay in Zürich while I was in Paris, became very irritated at my merry report and declared me to be "a shameless darling of fortune", as he obviously looked upon it as a disaster that he should be confined to his "Zürich hole".

How I had to smile inwardly at his envy of my "good fortune"! My financial dealings proceeded sluggishly onward, for my operas had by now been sold to most every possible theater, and nothing remained to me of the original capital sums received for them. Inasmuch as I heard nothing of these performances of my operas, save for the small sums they brought me, I got the idea of bringing *Rienzi* back to market, on the grounds that it was really rather well suited for our bad theaters: to get started in this, a reintroduction of the work in the Dresden repertory was desirable; but that was prevented by the alarm caused by Orsini's assassination attempt – at least that is what I was told. So I continued to work at the orchestration of the first act of *Tristan* and could scarcely conceal to myself as time went on that the excuses offered to prevent its rapid diffusion in our theaters were likely to be other than merely political. Thus I worked on, toward a future that seemed inherently hopeless.

In the month of March Frau Wesendonck disclosed to me her desire to celebrate her husband's birthday with some kind of music in her house; she had hit upon this idea as a result of a little musical matinée I had arranged for her own birthday in the course of the winter with the neighborly help of eight cooperative Zürich musicians. The pride of the Villa Wesendonck, it must be noted, consisted of a relatively not unspacious hall, elegantly decorated by Parisian plasterers, of which I had once remarked that music would not sound at all badly there. This had been tested in miniature on that previous occasion and was now to prove itself on a larger scale. I offered to put together a decent orchestra and perform fragments of Beethoven symphonies, consisting chiefly of the more cheerful movements, for social entertainment. The requisite preparations took some time, however, and the date of the birthday had to be overstepped. Thus we reached Easter time, and our concert took place on one of the last days of March.[1] This household music festival actually went quite well; an orchestra manned sufficiently to do justice to Beethoven's instrumentation played a combined selection of symphony excerpts under my direction to the guests scattered throughout the adjoining rooms, and with the best of success. The unheard-of nature of such a domestic concert seemed to put everybody in an excited mood; at the beginning of the concert I was presented by the daughter of the house with a lovely baton made of carved ivory from a design by Semper (the first and only one I have ever received as a ceremonial gift). There was no dearth of flowers and plants surrounding the place where I stood to conduct, and when we closed, in accordance with my taste for the effect of such a performance, not with a rip-roaring piece, but rather with the deeply tranquil Adagio from the Ninth Symphony, people could justifiably say that Zürich society had experienced something that was not entirely run-of-the-mill.

My friends, upon whom I had bestowed this mark of distinction, were also profoundly touched by it. This festivity affected me in a melancholy way, as if it constituted some kind of symbolic high point of a life's relationship, and indeed as if its actual capacity had been overtaxed and the string of the bow pulled too taut. Frau Wille told me later that she had also been possessed by similar feelings on that evening. On April 3rd I dispatched the manuscript score of the first act of *Tristan und Isolde* to Leipzig to be engraved; I sent to Frau Wesendonck the pencil sketches for the instrumentation of the prelude, which I had previously promised to her, accompanied by a little note in which I calmly and earnestly described my prevailing state of mind at this moment. For some time my wife had been brooding on her relationship with Frau Wesendonck; she complained more and more fretfully about not being treated by her with the attentiveness due to the wife of a man who was always made so welcome; and in general she found that whenever we got together socially our lady friend was more interested in visiting me than her. However, she had not yet indulged in any open expression of suspicion. Being by chance in the little garden at the time, she intercepted my communication on that morning, took it away from the servant, then broke the seal and opened the letter.[1] As it was entirely impossible for her to comprehend the mood which had brought forth these lines, she clung all the more fixedly to a trivial interpretation of the words and thought herself entitled to burst into my room and attack me with the most extraordinary reproaches about the terrible discovery she had made. She later admitted to me that nothing had infuriated her so much as my absolute calm and what struck her as the indifference with which I countered her foolish behavior. Actually I said not a word to her and simply let her leave the room, after scarcely moving from my chair. But to myself I said that this was the moment I had been expecting in one form or another, when I had to acknowledge frankly the intolerable conditions of the married life we had recommenced eight years before, and draw some conclusions as to my future life. By a most decided demand that she behave circumspectly and not be guilty of any rash acts, I tried to make Minna understand the real significance which this otherwise trifling event had assumed for us. She actually seemed to comprehend this and promised me to behave decorously and not to indulge her silly jealousy. Unfortunately the poor woman was already suffering from the effects of a serious worsening of her heart condition on her disposition; the characteristic pessimism and agonizing restlessness which such enlargements of the heart cause to those who suffer them could not be overcome: after a few days she found it necessary to give vent to her feelings, and the only way she felt able to accomplish this was to warn our neighbor, in her eyes a well-intentioned act, against the consequences of any indiscreet intimacies with me. Returning from a walk, I found Herr and Frau Wesendonck in their carriage, about to leave for a drive; I noticed her agitated look and, by contrast, the strangely contented smile on the countenance of her husband. I immediately realized what had happened; for I also found my wife in a markedly exhilarated mood; she offered me her hand in great probity and announced to me the renewal of her amity. To my question whether she might have broken her promise she replied confidently that, as a sensible woman, she had been obliged to set matters straight. I pointed out to her that she would probably have to bear some very severe consequences as a result of her breach of faith; but for the moment I thought it essential that she take those steps we had previously arranged to bolster her health somewhat and told her she should go to the recommended spa at Brestenberg on Lake Hallwyl as soon as possible. We had actually received splendid reports about cures for heart patients effected by the doctor there. Minna was also in agreement with the commencement of this treatment for her illness; and so I accompanied her together with her parrot a few days later, during which time I carefully avoided inquiring at the main house as to what had happened, to the pleasantly situated and well-equipped spa, scarcely a quarter day's journey away. When I left her there, at the moment of our farewell, she seemed suddenly to sense the painful seriousness of our situation; I could say very little to console her, except that I would try, in the interests of our future life together, to mitigate the consequences I feared from her broken promise.

Upon my return home I had to discover more precisely the unpleasant outcome of my wife's conduct toward our neighbor. In her crude misinterpretation of my purely friendly relationship to the young lady, who was always deeply concerned for my well-being and my tranquillity, Minna had gone so far as to threaten to tell her husband and by this had so profoundly insulted her, being really unaware of having done wrong in any way, that she even began to have doubts about me, as she did not understand how I could have permitted my wife to nurture such a misconception. The upshot of this disturbance was that, thanks to the discreet mediation of our good friend Frau Wille, I was eventually absolved of any responsibility for my wife's conduct. Yet I was given to understand that henceforth it would be impossible for the insulted lady to set foot in my house, or to continue any association with my wife. They did not seem to realize clearly enough, or want to admit, that I could only respond to this by giving up my dwelling and leaving Zürich. And since, although my relations with this friendly family had been shaken, they had not been actually undermined, even I at length developed the conviction that all this confusion would sort itself out in some way calmly enough. To this end I had to count above all on an improvement in my wife's condition, through which she would be enabled to understand how foolish she had been and bring herself to the point of resuming relations with our neighbors on a sensible basis.

Some time elapsed, during which the Wesendonck family took a pleasure trip of several weeks to Northern Italy. The arrival of the Erard piano I had been promised made me feel almost sad; I suddenly realized what a toneless instrument my old Breitkopf & Härtel "Kapellmeister grand" had been during all the years I had relied on it and consigned it at once to the basement, where my wife, who was careful to store things, had asked that it be placed. (She later took it with her to Saxony and sold it, I think, for one hundred talers.) The new piano flattered my musical sensibility uncommonly, and while improvising I effortlessly drifted into the soft nocturnal sounds of the second act of *Tristan*, the composition of which I now actually began early in May.

In this work I was interrupted unexpectedly by an invitation from the Grand Duke of Weimar to visit him on a specific day in Lucerne, where he was going to stop off on his return from a trip to Italy. I accepted this invitation and thus was accorded a lengthy interview with my former purported patron at a hotel in Lucerne in the room of the Court Chamberlain von Beaulieu, whom I had met at the time of my flight. I gathered from this conversation that my dealings with the Grand Duke of Baden regarding a performance of *Tristan* in Karlsruhe had made some impression on the court in Weimar. In expressly mentioning these dealings, Karl Alexander had it in mind to gain my assurance, in return for his expressions of continuing interest in regard to my Nibelung works, that I would be willing to designate this work for performance in Weimar. I had no trouble reassuring him on this point. Beyond that I was entertained by the whole personality of this reigning prince, who chatted with uninhibited amiability while we were seated together on a narrow couch, while on the other hand obviously trying to give me a favorable impression of his culture by his oddly eclectic use of language and terminology. It was noticeable that his dignity was not at all disturbed by the fatuous remarks that Herr von Beaulieu interjected in our conversation in an extremely dry tone of voice. After the Grand Duke had interrogated me in carefully chosen words as to my "real opinion" of Liszt's compositions, I was then utterly amazed to find him not in the slightest put out when his Chamberlain bluntly expressed extremely derogatory opinions of the man who was the Duke's highly esteemed friend, claiming in particular that Liszt's composing was nothing more than a whim of the great virtuoso. This afforded me an interesting insight into this princely relationship of my friend, while I had some difficulty keeping the conversation in a serious vein the whole time. On the following morning I had to pay one more visit on the Grand Duke; this time I found him without his chamberlain, which had a decidedly favorable effect on the warmth of his remarks concerning his friend, about whom, now that we were alone, he could not say enough as to his advice and the inspiring nature of his association with him. I also had the surprise of seeing the Grand Duchess enter the room and receive me with a very civil bow, which in its disciplined precision has remained unforgettable to me. My encounter with these exalted personages made a very pleasant adventure of my trip; for the rest, I have never heard anything from either of them again.*[1] When I later visited Liszt in Weimar before his departure from there, he found it impossible to induce the Grand Duke to receive me!

Shortly after[2] I had returned from this excursion, Karl Tausig[3] showed up one day at my dwelling, armed with a letter of recommendation from Liszt. He was sixteen years old at the time and, though physically very delicate, surprised everybody by the uncommon precocity of his understanding and general deportment. He had already been hailed as a future Liszt as a result of his public debut as a pianist in Vienna. That was about the way he behaved as well; he insisted at this tender age on smoking the strongest cigars procurable, so that I really became incensed about it. On the other hand, I was pleased at his decision to spend some time in my company, and all the more so when I found that, apart from his amusing, half-childish yet perceptive and already even sly personality, he could play the piano in an extraordinarily mature way and possessed a quick faculty of musical understanding. He played every conceivable piece at sight and knew how to employ his unusual ability in the most

---

* Footnote in the original edition: "(This was dictated in 1868)". [Editor's note: Probably dictated in 1869, in fact. We know from Cosima's diaries that the passage about Schopenhauer, on pp. 508–10, was dictated on January 1st 1869.]

extravagant tricks for my entertainment. He immediately moved into a place in my immediate vicinity, was my daily guest at mealtimes, and also had to accompany me on my regular walks in the Sihltal, an obligation from which he soon tried to extricate himself. He also had to accompany me on a visit to Minna at Brestenberg; when I began repeating these visits on an almost weekly basis in the hope of contributing to the success of the cure, Tausig also tried to extricate himself from this duty as well, for neither Brestenberg nor the company of Minna seemed to agree with him.

But he could not avoid a further encounter with her when she interrupted her cure at the end of May and, worried about housekeeping problems, came back to me for a few days. From her conduct I noted that she did not feel obliged to attribute any lasting significance to the recent domestic upheaval, as she seemed to be of the opinion that the whole thing had been a "little love affair" which she had put in order. As she expressed herself on this subject with a certain unpleasant flippancy, I had to let her know how things stood clearly and distinctly one evening, despite my desire to forbear as much as possible in consideration of the condition of her health. As a result of her disobedience and her foolish behavior toward our neighbor, I told her, the possibility of our staying in this hard-won and newly furnished refuge now appeared highly dubious to me, and thus I had no choice other than to prepare her to consider the necessity for a separation, as in the event this move took place, I was disinclined to set up any other common household anywhere else. The earnestness with which I dwelt on our past life together appeared to shake her sufficiently on this occasion, particularly at the realization that she was responsible for the potential collapse of our last and painfully constructed chance of a respectable life in financial security, so that I heard her here, for the first time in our life, utter a gentle and dignified lament. For the first and only time she gave me a sign of affectionate humility by kissing my hand when I withdrew from her late in the night. This touched me very much and quickly awakened in me the hope for a decisive transformation in the character of the poor woman; and that in turn induced me to hope for a satisfactory continuation of the kind of life we had recently made for ourselves.

Everything augured well at the present time for the bolstering of this hope: my wife returned to Brestenberg to complete the second half of her cure; the most luxuriant summer weather favored my inclination to work on the second act of *Tristan*; the evenings with Tausig entertained me; my relations with my neighbors, who had never shown me any hostility, seemed to be evolving in the manner I thought suitable and desirable for our future association. It was easy to assume that, if my wife would visit her relatives in Saxony for a period after the end of her cure, the passing of time would finally let everything that had happened be forgotten, so that her own future conduct, as well as the changed mood of our neighbor who considered herself so deeply offended, would make it possible for us to renew our mutual relationship in an irreproachable way.

This halcyon mood was brightened still further by the expectation of other welcome visitors as well as the development of favorable relationships with the two most important German theaters. In June the Berlin intendant approached me about *Lohengrin*, and we soon came to an agreement. But in Vienna, as well, *Tannhäuser*'s taking of the city by storm had had its effect on the attitude previously held by the management of the court theaters; a short time before, the well reputed conductor Karl Eckert[1] had been entrusted with the technical direction of the opera house: he now seized upon the happy conjunction of two circumstances, the presence of a fine resident company of singers, and the closure of the theater for necessary redecoration and the consequent temporary cessation of performances, which thus presented an ideal period of free time in which to study a difficult new work, to push the acceptance of my *Lohengrin* through the court authorities. He now made me his offer. I wanted to insist on authorial rights, such as were granted by Berlin; Vienna maintained it could not offer these to me, on the grounds that the present, elderly theater building, with its extremely limited capacity, brought in only scanty receipts. And then one day I saw Kapellmeister Esser,[2] dispatched from Vienna especially for this purpose, appear at my door to arrange everything very nicely by paying me at once in the name of the management one thousand guilders for the first twenty performances of *Lohengrin*, and agreeing to pay another thousand guilders after these twenty had been completed. The congenial and amicable attitude of this honest musician won me over immediately, and without delay I concluded the agreement with him, with the result that Esser immediately went through the score of *Lohengrin* with me zealously and scrupulously, noting all my specific wishes for his guidance. When he departed to begin work in Vienna at once I could have full confidence in the success of the venture.

I was thus in good spirits early in July, as I finished the composition sketches for the second act of *Tristan* and began working out the final version of it, but without getting much beyond the first scene, for from this point on I was exposed to continual interruptions in my work. First, Tichatschek showed up for another visit and established himself in my little guest room in order, as he put it, to recuperate somewhat from his latest exertions; for he could boast of having brought my operas back into the Dresden repertory, after they had been repeatedly forbidden for a considerable period, and of having performed in them triumphantly. *Lohengrin* was also due to be given there soon. While this was all very heartening, I really didn't know what to do with this good fellow at close quarters. Fortunately I could consign him to Tausig; he understood my problem and took charge of Tichatschek for more or less the whole day by playing cards with him. Soon the young tenor Niemann[1] also arrived, together with his bride, the excellent actress Seebach:[2] his great talent had been highly praised to me and now by his almost superhuman stature he immediately struck me as if destined to be my Siegfried. Having two famous tenors in my house simultaneously caused a misfortune in that neither would sing for me, for they were ill at ease in each other's presence. But of Niemann I had every confidence that his voice would be commensurate with his imposing personality.

I then went to pick up my wife at Brestenberg on July 15th to bring her home. During my brief absence my servant, a wily Saxon, had felt obliged to lend some solemnity to the return of the mistress of the house by erecting a kind of triumphal arch. This led to great misunderstandings: Minna became immediately convinced to her vast satisfaction that this flower-bedecked arch would necessarily impinge strongly on the notice of our neighbors, and felt that this was a good way of letting them know that her return to the house could by no means be considered as readmission on terms that might be considered humiliating to herself. With triumphant satisfaction she insisted that the ceremonial decoration be not removed for several days. At this same period, faithful to their promise, the Bülows arrived for another visit with me, but confounded Tichatschek kept delaying his departure and thus continued to commandeer the sole tiny guest-room, so that I had to leave my friends in the hotel for several days. However, the visits they paid to the Wesendoncks, as well as to me, soon afforded me an opportunity to learn, much to my surprise, of the effect the triumphal arch had produced on our neighbor's young wife, who was still nursing her injured feelings. When I was notified of the excesses of emotion in that quarter, I now saw to what a sorry state of confusion things had come and immediately abandoned all hope of a peaceful resolution to the tangled situation.

These were days of the most unbearable discord: I wished I were as far away as possible in some desert seclusion, but at the same time I was in the curious position of making my home hospitable to one guest after another. Finally Tichatschek at least went away, and though I was obliged to stay there I could at least devote myself to the pleasant task of welcoming my treasured guests under my roof. The Bülows were really a godsend and ideally suited to put a damper on the horrible agitation raging in my house. Hans put a good face on things when, on the day he arrived, he found me in the middle of a horrible scene with Minna; for I had told her plainly that, as I saw the situation, there was no likelihood that we would be staying here for long, and I was only delaying my departure for the sake of our young friends. This time I had been obliged to admit to her that the reasons for my despair were not entirely attributable to her behavior alone. We spent a full month together in this manner in the house I had so innocently christened my last refuge: it was a long, extremely painful period; for each day, by the experiences it brought, could only strengthen my determination to give up this establishment. My young guests suffered no less under these circumstances; my misery communicated itself to everyone who seriously sympathized with me. To these friends Klindworth was soon added for, as if to fill the cup of joylessness in our strange house-party, he arrived from London for a visit. Thus the house was packed every day, and our table crowded with fearful, concerned and uneasy guests, while every pain was taken to entertain them by their hosts, who were about to give up this household forever.

It seemed to me there simply had to be a person quite outstandingly capable of bringing light and reconcilement, or at the very least a tolerable order in the confusion surrounding us. And Liszt had promised me a visit: he stood so happily aside from all these damaged relationships and deteriorating circumstances, was so much a man of the world, and possessed to such a high degree that which is called personal "aplomb", that I could not help regarding him as qualified to find a sensible way to counter the forces of unreason at work here. I was almost inclined to make my final decisions dependent upon the effect of his forthcoming visit. We vainly tried to induce him to hasten his trip: in response he offered me a rendezvous on Lake Geneva a month later! At that I lost all courage. Living together with my friends no longer offered me consolation; for, while on the one hand no one could understand how I could be driven out of a home that suited me so well, it was nonetheless perfectly clear that I could not stick it out here as things were. We made music now and then, but only very distractedly and half-heartedly. As if to make my stupefaction complete, we faced at that time the calamity represented by a Swiss Song Festival, during which I had to ward off all sorts of importunities, not always as amiably as could be wished. Among other things, I had to decline to see Franz Lachner, who was functioning as an honored guest in these proceedings, and I did not return his call. Tausig, it is true, managed to amuse us by singing Lachner's *Old German Battle Song*, composed especially for this festival, an octave higher than it was written, which his boyish falsetto enabled him to do; yet even his pranks could not cheer us up any longer. Everything that in other circumstances could have made this summer month one of the most stimulating of my life combined to emphasize the discomforts of the period: it was that way with the visit of the Comtesse d'Agoult[1] as well, who came to visit her daughter and son-in-law, and joined our circle during this time. By way of filling the house to the brim, Kárl Ritter also arrived, after a long period of sulking and grumbling, and once again proved himself to be an unusual and interesting person.

As the time for a general departure at last drew near, I was obliged to make the arrangements necessary for the dissolution of my household. I handled this by a personal visit to Wesendonck, and took leave of his wife in the company of Bülow. Despite the enduring confusion in her ideas of what had happened, she now seemed to be reproaching herself for the injustice she had done, and recognizing that it was that which necessarily entailed the end of my residence there. All my friends bade me farewell in painful emotion, while I could respond to their expressions of sorrow with little more than apathy. On August 16th the Bülows also left, Hans in tears and Cosima in gloomy silence. I had arranged with Minna that she should remain behind me for a week or so to clear out the house and dispose of our few belongings as she thought best. I had in fact advised her to delegate this job to someone else, because I could not understand how she would possibly wish to undertake such a wretched task in such dismal circumstances. But she didn't agree and felt it would be terrible if, with all our misfortunes, we also abandoned our property; there had to be order at all costs! To my dismay I later learned that she carried out the removal of our goods and her own departure with painstaking formality, advertising in the daily newspapers that the personal effects would be sold at bargain prices owing to the sudden departure, and thereby exciting so much curiosity that everybody became alarmed and began asking questions and spreading rumors, with the result that the whole affair received the scandalous taint which ever since has caused me and the Wesendonck family such pain and unpleasantness.

On August 17th, the day after the Bülows' departure – for only the presence of these friends had held me in Zürich – I got up at the crack of dawn after a sleepless night and went down to the dining room, where I found Minna already waiting for me with breakfast, for I intended to leave by the five o'clock train. She was calm; it was only when she accompanied me in the carriage to the station that the emotions of this sad hour overwhelmed her. It was a glorious summer day, the sky cloudless and bright; I remember that I did not look back even once or shed a tear at our leave-taking, and this almost frightened me. But as the steam locomotive carried me away, I could not conceal from myself an increasing sense of well-being; it was obvious that the absolutely pointless misery of the recent past had been endurable no longer, and that my life's impetus and its purpose demanded complete severance from all those circumstances that had produced such suffering. On the evening of that same day I arrived in Geneva; I wanted first of all to rest there a little and collect myself in order to be able to prepare the next moves in my life's plan calmly and sensibly. As I intended to make a renewed attempt to settle in Italy, I proposed, guided by my prior experience, to await the cooler autumn weather, in order that I would not again be subjected to the malign influence of a sudden change of climate. I rented quarters in the Maison Fazy for an entire month and tried to persuade myself that things would be very tolerable there for a time. I notified Karl Ritter in Lausanne of this decision and my plans for Italy: to my amazement I received from him in reply the announcement that he too was planning to give up his residence and to go to Italy alone, as his wife was about to visit her family in Saxony for the winter. He offered to be my traveling companion. This was quite all right with me, and as Ritter assured me at the same time that the climate of Venice, which he had gotten to know the year before, was entirely suitable at this time of year, I was thereby induced to hasten my departure. But I still had to make certain that my passport was in order; I expected, that is, the appropriate embassies in Berne to confirm to me that, as a political refugee, I would still have nothing to fear in Venice, which belonged to Austria, but not to the German Federation. Liszt, to whom I had turned for advice in the matter, felt impelled to warn me against Venice; yet the report one of my friends recieved from the Austrian Ambassador in Berne was completely innocuous, and so

I told Karl Ritter, after scarcely a week in Geneva, that I was ready to go, and then went to pick him up at his curious little villa near Lausanne to begin our journey together.

When he said good-bye to his wife it was clear to me that all was not well between them. After Ritter had taken leave of his wife in Lausanne with great coldness and constraint, he disclosed to me in the mail coach with sudden and vehement volubility that he had just left her for good: over the years since his marriage, he said, he had endured just about everything a human being could, but now it was over; until now he had withdrawn from all social activities to spare himself the embarrassments caused by the conduct of his wife: but recently she had been tormenting him even in their isolation through personal jealousy, and this had proved so intolerable, he added, that he had been obliged to decide upon a formal separation, if not a divorce. As a husband of very recent date he considered himself to be in a position similar to what he understood mine to be, and this supposed equality made him very companionable and devoted to me.

We didn't say much more about these matters and abandoned ourselves silently to the impressions of the journey. This took us over the Simplon to Lago Maggiore, where I again visited the Borromean Islands from Baveno. Here, on the terrace garden of Isola Bella, I enjoyed a marvelous late summer morning in the company of my young friend, who was never obtrusive but perhaps almost too taciturn; for the first time I felt I had regained my peace of mind and was filled with hope for a new and harmonious future. We continued our trip via Sesto Calende by mail coach to Milan; Karl scarcely gave me time to admire the famous cathedral, so strongly was he pulled toward the Venice he loved so much; and it was all right with me to be driven along by this feeling. At sundown on August 29th, when we were looking down from the causeway at the image of Venice rising reflected from the waters beneath, Karl suddenly lost his hat out the railway car window when leaning out in delight. I thought I should follow suit and threw my hat out as well: thus we both arrived bare-headed in Venice and immediately got into a gondola, to proceed along the entire Canale Grande to the Piazzetta beside San Marco. The weather had suddenly turned somewhat unpleasant, and the sight of the gondola itself had shocked me a bit; for despite all I had heard of these conveyances, painted black on black, the actual sight of one was still a rude surprise: when I had to go under the black awning, my first thought was a revival of a fear of cholera that I had previously mastered; it decidedly seemed to me as if I were taking part in a funeral procession during an epidemic. Karl assured me that this was how most people felt, but that one got used to it very quickly. Now came an extremely long trip round the many bends of the Canale Grande: the impressions made by all this were not sufficient to dispel my anxious mood. Whereas Karl had eyes only for a Ca d'oro belonging to Fanny Elssler[1] or some other famous palace between the deteriorating walls, my melancholy glance fell solely on the crumbling ruins between these interesting buildings. At length I fell silent and offered no objection to getting out at the world-famous Piazzetta to be shown the Palace of the Doges, though I reserved the right to admire it until such time as I had freed myself of the melancholy mood which my arrival in Venice had produced.

Starting out the next day from the Hotel Danieli, where we had found only some dark quarters in rooms overlooking narrow and tiny canals, I first hunted for a suitable place to live for my longer stay. I heard that one of the three Giustiniani palaces, not far from the Palazzo Foscari, was at present almost free of lodgers as a result of a location deemed not very suitable for the winter season: I found some exceptionally big and imposing rooms there, being told that they would all remain unoccupied; thus I rented a large and stately room, with a spacious adjoining bedroom, had my bags brought there quickly, and could tell myself by that evening of August 30th that I was now residing in Venice. The desire to be able to work here unmolested governed me in everything. I at once wrote to Zürich, requesting that my Erard piano and my bed be sent on after me, for as to the latter I had a feeling I would learn in Venice what it is to freeze. Furthermore, I soon found the grayish walls of my main room distasteful, as they were ill-suited to the ceiling, which was painted with what I considered a rather tasteful fresco. I decided to have the large room completely hung with an admittedly very cheap dark red wallpaper: this caused a lot of commotion at first; yet it seemed worth the effort to go through with it, as I could gaze down from my balcony at the wonderful canal with a gradually increasing sense of well-being and tell myself that here was the place I would complete my *Tristan*. I did some further decorating; I arranged to have dark red curtains, though of the cheapest calico, to cover the unworthy doors the Hungarian landlord had caused to be installed in the utterly dilapidated palace in place of the valuable originals, which had probably been stolen. Apart from that, the landlord had managed to get some showy furniture: there were some gilt chairs, though covered with cheap cotton plush, but above all a finely carved gilt table base,

upon which a common deal top had been placed; this I now had to cover
with a drape of a tolerable red. At last the Erard came; it was placed
in the center of the large room, and now it was time to storm this
wonderful Venice with music.

But soon the dysentery I had already gotten to know in Genoa made
its appearance and rendered me incapable of any intellectual activity for
weeks. I was already learning to appreciate the matchless beauty of
Venice, and I was full of hope that my delight in it would liberate
immense powers in my reawakened love of life as a creative artist. On
one of my first promenades on the Riva I had been approached by two
strangers, one of whom introduced himself as Count Edmund Zichy and
the other as a Prince Dolgorukov.[1] Both had left Vienna scarcely a week
before, where they had attended a performance of my *Lohengrin*: they
gave me the most encouraging reports of its success, and from their
enthusiasm I could see that the impression they had received had been
an inordinately favorable one. Count Zichy soon left Venice; but
Dolgorukov had elected to spend the entire winter there. While I was
definitely in the mood to avoid all social life, the Russian, who was about
fifty years of age, soon managed to make me yield on this point as far
as it concerned him. He had an earnest and extremely expressive
countenance (he prided himself on being of direct Caucasian descent)
and showed remarkable breadth of culture, a discriminating knowledge
of the world, and above all an understanding of music, in the literature
of which he was so well versed that it clearly constituted a special and
enduring passion on his part. I had told him immediately that on account
of my health I was obliged to renounce all social life and was greatly
in need of being alone; while it was obviously difficult to elude him
altogether on the constricted promenades of Venice, the restaurant in
the Albergo San Marco, where I met Ritter every day at the dinner hour,
provided another place for inevitable encounters with this stranger to
whom I eventually became sincerely attached, for he had taken up
residence in this hotel and I could hardly prevent him from taking his
meals there as well. During my stay in Venice we saw each other almost
daily and were truly congenial.

But I had a more serious surprise when I came back to my rooms one
evening and was notified that Liszt had just arrived in our palace. I
rushed eagerly to the room I was told he had taken, and found there
to my dismay the pianist Winterberger, who had introduced himself to
my landlord as a friend of Liszt and myself, and in the initial confusion
had misled him into believing that his new guest was Liszt himself. As

a matter of fact I had recently become acquainted with this young man as a member of Liszt's entourage during the time of his lengthy stay in Zürich; he was reputed to be an excellent organist and beyond that, when arrangements for two pianos were to be played, he served as a *secondo*. Except for some rather silly behavior on his part, I had taken little notice of him. Above all I was now amazed that he had taken lodgings in precisely my Venetian place of residence. He claimed he was only the advance guard for a Princess Gallitzin,[1] for whom he was to seek out winter quarters in Venice; inasmuch as he knew nobody here but had learned of my stay while still in Vienna, he felt it was only natural to turn first of all to my hotel. I denied flatly that it was a hotel, and told him that if a Russian princess had it in mind to settle next to me, I would move out at once. He then reassured me by admitting that by mentioning the Princess he had only wanted to impress the landlord; he believed that she had already rented rooms elsewhere. When I then asked him what he wanted for himself in the palace, also advising him that it was very expensive here and that I endured these big expenses solely because I wanted above all to live unmolested without neighbors and most definitely without hearing any piano-playing, he tried to pacify me with the assertion that he would definitely not get in my way; I should accept his presence in the same house for the time being, he implored, at least until he could find the funds to transfer to other lodgings. He next exerted himself to gain the good graces of Karl Ritter; the two set themselves up in a room in the palace at a sufficient distance from mine to be out of earshot. With that I consented to have this guest in my vicinity, but it was a long time before I permitted Ritter to bring him along one evening on a visit.

A Venetian piano teacher named Tessarin had better luck in winning my favor. He was a typically handsome Venetian, but with a strange stammer in his speech; he had a passion for German music, and was familiar with Liszt's more recent compositions and also my operas. He was the first to admit that, as far as music was concerned, he was a "rare bird" among Italians. His approach to me was also effected through Ritter, who seemed to devote himself in Venice more to the study of his fellow man than to serious work. He had rented a very modest little dwelling on the Riva dei Schiavoni that caught all the sun, and for this reason was never obliged to heat it. This served mainly as a repository for his scanty baggage, for he was almost never at home, chasing around after pictures and collections during the day and after people in the cafés of St Mark's Square at night. He remained the only person I saw regularly every day. Otherwise I rigorously avoided any other society or acquaintance. I was repeatedly requested by the private physician of the Princess Gallitzin, who actually did show up in Venice and seemingly began holding court there in a big way, to pay a visit on the lady; as I once found myself needing the vocal scores of *Tannhäuser* and *Lohengrin* and was told that the princess was the only person in Venice possessing them, I was bold enough to ask her for them, but without feeling obligated to visit her as a consequence. Only one other stranger penetrated my defenses, because, having met him in the Albergo San Marco, his countenance had pleased me: this was the painter Rahl from Vienna. For him, the Prince Dolgorukov and the piano teacher Tessarin I even arranged something resembling a musical soirée, when some things of mine were played. It was here that Winterberger made his debut in our circle.

All my social life during the seven months I spent in Venice was restricted to these few relationships, while my daily routine was maintained with scrupulous regularity the whole time. I worked until two o'clock, then stepped into a waiting gondola to voyage along the solemn Canale Grande to the bustling Piazzetta, whose unusually rich charms refreshed me every day anew. There I went to my restaurant on St Mark's Square, took a walk after the meal along the Riva, either alone or with Karl Ritter, to the Giardino Pubblico, the only place in Venice where there are any trees, and at nightfall I came back in the gondola down the canal, growing ever more silent and sombre, until reaching the point at which I could see my little lamp shining out at me, the only point of light in the nocturnal facade of the Palazzo Giustiniani. After I had done some more work, Karl would arrive regularly at eight p.m., his approach announced by the splashing of the gondola, and we would take our tea and chat for an hour or two. I interrupted this routine only rarely to visit one of the theaters, among which I decidedly preferred the plays in the Camploi Theater, where works by Goldoni were very well performed. I paid the opera, on the other hand, only transitory attention, enough to satisfy my curiosity. More frequently, and particularly when bad weather hindered our walks, we attended the popular plays produced every day at the Malibran Theater; there, for an entrance fee of six kreuzers, we could join a splendid audience (mostly in shirtsleeves), whose preference was for melodramas of knight-errantry. Yet one day I saw here to my amazement and utter delight the grotesque comedy *Le Baruffe Chiozziote*, which Goethe in his time had so much enjoyed at the same place, and which was given with greater verisimilitude than I have ever encountered anywhere else.

Beyond this there was little to attract my attention in the very oppressed and degenerate life of the Venetian populace, for as far as human activity in the glorious ruins of this wonderful city was concerned, the only impression I was able to form was that it was maintained as a bathing resort for tourists. Strangely enough, it was the thoroughly German element of good military music, so well represented in the Austrian army, that brought me here into a certain contact with public life. The bandmasters of the two Austrian regiments stationed in Venice got the idea of playing overtures of mine, such as those to *Tannhäuser* and *Rienzi*, and invited me to attend rehearsals at the barracks. Here I found the whole officer corps assembled, which on this occasion treated me very respectfully. The two bands took turns playing in the evening in the middle of a brilliantly illuminated St Mark's Square, which offered a truly superb acoustical setting for such music. Several times at the end of dinner I was surprised to hear my overtures all of a sudden; when I sat at the restaurant window abandoning myself to the impressions of the music, I did not know which dazzled me most – the incomparable square in its magnificent illumination filled with countless numbers of moving people, or the music which seemed to be wafting all these phenomena aloft in a resounding transfiguration. But there was one thing utterly lacking here which one would otherwise have certainly expected from an Italian audience: thousands of people grouped themselves around the band and listened to the music with intense concentration; but no two hands ever forgot themselves to the extent of applauding, for any sign of approbation for an Austrian military band would have been looked upon as treason to the motherland. All public life in Venice suffered from this strange tension between the populace and the authorities, and this was particularly obvious in the behavior of the people toward the Austrian officers, who floated about in public life in Venice like oil on water. The populace also behaved with equal reserve, and even hostility, to the clergy, whose members were in fact mostly of Italian descent. I once saw a procession of clerics crossing St Mark's Square in full ceremonial vestments to the accompaniment of unconcealed derision on the part of the people.

It was very difficult for Ritter to induce me to interrupt my daily routine even to visit a gallery or a church, although whenever we had to walk through the city I was always delighted anew by the untold manifold architectural peculiarities and marvels. But throughout my entire stay in Venice my principal recreation lay in the gondola trips to the Lido. Above all it was the homeward journey at sundown which invariably overwhelmed me by its incomparable impact. Right at the outset of our stay in September of that year we saw on such occasions the magical appearance of the great comet, which was at that time at its highest brilliance, and was generally held to be a portent of imminent catastrophe in war. Then there was the singing of a popular choral society, formed and directed by an official of the Venetian Arsenal, which sounded truly idyllic in the lagoon. These singers generally sang only three-part folksongs with simple harmonies. It was new to me to hear the top part not rising above the alto range, thus not touching the soprano at all and thereby imparting to the sound a quality of masculine youthfulness I had not known until then. On fine evenings they went along the Canale Grande singing in a big, illuminated gondola, stopping to serenade in front of certain palaces, no doubt prearranged and for pay, and usually attracting countless other gondolas as a retinue. On a sleepless night that drove me out on the balcony of my apartment at about three o'clock in the morning, I heard for the first time the famous old folksong of the gondolieri. I thought the first call, piercing the stillness of the night like a harsh lament, emanated from the Rialto, barely a quarter hour's distance away, or thereabouts; from a similar distance this would be answered from another quarter in the same way. This strange melancholy dialogue, which was repeated frequently at longish intervals, moved me too much for me to be able to fix its musical components in my mind. Yet on another occasion I learned that this folksong had an indisputably poetic interest. When I was riding back late one evening along the dark canal, the moon came out and illuminated, together with the indescribable palaces, the tall silhouette of my gondolier towering above the stern of his gondola, while he slowly turned his mighty oar. Suddenly from his breast came a mournful sound not unlike the howl of an animal, swelling up from a deep, low note, and after a long-sustained "Oh", it culminated in the simple musical phrase "Venezia". This was followed by some words I could not retain in my memory, being so greatly shaken by the emotion of the moment. Such were the impressions that seemed most characteristic of Venice to me during my stay, and they remained with me until the completion of the second act of *Tristan*, and perhaps even helped to inspire the long-drawn-out lament for the shepherd's horn at the beginning of the third act.

But these fruits of my mood were not easily won and could not be enjoyed continuously. Physical sufferings and those old worries which never quite left me often blocked and disturbed my work. I had scarcely arranged things comfortably in my rooms, so as to overcome their facing north and their exposure to frequent gusts of wind against which I had almost no protection in the form of heating, I had barely gotten over the demoralizing effects of dysentery, and was just about to take up the cruelly severed threads of my work on the second act, when I fell victim to a specifically Venetian sickness in the shape of a malevolent carbuncle on my leg, resulting from the drastic change of climate and air. This malady, which I first considered of no importance, soon grew extraordinarily painful, and I had to go to a doctor, who gave me careful treatment for four weeks. It was late in the autumn, toward the end of November, and Ritter left me during precisely that period to visit his relatives and friends in Dresden and Berlin; I thus remained alone during the entire time this sickness lasted, my sole society being confined to the simple servants of the house. Unable to work, I sought diversion in reading the history of Venice by Count Daru,[1] and being on the spot there myself derived great interest from it. In particular it made me lose some of my popular prejudices against the tyrannical mode of government in old Venice. The notorious Council of Ten and the State Inquisition now appeared to me in the light of a certain characteristic naivety, though certainly of a grim kind; the open admission that in the secrecy of its methods lay the guarantee of the power of the state seemed to enlist the citizens of this unusual republic so decidedly in its cause that the suppression of knowledge of governmental activities was quite reasonably made a real republican duty. True hypocrisy was thus entirely foreign to this state, just as the ecclesiastical element, though respectfully wedded to the secular power, never managed to exert such a degenerative influence on the character development of its citizens as in other parts of Italy. The ruthless calculations underlying reasons of state were converted into maxims of a character completely at one with the ancient, pagan world, with nothing dark or ominous about them, and which vividly recalled the same maxims which the Athenians, as we read in Thucydides, quite openly acclaimed as the basis of manly morality.

In addition to this I again took up for my recuperation, as I had so often done before, a volume of Schopenhauer, whom I learned once again to value from my heart, while I now had the uplifting experience of being able to remedy some alarming weaknesses in one aspect of his system, though solely by means of hints which he himself provided.

My few relationships with the world outside Venice settled down in a manner that gave me increasing reassurance during this time; only I was saddened one day to get a letter from Wesendonck telling me of the death of his four-year-old son Guido: it struck me to the heart to think that I had declined to stand godfather to the child on the improvised pretext that I might bring him bad luck. Moved by this event, and longing to be at peace with all the world, I got the idea of making a short excursion over the Alps to celebrate Christmas, perhaps, with my old friends in a spirit of cordiality that would benefit us all. I communicated this thought to Frau Wille, and curiously enough, instead of getting a reply from her, received a letter from her husband giving me an utterly unexpected report about the huge and highly distasteful uproar my departure from Zürich had caused, particularly by the way my wife had handled her part of the arrangements, and how the Wesendonck family had been harassed by all this. As I also learned, on the other hand, how wisely and responsibly Wesendonck had conducted himself throughout, the renewal of a friendly association, holding out the promise of better understanding in the future, came about virtually of its own accord. Minna's relations with me benefited greatly from the fact that, once back in Dresden, she moved calmly in the circle of our old acquaintances and, while I continued to show her every care and consideration, she showed good sense and restraint in her correspondence, thus strengthening the favorable impression she had made on me at the time of that touching nocturnal scene. I was also glad to offer her the prospect of a domestic reunion at some future point, but I saw this as feasible only on the establishment of a domicile that promised to be permanent, and this I could think possible only in Germany, preferably in Dresden itself. To get some idea how things stood in this direction, I did not fail to turn to Herr von Lüttichau himself, for I had received from Minna, who had gone to visit my old chief, the most favorable reports of his decent conduct, and even of his warm attachment to me. I went so far as to write him a comprehensive and cordial letter. But it was instructive for me to receive in reply only a few cursory lines in a dry, official style, whereby he let me know that for the present, with respect to my desire to return to Saxony, nothing could be done. On the contrary, I learned through the police authorities in Venice that the Saxon Ambassador in Vienna was doing his zealous best to drive me out of Venice. This did not succeed, for I was sufficiently protected by my Swiss passport, which the Austrian officials, to my great joy, honored very scrupulously. My only hope with respect to my wish to return to Germany lay with the friendly efforts of the Grand Duke of Baden on my behalf. Eduard Devrient, to whom I turned for more information on this point, particularly with regard to our plan for the first performance of *Tristan*, notified me that the Grand Duke regarded my presence at this as a foregone conclusion; but whether, if his direct intervention with the King of Saxony for permission to invite me remained fruitless, he was thinking of taking the step on his own in contravention of the laws of the federation, or however else he intended to arrange matters, was something Devrient could not tell me. Thus I recognized that my hopes of going back to Germany could be only very uncertain for the time being.

Besides this, a great deal of my time was taken up in regular correspondence concerning procurement of the necessary funds to maintain two separate households, a considerable task. Fortunately a few of the bigger theaters had been holding out against my operas the whole time, and therefore I could look forward to fees from them in the future, whereas those from the more eager theaters were already exhausted. Thus one day, the last major German theater to do so, the Stuttgart Court Theater, requested *Tannhäuser*. I had a particular affection for Stuttgart at that time for that very reason and this also went for Vienna, which had as yet only given my *Lohengrin*, and after its success now saw itself impelled to apply for *Tannhäuser*. My negotiations with Karl Eckert, its director at the time, quickly led to satisfactory results.

All this developed in the course of the winter until well into the spring of 1859. Apart from this, I lived in great tranquillity and under a strict routine in the manner I have described. After my leg infection was cured, I was able to resume my regular gondola trips to the Piazzetta, returning every evening, and at last get back to my musical work with some degree of continuity. I spent Christmas and New Year's Day entirely alone. Only at night did I find myself frequently in a large company of people, namely in my dreams, which were especially vivid during this period.

At the beginning of January 1859, Karl Ritter suddenly appeared once again on my threshold at the hour of the customary evening visit. In the interval, worries about the performance of one of his plays had driven him to the shores of the Baltic. This was a dramatic work he had completed a short time before, entitled *Armida*, much of which again testified to the great talent of the young man; while the nature of the work as a whole offered frightening glimpses into the soul of the poet and accordingly did not permit a favorable judgment as to many aspects of its execution, other parts, particularly the encounter between Rinaldo and Armida and the sudden blossoming of their love, were really well done and showed true poetic fire. As in all such works, which are always fundamentally flawed by their dilettante authors' reluctance to take pains, there was much in this drama that needed revision and better execution, if it were to be effective on the stage. But Karl wouldn't hear anything of this; in fact he believed he had found in an intelligent theater manager in Stettin just the man to look beyond all such scruples as I might have in the matter. In this he had also been proved mistaken and now, thwarted here as well, had returned to Venice in order to live more or less as he pleased. To be able to wander through Rome in the habit of a Capuchin monk and scrutinize art treasures by the hour was the kind of existence he seemed to prefer to any other. Refusing to consider any further adaptation of *Armida*, he declared his intention to start work on some new dramatic subject which he had extracted from Machiavelli's *Florentine Stories*. But he didn't want to be more specific for fear that I would advise against it on the grounds it contained only situations and no substance. He seemed disinclined to do any musical work, although a fantasia for piano he had composed soon after his arrival in Venice made the young man seem interesting to me from this side as well. Yet all the greater was Karl's interest in the continuing development of the second act of *Tristan*, on which I was now at last making steady progress. In the evenings I often played for him, together with Winterberger and also Tessarin, what I had just completed, and this invariably led to considerable excitement. During the previous period of interruption in my work, Härtels had already completed the engraving of the first act of my score, and Bülow had arranged it for piano. Thus a part of this work stood before me like a monument while I was still in a state of gestatory turmoil with regard to the execution of the whole. During the early months of the year the instrumentation of this act neared completion, and I could send off pages of score by the bundle to be engraved. I was able to dispatch the final packet of score sheets to Leipzig by the middle of March.

It now became necessary to make some new decisions in my plan of life, for the question was, where was I to compose the third act, as I intended to begin it only in a place where I had the prospect of finishing it undisturbed. It did not seem that this would be the case with Venice. My work would occupy me until well into the summer, and I did not think I ought to spend this season there, as the climate of the city in these months made it inadvisable for reasons of my health. I had already suffered the great disadvantage resulting from the lack of opportunity to take long walks. On one occasion, in order to be able to stretch my legs properly for once, I had traveled by rail in the middle of winter to Viterbo, and had tramped a few miles inland toward the mountains. But rough weather had impeded me in this; and other unfavorable circumstances contributed to my bringing back from this excursion a particularly favorable impression of the city of lagoons as a place of refuge against dusty roads and the spectacle of horses being maltreated. But it now turned out, moreover, that my further stay in Venice was not entirely a matter of my own choosing. I had recently been summoned most politely to see a police official, who informed me without mincing words that the Saxon Embassy in Vienna was agitating incessantly against my continued presence in a part of the Austrian state. When I responded by stating that I wished to prolong my stay only until the spring, I was advised to appeal to Archduke Max, who was residing in Milan at the time as Viceroy, to get permission to do so out of consideration for my health and based on a doctor's certificate. I did this and the Archduke issued immediate instructions to the Venetian authorities by telegraph to leave me alone.

Soon it became clear to me in any case that the political situation, which was putting all of Austrian Italy into a state of ferment, would result in renewed precautionary measures against foreigners. The outbreak of war with Piedmont and France became increasingly imminent, and the evidence of great turmoil in the Italian populace grew ever more palpable. One day when I was sauntering along the Riva with Tessarin we ran into quite a crowd of foreigners who were waiting in respectful curiosity to see Archduke Maximilian and his wife,[1] then paying a short visit to Venice, emerge from a building. I first learned this from a hefty shove from my Venetian pianist, who tried to pull me away from the scene by the arm, so that, as he put it, we would not have to take off our hats to the Archduke. When I saw the stately and winning form of the young prince striding out, I laughingly gave my friend the slip and was glad to be able to express gratitude to my protector by a greeting, though he could not know who I was. Soon everything assumed a more serious and ominous character, and day after day the Riva was so unduly crowded by newly disembarked troops that it became entirely impassable for the daily promenade. Their officers made a generally very pleasant impression on me, and the colloquial German of their casual conversation made me feel quite at home. Yet it was impossible to take a similar view of the troops, for in them I found mostly the rather dull and servile features typical of certain Slavic races within the Austrian Empire. There was no denying a certain massive strength in them, but on the other hand it was no less clear that they were entirely devoid of that simple but innate intelligence which so pleasantly distinguishes the Italian people. I could not easily accord that race the victory over the latter. The facial characteristics of these soldiers were forcibly recalled to me later in the autumn of that same year when I saw the French élite troops, the Chasseurs de Vincennes and the Zouaves, and could not help but compare them with those Austrian troops; I then suddenly understood, without any strategic knowledge of the subject, the battles of Magenta and Solferino.[1] For the moment I learned belatedly that Milan was already in a state of siege and virtually sealed off from visits by foreigners. As I had decided to look for a summer refuge in Switzerland on the Lake of Lucerne, this news impelled me to hasten my departure in order not to be cut off by the outbreak of war. So I packed my things, sent the Erard over the Gotthard again, and prepared to say good-bye to my few friends. Ritter had decided to stay in Italy, intending to go on to Florence and Rome, where Winterberger, with whom Karl had formed a strange friendship, had preceded him. The latter claimed, as a matter of fact, that one of his brothers had provided him with enough money to do what he wanted in Italy, which was just what he needed for rest and recuperation, though from what he was to recover remained unclear to me at any rate. Thus Ritter assumed that he would soon be able to leave Venice as well. I took a most cordial leave of the worthy Dolgorukov, who was in great suffering at the time, and embraced Karl at the railroad station, presumably for the last time, as since then I have been without direct communication from him and have not seen him again to this day.[2]

On March 24th, after some complications caused by examination of passports by the military, I arrived in Milan, where I accorded myself a three-day stay to see the sights. Without any official guide, I contented myself with following the simplest directions to visit the Brera, the Ambrosian Library, Leonardo de Vinci's *Last Supper*, and the cathedral, where I clambered up all its various roofs and towers. As always, it was the first impressions that remained the most vivid, and in the Brera I was particularly struck by two paintings that I saw as soon as I entered the building: Van Dyck's *Saint Anthony before the Infant Jesus* and Crespi's *Martyrdom of Saint Stephen*; there and then I realized that I would never be worth anything as a judge of paintings, for once the subject matter reveals itself to me clearly and agreeably, it settles my view and nothing else counts. Yet I gained a deeper insight into the effect produced by the purely artistic significance of a painting when I stood before Da Vinci's *Last Supper* and had the same experience as everyone else. The original work has deteriorated so badly that the paint is almost entirely ruined, yet after one has examined more closely the copies reconstructing the original, which are placed permanently alongside it, and then turns again from the copies to the ruin of the original, everyone experiences, as I did, that one's eye has become visionary, and one suddenly perceives with the greatest clarity what it is that cannot be copied. In the evening I hastened to the comedy I had become so fond of, given here in the tiny Teatro Re before a scanty public of the lowest rank, as today's Italians unfortunately have such a low opinion of the genre. The Goldoni plays were produced here as well, and with great gusto and skill, it seemed to me. On the other hand, at La Scala, surrounded by extraordinary external splendor, I had to suffer another act of witness to the great demoralization of Italian taste in art. Before as brilliant and animated an audience as could possibly be desired, this gigantic theater offered a production of an unbelievably worthless and incompetent operatic effort by a modern composer whose name I have forgotten. Yet I discovered on that same evening that the Italian public, reputed so passionately fond of the lyric art, already regarded the ballet as the main thing; for obviously the boring opera preceding it only served as a preparation for a huge choreographic extravaganza with nothing less than Antony and Cleopatra as its subject. In this work I even spotted that cool politician Octavian, who up to then had not wandered into any opera, even an Italian one, disporting himself in pantomime, while maintaining a modicum of diplomatic dignity. But the culmination was Cleopatra's funeral, which afforded the immense *corps de ballet* an opportunity to display the most varied and picturesque effects in spectacular costumes.

After absorbing all these enjoyable impressions alone, I journeyed on a gorgeous spring day via Como, where everything was exuberantly in bloom, and then via Lugano, which I already knew, and the Gotthard, which I had to cross in a little open sleigh between high walls of snow, until arriving in Lucerne, where, by contrast to the glorious spring I had left in Italy, I found the most inhospitable cold weather. The calculations which had led me to the decision to stay in this place were based upon the assumption that the big Hotel zum Schweizerhof there would be entirely empty until the beginning of the summer season, and that I could thus find commodious and noise-free lodgings without making further prearrangements. In this I was not proved wrong. Colonel Segesser, the humane keeper of the hotel, allotted me a whole floor in the left annex for my convenience, in the main rooms of which I could make myself comfortable without incurring overly large expense. However, as the hotel at this time of year had only a very small staff, I was obliged to make special arrangements for service; and for this purpose I found a meticulous and considerate woman to look after my comfort, whose excellent services, particularly after the hotel began filling up, I remembered very well, and many years later I engaged her as my housekeeper. Soon thereafter my things arrived from Venice. The Erard had been obliged to cross the snowy Alps again; when it was finally set up in my large main room, I told myself that all this effort and expense had been undertaken in order that I should at last compose the third act of *Tristan und Isolde*. At times this struck me as a wild presumption, for the difficulties standing in the way of the completion of my work seemed destined to prevail over it. I compared myself with Leto, who had been hounded around the world while searching for a place to give birth to Apollo and Artemis, until finally Poseidon had taken pity on her and caused the island of Delos to rise from the sea for this purpose.

I now wanted to consider Lucerne my Delos. But the pernicious influence of the weather, which continued intensely cold and wet until the end of May, depressed my spirits in the most disagreeable way. As this refuge had been gained by such great sacrifices, I considered every day uselessly frittered away and these sacrifices made in vain if I did not succeed in doing some work on my composition. Since the greater part of this third act was concerned with a subject sad beyond words, it came to such a pass that I can recall the first months of this temporary stay in Lucerne only with a shudder.

Only a few days after my arrival I visited the Wesendoncks in Zürich. Our reunion was melancholy but in no way constrained. I spent a few days at the home of my friends, saw my old Zürich acquaintances there again, and it was as if I looked out of one dream into another. In fact everything had grown insubstantial for me. I repeated the trip several times during my stay in Lucerne, and these visits were returned twice, once on my birthday.

Apart from the work with which I persisted in my then depressed frame of mind, I also had to worry about my wife's welfare. Voluntarily, and because it was incumbent upon me to do so, in consideration of the altered circumstances in which my friends the Ritters had been placed, I had already in Venice felt obliged to renounce the financial support they had loyally given me until then. The pitiful income from *Tannhäuser* and *Lohengrin* was now close to being exhausted, as they would not go on being performed much longer. As I would have to resume the composition of my *Nibelungen* after completing *Tristan*, I thought it my duty to try to find some way to do something for my future subsistence with this work. On the basis of his personal communications to me during the previous year, the Grand Duke of Weimar seemed to be favorably inclined toward it. I therefore wrote to Liszt and repeated my request to propose seriously to the Grand Duke that he purchase full proprietary rights to my work with the understanding that he would also undertake to find a publisher and then receive whatever income was generated in return. As a workable basis for this transaction I suggested the terms which had been worked out in the unsuccessful negotiations with Härtels. But Liszt soon gave me an embarrassed hint that the Grand Duke was really not very keen to take the bait, and this told me quite enough.

In addition to this, circumstances dictated that I try to come to some agreement with Meser in Dresden about the unhappy business of the ownership of the company set up to publish my three earlier operas, because one of my main creditors, the actor Kriete, was clamoring for repayment of his capital. A Dresden lawyer named Schmidt offered his services to settle the matter, and after a lot of irritating correspondence back and forth the upshot was that the successor of the recently deceased Meser, a certain Herr Müller, would take over as full owner of this publishing house. In this affair I was told of nothing but the continuing costs and outlays of my former partner in this venture; there was never any light shed on the subject of possible income, though the lawyer admitted to me that the late Meser must have managed to salt away several thousand talers, which could not be recouped inasmuch as he had left his heirs no capital whatsoever. To pacify the clamoring Kriete I had to agree to sell my share for precisely as much as was needed to repay their capital to him and a second, minor creditor, namely three thousand talers. With respect to accrued interest and interest compounded on past-due interest I remained personally in debt to Kriete; by 1864 this sum amounted to eighteen hundred talers, which was then infallibly demanded of me by court order. In the interests of my chief creditor, Pusinelli, who could only be accorded a token repayment on this occasion, I reserved to myself the French rights for my three operas, for the eventuality that this music might sometime be performed in France through my efforts and could then be sold to a French publisher. This reservation, according to the text of a letter from my lawyer Schmidt, was expressly recognized by the successor firm in Dresden. As Pusinelli made the friendly gesture of renouncing any claim he might have to repayment of his loan through income from this source, my future prospects in France and the hope that my operas might win acceptance there constituted the sole possibility of obtaining reimbursement for the expenses I had incurred in publishing them, the possibility of an actual profit being obviously out of the question. When I later came to make an agreement with the Paris publisher Flaxland, this Dresden successor to Meser nevertheless put forth a claim to exclusive rights over my operas, and actually succeeded in harassing Flaxland in his activities to the extent that he had to pay them six thousand francs to keep them quiet; this naturally induced Flaxland to refuse to recognize my ownership rights to these works for France. At this I made repeated appeals to that lawyer Adolph Schmidt, asking of him nothing more than that he would forward to me a copy of the correspondence referring to the rights I had reserved as set forth in the terms negotiated at Lucerne. To all the letters addressed to him on the subject, however, he obstinately refused an answer, and I learned later from a legal expert in Vienna that I would have to give up hope of obtaining such evidence, for I had no legal means of compelling the lawyer to produce it if he were not so inclined.

While I could do little to improve my future prospects in this way, I at least had the satisfaction of seeing the *Tannhäuser* score engraved at last. As the original lithographed edition, drawn from my autograph, had been exhausted, mainly as a result of Meser's wastefulness, I had already persuaded the Härtels, while I was still in Venice, to have the score engraved. Now that Meser's successor had acquired complete rights to the whole publication, it became a point of honor to them not to surrender the score to another publisher. Therefore the firm undertook the engraving at its own expense. Unfortunately, it turned out that I was destined scarcely a year later to recast the first two scenes completely and make a full-scale revision of the work. To this day I have regretted that this additional work did not go into the engraved score.

Still operating under the assumption that *Tristan* would be a good business proposition for theaters, the Härtels had their people work industriously at the engraving of the second act of the score while I was busy working on the third. The process of correcting the proofs of the second act, while I was simultaneously in the throes of composing the ecstasies of the third act, had the strangest, even uncanny, effect on me; for it was in just those first scenes of this act that I realized with complete clarity that I had written the most audacious and original work of my life in this very opera, which it was believed, quite unwarrantably, would turn out to be easy to produce. While I was working on Tristan's big scene I had to ask myself often enough whether I was out of my mind in thinking I could give such a thing to a publisher to be printed for use in the theater. And yet I did not want to part with a single accent of suffering, even though the whole thing tormented me myself to an intense degree.

I tried to overcome my abdominal troubles by resorting, among other things, to Kissingen water in moderate doses; as the walks that formed an indispensable part of this treatment as a relaxation made me tired, if I took them in the early morning, and incapable of working, I hit upon the idea of taking short horseback rides instead. The owner of my hotel accorded me for this ritual a twenty-five-year-old horse named Lise; I rode the animal every morning as long as she was inclined to keep moving: she never bore me very far, but rather turned back regularly at certain spots without paying the slightest attention to her rider's exhortations.

Thus the months of April, May and most of June passed without my completing more than half the composition of the third act, while I was struggling with my melancholy mood the whole time. Finally the tourist season opened; the hotel and its annexes began filling up, and it was no longer possible to think of maintaining any special privileges with respect to the use of such choice quarters. It was proposed that I move to the third floor of the main building, where only travelers on their way through Switzerland put up, and for no more than a night, while the annex housed people staying for longer periods, who used their rooms during the day as well. This arrangement actually worked out quite astonishingly well: from then on I was completely undisturbed during work hours in my smallish sitting room, with adjoining bedroom, as the rooms engaged for a night's sleep by transients were perfectly empty during the day. At last really splendid summer weather set in and provided two months of cloudless skies. I enjoyed the rare pleasure of being sheltered from the extreme heat by carefully keeping my little room cool and dark, surrendering myself to the summer air only in the evenings on my small balcony. A small number of very good horn players delighted me on such occasions by appearing almost every evening in a skiff on the lake and playing some simple folk tunes. In my work I had now fortunately got beyond the dreadful critical point, and in spite of the inherently melancholy character of that final part of my poem which remained to be mastered, its gentler mood produced in me an almost comforting and joyful state of exaltation, in which I completed the composition of the whole work by the beginning of August, except for some instrumentation remaining to be done.

Solitary as I was, the events of the Italian war, so exciting at the time, provided me with sufficient distraction. I followed this struggle in all its vicissitudes with the intense interest such an unexpected and meaningful matter deserved. Yet I did not remain entirely without company. In July Felix Draeseke,[1] who was unknown to me until then, arrived in Lucerne for a lengthy visit. After he had heard a performance of the prelude to *Tristan und Isolde* under Liszt's auspices, he had decided almost at once to get to know me personally. I was utterly abashed at his arrival and told him I didn't see how I could be of much service to him. And as he had a lot of facetious gossip about persons and things that really no longer interested me very much , he was at first something of a nuisance. To my surprise he noticed this and took it to heart so much that he became convinced after a few days he ought to leave. This in turn made me feel embarrassed; and from then on I did my best to erase any unfavorable impressions he might have formed of me. I soon got to like him; and for an extended period, until shortly before I left Lucerne, he was my daily companion, giving me a good deal of pleasure, as he was a very gifted and not uncultured musician.

My old Zürich acquaintance Wilhelm Baumgartner also came to Lucerne for a few weeks on my account. And finally Alexander Serov[2] arrived from St Petersburg in order to spend some time in my vicinity; he was a remarkable and intelligent man, and a vociferous partisan of Liszt and myself. He had heard my *Lohengrin* in Dresden and now wanted to learn more of my work, so I had to help out by performing *Tristan* for him in my characteristic summary way. I also climbed Mount Pilatus with Draeseke, on which occasion I again had to suffer sympathetic fears for a companion afflicted by vertigo. As a farewell I invited him to take an excursion to Brunnen and the Grütli; after this we parted for the time being, as his modest funds did not permit him a more lengthy stay, and I too was seriously contemplating my departure.

The only question was where I was to go. I had turned again to the Grand Duke of Baden, first by letter through Eduard Devrient, and then by addressing him directly, hoping to receive the assurance that I could now settle, if not in Karlsruhe itself, then at least in a small village nearby, for this would satisfy my now imperative need to have some association with an orchestra and singers, if only just to hear them. I learned later that the Grand Duke actually made written inquiries to the King of Saxony in this matter; but the answer always came back that they could not amnesty me but only pardon me, after I had placed myself at their disposal for judicial interrogation. Thus my wish had to remain unfulfilled, and I was now alarmed as to how the production of *Tristan*, which it was still intended to stage, could be arranged to take place under my personal supervision. I was continually assured that the Grand Duke would find his own means of settling this. Yet where was I to turn to find some kind of residence that promised the permanence I longed for? After deep thought I decided I had no alternative other than Paris, if only to assure myself of hearing a first-class orchestra or quartet from time to time; for the lack of this stimulus in Zürich had finally proved unbearable. Nowhere but in Paris, where, moreover, I would remain undisturbed, could I count with certainty on this form of artistic recreation at a sufficiently elevated standard.

Finally, I could not avoid feeling obliged to make also some arrangement with regard to my wife. We had now been separated for a whole year; after the harsh lessons she had received from me and which, as evidenced by her own letters, had not remained without effect on her, I could assume that we could once more live together in tolerable harmony. This also seemed to be dictated by the need to resolve the considerable difficulty of providing for her upkeep. We thus agreed that she should join me in Paris late in the autumn; until that time I volunteered to take care of the arrangements for establishing residence there, and to this end undertook to have all our furniture and household effects remaining in Zürich dispatched to Paris. My primary need in carrying out this plan was for financial means, and I was unable to look upon any of my current sources of income as likely to supply it. The proposition I had made to the Grand Duke of Weimar, namely purchase of the rights for my *Nibelungen* for publication purposes, I now broached with Wesendonck. He willingly acceded to my desires and was ready to pay me an amount for each of the completed parts of my work roughly equal to what I could expect to receive as a fee from a future publisher. In return I ceded the rights to him.

After that I could go ahead with my travel arrangements and left on September 7th, first making a three-day visit to my friends in Zürich. I spent these days well cared for in the home of the Wesendoncks and saw there my previous acquaintances, particularly Herwegh, Semper and Gottfried Keller, with whom I spent an evening marked by a fierce battle with Semper about the political events of the day. Semper professed to see in the recent defeat of Austria a blow to the German national principle; in the Latin element represented by Louis Napoleon

591

he recognized something resembling Assyrian despotism, the target of his hatred in politics as in art. He expressed himself about all this with such vehemence that he even provoked the normally silent Keller to lively argument, which in turn so irritated Semper that he finally reproached me rather desperately for having lured him into a trap by occasioning his invitation to the Wesendonck house. But we ultimately parted as friends, and when we have met on subsequent occasions our discussions have never again degenerated into such emotion. From Zürich I went out to visit the Sulzer family in Winterthur. I didn't find Sulzer himself there, but I did see his wife with a boy she had just borne him; both made a very touching and congenial impression, all the more so because I now obviously had to think of my friend, that remarkable possessor of so old a head on such young shoulders, as a happy father.

On September 15th[1] I reached Paris. I had intended to look for a place to live in the neighborhood of the Champs Elysées and thus hunted first for temporary lodgings in that area, finding somewhere in the Rue Matignon. My main objective was to find the quiet refuge I had been longing for in a little house away from the bustle of the city; I devoted all my initial efforts to discovering such a place. In so doing I thought I should exploit all my previous acquaintances. But the Olliviers were not in Paris at the time; Mme d'Agoult was sick, about to leave for Italy, and couldn't receive me; instead she referred me to her daughter Countess Charnacé,[2] whom I looked up but without being able to make clear to her what I was after. I also visited the Hérold family, who had been so attentive to me during my visit when I was last in Paris; but I found Mme Hérold in a strange state of nervous distraction, so that instead of discussion of my problem with her, it seemed better to try to calm her down and not excite her by any kind of request. In my intense eagerness to find a place to live I therefore set out by myself without any further assistance and finally discovered near the Barrière de l'Etoile, in the Rue Newton, an incomplete side street off the Champs Elysées, a nice little villa with a small garden. This I rented on a three-year lease at four thousand francs annually. Here I expected absolute tranquillity above all else, and an utter absence of street noise. This alone predisposed me in favor of the new domicile. The well-known author Octave Feuillet,[3] at that time a protégé of the Imperial Court, had been living there previously. Only I was a bit surprised that the interior seemed so badly neglected, even though it was not an old building. The owner could in no way be persuaded to do anything to restore the place to make it more habitable, even if I had been willing to pay higher rent.

The reason for this became clear to me a short while later: the place was to be condemned in the wake of new construction plans being carried out by the city of Paris, and the house was scheduled for demolition before long; but the time had not yet come to notify the owners officially of this intention, for had this been done their claims for compensation would have become valid at once. As a result of all this, I remained innocently convinced that everything I was spending on interior decoration and repairs would benefit me over a series of years; I therefore made haste to give the necessary orders to have this work done, had my furniture sent from Zürich, and thought myself now entitled, as fate had forced me to make the choice, to consider myself a resident of Paris for the rest of my life.

While these decorations were being carried out I tried to get a more accurate idea of what I could expect for my future situation from the signs I had noted to date of the popularity of my works. I first looked up young M. de Charnal, the man I had entrusted with the adaptation of my *Rienzi*, to get a report on this matter. It turned out that M. Carvalho, director of the Théâtre Lyrique, would hear of absolutely nothing but *Tannhäuser*. I then induced this gentleman to visit me himself so that we could discuss the matter together. He confirmed that he was most decidedly inclined to perform one of my operas; only it would have to be *Tannhäuser*, for this name, he said, was inextricably identified with mine by the Parisian public, who would regard it as utterly absurd to perform any other work under the name "Wagner". With respect to the man I had chosen to adapt the poem of this opera, he seemed to harbor grave doubts, as if I had made a serious mistake. I then tried to get somewhat more precise information about the capacities of M. de Charnal and discovered to my horror that this youthful and very pleasant fellow, who was proud of his recent collaboration on a melodrama called *Schinderhannes* (which he deemed a romantic German piece), hadn't the slightest conception of the nature of the work he was supposed to do. As his enthusiasm touched me, I nonetheless tried to shape some verses with him suitable for the music, but these efforts soon bogged down and I found them to be fruitless.

I had been recommended by Bülow to a young doctor who was no longer practising medicine named Auguste de Gaspérini, whose acquaintance he had made in Baden-Baden and in whom he had recognized a remarkable liking for my music. I had called on him without delay and, finding him away from Paris at the time, had contacted him by letter. In response he now sent me, together with a letter of recommendation, his friend Leroy, a well-schooled Paris music teacher who soon won my approbation by his genial character and inspired my confidence by immediately advising me against having anything to do with an obscure theatrical journalist, as M. de Charnal eventually turned out to be. Instead, he recommended that I get in touch with Roger,[1] a highly gifted and experienced opera singer, who was a favorite of the Parisians and who knew German well. This took a load off my mind; I accepted an invitation to Roger's country estate, arranged by Leroy with the help of another friend, and one day found myself being conducted to a meeting with him there. I have forgotten the name of the proud estate of this celebrated Parisian tenor; it was the former chateau of a marquess and in the most seigneurial of styles, surrounded by a gigantic hunting reserve. It was his desire to handle a gun and do justice to this park that had inflicted upon the amiable singer a terrible accident, which had shattered his right arm. I met Roger several months after the accident, when he was completely recovered; but he had lost his right forearm, and now it was a question whether a well-known mechanic, who had promised to produce a perfect substitute for the lost limb, could do the job and thus permit him to go back on the stage. In this he succeeded quite well, as I soon had occasion to observe; I saw Roger appear in a benefit performance put on for him at the Opéra and use his right arm so ingeniously that he was rewarded with tumultuous applause specifically for it. Yet he soon had to recognize that he was considered an invalid and his career at the Opéra had come to a close. For the moment he seemed pleased to be able to assure himself some form of literary activity by accepting the task I offered him. He joyfully accepted my suggestion that he should make a singable translation of *Tannhäuser*, and having already produced a French text for some of the main passages, sang some of them for me, much of which struck me as highly accomplished. After resting up for a night, I thus left the chateau of this singer who had hitherto been so popular and now had only a sad decline before him, in a cheerful and confident frame of mind, for his intelligent approach to my opera had given me a hopeful idea of the possibilities of cultivating the French spirit. That I nonetheless was soon compelled to renounce the collaboration with Roger resulted from the fact that he was first compelled to look after his own situation and try to do something about the sad circumstances into which he had fallen. This took up all his time for a long period, and thus he could scarcely respond adquately to my suggestion. I thereby lost sight of him altogether for the time being.

But* even my attempt with Roger had been inherently more of a casual coincidence rather than something I had felt impelled to do. I still clung to my plan to find in Paris a suitable place to live, whereas my serious artistic undertakings would always remain directed towards Germany, which however remained inaccessible to me. But soon everything took on a different coloring when the proposed performance of *Tristan* in Karlsruhe, on which I was still counting, was finally definitely canceled. For a long time I continued to be uncertain as to the true reasons why this seemingly cast-iron commitment had been abandoned. Eduard Devrient notified me that all attempts to engage a singer suitable for Isolde had foundered on my refusal to accept Garrigues[1] (who at that time was already married to young Schnorr), and that he felt all the more keenly his inability to figure out what to do about all the other problems, inasmuch as even the tenor Schnorr, who was so devoted to me, was himself in despair at the difficulty of executing the task represented by the last part of his role. I recognized at once that there was confusion here, whose ill-effects I could easily have ameliorated if I had been permitted to get to Karlsruhe myself even for a brief period. But my mere reiteration of this wish seemed to arouse the bitterest feelings against me; Devrient expressed his own reaction with so much vehemence and harshness that I inevitably began to believe what kept me out of Karlsruhe was mainly his personal disinclination to have me interfere in the management of his theater; or else, as a milder interpretation, I could conclude that the Grand Duke felt embarrassed at not being able to fulfill the prospects he had previously held out to me of a visit to his seat in Karlsruhe, and that now it appeared almost preferable to him if the pretext for any such visit were eliminated for other reasons. At the same time I received from Bülow, who had been repeatedly in Karlsruhe, more than enough hints about Devrient's attitude in this whole affair. Full light was shed on the matter only at a later date; meanwhile it was of the utmost importance for me to face the fact that I remained completely cut off from Germany and would have to think of new terrain for the object I had so very much at heart, the production of *Tristan*. I quickly sketched a plan for the establishment of a German theatrical venture in Paris itself of the kind which had already existed in the past, particularly in association with Frau Schröder-Devrient. I thought I could safely rely on the finest German singers known to me to follow me willingly if I were to invite them to

* At the start of this paragraph, in Cosima's hand: "(July 31st 1872)".

participate in such an undertaking in Paris; and I actually received acceptances at once from Tichatschek, Mitterwurzer, the tenor Niemann, and also from Luise Meyer[1] in Vienna, in the event I were to succeed in launching a German opera season in Paris. Thus my immediate and sizeable worry was to find a suitable man in Paris itself who would be ready to carry out this plan at his own risk. My idea was to secure the Salle Ventadour for a spring season lasting two months after the Italian opera season had ended. There would then be performances by a select ensemble and chorus of German singers, first of *Tannhäuser* and *Lohengrin*, and finally of *Tristan*, which would be done as much for me as for the Parisians.

With this plan in mind, my efforts took an entirely different direction from that toward which they had tended when I had first settled in Paris again; to cultivate acquaintanceships, particularly among people of influence, was now of paramount importance for me. Thus, I was very glad to see Gaspérini, with whom I had previously had the most fleeting of acquaintances, return to Paris for a lasting duration, and through his good offices, after I had at once communicated my new plan to him, to be introduced in a most cordial manner to a certain M. Lucy, a rich man who was especially well disposed toward him, and not without influence, being farmer-general in Marseille at the time. The upshot of our discussions was always the acknowledgement that our most important need was to find a man who would serve as the indispensable financial guarantor of the projected undertaking. My friend Gaspérini could scarcely object to my natural assumption that in the circumstances as he had described them to me M. Lucy should be considered the ideal man for this purpose; yet he deemed it advisable to put our wishes before his friend very circumspectly, for although M. Lucy had a great "chaleur de coeur", he was still above all else a businessman and knew little about music. Above all else, it therefore seemed necessary to acquaint Paris with my music and myself in no uncertain manner, in order to lay the foundation for the success of our subsequent undertakings. With this intention in mind, I decided first of all to give several major concerts. To this I had immediately to take my old friend Belloni, Liszt's former secretary, into the circle of people I was cultivating. He at once enlisted a companion in the cause, a very intelligent and, as far as I always knew, well-intentioned fellow named Giacomelli. He was the editor of a theatrical journal and was commended to me by Belloni for his "beautiful French" as well as his exceptional energy. The odd editorial office of my new protector henceforth became one of our most important centers, where I went almost daily to encounter all the strange creatures one is forced to deal with in theatrical matters and related business in Paris.

The first problem was to obtain the most suitable hall for my intended concerts. It was obvious that I would appear to greatest advantage before the Parisian public if I could secure the theater and orchestra of the Opéra itself. For this I had to petition the Emperor Napoleon, which I did in a forthright document drafted by Gaspérini. In this connection I had to beware of the hostility of Fould,[1] at that time Napoleon's Minister of State and of the Royal Household, resulting from his friendly relationship with Meyerbeer. The damaging influence we feared from him would, we hoped, be countered by that of M. Mocquard, who was Napoleon's secretary and, Ollivier asserted, his speechwriter as well. In an "élan" of fiery generosity, M. Lucy decided to turn to the friend of his youth – for M. Mocquard lived in his memory as such – and address him a personal letter of recommendation about the matter. Inasmuch as no reply whatever emanated from the Tuileries even to this, I grew increasingly skeptical, in my daily consultations with my practical friends Belloni and Giacomelli, that we could do anything about the Minister of State and therefore opened negotiations with M. Calzado, the director of the Italian Opera. At first we got a flat rejection, whereupon I finally set off to see this man personally. Through powers of persuasion at which even I was surprised, and particularly through holding out to him the possibility of a great success in a future performance of my newest opera *Tristan* by the Italians, I at least succeeded in extracting his consent to rent the Salle Ventadour to me for three evenings, each to be spaced a week apart; but even my most impassioned eloquence, which Giacomelli extolled to the skies on our way back, could not persuade him to lower the rent, which he fixed at four thousand francs per evening, including only the hall itself and the illumination.

Now the most important thing was to get together an excellent orchestra and engage it for my concerts, a task with which my two agents were kept very busy for the time being. As a result of their efforts in this regard, I now began to notice the first signs of a hitherto unsuspected hostile attitude on the part of my old friend Berlioz toward me and my undertaking.

Still under the spell of the favorable impression my London meetings with Berlioz in 1855 had left with me, and which had been strengthened by the friendly correspondence we had kept up for a time, I had gone straight to his apartment after my arrival on this occasion; as I did not find him at home, I had gone back down to the street, where I met Berlioz on his way home and could not help observing that the sight of me caused him a twinge of pain horrifyingly evident in his countenance and whole physical bearing. I saw at a glance how matters stood between us but concealed my own uneasiness under an expression of natural concern for his condition, as to which he immediately assured me that he was suffering severely, and that he could only bear up against vehement attacks of neuralgia by electric shock treatment, from a session of which he was just returning. In order not to make his pain any worse I offered to take my leave at once, but this made him feel so ashamed that he implored me to come up with him to his apartment once again. Here I succeeded in making him somewhat more amicably disposed by describing my true intentions in coming to Paris: even the concerts I proposed to give, I told him, were merely designed to attract the attention of the public to the extent that a German opera company could be established that would enable me to perform works of my own I had not yet heard; as to a French production of my *Tannhäuser*, which M. Carvalho seemed to have in mind, I was entirely willing to do without it. As a result of these disclosures my relations with Berlioz remained good for a time and were even seemingly very friendly. I consequently thought that, with respect to the recruitment of the necessary orchestral musicians, I would do well to refer my agents in this matter to my experienced friend, whose advice would surely prove invaluable. They told me that Berlioz had shown himself to be very obliging at first, but that all this had changed completely when one day Mme Berlioz had entered the room during their discussions and had exclaimed in irritated astonishment: "Comment, je crois que vous donnez des conseils pour les concerts de M. Wagner?" In regard to this lady, Belloni had learned that she had just been sent an expensive bracelet from Meyerbeer. "Don't count on Berlioz!" With this warning my knowledgeable agent put this whole affair on a sounder footing.

From this time forward I saw Belloni's normally beaming countenance invariably covered by clouds of deepest anxiety. He thought he had discovered that the whole of the Parisian "press" was exceedingly hostile toward me, and he did not entertain the slightest doubt that this was the result of the tremendous excitation endured by Meyerbeer in Berlin at the present time. He knew of an agitated correspondence going on between Berlin and the principal Parisian journalists, and that the notorious Fiorentino[1] had exploited Meyerbeer's dismay at my Paris plans by a threat to find my music good; this in turn must naturally drive Meyerbeer to pay out the most monstrous bribes. All this increased Belloni's anxiety and he now advised me above all to secure strong financial backing for my venture or else, if the prospects in this regard remained poor, my only hope lay in doing my utmost to secure the support of the Emperor. He asseverated that the concerts must on no account be risked without financial backing, for everything was at stake for me in giving them, and his warnings necessarily made me cautious, for in the wake of my relocation to Paris and the establishment of a new domicile, all my sources of monetary assistance had been utterly exhausted. Thus I was forced to take up again with renewed energy my negotiations with the Tuileries concerning the possibility of my securing the Opéra and its orchestra free of charge. Ollivier assisted me in this endeavor with judicious advice and imaginative introductions, bringing me into some very exotic contacts, even if only fleetingly; thus, for example, I penetrated to the office of M. Camille Doucet (a high official in Fould's ministry and also a playwright), always with the intention of getting at the unapproachable and much-feared minister and Meyerbeer-admirer himself. As a result of one of these introductions I also formed a lasting, close friendship with M. Jules Ferry,[1] though it was of no consequence to the purpose immediately at hand. The Emperor and his secretary remained obstinately silent, even after I had obtained from the Grand Duke of Baden an intercession by his ambassador on my behalf as well as that of the Swiss ambassador Dr Kern, whose combined forces would nevertheless at best have enlightened me, and probably the Emperor as well, about the formidable Fould. But it was in vain: there was no response.

In these circumstances I regarded it as a rather odd stroke of fate that Minna should choose precisely this time to announce her readiness to rejoin me in Paris, and that I should expect her shortly. In the selection and fitting-out of the little house in the Rue Newton I had made my provisions with a very special eye to our future life together; my living room was separated from hers by a staircase, and I had made certain that her part of the house lacked nothing in comfort. But above all I had also indulged the inclination I had felt since my last reunion with her in Zürich to furnish the house with that degree of special comfort which was to bring me reproaches of love of luxury, as if thereby it would be more bearable to live together with a woman who was becoming increasingly alien to me. Beyond this, the little house in the Rue Newton offered the opportunity to create a salon, and while I did not want to go about this extravagantly, it eventually turned out that, in addition to the horrendous difficulties of interminable dealings with unreliable Parisian workers, I also got into unanticipated expenses. Yet I consoled myself with the reflection that, if this was the way it had to be, Minna would at least be put in a good mood upon entering the house she would henceforth have to manage. I also in particular thought it necessary to get a maid for her, and took on an apparently highly suitable person recommended to me by Mme Hérold for this purpose. In addition I had engaged a manservant immediately upon my arrival, and although he was a rather foolish native of Valais and a former Papal guard, he soon became apparently quite devoted to me.

On top of this staff, Minna now brought along her former Zürich cook, by whom she was accompanied when it was at last time for me to go and meet her on the railway-station platform on November 17th. Here Minna immediately handed me the parrot and her dog Fips, which involuntarily reminded me of her arrival at the dock in Rohrschach ten years before. Just as she had done then, she now gave me to understand at once that she was not coming back to me out of any sense of need, and that if I were to treat her badly, she knew quite well where she could return. Apart from this, I could not fail to notice that a great change had taken place in her compared with that earlier time; she confessed to me that she was filled with the anxieties and uneasiness comparable to those of a person commencing a new job and not knowing whether it would work out well enough. I sought to distract her by acquainting her with my external situation and expected to enlist her support. Unfortunately she showed not the slightest sympathy or interest; instead her entire attention was immediately absorbed by the domestic amenities of our house. The fact that I had taken a manservant filled her with scorn; but that, under the title of lady's maid, I had provided her with what I really considered a necessary attendant, made her instantly furious. This girl, whom Mme Hérold had recommended to me with the assurance that she had shown angelic patience in the care of her aged and very sick mother, was soon so demoralized by Minna's behavior to her that after a very short period I took it upon myself to dismiss her; on this occasion I reaped vehement reproaches for having accorded her a small gratuity. Minna succeeded to an even greater extent in utterly discomposing my manservant, who finally stated that he would accept no more commands from my wife and, after my expostulations with him on the subject, began behaving insolently to me, so he also had to be dismissed after a short time. He left me with a very fine set of livery which I had just purchased for him at a considerable cost, and which henceforth hung unused, as I had no inclination to put another manservant into it. On the other hand, I must give the Swabian girl Therese, who thenceforth took care of all the domestic chores during my entire stay in Paris, the highest testimonial for her achievement. This girl, gifted with an uncommon innate intelligence, was also able to grasp my painful position vis-à-vis her mistress, understood her weaknesses, and succeeded in neutralizing their ill effects on my behalf and that of the household as well by her indefatigable activity.

Thus, through this last reunion with Minna, I again entered a cycle of life which I had known many times before and which I now seemed destined to relive from beginning to end. This time it was almost a blessing that there was no question of quiet seclusion, but that on the contrary we were involved in an endless succession of external relationships and activities, to which I had again been driven by my destiny entirely against my choice and inclination.

At* the outset of 1860 a quite unexpected turn of events made it appear that my undertakings might meet with success. From Vienna the conductor Esser transmitted to me a request from the music dealer Schott in Mainz to obtain a new opera of mine for publication. At that moment I had nothing to offer but *Das Rheingold*; the special nature of this work, designed as it was solely as a prelude to the vast *Nibelungen* trilogy, made it difficult for me to offer it simply as an "opera" for this purpose. Yet Schott's eagerness to have a new work of mine, whatever it might be, in his catalogue appeared to be so great that I finally overcame all scruples and, without trying to gloss over the difficulties involved in the popularization of this work, offered it to him against payment of ten thousand francs. At the same time I assured him of the right to acquire each of the remaining three works at the same price. At once I conceived the plan, in the event Schott agreed to my demands, to spend this unexpected income in furtherance of my Paris undertaking. Worn down by the obstinate silence maintained by the imperial secretariat, I now authorized my agents to make a deal with Signor Calzado to obtain the Italian Opera House for three concerts, as well as to engage the necessary orchestral players and singers. While all this was going on, I was again beset by worries arising from Schott's hesitant alternative offers; in order not to scare him off, however, I wrote to the conductor Schmidt in Frankfurt, authorizing him to continue these

---

* Note in the margin of the manuscript, in Cosima's hand: "Resumed March 4th 1873, Dammallee, Bayreuth".

negotiations based on a lower demand on my part. I had scarcely dispatched this letter when an answer from Schott arrived, finally expressing his willingness to pay me ten thousand francs. This elicited a hasty telegram from me to Schmidt, quickly canceling the authorization I had given him.

With renewed confidence my agents and I now pursued our concert plans, the preparations for which absorbed all my energies. I had to find a chorus, and found it necessary to augment expensive personnel from the Italian Opera with a group of German singers under the direction of a certain Herr Ehmant, which had been recommended to me. In order to ingratiate myself with its members, I had to show myself at their clubroom in the Rue du Temple one evening and cheerfully accommodate myself to the smell of beer and the fumes of tobacco in the midst of which these sturdy Germans were to disclose their art to me. I was also put into contact with a M. Cheré, instructor and director of a French glee club, whose rehearsals took place in the Ecole de Médecine. In him I came upon a strange enthusiast, who wanted to achieve by his method of teaching people to sing without reading notes no less than a regeneration of the authentic French spirit. But the worst trouble was caused by the need to have the orchestral parts for the excerpts I was going to perform copied out for me. For this job I hired several poverty-stricken German musicians, who stayed at my house from morning till night to carry out this often difficult task under my direction and supervision.

In the middle of all these impassioned activities, Hans von Bülow now turned up, and his purpose in coming to Paris, as was demonstrated by the degree of success, was more to assist me in my undertaking than to follow his own interests as a concert virtuoso. He lived at the house of Liszt's mother but spent most of the day with me, to help in every way he could, as with the preparation of the orchestral parts. His active involvement was extraordinary in every aspect; he especially seemed to have set himself the task of making certain social connections he and his wife had formed during their previous visit to Paris redound to my advantage. The result of this was felt in due course; meanwhile he helped me to arrange the concerts themselves, for which the rehearsals now began.

The first of these rehearsals took place in the Salle Herz and led to such agitation on the part of the musicians against me that it almost resembled a mutiny. I was continually obliged to remonstrate with them over some habits of theirs I could not indulge, while making every effort to explain my reasons. They were particularly incensed at the way I took my 6/8 time, which I beat according to the pattern of 4/4 measure while they all protested tumultuously that it should be taken *alla breve*. When I called them sharply to order and asked them to show the discipline of a well-ordered orchestra, I got the reply that I was not dealing with Prussian soldiers but with free men. At length I perceived that one of the chief difficulties lay in the deficiencies of the seating-plan and so I hatched a scheme for the second rehearsal. After consultation with my friends I went to the concert hall early on the morning when it was scheduled, made sure that the desks were arranged according to my own idea of what was practical, and above all ordered a copious breakfast for all the musicians, to which I invited them at the beginning of the rehearsal in the following manner: I told the musicians that the giving of the concerts depended on the results of our work today; we should not leave the concert hall until we had come to some clear resolution; I therefore requested the gentlemen first to ündertake a two-hour rehearsal and then to proceed to the adjoining room for a frugal breakfast already awaiting them, whereupon we would immediately commence a second rehearsal, for which I would also pay them. The effect of this proposition was quite extraordinary: the advantageous lay-out of the orchestra helped to sustain the good mood; the favorable impression the prelude to *Lohengrin* now produced on everybody finally evoked real enthusiasm, so that by the end of the first part of the rehearsal both players and listeners, among whom was Gaspérini, were completely won over to my cause. This friendly atmosphere carried over most gratifyingly to the stage of the Italian Opera House, where the final rehearsal was held; I had now gained sufficient control to eject a sloppy trumpeter from the orchestra with a harsh reproof, without suffering the slightest setback from any spirit of camaraderie.

The first concert took place at last on January 25th (1860); the reception accorded by the public to the selections I had culled from my various operas up to *Tristan und Isolde* was entirely favorable, even enthusiastic. I had the experience of hearing one of my pieces, the march from *Tannhäuser*, interrupted by stormy applause, for the apparent reason that the audience was joyfully surprised to find my music, about which so many derogatory reports had been heard, was not without sustained melody.

Well satisfied with the manner in which the concert had been given as well as with its reception, I had to overcome some quite different feelings aroused in me during the next few days by the way the newspapers gave vent to their views on the subject. It turned out that Belloni had been entirely right and that our refusal to invite the press, which had been based on his appreciation of the situation, had merely roused our opponents to greater fury. As the whole undertaking had been designed more to enlist help from interested parties rather than to secure the praise of music critics, I was much less disturbed by the blustering of these gentlemen than by the absence of any sign of this interest from other quarters. Above all I was concerned that the apparently packed house had not brought us higher receipts than was actually the case. We had taken between five and six thousand francs, but the costs had been over eleven thousand francs. These could be recouped to some extent, however, if we could achieve higher receipts from the less expensive second concert. But Belloni and Giacomelli hung their heads in despair; they felt they could not close their eyes to the fact that concerts were really not the right genre for the French, who always demanded some dramatic element, i.e. costumes, decorations, ballet and so forth, if they were to feel satisfied. The poor advance sale for the second concert, which was given on February 1st, had even compelled my agents to fill the house artificially in order to save face; I had to give them a free hand in all this and was later astonished to see how they had managed to fill the front rows of this aristocratic theater in such a way that everyone, including our enemies, was deceived. The true receipts amounted to little more than two thousand francs, and now it required all my determination and contempt for the miseries that might result to prevent canceling the third concert scheduled for February 8th.

My fee from Schott, part of which I had been obliged to expend for the maintenance of my again troubled domestic existence, was now exhausted, and I had to look around for a subsidy. This I obtained with great effort, through Gaspérini's good offices, from the man on whose support in the widest sense the whole undertaking had been founded in the first place. This was the aforementioned farmer-general from Marseille, M. Lucy, who was expected to arrive in Paris at the time of my concerts, and of whom my friend Gaspérini thought he could assume that a major success on my part with the French public would move him to the generous decision to finance my project for the establishment of a German opera in Paris. Instead, M. Lucy failed to show up for the first concert at all and was present only for part of the second, during which he fell asleep. The fact that he was now called upon to advance several thousand francs for the third concert naturally seemed to shield him from any further demands on our part, and he felt a certain satisfaction in buying an exemption from all further participation in my plans at the price of this loan. Whereas this third concert necessarily now seemed intrinsically unavailing, even to me, I was nevertheless very pleased with it, not only at the excellent spirit of the performance itself, but also at its splendid reception by the audience, which my agents had again been obliged to supplement to make the hall appear full but which nonetheless actually showed a marked increase in paid admissions.

The realization of the deep impression produced on a number of people had a greater impact on me than my dejection at what was, from all outward appearances, a failed undertaking. Undeniably the direct sensation produced by the concerts, as well as the indirect effects of what the press had insisted on saying about them, had aroused extraordinary interest in me. My refusal to invite any music critics seemed to be regarded on all sides as an admirable piece of audacity on my part. I had easily predicted the attitude likely to be adopted by the majority of the critics; yet I regretted that even such men as M. Franc-Marie, the critic of the *Patrie*, who at the end of the first concert had come forward to thank me in deepest emotion, had nonetheless found themselves obliged to bow to the dictates of professional solidarity, and thus in the end were driven so far as to utterly deny their favorable inclinations toward me. But Berlioz stirred up a truly infuriating hubbub with an article in the *Journal des Débats* that began with a lot of circumlocutions but finally indulged some flagrantly perfidious suppositions about me. I decided not to let my old friend get off so easily for his bad behavior and answered him with a letter I caused to be meticulously translated into good French and sent to the *Journal des Débats*, together with a formal complaint. It so happened that this very letter had the effect of attracting those upon whom my concerts had already made a favorable impression all the more strongly to me. Among others, a M. Perrin[1] introduced himself to me; he had formerly been director of the Opéra Comique, was now a wealthy bel esprit and painter, and was nevertheless subsequently to become director of the Opéra. He had heard *Lohengrin* and *Tannhäuser* in Germany and expressed himself in such a way as led me to assume that he would make it a point of honor to bring these operas to France, if he were ever in a position to do so. A Count Foucher de Careil[2] had also acquainted himself with my operas in the same way by seeing them performed in Germany, and he too became a distinguished and enduring friend. He had made a name by various writings on German philosophy, and particularly by an edition of the works of Leibniz, and it inevitably proved interesting to me to be brought into contact through him with an aspect of French thought hitherto unknown to me.

If I omit to mention a number of fleeting acquaintances, among whom a Russian Count Tolstoi distinguished himself especially, I must nonetheless testify to the splendid impression which the novelist Champfleury[1] made on me by his enchanting and admirable pamphlet about me and my concerts. In a series of what appeared to be quickly improvised aphorisms, he displayed such great comprehension of my music and even of my personality as I had previously encountered only in Liszt's remarks on *Lohengrin* and *Tannhäuser* but never again since then in such spirited and pithy form. My ensuing personal acquaintance with Champfleury introduced me to a very straightforward and in a certain sense congenial fellow, whose like is only rarely found as he belonged to a type of Frenchman rapidly becoming extinct.

Still more significant in its way was the approach to me by the poet Baudelaire. My acquaintance with him began by a letter in which he described the impression made by my music on a person who hitherto had believed his sensibility responsive to colors and not to sounds. His opinions on the matter, expressed with conscious boldness in the most bizarre flights of fantasy, showed me at once that I was confronted here by a person of an extraordinary mind, who was capable of pursuing the impressions he had received from me to their ultimate conclusions with unbounded vigor. He explained that he had intentionally omitted to put his return address under his signature in order that I should not get the idea that he wanted anything from me. It goes without saying that I soon managed to find him and include him in that circle of acquaintances to whom I announced my intention of being at home every Wednesday evening to receive them.

I had been told by my older Parisian friends, among whom I continued to count the faithful Gaspérini, that this was the right thing to do in Paris; and thus I came to hold a salon in my little house on the Rue Newton, quite in accordance with the most fashionable dictates, whereat Minna, though she knew only a few miserable scraps of French, felt herself to be in a very respectable position. This salon, attended by the Olliviers among others, was peopled over a time with an ever-growing influx of guests. Here an earlier acquaintance of mine, Malwida von Meysenbug,[2] also joined me again, to remain thereafter a close friend for life. I had met her once before, during my stay in London in 1855, after she had previously written me a letter expressing enthusiastic agreement with my book *The Art-Work of the Future*. During that time in London, when we met one evening at the home of a family called Althaus, I found her full of all kinds of plans to reform humanity similar to those I had set forth in that book, but which I had by then, under the influence of Schopenhauer and through recognition of the deep tragedy of the world and the nothingness of its phenomena, abandoned almost with a sense of irritation. When discussing all this it was painful for me not to be understood by my enthusiastic friend and to appear to her as a renegade from a noble cause. We parted on very bad terms. I almost retreated in alarm when I met Malwida again in Paris; yet soon all memories of those painful London debates were effaced, for she at once declared that our dispute had produced the decided success of forcing her to read Schopenhauer without further delay. After she had become familiar with his philosophy through serious study, she had at any rate perceived that her views concerning the way to make everybody happy must necessarily have appeared extremely distasteful to me on account of their shallowness. She now considered herself my most fervent convert and interpreted this as involving her in continuing solicitude for my well-being. While propriety required me to place her at first in the position of being a friend to my wife, she could not help noticing at a glance the miseries of our now only outwardly conjugal life, and, realizing how difficult the situation was, made it her business to intervene with affectionate solicitude against all the unpleasantnesses that were caused by it. In the same way, she also could not help realizing at once the difficulties of my financial situation in Paris, given the almost indeterminate nature of my undertakings and the complete absence of a material foundation for my existence. The vast expenses arising from the three concerts could not remain a secret from any of those concerned about me; Malwida too had soon guessed the difficulties I was in, for there seemed to be no prospects in any quarter for a practical success in my previous ventures or for anything that could be considered compensation for the sacrifices I had made in carrying them out. Entirely of her own accord she felt herself obliged to look for help on my behalf, and to this end sought to provide me with an introduction to a Mme Schwabe,[1] the widow of a rich English tradesman in whose house she had found employment as governess to the elder daughter. She did not conceal from herself or from me the disagreeable interpretations that would be put upon my cultivating this relationship; she nevertheless counted on the kindness she believed this rather grotesque woman to possess, as well as her vanity, which would surely induce her to try to compensate me for the distinction conferred by an invitation to my salon.

The truth was that my money had entirely run out; and I only found the courage to deny my poverty-stricken condition when I learned to my dismay that people were running around among the Germans in Paris arranging to pass the hat to indemnify me for the costs of my concerts. At this news I came forward at once with an announcement that the assumption that I was in need as a result of losses rested on false rumors, and that I would have to reject any assistance of this kind. Mme Schwabe, who also came regularly to my soirées and went to sleep just as regularly whenever we made music, was now induced, by careful prompting on the part of Malwida, to offer me her personal help. This amounted to approximately three thousand francs, which at that moment were in fact desperately needed; as I did not want to accept the money as a gift, I gave the lady, who had by no means demanded it, a bill of exchange due and payable a year later. She accepted this good-naturedly, not as security but merely in order to assuage my feelings. When this bill subsequently fell due, I found it impossible to make the payment and again turned to Malwida, who was still in Paris, and asked her to tell Mme Schwabe, who was out of town, how things stood and request a prolongation of the bill for another year. Malwida earnestly assured me that I need not trouble myself even to make such a request, as Mme Schwabe had never looked upon this sum as other than a voluntary contribution toward my Paris undertakings, in which she was proud to take an interest. How the case really stood will be seen later.[1]

During this strangely exciting time I was as much touched as surprised to receive a present from an admirer in Dresden named Richard Weiland; it was a piece of not inartistically wrought silver, representing a sheet of music surrounded by a crown of laurel, on which the opening bars of the main themes from my operas up to *Rheingold* and *Tristan* were engraved. This modest man visited me later on one occasion and told me he had been traveling around almost incessantly attending performances of my operas at various places, pointing out that he recalled a production of *Tannhäuser* in Prague in which the overture had lasted twenty minutes, whereas under my baton in Dresden it had taken only twelve.

I received an equally agreeable fillip, of a different kind, from an incident involving me with Rossini. Some comedian in one of the papers had attributed to him a "bon mot", according to which he had served his friend Caraffa, who had declared himself an admirer of my music, some fish without sauce at dinner, telling him that this was appropriate for a man who liked music without melody. Rossini now published a formal and earnest protest against this story, terming it a "mauvaise blague", and stating at the same time that he would never permit himself such jokes at the expense of a man who was trying to widen the frontiers of his art. As soon as I learned of this I didn't hesitate a minute in looking up Rossini, being received most cordially in the manner I subsequently described in an essay devoted to my recollections of him. I was no less pleased to learn, with respect to my old acquaintance Halévy, that he had taken my side in the dispute about my music. I have described my visit to him and the conversation we had on this occasion on an earlier page.

Despite all these for the most part friendly and encouraging encounters, nothing developed that offered anything resembling a prospect of making my situation more secure. I was still kept in suspense as to whether I would receive an answer to the appeal I had submitted to the Emperor Napoleon, granting me the use of the Opéra for the repetition of my concerts. Only by obtaining this concession, with no requirement for financial outlays on my part, could I gain the benefit I needed more sorely every day. It remained beyond all doubt that Minister Fould was working against me with the Emperor as fiercely as he could. As I had now made the surprising discovery that Marshal Magnan[1] had been present at all three of my concerts, I thought I could count on this gentleman, to whom the Emperor was particularly indebted for services at the time of the December 2nd coup d'état, to be not unfavorably disposed toward my cause. I was utterly determined to get at this detestable M. Fould, and therefore made my approach to the Marshal, whereupon I had the huge surprise one day to see a hussar ride up to my house, ring the bell while still on horseback, and hand my astonished servant a letter from Magnan summoning me to his presence. I was duly received at the headquarters of Paris Command by this great soldier, whose air was almost that of a grandiose desperado: he chatted very understandingly with me, frankly confessing his delight in my music, and listened attentively to my report about the conspicuously futile attempts I had made with the Emperor, as well as to the suspicion I voiced concerning M. Fould. It was later reported to me that he confronted Fould in the Tuileries that very evening with some sharp words with respect to my cause.

At any rate, it is certain that from this moment on I noticed my affairs taking a more favorable turn in those quarters. Yet the deciding factor was produced by a movement in my favor from an entirely unexpected direction. His interest in the outcome of all these plans had kept Bülow in Paris long after he should have departed. He had arrived there with letters of introduction from the then Princess Regent of Prussia[1] to the ambassador, Count Pourtalès.[2] His expectation that the latter might eventually express the desire to have me introduced to him had remained unfulfilled up to then. To compel him to make my acquaintance, he finally hit upon the plan of inviting the Prussian ambassador and his attaché, Count Paul Hatzfeld,[3] to dine at Vachette's, a superb restaurant to which I would then accompany him. With an inscrutable smile he showed me the readily forthcoming notes of acceptance from the two gentlemen. Above all, Bülow took care of the main attraction by ordering a particularly tasty repast. The success of this meeting was everything that could be desired; Count Pourtalès pleased me especially by the great simplicity and undisguised warmth of his conversation, as well as by his conduct toward me. From then on, Count Hatzfeld visited me regularly, also attending my Wednesday receptions, and at length brought me news that there were distinct stirrings in my favor at the court in the Tuileries. Finally, he requested me to accompany him on a visit to Count Bacciochi,[4] the Emperor's principal chamberlain. From him I got the first sign of an imperial reaction to my former appeals: the question was why I was insisting on a concert to be given at the Opéra; such a thing could not seriously interest anyone, nor could it bring me any further success; it would probably be better, I was advised, if the director of this imperial institution, M. Alphonse Royer, were to be induced to come to an agreement with me concerning an opera to be composed for Paris. As I wouldn't hear of any such thing, several further such conferences remained fruitless; I was accompanied to one of them by Bülow, on which occasion we noticed to our amusement that this strange count, whom Belloni claimed to have known in his youth as a ticket-taker at La Scala in Milan, was trying to conceal spastic movement of his hand, the result of a not very creditable infirmity, by playing continually with a little wooden stick, which he caused to jump up and down with pretended affectation. Even after I had thus gained access to the imperial officials, it appeared as if next to nothing would be done on my behalf, when suddenly one morning Count Hatzfeld overwhelmed me with the news that the Emperor had given orders the night before for a performance of my *Tannhäuser*. The decisive word in the matter, he told me, had been spoken by the Princess Metternich.[5] At a moment when I was being talked about in the presence of the Emperor she had joined the circle, and on being asked her opinion had spoken of this opera, which she had seen in Dresden, with such enthusiasm that the Emperor had immediately given her his promise to order a production of it to be mounted. Fould, it is true, had exploded in anger when receiving the imperial order that same evening, but Napoleon had informed him he could not go back on his word to Princess Metternich. Now I was again led to Bacciochi, who received me this time with very solemn mien, and first of all directed to me the singular question as to what my opera was all about. I gave him a summary, and when I had finished he breathed a sigh of relief: "Ah! Le pape ne vient pas en scène. C'est bon! On nous avait dit que vous aviez fait paraître le Saint-Père, et ceci, vous comprenez, n'aurait pas pu passer. Du reste, Monsieur, on sait à présent que vous avez énormément de génie; l'empereur donne l'ordre de représenter votre opéra." He further assured me that henceforth everything would be done to satisfy my wishes; I need deal solely with M. Royer in the matter from now on.

This turn of events threw me into a state of numbed confusion, for my inner voice told me I owed all this to a series of misunderstandings. Certainly all hope of being able to carry out my original plan of producing my works with a select German troupe in Paris had disappeared, and I could not conceal from myself that my only chance now was the luck of an adventurer. Several conferences with M. Royer sufficed to enlighten me as to the character of this my new undertaking. Nothing caused him so much worry as to convince me of the need to change the second act, as the insertion of a big ballet at this point was absolutely unavoidable. To this and similar proposals I made virtually no reply, and on the way home could only ask myself what would become of me if I were to refuse the performance of my *Tannhäuser* at the Opéra.

Meanwhile other and more immediate cares connected with my personal affairs became so pressing that I was obliged to devote my full attention to them. For this reason I decided to carry out a venture suggested by Giacomelli and repeat my concerts in Brussels. A contract was concluded with the Théâtre de la Monnaie for three concerts, half of the receipts to be left to me, after deduction of all the costs. In the company of my agent I then traveled on March 19th to the Belgian capital to see if I could succeed there in recouping the money I had lost in Paris. Under the guidance of my mentor I found myself impelled to call on all sorts of newspaper editors and, among other Belgian notabilities, M. Fétis *père*. Of him I knew that he had let himself be bought by Meyerbeer against me years ago, and I now found it amusing to enter into a discussion with this autocratically posturing man, in the course of which he finally declared himself to be entirely of my opinion.

Here I also made an unusual acquaintance in Councillor of State Klindworth,[1] whose daughter, or as some said, his wife, had previously been recommended to me by Liszt on the occasion of my stay in London; but she had never appeared, and I now had the pleasant surprise of receiving an invitation from her in Brussels. While she treated me in an extraordinarily cordial way, Herr Klindworth himself was a source of inexhaustible conversation with stories of his bizarre career as a diplomatic agent in all kinds of affairs that remained obscure to me. I dined with them on several occasions and was introduced there to Count and Countess Coudenhove,[2] the latter being the daughter of my older friend Mme Kalergis. Herr Klindworth took a keen and continuing interest in me, which even prompted him to press upon me a letter of recommendation to Prince Metternich, with whose father he claimed to have been on close terms. He had a curious habit of interlarding his otherwise frivolous maxims with continual references to an omnipotent providence governing all things, and when, during one of our last conversations, I once hazarded an irritated retort, he utterly lost his temper, and I thought he was on the point of breaking with me completely, something which nonetheless seemed destined not to happen, then or later. Apart from these interesting acquaintances, I gained nothing in Brussels but trouble and useless effort. The first concert, non-subscription, was very well attended. But according to a clause in the contract, which I had misconstrued, all the costs of the actual performance fell upon me alone, and the concert managers now interpreted this so rigidly that there were virtually no profits left for me; this was supposed to be remedied at the second concert, but that was a subscription performance; beyond the subscribers, who, I was told, practically filled the house, there were few paying customers, so that there was not even enough left .to pay my travel and living expenses, increased as they were by the presence of an agent and a servant. I therefore decided to renounce a third concert and, having been presented with a Bohemian glass vase by Mrs Street, the aforementioned daughter of Klindworth, set off back to Paris in a less than cheerful frame of mind. Nevertheless, my stay had involved a pleasant diversion in the form of a very brief trip to Antwerp. By no means inclined to devote the little time available to me to look at art treasures, I contented myself with a tour of its external sights, which seemed to offer less of antiquarian interest than I had expected. I was especially disconcerted at the placement of the famous citadel. In conceiving the scene for the first act of my *Lohengrin*, I had assumed that this citadel, which I envisioned as the old castle of Antwerp, would necessarily be a prominent sight when beheld from beyond the Scheldt; instead, nothing could be seen except a flat and unremarkable plain, with fortifications dug into the ground. After this, whenever I saw *Lohengrin* I usually had to smile at the scene-painter's castle, perched high in the background on top of a stately hill.

Upon returning to Paris at the end of March my sole worry was how to repair my impecunious and seemingly hopeless situation. The pressure of these monetary cares seemed all the more incongruous in view of the fact that my notoriety had made me very fashionable; I kept up appearances and my Wednesday receptions became increasingly brilliant; interesting strangers began looking me up in the hope of being blessed with similar fortune; Fräulein Ingeborg Stark,[1] later the wife of the young Hans von Bronsart, came as a vision of elegance to play the piano for us, with modest assistance from Fräulein Aline Hund from Weimar; a highly gifted young French musician, Camille Saint-Saëns, took a most agreeable part in our musical activities, and a most valuable addition to my circle of French acquaintances was made in M. Frédéric Villot. He was curator of paintings at the Louvre, an extremely sensitive and cultured man whom I had met one day at the shop of the music dealer Flaxland, with whom I had some not unimportant business, where he had come to inquire as to the whereabouts of the score of *Tristan* which he had ordered; quite amazed by this, I had asked him, after we were introduced and I had learned that he possessed the scores of my earlier operas as well, how he could derive enjoyment from my dramatic compositions without a command of the German language, as I could not understand how he could otherwise make much sense of music so closely interwoven with the poetry; he responded with the spirited remark that it was precisely my music which served as the best possible guide to a comprehension of the drama, whereupon I formed a strong attachment to the man and was very pleased to be able to maintain a stimulating association with him. When I subsequently produced a very comprehensive preface to the translation of my operatic poems, I could think of no one to whom it could more worthily be dedicated. The scores of my operas, which he did not know how to play on his own, were played for him by the aforementioned young musician Saint-Saëns, who seemed something of a protégé of his. I soon learned to appreciate the consummate skill and talent Saint-Saëns evinced in so doing and was really amazed by him; with his unsurpassable assurance and rapidity in taking in the most complex orchestral scores at a glance, the young man combined a no less admirable memory; he not only knew how to play my scores, which now included *Tristan* as well, by heart, but also how to bring out essential and less essential details with such accuracy that one might easily have thought he had the full score continually before his eyes. I later discovered that this dimwitted receptivity in grasping the technical aspects of music was not accompanied by corresponding intensity of productive power, so that as he persisted with his efforts to make a mark as a composer himself I quite lost sight of him.

I now had to enter into closer consultation with the director of the Opéra, M. Royer, about the production of *Tannhäuser* he had been commanded to undertake. Two months went by before I was able to make up my mind whether to say yes or no to the whole business. At no single interview did the man fail to press upon me the need to insert a ballet into the second act; I may have benumbed him with my eloquent protestations, but I never managed to convince him. Meanwhile, I could not refuse to consider the need for a practicable translation of the libretto.

The progress made on this work so far was hardly worthy of the name. I have already recounted how I found Charnal altogether incompetent, Roger vanished from my horizon, and Gaspérini disinclined to accept the task; then a certain Herr Lindau[1] (with the first name Paul, if I remember rightly) had turned up at my house, confidently stating that he could produce the right translation of *Tannhäuser* in collaboration with the young Edmond Roche. This Lindau, a native of Magdeburg who had fled from Prussian military service, had been recommended to me by Giacomelli as a worthy substitute to sing my "Etoile du soir"[2] at one of my concerts, when the French singer he had engaged suddenly canceled. He had at once agreed to do the song without rehearsal, on the grounds that he was already "very well acquainted with it", and this had induced me to regard him as a good genius sent from heaven. My utter astonishment at the unprecedented presumption of the man knew no bounds when on the evening of the concert he executed his task with the most amateurish timidity, without managing to get a single bar of the song clearly across to the audience, whose stupefaction at this seemed to be the only thing that prevented a general outburst of voluble discontent. Nevertheless Lindau, who found all sorts of excuses and explanations for his misdeed, managed to insinuate himself as a friend of the house, if not as a decent singer then at least as a faithful friend, being particularly successful in winning the favor of my wife, and gradually becoming an almost daily guest; in spite of inner misgivings that would not be silenced, I treated him with tolerant good-nature, not so much on account of the "fabulous connections" he boasted of, but rather because he showed himself to be most obliging in running errands for us.

But the factor that finally induced me to let him participate in the translation of *Tannhäuser* was his suggestion that Edmond Roche collaborate in the job.

I had become acquainted with Roche immediately upon my arrival in Paris (in September of the previous year) in the most unusual and winning way. In order to take delivery of my furniture after its arrival from Zürich, I had to go to an office of the Bureau of Customs; there I was referred to a pale, shabby but lively looking young fellow, with whom I was to settle the matter; as I was about to give my name, he interrupted me enthusiastically: "Oh, je connais bien M. Richard Wagner, puisque j'ai son portrait suspendu au-dessus de mon piano." Greatly astonished, I asked what he knew about me and learned that through close study of the vocal scores of my operas he had become a fervent admirer. After he had helped me take care of my tiresome customs problems with the most gratifying selflessness, I made him promise to visit me; he did so, and I was able to gain a clearer insight into the difficult situation of this poor fellow, who evinced, as far as I could judge, considerable poetic talent. He told me that he had tried to make his way as a violinist in the orchestras of the little vaudeville theaters, but he had been so bad at it that out of consideration for his family (for he was already married), he had been obliged to settle for a lowly position in the civil service with a secure salary and the prospect of advancement. That he actually understood my music very well was soon clear to me; he asserted it constituted the sole consolation in his sad existence. As far as his poetic efforts were concerned, Gaspérini and some other competent judges could say that they represented good verses at the very least. I had already thought of him as a possible translator for *Tannhäuser* and when his ignorance of German, the only obstacle to his doing the work, had been offset by Lindau's offer of collaboration, this arrangement induced me to accept the latter's proposal at once.

We agreed the first thing to be done was a straight prose translation of the whole thing, and this task I naturally entrusted to Lindau alone. There was a considerable delay before this came to hand, subsequently explained by the fact that Lindau was quite unable to produce even this literal version and had delegated the work to another man, an indigent Frenchman who knew German, whom he induced to take it on by promising a fee to be squeezed out of me at some future date. At the same time Roche had put a few of the main stanzas of my poem in verses which pleased me considerably, and with this evidence of the capabilities of my collaborators I now went to Royer to get his consent to give them a formal commission for the work. He didn't seem to like the idea of giving the job to two unknowns; but I insisted on giving them a chance at least. Stubbornly determined not to let Roche be deprived of the commission, I myself began participating in the task, as I soon saw that Lindau was hopelessly incapable of any real help. The two often sat with me for four hours at a stretch in order to produce only a few lines, on which occasions I was usually tempted to throw Lindau out of the house, as he didn't even show any understanding of the German text yet was always ready with the most incongruous suggestions. It was only because I could not think of any other way to keep poor Roche in the work that I endured such an absurd association and its constant irritations.

These onerous labors lasted several months, during which I was occupied by further negotiations with Royer concerning preparations for the performance, particularly as to casting the roles. It struck me as odd that hardly any of the singers at the Opéra were suggested by its director for this purpose; most of them were unsuitable in my eyes anyway, with the exception of a Mme Gueymard,[1] whom I would gladly have seen as Venus, but who was refused to me on grounds that remained obscure. Meanwhile, in order to get some idea of the abilities of the ensemble, I had to attend several performances of such operas as *Il trovatore*, *La favorite*, and *Semiramide*, on which occasions my inner voice told me clearly that I was on a hopelessly wrong path, with the result that on my way home every time I came to the conclusion that I should give up the whole thing. On the other hand, I was continually seduced by the way Royer, who had full authority to do so, generously offered to engage any guest singer I might desire. The main question in this regard was a tenor for the title role: for this I could think of no other but Niemann from Hanover, whose praises were sung to me on all sides. Even Frenchmen such as Foucher de Careil and Perrin, who had heard him in my roles, affirmed his special quality; the director thought such an arrangement definitely advantageous for his theater, and so Niemann was invited to Paris for the purpose of negotiating a contract as guest singer. Beyond this, M. Royer wanted me to opt for a certain Mme Tedesco as Venus, as she was supposedly a "tragédienne" and on account of her beauty would be a very valuable addition to the company. Without knowing the lady I gave my consent to this splendid piece of advice, and moreover willingly agreed to the engagement of a Mlle Sax,[1] a yet unspoiled young singer with a very lovely voice, as well as an Italian baritone named Morini,[2] whose sonorous vocalism had decidedly pleased me in those performances I had attended, particularly as contrasted with the puny French singers in this category. By these arrangements I thought I had done all that was necessary at the moment in the best possible way, but I still didn't really believe in the venture.

Amid these doings I passed my forty-seventh birthday in a far from happy frame of mind, to which, however, on that evening the particularly bright glowing of Jupiter offered an omen of better things to come. The better weather appropriate for this time of year, which is never favorable for doing business in Paris, only served to heighten my miseries: I was and remained continuingly without prospect of meeting my household expenses, which had meanwhile become quite heavy. Still trying, amid all the other worries, to find some remedy for this, I had contracted with the music dealer Flaxland for the sale of all the French rights to my operas *Der fliegende Holländer*, *Tannhäuser* and *Lohengrin*, so as to make the best use I could of them. This contract stipulated that the publisher would pay me one thousand francs for each of the three operas at once, further payments to be made only after performances at a Paris theater, whereupon I would get an additional thousand francs after the first ten performances, and an equal amount for the following performances up to the twentieth. I immediately notified my friend Pusinelli of this contract, having reserved these rights in his interest when selling out to Meser's successor, so as to be able to repay the loan he had made me at the time of their original publication. At the same time I asked him to let me retain the initial payment by Flaxland, as I would otherwise have no funds to support my efforts to make these operas popular in Paris. My friend approved all these dispositions. The Dresden publisher, on the other hand, was all the more disagreeable and complained at once that I was infringing upon his rights in France, pestering Flaxland to the extent that the latter felt justified in henceforth creating all kinds of difficulties for me.

I had almost become ensnared in additional unpleasant complications in this respect, without doing myself any good in the process, when one day Count Paul Hatzfeld appeared at my door with an invitation to visit Mme Kalergis, who had just arrived in Paris, as she had something to tell me. This was the first time that I had seen her since my stay in Paris with Liszt in 1853, and I was received by her with a declaration that she regretted not having been present at my concerts the previous winter all the more keenly, because she had thereby lost an opportunity to be helpful to me in a time of great difficulty. She had learned, she said, that I had suffered great losses, estimated to her at ten thousand francs, and now she requested me to accept that sum from her to make my deficit good. Whereas I had felt it proper to deny the existence of any such losses to Count Hatzfeld, for even the Prussian Legation had been approached by the people who had wanted to make that abhorrent collection on my behalf, I now found not the slightest grounds for hiding the truth from this noble-hearted woman. To me it was only as if something were being done which I had every right to expect the whole time: and what I felt immediately in response was solely the need to make some commensurate return to this rare lady, at least to mean something to her. All the anxieties I was caused by my subsequent relationship with her were traceable to my inability to fulfill this one wish, which was in turn caused by her strange character and unsettled way of living. For the present I tried to do something that would evidence the sincerity of my desire in this regard. Especially for her I improvised a hearing of the second act of *Tristan*, at which Mme Viardot, whom I got to know better on this occasion, shared the vocal parts with me, while for the piano I had Klindworth come over from London at my expense. This highly unusual and intimate performance took place at the home of Mme Viardot; apart from Mme Kalergis, for whom alone it was being given, Berlioz was the only other listener. His inclusion had been instigated by Mme Viardot, seemingly in the determination of easing the strained relations between Berlioz and myself. I really don't know what effect was produced on the participants and the listeners by the performance of this extraordinary fragment in such peculiar circumstances; Mme Kalergis said nothing, while Berlioz merely expressed himself favorably as to the "chaleur" of my delivery, which may very well have afforded a strong contrast with that of my partner, who rendered most of the part with half voice. This situation seemed to anger Klindworth particularly; he had in fact done his part superbly but told me he had been consumed with fury when he observed Viardot's lukewarm delivery, which was probably determined by the presence of Berlioz. By contrast, we had a much better time one evening when we went through the first act of *Die Walküre* at my home, on which occasion, in addition to Mme Kalergis, the singer Niemann was also present.

Niemann had come to Paris at the invitation of Royer to conclude a contract. Unfortunately, the impression he made on me when I first saw him again was by no means as favorable as when he had visited me in

Zürich several years before: I was shocked by the crude air of cynicism
he had put on, greeting me at the very threshold with the question:
"Well, do you want me or not?" By contrast, he pulled himself together
splendidly for our communal meeting in the office of the director in order
to produce a good effect. In this he succeeded admirably, for everybody
was astounded at the phenomenon of a tenor of such physical immensity.
Nonetheless he had to submit to an audition for form's sake, for which
he chose Tannhäuser's narration of his pilgrimage, singing and acting
it on the stage of the Opéra. Mme Kalergis and Princess Metternich,
who had attended in secret, were both immediately taken by Niemann,
and the management of the theater no less so. He was engaged for eight
months at a monthly salary of ten thousand francs, and this engagement
was solely for *Tannhäuser*, as I felt obliged to protest against his
appearing in any other operas beforehand.

It was the concluding of this engagement and the remarkable
circumstances that had brought it about which filled me with a hitherto
unknown sense of power suddenly placed in my hands. I had also been
drawn into closer association with Princess Metternich, who had to be
considered my protectress in the whole affair, and I found myself warmly
received by her husband, as well as the wider diplomatic circles to which
they both belonged. Everybody seemed to attribute to the princess
almost omnipotent influence at the imperial court; the otherwise mighty
Minister of State, Fould, seemed unable to do anything against her in
matters pertaining to me. She had instructed me to take any problems
I might have to her alone: she would know how to get things done, which
seemed to be particularly important to her, as she no doubt could see
that I still had no real faith in the whole enterprise.

Under these more hopeful auspices it looked as though the months
from summer to autumn, when the rehearsals were scheduled to begin,
would be pleasant ones for me. It was especially valuable to me to be
in a position at just that time to do something for Minna's health, as
the doctors had urgently prescribed a cure for her at the spa in Bad Soden
near Frankfurt; she proceeded there at the beginning of July, and I
promised to come and pick her up when her cure was over, for I now
had the opportunity of making a visit to the Rhine.

My relations with the King of Saxony, who had stubbornly refused
me amnesty "for juridical reasons", had undergone a change for the
better. I owed this to the growing interest taken in me by the other
German legations, especially those of Austria and Prussia. Herr von
Seebach, the Saxon Ambassador and husband of a cousin of my

magnanimous friend Mme Kalergis, had also shown considerable interest in me and had seemingly grown tired of being continually interpellated by his fellow diplomats about my status as a "political refugee". Accordingly, he had made it his business to mediate on my behalf with the Saxon Court. In this he seems to have been seconded by the then Princess Regent of Prussia, again at the instigation of Count Pourtalès. I learned that, on the occasion of a meeting between the German princes and Emperor Napoleon in Baden,[1] she had used the opportunity to put in a good word for me with the King of Saxony. The upshot was, after we had disposed of a number of ludicrous conditions which Herr von Seebach was obliged to impose, he at length was able to report that, although King Johann could not pardon me or permit my return to the Kingdom of Saxony, he would nonetheless raise no further objections to my staying in any other state of the German Federation which I might wish to visit for artistic purposes, provided that state itself had no objections to my presence. Herr von Seebach then hinted that I should take the opportunity of presenting myself to the Princess Regent on my first visit to the Rhenish provinces, in order to express my gratitude for her intercession, something which the King of Saxony seemed to desire as well.

Before I could carry out this intention I had to endure the most wearisome torments with the translators of my *Tannhäuser*. Amid these anxieties and throughout the previous worries I again suffered a recurrence of the old malady which seemed to be settled in my abdomen. As a remedy I was advised to ride horseback; the painter Czermak,[2] a friendly young man whom Fräulein Meysenbug had introduced to me, now offered to help me with these riding exercises. For this purpose I had to contract for a series of rides with a livery stable, as a result of which my companion and I found ourselves mounted one day on the most peaceable nags available, as we had specifically requested. We then ventured forth with utmost caution for a ride in the Bois de Boulogne, choosing the early morning hours in order not to bump into the elegant chevaliers of high society. As I was relying on Czermak's experience, I was amazed to find myself outdoing him on this occasion, if not in horsemanship then at least in daring, for I was able to endure the extremely uncomfortable trot of my horse, whereas he loudly swore he would never go through such an exercise again. Emboldened by this, I decided to ride out alone the following day; the stable-boy who brought me my horse prudently kept an eye on me as far as the Barrière de l'Etoile, as he was skeptical of my ability to take the horse beyond this point: when I approached the Avenue de l'Impératrice my steed stubbornly refused to go àny further, balking and side-stepping and finally coming to a complete standstill, until I finally elected to turn back, upon which the solicitous stable-boy luckily came to my rescue; he helped me off my horse in the middle of the street and led it home with a smirk. This was my last attempt to master the equestrian art; it cost me a subscription for ten rides, the vouchers for which reposed unused in my desk.

By way of compensation, I found abundant recreation in my solitary walks in the Bois de Boulogne accompanied by my cheerful little dog Fips, during which I learned to treasure anew the splendors of this park. Life also became quieter, as is usual in Paris at this time of year. After having experienced the spectacular outcome of the dinner he had arranged at Vachette's, represented by the imperial command to give *Tannhäuser*, Bülow had long since gone back to Germany; and in August I too set out on the carefully planned expedition to the German provinces of the Rhine, first proceeding via Cologne to Koblenz, where I expected to find Princess Augusta of Prussia. But I learned that she was staying in Baden, and therefore made my way there via Bad Soden, where I collected Minna for the rest of the trip, to be made in the company of her recently acquired friend, Mathilde Schiffner. On the way we stopped at Frankfurt, where I saw my brother Albert again for the first time since leaving Dresden, as he also happened to be passing through.

While there it occurred to me that I was in a city where Schopenhauer resided; but a strange diffidence prevented me from visiting him; I was much too distraught and too far removed from that sole issue which would have made a meeting with Schopenhauer significant for me, even if I had felt myself entirely up to a discussion with him. As with so many other things in my life, I again deferred one of its priceless opportunities for "some other time", which, as I hoped, would surely present itself soon. When, a year after this fleeting visit, I came back to Frankfurt to work on my *Meistersinger*, the time would have been ripe for such an encounter: yet Schopenhauer had died in that very year[1] – a fact which led me to ponder the vagaries of fate in self-reproach.

Meanwhile yet another fondly cherished hope came to nothing; I had flattered myself into believing I could persuade Liszt to meet me here in Frankfurt; but there I found only his letter, telling me it was impossible for him to fulfill my request. From here we went on to Baden-Baden where, while Minna and her friend were being seduced by the pleasures of the roulette table, I tried to gain an audience with Her

Royal Highness by means of a letter of recommendation from Count Pourtalès to Countess Hacke, lady-in-waiting to my exalted benefactress. After some delay, I duly received an invitation to meet her in the Pump Room at five o'clock in the afternoon. It was a cold and rainy day, and the whole place seemed absolutely deserted when I repaired to the Pump Room in which Augusta and the Countess Hacke were promenading up and down. They halted graciously as they came by me. The highly winsome impression she had made on that evening when her husband had presented me to her in her box at the Berlin Court Theater was in no way to be recaptured; she spoke in a very affected manner and reminded me in this respect of her exalted brother, the Grand Duke of Weimar, whom I had met several years before in Lucerne. Her conversation consisted almost exclusively of assurances that she was entirely powerless in every respect to do anything, in reply to which I somewhat imprudently brought up that from the hint I had received from the King of Saxony I had to thank her for the concession granted to me. This seemed quite openly to displease her, and she dismissed me with some rather banal remarks indicating only the most generalized kind of interest. My old friend Alwine Frommann told me later she didn't know what it was about me that had displeased the Princess, and thought it might have been my Saxon accent. Thus I left the much-praised Baden paradise without carrying away any congenial impressions, boarded a steamship at Mannheim with Minna alone, and went on a trip down the Rhine for the first time, during which it occurred to me that I had crossed the Rhine repeatedly without ever having become acquainted with this most characteristic thoroughfare of medieval Germany. A speedy return via Cologne concluded this excursion, which had lasted only a week, for I now had to face and resolve the mounting problems of my Paris undertaking.

One factor that seemed likely to alleviate the difficulties confronting me was the friendly relationship which the young banker Emil Erlanger was disposed to enter into with me. I owed this primarily to a strange fellow named Albert Beckmann, formerly a revolutionary in Hanover, subsequently private librarian to Prince Louis Napoleon, and at present press agent for several interests I could never quite identify; having declared himself one of my partisans, he had known how to make my acquaintance, and had always shown himself to be most obliging. He now announced to me that Herr Erlanger, one of those whom he represented in press matters, also wanted to meet me; I was on the point of turning him down with the remark that I needed nothing of a banker except his money; but he responded to this joke by telling me in all seriousness that it was precisely in this respect, where I so obviously had need of it, that Erlanger wanted to serve me. Thus I got to know a really charming person, who had first been attracted to me by a genuine love for my music, which he had frequently heard in Germany. He expressed the frank request that I put my financial affairs in his hands, which initially could only mean that he would be responsible for subsidizing me to whatever extent necessary while I was in Paris, in return for which I would assign to his administration all the eventual receipts of my Paris undertakings: in short, he wanted to be my banker in Paris. This offer was as new to me as it was exactly suited to my needs in my curious situation; and in fact, as far as my financial position was concerned, I had no further troubles until my Paris destiny was finally decided. Although my dealings with Herr Erlanger were necessarily accompanied by the many annoyances which a man's kindliness alone cannot dispel, I found him at all times a true friend, as concerned for my well-being as for the success of my undertaking.

This eminently satisfactory turn of events, which in other circumstances would have served to inspire me with the utmost confidence, was not able, however, to help me develop the slightest enthusiasm for an undertaking whose hollowness and unsuitability for my purposes was clear to me at almost every contact with it. I went about meeting the demands placed upon me by the undertaking in a disgruntled way, despite its being the foundation of the trust reposed in me. But a new and pleasant acquaintance it brought me managed to make me close my eyes once more to the true nature of my enterprise, and so my spirits were restored. M. Royer notified me that the translation I had taken infinite pains to bring into existence through my two volunteers was not satisfactory, and he most urgently recommended a complete revision by M. Charles Truinet,[1] whose pen name was Nuitter. This was a still young man of uncommonly winning and open character. He had called on me a few months before upon recommendation of Emile Ollivier, a fellow attorney at the Paris bar, to offer his services in the translation of my operas. Proud of my connection with Lindau, however, I had rejected him: but now the time had come, following Royer's proposal, to consider Truinet's renewed offer. He knew no German, but maintained that as far as that was concerned he could rely on his aged father, who had traveled for a long time in Germany and had acquired a sufficient smattering of our language. Indeed, a mastery of German didn't seem to be what was required to give a freer French gloss to the verses poor

Roche had anxiously put together under the shameless domination of Lindau's vaunted superior knowledge. The inexhaustible patience evinced by Truinet in making one change after another to meet the requirements of my musical phrasing as well soon disposed me in favor of this final collaborator. From this time forward we had to keep Lindau, his utter incompetence clearly recognized, from taking any part in the revision, whereas Roche was retained on the job insofar as his work served as the basis for the new versification. As he had difficulty getting away from the Bureau of Customs, Roche remained largely exempted from further exertions, for Truinet was completely free and could be with me every day. I now saw that Truinet's law degree was merely ornamental, and that he had never really thought of accepting a brief, for his main interest lay in the administration of the Opéra, to which he was moreover attached as keeper of the archives. With one collaborator or another he also devised pieces for the vaudeville and other theaters of low degree, even including the "Bouffes Parisiens", though he was always very embarrassed and evasive in regard to this latter activity. While I was greatly obliged to him for producing a French text of *Tannhäuser* which was actually singable and was generally judged "acceptable", I do not remember being carried away by his poetic or even aesthetic gifts; yet he proved his worth as a well-informed, warm-hearted and staunch friend at all times, especially when things were at their worst. I can scarcely recall another person of such delicate judgment on the most difficult matters, who at the same time was so ready and willing to stand up for the view I was advocating whenever the time came to do so.

We first had to join forces to do an entirely new piece of work. In accordance with a need I had always felt, I had seized the opportunity presented by this carefully prepared production of *Tannhäuser* to expand significantly the first scene with Venus. For this purpose I drafted a German text in free verse, leaving the translator full freedom to find a suitable French version: I was assured Truinet's verses were not at all bad, and based on these I now executed the scene musically, adapting the German text to it only subsequently. Apart from this, my annoying arguments with the management concerning a ballet had also induced me to extend the introductory Venusberg scene to a length far greater than it had previously possessed, whereby, as far as I could see, the *corps de ballet* was afforded such a vast choreographic challenge that there would no longer be any grounds for complaint about my lack of compliance in the matter. Writing the music for these scenes took most of my time during the month of September, while at the same time I also began piano rehearsals in the foyer of the Opéra.

The company, part of which had been newly engaged for this purpose, was now completely assembled, and I was interested to see how a new work was taken in hand at the Opéra. The best description of this would be highest precision combined with maximum dispassion; the chorusmaster M. Vauthrot excelled in both respects. He was a man I could not help regarding as hostile to me, for I could never elicit a single sign of enthusiasm from him, yet on the other hand he proved how seriously he took the work by the most punctilious solicitude in this respect. He insisted on some significant changes in the text on grounds of singability. My knowledge of the scores of Auber and Boïeldieu had misled me into believing that the French were entirely indifferent whether the mute syllables in poetry and song should be sounded or not; Vauthrot asserted that was the case only with composers, not with good singers. I countered his frequently expressed misgivings about the length of the work with the remark that I could not comprehend how he could be afraid of boring any public that had become habituated to Rossini's *Semiramide*, which was frequently performed at that period; he weighed this point and admitted I was correct with respect to the music and to the plot; but I had forgotten, he asserted, that the public cared neither for music nor plot, but concentrated its attention solely on the virtuoso performances of the singers. However, *Tannhäuser* offered little scope for that sort of thing, and neither was it within my powers to provide it: the only virtuoso among the singers I had been given was a rather grotesque but voluptuous Jewess, Mme Tedesco, who had recently returned from triumphs in Italian operas in Portugal and Spain; she seemed very pleased at my involuntary choice of her for Venus, for the reason that this had brought her an engagement at the Opéra. She made every conceivable effort to solve what was for her an entirely alien challenge, as the role was suitable solely for an authentic tragic actress, and for a time it appeared her efforts would be successful, especially as it was obvious that in the frequent rehearsals for her and Niemann alone a strong attraction had sprung into being between "Venus" and "Tannhäuser". As Niemann had mastered the French language with great skill, these rehearsals, in which Mlle Sax also proved her worth, took a truly hopeful course, which continued undisturbed for a time as I did not yet have to deal with M. Dietzsch;[1] for according to the traditions of the house, as *chef d'orchestre* and the eventual conductor of the opera, he was obliged to be present only at the piano rehearsals to acquaint himself with the intentions of the singers. I was even less disturbed by M. Cormon, the stage director for the opera, who was also present at these rehearsals, and who conducted some preliminary discussions concerning the blocking of the scenes with the customary French liveliness and skill. Even when M. Cormon or others did not understand me, they were always willing to accede to my wishes, for I continued to be regarded as all-powerful, and they all thought I could get whatever I wanted done through Princess Metternich. Several signs reinforced this belief: for instance, I had learned that Prince Poniatowsky[1] was threatening to place a serious obstacle in the path of our rehearsals by insisting upon a revival of one of his own failed operas; my complaint about this was instantly acted upon by the undaunted princess and resulted in a command according to which the princely opera was postponed. This naturally did not ingratiate me with the prince, as he made rather clear to me on the occasion of a visit I paid him.

In the midst of this activity I was diverted for a time by a visit from my sister Luise and part of her family. I could entertain her at my own home only with the greatest difficulty, as extraordinarily enough it had become mortally dangerous to reach my house at all; it was now perfectly clear why the landlord had insisted upon a long lease at the time I took the place yet had refused to make any repairs to it; for it had already been decided by the Paris planning authorities to clear the Rue Newton, together with all its side streets, so as to open up a broad boulevard from one of the bridges to the Barrière de l'Etoile. The existence of this plan had been disavowed up to the last minute, however, in order to postpone for as long as possible the need to pay compensation for expropriated sites. To my astonishment I found the street being dug up right at my doorstep and quite deeply as well; at first no carriages could get through, and before long no one could get there on foot either. Under these circumstances, the owner of the house had no objection to my leaving it forthwith, demanding only that I sue him for damages, as this would be the sole way he himself could get anything back from the government. At this time my friend Ollivier had been disbarred for three months on account of some parliamentary misdemeanor; he referred me to his friend Picard for the prosecution of my case. As I saw later from the record of the proceedings, this man fulfilled his task with much spirit. Yet no compensation was forthcoming for me (though I do not know whether the proprietor got anything), and I had to content myself with being released from the remaining obligations under my lease. Thus I had permission to hunt for another place to live, not too far removed from the Opéra, and eventually found a rather shabby and cheerless abode in the Rue d'Aumale. Late that autumn in raw weather we made the laborious transfer, at which time Luise's daughter, my niece Ottilie, provided friendly help, capable child that she was. Unfortunately I had caught a very severe cold in the course of moving, and taking no precautions against it, again plunged into the growing excitement of the rehearsals, with the result that I was eventually struck down by typhoid fever.

We had reached the month of November, and my relatives had to return home leaving me behind in a state of unconsciousness, in which I was consigned to the care of my friend Gaspérini. In my fevered paroxysms I insisted on his calling in all kinds of medical assistance, and Count Hatzfeld actually brought in the doctor attached to the Prussian Legation. The injustice thus done to my friend was by no means attributable to any mistrust but rather to the feverish hallucinations filling my brain. In this condition I imagined that Princess Metternich and Mme Kalergis were setting up a complete court for me, to which I would also invite the Emperor Napoleon, and I actually requested that Emil Erlanger should be brought, as I could not conceive of ever getting well in the dank hole where I was located. Finally, I insisted on being taken to Naples, where I promised a speedy recovery if I could only have an unlimited association with Garibaldi. Gaspérini patiently endured all this nonsense; he and Minna managed to restrain me in spite of my enraged struggles in order to put the requisite mustard plasters on the soles of my feet. During bad nights later in my life I have been visited by similar vain and extravagant fantasms, and upon awakening have realized with a shudder that they were akin to those born to me in that period. After five days the fever was mastered; but I now seemed about to go blind and was extremely weak. At last the effect on my sight went away, and after a few weeks I again trusted myself far enough to creep along the few streets between my house and the Opéra to alleviate my worries about the continuation of the rehearsals.

People there seemed to have thought me on my death-bed, and this had induced the strangest emotions in them; I learned that the rehearsals had been needlessly suspended. Furthermore, I realized from one sign after another that the heart had gone out of the affair, a fact I tried to conceal from myself as best I could, in my sore need of recuperation. Instead I took special pleasure in the publication of a translation of my four earlier operatic poems, for which I had written a very comprehensive preface addressed to M. Frédéric Villot. The translation of all these had been taken care of by M. Challemel-Lacour,[1] a man whom I had known casually at Herwegh's house in bygone years when he was a political refugee. He did such admirable service as a brilliant translator that everybody recognized the value of his work. I had sent the original German text of the preface to the publisher J. J. Weber in Leipzig for publication under the title *Music of the Future*. This pamphlet now arrived and gave me great satisfaction, as I had the feeling it would be the sole profit I would have from this Paris undertaking, for all its outward brilliance. Meanwhile I managed to complete the new music for *Tannhäuser*: the big choreographic scene in the Venusberg had remained to be done, and I completed it one sleepless night at 3 a.m., at just the moment Minna came home from the grand ball at the Hôtel de Ville, which she had attended with one of her lady friends. I gave her reasonably lavish presents at Christmas, while I continued my long recuperation with a regimen prescribed by my doctors consisting of beefsteak in the morning and a glass of Bavarian beer before bedtime. We didn't celebrate New Year's Eve this time, and I slept calmly into the year 1861.

At the outset of the year the laxity with which the rehearsals had been conducted since I had fallen ill was transformed into a more decisive effort to cope with all aspects of the production. But at the same time I could not help noticing that the mood of all the participants had undergone a basic change. The inordinate number of rehearsals gave me the impression that the management was motivated more by the determination rigorously to carry out a command than by any real hope of success. And as time went on I gained an increasingly clear insight into how things actually stood. With regard to the press, which was entirely in the hands of Meyerbeer, I had known long ago what to expect. Now the management, no doubt after trying to placate the leaders of the pack, had also come to the conclusion that this daring venture with *Tannhäuser* would get a hostile reception from that quarter. This view penetrated to the highest circles, and there seemed to be some attempt to find a way to win over to my cause that part of the opera-going public which could decide the matter. Prince Metternich invited me one day to be presented to the new Minister of State, Count Walewsky;[2] this took place with a good deal of ceremony, as represented in particular by a highly persuasive speech directed at me by the Count, attempting to assure me that my good fortune was his abiding concern and that people desired to help me achieve a brilliant success: it was in my hands to achieve this, he concluded, if only I would consent to insert a ballet in the second act of my opera; this would not be any paltry affair, he assured me: I could have my pick of the most famous ballerinas from Petersburg and London; they would be immediately engaged as soon as I consented to entrust my success to them. In declining all these propositions I believe I was no less eloquent than he in making them; that I completely failed to convince him was due to the fact that I did not seem to understand him when he insisted that a ballet in the first act counted for nothing, because those habitués who went to the opera solely on account of the ballet were now accustomed to dining at around 8 p.m., and thus could get to the theater only at about 10 p.m., or right in the middle of the performance. I objected that, even if I could do nothing for these gentlemen, I might still make a proper impression on another part of the audience, but he countered with unshakable solemnity that these gentlemen were the only ones who could be counted on to produce a favorable outcome, as they alone had enough power to offset even the hostility of the press. When I turned a deaf ear to all this and offered instead to withdraw my work completely, I was assured with the utmost seriousness that, according to the command of the Emperor, which everyone had to obey, I was the person in charge; my wishes would be followed in everything and, he added, his advice had only been intended as a friendly service.

The consequences of this conversation soon became evident to me in many ways. I threw myself enthusiastically into the task of setting up the huge and unconventional dance scenes of the first act, for which I now tried to win the sympathy of the ballet-master Petitpas;[1] what I demanded was unheard-of and departed radically from traditional choreographic practices; I drew attention to the dances of the Maenads and the Bacchantes, but only astounded Petitpas by my assumption that such things, which he well comprehended, could be done by his little dancing pupils: for, as he revealed to me, by placing my ballet in the first act, I had in effect renounced the services of the main *corps de ballet*; by way of compensation he could offer me only the additional engagement of three Hungarian dancers, who up to then had been dancing in the *féeries* given at the Porte St Martin,[2] to perform as the Three Graces. While I was quite content to be spared the need to have anything to do with the prima ballerinas, I was all the more determined to have the *corps de ballet* itself execute some significant movements. I wanted the male component brought up to a respectable strength, but was told that, apart from a few skinny youths who, for fifty francs a month, hovered uselessly round the edge of the stage during the performances of the solo dancers, nothing could be done. Finally, I tried to produce my effects by means of costumes and asked for a special allocation of funds for that purpose, only to be told by my good friend Truinet, after being worn down by official evasions, that the management was determined not to spend a sou on the ballet, which it regarded as a hopeless undertaking. This was the first of the signs by which I became aware of the fact that even in the circles of the theater management itself, *Tannhäuser* was already considered a lost cause and a waste of effort.

The gloom created by this conviction henceforth weighed with increasing pressure upon all the preparations for the performance, which was now always being put off for some new reason. By the beginning of the year the rehearsals had reached the point at which scenes could be set up and orchestral practice commenced. Here everything was handled with an assiduity which initially struck me as very pleasing, until it eventually became burdensome to me, because I could see that the constant repetitions sapped everyone's powers, whereas I was now once again well enough, if I had had everything in my own hands as I would have liked, to pull the matter quickly through to a conclusion as best I could. But it was not fatigue from repeated rehearsals that made Niemann, the pillar of this production, recoil from the task he had begun with such encouraging energy. Having felt[1] it necessary to devote part of his emoluments in Paris to an effort to conciliate the chief Parisian critics, he had been apprised in the course of these attempts at bribery that the downfall of my work had been sworn, and that he could save his own skin solely by desertion and subsequent appearance in operas of Meyerbeer. From this time on he had become moody, while toward me he tried to assume a certain demonic air; he asserted that he saw a dark future, and in the course of this brought forth some quite sensible criticism, especially of the whole Opéra as an institution, its public, and the quality of its singers, of whom none were really suited for my roles, as I had conceived them. Beyond that, he inveighed against all those things I could scarcely conceal from myself as soon as I had any dealings with regard to my work with the chorusmaster, the stage director, the ballet-master, or, especially, the conductor. Above all, Niemann, who at the outset had openly insisted on maintaining the integrity of the part, now began demanding certain cuts; he met my astonishment at this by the statement that I should surely not pretend any particular passage mattered very much; we were in an undertaking, he said, that could not be over quickly enough. When he again demanded the excision of the adagio passage in the second act finale which I knew to be of crucial importance, and which he had sung in several early rehearsals to the great emotion of all those present, he responded to my protest with a letter stating he had no desire to hazard his voice and reputation on my account; if I didn't want to cut the piece, he wrote, I should find whoever else I could to sing it. I knew from that point on I was dealing with a beast driven wild by cowardice, and gave my knight, who no longer even had the courage to dally with Venus, no further attention with respect to his performance.

In these scarcely auspicious circumstances, the preparations for *Tannhäuser* shuffled toward the so-called "general" rehearsals. From all directions friends of bygone days streamed into Paris to experience the "glory" of the first performance. Among them were Otto Wesendonck, Ferdinand Praeger, the hapless Kietz, whose travel and hotel costs I had to pay to boot, and, more happily, M. Chandon from Epernay as well, together with a hamper full of Fleur du Jardin, his best brand of champagne, to be drunk to *Tannhäuser*'s success. But Bülow came too, depressed and saddened by the troubles of his own life, and hoping to gather courage and renewed vitality from the success of my work. I didn't dare tell him in so many words how badly things stood; on the contrary, noticing his discouragement, I tried to put a good face on things; yet from the first rehearsal he attended he did not fail to grasp what was going on; and I too no longer concealed anything from him. Thus we kept each other melancholy company until the performance, which continued to be postponed again and again, and it was only his unflagging efforts to be helpful to me in any way he could that prevented us from sinking into complete inertia. From whatever side we regarded our grotesque undertaking we found incongruousness and incompetence: it was impossible, for example, to assemble in all of Paris the twelve hunting horns which in Dresden had so splendidly produced the hunting calls at the end of Act One; in this matter I had to deal with a frightful fellow, the famous instrument-maker Sax,[1] who had to help me out with all kinds of surrogates in the form of Saxophones and Saxhorns. To top it off, he was officially charged with the direction of this music behind the scene. It was never possible to get it properly played.

But our deepest misery arose now from the hitherto unsuspected incompetence of the conductor M. Dietzsch. In the countless orchestral rehearsals we had held, I had become accustomed to using this man like a machine; from my customary position on the stage, right in front of his desk, I had conducted the orchestra along with him, and in doing so had above all insisted on my tempi in such a way that I had no doubt they would be firmly maintained after I was no longer in the middle of things. Yet I now found that as soon as Dietzsch was left to his own devices, everything began to waver, in that no tempo or nuance was strictly or consciously preserved. Now I recognized the worst of the dangers in which we found ourselves. Granted that the singers were not suited for their roles and thus could not be expected to produce the intended effect; granted that the ballet, the mainspring of the Opéra at that time, however sumptuously it was staged, could contribute nothing, or at best only a little, to the whole; granted that the spirit of the poem, and that certain something which touched a familiar chord in the public in even the worst performances of the work in Germany, would necessarily seem alien or at best only peculiar here: in the last resort the character of the music itself, as expressed in the orchestral score, still allowed the hope that it could make an impression even on the Parisian public, provided it was performed with sufficient conviction. It was precisely in this area, however, that I saw everything now sinking into a colorless chaos and every clear line effaced; the singers, moreover, began to grow insecure, and even the poor little girls in the ballet couldn't follow the beat for their trivial steps; and thus at last I felt I had to step in and state that the opera needed a different conductor, offering my own services in this capacity if need be. This declaration brought the confusion developing around me to a climax; even the orchestra members, who had long since recognized their incompetent conductor for what he was and openly made mock of him, took sides against me, now that it was a question of defending their official superior; the press raged at my "arrogance", and in the midst of all the uproar Napoleon III could only advise me to abandon my demand, as otherwise I would endanger my own position and the work to an extreme degree. In return, it was conceded that I could hold yet more rehearsals and repeat them until I was satisfied.

This way out of the impasse could lead to nothing but increased fatigue for me as well as for all those actively engaged in the performance, while at the same time it made no difference whatever to M. Dietzsch, whose understanding of tempo remained utterly unreliable. When I finally had to resort to the appearance of enforcing correct interpretations to help along the unavoidable performance, opposition at last broke out among the impetuous musicians of the orchestra against this "excessive" rehearsing. From this I could see the assurances of unlimited power I had received from the management had not been altogether in good faith, and gradually came to the conclusion, given the growing exhaustion on all sides, that I should, as it was termed, "withdraw my score", i.e. renounce the performance of the opera. I addressed a very specific memorandum on this subject to the Minister of State, Count Walewsky, but in response received only a laconic answer that my demand could not be granted, if only because of the substantial costs the preparations for my opera had already entailed. I refused to accept this decision and called a conference of those who were interested in my undertaking, among them Count Hatzfeld and Emil Erlanger, in order to consider all available means of preventing the performance of *Tannhäuser* at the Opéra. (By chance, Otto Wesendonck was also present at this conference; he was still in Paris awaiting the pleasure of attending the first performance; but here he must have realized how hopeless the whole thing was and delayed no longer but fled back to Zürich. The same thing had already happened with Praeger; Kietz alone held out, as he was busy trying to scrape together some money in Paris to support his further earthly existence, and despite his difficulties in doing so remained there the whole time.) The result of this conference was a renewed appeal to the Emperor Napoleon, but this met with the same gracious reply as before, in that I was merely authorized to hold more rehearsals; at last, weary to the depths of my soul, I decided to let things take their own course, being already completely without illusions as to the outcome.

Once I had given my consent to fix the date for the first performance of the opera, I was assailed from yet another quarter in the most extraordinary way. All of my friends and partisans demanded good seats for the first performance; on the other hand the management had informed me that the decision as to how to fill the house on such occasions lay in the hands of the imperial court and its satrapies. I was soon to realize clearly enough who would be getting preferential treatment; meanwhile I had to face fierce complaints from many of my friends for being unable to give them what they wanted. Some of them were extraordinarily quick to resent what they considered intentional neglect on my part: Champfleury complained by letter of a flagrant breach of friendship; Gaspérini commenced an open feud on the grounds that I had not reserved one of the best boxes for his patron and my creditor, M. Lucy, the farmer-general from Marseille. Even Blandine, who had been inspired with the most generous enthusiasm for my work by the rehearsals she had attended, could not suppress the suspicion that I was guilty of maltreating my best friends by giving her and her husband Ollivier no more than two orchestra stalls. She was deeply offended, and it took all Emil Erlanger's cool-headedness to induce her to admit the justice of my assurances that I was in an impossible situation and being betrayed on all sides. Poor Bülow alone understood everything; he suffered with me and made every conceivable effort to help me in these miseries. The reception accorded the first performance on March 13th made things clear for everybody, and my friends in particular then understood that it had never been a question of inviting them to celebrate one of my triumphs.

As to the way that evening went, I have reported it sufficiently elsewhere;[1] I was justified in flattering myself that in the end a favorable view of my opera prevailed. The real intention of my opponents had been to break up the performance completely, and this they had been unable to do. But I was dismayed the next day to hear nothing but reproaches from my friends, headed by Gaspérini, for having allowed the power of filling the house at the first performance to be wrenched from my hands; Meyerbeer, they told me, had always known better, and since his earliest days in Paris had never permitted the production of a single one of his operas without first assuring himself of the right to pack the house on opening night right down to the remotest corner. Because I had not looked after my best friends, such as M. Lucy, the failure we had experienced, Gaspérini asserted, could be booked to my account. I had to spend the whole day writing letters and trying to conciliate all sorts of people in these and similar matters. Above all, I was besieged with advice as to how I might recover the lost ground at the next performances; as the management placed only a very limited number of free seats at my disposal, funds had to be found to purchase tickets. I shrank from approaching Emil Erlanger or anyone else in this painful matter, to which my friends devoted themselves with holy zeal; Giacomelli had found out that a business friend of Wesendonck by the name of Aufmordt had offered to help out to the extent of five hundred francs. I now allowed these custodians of my welfare to proceed as they wished, curious to see what assistance I would derive from the adoption at this stage of the measures I had neglected earlier.

The second performance took place on March 18th, and the first act went very well indeed; the overture was applauded tumultuously and without opposition, and Mme Tedesco, whose heart had been finally won for the part of Venus by a gold-powdered wig she was given to wear, called up to me in the director's box, after the so-called "septuor" of the first-act finale had also been applauded in a most vigorous way, that everything was now in order and we had carried the day. But when shrill whistles were suddenly heard in the middle of the second act, M. Royer turned to me with an air of complete resignation and said: "Ce sont les Jockeys; nous sommes perdus." Apparently, there had been extensive negotiations at the behest of the Emperor with these gentlemen of the Jockey Club, who exercised final control within the theater, as to the fate of my opera; they had been requested to allow at least three performances to take place, after which, it was promised them, the opera would be cut sufficiently to permit it to function as a curtain-raiser for an ensuing ballet. But the gentlemen had not accepted this proposal: in the first place my attitude during the stormily contested first performance had not struck them as that of a person who would be willing to give his consent to such a procedure; and in the second place, it was to be feared that, if this opera were accorded two undisturbed performances, it might acquire so many admirers that it would be served up to the ballet fans thirty times running. This they were determined to block in good time. That they meant business was immediately recognized by the worthy M. Royer; and from that moment on he abandoned all resistance, in spite of the support of the Emperor and his consort, who stoically kept their seats throughout the uproar caused by their own courtiers.

These scenes had a shattering effect on my friends; Bülow embraced Minna after the performance, sobbing; she herself had not been spared insults from her neighbors, after she had been recognized as my wife; our faithful servant girl, the Swabian Therese, had been jeered at by one of these raging hooligans, but as she noticed that he understood German, she had quieted him for a time with a resounding "Schweinhund"; Kietz had been struck dumb, and Chandon's Fleur du Jardin reposed unopened in the storeroom.

When I learned that in spite of all this a third performance had nevertheless been scheduled, I was confronted by the alternative of again attempting to withdraw my score, or else demanding that my opera be given on a Sunday; the latter course would mean a performance outside the subscription scheme and I assumed that would ensure its not being regarded as a provocation by the habitués, who were accustomed to leave their boxes available at such performances to such of the public as wished to purchase tickets. My proposed strategem seemed to please both the management and the Tuileries; it was adopted, only my request that this be labeled the third and last performance was denied. Minna and I stayed away from it. It was just as repugnant to me to see my wife insulted as to see the singers abused. As far as the singers were concerned, I learned that Niemann had found a way to protect himself in need; when he found himself subjected to persistent insults by the audience, he simply shrugged his shoulders and as an excuse gestured toward the proscenium box, in which I was supposed to be sitting. I therefore reserved my sincere sorrow for Morelli and Mlle Sax, who had proved unshakably devoted to me. After the first performance, I had met Mlle Sax in the corridor on her way home and had jokingly made fun of her for being whistled off the stage; with proud dignity she replied: "Je le supporterai cent fois comme aujourd'hui. Ah, les misérables!" Morelli was caught in a curious conflict with himself when he had to sustain the onslaught of the hooligans. I had explained to him down to the minutest detail how he should act his part from the time Elisabeth disappears in the third act to the beginning of his song to the evening star; he was on no account to quit his seat on the rock, from which, half turned to the public, he was to address his farewell to her. It had been difficult for him to accept these instructions, as he asserted it was against all traditions in opera that a singer should not deliver such an important passage straight into the audience from the very front of the stage. When in the course of the actual performance he picked up his harp to commence the song, a voice called out from the audience: "Ah! il prend encore sa harpe", whereupon the public dissolved in howls of laughter. This was followed by a renewal of sustained whistling, so that Morelli at last boldly decided to put down his harp and step forward to the proscenium in the usual way. He then resolutely sang his evening fantasy without accompaniment (for Dietzsch found his place only at the tenth bar), during which everyone fell silent, finally listening breathlessly and at the end showering the singer with applause.

As the singers showed the courage to face new onslaughts, I could not object, but at the same time I could not endure being in the position of a passive spectator suffering such indignities helplessly. For this reason, since the outcome of the third performance was also highly doutbful, I remained, as aforementioned, at home. Between the acts messengers came to us with reports: Truinet had already come round to my point of view by the end of the first act, recommending that the score be withdrawn at all costs; it had turned out that the members of the Jockey Club had not, as was their usual habit, remained away from the Sunday performance, but on the contrary had made a point of being there in order not to let a single scene go by uncontested. I was told that during the first act alone there had been two fights lasting fifteen minutes each and causing the performance to come to a standstill. By far the greater part of the public stubbornly took my part against the juvenile conduct of the hooligans, though without necessarily intending their action to express a judgment of the opera, but they were at a huge disadvantage: when everybody on my side was utterly exhausted by shouting and clapping and calling for order and it appeared as if peace had been restored once more, the Jockeys could effortlessly again begin blowing their hunting whistles and flageolets, so that they won every round. In the interval between acts one of these gentlemen entered the box of a noble lady, who, seething with fury, introduced him to one of her friends with the words: "C'est un des ces misérables, mon cousin"; the fellow was utterly unabashed and replied: "What do you want me to do? I am actually beginning to like the music; but you will understand one has to keep one's word. Permit me to get back to work!" With these words he withdrew. The following day I found the amiable Saxon Ambassador Herr von Seebach completely hoarse; he and all his friends had utterly lost their voices in the nocturnal uproar. Princess Metternich had remained at home; during the first two performances she had been compelled to bear the openly expressed contumely of our opponents. She described the fury unleashed by these events by mentioning some of her best friends, with whom she had engaged in such a virulent argument that she had said: "You can have your French freedom! In Vienna, where there is some real nobility, it would be unthinkable for a Prince Liechtenstein or Schwarzenberg to whistle from his box during *Fidelio* and demand a ballet." I think she also put the same case to the Emperor and forced him to consider whether police intervention might be advisable to set some limit on the activities of these people, most of whom unfortunately belonged to the imperial court itself. There had been talk of this, and my friends had really believed that victory was assured when they saw the corridors of the Opéra strongly manned by police for the third performance; but it turned out later that these measures had been undertaken for the protection of the Jockeys themselves, for it was feared they might be attacked by the public in punishment for their insolence. Apparently this performance, which at any rate was again carried through to the end, was accompanied from start to finish by an unending tumult. After the second act the wife of the Hungarian revolutionary minister, von Szemere,[1] joined us, completely distraught and with the statement that what was going on in the theater was unbearable. Nobody seemed able to tell me anything coherent about the course of the third act; it appears to have resembled a continuing battle clouded by the smoke of gunpowder.

I summoned my friend Truinet for the next morning, and together we drafted a note to the management, in which I stated that, for the protection of the singers, whom I could no longer permit to be abused on my behalf by a section of the public, and since the imperial authorities could not enforce any safeguards to prevent such abuse, I withdrew my score and, as its author, forbade any further performance of it. Amazingly enough, this did not constitute an act of empty bravado on my part; for a fourth and fifth performance had already been scheduled, and the management objected that it too had obligations toward the public, which was clamoring to attend these performances. I arranged through Truinet for my letter to be published the next day in the *Journal des Débats*, and then after some additional delay there followed an announcement from the management agreeing to the withdrawal of my work.

With this conclusion, a lawsuit in which Ollivier acted for me against that Herr Lindau also came to an end. He had sued for a share in the author's rights of the text, in which he claimed to have been a collaborator on an equal footing with the other two. His lawyer, Maître Marie, based his plea on the principle, attributed to me, that I was not concerned with melody but merely with the precise declamation of the words of the text, which obviously neither Roche nor Truinet could have ensured, given the fact that neither knew German. Ollivier's plaidoyer on my behalf on this point was so fervent that he seemed on the point of trying to prove the purely musical essence of my melody by singing the song to the evening star. Carried away by this, the judges rejected the claim of my opponent, but requested me to pay him a token sum, for he appeared to have had some part in the work from the beginning. I could not, however, have paid this out of the income from the Paris performances of *Tannhäuser*, as Truinet and I had agreed, upon withdrawal of the opera, to transmit all the proceeds deriving from my rights of authorship, both for libretto and music, to poor Roche, to whom the failure of my work meant the abandonment of his sole hope for improvement of his sad situation.

Various other connections I had formed were severed immediately after this outcome to things. During the past months I had also been busying myself with a "cercle artistique": this club had been established in aristocratic circles, apparently with the strong support of the German legations, with the purpose of promoting good performances of good music in other venues than theaters, and stimulating interest in this cause in good social circles. Unfortunately, in the brochure the "cercle" published setting forth its goals, there was a comparison of its efforts on behalf of good music with those of the Jockey Club in the breeding of good horses. Be that as it may, the object was to enlist everybody who had a name in music, and thus I could not really avoid becoming a member at yearly dues of two hundred francs. For this, I was elected, together with M. Gounod and several other Paris notables, to an artistic committee of which Auber was made President. The society often held its meetings at the house of a certain Count d'Osmond, a lively young man who had lost an arm in a duel and was also an amateur musician. In this way I also got to know a young Prince Polignac,[1] who interested me principally on account of his brother, to whom the world was indebted for a complete translation of *Faust*. I had to lunch with him one morning, and here he revealed himself as a musical fantast: he insisted on trying to convince me of the correctness of his interpretation of Beethoven's Symphony in A major, the final movement of which he contended described a shipwreck, phase by phase. Our committee meetings, which were at first concerned with arrangements and preparations for a big concert of classical music, for which, however, I too was expected to write something, were enlivened only by the pedantic zeal of Gounod, who performed his secretarial duties with tireless and luxuriant garrulity, while Auber interrupted rather than governed the proceedings, never contributing anything but little witticisms, which were not always very delicate and which were plainly intended to hasten the discussion to a close. I actually received an invitation to attend another of these meetings even after the decisive failure of *Tannhäuser*, but I never went again and submitted my resignation to the President of the society on the grounds that I would probably be returning to Germany very shortly.

It was only with Gounod that I continued on friendly terms. I had heard he had been a strong advocate for me in society; he is supposed to have exclaimed: "Que Dieu me donne une pareille chûte!" As a reward for this I gave him a copy of the score of *Tristan und Isolde*, being all the more gratified by his conduct because no considerations of friendship had ever been able to induce me to hear his *Faust*.[2]

I now became aware of many enthusiastic partisans of my cause; I was especially celebrated in the columns of those smaller journals which Meyerbeer had as yet neglected, and many good phrases were coined. I read somewhere that my *Tannhäuser* was "la symphonie chantée". Baudelaire distinguished himself by an extremely witty and apt brochure on the same subject; and finally even Jules Janin surprised me by an article in the *Journal des Débats*, in which he gave an indignant account of these events in his typically discursive manner. Parodies of *Tannhäuser* were given in the theaters for the delectation of the public, and Musard[1] thought he could find no better way to attract larger audiences to his concerts than by daily placards announcing the overture to *Tannhäuser* in enormous lettering. Pasdeloup[2] also frequently gave pieces by me to demonstrate his own view. To top it off, the wife of the Austrian Military Plenipotentiary, Countess Löwenthal, gave a huge matinée, at which Mme Viardot had to sing various passages from *Tannhäuser*, for which she received five hundred francs. Curiously enough, people seemed to link my fate with that of a certain M. de la Vaquerie,[3] who had also suffered defeat in a similarly scandalous way with a drama entitled *Les funérailles de l'honneur*. His friends gave a banquet for him to which I was also invited; he and I were enthusiastically fêted, there were fiery speeches about the "encanaillement" of the public and political matters were touched upon, in all likelihood because my fellow guest of honor was a relative of Victor Hugo. Unfortunately my special devotees had procured a pianino, on which I was then compelled, virtually by force, to play some of the more popular pieces from *Tannhäuser*, with the result that the occasion was transformed into a tribute to me alone.

But a much more important result of the bizarre popularity I was widely recognized to possess was the planning of far greater undertakings. The director of the Théâtre Lyrique began looking everywhere for a tenor suitable for Tannhäuser, and it was only his inability to find such a man that made him renounce his intention to produce my opera again at once. M. de Beaumont, Director of the Opéra Comique, was on the verge of bankruptcy and hoped to save himself with *Tannhäuser*, in which intention he bombarded me with the most urgent proposals. Admittedly he was hoping at the same time to obtain the intervention of Princess Metternich on his behalf with the Emperor, who he counted on to help him out of his troubles. He coldly rebuked me when I failed to be carried away by his prognostications of glory, to which indeed I was little inclined to listen. But I was nonetheless not uninterested to learn that Roger, who was now with the Opéra Comique, had shortly thereafter interspersed an excerpt from the last act of *Tannhäuser* in a concert given in his benefit, whereby he had called down upon his head the fury of the press while gaining a good reception from the public. The projects multiplied. A certain M. de Chabrol, whose pen name was Lorbac, now announced himself to me on behalf of a society headed by a tremendously rich man for the purpose of founding a "Théâtre Wagner". I wouldn't hear of this, except on the condition that a reputable and experienced man could be found to be its director. M. Perrin was selected as the right man. He had been living for years in the firm expectation of being appointed to head the Opéra, and thought he ought not to compromise himself in this way. As a matter of fact, he attributed the failure of *Tannhäuser* solely to the incompetence of M. Royer, whose business it should have been to win over the press: to prove that, if he took the matter in hand, events would take a different course and *Tannhäuser* would succeed, represented a considerable temptation for him to participate; yet, being extremely cool and circumspect, he thought he could detect substantial weaknesses in the propositions of M. Lorbac; as the latter tried to negotiate with him about certain provisions, Perrin immediately thought he recognized an unsavory speculation and declared that, if he were to found a Wagner-Theater, he would find the necessary funds in his own way. To this end he actually began weighing the possibility of acquiring a big coffee-house called "Alcazar", and on another occasion the "Bazar de la Bonne Nouvelle", for such a theater. Now it even looked as though the right capitalists might be found to participate in his undertaking; M. Erlanger thought he could definitely induce ten bankers to subscribe for fifty thousand francs worth of shares in the venture, producing a fund of five hundred thousand francs which could then be turned over to M. Perrin to run. But he soon lost courage when he realized the gentlemen he was dealing with were only interested in using their money for a theater for their own personal amusement, and not for the serious purpose of establishing my works in Paris.

After this depressing experience M. Erlanger withdrew from further participation in my fate. As a businessman, he regarded the contract he had made with me as a financial risk that had simply not turned out well. Thus the job of bringing order to my financial affairs seemed likely to devolve upon other friends, and for this purpose the German embassies, who had been told to do so by Count Hatzfeld, approached me with great delicacy to find out what my needs might be. My own view of the situation was simply that, following the emperor's command for a performance of my opera, I had wasted a lot of time on an undertaking, the fruitless outcome of which was not my fault. With some justice my friends pointed out to me that I had been negligent in not insisting on certain compensatory stipulations at the outset, a demand which the practical mind of a Frenchman would have recognized as reasonable and obvious. As a matter of fact, I had not made conditions requiring payment for my time and trouble, and thus remained dependent solely on the author's rights which would have come to me in the event of a success. As I found it impossible to turn to the management of the Opéra or to the Emperor to seek personal redress for my own neglect, I was content to let Princess Metternich intercede on my behalf. Count Pourtalès had just gone to Berlin for a time to try to persuade the Prince Regent of Prussia to order a performance of *Tannhäuser* for my benefit. Unfortunately the Regent had not been able to carry through his command against the opposition of the intendant of his theater, Herr von Hülsen, who was thoroughly hostile to me. As I foresaw a long period of complete helplessness, I thus necessarily had to leave it to my noble patroness to represent my claims for compensation, and departed on April 15th (for all these postludes had taken place within the brief span of a month after the *Tannhäuser* performances) to make a short trip to Germany, where I hoped to win some solid ground under my feet for the future.

The only person who had really understood my true situation, in the midst of all the uproar in Paris, had preceded me on this same path: Bülow had now sent me news from Karlsruhe that the grand-ducal family was favorably disposed toward me, and I promptly formed the plan of getting the people there to take the production of my *Tristan* seriously in hand, after having so lamentably delayed it in the past. Accordingly I arrived in Karlsruhe,[1] and if anything was calculated to strengthen me in my resolve to carry out my hastily conceived plan, it was the uncommonly frank reception I received from the Grand Duke of Baden. This exalted gentleman seemed to feel a hearty desire to awaken my confidence in him; in an extremely intimate conversation, in which his young wife also participated, the Grand Duke spared no pains to let me know that his interest in me was not rooted in my operas, which he did not presume to judge, but rather in the man who had been obliged to suffer greatly for his independent and patriotic views. As I naturally could not attach much importance to the political significance of my past career, he interpreted this as distrustful reticence on my part, and he tried to encourage me by the assurance that, if severe mistakes and even great misdeeds had occurred in this area, these had principally affected the people who had stayed in Germany and, remaining miserable, had certainly atoned by their inner sufferings as well; by contrast, it was now the obligation of the guilty to redress the wrongs they had done to those driven into exile at the time. He willingly placed his theater at my disposal and issued the necessary commands to its director. This was my old "friend" Eduard Devrient, whose painful embarrassment upon my arrival amply justified all that Bülow had said about the utter worthlessness of those sentiments of sincere sympathy he had previously affected. But in the cheerful frame of mind produced by the Grand Duke's gracious reception, I was soon able to bring Devrient around, at least apparently, to where I wanted him. He had to begin serious discussion with me on the intended performance of *Tristan*, and as it did not occur to him to deny that, particularly after the departure of Schnorr to Dresden, he didn't have the requisite singers for my work, he referred me to Vienna; in doing so he did not fail to express his amazement that I did not want to bring all my operas to performance there, where all the resources were available. It cost me considerable effort to explain to him why I preferred some exceptional performances of my work in Karlsruhe to its possible inclusion in the repertory of the Vienna Opera House. I thus got approval for my proposal to seek in Vienna for the other singers who would be needed for this "model performance" in Karlsruhe, in addition to Schnorr, who would in any case be invited to Karlsruhe to take part in it.

Thus my sights were set on Vienna and first I had to return to Paris to settle my affairs there in such a way as to arm me for the execution of my latest project. Returning there after an absence of only six days, I unfortunately had to occupy myself exclusively with finding the necessary funds for my needs. Under these circumstances some of the sympathetic approaches and assurances I was accorded with increased warmth by such people as Frau von Seebach were as disquieting as they were unhelpful. In the meantime the operations undertaken by Princess Metternich to secure me some compensation on a larger scale ran their mysterious slow course, and it was a merchant named Stürmer, whom I had previously known in Zürich, and who had shown me a cordial concern the whole time in Paris, through whose assistance I was now enabled to arrange my household affairs and then set off for Vienna. Liszt had been expected in Paris for some time, and during the fateful period I had been through I had often fervently longed for his presence, for it seemed obvious that, with the esteem in which he was now held in French high society, he could have been extremely helpful in unravelling the tangled situation. But in response to my repeated inquiries concerning his delayed arrival, all I got was a secretive epistolary shrug of the shoulders. It seemed ironic that, just as I had arranged everything for my journey to Vienna, I got word that Liszt would be arriving in Paris within a few days. As I had no choice other than to do my best to improve my situation, which demanded that I at once begin picking up new threads in my plan for life, I left Paris in the middle of May without awaiting the arrival of my old friend.

I stopped first of all at Karlsruhe for another interview with the Grand Duke, was accorded the same friendly reception, and got permission to engage in Vienna those singers I might need for a model performance of *Tristan* at the theater in Karlsruhe. Armed with this command, I went on to Vienna, where I stayed at the Archduke Karl and awaited the fulfillment of a promise Kapellmeister Esser had made by letter to put on a few performances of my operas for me. It was here I first heard my *Lohengrin* performed on the stage. Although the opera had already been given very frequently, the whole ensemble got together for the complete rehearsal I had requested. The orchestra immediately played the prelude with such beauty and warmth, and the voices of the singers and their other good qualities were displayed to such good advantage in the performance of a work they already knew well that, overcome by these impressions, I lost all inclination to criticize any aspect of the production. People seemed to notice how deeply moved I was, and to Dr Hanslick this no doubt appeared the proper moment to have himself amicably introduced to me, while I was sitting on the stage and listening; I greeted him shortly as if he were entirely unknown to me, whereupon the tenor Ander[1] introduced him to me again with the comment that this was my old acquaintance Dr Hanslick; I replied laconically that I remembered Dr Hanslick very well, and turned back to the rehearsal. It seems my Viennese friends now had the same experience as previously my London acquaintances, when they had tried to direct my attention to the most fearsome critic and found me disinclined to any such gesture. This fellow, who, then still a young student, had attended one of the first performances of *Tannhäuser* in Dresden and had written about the work with glowing enthusiasm, had since developed into one of the most vicious opponents of my work, as had been amply demonstrated on the occasion of productions of my operas in Vienna. Those members of the opera company well disposed toward me seemed henceforth to have no greater concern than to effect a reconciliation between me and this critic; as they did not succeed, those who ascribed to the enmity thus aroused the ensuing failure of every undertaking in which I counted on Viennese support may not have been far wrong.

But for the present it seemed as if the flood of enthusiasm for me would sweep away all unpleasantness. The performance of *Lohengrin* I attended turned into one of those unending and fervent ovations such as I have only experienced at the hands of the Viennese public. They wanted to put on my two earlier operas in the same way; but I felt a certain shyness about a repetition of what I had experienced on that night; as I had also been informed of serious weaknesses in the production of *Tannhäuser*, I accepted only a further performance of the more modest *Der fliegende Holländer*, mainly because I was anxious to hear the singer Beck,[1] who excelled in this opera. Once again the public indulged in the same expressions of delight, and thus, borne on the crest of this general favor, I was able to go about the real business I had in mind. The academic young of Vienna had wanted to do me the honor of a torchlight procession, but I declined this, thereby gaining Esser's wholehearted approval, in particular. Together with the highest authorities at the Opera, he began considering how these triumphs could be exploited. I presented myself to Count Lanskoronsky,[2] Comptroller of the Imperial Court, who had been described to me as a strange man who knew absolutely nothing about art and its requirements. When I submitted my appeal that he should give the principal singers at his opera house, namely Frau Dustmann (formerly Luise Meyer), Herr Beck, as well as possibly Herr Ander, leave at some future time to participate in the performance of *Tristan* I was planning for Karlsruhe, the old gentleman replied dryly that this would not be possible. He thought it far more reasonable, given the fact that I was satisfied with his ensemble, to give my new work in Vienna. I promptly lost the courage necessary to oppose this proposition.

As I was descending the steps of the Hofburg meditating about this new turn of events, I was met at the gate by a stately gentleman of unusually sympathetic countenance, who offered to conduct me in his carriage to my hotel. This was Joseph Standhartner, a famous society doctor and an earnest devotee of music, destined henceforth to be a staunch friend for life. By this time Karl Tausig had also found his way to me, as he had thrown himself upon Vienna with the purpose of conquering this terrain for Liszt's compositions, having opened his campaign the previous winter with a series of orchestral concerts arranged and conducted by himself. He also brought me Peter Cornelius, who had also been drawn to Vienna and whom I had met previously only on that occasion in Basel in 1853. Both were revelling at the time in Bülow's recently published piano arrangement of *Tristan*. In my hotel, to which Tausig had delivered a Bösendorfer grand piano, the musical temperature soon ran high: they would have been glad to start the rehearsals for *Tristan* at once: at any rate, I was urged so strongly to accept the proposal that my work be performed here that I finally left Vienna only after promising to return in a few months to begin the preliminary study.

I was somewhat embarrassed by the need to tell the Grand Duke of Baden I had changed my mind; so I readily yielded to an impulse to go to Karslruhe only by an oddly roundabout route. As my birthday fell just at the time of this return trip, I resolved to celebrate it in Zürich. I went without delay via Munich to Winterthur, hoping to find my good friend Sulzer there; unfortunately he was away, and I only saw his wife, who, together with their little son, an attractive and lively boy, made a touching impression on me. I knew I would be able to locate Sulzer in Zürich the following day, May 22nd, and spent the not insignificant remainder of the day chained in a tiny hotel room by my travel reading, Goethe's *Wanderjahre*, experiencing for the first time complete understanding of this strange work. In particular, I was captivated by the poet's description of the way the journeymen set out in which a kind of wild lyricism predominates, and this brought me close to the spirit of the poet in this work as well. The next morning I got to Zürich at early dawn. It was a gloriously clear morning and I decided to take a circuitous path through the Sihltal I knew so well up to the estate of the Wesendoncks. My arrival there was completely unannounced; I inquired about the habits of the house and learned that Wesendonck usually came down to the dining room to take breakfast alone at this time. I sat down in a corner and awaited this big, good-natured fellow, until at length he stepped silently into the room to get his coffee and burst into expressions of hearty astonishment at finding me there. The day went very sociably; Sulzer, Semper, Herwegh, and also Gottfried Keller were summoned, and I had the satisfaction of having produced a well-contrived surprise in exceptional circumstances, as my recent doings had been the daily topic of animated discussion among these friends.

The next day I hurried on to Karlsruhe, where my news was received by the Grand Duke with amicable acquiescence. I could rightly tell him that my request for leave of absence for the singers had been rejected and the projected performance in Karlsruhe thereby rendered impossible. Eduard Devrient accepted this turn of events not only without sorrow but with undisguised satisfaction, and he wished me a brilliant future in Vienna. Here Tausig overtook me, having already decided in Vienna to go to Paris in order to meet Liszt there, and together we continued the journey via Strassburg.

When I reached Paris I found my household already close to disbandment. My only anxiety in this regard was to procure the means to get away from the city and to make some immediate arrangements for what appeared an entirely blank future. Meanwhile, however, Minna still had the opportunity to display her talents as a housekeeper. Liszt was already swept up in his usual social routine, and even his daughter Blandine could only manage to get a word with him in the carriage in which he drove from visit to visit. Out of the goodness of his heart however, he found time to invite himself once to my house for a beefsteak party; in fact he even managed to devote a whole evening to me, volunteering to take care of a few obligations on my behalf. In the presence of some of the friends who had shared the bad times of the past with us, he also played the piano that evening; thus it happened that poor Tausig, who in a lonely hour on the previous day had played Liszt's fantasia on the name BACH in a way that had truly astonished me, now literally shriveled before Liszt when he happened to play the same piece with an almost casual air, caught in the absolutely crushing feeling of helplessness when confronted by this colossus, who rose so far above the merely astonishing. Another day we met for breakfast at the home of Gounod, where we had an uncommonly dull time enlivened solely by the almost desperate humor of poor Baudelaire. This man, "criblé de dettes" as he told me, was compelled daily to think up the most extravagant measures to obtain a bare subsistence. He kept approaching me with the wildest schemes to exploit my notorious fiasco. While quite incapable of entering into any of these, I was now delighted to see this brilliant person take refuge under the eagle-wing of Liszt in his ascendancy. Liszt introduced him in all those places where there was some hope of meeting success and favor; whether this helped him in any way I never knew. I learned only that he died not long afterward[1] and, I believe, not in any excess of good fortune. Apart from this festive morning I met Liszt once again at a dinner at the Austrian Embassy, an occasion which my friend used quite prettily to demonstrate his sympathy for me by playing some passages from *Lohengrin* in the presence of Princess Metternich. He was also summoned to a dinner at the Tuileries, to which, however, it was not thought necessary to invite me to accompany him; he thereafter reported to me a most decorous conversation with the Emperor Napoleon concerning the *Tannhäuser* affair in Paris, the upshot of which seems to have been that my work was simply out of place at the Opéra. Whether Liszt ever discussed these matters with Lamartine I do not know; but I do know that he was several times detained by this older friend from meetings I had requested with him. Tausig, who at the outset had spent most of his time with me, soon lapsed back into his natural dependence on his master, so that he finally disappeared from my horizon entirely, he and Liszt departing for Brussels to visit Mme Street.

I was now longing to get away from Paris. Fortunately I was able to get rid of my house in the Rue d'Aumale by successfully subletting it, a transaction facilitated by a gift of one hundred francs to the janitor: now it was merely a question of waiting to hear from my benefactors. As I could not press them, my situation prolonged itself in a way that caused me the greatest difficulties, although it did not lack alleviation in the form of droll incidents. For example, I had gained the rather strange partisanship of an old niece of Meyerbeer named Fräulein Eberty; she had been through the *Tannhäuser* brouhaha in almost raging devotion to my cause and now seemed very concerned to find a way to make my unhappy situation more cheerful: to this end she arranged a really charming dinner in the best spring weather in a first-class restaurant in the Bois de Boulogne for us and Kietz, who was still sticking to us. In addition, the Flaxland family, with whom I had gotten into a quarrel of sorts over the publication of *Tannhäuser*, now exerted themselves in every possible way to show me kindness, although I could have wished there had been no reason for them to do so.

At any rate, it remained a settled matter that we had to leave Paris very soon. Minna proposed to continue her treatment of the previous year at Bad Soden, after which she would visit her old friends in Dresden, while I was biding my time until returning to Vienna to begin preparations for my *Tristan*. We decided to leave all our household goods well packed in the hands of a Paris forwarding agent. While thus preoccupied with thoughts of our departure, the postponement of which was causing so much awkwardness, we also considered how best to transport our little dog Fips by railroad. One day, June 22nd, my wife returned to the house with the dog which had suffered some mortal harm while they were out, for which there was no explanation; from Minna's account, the only thing we could think of was that the dog had swallowed some virulent poison spread on the street; his condition was pitiable; without showing the slightest sign of external injury, he was breathing in such a convulsive manner that we concluded he must have damaged his lungs; in his first frantic pangs he had bitten Minna severely in the mouth, so that I quickly summoned a doctor, who then dispelled our fears that the injury had been caused by a rabid dog. But there was nothing we could do for the poor animal, who lay silently curled up while his breath grew steadily shorter and more convulsive. Toward eleven o'clock in the evening he seemed to have fallen asleep under Minna's bed, but when I pulled him out he was dead. The effect of this melancholy event on Minna and myself found no verbal expression. In our childless life together the presence of domestic pets had taken on great significance; the sudden death of this lively and lovable animal constituted a final breach in a union that had long ago become impossible. For the moment my most urgent worry was to rescue the body from the usual fate accorded dead dogs in Paris, that of being pitched out into the street and gathered up in the morning by the garbage collector. My friend Stürmer had a small garden nearby, behind his house in the Rue de la Tour des Dames, where I wanted to bury Fips the next day; but it cost me an inordinate expenditure of persuasion to convince the absent owner's housekeeper to give me permission to do so. But finally, with the help of the janitor, I dug as deep a grave as possible among the garden bushes to receive the body of our poor little dog. When this melancholy job was completed, I smoothed over the grave-site very carefully and tried to make the spot as indistinguishable as possible; for I suspected that Herr Stürmer might object to harboring the animal's body and have it carted away, a regrettable outcome I thereby strove to prevent.

At last Count Hatzfeld announced to me in the kindliest possible manner that some friends of my art, who wished to remain unidentified, were united in sympathy for my unmerited troubles and had resolved to offer the necessary means to relieve me of these onerous difficulties. I considered it fitting to express my thanks for this happy resolution solely to my patroness Princess Metternich, and now set about making final arrangements for the discontinuation of my Paris establishment. My first care, as soon as all the tedious arrangements in this regard had been made, was to see that Minna departed for Germany at once to continue her treatment. By contrast, I saw no more urgent objective there for myself than a visit to Liszt in Weimar, where a German musicians' congress was to be held that August with farewell performances of Liszt's works. Apart from this, Flaxland, who had summoned up the courage to publish my other operas in French, wanted to detain me in Paris until I had completed the translation of *Der fliegende Holländer* in collaboration with Truinet. For this I required a few more weeks, which I could not possibly spend in our house, now entirely stripped of furniture. Upon hearing of this, Count Pourtalès invited me to take residence in the Prussian Embassy for this period, a remarkable and indeed, in my life, unprecedented act of kindness, which I accepted with gratitude and, be it said, some trepidation. On July 12th I saw Minna off to Bad Soden and that same day went to reside at the embassy, where I was given a cozy room looking out upon a garden and with a view of the Tuileries in the distance. Two black swans were swimming in the little garden pool, and I was drawn to them in a dream-like manner. When young Hatzfeld first looked me up in my room to inquire on behalf of my benefactors as to my needs, I was overwhelmed for the first time in many years by a strong and deep sense of well-being arising from my complete lack of any possessions and detachment from all those things which are normally considered necessary for a permanent way of life.

I asked permission to have my Erard, which I had not suffered to be packed away with the rest of my furniture, brought to the embassy, where a handsome room was set aside for it on the *piano nobile*. Here I worked during the mornings on the translation of *Der fliegende Holländer* and composed two musical album pieces, one of which, later published, was dedicated to Princess Metternich and contained a pleasant theme that had been in my mind for some time. A similar one for Frau Pourtalès has been lost. My association with the family of my host not only had a soothing influence but also a truly gratifying effect on me; we took our meals together every day, and frequently the family's midday meal developed into a diplomatic dinner party. I became acquainted with the former Prussian minister Bethmann-Hollweg,[1] the father of Countess Pourtalès, with whom I was able to discuss in detail my conception of the relationship of art to the state. When I succeeded in making my views clear to the minister, the immediate, desperate response was that no such understanding could ever be reached with the head of state, as to him art belonged exclusively in the realm of entertainment. Apart from Count Hatzfeld, the two other attachés, a Prince Reuss and Count Dönhoff, often took part on these domestic occasions. The former was apparently the political intriguer of the legation and was particularly commended to me on account of the intense and skillful efforts he had made on my behalf at the imperial court. By contrast, the latter impressed me simply by his countenance and his straightforward friendliness. Here, too, I was brought into contact once more with Prince and Princess Metternich. I could not help noticing that a certain reserve had crept into our relations; by the princess's fierce partisanship in the *Tannhäuser* fiasco she had brought upon herself not only the coarsest treatment at the hands of the press, but also the most malign and unchivalrous aspersions of so-called high society: her husband seemed to have taken it all very well, yet without doubt he had also gone through some bad moments. I couldn't quite figure out what compensation the Princess could have found in my art for all she had been obliged to endure; most people considered her only a very flighty woman, adept at keeping herself in the public eye. It had never been possible for me in my previous association with her to find any mutual ground: all I could see in her was a pert self-confidence, a great vitality springing from this, and a sharp and practised eye in judging how things really stood. I never entirely fathomed what she meant when she said to me one day rather shamefacedly that she particularly liked to hear "fugues". As for the Prince himself, a rather cold and dry character, he seemed drawn to me by his own inclination to learn how to compose; yet he was smart enough never to bother me with this, while I found occasion to appreciate his balanced judgement in political matters, a quality which he seemingly owed more to the instinct imbued by his birth and position rather than to any development of natural talents. After I had spent many pleasant evenings in intimate association with my cordial hosts and even found myself impelled to try to preach Schopenhauer to them, we had one big soirée which led to utterly intoxicating excitement. Before a circle of devoted friends, some pieces from several different works of mine were played in a vivid way; Saint-Saëns took over at the piano, and I had the strange experience of hearing the Neapolitan Princess Campo-Reale sing Isolde's closing scene to that excellent musician's accompaniment with lovely German enunciation and a surprising accuracy of intonation.

While I thus passed three weeks pleasantly resting up, Count Pourtalès procured for me a splendid Prussian ministerial passport for my forthcoming trip to Germany, his attempt to get me a Saxon passport having foundered on the pusillanimity of Herr von Seebach. Before I left Paris this time, thinking it would be for ever, I felt impelled to bid an intimate farewell to the few French friends who had stood by me loyally in all the vicissitudes I had suffered. I got together with Gaspérini, Champfleury, and Truinet in a café in the Rue Lafitte; we talked until far into the night, and when I was about to get started on my way back to the Faubourg St Germain, Champfleury, who lived on the heights of Montmartre, announced his insistence on taking me home, on the grounds that we could not know whether we would ever see one another again. I enjoyed the exquisite effect of the bright moonlight on the now deserted streets of Paris; only the huge business firms, particularly those dominating the Rue Richelieu, seemed to turn night into day by the hectic activities going on right up to the top floors of the buildings. Champfleury smoked his little pipe and conversed to me about the prospects for French politics: his father, he said, was an old

Bonapartist of the first water; yet recently, after reading the papers day after day, he had been obliged to exclaim: "Pourtant, avant de mourir je voudrais voir autre chose." We parted very affectionately at the door of the embassy.

There was an equally friendly farewell from another young French friend whom I have not yet mentioned. This was Gustave Doré, who had been sent to me by Ollivier at the outset of my appearance in Paris; he had proposed to make a fantastic sketch of me in the act of conducting. But for some unknown reason this was not done, most probably because I didn't show any great enthusiasm for the idea. Yet Doré remained a staunch friend, and now he was one of those few people who made a point of evidencing their friendship for me in their intense indignation at the outrage perpetrated against me. This extraordinarily productive artist also proposed to include the *Nibelungen* among his many subjects for illustration; I therefore wanted him to become acquainted with my conception of this cycle of myths, but this was very difficult; as he assured me he had a friend well versed in the German language and its literature, I permitted myself to present him a copy of the vocal score of *Rheingold* which had recently been published, as its text would give him the clearest idea of how I had shaped the material. By this means I simultaneously returned the compliment of his having presented me a copy of his illustrations for Dante, which had also just appeared.

Replete with pleasant and agreeable impressions, which constituted the only gain of any real worth extracted from my arduous Paris undertaking, I left the beneficent refuge provided by my Prussian friends during the first week in August, proceeding first via Cologne to Bad Soden. Here I found Minna in the company of the aforementioned Mathilde Schiffner, who seemed to have become indispensable to her as an easy person to tyrannize. I spent two extremely painful days devoted to the task of making the poor woman understand that she would have to settle in Dresden, where I was not yet allowed to stay, whereas I would have to look around in Germany, but first in Vienna, to find a new base of operations. Upon hearing of my plans and my promise to make certain that in any event she would receive one thousand talers a year from me, she glanced at her friend in strange satisfaction. This bargain set the standard for my relationship with her for the rest of her life. As I was now turning to Weimar for the moment, she accompanied me as far as Frankfurt, where we parted. Schopenhauer had died there a short time before.

PART FOUR

1861–4

And* so I crossed Thuringia again, passing the Wartburg which, whether I visited it or just saw it in the distance, seemed to have so strange a significance for my departures from Germany as well as my returnings. I arrived in Weimar[1] at two o'clock at night, to be conducted the next day to rooms that Liszt had specified for my use in the Altenburg. Investing his words with significance, he told me that these were the rooms of Princess Marie. This time, however, there were no ladies to entertain us; Princess Karoline was already in Rome, and her daughter had married Prince Konstantin Hohenlohe and gone to live in Vienna. Only Miss Anderson, Marie's governess, had remained behind to help Liszt take care of his guests. Indeed, I found the Altenburg on the point of being shut up; Liszt's youthful uncle[2] Eduard had come from Vienna for this purpose, and was taking inventory of its contents. But at the same time there was unusual conviviality, for a congress of musicians[3] was about to begin, and Liszt was quartering a large number of the participants in his home. Bülow and Cornelius were included among these; it struck me as a bit odd that they all, even Liszt, went around wearing traveling caps on their heads, thereby emphasizing, or so I speedily concluded, the lack of ceremony surrounding this music festival in rural Weimar. On the top floor of the house Franz Brendel and his wife were installed in some splendor; the place was soon teeming with musicians, among whom I met my old acquaintance Draeseke as well as a young man called Weissheimer,[4] whom Liszt had once sent to see me in Zürich. Tausig also showed up, but absented himself from our free and easy gatherings most of the time in order to pursue a love affair with a young lady. Liszt gave me Emilie Genast[5] as a companion on one or two short excursions, an arrangement that caused me no complaint, as she was both understanding and witty. I also got to know the violinist and musician Damrosch.[6] It was a great pleasure to see my old friend Alwine Frommann once again, though there was some tension between her and Liszt at the time. When Blandine and Ollivier finally arrived from Paris and became my neighbors in the Altenburg, the days, lively enough before, now became almost boisterously merry. Bülow, who had been designated to conduct Liszt's *Faust* Symphony, seemed to me the most exuberant of all. His energy was utterly extraordinary; he had learned the score entirely by heart and, with an orchestra by no means representing the élite of German musicians, produced it with extreme precision, delicacy and ardor. Next to this symphony, the best

* Note in the margin of the manuscript, in Cosima's hand: "Continuation January 10th 1876"; and below, referring to the content: "August 1861".

performance was the music for *Prometheus*; but I was especially touched by a performance of a song cycle composed by Bülow himself, entitled *Die Entsagende*, which was sung by Emilie Genast. Apart from this, the festival concerts offered little of value; a cantata by Weissheimer called *Das Grab im Busento* passed muster, but a German March composed by Draeseke caused a real scandal. This truly miserable product of an otherwise highly gifted person, apparently an exercise in self-mockery, was for some scarcely comprehensible reason strongly sponsored by Liszt in a most provocative way; as Draeseke proved ludicrously incompetent to conduct his own composition, Liszt insisted, against the advice of all his friends, upon the performance of the march under Bülow's baton. Hans succeeded in doing this, and by heart to boot; but the whole thing ended in a preposterous scene. Liszt, who could not be persuaded to respond to the jubilant reception accorded his own works by bowing to the public on a single occasion, appeared in the proscenium box at the close of Draeseke's march, which had been greeted by the martyred audience with prolonged dissatisfaction, to applaud his protégé's work, clapping with hands ostentatiously out-stretched and shouting thunderous "bravos". A real battle set in between Liszt, whose face was flushed with anger, and the audience. Blandine, who was sitting next to me, was in abject despair, as I was, at the outrageously provocative conduct of her father, and it was a long time before we calmed down after the incident. We couldn't get very much out of Liszt on the subject; we heard him make a few furiously deprecatory remarks about the public, for whom he alleged this march was too good; I heard from another quarter that it all arose out of rancor against the regular Weimar public, which was very strange because they were not represented on this occasion. Liszt seemed to think it a good opportunity to avenge Cornelius, whose opera *Der Barbier von Bagdad* had been produced a short time before under Liszt's direction and had been hissed by the Weimar audience. In addition, I could see that Liszt was plagued by all sorts of other worries. As he himself admitted to me, he had been trying to induce the Grand Duke of Weimar to offer me some particular mark of distinction; he wanted to see me invited to dine at court with him; but as the Duke had qualms about entertaining a person who was still banned from his native Saxony as a political exile, Liszt thought he could at least get the Order of the White Falcon for me. But this too was rejected. As his exertions at court had proved so fruitless, he was now bent on seeing the citizens of the ducal seat do their part in celebrating my presence; it was decided to put on a torchlight procession in my honor. When I got wind of it, I did my very best to undermine the initiative; in this I was successful. But I was not to get off without any ovation at all; one morning Councillor Gille of Jena arrived under my window with a group of six students to render a nice little choral society song, a courtesy to which I responded in heartiest gratitude. A contrast to this was presented by a big banquet attended by all the musicians. I sat between Blandine and Ollivier, and the feast developed into a really cordial ovation for the composer of *Tannhäuser* and *Lohengrin*, whom they could now welcome back to Germany after winning their esteem and becoming famous during the period of his exile. Liszt's speech was short but fiery, and I had to respond at greater length, following a special orator chosen for the ceremony. I also found the select gatherings at Liszt's own luncheon table very pleasant, and I toasted the absent hostess of the Altenburg on one such occasion. Once we had our meal in the garden, and on that occasion I was delighted to see my old friend Alwine Frommann reconciled with Liszt and chatting very intelligently with Ollivier.

After a week of manifold and stimulating experience, the day of separation came for us all. By a happy chance the greater part of my prearranged trip to Vienna could be made in the company of Blandine and Ollivier. These two had decided to visit Cosima in Bad Reichenhall, where she was taking the cure. When we all bade farewell to Liszt at the railroad station we also thought of Bülow, who had distinguished himself so nobly during the days just past, and who had left a day earlier; we outdid ourselves in encomiums for him, though I added a little jesting remark that he really had not been obliged to marry Cosima as well; to which Liszt responded with a little bow: "That was a luxury."

We travelers, Blandine and I in particular, now fell into a merrily exuberant mood, much intensified by Ollivier's continual query, "Qu'est ce qu'il dit?", repeated every time we were seized by a gust of laughter. He had to submit good-humoredly to our incessant joking in German; yet we always responded in French to his frequent requests for "tonique" or "jambon cru", which seemed to constitute the principal elements of his diet. We arrived in Nuremberg, where we were compelled to stop for the night, well after midnight and were laboriously conveyed to a hotel, which opened its doors only after a long delay. A fat old innkeeper acceded to our pleas to provide us with rooms, late as it was; in order to accomplish this, however, after much anxious cogitation, he left us to wait in the hall for a long time, while he vanished down a side corridor, where we heard him call the name "Margarethe"[1] in bashful tones through a bedroom door. He repeated this several times, adding that there were guests waiting; he was answered from within by a woman's voice. After many entreaties by the innkeeper, Margarethe finally emerged en déshabille and brought us, after a whispered conference with him, to the rooms selected for our use. The humor of the affair lay in the fact that neither the innkeeper nor his maid seemed to take any notice of the uproarious laughter in which we three were indulging the whole time. The next day we went to see some of the sights of the town, last of all the Germanic Museum, which was in such wretched condition at the time that it earned the contempt of my French friend; though the large collection of instruments of torture, notably a box studded with nails, filled Blandine with disgust blended with compassion.

That evening we reached Munich, inspecting it the next day, after provisioning ourselves with "tonique" and ham, to our mutual delight and that of Ollivier in particular. He found that the classical style represented by the buildings constructed under the aegis of King Ludwig I[1] contrasted favorably with those with which Louis Napoleon, much to Ollivier's disgust, had elected to fill Paris. He assured us he would be heard from in Paris on the subject. Here I also met by chance my young former acquaintance, Robert von Hornstein; I introduced him as "Baron" to my friends: his quaint form and fatuous conduct aroused their merriment, which turned into something of a riot when "le baron" thought it necessary, before we started on our overnight journey to Bad Reichenhall, to take us to a brewery located some distance away. This took place in darkest night; apart from the stump of a candle with which "le baron" himself descended into the cellar to bring up the beer, there was no lighting whatever; yet the beer seemed to taste particularly good, and after Hornstein had repeated his descent into the cellar several times, and it became necessary for us to make all speed as we retraced on foot the uncommonly difficult path across fields and ditches to get back to the station, we realized that the unaccustomed potation had somewhat befogged us. Blandine fell into a deep sleep as soon as we climbed aboard the carriage, waking only at daybreak when we reached Bad Reichenhall, where Cosima met us and took us to the rooms prepared for us.

We were first of all very pleased to find Cosima's state of health much less alarming than we, and particularly I myself, had previously assumed it to be. A whey cure had been prescribed for her here. The next morning we actually participated in a promenade to the dairy; Cosima appeared to attribute less importance to this medicine than to the walks and the bracing mountain air. Ollivier and I, however, were mostly excluded from the hilarity that soon set in here as well, as the two sisters, who laughed so incessantly that their presence could be determined from far away, usually locked themselves away in their rooms for privacy, so that I could only resort to conversations in French with my political friend. Yet I found a way to gain admission to the sisters several times, announcing to them, among other things, my intention to adopt them, on the grounds that their father was no longer paying attention to either of them. This was greeted with more mirth than credence. I complained once to Blandine about Cosima's wild ways; at first she didn't seem to want to understand me, but in the end decided to interpret my words as being themselves the expression of a "timidité d'un sauvage". After a few days, however, I had to think of continuing my journey, after this pleasant interruption; I took leave of them in the hall and caught a look of almost timid inquiry from Cosima.

I first drove down the valley to Salzburg in a one-horse carriage. At the Austrian border I had to go through a scene with the customs officials. Liszt had presented me in Weimar with a box of the most exquisite cigars, which he himself had received from Baron Sina;[1] being well aware, from my stay in Venice, of the incredible formalities attendant upon the importation of these articles into Austria, I had hit upon the idea of concealing the cigars among my clothing and in my coat pockets. The customs officer, an old soldier, seemed well prepared to counter such measures and drew the "corpora delicti" singly from all the folds of my little valise. I had tried to bribe him by a little tip; he had actually pocketed this sum, and thus I was all the more furious when he denounced me to the office. Here I was obliged to pay a large fine, but received permission to buy back the cigars, something I furiously declined to do; when I received the receipt for the fine I had paid, I was also reimbursed with the Prussian taler that the customs officer had previously pocketed. When I got back into the carriage to continue the trip, I saw this official seated calmly in front of a glass of beer, eating his bread and cheese; he greeted me politely and I offered to return the taler to him, but this time he refused to accept it. I have often been angry with myself for not getting this man's name, as I was left with the idea that he would make an excellent, trustworthy servant, and I would like to have engaged him as such later on.

I spent the night in Salzburg, arriving there soaked by floods of rain, and on the following day at last reached Vienna, my destination for the present. Here I proposed to accept the hospitality of Kolatschek, who had been among my friends in Switzerland; he had long since been amnestied by Austria, and on my last visit to Vienna had called on me to offer the hospitality of his house if I should ever return for a longer stay, in order to spare me the unpleasantness of residing in a hotel. For reasons of economy alone, very urgent at the time, I had willingly accepted this offer, and now drove with my luggage directly to the address he had given me. To my astonishment I discovered at once that it was in a very remote suburb, virtually without any transport to Vienna. Moreover, the house was quite deserted, for Kolatschek had gone off with his family for a summer vacation in Hütteldorf; with some difficulty I unearthed an old servant who had been given some vague idea by her employer that I was to be expected. She showed me to a little room where I was to sleep, if I wanted; there appeared to be no arrangements for laundry or any other service. Greatly put out by this disappointment, I first went back into the city in order to wait for Kolatschek in a café near St Stephan's square where, according to the maid, he would show up at a particular hour. I sat there for a long time, repeatedly asking after the man I expected to meet, when suddenly I saw Standhartner come in. His utter amazement at finding me here was intensified, as he told me, by the fact that he had never before entered this particular café. It was only a peculiar coincidence that had led him there on this day and at that time. When I informed him of my situation he at once became incensed that I should be living in the most remote part of Vienna when I had such urgent business in the middle of the city, and he immediately offered me his own home, which he was about to leave for six weeks with his family, as a temporary abode. An attractive niece, who was living in the same house with her mother and sister, would take care of breakfast and the necessary services. I would thus be able to make myself comfortable with the whole house at my disposal. He jubilantly led me to the house, which had already been vacated by his family to spend their summer holidays in Salzburg. Kolatschek was notified, my bag brought in, and for several days I enjoyed Standhartner's company as well as his splendid hospitality. But I also had to recognize a number of new complications for my situation in the further news my friends gave me. The rehearsals scheduled the previous year for this time (I had arrived in Vienna on August 14th) had already been postponed indefinitely, because the tenor Ander had reported trouble with his voice. Upon hearing this I at once came to the conclusion that my stay in Vienna would be pointless; yet I could not think anybody would have any idea where I should turn to pursue any constructive purpose.

My situation, as it only now became clear to me, was entirely hopeless, for it appeared I had been abandoned by everybody. A few years before I might have flattered myself in a similar case that Liszt would be pleased to have me in Weimar during an interim period, but upon my return to Germany I had found his house, as aforementioned, in the process of being boarded up. Thus my main concern was to find an agreeable refuge somewhere. With virtually this sole purpose in view I turned to the Grand Duke of Baden, who had greeted me with such friendly sympathy a short time before. I wrote him a beseeching letter explaining my situation, assuring him that above all I needed a place of refuge, however modest, and imploring him to enable me to find one in or near Karslruhe, by granting me a yearly pension of twelve hundred guilders. How astonished I was to receive in reply a letter merely signed by the Grand Duke and not in his own hand, arguing that if my request was granted I would soon be meddling in the affairs of the theater and thus predictably embroiled in battles with its director, my old friend Eduard Devrient, whose solicitude for me I could now see for myself; as in such cases the Grand Duke would probably be compelled, as he put it, to "exercise his prerogatives of justice", possibly to my disadvantage, he felt obliged, on careful consideration, to decline my request.

Princess Metternich, who had sensed my difficulty in these matters when I left Paris, had recommended me most heartily in Vienna to the family of Count Nakós, of whose wife she had spoken to me with particular emphasis. I had now also made the acquaintance through Standhartner, during the few days I spent with him before he left, of young Prince Rudolf Liechtenstein, known to his friends solely as "Rudi". He had been commended warmly to me as a fervent admirer of my music by his doctor, with whom he was on close terms. I often met him for meals at the Archduke Karl after Standhartner had rejoined his family, and there we agreed upon a plan to visit Count Nakós at his estate, Schwarzau, some distance away. The journey was made in the most comfortable fashion, partly by rail and in the company of the prince's young wife. They then introduced me to the Nakós family at Schwarzau: the count proved to be a splendidly handsome man, while by contrast she was a sort of cultured gypsy, whose painting talent was evidenced most obtrusively by huge copies of Van Dycks hanging everywhere on the walls. Her piano playing, on the other hand, was a bit harder to bear, as she played only gypsy melodies with an authenticity, as she contended, of which Liszt was incapable. The music of *Lohengrin* seemed to have predisposed them all in my favor; this appreciation was confirmed by some other magnates who were visiting there, among them

Count Edmund Zichy whom I had known in Venice. I was thus able to apprehend at close quarters the generosity of Hungarian hospitality, though without being especially edified by the conversation. Unfortunately I soon had to begin asking myself what I was really up to among these people. I had been accorded a nice room for the night, and the next day I took an early opportunity to look around the beautifully maintained grounds of the stately castle with the thought of finding some part of it that might be placed at my disposal for a more lengthy visit. But my laudatory remarks about the size of the building were met at breakfast with the assurance that it scarcely sufficed for the needs of the count's family, as the young countess and her servants needed particularly lavish accommodation. It was a cold September morning, and we spent it in the open air; my friend "Rudi" seemed to be in a bad mood; I was freezing and soon took leave of this rich men's table with the consciousness of seldom having found myself in the company of such nice people, but without the faintest idea what I might have in common with them. This feeling grew into positive revulsion when I traveled with several of these "cavaliers" as far as the railroad station at Mödling and was reduced to absolute silence for an hour while they conversed about literally nothing but horses, a topic that by this time I knew quite well enough.

I got out at Mödling to visit the tenor Ander, having invited myself for the day with the intention of going through *Tristan* with him. It was still quite early on a bright morning, and the day was growing steadily warmer; I decided to take a walk in the lovely Brühl park before looking up Ander. There I ordered a second breakfast in the garden of a beautifully situated inn and enjoyed an extremely refreshing hour of complete solitude. The woodbirds had already fallen silent, but a flock of sparrows, which swelled to a tremendous horde, came to share my meal; when I fed them with breadcrumbs they finally became so tame they settled in swarms on the table in front of me to seize their booty. This recalled that morning in Montmorency at the restaurant of the innkeeper Homo. Here as well, after I had shed some tears, I burst out laughing and set off for Ander's summer retreat. Unfortunately his condition confirmed to me that his vocal trouble was no mere pretext. At any rate I soon had to admit to myself that this paltry fellow, although worshipped as a demigod in Vienna, would never be capable of rising to the challenge posed by the role of Tristan. Yet now that I was here, I did my best to make my whole *Tristan* clear to him in the manner that always caused me so much excitement; he responded with the statement that the role fitted him like a glove. I had arranged for Tausig and Cornelius, whom I had again met in Vienna, to come out to Ander's house for the day, and together we went back to Vienna that evening.

I spent a good deal of time with these two, who were worried about me and did their best to cheer me up; Tausig, it is true, was a bit more reserved, as he had certain aspirations in high places at that time. Yet this young friend also accepted invitations that brought all three of us to the house of Frau Dustmann, who was spending the summer in Hietzing. We had several dinner parties as well as a few vocal rehearsals for the role of Isolde, a part for which her voice and her spiritual capacity seemed to suit her. There I again read my poem for *Tristan*, always in the conviction that I would somehow find a way, given patience and enthusiasm, to make a performance possible. Meanwhile, however, I needed the former quality most of all, for there was little to be achieved with the latter; Ander was and remained vocally indisposed, and no doctor would predict the time when he might recover from his malady.

I got through the time as best I could and hit upon the idea of translating the French text of the new scene in *Tannhäuser* written for Paris back into German. Cornelius had to make a copy for my use, as the original score was now very dilapidated; I appropriated his copy without inquiring after the original, which remained in his hands: what came of this will be seen later.

We were joined by the musician Winterberger, whom I had known some time before and whom we found in what I considered an enviable position. Countess Banffy, an old friend of Liszt, had taken him into her very pleasant house in Hietzing; he was living there comfortably without a worry in the world, for the kindly lady regarded it as her duty to see that he lacked nothing, despite the fact that he had never accomplished very much. Through him I again got news of Karl Ritter. As far as I could gather, Winterberger had played the cavalier in Rome and Naples at Karl's expense, having love affairs with young princesses and making such heavy inroads on Ritter's capital that the latter was now obliged to accept room and board from a piano maker in Naples in return for giving lessons to the children of the house. After running through all this money, Winterberger had embarked upon further adventures in Hungary, seemingly on the basis of some introductions from Liszt; this did not seem to have gone according to plan, but he now found himself well recompensed by his stay in the house of the good countess. I met another house guest of this lady in Fräulein Mössner, an excellent harpist; by order of the countess she was supposed to play the harp in the garden and there, whether at or with her instrument, she looked very pert and pretty, and made an enduringly favorable impression. Unfortunately I became involved in a quarrel with the young lady because I didn't want to compose a solo for her instrument; from the moment I definitively refused to foster her ambition in this way she no longer took any notice of me.

Among the special acquaintances I made in Vienna in this difficult period the poet Hebbel must also be mentioned. As it seemed not unlikely that I would have to make Vienna my base of operations for an extended period, I found it advisable to become more closely acquainted with the local literary lights. I prepared myself for a meeting with Hebbel by a prior reading of his plays, whereby I did my level best to find them good and convince myself that a closer association with Hebbel would be desirable. Although I soon realized the great weaknesses of his works, particularly the unnaturalness of his conceptions and the generally commonplace level of his diction, however recherché he tried to make it, I was now not to be deterred from carrying out my plan. I visited him only once and on this occasion did not converse with him for any extended period. I found no trace in the personality of the poet of the eccentric force which seemingly threatens to explode in ·most of his dramatic figures; when I heard some years later[1] that Hebbel had died of a bone disease I understood what had made such a disquieting impression on me. He chatted with me about the Viennese theatrical world with the air of an amateur who feels neglected but still persists in his efforts. I did not feel particularly stimulated to repeat my visit, especially when he left a card after returning the call at my residence in my absence, announcing himself as "Hebbel, chevalier *des* plusieurs ordres".

I found my old friend Heinrich Laube long since well established as director of the Imperial and Royal Court Theater. At my first visit the previous spring he had already felt it his duty to introduce me to Viennese literary celebrities; being of a practical turn of mind, he counted chiefly journalists and critics among these. Thinking I would be especially interested, he had invited Dr Hanslick to a big dinner party, and was immediately astonished when I had not a word to say to him. This led him to predict that I would have a tough time in Vienna if I really wished to make it a center of my artistic efforts. Upon returning this time I was welcomed simply as an old friend, and he gave me a standing invitation to luncheon; as he was a passionate hunter, his table was richly provided with fresh game. I did not take advantage of this invitation very often, however, as the conversation, which was enlivened solely by routine theater gossip, did not attract me. After the meal it was customary for actors and literary people to assemble around a large table for coffee and cigars, during which time, while Laube rested silently in a cloud of cigar smoke, his wife usually held court. For his sake she had become a directrix at the theater and found it necessary to hold forth in lengthy speeches about things of which she had not the remotest inkling; in this my only pleasure lay in observing once more the good nature I had esteemed in her in former times, for she responded to my entirely uninhibited criticisms, whenever none of the courtiers was bold enough to correct her, with unconcealed merriment. To her and her husband I probably seemed some kind of brilliant buffoon and nothing more, for my conversation consisted almost exclusively of jokes and witticisms, given the fact that I was indifferent to the things they took seriously. When I later gave my Vienna concerts, Frau Laube expressed friendly amazement that I seemed to be able to conduct very well, contrary to what she had expected from reading some newspaper report.

In one matter Laube's practical knowledge proved not unimportant, for he was able to tell me all about the nature of the higher officials at the Imperial and Court Theater. It turned out that an Imperial Councillor von Raymond was of the most immense significance; the old Count Lanskoronsky, who was otherwise very jealous of his authority as Supreme Court Chamberlain, could not trust himself to come to any decision in money questions before consulting the former, who had the reputation of being an expert. Raymond himself, whom I soon found to be a model of philistinism, had become hesitant with regard to my project of performing *Tristan*, particularly as a result of the continuing hostility of the Viennese press, and tended to procrastinate. My official contact with the theater remained solely the director of the opera house, Herr Salvi, the former singing teacher of a lady-in-waiting to the Archduchess Sophie; this man, utterly ignorant and incompetent, now had to pretend to me that, in accordance with the command from on high, nothing was more important to him than to foster the production of *Tristan*. Accordingly he tried, by an incessant display of zeal and solicitude, to conceal from me the mood of doubt and hesitation spreading within the company.

I discovered how things stood one day when a group of our singers went with me to the country estate of a Herr Dumba, who had been introduced to me as an enthusiastic well-wisher. Herr Ander had brought along his working score for the role of Tristan as if to demonstrate that he couldn't be separated from it for as much as a day. Frau Dustmann was irritated at this and accused Ander of playing games in order to deceive me; for Ander, she said, knew as well as anybody that he would never sing the role, and that he was only looking for a chance to find a way to blame her, Frau Dustmann, for the prevention of the performance. Salvi always tried to intervene to counteract such dispiriting insights. He recommended that I look over the tenor Walter;[1] he was most distasteful to me and I rejected him, so Salvi referred me to singers at other theaters, whom he was willing to engage as guests. At this point it actually came to a few guest performances for testing purposes, and a Herr Morini seemed to offer the best prospects. I was really so deeply depressed and driven by the desire to do something for my work at any price that I went with Cornelius to a performance of Donizetti's *Lucia* and even tried to persuade my friend of the excellence of this singer. Cornelius, who was completely absorbed in listening, suddenly realized that I was looking at him expectantly and burst out with "Dreadful! Dreadful!", whereupon we both had to laugh so much that we soon left the theater in a most cheerful mood.

As he seemed an honest man of the theater, I finally wound up dealing solely with the conductor Heinrich Esser. He had worked his way into *Tristan* with great diligence, though it was a difficult task for him, and he never lost hope that the performance might be possible, if only I would agree to Walter in the title role; despite my continuing refusal to avail myself of the services of this singer, we remained good friends. As he was a good walker we often perambulated through the woods surrounding Vienna, our conversation being animated on my part and serious and well-meant on his.

While this whole *Tristan* affair was running its endless course like some chronic illness, Standhartner had returned at the end of September with his family. Consequently the next thing I had to do was to look about for a residence, which I found in the Hotel Empress Elisabeth. Through my cordial association with my friend's family, I got to know his wife and three sons, as well as a daughter from her first marriage, plus another daughter from her second with Standhartner. With regard to my stay in this congenial house, I would henceforth greatly miss the kindly care devoted to me by the aforementioned niece Seraphine,[2] who was not only tireless in her solicitude but also an amusing companion. Because of her dainty figure and hair always curled "à l'enfant", I had named her "the doll". Now I found it more difficult to get along in a gloomy hotel room. My living expenses also increased severely. As for royalties, I recall receiving at this time only twenty-five or thirty louis d'or for *Tannhäuser* from Brunswick. On the other hand I got from Minna in Dresden a few sprigs from a silver-spangled wreath which some friends of hers had given her on November 24th, the date of her silver wedding. I could hardly wonder that there was no dearth of bitter reproaches accompanying this shipment; in response, I tried to give her hope for a golden wedding. For the moment, sitting so purposelessly in an expensive Vienna hotel, I did my best to open some prospects for the performance of *Tristan*. I turned to Tichatschek in Dresden, but naturally without success in obtaining his acceptance. I tried the same with Schnorr, and with the same result. And so I had to confess that my situation was pretty miserable.

In a casual communication to the Wesendoncks I had made no secret how things stood; apparently with the objective of cheering me up, they invited me to meet them in Venice, where they were just about to go on a pleasure trip. Heaven knows what I had in mind when I set off one gray November day to go by rail via Trieste, and from there with a steamboat, which made me sick, to reach Venice and proceed to my little room in the Hotel Danieli. My friends, whom I found in flourishing circumstances, were reveling in enjoyment of the paintings and seemed to have it in mind to dispel my depression by sharing these delights. They seemed disinclined to realize what my position was in Vienna, and indeed, after the failure of the Paris venture that had been attended by so many glorious hopes, I increasingly found that most of my friends had tacitly abandoned hopes for my future success. Wesendonck, who was always armed with a huge opera glass, ready to inspect works of art, managed to induce me only once to visit the Palace of the Doges,[1] a building which I had known only from the outside on my former visit to Venice. I have to admit that despite all my apathy Titian's *Assumption of the Virgin* in the great hall of the Doges[2] made a most exalting impression upon me, so that by this inspiration I found my old creative powers awakening within me with almost their original primordial power.

I decided to write *Die Meistersinger*.

After a frugal dinner with my old acquaintance Tessarin and the Wesendoncks, whom I had invited to the Albergo San Marco, and after exchanging friendly greetings with Luigia, my former attendant at the Palazzo Giustiniani, I suddenly left Venice, much to the amazement of my friends. I had spent four externally dreary days there, and now started my long and dismal trip back by train on the roundabout land route to Vienna. During this journey I first thought of the musical treatment of *Die Meistersinger*, the poem for which I had retained in my mind only in its earliest form; I conceived the main part of the overture in C major with the greatest clarity.

Given these last impressions, I got back to Vienna in a truly comfortable frame of mind. I immediately announced my return to Cornelius by sending him a model of a gondola I had bought for him in Venice and which I accompanied with a little canzona in nonsensical Italian. When I told him of my plan to do *Die Meistersinger* he was beside himself with delight. He remained in a state of delirious excitement right up to my departure from Vienna. I at once enlisted my friend to help procure the material necessary to master the *Meistersinger* subject. My first idea was to undertake a thorough study of Grimm's polemic[1] on the masters' way of singing; then I had to get hold of old Wagenseil's[2] *Chronicle of Nuremberg*; Cornelius accompanied me to the Imperial Library for this purpose; we were lucky to find the book, but to get permission to take it out my friend had to pay what he described to me as a very disagreeable visit to Baron Münch-Bellinghausen (Halm).[3] Then I sat down eagerly in my hotel and appropriated excerpts from the *Chronicle*, which I soon used in my libretto in a manner that astonished those who knew nothing of the subject.

Now it was a question of finding some means of subsistence during the time I was completing the work. I applied first to the music dealer Schott in Mainz, to whom I offered *Die Meistersinger* if he would advance me the necessary cash. Driven by the need to provide myself with funds for as long a period as possible, I went so far as to offer him not only the copyright but also the performance rights against a payment of twenty thousand francs. A telegram from Schott conveying an absolute refusal destroyed all my hopes for the moment. Finding myself compelled to look to other sources, I decided to turn to Berlin. Bülow, who was always exerting himself on my behalf, had intimated that I might be able to raise a sizeable sum of money if I conducted a big concert there; as I longed at the same time for a place to stay among friends, Berlin seemed to beckon as a last resort. I was within hours of leaving for there one evening when at midday a letter from Schott arrived on the heels of the telegram of rejection, holding out somewhat more cheering prospects; he offered to take over the publication of the vocal score of *Die Walküre* and advance me fifteen hundred guilders at once on open account. The joy of Cornelius at what he considered the salvation of *Die Meistersinger* was unbounded. Bülow meanwhile wrote me from Berlin, dejectedly and highly indignant, of his miserable experiences resulting from the preliminary arrangements for my concert. Herr von Hülsen had told him he would not receive me if I came to Berlin, and upon closer consideration Bülow had been obliged to conclude that a concert in the big Kroll auditorium would not be feasible.

While I was busily engaged working out a detailed scenario of my *Meistersinger*, the arrival of Prince and Princess Metternich in Vienna brought a new and seemingly auspicious development for me.

The concern of my Paris patrons for me and my situation was indisputably real; to show some sign of appreciation I persuaded the management of the Opera House to permit me to invite the superb orchestra to the theater to play a few excerpts from *Tristan* during some morning hours, as if it were a rehearsal. The orchestra and Frau Dustmann were entirely willing to accede to my wish: Princess Metternich and some of her acquaintances were invited to this audition, in which my performance of three sizeable fragments, the prelude to the first act and the beginning and middle of the second, after going through them only once with the orchestra, and with Frau Dustmann at hand to render the vocal part, was so successful that I felt fully justified in believing I had made the most splendid impression. Herr Ander had showed up here as well, but without trying as much as a note or indicating he even knew one. My princely friends, and, curiously enough, the prima ballerina Fräulein Couqui, who had attended the audition surreptitiously, were lavish with their praise.

One day, having learned of my desire for a place of refuge where I could carry out my new work undisturbed, the Metternichs announced that they could provide just such a quiet retreat in Paris: the prince had now completely furnished his spacious embassy and could provide me with a pleasant room opening out on a tranquil garden, similar to the one I had occupied in the Prussian Embassy; my Erard was still in Paris, they reminded me, and if I got there by the end of the year I would find everything ready for me to begin my work. I accepted this delightful invitation with undisguised joy, and from then on my only worry was to arrange things so that I could leave Vienna and transfer to Paris in a dignified way. In this, an arrangement made through Standhartner's intermediation, involving an offer by the management to pay me a part of the fee stipulated for *Tristan*, seemed to afford some help. Yet as I was to receive five hundred florins only under terms and conditions that looked very like absolute repudiation of the whole transaction, I immediately rejected this offer. However, this did not prevent the newspapers, which were always in cahoots with the management, from loudly proclaiming that I had accepted a fee for the non-performance of *Tristan*. Fortunately I was able to counter this calumny by producing proof of what I had actually done in the matter. The negotiations with Schott now began to drag a bit, for I didn't want to accept his offer for *Die Walküre*; I stuck to my offer of the new opera *Die Meistersinger* and finally got the payment of fifteen hundred guilders originally offered for *Die Walküre*[1] booked as an advance for my new work. As soon as I received the bill of exchange I started packing, when a telegram arrived from Princess Metternich, who had already returned to Paris, asking me to postpone my arrival until January 1st. In order to get away from Vienna, I decided not to be deterred in my plans and went first to Mainz to negotiate further with Schott. My farewell at the railway station was especially enlivened by Cornelius, who whispered to me in mystical exaltation a stanza for Sachs I had already communicated to him; this was the verse:

> The bird who sang today
> His throat rang proud and true
> Though the Masters were in dismay[2]
> Hans Sachs loved it through and through.

In Mainz I now got to know the Schott family, who had already crossed my horizon in Paris, somewhat better. The young musician Weissheimer was also a daily guest at their house, being at the outset of his career as assistant conductor at the local theater. At luncheon one day another young man, the lawyer Städl, brought forth a truly remarkable toast, together with a hyperbolic speech that surprised me considerably. Despite all this my negotiations with the highly odd fellow I now discovered Franz Schott to be proceeded with uncommon difficulty. I insisted on carrying out my first proposal, which involved his providing me with the necessary funds for two years in succession, so that I could complete my work without interruption. He tried to put his unwillingness to do that in a good light by asserting that it was against his instincts to barter as it were with a man like me, not only buying my work from me for a given sum, but also my rights as author in respect of theatrical performances; he was a music publisher, he said, and wanted to remain just that and nothing more. I responded that he need only advance me the necessary funds in the form I requested, and that repayment of the part deemed to be for the literary property would be guaranteed through future theatrical receipts, which were pledged to him. It took a long time to bring him to the point of making me advances against "compositions to be delivered", an arrangement I finally accepted but with the insistence that I had to be able to count on consecutive payments totaling twenty thousand francs. As I needed money there and then after the settlement of my Vienna hotel bill, Schott now gave me a bill of exchange drawn on Paris. From there I received a letter of Princess Metternich, whose significance I could not entirely fathom, stating that her mother, Countess Sandor, had died, and that this produced a change in her family situation.

Once again I pondered whether it was advisable to try my luck in Karlsruhe, taking some modest lodgings there or in the vicinity, and seeing whether in the course of time it might develop into a permanent establishment. As far as the difficult matter of Minna's support in Dresden was concerned, obliged as I was to come up with one thousand talers a year in accordance with my promise, it appeared more sensible and indeed more economical for me to summon my wife to share this abode with me. But a letter arriving from her at that time, which really consisted of nothing more than an attempt to incite me against my friends, scared me away from any thought of a reunion and determined me to carry out my Paris plans in order to stay as far away from her as possible.

So I started for Paris toward the middle of December, where I first settled at the unpretentious Hotel Voltaire on the *quai* of the same name, with a modest room but a pleasant view. Here I wanted to collect myself for my work and live incognito as long as possible until, as she had previously requested, I could present myself to Princess Metternich at the beginning of the new year. In order not to embarrass Pourtalès and Hatzfeld, who were close friends of theirs, I pretended I hadn't yet come to Paris as far as they were concerned, and looked up solely my old acquaintances Truinet, Gaspérini, Flaxland, and the painter Czermak, all of whom had nothing to do with that particular circle. I met Truinet and his father again regularly for evening meals at the Taverne Anglaise, to which I slunk unnoticed through the old familiar streets as soon as night had fallen. Suddenly one day I was struck upon opening a newspaper there by an announcement of the death of Count Pourtalès. My distress was vast, and particularly my regret at having neglected to visit this man, who had been such a staunch friend, through my strange consideration for the Metternichs. Now I went to see Count Hatzfeld, at least, who confirmed the sad news and told me the circumstances of his unexpected demise, the result of a heart disease his doctors had not discovered until the very last minute. At the same time I learned the true facts about the situation in the Metternich establishment. The death of Countess Sandor, of which Princess Pauline had written me, had the following significance: the Count, that notorious Hungarian madcap, had up to then been kept confined as a lunatic by his wife for the sake of the whole family; after her death the family now feared the most immense trouble from the Count, who was no longer being watched over. For this reason the Metternichs felt it necessary to take him under their supervision in Paris and provide him with the requisite care. For this purpose the Princess had immediately allocated as solely suitable the rooms she had previously offered to me; thus I now recognized there was no longer any thought of taking me into the Austrian Embassy, and I was left to reflect on this bizarre stroke of fate that had again cast me adrift in ill-omened Paris.

For the moment I had no alternative other than to keep my not very expensive accommodation in the Hotel Voltaire until I had completed my *Meistersinger* poem, and while I was doing that to think exhaustively about my next move, and keep my eyes open for somewhere to turn in search of the refuge I had already tried so hard to find for the creation of my new work. It wasn't easy; my name and person were involuntarily regarded in the dubious light of my Paris failure by everyone I met, and seemed to be surrounded by a mist, which made me unrecognizable even to old friends. I almost felt that even the Olliviers had been affected by all this distrust, to judge from the reception they accorded me at their home: at any rate, they regarded it as more than ill-advised of me to appear in the Paris arena again so soon. I had to explain the odd circumstances that had brought me here again, and assure them I had no intention of prolonging my stay. Beyond this surely deceptive impression, I now soon recognized the change that had taken place within the bosom of the family. The grandmother was laid up with a broken leg, incurable at her age; Ollivier had taken her into his rather small home to care for her, and we assembled for dinner about her bed in a little room. Blandine seemed to have changed markedly since the summer and had a sorrowful, grave air about her; I formed the impression that she was with child. Emile, in his dry and laconic way, gave me a single piece of useful advice: when that Richard Lindau sent me a threatening communication, through his lawyer, requesting the compensation the court had accorded him for his imaginary work on *Tannhäuser*, I showed Ollivier the letter and asked him what to do. "Ne répondez pas" was all he said; and his advice was as good as it was easy to follow: I never heard anything from that quarter again. I sorrowfully made up my mind not to bother the Olliviers any longer; Blandine bade farewell to me with a look of infinite melancholy.

Instead I became involved in an almost regular association with Czermak, joining him nearly every evening, at either the Taverne Anglaise, where I could always be sure of finding the Truinet family, or some other equally inexpensive restaurant. We usually went on to one of the small theaters which I had entirely neglected during the period of stress. The best of these was the Gymnase, where a superb troupe played pieces that were almost all excellent. Among these I recall a particularly tender and touching one-acter entitled *Je dîne chez ma mère*. In the Théâtre du Palais Royal, where things were not so refined, as well as in the Théâtre Déjazet, I discovered the archetypes of all those farces with which the German public is entertained year in and year out, in feeble adaptations and incongruous relocations. Beyond this I sometimes attended the luncheon table of the Flaxland family, who, astonishingly enough, still refused to despair of my ultimate success in Paris; in the meantime my Paris publisher continued to issue *Der fliegende Holländer* as well as *Rienzi*, for which he even gave me a small fee of fifteen hundred francs, as these works had not been included in the original sale.

The reason for the almost cheerful enjoyment with which I managed to regard my difficult situation in Paris this time, and which has enabled me since to look back on it as a pleasant memory, lay in the fact that my *Meistersinger* poem swelled daily as the couplets flooded in. How could I help being put in a good humor, when I looked down from my third-floor hotel window on the tremendous bustle on the quaysides and over the various bridges, with a view of the Tuileries, the Louvre, stretching all the way to the Hotel de Ville, whenever I raised my eyes from the manuscript, after pondering the quaint verses and sayings of my Nuremberg masters!

I had already gotten quite far into the first act when the fateful New Year's Day of 1862 arrived and I now paid my long-delayed visit to Princess Metternich. She was naturally quite embarrassed, and in response to her repeated asseverations of remorse at the necessity of revoking my invitation by reason of the circumstances known to me, my only course was to reassure her most cheerfully. I asked Count Hatzfeld to let me know when the now widowed Countess Pourtalès would feel well enough to receive my visit.

And so I continued working on my *Meistersinger* poem through the month of January and finished it in precisely thirty days. The melody for that fragment from Hans Sachs' poem saluting the Reformation, with which I have the people greet their beloved master in the last act, occurred to me on the way to the Taverne Anglaise as I was walking through the galleries of the Palais Royal; I found Truinet waiting for me and asked him for a pencil and a piece of paper to jot down my melody, covertly singing it to him as I did so. I usually accompanied him and his father along the boulevards to his flat in the Faubourg St Honoré, and on that evening he could do nothing but exclaim: "Mais, quelle gaîté d'esprit, cher maître!"

The closer I got to the end of my work, the more seriously I had to worry about where to go next; I still clung to the hope that something similar to what I had lost when Liszt relinquished the Altenburg would fall to my lot. I then remembered that during the previous year I had received a most fervent invitation from Mrs Street to stay with her and her father in Brussels; I now made reference to this in asking whether she could offer me modest shelter for a time: the necessity of declining to do so cast them into "désolation". I also turned to Cosima in Berlin with a similar inquiry, at which she really seemed to be horrified; but I quite understood the reason for her reaction later when I visited Berlin and saw how Bülow lived. It struck me as highly remarkable, however, that my brother-in-law Avenarius, of whom I learned that he was living in Berlin in comfortable circumstances, responded very earnestly to my request and asked me at the very least to come and stay with him to judge for myself whether it would be feasible to remain there for a longer period. My sister Cäcilie, however, forbade me to take Minna along, though she thought she could find a suitable place for her in the neighborhood in the event of a visit. To her misfortune poor Minna could do nothing better than write me a furious letter complaining of the insulting behavior of my sister: the possibility of being caught in the cross-fire of the old squabbles was enough to make me decline my brother-in-law's invitation at once.

And so I finally hit on the idea of looking for a quiet retreat in the vicinity of Mainz, under the financial protection of Schott. He had told me of a nice country estate located in this area belonging to young Baron von Hornstein; I believed I was really doing the latter an honor when I wrote him in Munich and asked for permission to stay for some time at his place in the Rheingau. Accordingly, I was greatly dismayed to get an answer indicating only alarm at my presumption. I then decided to go directly to Mainz, where I dispatched all our household effects that had been stored in Paris for nearly a year. Before I left Paris after making all these decisions I was afforded the consolation of a lofty admonition to face everything with resignation and fortitude. I had also written Frau Wesendonck about my chief concern, but only as one communicates such things to close friends; she responded to this by sending me a little cast-iron paperweight she had bought for me on that visit to Venice; it represented the Lion of St Mark with its paw on the book and was supposed to suggest that I should imitate this lion in some way. At any rate, they hadn't had the idea of offering me what I was looking for.

On the other hand, Countess Pourtalès finally permitted me to visit her. In spite of being in mourning after her profound loss, she did not wish to leave her great sympathy for me unexpressed; when I told her what I was working on, she asked about my libretto: she countered my regret that she would certainly not find the lively and humorous character of my *Meistersinger* to her taste at this time with a friendly request that I read it to her, for which purpose she invited me to spend the evening with her. She was the first person to whom I had the opportunity to read my completed text, and it made such a significant impression on us both that we often could not help bursting out into hearty laughter.

On the evening of my departure on February 1st, I invited my friends Gaspérini, Czermak, and the Truinets to a farewell meal at my hotel. Everybody was in high spirits, and particularly cheered by my own good mood, although none of them could entirely grasp the significance of the subject of the poem I had just finished and the further execution of which I promised myself would do so much good for Germany.

Still worried about choosing the right place for the refuge I now needed so badly, I at first again directed my steps toward Karlsruhe. Once more I was received cordially by the grand-ducal couple and was asked about my further plans. But there was no hint in any way that the residence I was hunting for could possibly be made available in Karlsruhe. I found it remarkable that the Grand Duke expressed apparently sympathetic concern as to how I found money to pay the costs of my unsettled life, even counting only my travel expenses; I tried to reassure him on this cheerfully enough by referring to my contractual relationship with Schott, who was to provide me with the requisite funds in the form of advances against completion of my *Meistersinger*. This seemed to console him. I later learned from Alwine Frommann that the Grand Duke had once commented that I had behaved a bit prudishly to him after he had offered, like a true friend, to open his purse on my behalf. But I had noticed no such thing; in our discussion it was only a matter of my possibly coming back to Karlsruhe to rehearse and conduct one of my operas, perhaps *Lohengrin*.

At any rate I continued my journey to Mainz, arriving there on February 4th during a major flood. Owing to a premature thaw, the Rhine had overflowed its banks to an unusual extent; I could only reach Schott's place at considerable risk; nonetheless I had agreed to read the *Meistersinger* there on the evening of the 5th, and for this occasion had summoned Cornelius to come from Vienna, arranging in Paris for a remittance of one hundred francs to cover his travel expenses. I had received no answer from him, and as I learned upon arrival in Mainz that the same flooding had affected all rivers in Germany and was blocking rail traffic, I no longer counted on Cornelius to appear. Yet I still delayed the beginning of the reading until the appointed hour; and lo and behold at seven o'clock sharp, Cornelius entered the room. He had been through the most arduous adventures, even losing his overcoat on the way, and had just arrived at his sister's house a few hours before, half frozen to death. The reading of my poem put us all into good spirits here as well; I was only saddened that I could not shake Cornelius in his resolve to return at once the following day: he regarded the punctilious effectuation of his plan to come to Mainz solely for a reading of *Die Meistersinger* as essential, if the event was to preserve its special character. He actually went back to Vienna the next day, despite floods and ice-floes.

As agreed, I now set about with Schott to look for a dwelling on the opposite bank of the Rhine. We had Biebrich in mind for this purpose; as I didn't find anything suitable, we also considered Wiesbaden itself; at last I decided to take temporary quarters in the Europäischer Hof in Biebrich and continue my search from there. As I was always particularly concerned to dwell somewhere isolated and, in particular, undisturbed by any unmusical noises, I elected to rent a very small apartment, which nonetheless exactly suited my needs, in a large summer house built close to the Rhine by the architect Frickhöfer. I had to await my household goods from Paris before furnishing it; these arrived, and at endless trouble and expense were duly unloaded at the Biebrich Customs House, where I managed to take possession of the things I needed most.

I kept only what was absolutely necessary for Biebrich, whereas the greater part was to be sent on to my wife in Dresden. I had notified Minna of this, and she at once became very worried about the possibility that in my haphazard unpacking I might damage or even lose things. After a week I had scarcely settled down with my newly retrieved Erard, when

Minna suddenly showed up in Biebrich. At first I felt nothing but sincere pleasure at her healthy appearance and inexhaustible energy in the practical handling of things: at the outset I even thought it might be best to let her settle at my side. But unfortunately my good mood was not allowed to last long, for the old scenes soon began to recur: when we went to the Customs House to undertake the palpable and visible separation of "meum" and "tuum", she could not contain her anger that I had not awaited her arrival and had on my initiative removed some things for my own use. As she nevertheless thought it only proper that I should be provided with certain household effects, she gave me four sets of knives, forks, and spoons, a few cups and saucers, and plates to match. She then superintended the packing of the not inconsiderable remainder of our goods, and after everything had been taken care of the way she wanted it, returned after a week to Dresden. She now flattered herself with the hope that her establishment there would be sufficiently well furnished to receive my visit, which she expected in the near future; with this idea in mind she had taken the necessary steps with higher government officials, who had been able to obtain a decree from the minister to the effect that, if I now petitioned the King for amnesty, nothing would stand in the way of my return to Dresden.

I was very hesitant to do anything in that direction. Minna's presence had only exacerbated the disruption of my previous mood, which had already been disturbed by recent events; the raw weather, defective heating, a badly managed household, heavy expenses, particularly those for Minna's support, all combined to deprive me for the moment of all joy in continuing the work begun in the Hotel Voltaire. With the presumable intention of providing me a pleasant diversion, the Schott family invited me to Darmstadt to a performance of *Rienzi* with Niemann: fearing that a possible demonstration at the theater in my honor might offend the sensibilities of the Grand Duke, the then Minister von Dalwigk[1] met me at the station and conducted me to his own box, where he could give the impression that I was being presented to the public on behalf of the Duke. In this manner everything went quite nicely and agreeably. The performance itself, in which Niemann showed himself in one of his best roles, was of interest to me furthermore in that they cut as much of the opera as they could, presumably in deference to the taste of the Grand Duke, so as to extend the ballet as much as possible by repeating its most trivial parts.

To get back from this expedition, I once again had to brave the ice-floes of the Rhine. In very low spirits I tried to introduce some comfort in my establishment and to this end hired a servant girl who also made my breakfasts; I took my other meals in the Europäischer Hof.

But when I found that I still couldn't recover my working mood and that I had succumbed to a certain restlessness, I offered the Grand Duke of Baden to fulfill my promise by paying him another visit, in order to read my *Meistersinger*. The Grand Duke answered me cordially with a personally signed telegram, whereupon I went to Karlsruhe on March 7th and read my manuscript to the grand-ducal pair. For this reading they had thoughtfully selected a salon where there hung a large historical tableau painted by my old friend Pecht, showing the young Goethe reading the first fragments of his *Faust* to the ancestors of the ducal family. My piece was very kindly received, and it seemed quite appropriate that at the close the Grand Duchess expressed particular interest in the musical treatment to be accorded the worthy Pogner, a graceful admission of embarrassment that a plain citizen could often be more zealous on behalf of the arts than many a prince. We again discussed a performance of *Lohengrin* under my baton, and for this purpose I was again referred to Eduard Devrient. Unfortunately, he now made a terrible impression on me through his production of *Tannhäuser* at the theater. I was compelled to witness this performance at his side and was astonished to find that this man I had once deemed so experienced a dramaturg had sunk to the lowest levels of theatrical vulgarity. To my amazement at the most hair-raising transgressions in the production he responded with even greater surprise and haughty indignation that I could make a fuss about the matter, as I knew very well that that was how things were done in the theater. Nonetheless it was still agreed that there would be a model performance of *Lohengrin* the following summer with the Schnorr couple in the leading roles.

A much pleasanter impression was derived from a play I saw on the way through Frankfurt, a nice little comedy at the local theater in which Friederike Meyer, the sister of my Vienna singer Frau Dustmann, attracted my attention by acting that was more subtle and delicate than I was accustomed to see from German actors. I now began to consider the possibility of gathering a few suitable friends in the neighborhood of Biebrich, so that I would not be entirely dependent on the Schott family or the innkeeper for company. Thus, I had already looked up the Raff[1] family in Wiesbaden. Frau Raff, a sister of Emilie Genast, who had made a favorable impression on me in Weimar, was engaged as an actress at the Wiesbaden theater. It was said of her that by extraordinary thrift and orderliness she had transformed the condition of her husband, who had hitherto neglected his affairs, into a thriving prosperity. Raff himself, who had been represented to me by various sources as an eccentric yet gifted fellow who had been up to all sorts of mischief under the protection of Liszt, disappointed me immediately in that I found him to be a rather cold and dry man, full of conceit and yet without any broader vision of things. Taking advantage of the position his wife's care had procured for him, he thought he was entitled to offer me patronizing advice as to my own situation; he told me it would be beneficial if I paid more attention to prevailing conditions as far as my music dramas were concerned, and in this connection referred to *Tristan* as an excrescence of idealistic extravagance. In the course of my rambles around Wiesbaden, I liked to call on Raff's wife occasionally, though she was basically a rather insignificant person, whereas I soon became extraordinarily indifferent to Raff himself. Still, when he got to know me better, he began modifying his oracular sayings, and eventually seemed to develop a certain wariness in regard to my jovial humor, against which he felt himself defenseless.

In Biebrich, on the other hand, Wendelin Weissheimer, whom I had known previously only slightly, began calling on me frequently. He was the son of a rich farmer in Osthofen, who to the astonishment of his father insisted on making music his profession. He was very anxious to introduce me to his father in order to give him a favorable idea of his choice of an artistic career. This led me to excursions to that area, while I had an opportunity to judge young Weissheimer's talent as a conductor through a performance of Offenbach's *Orpheus* in the theater in Mainz, where he had so far risen to only a subordinate position. I was appalled at finding myself dragged down by my sympathy for this young man into attending such an abomination, and for a long time I could not help letting Weissheimer feel my displeasure about it.

I tried to find nobler entertainment by writing to Friederike Meyer in Frankfurt and asking her to let me know when there would be a repetition of Calderón's comedy *The Open Secret*, the announcement of which I had noticed too late. Delighted by my interest, she let me know that, although that play would not be given again in the near future, I could look forward to Calderón's *Don Gutierre*. I went to Frankfurt again for the performance of this play, got to know this interesting actress personally, and all things considered had every reason to be pleased with the production of Calderón's tragedy, although, as the female lead, this brilliant actress[1] was completely successful only in the more tender parts of her role, whereas her powers were insufficient for the great tragic moments. She told me she often visited a family she knew in Mainz, and I responded by expressing the wish that she should look me up in Biebrich: she promised to do so.

A grand soirée given by the Schotts for their acquaintances in Mainz was the occasion of my making friends with Mathilde Maier, whom Frau Schott had especially selected to be my neighbor at table on account of her "cleverness", as she termed it; her intelligent and sincere manner, to which her Mainz dialect seemed particularly suited, distinguished her favorably from the rest of the company, without making her in any way obtrusive. I promised to visit her at her family house and here discovered an urban idyll such as I had not encountered before. Mathilde, the daughter of a lawyer who had died leaving a modest amount of money, lived with her mother, two aunts, and a sister in restricted but neat domesticity, whereas her brother, who was studying commerce in Paris, caused her continual worry. For it was she with her common sense and capable mind who took charge of all the family's affairs, and, seemingly, to the satisfaction of all of them. I was received there with uncommon cordiality whenever I came to Mainz on business, which generally happened once a week, and was invariably pressed to take a little meal with them. As the family also had a wide circle of acquaintances, including among others an old man who had been the sole friend of Schopenhauer, I often met Mathilde elsewhere as well, as for instance at the Raffs' house in Wiesbaden, from where she and an older friend Luise Wagner would accompany me home, just as I would sometimes go on with them to Mainz.

As the fine season of the year now approached, such agreeable impressions, to which frequent walks in the lovely park of Biebrich Castle also contributed their share, now finally rekindled my inclination to do creative work. During a beautiful sunset which transfigured the light as, from the balcony of my apartment, I contemplated a splendid view of "Mainz the Golden" and the majestic Rhine streaming past it, the prelude to my *Meistersinger*, just as I had once previously seen it as a distant apparition rising from a mood of despair, now returned suddenly clear and distinct to my soul. I set about putting the prelude on paper and wrote it down precisely as it is in the score today, with all the main themes of the whole drama already definitively formed. From there I went on in the text, working on the ensuing scenes consecutively.

I was in such a good mood that I also paid a call on the Duke of Nassau.[1] He was my neighbor, and I had seen him so often during my solitary walks in the park that I considered it only proper to introduce myself. Unfortunately nothing much seemed to develop from our conversation; he was a good-natured but limited person, who excused himself for continuing to smoke his cigar in my presence by contending that he could not survive without them. For the rest, he expressed a preference for Italian opera which I was quite content for him to retain. Yet I had a secret purpose in trying to win his favor. In one of the secluded parts of his park, next to a pond, stood an ancient-looking little castle, which was something of a picturesque ruin and at the time was serving as a sculptor's studio. I conceived the bold idea of seeking to have this small and crumbling building allocated to me for the rest of my life; for even now I had begun to worry how long I would be able to hold out in my present flat, because the greater part of the floor on which I occupied two rooms had been rented out for the summer to a "family", of whom I had learned that they would enter armed with a piano. But soon I was advised not to attempt to win the favor of the Duke of Nassau for my plan, as the little castle was very damp and would be injurious to my health.

Nevertheless, nothing could deter me from continuing my search for an isolated small house with a garden. On the excursions I often undertook for this purpose I was frequently accompanied not only by Weissheimer but also that young lawyer Städl, who had made at Schott's house that nice toast I have previously mentioned. He was an odd fellow, whose often very excited temperament I could only explain by the fact that he was a compulsive gambler at the roulette table in Wiesbaden. He introduced me to a friend of his, a Dr Schüler from Wiesbaden who was a good musician as well: together with them both I now weighed all the possibilities of acquiring or even merely finding my little dream castle. To this end we once visited Bingen and climbed the famous old tower in which Emperor Heinrich IV had once been held prisoner. After we had mounted the rather steep cliff on which this tower stood, we found on the fourth floor a single room occupying the whole storey, with just one oriel window overlooking the Rhine. I recognized this as the ideal of all my conceptions of a place to live, and mentally constructed a number of small subsections separated by curtains, thus affording what I thought would become a glorious refuge for the rest of my days. Städl and Schüler did not think it would be necessarily impossible to see my wish fulfilled, as they were in contact with the owner of the ruin. They actually disclosed to me a short time later that the owner had nothing against letting this room for a low rent; yet the utter unfeasibility of carrying out my plan was immediately pointed out to me; nobody would be able to serve me there, they asserted, nor would anyone want to, for among other things the place had no well, and the only water, which was in any case bad, had to be brought up from a frightfully deep cistern beneath the tower keep. It did not require more than one such obstacle to make me give up all such extravagant projects. It went the same way with a large country estate in the Rheingau belonging to Count Schönborn, to which my attention had been drawn for the reason that it was unoccupied by its noble owners: here I found a lot of empty rooms, some of which I could have fitted out for my purposes; but after further investigation with the steward, who transmitted an inquiry to Count Schönborn in the matter, I was given a negative response.

A strange incident that occurred at about this time threatened to disturb me in the work I had resumed. Friederike Meyer kept her promise and visited me one afternoon in the company of a friend, on the way back from her customary expedition to Mainz. After staying only a short while she suddenly became very agitated and announced to the dismay of all that she was afraid she had contracted scarlet fever. As a matter of fact, her condition was soon alarming, so that she first had to take a room at the Europäischer Hof and summon a doctor. The certitude with which she at once identified the sickness befalling her, which in most cases is caught only from children, necessarily struck me as remarkable: but my amazement grew more intense when, early the next morning, Herr von Guaita, the Director of the Frankfurt Theater, rushed to her bedside upon hearing the news. The depth of his solicitude appeared attributable to an interest that went beyond mere professional concern. He took Friederike under his wing at once and treated her with the greatest care, thus relieving me of the pangs of anxiety caused by this strange case. I chatted a bit with Herr von Guaita about the possibility of producing one of my operas in Frankfurt, and on the second day helped conduct the sick lady to the railroad station, to which she was transported by Guaita, it seemed to me, with the most delicate fatherly concern.

Soon after this a Herr Bürde, husband of the well-known singer Ney and at the same time an actor at the Frankfurt Theater, paid me a call: I discussed Friederike Meyer's talent with him, among other things, and he told me she was generally believed to be the mistress of Herr von Guaita, who was greatly respected in the city as a result of his patrician position, and that she had received the present of a house from him in which she was now living. As Herr von Guaita had by no means made an agreeable impression on me, but on the contrary had filled me with uneasiness, this news caused me some worry. By contrast, my other acquaintances living in the proximity of my Biebrich refuge were all most cordial and friendly when I entertained this little circle in my apartment on the evening of my birthday, May 22nd. Mathilde Maier, together with her sister and friend, were most ingenious in utilizing my pitiful inventory of crockery, and in a certain sense she did the honors as mistress of the house.

But now an old source of disturbance was revived in the form of an exchange of increasingly ominous letters with Minna. Having set her up in Dresden, and at the same time wanting to spare her the humiliation of an open separation, I had found myself finally compelled to take the step she had instigated with the Saxon Minister of Justice: I had submitted a request for a complete amnesty and now received it, along with permission to settle in Dresden if I wished. Consequently, Minna felt herself entitled to rent a bigger flat, which could be well furnished with her share of our household effects, on the assumption that I would share it with her in time, at least periodically. I necessarily had to accede without protest to her demands for funds for this purpose and, among other things, try to scrape together the nine hundred talers she required. The more calmly I behaved in this matter, the more she seemed to take offense at my tranquil and dispassionate letters: reproaches for supposed injuries in the past and recriminations of all sorts issued from her at a faster rate than ever before. So I finally turned to my old friend Pusinelli, who for my sake had always stood loyally at the side of this intractable woman, and asked him to prescribe the strong medicine my sister Klara had previously suggested as the best means of curing her sufferings. I asked my friend to urge Minna to consider the necessity for a divorce. It seems to have been no easy matter for my friend to carry out this mission, given the way things stood. He reported to me that she had been greatly shocked but had emphatically refused to countenance the possibility of a divorce by mutual consent. But at any rate Minna's behavior now underwent a marked change, just as my sister had predicted; she ceased tormenting me and seemed to accept the situation. Pusinelli had suggested further treatment for her heart condition at Bad Reichenhall; I sent her the money for this, and she then spent the summer apparently in good spirits at the same place where I had met Cosima taking the cure a year before.

Once again I turned to my work, the best solace whenever such interruptions had been overcome. One night I was disturbed by a strange event. In the course of a pleasant evening I had sketched the agreeable theme of Pogner's words, "Day of St John, that welcome feast" etc., and while dozing off still had the melody floating in my consciousness, when I was suddenly fully awakened by the hysterical laughter of a woman somewhere above me in the house. The laughter grew increasingly wild, and finally turned into horrible whimpering and frightful howling. I sprang out of bed in alarm and then found that this uproar was being caused by my servant girl Lieschen, who was suffering hysterical convulsions in her room, directly above mine. My landlord's maid was there to help her; a doctor was summoned; while I was terrified at the thought that the girl would give up the ghost, I could not help wondering at the curious calm of the others present; I learned that such fits were quite frequent among young girls, particularly after an evening of dancing. For all that, I was held spellbound by the incident and its horrifying phenomena, and remained for a long time to witness the changes, similar to the ebb and flow of a tide, whereby what first seemed mere childish hilarity passed through various stages to the most brazen laughter and then finally to the screams of the damned. The girl ran through this gamut several times before her fit subsided somewhat, whereupon I went back to bed and the melody of Pogner's "Johannistag" returned and gradually dispelled those fearsome impressions.

Watching young Städl one day at the gaming tables in Wiesbaden, it struck me that his condition was somewhat similar to that of the unfortunate servant girl. Together with him and young Weissheimer, I had companionably taken coffee in the garden outside the casino, when Städl suddenly disappeared for a time; in order to find him, Weissheimer led me to the gaming tables. Seldom have I witnessed a more horrifying transmogrification in the countenance of a man as I now saw Städl in the grip of gambling mania. As before with poor Lieschen, a demon seemed to have taken possession of him – doing, as the popular expression has it, the devil's own work. No appeal, no shaming admonition of any kind could prevail upon the man, who was tormented by his losses, to pull himself together. As I remembered the compulsion to gamble I had felt in my own youth for a time, I spoke to young Weissheimer on the subject and offered to show him how I could rely on pure chance, but not on good luck. When a new round of roulette began, I told him in a voice of quiet certitude that number eleven would win: it did. I added fuel to the fire of his astonishment by predicting that number twenty-seven would win the next round, during which I recall feeling a kind of ecstatic transport: this number also won, and now my friend was in such a state of excitement that he fervently urged me to place a bet myself on one of the numbers I was foretelling. And I cannot help recalling the curious and very tranquil exaltation in which I explained to him that, as soon as I introduced my personal interests into the game, my gift of prophecy would disappear at once. I then drew him away from the table, and we went back to Biebrich together in a lovely sunset.

I now got into a very painful entanglement with poor Friederike Meyer: she wrote to tell me of her recovery and requested me to pay her a visit, as she felt it her duty to apologize for any inconvenience caused me. Since the short trip to Frankfurt often amused and diverted me, I gladly fulfilled her wishes, finding her in a state of convalescence but still weak and obviously concerned to dispel any unpleasant conceptions I might have about her. She spoke of her relationship with Herr von Guaita as if he were an almost over-tenderly solicitous father to her. She had left her family when very young, she told me, having in particular dissociated herself from her elder sister Luise, whom she considered as having compromised herself by marrying that distasteful Herr Dustmann, whose name she now bore. And thus, alone in the world, she had come to Frankfurt, where the fortuitous protection of Herr von Guaita, already a man of mature years, had proven very welcome to her. Unfortunately, she had suffered very much as a result of his protection, and in particular from the vile attacks upon her reputation made by his family, as they were obsessed by the idea that he might even want to marry her. In response to this revelation, I could not help letting her know that I had noticed a few signs of this enmity and went so far as to tell her about the rumors concerning the house she had supposedly received as a gift. This seemed to produce a quite extraordinary effect on Friederike, who had scarcely recovered from her illness; she expressed extreme indignation at these rumors, although she had been obliged to suspect that such slanders had been circulating about her for a long time: for this reason, she added, she had been considering abandoning the Frankfurt Theater and was now more than ever determined to do so. I saw no reason to doubt her veracity in all this. Moreover, since Herr von Guaita, in respect of his personality and also of what seemed to me at the time his incomprehensible conduct, struck me increasingly as a doubtful character, I became a strong partisan of this gifted girl's interests, threatened as they were by palpable injustice. I advised her to further her recuperation by arranging for a lengthy vacation to be spent near the Rhine.

In accordance with the instructions received from the Grand Duke,

Eduard Devrient now approached me with regard to the production of *Lohengrin* in Karlsruhe under my direction. The arrogant and downright angry tone of the reproach contained in his letter to me concerning my desire to have *Lohengrin* performed without cuts was admirably calculated to open my eyes about the person I had once so blindly esteemed. He wrote me that the orchestral parts had already been copied out, observing the cuts in the score used by Rietz[1] for his Leipzig performance, and that therefore all the parts I wished restored would have to be laboriously inserted in these copies, a demand which he regarded as nothing less than harassment on my part. I then recalled that the only production of *Lohengrin* that had almost immediately been removed from the boards because of its total lack of success had been precisely that one put on by Rietz in Leipzig, and now here was Devrient, who regarded Rietz as Mendelssohn's successor and the best musician of our time, concluding that this mutilated version of my work was the only one suited for Karlsruhe. I shuddered at the erroneous light in which I had almost forced myself to view Devrient for so long. I notified him at once of my anger about this and my decision to have nothing to do with *Lohengrin* in Karlsruhe, expressing my intention to explain my reasons to the Grand Duke at an appropriate time. I nonetheless learned soon thereafter that *Lohengrin* was to be produced in Karlsruhe in the usual manner, with the Schnorrs as guest singers. I greatly desired to get to know Schnorr and his capabilities; accordingly, I set off for Karlsruhe unannounced, obtained a ticket through Kalliwoda,[2] and thus attended the performance, paying no attention to anything else. I have described the impression made on me by Schnorr in my published recollections of him; I took him to my heart at once, and I sent him a request to spend an hour chatting with me in my hotel room after the performance.

I had heard so much about the poor state of his health that I was truly delighted to see him enter my room, though it was late at night and he had undergone no little strain, with beaming eyes and jaunty step. He met my spontaneous concern to spare him any kind of dissipation by readily accepting my offer to seal our new acquaintanceship with champagne. In the merriest mood we spent a good part of the night in what were for me highly instructive conversations about the character of Devrient, until finally I decided to stay the following day as well, in order to be able to accept his invitation to dine with him and his wife. As I had to assume that the Grand Duke would have learned of my now extended stay in Karlsruhe, I asked to see him the following day and was given an appointment for the afternoon. After talking at luncheon with Frau Schnorr, whom I found to possess a great and well-schooled theatrical talent, and after making the most astonishing discoveries about Devrient's behavior in the *Tristan* affair, the interview in the grand-ducal palace that followed it went off in an atmosphere of some mutual tension. I set forth the reasons why I had revoked my promise with respect to the performance of *Lohengrin* and openly declared my assumptions concerning the manner in which the production of *Tristan* had been undermined by Devrient. As Devrient had cleverly led the Grand Duke to believe in his profound friendship and genuine solicitude for me, all this obviously pained him very much; yet he seemed inclined to believe that it was simply a question of artistic differences between me and his theater director, because when dismissing me he expressed the wish to see these apparent misunderstandings resolved by mutual agreement. At this I told him flatly that I saw no possibility of doing anything together with Devrient. This then caused the Grand Duke to become truly angry; he had not believed, he asserted, I could possibly treat a proven friend so ungratefully. Given the earnestness of this rebuke, I could at first only tender my apologies for not having initially expressed my determination with the seriousness he had a right to expect, but rather only in a manner I had thought proper to the occasion; but inasmuch as the Grand Duke, by the very great importance he attached to the matter, had now seemingly justified me in giving my real opinion about this purported friend, I contended I could now quite properly tell him I wanted to have nothing more to do with Devrient. In response, the Grand Duke reverted to a kindly tone in trying to suggest that he would not regard my declaration as irrevocable, as after all it lay in his power to propitiate me. I departed with an expression of earnest regret that I could see no prospect for the success of any efforts undertaken in this direction by my patron.

I later learned that Devrient, who naturally had been told of the incident by the Grand Duke, saw in this an attempt on my part to remove him from his job and supplant him. As a matter of fact, the Grand Duke had set his heart on my conducting a concert, at which excerpts from my latest works would be played; Devrient was obliged to write me officially about this matter some time later, on which occasion he made it clear he felt himself to be the victor in the intrigues that I had conducted against him, by informing me that his distinguished patron nonetheless wished to carry out the projected concert, as from his lofty point of view he could "make a distinction between the art and the artist". To that I responded with a simple refusal.

I had a long conversation with the Schnorrs about this episode and arranged with them to visit me soon in Biebrich; I then returned there to receive the impending visit of the Bülows. Hans arrived at the beginning of July to look for a place for Cosima to stay, and she followed two days later. We were delighted to be reunited and exploited the opportunity to make all kinds of excursions in the friendly Rheingau. We took our meals together regularly in the dining room of the Europäischer Hof, where the Schnorrs also came to stay, and most of the time we were in high spirits. In the evening we made music. Alwine Frommann, who came through Biebrich on a trip, also attended a *Meistersinger* reading: they all seemed to be surprised at my newest libretto, particularly with regard to the merry popular style I had never employed before. The singer Frau Dustmann, who had been engaged for a guest role in Wiesbaden, also showed up; unfortunately I noticed in her a lively antipathy toward her sister Friederike whom she accused of a scandalous liaison. This strengthened among other things my conviction that it was high time for Friederike to sever all her ties with Frankfurt.

After Bülow's assistance had enabled me to let my friends hear that part of *Die Meistersinger* I had been able to compose, we also went though most of *Tristan*, whereby the Schnorrs had an opportunity to demonstrate how far they had already proceeded in mastering this challenge. On the whole I found that both were still very deficient in clarity of expression.

The arrival of summer brought an increasing flow of visitors to our area, among them many of my acquaintances: the concertmaster David[1] arrived from Leipzig, with his young student August Wilhelmj,[2] the son of a Wiesbaden attorney. Now we could really make music in a satisfactory manner, to which Alois Schmitt,[3] who was Kapellmeister in Schwerin, also made an odd contribution in the form of one of his compositions "taken from cold storage", as he put it. One evening we put on a real soirée, as the Schotts joined the rest of my friends, and the two Schnorrs delighted us with a rendition of the so-called love scene from the third act of *Lohengrin*.

We were all greatly moved one day to see Röckel suddenly enter the hotel dining room. After thirteen years of imprisonment within the confines of the Waldheim jail he had at last been released. But I was amazed to find in my old friend, apart from the fact that his hair had turned gray, no real change. He explained this to me by stating that he felt as if he had now emerged from a shell in which he had been enclosed for his own protection. When we were considering what kind of job he should now look for, I thought it best to advise him to ask for a position in the service of a benevolent and liberal prince like the Grand Duke of Baden. He did not think he could succeed in any ministry owing to his lack of legal knowledge; by contrast, he felt he was eminently qualified for work in prison administration, for he had gained a great deal of first-hand knowledge in this field and at the same time had recognized what reforms were most needed. He went off to the German riflemen's competition being held in Frankfurt at about this time and, in recognition of his martyrdom and unwavering conduct, was accorded a most flattering public ovation there. He remained in Frankfurt and its surroundings for some time.

Apart from this, my close friends and I were pestered by a painter named Cäsar Willich, whom Otto Wesendonck had commissioned to paint my portrait. His wife having just given birth at the time, Wesendonck had hit upon the idea of making her a truly expressive gift with my portrait. Unfortunately it proved impossible to lead the painter to any adequate conception of my physiognomy: although Cosima was present at nearly all the sittings and tried everything to put the painter on the right track, there finally remained no recourse other than to offer him only my profile, so that he could at least produce something remotely resembling me. After he had accomplished this to his own satisfaction, he made a copy out of gratitude as a present for me, which I sent immediately to Minna in Dresden, through whom it later went to my sister Luise. It was a terrible picture, which I encountered once again when it was put on display by the painter in Frankfurt.

I had a pleasant outing with the Bülows and Schnorrs to Bingen one evening; from Rüdesheim on the opposite bank, where she was enjoying her vacation, I fetched Friederike Meyer for the occasion and introduced her to my friends, Cosima in particular taking a friendly interest in this unusually gifted young woman. Our gaiety as we sat in the open air with our glasses of wine was heightened by an unexpected occurrence: we were accosted by a stranger who approached us respectfully from a distant table, and, extending his full glass toward me, delivered a very fervent and edifying greeting; he was a Berliner and an ardent enthusiast for my works. He spoke not only for himself but also on behalf of two of his friends, who thereupon came to sit at our table, where our high spirits finally seduced us into ordering champagne. A glorious evening with a wonderful moonrise consecrated the lovely mood in which we returned late at night from this agreeable excursion.

After we had visited Schlangenbad, where Alwine Frommann was staying, in equally fine humor, our exuberance now led us to an even longer expedition to Rolandseck. On this trip we first stopped at Remagen, where we visited the beautifully situated church where a young monk was preaching to a tremendous crowd, after which we took our midday meal in a garden on the banks of the Rhine. We put up for the night in Rolandseck, from where we went early the next day to climb the Drachenfels. There was an incident in connection with this ascent which had an amusing sequel. When we had arrived at the railroad station on the opposite bank of the Rhine after coming back down, I missed my wallet which had slipped out of my overcoat pocket, together with its contents, a hundred-guilder note: two gentlemen who had joined us at the Drachenfels immediately offered to retrace their steps, certainly an arduous undertaking, to search for the lost wallet. And after a few hours they actually returned, bringing me the wallet and its contents, which had been found at the top of the hill by two stone-knappers working there and immediately turned over to them. These honest people had been given, as I had instructed, a decent finder's reward, and now the happy outcome to this adventure had to be celebrated with a merry meal with the best of wines. The whole thing was capped for me many years later: when I entered a restaurant in Cologne in the year 1873, the manager introduced himself as the same man who had taken care of us in that tavern on the banks of the Rhine eleven years before, and who had received that aforementioned hundred-guilder note to make change; the following had happened with this note, he then told me: an Englishman to whom he had related this story that same day offered to buy the note at double its face value; he had declined the offer flatly, but instead let the Britisher have the note against the promise to provide champagne to all those present who had heard of the incident. This promise had then been fulfilled most generously.

A less satisfactory excursion was the result of an invitation from the Weissheimer family to Osthofen; there we were bedded down for the night after being compelled to take part the foregoing day in a country wedding feast that went on to all hours. Cosima was the only one who remained in good spirits throughout this trial, but while I stood by her in this as best I could, the discontent which had been accumulating in Bülow over a long period, at everything that happened to him in life, goaded him into several outbursts of rage. We tried to console ourselves that nothing like this could happen to us again. The following day, while I, brooding on other reasons for my discontent with my situation, prepared to return home, Cosima induced Hans to continue the trip as far as Worms, where he might find distraction and recreation in inspecting the old cathedral there. They later followed me to Biebrich.

Another little adventure we had at the gambling tables in Wiesbaden still lingers in my memory. I had just received a fee of twenty louis d'or from some theater for an opera; not really knowing what I could do with such a small sum, considering the fact that my financial situation was getting worse and worse, I ventured to ask Cosima to try our joint luck and risk half the sum at roulette. I looked on with amazement as she proceeded, without any knowledge of even the simplest rudiments of the game, to throw one gold piece after another on the table in such a manner that they never covered any specific number or color and regularly vanished behind the croupier's rake. I became worried and quickly disappeared to go to another table in order to offset Cosima's hapless and inept efforts. In this financial maneuver I was instantly favored by good fortune to the extent of immediately recouping the ten louis d'or my friend had lost, and this led to great merriment on our part.

The visit we paid together to Wiesbaden for a performance of *Lohengrin* turned out less happily. After we had been quite well satisfied and put into a good mood by the first act, the production lapsed throughout the rest of the work into such infuriating distortion as I had not believed possible; I left the theater in a rage before the performance was over, while Hans remained in martyrdom to the end at Cosima's behest in order to preserve appearances, though both were no less angry than I.

On another occasion I heard that the Metternichs had arrived at their Castle Johannisberg. Still preoccupied by my desire for a tranquil place in which to complete my *Meistersinger*, I immediately got the idea that the castle, which normally stood empty, might serve my purpose and got word to the Prince that I would like to visit him, upon which an invitation followed forthwith. The Bülows accompanied me to the railroad station. I had nothing to complain about as far as my reception by my patrons was concerned. They had already thought of the possibility of harboring me temporarily at Johannisberg Castle and had decided they could easily offer me rooms in the steward's quarters, although they felt it necessary to point out possible difficulties in procuring my meals. But the prince had been more concerned with another possibility, that of providing me with a permanent position in Vienna. He intended, he said, to speak to Minister Schmerling[1] on this matter on the occasion of his next stay in Vienna, as he considered him the best person to do something for me: he would understand me, he said, and perhaps be able to discover a suitable position for me in the higher sense of the term, and even interest the Emperor on my behalf. When I returned to Vienna I was simply to look up Schmerling, safe in the assumption that I had already been introduced to him by the Prince. The Metternichs soon left in response to an invitation to the ducal court at Wiesbaden, to which city I accompanied them and then rejoined the Bülows there.

When the Schnorrs had departed after a stay of two weeks, the time also approached when the Bülows would have to leave. I accompanied them to Frankfurt, where we stayed two days in order to attend a performance of Goethe's *Tasso*, which was supposed to be introduced by a rendition of Liszt's tone poem of the same title. The performance evoked mixed feelings in us. Friederike Meyer as the Princess, and especially a Herr Schneider as Tasso, appealed to us greatly, but Hans, in particular, could not get over the scandalous treatment accorded Liszt's work by the conductor Ignaz Lachner.[1] Friederike gave a luncheon for us in the restaurant at the Botanical Gardens before the performance, at which the mysterious Herr von Guaita also eventually made an appearance. To our astonishment, from this point on the conversation became a duologue for the two of them while we perforce listened uncomprehendingly, able to discern only his intense jealousy and Friederike's witty and scornful defense against it. Yet for all his excitement Guaita pulled himself together somewhat when he discussed with me his project to produce *Lohengrin* under my direction in Frankfurt. I was favorably inclined to this plan, as I saw in it an opportunity for another get-together with the Bülows and the Schnorrs. The Bülows promised to come, and I got after the Schnorrs to consent to be in the cast. And so we thought we could bid one another farewell cheerfully this time, even though the increasing and often excessive ill temper of Hans had drawn many an involuntary sigh from me, as he seemed always to feel tormented by something or other. On the other hand, Cosima appeared to have lost the shyness she evinced toward me during my visit to Bad Reichenhall the previous year in a most agreeable sense. When I had played and sung "Wotan's Farewell" for my friends one day in my own special way, I noticed on Cosima's countenance the same expression she had showed me, much to my surprise, at that leave-taking in Zürich; but this time the ecstasy had dissolved into a serene transfiguration. Here everything was silence and mystery, only now the belief in her belonging to me came over me with such certitude that in my eccentric exuberance I got a wild idea. When I was conducting Cosima across an open square back to her hotel it occurred to me to dare her to jump into a wheel-barrow which stood empty nearby so that I could wheel her back to the hotel: she was game for it at once, whereas I, again struck by astonishment, lost the courage to carry out my mad project. Following behind us, Bülow had witnessed the incident; Cosima explained to him unabashedly what it was all about, but unfortunately it did not appear that he could share our high spirits, for he cautioned his wife to be more careful in such things.

On returning to Biebrich I was confronted by grave problems. After a long delay Schott finally refused flatly to give me any further cash advances. Yet I had been paying all my expenses since shortly after leaving Vienna by these advances from my publisher alone. These expenses included the settlement of my wife in Dresden, and my own move to Biebrich, which of course I had made via Paris, where I had to satisfy many hidden creditors. Despite this onerous beginning, which in fact had swallowed up more than half the total sum we had agreed upon for *Die Meistersinger*, I now thought I could manage to complete the work in tranquillity with the rest of the amount due me. But since then Schott had been putting me off with consolatory references to settlement dates with his retailers. I had already had to take some difficult steps to help myself: everything seemed to depend on whether I could soon deliver a complete act of *Die Meistersinger* to Schott. In this I had reached the scene where Pogner is about to present Walther to the masters, when, in about mid-August and while the Bülows were still there, I became the victim of what was in itself a minor accident, but which nonetheless managed to make it impossible for me to write for a full two months. My surly landlord had a bulldog named Leo which he kept chained up, and this cruel neglect on the part of his master had made me continually sorry for him. Thus one day I wanted to help free him of lice and, in order that the servant-girl would not be frightened while doing this, held his head: despite the great affection the dog had formed for me, he once snapped involuntarily and bit me, apparently only superficially, in the upper joint of my right thumb; there was no visible wound, yet it soon turned out that the flesh surrounding the bone had become inflamed as a result of the contusion. The more I used the thumb, the greater the pain became, and I was ordered not to use the hand to write until my hand had healed completely. While newspapers reported that I had been bitten by a mad dog, the case was bad enough, though not as ominous as that, to make me reflect seriously on human fragility. To complete my work I thus needed not only a sound mind, good ideas and other skills I had acquired, but also a healthy thumb to write with, for here it was not a question of dictating a poem but creating music no one else could write down.

In order to be able to deliver something commercially viable for Schott to be going on with, I took the advice of Raff, who thought a sheaf of songs by me would be worth one thousand francs, and offered him the five poems by my friend Frau Wesendonck which I had set to music based largely on my studies for *Tristan* at the time. The songs were accepted and published, but seemingly without achieving any favorable impact on Schott's overall frame of mind. I had to conclude that he had been the victim of some slander against me: to get to the bottom of it I went myself to Bad Kissingen, where he was taking a cure. But I was stubbornly denied a talk with him, as Frau Schott was posted outside his door like a guardian angel to inform me that a bad liver ailment prevented her husband from seeing me. This told me enough, and so I got some money for the interim from young Weissheimer, who was supported by his rich father and was glad to do me this favor, and began considering what my next alternative would be, inasmuch as I could no longer count on Schott and thus could not think of finishing *Die Meistersinger* unimpeded.

Under these circumstances I was greatly surprised to receive a renewed official invitation to Vienna to supervise the production of *Tristan*. I was informed that all obstacles had been removed, for Ander had completely recovered from his vocal troubles. I was honestly amazed at all this, and upon closer inquiry arrived at the following interpretation of the events that had transpired in Vienna since my departure. Before I had left there the last time, Frau Luise Dustmann, who seemed to have been really struck by the part of Isolde, had tried to do away with the real hindrance to my undertaking by persuading me to attend an evening party at which she wanted to bring me together with Dr Hanslick again. She knew that unless this gentleman could be brought around to my cause, nothing could be done for me in Vienna; my good mood made it easy for me on that evening to treat Hanslick for some time as a casual acquaintance up to the point when he took me aside for an intimate talk and assured me, with tears and sobs, that he could no longer bear it to see himself misunderstood by me; the blame for anything untoward in his judgments about me, he averred, was certainly not rooted in a malevolent intention but solely in a limitation of the individual, and he would like nothing better than to have the boundaries of his knowledge extended by my instruction. These declarations were made with such an explosion of emotion that I could feel no wish other than to soothe his pain and promised him my undivided sympathy in his further pursuits. Shortly before my departure from Vienna I had actually learned that Hanslick was running around among my acquaintances praising me and my kindliness to the skies. This transformation had duly affected the singers of the Opera House, and especially Councillor Raymond, the adviser to the Imperial Court Chamberlain, in such a way that finally the official higher view was said to be that the production of *Tristan* was a point of honor for Vienna. This was the reason for my renewed summons.

At the same time young Weissheimer notified me from Leipzig, to which he had repaired, that he thought he could arrange a good concert there if I would support him with the performance of my new prelude to *Die Meistersinger* as well as the *Tannhäuser* overture. He was sure this would attract so much attention that he could raise the price of admission, and after selling out the house and deducting only the costs, he would be able to place a not insignificant sum at my disposal. In addition to this, I could scarcely renege on my promise to Herr von Guaita with regard to the production of *Lohengrin* in Frankfurt, despite the fact that the Schnorrs had been obliged to decline my invitation to participate. Weighing all these requests, I now planned to put *Die Meistersinger* aside for the time being and try to make enough from these outside activities to enable me to take up the work again the following spring and complete it irrespective of Schott's tergiversations. Therefore I decided to retain my congenial apartment in Biebrich at all costs. Minna, on the other hand, had been pressing me to send her some of the furniture including my bed and other objects which I had grown accustomed to, in order that her Dresden establishment would be complete, and "so that I would find everything in perfect order when I got there". If I were not to act in contravention of the established fiction that facilitated her separation from me, I had no choice other than to send her what she demanded, and so I re-equipped my Rhenish retreat with the help of a Wiesbaden furniture manufacturer, who offered me long-term credit for this purpose.

At the end of September I went to Frankfurt for a week to take command of the rehearsals for *Lohengrin*. Here again I went through the same experience as so often before: after the first contact with the company I was ready to give up the whole undertaking immediately; but then the general consternation and the entreaties to persevere had their effect, and I succumbed to their influence until I finally began to take an interest in the effect to be achieved by an uncut performance, correct tempi, as well as proper scenic direction, and tried to ignore the miserable singers. Yet Friederike Meyer was probably the only one who felt this effect to the full; the public was as "animated" as usual, but I was told later that the subsequent performances directed by Herr Ignaz Lachner, who was held in the highest esteem in Frankfurt and was an utterly wretched and incompetent conductor, fell off so badly in their effect that, in order to keep the opera on the boards, the old butchery had to be resumed.

The impact of all this was all the more depressing because even the Bülows had been unable to be among the guests. Cosima, I now learned, had been obliged to rush through on her way to Paris in order to be with her bedridden grandmother, who had just received a new and most distressing shock. Blandine had died in childbirth, after having had to endure her confinement in St Tropez. Now I locked myself away for some time in my apartment in Biebrich when the raw weather began and managed to compel my very carefully guarded thumb to function in the instrumentation of some passages of *Die Meistersinger* for use in concert form. I sent the prelude to Weissheimer at once to have the parts copied in Leipzig, and also adapted the "Assembly of the Masters" as well as "Pogner's Address" for the orchestra.

By the end of October I was finally ready to begin my journey to Leipzig. During the trip I was once again induced to visit the Wartburg in strange circumstances: in Eisenach, where I had stepped out of the railway carriage for a few minutes, the train had suddenly begun to pull out just as I was hurriedly trying to climb back aboard; I instinctively ran after the departing train with a hasty yell to the conductor, but naturally without being able to halt it. There was a rather large crowd at the station assembled to attend the departure of a prince, and these people now broke out into loud laughter at my plight; I asked them whether they were actually amused to see this happen to me. "Yes, we are very amused", came the reply. From this incident I derived the axiom that one can at least help to amuse the German public by one's own misfortunes. As the next train to Leipzig was not scheduled for another five hours, I telegraphed my brother-in-law Hermann Brockhaus, whom I had asked to put me up, to notify him I would be late and then let myself be persuaded by a guide who introduced himself to me to visit the Wartburg. There I inspected the partial restorations undertaken at the behest of the Grand Duke, including the hall with its pictures by

Schwind.[1] But it all left me rather cold, and I then went to the restaurant of this Eisenach playground, where I saw various good ladies engaged in knitting stockings. The Grand Duke of Weimar assured me later that *Tannhäuser* enjoyed immense popularity throughout Thuringia right down to the last peasant boy: but neither the host nor my guide seemed to know anything about it; I entered my full name in the guest book and added a few remarks concerning the pleasant salutation I had received at the railroad station. I have never learned whether anybody noticed this.

Hermann Brockhaus, who had aged somewhat and grown fat, gave me a most cheerful reception when I arrived in Leipzig late that night, conducting me to his house where I found Ottilie with her family and was comfortably installed with them. We had much to talk about, and my brother-in-law's characteristic high spirits in participating in such conversations often kept us enthralled until all hours of the morning. My association with the entirely unknown young composer Weissheimer aroused some misgivings: his concert program was in fact packed with a large number of his own compositions, among which was included his recently completed tone poem *Der Ritter Toggenburg*. If I had attended the rehearsals in a dispassionate mood, I would no doubt have objected to the carrying out of this program in full; but on the contrary, the hours I spent in the concert hall belong to the most treasured and intimate memories of my life, for it was there I met the Bülows again. Hans had felt it his duty to support me in consecrating Weissheimer's debut by performing a new piano concerto by Liszt at the concert. The mere act of entering the old familiar Gewandhaus hall, along with the task of introducing myself to the members of the orchestra as if I were a complete stranger, for none of them seemed to know me, was enough to make me feel ill-at-ease and captious. But suddenly I felt utterly transported by the sight of Cosima, sitting in a corner of the hall, very pale and in deep mourning yet smiling at me warmly. She had just returned from Paris from the bed of her incurably sick grandmother, filled with grief at the inexplicably sudden death of her sister, and thus she now appeared to me as if stepping toward me from another world. Our emotions were so solemn and so deep that only our absolute surrender to the joy of meeting again could help us bridge that abyss. All the events of the rehearsals struck us as an oddly amusing magic lantern show, at which we looked on like laughing children. Hans was also in good spirits, for we all thought of ourselves as being involved in an adventure worthy of Don Quixote, and at one point he called my attention to Brendel, who was sitting quite near us and seemed to expect me to greet him. I found it amusing to prolong his suspense by pretending not to recognize him; this seems to have wounded the poor man so greatly that, in order to make amends for this mean trick, I made a point of alluding specially to Brendel's achievements when I later discussed *Judaism in Music* in a public forum. This was my way of atonement to a man deceased by then.

The arrival of Alexander Ritter with my niece Franziska[1] also contributed to our general merriment; this was continually stimulated by the monstrosities of Weissheimer's compositions; Ritter, who already knew the text of my *Meistersinger*, described a deeply melancholy and highly incoherent melody for the contrabasses in *Der Ritter Toggenburg* as "the lonely glutton tune". Our good spirits might have failed us in the end, however, had it not been for the impressions produced by the successful rendition of the *Meistersinger* prelude as well as the new composition by Liszt with Bülow's glorious performance at the keyboard, all of which nobly refreshed our mood. The concert itself finally confirmed the chimerical quality of the entire adventure, in the anticipation of which we had felt such pleasant enjoyment. To the consternation of Weissheimer, the Leipzig public stayed away in droves, and indeed the sponsors of the subscription concerts seem to have instructed people to do so. I have never seen such an empty hall for any similar occasion: apart from my family, among whom my sister Ottilie was distinguished by a very eccentric hat, there were only a few rows filled with some visitors from out of town who had come to attend this concert. Prominent among them were my Weimar friends: the conductor Lassen[2] and Councillor Franz Müller, as well as Richard Pohl who never failed, and Judge Gille, all faithfully put in an appearance. In addition, and much to my astonishment, I also noticed old Councillor Küstner, the former intendant of the Berlin Court Theater, to whose greeting and amazement at the incomprehensible emptiness of the hall I had to return a civil answer. The people of Leipzig were represented solely by some special friends of my family, who otherwise never went to concerts, among them my devoted admirer Dr Lothar Müller, the son of Dr Moritz Müller, an allopathist I had known and liked in early youth. In the middle of the hall there was only the bride of the concert-giver, together with her mother; during the course of the concert I took my place some distance away from them together with Cosima, and this seemed to annoy the members of my family, who were observing us from afar and could not comprehend why we were incessantly laughing, while they sat there in high dudgeon. As to the prelude to *Die Meistersinger*, it produced such a favorable effect on the few friends constituting the public that we had to repeat it then and there, which pleased even the orchestra. Indeed, this seemed to break the ice of their artificially nurtured distrust of me; for when I closed the concert with the *Tannhäuser* overture, the orchestra celebrated my recall to the podium with a tremendous flourish from all instruments, which especially delighted my sister Ottilie beyond measure, for she asserted that this honor had previously been accorded only to Jenny Lind. My friend Weissheimer, who had really exhausted everybody's patience in a most irresponsible way, gradually developed a feeling of resentment toward me dating from this period: he felt entitled to contend that he would have done better not to have included my brilliant orchestral works but rather to have offered solely his own compositions to the public at reduced prices. As it was, he had to bear the losses, much to the disappointment of his father, and also overcome the unnecessary humiliation of being unable to offer me any profits.

My brother-in-law was undeterred by these painful impressions from carrying out the domestic celebrations prearranged in expectation of our triumph. The Bülows also attended this banquet. There was an evening party at which I read the *Meistersinger* libretto to excellent effect before a stately assemblage of professors. Here I renewed my acquaintance with Professor Weiss, who interested me very much, as I remembered him as a friend of my uncle. He expressed particular amazement at my artistry as a reader.

By then the Bülows had unfortunately returned to Berlin; we had seen each other once again on a very cold day on the street in unfavorable circumstances, as they were going about the ritual of paying return calls, and during our short leave-taking the general depression that weighed on us seemed more noticeable than the fleeting high spirits of the last few days. My friends were also undoubtedly well aware of the utterly forlorn and terrible position in which I found myself. I had been so foolish as actually to delude myself that the receipts from my Leipzig concert undertaking would at least provide me with enough money to tide me over for the moment. In this regard, I was first of all embarrassed by being unable to pay the rent due my landlord in Biebrich punctually, for I was staking everything on being able to retain this place of refuge for another year, and in him I was compelled to deal with an obstinate, ill-tempered fellow whom I thought I could induce to grant me an extension of the lease only by prepayment. As I was also obliged to take care of Minna by sending her quarterly remittance at this time, help

provided by Councillor Müller acting on behalf of the Grand Duke of
Weimar seemed truly heaven-sent. After I had given up entirely on
Schott, I had turned in my distress to this old acquaintance and asked
him to discuss my situation with the Grand Duke in the hope of
persuading him to help, possibly in the form of an advance payment for
my new operas. In response to this I now received through Müller the
remarkable and unexpected sum of five hundred talers. It was only later
that I accounted for this friendly gesture on the part of the Grand Duke
by the explanation that it had constituted a deliberate attempt to
influence Liszt, whom he wanted to lure back to Weimar at all costs;
His Highness was certainly not mistaken in his assumption that obliging
and generous conduct toward me would have a splendid effect on our
mutual friend.

Thus, I was now in a position to go to Dresden for a few days, in
order to supplement the financial assistance I was giving Minna by
paying her the honor of the visit she believed to be essential if she were
to maintain her difficult position. Minna met me at the railroad station
and conducted me to the flat she had taken and furnished in the
Walpurgisstrasse, a street which had not existed at the time I left
Dresden. She had set up her household once again in her usual skillful
manner and with the intention of making me feel at home in it; at the
entrance was a little doormat on which she had embroidered the word
"Salve". I recognized our Paris drawing room at once in the red silk
curtains and the furniture. I was to have a stately bedroom, as well as
an exceedingly comfortable adjoining study, which, together with the
salon, were to be for my exclusive use, while Minna installed herself in
one small room with alcoves, overlooking the courtyard. The study was
adorned by the magnificent mahogany bureau custom-made for me when
I became a conductor at Dresden, but which had been bought by the
Ritter family at the time of my flight and given to their son-in-law
Kummer; Minna had procured this from him on loan, and now
suggested I buy it back for sixty talers: when I did not respond warmly
to the idea, her mood became gloomier. Oppressed by the anxiety and
tension she felt at being alone with me, she had invited my sister Klara
to come from Chemnitz to visit us and shared her small quarters with
her. Klara proved here as before most discreet and discerning: she no
doubt pitied Minna and wanted to help her over a difficult period, yet
always in the intention of strengthening her in the conviction that our
continued separation was necessary. Precise awareness of my very

precarious position was needed to foster this conviction: the money worries were so overriding that they served as a counterweight to Minna's other distraught ideas. But I did succeed in avoiding all arguments with her, which was in part attributable to the fact that we spent most of our time in the company of others, the chief occasions being a reunion with the family of Fritz Brockhaus along with his married daughter Klara Kessinger, as well as with the Pusinellis, old Heine, and finally both the Schnorrs.

I spent the mornings paying visits, and when I set out to pay my respects to Minister Bär in gratitude for my amnesty, and thus found myself promenading through the streets of Dresden for the first time again, the initial impression was one of boredom and emptiness, for I had seen them last in a fantastically barricaded state which had made them much more interesting. I knew none of the people I passed; even the glover, whose shop I had always patronized and where I was now obliged to go once again, did not seem to know me, until suddenly, while I actually stood in the shop, an elderly man rushed in from the street in highest excitement and with tears in his eyes: it was the now greatly aged Karl Kummer, the greatest oboe player I have ever encountered and to whom I had been almost affectionately devoted as a result. We embraced in great joy, and I asked if he were still producing such wonderful sounds with his instrument, whereupon he replied that, ever since I had left, the oboe hadn't really appealed to him: he had permitted himself to be pensioned off long ago. In response to my inquiries he told me that all my old stalwarts in the orchestra, including the tall contrabassist Dietz, had died or been pensioned, while both von Lüttichau and Reissiger had died, Lipinsky had long since returned to Poland, and Concertmaster Schubert was no longer fit for work; thus everything seemed colorless and new to me. Minister Bär expressed considerable reservations about my amnesty, which he had nonetheless dared to sign himself even though he was still afraid that in view of my great popularity as a composer of operas I could be the cause of some annoying demonstrations. But I consoled him in this regard with the assurance that I would be here for only a few days, and would not go to the theater: at this he sighed deeply and dismissed me with an exceedingly grave look. My reception by Herr von Beust contrasted sharply with this: with smiling elegance he chatted with me, suggesting that I could not possibly be as innocent as I seemed to consider myself; he pointed out to me a letter which had been found in Röckel's pocket in those days: this was new to me, and I readily conceded I felt obliged to regard the amnesty I had received as a pardon for past imprudence. We parted with the most cordial expressions of friendship.

We had one more evening party in Minna's salon, where I again read *Meistersinger* for the benefit of those who did not yet know it. After I had provided Minna with enough money for quite a long period, she accompanied me on the fourth day to the railroad station, where she took an anguished leave of me with anxious forebodings that she would never see me again.

In Leipzig I stopped off for a day at a hotel where I met Alexander Ritter again and spent a pleasant evening with him over some punch. My reason for this short visit was that I had been assured that a concert exclusively devoted to my own works would attract an exceptional crowd: considering my need for money, I had also examined this possibility but now found that such an undertaking would by no means be financially secure and hastened back to Biebrich, where I had to put my household matters in order. Here to my great annoyance I found my landlord in an increasingly difficult mood; he seemed unable to forget that I had criticized him for the way he treated his dog and had taken the part of my servant-girl when he had been angry about her love affair with a local tailor. Despite payment and promises, he remained intractable and insisted he would have to move into my part of the house for health reasons no later than the following spring. While I was able to compel him by means of a prepayment to leave my household as it stood at least until Easter, I again set about, under the guidance of Dr Schüler and Mathilde Maier, to search the Rheingau for a suitable place to live for the next year. The time being so short, however, I met with no success, though my friends promised to hunt untiringly for what I needed.

In Mainz I saw Friederike Meyer again. Her position in Frankfurt seemed to have become even more intolerable; when she heard I had turned away Herr von Guaita's stage director when he had come to Biebrich some time before under instructions to pay me fifteen louis d'or for conducting *Lohengrin*, she strongly approved my action; she herself, it seemed, had broken completely with that gentleman, had insisted on being released from her contract, and was now about to take up an engagement promised her at the Vienna Burgtheater. By her action and determination she gained my sympathy anew, for I considered all this a strong rebuttal to the slanders to which she had been subjected. As I was also about to leave for Vienna, she was pleased to be able to make part of the journey with me, because she expected to stop for one day in Nuremberg where I could meet her for the rest of the trip. This we did and arrived in Vienna together, where she went to the Hotel Munsch, while I again took up residence in my already familiar Empress Elisabeth. This was on November 15th.[1] I looked up Herr Esser at once and learned from him that everybody was working very zealously on *Tristan*; but my easily misinterpreted relationship to her sister soon caused me extremely unpleasant quarrels with Frau Dustmann. I simply couldn't explain things to her satisfaction, as she considered her sister as being involved in a scandalous affair with Herr von Guaita and thus a disgrace to her family, the upshot being that she felt compromised by her presence in Vienna. To top it off, Friederike's own condition soon aroused my most intense concern. She had contracted for three guest performances at the Burgtheater without bearing in mind how unfit she was at that time to make a favorable impression in the theater, particularly before a Viennese audience; the severe sickness from which she had recovered only in the most turbulent circumstances had disfigured her by making her unduly thin; in addition, her head had grown virtually bald, and yet she insisted on refusing to use a wig. The enmity of her sister had alienated the members of the Burgtheater company, and as a result of all this, as well as an inept choice of roles, her appearances were a failure, and there could be no question of a permanent engagement. Although she grew steadily weaker and suffered from constant insomnia, she still tried to conceal her true situation from me out of courageous reticence. At a somewhat cheaper inn, The City of Frankfurt, she now intended, as she did not seem to be embarrassed for funds, to spare her nerves as much as possible and await an improvement: at my request she summoned Standhartner, who didn't seem to be able to help her very much. As the climate now became extremely raw – for it was the end of November and the beginning of December – I got the idea, inasmuch as she had been told to exercise a good deal in the open air, to recommend to her a lengthy stay in Venice. She also seemed to have plenty of money for this: she followed my advice and on an icy cold morning I accompanied her to the station, where I abandoned her, together with the faithful maid who had been with her, to what I hoped would be a better fate. I had the satisfaction of soon receiving encouraging reports from her from Venice, especially concerning her health.

While these matters involved me in all sorts of difficult complications, I had been keeping up my old acquaintances in Vienna. A strange incident[1] had occurred at the outset of this visit. I was to read my *Meistersinger* for the Standhartner family, just as I had done everywhere else: since Herr Hanslick was now considered a friend of mine, they thought it would be a good idea to invite him as well; but here we noticed in the course of the reading that this fearsome critic became constantly paler and angrier, and remarkably enough, when the reading was over he could not be persuaded to remain for a time, but departed at once in obvious vexation. My friends all concluded that Hanslick had interpreted the entire libretto as a pasquinade directed at him and our invitation to the reading as an insult. And the critic's attitude toward me indeed underwent a highly noticeable change from that evening forward and turned into bitter enmity, the results of which we were soon to see.

Cornelius and Tausig had meanwhile showed up again. First of all I had to vent my sincere displeasure with them for their behavior the previous summer: when I had seen the prospect of uniting the Bülows and the Schnorrs with me at Biebrich, my hearty liking for these two young friends had made me invite them as well. I had received an acceptance from Cornelius at once, and was thus all the more astonished one day to get a letter from him in Geneva, where Tausig, who seemed suddenly to have plenty of money, had lured him for what was apparently a more promising and agreeable summer excursion. Without the slightest expression of regret at not being able to meet me that summer, it was only reported to me that both had just jubilantly "smoked a glorious cigar to my health". When both now arrived in Vienna it remained impossible for me to refrain from pointing out to them how insulting their behavior had been, although they couldn't seem to grasp why I would object to their having chosen a lovely excursion through French Switzerland in preference to a visit to Biebrich. They obviously considered me a tyrant. Tausig also became suspect to me through his odd conduct in my hotel. I learned that he usually took his meals in the restaurant on the ground floor, and then invariably went up to the fourth floor, avoiding my rooms entirely, to visit a Countess Krockow.[2] When I asked him about this and learned that this lady was also well acquainted with Cosima, I expressed my amazement that he had not introduced me to her as well; with singularly incoherent excuses he continually avoided following my suggestion; when I began teasing him about a supposed love affair, he told me there could be no question of that, for the lady was already quite old. So I let him alone, but my astonishment at Tausig's strange conduct increased when I got to know Countess

Krockow in later years. I found she was an earnest admirer of mine and learned that she had wanted nothing more intensely at that time than to make my acquaintance, which Tausig had stubbornly refused to arrange, upon the pretext that I did not enjoy the company of women.

But we eventually resumed our lively, friendly association when I began seriously considering the execution of my plan to give concerts in Vienna. While I left the piano rehearsals for the vocal roles in *Tristan* in the hands of the conscientious conductor Esser, who seemed to be handling them very industriously, my mistrust as to the actual success of these preparations remained undispelled. It was less a matter of doubting the capabilities of the participants than their good faith in the whole affair. The absurd behavior of Frau Dustmann, in particular, had managed to make me forgo frequent attendance at the rehearsals. By contrast, I promised myself a favorable effect from concerts consisting of fragments from new works of mine still unknown in Vienna, because I thought I could thereby show my hidden enemies that there were other means at my disposal to bring my more recent works before the public beside theatrical performances which it was so easy for them to impede. In all practical matters pertaining to this project Tausig was a great help. We decided to rent the Theater an der Wien for three evenings, the idea being to give a concert there at the end of December and repeat it twice at intervals of a week. The first task was to copy the orchestral parts for the fragments I took from my scores for this concert: these consisted of two fragments from *Das Rheingold*, two from *Die Walküre* and two more from *Die Meistersinger*, whereas I withheld the prelude to *Tristan* in order not to prejudice the performance of the whole work in the opera house, which was still scheduled for a subsequent date. With the help of some assistants, Cornelius and Tausig now got to work on this job, which could only be accomplished by people experienced in reading scores if the necessary musical correctness were to be achieved. They were joined by Weissheimer, who had arrived in Vienna for the purpose of attending this concert. Tausig now notified me that Brahms, whom he commended as "a very fine fellow", was quite willing, despite the fact that he was already so famous, to take over some of the work himself: he actually received a part of *Die Meistersinger* to copy. Brahms behaved here in a truly modest and good-natured way; only he showed little vivacity, so that in our gatherings he often went almost unnoticed. I also ran across Friedrich Uhl again, an old acquaintance who was now editing, together with Julius Fröbel, a political journal called *Der Botschafter* under Schmerling's auspices. He placed the columns of his journal at my disposal and induced me to give him the first act of the *Meistersinger* libretto for his feuilleton: my friends insisted they noticed Hanslick growing more and more venomous.

While my companions and I were deeply mired in the preparations for the concert, a certain Herr Moritz popped up one day, whom Bülow had already introduced to me in Paris as a silly fellow. His clumsy and importunate conduct, combined with obviously fictive reports of things Bülow wanted me to do, impelled me, spurred by Tausig's impatience with him, to show this unwanted intruder the door. He reported this to Cosima in a manner so insulting to Bülow that she in turn found it necessary to write me expressing her intense indignation at such thoughtless behavior on my part toward my most proven friends. I was so amazed and dumbfounded by this strange and incomprehensible event that I handed Tausig Cosima's letter without a word, only asking him what could be done to combat such nonsense: he at once undertook to clarify the matter for Cosima and resolve the misunderstanding; I soon had the pleasure of finding he had been successful in this mission.

We* now got to the rehearsals for the concert; I obtained the singers I needed from the ensemble of the Court Opera in order to be able to perform the excerpts from *Rheingold*, *Walküre*, and *Siegfried* (the two forging songs), along with "Pogner's Address" from *Die Meistersinger*. I had to resort to amateurs only for the three Rhine Maidens. The concertmaster Hellmesberger[1] was a great help to me in this matter as in every other way, and by his superb playing and demonstrations of enthusiasm set a splendid example to the other musicians.[2] After the deafening preliminary rehearsals in a little music room in the opera house, where the volume of sound created put Cornelius in a state of perplexity, we got to the stage of the Theater an der Wien itself, where in addition to the high rent for the premises I also had to absorb the cost of setting up the podium for the orchestra. The playing area, which was behind a proscenium arch and surrounded by coulisses, still remained extraordinarily unfavorable acoustically; yet I really didn't feel bold enough to erect sounding boards at my own expense. Although the first concert on December 26th drew a large audience, it brought me nothing but unduly heavy expenses and great dissatisfaction owing to the poor effect produced by the orchestra as a result of the acoustical problems. Despite the bad prospects I decided to bear the cost of building an acoustic shell in order to improve the effect of the next two concerts. In this I flattered myself that I might count on the success of the efforts

---

* In the margin of the manuscript, in Cosima's hand: "March 20th 1880. Villa d'Angri".

being made to arouse interest in the highest circles. My friend Prince Liechtenstein thought this was by no means impossible: he believed he could manage to interest the Imperial Court through Countess Zamoiska, the lady-in-waiting; he conducted me to her one day through the countless corridors of the Imperial Palace. As later became clear to me, Madame Kalergis had done some spade-work here as well; but she apparently succeeded only in winning over the young Empress,[1] who appeared alone with no entourage whatever at the concert. But I suffered every conceivable disappointment at the second concert, which I had insisted on scheduling, despite many warnings, on New Year's Day 1863: the hall was very sparsely filled, and my sole consolation was the fact that the orchestra now produced a superb effect through the acoustical improvements to the platform. As a consequence, the pieces were so well received that I was able to give a third concert on January 8th before a packed house. On this occasion I got gratifying evidence of the great musical gifts of the Viennese public: the by no means spectacular introduction to "Pogner's Address" had to be encored at once in response to stormy ovations, despite the fact that the singer had already risen to commence his part. At this moment I happened to behold in one of the boxes a favorable omen for my present position: I recognized Mme Kalergis, who had just arrived to spend some time in Vienna, being motivated, I fondly hoped, by the desire to do something for me as well. As she was also a friend of Standhartner, she got together with him at once to consider how I could be helped out of the critical situation I was in once again as a result of the heavy expenses of the concerts. She herself had stated to our mutual friend that she had no funds at her disposal and could only meet special expenditures by going into debt. Thus, richer patrons needed to be enlisted. Chief among these was Baroness von Stockhausen, wife of the Hanoverian minister: as a very intimate friend of Standhartner, she was warmly attached to my cause, and also won over Lady Bloomfield together with her husband, the English ambassador. There was a soirée at the residence of the latter, as well as several evening parties at the house of Frau von Stockhausen. One day Standhartner delivered five hundred guilders to me from an anonymous donor to help cover my expenses. Mme Kalergis managed to scrape together one thousand guilders, and these were also turned over to me by Standhartner for my subsequent needs. In her efforts to interest the court in me, however, she remained unsuccessful, despite her close friendship with Countess Zamoiska. To my misfortune a member of the Könneritz family from Saxony turned up as ambassador and was able to suppress any initiative that might have been taken on my behalf by the highly influential Archduchess Sophie with the assertion that in bygone days I had put the castle of the King of Saxony to the torch.

But undaunted my patroness still searched in every direction for ways to help me. To fulfill my greatest wish, to be harbored in a peaceful dwelling for a time, she had conceived the idea of procuring for me the residence of an attaché at the English embassy, the son of the famous Lytton Bulwer. He had been recalled but retained his quarters for a lengthy period. She introduced me to this youthful and very obliging person; together with Cornelius and Mme Kalergis, I had dinner at his house one evening, after which I got started on a reading of *Götter-dämmerung*, but seemingly without being able to gain an attentive hearing; noticing this, I broke off and departed with Cornelius, while Mme Kalergis remained behind alone with Bulwer. Cornelius thought the only way to interpret this was that we had constituted an obstacle to a more intimate conversation, and I confess I was misled this time by earlier albeit quite unwarranted suspicions to the extent of responding to my friend's wild laughter with no more than a jest. We were very cold on the way home; Bulwer's rooms had also struck us as very poorly heated: we took refuge in a restaurant to warm ourselves with a glass of punch, an occasion that has remained in my memory because I saw Cornelius for the first time in a really quite ungovernable, eccentric mood. While we were letting ourselves go in this way, Mme Kalergis, as I later realized, was using her powers as a powerful and irresistible feminine advocate to induce Bulwer to take a possibly decisive interest in me. The upshot was that I at least received an offer from him to place his dwelling unconditionally at my disposal for nine months. But on closer consideration I really didn't know what advantage this would bring me, as I could not see any prospect of earning any further money for my subsistence in Vienna.

My plans were then decisively affected by an invitation from St Petersburg to conduct two concerts there in March for a fee of two thousand silver roubles. Mme Kalergis, whose efforts on my behalf I could see in this invitation as well, urged me to accept at all costs, and held out the prospect of further augmenting my receipts by giving an additional concert on my own initiative, a venture which would prove very lucrative. The only thing that could have held me back from accepting this invitation would have been the certainty of being able to produce *Tristan* in Vienna in the course of the next few months; but renewed illness on the part of the tenor Ander had caused the preparations to bog down again; and I had lost faith entirely in the assurances that had brought me back to Vienna. The outcome of my visit to Minister Schmerling shortly after my arrival had contributed to this view of things. He was highly surprised when I referred to the recommendation of Prince Metternich; for according to the minister, the latter had not said a word to him about me. Yet he very gallantly continued with the declaration that a man of my accomplishments needed no such introduction to enlist his interest. When I then mentioned the idea Prince Metternich had been kind enough to put forward that I might be accorded some special position in Vienna by the Emperor, he hastened to assure me that he had not the slightest influence on any decision of the Emperor. These revelations by Minister Schmerling served very well to shed light on the conduct of Prince Metternich, and I concluded that the latter had preferred to attempt to influence the Imperial Court Chamberlain on behalf of a serious resumption of the *Tristan* project rather than to undertake fruitless exertions with the Minister.

But since this prospect, as aforementioned, now receded into the distance, I accepted the invitation to St Petersburg. First of all it was necessary to provide myself with funds, and it looked as though these would be forthcoming from a concert that Heinrich Porges[1] had arranged for me in Prague. Accordingly, I went to Prague early in February and had every reason to be delighted with my reception. Young Porges, a fervent partisan of Liszt and myself, pleased me personally and also by the zeal he demonstrated. The concert, which included a Beethoven symphony as well as fragments from my newer works, took place in the Sophieninsel Hall and went off very well. When Porges came to pay me a thousand guilders the next day, with the prospect of supplementary remittances later, I laughingly assured him that this was the first money I had ever earned by personal endeavor. In addition he introduced me to several very devoted and cultured young people of the German as well as the Czech party, among whom a mathematics teacher named Lieblein and a writer named Musiol stood out as particularly agreeable. I was moved to see Marie Löw,[2] whom I had known in my earliest youth, once again after so many years. She had ceased singing and taken up the harp, and now she participated in my concert as a member of the orchestra playing this instrument. On the occasion of the first performance of *Tannhäuser* in Prague, she had sent me an enthusiastic report about it; these feelings were now strengthened and she remained for many ensuing years strongly devoted to me. Highly satisfied and replete with new hope, I hurried back to Vienna again to see what could be done to come to a definite decision about *Tristan*. Another piano rehearsal of the first two acts was arranged for me, and I was astonished at the entirely passable achievements of the tenor, while I could not withhold from Frau Dustmann my sincerest congratulations at her admirable execution of her difficult part. Thus, it was now agreed that my work would be performed probably after Easter, which fitted well with my scheduled return from Russia.

The hope of gleaning greater earnings there led me to revive my former plan to settle permanently in my tranquil Biebrich. As there was still time before my trip to Russia, I returned to the Rhine to put things in order there. Once again I lodged in Frickhöfer's house, while searching the Rheingau in the company of Mathilde Maier and her friend Luise Wagner for the place of refuge I longed for; but not finding what I wanted, I even began negotiating with Frickhöfer to put up a small cottage on a little plot of land I proposed to buy near his villa. Herr Schüler, whom I had gotten to know through young Herr Städl, was to take the matter in hand, as he had both legal and business experience; a cost estimate was prepared, and it now depended entirely on the size of my Russian receipts whether the undertaking could go forward the following spring or not. As I had to vacate Frickhöfer's apartment by Easter at any event, I now had all my household effects taken away and placed in storage with the furniture dealer in Wiesbaden to whom I was still in debt for most of it.

And so I set out in the best of spirits, calling first in Berlin, where I at once announced myself at Bülow's apartment. Cosima, who was soon to give birth,[1] could not be prevented, in her delight at seeing me again, from conducting me to the music school, where we would find Hans. I entered a long room, at the far end of which Bülow was giving a piano lesson; I remained by the door for a time without speaking until Hans leapt up and went angrily after the intruder, only to break out in all the more joyous laughter when he recognized me. We arranged to take luncheon together, and with Cosima alone I set out in a splendid shared humor on a drive in a beautiful carriage from the Hotel de Russie, whose gray silk upholstery gave us incessant pleasure. Bülow had been worried about my seeing his wife while she was pregnant, for I had once made some critical remark about another woman of our acquaintance in this condition. We were pleased to be able to reassure him as to the present case since nothing about Cosima could possibly upset me. Sharing my hopes and rejoicing at this turn in my fortunes, these two friends accompanied me to the Königsberg railroad station and bade me farewell as I departed into the night on the next stage of my journey.

In Königsberg I had to wait half a day and a night, spending the time quietly in a hotel room, as I felt no desire to revisit the localities of a place that had once been so fateful for me, and did not even pay any attention to the precise position of the hotel. I continued my trip early in the morning across the Russian border. Prey to a certain unease at my recollections of my former illicit crossing of the border, I scanned the faces of my fellow travelers closely during the long trip. Among them I was especially struck by a Latvian nobleman of German descent, who expressed his distaste at the emancipation of the serfs by the Tsar in the harsh tones of a German Junker: from this it was clear to me that Russian freedom movements would not receive much support from our German nobility living among them. When we were approaching St Petersburg, I was startled to see the train suddenly stopped for close inspection by police. I was told they were searching for persons suspected of participating in the most recent Polish revolt, which had just broken out. Not far from the capital the empty seats suddenly filled with people whose large Russian fur hats made me all the more suspicious, inasmuch as the wearers fixed me with an incessant stare. But suddenly the face of one of them lit up in transfiguration, and he hailed me enthusiastically as the man whom he and several other members of the Imperial Orchestra had come out to greet. They were all Germans, and on our arrival at the St Petersburg station, they jubilantly introduced me to a large contingent from the orchestra, with the Committee of the Philharmonic Society at their head. As a suitable place to stay, I had had recommended to me a German boarding house in a building on the Nevsky Prospect. Here I was very graciously received and cared for by Frau Kunst, the wife of a German businessman, and given a superb salon overlooking the bustling boulevard. I took my meals together with the other boarders and regular diners, usually inviting Alexander Serov, whom I had met in Lucerne, to join us as my guest. This man, who showed up at once on my arrival, I now found to be earning a meager living as a censor of German newspapers. Looking a bit down at heel, sickly and having a difficult time of things, he won my esteem by his great independence of mind and truthfulness, qualities which, combined with a sharp intellect, had made him, as I soon learned, one of the most influential and feared critics. This became clear to me when I was approached from people in the highest circles to use my influence with Serov to modify his relentless hounding of Anton Rubinstein,[1] who was being sponsored most arduously at the time. When I approached him on this subject, and he told me all the reasons why he considered Rubinstein's activities in Russia as an artist so pernicious,

I asked him at least for my sake, as I did not want to be considered Rubinstein's rival during my short stay in St Petersburg, to restrain his attacks somewhat; to this he responded with the vehemence of convulsive suffering: "I hate him and can make no concessions". By contrast he was most congenial with me; he understood me and my nature so completely that almost all our conversation could be conducted in jest, as we were in complete agreement on all serious matters. There is nothing to which I can compare the solicitude with which he helped me in all directions. He took care of the necessary translation into Russian of the program notes for my concerts, as well as for the vocal texts of the fragments from my operas. He also displayed the most splendid insight into helping me secure the most qualified singers. For all this he seemed to find abundant recompense by attending the rehearsals and the performances. His radiant face beamed encouragement and stimulation at me everywhere.

The orchestra itself, which assembled around me in the vast and lovely hall of the Society of Nobles, satisfied me eminently; it had been put together from one hundred and twenty hand-picked musicians of the Imperial Orchestra and consisted mainly of capable artists who, because they were usually employed solely in Italian opera and ballet, were now delighted at the prospect of occupying themselves with nobler music under the kind of direction I was capable of providing.

After the marked success of my first concert, I received some approaches from those circles to which, as now became clear to me, I had been secretly but strongly recommended by Marie Kalergis. My unseen patroness had most circumspectly prepared my introduction to the Grand Duchess Helene.[1] I was instructed first of all to make use of a recommendation from Standhartner to the Grand Duchess's personal physician, Dr Arneth, whom he had known in Vienna, and who in turn could introduce me to her most trusted lady-in-waiting, Fräulein von Rhaden. I would have been well content to make the acquaintance of this lady alone, for in her I found a woman of wide culture, great intelligence and noble bearing, whose increasingly earnest interest in me was admixed with a certain anxiety, which seemed to pertain to some worry about the Grand Duchess. It struck me that she felt something more should be done for me than could plausibly be expected from the Grand Duchess, her temperament and character being what they were. I was still not admitted directly to this exalted person, but rather received first an invitation to an evening party in the quarters of the chief lady-in-waiting, at which among others the Grand Duchess would also be present. Here Anton Rubinstein did the artistic honors; after he had introduced me to the chief lady-in-waiting, this person ventured to introduce me to her mistress, the Grand Duchess herself. This seemed to go quite well, and accordingly I soon received a direct invitation to participate in an intimate afternoon tea circle with the Grand Duchess. Here I met, apart from Fräulein von Rhaden, the lady-in-waiting next to her in rank, Fräulein von Stahl, as well as a genial old man who was introduced to me as General von Brebern, a long-standing friend of the duchess. Fräulein von Rhaden seemed to have made extraordinary efforts on my behalf, the outcome of which was an express request by the Grand Duchess for me to acquaint her with my *Nibelungen* poem. As I had no copy of it with me, but knew that the edition being issued by Weber in Leipzig ought to have been finished by now, I was prevailed upon to telegraph Leipzig at once to demand that the completed sheets be dispatched to the court of the Grand Duchess forthwith. Meanwhile, my patrons had to content themselves with a reading of *Die Meistersinger*. This occasion was graced by the presence of Grand Duchess Marie,[1] the extremely stately and still beautiful daughter of Tsar Nicholas and a woman known for her rather passionate life. As to what this lady could make of my libretto, I was only told later by Fräulein von Rhaden she had been very worried that Hans Sachs would marry Eva in the end.

After a few days several packets containing my *Nibelungen* proof sheets began arriving, and the intimate tea circle of the Grand Duchess enclasped me on four successive occasions to hear my readings; General von Brebern also showed up regularly in order, as Fräulein von Rhaden put it, "to bloom like a rose" in ever deeper sleep. This evoked exuberant witticisms from the merry and pretty Fräulein von Stahl when I accompanied the two ladies-in-waiting from the spacious salon along endless corridors and staircases to their distant quarters each night.

Among people of high rank and influence the only other person I got to know was Count Wielhorsky, who held a position of high trust at the Imperial court and was deemed to be a patron of music, inasmuch as he felt himself distinguished by his ability to play the cello. The old gentleman appeared well disposed toward me and seemingly liked my concerts; indeed, he assured me he had first understood Beethoven's Eighth Symphony (in F major) through my interpretation. He also considered that he had fully grasped my prelude to *Die Meistersinger*; by contrast, he thought Grand Duchess Marie pretentious for having said she had been enraptured by the prelude to *Tristan* while finding that to *Meistersinger* incomprehensible, as he himself had been able to understand the former work only by exertion of all his musical powers. When I told this to Serov, he burst out: "Ah! l'animal de Comte! Cette femme connaît l'amour!"

The Count gave a splendid dinner in my honor, at which Anton Rubinstein and Madame Abaza were present. When I requested Rubinstein to play for us after dinner, Madame Abaza insisted on singing his *Persian Songs*,[1] which appeared to irritate the composer as he no doubt felt he had written many other lovely things. Yet both the composition and its rendition gave me a very favorable opinion of the talent of the two artists. Through the singer, who had originally been in the employ of the Grand Duchess in that capacity but who was now married to a rich and cultured Russian gentleman, I was introduced to the home of Herr Abaza himself and received there with exceptional courtesy. In addition, a Baron Vietinghoff, being an amateur musician and an admirer, had commended himself to me and honored me with invitations to his house, where on one occasion I again met Ingeborg Stark, the beautiful Swedish pianist and composer of sonatas. She startled me by the uninhibited gusto with which she loudly chortled when playing the compositions of the Baron. She also put on a serious air for, as she informed me, she was now engaged to Hans von Bronsart.

Rubinstein himself, with whom I exchanged some friendly visits, behaved in a completely honorable manner, though there was an element of strain in his conduct toward me, for he made no bones about the fact that Serov's enmity had made him decide to give up his position in St Petersburg. It was also thought advisable to introduce me to the commercial circles in St Petersburg, with a view toward helping my forthcoming benefit concert; for this purpose I was invited to a concert being given in the hall of the Chamber of Commerce. I was received there on the steps by an extremely drunken Russian, who introduced himself to me as the conductor. With a small group of musicians from the Imperial Orchestra he conducted among other pieces the overtures to Rossini's *William Tell* and Weber's *Oberon*, for the execution of which the timpani had been replaced by a little military drum. This produced some strange effects, particularly in the lovely transfiguration passage of the *Oberon* overture.

While I was well equipped for my concerts as far as the orchestra was concerned, I had tremendous difficulty in securing adequate singers. There was a quite passable soprano in Fräulein Bianchi: but for the tenor parts I had to content myself with a certain Herr Setov, who had a lot of courage but very little voice; yet he made it possible for me to perform the forging songs from *Siegfried*, as by his presence he at least gave the appearance of singing, even if in reality the task was carried out by the orchestra alone. After completing the two Philharmonic Society concerts, I had to make preparations for my own concert at the Imperial Opera House, in the arrangements for which I was assisted by a retired musician who, together with Serov, spent long hours in my well-heated room without ever removing his enormous fur coat; as we also had great difficulty with him owing to his incompetence, we termed him "the sheep in wolf's clothing". The concert itself succeeded beyond expectation, and I do not ever recall being received more enthusiastically by an audience than was the case here, for even the initial applause was so stormy and lasted so long that it overwhelmed me, something which was otherwise not easy to achieve. The fiery devotion of the orchestra itself seems to have contributed greatly to the enthusiasm of the public. For it was my one hundred and twenty musicians themselves who repeatedly instigated the tempestuous outbursts of applause, an event that appeared unprecedented in St Petersburg. From some of them I heard such exclamations as: "Let us admit we didn't know until now what music is!" These extremely favorable circumstances were now exploited by their regular conductor, Herr Schuberth,[1] who had been helpful to me with his sound advice throughout, to request me to conduct at the forthcoming concert to be given for his benefit. Somewhat peevishly, as I could see it was a question of taking money from my pocket and putting it into his, I agreed to this, inasmuch as all my other friends recommended I do so. Thus, I repeated a week later the most popular pieces from my program before an equally large audience and with the same success, except that this time the handsome receipts of three thousand roubles were allocated to the support of a rather feeble fellow, who in unexpected retribution for his encroachment on my preserve was summoned to the next world that very year.

To balance this, I now had the prospect of further success and income from a contract concluded with General Lvov, intendant of the theater in Moscow. I was to give three concerts in the Bolshoi Theater, receiving half the receipts of each and a guarantee of one thousand roubles at a minimum. I arrived there miserable, uncomfortable and suffering from a cold, in weather alternating between frost and thaw, to take up residence in a poorly located German boarding house. After I had made the necessary preliminary arrangements with the intendant, who struck me as rather paltry despite the orders hanging round his neck, and after I had also reached an understanding with a Russian tenor and a superannuated

Italian lady concerning the difficult choice of vocal excerpts, I commenced the orchestral rehearsals at once. Here I got to know the younger Rubinstein, Anton's brother Nikolaus,[1] who in his capacity as director of the Russian Musical Society represented the chief authority in his field in Moscow and behaved to me modestly and pleasantly throughout. The orchestra consisted of a hundred musicians, which served the imperial purposes for Italian opera and ballet and was of far lesser quality than the one in St Petersburg. Yet here, too, I found a small number of very able string players, all of them passionately devoted to me, and including an old acquaintance from my time in Riga, the cellist von Lutzau, who in those days used to distinguish himself by his ready wit. But I had the greatest joy of a violinist, one Albrecht, brother to the man who had given me such a fright with his Russian fur hat before my arrival in St Petersburg. This mere handful of players, however, was not enough to dispel my feeling that my association with the Moscow orchestra represented an abrupt drop in artistic standards. I struggled along without deriving any real satisfaction, to which was added my exasperation with the Russian tenor, who appeared at the rehearsals in a red shirt, to demonstrate his patriotic resistance to my music by singing Siegfried's forging songs in Russian in the insipid manner he had learned from the Italians. On the morning of the first concert I was obliged to report sick as a result of a severe, feverish cold and thus have it canceled. With the streets of Moscow lying deep in filthy slush, there seemed to be no arrangements for getting news of such things to the public, and I learned that many brilliant carriages had driven up to the theater only to be turned back too late, a source of considerable angry comment. After I had rested for two days, I insisted on giving the three contractual concerts within a period of six days, an exertion to which I was spurred by the desire to be done with an undertaking I felt unworthy of me. Although the Bolshoi Theater was filled each time with an audience more splendidly dressed than any I have ever seen since, I was told that, according to the calculations of the imperial intendancy, the receipts did not exceed the guaranteed amount. Yet I felt sufficiently compensated by the invariably magnificent reception accorded my efforts, and above all by the enthusiasm of the musicians that was forthcoming here as well. A deputation of the musicians requested me to give a fourth concert; when I refused, they tried to persuade me to give at least one more "rehearsal", a proposal I smilingly turned down as well. The orchestra nonetheless honored me with a banquet, on which occasion, after Nikolaus Rubinstein had delivered a very warm and appropriate speech, things eventually became very boisterous. Somebody picked me up and carried me around the room on his back; and then a universal outcry ensued, as everybody wanted to do me the same service. Here I was also presented with a gift, purchased with funds raised among the orchestra members, in the form of a gold snuff-box on which were engraved Siegmund's words from the *Walküre*: "Yet one has come". I returned the compliment by presenting the orchestra with a large photograph of myself, on which I wrote the words preceding that line: "No one has gone".

Apart from the musical world, I became acquainted through the strong urging and recommendation of Mme Kalergis with a Prince Odoyevsky.[1] According to my friend, this was a man of the noblest possible sort and would understand me completely. After an arduous drive of many hours duration, I reached his modest dwelling and was received with patriarchal simplicity at his family dinner table. It was very difficult for me to give him any idea of what I was or what I wanted; for his part, in order to make an impression, he relied entirely on the effect to be produced by looking at a huge instrument resembling an organ, which he had invented and caused to be installed in one of the larger rooms. Unfortunately there was no one there who could play it; but I could not help forming an idea of the divine service, conducted according to his own system, which he inflicted with the aid of this instrument on his relatives and acquaintances there every Sunday. Always mindful of my kindly patroness, I nonetheless tried to give the genial prince some insight into my situation and the goal of my efforts; with apparent emotion he exclaimed: "J'ai ce qu'il vous faut. Parlez à Wolffsohn!" On further inquiry I learned that this guardian spirit he was recommending to me was by no means a banker but a Russian Jew who wrote novels.

From all these activities there seemed to be enough income, if I counted possible additional, large receipts in St Petersburg, to consider carrying out my project to build a house in Biebrich. For this reason, and even before leaving Moscow after a ten-day stay, I sent my agent in Wiesbaden a telegram on the matter. And to Minna as well, who was now complaining of the high cost of her move to Dresden, I sent one thousand roubles.

However, on my return to St Petersburg I was at once subjected to great annoyances. Everybody advised me against giving the benefit concert I had scheduled for the second day of Easter, as this day was habitually given over to private social gatherings. In addition, I had not been able to avoid consenting to give another concert on the third day after the date announced for my own as a benefit for the inmates of St Petersburg debtors' prison, for the Grand Duchess Helene had strongly recommended I do so. The whole of St Petersburg made it a point of honor to support this latter undertaking, as it took place under the highest auspices, and whereas seats for it were sold out in advance, I had to content myself with a very empty hall at the Casino of the Nobles and receipts which fortunately just sufficed to cover my costs. By contrast the mood was all the more festive at the concert for the debtors: General Suvorov,[1] a gloriously handsome man and Governor of St Petersburg to boot, presented me on behalf of the beneficiaries with a beautifully wrought silver drinking-horn.

I now set about paying farewell calls, in the course of which Fräulein von Rhaden distinguished herself by particular solicitude for me. Through her, in order to compensate me for the lost income at my last benefit, the Grand Duchess sent me one thousand roubles, with the hint that she might repeat it every year until my situation improved. With things turning out so well, I could only regret that the relationship thus established could not have more stable and fruitful results. I suggested to the Grand Duchess through Fräulein von Rhaden that she invite me to come to St Petersburg annually for three months to place myself fully at her disposal for concerts as well as theatrical performances, in return for which she would have to pay me a no more than adequate yearly salary. On the day before my departure I told my kindly advocate of my plan to settle in Biebrich but without hiding from her my anxiety that, if I used the money earned in Russia for this purpose, my situation would be the same as before; this made me worry whether I would not be better advised to drop the plan to build a house: in response I got the ardent reply: "Build and hope!" At the last moment before leaving for the railroad station I responded gratefully to her in a similar tone that I now knew that I had to do. And so I left at the end of April, to a rousing send-off by Serov and the musicians of the orchestra, crossing the Russian wilderness without stopping at Riga, where I had been invited to give a concert, and finally arriving at the border town of Wirballen, where a telegram sent after me by Fräulein von Rhaden caught up with me. With reference to the last message I had sent her, she now felt impelled to add the words "Not too rashly!" This was quite enough to revive my doubts as to the wisdom of carrying out my house-building plans.

Without any further delay I got to Berlin, where I proceeded at once to the Bülows' apartment. I had received no news of Cosima over the intervening months and now announced myself at the door, full of anxiety about her. The servant girl didn't want to let me in; "The lady is not well." When I asked, "Is she really sick?" I got an evasive smile for an answer and realized at once how things stood, so I rushed in joyfully to greet Cosima, who had already given birth to her daughter Blandine some time before and was now on the high road to recovery, but was not receiving casual visitors. Everything seemed to be going well, and Hans too was in high spirits, as he thought the success of my Russian trip would free me from worries for a long time. But I knew that this assumption was only justified if my wish to be invited annually to St Petersburg to resume my efforts there were granted. Yet as to this, I received an instructive letter following that telegram from Fräulein von Rhaden, informing me that I could not count on the prospect at all. This clear statement compelled me to balance my Russian receipts very closely, and after deduction of hotel and travel expenses, the money sent to Minna, and certain payments to my Wiesbaden furniture dealer, the receipts amounted to little more than four thousand talers, whereupon the plan to buy a plot of land and build a house necessarily had to be given up. Cosima's splendid condition and cheerful mood made me supress all worries for the moment, and once again we exuberantly drove in a splendid carriage along the avenues of the Tiergarten, dined at the Hotel de Russie to our heart's content, while pretending the bad times were gone forever.

Meanwhile I had to go back to Vienna in any event. As a matter of fact, I had recently received word from there that *Tristan* had had to be postponed again, this time as a result of the poor health of Frau Dustmann. To keep a closer watch on this important affair, and also no doubt because I had formed no such intimate artistic ties with any other German city as with Vienna, I clung to this as the most appropriate place to stay. Tausig, whom I now found flourishing there, entirely confirmed me in this view and fortified me in my resolve by pledging himself to find me in the vicinity of Vienna the pleasant and tranquil dwelling I had set my sights upon. He succeeded in this quite admirably through the services of his own landlord. The very agreeable house of an old Baron von Rackowitz[1] in Penzing, in which I was offered the whole top floor and exclusive use of a shady and fairly large garden, gave me the most delightful accommodation for a yearly rent of twelve hundred guilders.

In the housekeeper Franz Mrazek I found a very obliging man whom, together with his wife Anna, a very talented and ingratiating lady, I at once took into my personal service, in which they remained for many years through all sorts of vicissitudes. Then it became a question once more of spending money to furnish my longed-for refuge so that I could rest and work there in comfort. I had the remainder of my household effects sent on from Biebrich, together with the new furniture I had found it necessary to buy and my Erard piano. In lovely spring weather I entered my new residence on May 12th and at first wasted a good deal of time through the excitement in which I was plunged by the job of fitting out my comfortable rooms. It was at this juncture that the foundations were laid of my relationship with the company of Philipp Haas & Sons, which took on an ominous aspect as time went on. Meanwhile, all my efforts on behalf of what I considered a very auspicious establishment put me into the best of moods. The music room, with the piano that had meanwhile arrived and various Raphael prints that had fallen to me in the division of our property at Biebrich, was completely ready by the time I celebrated my fiftieth birthday on May 22nd. On this evening I was accorded a serenade with little lanterns by the businessmen's glee club, in which a deputation of students also joined and offered me an ardent greeting. I had taken care of the wine, and everything went splendidly. The Mrazek couple took care of my domestic needs quite nicely; Anna's culinary artistry even made it possible for me to invite Cornelius and Tausig to dinner frequently enough.

Unfortunately, Minna began causing me great trouble again by bitter reproaches about everything I was doing. As I had now decided never to answer her directly, I wrote on this occasion to her daughter Nathalie, to whom she was still concealing her true relationship, and called her attention to the arrangement we had made the previous year. How much I now needed a woman's attention and care in the management of my household became clear to me when I wrote Mathilde Maier in Mainz and expressed the straightforward wish that she would come to me and make up for what was lacking in her skillful manner. I was sure that my good friend was sensible enough to interpret my meaning correctly and not feel ashamed in any way. In this I was most probably correct, but I had not made sufficient allowance for her mother and her bourgeois surroundings in general. She seems to have been greatly agitated by my invitation, until her friend Luise Wagner managed at length to calm her sufficiently to be able to write and advise me frankly, with middle-class shrewdness and precision, that I should divorce my wife, after which everything would easily take care of itself. Greatly startled by this, I immediately withdrew my invitation as ill-considered and tried to calm everyone down as best I could.

On the other hand, Friederike Meyer's incomprehensible fate continued to cause me, even if against her own will, considerable anxiety. After she had spent several months in Venice the previous winter, seemingly to her benefit, I had communicated to her from St Petersburg the wish that she would join me in Berlin with the Bülows. In making the suggestion I had carefully considered the kindly interest Cosima had taken in her and thought we could mutually consider how to help our friend bring order into her notably chaotic life. She did not appear, however; instead, she announced to me that, inasmuch as her poor health was hampering her theatrical career, she had settled with a lady friend in Coburg, and would try to earn a living by occasional appearances at the small theater there. For many reasons I could not extend to her the kind of invitation I had sent to Mathilde Maier. She, for her part, vehemently wished to get together with me again for a short time, whereafter, she assured me, she would leave me in peace. I was in no doubt that it would be purposeless and risky to accede to this request at once; yet I offered the possibility as a prospect for some future date. In the course of the summer she repeated the request from several different places, until finally, as I was scheduled to give a concert late that autumn in Karlsruhe, I suggested to her that we meet at that time and place. From then on I never received the slightest further communication from this strange and interesting lady, so that I soon had to regard our relationship as severed, particularly as I had no idea where she had gone. Not until several years later was the secret of her difficult position revealed to me, and according to this information I was obliged to conclude that she had been reluctant to tell me the truth about her relationship to Herr von Guaita. He seems to have had far greater claims on her affections than I had presumed, and now she had been compelled, apparently by the hardships of her situation, to surrender herself to him, who still seriously cared for her, as her last friend in the world. I learned that she was living in seclusion with two children, secretly married to Herr von Guaita as people guessed, withdrawn not only from the theater but also from the world at large, on a small estate near the Rhine.

I had still not yet succeeded in achieving the tranquillity needed for my work, despite all my elaborate and ceremonial preparations. A burglary in the house, which deprived me of the gold snuff-box presented to me by the musicians in Moscow, renewed my old desire for a dog: to this end my friendly old landlord let me have an ancient gun-dog, one which he already neglected, with the name Pohl, one of the most loveable and excellent animals that ever became attached to me. In his company I undertook long walks every day, for which the extremely pleasant neighborhood afforded admirable opportunities. Otherwise I remained more or less alone for a time, as Tausig had been confined to his bed by a severe illness for an extended period, and Cornelius was suffering from an injured foot as a result of having jumped down carelessly from an omnibus when visiting Penzing. I continued my amicable association with Standhartner and his family; I also had frequent visits from Fritz Porges, the younger brother of Heinrich, who had just commenced practising as a doctor. He was a really nice fellow, whose acquaintance with me dated from that serenade by the businessmen's glee club, of which he had been the instigator.

I had become convinced that there was no longer any likelihood that *Tristan* would be produced at the Opera House, as I learned that the illness of Frau Dustmann was merely a pretext, while Ander's complete loss of voice had been the true reason for the most recent interruption in the rehearsals. The good Esser tried hard to persuade me to give the role of Tristan to another tenor in the company by the name of Walter; but he was so antipathetic to me that I couldn't even bring myself to hear him in *Lohengrin*. So I just let the whole affair drop and tried to get in the mood to resume my work on *Die Meistersinger*. Accordingly, I first began work on the instrumentation of the part of the first act I had already composed, having up to then scored only a few fragments for concert purposes. But as summer approached, however, the old worries about my future subsistence began to pervade all my thoughts and feelings about the present: it was clear to me that, if I were to fulfill my commitments, and particularly those to Minna, I would have to look around for remunerative work again soon.

It was therefore most opportune when I received an unexpected invitation from the management of the National Theater in Pest to give two concerts there. In response to this I went to the Hungarian capital at the end of July, was received by the intendant, Radnotfay, like an unknown, and was enlightened by Réményi,[1] an erstwhile protégé of Liszt who was in fact a not untalented violin virtuoso and displayed a boundless passion for myself, that he had instigated the invitation to me entirely on his own initiative. While there was little prospect of earning much money there, as I had expressed willingness to content myself with five hundred guilders for each of the two concerts, I nonetheless had reason to be pleased by the success of the concerts themselves and the great interest evinced by the public. In this city, where the Magyar opposition to Austria was still at its most adamant, I made the acquaintance of some highly gifted and distinguished-looking young men, among whom Herr Rosti remains pleasantly in my memory. They organized a truly idyllic celebration for me in the form of a banquet on an island in the Danube attended only by a few initiates. Under an age-old oak tree we settled down as if to a patriarchal feast. A young lawyer whose name I have unfortunately forgotten made the principal speech, and held me rapt and amazed not only by the ardor of his delivery but also particularly by the exalted earnestness of his views, which were based on a comprehensive knowledge of my works and activities. We returned down the Danube in the fast skiffs of the Rowing Club to which my hosts belonged, and on the way we had to go through a thunderstorm which approached hurricane force and turned the mighty river into a seething cauldron. There was only one woman in our party, the Countess Bethlen-Gabor,[1] and she was together with me in a small craft being rowed by Rosti and a friend. These two were in agonies of fear that their boat would be shattered by a collision with one of the rafts toward which we were being driven by the current. They therefore struggled desperately to keep us away from these rafts, whereas I saw the only hope of saving ourselves and in particular the lady, who was seated beside me, was in boarding one of them. To accomplish this in spite of the objections of our oarsmen, I seized a projecting peg on a raft we were brushing against and thus held our little boat firmly in position; while the two oarsmen screamed that the *Ellida* would now be lost, I quickly hoisted the lady out of the skiff and on to the raft, across which we walked to the shore, leaving our friends to save the *Ellida* as best they could. We two then walked through the blinding rainstorm, yet safe and sound, back to the city. My conduct in the presence of this danger did not fail to increase somewhat the esteem in which I was held by my friends; there followed yet another ceremonial banquet in a public garden with a vast number of participants. Here I was treated in true Hungarian style. There was an enormous gypsy band and my approach was greeted by the Rákóczy march, to the accompaniment of stormy yells of "Eljen" by the assembled guests. Here as well there were fiery orations and appreciative allusions to me and to the fact that my influence now extended far beyond the borders of Germany. The introductory remarks for these speeches were always given in Hungarian, as if to excuse the fact that the main oration would be in German for the sake of the guest. And here I was never referred to as Richard Wagner, but always as "Wagner Richard".

Even the highest military authorities insisted on offering me a tribute through the good offices of Field Marshal Coronini:[1] I was invited by the Count to a performance of the combined military bands at Buda Castle, where I was graciously received by him together with his family, treated to ices, and led to a balcony to listen to a concert given by this massive chorus of musicians. The effect of all these demonstrations was exceedingly refreshing, so that I was almost sorry to be obliged to leave the rejuvenating atmosphere of Pest and return to my dull and musty refuge in Vienna. On the way back at the beginning of August I was joined for part of the journey by Herr von Seebach, whom I had known in Paris as the congenial Saxon ambassador. He complained to me of the enormous losses he was incurring through difficulties in administering the estates in Southern Russia he had acquired through marriage, as he was just returning from a visit there; by contrast, I tried to reassure him as to my own position, and this seemed to please him.

The meager receipts from my Budapest concerts, of which in fact I had been able to carry away only half, were not calculated to dispel my anxieties about the future. Having staked everything on what I trusted would be a permanent establishment, the first question was how to secure an annual earned income which would at least be certain even if not overly large. While I did not consider it necessary to abandon my connections with St Petersburg and the plans I had based upon them, I nonetheless felt I should not entirely ignore the assurances given me by Rémenyi, who had boasted to me of his great influence with Hungarian magnates. He had told me that it would certainly not be a difficult matter to obtain for me a similar pension in Pest in return for the kind of services I had in mind to do in St Petersburg. He actually visited me in Penzing shortly after my return, accompanied by his adopted son, young Plotényi, whose extraordinary good looks and amiability made a very good impression on me. As for the father himself, although he won my warm approbation for his brilliant performance of the Rákóczy march on the violin, I quickly perceived that his glowing promises had been intended more to produce an immediate effect on me rather than to achieve any permanent result. In accordance with his own desire, I soon lost track of him altogether.

While I was compelled to busy myself with plans for further concert tours, I was able for the present to luxuriate in the pleasant shade of my garden in the intense heat, and every evening I set off on long rambles with my trusty dog Pohl, the most refreshing being those to the dairy-farm at St Veit where I enjoyed the fresh milk. My little circle of friends was restricted still to Cornelius and Tausig, who had eventually recovered his health, though he disappeared from my sight for some time again owing to his association with rich Austrian officers. On the other hand, the elder Porges brother now joined the younger one quite frequently in accompanying me on little excursions. My niece Ottilie Brockhaus, who was living with the family of her mother's friend Heinrich Laube, also gave me the pleasure of a visit from time to time.

But whenever I settled down to serious work, I was goaded anew by worry and fear as to how I would continue to support myself. As another expedition to Russia was out of the question until Easter of the following year at the earliest, I could only consider German cities for my purposes. From some quarters, Darmstadt for example, I got absolute rejections; from Karlsruhe, after I had applied directly to the Grand Duke, I received an indefinite response. But my confidence was shaken more severely by the absolute rejection that came in response to the inquiry I finally made to St Petersburg, concerning the plan which, if it had gone through, would have provided me with a regular salary. The Polish revolution that had broken out in the course of the summer, I was assured, had crippled all artistic enterprises there. I got better news from Moscow, where they held out the prospect of some good concerts in the following year. Next, I recalled that the singer Setov had confidently recommended Kiev to me as extremely rewarding terrain. There was an exchange of correspondence about this, and I was again put off until the following Easter, when all the nobility of Little Russia were to gather there. These were all plans for the future which, whenever I worried about how to carry them out, robbed me of all the equanimity needed for my work. At any rate there was a long intervening period during which I would have to take care of myself, and of Minna as well. Any prospect of a position in Vienna had to be handled with the greatest circumspection, and the result was that with the approach of autumn there was nothing for me to do but borrow money, a process in which Tausig assisted me, as he was extraordinarily well versed in such matters.

I could not help wondering whether I should give up my establishment in Penzing; but the question always remained where to go from there. Every time I was stirred by the desire to compose, money worries always supervened and drove me, as it was a question of merely getting from one day to the next, to take refuge in reading Duncker's[1] *History of the*

Ancient World. Eventually all my time was taken up by correspondence about concerts. First, I commissioned Heinrich Porges to do what he could about another visit to Prague; however, he also proposed that I should give a concert at Löwenberg, where the very favorable dispositions of Prince von Hohenzollern[1] offered an excellent prospect. I was also referred to Hans von Bronsart, who was directing a private orchestral society in Dresden at the time. He responded with great fervor to my suggestions, and we came to an agreement as to the time and program of a concert I would conduct in Dresden. As the Grand Duke of Baden had also placed his theater in Karlsruhe at my disposal for a concert to be given in November, I thought I had done enough in this regard for now to permit myself an initiative in another direction. I wrote a lengthy article for the Uhl-Fröbel journal *Der Botschafter* about the Imperial Court Theater of Vienna, in which I advanced a number of suggestions for the thorough reform of this badly mismanaged institution. Even the press generally acknowledged the soundness of my proposals, and there were also apparently some reverberations in high administrative circles; for I soon learned through my friend Rudolf Liechtenstein that he had been approached concerning the possibility of his assuming the management of the theater, and in this connection there was some thought of asking me to head the Opera House. Among the reasons causing this project to be dropped was the fear, as Liechtenstein told me, that under his management people would hear nothing but "Wagnerian opera".

In the end it was a pleasure to escape the oppression of my situation by setting forth on my concert tours. First, at the beginning of November, I went to Prague to try my luck there again in the hope of big receipts; unfortunately Heinrich Porges had not been able to handle the preliminary arrangements himself, and his deputies, being busy schoolteachers, were not equally up to the task. Costs had gone up, but income had gone down for the reason that they did not dare ask such high prices as before. I wanted to remedy that by giving a second concert a few days later: I insisted on doing this although I was advised against it, whereby my friends were proven right. The receipts scarcely covered the costs on this occasion, and as I had been compelled to send the funds earned from the first concert to Vienna to redeem a bill of exchange I had left behind, to avoid embarrassment I had to take advantage of an offer by a local banker and would-be patron in order to pay my hotel bill and subsequent travel expenses.

In a mood reflecting these events I made my way to Karlsruhe via

Nuremberg and Stuttgart under conditions of extreme hardship, in bitter cold and constant delays. In Karlsruhe a number of friends now gathered around me, attracted by the reports of the venture. Richard Pohl, who never failed, from Baden, Mathilde Maier, Frau Betty Schott, the wife of my publisher, and even Raff from Wiesbaden, as well as Emilie Genast and Karl Eckert, who had just been appointed Kapellmeister at Stuttgart, all found their way to join me. For the first concert on November 14th I had immediate trouble with the singers, as the baritone Hauser, who was scheduled to sing "Wotan's Farewell" and the "Cobbler's Song" of Hans Sachs, fell sick and was replaced by a voiceless though practised vaudeville singer. According to Eduard Devrient, this didn't make any difference. My relations with him were strictly official, but he certainly carried out my instructions for the construction of the orchestra podium to the letter. As far as the orchestra were concerned the concert went very well, so that the Grand Duke, who had received me cordially in his box, requested a repeat performance a week later. I at once expressed my doubts, as experience had already taught me that good attendance at such concerts, particularly considering the high prices, could only be attributed to the curiosity of listeners who often came from far away, whereas those who really understood art and were interested in the music itself always formed a small minority. Yet the Grand Duke insisted, because he wanted to offer a taste of my work to his mother-in-law, Queen Augusta, who would be arriving a few days later. I was particularly miserable at the prospect of spending this period alone in my Karlsruhe hotel, when Marie Kalergis, who had just recently become a Muchanov by marriage, and who had also showed up at the concert much to my delight, now invited me to Baden-Baden, where she was residing. My friend was at the station to meet me and offered to conduct me into the town, a gesture I felt it proper to decline on the grounds that with my old "robber's hat" I would not look respectable enough; but she took me by the arm and assured me, "we all wear such things here". Thus we proceeded to the villa of Pauline Viardot, where we had to take our dinner as my friend's own house was not adequately set up as yet. At the side of my old acquaintance I now got to know the Russian writer Turgenev; Mme Muchanov presented her husband to me somewhat gingerly, wondering what I would make of this marriage. Supported by her companions, who were all cosmopolitans, she endeavored to create pleasant diversions during the time we spent together. Well satisfied by the admirable intention of my friend and benefactress, I left Baden and filled the interim with a little side trip to

Zürich, where I tried to relax for a few days in the home of the Wesendonck family.[1] The idea of assisting me in any way did not seem to dawn on them, even though I described my situation quite frankly. And so I turned back to Karlsruhe, where I gave my second concert on November 29th[2] to a sparsely filled house, just as I had foreseen. According to the view of the grand-ducal couple, the presence of Queen Augusta alone should have been sufficient to counterbalance any less pleasant impressions: I was again invited to the royal box, where I found all the royal highnesses grouped around the Queen who, with a blue rose on her forehead, proceeded to speak some words of praise to which the Baden court listened with breathless attention; but after the royal lady had made a few general remarks and was supposed to go into greater detail, she delegated the task to her daughter, on the grounds that she understood more about the subject. The next day I received my share of the profits, which had been fixed at half the receipts after deduction for costs. It came to one hundred guilders, with which I at once bought a fur coat originally priced at one hundred and ten guilders but reduced by ten guilders after I explained the precise amount I had received. There was still the Grand Duke's personal gift to come, consisting of a gold box with fifteen louis d'or in it. I had to thank him for this in writing and then try to decide whether, after the bother and fatigue of the last few weeks, I should now add to the long series of disappointments by giving a concert in Dresden. Many considerations, and indeed practically everything connected with a visit to Dresden, moved me to summon the courage to tell the friendly and considerate Hans von Bronsart not to expect me and to cancel the concert. Although this no doubt caused him great inconveniences, he took it in very good grace.

I still wanted to make an attempt on the firm of Schott in Mainz and therefore traveled by night to Mainz, where the family of Mathilde Maier insisted on harboring me nicely in their little home while I was there. During the day and night I spent here in the narrow Karthäusergasse I was waited upon with the greatest solicitude, and from this base I undertook a new assault on the publishing house of Schott, but without securing any great booty, as I declined to permit the excerpts from my new works, that had been prepared for concert purposes, to be published separately for use in the concert hall.

As my only remaining source of profit was now the concert at Löwenberg, I turned my steps in that direction, but in order to avoid Dresden made a little detour to Berlin, where I arrived, utterly exhausted after traveling through the night, early on November 28th. I was met, as I had requested, by the Bülows, but they at once persuaded me to postpone my immediate departure for Silesia for a day and devote this time to them. Hans probably wanted me above all to attend a concert to be given that evening under his direction, and of course this then induced me to stay. In cold, raw and dank weather we spent our time as cheerfully as possible conversing about my miserable situation. To augment my funds, it was decided to hand over the Grand Duke of Baden's gold box to our old friend, the worthy Weitzmann,[1] to be sold. The proceeds of this transaction, amounting to about ninety talers, were brought to me at the Hotel Brandenburg, where I was dining with Bülow, and there was no lack of jokes concerning this buttressing of my existence. As Bülow had to make some preparations for his concert I again went for a drive in a handsome carriage alone with Cosima. This time we fell silent and all joking ceased. We gazed mutely into each other's eyes and an intense longing for the fullest avowal of the truth forced us to a confession, requiring no words whatever, of the incommensurable misfortune that weighed upon us. With tears and sobs[2] we sealed a vow to belong to each other alone. It lifted a great weight from our hearts. The profound tranquillity which ensued gave us the serenity to attend the concert without any sense of oppression. As a matter of fact, a sensitive and buoyant performance of Beethoven's smaller concert overture (in C major), together with the very clever arrangement by Hans of Gluck's overture to *Paris and Helen*, even managed to attract my close attention. We saw Alwine Frommann in the audience and met her during the intermission on the grand staircase of the concert hall; after the second part had begun and the stairs were empty, we sat together on the steps for some time chatting gaily and intimately with our old friend. After the concert we had to attend a supper at the home of the worthy Weitzmann, the inordinate copiousness of which reduced us, who were so in need of the profoundest peace, to almost frantic despair. But then the day was over, and after spending a night under Bülow's roof, I recommenced my journey, and our farewell reminded me so vividly of that first marvelously touching parting from Cosima in Zürich that the intervening years vanished like a confused dream separating two of life's most momentous days. If then what we sensed but did not understand had compelled silence, it was now no less impossible to express in words what was tacitly acknowledged.

I was met at a Silesian railroad station by the Prince's Kapellmeister Herr Seifriz,[3] who accompanied me in one of the royal carriages to Löwenberg.

The old Prince of Hohenlohe-Hechingen, already well disposed toward me as a result of his friendship with Liszt, had been told about my situation by Heinrich Porges, who had been in his employ for a short time, and he had now invited me to give a concert at his modest castle to an audience composed exclusively of invited guests. After being comfortably accommodated in some rooms on the ground floor of his house, to which he had himself rolled in his wheel-chair on frequent occasions from his own rooms just opposite, I could feel not only quite at ease but also somewhat hopeful. I immediately set to work rehearsing the excerpts I had selected from my works with the perfectly adequate private orchestra maintained by the Prince, and these sessions were invariably attended by my host to his great satisfaction. We took our meals together in a very congenial atmosphere; on the day of the concert performance itself we had something of a gala dinner, at which occasion I was surprised to meet the sister of Frau Wille of Mariafeld, Henriette von Bissing, whom I had known very well in Zürich. Possessor of an estate near Löwenberg, she too had been invited by the Prince and now proved to be the same enthusiastic admirer as of old. Very intelligent and witty, she immediately became my preferred companion. After the concert had come off quite well, I had to fulfill another request of the Prince the next day by performing Beethoven's C minor Symphony privately for him; this was also attended by Frau von Bissing, who had been widowed some time before, and she now indicated her intention to come to my concert in Breslau as well. Before my departure from Löwenberg, Herr Seifriz brought me a fee of fourteen hundred talers on behalf of the Prince, and with an expression of regret, moreover, that he could not acknowledge my services more generously. After all my previous experiences I was truly astonished and contented by this, and it was a pleasure for me to be able to offer this sterling Prince my heartfelt thanks with all the eloquence at my command.

And so I went on to Breslau, where the concertmaster Damrosch, whose acquaintance I had made during my last stay in Weimar and who had been recommended by Liszt, had arranged another concert for me. Unfortunately everything here struck me as extraordinarily dismal and depressing: the whole affair, as could only be expected, had been planned on the most paltry scale. A perfectly ghastly concert room, which usually served as a beer hall and gave out on a small vaudeville theater, separated from it only by an unspeakably vulgar curtain hanging down in front, repelled me so strongly that I at first wanted to dismiss the seedy-looking musicians at once. In addition, it was clear I would first have to procure a raised wooden platform for the orchestra. My anxious friend Damrosch had to promise at the very least to arrange to neutralize the horrible stench of tobacco imbuing the place. As he could offer no guarantee as to the size of the receipts, I was only induced to go on with the enterprise in the end by the desire not to compromise him too severely. To my dismay I saw almost the whole place, particularly the front part, occupied only by Jews, and the fact that I owed whatever success I achieved to the sympathetic interest of this segment of the population became clear to me the next day, when I went to a dinner at midday arranged by Damrosch in my honor, which solely Jews attended. Like a ray of light from a better world, the appearance of Fräulein Marie von Buch[1] as I was leaving the concert hall had cheered me up. Together with her grandmother, she had hurried over to my concert from the Hatzfeld estates, and after it was over had lingered in the improvised board partition serving as a box until the public had left and I emerged. This young lady also came up to me again, dressed in traveling clothes, at the close of the Damrosch dinner and tried to make me feel better about my obviously depressing situation by a number of kindly and sympathetic remarks. After my return to Vienna, I thanked her in writing for this gesture, and in response she asked me for a folio for her album; remembering how shaken I had been upon my departure from Berlin, and attempting also to communicate my innermost feelings to a woman not unworthy of this confidence, I wrote on it Calderón's words: "Things impossible to conceal and impossible to reveal", whereby I felt I had felicitously conveyed to a friend, though she could not understand, an idea of the only thing that lived in me, of which I alone had cognizance.

My renewed meeting with Henriette von Bissing had entirely different results. She had followed me to Breslau and put up at the same hotel. My sickly appearance seemed to inspire her with great sympathy for me and for my situation. I described the latter to her quite frankly, telling her of the disruption of the even and orderly flow of life so necessary to me and to my work that dated from my departure from Zürich in 1858, as well as of my repeated but hitherto vain struggles to bring permanent order into my financial affairs. My friend did not hesitate to blame what she called Frau Wesendonck's childish and impulsive behavior towards my wife, which she now felt herself called upon to expiate. She approved of my settling down in Penzing and only wished that no outside enterprise would diminish its beneficial effect on me. She absolutely would not hear of my plan for touring Russia during the coming winter to earn some necessary money, but rather undertook to provide from her own, admittedly very significant fortune the by no means small sums necessary to maintain me in an independent position for a long time to come. For some time to come I would still have to look after myself as best I could, she said, because raising the promised funds to place at my disposal would probably require a good deal of effort on her part.

Greatly consoled by the prospects opened up by this encounter, I returned to Vienna on December 9th. While still at Löwenberg I had been obliged to remit most of the Prince's gift, partly for Minna and partly to pay fresh debts in Vienna. With little cash in hand but with new firmly based hopes for the future, I could now greet my few friends in tolerably good spirits. Among these, Peter Cornelius began dropping in every evening, and as we were usually joined by Heinrich Porges and Gustav Schönaich,[1] we constituted a customary little circle of familiar friends. I invited them all to spend Christmas Eve with me, and under a lighted Christmas tree bestowed an appropriate trifle on each of them. Some work also came my way again, as Tausig asked me to help him out with a concert he was to give in the Redoutensaal. In addition to a few excerpts from my operas, I also performed the overture to *Freischütz* in precisely my way and to my special satisfaction, and its effect was surprising even to the orchestra. But there was still not the slightest sign of official recognition for my efforts; I was and continued to be ignored in high places. Moreover, Frau von Bissing's communications gradually revealed difficulties she was encountering in making good her promise: yet as the letters were still hopeful in tone, I was able to spend New Year's Eve with the Standhartners in a confident mood and enjoy a poem specially written for the occasion by Cornelius, which was equally humorous and appropriate.

But the new year of 1864 soon assumed an increasingly ominous aspect. I fell ill with a rapidly worsening, painful catarrhal malady, which necessitated my making frequent demands on Standhartner's care. But I was more seriously threatened by the turnabout evidenced by the communications of Frau von Bissing. It seemed that she could not raise the money she had promised me without the help of her Hamburg family, the Slomans, who were shipowners, and from them she was meeting violent opposition, peppered with slanderous charges against me. I was so upset by these circumstances that I wanted to be in a position to renounce the lady's help entirely and therefore began seriously reconsidering my former plans for a Russian tour. Fräulein von Rhaden, to whom I again applied, now felt it necessary to advise me urgently against any attempt to visit St Petersburg, not only because I would find the route blocked by the disturbances resulting from the war in the Polish provinces, but also because nobody would pay any attention to me if I got there. On the other hand, a visit to Kiev, with the prospect of a profit of five thousand roubles, was considered entirely feasible. Focusing my thoughts on this, I drew up a plan together with Cornelius, who intended to accompany me, calling for a voyage over the Black Sea to Odessa, in order to proceed from there to Kiev. For this purpose we decided to provide ourselves with the requisite fur coats. Meanwhile, I had no alternative other than to float short-term bills of exchange in order to redeem other such short-term bills that were falling due. By this I got into an economic system which, leading as it would to obvious and inevitable ruin, could only be resolved by timely and fundamental financial assistance. In these straits I was at last obliged to request a clear declaration from my lady friend, not so much as to whether she could help me immediately, but whether she really wanted to do so at all, as I was no longer capable of preventing my complete ruin. She must have been extremely offended by this for some reason or other, for she went so far as to respond to me in words of this variety: "You want to know finally whether I will or not? Well then, in God's name: No!" This reply seemed quite incomprehensible at the time and attributable solely to the weakness of her not very independent character; but not long afterwards I received from her sister a very surprising explanation: Frau Wille confessed to me, in great agitation as a result of my probings on the subject, that her sister had said to herself: "Even if I save Wagner, in the end he will still love only that Wesendonck woman!..."

Amid these vicissitudes the month of February came to an end, and while Cornelius and I were busily working out the details of our Russian trip, I got news from Kiev and Odessa that it would be inadvisable to attempt any artistic ventures there this year. Now it became clear to me that under these circumstances I could no longer maintain my position in Vienna or my establishment in Penzing, because there was not only no prospect of earning any money even on a temporary basis, but also my short-term debts had mounted to such an ominous height under the well-known system of usury that without some extraordinary assistance my very person was actually threatened. In this situation I turned in utter frankness, at first only for advice, to Eduard Liszt, the youthful uncle of my old friend Franz and a judge at the Imperial Provincial Court. During my first stay in Vienna he had commended himself to me as a warmly devoted friend, who would always be willing to do me a favor. As far as the redemption of my short-term bills was concerned, he could see no way out other than to find a rich benefactor who would settle with the creditors. For a time he believed that a certain Madame Schöller, a devoted admirer of mine and also the wife of a rich merchant, not only possessed the means but the willingness to use them on my behalf. Standhartner, from whom I concealed nothing, also thought he could do something for me in this regard. By these efforts my situation was held in a state of suspension for a few more weeks, until it eventually turned out that the best my friends could do for me was to provide enough money to take what seemed the absolutely necessary step of fleeing to Switzerland, where I would be personally protected until such time as I could raise funds to redeem my bills. To the lawyer Eduard Liszt, this way out of the predicament seemed particularly advisable, as he would then be in a position to punish those who had victimized me with their unconscionable usury.

During the anxious period of the past few months, pervaded as they were by some indefinite hopes, my association with my few friends had been animated throughout. Cornelius still turned up regularly every evening, being joined by Otto Bach[1] as well as little Count Laurencin,[2] and on one occasion Rudolf Liechtenstein. Together with Cornelius, I began re-reading the *Iliad*:[3] when I got to the Catalogue of Ships, I wanted to skip the passage; but Peter insisted on it and offered to read it himself. I do not recall whether we finished it. My own reading material consisted of Chateaubriand's *La vie de Rancé*,[4] which Tausig had brought me, whereupon he himself disappeared, only to reemerge after a certain interval as the affianced husband of a Hungarian pianist. I was unwell the whole time and suffered greatly from severe catarrhal troubles. Thoughts of death gripped me so tightly that I lost all desire to shake them off. I set about bequeathing my books and manuscripts, of which Cornelius was to receive a share. Some time previously I had taken the precaution of commending my household effects remaining in Penzing, now no longer secure, to the protection of Standhartner. As my friends now most urgently recommended that I get ready to flee, I had turned to Otto Wesendonck, given the fact that my path would take me to Switzerland, and asked him to shelter me in his house. He rejected my request categorically: in response I could not avoid pointing out how shabbily he was behaving. Now it was a question of arranging my departure so that it would appear I would be coming back in the near future. In his great anxiety to cover up my departure, Standhartner had me come to dine at his house, where my servant Franz Mrazek brought me my luggage. I bade a very distressed farewell to him, his wife Anna, as well as my good dog Pohl. Standhartner's stepson Karl Schönaich, who wept from grief, and Cornelius, who by contrast was in a frivolous mood, accompanied me to the station, where I departed on the afternoon of March 23rd, to go first of all to Munich, where I hoped to be completely unnoticed and have a chance to recuperate for two days from the frightful strain of the recent past. I spent those days in the Bayerischer Hof, from which I undertook a few walks through the city. It was Good Friday: the weather was very bad and seemed to reflect the mood of the entire populace, whom I saw proceeding from one church to another in deepest mourning. King Maximilian II, whom the Bavarians had grown to love, had died a few days before, leaving his son to ascend the throne at the youthful but still legitimate age of eighteen and a half. In a display window I saw a portrait of the young king Ludwig II, and felt that special emotion awakened in us by the sight of beauty and youth being placed in what will presumably be a very difficult situation. Here I wrote a humorous epitaph[1] for myself and then journeyed unmolested over Lake Constance, a refugee once again and in need of shelter, and on to Zürich, from where I immediately proceeded to the estate of Dr Wille at Mariafeld.

I had already written to Frau Wille to ask her to put me up for a few days, having gotten to know her very well during my previous stay in Zürich, while I had never become a very close friend of her husband. I wanted to use this time to hunt for a suitable place to stay in one of the towns bordering on Lake Zürich, and to this she had kindly consented. I did not find Dr Wille there, as he was away on a pleasure trip to Constantinople. It was not difficult to bring my friend to understand my situation, and I found her entirely willing to help me. First of all, she gave me some rooms in an adjoining building previously occupied by Frau von Bissing, from which, however, the rather comfortable furniture had been removed. I wanted to take care of my own meals but had to yield to her request to assume that responsibility. As furniture was lacking, she felt justified in turning to Frau Wesendonck in this regard, who at once sent over some things she could spare from her own household, together with a pianino. In order to avoid any appearance of unpleasantness, she also wanted me to pay a visit to my old Zürich friends; but continual illness, augmented by the difficulty in heating my rooms adequately, kept me from doing so for so long that Otto and Mathilde finally came to see us in Mariafeld. The tense and uncertain demeanor of this couple was not entirely incomprehensible to me, but I behaved as if I didn't notice it. My catarrhal trouble, which rendered me incapable of looking around for a house in the surrounding district, was continually aggravated by the bad weather and my own deep depression. Wrapped in my Karlsruhe fur coat from morning till night, I spent these gruesome days benumbing myself by reading the volumes Frau Wille sent over to me one after another in my seclusion. I read Jean Paul's *Siebenkäs*, Frederick the Great's diary, Tauler,[1] novels by George Sand, Walter Scott, and finally *Felicitas*, a work from the pen of my sympathetic hostess. Nothing reached me from the outside world except a passionate lament from Mathilde Maier, and a most unexpected but pleasant surprise, in the form of a remittance of seventy-five francs sent me by Truinet, representing my Paris royalties. At this, I got into a conversation with Frau Wille, replete with a strange mixture of whimsy and gallows humor, as to what I would have to do to extricate myself completely from my wretched situation in life. Among other things we concluded it would be necessary for me to get a divorce from my wife in order to contract a rich marriage. As this seemed perfectly sensible and not implausible, I actually wrote to my sister Luise Brockhaus and asked her if she could not have a talk with Minna and persuade her to be content with the yearly allowance and no longer cling to my person; in response I received emotionally worded advice to think first of shoring up my reputation, and by means of a new work to ensure unassailable credit for myself, whereupon my situation would improve without resorting to any drastic measures: in any case, I was told, I would do well to apply for the conductorship that had recently become vacant in Darmstadt.

I got very bad news from Vienna: to protect the household effects I had left behind in my apartment there, Standhartner had gone so far as to sell them to a Viennese agent, reserving the right to repurchase. To this I responded in extreme indignation, as I saw my landlord, to whom I had to pay rent within a few days, compromised by this action. Through Frau Wille I managed to obtain the money needed to meet this obligation and forwarded it at once to Baron Rackowitz. Unfortunately I learned that Standhartner and Eduard Liszt had done a thorough job of things, having already paid the rent from the proceeds of the furniture and thereby cutting off all possibility of my returning to Vienna, which both believed would be ruinous for me. But when I heard at the same time from Cornelius that Tausig, who was then in Hungary and had previously added his endorsement to one of my demand notes, now felt himself prevented by me from going back to Vienna as he wished, I was so deeply upset that I decided on the spot to return there, no matter how great the danger might be. I notified my friends there of this but decided first to try to provide myself with enough money to be able to offer my creditors a settlement of sorts. For this purpose I had written most urgently to Schott in Mainz, not sparing him some vehement reproaches about his conduct toward me. I now decided to leave Mariafeld and go to Stuttgart, where I could press these efforts and await their outcome in closer proximity. But there were also other motives for this diversion, and these were as follows.

Dr Wille had returned, and I could see at once from his demeanor that my presence at Mariafeld alarmed him, as he no doubt feared I was counting on him too for help. In some embarrassment, occasioned by the attitude I had adopted in response to all this, he admitted in an unguarded moment that his feelings toward me were rather strained, but pardonably so in that he was confronted by a man to whom he felt inexplicably inferior, whereas he had always considered himself a man among men: "After all, a man wants to be something in his own house, and here especially doesn't want to serve as a mere foil for another man." Foreseeing her husband's state of mind, Frau Wille had made an arrangement with the Wesendonck family whereby they were to give me a monthly allowance of one hundred francs during the period of my stay in Mariafeld; when I got wind of this I had no alternative other than to write Frau Wesendonck that I would be leaving Switzerland immediately and request her in the kindest possible way to consider herself relieved of any anxiety about me, on the grounds that I had taken steps to arrange everything in accordance with my own desires. I learned later that she had returned this letter unopened to Frau Wille, probably believing it compromised her in some way.

Meanwhile I left for Stuttgart on April 30th; I knew that Karl Eckert had been settled there for some time as conductor at the Royal Court Theater, and I had reason to believe this good-natured fellow to be unreservedly well-disposed toward me, not only because of his admirable behavior to me when he was director of the Vienna Opera, but also in view of the enthusiasm he had showed when he came to my Karlsruhe concert the year before. I expected nothing more of him than to assist me to look for a quiet place to spend the coming summer, possibly in Cannstatt or some such town near Stuttgart. Here I wanted above all to complete the first act of *Die Meistersinger*, in order to be able at last to send Schott a part of the manuscript, as I had promised him I soon would when I had gone after him about the cash advances he had been denying me for so long. Thereafter I intended to live in great seclusion and, I hoped, obscurity as well, in order to try to assemble the funds to pay my Viennese debts. Eckert received me in an extremely cordial manner. His wife, who had been one of the great beauties of Vienna, had given up a very advantageous position out of some fanciful desire to be married to an artist, and she had retained enough money to enable her to provide the mere conductor with a comfortable and hospitable home, of which I now gained a pleasurable impression. Eckert considered it his absolute duty to take me to the manager of the theater, Baron von Gall:[1] the latter alluded quite sensibly and sympathetically to my difficult situation in Germany, where everything would continue to remain closed to me, he believed, as long as the ubiquitous Saxon diplomats and agents went around trying to injure me by spreading all kinds of suspicion. After getting to know me better, he thought he might be able to intervene on my behalf at the Württemberg Court. While I was talking over these matters rather late in the evening of May 3rd at the Eckerts' house, a card was brought to me, left by a gentleman with the title "Secretary to the King of Bavaria". Disagreeably surprised that my presence in Stuttgart was already known to people passing through, I asked that he be told I wasn't there, after which I withdrew to my hotel, only to be informed by its proprietor that a gentleman from Munich wished to speak to me on an urgent matter. I agreed to an appointment for ten o'clock the following morning and spent a restless night, preparing myself, as always now, for the worst. The next day I received Herr Pfistermeister,[2] the Cabinet Secretary of His Majesty the King of Bavaria, in my room. He began by expressing his great pleasure at having found me here thanks to some fortuitous directions, after having hunted for me in vain in Vienna and finally even in Mariafeld on Lake Zürich. He brought me a note from the young King[3] of Bavaria, together with a portrait and a ring as a present. In words which, though few, penetrated to the core of my being, the young monarch avowed his great admiration for my art and his firm resolve to keep me at his side as a friend for ever, to spare me any malignant strokes of fate. At the same time, Herr Pfistermeister notified me that he had instructions to conduct me to the King at once, and asked for my permission to announce to his master by telegram that I would be there the following day. I had been invited to lunch at the Eckerts' house; Herr Pfistermeister was obliged to decline to accompany me there. My friends, who had meanwhile been joined by young Weissheimer from Osthofen, were understandably amazed and overjoyed at the news I brought them. While we were at lunch Eckert was informed by telegram that Meyerbeer had just died in Paris:[1] Weissheimer burst out into boorish laughter at the strange coincidence that this operatic master, who had done me so much harm, should not have lived to see this day. Herr von Gall also made an appearance, to admit, in friendly astonishment, that I would certainly no longer be in need of his good offices. He had already given the order for a production of *Lohengrin* and now paid me the stipulated sum on the spot. At five o'clock that evening I met Herr Pfistermeister at the railroad station to travel with him to Munich, where my visit to the King had already been announced for the following day.

On the same day I had received the most urgent warnings from Vienna not to return there. But my life was to have no more of such alarms. The dangerous path on which destiny now beckoned me to the highest goals would not be free of worries and troubles of a kind hitherto unknown to me; but under the protection of my exalted friend the meanest cares of subsistence were never to touch me again.

AFTERWORD

It is not always the case with Wagner's autobiography that the evidence is as reliable as that concerning the writing of it. There are two sources which confirm the date when it was started: the first page of the manuscript bears the inscription "Munich July 17th 1865" and the entwined initials R. C. W., standing for Richard Wagner and Cosima von Bülow (as she still was at that date); July 17th was the date on which Wagner began to dictate his memoirs to Cosima, in his house in Munich, using notes he had made previously to assist his memory. Then there is a letter dated July 21st which Wagner wrote to King Ludwig II of Bavaria, who was out of Munich at the time: "What do you think I was doing when your letter of yesterday arrived? To save you guessing, I will tell you: I was dictating my biography! Our friend Cosima does not cease to remind me of our king's wish." In the preface which he wrote at a later date Wagner mentions only Cosima's desire that he would tell the story of his life, but that is likely to be one of the inexactitudes, the bland artifices, that we encounter in dealing with this book. King Ludwig had already expressed his wish that the composer he idolized would write his autobiography, in a letter dated May 28th 1865: "You would cause me inexpressible happiness if you were to give me an exhaustive description of your intellectual and spiritual development and of the external events of your life as well! May I nurture the hope of seeing this wish of mine fulfilled one day?" He was not to plead in vain. Only a few weeks after Hans von Bülow had conducted the première of *Tristan und Isolde* in Munich, his wife Cosima began to take down, from Wagner's dictation, one of the most exciting, and most controversial, of all autobiographies. It is a work which bursts all normal bounds as emphatically as almost everything else undertaken by that remarkable man of genius, in whom immense vitality was partnered by a delicate physical constitution; it is a panorama of its age, epic in its proportions, a paradigm of nineteenth-century literary composition, adventurous and indefatigable. And the course this autobiography took as a printed book was to be no less full of incident than the story it tells.

This "afterword" will give a brief account of that course, and outline the two difficulties in regard to this self-portrait that have always confronted readers who set store by reliability: establishing the authentic text and accounting for the errors that crept in during the writing.

Wagner was not the victim of any flagrant self-deceptions or misapprehensions, apart from a few tricks his memory played him. His narration was affected, however, unconsciously or semi-consciously, by attempts to stylize his story, to regularize its course and attune it to the way of the world, such as are only to be expected when the tale itself is so incredible and so improbable. The book was written while the life it describes was still in mid-career. All the time that Wagner was dictating *Mein Leben*, he was simultaneously living through his dramatic months in Munich, the Bülow affair, the eventual union with Cosima, the relationships with King Ludwig and with Nietzsche – both of which veered at different times from the warmest enthusiasm to the most awkward estrangement, the crises and the triumph of his festival project; and even after 1876, as the autobiography drew near to completion, the future of the Bayreuth undertaking was by no means assured. Depression and dejection, doubt as to the realization of his plans, may have dogged Wagner; personal slights and offenses – even if imagined – had coloured his recollections, and continued to alter them, clouding his view while he dictated.

He was also affected by the influence of the two people who had asked him to write his autobiography: King Ludwig and Cosima. For Wagner, the King was always to remain his saviour in the hour of need, the person to whom he owed the decisive change in his fortunes, and who had rescued him from the utmost misery and despair and made possible the realization of his ideas and his goals. The final sentence of *Mein Leben* acknowledges his debt. But in Cosima he saw the helper and diplomat who smoothed his path, and at the same time was everything he desired his life's partner to be: cultivated, passionate in her enthusiasms, and competent to organize and improve the running of his life. These were the two people who were now closest to him, it was for them, in the first place, that this account of his life was intended, and it may have been the sense of gratitude toward them which moved Wagner on occasion to play down the influence and help he received from others.

The representation of his relationship with the Wesendoncks could have been affected by that consideration – he made some scathing remarks about Otto Wesendonck, some of which were then cut from the first edition of *Mein Leben* to be made available to the general public. (The present edition has restored them.) The act of dictation made it necessary to take the amanuensis into account: Cosima might have been offended or hurt if he had lingered over other, no less passionate love affairs. Wagner's feelings for Mathilde Wesendonck are hardly hinted at in *Mein Leben*, while he had told Eliza Wille, on June 5th 1863, that Mathilde Wesendonck "is and remains my first and only love! I feel that now with more and more certainty!" It is astonishing to discover him later, in conversations with Cosima that she recorded in her diaries, explaining the whole affair away as a misunderstanding, as if it had existed only in Mathilde's fervid imagination. His relationship with Friederike Meyer is another on which he proves evasive; he confessed to a love affair with her in a letter to Hans von Bülow (February 16th 1863), but there is no mention of it in *Mein Leben*.

The way Wagner makes light of his involvement in the Dresden uprising can perhaps be set down to the King's account. Even if we accept his plea that he was concerned more with artistic revolution, and hence with revolution for the sake of art, than with social reform; even if the obvious opposition shown by the Dresden court to his artistic plans and desires caused personal, subjective feelings to dominate his motives; even if he could later represent his role in the revolution as being primarily a matter of general, human interest (which was for him, we may accept, synonymous with artistic interest), without diverging too far from the absolute truth: in spite of all these allowances, the picture *Mein Leben* gives of Wagner's thoughts and actions before and during the uprising is not complete. Far more is to be learned from his letters, especially those addressed to his Dresden friend Theodor Uhlig. The following excerpt from one of these letters was published for the first time in *Bayreuther Blätter* in 1892 (an edition of the letters published in 1888 suppressed substantial portions of them): "I cannot conceive of a *performance* until *after the revolution*, only the revolution can bring me the artists and the audiences, the next revolution must necessarily mean the end of the whole of our *theatrical set-up*; our theaters must all collapse, they will, it's inevitable. Out of their ruins I will then summon forth what I need, and I will obtain *then* what I need. Then I will erect a theater beside the Rhine and issue an invitation to a great dramatic festival: after a year of preparation I will then perform my entire work in the course of *four* days. Through it I will enable the men and women of the revolution to perceive the *meaning* of that revolution in its noblest sense. *That public* will understand me; the present-day public is incapable of doing so." If he thought like that after his flight (November 12th 1851), how serious will he not have been before it? *Mein Leben*, on the other hand, gives the impression that he merely allowed himself to be swept along in the current of the revolution as an inquisitive observer and only incidentally a participant, inasmuch as he was already conscious that his position in Dresden was untenable and that he was only breaking behind him bridges that no longer supported his weight in any case.

The letters first published with the Burrell Collection in 1950 have also emended somewhat the impression that the autobiography makes of Minna Wagner. It was an unhappy marriage from the start, and yet Wagner obviously felt more closely bound to Minna than he was prepared to admit in *Mein Leben*, where he regularly complains of the defects of her character. Yet enduring the bad, the truly wretched times in Königsberg, Riga, Paris and Dresden, at the side of this monster of a monologuist, required a readiness for self-sacrifice and a tolerance on her part which Wagner never forgot, at least so long as she was alive. She would after all have preferred a celebrated Kapellmeister with a few more successful operas like *Rienzi* to his name and a safe position in a court theater. And had there not been a particular point beyond which she was incapable of understanding his art and appreciating his stature – hard to judge from the very close quarters at which she saw him – her portrait in *Mein Leben* might well be different.

The subjective quality of Wagner's autobiography emerges most clearly, perhaps, in the casual and in some cases condescending tone he adopts towards contemporaries, affecting to have difficulty in remembering the names of well-known and well-regarded people; and it is also present in the attacks on other composers of the age, above all on Meyerbeer. Wagner had little grounds for complaint after his first encounter with Meyerbeer, even if success and fame had spoiled him; he turned to Meyerbeer for help and relied on letters of introduction from him on repeated occasions. But since the artistic arguments were all on Wagner's side – history has proved him right on every point – the relationship between the aspiring musical revolutionary and the established "operatic master" of the day was bound to turn into profound antipathy before long. It is an instance in which we can observe a process that was typical of Wagner: the interpretation of the world from one monomaniac standpoint alone. For the outcome was that unpleasant essay *Judaism in Music* of 1850. As soon as one starts to investigate Wagner's antisemitism one comes upon those concealed motives which manifest themselves by transforming a subjective resentment into an ideology. In Meyerbeer's case, Wagner went so far as to place the news of his death and that of his own elevation together in an unsavory juxtaposition on the last page of his autobiography, even if he then takes care to attribute the unsavoriness to the "boorish laughter" of

Weissheimer. Becoming ever more obsessed with the idea of a "Jewish conspiracy" against himself and his work, Wagner willfully forgot that some of his closest and most intimate friends were Jews: Samuel Lehrs, Josef Rubinstein, Tausig, whom he loved tenderly, and Angelo Neumann; and that many of those who purchased patronage vouchers as a contribution to the financing of the first Bayreuth Festival were Jews, including Alfred Pringsheim, professor of mathematics at the University of Munich, who would one day convert his son-in-law Thomas Mann to a passion for the creator of the *Ring* and for the nervous, psychological intensity of the music of *Tristan* which was to yield a further creative harvest. But *Parsifal* was conducted by a man with the name of Levi, and Wagner's determination on that point was not shaken by the receipt of anonymous antisemitic missives insisting that he preserve the "purity" of his work and not allow it to be conducted by a Jew.

These instances should be enough to demonstrate the incalculable formula governing the mixture of the subjective and the tendentious, reliable narration and self-justifying defamation in the text of this book.

Wagner unfolded the story of his life from earliest infancy to the eve of his fifty-first birthday. He devoted particular care and detail to the description of his professional and musical development. The work is always in the foreground and determines the pattern according to which the life (and the *Life*) is woven. The most is made of the peaks and of the deeps: to use a musical analogy, there are places scored as skillfully as anything Wagner wrote for the stage. The melancholy beauty of his writing for the strings in a scene like the meeting of Senta and the Flying Dutchman is paralleled in the richness of his descriptions of his despairs and disasters – which are followed, always, by regeneration, revival, scored for full orchestra. Observe the artistry with which he directs his own role in the ceremony when Carl Maria von Weber's remains are brought back to Dresden: muted brass and woodwind. The rehearsal of the funeral music, which he composed, cannot have been as beautiful as it becomes in his description. At the graveside: a great actor listens to his own words, self-absorbed and abstracted, he falls silent, and only the silence prompts him to resume talking, so that at the end even the actor Emil Devrient assures him that he was impressed by the ceremony as a performance as much as a rite. How much art and humor there is in the account of the performance of that youthful symphony with the fatal, recurrent drum-beat, or the raging of *The Battle of Vittoria*, which drove the audience from the hall! The culminating passage is the monument to Spontini, larger than lifesize – swollen indeed to something just short of bursting-point, a satirical portrait of the first rank, the intentionality of which does not strike the reader until it is over. A whole world is used as the background to a self-portrait. What a spectacle! And what the work may lose in accuracy is made up for by its compositional skill: the forms of the dramatic structure, the climaxes, the act-closes are planned and executed with the utmost precision. If a storm blows up, Schopenhauer wrote, the experienced sailor furls his sails: Wagner crowds on every scrap of canvas! Driven onto the rocks with his ship, he jumps clear at the right moment and always survives: his restless nature, forever creating obstacles for itself, is faithfully reflected in this book. And then, finally, there are the solos for cor anglais: the incessant desertions, the mourning over the faithlessness of friends, the old, sad song of the outcast, wounded incurably by the longing for a better, more ideal world full of love and art – all of this interspersed with hoaxes and *con fuoco*, one flight after another, and a rumbustiousness in the action and the adventures that would be the envy of a novelist. Failure, unhappy speculations with expected but unrealized income, new debts, did nothing to diminish the man's self-confidence. *He was somebody*, he had the right to expect things, even when looking back, as though the world should already have recognized him for what he was in his youth. The autobiography also bears witness to the consistency – or better, the unthinking, reckless instinct and courage – with which this musician of the nineteenth century, the patchily educated scion of a large, and not rich, middle-class family, overcame all obstacles and, ignoring what was feasible in his time, realized his artistic ambitions. For all the monstrousness that is an essential ingredient in this wide-ranging and discursive life, provoked though the reader may be by the solipsism and insufferableness of the author – Wagner's autobiography is the record of a battle for self-realization in which the original ideal was never abandoned, and as a "drama" it is not the least considerable of his works.

Its composition ran parallel with that of *Siegfried*, *Die Meistersinger*, *Götterdämmerung* and *Parsifal*. At first the dictation proceeded at a handsome pace. After less than a week, Cosima had already filled forty sides when the news of the death of Ludwig Schnorr von Carolsfeld caused the first break in the dictation on July 21st 1865. Subsequent progress is easy to trace, from the dates noted in the margin by Cosima (given in foot-notes in the present edition), and from the numerous references to the work in letters. Writing to King Ludwig from Tribschen on May 18th 1866, Cosima announced: "Yesterday we took up the biography again. In the mornings I write it out, in the evenings our friend dictates." From this we learn that at least the early part of the manuscript, which is the easiest part to read, is a fair copy from what she took down at the moment of dictation. In October 1866 she wrote to the king again: "In the evenings after tea our friend dictates the biography to me. We have now arrived in Paris at the time when the *Faust* Overture was written (1839–40). I cannot tell you how it distresses me to learn exactly what that dreadful time was like, and how moved I am by the leniency with which our friend judges the abominable treatment he received on all sides." Early in February 1867: "We are working on the biography now as assiduously as ants." The most important caesuras are the birth of her and Wagner's daughter Eva (February 17th 1867), the writing down of the so-called "Annals" in February 1868 and the start of work on Part IV (January 10th 1876), which took until 1880 to finish.

As soon as Wagner had finished a sizeable section of his autobiography he went over it, correcting and revising it in his own handwriting. Early in 1867 Cosima wrote to King Ludwig, from her home in Munich: "He feels good on Tribschen and is at present correcting the biography." Wagner was determined to distribute his autobiography to a few friends and relations, and of course to the king, in a very expensive privately printed edition. He mentioned the matter to Otto Wesendonck, writing from Tribschen on January 5th 1870: "In order to preserve this manuscript against loss, I recently hit upon the idea of having perhaps half a dozen copies of it printed at my expense. I enclose one of the first specimen sheets, which have just arrived, but I beseech you not to interpret this as any kind of bid for your interest." It is of some importance to realize that the plan to print the text privately took clearly defined shape at a very early stage, although there was no thought of publication. Writing from Geneva on January 3rd 1866, he told his sister Luise Brockhaus: "Of course this dictation is not intended for the general public: its only purpose is, after my death, to serve as a truthful point of reference for him who may be called to tell the world about my life." But the author's eye was already drawn toward his potential readers while he was dictating; there is no other interpretation to put on the give-away comment that Ferdinand Hiller "will perhaps consider me deceitful if he now learns that I concealed" a source of historical information that could have been useful to Hiller in an opera. And Cosima's diaries contain the remark that Siegfried would be able to make a nice sum of money one day, if he had the book published. Nobody tells a story at such length without thinking of readers, and so ulterior motives insinuate themselves: the intention of providing "a truthful point of reference" for a biographer goes by the board. Pierre Boulez has rightly remarked of Wagner's autobiographical writings that their content is not insincere, but "where Wagner regards himself as a figure of public interest even his most personal writings seem to be written with an eye to posterity" ("Divergences: the man and his work", in *Wagner, a documentary study*, ed. by H. Barth etc., London, 1975). This does not mean to say that Wagner's relationship with those he was directly addressing was a sham, but it contained a degree of calculation that nevertheless did not exclude ironic self-deception and involuntary self-revelation: as for example in the account of his wedding to Minna, when he in all seriousness understood the preacher's mysterious allusion to "a friend" to refer to some as yet unknown patron, only to discover, disappointedly, that it was – Jesus. Wagner's autobiography is not an edifying story. Cosima told the king how she regarded it: "Had I not constantly begged him to say everything, however painful it might be, there is quite a lot that he would not have set down. I was bold enough to assert that you too would have asked him to do it, and so he plunges deep into a sea of unedifying memories." There is certainly no lack of those – it is rare for an autobiography to be quite so merciless as this is in some respects. Indeed, one reader was later to conclude, as we shall see, that the whole thing was a vile forgery by his enemies. And having set down on paper all the crises and triumphs of his stranger-than-fiction life, he sent it off immediately to a printer: and that is where the history of this book really begins.

It begins inauspiciously. The first three parts of the manuscript were sent in installments to an Italian printer in Basle, Bonfantini. But the compositors had great difficulty in deciphering the copy and the client was too far away – at first in Lucerne, later in Bayreuth – to be consulted about every single doubtful passage. And so this private edition contains mistakes that distorted the meaning and moreover persisted through the subsequent editions. Names of places and people were changed, words were altered to other words that look very similar in handwriting: "Ausbrüche" (outbreaks) became "Ausdrücke" (expressions), "ernüchtert" (sobered) became "ermüdet" (wearied), "naiver" (naive) became "seiner" (his), "Sommer" (summer) became "Januar" (January), while the compositor transformed the "universal" bedroom in the Wagners' Paris lodgings into a "miserable" one, and so on. In the last part of the manuscript Cosima's handwriting was far worse, so that it is some kind of miracle that decipherment produced any sense at all. On top of all this, Friedrich Nietzsche, entrusted with the job of overseeing the production of the first volumes, evidently undertook some stylistic revision, and in doing so he must have frequently tampered with Wagner's German. Cosima wrote to him from Tribschen on June 2nd 1871: "Herewith a Lamentation from Bonfantini with head-shakings from the Master over the philology!" But which of them raised objections, and to what? The answer will never be known, for the proofs have vanished.

In spite of all that the differences between the private printing and the manuscript are irrelevant to the passing of judgment on Wagner. Very few words are actually missing from the private edition, and those are small sections of sentences; perhaps the most interesting is the remark about how a certain Herr von Einsiedel had his way with the inexperienced Minna Planer: we read in the manuscript that it was accomplished "half by force and half by seduction".

A number of inaccurate assertions have been made about the manuscript and the private edition, and the mystification was made worse by scandal-mongering. Thus the two Americans, Philip Dutton Hurn and Waverley Lewis Root, in their polemic *The Truth about Wagner* (1930), cited Nietzsche as their authority for the claim that on the first page of the private edition Wagner identified Ludwig Geyer as his father and not Friedrich Wagner. This turns out to be a complete fabrication.

It was November 1870 before the first volume of the private edition was ready. The publication of the Burrell Collection (of which more below) revealed for the first time the number of copies printed and the terms on which Bonfantini was given the work; they must have struck him as highly baffling and mysterious. First a letter from Wagner to Bonfantini, dated July 7th 1870: "I return herewith the corrected proofs. You can easily hire a German compositor for the work. In the agreement we concluded the most important condition is that you keep a strict watch that no proof and certainly no printed copy of the book reach the public, since I am bearing the expenses of printing fifteen copies of this autobiography with the sole purpose of avoiding the possible loss of my manuscript, and of putting the copies into the hands of faithful and responsible friends who must keep them for a more distant future. Instead of spending money on having them printed, I could make a lot if I was ready to sell the manuscript to a publisher for publication. Thus the foundation of our agreement is the greatest discretion on your part. You must know whether you can entrust the work to a compositor with a command of German, since the essential point is that you watch that neither the manuscript nor a single page of the printed material be removed, which will be prevented if you scrupulously destroy every corrected proof, and if you comply with our agreement conscientiously and don't print more than fifteen copies, which should be sent to me immediately after they are printed off. You know that of the first four sheets I have received only a single copy. In addition to that, pages 65–96 are missing from the manuscript which was returned. Would you please find out if perhaps Herr Nietzsche has them." Wagner returned the last proofs to Bonfantini on November 21st: "On the title I ask you please to remove the name of your printing establishment, since that would give my manuscript the character of a publication, which I want to avoid by all means. Instead of that please put the coat of arms at the place I have indicated on the proof. If it is your ambition (which flatters me) to be known by my descendants as the printer of my autobiography, you can set your name in small type at the foot of the last page, as is the usual practice." Bonfantini did as he was asked. The coat of arms is placed at the head of the first page of text in each volume, and the following imprint appears on the last page of each of the first three volumes: "Basel – Druck von G. A. Bonfantini".

Wagner was able to send the first volume of his memoirs to a small number of friends and intimates for Christmas 1870: King Ludwig, Franz Liszt, Countess Marie von Schleinitz, Otto Wesendonck and another Zürich friend, Jakob Sulzer. As we learn from a letter Sulzer wrote to Mathilde Wesendonck in August 1887, which first came to light in 1976, Wagner gave Sulzer the imposing octavo volume while he was paying a Christmas visit to Tribschen, on the strict condition that it was to remain sealed to all eyes but his own. Sulzer goes on: "But a few days later I received a note – which I attributed at the time to his wife's intervention – asking me to send the *mysterium* back. The first *circa* eighty pages, which I had read by then, do not get anywhere near the time in Zürich." This led Sulzer to surmise, quite correctly, that what he had in his hands was no more than the first volume of several. He was asked to return it, without any precise explanation, on January 10th 1871. Otto Wesendonck upset the Wagners by acknowledging his gift with the suggestion that henceforth Wagner should not go into such minute detail: the advice suggests a not unfounded fear of indiscretion, but it was at once interpreted in Tribschen as unwarranted interference. The recipients all faithfully kept silent about the content of the book, so much so that even in 1887 Sulzer could ask Frau Wesendonck: "Can it be that, although of all living beings you unquestionably have the first

right to the knowledge, you have never heard of [the memoirs']
existence?" It seems as though Wagner did not deceive himself when
he wrote in his preface of his confidence that his friends would not
communicate anything from the book to persons whose interest in the
subject was less "pure" than their own.

The correspondence with Bonfantini about the proofs of the second
volume stretched out over the whole of 1871 until August 22nd 1872,
when Wagner told Bonfantini that he was at the end of the manuscript
material for the second volume, which was ready in December 1872. A
letter of January 12th 1873 refers to a total of eighteen copies, and so
does another, dated November 10th 1873, in which Wagner asks
Bonfantini if he is willing to print off the third volume. Wagner sent
the last proof-corrections and some minor emendations to the third
volume on June 29th 1874, and added his thanks for Bonfantini's
discretion. Volume three was printed off in 1875 (Wagner acknowledged
it on April 4th), and at Christmas that year Wagner gave the first three
volumes of his autobiography to King Ludwig with a dedicatory
inscription which once again indicates that the memoirs were ultimately
intended for the author's son Siegfried. "With trust in the royal favor
and grace, the account of his life, written that his son may value it one
day, and contained in these three volumes, is presented to his sublime
benefactor, King Ludwig II of Bavaria, for his sole possession and
sympathetic reception, by Richard Wagner."

Thus, under conditions of the strictest secrecy, the first three volumes
of the biography were already complete by the time Wagner started
dictating the last part in January 1876, finishing it in 1880. The last
volume was printed in Bayreuth, by the firm of T. Burger. Wagner gave
the king his copy on August 25th 1880.

With this, one might suppose, the history of the book was at an end.
But after Wagner's death Cosima asked all the recipients to return the
volumes (if not earlier – 1878 in the case of Mathilde Maier), and most
of the copies were destroyed. Even the king returned his four volumes,
which were kept in Wahnfried but disappeared at some later date. Thus
for a long time the very existence of the autobiography was virtually
unknown. Jakob Sulzer for one never heard of it again and told Mathilde
Wesendonck of his curiosity as to "whether it still exists and whether
it will ever come to light in its authentic shape. The latter is something
I would not wish for." He was probably afraid – as she was – that "in
the nature of its psychological origin" the truth would not be well served
in it: "Wagner was an extremely subjective nature, his entire knowledge

of the world, the entire knowledge that he wanted of the world, was what he got from the arbitrary reflection of it that he carried in his own consciousness." It could hardly be more accurately or more carefully expressed: Sulzer's personal integrity was not compromised by his loyalty to Wagner.

The English enthusiast Mary Burrell, having collected all the documentary material she could find outside Bayreuth, formed quite different conclusions. She set herself the notable and commendable goal, like many another after her, to correct the cliché-ridden and implausible pictures composed by contemporary biographers and by Wagner's enemies and critics. In pursuit of her aim, in 1892 she sought out the widow of Bonfantini. The printer had possessed ambition and some of the other very human attributes of his trade. What does a printer do when he is commanded with such insistence to destroy all corrected proofs? He keeps a copy for himself, of course. This one proof copy, and the letters quoted above, were purchased by Mrs Burrell on October 1st 1892 from the printer's widow, Thekla Bonfantini Stuckert. And Mrs Burrell simply could not believe what she read: either the autobiography was a forgery, the malicious fabrication of his enemies, or Wagner was not to be held fully responsible for its composition or its contents. She decided to be as silent on the subject as all its previous readers.

But the myth grew, and even Wahnfried could not remain indifferent to the rumours for ever. On the one hand it was said that the truth about Wagner was being suppressed, and on the other that the document had either disappeared or existed only in one single copy of the private printing, and that that was inaccessible. In fact, the Wagner Archive at Bayreuth has only two complete copies and one incomplete. In the end, twenty-eight years passed after Wagner's death before the first public edition appeared – and gave rise to a lot of new speculation.

We now know that the edition of 1911 differed from the privately printed edition in respect of seventeen passages which had been modified by omission or rewriting. The blue pencil had been drawn through some indiscreet remarks about Wagner's friend Karl Ritter and his unhappy marriage and through disparaging remarks about Felix Draeseke and Luise Meyer's husband. In the case of Draeseke, Liszt had insisted on promoting a march he had written at the 1861 musicians' congress in Weimar, which is described in the 1911 edition of *Mein Leben* as a "curious composition", but in the original printing the words "truly miserable" were used. The comment on Friederike Meyer's relationship with her sister Luise, "whom she considered as having compromised herself by marrying that distasteful Herr Dustmann, whose name she now bore", is omitted altogether. Other omissions are longer. The manuscript and the private edition contain a bitter attack on the tenor Albert Niemann for the role he played during the preparations for the Paris production of *Tannhäuser*. "He had been apprised that the downfall of my work had been sworn" is all that remains in the 1911 edition of the first sentence of this attack, which, in full, reads as follows: "Having felt it necessary to devote part of his emoluments in Paris to an effort to conciliate the chief Parisian critics, he had been apprised in the course of these attempts at bribery that the downfall of my work had been sworn, and that he could save his own skin solely by desertion and subsequent appearance in operas of Meyerbeer" (p. 630 of this edition). A further cut was made a few sentences later: "When he [Niemann] again demanded the excision of the adagio passage in the second act finale which I knew to be of crucial importance, and which he had sung in several early rehearsals to the great emotion of all those present, he responded to my protest with a letter stating he had no desire to hazard his voice and reputation on my account; if I didn't want to cut the piece, he wrote, I should find whoever else I could to sing it. I knew from that point on I was dealing with a beast driven wild by cowardice, and gave my knight, who no longer even had the courage to dally with Venus, no further attention with respect to his performance." If we take into account the fact that Niemann was later one of Wagner's most dedicated exponents, we need seek no further for a reason for these particular cuts.

Other cuts include part of the remarks about Mme Kalergis (p. 504: the complete sentence beginning "The rumors reaching me..."); a comment on Karl Ritter and his wife (p. 529: the complete sentence beginning "His young and rather uncultivated wife...") and an entire paragraph about their marriage (p. 572: from "When he said goodbye..." to "...companionable and devoted to me"); the reference to "a particularly tasty repast" ordered by Bülow for some Prussian diplomats (p. 610); another damaging remark about Albert Niemann (pp. 635–6: the complete sentence beginning "As far as the singers were concerned..."); the phrase "by such people as Frau von Seebach" (p. 643); and the revelation of Frau von Bissing's feelings about him (p. 733: from "Frau Wille confessed to me..." to the end of the paragraph; other single words are also omitted from this passage).

Some of the changes were made to temper the derogatory nature of Wagner's remarks about the Wesendoncks, especially Otto. At best the text of *Mein Leben* does not do justice to the help and practical proofs of friendship Otto Wesendonck gave to Wagner, and it was some small amends if the reference to his lack of cultivation was changed to an attribution of "artlessness" ("Offenheit", p. 552). When Wagner was preparing to flee from Vienna in 1864, he asked Wesendonck "to shelter me in his house", but the request was refused. The editors of the 1911 edition must have recognized that it did not become Wagner to admit that thereupon he told Wesendonck "how shabbily he was behaving", and had him reproach him for "his wrong" instead ("sein Unrecht", p. 734). The sentence "At any rate, they hadn't had the idea of offering me what I was looking for" (p. 675) was completely cut, as was the description of Mathilde Wesendonck's behavior toward Minna as "childish and impulsive" (p. 731).

There are two more passages toward the end of the book which were omitted for a somewhat different reason, as they concern Wagner's relationship with Cosima. The first comes at the end of the description of an incident in 1862, when Wagner and the Bülows were paying a short visit to Frankfurt, and Wagner invited Cosima to allow him to push her across the square to the hotel in a wheel-barrow (p. 693). "Following behind us, Hans had witnessed the incident; Cosima explained to him unabashedly what it was all about, but unfortunately it did not appear that he could share our high spirits, for he cautioned his wife to be more careful in such things." The editors of the 1911 edition decided that this admission that Hans von Bülow's jealousy had been aroused as early as 1862 ought to be cut. The Bülows were not divorced until 1870, but Richard and Cosima had long decided to live together at a time when they were still vehemently denying the very existence of a liaison to the king and the world in general. The private edition also includes, a few pages before the end, in the description of Wagner's visit to Berlin, when he and Cosima went for a drive while Hans was rehearsing for a concert, the famous sentence which continued to be whispered about even though it was cut from the 1911 edition: "With tears and sobs we sealed a vow to belong to each other alone" (p. 729). That was on November 28th 1863. The *Annals* state merely: "Night journey via Frankfurt to Berlin: Bülows at station. Stay one day. Concert. (Frommann on the stairs.) Waitzmann. (28 Nov:) – Löwenberg." But there can be no doubt that the decision that changed their lives was made on that day; as Cosima's diaries reveal, the anniversary was celebrated every year.

Thus to the numerous printer's errors of the private printing and the minor nonsense that resulted from them were added the omissions and alterations of the 1911 edition, all of them to be inherited by subsequent editions. Daniela Thode, Wagner's step-daughter, pointed out that the "bibliographical remark" in the "popular" edition of 1914, which speaks of the "most faithful possible reproduction of the manuscript", refers to the "small number of isolated omissions", "which had to be undertaken out of consideration for those yet living and their relatives". She told Wilhelm Altmann, who assumed responsibility for the "critical" edition of 1923 but evidently never saw the manuscript, that she very much regretted, "for the Master's sake, that more such omissions had not been made". As a result none of the subsequent editions were either complete or reliable; indeed, adding new errors to the old, they introduced the form "Bertz" for the spelling of Wagner's mother's maiden name.

The further the distance traveled from the original, the less firm the ground underfoot became. The text became the object of the wildest speculation, and what was far worse than the actual errors and omissions was the sense of uncertainty: nobody knew what lay concealed in the manuscript. Would it not have been simpler to go back to the manuscript and follow that? But for a time even the manuscript was incomplete. There were two lacunae in it in 1933; as Dr Otto Strobel confirmed at the time, fifteen pages were in private hands in Nuremberg, while the other pages missing were believed irretrievably lost. Since then the manuscript has been restored complete: the fifteen sheets in Nuremberg were purchased by the municipality of Bayreuth and given to the Wagner Archives, while the second batch of missing pages was found during a systematic search of all the crates and trunks in the attic of Wahnfried.

Mein Leben ends in May 1864. The story it tells was continued, not in the *Annals* or anywhere else in the *Brown Book*, but in the diaries that Cosima began to keep on January 1st 1869. In the letter of July 21st–22nd 1865 that was quoted above, Wagner told King Ludwig: "We have decided to carry the dictation up to my union with you, dear, glorious Prince; from that point onward Cosima shall continue the biography on her own, and, it is to be hoped, complete it one day. She is the best person for the task, and will carry it out splendidly." But the four years following the "union" with King Ludwig in May 1864 were too agitated and eventful for Cosima to be able to start on her part of the biographical work. It was only after she had moved to Tribschen to live with Wagner for good that she was able to begin the journal that she then kept for over fourteen years. The couple certainly considered the idea of continuing dictation so as to take the story up to the end of 1868, the time of their own "union"; not only is there a reference to the possibility in her diary, but Wagner also mentioned it to the King in a letter of January 25th 1880; he had promised his wife, he said, that while they were in Naples he would dictate something from his life to her every day if possible, "with the intention of continuing what has already been recorded up to the moment when at last Fate permitted our complete union, and since when she herself has been writing down the most meticulous records about me, my daily life and activities, in order that after my death my son will have in his possession the story of my entire life with no lacunae". But Siegfried was not to be so fortunate, for one reason or another. The fate of Cosima's diaries was even more contentious than that of the autobiography; by her will Eva Chamberlain put an embargo on them that lasted until 1972, and it was only after legal proceedings lasting several years that they were published, in 1976–7.

There is a curious irony in the fact that, with all Wagner's readiness to tell his story, the two great testimonies that in his opinion represented him best reached posterity only after such delays. Whatever the balance of truth and self-stylization in them, the diaries and the autobiography contain Wagner entire. In *Mein Leben* he is no longer quite the assured stylist of the letters and journalism from Paris; the Heine-like irony flashes less often, muffled in the folds of satin and velvet – but what life there is behind the flowery language, what fire burns behind the prematurely assumed mask of a reflective old age! Finally, the position that this autobiography can claim as a primary source for the history of German art and society between the age of Goethe and the age of Bismarck is unaffected by the storms that still rage around the creative phenomenon that was Richard Wagner.

Martin Gregor-Dellin
1976

In 1963 the Munich publishing house of Paul List published the first complete and authentic edition of *Mein Leben*, edited by Martin Gregor-Dellin, and based on the manuscript now preserved in the Wagner Archives in Bayreuth (the transcript was by Gertrud Strobel); a second, less luxurious edition in two volumes appeared in 1969 and was reissued in one volume, with minor corrections (of literals, for example) and fuller annotation, in 1976. The editor's "Afterword" was also modified to take account of the quantities of Wagner documents that had been published for the first time since 1963. The text in these three editions represented that of the manuscript as it was after Wagner had gone through it making additions and alterations to the text that Cosima had taken down from his dictation. Correction of Wagner's slips of memory, including those affecting personal names, was consigned to the annotation at the end of the book, while some insignificant instances of unconventional orthography were discreetly corrected by the editor on the page, with a comment in the annotation in a few cases of grammatical error. The German editions contained foot-notes reproducing the few foot-notes in the original, private edition, and the occasional marginal notes found in the manuscript; they also followed the private edition in the matter of italicization.

This English edition follows the 1976 printing. The correction of Wagner's slips of memory is again to be found in the annotation at the end, while the grammatical corrections undertaken by Martin Gregor-Dellin were adopted without special notice in the translation. The convention of printing proper nouns in italics has been ignored, and the dashes that subdivide Wagner's long paragraphs, according to German convention, have been used as a guide in setting shorter paragraphs in accordance with English conventions. The running heads from the privately printed edition, which were a feature of the 1963 edition but were omitted from those of 1969 and 1976, have been reintroduced to act as signposts in a text whose only subdivisions are the four parts.

The annotation, including the foot-notes, in this English edition is based on that in the 1976 German edition, but adapted to some extent to the needs of non-German readers. It follows the German edition in including the texts of two letters written by Wagner, one to his sister Rosalie in December 1833, when he had just finished *Die Feen*, and the other the fateful letter to Mathilde Wesendonck of April 7th 1858, which was intercepted by his wife Minna. As Martin Gregor-Dellin has remarked, the letter to Rosalie (which Wagner obviously intended to append to the private edition of *Mein Leben*, though the intention was not carried out) is extremely informative about the twenty-year-old Wagner, "his plans, his tastes, his artistic ideas and his relationship to his family".

Apart from brief cuts in Martin Gregor-Dellin's "Afterword" of matter germane to the German edition, the only major omission here from the material appended to the 1976 edition consists of the text of the *Annals* from May 5th 1864 to December 31st 1868. The intention of reproducing this last section of the autobiographical notes Wagner wrote down in his *Brown Book* in 1868 was to bridge the gap between the end of the autobiography he actually wrote and the beginning of the diaries Cosima kept from January 1st 1869 to the eve of his death, February 12th 1883, using a text composed by Wagner himself. But while the *Annals* are valuable material for the biographer, they do not constitute autobiography. Except for the reader who is already familiar with Wagner's life, many of the entries are incomprehensible without very full annotation, and the need for annotation is compounded in translation, where often the interpretational options open to the reader are necessarily pre-empted.

Moreover, since the first complete edition of *Mein Leben* appeared in 1963, the *Brown Book* has also been published (edited by Joachim Bergfeld, Zürich, 1975), including the complete *Annals*, 1846–68; the English translation by George Bird appeared in 1980. Cosima Wagner's diaries, edited by Martin Gregor-Dellin and Dietrich Mack, have also been published in German (Munich, 1976–7) and in Geoffrey Skelton's English translation, and so only the authentic text of *Mein Leben* has been lacking to give English-language readers, as nearly as possible, Wagner's entire life-story in his own words.

The anonymously prepared German edition of *Mein Leben* that issued from Wahnfried in 1911 was matched with an equally anonymous English translation authorized by the same source. Remarkably that edition has been allowed to stand unchallenged for seventy years, despite its incompleteness, its inaccuracies and its failure to reproduce Wagner's tone of voice. The cadences of Wagner's German are those of speech, and long though they may be at times, the periods of *Mein Leben* were originally spoken aloud. To reproduce that tone of voice, combined with strict accuracy in translation, has been the mutual objective of the undersigned.

Andrew Gray   Mary Whittall
October 1982

NOTES

Foreword   "friend and wife": Cosima von Bülow, née Liszt, who married Wagner in Lucerne, August 25th, 1870.

p. 3   1   "christened": Wagner was not christened until August 16th 1813.

   2   "My father": Friedrich Wagner born June 18th 1770, died November 22nd 1813.

   3   "his own father's": Gottlieb Friedrich Wagner (1736–95), a tax collector, married in 1769 to Sophie Eichel, daughter of a schoolmaster.

   4   "Adolf": Adolf Wagner (1774–1835), independent scholar, writer, and translator.

   5   "My mother": Johanna Rosine born September 19th 1778, daughter of the master-baker Pätz in Weissenfels, married Friedrich Wagner in 1798 and died January 9th 1848.

   6   "actress of the day": Friederike Wilhelmine Hartwig, née Worthon (1777–1849), the first Joan in Schiller's *Maid of Orleans*.

   7   "Ludwig Geyer": born January 21st 1778, actor, dramatist, and portrait painter, he married Wagner's mother on August 28th 1814 and died September 30th 1821. There is no evidence for the assertion that Geyer was Wagner's real father.

p. 4   1   "seven surviving children": Albert (1799–1874), Rosalie (1803–37), Julius (1804–62), Luise (1805–71), Klara (1807–75), Ottilie (1811–83), and Richard. Wagner does not mention two children who died early – Gustav (1801–4) and Theresia (1809–14).

   2   "Cäcilie": Cäcilie Geyer (1815–93).

p. 5   1   "Kotzebue's": August von Kotzebue (1761–1819), dramatist and diplomat.

   2   "the pastor": Christian Ephraim Wetzel (1776–1823).

p. 7   1   "visit it again": this visit did in fact take place in 1873 and is described in Cosima Wagner's diaries.

p. 8   1   "Ypsilanti Waltz": Alexander Ypsilanti (1792–1828), a Greek freedom fighter against Turkish domination.

p. 9   1   "Titus wig": a Titus cut was a short crop, named after the Roman emperor.

p. 10   1   "*Parnasso Italiano*": an anthology of Italian poems.

p. 11   1   "really 'Petz'": actually Pätz – in the manuscript the "e" was originally an "ä". In most editions of *My Life* it is mistakenly printed as "Bertz".

   2   "a Weimar prince": Prinz Konstantin of Saxe-Weimar, brother of Karl August, who possibly discovered the theatrically talented young girl in Weissenfels and had her educated in a Leipzig institute. There is no basis for the belief that he was Johanna Rosine's natural father.

p. 16   1   "August Apel's": Johann August Apel (1771–1816) wrote plays and stories and was, with Friedrich Laun, editor of the "Book of Ghosts" in which the novella *Der Freischütz* appeared.

p. 17   1   "Count Pachta": Johann Joseph, Count Pachta was President of the Prague Conservatory. His natural daughters were Jenny and Auguste Raymann.

p. 19   1   *"Genovefa"*: a folktale based on a French legend. The virtuous Genovefa is calumniated by Golo, who has failed to seduce her while her husband, the Count Palatine, is away on a crusade.

p. 23   1   "sister of...Wendt": Sophie (1792–1860), author; sister of Amadeus Wendt, a professor at Göttingen.

p. 25   1   "lost": in 1891 Mrs Burrell purchased the manuscript from Nathalie Bilz-Planer. It is now in the Wagner Archives.

p. 27   1   "Mieksch": Johann Aloys Mieksch (1765–1845).

p. 30   1   "Prince Anton": Prince Anton (1755–1836), brother of Friedrich August I.

        2   "Ostallee": actually the Ostraallee.

        3   "his death": Beethoven had died on March 26th 1827.

p. 31   1   "Logier's": Johann Bernhard Logier (1777–1846), a German music teacher active in England and Ireland.

        2   "Friedrich Wieck": Friedrich Wieck (1785–1873), a German piano and singing teacher, father of Clara Wieck.

p. 32   1   "Staerkel, Stamitz, and Steibelt": Johann Franz Xaver Sterkel (1750–1817), a composer; Johann Stamitz (1717–57), composer of the Mannheim school; Daniel Steibelt (1765–1823), composer and pianist.

p. 34   1   "singer Wolfram": Heinrich Wolfram, later engaged in commerce, married Wagner's sister Klara in 1828.

        2   "Kühnlein": actually Johann Christoph Kienlen (1784–1830?), a composer, conductor, and singing teacher.

p. 36   1   "Schott": Franz Schott (1811–74), music publisher and from 1855 sole proprietor of the business.

        2   "Sipp": Robert Sipp (1806–99).

        3   "Mayseder": Joseph Mayseder (1789–1863), Austrian violin virtuoso and composer.

p. 37   1   "Wilhelmine Schröder-Devrient": Wilhelmine Schröder-Devrient (1804–60), operatic singer who became famous as Leonore in *Fidelio*.

p. 39   1   *"Universal History"*: The *Weltgeschichte für Kinder und Kinderlehrer* (nine vols.) by Karl Friedrich Becker (1777–1806), a German historian.

        2   "July revolution": rising of the people against the Bourbon regime at the end of July 1830.

        3   "King of France": Charles X (1757–1836), on the throne from 1824, forced to go abroad.

        4   "Lafayette": Marie-Joseph, Marquis de La Fayette (1757–1834), liberal royalist who later emigrated.

        5   "a new king": the "bourgeois king" Louis-Philippe of Orléans (1773–1850), reigned until 1848.

p. 40   1   "Rector Krug": Traugott Krug (1770–1842), a philosopher of the Kantian school.

p. 51   1   "Heinrich Dorn": Heinrich Dorn (1804–92), a conductor; in Leipzig in 1829; became director of church music (1833) and later theatre music (1839) in Riga; later in Berlin; he was a composer and wrote reminiscences of his meetings with Wagner.

p. 54   1   "a man named Weiss": Christian Hermann Weisse (1801–66), philosophical writer and translator.

        2   "Theodor Weinlich": actually Weinlig (1780–1842).

        3   "Padre Martini": Giambattista Martini (1706–84), Italian music theorist, composer, and priest.

p. 56   1   "Pleyel": Ignaz Pleyel (1757–1831), Austrian composer who was a pupil of Haydn. He was a piano teacher, and later ran a music shop and piano factory in Paris.

        2   "Breitkopf und Härtel": music publisher in Leipzig, from 1835 run by Hermann Härtel (1803–75) and Raymund Härtel (1810–88).

        3   "Mathäi": Heinrich August Matthäi (17?–1835), concertmaster since 1817.

        4   "Pohlenz": Christian August Pohlenz (1790–1843), conductor, singing teacher, and composer of songs. Conductor of the Leipzig Gewandhaus 1827–1835.

        5   "annual performance": this is inaccurate – the symphony was performed three times in 1826, and once each in the years 1828–30 and 1834–7.

p. 57   1   "Palazzesi": Mathilde Palazzesi, singer at the Dresden Court Theater.

        2   "Raupach's": Ernst Raupach (1784–1852), a German Late Romantic dramatist with 117 historical dramas to his credit.

p. 58   1   "not announcing it": on the theater poster for March 16th 1832 Wagner is named.

        2   "Rochlitz": Johann Friedrich Rochlitz (1769–1842), writer on music and editor of the *Allgemeine musikalische Zeitung* in Leipzig.

p. 60   1   "General Bem": Joseph Bem (1791–1850), promoted to general in the Polish uprising, he fought against the Habsburgs in Hungary (1848–9).

p. 61   1   "The Third of May": a Polish freedom song stemming from 1792, which referred to the constitution agreed in 1791.

p. 62   1   "Strauss": Johann Strauss the Elder (1804–49).

        2   "*Fortunato's Adventures...*": presumably the farce *The Barometer-maker on the Magic Island* by Ferdinand Raimund (1790–1836).

        3   "Wild...Binder": Franz Wild (1792–1860), tenor; Josef Staudigl (1807–61), bass-baritone; Sebastian Binder (1800–45), tenor.

        4   "*Zampa*": opera by Hérold.

p. 64   1   "Dionys Weber": Bedřich Diviš Weber (1766–1842), music theorist and composer, first director of the Prague Conservatory.

        2   "Moritz": Heinrich Moritz (1800–67), character actor and director.

        3   "Kittl": Johann Friedrich Kittl (1806–68), Weber's successor as director of the Prague Conservatory.

p. 65   1   "Lindpaintner": Peter Josef Lindpaintner (1791–1856), conductor, and composer of operas and *Singspiele*.

p. 66   1   "Theodor Apel": 1811–67, son of the writer Johann August Apel, and himself a writer.

        2   "*Glockentöne*": actually *Abendglocken*.

        3   "Büsching's book": *Ritterzeit und Ritterwesen* by the Breslau antiquary Johann Gustav Gottlieb Büsching (1783–1829).

p. 70   1   "Heinrich Laube": 1806–84, dramatist and journalist on *Junges Deutschland*. He wrote the epistolary novel *Das junge Europa* and from 1849 to 1869 was director of the Hofburgtheater in Vienna.

        2   "Börne": Ludwig Börne (1786–1837), writer and political journalist who emigrated to Paris in 1830.

        3   "Ludwig Robert": 1778–1832, a writer and brother of Rahel Varnhagen von Ense.

p. 71   1   "Kocziusko": Tadeusz Kocziusko (1746–1817), Polish patriot.

p. 73   1   "Casper Hauser": a foundling who appeared from nowhere in Nuremberg on May 26th 1824, and whose origins aroused fanciful conjectures.

2   "Paër": Ferdinando Paër (1771–1839), Italian court Kapellmeister in Dresden and later in Paris. Opera composer.

p. 74   1   "Valentin Hamm": Johann Valentin Hamm (1811–75), wrote one opera and light music.

p. 78   1   "Copy of the letter" both in the manuscript and in the privately printed edition an asterisk appears here. The footnote in the printed edition reads "See the letter in the appendix"; however this is not provided. The letter in question, sent to Rosalie from Würzburg on December 11th 1833, is now reproduced in full:

Würzburg. December 11th 1833

I must confess to you, my one and only Rosalie, that your letter made an immeasurable impression on me, as it came at a time when the sole reason for my silence toward all of you was that I felt ashamed somehow and didn't know how to approach you. I was very close to supposing that, after all the sacrifices you had all made for me, it must be extremely disagreeable to see that their purpose had not been attained, and that you might even be angry with me for the way I gave you the news of the disappointment. Oh, I was so depressed in a way whenever I thought of you, believing I could sense how you pictured the purpose of my stay here, as to the outcome of which you could not possibly have any idea. I simply can't describe how much I was tormented with such anxious visions, all the more so because of the contrast between them and the feelings derived from my daily work on my opera. Praise God – or, better, praise You! From many such anxieties your – how shall I term it? – your wonder-working letter has liberated me, while on the other hand it has caused me fresh uneasiness – because after I had read it through I couldn't work for several days. I wanted to write back to you at once – but – the last act of my opera still lacked its finale; the day before yesterday I completed it – and thereby the whole opera; it was precisely 12 noon, and church bells were ringing from every tower when I wrote "finis" under it – that gave me a lot of pleasure!

Now dearest, the composition of my opera is done, and I have only the instrumentation of the last act to do! My rather pedantic manner of writing out the score at once as neatly and cleanly as possible has made the instrumentation the slowest part of my work; still I think, if I really keep at it, I will have finished this last work on my opera in about 3 weeks and thus will be able to leave here in about 4 weeks' time. But how shall I describe to you the mood in which I have been working in these last few days! How I have thought of you all – oh, of *you*, Rosalie – at almost every note, and this was a feeling that no doubt spurred me on – but also often came over me so strongly that I couldn't go on working but had to get up and go out. It happened so often, and I always took it as a joyful anticipation, oh, and how it delighted me that your letter shows a similar sympathy! God grant that I do not disappoint you in your joyful expectations; but it can't really be so – after all, everything just flowed from my innermost soul – and the saying is – that that's how to reach the souls of others.

Tomorrow there is a concert, for which I have been requested to provide some numbers from my opera. An amateur with a lovely voice will sing Ada's big aria, and then the same singer together with Albert and a young basso will sing the trio that leads on from the introduction to the second act, and concerns the situation when Arindal returns to his domain with Morald and is received by his sister Lora. The chorus hails him jubilantly as king, but he interrupts with expressions of anguish: "O cease these tones of rejoicing, they fill me with foreboding; for my royal mantle is my father's shroud!" He is over his dreams of the spirit world and finds everything in his country laid waste and desolate; everything reminds him of his father who died of grief for him, and over and above all this there is Ada's prophecy of the terrors awaiting him on this day; thus the transition is prepared to that mood in which he approaches Ada in the finale. By contrast Lora and Morald are given new strength by Arindal's return and look forward to a happy outcome of the struggle. This mood is reflected in the theme of the ensuing allegro, whose solemn exaltation so moved Albert in the rehearsal, he assured me, that he had to stop singing. This interruption pleased me more than if he had gone on merrily singing. And this is basically one of the less significant numbers: for instance, I've a trio in the third act in which Arindal is aroused from his madness and gradually senses that it yielded to a call from his wife; whereupon he is encouraged by the two spirits to liberate Ada, at last takes up his arms and hurries off in ecstasy to free her – I am counting on a good deal more from that!

How I run on about all these things! It is only the longing to tell you everything! God, God – the time is not so far away – soon I will really be with you all – with *you*, Rosalie! Yet I cannot abandon myself to it to any extent, as otherwise I couldn't write another word – and I would have so much to tell you if I could only get everything straight! I am in such a continuous state of excitement at the moment – I couldn't sleep last night again – oh, what am I saying – I have long since had to give up restful nights – I am always thinking of you all – and – about my opera, immodestly enough! I have been dreaming of you all a lot, and how I would arrive at the house, and how I would be received! Strange! My dreams of this kind have been like a steadily rising climax – in the first one my reception at your hands was nothing special – cold and ordinary – but later it got more intimate – warmer – and now in my dreams it is everything I could want it to be in reality. I hope it doesn't mean anything; you will all be good to me no doubt, even if I have scarcely earned it beforehand.

What you write about the acceptance and production of my opera in Leipzig suits me very well, and I thank you for your efforts to prepare the ground. I would think it should all go well – no, I don't just think it – I hope for it and would be very much upset if this hope were disappointed! But tell me, you write among other things that *Hans Heiling* is such a success and is packing the house; I must admit that this news was very welcome to me in a certain respect. We have produced the opera here as well, and I also find the music really quite nice, particularly the individual numbers; but I have never seen such a complete lack of overall effect in any other Marschner opera. I don't know why, but he has allowed the best effects to go by entirely unexploited – what kind of act-finales are these! – what tuneless choruses! In the second-act finale he treats the culmination of the whole thing: "He comes from the realm of gnomes and dwarves, he is the prince of the mountain spirits!" so sloppily and produces so little in the way of a climax that you would think something of no significance whatever was going on! In short, not a single number communicates any excitement! I must confess, it might even lead me to entertain conceited hopes for my own opera!

I'm sorry your sopranos are in such a sad way – I shall certainly need a reliable voice and exciting acting talent – something like Devrient would be no bad thing! From what I know of Gerhardt her voice may well be too weak – that she nonetheless seems to have been good in *Alice* gives me hope. Above all it is necessary that Eichberger stays, because the tenor has indisputably the biggest and also the most grateful role – if he were to leave it would be a tremendous blow for me! Albert very much wants to do the part and would certainly be excellent in it – perhaps, if he ever gives guest performances in Leipzig! As for the rest of what you write me – dearest Rosalie – let me say nothing about it for now – it has all touched me too unpleasantly and wounded me on the raw too much for me to be able to communicate with you on so many of these topics; I'll be with you soon, and I now believe I have enough of a gift to at least alleviate some of your own anxieties – and relieve our good mother of some of her crazy notions! I thank you for those confidences – the source from which they flowed, your loving trust in me, honors me greatly!

What is Mother doing, what are you all up to? Oh, I will see you all again soon! I am really a very pampered child, and it upsets me all the time when I am away from you! I hope, my Rosalie, we two will be together *very often* in this life! Do you want that? At any rate, I am tremendously delighted that everything is going quite well with all of you, greet everyone for me, and don't let them worry about my arrival. I will have been away from you for nearly a year – God grant that it pays dividends! I see I am becoming very disorderly at the close of my letter, and you can chalk that up to my continuing disquiet and excitement, which gets the better of me all the time and particularly when I think of you and my return – everything spins round together in my head, and it is high time I get my opera finished, as otherwise my objectivity will be in bad shape. Therefore, God willing, I'll be done in 3–4 weeks – and then onward to you all!

Albert writes too – how happy I am that he has taken over on my behalf something that I can only think of with terror! I can do no more than beg all of you most deeply for your kindness and indulgence in all things! God, I am only 20 years old! Greet everybody again, and above all my mother with all, *all* my heart and tell them a lot about their Richard, who causes them so much trouble and misery. But you – are still my angel, my good and only Rosalie! Always remain so!

Your Richard.

p. 79   1   "Ringelhardt": Friedrich Sebald Ringelhardt (1785–1855), actor and theater director in Leipzig 1831–44.

        2   "Stegmayer": Ferdinand Stegmayer (1803–63), Austrian composer. He was a conductor in Leipzig, Bremen, and Vienna where he also taught singing at the Conservatory.

        3   "Hauser": Franz Hauser (1794–1870), Bohemian singer, director, and music teacher. Taught singing in Vienna in 1837 and was director of the Munich Conservatory 1846–64.

p. 80   1   "Bierey": Gottlob Benedikt Bierey (1772–1840).

        2   "Heinse's *Ardinghello*": *Ardinghello und die glückseligen Inseln*, a "Sturm und Drang" novel by Johann Jakob Wilhelm Heinse (1749–1803) which first appeared in 1787.

p. 81   1   "Will's absence": this refers to Wagner's departure from Munich on December 10th 1865, forced upon him by his enemies. Following Schopenhauer's *Die Welt als Wille und Vorstellung*, Wagner liked to describe himself in connection with Cosima as "Will"; Cosima bore the name "Vorstel".

p. 83   1   "*La muette de Portici*": an opera by Auber.

2   "Sicilian Vespers": the rising of the Sicilians against the French in 1282. Verdi's opera of the same name did not appear until 1855.

p. 86   1   "Heinrich Bethmann": 1774–1857.

2   "actress Bethmann": Friederike Unzelmann, née Flittner (17?–1815).

3   "King of Prussia": Friedrich Wilhelm III (1770–1840).

p. 87   1   "Herr Schmale": Wilhelm Schmale, a stage director in Magdeburg and Schwerin.

p. 89   1   "*Lumpaci Vagabundus*": farce by Johann Nepomuk Nestroy (1801–62), the Austrian dramatist.

2   "Friedrich Schmitt": 1812–84, singer and singing teacher. In Magdeburg 1834–5, and later in Leipzig, Dresden, Munich, Vienna, and Berlin.

p. 91   1   "Herr von O.": presumably Otterstedt, the painter of the earliest portrait of Minna.

p. 94   1   "Mme Haas": Mathilde Haas (1803–37), actress in Magdeburg from 1834. She was the lover of Heinrich Laube.

p. 97   1   "Ludwig Meyer": 1802–62, actor and director, in Leipzig in 1834 and Magdeburg in 1835.

p. 100   1   "Livia Gerhart": alternatively Gerhard (1818–91), married to the Leipzig banker Woldemar Frege, she made her debut when she was only fifteen.

p. 101   1   "Friedrich Schneider": 1786–1853, composer of oratorios and court Kapellmeister in Dessau.

p. 104   1   "*Die Schweizerfamilie*": an opera by the Viennese composer and court Kapellmeister Joseph Weigl (1766–1846).

p. 105   1   "Lablache": Luigi Lablache (1794–1858), an Italian singer of French origin, in Italy and Vienna until 1830, later in Paris, London, and St Petersburg.

p. 108   1   "red portfolio": Wagner drew on the notes in this document for his account of the first thirty-three years of his life, and it is believed he then destroyed it. Four pages (covering 1813–39) survive in the Wagner Archives and were published, first in 1936 in the *Allgemeine Musikzeitung*, and then in the first volume of Wagner's *Sämtliche Briefe* (Leipzig, 1967).

2   "Guhr": Karl Wilhelm Guhr (1787–1848), composer and conductor, in Frankfurt am Main 1821–48.

p. 109   1   "née Zeibig": Karoline Pollert, née Zeibig, a singer in St Petersburg 1835–6, and later in Magdeburg and Königsberg.

2   "Krug": Friedrich Krug (1812–92), a bass-baritone in Leipzig and Magdeburg who later became the theater director in Kassel.

p. 119   1   "Schreiber": a tenor in Magdeburg, who was engaged for a time to Minna Planer's sister, Amalie.

p. 122   1   "Cerf": Karl Friedrich Hirsch, known as Cerf (1782–1845). He was a horse trader, a member of the war commission, and from 1822 a theater director in Berlin. "Hirsch" means "stag" in German, as does "cerf" in French.

2   "Gläser": Franz Gläser (1798–1861), a Bohemian composer and conductor, in Vienna, Berlin, and Copenhagen.

p. 126   1   "Louis Schubert": 1806–50, a conductor who worked in Königsberg, and later Oldenburg and St Petersburg.

p. 129   1   "a daughter": Nathalie Planer (later Bilz), 1826–92.

p. 136   1   "Holtei": Karl von Holtei (1798–1880), German dramatist and writer of *Singspiele* and novels.

p. 142   I   "Bulwer's novel": *Rienzi, the last of the Tribunes*, by Edward Bulwer-Lytton (1803–73), the English novelist and politician. He changed his name from Bulwer to Bulwer-Lytton in 1843.

p. 143   I   "Scribe": Eugène Scribe (1791–1861), French dramatist and opera librettist.

        2   "König": Heinrich König (1790–1869), German writer whose novel *Die hohe Braut* appeared in 1833.

        3   "Amalie Planer": the sister of Wagner's first wife Minna, she was married in 1839 to the Russian cavalry captain and later general Carl von Meck.

p. 144   I   "Holtei's first wife": Luise Rogé (17?–1825), an actress.

        2   "Henriette Sontag": 1806–54, concert and opera singer who from 1828 was married to the Sardinian diplomat Count Rossi.

        3   "Bürger's ballad": Gottfried August Bürger (1747–94), pioneer of the modern literary ballad.

p. 145   I   "Carl Blum": Karl Ludwig Blum or Blumer (1786–1844), a stage director at the Berlin opera, and composer and librettist of over fifty stage works.

        2   "Löbmann": Franz Löbmann (1811–78), conductor and violinist.

p. 151   I   "death...Rosalie": on October 12th 1837.

p. 153   I   "Joseph Hoffmann": actually Johann Hoffmann (1805–65); a singer. He was temporary manager of the Riga theater in 1839, and in 1855 became director of the Josephstädter-Theater in Vienna.

p. 154   I   "'the music of the future'": coined by the Cologne music critic Ludwig Bischoff with reference to Wagner's essay *The Artwork of the Future* (see note 2 to p. 467).

p. 156   I   "Wilhelm Taubert": 1811–91, conductor, pianist and composer. He was director of the Berlin court concerts and Kapellmeister of the court opera.

p. 160   I   "had a bust of the nymph at the bowsprit": In German this is "hatte das Brustbild der Nymphe an der Puppe aufgesteckt", which means, literally, "had a bust of the nymph at the doll (*or* pupa)". One may perhaps take this to mean "...as a figurehead", but that is not a connotation normally carried by "Puppe", and does not account for the preposition. Wagner's description of the Thetis is too cursory for the National Maritime Museum to be able to say more than "it is possible to have figures in other places on board ship, possibly for example round the stern, or at the break of the poop, though whether a small Baltic trader would do so is a point". One may otherwise postulate a break in dictation while Richard and Cosima wonder what to call the sharp, or perhaps the blunt, end of the ship. Cosima (who grew up in France) ventures "la poupe"; Richard exclaims "la poupée!"; they laugh heartily, she writes down "Puppe" as a temporary expedient and forgets to check it.

p. 162   I   "furled the sails": literally "raised" – "aufhisste". The National Maritime Museum writes that the notion "that the sails would be lowered seems more likely, but if they were square sails they would have been furled or 'rolled up'".

p. 166   I   "Sir John Smart": actually Sir George Smart (1776–1867), founder member and conductor of the Philharmonic Society.

p. 167   I   "Lord Melbourne": William Lamb, Viscount Melbourne (1779–1848), leader of the Whigs and prime minister in 1834 and 1835–41.

        2   "Brougham": Henry Lord Brougham and Vaux (1778–1868), Whig politician and writer.

        3   "Bishop of London": Charles James Bloomfield (1786–1857).

p. 169   I   "Habeneck": François Antoine Habeneck (1781–1849). Director and conductor of the Paris Grand Opéra. Of German origin.

2   "Moscheles": Ignaz Moscheles (1794–1870), pianist and composer who taught Mendelssohn. From 1846 at the Leipzig Conservatory.

3   "Mlle Blahedka": Marie Leopoldine Blahedka (1811–87), a pianist.

p. 170   1   "to marry": this did not take place until March 1840.

2   "E. G. Anders": Gottfried Engelbert Anders (1795–1866), an aristocrat by origin, he lived under this name in Paris where from 1833 he was an employee of the Bibliothèque Nationale.

p. 171   1   "Maurice Schlesinger": 1797–1871, German music publisher. He was editor of the *Gazette musicale de Paris* (later the *Revue et Gazette musicale de Paris*).

2   "philologist Lehrs": Samuel Lehrs (1806–43).

p. 172   1   "Dumersan": Marion Dumersan (1780–1849), French dramatist.

p. 173   1   "Lewald's": August Lewald (1792–1849), writer and editor of the Stuttgart weekly periodical *Europa*.

p. 174   1   "Panofka": Heinrich Panofka (1807–87), violinist and singing teacher.

2   "Pauline Viardot": 1821–90, daughter of the Spanish singer and composer Manuel Garcia and married to the French historian and writer Louis Viardot, she was known as Pauline Viardot-Garcia. From 1840 mezzo-soprano at the Italian opera in Paris, and from 1849 at the Grand Opéra.

p. 176   1   "Mme Dorus-Gras": Julie Aimée Josephe Dorus-Gras (1805–96), French singer, from 1830 to 1850 first coloratura soprano at the Grand Opéra.

p. 178   1   "Ernst Kietz": Ernst Benedikt Kietz (1816–92), a pupil of Delaroche.

2   "Delaroche": Paul Delaroche (1797–1856), French history painter.

p. 179   1   "Before...year": a mistake, see p. 170, note 1.

p. 180   1   "Prince Pückler": Hermann, Prince of Pückler-Muskau (1785–1871) known as a landscape gardener and travel writer.

p. 182   1   "Edouard Monnaie": actually Monnais (1798–1868), French theater director and editor of the periodicals *La Revue musicale* and *La Gazette musicale*.

p. 183   1   "Zschokke": Heinrich Zschokke (1771–1848), German-Swiss writer and politician.

2   "Laffitte": probably the French banker Jacques Lafitte (1767–1844).

p. 184   1   "Pecht": Friedrich Pecht (1814–1903), history and portrait painter, in Munich from 1855 where he edited the periodical *Kunst für alle*.

p. 185   1   "When...1848": actually this occurred in 1849.

p. 186   1   "Lvov": Alexey Fyodorovich Lvov (1799–1870), composer and collector of Russian church music.

2   "Léon Pillet": from 1841 director of the Grand Opéra.

p. 188   1   "Tichatschek": Joseph Aloys Tichatschek (1807–86), Bohemian tenor, at the Dresden Court Opera 1838–72. He was the first Rienzi and Tannhäuser.

2   "Councillor Winkler": Theodor Winkler (1775–1856), whose pseudonym was Theodor Hell, a dramatist and editor of the Dresden *Abendzeitung* and of the posthumous writings of Weber.

3   "Reissiger": Karl Gottlieb Reissiger (1798–1859), conductor and composer.

4   "Herr von Lüttichau": August Freiherr von Lüttichau (1786–1863), general director of the Dresden Court Theater 1824–62.

5   "Heinrich": Heinrich Brockhaus (1804–74), publisher and brother of Friedrich and Hermann Brockhaus. Proprietor (from 1829 with Friedrich but from 1850 on his own) of the publishing house F. A. Brockhaus. After 1849 he seized Wagner's Dresden library.

p. 194   1   "quadruple alliance": the 1840 alliance of England, Russia, Austria, and Prussia.

         2   "Thiers": Adolphe Thiers (1797–1877), French statesman who became first president of the Third Republic in 1871.

p. 198   1   "Scheuerlin": actually Georg Scheurlin (1802–72).

p. 199   1   "Paul Foucher": 1810–75, French writer.

p. 204   1   "Proudhon": Pierre Joseph Proudhon (1809–65), utopian socialist and political theorist, of some influence on the young Wagner.

         2   "Berlin Court Theater": in fact it was sent directly to Meyerbeer.

p. 207   1   "Lachner": Franz Lachner (1803–90), German composer and conductor. From 1832 he was Kapellmeister and from 1852 to 1865 general music director in Munich.

         2   "Küstner": Karl Theodor von Küstner (1784–1864), director of the Leipzig Stadttheater (1817–28), of the court theater in Munich (1833–42), and until 1851 general director of the royal theaters in Berlin.

         3   "Saint-Georges": Jules de Saint-Georges (1801–75), French dramatist and librettist.

p. 210   1   "Raumer's": Friedrich von Raumer (1781–1873), German historian who wrote, in the wake of Romanticism, the *Geschichte der Hohenstaufen und ihrer Zeit* (6 vols., 1823–5).

p. 213   1   "Lukas's": C. T. L. Lucas attempted to show in the *Proceedings of the Royal German Society of Königsberg* in 1838 that Heinrich von Ofterdingen and Tannhäuser were identical – in reality an untenable view.

         2   "Herr Dessauer": Josef Dessauer (1798–1876), a Bohemian composer who wrote songs, operas, and instrumental works.

         3   "Dietsch": Pierre Louis Philippe Dietsch (1808–65), French conductor and composer.

p. 214   1   "chorusmaster Fischer": Wilhelm Fischer (1789–1859).

         2   "Count Redern": Friedrich Wilhelm, Count Redern (1802–83), director of the court theater in Berlin (1828–42) and, after Küstner's appointment, nominal general director of court music.

p. 215   1   "Schletter": Heinrich Schletter (1793–1853), a silk merchant.

p. 219   1   "Despléchin": Edouard Désiré Joseph Despléchin (1802–70), scene painter for the Paris opera.

p. 221   1   "Rellstab": Ludwig Rellstab (1799–1860), Berlin theater and music critic.

p. 224   1   "Johanna": Johanna (1826–94) was a singer, who, after losing her voice, became an actress. She married the district magistrate Alfred Jachmann.

p. 228   1   "Kriethe": actually Hans Kriete, from 1827 to 1858 an actor at the Dresden Court Theater. In 1843 he married Henriette Wüst, a soprano at the court theater, who sang Irene in the first performance of *Rienzi*.

         2   "Kittl": Johann Friedrich Kittl (see note 3 to p. 64).

p. 234   1   "Julius Mosen": 1803–67, a lawyer and later "Dramaturg" in Oldenburg who wrote novellas and folk poems.

p. 235   1   "Carl Bank": actually Karl Banck (1809–89), musicologist, critic, composer, and contributor to the *Neue Zeitschrift für Musik* founded by Schumann in 1834.

         2   "Julius Schladebach": 1810–72, a doctor of medicine and editor of the *Neues Universallexikon der Tonkunst*.

p. 236   1   "Rastrelli": Joseph Rastrelli (1799–1842), music director in Dresden from 1829; he wrote operas and masses.

         2   "Wächter": Johann Michael Wächter (1794–1853), an opera singer. From 1827 bass-baritone at the Dresden Court Theater, he sang in the first

performances of *Rienzi* (Orsini), *Flying Dutchman* (Dutchman), and *Tannhäuser* (Biterolf).

3   "Sophie Schröder": 1781–1868, née Burger, an actress.

p. 244 1   "present King of Prussia": Wilhelm I (1797–1888), reigned from 1861; he became German emperor in 1871.

p. 245 1   "Morlacchi": Francesco Morlacchi (1784–1841), Italian conductor and composer, from 1810 conductor of the Italian opera in Dresden.

p. 246 1   "brother Johann": Prince of Saxony (1801–73). He succeeded his brother Friedrich August as king in 1854.

p. 251 1   "Karl Lipinsky": actually Karol Józef Lipiński (1790–1861), Polish violinist and composer who was from 1839 to 1861 the first concertmaster of the Dresden Court Orchestra.

p. 255 1   "Ida Hahn-Hahn": 1805–80, a novelist.

p. 257 1   "court lithographer Fürstenau": Moritz Fürstenau (1824–89), flautist and, from 1852, curator of the royal music collection in Dresden.

p. 258 1   "Herr Ferdinand Hiller": 1811–65, a conductor and composer of operas, oratorios, orchestral and chamber music. Conductor of the Leipzig Gewandhaus (1843–4), in Dresden 1844–7, and later in Düsseldorf and Cologne.

     2   "Rietschel": Ernst Rietschel (1804–61), a classical sculptor, who became a professor in Dresden in 1832.

p. 261 1   "Kummer": a member of a family of musicians who flourished in Saxony in the 18th and 19th centuries; for the history of the writing desk see p. 700.

     2   "Cornelius": Peter Cornelius (1783–1867), a painter, uncle of the composer of the same name.

p. 263 1   "Henning": actually Carl Wilhelm Hennig (1784–1867), a conductor and composer of theater music. He was music director of the Berlin Court Orchestra from 1836, and Kapellmeister in Berlin 1840–8.

p. 266 1   "Professor Werder": Karl Friedrich Werder (1806–91), pupil of Hegel, an aesthetician and dramatist.

     2   "Cornet": Julius Cornet (1793–1860), a singer and until 1857 Court Opera director in Vienna.

p. 267 1   "Wurda": Joseph Wurda (1807–?), a tenor, singing teacher, and for ten years a director at the Hamburg theater.

p. 269 1   "which could be heard nowhere else": with the exception of Hamburg.

p. 270 1   "Alwine Frommann": 1800–75, a painter; she was to be a good friend – see pp. 487–8, 511, for example.

     2   "Herr Eduard Devrient": 1801–77, director, theater manager, and writer. In Dresden 1844–6, and Karlsruhe 1852–70.

p. 277 1   "I made no effort": this is incorrect – Wagner spoke at length with Meyerbeer.

p. 287 1   "le Vorhalt? de la Sexte": thus in the manuscript; evidently Wagner could not recall Spontini's exact word, which must have been "la suspension".

p. 292 1   "Karl Golmick": actually Carl Gollmick (1796–1866), pianist, composer, and writer of comedies.

     2   "Mitterwurzer": Anton Mitterwurzer (1818–76), an Austrian baritone at the Dresden Court Theater 1839–70.

     3   "Frau Spatzer Gentiluomo": actually Spitzer-Gentiluomo, a singer at the Dresden Court Theater 1842–6.

p. 293 1   "Becker's song": poem by Nikolaus Becker (1809–45) which arose out of the threat of war between France and Germany in 1840.

p. 296   1   "St Paul's Church": the Catholic chapel in Moorfields.

p. 298   1   "the following morning": December 15th 1844.

p. 299   1   "Emil Devrient": 1803–72, a German actor at the Dresden Court Theater from 1831. He was the brother of Eduard Devrient.

p. 301   1   "Simrock": Karl Simrock (1802–76), a writer and scholar of German literature who was a professor at Bonn. In his *Heldenbuch* (6 vols, 1843–9), he translated folk epics from the German Middle Ages as well as the *Nibelungenlied*.

p. 302   1   "San Marte": the pseudonym of Albert Schulz (1802–93), originally a lawyer, and later a scholar of German literature and myths. He published a two-volume "life and works" of Wolfram von Eschenbach (1836–41).

         2   "Görres": Joseph Görres (1776–1848), a German political journalist whose work has a Romantic-Catholic stamp.

p. 303   1   "Gervinus": Georg Gottfried Gervinus (1805–71), a liberal scholar and literary historian and in 1848 a member of the Frankfurt National Assembly. His *Geschichte der poetischen National-Literatur der Deutschen* appeared 1835–42.

p. 310   1   "Princess Augusta": Augusta of Saxe-Weimar-Eisenach (1811–90), married in 1829 to Prince Wilhelm of Prussia, later King and Emperor Wilhelm I.

p. 313   1   "Czersky and Ronge": Johannes Czersky and Johannes Ronge were two priests who led a reform movement opposed to papal absolutism, celibacy in the priesthood, and other religious extremes.

p. 318   1   "Herr von Falkenstein": probably Johann Paul Freiherr von Falkenstein (1801–82), later a minister in the Saxon government.

         2   "Bendemann": Eduard Bendemann (1811–89), a painter of historical scenes who decorated the palace in Dresden with frescoes, 1838–59.

         3   "Hübner": Julius Hübner, a painter of predominantly religious subjects.

p. 319   1   "Reinecke": actually Robert Reinick (1805–52), a painter and writer of late Romantic childrens' books.

p. 320   1   "Hebbel": Friedrich Hebbel (1813–63), dramatist, poet, and prose writer.

         2   "Julius Schnorr": Julius Schnorr von Carolsfeld (1794–1872), a history painter and director of the Dresden Picture Gallery 1846–71.

         3   "Hänel": actually Ernst Hähnel (1811–91), a sculptor responsible for the Romantic statue of Raphael and the bronze statue of Beethoven in Bonn.

p. 321   1   "Gutzkow": Karl Gutzkow (1811–78), a German dramatist and romance writer who was a leading figure in "Junges Deutschland".

p. 324   1   "Berthold Auerbach": 1812–82, a dramatist and writer of folk tales about village life; the most popular prose writer of his time.

         2   "Duke of Weimar": Karl Alexander (1818–1901), succeeded in 1853.

p. 327   1   "Adolf Stahr": 1805–76, a philologist in Oldenburg and later Berlin. He married the novelist Fanny Lewald (1811–89) and wrote several works on the German classics.

p. 329   1   "Leipzig Concert Society": This is a mistake. Leipzig in fact refused, and the parts were borrowed from the Berlin Royal Orchestra.

p. 331   1   "Anacker": August Ferdinand Anacker (1790–1854), a composer who wrote among other things a cantata *Bergmannsgruss*.

p. 332   1   "Dreissig singing academy": this was the Dresden singing academy named after the court organist Anton Dreyssig (1776–1815).

         2   "Gade": the Danish composer, Niels W. Gade (1817–90).

         3   "Köchly": Theodor Köchly (1815–76), a teacher at the Dresden Kreuzschule, and later Professor of Classical Philology in Zürich.

p. 338   1   "Kaskel": he was the first husband of Bülow's mother, Franziska, née Stoll.

p. 342   1   "Droysen's": Johann Gustav Droysen (1808–84), historian, member of the Frankfurt National Assembly, who translated Aeschylus and Aristophanes, and later devoted himself to Prussian history.

p. 343   1   "Niebuhr": Berthold Georg Niebuhr (1776–1831), historian and Prussian politician; *Römische Geschichte* (1828–32).

        2   "Mone's": Franz Josef Mone (1796–1871) a German scholar of language, myth, and history, who in 1836 published *Untersuchungen zur Geschichte der teutschen Heldensage*.

p. 347   1   "untalented tenor": Julius Pfister (1817–?), sang in Breslau and Berlin.

p. 348   1   "Albert Franck": It is to be assumed that Wagner is actually speaking of Hermann Franck, whose brother Albert was a bookseller (see pp. 316 and 425).

p. 349   1   "Bernhard Marx": Adolf Bernhard Marx (1799–1866), a music teacher, from 1830 Professor and Director of Music at Berlin University.

p. 350   1   "Ernst Kossak": 1814–80, philologist and writer on music. He was founder of the Berlin music periodical *Echo* and of the *Zeitungshalle*.

        2   "Hieronymus Truhn": Friedrich Hieronymus Truhn (1811–66), composer and writer on music.

        3   "Lutter and Wegener's": a Berlin wine cellar, specially favored by E. T. A. Hoffmann.

p. 351   1   "Eduard von Bülow": 1803–53, translator and writer, who for his second wife took the daughter of General Count Bülow von Dennewitz.

p. 352   1   "Prince of Prussia": later King and Emperor Wilhelm I.

p. 353   1   "death of Mendelssohn": on November 4th 1847.

p. 358   1   "my mother's death": on January 9th 1848.

p. 359   1   "'Sonderbund' war": waged and won by the more liberal cantons against the original Catholic cantons who had formed a "separate confederation".

        2   "Republic in Paris": February 24th 1848.

p. 360   1   "dismissed...ministers": March 16th 1848.

p. 361   1   "Vienna and Berlin": the Chancellor Metternich fell from power on March 13th 1848, and on March 18th there was a rising in Berlin.

        2   "Jessie Laussot": née Taylor, after her separation from the businessman Eugène Laussot, she married the historian and journalist Karl Hildebrand and moved with him to Florence.

p. 366   1   "Mosewius": Johann Theodor Mosewius (1788–1858), a writer on music, singer, founder of the Breslau singing academy (1825), and university music director (1832).

p. 367   1   "Professor Fischhof": Josef Fischhof (1804–57), pianist and professor at the Vienna Conservatory.

        2   "Herr Vesque von Püttlingen": Johann Freiherr Vesque von Püttlingen (1803–83), an official in the Austrian Foreign Ministry. He was a pianist and, under the pseudonym J. Hoven, published six operas.

p. 368   1   "Herr Theodor Uhl": actually Friedrich Uhl (1825–1906), journalist and novelist.

        2   "Herr Franck": actually Ludwig August Frankl (1810–94), writer of epics and editor of the periodical *Sonntagsblätter*. The author of the poem *Der Tannhäuser* (1854) mentioned by Wagner was however Adolf Franckel (1823–96).

        3   "Dr Pacher": actually Bacher, a journalist.

        4   "Dr Becher": Alfred Julius Becher (1803–48), an Austrian journalist and

democratic politician, who at the end of 1848 was executed by the authorities.

5 "Franz Grillparzer": 1791–1872, Austrian playwright whose work effectively spanned the entire Romantic range from faerie to historic costume drama. The nature of *Die Ahnfrau* is such that it could have been yet another influence on *Leubald und Adelaïde*.

6 "Bauernfeld": Eduard von Bauernfeld (1802–90), an Austrian writer of comedies, and feuilletonist.

p. 369 1 "October days": by the beginning of November the Vienna uprising had been crushed by the army of Field-Marshal Prince Alfred Windischgrätz, and there were many executions.

2 "Count Albert Nostitz": 1807–71, an Austrian privy councillor and politician.

p. 372 1 "*Das Volksblatt*": Wagner was a contributor to this and even edited it for a short time.

p. 374 1 "Herr von der Pfordten": Ludwig von der Pfordten (1811–80), who was later prime minister of Bavaria.

p. 375 1 "Herr von Trütschler": Wilhelm Adolf von Trütschler (1818–49), member of the Dresden court of appeal and, in 1848, of the Frankfurt National Assembly. As a participant in the Baden uprising he was executed by the authorities in Mannheim on August 14th 1849.

p. 376 1 "priest Lambert": Pfaffe Lamprecht, a German priest of the early twelfth century who was a poet and translator.

p. 378 1 "Fröbel": Julius Fröbel (1805–93), journalist and politician, a member of the Frankfurt National Assembly. He was sentenced to death in Vienna but later pardoned.

2 "Blum": Robert Blum (1807–48), democratic politician, leader of the left-wing faction in the Frankfurt Parliament. He was sentenced to death in Vienna and shot on November 9th 1848.

3 "Archduchess Sophie": princess of Bavaria (1805–72), mother of Emperor Franz Joseph (1848–1916).

p. 379 1 "the son of my old friend": Wilhelm Heine (1827–85), painter and travel writer.

p. 384 1 "Georg Herwegh": 1815–75, revolutionary poet, who took part in the Baden uprising of 1848 and later fled to Switzerland.

p. 390 1 "Liszt...March": this is a mistake; Liszt told him of the performance on February 9th 1849.

2 "Beust": Friedrich Ferdinand Freiherr von Beust (1809–86) was Saxon Foreign Minister from 1849 until 1866. He was an opponent of the unification policy of Bismarck, and later became the Austrian Foreign Minister and Imperial Chancellor until 1871.

p. 393 1 "Thursday May 4th": from here on the dating is faulty. Thursday was May 3rd, but the scene on the barricades probably did not take place until the Friday.

p. 395 1 "(Friday May 5th)": actually Friday May 4th.

p. 396 1 "Heinz": actually Lieutentant-Colonel Heinze, previously an officer in the service of Greece, a landowner, a member of the upper chamber and in May 1849 commander of the Communal Guard.

p. 397 1 "(May 5th)": actually Friday May 4th.

2 "(May 6th)": actually Saturday May 5th.

p. 398 1 "Heubner": Otto Leonhard Heubner (1812–93), chairman of the Freiberg district council, member of the Frankfurt National Assembly and Saxon diet, he was captured and sentenced to life imprisonment. In 1859 he was released and later became a lawyer and a member of parliament once again.

2 "Todt": Karl Gotthelf Todt (1803–52), Saxon envoy to the German Confederation in 1848, who fled to Switzerland in 1849.

3 "Tzschirner": Samuel Erdmann Tzschirner (c. 1812–70), lawyer and member of the Saxon diet, he represented the extreme left-wing faction in the provisional government and supported Bakunin. He fled with Todt to Switzerland but returned after the 1865 amnesty.

p. 399   1   "Sunday May 7th": actually May 6th.

p. 401   1   "Monday May 8th": actually May 7th.

p. 404   1   "Tuesday May 9th": actually May 8th.

p. 407   1   "postal secretary Martin": Heubner's adjutant.

2 "Metzdorff": after the uprising he fled to Paris where he supported himself by teaching and was expelled as a German in 1870. He met Wagner on the streets of Lucerne on August 19th 1870 (see Cosima's diaries).

p. 409   1   "Stephan Born": 1824–98, a social reformer who later became Professor of Literature at the University of Basle.

p. 412   1   "Genast": Eduard Genast (1797–1866), singer, actor, and stage director, from 1829 at the Weimar Court Theater, and 1833–51 also an opera director.

2 "Princess von Wittgenstein": Carolyne or Karoline von Sayn–Wittgenstein, née von Ivanovska (1819–87), friend and life companion of Franz Liszt in Weimar.

p. 413   1   "Stör": Karl Stör (1814–89), later court Kapellmeister.

2 "Goetze": Franz Goetze (1814–88), violinist, lyric tenor at the Weimar court theatre (1836–52), and later a singing teacher at the Leipzig Conservatory.

3 "Grand Duchess of Weimar": Maria Pavlovna, née Grand Princess of Russia, daughter of Paul I and wife of the reigning Grand Duke Karl Friedrich (1783–1853).

p. 414   1   "Kühmstedt": Friedrich Kühmstedt (1809–58), a composer of organ music.

2 "von Watzdorf": Christian Bernhard von Watzdorf (1804–70), from 1843 a minister in the Saxe-Weimar-Eisenach government responsible for foreign affairs and justice.

p. 415   1   "Professor Wolff": Oskar Ludwig Berhard Wolff (1799–1851), Professor of Modern Languages in Jena.

2 "Professor Widmann": Christian Adolf Widmann (1818–78), writer, politician, and political economist.

p. 416   1   "mail coach": the manuscript reads "by rail" but this was corrected in the privately printed edition.

p. 420   1   "Lamartine's": Alphonse de Lamartine (1790–1869), French liberal politician, historian, and Romantic poet, who after the revolution of February 1848 temporarily became Foreign Minister.

2 "Ledru-Rollin": Alexandre-August Ledru-Rollin (1808–74), French left-wing democrat who was Minister of the Interior in 1848 and leader of the Paris uprising in June of that year.

p. 423   1   "Alfred Escher": 1819–82, Swiss politician who promoted the construction of railways.

p. 425   1   "Professor Ettmüller": Ernst Moritz Ludwig Ettmüller (1802–77), writer, editor, and authority on medieval German literature. He was a professor in Zürich from 1833.

p. 426	1	"Görgey's surrender": the Hungarian rising against the Habsburgs ended with the capitulation of General Arthur Görgey on August 13th 1849.
	2	"Genelli": Bonaventura Genelli (1798–1868), a painter and illustrator of Dante and Homer who lived in Germany.
p. 427	1	"her painful death": Wilhelmine Schröder-Devrient died in Coburg on January 26th 1860.
p. 429	1	"Gustav Schlesinger": actually Gustav Schlesier (1811–?), a writer and journalist, who worked on Laube's *Zeitung für die elegante Welt* and then for Lewald's weekly *Europa*.
p. 432	1	"the French poet": the above mentioned Gustave Vaisse.
p. 435	1	"Adolph Kolatschek": published *Art and Climate* in his *Deutsche Monatschrift* in 1850.
p. 439	1	"Röckel, Bakunin, and Heubner": these executions were never carried out, in fact.
p. 457	1	"von Poissl": Johann Nepomuk Freiherr von Poissl (1783–1865), first intendant of the Court Theater and of court music in Munich.
p. 458	1	"Platen's": Count von Platen-Hallermund (1796–1835), German neo-classical poet.
p. 461	1	"Bernhard Spyri": also town clerk, and married (1852) to the successful author Johanna Spyri, née Heusser.
	2	"Abt": Franz Abt (1819–85), composer of folk-songs and choruses for male choirs.
p. 462	1	"Reinhold Solger": 1817–66, writer and politician, who later wrote a history of the American civil war.
p. 463	1	"Franz Dingelstedt": 1814–81, a poet and dramaturg. He was successively intendant of the Munich Court Theater, general intendant of the Court Theater in Weimar and director of the Vienna Court Opera and the Burgtheater.
p. 464	1	"Robert Franz": 1815–92, University music director at Halle an der Saale and a composer of Romantic songs.
	2	"Frau Birch-Pfeiffer": Charlotte Birch-Pfeiffer (1800–68), actress, short story writer and author of countless sentimental plays.
p. 467	1	"with a pseudonym": K. Freigedank ("free-thought"). The essay appeared in Brendel's journal in 1850.
	2	"Bischoff": Ludwig Friedrich Christian Bischoff (1794–1867), a music critic who founded the *Rheinische Musikzeitung* and later the *Niederrheinische Musikzeitung*.
p. 471	1	"Priessnitz": Vinzenz Priessnitz (1799–1852), a farmer and naturopath.
	2	"Court Councillor Carus": Carl Gustav Carus (1789–1869), physician, psychologist, writer, and landscape painter in Dresden.
p. 473	1	"Albisbrunn": in the manuscript and privately printed edition spelt "Albisbrunner"; Swiss place names are occasionally spelt inaccurately.
p. 476	1	"Blandine Ollivier": 1835–62, Liszt's oldest daughter from his relationship with the Countess Marie d'Agoult. She was Cosima's sister and married the French lawyer and politician Emile Ollivier (see note 2 to p. 555).
p. 478	1	"December 2nd": on December 2nd 1851, the President of the Republic Louis Napoleon Bonapate (later Emperor Napoleon III), seized power by dissolving the National Assembly.
p. 479	1	"Wesendonck": Otto Wesendonck (1815–96), a textile merchant, married Mathilde, née Luckemeyer (1828–1902) in 1848. Mathilde wrote the words to many songs and after 1865 historical dramas. The couple came from Düsseldorf and lived in Zürich from 1852. Later they went to New York,

returned to Zürich, and from 1871 settled in Dresden. Their name was always spelt by the couple themselves, and by Wagner and Cosima, "Wesendonck" (that is to say with the "c"), which seems a good reason for using it in this edition of Wagner's autobiography.

2 "Osenbrück": actually Eduard Osenbrüggen (1809–79), a teacher of criminal law at the University of Zürich.

p. 482 1 "so I set...mid July": for Interlaken on July 12th, and Faulhorn and Meiringen on July 13th.

p. 486 1 "Dr François Wille": 1811–96, a political journalist.

2 "by his wife": Eliza Wille 1809–93, a novelist. In 1851 the Willes, who were politically active in Hamburg and Holstein, left Germany and settled on their estate Mariafeld near Zürich.

3 "Sloman": R. M. Sloman (?–1867), an Englishman who married into a Hamburg family.

4 "General Haynau": an allusion to the Austrian general Julius Jakob Freiherr von Haynau (1786–1853), notorious for the cruelty with which he crushed nationalist movements in Hungary and Italy.

p. 487 1 "Louis Schindelmeisser": 1811–64, Heinrich Dorn's stepbrother, German conductor and composer who wrote operas, instrumental and vocal works. He worked in Berlin, Budapest, Darmstadt, Frankfurt am Main.

2 "Herr von Hülsen": Botho von Hülsen (1815–86), a lieutenant in the guards, he became general intendant of the Berlin Court Theaters.

p. 490 1 "Frau von Bissing": Henriette von Bissing, née Sloman (1798–1879), a novelist.

p. 491 1 "I inquired of Herr Härtel": not until April 5th 1856, in fact. Uhlig's *Musikalische Schriften* were published in Regensburg in 1913.

p. 493 1 "*A Theater in Zürich*": published in the early part of 1851.

p. 494 1 "wife of Herr Heim": Emilie Heim, a soprano and friend of Wagner.

p. 495 1 "Now...weeks": Wagner has evidently fused the two visits by Liszt to Zürich in 1853 and 1856 into one. In 1853 the *Faust Symphony* had not yet been composed (in the *Annals* for this year Wagner struck out the word "Faust". Even the letter to Marie von Wittgenstein *Über Franz Liszts Symphonische Dichtungen* was only written *after* Liszt's second visit and not completed until February 15th 1857.

2 "Frau Stockar-Escher": Clementine Stockar-Escher (1816–86), painted water-colours of Richard and Minna Wagner in 1853.

3 "Marie von Wittgenstein": Princess Marie von Sayn-Wittgenstein (1837–97), daughter of Princess Carolyne and Prince Nikolaus von Sayn-Wittgenstein, married (1859) to Prince Konstantin Hohenlohe-Schillingsfürst, Lord High Steward at the Vienna court and brother of the German Imperial Chancellor, Clodwig Hohenlohe.

p. 497 1 "Daumer's version of Hafiz": Georg Friedrich Daumer (1800–75), German poet and religio-philosophical writer; his *Hafiz* (Persian lyrics from the 14th century) appeared in 1846.

p. 498 1 "where I now...Italy": Wagner inserted this phrase himself. The original text, later crossed out by him, ran "From there my wife made her way to the warm spas at Baden am Stein, where even I on a number of visits took the waters, which, however, only led to the ever increasing irritation of my nerves." Minna had however gone to Baden only for a week at the beginning of August; she took the waters there in September.

2 "September...at last": Wagner departed on August 24th in fact, was in Genoa on 31st and in Spezia on September 3rd.

p. 500   1   "Peter Cornelius": 1824–74, composer and writer. His operas include *Der Barbier von Bagdad* (1858) and *Der Cid* (1865).

         2   "Richard Pohl": 1826–96, writer on music and composer, closely connected with Liszt during the latter's Weimar period and an enthusiast for Wagner's music.

         3   "Dionys Pruckner": 1834–96, pianist and pupil of Liszt.

p. 503   1   "an evening with his children": Blandine (1835–1862), Cosima (1837–1930), Daniel (1839–1859).

         2   "Jules Janin": 1804–74, French drama critic, novelist, feuilletonist.

p. 504   1   "General Cavaignac": Louis Eugène Cavaignac (1802–57), a governor general of Algeria and war minister who ruthlessly crushed the uprisings of 1848 in Paris.

p. 509   1   "Herr Frauenstädt": Julius Frauenstädt (1813–79), an author of philosophical works, disciple of Schopenhauer and heir of his literary estate.

         2   "an English critic": John Oxenford, whose article "Iconoclasm in German philosophy" had been published in German shortly after its first appearance in the *Westminster and Foreign Quarterly Review* in April 1853.

p. 510   1   "Yet I...later": According to Cosima's diaries (Jan. 16th 1869) Schopenhauer said to Karl Ritter, "I admire the way Wagner in his *Nibelungen* has made shadowy mythical figures human for us." Then he added "He is a poet but no musician."

p. 513   1   "the first performance": this is a mistake; Wagner conducted the third performance on February 23rd 1855.

p. 514   1   "March 2nd": actually March 4th.

         2   "Ferdinand Praeger": 1815–91, composer and writer on music.

         3   "Mr Costa": Michele Costa (1808–84), an opera and oratorio composer of Italian origin, whose name was anglicized as (Sir) Michael Costa. It was his sudden resignation from the Philharmonic Society Concerts which led to Wagner's invitation to London.

p. 515   1   "Sainton": Prosper Sainton (1813–90), violinist and composer.

p. 518   1   "Karl Klindworth": 1830–1916, pianist and piano teacher in London, Moscow, and Berlin. A pupil of Liszt, he made vocal scores of Wagner's works. His adopted daughter Winifred Williams (born 1897) married Wagner's son, Siegfried.

p. 519   1   "a coachman...Queen": In his *Life of Wagner* (vol. 2 pp. 458–9) Ernest Newman wonders if this is not Wagner's misinterpretation of "Master of the Horse".

p. 521   1   "Mr Ellerton": John Ellerton (1807–73), English composer of operas and string quartets.

         2   "Potter": Philip Cipriani Potter (1792–1871), Principal of the Royal Academy of Music, 1832–59.

p. 522   1   "Mr MacFarren": George Alexander MacFarren (1813–87), English composer and writer on music. He was not Scottish as Wagner thought.

         2   "*Steeplechase*": actually it was entitled *Chevy Chace* (sic).

         3   "German mile": seven and a half kilometers.

p. 523   1   "M. Fétis": François-Joseph Fétis (1784–1871), a Belgian music teacher, organist and composer of church music and operas. In 1827 in Paris he founded the *Revue musicale*; he wrote a history of music and held German music in particularly high esteem.

p. 525   1   "Miss Curshman": Charlotte Saunders Curshman (1816–76), in fact an English singer and actress.

p. 528   1   "Jandala maiden": one of the lower castes in India.

p. 531   1   "Goethe's outburst": "Do they say the Swiss are free? Free? These well-to-do bourgeois safely locked up in their cities?"

p. 532   1   "Theodor Kirchner": 1823–1903, German composer and conductor.

p. 538   1   "Domenico": St Dominic (1170–1221), founder of the Dominican order.

p. 539   1   "Winterberger": Alexander Winterberger (1834–1914), pianist and composer.

     2   "Moleschott": Jakob Moleschott (1822–93), a Dutch psychologist and philosopher who was a professor in Zürich, and later Turin and Rome.

p. 540   1   "Hoffmann von Fallersleben": August Heinrich Hoffmann von Fallersleben (1798–1874), a German writer of well-known, even revolutionary songs, including "Deutschland, Deutschland über alles". In 1830 he became Professor of German Language and Literature in Breslau, and later spent much time traveling.

p. 546   1   "I complained...Liszt": this occurred on December 16th 1856 before the negotiations with the publisher.

     2   "Liszt understood me well": This sentence was revised by Wagner himself. Originally it ran "Liszt understood me well, but after some time he replied that His Royal Highness regarded the affair as a dish of which he did not at all like the taste, [and] that sufficed for me to drop the matter immediately."

p. 547   1   "on Good Friday I awoke": a slip of the memory since Good Friday occurred on April 10th and moving into "Asyl" only took place on April 28th 1857. Presumably Wagner was only in the house to reassure himself that the building alterations were continuing.

p. 548   1   "I went...Siegfried": on May 22nd 1857.

     2   "Refuge": "Asyl".

     3   "Ferreiro": which means more or less "The Iron Man". This Brazilian living in Dresden was in fact called Dr Ernest Ferreira-França.

     4   "Emperor of Brazil": Emperor Dom Pedro II (1825–91) reigned from 1831 (under a regency until 1840), and was overthrown in 1889. Eight years after the dictation of this sentence, on August 13th 1876, he came to the first performance of Das Rheingold at Bayreuth and visited Wagner in Wahnfried.

p. 549   1   "beginning of July": Devrient's visit took place from June 30th to July 3rd 1857.

p. 551   1   "Schnorr": Ludwig Schnorr von Carolsfeld (1836–65), son of the painter Julius, revered by Wagner as a model for all his singers.

     2   "beginning of August": August 9th 1857.

p. 553   1   "beginning of October": the composition sketch was begun on October 1st.

p. 554   1   "four hundred louis d'or": actually six hundred.

     2   "Schack's work": Adolf Friedrich, Count von Schack (1815–94) wrote a history of dramatic literature and art in Spain, translated oriental literature, and used his own collections as the basis for a picture gallery in Munich.

p. 555   1   "M. Carvalho": Pseudonym of Léon Carvaille, director of the Théâtre Lyríque in Paris.

     2   "Emile Ollivier": 1825–1913, a French politician. In 1870 he formed the first parliamentary ministry of Napoleon III as an advocate of the concept of a liberal empire; he was however driven into the war, became information minister, and resigned on August 9th 1870.

p. 557   1   "Orsini's...attempt": on January 14th 1858 Italian revolutionaries under Felice, Count Orsini, attempted to assassinate Napoleon III.

Sebastian Erard (1752–1831), Pierre Erard had died in 1855.

which Minna opened and kept to her death, and which assumed such
enormous importance for Wagner's marriage and for his later relations with
the Wesendoncks, has become known through being published with the
Burrell Collection. It is reproduced here in full:

Madame Mathilde Wesendonck

Just out of bed.

Morning confession.

Oh, no! no! It isn't de Sanctis I hate, but myself, that I always keep
surprising my own poor heart in such weakness! Shall I excuse myself with
my indisposition, and the sensitivity and irritability it nourishes? Let's see
how it goes. The day before yesterday an angel came to me at noon, blessed
and comforted me; that made me feel so well and serene that I felt a hearty
need for the company of friends that evening, in order to let them partake
of my inner happiness; I knew I would be really friendly and congenial.
Then I hear that it was thought inadvisable in your house to deliver my
letter to you because de Sanctis was with you. Your husband remained of
the same opinion. I waited in vain and finally had the pleasure of receiving
Herr von Marschall, who settled in with us for the evening and with every
one of his words filled me with a terrible hatred for all the de Sanctises
of this world. The fortunate fellow – he kept her away from me! And by
what gift? Only through her patience. I couldn't blame him for being so
serious with you; everybody who has anything to do with you takes it so
seriously! How earnestly I take it after all – to the point of suffering
torments for you! But why does she nurse these pedantic fetters? What
does she care for things Italianate? Well, I could answer that for myself.
But the better I could the more irritable I became with that burdensome
fellow; in my dreams he blended into Marschall, and thus formed a shape
in which I recognized all the misery the world holds for me.

That's the way the night went. In the morning I got reasonable again,
and could pray to my angel right heartfully; and this prayer was love! Love!
Joy at this love, the source of my redemption, reigned in the depths of my
soul! Then came the day with its bad weather and the pleasures of your
garden were denied me; and nor could I get anywhere with my work. So
my whole day was a struggle between chagrin and longing for you; and
whenever I felt this longing the most intensely our boring pedant always
seemed to be in the way, stealing you from me, and I had no alternative
but to admit to myself that I hated him. Oh, what a wretch I am! I had
to tell you so; I had no choice. But it was a mean thing to do, and I have
deserved an appropriate punishment. What shall it be? Next Monday I
will come to tea a little late and will be very pleasant to de Sanctis the whole
evening, and I will speak French in a manner that will bring joy to all who
hear it.

What was that stupid quarrel about Goethe yesterday? That Goethe
could be manipulated to serve philistine accommodation to the world rests
in the end, to be sure, on a misunderstanding of the poet; but that it could
happen *at all* puts me on my guard toward him and in particular toward
his interpreters and emendators. Now, you know, I didn't object to

anything yesterday, and especially not to your great pleasure in *Faust*; but to be obliged to hear again and again that Faust himself is the most significant human type that any poet has yet created, that made me – (very foolishly!) – angry. I can't let anyone I know harbor illusions on this point. Faust's despair with the world is based in the beginning either on knowledge of the world – in which case it is pitiful of him to plunge with great ostentation, upon his transformation, into the world he despises, and is to be counted in my eyes among those misanthropes who nonetheless know of no greater ambition throughout their lives than to deceive people and let themselves be admired by them; or – and this is probably the case – Faust is nothing more than an academic with some crazy notions, and he has as yet never explored the real world with any emotional understanding; in that case he is just cripplingly underdeveloped, and one can say that it is good for him to be sent out into the world to learn something. If so, it would be better for him to really learn what there is to be learned, and indeed at the first, wonderful opportunity, the love of Gretchen. But oh, how happy the poet is, when he has gotten him out of the depths of this love, to let him wake up one fine morning with not a trace of the whole affair remaining in his memory, so that the authentic great world, the classical world of art, the practical world of industry, can be *played out* before his decidedly objective scrutiny in the greatest possible comfort. Thus for me Faust really signifies only a wasted opportunity; and this opportunity was nothing less than the only one he had of salvation and redemption. The old sinner feels this himself in the end and tries to make up for it in the final tableau – outside the whole affair, so to speak, after death, when it doesn't bother him any more but can only be very pleasant to be taken up in the arms of an angel and even, no doubt, awoken to a new life.

Now I call all this fine and good, and Goethe remains just as great a poet for me, for he is always truthful and can be no other; people may well also call it objective that the subject never gets to take up the object, the world, into himself (which can only be done by active *sympathy*), but only displays the object for his own scrutiny, and loses himself in it in contemplation, not in sympathy (for that would make him become the world – and the subject's becoming the world is a matter that concerns the saint, and not the poet of *Faust*, who has ended up as a paragon for philistines); in the end I am always pleased with Goethe for always sensing that something was wrong with his activity and yet not taking comfort in his ability to keep his own sympathy at arm's length – and, as I said, to me Goethe is a gift of nature, through whom I get to know the world as through few others. He did what he could and – honor to him! But try to make his miserable Faust the noblest form of man? That's because the world gets anxious when it contemplates the abyss of the great problem of existence; what a comfort it is to people that Faust jumps back at the last moment and decides, inasmuch as he can't leave the world alone, to take it as it is. Yes, if you only knew that from then on he has only Mephistopheles for guide, if you could only face being tormented eternally by the father of lies, after the blessed redemptress, the noble Gretchen, has turned her back on you in painful exaltation. No doubt Goethe knew that; but you should know it too!

What is this nonsense I am talking here! Is it the pleasure of talking to myself, or the joy of talking to you? Yes, to you! But if I see your eyes

I cannot talk any more; then everything I could say becomes utterly insignificant! You see, then everything seems so indisputably true to me, then I am so sure of myself, whenever your wonderful, sacred eyes rest upon me, and I sink into them! Then there are no more objects and subjects; then everything is one and the same, deep and immeasurable harmony! Oh, that is tranquillity, and in this tranquillity is the highest and most complete life! He is a fool who tries to win the world and this peace from outside! A blind man, if he has not recognized your eyes and not found his soul within them! Only inside, within us, only in the depths is salvation to be found! I can only speak and explain myself to you when I don't see you or – am not permitted to see you.

Be kind to me and forgive me my childish behavior yesterday: you were quite right to call it that!

The weather seems mild. I'll come into the garden today; as soon as I see you, I'll be hoping to find you undisturbed for a moment!

Take my whole soul as a morning greeting!

p. 565 1 "never heard...again": the Grand Duke Karl Alexander of Saxe-Weimar arrived in Bayreuth as a festival guest on August 12th 1876 and visited Wagner at Wahnfried on August 17th.

2 "Shortly after": a number of slips of the memory; the Lucerne encounter with the Grand Duke occurred on June 23rd, while Tausig had arrived on May 20th.

3 "Karl Tausig": 1841–71, a pupil of Liszt and one of the founders of the patrons' society formed to pay for the building of the Festspielhaus.

p. 567 1 "Karl Eckert": 1820–79, accompanied Henriette Sontag in the U.S.A. (see note 2 on p. 144), and after that a conductor in Stuttgart. He became court Kapellmeister in Berlin from 1869 and music director in Vienna.

2 "Esser": Heinrich Esser (1818–72), composer and conductor; from 1847 Kapellmeister at the Court Opera in Vienna. It was he who brought Franz Schott and Wagner together.

p. 568 1 "Niemann": Albert Niemann (1831–1917); a member of the Berlin Opera who sang in the Paris *Tannhäuser* of 1861, and in the performance of Beethoven's Ninth Symphony at the laying of the foundation stone for the Festspielhaus in 1872; he sang Siegmund in the first festival.

2 "Seebach": Marie Seebach (1830–97), who was married to Niemann 1859–68; she was a famous Gretchen in *Faust*.

p. 570 1 "Comtesse d'Agoult": Marie Cathérine Sophie, Comtesse d'Agoult (1805–1876), née Flavigny, daughter of the Vicomte Alexandre de Flavigny and Marie Bethmann from the Frankfurt banking house Bethmann. In 1827 she married the Comte d'Agoult and was the focal point of a literary salon. An affair with Liszt lasted from 1834 to 1839. Under the pseudonym Daniel Stern she wrote novels and works of history; after 1848 she turned to political subjects.

p. 573 1 "Fanny Elssler": 1810–84, a Viennese dancer renowned throughout Europe.

p. 574 1 "Prince Dolgorukov": this may refer to a Peter Vladimirovich Dolgorukov who was banished from Russia, lived in Paris for a while, became known as an author and died in Geneva in 1868.

p. 575 1 "Princess Gallitzin": a member of the Russian nobility.

p. 579 1 "Count Daru": Pierre Antoine Bruno, Comte Daru (1767–1829), a French politician who wrote *Histoire de la république de Venise*.

p. 583 1 "Maximilian and his wife": Ferdinand Maximilian (1832–67), younger brother of the Emperor Franz Joseph of Austria. He was governor of Lombardy and in 1864 assumed the imperial crown of Mexico. He was defeated by the republicans, taken prisoner, and shot; his wife Charlotte (1840–1927), born a princess of Belgium, became insane.

p. 584   1   "Magenta and Solferino": defeats of the Austrians on June 4th and 24th 1859.

2   "again to this day": they were never to meet again although Wagner found where Karl was living in Venice in April 1882 (see Cosima's diaries).

p. 590   1   "Felix Draeseke": 1835–1913, musician and music theorist; a pupil of Liszt, he composed symphonies and choral works.

2   "Alexander Serov": 1820–71, a Russian writer on music and opera composer; his name is usually written as "Seroff" by Richard and Cosima Wagner.

p. 592   1   "September 15th": this is inexact; Wagner probably arrived several days earlier.

2   "Countess Charnacé": Claire Christine Charnacé, née d'Agoult, Cosima's half-sister, married from 1849.

3   "Octave Feuillet": 1821–91, French author of salon novels and dramas.

p. 594   1   "Roger": Gustave Hippolyte Roger (1815–79), a French tenor and later singing-teacher.

p. 595   1   "Garrigues": Malwina Garrigues (1825–1904).

p. 596   1   "Luise Meyer": 1831–99; after Emperor Franz Joseph heard her as Elisabeth, she was engaged to sing Elsa at the Vienna Court Opera.

p. 597   1   "Fould": Achille Fould (1800–67), a French financier and several times finance minister under Napoleon III.

p. 598   1   "Fiorentino": Pier Angelo Fiorentino (1806–64), Italian novelist and critic.

p. 599   1   "Jules Ferry": 1832–93, French journalist and lawyer; he was later prime minister during the colonial era in the 1880s.

p. 605   1   "M. Perrin": Emile Perrin who appears as the leader of the chorus in Wagner's *Eine Kapitulation* (1870).

2   "Count Foucher de Careil": Louis Alexandre, Count Foucher de Careil (1826–91), a philosophical writer, politician, and editor of Leibniz's work in France; he also wrote about Hegel, Schopenhauer, and Goethe.

p. 606   1   "Champfleury": Jules Fleury-Husson, known as Champfleury (1821–89), a French writer (*Richard Wagner*, 1860), sculptor and painter.

2   "Malwida von Meysenbug": a German author who wrote short stories and a set of "memoirs of an idealist". She campaigned for workers' and women's education, was exiled from Berlin in 1852 and lived at various times in London, Paris, Florence, and Rome. From 1872 she was a frequent visitor to Bayreuth.

p. 607   1   "Mme Schwabe": in the manuscript before the word "widow", the word "Jewish" has been crossed out.

p. 608   1   "How...later": the bill from Mme Schwabe, amounting to 2400 guilders, was purchased by Wagner's enemies and presented on May 15th 1865. The autobiography contains nothing about this, and it is only recounted in the 1865 Annals. The remark is either the result of an oversight at the time or indicates that while dictating the year 1860 for the autobiography Wagner still intended to continue it.

p. 609   1   "Marshal Magnan": Bernard Pierre Magnan (1791–1865) crushed the uprising caused by the coup d'état of December 2nd 1851. As a result, he was appointed senator, and then Marshal of France by Napoleon III.

p. 610 1 "Princess...Prussia": Princess Augusta (cf. note 1 to p. 310); her husband was Regent on behalf of his insane brother.

2 "Count Pourtalès": Albert, Count Pourtalès (1812–61), a Prussian diplomat of French-Swiss parentage.

3 "Count Paul Hatzfeld": Paul, Count von Hatzfeld-Wildenburg (1831–1901), a Prussian and later German diplomat, for many years ambassador to London.

4 "Count Bacciochi": Felice, Count Bacciochi (1803–66), a close friend of Napoleon III, of Corsican origin. He was extraordinary ambassador and later the general director of the theater in Paris.

5 "Princess Metternich": Pauline, Princess Metternich (1836–1919), née Countess Sandor, married to Chancellor Metternich's son, the Austrian ambassador, Richard, Prince Metternich-Winneburg (1829–95).

p. 612 1 "Klindworth": Georg Heinrich Klindworth (1795–1882), journalist, actor, member of the council of state, and secret agent for Austria and Prussia; his daughter Agnes Denis-Street, was a pupil and later an intimate friend of Liszt.

2 "Count and Countess Coudenhove": Austrian aristocracy who originated in Brabant.

p. 613 1 "Ingeborg Stark": 1840–1913, a pianist (pupil of Liszt) and successful composer. In 1862 she married the composer and later intendant of the Hanover and Weimar Court Theaters Hans Bronsart von Schellendorf (1830–1913).

p. 614 1 "Herr Lindau": Richard Lindau (1831–1900), later in the consular service, was the brother of the writer and theater intendant Paul Lindau and of the writer Rudolf Lindau. Wagner later (p. 672) refers to him as Richard.

2 "Etoile du soir": "O du mein holder Abendstern" from *Tannhäuser*.

p. 616 1 "Mme Gueymard": presumably the wife of the influential French tenor Louis Gueymard (1822–?).

p. 617 1 "Mlle Sax": possibly the daughter of the Parisian instrument maker and teacher, Adolph Sax (see note 1 to p. 631).

2 "Morini": actually Morelli.

p. 620 1 "Baden": June 15th–17th 1860.

2 "Czermak": Jaroslaw Czermak (1831–78), a Czech painter who studied in Antwerp and lived in Paris.

p. 621 1 "Schopenhauer...year": on September 21st 1860.

p. 623 1 "Charles Truinet": 1828–99, French librettist and translator, who founded and ran the archives of the Grand Opéra in Paris.

p. 625 1 "M. Dietzsch": the same Pierre Louis Philippe Dietsch referred to on p. 213.

p. 626 1 "Prince Poniatowsky": Joseph, Prince Poniatowski (1816–73), a diplomat and senator of Polish aristocratic stock who composed several operas.

p. 628 1 "M. Challemel-Lacour": Paul Amand Challemel-Lacour (1827–96), French republican, who after the 1851 coup d'état was banished (1852–9) and became Professor of French Literature in Zürich.

2 "Count Walewsky": Alexander, Count, later Duke Walewski (1810–68), illegitimate son of Napoleon I, who was a diplomat and minister of state under Napoleon III.

p. 629 1 "Petitpas": actually Marius Petipa (1822–1910), the French choreographer.

2 "Porte St Martin": a theater in the Parisian suburbs.

p. 630   1   "Having felt": this entire sentence ran in all editions from 1911 to 1958 as follows: "He had been apprised that the downfall of my work had been sworn." (See Afterword.)

p. 631   1   "Sax": Adolphe Sax (1814–94), an instrument maker and teacher at the Paris Conservatoire. He invented a number of wind instruments, among them the saxophone.

p. 634   1   "I have…elsewhere": in the *Deutsche Allgemeine Zeitung* for March 27th 1861.

p. 637   1   "Szemere": Batholomew Szemere (1812–69), a Hungarian politician and writer, who decided with Kossuth in favor of revolution, in 1849 fled to Constantinople and, later, Paris.

p. 639   1   "Prince Polignac": Jules Armand Jean Melchior, Duc de Polignac (1817–?); of French parentage, he served in the Bavarian army and lived in Paris.

        2   "his *Faust*": Wagner heard the opera in Wiesbaden on February 9th 1862.

p. 640   1   "Musard": In fact, Philippe Musard, founder of the popular "Concerts Musard", was dead by 1861.

        2   "Pasdeloup": Jules Etienne Pasdeloup (1819–87), teacher at the Paris Conservatoire and founder of the "Concerts populaires de musique classique" in which many of Wagner's works were played in the 1870s.

        3   "M. de la Vaquerie": Auguste Vaquerie (1819–95), French poet, dramatist, and essayist, brother of a son-in-law of Victor Hugo.

p. 642   1   "Accordingly…Karlsruhe": This phrase, in Wagner's hand in the manuscript, replaces the following passage, which he himself crossed out: "True, Schnorr had left Karlsruhe for Dresden, and it appeared altogether as though the singers there had nothing to offer me. On the other hand, after all the reports I had heard of her, I had formed a very favorable opinion of the soprano Luise Meyer, now Frau Dustmann and working in Vienna. Thus it was with a view to procuring her services that I intended to make Vienna the ultimate destination of my journey, while transferring the base of my future operations to Karlsruhe. Accordingly I made my first stop there…"

p. 644   1   "Ander": Alois Ander (1821–64).

p. 645   1   "the singer Beck": Johann Nepomuk Beck (1827–1904).

        2   "Count Lanskoronsky": actually Lanckoronski.

p. 647   1   "not long afterward": Baudelaire died on August 31st 1867.

p. 650   1   "Bethmann-Hollweg": Moritz August Bethmann-Hollweg (1795–1877), lawyer and liberal politician; Prussian minister of culture 1858–62.

p. 655   1   "I arrived in Weimar": on August 2nd 1861.

        2   "Liszt's youthful uncle": Eduard Liszt, a Viennese teacher of penal law and criminologist, actually younger than his nephew Franz.

        3   "a congress of musicians": first meeting of the Allgemeiner Deutscher Musikverein, in the founding of which Liszt was a prime mover.

        4   "Weissheimer": Wendelin Weissheimer (1838–1910), a conductor, music teacher and composer.

        5   "Emilie Genast": a singer and actress, daughter of the actor and director Eduard Genast.

        6   "Damrosch": Leopold Damrosch (1832–85), a composer and conductor as well as violinist who later exerted a great influence on musical life in U.S.A.

p. 657   1   "Margarethe": the editions of 1911 and later change the name for some unknown reason to "Magdalene".

p. 658   1   "King Ludwig I": King of Bavaria (1786–1868); he had to abdicate in 1848.

p. 659   1   "Baron Sina": a Viennese banker.

p. 664   1   "some years later": Hebbel died in Vienna in 1863.

p. 666   1   "Walter": Gustav Walter (1836–?), who from 1856 sang Verdi and Wagner roles at the Vienna Court Opera.

         2   "Seraphine": Seraphine Mauro.

p. 667   1   "Palace of the Doges": corrected in the privately printed edition to "Academy of the Arts".

         2   "in the...Doges": deleted in the privately printed edition.

p. 668   1   "Grimm's polemic": *Über den altdeutschen Meistergesang* (1811).

         2   "Wagenseil's": Johann Christoph Wagenseil (1633–1705) a professor in Altdorf who wrote on the mastersingers in an appendix to his Nuremberg chronicle.

         3   "Baron Münch-Bellinghausen (Halm)": Eligius Franz Joseph Freiherr von Münch-Bellinghausen, an Austrian dramatist who wrote under the name of Friedrich Halm. He was general intendant of the Vienna Court Theater 1867–70.

p. 670   1   "payment...*Die Walküre*": Wagner offered *Die Walküre* to Schott on October 17th 1861, and acknowledged the advance on October 30th.

         2   "'Though...dismay'": the line is quoted here as "ward auch den Meistern dabei bang" (the word "dabei" being inserted in Wagner's hand in the manuscript), which differs slightly from the text of *Die Meistersinger*: "macht er den Meistern bang".

p. 677   1   "von Dalwigk": Karl Friedrich Reinhard Freiherr von Dalwigk (1802–80), prime minister in Hesse-Darmstadt and opponent of Bismarck's policy of German unification.

p. 678   1   "Raff": Joachim Raff (1822–82), musician and composer, taught piano in Wiesbaden and later became the director of the Hoch Conservatory in Frankfurt. In 1859 he was married to the actress Doris Genast (1826–1912).

p. 679   1   "as the female...actress": inserted later by Wagner in the manuscript to replace "this artist".

p. 680   1   "Duke of Nassau": Adolf (1817–1905), reigned from 1839 and was deposed by Prussia in 1866. He later became the Grand Duke of Luxembourg.

p. 686   1   "Rietz": Julius Rietz (1812–77), cellist, conductor, and composer; a teacher at the Leipzig Conservatory and conductor of the Gewandhaus concerts. He was later general music director in Dresden.

         2   "Kalliwoda": Wilhelm Kalliwoda (1827–93), court Kapellmeister in Karlsruhe; son of the Czech composer Johann Wenzel Kalliwoda.

p. 688   1   "David": Ferdinand David (1810–73), concertmaster of the Leipzig Gewandhaus from 1836; he taught at the Conservatory and wrote violin concertos (dedicatee of the Mendelssohn E minor Concerto).

         2   "August Wilhelmj": 1845–1908, violin virtuoso and teacher; concertmaster at the first Bayreuth festival.

         3   "Alois Schmitt": actually Aloys Schmitt (1788–1866), a music teacher and composer.

p. 691   1   "Minister Schmerling": Anton von Schmerling (1805–93), Austrian minister of state 1860–5.

p. 692   1   "Ignaz Lachner": 1807–95, German violinist and conductor, and composer; brother of the composer Franz Lachner. He was an infant prodigy and later held appointments in Stuttgart, Munich, Hamburg, and Frankfurt.

p. 697   1   "Schwind": Moritz von Schwind (1804–71), Munich painter and draughtsman.

p. 698   1   "Alexander Ritter...Franziska": Alexander Ritter (1833–96), violinist and composer, younger brother of Karl Ritter; he was conductor at Schwerin from 1856. In 1852 he married the daughter of Wagner's elder brother Albert, Franziska (1829–95).

         2   "Lassen": Eduard Lassen (1830–1904), a Belgo-Danish musician who wrote incidental music to Goethe's *Faust*. He succeeded Liszt as court Kapellmeister in Weimar in 1858.

p. 703   1   "November 15th": the arrival took place on November 14th.

p. 704   1   "A strange incident": this took place on the evening of November 23rd.

         2   "Countess Krockow": Elisabeth von Krockow, a member of the Pomeranian nobility.

p. 706   1   "Hellmesberger": Joseph Hellmesberger (1829–93) the Elder, an Austrian violinist and conductor.

         2   "to...other musicians": in the manuscript there follows a sentence later crossed out: "He provided me with the three Rhinedaughters from among the pupils of the singing teacher Marchesi; unfortunately one of them was a very unpleasant Jewess whom I could not reject because her alto part could not be filled by anyone else."

p. 707   1   "young Empress": Elisabeth (1837–98), of the Bavarian royal family, married in 1854 to Emperor Franz Joseph I of Austria.

p. 709   1   "Heinrich Porges": 1837–1900, writer on music and choir conductor, in Munich from 1867.

         2   "Marie Löw": Maria Lehmann, née Loew (1807–83), a singer at the Leipzig theater. She was the mother of the singers Lilli and Maria Lehmann who took part in the first Bayreuth festival.

p. 710   1   "Cosima...birth": Cosima and Hans von Bülow's second daughter, Blandine, was born on March 20th 1863.

p. 711   1   "Anton Rubinstein": 1829–94, Russian pianist and composer, who from 1862 was director of the St Petersburg Conservatory.

p. 712   1   "Grand Duchess Helene": Helene Pavlovna (1807–73), née Princess of Württemberg, widow of the Grand Duke Mikhail Pavlovich, brother of Nicholas I.

p. 713   1   "Grand Duchess Marie": Maria Nikolayevna (1819–76), Duchess of Leuchtenberg.

p. 714   1   "*Persian Songs*": twelve songs to words by Mirza Shafi in a German translation by Friedrich Bodenstedt.

p. 715   1   "Herr Schuberth": Karl Schuberth (1811–63).

p. 716   1   "Nikolaus": Nikolay Rubinstein (1835–81), pianist and conductor; founder of the Moscow Conservatory.

p. 717   1   "Prince Odoyevsky": Vladimir Fedorovich Odoyevsky (1803–69), Russian poet and writer on music; author of *Russian Nights*.

p. 718   1   "General Suvorov": Alexander Arkadyevich Suvorov-Rymnikski, a diplomat and general who was military governor of St Petersburg 1861–6.

p. 719   1   "Baron von Rackowitz": probably actually Rachowin or Radowitz.

p. 722   1   "Réményi": Ede Réményi (1828–98), had in common with Wagner the experience of exile, following his part in the Hungarian uprising against Austria in 1848–9. Made a career as a virtuoso, and held the post of solo violinist to Queen Victoria 1854–9. Allowed to return to Hungary in 1860, but took up residence in the United States in the last twenty years of his life.

p. 723   1   "Countess Bethlen-Gabor": member of a noble Transylvanian–Hungarian family.

p. 724   1   "Coronini": Johann Baptist Alexius, Count of Coronini-Cronberg (1794–1876), Austrian Director of Ordnance.

p. 725   1   "Duncker's": Max Wolfgang Duncker (1811–86), historian and liberal politician, a member of the Frankfurt National Assembly and Professor of Political History in Tübingen. The *Geschichte des Altertums* dates from 1852.

p. 726   1   "Prince von Hohenzollern": Friedrich Wilhelm Konstantin, Prince von Hohenzollern-Hechingen (1801–69), renounced sovereignty in 1849 and lived in Silesia where he fostered musical life.

p. 728   1   "Wesendonck family": in the original form this appears as "in the home of my friends the Wesendoncks".

      2   "November 29th": actually November 19th.

p. 729   1   "Weitzmann": Karl Friedrich Weitzmann (1808–80), composition teacher, conductor and writer on music.

      2   "With tears and sobs": this sentence is missing in all editions before 1963 (see Afterword); the meeting took place on November 28th 1863.

      3   "Seifriz": Max Seifriz (1827–85), German conductor, court Kapellmeister at Stuttgart from 1871.

p. 731   1   "Marie von Buch": 1842–1912; from 1865 to 1885 married to the Prussian minister Alexander, Count von Schleinitz. She appears as the Countess Marie von Schleinitz in Cosima's diaries; in 1886 she married the Austrian diplomat Anton, Count von Wolkenstein; she supported Wagner and was an influential figure in Berlin society in the 1870s.

p. 732   1   "Gustav Schönaich": 1840–1906, stepson of Dr Joseph Standhartner; later he became a journalist and writer.

p. 734   1   "Otto Bach": 1833–93, Austrian conductor, music teacher, and composer; director of the Salzburg Mozarteum from 1868.

      2   "Count Laurencin": 1819–90, a writer on music.

      3   "re-reading the *Iliad*": in the translation by Johann Heinrich Voss.

      4   "*La Vie de Rancé*": a biography of the founder of the Trappist order of monks.

p. 735   1   "humorous epitaph": "Hier liegt Wagner, der nichts geworden, nicht einmal Ritter vom lumpigsten Orden; nicht einen Hund hinterm Ofen entlockt er, Universitäten nicht mal 'nen Dokter." "Here lies Wagner, who never throve, tempted no dog from behind the stove, earned not the shabbiest star or garter, honored by no Alma Marter." (sic)

p. 736   1   "Tauler": Johannes Tauler (*c.* 1300–61), a mystic.

p. 738   1   "Baron von Gall": Ferdinand Freiherr von Gall (1809–72), writer and theater intendant in Oldenburg and Stuttgart.

      2   "Herr Pfistermeister": Franz Seraph von Pfistermeister (1820–1912), later one of Wagner's chief opponents in Munich.

      3   "a note...King": in fact the communication was oral not written.

p. 739   1   "Meyerbeer...Paris": on May 2nd 1864.